European Union Law

EDITED BY

CATHERINE BARNARD

AND

STEVE PEERS

OXFORD

UNIVERSITY PRESS

OXFORD
UNIVERSITY PRESS

Great Clarendon Street, Oxford, OX2 6DP,
United Kingdom

Oxford University Press is a department of the University of Oxford.
It furthers the University's objective of excellence in research, scholarship,
and education by publishing worldwide. Oxford is a registered trade mark of
Oxford University Press in the UK and in certain other countries

Published in the United States of America by Oxford University Press
198 Madison Avenue, New York, NY 10016, United States of America

British Library Cataloguing in Publication Data
Data available

Library of Congress Control Number: 2013957440

ISBN 978-0-19-968611-7

Printed in Great Britain by
Ashford Colour Press Ltd, Gosport, Hampshire

Preface

It is hard to be neutral about the EU. It provokes strong views and passions. Yet in the tumult of Treaty reform, case law, legislation, theory, and empirical research lies a core subject that must be taught to students. How to fashion the material in a way that is engaging and accessible? How is it possible in one course to convey EU constitutional, administrative, tort, contract, and criminal law, subjects that command whole courses of their own in domestic legal systems, each one taught by a range of experts? This book tries to address the conundrum in two ways.

First, it provides thorough but realistic coverage of the main topics taught on undergraduate courses (constitutional and institutional law, remedies, four freedoms, competition law). However, it then supplements those topics with chapters on specific subjects (eg consumer law, health law, social law, environmental law, criminal law) which are intended to illustrate how the core topics apply to those specific subject areas, as well as whetting the readers' appetite for more. Finally, it introduces the readers to the rapidly developing and increasingly important subject of public services and EU law; a subject we believe may become the battleground on which ever more of the EU/Member State turf wars are fought.

Secondly, it brings a range of voices to the subject. This makes it unique in textbooks on EU law. Each chapter is written by a different author, enabling readers to learn from the experts within each field. Some of the chapter authors also work for (or have worked for) EU institutions. This brings a different perspective to their work. The authors are also all experienced teachers. Between them they have decades of practice explaining complex subjects to students. This experience has shaped their presentation of each topic. The authors are also distinguished researchers and their research has helped to frame the themes which are woven into each chapter. The authors come from a number of different countries (Belgium, the Czech Republic, Germany, Finland, Ireland, Italy, Luxembourg, the Netherlands, Spain, Sweden, the UK). This reflects the diverse membership of the EU, and the diverse legal heritage into which EU law must fit and from which EU law develops.

Of course, with such diversity comes the risks of lacunae or repetition. Our job, as editors, has been to minimize such risks, by coordinating the different contributions in order to keep overlaps, conflicts, and omissions to a minimum. We have also benefited from the substantial input of Abbey Nelms, our editor at OUP, and her team of anonymous referees, both academic and student, who have commented on every chapter, and helped to check not only for quality but also that the coverage is thorough but manageable.

That said, the close connections between the subject matter of the different chapters, which is inherent in the nature of EU law as a subject means that some crossover between chapters is inevitable. We thought it was useful, for instance, that some chapters included a case study of the same case, but from different perspectives (see eg the case studies in chapters 8 and 9), in order to allow the same issue to be viewed through various lenses. Our aim was to balance the twin objectives of uniformity and diversity. And while each author has painted a different picture of their particular aspect of EU law, we have assembled these separate images into a mosaic depicting the subject as a whole.

All of this has been done with the image of the student firmly in mind. So each chapter has an introduction which sets out the main themes relevant in the subject area and an outline of what is to follow, and a list of further reading at the end of each chapter enabling the student to take the material further. Each chapter also contains a case study which may develop the ideas in the chapter or highlight a particular topic which merits further attention. Where appropriate, diagrams have also been included to provide a visual summary of complex points of law.

We are hugely grateful to the team at OUP: to Abbey Nelms, our publishing editor, for her patience and considerable support, to Sarah Stephenson, our magnificent production editor, to Joy Ruskin-Tompkins for her excellent work as our copy-editor, and to Philip Moore for careful proofreading. We also owe a debt of gratitude to the authors for taking on the challenge of writing for this book and who have patiently put up with our streams of emails and questions, to the many referees for doing such a thorough job, and to our long-suffering families who have put up with us.

CSB
SP
2 December 2013

Outline contents

Detailed contents

Notes on contributors

Editors

Catherine Barnard is Professor of European Union Law and Labour Law and Fellow of Trinity College, Cambridge.

Steve Peers is Professor of Law at the University of Essex.

Contributors

Albertina Albors-Llorens is a University Senior Lecturer and Fellow of Girton College, Cambridge.

Michal Bobek is Professor of European Law at the College of Europe. He is also Research Fellow at the Institute of European and Comparative Law, University of Oxford.

Kieran St C Bradley is a Judge at the European Union Civil Service Tribunal and former Director in the Legal Service of the European Parliament.

Paul Craig is Professor of English Law and Fellow of St John's College, Oxford.

Geert De Baere is Assistant Professor of International and EU Law at the University of Leuven, Belgium, where he is also Senior Member at the Leuven Centre for Global Governance Studies.

Bruno de Witte is Professor of European Union Law at Maastricht University, and part-time Professor at the European University Institute (EUI) in Florence.

Leo Flynn is a Member of the Legal Service of the European Commission and Visiting Lecturer in Law at King's College London.

Leigh Hancher is Professor of European Union Law at the Tilburg University and is Of Counsel at the Amsterdam office of Allen & Overy LLP.

Tamara Hervey is Jean Monnet Professor of European Union Law at the University of Sheffield, where she is also Head of the School of Law.

Alicia Hinarejos is a University Lecturer in Law and Fellow of Downing College, Cambridge.

Herwig CH Hofmann is Professor of European and Transnational Public Law and Jean Monnet Chair in European Public Law at the University of Luxembourg.

Geraint Howells is Professor of Law and Head of School at the University of Manchester.

Alison Jones is Professor of Law at King's College London and a solicitor at Freshfields Bruckhaus Deringer LLP.

Martín Martínez Navarro is a Legal Officer at the European Ombudsman and Lecturer at the Université Libre de Bruxelles.

Elisa Morgera is Senior Lecturer in Global Environmental Law at the University of Edinburgh and Co-Director of the University's Europa Institute.

Niamh Nic Shuibhne is Professor of European Union Law at the University of Edinburgh and Visiting Professor at the College of Europe, Bruges.

Peter Oliver is Visiting Professor at the Université Libre de Bruxelles and a former Legal Advisor to the European Commission in Brussels.

Mia Rönnmar is Professor in Private and Labour Law at Lund University, Sweden.

Wolf Sauter is Professor of Healthcare Regulation at Tilburg University and Competition Expert for the Dutch Healthcare Authority.

Robert Schütze is Professor of European Law and Co-Director of the Global Policy Institute at Durham University.

Jukka Snell is Professor of European Law at the University of Turku, Finland and at Swansea University, UK.

Eleanor Spaventa is Professor of European Union Law at Durham University.

John R Spencer is Fellow of Selwyn College, Cambridge, and until his retirement was a Professor in the Law Faculty. He is also President of the European Criminal Law Association (UK).

Christopher Townley is Senior Lecturer in Law at King's College London. He previously worked as a solicitor at Clifford Chance LLP and at the Office of Fair Trading.

Table of abbreviations

AG	Advocate General
All ER	All England Law Reports
ATP	absolute territorial protection
AVC	average variable costs
BVerfGE	Entscheidungen des Bundesverfassungsgerichts (Reports of the Decisions of the [German] Federal Constitutional Court)
BRIC	Brazil, Russia, India, and China
CCP	Common Commercial Policy
CCS	carbon capture and storage
CEAS	Common European Asylum System
CEE	charge of equivalent effect
CFSP	Common Foreign and Security Policy
Ch	Chancery Division Reports
CIS	Common Implementation Strategy
CISA	Convention Implementing the Schengen Agreement
CMLR	Common Market Law Reports
CRD	Citizens' Rights Directive 2004/38
CSDP	Common Security and Defence Policy
CSOH	Court of Session, Outer House Reports
EAEC	European Atomic Energy Community
EAW	European Arrest Warrant
EC	European Community
ECB	European Central Bank
ECHR	European Convention on Human Rights
ECHRR	European Court of Human Rights Reports
ECmHRR	European Commission on Human Rights Reports
ECN	European Competition Network
ECtHR	European Court of Human Rights
ECJ	European Court of Justice
ECR	European Court Reports
ECSC	European Coal and Steel Community
EDC	European Defence Community
EEA	European Economic Area
EEAS	European External Action Service
EEC	European Economic Community

EEIG	European Economic Interest Grouping
EES	European Employment Strategy
EFSF	European Financial Stability Fund
EFSM	European Financial Stability Mechanism
EFTA	European Free Trade Area
EHRR	European Human Rights Reports
EMA	European Medicines Agency
EMS	European Monetary System
EMU	economic and monetary union
EPC	European Political Community
EPPO	European Public Prosecutor's Office
ESCB	European System of Central Banks
ESM	European Stability Mechanism
ETS	Emission Trading Scheme
EU	European Union
Euratom	European Atomic Energy Community
Europol	European Police Office
EWCA Civ	England and Wales Court of Appeal (Civil Division) Reports
EWCA Crim	England and Wales Court of Appeal (Criminal Division) Reports
EWHC (Admin)	England and Wales High Court (Administrative Division) Reports
GDP	gross domestic product
ICH	International Conference on Harmonisation of Technical Requirements for Registration of Pharmaceuticals for Human Use
ICT	information communication technology
IGC	intergovernmental conference
ILM	International Legal Materials
ILO	International Labour Organization
IMF	International Monetary Fund
INP	innominate non-legislative procedure
JHA	Justice and Home Affairs
MEE	measure of equivalent effect
MEP	Member of the European Parliament
NATO	North Atlantic Treaty Organization
NCA	national competition authority
NGO	non-government organization
nyr	not yet reported
OCT	overseas country or territory
OECD	Organisation for Economic Co-operation and Development
OEEC	Organisation for European Economic Co-operation
OJ	*Official Journal of the European Union*

OLAF	l'Office européen de lutte anti-fraude (European Anti-Fraud Office)
OLP	ordinary legislative procedure
ORRPI	overriding reasons in the public interest
PCT	Primary Care Trust
PIM	person of independent means
PJCCM	Police and Judicial Cooperation in Criminal Matters
PLR	prior lawful residence
PSO	public service obligation
QMV	qualified majority voting
QR	quantitative restriction
REIO	regional economic international organization
SA	social assistance
SCE	Societas Cooperativa Europaea (European Cooperative Society)
SE	Societas Europaea (European Company)
SEA	Single European Act
SG&L	student grants and loans
SGEI	service of general economic interest
SGI	service of general interest
SIS	Schengen Information System
SLP	special legislative procedure
SPE	Societas Privata Europaea (Private European Company)
SPS	sanitary and phytosanitary measures
SSGI	social service of general interest
Stat	Statutes at Large
TCN	third-country national
TEU	Treaty on European Union
TFEU	Treaty on the Functioning of the European Union
TRIPS	Trade-Related Aspects of Intellectual Property Rights
TSCG	Treaty on Stability, Coordination and Governance in the EMU
UKAIT	UK Asylum and Immigration Tribunal Reports
UKSC	United Kingdom Supreme Court Reports
UN	United Nations
UNTS	United Nations Treaty Series
USO	universal service obligation
VIS	Visa Information System
WEU	Western European Union
WFD	Water Framework Directive 2000/60/EC
WHO	World Health Organization
WTO	World Trade Organization

Table of legislation

Recommendations

Regulations

Rules

Decisions

Statutory Instruments

Table of cases

Court of Justice cases - Numerical

Commission cases

ECtHR cases

Tables of equivalences[1]

TREATY ON EUROPEAN UNION

Old numbering of the Treaty on European Union	New numbering of the Treaty on European Union	Old numbering of the Treaty on European Union	New numbering of the Treaty on European Union
TITLE I	**TITLE I**		Article 11
Article 1	Article 1		Article 12
	Article 2	**TITLE III**	**TITLE III**
Article 2	Article 3	Article 9 (repealed)[8]	Article 13
Article 3 (repealed)[2]			Article 14[9]
	Article 4		Article 15[10]
	Article 5[3]		Article 16[11]
Article 4 (repealed)[4]			Article 17[12]
Article 5 (repealed)[5]			Article 18
Article 6	Article 6		Article 19[13]
Article 7	Article 7	**TITLE IV**	**TITLE IV**
	Article 8	Article 10 (repealed)[14]	
		Articles 27a to 27e (replaced)	
TITLE II	**TITLE II**	*Articles 40 to 40b (replaced)*	Article 20[15]
Article 8 (repealed)[6]	Article 9	*Articles 43 to 45 (replaced)*	
	Article 10[7]		

[1] Tables of equivalences as referred to in Article 5 of the Treaty of Lisbon. The original centre column, which set out the intermediate numbering as used in that Treaty, has been omitted.

[2] Replaced, in substance, by Article 7 of the Treaty on the Functioning of the European Union ('TFEU') and by Articles 13(1) and 21, paragraph 3, second subparagraph of the Treaty on European Union ('TEU').

[3] Replaced Article 5 of the Treaty establishing the European Community ('TEC').

[4] Replaced, in substance, by Article 15.   [5] Replaced, in substance, by Article 13, paragraph 2.

[6] Article 8 TEU, which was in force until the entry into force of the Treaty of Lisbon (hereinafter 'previous'), amended the TEC. Those amendments are incorporated into the latter Treaty and Article 8 was repealed. Its number was used to insert a new provision.

[7] Paragraph 4 replaced, in substance, the first subparagraph of Article 191 TEC.

[8] The previous Article 9 TEU amended the Treaty establishing the European Coal and Steel Community. This latter expired on 23 July 2002. Article 9 was repealed and the number thereof was used to insert another provision.

[9] – Paragraphs 1 and 2 replaced, in substance, Article 189 TEC;
– paragraphs 1 to 3 replaced, in substance, paragraphs 1 to 3 of Article 190 TEC;
– paragraph 1 replaced, in substance, the first subparagraph of Article 192 TEC;
– paragraph 4 replaced, in substance, the first subparagraph of Article 197 TEC.

[10] Replaced, in substance, Article 4.

[11] – Paragraph 1 replaced, in substance, the first and second indents of Article 202 TEC;
– paragraphs 2 and 9 replaced, in substance, Article 203 TEC;
– paragraphs 4 and 5 replaced, in substance, paragraphs 2 and 4 of Article 205 TEC.

[12] – Paragraph 1 replaced, in substance, Article 211 TEC;
– paragraphs 3 and 7 replaced, in substance, Article 214 TEC.
– paragraph 6 replaced, in substance, paragraphs 1, 3 and 4 of Article 217 TEC.

[13] – Replaced, in substance, Article 220 TEC.
– the second subparagraph of paragraph 2 replaced, in substance, the first subparagraph of Article 221 TEC.

[14] The previous Article 10 TEU amended the Treaty establishing the European Atomic Energy Community. Those amendments are incorporated into the Treaty of Lisbon. Article 10 was repealed and the number thereof was used to insert another provision.   [15] Also replaced Articles 11 and 11a TEC.

Old numbering of the Treaty on European Union	New numbering of the Treaty on European Union	Old numbering of the Treaty on European Union	New numbering of the Treaty on European Union
TITLE V	**TITLE V**		Article 45
	Chapter 1		Article 46
	Article 21		
	Article 22	**TITLE VI (repealed)**[17]	
	Chapter 2	Article 29 (replaced)[18]	
	Section 1	Article 30 (replaced)[19]	
	Article 23	Article 31 (replaced)[20]	
Article 11	Article 24	Article 32 (replaced)[21]	
Article 12	Article 25	Article 33 (replaced)[22]	
Article 13	Article 26	Article 34 (repealed)	
	Article 27	Article 35 (repealed)	
Article 14	Article 28	Article 36 (replaced)[23]	
Article 15	Article 29	Article 37 (repealed)	
Article 22 (moved)	Article 30	Article 38 (repealed)	
Article 23 (moved)	Article 31	Article 39 (repealed)	
Article 16	Article 32	Article 40 (replaced)[24]	*Article 20*
Article 17 (moved)	*Article 42*	Article 40 A (replaced)[24]	*Article 20*
Article 18	Article 33	Article 40 B (replaced)[24]	*Article 20*
Article 19	Article 34	Article 41 (repealed)	
Article 20	Article 35	Article 42 (repealed)	
Article 21	Article 36		
Article 22 (moved)	*Article 30*	**TITLE VII (replaced)**[25]	**TITLE IV**
Article 23 (moved)	*Article 31*	Article 43 (replaced)[25]	*Article 20*
Article 24	Article 37	Article 43 A (replaced)[25]	*Article 20*
Article 25	Article 38	Article 43 B (replaced)[25]	*Article 20*
	Article 39	Article 44 (replaced)[25]	*Article 20*
Article 47 (moved)	Article 40	Article 44 A (replaced)[25]	*Article 20*
Article 26 (repealed)		Article 45 (replaced)[25]	*Article 20*
Article 27 (repealed)		**TITLE VIII**	**TITLE VI**
Article 27a (replaced)[16]	*Article 20*	Article 46 (repealed)	
Article 27b (replaced)[16]	*Article 20*		Article 47
Article 27c (replaced)[16]	*Article 20*	Article 47 (replaced)	*Article 40*
Article 27d (replaced)[16]	*Article 20*	Article 48	Article 48
Article 27e (replaced)[16]	*Article 20*	Article 49	Article 49
Article 28	Article 41		Article 50
	Section 2		Article 51
Article 17 (moved)	Article 42		Article 52
	Article 43	Article 50 (repealed)	
	Article 44	Article 51	Article 53
		Article 52	Article 54
		Article 53	Article 55

[16] The previous Articles 27a to 27e, on enhanced cooperation, were also replaced by Articles 326 to 334 TFEU.

[17] The previous provisions of Title VI of the TEU, on police and judicial cooperation in criminal matters, were replaced by the provisions of Chapters 1, 4 and 5 of Title IV of Part Three of the TFEU.

[18] Replaced by Article 67 TFEU.   [19] Replaced by Articles 87 and 88 TFEU.

[20] Replaced by Articles 82, 83 and 85 TFEU.   [21] Replaced by Article 89 TFEU.

[22] Replaced by Article 72 TFEU.   [23] Replaced by Article 71 TFEU.

[24] The previous Articles 40 to 40b TEU, on enhanced cooperation, were also replaced by Articles 326 to 334 TFEU.

[25] The previous Articles 43 to 45 and Title VII of the TEU, on enhanced cooperation, were also replaced by Articles 326 to 334 TFEU.

TREATY ON THE FUNCTIONING OF THE EUROPEAN UNION

Old numbering of the Treaty establishing the European Community	New numbering of the Treaty on the Functioning of the European Union	Old numbering of the Treaty establishing the European Community	New numbering of the Treaty on the Functioning of the European Union
PART ONE	**PART ONE**	Article 17	Article 20
Article 1 (repealed)		Article 18	Article 21
	Article 1	Article 19	Article 22
Article 2 (repealed)[26]		Article 20	Article 23
	Title I	Article 21	Article 24
	Article 2	Article 22	Article 25
	Article 3	**PART THREE**	**PART THREE**
	Article 4		Title I
	Article 5	*Article 14 (moved)*	Article 26
	Article 6	*Article 15 (moved)*	Article 27
	Title II	**Title I**	**Title II**
	Article 7	Article 23	Article 28
Article 3, paragraph 1 (repealed)[27]		Article 24	Article 29
		Chapter 1	Chapter 1
Article 3, paragraph 2	Article 8	Article 25	Article 30
Article 4 (moved)	*Article 119*	Article 26	Article 31
Article 5 (replaced)[28]		Article 27	Article 32
	Article 9	*Part Three, Title X (moved)*	Chapter 2
	Article 10		
Article 6	Article 11	*Article 135 (moved)*	Article 33
Article 153, paragraph 2 (moved)	Article 12	Chapter 2	Chapter 3
		Article 28	Article 34
	Article 132[29]	Article 29	Article 35
Article 7 (repealed)[30]		Article 30	Article 36
Article 8 (repealed)[31]		Article 31	Article 37
Article 9 (repealed)		**Title II**	**Title III**
Article 10 (repealed)[32]		Article 32	Article 38
Article 11 (replaced)[33]	*Articles 326 to 334*	Article 33	Article 39
Article 11a (replaced)[33]	*Articles 326 to 334*	Article 34	Article 40
Article 12 (repealed)	*Article 18*	Article 35	Article 41
Article 13 (moved)	*Article 19*	Article 36	Article 42
Article 14 (moved)	*Article 26*	Article 37	Article 43
Article 15 (moved)	*Article 27*	Article 38	Article 44
Article 16	Article 14	**Title III**	**Title IV**
Article 255 (moved)	Article 15	Chapter 1	Chapter 1
Article 286 (moved)	Article 16	Article 39	Article 45
	Article 17	Article 40	Article 46
PART TWO	**PART TWO**		
Article 12 (moved)	Article 18		
Article 13 (moved)	Article 19		

[26] Replaced, in substance, by Article 3 TEU.
[27] Replaced, in substance, by Articles 3 to 6 TFEU.
[28] Replaced, in substance, by Article 5 TEU.
[29] Insertion of the operative part of the Protocol on protection and welfare of animals.
[30] Replaced, in substance, by Article 13 TEU.
[31] Replaced, in substance, by Article 13 TEU and Article 282, paragraph 1, TFEU.
[32] Replaced, in substance, by Article 4, paragraph 3, TEU.   [33] Also replaced by Article 20 TEU.

Old numbering of the Treaty establishing the European Community	New numbering of the Treaty on the Functioning of the European Union
Article 41	Article 47
Article 42	Article 48
Chapter 2	Chapter 2
Article 43	Article 49
Article 44	Article 50
Article 45	Article 51
Article 46	Article 52
Article 47	Article 53
Article 48	Article 54
Article 294 (moved)	Article 55
Chapter 3	Chapter 3
Article 49	Article 56
Article 50	Article 57
Article 51	Article 58
Article 52	Article 59
Article 53	Article 60
Article 54	Article 61
Article 55	Article 62
Chapter 4	Chapter 4
Article 56	Article 63
Article 57	Article 64
Article 58	Article 65
Article 59	Article 66
Article 60 (moved)	*Article 75*
Title IV	**Title V**
	Chapter 1
Article 61	Article 67^{34}
	Article 68
	Article 69
	Article 70
	Article 71^{35}
Article 64, paragraph 1 (replaced)	Article 72^{36}
	Article 73
Article 66 (replaced)	Article 74
Article 60 (moved)	Article 75
	Article 76
	Chapter 2
Article 62	Article 77
Article 63, points 1 and 2, and Article 64, paragraph 2^{37}	Article 78
Article 63, points 3 and 4	Article 79
	Article 80
Article 64, paragraph 1 (replaced)	*Article 72*
	Chapter 3

Old numbering of the Treaty establishing the European Community	New numbering of the Treaty on the Functioning of the European Union
Article 65	Article 81
Article 66 (replaced)	*Article 74*
Article 67 (repealed)	
Article 68 (repealed)	
Article 69 (repealed)	
	Chapter 4
	Article 82^{38}
	Article 83^{38}
	Article 84
	Article 85^{38}
	Article 86
	Chapter 5
	Article 87^{39}
	Article 88^{39}
	Article 89^{40}
Title V	**Title VI**
Article 70	Article 90
Article 71	Article 91
Article 72	Article 92
Article 73	Article 93
Article 74	Article 94
Article 75	Article 95
Article 76	Article 96
Article 77	Article 97
Article 78	Article 98
Article 79	Article 99
Article 80	Article 100

[34] Also replaced the previous Article 29 TEU.   [35] Also replaced the previous Article 36 TEU.
[36] Also replaced the previous Article 33 TEU.
[37] Points 1 and 2 of Article 63 EC were replaced by paragraphs 1 and 2 of Article 78 TFEU, and paragraph 2 of Article 64 was replaced by paragraph 3 of Article 78 TFEU.
[38] Replaced the previous Article 31 TEU.   [39] Replaced the previous Article 30 TEU.
[40] Replaced the previous Article 32 TEU.

Old numbering of the Treaty establishing the European Community	New numbering of the Treaty on the Functioning of the European Union
Title VI	Title VII
Chapter 1	Chapter 1
Section 1	Section 1
Article 81	Article 101
Article 82	Article 102
Article 83	Article 103
Article 84	Article 104
Article 85	Article 105
Article 86	Article 106
Section 2	Section 2
Article 87	Article 107
Article 88	Article 108
Article 89	Article 109
Chapter 2	Chapter 2
Article 90	Article 110
Article 91	Article 111
Article 92	Article 112
Article 93	Article 113
Chapter 3	Chapter 3
Article 95 (moved)	Article 114
Article 94 (moved)	Article 115
Article 96	Article 116
Article 97	Article 117
	Article 118
Title VII	Title VIII
Article 4 (moved)	Article 119
Chapter 1	Chapter 1
Article 98	Article 120
Article 99	Article 121
Article 100	Article 122
Article 101	Article 123
Article 102	Article 124
Article 103	Article 125
Article 104	Article 126
Chapter 2	Chapter 2
Article 105	Article 127
Article 106	Article 128
Article 107	Article 129
Article 108	Article 130
Article 109	Article 131
Article 110	Article 132
Article 111, paragraphs 1 to 3 and 5 (moved)	*Article 219*
Article 111, paragraph 4 (moved)	*Article 138*
	Article 133
Chapter 3	Chapter 3

Old numbering of the Treaty establishing the European Community	New numbering of the Treaty on the Functioning of the European Union
Article 112 (moved)	*Article 283*
Article 113 (moved)	*Article 284*
Article 114	Article 134
Article 115	Article 135
	Chapter 4
	Article 136
	Article 137
Article 111, paragraph 4 (moved)	Article 138
Chapter 4	Chapter 5
Article 116 (repealed)	
	Article 139
Article 117, paragraph 2, first five indents (moved)	*Article 141, paragraph 2*
Article 117, paragraphs 1, 2, sixth indent, and 3 to 9 (repealed)	
Article 121, paragraph 1 (moved)	
Article 122, paragraph 2, second sentence (moved)	Article 140[41]
Article 123, paragraph 5 (moved)	
Article 118 (repealed)	
Article 123, paragraph 3 (moved)	Article 141[42]
Article 117, paragraph 2, first five indents (moved)	
Article 124, paragraph 1 (moved)	Article 142
Article 119	Article 143
Article 120	Article 144
Article 121, paragraph 1 (moved)	*Article 140, paragraph 1*
Article 121, paragraphs 2 to 4 (repealed)	
Article 122, paragraphs 1, 2, first sentence, 3, 4, 5 and 6 (repealed)	
Article 122, paragraph 2, second sentence (moved)	*Article 140, paragraph 2, first subparagraph*
Article 123, paragraphs 1, 2 and 4 (repealed)	
Article 123, paragraph 3 (moved)	*Article 141, paragraph 1*
Article 123, paragraph 5 (moved)	*Article 140, paragraph 3*
Article 124, paragraph 1 (moved)	*Article 142*

[41] – Article 140, paragraph 1, took over the wording of paragraph 1 of Article 121.
    – Article 140, paragraph 2, took over the second sentence of paragraph 2 of Article 122.
    – Article 140, paragraph 3, took over paragraph 5 of Article 123.

[42] – Article 141, paragraph 1, took over paragraph 3 of Article 123.
    – Article 141, paragraph 2, took over the first five indents of paragraph 2 of Article 117.

Old numbering of the Treaty establishing the European Community	New numbering of the Treaty on the Functioning of the European Union
Article 124, paragraph 2 (repealed)	
Title VIII	**Title IX**
Article 125	Article 145
Article 126	Article 146
Article 127	Article 147
Article 128	Article 148
Article 129	Article 149
Article 130	Article 150
Title IX (moved)	*Part Five, Title II*
Article 131 (moved)	*Article 206*
Article 132 (repealed)	
Article 133 (moved)	*Article 207*
Article 134 (repealed)	
Title X (moved)	*Part Three, Title II, Chapter 2*
Article 135 (moved)	*Article 33*
Title XI	**Title X**
Chapter 1 (repealed)	
Article 136	Article 151
	Article 152
Article 137	Article 153
Article 138	Article 154
Article 139	Article 155
Article 140	Article 156
Article 141	Article 157
Article 142	Article 158
Article 143	Article 159
Article 144	Article 160
Article 145	Article 161
Chapter 2	**Title XI**
Article 146	Article 162
Article 147	Article 163
Article 148	Article 164
Chapter 3	**Title XII**
Article 149	Article 165
Article 150	Article 166
Title XII	Title XIII
Article 151	Article 167
Title XIII	Title XIV
Article 152	Article 168
Title XIV	Title XV
Article 153, paragraphs 1, 3, 4 and 5	Article 169
Article 153, paragraph 2 (moved)	*Article 12*

Old numbering of the Treaty establishing the European Community	New numbering of the Treaty on the Functioning of the European Union
Title XV	**Title XVI**
Article 154	Article 170
Article 155	Article 171
Article 156	Article 172
Title XVI	**Title XVII**
Article 157	Article 173
Title XVII	**Title XVIII**
Article 158	Article 174
Article 159	Article 175
Article 160	Article 176
Article 161	Article 177
Article 162	Article 178
Title XVIII	**Title XIX**
Article 163	Article 179
Article 164	Article 180
Article 165	Article 181
Article 166	Article 182
Article 167	Article 183
Article 168	Article 184
Article 169	Article 185
Article 170	Article 186
Article 171	Article 187
Article 172	Article 188
	Article 189
Article 173	Article 190
Title XIX	**Title XX**
Article 174	Article 191
Article 175	Article 192
Article 176	Article 193
	Title XXI
	Article 194
	Title XXII
	Article 195
	Title XXIII
	Article 196
	Title XXIV
	Article 197
Title XX (moved)	*Part Five, Title III, Chapter 1*
Article 177 (moved)	*Article 208*
Article 178 (repealed)[43]	
Article 179 (moved)	*Article 209*
Article 180 (moved)	*Article 210*
Article 181 (moved)	*Article 211*
Title XXI (moved)	*Part Five, Title III, Chapter 2*
Article 181a (moved)	*Article 212*

[43] Replaced, in substance, by the second sentence of the second subparagraph of paragraph 1 of Article 208 TFEU.

Old numbering of the Treaty establishing the European Community	New numbering of the Treaty on the Functioning of the European Union	Old numbering of the Treaty establishing the European Community	New numbering of the Treaty on the Functioning of the European Union
PART FOUR	**PART FOUR**	**PART FIVE**	**PART SIX**
Article 182	Article 198	Title I	Title I
Article 183	Article 199	Chapter 1	Chapter 1
Article 184	Article 200	Section 1	Section 1
Article 185	Article 201	Article 189 (repealed)[45]	
Article 186	Article 202	Article 190, paragraphs 1 to 3 (repealed)[46]	
Article 187	Article 203	Article 190, paragraphs 4 and 5	Article 223
Article 188	Article 204		
	PART FIVE	Article 191, first paragraph (repealed)[47]	
	Title I	Article 191, second paragraph	Article 224
	Article 205		
Part Three, Title IX (moved)	**Title II**	Article 192, first paragraph (repealed)[48]	
Article 131 (moved)	Article 206	Article 192, second paragraph	Article 225
Article 133 (moved)	Article 207	Article 193	Article 226
	Title III	Article 194	Article 227
Part Three, Title XX (moved)	Chapter 1	Article 195	Article 228
Article 177 (moved)	Article 208[44]	Article 196	Article 229
Article 179 (moved)	Article 209	Article 197, first paragraph (repealed)[49]	
Article 180 (moved)	Article 210	Article 197, second, third and fourth paragraphs	Article 230
Article 181 (moved)	Article 211		
Part Three, Title XXI (moved)	Chapter 2	Article 198	Article 231
Article 181a (moved)	Article 212	Article 199	Article 232
	Article 213	Article 200	Article 233
	Chapter 3	Article 201	Article 234
	Article 214		Section 2
	Title IV		Article 235
Article 301 (replaced)	Article 215		Article 236
	Title V	Section 2	Section 3
	Article 216	Article 202 (repealed)[50]	
Article 310 (moved)	Article 217	Article 203 (repealed)[51]	
Article 300 (replaced)	Article 218	Article 204	Article 237
Article 111, paragraphs 1 to 3 and 5 (moved)	Article 219	Article 205, paragraphs 2 and 4 (repealed)[52]	
	Title VI	Article 205, paragraphs 1 and 3	Article 238
Articles 302 to 304 (replaced)	Article 220	Article 206	Article 239
	Article 221	Article 207	Article 240
	Title VII	Article 208	Article 241
	Article 222		

[44] The second sentence of the second subparagraph of paragraph 1 replaced, in substance, Article 178 TEC.
[45] Replaced, in substance, by Article 14, paragraphs 1 and 2, TEU.
[46] Replaced, in substance, by Article 14, paragraphs 1 to 3, TEU.
[47] Replaced, in substance, by Article 11, paragraph 4, TEU.
[48] Replaced, in substance, by Article 14, paragraph 1, TEU.
[49] Replaced, in substance, by Article 14, paragraph 4, TEU.
[50] Replaced, in substance, by Article 16, paragraph 1, TEU and by Articles 290 and 291 TFEU.
[51] Replaced, in substance, by Article 16, paragraphs 2 and 9 TEU.
[52] Replaced, in substance, by Article 16, paragraphs 4 and 5 TEU.

Old numbering of the Treaty establishing the European Community	New numbering of the Treaty on the Functioning of the European Union	Old numbering of the Treaty establishing the European Community	New numbering of the Treaty on the Functioning of the European Union
Article 209	Article 242	Article 236	Article 270
Article 210	Article 243	Article 237	Article 271
Section 3	Section 4	Article 238	Article 272
Article 211 (repealed)[53]		Article 239	Article 273
	Article 244	Article 240	Article 274
Article 212 (moved)	*Article 249, paragraph 2*		Article 275
Article 213	Article 245		Article 276
Article 214 (repealed)[54]		Article 241	Article 277
Article 215	Article 246	Article 242	Article 278
Article 216	Article 247	Article 243	Article 279
Article 217, paragraphs 1, 3 and 4 (repealed)[55]		Article 244	Article 280
		Article 245	Article 281
Article 217, paragraph 2	Article 248		Section 6
Article 218, paragraph 1 (repealed)[56]			Article 282
		Article 112 (moved)	Article 283
Article 218, paragraph 2	Article 249	*Article 113 (moved)*	Article 284
Article 219	Article 250	Section 5	Section 7
Section 4	Section 5	Article 246	Article 285
Article 220 (repealed)[57]		Article 247	Article 286
Article 221, first paragraph (repealed)[58]		Article 248	Article 287
Article 221, second and third paragraphs	Article 251	Chapter 2	Chapter 2
			Section 1
		Article 249	Article 288
Article 222	Article 252		Article 289
Article 223	Article 253		Article 290[60]
Article 224[59]	Article 254		Article 291[60]
	Article 255		Article 292
Article 225	Article 256		Section 2
Article 225a	Article 257	Article 250	Article 293
Article 226	Article 258	Article 251	Article 294
Article 227	Article 259	Article 252 (repealed)	
Article 228	Article 260		Article 295
Article 229	Article 261	Article 253	Article 296
Article 229a	Article 262	Article 254	Article 297
Article 230	Article 263		Article 298
Article 231	Article 264	Article 255 (moved)	*Article 15*
Article 232	Article 265	Article 256	Article 299
Article 233	Article 266		Chapter 3
Article 234	Article 267		Article 300
Article 235	Article 268	Chapter 3	Section 1
	Article 269	Article 257 (repealed)[61]	

[53] Replaced, in substance, by Article 17, paragraph 1, TEU.

[54] Replaced, in substance, by Article 17, paragraphs 3 and 7, TEU.

[55] Replaced, in substance, by Article 17, paragraph 6, TEU.

[56] Replaced, in substance, by Article 295 TFEU.   [57] Replaced, in substance, by Article 19 TEU.

[58] Replaced, in substance, by Article 19, paragraph 2, first subparagraph of the TEU.

[59] The first sentence of the first subparagraph was replaced, in substance, by Article 19, paragraph 2, second subparagraph of the TEU.   [60] Replaced, in substance, the third indent of Article 202 TEC.

[61] Replaced, in substance, by Article 300, paragraph 2 of the TFEU.

Old numbering of the Treaty establishing the European Community	New numbering of the Treaty on the Functioning of the European Union	Old numbering of the Treaty establishing the European Community	New numbering of the Treaty on the Functioning of the European Union
Article 258, first, second and fourth paragraphs	Article 301	Article 280	Article 325
Article 258, third paragraph (repealed)[62]			Title III
Article 259	Article 302	*Articles 11 and 11a (replaced)*	Article 326[65]
Article 260	Article 303	*Articles 11 and 11a (replaced)*	Article 327[65]
Article 261 (repealed)		*Articles 11 and 11a (replaced)*	Article 328[65]
Article 262	Article 304	*Articles 11 and 11a (replaced)*	Article 329[65]
Chapter 4	Section 2	*Articles 11 and 11a (replaced)*	Article 330[65]
Article 263, first and fifth paragraphs (repealed)[63]		*Articles 11 and 11a (replaced)*	Article 331[65]
Article 263, second to fourth paragraphs	Article 305	*Articles 11 and 11a (replaced)*	Article 332[65]
Article 264	Article 306	*Articles 11 and 11a (replaced)*	Article 333[65]
Article 265	Article 307	*Articles 11 and 11a (replaced)*	Article 334[65]
Chapter 5	Chapter 4	**PART SIX**	**PART SEVEN**
Article 266	Article 308	Article 281 (repealed)[66]	
Article 267	Article 309	Article 282	Article 335
Title II	Title II	Article 283	Article 336
Article 268	Article 310	Article 284	Article 337
	Chapter 1	Article 285	Article 338
Article 269	Article 311	Article 286 (replaced)	*Article 16*
Article 270 (repealed)[64]		Article 287	Article 339
	Chapter 2	Article 288	Article 340
	Article 312	Article 289	Article 341
	Chapter 3	Article 290	Article 342
Article 272, paragraph 1 (moved)	Article 313	Article 291	Article 343
Article 271 (moved)	*Article 316*	Article 292	Article 344
Article 272, paragraph 1 (moved)	*Article 313*	Article 293 (repealed)	
Article 272, paragraphs 2 to 10	Article 314	Article 294 (moved)	*Article 55*
Article 273	Article 315	Article 295	Article 345
Article 271 (moved)	Article 316	Article 296	Article 346
	Chapter 4	Article 297	Article 347
Article 274	Article 317	Article 298	Article 348
Article 275	Article 318	Article 299, paragraph 1 (repealed)[67]	
Article 276	Article 319	Article 299, paragraph 2, second, third and fourth subparagraphs	Article 349
	Chapter 5	Article 299, paragraph 2, first subparagraph, and paragraphs 3 to 6 (moved)	*Article 355*
Article 277	Article 320		
Article 278	Article 321		
Article 279	Article 322		
	Article 323		
	Article 324		
	Chapter 6		

[62] Replaced, in substance, by Article 300, paragraph 4 of the TFEU.
[63] Replaced, in substance, by Article 300, paragraphs 3 and 4, TFEU.
[64] Replaced, in substance, by Article 310, paragraph 4, TFEU.
[65] Also replaced the previous Articles 27a to 27e, 40 to 40b, and 43 to 45 TEU.
[66] Replaced, in substance, by Article 47 TEU.   [67] Replaced, in substance by Article 52 TEU.

Old numbering of the Treaty establishing the European Community	New numbering of the Treaty on the Functioning of the European Union	Old numbering of the Treaty establishing the European Community	New numbering of the Treaty on the Functioning of the European Union
Article 300 (replaced)	*Article 218*	Article 310 (moved)	*Article 217*
Article 301 (replaced)	*Article 215*	Article 311 (repealed)[68]	
Article 302 (replaced)	*Article 220*	*Article 299, paragraph 2, first subparagraph, and paragraphs 3 to 6 (moved)*	Article 355
Article 303 (replaced)	*Article 220*		
Article 304 (replaced)	*Article 220*		
Article 305 (repealed)		Article 312	Article 356
Article 306	Article 350	Final Provisions	
Article 307	Article 351	Article 313	Article 357
Article 308	Article 352		Article 358
	Article 353		
Article 309	Article 354	Article 314 (repealed)[69]	

[68] Replaced, in substance by Article 51 TEU.   [69] Replaced, in substance by Article 55 TEU.

1

Introduction

Catherine Barnard and Steve Peers

1 Introduction

For many people European Union (EU) law interferes with too many aspects of their lives. This was summed up by the headline in a UK paper: 'Bog standard: Brussels demands the same toilet flush across the Continent after discovering Brits use the most water'.[1] This story has it all: mad Brussels bureaucrats excessively regulating even how we go to the toilet; 'Loo couldn't make it up' said UK tabloid *The Sun*. Yet a closer look reveals a different picture. As the European Commission pointed out,[2] toilet flushing accounts for about 30 per cent of total household water consumption in the UK. Much of this water use is unnecessary. So an eco-label can help buyers choose loos that will save water and money. Eco-labelling measures already exist for washing machines and dishwashers and it is perfectly logical to take steps to help people buy more efficient toilets. In a single market where products are being sold across borders, this is best done at EU level.[3] The question, then, is who is right: *The Sun* or the Commission?

The story about the loo flush raises in microcosm some of the biggest questions facing the EU today: what should it be doing, how should it be doing it, and how should it be communicating what it is doing. A bottom-up approach (no pun intended) would suggest that loo flushing should be a matter for national law; a top-down single market perspective would suggest that the EU should intervene when the movement of goods across borders is affected. If the EU does act, how intensive should that action be? The eco-labelling award scheme reveals an imaginative approach to regulation. The use of these eco-labels is

---

[1] http://www.dailymail.co.uk/news/article-2480829/Bog-standard-Brussels-demands-toilet-flush-Continent-discovering-Brits-use-water.html#ixzz2llsEoH4v

[2] http://ec.europa.eu/unitedkingdom/blog/

[3] A Commission study estimates that even with only 10 per cent market penetration for eco-label toilets, the cumulative savings for households alone across the EU would exceed £330 million (€388.5 million). With 20 per cent market penetration, that figure would roughly double. Pro rata that would mean roughly £70 million in the UK, with at least as much again saved by non-household users.

voluntary:[4] industries apply for the label if they want to get it and the beneficial reputational kudos that goes with it. They may choose not to. However, if they do apply, their product needs to comply with the criteria set for each product group (eg washing machines, fridges, and now toilets) by a Commission Decision[5] adopted under powers conferred by Council Regulation 1980/2000.[6]

Thus, contrary to popular misconception, EU rules are not all of the command and control kind (all bananas must be straight). The EU has experimented with different types of regulation to create flexibility in the operation of its rules. This flexibility is provided by the law and, as this book will show, the law is central to the operation of the EU.

Indeed, the EU itself is a legal construct.[7] It was born out of treaties and its subsequent development has been marked by successive Treaty amendments. One of the earliest major research projects on the EU described the process as 'integration through law';[8] and the Court of Justice, the supreme court of the EU, has been in the engine room of that process. Of course, law and politics go hand in hand and no lawyer would deny the important role played by politicians in both driving forward and shaping the development of the EU, particularly faced with seismic geopolitical forces – the fall of the Berlin Wall, 9/11, and the sovereign debt crisis. Although the hegemony of law may have waned over recent years, as problems have arisen which are not immediately amenable to legal resolution, law remains central to the EU project. And it is the law, set in this broader political context, which is the subject matter of this book.

2 The development of EU law

In the early days, the EU focused upon economic integration: the free movement of goods, persons, capital, and services,[9] collectively known as the four freedoms, along with competition law and control of government support to industry, known as 'State aid'.[10] The basic idea was simple but fundamental: due to closer trade ties States would become dependent on each other and thus the imperative to go to war would be reduced.

However, the material scope (ie the subject matter) of EU law has been widening beyond these issues for many years.[11] For example, the original Treaty establishing what was then the European Economic Community (EEC) already made some reference to social policy, but due to concerns about the impact of economic integration upon social standards, the EU has since developed a significant body of law in this area.[12] Owing to growing concern about environmental protection and consumer protection, including the possible impact of economic integration upon national environment and consumer law, the EU has also developed law in these areas too.[13] Even an area of law which in principle the EU largely leaves to the Member States to regulate – health care – is significantly affected

---

[4] http://ec.europa.eu/environment/ecolabel/information-and-contacts.html

[5] See eg Commission Decision 2000/45 establishing the ecological criteria for the award of the Community eco-label to washing machines (OJ [2000] L16/74). [6] OJ [2000] L237/1.

[7] This phrase was used by the British Attorney General, Dominic Grieve, in a newspaper interview http://www.telegraph.co.uk/news/politics/10469453/Dominic-Grieve-were-a-changing-nation-but-Im-an-optimist.html

[8] M Cappelletti, M Seccombe, and JHH Weiler (eds), *Integration through Law* (Berlin: De Gruyter, 1985).

[9] For details, see chapters 11–16. [10] See respectively chapters 17 and 18.

[11] For a more detailed overview of the development of the EU, see chapter 2.

[12] For details, see chapter 20. [13] For details, see chapters 22 and 23.

by the economic integration process.[14] This is the spillover effect which Jean Monnet, one of the founding fathers of the EU project, hoped would occur once the process of integration had started. As the theory of neofunctionalism describes it, integration in one sector necessitates integration in another sector to ensure that the advantage of integration in the first sector is maximized. So Member States could legitimately obstruct the free movement of goods due to concerns about consumer protection or the environment.[15] This necessitates harmonization in these sectors in order to facilitate free movement of goods.

Taking this one stage further, if exporters of goods within the EU are really to benefit from the economies of scale offered by the single market, then they need to enjoy the certainty offered by having a single currency. It was this biggest step of all that was launched by the Maastricht Treaty in 1992, which set out a framework for the EU to create an economic and monetary union (EMU). The majority of Member States now share a single currency, and in connection with this, the EU coordinates Member States' fiscal and economic policies. The intensity of this coordination has strengthened since the single currency project began to face increasing difficulties in light of the economic crisis, beginning in 2008, and it became necessary for some Member States to 'bail out' other Member States in order for the currency to survive.

Discussions are now underway for ever-closer integration of Member States' economic policies and greater political control of those policies by the EU institutions, at least in the case of eurozone States.[16] The centripetal forces at play point to ever-greater centralization – at the very time when citizens in a number of countries are calling for a repatriation of powers to the Member States. This tension between the needs for effective governance of the European project while respecting State autonomy and diversity at national level has tormented the EU since its inception. For some, this tension is creative and leads to better solutions in the longer term, preventing the EU from overreaching itself. For others, it has handicapped the EU in its ability to respond to the crisis – the German refusal to agree to Eurobonds (the joint pooling of some or all of the eurozone States' government debt), widely seen as an important pillar in resolving the crisis, is a case in point. The German refusal, wholly comprehensible in terms of domestic politics, shows that neofunctionalism is too simplistic a theory to describe the complex interactions in the EU. Governments, particularly in Germany and France, continue to call the shots when it really matters and this intergovernmentalism is reflected in the role of the European Council, now one of the most important EU institutions.[17]

The EU has also become a major forum for integration as regards issues which, at first sight, are non-economic. While the EU always had a common policy on trade with third (ie non-EU) countries, known as the 'common commercial policy', and many of its internal policies have a significant external dimension (eg EU environment policy), the EU has also taken steps towards creating a Common Foreign and Security Policy, including defence issues.[18] In addition, the EU has increasingly addressed issues within the scope of justice and home affairs, matters traditionally seen as lying at the heart of national sovereignty, in particular criminal law and immigration and asylum matters.[19] In practice, even these issues have important links with economic integration, since the abolition of border controls between most Member States has meant that it is easier for alleged criminals to flee

---

[14] For details, see chapter 21.
[15] For details, see chapters 12 and 16. For more on the concept of neofunctionalism, see chapter 2.
[16] For details, see chapter 19.   [17] For details, see chapter 3.
[18] On all of these issues, see chapter 24.   [19] For details, see respectively chapters 25 and 26.

from one Member State to another, and harder to apply a purely national policy on asylum and immigration.

Along with this widening of the material scope of EU law, the EU's territorial scope has widened greatly too, with its membership expanding from six to 28 Member States.[20]

The ever-growing impact of EU law has also been accelerated by the very nature of EU law, because (for many Member States) EU law has a much greater force within national legal systems than most other international treaties.[21] Indeed, there is an important debate as to whether EU law can still be regarded as a form of international law at all, or whether it has become *sui generis* (meaning, 'in a class by itself').[22]

Over the years, EU law has not just widened its material and territorial scope, but it has also developed a complex institutional framework for the adoption and enforcement of its law, establishing both a political and a judicial system to that end.[23] Like any complex legal system, the EU has developed basic principles that govern the application of that system, as well as rules which govern its administration.[24] One of these key principles is the requirement to protect human rights,[25] which has become increasingly important as (for example) EU law concerns itself with more issues (eg criminal law and asylum) that impact upon civil liberties,[26] and as EU austerity policies (intended to address the economic and financial crisis linked to EMU) have an ever-greater impact upon social rights.[27]

More broadly, the constitutional and administrative law of the EU as a whole raises questions about the nature of national sovereignty in the EU legal order and the EU's fidelity to basic constitutional principles, such as the separation of powers.[28] This raises even more fundamental questions – does the EU have a constitution, following the demise of the Constitutional Treaty,[29] and if so, what sort? How does the EU's special brand of constitutionalism accommodate uniformity and diversity, as well as the role of the centre and that of national and sub-national actors? This has led to an increasingly sophisticated debate about the role of multi-level governance (the idea that there are various interacting authority structures at work) *within* the EU. But it also raises questions as to how the EU relates to other major international bodies *outside* its own sphere of influence.[30] The United Nations (UN) is a prime example, as featured in the terrorist asset-freezing cases.[31] How open can and should the EU be to these external bodies?

3 Themes

The chapters of this book are linked by overarching themes, which can be introduced in the form of two questions: 'What should the EU be doing?' and 'How should the EU go about doing it?'

The question of *what* the EU should do is linked to the concept of '*output* legitimacy', that is, the EU proving its value to the public by showing that it is effective in contributing to the achievement of objectives which have wide public support (eg economic growth and job creation). The question of *how* the EU should accomplish these tasks is linked to

---

[20] For an overview of EU enlargement, see chapter 2.   [21] For details, see chapter 6.

[22] For details of this debate, see chapter 7.

[23] On the political system, see chapter 3; on the judicial system, see chapter 10; and on the decision-making process, see chapter 5.   [24] For details, see chapter 8.

[25] For details, see chapter 9.   [26] See chapters 25 and 26.

[27] See chapters 19 and 20.   [28] For a detailed discussion, see chapter 4.

[29] On the failed attempt to draw up a Constitutional Treaty for the EU, see further chapter 2.

[30] See further chapter 24.   [31] See the case studies in chapters 8 and 9.

the concept of '*input* legitimacy', that is, how fair and democratic is the process by which the EU takes decisions. These two types of legitimacy are linked, because if the EU tries to do more things, more questions are likely to be raised about its democratic credentials.[32] Indeed, the two forms of legitimacy might come into direct conflict, where, for instance, an attempt to make the EU more effective by removing Member States' vetoes over a policy area (which will make it easier for the EU to take decisions) could be seen as a reduction in democratic legitimacy, from the point of view of a national parliament (which will no longer have full sovereignty over decisions in that policy area).

3.1 Input legitimacy

The EU has various systems in place to help achieve input legitimacy: the doctrines of separation of powers,[33] the vertical division of competences between the States and the EU,[34] and a powerful judicial system[35] which has been active in developing the 'general principles of EU law' (including the principles of proportionality, the rule of law (transparency, legality, legal certainty, and legitimate expectations), good administration, information-related rights (freedom of information and data protection), and procedural rights (the right to be heard, the right to an effective judicial remedy, and additional rights of the defence)) as tools to review the activities of the EU legislature and executive, as well as those of the Member States when acting within the scope of EU law.[36]

These principles are linked to the broader system for the protection of human rights in the EU legal order, which was restructured in 2009 to provide for a binding EU Charter of Fundamental Rights and an obligation for the EU to sign up to the European Convention on Human Rights, which has now resulted in a draft treaty to this end.[37] Specific tensions between human rights and security objectives can be seen in the regulation of immigration and asylum law (ie the entry and residence of non-EU citizens) by the EU[38] and between human rights and the power for national authorities to decide which citizens of other EU Member States can come into the territory and stay there.[39] The protection of human rights has become directly linked to the creation of EU citizenship: the introduction of EU citizenship has profoundly altered the way in which the Court of Justice has viewed nationals of one Member State who move to another Member State.[40] This, in itself, has raised further questions about the legitimacy of the Court of Justice within the EU system with notions of separation of powers.

Moreover, these fundamental questions about the EU's legitimacy raise a further set of questions, in particular: 'How much should the EU do, as compared to its Member States?' and 'How should EU law reconcile tensions between different objectives – particularly between economic and non-economic objectives?' Of course, the answers to these questions might change over time, or be different in varied policy fields. Again, the two questions are necessarily linked: the more that the EU gets involved with a particular policy area, the less capacity for Member States to make their own individual decisions about how to balance economic and non-economic objectives in that area. These questions could be described as raising respectively a *vertical* issue – the 'division of powers' between the EU and its Member States – and a *horizontal* issue – regarding the relative priority of economic over non-economic objectives.

---

[32] For details, see chapter 2.   [33] For details, see chapter 4.   [34] For details, see chapter 5.
[35] For details, see chapter 10.   [36] For details, see chapter 8.
[37] For further details, see chapter 9.   [38] For further details, see chapter 26.
[39] For further details, see chapters 13 and 16.   [40] For further details, see chapter 13.

In respect of the vertical question of how much should the EU do, the Member States are inevitably conflicted. This can be seen in the field of external relations where Member States want to maintain control over EU external policies while at the same time aspiring to make them more effective.[41] Likewise, in the field of EU criminal law, Member States are torn between a desire to reap the practical benefits of cooperation in matters of criminal law and their concern about the loss of sovereignty in this sensitive field.[42] A similar dynamic applies in immigration and asylum law.[43] If the EU does act and a Member State objects, then it is the Court of Justice which polices the boundary. Its decisions have influenced the level of EU intervention: the more the Court checks whether the criteria for EU action have been satisfied, the more likely it is to strike down a measure. In practice, its review has been generally light touch, with one notable exception, the decision in *Tobacco Advertising I*.[44] This highlights the tension between input and output legitimacy: if the EU wants to deliver in a particular policy area it needs to have the powers and to exercise them in the way that it chooses. However, this may come at the price of national sovereignty.

What if individuals object about what the EU is doing? Do they have a voice? If that voice means bringing a case to court to challenge the EU's use of its powers, the Court of Justice has made it difficult for individuals to do so directly before the EU Courts.[45] If that voice means voting in parliamentary elections, then many think their voice is drowned out or the politicians are not responding to what they want. In some Member States this has led to growing support for extremist parties and in other States to a move towards exit. The EU has failed to inspire much loyalty or love. This maybe because it is hard to love a customs union or a common market on which much of the EU's output legitimacy is based.

3.2 Output legitimacy

The EU's output legitimacy is explicitly or implicitly linked to its achievements in substantive EU law – beginning with the original core issues of economic integration,[46] as extended to economic and monetary union,[47] and to other policy areas such as health care and social policy.[48] Successful delivery of these policies has been backed up by the creation – by the Court of Justice – of a system of remedies at domestic level.[49] For some this is judicial activism; for others this is a necessary corollary to ensure the effective application of the rules Member States voluntarily signed up to.

And the EU has reinforced its internal policies through parallel action on the external stage. Reforms to the EU's competence in this field have strengthened the EU's ability to negotiate international agreements, particularly as regards international trade.[50] Paradoxically, the EU's success in achieving the four freedoms (free movement of goods, persons, services, and capital) has raised fundamental questions as to the ability of nation-States to control their own borders and keep out goods (horsemeat), persons (large-scale immigration from the East, the Polish plumber), and capital (foreign ownership of key industries) they do not want.[51] Nationals in some Member States want to pull the drawbridge up and keep out all that is foreign. EU law stops their governments from doing this.

However, the biggest challenge to the EU's claims for output legitimacy – that it is able to deliver growth and prosperity – have come with the crisis. Some blame EU policies for contributing to the crisis in the first place; others criticize the EU's laggardly, piecemeal

---

[41] For further details, see chapter 24.   [42] For further details, see chapter 25.
[43] For further details, see chapter 26.   [44] For details, see chapter 11.
[45] For details, see chapter 10.   [46] For details, see chapters 11–18.
[47] For details, see chapter 19.   [48] For details, see chapters 20–26.
[49] For details, see chapter 6.   [50] For details, see chapter 24.   [51] For details, see chapter 16.

response to the crisis for making a bad situation worse. Those living in countries in receipt of a 'bail-out' blame the EU/IMF (International Monetary Fund) for the pain they are currently suffering as a result of the austerity policies which have been imposed on them as a condition of receiving financial assistance. Nevertheless, even in these countries the majority view is that they would prefer to remain within the EU than out. This must say something about the safety net the EU continues to offer.

The crisis has also posed major challenges to the welfare state. Traditionally seen as an area of national competence, EU law and policies are increasingly having a direct or indirect impact. First, austerity measures have led to significant cuts in pension and social welfare provision, whether it be care for the elderly, social benefits, or health care.

Secondly, eurozone countries which are no longer free to devalue their currencies in order to regain competitiveness have been forced into a cycle of 'internal devaluation', a euphemism for cuts to wages and labour standards; standards which have often been the result of decades of struggle by the trade union movement and the International Labour Organization. This is a direct challenge to the European Social Model, which has long been regarded as one of the proudest achievements of European Member States.[52] This is not the first challenge to the EU's social model. The enlargement of the EU to include the Eastern European States created opportunities for workers from those States but risks for workers from wealthier States who saw their wages being undercut by EU migrant workers.

Thirdly, as the control on the use of public money gets tighter, there is ever-greater pressure from the EU for States to open up the provision of public services to competition in order to obtain value for money. For some States, this has long been public policy; for others it is a recent development. Increasingly the Court of Justice has been applying pressure on national systems: it has ruled that the four freedoms and competition rules, including State aids, apply to public services where those services are seen as an economic activity.[53] However, there has been some sensitivity to the necessity, particularly in the case of SSGIs – social services of general interest (eg home care for the elderly) – that EU law should not interrupt the provision of quality services. So EU law has carved out some exceptions to the rules.[54]

This tension between the economic and non-economic objectives of the EU can be seen played out in other areas too. For example, in the field of environmental law, where initially there was a perceived conflict between environmental and economic objectives, EU law now attempts to reconcile these objectives, either by trying to strike a balance between competing environmental and economic objectives or by integrating environmental and economic objectives through market-based mechanisms and other innovative regulatory approaches.[55]

4 Conclusion

The EU has fundamentally changed the relationship between States and their citizens. It has also delivered reforms in major policy areas and improved the daily quality of life for individuals – just think about low-cost air travel; the ready availability of abundant, good, varied food (pasta, panettone, pancetta); cheap(er) roaming charges. However, national politicians have been woefully bad at explaining the benefits of EU membership; and very quick to blame the EU for things that go wrong.

---

[52] For details, see chapter 20.   [53] For details, see chapters 18 and 21.   [54] See chapter 21.
[55] For further details, see chapter 22.

The EU, too, has also been poor at making a successful case for its own existence (and financial skulduggery has sullied its own image and undermined trust in the EU). The justification for the existence of the EU based on delivering peace in Europe no longer seems relevant to younger generations. So a case based on output legitimacy needs to be made all the more strongly. And when the EU fails to deliver on this, this precipitates a crisis in confidence in the EU. What has the EU ever done for me?

But let's consider the counter-factual. What if the EU did not exist, would there be a need for an equivalent body today? In a highly interrelated globalized world with two power blocs, the US and China, and with the other BRICs (Brazil, Russia, India, and China) coming up fast behind, European States would need to form some kind of unit to get their voice heard on the global stage. It may be that if the EU was built today, it wouldn't have started from where we are now. But it is very likely that some pan-European body would have been created (as can be seen with newly created customs unions emerging across the globe, such as the one between Russia, Belarus, and Kazakhstan, and the East African Community). The question then is, what would the European version have looked like – and how different would it be from the EU we have today? The aim of this book is to help readers understand what the EU is and why. They can then decide for themselves whether it is a good thing – or not.

2

Development of the EU

Paul Craig

1 Introduction

This chapter charts the development of what is now the EU. It is a complex and interesting story, and one that is still unfolding. It cannot be understood without an appreciation of the proximate connection between the rise of nationalism in the nineteenth century, its excesses in the twentieth, and the movement towards European integration. This is considered in the next section, which is followed by analysis of the first concrete steps towards European integration in the form of the European Coal and Steel Community in 1951 and the way in which this led towards creation of the European Economic Community in 1957, after the failure of more ambitious attempts at integration in the mid-1950s. The period thereafter was relatively stable, in the sense that there were no major amendments to the original EEC Treaty until the passage of the Single European Act 1986. The rationale for this reform is examined in section 4, and is followed in section 5 by consideration of the Treaty amendments that occurred between 1986 and the end of the millennium, the Maastricht Treaty, the Treaty of Amsterdam, and the Treaty of Nice. The dawn of the new century seemed at the time to herald the prospect of yet more piecemeal Treaty reform, but this expectation was undermined by the determination to press forward with efforts at more comprehensive Treaty reform. The story of these reform efforts, including the drafting and demise of the Constitutional Treaty in 2004, followed by the successful ratification of the Lisbon Treaty in 2009, is told in section 6. The hope that an expanded EU might develop in relative calm was, however, undermined by the financial crisis that sent shockwaves through the Union that continue to reverberate to the present day. No account of the development of European integration can be complete without being cognizant of this, which is discussed in section 7. The chapter concludes by introducing theories that seek to explain why integration has occurred.

There are a number of related themes that are central to the emergence and development of the EEC from its inception to the EU as it currently exists. Three are especially noteworthy. There is, first, discourse concerning the motivation behind European integration, and the relative influence in that respect of Member States and the very Institutions that they created, which has been at the centre of much of the theorizing concerning the EU.

A second theme concerns the relative importance of what are termed output and input legitimacy. The former sees the EU's legitimacy primarily in terms of the beneficial outcomes that flow from its existence. This was the traditional conception of legitimacy that underpinned the vision of those who created the EEC, with peace and prosperity being seen as the positive outcomes from integration. By the 1980s political and academic commentators were increasingly concerned with input legitimacy. It was clear that the European Community (EC) was wielding considerable power over significant areas, which was not purely economic. This led to greater attention being placed on the extent to which the choices thus made, whatsoever they might be, had democratic legitimacy. There was a growing literature on the EC's democratic deficit, and the extent to which increase in the power of the European Parliament might alleviate this problem. Enlargement from an EEC with six Member States, to an EU of 28 was another factor in the shift to concern over input legitimacy, with discussion as to how decision-making procedures in the Commission, Council, and the European Parliament would have to be modified to render the EU governable and workable. The relative shift in focus from output to input legitimacy has been further fuelled by the financial crisis and subsequent euro crisis, which has cast a long shadow over the promise that the EU will deliver prosperity.

The third theme is related to the second, albeit distinct. It concerns the balance between economic and social objectives within EU integration. There is little doubt that the initial focus of the EEC was on economic integration, as evidenced by the very name European Economic Community. The original Treaty of Rome that established the EEC was not, however, solely concerned with economic matters, and this has been reinforced by many subsequent Treaty amendments that deal with matters that are as much social as they are economic, and by the subsequent change in nomenclature from EEC to EC, European Community, and then to EU, European Union. The balance between the economic and the social within the EU nonetheless remains contestable, ever more so in light of the financial crisis, where austerity measures at EU and national level have had a significant impact on the social dimension of EU policies.

Alongside the five major amendments to the Treaties that are the foundation of EU law (and previously EEC/EC law), there have been seven enlargements of the EU over the years. These key steps in the EU's development can be visualized in the form of a timeline.[1]

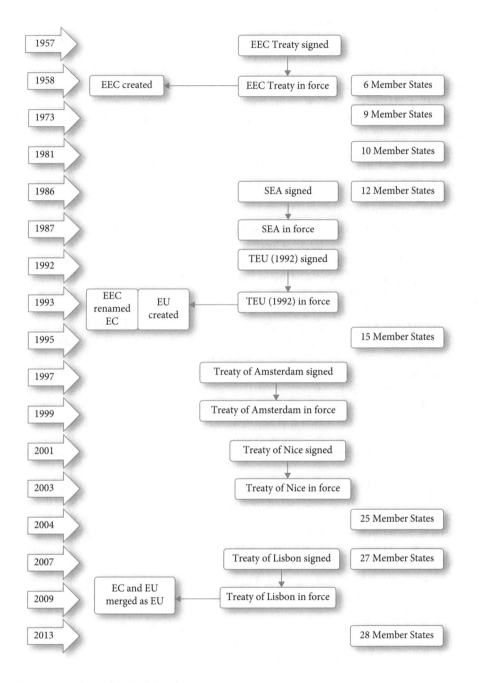

Fig 2.1 Timeline of the EU's development

---

[1] For more detail, see the interactive map and timeline of the EU's development, which can be found on the Online Resource Centre which accompanies this book.

2 Nationalism and the origins of the EU

There is no doubt that viewed from an historical perspective ideas of European unity can be traced to the late seventeenth century, when a prominent English Quaker, William Penn, called for a European Parliament.[2] There is, however, also little doubt that the more immediate push for some form of European integration can be dated to the nineteenth century. It is worth recalling that, for example, Germany and Italy only became unified States in 1871, drawing together what had hitherto been groups of smaller States, duchies, or principalities, some of which were ruled by foreign powers. A powerful factor in the unification process in both countries was the surge in nationalist sentiment, which resonated in politics, philosophy, and literature. Fichte in Germany and Manzoni in Italy were but two prominent proponents of this nationalist ethos. It can be traced back to the beginnings of the nineteenth century, in reaction to French dominance of Europe and the privations that resulted from Napoleonic campaigns in Central Europe.

There was much that was positive about this nationalist sentiment, which was initially directed towards attainment of unified States from disparate principalities and the like, combined with the desire to be rid of foreign control. It was driven, moreover, by the strong feeling that those who shared a common language and culture should naturally coexist in a single political entity, the corollary being that pre-existing boundaries between principalities were 'unnatural' and should not be allowed to impede the natural joinder of those who shared a common linguistic and cultural identity.

The darker side of nationalism became apparent towards the end of the nineteenth and the beginning of the twentieth century. It was driven in part by economic imperatives, but in part also by the desire to assert the prominence of a particular national identity. The battles were initially fought on borrowed terrain, with the main nation-States in Europe engaged in the carving up of Africa. The First and Second World Wars brought the clash of nation-States to the very forefront of the European stage, made yet worse by the increased capacity for death and destruction resulting from technological 'advances' in weaponry. While there is, of course, considerable debate about the causes of both conflicts, the aggressive and external effects of nationalism were significant in relation to both conflicts.

The culmination of the Second World War generated a widespread feeling that there had to be a way of organizing international affairs so as at least to reduce, if not eradicate, the possibility of such national conflict recurring on this scale. This explains the founding of the United Nations in 1945, where the guiding rationale was to provide a forum in which disputes could be resolved through dialogue, rather than conflict, and to institutionalize a regime of international peacekeeping and dispute settlement where force was required. The guiding rationale for the establishment of the UN remains relevant, notwithstanding debates as to its subsequent successes and limitations.

The founding of the EEC was another response to the horrors of two world wars, although it was to be over a decade before it became a reality. During the war, the Resistance movement had strongly supported the idea of a united Europe, to replace the

---

[2] D Urwin, *The Community of Europe: A History of European Integration* (2nd edn, London: Longman, 1995); J Pinder and S Usherwood, *The European Union: A Very Short Introduction* (3rd edn, Oxford: Oxford University Press, 2013).

destructive forces of nationalism.[3] However, the integration movement faltered after the war, especially after the electoral defeat in the UK of Churchill, who had been a strong proponent of European unity. There were nonetheless other moves towards European cooperation. The US in 1947 introduced the Marshall Plan to provide financial aid for Europe, which was administered in 1948 by the Organisation for European Economic Co-operation (OEEC) and in 1960 the Organisation for Economic Co-operation and Development (OECD). Cooperation in defence was furthered by the creation of the North Atlantic Treaty Organization (NATO) in 1948 and the Western European Union (WEU) in 1954. The Statute on the Council of Europe was signed in 1949, providing for a Committee of Ministers and a Parliamentary Assembly. The international organization is best-known for the European Convention on Human Rights (ECHR), which was signed in 1950 and came into force in 1953. We can now consider the more concrete moves towards the founding of the EEC.

3 From ECSC to EEC

3.1 European Coal and Steel Community: ECSC

The UK was unwilling to participate in potentially far-reaching plans for European integration in 1948, and this led to more modest, albeit important, proposals advanced by the French foreign minister that France and Germany should administer their coal and steel resources pursuant to an international agreement in which supervisory authority was given to a body termed the High Authority. The proposal was framed so that other States could also join the international agreement. The detailed plan was drafted by Jean Monnet, a committed federalist. The focus on coal and steel was in part economic, but also in large part political. Coal and steel were still the principal materials for waging war. Placing production of such material under an international body was therefore consciously designed to assuage fears that Germany might covertly rearm. By assuaging such fears it was hoped to bring Germany back into the mainstream European fold, more especially because the political architecture in Europe had changed dramatically after 1945, with Russian dominance of Eastern Europe and the emergence of the cold war.

The European Coal and Steel Community (ECSC) Treaty was signed in 1951 by France, Germany, Italy, Belgium, Netherlands, and Luxembourg. It had a lifespan of 50 years to expire in 2002, and established a common market in coal and steel. There were four principal institutions. The High Authority, composed of nine independent appointees of the six Member State governments, was the main executive institution with decision-making power; an Assembly made up of national parliaments' delegates had supervisory and advisory powers; a Council composed of a representative from each national government had limited decision-making powers and a broader consultative role; the fourth institution was the Court of Justice composed of nine judges. Although the remit of the ECSC was limited to coal and steel, its proponents always saw it as a supranational authority, in which the High Authority could adopt decisions other than by unanimity, which could then serve as the first step towards broader European integration.[4]

---

[3] W Lipgens (ed), *Documents of the History of European Integration* (Florence: European University Institute, 1985).

[4] F Duchêne, *Jean Monnet: The First Statesman of Interdependence* (London: Norton, 1994) 239.

3.2 European Defence Community and European Political Community: EDC and EPC

The 1950s also witnessed setbacks in the moves towards European integration, which were nonetheless important in the overall story of the creation of the EEC. The central proposals that failed to come to fruition were the European Defence Community (EDC) and the European Political Community (EPC).

The proposal for the EDC had its origins in French opposition to German membership of NATO. The French alternative outlined in the Pleven Plan in 1950 was for the EDC, which would have a European army, a common budget, and joint institutions. The EDC Treaty was signed in 1952 by the six ECSC States, but Britain refused to participate, and progress towards ratification was slow. It was felt that the existence of a European army required some form of common European foreign policy, and this was the catalyst for the plans to establish the EPC. The 1953 EPC draft statute was crafted by the ECSC Assembly as reinforced by certain additional members, with the principal work being carried out by a Constitutional Committee. It produced far-reaching plans for a federal, parliamentary-style form of European integration, in which there would be a bicameral ('two-level') parliament, with one chamber elected by direct universal suffrage, and the other senate-type body being appointed by national parliaments. The parliament thus constituted would have real legislative power. There was also to be an Executive Council, which would in effect have been the government of the EPC, with responsibility to the Parliament. The draft statute also contained provision for a Court of Justice and an Economic and Social Council. Although the draft received almost unanimous support in the ECSC Assembly, the reaction of the six foreign ministers of the ECSC was more circumspect, and there was significant opposition to the degree of parliamentary power that existed under the draft EPC statute.

The fate of the EPC was, however, inextricably linked with that of the EDC. The latter failed when the French National Assembly refused to ratify the EDC in 1954, opposition coming from both the French right and left wing, albeit for very different reasons.[5] This resulted in a major setback for the integration process and the shelving of plans for defence and political union. It would be 39 years before the Member States ratified another treaty, signed at Maastricht in 1992, purporting to establish a 'European Union'.

3.3 European Economic Community: EEC

Movement towards European integration was not, however, halted by the failure of the EDC/EPC. Indeed, the very demise of these ambitious projects led proponents of European integration to focus more directly on the economic rather than the political, while drawing on ideas that had been discussed when the EPC was being drafted. Thus the Netherlands had sought to include in the EPC proposals the idea of a common market in which products would be able to move freely under the guarantee of a supranational authority. This was felt to be too risky for several countries in the early 1950s, since they had protectionist traditions that they were unwilling to relinquish. It was nonetheless this very idea of a common market in which goods and services would be traded freely across a level playing field consisting of the territories of the Member States that was to resurface. A conference of foreign ministers of the six Member States of the ECSC was held in Messina in Italy in 1955. A committee chaired by Paul-Henri Spaak, Belgian Prime Minister and a

---

[5] J Pinder, *The Building of the European Union* (3rd edn, Oxford: Oxford University Press, 1998).

strong advocate of integration, published its report in 1956, which contained the basic plan for what became the European Atomic Energy Community (Euratom) and the EEC. The underlying long-term objective may well have been political, but the initial focus was nonetheless economic. There was no temporal limit to the EEC Treaty: the Treaty of Rome was signed in March 1957 and came into effect in January 1958. There were six Member States: France, Germany, the Netherlands, Belgium, Italy, and Luxembourg. The same Member States were signatories of the Euratom Treaty, which came into effect at the same time as the EEC Treaty.

In economic terms, the idea of a common market connotes the removal of barriers to trade, such as tariffs, which increase the cost of imports, or quotas, which limit the number of imports of a certain type of product. These barriers to trade were to be abolished and a common customs tariff was to be set up. The common market was to be established over a transitional period of several stages, during which tariff barriers would be removed and the common external customs tariff established. A common market connoted, however, more than the removal of tariffs and quotas. It also entailed the free movement of the economic factors of production in order to ensure that they were being used most efficiently throughout the Community as a whole. This explains the centrality to the Community of the 'four freedoms', which are often regarded as the core of its economic constitution: free movement of goods, workers, capital, and establishment and the provision of services (see further chapters 11 to 16). The idea was therefore that if, for example, a worker could not obtain a job in a particular country, because unemployment levels were high, he or she should be able to move freely within the EEC to search for employment within another country where there might be an excess of demand over the supply for labour, with the consequence that the value of the labour resource within the Community as a whole was enhanced. The Treaty also contained key provisions to ensure that the idea of a level playing field was not undermined by the anti-competitive actions of private parties, or by national action that favoured domestic industry (see further chapters 17 and 18). The Treaty of Rome was in addition designed to approximate the economic policies of the Member States, to promote harmonious development of economic activities throughout the Community, to increase stability and raise the standard of living, and to promote closer relations between the Member States. There were common policies in agriculture and transport. A European Social Fund was established to improve employment opportunities, and an Investment Bank to give loans and guarantees and to help less developed regions or sectors. A European Development Fund for overseas countries and territories of some of the Member States was also established.

In institutional terms the Treaty of Rome was a mixture of continuity with the past in terms of the institutional ordering under the ECSC, combined with novel arrangements devised for the EEC. The Parliamentary Assembly and the Court of Justice were shared with the ECSC. There was, however, a separate Council of Ministers consisting of a national representative from each Member State, which represented its interest in the Council, and a separate executive authority, the Commission, which was composed of members drawn from the Member States, who had an obligation of independence and who were to represent the Community rather than the national interest. It was not until the Merger Treaty in 1965 that these Institutions were merged and shared by the three Communities. An Economic and Social Committee with advisory status was set up, to be shared with the Euratom Community.

The location of legislative and executive power was crucial to the arrangements put in place by the Treaty of Rome (on the Institutions, see further chapters 3 and 4). It will be recalled that the draft statute for the European Political Community had been parliamentary in its orientation, giving very considerable power to the proposed bicameral legislature.

It will also be recalled that this aroused considerable opposition from the Member States of the ECSC. The same unwillingness to accord power to parliamentary Institutions was evident in the Treaty of Rome. The legal and political reality was that legislative power was divided between the Commission, which proposed legislative initiatives, and the Council of Ministers, which voted on them. The Parliamentary Assembly, which changed its name to the European Parliament in 1962, had a bare right to be consulted, and that was only where a particular Treaty article mandated such consultation. Voting procedure varied according to the nature of the issue: in some limited instances voting was by simple majority, in many others it was by 'qualified majority', while in yet others unanimity was required. Where qualified majority voting applied, voting in the Council was weighted to give greater weight to the larger Member States than the smaller, in order to reflect differences in population, although the weighting was not perfectly proportional in this respect.

Executive power was also divided in the original Treaty of Rome, although the Commission was given considerable power in this respect. Thus it was the Commission that was accorded the role of 'watchdog' to ensure that Member States complied with the Treaty; it was the Commission that had responsibility to ensure that regulations, directives, and decisions enacted pursuant to the Treaty were effectively implemented; and it was the Commission that was the principal negotiator of international agreements on behalf of the Community. The Council nonetheless exercised certain executive responsibilities in relation to, for example, the conclusion of international agreements, the planning of the overall policy agenda, and the Community budget. The Assembly was also given some power over the budget, and in addition possessed a strong but never-used power of censure, despite the tabling of many motions of censure over the years, including one shortly before the dramatic resignation of the Commission in 1999.[6]

4 From EEC to the Single European Act

4.1 Tensions within the Community

The Treaty of Rome continued to provide the legal framework for the EEC for almost 30 years, subject to the Merger Treaty of 1965, which came into effect in 1967, and which merged the executive organs of the ECSC, Euratom, and the EEC. The lack of other Treaty amendment during this period is all the more remarkable given that the years after the Single European Act 1986 (SEA) have seen an almost continuous process of Treaty reform. There were nonetheless important developments in the period between the EEC Treaty and the SEA.

The Community expanded through accession of new Member States. The UK had chosen to remain outside the EEC when it was initially established. It made its first application to join in 1961, but the French President, Charles de Gaulle, vetoed UK membership in 1963, and also a second UK application in 1967. It was not until de Gaulle's resignation that Britain's application for membership was accepted, together with those of Ireland and Denmark in 1973. Greece became a member of the EEC in 1981, followed by Spain and Portugal in 1986.

The almost 30-year period between the EEC and the SEA revealed, moreover, tensions between an intergovernmental view of the Community, championed initially by President de Gaulle of France, in which State interests were regarded as paramount, and a more supranational perspective espoused initially by Walter Hallstein, the Commission President, in

---

[6] K Bradley, 'The Institutional Law of the EU in 1999' (1999/2000) 19 *Yearbook of European Law* 547, 584.

which the overall Community good was perceived as the primary objective, even if this required sacrifice by particular Member States. The tension surfaced in 1965, at the time when the transitional provisions of the Treaty dictated a move from unanimous to qualified majority voting in the Council, which would have affected many, although not all, areas of decision-making. De Gaulle objected to a Commission proposal that the Community should be able to raise its own resources from agricultural levies and external tariffs, rather than national contributions.[7] When compromise in the Council proved to be impossible, France refused to attend further Council meetings and adopted what became known as the 'empty-chair' policy. This lasted for seven months, from June 1965 until January 1966, after which a settlement was reached, which became known as the Luxembourg Compromise or the Luxembourg Accords. They were essentially an agreement to disagree over voting methods in the Council. The French asserted that even in cases where the Treaty provided for majority decision-making, discussion must continue until unanimity was reached whenever important national interests were at stake. The other five Member States declared instead that in such circumstances the Council would 'endeavour, within a reasonable time, to reach solutions which can be adopted by all'.[8] It seems nonetheless that the French view prevailed, such that if a State pleaded that its 'very important interests' were at stake, then this was akin to a veto, which the other Member States would respect.

The period between the EEC Treaty and the SEA also saw other developments that enhanced Member State power over decision-making and intergovernmentalism. In 1970 the Davignon Report recommended the holding of quarterly meetings of the foreign ministers of the Member States, which became an intergovernmental forum for cooperation in foreign policy. In 1973 this became known as European Political Co-operation, which enabled the EEC to be represented as one voice in other international organizations in which all Member States participated, but also enhanced intergovernmentalism.

In 1974 the European Council was established to regularize the practice of holding summits. This body consists of the heads of government of the Member States, with the President of the Commission attending its biannual meetings. The European Council's 'summitry' provided the Community with much-needed direction, but represented to some a weakening in the supranational elements of the Community. The European Council was not within the framework created by the Treaties, and it was not until the SEA that it was recognized in a formal instrument. European Political Co-operation and the European Council enabled Member State interests at the highest level to impact on matters of political or economic concern, and their decisions, while not formally binding, would normally constitute the frame within which binding Community initiatives would be pursued. The Member States also assumed greater control over the detail of Community secondary legislation, through the creation of what became known as comitology. This enabled Member States to influence the content of secondary Community legislation in a way that had not been envisaged in the original EEC Treaty. Commentators lamented the dilution of the EEC's supranational dimension and regarded it as a principal reason why legislative initiatives to flesh out the requirements of Treaty articles were not being enacted, or that this only occurred after significant delay.[9]

There were, however, also developments during the period between the EEC and the SEA that enhanced supranationalism. Thus 1976 saw agreement on direct elections to

---

[7] The EEC achieved its own resources through the Treaty of Luxembourg 1970 (known as 'the first budgetary treaty'), which entered into force in 1971.   [8] Bull EC 3-1966, 9.

[9] P Dankert, 'The EC – Past, Present and Future' in L Tsoukalis (ed), *The EC: Past, Present and Future* (Oxford: Basil Blackwell, 1983). For more on the European Council as an EU Institution, see chapter 3, and for more on the comitology procedure, see chapter 5.

the Assembly, and the first such elections took place in 1979. It provided the EEC with a direct electoral mandate that it had lacked hitherto, but the downside of this development was that voter turnout was low, and elections were often fought on national rather than Community issues.[10] Moreover, the direct electoral mandate served to highlight the fact of the Assembly's limited power in the legislative process. The supranational dimension to the Community was more unequivocally enhanced by developments relating to resources and the budget. In 1969 agreement was reached on funding from the Community's own resources rather than from national contributions, and on the expansion of the Parliament's role in the budgetary process. This thereby gave the Community greater financial independence and strengthened Parliament's role as a decision-maker. These developments were furthered in 1975 when a second budgetary treaty was adopted. The European Court of Justice (ECJ) also made important contributions to the supranational dynamic of the Community during this period. It used the doctrine of direct effect in the 1960s and 1970s to make Community policies more effective. It interpreted Treaty provisions broadly in order to foster the overall aims of the Community, such as the free movement of goods. It created the supremacy of Community law over national law to reinforce these judicial strategies (see further chapter 6; on the Court of Justice generally, see chapter 10).

While there were positive developments relating to the Community from a supranational perspective, it was nonetheless the case that the decade from the mid-1970s to the mid-1980s was perceived as a period of relative political stagnation in the EEC. This was epitomized by the Commission's difficulty in securing the passage of legislation through the Council, with the consequence that Community objectives were left unfulfilled or that progress was extremely slow. The malaise was recognized in high-level reports from the mid-1970s onwards, such as the Tindemans Report 1974–5 and that of the 'Three Wise Men' in 1978,[11] both of which recommended strengthening the supranational elements of the Community, and diminishing the impact of intergovernmentalism, but neither was acted on. The European Parliament proposed radical reform in 1984 in a 'Draft Treaty on European Union', but it too was largely ignored. The catalyst for change finally came from a meeting of the heads of State in the Fontainebleau European Council in 1984, which established two committees to consider Treaty revision and political integration. This in turn led the 1985 European Council in Milan to establish an intergovernmental conference (IGC) to discuss Treaty amendment. It was this IGC that generated the SEA. The impetus for reform was furthered by an extensive Commission 'White Paper' that set out a timetable for completion of the internal market, complete with a long list of barriers to be removed before a deadline of 1992.[12]

4.2 Single European Act: SEA

The SEA 1986 was a disappointment to those who advocated far-reaching reform of the kind posited by the European Parliament in its Draft Treaty on the European Union. It nonetheless had a far-reaching significance, and it still ranks as one of the most significant Treaty revisions in the history of the EU. This is because of the institutional and substantive changes that it introduced.

In institutional terms, the SEA made a number of changes. It gave a legal basis to European Political Co-operation and formal recognition to the European Council, although not within the Community Treaties. A Court of First Instance was created to assist the Court

---

[10] M Holland, *European Integration from Community to Union* (London: Pinter, 1994) 42.
[11] Bull EC 11-1979, 1.5.2.   [12] COM(85) 310.

of Justice. Lastly, the so-called 'comitology' procedure, under which the Council delegates powers to the Commission on certain conditions, was formally included within what was Article 202 EC.[13]

The most significant institutional change was, however, that the SEA began the transformation in the role of the European Parliament that continues to the present day. We have already seen that the Treaty of Rome gave it scant powers, and that its role in the legislative process was minimal, being limited to a right to be consulted and then only where a particular Treaty article so mandated. We have also seen that the role of parliamentary Institutions in the schema of European integration had been a contentious issue, as exemplified by the debates concerning the EPC and those concerning the Draft Treaty on European Union 30 years later. Viewed from this perspective, the change made by the SEA might, at the time, have appeared relatively minimal. A new legislative procedure was created, the 'cooperation' procedure, which applied to a defined list of Treaty articles. There is some evidence that this was regarded as a relatively minor change, accepted by the Member States that were drafting the SEA to compensate the European Parliament for the fact that its far-reaching reforms proposed in the Draft Treaty on European Union had been largely sidelined. The creation of the cooperation procedure was, however, to transform the Community decision-making process. Prior to the SEA, the approach to the passage of legislation was captured by the aphorism that the 'Commission proposes, and the Council disposes', revealing the Commission's role as initiator of legislation and the Council's role in voting on such measures. The change heralded by the SEA meant that the Commission would now have to take seriously the views of the European Parliament in the areas where the cooperation procedure applied. The enactment of legislation required input from three players, not two, more especially because the cooperation procedure meant that the European Parliament could in effect block legislative proposals provided that it had some support in the Council.

The impact of the cooperation procedure was enhanced because of the substantive changes made by the SEA, in particular the creation of what was initially Article 100a EEC and is now Article 114 TFEU, which is the main Treaty provision conferring power upon the EU to adopt legislation concerning the internal market. A word by way of explanation is required to understand the importance of this change. The completion of a common market requires not merely that trade barriers are prohibited, what is termed negative integration, but also that there should be European regulation of certain issues *in place of* national regulation, what is termed positive integration or harmonization. The latter is required because each country will have certain rules on, for example, banking that embody important public interests, such as the prevention of fraud, the safeguarding of deposits, and the like. These rules cannot be eradicated, nor should they be. It is nonetheless the case that the very multiplicity of such national rules can hamper the creation of a common market, because traders will then have to satisfy what may be a different set of such rules in each Member State, thereby adding significantly to the costs of business (see further chapter 11). A way of meeting this difficulty is for there to be one set of Community rules on such issues. This was recognized in the original Treaty of Rome, but the relevant provision conferring power to adopt legislation concerning the common market, what was Article 100 EEC and is now Article 115 TFEU, required unanimity in the Council. This was difficult to secure, ever more so in a Community with a growing number of Member States. This was the rationale for the enactment of Article 100a EEC, now Article 114 TFEU, which provided for the enactment of measures to approximate the laws of the Member States for this purpose. The cooperation

---

[13] The legal regime for dealing with these measures was altered by the Lisbon Treaty, Arts 290–291 TFEU. See further chapter 5.

procedure was applicable to this article and voting within the Council was by qualified majority, rather than unanimity. The European Parliament was thereby accorded a role in the legislative process and this role was applicable to the very Treaty article that was to be the foundation for the enactment of measures to complete the internal market. The SEA amended the Treaty of Rome to provide that the Community should adopt measures with the aim of 'progressively establishing the internal market over a period expiring on 31 December 1992', and defined the internal market as 'an area without internal frontiers in which the free movement of goods, persons, services and capital is ensured'.[14] What is now Article 114 TFEU became the principal vehicle for the enactment of measures to complete the internal market through the passage of legislation approximating Member State laws.

The impact of the SEA was not, however, confined to the above. The SEA also added new substantive areas of Community competence, some of which had already been asserted by the Institutions and supported by the Court, without any express Treaty basis. The additions covered cooperation in economic and monetary union (see chapter 19), social policy (see chapter 20), economic and social cohesion, research and technological development, and environmental policy (see chapter 22).

5 From the SEA to the Nice Treaty

5.1 Maastricht Treaty: the Treaty on European Union

The SEA reinvigorated the Community and many measures to complete the internal market were duly enacted in the period between 1986 and 1992. It would nonetheless be mistaken to think that the internal market could truly be 'completed' by 1992, or indeed any particular date thereafter. This is because factors such as technological change, industrial innovation, and changing patterns of consumer behaviour can generate the need for new measures enacted by the EU in order to eradicate or reduce obstacles to interstate trade. The momentum generated by the SEA continued after its adoption. A committee chaired by the President of the Commission, Jacques Delors, on economic and monetary union (EMU) reported in 1989 and set out a three-stage plan for reaching EMU. The European Council held an IGC on the subject, and a second IGC on political union. This led to a draft Treaty in 1991 and the Treaty on European Union (TEU) was signed by the Member States in Maastricht in February 1992.[15] It entered into force in November 1993 having survived constitutional challenge before the German Federal Constitutional Court.[16]

5.1.1 The three-pillar system

The TEU made a number of important changes to the Treaty of Rome, in both institutional and substantive terms. It was also significant in terms of the overall legal architecture, because it introduced what was known as the 'three-pillar' structure for what was to be the European Union, with the Communities as the first of these pillars, and the EEC Treaty was officially renamed the European Community Treaty.[17] The Second Pillar dealt with Common Foreign and Security Policy (CFSP) and built on earlier mechanisms for European Political Cooperation. The Third Pillar dealt with Justice and Home Affairs (JHA) and built on earlier informal initiatives in this area (see chapters 25 and 26). The pillar structure was preserved in

---

[14] Art 8a EEC.   [15] R Corbett, *The Treaty of Maastricht* (London: Longman, 1993).
[16] Cases 2 BvR 2134/92 and 2159/92 *Brunner v The European Union Treaty* [1994] 1 CMLR 57.
[17] D Curtin, 'The Constitutional Structure of the Union: A Europe of Bits and Pieces' (1993) 30 *Common Market Law Review* 17.

subsequent Treaty amendments, but was then removed by the Lisbon Treaty, although distinct rules still apply to the CFSP (see chapter 24). Title I of the TEU contained common provisions, which laid down basic principles for the 'Union', and set out its objectives.[18]

The EU was therefore given new responsibilities in relation to CFSP and JHA. The key issue is therefore why these new competences were not simply added to those already existing, in the same manner as had been done in earlier Treaty amendments, when the SEA added to the range of Community competence through new titles or chapters being inserted in the existing Treaty of Rome. The principal rationale for creating separate pillars for the CFSP and JHA was as follows. The Member States wished for some established mechanism through which they could cooperate in relation to CFSP and JHA. The absence of such an established mechanism meant that such meetings would have to be set up afresh to discuss each new problem. This was time-consuming and cumbersome. The Member States were not, however, willing to subject these areas to the normal supranational methods of decision-making that characterized the Community Pillar. They did not wish the Commission and the ECJ to be able to exercise the powers they had under the Community Pillar, because the Second and Third Pillars concerned sensitive areas of policy considered to be at the core of national sovereignty. The central distinguishing feature of decision-making under the Second and Third Pillars is that it was more intergovernmental, with the Member States in the Council and European Council retaining the primary reins of power. The other Community Institutions, the Commission, European Parliament, and ECJ, either had no role or one that was much reduced by way of comparison with the Community Pillar.

5.1.2 The Community Treaties

The Maastricht Treaty made a number of institutional changes to the Treaty of Rome, the most significant being the further increase in the Parliament's legislative involvement, by introducing the so-called co-decision procedure, which was amended and strengthened by the Treaty of Amsterdam. This allowed the European Parliament to block legislation of which it disapproved, if it was subject to this procedure. The Parliament was also given the right to request the Commission to initiate legislation and the power to block the appointment of the new Commission. There were other significant institutional changes: provision was made for a European System of Central Banks (ESCB) and a European Central Bank (ECB) to oversee economic and monetary union (see chapter 19), for a Parliamentary Ombudsman, and for a 'Committee of the Regions'.

The Maastricht Treaty also made significant substantive changes. It established the principle of subsidiarity. It was introduced to alleviate fears that the EC was becoming too 'federal' by distinguishing areas where action was best taken at Community level and national level.[19] A new concept of European citizenship was introduced, which was to become a fertile source for ECJ case law.[20] There were new provisions on economic and monetary union,[21] which laid the foundations for the introduction of the single currency.[22] The Maastricht Treaty also, like the SEA in the earlier decade, added new areas of competence to the EC, with new titles added to the Treaty in areas such as culture, public health (see chapter 21), consumer protection (see chapter 23), trans-European networks, and

---

[18] There were originally seven titles in the TEU: Title I included the 'common provisions', which set out the basic objectives of the TEU. Titles II, III, and IV covered the First Pillar amendments to the EEC, ECSC, and Euratom Treaties respectively. Title V created the Second Pillar of the Common Foreign and Security Policy, Title VI the Third Pillar of Justice and Home Affairs, and Title VII contained the final provisions.

[19] Art 5 EC. For more on the principle of subsidiarity, see chapter 5.

[20] Arts 17–21 EC. See chapter 13.   [21] Arts 98–124 EC. See chapter 19.

[22] J Pipkorn, 'Legal Arrangements in the Treaty of Maastricht for the Effectiveness of the Economic and Monetary Union' (1994) 31 *Common Market Law Review* 263.

development cooperation; and significant modifications made in relation to the titles on, for example, the environment (see chapter 22).

5.1.3 Common foreign and security policy

The CFSP Pillar created by the Maastricht Treaty was, as we have seen, distinct from the Community institutional and legal structure, such that decision-making was more intergovernmental and less supranational than under the Community Pillar. The CFSP Pillar established the objectives of EU action in this area, which included preservation of peace and international security, respect for human rights, and development of democracy. Each Member State had an obligation to inform and consult each other on any matter of common foreign and security policy that was of general interest, in order to ensure that the Member States' combined influence could be exercised as effectively as possible, through concerted and convergent action. Provision was made for the Council to define a 'common position' for the Member States on such issues. It was, however, the European Council, consisting of the heads of State and government of the Member States, which was to define the principles and general guidelines for the CFSP, with the Council having responsibility for decisions to implement it. The CFSP included all questions related to the security of the Union, including the eventual framing of a common defence policy. While decision-making was concentrated in the hands of Institutions in which Member State interests predominated, the Council and the European Council, there was nonetheless provision for the European Parliament to be kept informed about foreign and security policy, and the Commission was to be fully associated with work in this area.

5.1.4 Justice and home affairs

The JHA Pillar originally governed policies such as asylum, immigration, and 'third country' (non-EU) nationals, which were integrated into the EC Treaty by the Treaty of Amsterdam (see chapter 26). However, prior to the Lisbon Treaty the Third Pillar also included cooperation on a range of international crime issues and various forms of judicial, customs, and police cooperation, including the establishment of a European Police Office (Europol) for exchanging information (see chapter 25). National sensitivity about such issues meant that the Member States were not willing for them to be included within the ordinary Community Pillar and be subject to the supranational rules on decision-making. Decision-making was dominated by the Council, and the ECJ's powers were limited. The Lisbon Treaty has now brought the entirety of what was the Third Pillar into the general fabric of the Treaty.[23]

5.2 Treaty of Amsterdam

The process of Treaty amendment did not halt other important developments. Membership of the EU expanded shortly after the Maastricht Treaty, with Austria, Sweden, and Finland joining in 1995. An accession agreement was also negotiated with Norway, but a national referendum opposed membership of the EU, as it had done in 1973. An Agreement on the European Economic Area (EEA) was also made between the EC and the States that were party to the European Free Trade Association (EFTA), and came into force in 1994.[24]

---

[23] Arts 67–89 TFEU.

[24] It provided for free-movement provisions similar to those in the EC Treaty, analogous rules on competition policy, and 'close co-operation' in other policy areas, having been declared compatible with the EC Treaty by the ECJ, Opinion 1/91 [1991] ECR I-6079; Opinion 1/92 [1992] ECR I-2821; J Forman, 'The EEA Agreement Five Years On: Dynamic Homogeneity in Practice and Its Implementation by the Two EEA Courts' (1999) 36 *Common Market Law Review* 751. Since 1995, the non-EU parties to the EEA have been Iceland, Norway, and Liechtenstein. One country (Switzerland) remains a member of EFTA, but decided not to join the EEA; it has, however, entered into a number of separate bilateral treaties with the EU.

The ink was nonetheless scarcely dry on the Maastricht Treaty before plans were being made for an IGC between the Member States that would pave the way for the next round of Treaty reform, which was the Treaty of Amsterdam. It was signed in 1997 and came into effect on 1 May 1999. It was initially intended to prepare the Union for enlargement through accession of Eastern European countries, but this issue was postponed until the Nice Treaty. The result was that the Treaty of Amsterdam was a modest exercise in Treaty reform, but it did delete obsolete provisions from the EC Treaty, and renumber all the articles, titles, and sections of the TEU and the EC Treaty.

The 1990s saw a surge of debate, political and academic, concerning the legitimacy of the EU. This is the rationale for amendments introduced by the Treaty of Amsterdam designed to enhance the EU's legitimacy. The principle of openness was added, such that decisions were to be taken 'as openly as possible' and as closely as possible to the citizen.[25] Promotion of a high level of employment and the establishment of the area of 'freedom, security and justice' were added to the EU's objectives.[26] There were amendments the effect of which was that the Union was said to be founded on respect for human rights, democracy, and the rule of law.[27] Respect for these principles was a condition for EU membership.[28] On a related note, the Treaty of Amsterdam declared that the EU should respect the fundamental rights protected in the ECHR and in national constitutions,[29] and there was provision that if the Council found a 'serious and persistent breach' by a Member State of principles concerning the rule of law, human rights, and democracy, it could suspend some of that State's rights under the Treaty.[30]

The institutional changes made by the Treaty of Amsterdam were in large part an extension and consolidation of a reform process begun with the SEA. The co-decision procedure was amended to increase the European Parliament's power and the number of Treaty articles to which it was applicable was expanded. The cooperation procedure introduced by the SEA was virtually eliminated, apart from provisions on EMU. The increase in the European Parliament's power was also evident in the amendment whereby its assent was required for appointment of the Commission President.[31] There were, moreover, changes designed to enhance the Community's legitimacy in relation to its citizens. The same continuity with the past was evident in the trajectory of amendments concerning the scope of Community power. This was, as with the SEA and the Maastricht Treaty, further enhanced through the addition of new heads of competence, or the modification of existing heads.[32] There was also a new provision that conferred legislative competence on the Community to combat discrimination based on sex, racial or ethnic origin, religion or belief, disability, age, or sexual orientation.[33]

The Treaty of Amsterdam also amended the Second and Third Pillars. The changes made to the Second Pillar were modest, including the fact that the Secretary-General of the Council was nominated as 'High Representative' for the CFSP to assist the Council Presidency, and the Council was given power to 'conclude' international agreements,[34] whenever this was necessary in implementing the CFSP.

---

[25] Art 1 EU. On the transparency of the EU decision-making process, see chapters 3 and 8.

[26] Art 2 EU.   [27] Art 6 EU.   [28] Art 49 EU.

[29] Art 6(2) EU. This was subject to judicial oversight through Art 46 EU. See further chapter 9.

[30] Art 7 EU.   [31] Art 214(2) EC. See chapter 3.

[32] There was a new title on Employment, the provisions on Social Policy were modified, the title on public health was replaced and enhanced, and that on consumer protection was amended. See chapters 20, 21, and 23.

[33] Art 13 EC. See chapter 20.

[34] Art 24 EU; JW de Zwaan, 'Legal Personality of the European Communities and the European Union' (1999) 30 *Netherlands Yearbook of International Law* 75; K Lenaerts and E de Smijter, 'The European Union as an Actor under International Law' (1999/2000) 19 *Yearbook of European Law* 95. On the CFSP, see further chapter 24.

The changes made to the Third Pillar were more significant. The decision-making structure had been criticized on the ground that many JHA policies, such as immigration, asylum, and border controls, were unsuited to the intergovernmental processes established. The consequence was that those parts of JHA dealing with visas, asylum, immigration, and other aspects of free movement of persons were incorporated into Title IV EC, although the relevant legal provisions meant that decision-making was still more intergovernmental than in other areas, at least for a certain period of time (see chapter 26). The remaining Third Pillar provisions were subjected to institutional controls closer to those under the Community Pillar, and the Third Pillar was renamed 'Police and Judicial Cooperation in Criminal Matters'. The aim of the remodelled Third Pillar was to provide citizens with a high level of safety in an area of freedom, security, and justice, by developing 'common action' in three areas: police cooperation in criminal matters, judicial cooperation in criminal matters, and the prevention and combating of racism and xenophobia.[35] These objectives were pursued through legal instruments specific to the Third Pillar:[36] common positions, framework decisions, decisions, and conventions. The ECJ had some jurisdiction over certain measures adopted under this pillar,[37] thereby further eroding the distinction between the Community Pillar and the Third Pillar, although it was not equivalent to its jurisdiction under the Community Pillar.

5.3 Treaty of Nice

We have already noted the fact that the original Treaty of Rome remained largely unchanged for the first 30 years of the Community's existence. By way of contrast, the period from the mid-1980s onwards was dominated by Treaty reform or discussion about such reform.[38] The very fact that the Treaty of Amsterdam had failed to address the institutional structure pending enlargement meant that a further IGC to pave the way for Treaty amendment was inevitable, given that discussions for enlargement were underway. Such an IGC was convened in 1999 to consider composition of the Commission, the weighting of votes in the Council, and the extension of qualified majority voting. The Treaty of Nice was concluded in December 2000, and entered into force on 1 February 2003.[39]

The Treaty of Nice made a number of changes to the EC Treaty, in particular relating to the Community's institutional structure. This had been devised for a Community of six Member States, which had now expanded to 15. There was consensus on the need for reform of institutional arrangements pending enlargement. This was achieved and the Treaty provisions concerning the weighting of votes in the Council, the distribution of seats in the European Parliament, and the composition of the Commission were amended. These topics might sound dry, but the debates concerning reform were often fierce, precisely because the resolution of these issues raised broader considerations concerning the relative power of large, medium, and small States in the Community, and also raised

---

[35] Art 29 EU. On the revised Third Pillar, see further chapter 25.

[36] Art 34 EU.   [37] Art 35 EU.

[38] B de Witte, 'The Closest Thing to a Constitutional Conversation in Europe: The Semi-Permanent Treaty Revision Process' in P Beaumont, C Lyons, and N Walker (eds), *Convergence and Divergence in European Public Law* (Oxford: Hart Publishing, 2002) ch 3.

[39] OJ [2001] C80/1; K Bradley, 'Institutional Design in the Treaty of Nice' (2001) 38 *Common Market Law Review* 1095; R Barents, 'Some Observations on the Treaty of Nice' (2001) 8 *Maastricht Journal of European and Comparative Law* 121.

contentious issues as to the balance of power between the EU Institutions (see further chapter 3). The detailed provisions on these matters have been superseded by those in the Lisbon Treaty, but we shall see that the discourse concerning these changes was similarly contentious as those in the Treaty of Nice.

5.4 **Charter of Rights**

Parallel to the discussion that led to the Treaty of Nice, there was discourse that led to the EU Charter of Rights. The initial catalyst for this came from the European Council in 1999, which conceived of the Charter as important in itself and as a mechanism for enhancing the legitimacy of the EU. It established a 'body' which included national parliamentarians, European parliamentarians, and national government representatives to draft a Charter of fundamental rights for the EU.[40] This body, which renamed itself a 'Convention', began work early in 2000 and drew up a Charter by the end of 2000. The Charter received political approval of the Member States at the Nice European Council in December 2000.[41] It was drafted so as to be legally binding, and it was intended that this should be resolved when the Treaty of Nice was being deliberated. The Charter's legal status was not, however, resolved in Nice, and the decision on its legal status was placed on the 'post-Nice agenda' and post-poned until the 2004 IGC.

6 **From Nice to Lisbon**

6.1 **The Laeken Declaration**

The initial expectation following the Treaty of Nice was that there would be yet another round of piecemeal Treaty reform four years later in 2004. The agenda for that IGC had already been partly filled in, the intent being that it would consider issues addressed but not resolved in the discussion leading to the Treaty of Nice. These included the status of the Charter of Rights, the scope of Community competence, and the role to be played by national parliaments in the Community decision-making process. These issues were to be considered further at the Laeken European Council scheduled for December 2001. The nature of the reform process was, however, transformed during 2000, which was then reflected in the conclusions of the Laeken European Council.[42]

It came to be accepted that the topics left over from the Treaty of Nice were not discrete, but resonated with other issues concerning the institutional balance of power within the EU, and with the distribution of authority between the EU and the Member States. This in turn led to a growing feeling that there should be a more profound rethinking of the fundamentals of the EU. It was also accepted that if a broad range of issues was to be discussed, then the result should be legitimated by input from a broader 'constituency' than hitherto. This emerging consensus was reflected in the Laeken European Council,[43] which gave formal approval, through the Laeken Declaration, to the broadening of the issues left open post-Nice. These issues became the 'headings' within which a plethora of other questions were posed, concerning virtually every issue of importance for the EU. The Laeken Declaration also formally embraced the Convention model which had been used to draw

---

[40] G de Búrca, 'The Drafting of the EU Charter of Fundamental Rights' (2001) 26 *European Law Review* 126. See further chapter 9.   [41] OJ [2000] C364/1.
[42] P Craig, 'Constitutional Process and Reform in the EU: Nice, Laeken, the Convention and the IGC' (2004) 10 *European Public Law* 653.   [43] Laeken European Council, 14–15 December 2001.

up the Charter of Rights, and established a Convention on the Future of Europe, with a composition designed to enhance the legitimacy of its results.

6.2 Constitutional Treaty

The Convention[44] was composed of representatives from national governments, national parliaments, the European Parliament, and the Commission. The accession countries were also represented. The Convention was chaired by former French President Giscard d'Estaing, and there were two vice-chairmen, Giuliano Amato and Jean-Luc Dehaene. The executive role in the Convention was undertaken by the Praesidium.[45] It began work in 2002, making extensive use of Working Groups for consideration of particular topics.[46] The end result in 2003 was a proposal for a Constitutional Treaty, but it is important to understand that this was not preordained. The possibility of a constitutional text was mentioned only at the end of the Laeken Declaration, in the context of Treaty simplification, and the language was cautious. Many Member States felt that the Convention might just be a talking shop, which produced recommendations.[47] It was therefore something of a surprise when Giscard d'Estaing, in the Convention opening ceremony, announced that he sought consensus on a Constitutional Treaty for Europe. The Convention, once established, developed its own institutional vision. The idea took hold that the Convention should produce a coherent document in the form of a Constitutional Treaty. The Draft Treaty Establishing a Constitution for Europe[48] was duly agreed by the Convention in June 2003 and submitted to the European Council in July.[49]

The Member States in the European Council were, however, divided on certain issues and agreement on the Constitutional Treaty was only secured at the European Council meeting in June 2004.[50] It was still necessary for the Constitutional Treaty[51] to be ratified in accord with the constitutional requirements of each Member State. Fifteen Member States ratified the Treaty, but progress with ratification came to an abrupt halt when France and the Netherlands rejected the Constitutional Treaty in their referenda.[52] A number of Member States therefore postponed their ratification process. The European Council in 2005 decided it was best for there to be a time for 'reflection'. The Constitutional Treaty never 'recovered' from the negative votes in France and the Netherlands, and did not become law. However, the Lisbon Treaty, which was ratified in 2009, drew very heavily on the Constitutional Treaty and the great majority of the major changes in the Lisbon Treaty were taken over from the Constitutional Treaty without further debate.

---

[44] http://european-convention.eu.int.

[45] It was composed of the Convention Chairman and Vice-Chairmen, and nine other members.

[46] Working groups were established on subsidiarity; Charter of Rights; legal personality; national parliaments; competence; economic governance; external action; defence; Treaty simplification; freedom, security, and justice; and social Europe. The decision to create the first six groups was taken in May 2002; the remaining five groups were created later in autumn 2002.

[47] P Norman, 'From the Convention to the IGC (Institutions)' (2003) Federal Trust for Education and Research, Online Paper 28/03, 2.

[48] The Constitutional Treaty was divided into four parts: Part I dealt with the basic objectives and values of the EU, fundamental rights, competences, forms of law-making, institutional division of power, and the like; Part II contained the Charter of Rights, which had been made binding by Part I; Part III concerned the policies and functions of the EU; and Part IV contained the final provisions.

[49] CONV 850/03, Draft Treaty establishing a Constitution for Europe, Brussels, 18 July 2003.

[50] Brussels European Council, 17–18 June 2004, paras 4–5.

[51] Treaty Establishing a Constitution for Europe (OJ [2004] C316/1).

[52] R Dehousse, 'The Unmaking of a Constitution: Lessons from the European Referenda' (2006) 13 *Constellations* 151.

6.3 **Lisbon Treaty**

The failure of the Constitutional Treaty meant that the legal ordering of the EU continued to be based on the Treaty of Rome as amended by later Treaties, including the Treaty
of Nice. This Treaty architecture had to regulate an EU of 25 Member States, the result of
the 2004 enlargement that brought ten further States into the EU: the Czech Republic,
Estonia, Cyprus, Latvia, Lithuania, Hungary, Malta, Poland, Slovenia, and Slovakia.
Bulgaria and Romania joined the EU in 2007, and Croatia acceded in 2013, making 28
States.

Case study 2.1: Negotiation of the Lisbon Treaty

The preceding discussion revealed the delicate negotiations that often accompany Treaty
reform. This was, not surprisingly, evident also in relation to the Lisbon Treaty, more
especially so given the negative reaction to the Constitutional Treaty, which generated
academic debate as to what should happen to the 'constitutional' project.[53] The decision that there should be a 'period of reflection' after the negative results in the French
and Dutch referenda was sensible, given the justified concern that more States might
vote against the Constitutional Treaty. The calm phrase 'period of reflection' nonetheless concealed a far more troubled perspective in the EU institutions, which were at the
time unsure whether any of the content of the Constitutional Treaty could be salvaged.
The Member States were not, however, willing to allow the work that had been put into
the Constitutional Treaty to be lost. To this end, the European Council in 2006 com-
missioned Germany, which held the Presidency of the European Council in the first
half of 2007, to report on the prospects for Treaty reform. The choice of Germany was
not simply fortuitous, since it was felt that if matters could be moved forward, it would
have the organizational capacity and power to do so. In the first half of 2007 Germany
engaged in a series of bilateral discussions with other Member States, in order to determine whether an agreement could be brokered that would lead to some revised Treaty
reform. Germany's Presidency of the European Council culminated with the June 2007
European Council,[54] which considered a detailed mandate of the changes that should be
made to the Constitutional Treaty, in order that a revised Treaty could successfully be
concluded.

   This led to the birth of the Reform Treaty. The European Council concluded that 'after
two years of uncertainty over the Union's treaty reform process, the time has come to
resolve the issue and for the Union to move on'.[55] It was agreed to convene an IGC,[56]
which was to carry out its work in accord with the detailed mandate provided in Annex
I to the conclusions of the European Council, and finish its deliberations by the end of
2007.[57] The Reform Treaty was to contain two principal clauses, which amended respectively the TEU, and the EC Treaty, the latter of which would be renamed the Treaty on
the Functioning of the European Union, TFEU. The Union should have a single legal
personality and the word 'Community' throughout would be replaced by the word

---

[53] G de Búrca, 'The European Constitution Project after the Referenda' (2006) 13 *Constellations* 205; A Duff,
'Plan B: How to Rescue the European Constitution, (2006) Notre Europe, Studies and Research No 52; J Ziller,
'Une constitution courte et obscure ou claire et détaillée? Perspectives pour la simplification des traites et la
rationalisation de l'ordre juridique de l'union européenne' (2006), EUI Working Papers, Law 2006/31.
[54] Brussels European Council, 21–22 June 2007.   [55] Ibid, para 8.
[56] Ibid, para 10.   [57] Ibid, para 11.

'Union'.[58] There was a conscious decision to excise mention of the word 'constitution' from the Reform Treaty. The principal objective was to conclude this Treaty reform, and given that the constitutional terminology of the Constitutional Treaty was problematic for some Member States it was dropped. This was also the rationale for other terminological changes where the wording in the Constitutional Treaty was felt, whether correctly or not,[59] to connote the idea of the EU as a State entity. Thus the title 'Union Minister for Foreign Affairs' was replaced by 'High Representative of the Union for Foreign Affairs and Security Policy'; the terms 'law' and 'framework law' were abandoned; there was no flag, anthem, or motto; and the clause in the Constitutional Treaty concerning the primacy of EU law was replaced by a declaration.

Portugal held the Presidency of the European Council in the second half of 2007 and was keen that Treaty reform should be concluded during its Presidency so that the new Treaty could bear its name. Developments in the second half of 2007 were rapid. There was scant time for any detailed discussion or input into the draft Treaty that emerged from the IGC. What became the Lisbon Treaty was forged hurriedly by the Member States and Community institutions, since they were keen to conclude a process that had started shortly after the beginning of the new millennium. The desire to conclude the Lisbon Treaty expeditiously was, moreover, explicable, since it was the same in most important respects as the Constitutional Treaty. The issues had been debated in detail in the Convention on the Future of Europe after a relatively open discourse, and were considered once again in the IGC in 2004. There was therefore little appetite for those engaged in the 2007 IGC to reopen Pandora's box,[60] even if this could not be admitted too explicitly since they would be open to the criticism that they were largely repackaging provisions that had been rejected by voters in two prominent Member States, although it should also be noted that the negative votes in the French and Dutch referenda had relatively little to do with anything new in the Constitutional Treaty.[61]

The 2007 IGC produced a document that was signed by the Member States on 13 December 2007,[62] and the title was changed from the Reform Treaty to the Lisbon Treaty in recognition of the place of signature. The finishing post was in sight, but the Treaty required ratification by each Member State, and Ireland rejected it in a referendum. This obstacle was overcome by a second Irish referendum in October 2009, after concessions were made to Ireland. The final hurdle was the unwillingness of the Czech President to ratify the Lisbon Treaty, but he did so reluctantly after a constitutional challenge to the Treaty had been rejected by the Czech Constitutional Court, and after other Member States agreed to add at a later date a Protocol to the Treaties relating to the Czech Republic and the Charter of Rights (see chapter 9). The Lisbon Treaty entered into force on 1 December 2009.

[58] Brussels European Council, 21–22 June 2007, Annex I, para 2.

[59] S Griller, 'Is this a Constitution? Remarks on a Contested Concept' in S Griller and J Ziller (eds), *The Lisbon Treaty: EU Constitutionalism without a Constitutional Treaty?* (Vienna: Springer, 2008).

[60] G Tsebelis, 'Thinking about the Recent Past and Future of the EU' (2008) 46 *Journal of Common Market Studies* 265.

[61] See in general, R Dehousse, 'The Unmaking of a Constitution: Lessons from the European Referenda' (2006) 13 *Constellations* 151.

[62] Conference of the Representatives of the Governments of the Member States, Treaty of Lisbon Amending the Treaty on European Union and the Treaty Establishing the European Community, CIG 14/07, Brussels, 3 December 2007 (OJ [2007] C306/1).

6.3.1 Form

The Lisbon Treaty amends the TEU and the EC Treaty.[63] The Lisbon Treaty has seven articles, of which Articles 1 and 2 are the most important, plus numerous Protocols and declarations. Article 1 amended the TEU, and contained some principles that govern the EU, as well as revised provisions concerning the CFSP and enhanced cooperation. Article 2 amended the EC Treaty, which was renamed the Treaty on the Functioning of the European Union. The EU is henceforth to be founded on the TEU and the TFEU, and the two Treaties have the same legal value.[64] The Union replaces and succeeds the EC.[65] A consolidated version of the Lisbon Treaty contains the new numbering and references to the old provisions where appropriate.[66]

6.3.2 Substance

Part I of the Constitutional Treaty contained the principles of a constitutional nature that governed the EU. The Lisbon Treaty is less clear in this respect, although the revised TEU has some constitutional principles for the EU. This is especially true in relation to Title I – Common Provisions, Title II – Democratic Principles, and Title III – Provisions on the Institutions. There are nonetheless matters not included within the revised TEU, which had properly been in Part I of the Constitutional Treaty. Thus, for example, the main rules concerning competence are in the TFEU,[67] as are the provisions concerning the hierarchy of norms,[68] and those relating to budgetary planning.[69]

The Lisbon Treaty did, however, improve the architecture of the TFEU. The latter Treaty is divided into seven parts. Part One, entitled Principles, contains two titles, the first of which deals with Categories of Competence, the second of which covers Provisions having General Application. Part Two deals with Discrimination and Citizenship of the Union. Part Three, which covers Policies and Internal Actions of the Union, is the largest Part of the TFEU with 24 titles.[70] The provisions on Police and Judicial Cooperation in Criminal Matters, the Third Pillar of the old TEU, have been moved into the new TFEU.[71] Part Four of the TFEU covers Association of Overseas Countries and Territories. Part Five deals with EU External Action, bringing together subject matter with an external dimension. Part Six is concerned with Institutional and Budgetary Provisions, while Part Seven covers General and Final Provisions.

The Lisbon Treaty is not built on the pillar system, and in this sense the Treaty architecture that had prevailed since the Maastricht Treaty has now gone. There are nonetheless distinctive rules relating to the CFSP, which means that in reality there is still something akin to a separate 'pillar' for such matters. The approach to the CFSP in the Lisbon Treaty largely replicates that in the Constitutional Treaty, subject to the change of nomenclature,

---

[63] J-C Piris, *The Lisbon Treaty: A Legal and Political Analysis* (Cambridge: Cambridge University Press, 2010); P Craig, *The Lisbon Treaty: Law, Politics and Treaty Reform* (Oxford: Oxford University Press, 2010).

[64] Art 1, para 3 TEU.   [65] Art 1, para 3 TEU.

[66] Consolidated Versions of the Treaty on European Union and the Treaty on the Functioning of the European Union (OJ [2008] C115/1, OJ [2010] C83/1).   [67] Arts 2–6 TFEU. See further chapter 5.

[68] Arts 288–292 TFEU. See further chapter 5.   [69] Art 312 TFEU.

[70] I – Internal Market; II – Free Movement of Goods; III – Agriculture and Fisheries; IV – Free Movement of Persons, Services, and Capital; V – Area of Freedom, Security and Justice; VI – Transport; VII – Common Rules on Competition, Taxation and Approximation of Laws; VIII – Economic and Monetary Policy; IX – Employment; X – Social Policy; XI – The European Social Fund; XII – Education, Vocational Training, Youth and Sport; XIII – Culture; XIV – Public Health; XV – Consumer Protection; XVI – Trans-European Networks; XVII – Industry; XVIII – Economic, Social and Territorial Cohesion; XIX – Research and Technological Development and Space; XX – Environment; XXI – Energy; XXII – Tourism; XXIII – Civil Protection; XXIV – Administrative Cooperation.   [71] Part Three, Title V TFEU. See chapter 25.

from 'Union Minister for Foreign Affairs' to 'High Representative of the Union for Foreign Affairs and Security Policy'. Executive authority continues to reside principally with the European Council and the Council.[72] The ECJ continues to be largely excluded from the CFSP.[73]

7 Impact of the financial crisis

The Member States and EU institutional players that had finally secured the passage and ratification of the Lisbon Treaty hoped for a period of relative calm in which the new Treaty arrangements could bed down. This was not to be. The successful conclusion of the Lisbon Treaty overlapped with the beginnings of the financial crisis and related crisis with the euro that have had a profound political, economic, and social impact on the EU.[74]

The reasons for the crisis are complex and cannot be examined in detail here (see instead chapter 19), but some idea of the causes is nonetheless important.[75] The Maastricht Treaty introduced, as we have seen, the legal framework for economic and monetary union. The latter connotes the idea of a single currency overseen by a European Central Bank. The former captures the idea of control over national fiscal and budgetary policy, with the basic aim of ensuring that a Member State does not spend more than it earns. The rationale for these controls was that the stability of the euro could be undermined if the economies of the Member States that subscribed to the currency were perceived to be weak, and the financial markets might reach this conclusion if some Member States persistently spent more than they earned. The problem was that the two parts of the Maastricht settlement were out of sync.[76] EU control over national budgetary policy was relatively weak, and thus it was unable to exert the requisite control over national economic policy.

The specific problem for the EU began in earnest with the fact that Greece's credit rating to repay its debt was downgraded. This then led to problems for the euro, and to concerns about the budgetary health of some other countries that used the currency. The impact of these developments was downward pressure on the euro, which was only alleviated when euro countries provided a support package for Greece that satisfied the financial markets. The sovereign debt crisis was overlaid by, and interacted with, the banking crisis that affected some lending institutions that were heavily committed to economic sectors, such as housing, which were hit badly by the downturn in the economic markets.[77] The net effect was that a number of countries, in particular Greece, Ireland, and Portugal, have required very large amounts of assistance provided from funds financed by other Member States. Italy and Spain have also been on the 'danger list'. The assistance has been subject to 'strict

---

[72] Arts 22, 24 TEU. On the CFSP, see further chapter 24.

[73] Art 24 TEU, Art 275 TFEU. It does, however, have jurisdiction in relation to Art 40 TEU, which is designed to ensure that exercise of CFSP powers does not impinge on the general competences of the EU, and vice versa; the ECJ also has jurisdiction under Art 275 TFEU to review the legality of decisions imposing restrictive measures on natural or legal persons adopted by the Council under Chapter 2 of Title V TEU.

[74] M Adams, F Fabbrini, and P Larouche (eds), *The Constitutionalization of European Budgetary Constraints* (Oxford: Hart Publishing, 2014).

[75] http://ec.europa.eu/economy_finance/focuson/crisis/2010-04_en.htm; H James, H-W Micklitz, and H Schweitzer, 'The Impact of the Financial Crisis on the European Economic Constitution, (2010) EUI Working Papers, Law 2010/05.

[76] J-V Louis, 'Guest Editorial: The No-Bailout Clause and Rescue Packages' (2010) 47 *Common Market Law Review* 971.

[77] M Maduro, 'A New Governance for the European Union and the Euro: Democracy and Justice, (2012) European Parliament, Directorate-General for Internal Policies, Policy Department C: Citizens' Rights and Constitutional Affairs, PE 462.484.

conditionality', which means that the funding to the recipient States is contingent on their introducing far-reaching economic and social reforms, thereby increasing unemployment at a time when the general economic outlook has been bleak.

The economic and financial crisis has had profound effects on the EU, including its constitutional architecture.[78] Nor is the problem likely to go way in the short term. It has generated a complex array of political responses, some of which have been designed to provide assistance to ailing States, others of which have increased oversight of national economic policy. The measures have assumed varying legal forms, ranging from the enactment of ordinary EU legislation, albeit in an accelerated manner as warranted by the nature of the crisis, to intergovernmental agreements made outside the formal confines of the constituent Treaties. The constitutional implications of these developments continue to unfold, with profound consequences for the legal, economic, and political dimensions of the EU, and indeed for the balance between the 'economic' and the 'social', a theme that has run through the development of the EEC from its very inception. The social dimension of EU policy has been markedly affected by austerity policies at both EU and national level. The EU may weather this particular storm, but the nature of the polity that emerges thereafter remains to be seen.

8 Theories of integration

The discussion in this chapter has shown the way in which the EEC has changed since its inception. There is, however, a related but distinct issue, which is the rationale for this integration. The original EEC Treaty has been amended on many occasions and the subject matter over which the EU has competence has expanded very considerably. It is therefore important to consider the rationale for this. There is a wealth of literature, principally from political science, and there is not surprisingly debate as to the causes of integration (see also chapter 11).

8.1 Neofunctionalism

Neofunctionalism was the early ideology of Community integration.[79] The central tenet of neofunctionalism was the concept of 'spillover'. Functional spillover was based on the interconnectedness of the economy. Integration in one sphere created pressure for integration in other areas. Thus, for example, removal of formal tariff barriers would generate a need to deal with non-tariff barriers, which could equally inhibit realization of a single market. The desire for a level playing field between the States would then lead to other matters being decided at Community level, in order to prevent States from giving advantages to their own industries. Political spillover was equally important and involved the build-up of political pressure in favour of further integration. In integrated areas, interest groups would be expected to concentrate their attention on the Community, and apply pressure on those with regulatory power. Such groups would also become mindful of remaining barriers to interstate trade, which prevented them from reaping the rewards of existing integration, thereby adding to the pressure for further integration. The Commission was to

---

[78] P Craig, 'Economic Governance and the Euro Crisis: Constitutional Architecture and Constitutional Implications' in Adams, Fabbrini, and Larouche (n 74).

[79] E Haas, *The Uniting of Europe: Political, Social and Economic Forces 1950–1957* (Stanford, CA: Stanford University Press, 1958); L Lindberg, *The Political Dynamics of European Economic Integration* (Stanford, CA: Stanford University Press, 1963); L Lindberg and S Scheingold, *Europe's Would-Be Polity: Patterns of Change in the European Community* (Upper Saddle River, NJ: Prentice Hall, 1970); L Lindberg and S Scheingold, *Regional Integration* (Cambridge, MA: Harvard University Press, 1970).

be a major player in this political spillover, since it would encourage the beliefs of the State players. Neofunctionalism was to be the vehicle through which Community integration, conceived of as technocratic, elite-led gradualism, was to be realized. The idea of spillover reinforced the view that gradualism was a meaningful strategy for integration. Legitimacy was conceived of in terms of outcomes, increased prosperity, which was to be secured through technocracy, even if this meant a marginal role for elected bodies.[80]

Neofunctionalism was, however, challenged empirically and theoretically. The empirical challenge was based on its failure to explain the reality of the Community's development. The 1965 Luxembourg crisis had a profound impact, since Member State interests re-emerged with a vengeance. The resulting de facto unanimity principle signalled that Member States were not willing to allow Community development inconsistent with their vital interests. Decision-making for many years thereafter was conducted in the shadow of the veto. The Commission's role changed from emerging government for the Community to a more cautious bureaucracy.[81] Moreover, evidence of interest-group pressure for greater integration was found to be equivocal.[82]

The theoretical challenge to neofunctionalism was based on the fact that its failure to accord with political reality led to theoretical modification that rendered it increasingly indeterminate,[83] and on neofunctionalism's failure to relate to general themes within international relations, which sought to explain why States engaged in international cooperation. It would nonetheless be wrong to conclude that neofunctionalism has no explanatory value for EU integration, and it is arguable that functional spillover created impetus for further integration.[84]

8.2 Liberal intergovernmentalism

An alternative theory of integration is known as liberal intergovernmentalism, championed by Moravcsik.[85] His thesis is rooted in a branch of international relations theory. The central thesis is that States are the driving forces behind integration, that supranational actors are there largely at their behest and that such actors as such have little independent impact on the pace of integration.

The demand for integration is said to depend on national preferences, which are aggregated through their political institutions.[86] The increase in cross-border flows of goods and services create what are termed 'international policy externalities' among nations, which can have negative side effects on other States, thereby creating an incentive for policy coordination. The supply of integration is said to be a function of interstate bargaining and strategic interaction. Domestic preferences define 'a "bargaining space" of potentially viable agreements, each of which generates gains for one or more participants'.[87] Governments choose one such agreement, normally through negotiation. Integration is pursued through a supranational institution because it is felt to be more efficient. Constructing individual ad hoc

---

[80] Lindberg and Scheingold (n 79) 268–269.

[81] K Neunreither, 'Transformation of a Political Role: The Case of the Commission of the European Communities' (1971–2) 10 *Journal of Common Market Studies* 233.

[82] S George, *Politics and Policy in the European Union* (3rd edn, Oxford: Oxford University Press, 1996) 41–43.

[83] A Moravcsik, 'Preferences and Power in the European Community: A Liberal Intergovernmentalist Approach' (1993) 31 *Journal of Common Market Studies* 473, 476.   [84] George (n 82) 40–41.

[85] Moravcsik, 'Preferences and Power' (n 83); A Moravcsik, *National Preference Formation and Interstate Bargaining in the European Community, 1955–86* (Cambridge, MA: Harvard University Press, 1992); A Moravcsik, 'Negotiating the Single European Act: National Interests and Conventional Statecraft in the European Community' (1991) 45 *International Organization* 19.

[86] Moravcsik, 'Preferences and Power' (n 83) 481.   [87] Ibid, 497.

bargains between States can be costly.[88] This problem is obviated by a supranational structure such as the EU. The same basic driving force of efficiency is said to explain the decision-making procedures in the EU. Thus Member States carry out a cost–benefit calculation, with the decision to delegate or pool sovereignty signalling the willingness of national governments to accept an increased risk of being outvoted or overruled on any individual issue in exchange for more efficient collective decision-making.[89]

8.3 Multi-level governance

Liberal intergovernmentalism was predicated on the assumption that supranational institutions enabled national governments to attain policy goals that could not be obtained by independent action.[90] This State-centric view was challenged by those who saw the EU in terms of multi-level governance.

Thus Marks, Hooghe, and Blank argued that integration was a process in which authority and policy-making were shared across multiple levels of government – sub-national, national, and supranational.[91] National governments were major players, but did not have a monopoly of control. Supranational institutions, including the Commission, the European Parliament, and the ECJ, had influence in policy-making and could not merely be regarded as agents of national governments.[92] When competence over a certain subject matter has been transferred to the EU, proponents of multi-level governance contend that there are real limits to the degree of individual and collective State control over EU decisions.[93] Thus while Member States may play the decisive role in the Treaty-making process, they do not exert a monopoly of influence, and the day-to-day control exercised by the States collectively is less than that postulated by State-centric theorists. The ability of the 'principals', the Member States, to control the 'agents', the Commission and the ECJ, is limited by a range of factors, including the 'multiplicity of principals, the mistrust that exists among them, impediments to coherent principal action, informational asymmetries between principals and agents, and by the unintended consequences of institutional change'.[94]

8.4 Rational choice institutionalism

Rational choice institutionalism is a derivative of rational choice theory. The latter is premised on methodological individualism, whereby individuals have preferences, and choose the course of action that is the optimal method of securing them.[95] Rational choice institutionalists were critical of liberal intergovernmentalism because of the minimal role that the latter accorded to EU institutions,[96] although the gap between the two theories became narrower in the late 1990s.[97]

---

[88] J Buchanan and G Tullock, *The Calculus of Consent: Logical Foundations of Constitutional Democracy* (Ann Arbor, MI: University of Michigan Press, 1962).

[89] Moravcsik, 'Preferences and Power' (n 83) 509–510.

[90] A Milward, *The European Rescue of the Nation State* (Berkeley, CA: University of California Press, 1992); A Milward and V Sorensen, 'Independence or Integration? A National Choice' in A Milward, R Ranieri, F Romero, and V Sorensen (eds), *The Frontier of National Sovereignty: History and Theory, 1945–1992* (London: Routledge, 1993); P Taylor, 'The European Community and the State: Assumptions, Theories and Propositions' (1991) 17 *Review of International Studies* 109.

[91] G Marks, L Hooghe, and K Blank, 'European Integration from the 1980s: State-Centric v. Multiple-Level Governance' (1996) 34 *Journal of Common Market Studies* 341, 342.   [92] Ibid, 346.

[93] Ibid, 350–351.   [94] Ibid, 353–354.

[95] J Jupille, J Caporaso, and J Checkel, 'Integrating Institutions: Rationalism, Constructivism, and the Study of the European Union' (2003) 36 *Comparative Political Studies* 7.

[96] M Pollack, 'International Relations Theory and European Integration' (2000), EUI Working Papers, RSC 2000/55.

[97] This was primarily because Moravcsik modified his theory to acknowledge that supranational institutions might have greater powers over agenda-setting and the making of EU law outside major Treaty negotiations

Proponents of rational choice institutionalism acknowledged that institutions were important. Institutions constituted the rules of the game, thereby enhancing equilibrium, and they exemplified principal–agent analysis. Member State 'principals' delegated to supranational 'agents' to enhance the credibility of their commitments, and to deal with incomplete contracting, since Treaty provisions are often open to a spectrum of possible interpretations. Principal–agent literature focused on the controls that the principal might use to ensure that the agent did not deviate from the desired goals of the principal.[98]

8.5 Constructivism

Constructivists agree with rational choice institutionalists that institutions matter. They nonetheless dispute the foundations of much rational choice literature, more especially methodological individualism and the idea that individual or State preferences are 'given'. Constructivists contend that the relevant environment in which preferences are formed is inescapably social.[99] This inevitably impacts on, and thus constitutes, a person's understandings of their own interests. Institutions will embody social norms and will affect a person's interests and identity.

Thus whereas rational choice institutionalism regards institutions as rules of the game that provide incentives within which players pursue their given preferences, constructivists regard institutions more broadly to include 'informal rules and intersubjective understandings as well as formal rules, and posit a more important and fundamental role for institutions, which constitute actors and shape not simply their incentives but their preferences and identities as well'.[100]

There have been attempts to soften the divide between rational choice institutionalism and constructivism.[101] Thus, for example, many rational choice theorists accept that preferences may well be altruistic as opposed to egoistic, and that preferences may be constrained by social structure. There have, moreover, been moves to test the relative cogency of the two approaches through carefully crafted case studies.[102]

9 Conclusion

There will be no attempt to summarize the preceding analysis by way of conclusion. Two more general points should be borne in mind when reflecting on this material when reading later chapters in this book.

First, there have always been debates, both political and academic, as to why the EU has the array of powers that it currently possesses. This has been a theme in the contending theories of integration, and it has surfaced repeatedly in claims and counterclaims as to the

than he had posited in his earlier work: A Moravcsik, *The Choice for Europe: Social Purpose and State Power from Messina to Maastricht* (Ithaca, NY: Cornell University Press, 1998) 8.

[98] M Pollack, *The Engines of European Integration: Delegation, Agency, and Agenda Setting in the EU* (Oxford: Oxford University Press, 2003); Pollack (n 96).

[99] T Risse, 'Exploring the Nature of the Beast: International Relations Theory and Comparative Policy Analysis Meet the European Union' (1996) 34 *Journal of Common Market Studies* 53; J Checkel, 'The Constructivist Turn in International Relations Theory' (1998) 50 *World Politics* 324; T Christiansen, K Jorgensen, and A Wiener, 'The Social Construction of Europe' (1999) 6 *Journal of European Public Policy* 528.

[100] Pollack (n 96) 14–15.

[101] J Checkel, 'Bridging the Rational-Choice/Constructivist Gap? Theorizing Social Interaction in European Institutions, (2000) University of Oslo, ARENA Working Papers, WP 00/11.

[102] See eg the essays in (2003) 36 *Comparative Political Studies*.

relative degree of influence of the ECJ in furthering the integration process. A simple fact should nonetheless be borne in mind when thinking about this issue. It was the Member States acting by unanimity through a series of Treaty amendments spanning 30 years that decided to accord new heads of power to the EU. This should be borne firmly in mind when claims are made that the current disposition of power is the result of some 'smash and grab' operation by EU institutions.

Secondly, the balance between the 'economic' and the 'social' dimension of the EU has always been contentious. The successive Treaty amendments accorded the EU power over a broad array of subject matter – economic, social, and political in nature. While the EEC began with primarily economic aims, the establishment of a common market, the founding Member States were always alive to the interconnection between the economic, social, and political facets of society. They did not imagine that the economic dimension could be hermetically sealed, and this was symbolically reflected in the shift of nomenclature from EEC to EC. It also serves to explain the grant of social power to the EU, this being justified in part in order to prevent the balance between the economic and the social within the EU being tilted too greatly in favour of the former. A danger of the financial crisis is, however, that the social dimension will be sidelined as a result of the prominence given to resolution of economic problems.

Further reading

M Bond and K Feus, *The Treaty of Nice Explained* (London: Federal Trust, 2001)

D Chryssochoou, *Theorizing European Integration* (Thousand Oaks, CA: Sage, 2001)

R Corbett, *The Treaty of Maastricht* (London: Longman, 1993)

P Craig, *The Lisbon Treaty: Law, Politics, and Treaty Reform* (Oxford: Oxford University Press, 2010)

A Duff (ed), *The Treaty of Amsterdam* (London: Sweet & Maxwell, 1997)

N MacCormick, *Who's Afraid of a European Constitution?* (Exeter: Imprint Academic, 2005)

A Moravcsik, *The Choice for Europe* (London: University College London Press, 1999)

D O'Keefe and P Twomey (eds), *Legal Issues of the Amsterdam Treaty* (Oxford: Hart Publishing, 1999)

P Norman, *The Accidental Constitution, The Making of Europe's Constitutional Treaty* (Brussels: EuroComment, 2005)

J-C Piris, *The Constitution for Europe: A Legal Analysis* (Cambridge: Cambridge University Press, 2006)

J-C Piris, *The Lisbon Treaty: A Legal and Political Analysis* (Cambridge: Cambridge University Press, 2010)

J Winter, D Curtin, A Kellermann, and B de Witte, *Reforming the Treaty on European Union: The Legal Debate* (Alphen aan den Rijn: Kluwer, 1996)

J Ziller, *La nouvelle Constitution europeene* (Paris: La decouverte, 2005)

3

The EU's political institutions

Steve Peers

1 Introduction

> It has been said that democracy is the worst form of government except all the others that have been tried.
>
> Sir Winston Churchill

All of the EU's Member States are representative democracies. Furthermore, according to Article 10(1) TEU, as revised by the Treaty of Lisbon, 'the functioning of the Union shall be founded on representative democracy' (ie the concept that decisions are taken by politicians who have a democratic mandate). More precisely, Article 10(2) TEU specifies that the European Parliament is directly elected, the Council consists of Member States' ministers, and the European Council (which should be distinguished from the Council) consists of heads of State or government – the latter two groups being accountable to the voters or parliament of each individual Member State. But despite this, there is a widespread perception that the EU is highly undemocratic.

Another key feature of the EU's system is the attempt to ensure that EU law is effective. This depends on there being EU measures in existence in the first place – and therefore upon the effective functioning of the EU's political institutions, since they are the main source of such EU measures. To that end, the Treaties provide that Member States' governments usually do not have a veto over the adoption of EU measures. But, for those citizens who believe that, at least for some matters, only the decisions of their *national* politicians can be regarded as democratic, this is a fundamental problem. Again, as discussed in chapter 1, we see a tension, at least on some occasions, between different concepts of legitimacy: input legitimacy (public acceptance of the procedures which lead to the adoption of decisions) on the one hand, and output legitimacy (public approval of the substantive outcome of the decision-making process) on the other.

This chapter examines this possible tension between democracy and effectiveness in the context of the EU's political institutions: the European Parliament, the European Council, the Council, and the Commission. To this end, it examines in turn the composition, powers, and functioning of each of these institutions, comparing them to national systems and assessing their democratic accountability and the effectiveness of their functioning. Some key aspects of their powers (the adoption of legislation and other measures) are discussed in more detail in chapter 5,[1] and the details of their functioning in certain specific areas is discussed in other chapters (eg chapter 17 as regards competition law).

It will be seen that, largely to address concerns about democratic accountability, the role of various EU institutions has evolved over time – in particular to strengthen the legislative role of the European Parliament, and that body's control over the Commission. Similarly, the European Council has been enhancing its position as an EU institution, at the Commission's expense. These developments might have cumulatively increased the democratic legitimacy of the EU system, but decreased its efficiency. Conversely, as regards the Council, there has been a long-term shift towards increasingly using a form of majority voting instead of unanimous voting of Member States, thereby increasing the efficiency of the EU (ie its capacity to take decisions) at the possible cost of democratic legitimacy (because the democratic governments of Member States can be outvoted more often).

Although, according to Article 13(1) TEU, there are three other official EU institutions – the Court of Justice, the European Central Bank, and the Court of Auditors – this chapter focuses upon the institutions which have essentially political tasks. The rules governing some of the EU's other institutions, and the EU's offices, bodies, and agencies generally, are discussed elsewhere in this book.[2]

---

[1] On the democratic context of the EU's decision-making rules, see particularly section 11 of that chapter.

[2] On the Court of Justice, see chapter 10; on the European Central Bank, see chapter 19; on the agencies, see generally chapter 8. The EU also has two advisory bodies, the Economic and Social Committee and the Committee of the Regions (see Art 13(4) TEU and Arts 300–307 TFEU), which are not further discussed here.

2 The concept of representative democracy

In theory, representative democracy is simple. The public decides which politicians (who usually group themselves into political parties) they wish to vote for at each election, judge the performance of the successful politicians (ie the public's representatives) while in government, and then decide at the next election whether they wish to re-elect the same politicians or to vote for someone else.

But in practice, when it comes to designing a system for representative democracy, questions soon arise. What voting system should be used? Who gets to vote in elections? In the modern day, no one denies that women should have the right to vote, or argues that people should be excluded from voting because they do not have enough property, but what about foreigners? When should they be allowed to vote – if ever?

Furthermore, most modern political systems are more complex than the simple example given earlier – comprising only a single level of government with one legislative chamber. The larger and more diverse the groups of people voting (ie the electorate), the more likely that these groups (as defined, eg by language, region, class, or ethnicity) have a conflicting point of view on some key issues. If the country being governed is fairly large and/or diverse, an obvious way to address this is by providing for multiple levels of government, so that at least as regards some issues (eg education or criminal law) different parts of the country can decide to have different policies if the electorates vote for this. So, a country can be established as a federal State like Germany (or, outside the EU, the US, Canada, or Australia). As discussed further in chapter 4, a 'federal' State is one which divides powers between the central ('federal') government level and the sub-federal level (known, eg as states, provinces, or Länder). The opposite situation, where all powers in principle are held by the central government, is known as a 'unitary' State – for example, Ireland or the Netherlands.

However, there are other ways of dividing power between different levels of government. While the UK is in principle a unitary State, it has devolved power to some of its regions (Scotland, Wales, and Northern Ireland), and many unitary States give a significant role to local governments (ie the governments of cities, towns, and counties). Having said that, at least in principle, the central governments of unitary States could take such powers away from devolved or local governments, although that might prove difficult in practice. For instance, any attempt by the UK's central government to abolish the Scottish parliament without the consent of the Scottish people in a referendum would probably lead to increased support for Scottish independence. On the other hand, the division of powers between the two levels of government in federal States is, as discussed in chapter 4, entrenched by a constitution which has a higher rank than ordinary law, and cannot be amended without the consent of (usually) both levels of government.

Another way of addressing regional concerns, or the concerns of other diverse groups in society, is by establishing a second parliamentary chamber (ie a 'bicameral legislature'; again see further chapter 4). The majority of EU States, like the UK (ie the House of Commons and the House of Lords), Germany (the Bundestag and Bundesrat), and France (the National Assembly and the Senate), have established such a two-chamber legislature. As the German example shows, it is common for federal States to have a bicameral legislature.

Moreover, as discussed in chapter 4, government does not consist of legislatures only, but has two other branches: the executive and the judiciary (on the latter, see further chapter 10). Political systems usually make some form of attempt to allocate specific functions between these three branches (the principle of separation of powers). The executive is made up of a core group of individuals, namely a president or prime minister, along with a cabinet and support staff. The executive (usually) drafts bills for the parliament to vote on, and determines the detail of government policy on a day-to-day basis. It includes a permanent administration (ie a bureaucracy, or civil service), with the task of advising the government and applying the law on an individual basis, for instance processing applications for passports and student loans.

2.1 Representative democracy and the EU

As a rough starting point, it is useful to compare the EU's political institutions to the political institutions of States on a practical level (for a more theoretical version of this comparison, see chapter 4). The Commission can broadly be compared to the executive and administration (civil service) of the EU, while the Council and European Parliament can be compared to a two-chamber (bicameral) legislature, as described in the previous section. As in many bicameral systems, the lower house, in this case the European Parliament, is directly elected (like the House of Commons in the UK, or the Bundestag in Germany), but the upper house, in this case the Council, is not directly elected (like the House of Lords in the UK, or the Bundesrat in Germany). However, some executive powers have been conferred upon the Council and European Council.

Furthermore, as we will see in chapter 4, a key feature of the EU's political and legal system is that the division of powers between the EU and its Member States is comparable to the division of powers within federal States, as described previously. The system for the division of powers between the EU and its Member States is referred to as the rules on EU 'competences', and this system is discussed in detail in chapter 5. This current chapter sets out the institutional context of the EU's system of divided powers.

Another key feature of the EU system is that EU law is almost entirely administered by Member States, that is, it is national civil servants who, for instance, take action to enforce environmental law (see chapter 22), or who decide on the merits of asylum applications (see chapter 26), even though the substantive decisions which they make are largely determined by EU law. This is different to the approach in most federal States, although it is similar to the system in Germany, the EU's biggest federal State. For example, in the US the laws adopted by the federal government are often applied by federal agencies – the individual states cannot be ordered to act by the federal government (although they can be encouraged through the use of financial incentives). Within the EU system, this delegation of power is recognized expressly by the Treaty, which states that 'Member States shall adopt all measures of national law necessary to implement legally binding Union acts';[3] it is also reflected by the use of directives (which must be implemented by means of national law) to apply many EU policies,[4] and the role of national courts in the implementation of EU law.[5] Even where the EU institutions have traditionally taken the main role administering EU law, in recent years that administration has also been decentralized.[6]

The relationship between the EU institutions can be seen in Figure 3.1.

---

[3] Art 291(1) TFEU.   [4] See further chapters 5 and 6.   [5] See further chapter 10.
[6] See eg chapter 17, as regards competition law.

Fig 3.1 The relationship between the EU institutions

3 Commission

3.1 Introduction

Our examination of the EU's political institutions starts with the Commission, since most EU measures (as we will see) are either adopted by the Commission, or begin life as a Commission proposal. The Commission's role in the EU political system often attracts strong criticism. This is because it has a great deal of power – although the extent of that power is often misunderstood and overstated –and because many believe that it is not sufficiently democratically accountable. In particular, as noted already in section 2.1, the Commission constitutes an important part of the executive, and is responsible for almost all of the day-to-day administration of the EU (ie applying EU law to individual cases) – although it should not be forgotten that most EU law is administered by Member States. The key provisions on the composition, powers, and functioning of the Commission are in Article 17 TEU, and further rules are set out in Article 18 TEU, as regards the EU's High Representative for its common foreign and security policy (the 'High Representative'), and Articles 244–250 TFEU.

3.2 Composition

The Commission consists first and foremost of a 'college of Commissioners', which includes two particularly important Commissioners discussed separately – its President (section 3.2.2) and the EU's High Representative for its common foreign and security policy (section 3.2.3). But the Commission also consists of thousands of permanent administrative staff (see further later in the section).

3.2.1 Number of members

The Commission initially consisted of one member from each Member State and one extra member from each of the five largest Member States (the UK, France, Germany, Italy, and Spain). However, there were concerns that the number of Commissioners would become unmanageable after the extensive enlargement planned to the East (which was ultimately carried out in 2004). But while a reduction in the number of Commissioners would probably improve the efficiency of that institution, there was a contrary concern that if the Commission did not include at least one Commissioner from each Member State, it would lose some of its legitimacy.

The debate concerning the number of Commissioners ultimately became bound up with the even more difficult debate concerning the weighting of Member States' votes in the Council (see section 5), because the larger Member States did not want to give up their extra Commissioner unless they were given extra votes in the Council as a quid pro quo. It proved impossible to agree on these two issues during the negotiation of the Treaty of Amsterdam (in force 1999), so instead a Protocol was attached to the Treaties, stating that as of the next enlargement of the EU, there would be one Commissioner per Member State, provided that the weighting of votes in the Council had been adjusted 'in a manner acceptable to all Member States', in particular 'compensating' those Member States which lost a Commissioner.

It was no longer possible to put off this issue when negotiating the Treaty of Nice (in force 2003), given the imminence of enlargement. So this Treaty provided that there would be only one Commissioner per Member State as from 1 November 2004 (the start of the next Commission's term).[7] To increase efficiency, once the EU had 27 Member States (which occurred in 2007), the next Commission to take office (ie as from 1 November 2009) would have fewer Commissioners than the number of Member States. But the Treaty negotiators could not agree how this would take place, so left it up to the Council to decide on the details, including the exact number of Commissioners and which Member States would lose a Commissioner at any given time.

So there has been one Commissioner per Member State since 2004. However, the rules providing for a further reduction in the number of Commissioners from 2009 never came into effect, because the relevant provisions in the Treaties were amended again with the Treaty of Lisbon (in force 2009). Now the Treaties provide that the Commission remains at one Commissioner per Member State until 1 November 2014.[8] After that point, only two-thirds of Member States will have a Commissioner at any one time, although it is up to the European Council to adopt detailed rules on the exact system of rotation of Commissioners between Member States. However, the European Council (see section 6) also has the option to alter the number of Commissioners.[9]

In practice, the rules providing for a further reduction in the number of Commissioners from 2014 will not come into effect either, at least initially. This is because one reason that Irish voters initially voted against the Treaty of Lisbon in 2008 was their concern about losing a Commissioner. So as part of the deal to encourage Irish voters to vote in favour of the Treaty, EU leaders promised in December 2008 that if the Treaty of Lisbon were ratified, the European Council would decide to retain one Commissioner per Member State even after November 2014. Following the positive vote of the Irish public, and the

---

[7] On the parallel changes to Council voting, see section 5.   [8] Art 17(4) TEU.
[9] Art 17(5) TEU; see also Art 244 TFEU.

subsequent entry into force of the Treaty of Lisbon, the decision to this effect was formally adopted in 2013.[10]

3.2.2 The President

As noted already, a key role in the Commission is the job of President.[11] According to the Treaty, he or she lays down the guidelines for the Commission's work; decides on the internal organization of the Commission, ensuring its efficiency, consistency, and collegiality; and appoints Vice-Presidents from among the Commission's members. These Vice-Presidents are in addition to the High Representative for the EU's foreign policy, who is always a Vice-President.

The President can reshuffle the Commission, and require a Commissioner to resign, so on paper at least he or she has powers similar to a prime minister over his or her cabinet (ie the executive of a Member State). But historically the President did not have such powers,[12] and in fact there has never been a major reshuffle of the sort seen in (for instance) British politics. The President does not have any kind of veto over Commission proposals, or over anything else. Having said that, the President usually has significant influence over the rest of the Commission, and some Presidents (Walter Hallstein, President from 1958 to 1967, and Jacques Delors, President from 1995 to 2005) have had a major impact on the EU integration process. Indeed, each Commission is named in practice after its President (at the time of writing, the 'Barroso Commission', serving from 2010 to 2014).

3.2.3 High Representative

The job of High Representative[13] was created, in its initial form, by the Treaty of Amsterdam in 1999. At this point, the post was part of the Council, not the Commission. The creation of the post was intended to simplify the Union's representation as regards foreign policy, which had previously been in the hands of the rotating Council Presidency (see section 5). However, this just raised more questions, since the rotating Council Presidency continued to exist, and there was also a Commissioner for external relations.

To reduce the complexity of the system, the Treaty of Lisbon recast the role of the High Representative. He or she is a Commissioner (indeed a Commission Vice-President) but is also, as regards his or her foreign policy tasks, answerable to the Council (on those tasks and on the High Representative's appointment and role in practice, see the following section and chapter 24).

3.2.4 Appointment

Historically, the Commission President, and then the rest of the Commission, was appointed by the Member States 'by common accord' (ie unanimously, with no abstentions possible). In practice, the only debate was over the name of the Commission President; otherwise Member States just accepted each other's nominees. After all, if (for example) the UK had vetoed a French nominee, the French government would, in all likelihood, have vetoed a British nominee in retaliation. Each Member State normally nominated an individual from the governing political party (or the main governing party, in the event of a coalition). Due to the Commission's independence, however (see section 3.4), that individual

---

[10] OJ [2013] L165/98. Art 2 of this decision provides that it will be reviewed before the appointment of the next Commission, in 2019, 'in view of its effect on the functioning of the Commission'.
[11] Art 17(6) TEU and Art 248 TFEU.   [12] They only date back to the Treaty of Nice.
[13] See Art 18 TEU.

would remain a Commissioner for the Commission's full term even if the appointing government changed hands. For instance, the British Commissioner until November 2014 is a supporter of the Labour Party, since she was appointed when the Labour Party was in government – even though a Conservative/Liberal Democrat coalition took office only a few months after her appointment.

There is also the question of which posts go to which Commissioner, given that some jobs in the Commission (eg being in charge of competition or external trade) are perceived to be better jobs than others (eg being in charge of administration). The appointment system meant (and still means) that the Commissioners came from diverse political backgrounds, as compared to national politics, where cabinet ministers are all members of the party (or coalition parties) which has (or have) a parliamentary majority. Usually, Commissioners are (or have recently been) senior cabinet ministers in their national governments; indeed since 1995, Commission Presidents have all been sitting prime ministers in a Member State at their time of election.[14] For that reason, Commissioners are sometimes described derisively as 'failed politicians', although some of them do return successfully to national political life after their term(s) in the Commission.[15] In fact, there is usually a mini-exodus of Commissioners in the final year of a Commission's term, as cabinet posts and other desirable appointments in their respective national systems become available.

Over the years, in order to address concerns about the Commission's democratic accountability, the role of the European Parliament in the Commission's appointment was enhanced considerably. The Parliament was first of all given the power to approve the appointment of the Commission as a whole (Maastricht Treaty), and then the Commission President (Treaty of Amsterdam). From 1995, the Commission's term of office (originally four years) was changed to five years,[16] in order to align it with the European Parliament terms. So a new Commission takes office every five years (the next Commission will take office on 1 November 2014), not long after the election of a new European Parliament (as discussed in section 4, the next election is in May 2014).

Since the Treaty of Lisbon, the Treaties state that the Parliament, by a majority of its members (not just a majority of the votes), has the power to 'elect' the Commission President, although the European Council must first (by a qualified majority vote) nominate a single candidate for the Parliament's approval, 'taking account of' the results of the European Parliament election which has just been held.[17] The current Commission President, Jose Manuel Barroso, was (re)appointed in September 2009, before the Treaty of Lisbon came into force, so the new procedure has not been applied yet. From one point of view, the new procedure looks the same as the old one (where the European Parliament approved an appointment to be made by the European Council), but the reference to the Parliament electing the Commission President and taking account of the results of the elections to the Parliament suggest that a stronger link between those election results and the selection of the Commission President can be made.

In practice, it was already assumed in 1999, 2004, and 2009 that, in light of the Parliament's veto power over the appointment, the next Commission President had to come from the same political background as the largest party in the Parliament. But the names of potential candidates were only really discussed *after* the elections to the Parliament – meaning that the public voted in those elections without any discussion of who the next Commission

[14] eg the current Commission President was the sitting Prime Minister of Portugal.
[15] eg Peter Mandelson left the Commission in order to resume a post as a British cabinet minister when Gordon Brown was prime minister.
[16] See now Art 17(3) TEU. [17] Art 17(7) TEU.

President might be.[18] For the 2014 elections, though, the largest parties intend to decide in advance who their preferred candidates are for the post of the Commission President.[19] This can obviously be compared to the election process in many Member States, where voters know that their (collective) vote for a particular political party will in effect determine who becomes (or remains) the prime minister after the elections. Time will tell whether this planned change will increase interest in the European Parliament's elections and the legitimacy of the Commission President – assuming that the European Council is willing to accept the person concerned as their nominee.

After the election of the President, the other Commissioners are then appointed, on the basis of Member States' proposals, by agreement with the Commission President, by a qualified majority vote of the European Council and the approval of the European Parliament. The current Commissioners (other than the President) were appointed early in 2010, pursuant to the new rules established by the Treaty of Lisbon.[20]

A special rule applies to the appointment of the High Representative. The holder of this post is selected by the European Council by a qualified majority vote, with the agreement of the Commission President. The High Representative is also subject to the vote of the European Parliament as regards the entire Commission. The first person to hold this post (Catherine Ashton) was appointed by the European Council with effect from 1 December 2009.[21]

Since the Treaty of Lisbon, there are three important EU posts to fill at the same time, every five years (Commission President, High Representative, and European Council President – on which, see section 6). The posts are decided as part of a 'package deal'. Declaration 6 to the Treaty of Lisbon refers to the need to consider 'geographical and demographic diversity' (ie the size and location of Member States) when making the appointments, but in 2009 the European Council also considered political background and gender, wanting to balance a conservative man (European Council President; see section 6) with a socialist woman (High Representative).

While technically the European Parliament can only choose whether to vote for the entire Commission, not individual Commissioners, since 2004 it has found a way of rejecting individual nominees. When it was unsatisfied, in 2004 and 2009, with the credentials or policies of a few of the would-be Commissioners, the Parliament simply threatened to reject the whole lot, and the targeted individuals then withdrew their names from contention.

3.2.5 Control of the Commission

The basic question as regards political accountability can be summarized simply as, 'Can we throw the rascals out?' So how can the Commission be removed? Within the Member States, a government usually has to resign if it loses a no-confidence vote in parliament. Following that, fresh elections are held, or another party or parties are given a chance to form a government. Similarly, the EU Treaties have always provided for the possibility for the European Parliament (but not the Council, or the European Council) to remove the entire Commission, by means of a 'censure' vote. But this is difficult to apply, as it requires a two-thirds vote of Members of the European Parliament (MEPs) in favour, including a majority of the members of the Parliament (ie an absence or abstention effectively counts as

---

[18] One of the leading candidates *was* known in the 2009 elections – but only because he was the sitting President, and it was clear that the national governments where his party, the 'European People's Party', was in power, would nominate him for a new term if (as happened) that party was again the largest party following the elections.

[19] See the Commission recommendation on the conduct of the elections (OJ [2013] L79/29).

[20] OJ [2010] L38/7. The appointment of the Commission was delayed due to the delay in the entry into force of the Treaty of Lisbon.   [21] OJ [2009] L328/69. On the terms of the job, see OJ [2009] L322/36.

a vote to keep the Commission in office).[22] Even if one were passed, the High Representative would remain in office as regards her responsibilities to the Council.

Indeed, no censure vote ever has been passed. On the one occasion (in 1999) when a censure vote was absolutely certain to pass – every political party in the Parliament having declared its support, due to concerns that allegations about fraud and nepotism as regards certain Commissioners had not been adequately investigated – the Commission simply jumped before it was pushed, with the Commissioners resigning en masse before they could be censured. The Treaties provide that in the event of censure or mass resignation, the Commissioners continue to remain in office until they are replaced.[23] This might take some time, and it potentially damages the EU's legitimacy that such 'guilty' individuals still retain their jobs. While it is sometimes claimed that the European Council could then simply reappoint the same 'censured' Commissioners again, this is clearly not politically realistic – as the Parliament would then obviously use its powers to reject the proposed Commission.[24]

Sometimes, of course, individual Commissioners are considered to be poor at their job, or otherwise unsuitable for it. In fact, the Parliament's planned censure vote of 1999 was essentially aimed at only a small number of the Commissioners then in office. But there was no way for the Parliament to remove those individual Commissioners. The Treaties do provide for the removal of individual Commissioners who are 'guilty of serious misconduct' or cannot do their job, by the Court of Justice on application by the Council or Commission, but this procedure was not used in 1999 or since.[25]

It is now possible, as mentioned already, for the Commission President to force a Commissioner to resign, or to reshuffle the Commission. This is equivalent to the powers enjoyed by prime ministers over their cabinets; and in national politics, sustained serious criticism of a particular cabinet minister will probably sooner or later lead to his or her (forced) resignation, sacking by the prime minister, or removal from the cabinet or demotion to a lesser job at the time of the next reshuffle. But as noted already, no Commission President has ever reshuffled the Commission in a major way. Nor has any Commission President fired an individual Commissioner – although the existence of this power might have led to some Commissioners jumping before they were pushed (eg a Maltese Commissioner facing a public scandal resigned in 2012, in the same way that cabinet ministers facing similar scandals in Member States sometimes resign). Moreover, the European Parliament still cannot demand the removal of individual Commissioners. Yet perhaps a threat to use the censure vote would, by analogy with its previous threats to block the appointment of a new Commission, induce the Commission President to fire the Commissioner(s) concerned. By way of exception, the High Representative can lose her job, as the European Council can end her appointment by the same procedure which applies to her appointment.[26]

An individual vacancy in the Commission is filled by the Council, after consulting the European Parliament, with the agreement of the Commission President.[27]

3.3 **Powers**

Article 17(1) TEU sets out a very lengthy list of the Commission's tasks:

- to 'promote the general interest' of the EU and 'take appropriate initiatives to that end';

---

[22] See Art 17(8) TEU and Art 234 TFEU.   [23] Arts 234 and 246 TFEU.
[24] Even before it obtained such powers, the Parliament would obviously have used its powers to *censure* that reappointed Commission as soon as it could.   [25] See Art 17(8) TEU and Art 234 TFEU.
[26] Art 18(1) TEU.   [27] Art 247 TFEU.

- to 'ensure the application of the Treaties' and measures giving effect to them;
- to 'oversee the application' of EU law, subject to the Court of Justice;
- to 'execute the budget and manage programmes';
- to exercise 'coordinating, executive and management functions';
- to 'ensure the Union's external representation', except as regards EU foreign policy (where the High Representative has this task);
- to 'initiate the Union's annual and multi-annual programming'.

Starting with the Commission's executive tasks, first of all, as Article 17(2) TEU provides, it has a near-monopoly on introducing proposals for EU legislation, meaning that EU legislation cannot possibly be adopted unless the Commission initially proposed it. Furthermore, many non-legislative acts can only be adopted on the basis of a Commission proposal.[28] Of course, it cannot be forgotten that the proposed laws must then be agreed by the Council and the European Parliament.

Similarly, the Commission has a monopoly on negotiating international treaties on behalf of the EU, and otherwise representing the Union on the international level, with the exception of foreign policy (mentioned already) and treaties related to monetary issues (where the Council decides on a case-by-case basis who the negotiator will be).[29] Again, however, any treaties negotiated by the Commission must then be approved by the Council (and usually also the European Parliament) to come into force, and before the Commission can start to negotiate, it must be granted authority to do so by the Council.

Another key executive task is the power to adopt delegated acts or implementing measures, that is, sub-legislative acts which set out further details of EU policies. Delegated acts, which supplement or amend non-essential elements of EU legislative acts, can only be adopted by the Commission, although its adoption of such measures is subject to control by the Council and the European Parliament.[30] Implementing measures can be adopted when 'uniform conditions for implementing [EU acts] are needed'. Usually implementing measures can only be adopted by the Commission as well, but the Council adopts such measures as regards foreign policy and possibly as an exception in other cases.[31] The Commission's adoption of implementing measures is controlled by committees composed of Member States' officials.

These two tasks can be compared to the powers that are delegated to the executive and to civil servants in the Member States by acts of parliament in order to implement legislation (often known as 'delegated legislation', although that term is not used as regards the EU measures). However, the grant of power to the Commission is not usually as far-reaching as the grant of power to national executives and administrations. After all, as mentioned already, it is primarily up to Member States to implement EU law.

Next, the Commission has the legal right to take infringement actions against Member States which have not met their obligations under EU law.[32] This is an important means of ensuring the effective application of EU law, although it is also possible for individuals to use other means to enforce their EU law rights in the national courts (see chapter 6).

---

[28] There are limited derogations from the Commission's monopoly on making legislative proposals. For further discussion, see chapter 5.

[29] Arts 218 and 219 TFEU. For further discussion, see chapter 24.

[30] Art 290 TFEU. For further discussion, see chapter 5.

[31] Art 291 TFEU. For further discussion, see chapter 5.

[32] Arts 258 and 260 TFEU; see further chapter 10.

As for its administrative tasks, the Commission has the role of administering the EU's budget,[33] although the amount of each annual budget, and the multi-annual budget framework, is decided on first by the Council and the European Parliament.[34] The Commission is also subject to financial regulations adopted by those legislative bodies, and is supervised by the European Parliament as regards its budgetary management.[35]

Another key administrative job is to apply EU law in individual cases, for example as regards EU competition law, where the Commission investigates cartels (ie groups of companies setting prices etc together) and monopolies (a single company controlling most or all of a market), and EU law on State aids (ie money given by governments to companies), where the Commission has the power to decide that such money must be repaid. But as noted already, the power to apply EU competition law has been decentralized, and most areas of EU law are implemented entirely by Member States.[36]

As for the High Representative, her job is to conduct the EU's foreign policy, and to make proposals regarding that policy, 'as mandated by the Council'.[37] In addition, she chairs the EU's Foreign Affairs Council (ie meetings of Member States' foreign ministers; see section 5).[38] But the High Representative also sits in the Commission and coordinates the Commission's overall external activity (ie trade, development, enlargement, etc).[39]

3.4 Functioning

The key feature of the Commission's functioning is that it is 'completely independent', and cannot take instructions from governments or any other body.[40] There is an obvious tension between this rule and the objective of ensuring the Commission's accountability, but its independence does not constrain the other EU institutions as regards whether to accept Commission proposals (for instance). Nor does it prevent the application of the rules (discussed previously) which provide that individual Commissioners could possibly be fired, or that the entire Commission could be censured. In any event, it is widely believed that many individual Commissioners have a closer relationship with the Member State that nominated them than the letter of the Treaty would allow.

As an exception, as noted already, the High Representative is accountable to the Council, as far as foreign policy is concerned, but as regards her other tasks, must be as independent as the rest of the Commission.

The college of Commissioners makes decisions by a qualified majority, and in accordance with the Commission's rules of procedure.[41] For its administrative tasks, the Commission is organized into Directorates-General, each responsible for a particular subject, and usually presided over by a particular Commissioner. Since Commission proposals often impact on more than one subject, there are sometimes 'turf battles' between the Commissioners and Directorates-General. In some cases, these battles are resolved by two Commissioners making a joint proposal.[42] In these and many more cases, there are extensive 'inter-service consultations' between different Directorates-General before a proposal is made. For instance, the 2013 proposal for new EU legislation on the admission of students, researchers, and other persons from non-EU countries was made by the Home Affairs Commissioner,[43] but

---

[33] Art 317 TFEU.   [34] Arts 311, 312, and 314 TFEU.   [35] Arts 319 and 322 TFEU.

[36] eg the Commission cannot issue injunctions to enforce EU consumer law (see chapter 23), or European Arrest Warrants (see chapter 25), or decide on applications for asylum or residence permits (see chapter 26).

[37] Art 18(2) TEU.   [38] Art 18(3) TEU.   [39] Art 18(4) TEU.

[40] Art 17(3) TEU and Art 245 TFEU.

[41] Arts 249 and 250 TFEU. For the current rules of procedure of the Commission, see OJ [2010] L55/60.

[42] eg the proposal for legislation on fraud against EU financial interests (COM(2012) 363, 11 July 2012).

[43] COM(2013) 151, 25 March 2013.

doubtless was discussed with the Commissioners responsible for education and research (among others) beforehand.

As regards the High Representative, a special rule in the Treaties requires a particular administration – the European External Action Service – to be set up (see further chapter 24).

4 European Parliament

4.1 Introduction

The European Parliament is perhaps the most familiar EU political institution for those searching for parallels between the EU political system and national political systems. Like the lower legislative chamber (if there are two legislative chambers) or the only legislative chamber (if there is only one such chamber) of every democratic country, it is elected by popular vote at regular intervals. Indeed, from the very foundation of the European Communities (as they then were) in the 1950s, the intention was to elect the members of the European Parliament – although the first such elections were not arranged until 1979. Before that point, the Parliament was made up of part-time members whose main job was serving in national parliaments.

Also like national parliaments, the European Parliament's main tasks are to participate in the legislative and budgetary process and to hold the executive to account – although the latter task in particular is complicated by the complex structure of the EU, where the tasks of the executive are spread among three different institutions.

In addition to the Treaty provisions on the European Parliament,[44] there are also some important secondary measures which regulate its composition and functioning. In particular:

(a) Article 223 TFEU provides for the adoption of a Council decision on the procedure for elections to the European Parliament and for European Parliament regulations on the statute of its members (ie the pay and expenses of those members);[45]

(b) Article 14(2) TEU provides for the European Council to adopt a decision on the 'composition' of the European Parliament (ie allocating the number of seats per Member State); and

(c) Article 22(2) TFEU provides that every EU citizen living in another Member State can vote or stand for election to the European Parliament, subject to the adoption of detailed measures to that end by the Council.

Also, Article 224 TFEU provides for the adoption of regulations on European political parties, which broadly correspond to the political groups which sit in the European Parliament. Although the political parties as such do not impact on the functioning of the European Parliament, the political groups are a crucial part of the Parliament's day-to-day activities (as discussed in section 4.4). According to the Treaties, European political parties 'contribute to forming European political awareness and to expressing the will of citizens of the Union'.[46] The legal rules governing the parties' functioning are set out in legislation adopted in 2004, and amended subsequently.[47]

---

[44] Art 14 TEU and Arts 223–234 TFEU.   [45] For the text of this statute, see OJ [2005] L262/1.

[46] Art 10(4) TEU.

[47] Regulation 2004/2003 (OJ [2004] L297/1), as amended by Regulation 1524/2007 (OJ [2007] L343/5). A further proposed amendment is under discussion at time of writing: COM(2012) 499, 12 September 2012. See Art 224 TFEU.

4.2 **Composition**

4.2.1 Number of members

As the EU enlarged, the number of MEPs has been adjusted upwards over the years to match. The Treaty of Lisbon raised the normal ceiling to 751 MEPs. A key question is the distribution of the seats in the European Parliament between Member States. The Treaties require the seats to be allocated on the basis of 'degressive proportionality', that is, giving small Member States more weight (relative to their population) than large Member States, with no Member State having more than 96 seats or fewer than six seats.[48] As discussed in chapter 4, this has been criticized in some quarters because it does not adhere to the principle of 'representation by population' (ie the equal voting weight of each voter) which usually applies to the election of the lower house of parliament in federal systems. The exact allocation of seats between Member States is decided by the European Council.[49]

4.2.2 Elections

As Article 14(3) TEU states, the European Parliament is elected for five-year terms. This electoral term has been applied since the first direct election in 1979, and so the next election (at the time of writing) is due in May 2014. Also, the European Parliament's term is absolutely fixed, meaning that unlike in some countries, it is not possible to dissolve the entire parliament and hold early elections, even if the Commission has had to resign due to vote of censure by the Parliament (see section 3). This is different from the rules in most national political systems, which usually require fresh parliamentary elections if a government loses a 'no-confidence' vote and no alternative government can be formed (see eg the early elections following no-confidence votes in Ireland in 2011, Germany in 2005, and the Netherlands in 2012).

Originally, the Treaties provided for the adoption of a 'uniform procedure' for elections to the European Parliament.[50] While a Council Act on the election of MEPs was adopted in 1976,[51] this measure left open the adoption of a common electoral procedure for a later date, confining itself to defining issues like the dates of elections, and leaving the electoral system to be defined by 'national provisions' until then.[52]

The Treaty of Amsterdam (in force 1999) changed the rules, so that the electoral law could instead be based on 'principles common' to all Member States.[53] This allowed for the amendment of the Council Act in 2002.[54] The 2002 measure provides that voting must take place on the basis of 'proportional representation', that is, the seats must be allocated in principle according to the percentage of the vote obtained by each political party, rather than the system used in the UK for general elections (where the winning candidate in each constituency is the person with the greatest number of votes, meaning that a party can win a majority of the seats in parliament with only a minority of the votes in the election).

However, there is still flexibility for Member States as to whether to have several large constituencies in that Member State, as long as the system is still proportional,[55] and as regards other aspects of the voting system.[56] The fixed date of elections can be altered

---

[48] Art 14(2) TEU.
[49] OJ [2013] L181/57. This decision includes a more detailed definition of 'degressive proportionality'.
[50] See Art 138 of the original EEC Treaty, since repealed.   [51] OJ [1976] L278/1.
[52] Arts 7 and 9, 1976 Act.   [53] Art 223(1) TFEU.
[54] Decision 2002/772/EC (OJ [2002] L283/1).
[55] Art 2, 1976 Act as amended. On this basis, the UK provides for large multi-member constituencies such as London and Scotland, with the seats for each of these constituencies being allocated on a proportional basis, ie a party getting 30 per cent of the vote in a ten-seat constituency should get three of the seats.
[56] Arts 1(1) and (2) and 2A, 1976 Act as amended.

slightly, by deciding to hold an election up to two months before or one month after the normal period in early June.[57] Elections take place between Thursday and Sunday of the same week, reflecting the different traditions of Member States (eg UK elections are always held on Thursdays), but results cannot be made public in any Member State until all voting is finished.[58]

Being an MEP is incompatible with holding posts in other EU institutions or certain EU bodies, holding a national government post, or (since the 2002 amendments to the electoral act) being a member of a national parliament.[59]

While, as noted previously, there are European political parties, voting in European Parliament elections takes place on the basis of national political party affiliation, and is seen as a verdict by voters on national governments. In each successive election (at least up until 2009, the last election at the time of writing) the voter turnout for European Parliament elections has dropped, even as the European Parliament's powers (see section 4.3) have increased. This may be because in the absence of a direct link between the result of the European Parliament elections and the government of the EU, it is hard for voters to understand what they are voting for. It remains to be seen if the planned prior nominations by European political parties of their preferred candidates for Commission President (see section 3) changes this situation.

Turnout may also be dropping because of the remoteness of the European Parliament, both literally (ie the distant location of its meetings) and as regards individual MEPs (ie the size of the Parliament's constituencies as compared to the size of national parliamentary constituencies). Another factor may be public irritation about the cost of the European Parliament, since the Treaty requires it to meet in both Strasbourg and Brussels, and there are well-publicized scandals about the expenses of MEPs – although, of course, national parliamentarians are not scandal-free either. Similarly, the drop in turnout may also mirror the decline in turnout for national elections, given diminished public enthusiasm for politics in general.

The eligibility to vote in European Parliament elections and to run for office in the European Parliament is partly defined by EU law, which specifies that EU citizens who live in another Member State can in principle vote and run for election in European Parliament elections in that State, on the same conditions as nationals of that State.[60] Otherwise, the Court of Justice has ruled that the eligibility to vote and stand for election is defined by national law, subject to compliance with EU law. So while Member States may confine the right to vote in European Parliament elections to their national residents, they cannot discriminate by giving their citizens who reside in third countries the right to vote in those elections, while denying that right to their citizens who reside in their associated territories.[61] Member States also have discretion to allow citizens of third countries to vote in European Parliament elections.[62] In addition, they have obligations pursuant to the European Convention on Human Rights to permit the residents of their quasi-colonies to vote in European Parliament elections, if a sufficient proportion of EU law applies to the territory of those entities.[63]

---

[57] Art 10, 1976 Act as amended.   [58] Art 9, 1976 Act as amended.

[59] Art 6, 1976 Act as amended.

[60] Art 22(1) TFEU; see Directive 93/109 (OJ [1993] L329/34), as amended by Directive 2013/1 (OJ [2013] L26/27).   [61] Case C-300/04 *Eman and Sevinger* [2006] ECR I-8055.

[62] Case C-145/04 *Spain v UK* [2006] ECR I-7917.

[63] *Matthews v UK* (Appl No 24833/94), ECtHR, 1999.

4.3 **Powers**

Article 14(1) TEU lists two main categories of powers for the European Parliament: 'legislative and budgetary functions', which it exercises 'jointly with the Council'; and powers of 'political control and consultation'. The first category of powers is paralleled by the description of the first category of powers conferred upon the Council (see Article 16(1) TEU, discussed in section 5.3). As noted in the introduction, this wording reflects the two-chamber parliamentary system which the EU has developed.

Originally, the European Parliament was only consulted on a selection of draft measures. Following the first direct elections to the chamber in 1979, all five subsequent major Treaty amendments have expanded the Parliament's decision-making powers considerably, so that it now has equal legislative and budgetary power with the Council in a large majority of areas.[64]

First of all, the Single European Act (SEA) (in force 1987) created a procedure called the 'cooperation procedure', which gave the Parliament some additional influence over the legislative process in some areas. Secondly, the Maastricht Treaty (in force 1993) created a new procedure, known in practice as the 'co-decision' procedure, which put the Parliament and the Council broadly on the same footing as regards legislation in certain areas. That Treaty also extended the cooperation procedure to new areas.

Thirdly, the Treaty of Amsterdam (in force 1999) both extended the co-decision procedure to many new areas and streamlined that procedure, putting the Council and Parliament on an entirely equal footing within it.[65] That Treaty also curtailed the use of the cooperation procedure. Fourthly, the Treaty of Nice (in force 2003) extended the co-decision procedure to a small number of new areas.

Finally, the Treaty of Lisbon (in force 2009) dramatically expanded the use of the co-decision procedure, renaming it the 'ordinary legislative procedure' and specifying that a number of residual cases with different rules for adopting legislative acts had to be regarded as 'special legislative procedures'.[66] Although most special legislative procedures entail consultation of the European Parliament only, in some cases it has the power of 'consent', that is, it can veto the proposal in question.

As for the second category of the Parliament's powers ('political control and consultation'), its most important power of political control – as regards the appointment and dismissal of the Commission President and the rest of the Commission – has already been discussed in section 3. The Parliament also has political control as regards the Commission's delegated acts, as discussed already in section 3. It also has political control, in the form of the power of consent, as regards the following decisions:

- sanctions against Member States for breach of human rights;[67]
- the European Council's decision on the Parliament's own composition;[68]
- some aspects of Treaty amendment;[69]

---

[64] Although Arts 14(1) and 16(1) TEU refer to legislative and budgetary functions, in fact EU measures on the annual budget and multi-annual budget framework are legislative acts (see Arts 311, 312, and 314 TFEU), so are not discussed here separately. The European Parliament has the main role giving discharge to the Commission as regards its implementation of the budget (see Art 319 TFEU).

[65] So unlike, eg the UK's *Parliament Acts*, it is not possible for either legislative chamber in the EU system to overrule the other one, where the co-decision system (now the ordinary legislative procedure) applies.

[66] On legislative procedures generally, see Art 289 TFEU; on the ordinary legislative procedure, see Art 294 TFEU. For discussion of the details of these procedures, see chapter 5.   [67] Art 7(1) and (2) TEU.

[68] Art 14(2) TEU.

[69] The Parliament has to consent if the European Council does not want to hold a 'convention' before amending the Treaty according to the ordinary Treaty amendment procedure (Art 48(3) TEU), and to any

- enlargement of the EU;[70]
- treaties concerning the withdrawal of a Member State from the EU;[71]
- extensions of EU competence over criminal law;[72]
- the conclusion of most international agreements;[73]
- approval of enhanced cooperation (ie a group of some Member States going ahead without some others to adopt EU law).[74]

The Parliament also attempts to exert its power of control via means of parliamentary questions, committees of enquiry, petitions, and the European Ombudsman, who can investigate alleged maladministration by the EU's institutions, offices, bodies, and agencies (Articles 226–228 TFEU).

As for the Parliament's power of consultation, it applies to various other 'innominate non-legislative procedures' (ie cases where the Treaties provide for the EU institutions to adopt non-legislative acts),[75] for instance as regards appointments, the adoption of rules on competition or State aid law, the creation of committees, or changes in decision-making rules.[76] In some cases, there is only an obligation to inform the European Parliament once measures are adopted.[77] The European Parliament's role in relation to EU foreign policy is particularly weak: there is only an obligation for the High Representative to consult it on 'the main aspects and the basic choices' of EU foreign policies, and to inform it of 'how those policies evolve'.[78]

It should be noted, however, that like national parliaments, the European Parliament has long found ways of enhancing its powers beyond the strict letter of the law.[79] For instance, often closely related EU measures are proposed and adopted in a 'package', which sometimes includes non-legislative measures and measures subject to a special legislative procedure alongside measures subject to the ordinary legislative procedure. When this happens, the European Parliament invariably tries to use its leverage over the measures which must be adopted pursuant to the ordinary legislative procedure to influence the content of the other measures as well.[80] As regards international treaties, the Parliament's lack of power over the authorization and content of negotiations, and over the decision to sign the treaty (and perhaps apply it provisionally), is compensated for by its power (in most cases) to veto the final conclusion of the treaty concerned by the EU. If the Parliament indicates in a non-binding vote, while the treaty is being negotiated, that it is inclined to vote against the treaty when the time comes, or at least that it objects to that treaty unless certain changes are made to the intended text, the EU's negotiators (and the Council) must logically consider the Parliament's point of view, or risk the rejection of that treaty by the Parliament.

simplified Treaty amendments extending the use of qualified majority voting or the ordinary legislative procedure (Art 48(7) TEU). For more discussion of the Treaty amendment procedures, see chapter 5.

[70] Art 49 TEU.   [71] Art 50(2) TEU.   [72] Arts 82(2)(d), 83(1), and 86(4) TFEU.
[73] Art 218(6)(a) TFEU. See further chapter 24.   [74] Art 329(1) TFEU. See further chapter 5.
[75] On this concept, see further chapter 5. I am grateful to the author of that chapter, Kieran Bradley, for coining this term.
[76] Arts 74, 78(3), 81(3), 95(3), 103(1), 109, 125(2), 126(14), 128(2), 129(4), 140(2), 148(2), 150, 153(2), 160, 188, 192(2), 203, 218(6)(b), 219(1), 246, 283(2), 286(2), 322(2), 332, and 333(2) TFEU, and Arts 27(3), 41(3), 48(3), and 48(6) TEU. On the substance of the competition and State aids rules, see chapters 17 and 18.
[77] Arts 70, 71, 121(2), 122(2), 126(11), 134(3), 155(2), 156, 168(2), 173(2), 181(2), 215(1), 218(10), 219(2), 222(3), and 329(2) TFEU.   [78] Art 36 TEU.
[79] See similarly the Parliament's use of its powers as regards appointments to the Commission, discussed in section 3.
[80] A good example is the 'six-pack' legislation on economic governance, discussed in chapter 19.

When negotiations with the Council are particularly tough, but the Parliament is particularly committed to achieving its objectives, it sometimes 'freezes' EU funds, or other proposed legislation, in order to place pressure on the other EU institutions. For instance, when negotiating the 'Returns Directive' on the legal position of unauthorized (sometimes called 'illegal') immigrants, it blocked the release of EU money intended to help the Member States with the cost of dealing with such persons, until the negotiations were completed.[81] More recently, when negotiating legislation on the possible reintroduction of internal border controls by 'Schengen' Member States, the Parliament objected both to the content of changes to the Commission's proposals made by the Council, and the Council's decision to reclassify a proposal covered by the ordinary legislative procedure as a non-legislative act on which the Parliament would only be consulted. It therefore refused to adopt legislation on five other security-related measures until it reached an agreement on these proposals with the Council.[82] At the time of writing, the European Parliament strongly supported a Commission proposal on data protection in law enforcement institutions, but the Council was much less enthusiastic. Possibly the Parliament will ultimately find it necessary to freeze other proposals in order to force the Council's hand.

Furthermore, the Parliament is able and willing to resort to court action in order to pursue its legal arguments about EU measures.[83] Most obviously, it has brought cases arguing that EU measures were adopted on the wrong 'legal basis', that is, that the Council adopted a measure on the basis of a clause in the Treaties that gave the Parliament limited powers, but it should have instead adopted a measure on the basis of a clause in the Treaties which gives the Parliament more powers.[84] It has also challenged non-legislative measures that it believes should have been adopted as legislative measures.[85]

4.4 Functioning

Even though (as discussed in section 3), the European Parliament must approve the appointment of the Commission, and can remove the Commission by means of a censure motion, the link between the parliament and the executive in the EU system is much weaker than in most national systems. Put simply, unlike in many countries, the European Parliament does not need to 'support' the Commission as the government of the EU, because the removal of the Commission will not result in early elections to the European Parliament.

The consequence of this is that there is no parliamentary majority party (or parties), and therefore no 'opposition parties'. Instead, there are 'political groups', which bring together MEPs who are members of similar national parties in different Member States. For instance, the 'Party of European Socialists' political group consists of MEPs affiliated to the UK Labour Party, the French Socialist Party, the German Social Democratic Party, and a number of other centre-left parties across the EU. Although, due to the Commission's near-monopoly on proposing legislation (see section 3), MEPs do not have the right of

---

[81] On the content of this legislation, see case study 26.1 in chapter 26.

[82] In practice, this was known as the 'Schengen freeze'. On the content of the border control legislation, see again chapter 26.   [83] See further chapter 10.

[84] For recent examples of successful and unsuccessful claims of this sort, see respectively Case C-490/10 *European Parliament v Council*, judgment of 6 September 2012, nyr, and Case C-130/10 *European Parliament v Council*, judgment of 19 July 2012, nyr. On the concept of 'legal basis', see further chapter 5.

[85] For a recent example of a successful claim of this sort, see Case C-355/10 *European Parliament v Council*, judgment of 5 September 2012, nyr, which is the subject of case study 5.2 in chapter 5.

legislative initiative (ie there are no 'private member's bills'),[86] each political group decides whether it will vote in favour of 'government bills' (ie Commission proposals) or not, on a case-by-case basis. This means that a large number of political groups often work together to achieve the necessary majorities, even if the MEPs in those groups are linked to national political parties (eg the main socialist and conservative parties) which would rarely form coalitions at a national level.

As with many national parliaments, the day-to-day work of the European Parliament is largely carried out in committees. The Parliament's committees broadly reflect the tasks of individual Commissioners and Directorates-General (see section 3) and Council configurations (see section 5), and again there are sometimes turf battles. For instance, in 2013 after months of disputes between the budgetary control committee and the civil liberties committee as to which would be responsible for a proposal on EU fraud, it was finally agreed that both committees would work together.

Shortly after each legislative proposal or other measure which the Parliament examines, it allocates a 'rapporteur' in the relevant committee for the subject. The rapporteur is responsible for drafting the European Parliament's position on the measure and will be (where relevant) in charge of negotiations with the Council. These positions are allocated based on each political group's share of the seats in the Parliament, although of course each rapporteur will need to obtain support from other political groups (by taking account of their opinions when drafting a position and negotiating with the Council, and by accepting some proposed amendments suggested by other political groups) in order to obtain a majority in support of a proposal.

5 Council

5.1 Introduction

The Council is the EU's main decision-making organ, although to a large extent it now shares this role with the European Parliament. It is usually made up of ministers from Member States' governments,[87] so unsurprisingly it is one of the most 'intergovernmental' institutions (ie an institution dominated by Member States' governments). As mentioned at the outset of this chapter, it is crucial to keep in mind that the Council is a distinct body from the *European* Council, which is made up of Member States' presidents and prime ministers (see section 6). The basic rules on the composition and functioning of the Council are set out in Article 16 TEU, and further detailed rules are set out in Articles 237–243 TFEU and in the Council's rules of procedure.[88]

As noted already, the Council is, to a certain extent, comparable to the upper chamber of a two-chamber legislative system. In particular, it can be compared to the upper chamber in countries such as Germany (the Bundestag) and the US (the Senate), where membership of the chamber is directly linked to the division of the country into Länder (Germany) or states (the US). However, this comparison is only partly useful, since the Council has executive functions as well as legislative ones, and the members of the Council do not sit in Brussels as full-time 'senators'. Rather, their main job is as ministers in their national

---

[86] However, the Parliament as a whole can propose legislation in a few areas: for details, see chapter 5. It can also request the Commission to make a legislative proposal (Art 225 TFEU).

[87] It is possible that ministers from regional or state governments can attend the Council, although in that case they are still representing that Member State as a whole (Art 16(2) TEU).

[88] OJ [2009] L325/35.

governments. Moreover, as we shall see, different people serve in the Council depending on the subject matter of the issues under discussion.

As we saw at the outset of this chapter, Article 10(2) TEU states that the Council's democratic legitimacy is based on each *individual* minister's democratic accountability to the electorate or parliament of each Member State. There is no collective legitimacy of the Council as regards the EU as a whole.[89]

5.2 Composition

The Council consists of national ministers who represent their Member State's government, who can commit their government and cast a vote on its behalf.[90] It is therefore for the government of each Member State to decide who will appear in the Council to represent that government; this will depend on the results of elections, coalition negotiations, and cabinet reshuffles.

As noted already, the Council does not have a fixed membership. Rather, it is made up of different ministers depending on the subject matter being discussed. In this context, Article 16(6) TEU refers to the different 'configurations' of the Council. This Treaty provision refers to two specific such configurations. First of all, the General Affairs Council (usually made up of Member States' European Affairs Ministers), which is

> responsible for overall coordination of policies, institutional and administrative questions, horizontal dossiers which affect several of the European Union's policies, such as the multiannual financial framework and enlargement, and any dossier entrusted to it by the European Council.[91]

Secondly, the Foreign Affairs Council (obviously made up of Member States' foreign ministers), 'elaborates' the EU's external actions. More precisely, it is

> responsible for the whole of the European Union's external action, namely common foreign and security policy, common security and defence policy, common commercial policy, development cooperation and humanitarian aid.[92]

Otherwise, the list of Council configurations is adopted by the European Council.[93] Currently, there are eight other configurations: Agriculture and Fisheries; Justice and Home Affairs; Economic and Financial Affairs; Employment, Social Policy, Health and Consumer Affairs; Competitiveness (Internal Market, Industry, Research and Space); Education, Youth, Culture and Sport; Transport, Telecoms and Energy; and Environment. In practice some are subdivided (ie transport, telecoms, and energy ministers actually meet separately). The subject matter that each of these configurations deals with is not precisely defined, and there are occasionally 'turf battles' as to which Council configuration is in charge of a particular 'dossier'.

In practice, the General Affairs, Foreign Affairs, Agriculture and Fisheries, and Economic and Financial Affairs Councils usually meet every month, while the other Councils meet every two or three months.

---

[89] On the implications of this for the democratic credentials of the EU, see further chapter 4.

[90] Art 16(2) TEU.

[91] Art 2(2), Council rules of procedure. The General Affairs Council also has a role preparing and following up the European Council: see further section 6.   [92] Art 2(5), Council rules of procedure.

[93] Art 236(a) TFEU. For this list, see OJ [2009] L315/46, amended by OJ [2010] L263/12.

5.3 **Powers**

Article 16(1) TEU points out that the Council has two main categories of powers: 'legislative and budgetary functions', which it exercises 'jointly with the European Parliament'; and 'policy-making and coordinating functions'. As we have seen (section 4), the first of these powers matches the first of the European Parliament's main powers (as described in Article 14(1) TEU), but the second category of powers is obviously rather different from the Parliament's further powers of 'political control and consultation'.[94]

The Council's role in legislative procedures is discussed in detail in chapter 5; but it should be recalled (as discussed in section 4) that its role in the ordinary legislative procedure is exactly equal to that of the European Parliament. As regards special legislative procedures, most of these provide for the Council to adopt legislation with a requirement only to *consult* the Parliament. The two different roles of the Council are expressly provided for in the Treaties: Article 16(8) TEU requires the Council to meet in public when discussing legislative acts,[95] and to divide the agenda of each of its meetings between legislative and non-legislative acts.

As regards its 'policy-making and coordinating' functions, the Council's policy-making role is most obviously manifest in relation to the areas where it can adopt 'innominate non-legislative acts', that is, where the Treaties provide for the Council to adopt acts which are not legislative, in areas such as competition and State aids rules, or foreign policy measures.[96] It also has the lead role regarding international treaties, deciding on whether to give the Commission a mandate to negotiate, deciding on the content of that mandate, overseeing the negotiations in a special committee, and then deciding to sign and conclude the agreement. But the European Parliament's power to consent to most such treaties, and the Commission's (or High Representative's) power to negotiate them, cannot be forgotten.[97] The Council also has the power to suspend such treaties and to define the EU's position as regards implementing them.

In a limited number of cases, the Council also has the power to adopt implementing measures – namely where the EU acts concerned confer such power upon it, and concerning the implementation of foreign policy acts.[98]

As regards its coordination power, the Council has the power to coordinate, in particular, Member States' economic, employment, and social policies (see Article 5 TFEU). This process is often referred to as the 'open method of coordination', and results in measures which are often called 'soft law'.[99] In the area of economic policy coordination, however, the legal effect of the coordination has in principle been enhanced since 2011, in light of the economic and financial crisis.[100]

---

[94] Yet it should be recalled that the Council, like the Parliament, has the power of political control as regards delegated acts of the Commission: see section 3.

[95] For more on the transparency of the legislative process, see section 7.

[96] On this concept, see chapter 5. On the substance of such rules, see eg chapters 17, 18, and 24.

[97] On Art 218 TFEU, see further sections 3.3 and 4.3, and the analysis in chapter 24.

[98] According to Art 291(2) TFEU, the Council can only be given such powers in 'duly justified specific cases', and as regards foreign policy. The Council cannot create new types of legislative procedures which give it further power to adopt measures: see Case C-133/06 *European Parliament v Council* [2008] ECR I-3189. For more on implementing measures, see chapter 5.   [99] For more detail, see chapter 5.

[100] For more detail, see chapter 19.

5.4 **Functioning**

5.4.1 Voting in the Council

The most controversial question concerning the functioning of the Council has been its voting procedures. There are two key issues here: (a) whether the Council votes by unanimity, or by a 'qualified majority' (ie a majority vote in which Member States have different weights due to the size of their population); and (b) how to calculate a 'qualified majority' when such a vote must be held. A qualified majority vote is the default rule;[101] but there are also a few minor cases where only a simple majority of Member States (ie 15 out of 28 Member States at present) can adopt a measure.[102]

On the first point, it is obviously difficult to obtain unanimity in the Council, and inevitably it has been getting more difficult as the EU has enlarged. To address this, all five major Treaty amendments have expanded the use of qualified majority voting (QMV) in the Council. For instance, the SEA (in force 1987) introduced QMV for many measures related to completion of the internal market (eg Article 114 TFEU), including in flanking areas such as sea and air transport (see now Article 100 TFEU). This has facilitated (inter alia) the adoption of most of the legislation on consumer law discussed in chapter 23 – when unanimity had applied, it had taken many years to negotiate measures such as the Product Liability Directive. The Maastricht Treaty introduced QMV as regards (inter alia) environmental law, facilitating the adoption of much of the legislation discussed in chapter 22, while the Treaties of Amsterdam, Nice, and Lisbon gradually extended QMV as regards (inter alia) immigration law, facilitating the adoption of much of the legislation discussed in chapter 26. The Treaty of Lisbon introduced QMV for (inter alia) most criminal law and policing measures, making it easier in particular to adopt legislation on criminal suspects' rights, which had previously been blocked by national vetoes (see further chapter 25).

However, unanimous voting still remains in the Council for sensitive issues such as taxation, certain aspects of employment law and environmental law (see further chapters 20 and 22), or the possible creation of a European Public Prosecutor (see further chapter 25). While QMV is always used in the context of the ordinary legislative procedure, and usually applies when the Council adopts innominate non-legislative procedures (which were explained in section 4), unanimity usually applies as regards special legislative procedures. It should be noted that abstentions do not prevent the adoption of acts by unanimity.[103]

Sometimes a Member State which has been outvoted pursuant to a qualified majority vote argues that the measure concerned was adopted on the wrong 'legal basis' (see section 4), and so unanimous voting should have applied. Then again, sometimes the argument is the other way around – that a legal base entailing qualified majority should have been used, instead of a legal basis entailing unanimity (usually it is the Commission which makes this argument). These disputes often lead to legal challenges to the measures concerned, which are brought before the Court of Justice. For instance, the UK government brought a challenge (unsuccessfully) against the adoption of the EU's 'Working Time' Directive, which provides (among other things) for a maximum 48-hour week for workers in the Member States. The UK argued that this directive should have been adopted under Article 100 EC rather than 118a EC (under the 'old' Treaty numbers), which would have given the UK a veto.[104]

---

[101] Art 16(3) TEU.　　[102] Art 238(1) TFEU.　　[103] Art 238(4) TFEU.
[104] Case C-84/94 *UK v Council* [1996] ECR I-5755, concerning Directive 93/104 (OJ [1993] L307/18). On this directive, see further chapter 20. The relevant Treaty provisions are now Arts 115 and 153 TFEU.

In the event of a persistent veto, it is possible for a group of the Member States in favour of the measure in question to circumvent that veto by adopting the measure pursuant to the rules on 'enhanced cooperation', for instance as regards the adoption of legislation on EU patents in 2011 (despite Spanish and Italian opposition), provided that there is a qualified majority vote in Council in favour of using this process and other procedural and substantive rules are satisfied.[105]

On the second point, as with the European Parliament (see section 4) votes have always been weighted in the Council in the form of 'degressive proportionality', that is, giving small Member States more weight (relative to their population) than large Member States. The crucial question was always how to put together a 'blocking minority', that is, a combination of Member States with enough votes to block a decision from being adopted.

For many years, the Member States had between two votes (Luxembourg) and ten votes (the four biggest Member States) in the Council, with the blocking minority adjusted with every enlargement of the EU.[106] So, for instance, between 1995 and 2004, 26 votes were needed to block a decision. This could consist of two large Member States (which had ten votes each) and Spain (which had eight votes), or two large Member States and (in most cases) two smaller Member States. However, with the planned enlargement to include a number of small and medium-sized Member States in the East and the Mediterranean, the larger Member States were concerned that they would no longer be able to form blocking minorities as easily as they had in the past. So, before this major enlargement could go ahead, the larger Member States insisted that the system of Council voting should be reweighted, to give them more relative weight than they would enjoy if the then-current system were simply extended to cover the new Member States *mutatis mutandis*. In particular, Germany preferred to switch to a 'dual majority' system, meaning a measure would need to receive backing from a majority of Member States which also represent a majority of the total EU population; this would reflect Germany's de facto increase in population since its unification in 1990.

As noted previously (see section 3.2), this dispute became connected with the question of the number of Commissioners, since the large Member States did not want to give up their extra Commissioners without an increase in their relative voting weight in the Council. We have seen already that it was impossible to agree on these issues when negotiating the Treaty of Amsterdam, but a deal was reached as part of the Treaty of Nice.

This reweighting, which took effect from 1 November 2004, provides that (as adjusted for the 2007 and 2013 enlargements) a 'qualified majority' is achieved when there are 260 votes in favour out of 352 votes cast (so 93 votes are needed for a blocking minority).[107] As before, large Member States have more votes than small Member States, but the distribution of the votes is not fully proportionate to population. However, that distribution is more proportionate than it used to be. For instance, there are 29 votes each for the UK, Germany, France, and Italy; 27 votes for Spain and Poland; 4 votes each for Luxembourg,

---

[105] For more on this process, see chapter 5. In a few cases, enhanced cooperation can be 'fast-tracked' in the event of a veto, dispensing with these additional requirements: see Arts 86 and 87 TFEU.

[106] Before the first enlargement in 1973, Luxembourg had one vote and the largest Member States had four. Upon that enlargement, the number of votes were changed to benefit the medium-sized and large Member States slightly.

[107] For details, see Art 16(5) TEU and Art 3(3), Protocol 36 on transitional provisions. Note that an abstention effectively counts as a vote *against*.

Latvia, Estonia, Slovenia, and Cyprus; and 3 votes for Malta. It can be seen that a blocking minority can consist of (for instance) three large Member States plus any other Member State opposed (unless the other Member State is one of the five States with only three or four votes).

In addition, there is a requirement of 'dual majority' in favour of a measure: a proposal must also be supported by a majority of Member States, and by Member States representing 62 per cent of the EU population. Usually, the latter criterion would only come into play if Germany (and several other countries) opposed a proposal.

Due to concerns (which have not been borne out in practice) that these rules would make it too difficult to adopt EU measures, the Treaty of Lisbon altered the Council voting rules again, as from 1 November 2014. In principle, there is a simple move to a dual majority system: a proposal will need the support of 55 per cent of Member States (currently 16 out of 28 Member States) with 65 per cent of the EU population. A blocking minority will have to consist of at least four Member States.[108]

In principle, the new rules will make it easier to adopt measures. However, there is a transitional rule: until 31 March 2017, any Member State can insist that the old rules apply when a vote is taken. Effectively, the new and old rules will coexist.[109] This benefits particularly Poland and Spain (in fact, Poland insisted upon this rule), which had a larger share of the votes under the pre-2014 rules.

A further limit on the use of the revised QMV rules after November 2014 is a Council decision which provides that discussions must continue if a proportion of Member States falling short of a blocking minority insist upon this.[110] The Council must try to reach a 'satisfactory' solution' to these States' concerns within a 'reasonable time'.

There are also two variants on QMV. First of all, where the proposal in question was not made by the Commission (eg it was proposed by a group of Member States, or another EU institution or body: see chapter 5, section 7.1.1), two-thirds of Member States (currently 19 countries) must vote in favour.[111] As from 1 November 2014, in such cases 72 per cent of Member States (currently 21 countries) must vote in favour.[112]

Secondly, where not all Member States participate in an EU measure, due to opt-outs or the use of enhanced cooperation (see further chapter 5, section 9), the relevant Member States do not participate in the Council vote, so the voting rules have to be recalculated to apply to the participating Member States only.[113]

Finally, it should be noted that in a few sensitive cases (social security, foreign policy implementing measures, and aspects of criminal law), Member States with profound objections to a measure which could be adopted by a qualified majority can stop its adoption by means of a so-called 'emergency brake' procedure.[114]

5.4.2 Council Presidencies

A key feature of the functioning of the Council is its Presidency. Historically, before the entry into force of the Treaty of Lisbon, the Presidency was held by each Member State in

---

[108] Art 16(4) TEU.   [109] Art 3(2), transitional Protocol.

[110] OJ [2009] L314/73. Before 31 March 2017, this clause can be triggered by a group of Member States which either have 75 per cent of the population or 75 per cent of the numbers necessary to constitute a blocking minority. After that date, these percentages drop to 55 per cent.

[111] Art 3(3), transitional Protocol.   [112] Art 238(2) TFEU.

[113] Art 3(4), transitional Protocol and Art 238(3)(a) TFEU. Where both of these variants apply simultaneously (ie where a group of Member States make a criminal law proposal, and not all Member States participate in it), see the rule in Art 238(3)(b) TFEU.   [114] See further chapter 5, section 7.1.

turn for a period of six months. This system was then amended by the Treaty of Lisbon to provide that the Foreign Affairs Council is chaired by the High Representative (see section 3).[115] Similarly, before the Treaty of Lisbon, each Member State holding the Council Presidency also chaired the European Council, but now that body has its own full-time President (see section 6.2).

For the remaining Council configurations, according to Article 16(9) TEU, this role must still be taken by Member States on the basis of 'equal rotation', in accordance with a decision adopted by the European Council by a qualified majority.[116] According to this European Council decision, the Presidency is nominally held by groups of three Member States working together; these groups are chosen on the basis of their 'diversity and geographical balance'.[117] This means that each group of three contains a large, medium, and small State, and States from different parts of the EU; obvious groupings like the Baltic States or the Benelux States are avoided. However, in practice (as before) each of these three States takes the main role for a period of six months (ie Italy in the second half of 2014, Latvia in the first half of 2015, and Luxembourg in the second half of 2015), on a revolving basis, with the other members of the group assisting the lead Member State on the basis of a common programme.[118]

Holding the Presidency means that the Member State in question is responsible for scheduling and chairing all of the Council meetings planned for the six-month period (except for the Foreign Affairs Council), as well as the meetings of the Council's 'preparatory bodies', that is, its committees and working parties (see section 5.4.3).[119] As an exception, a representative of the High Representative chairs those preparatory bodies which are related to the foreign policy and defence aspects of the Foreign Affairs Council,[120] and certain other working groups or committees have a fixed chair who is elected (ie by his or her peers on that committee) or are chaired by the Council's General Secretariat (on which, see later).[121] Before the Treaty of Lisbon, the Council Presidency also had a significant role as regards EU foreign policy (ie representing the EU at the United Nations and other international meetings relating to foreign policy), but this task has effectively been taken over by the High Representative.

Even though the Treaty of Lisbon reduced its significance, the Council Presidency is in practice still an important part of the EU. The Member State which holds the Presidency is able to set the agenda for six months and usually selects certain outstanding disputes over policy or legislation that it will try to solve, between Member States and/or between the Council and the European Parliament (the Presidency is in charge of negotiating legislation with the European Parliament on behalf of the Council). In practice, though, the Presidency's flexibility is usually constrained by the agenda and deadlines set by the European Council (see section 6), as well as by the timetable of events. The following case study of a successful Council Presidency illustrates the continuing importance of this office.

---

[115] However, a footnote to Art 2(5) of the Council's rules of procedure indicates that when discussing trade issues, the High Representative will delegate chairing the Foreign Affairs Council to the rotating Council Presidency.

[116] Art 236(a) TFEU. For this decision, see OJ [2009] L315/50. A further Council decision sets out additional details: OJ [2009] L322/28.   [117] Art 1(1), European Council Decision OJ [2009] L315/50.

[118] Ibid, Art 1(2). The following 'trio' Presidencies will be the Netherlands, Slovakia, and Malta in 2016–17, then the UK, Estonia, and Bulgaria in 2017–18: Annex I, Council Decision OJ [2009] L322/28.

[119] Art 2, European Council Decision OJ [2009] L315/50.

[120] Annex II, Council Decision (OJ [2009] L322/28).   [121] Ibid, Annex III.

Case study 3.1: The Irish Council Presidency of 2013

The Irish government held the office of Council Presidency in the first half of 2013, following Denmark and Cyprus in 2012, and before Greece and Lithuania in 2013–14. The most crucial task for the Presidency was to reach agreement between the Council and European Parliament over the proposed legislation establishing the EU's multi-annual spending and revenue, since the existing multi-annual budget rules expired at the end of 2013. A failure to reach a deal would not have quite as drastic an effect as the periodic shutdowns of the US government over budget disputes, since it is legally possible for the EU to continue with the previous multi-annual budget framework, if no new framework can be agreed (see Article 312(4) TFEU). But it is much easier for the EU to function with a new multi-annual financial framework, and it has adopted such a new frameworks at regular intervals since the mid-1980s.

Negotiations for the new multi-year financial framework first of all took place between Member States, since the framework takes the form of a 'special legislative procedure' which has to be agreed unanimously in the Council. This part of the talks were in part conducted by the Council Presidency, and in part by the President of the European Council (see section 6), given that in practice the final, most controversial, details of these frameworks are always agreed by the European Council. The European Council reached a deal in February 2013, but this was not the end of the story, because the European Parliament has to give its consent to the adoption of the legislation concerned. It was up to the Irish Presidency to reach a deal between the Parliament and the Council, which it did by June 2013. However, the Parliament then imposed a 'freeze' (see section 4.3) and delayed its formal vote of approval of this legislation, because it wanted to plug gaps in the 2013 budget and influence the content of the 2014 annual budget too. So it fell to the subsequent Lithuanian Presidency to negotiate these issues with the European Parliament, and it reached a deal finally in November 2013.[122]

The negotiation of the multi-annual financial framework was only part of the picture. About 70 more legislative measures set out the details of the EU's multi-annual spending in specific fields (eg agriculture, fisheries, and research). So the Council Presidency was also responsible for concluding negotiations on as much as possible of this legislation. It was able to reach agreement between the European Parliament and the Council on a large majority of the measures concerned, with the main exception of external relations and Justice and Home Affairs spending, which the Lithuanian Presidency then had to negotiate on.

The Irish Presidency completed negotiations between the Council and European Parliament on other major issues as well. These included the reform of the EU's fisheries and agricultural policies, which were closely linked to the revision of the EU's funding legislation on those issues. It also negotiated a deal on the remaining legislation to establish the second phase of the Common European Asylum System, which had been under discussion since 2008–9. Furthermore, the Presidency agreed a deal with the European Parliament on reform of the 'Schengen' rules on external border controls (see further chapter 26), thereby 'unfreezing' the legislative proposals which the European Parliament had been blocking (see section 4). In the area of economic and monetary union, the Presidency negotiated deals on the transfer of banking supervision tasks to the European Central Bank, on the 'two-pack' legislation on the fiscal policies of eurozone Member States (see further chapter 19).

The Presidency also reached deals within the Council on new legislation on winding up failing banks and on a mandate for the Commission, on behalf of the EU, to negotiate a free

---

[122] OJ [2013] L347/884.

trade deal with the US (see further chapters 19 and 24). But in the former case, it then fell to the subsequent Presidency (Lithuania) to negotiate a deal with the European Parliament on the legislation to wind up banks, and to a succession of future Presidencies to address disputes that are likely to arise during the trade negotiations with the US.

While the Irish Presidency's achievements reflect that country's interests as an agricultural exporter, its good relations with the US, and its troubled banking industry,[123] any Member State holding the Presidency at that time would probably have tried to address the same issues. It is notable that some of the Presidency's successes concern issues in which it did not even participate (asylum and border control legislation); perhaps in those cases it was successful precisely because Ireland did *not* have a national interest at stake, and so could be a neutral mediator.

The EU judges Council Presidencies by how much EU business they are able to conclude successfully, that is, how efficient they are. By that standard, the Irish Presidency was judged a great success. For comparison's sake, it is useful to contrast it to a particularly *unsuccessful* Presidency. The Italian Presidency in the second half of 2003 not only failed to agree legislation establishing the *first* phase of the Common European Asylum System,[124] but also presided over the collapse of both the EU's economic governance system[125] and of negotiations to amend the Treaties to establish a Constitutional Treaty.[126] Possibly Italian Prime Minister Silvio Berlusconi was paying more attention to his own colourful personal life.

5.4.3 Other aspects

For all EU measures, the Council is assisted by a Committee of Permanent Representatives (ambassadors) of the Member States to the EU, known as 'Coreper'.[127] Coreper meets in two different formats: Coreper II deals with the business of the General Affairs, Foreign Affairs, Justice and Home Affairs, and Economic and Financial Affairs Council (ie the economic, foreign policy, political, and security issues that political scientists often refer to as 'high politics'), while Coreper I deals with the subject matter of the six other Council configurations[128] (ie the issues that political scientists often refer to as 'low politics'). Both Coreper I and Coreper II meet most weeks for one or two days each. Coreper cannot take legally binding decisions, but can take purely procedural decisions.[129] The national civil

---

[123] Once the European Central Bank begins to supervise banks, it is possible that some of the debt which Ireland incurred to bail out its banking system will be transferred to the European Stabilisation Mechanism, thus reducing the Irish national debt and to some extent sparing the Irish government from having to increase taxes and cut back government spending even more than it has already. See further chapter 19.

[124] These negotiations were then concluded successfully under the following Irish Presidency. For the substance of the law, see chapter 26.

[125] This led to a weakened system for control of Member States' excessive deficit spending, which some blame (at least in part) for the difficulties faced by the EU's economic and monetary union since 2008. See further chapter 19.

[126] As noted in chapter 2, these negotiations were resumed successfully under the following Presidency (the Irish again!), but the ensuing Constitutional Treaty was then not ratified by all Member States, and so did not come into force. However, the Treaty of Lisbon, which included much of the same text as the Constitutional Treaty, was later negotiated and ratified instead.   [127] Art 240(1) TFEU.

[128] The configurations dealt with by Coreper I are Agriculture and Fisheries; Employment, Social Policy, Health and Consumer Affairs; Competitiveness (Internal Market, Industry, Research and Space); Education, Youth, Culture and Sport; Transport, Telecoms and Energy; and Environment. See section 5.2.

[129] See Case C-25/94 *Commission v Council* [1996] ECR I-1469. See the Council's rules of procedure (OJ [2009] L325/35).

servants from the permanent representations in Brussels who deal with specific subjects sometimes meet separately to discuss those issues (eg in the form of 'Justice and Home Affairs Counsellors').

Beneath the level of Coreper, the Council is assisted by a number of working groups and committees; some (but not all) of the committees are referred to expressly in the Treaty. For instance, Article 207 TFEU refers to a committee on external trade matters, which plays a key role in the development of the EU's common commercial policy (see chapter 24). Like Coreper, the working groups and committees prepare the Council's work, and cannot take legally binding decisions. They agree in principle on the large majority of the texts of proposed EU measures. The provisions of those texts which are politically more difficult to agree are discussed by Coreper, which usually reaches agreement upon them. If Coreper cannot agree due to the great political sensitivity of a particular issue, then Member States' ministers must discuss that issue in Council. Of course, it should not be forgotten that if the measure concerned is subject to the ordinary legislative procedure, the Council must also negotiate a deal with the European Parliament.

The Council has a permanent staff who assist it with its tasks. They are organized in the form of a General Secretariat, which is divided into Directorates-General, rather like the Commission (see section 3). This administration is presided over by a Secretary-General.[130]

6 European Council

6.1 Introduction

The final political institution is the European Council, which consists primarily of the heads of State or government of each Member State. Like the Council (which, as pointed out previously, is comprised of national *ministers*), the members of the European Council can each individually refer back to a democratic mandate conferred by the voters or parliament of each individual Member State, but they do not have any collective mandate conferred by the EU electorate as a whole.[131] As we shall see, while the European Council is a weak institution in legal terms, its role is far more significant in practice. The rules governing the European Council are set out in Article 15 TEU and Articles 235–236 TFEU.

6.2 Composition

As with the Council, it is up to each Member State to decide who attends as its representative in the European Council. Since the European Council is a working political institution, those heads of State whose job is purely or largely ceremonial (eg the monarch, in the case of seven Member States, or the presidents of Ireland and Germany) do not attend. Instead, the European Council consists of prime ministers or their equivalents (eg the German chancellor, the Irish Taioseach) and the presidents of those countries (like France) where the president is the most important politician.

The High Representative (see previously) also takes part in the work of the European Council,[132] and the President of the European Council (see later) and the President of the Commission are also members of it. However, only the Member States' heads of State or government can vote.[133]

---

[130] Art 240(2) TFEU. For details of the current organization of the Secretariat-General, see http://www .consilium.europa.eu/media/1884553/gsc_organisation_chart_en.pdf, accessed 8 August 2013.
[131] See again Art 10(2) TEU.   [132] Art 15(2) TEU.   [133] Art 235(1) TFEU.

Up until the Treaty of Lisbon, Presidency of the European Council was held by a rotation of Member States for six-month periods (with the Member State holding both the Presidency of the Council (see section 5.4.2) and the Presidency of the European Council). The Treaty of Lisbon created the post of President of the European Council, which replaced this rotation system. The President is appointed by the European Council for two-and-a-half years, renewable once, by a qualified majority vote;[134] there is no role for any other EU institution (or the general public) in his or her appointment. The first full-time President, appointed as from 1 December 2009 when the Treaty of Lisbon entered into force, is Herman van Rompuy, the former Prime Minister of Belgium; his term was renewed in 2012, so will expire at the end of November 2014.[135] For a long time, former British Prime Minister Tony Blair had been the front runner for this job, but ultimately other EU leaders began to have misgivings about appointing him.

It should be noted that, despite some confusion in the press, the President of the European Council is not the 'President of the EU', but only the President of one of its institutions. As compared to powerful presidencies like those in France or the US, the powers of the President of the European Council are quite limited.[136] As noted already, the President does not vote at the European Council; and since the European Council does not have a legislative role, the President of the European Council cannot veto legislation (eg unlike the President of the US). Nor can he or she issue instructions to the European Council (or other EU institutions), or adopt binding measures (although the European Council *itself* can adopt binding acts, as discussed later). Rather, the President chairs the European Council and drives forward its work,[137] ensures its preparation and continuity,[138] aims to facilitate 'cohesion and consensus', reports regularly to the European Parliament, and represents the EU 'at his [or her] level' as regards foreign policy, without prejudice to the role of the High Representative (discussed previously). In practice, in light of the economic and financial crisis since van Rompuy took office, the external role of the first full-time President of the European Council has been limited.

While the President of the European Council cannot hold a national office, he or she is not banned from holding another EU post, although it would be awkward to hold the Presidencies of both the European Council and the Commission simultaneously – due to the differences in the appointment process and the degree of independence of these two offices. Similarly, it would be difficult in practice for the President of the European Council to hold another post in the Commission or the European Parliament.

In the absence of any legal powers for the President of the European Council, it is hard to judge the impact of creating the post. But it is clear that the post is not purely ceremonial: President van Rompuy is politically highly involved, and can hardly be compared to the UK's Queen, or the President of Germany. The European Council has been intensively involved in crisis management relating to the EU's economic and monetary union in recent years, and it is likely that the President played some role in facilitating agreement

---

[134] Art 15(5) TEU. This vote is calculated the same way as for the Council (see section 5). The European Council can dismiss its President (by the same voting rule) in the event of 'impediment or serious misconduct'.

[135] OJ [2009] L315/48; OJ [2012] L77/17. On the President's terms of office, see OJ [2009] L322/35.

[136] Art 15(6) TEU.

[137] The President of the European Council sets the agenda of meetings and draws up draft conclusions and decisions, but these must be discussed first in the General Affairs Council (see Art 3, European Council rules of procedure).

[138] On this point, the President of the European Council must cooperate with the President of the European Commission and acts 'on the basis of the work of the General Affairs Council'. See also Art 16(6) TEU, which provides for the General Affairs Council to ensure the follow-up to European Council meetings, in conjunction with the President of the European Council.

on the measures to be taken. Under the pre-Lisbon system, the president or prime minister of the rotating Member State which held the Presidency would of course have tried to achieve the same results, but given the length and complexity of the crisis it is probable that the EU benefited from having a single individual focus largely on this task for five years.

Conversely, the prime minister or president of the Member State which holds the Council Presidency has very little to do;[139] as compared to the pre-Lisbon situation, when he or she chaired the meetings of the European Council. The foreign minister of the Member State holding the Council Presidency also now has little to do, given that the Presidency no longer has an external relations role (see section 5.3).

6.3 Powers

6.3.1 Historical background

Unlike the EU's other political institutions, the European Council has not existed from the very beginning of the EU's Treaties. Rather, after several sporadic previous summit meetings of heads of State and government, it was created in 1974, but on an informal basis (ie not on the basis of a treaty or any legally binding text). The original intention of these summit meetings was to adopt 'an overall approach to the internal problems involved in achieving European unity and the external problems facing Europe', and 'to ensure progress and overall consistency in the activities of the Communities and in the work on political cooperation (ie foreign policy).'[140]

Despite its informal basis, the European Council quickly became the main venue for discussing and deciding upon the key issues facing the EU, such as enlargement, budget disputes, Treaty amendments, high-profile external relations issues, and major political initiatives. It met at least twice a year and, until the Treaty of Lisbon, the Presidency of the European Council matched the Presidency of the Council (see section 5.4.2). So, for instance, the UK last held the Presidency of the European Council in the second half of 2005, and the President of the European Council during that period was then-Prime Minister Tony Blair. The biggest task for that Presidency (which it achieved) was to reach agreement on the next multi-annual budget for the EU (which applied from 2007–13). The main European Council meeting was always held at the end of each six-month Presidency, although there were often one or two others held before that.

In purely legal terms, the role of the European Council before the Treaty of Lisbon was modest. This body was formally established in the SEA (in force 1987), which simply provided for the existence of the European Council in the form of heads of State and government, assisted by the Commission President and Member States' foreign ministers, to meet at least twice a year.[141] Subsequently, the original Treaty on European Union (Maastricht Treaty) specified that the task of the European Council 'shall provide the Union with the necessary impetus for its development and shall define the general political guidelines thereof'. It also confirmed that the European Council was chaired by the Member State holding the Council Presidency (which was already the existing practice), and that it would send the European Parliament a report

---

[139] The prime minister or president of the Member State holding the Council Presidency can fill in for the President of the European Council only in limited circumstances (see Art 2(4) European Council rules of procedure), namely where the President is ill, has died, or been removed from office, and only until the European Council selects a replacement. Also he or she reports to the European Council on the work of the Council (Art 4(1), European Council rules of procedure).

[140] Final communique of Paris summit, 9–10 December 1974.   [141] Art 2 SEA.

after each of its meetings and an annual report on the development of the EU.[142] The Maastricht Treaty also provided for a few formal roles for the European Council, for instance to 'define the principles of and general guidelines for the common foreign and security policy',[143] and to discuss the broad guidelines for Member States' and the EU's economic policy.[144] However, it was still left to the Council to adopt binding decisions, although as regards the start of EMU (and admitting new States to the EMU) the Council had to do so in the formation of heads of State and government.[145] Moreover, some decisions were to be made by the heads of State and government as such, as distinct from the European Council.[146]

Subsequently, the Treaty of Amsterdam gave the European Council the power to adopt 'common strategies' in the area of foreign policy (although the legal status of these acts was not defined),[147] a decision establishing a 'common defence' for the EU (subject to ratification by Member States),[148] and decisions settling a dispute over the start of 'closer cooperation' (now called 'enhanced cooperation') in the field of policing and criminal law.[149] However, the Treaty of Amsterdam still also provided for action by the Council, meeting at the level of heads of State and government,[150] and for mere 'conclusions' of the European Council on the employment situation.[151]

Next, the Treaty of Nice (in force 2003) included a declaration on the 'venue' of European Councils, providing that once the EU had 18 or more Member States (ie from May 2004), all its meetings would be held in Brussels, rather than (as before) in the Member State holding the Presidency. This was a precursor to the Treaty of Lisbon, which broke the link between the European Council Presidency and Member States.

6.3.2 Treaty of Lisbon

In total, the Treaty of Lisbon made three significant changes to the status and functioning of the European Council. First of all, that Treaty made the European Council an official Institution of the EU.[152] This means that the European Council can sue and be sued,[153] and has its own rules of procedure.[154]

Secondly, the role of the European Council was enhanced, by providing that it could adopt a much wider array of formal decisions, including decisions previously taken by heads of State and government (or by the Council in that composition). These mainly comprise decisions

---

[142] Art D TEU (OJ [1992] C191), renumbered Art 4 TEU by the Treaty of Amsterdam (OJ [1997] C340), in force 1997.   [143] Art J.8(1) TEU, renumbered Art 13(1) TEU by the Treaty of Amsterdam.

[144] Art 103 EC, renumbered Art 99 EC by the Treaty of Amsterdam.

[145] Arts 109j and 109k EC, renumbered Arts 121 and 122 EC by the Treaty of Amsterdam.

[146] Arts 109a and 109f EC, renumbered Arts 112 and 117 EC by the Treaty of Amsterdam, concerning appointments to the European Central Bank and its precursor body, the European Monetary Institute.

[147] Art 13(2) TEU (Treaty of Amsterdam version). Only three such measures were ever adopted, concerning Russia, Ukraine, and the Mediterranean (for the last such measure, see OJ [2004] L337/72).

[148] Art 17(1) TEU (Treaty of Amsterdam version). On the EU's defence policy, see chapter 24.

[149] Art 40(1) TEU (Treaty of Amsterdam version). For more on enhanced cooperation, see chapter 5.

[150] Art 11(2) EC (Treaty of Amsterdam version), which applied in the event of a dispute over launching 'closer cooperation' as regards EC law. In that case, the Council, in that special composition, could take a decision unanimously. Also, Art 7(1) TEU (Treaty of Amsterdam version), provided for the Council, in that special composition, to adopt decisions sanctioning Member States for serious and persistent breaches of human rights.   [151] Art 128 EC (Treaty of Amsterdam version).

[152] See the list of institutions in Art 13(2) TEU.

[153] Arts 263 and 265 TFEU (on actions for annulment and failure to act) refer expressly to the European Council. Implicitly, it is one of the 'institutions' whose acts can be the subject of references from national courts to the Court of Justice, for a ruling on those acts' validity and interpretation (Art 267(b) TFEU); this has been confirmed by the Court (Case C-370/12 *Pringle*, judgment of 27 November 2012, nyr). On the Court's jurisdiction, see further chapter 10.   [154] OJ [2009] L315/51.

on major appointments,[155] its own functioning,[156] the composition and functioning of other institutions,[157] and the Treaty amendment process,[158] along with other sundry powers.[159]

The European Council also retained its power to decide on sanctions against Member States and to adopt strategic foreign policy decisions and a decision establishing a common defence.[160] Its role in giving general guidance (as distinct from binding decisions) has also been retained, as regards the discussion of economic policy guidelines, its involvement in the adoption of the euro by more Member States, and the adoption of conclusions on the employment situation.[161] This general guidance power has also been enhanced, both generally[162] and as regards the specific areas of foreign policy,[163] justice and home affairs,[164] dispute settlement in sensitive areas,[165] enlargement,[166] and problematic Treaty ratifications.[167]

Significantly, the Treaties also set out one thing the European Council *cannot* do: it 'shall not exercise legislative functions'.[168] So formally at least, the legislative process only involves the other three political institutions (the Commission, the European Parliament, and the Council). However, the work of the European Council necessarily impacts upon the legislative process, for instance as regards multi-annual budget legislation (as seen in case study 3.1), and the European Council sometimes sets deadlines to adopt legislation or adopts broad guidelines as to its content (eg as regards much of the recent legislation on EMU, discussed in chapter 19).

Despite the significant changes to the Treaty provisions on the role of the European Council, the legal position according to the Treaty still understates its practical significance.

---

[155] See Art 17(7) TEU (nomination of candidate for Commission President, appointment of Commission); Art 18(1) TEU (appointment of High Representative); and Art 283(2) TFEU (appointments to the European Central Bank). On the Commission, see section 3; on the Central Bank, see OJ [2011] L173/8 and OJ [2012] L336/80.

[156] Art 15(5) TEU (appointment of its President); Art 235(3) TFEU (adoption of rules of procedure).

[157] See Art 14(2) TEU (composition of the European Parliament); Art 17(5) TEU (number of members of the European Commission); Art 236 TFEU (list of Council configurations and rotating Council Presidencies); and Art 244 TFEU (system for rotation of Commissioners). See sections 3, 4, and 5.

[158] See, in particular, Art 48 TEU, and the discussion of the Treaty amendment process in chapter 5.

[159] The European Council must be informed as regards the withdrawal of a Member State from the EU, and can decide to extend the time period to negotiate a treaty of withdrawal (Art 50 TEU). It can also extend the scope of crimes over which the future European Public Prosecutor has jurisdiction (Art 86(4) TFEU), and decide on removing the UK and Ireland from their participation in certain Justice and Home Affairs matters (Art 5(4) Protocol on the Schengen *acquis*). None of these powers have yet been used.

[160] See respectively Arts 7(2), 22(1), and 42(2) TEU.

[161] See respectively Arts 121(2), 140(2), and 148(1) TFEU.

[162] In place of the previous reference to 'general political guidelines', Art 15(1) TEU now provides for the European Council to 'define the general political direction and priorities' of the EU.

[163] Art 15(1) TEU.

[164] Art 68 TFEU provides for the European Council to 'define the strategic guidelines for legislative and operational planning within the area of freedom, security and justice'. See most recently the Stockholm programme (OJ [2010] C115).

[165] While there is no longer a role for the European Council as regards disputes over launching enhanced cooperation, it has a formal role in the event of disputes over proposed legislation concerning social security (Art 48 TFEU) or aspects of criminal law and policing (Arts 82(3), 83(3), 86(1), and 87(3) TFEU). These provisions have not yet been invoked.

[166] Art 49 TEU now requires the Council to take into account the 'conditions of eligibility' for EU membership which the European Council has agreed upon. This confirms the prior practice as regards the so-called 'Copenhagen criteria' for membership, which were agreed in 2002.

[167] See Art 48(5) TEU. This confirms the European Council's prior role as a venue for resolving problems relating to the ratification of the Maastricht, Nice, and Lisbon Treaties, and for restarting the Treaty amendment process after the failure of the Constitutional Treaty. See further chapter 2.

[168] Art 49 TEU now requires the Council to take into account the 'conditions of eligibility' for EU membership which the European Council has agreed upon. This confirms the prior practice as regards the so-called 'Copenhagen criteria' for membership, which were agreed in 2002.

For instance, in relation to enlargement, the European Council does not merely decide on eligibility criteria, but in practice decides when the EU is willing to open negotiations for particular countries to join. For instance, the European Council of June 2013 decided to open accession talks with Serbia. As regards major Treaty amendments, the European Council is the venue for the final phase of the negotiations in each intergovernmental conference, where the most difficult issues are settled. As for the multi-year EU budget process, the European Council is (as noted already) the venue for agreeing the most difficult issues as between Member States.

Since the Treaty of Lisbon, though, the European Council has mainly focused upon addressing the results of the ongoing economic and financial crisis, and in particular its effect upon EMU.

Finally, the third major change brought about by the Treaty of Lisbon was the appointment of a full-time President of the European Council (discussed at section 6.2).

Taken as a whole, then, the Treaty of Lisbon has increased the efficiency of the European Council, by creating the office of full-time President and by conferring more legal powers upon that body. However, the effect of these changes is to detach individual Member States from the workings of the EU, by divesting the prime ministers of the Member State holding the Council Presidency from their previous role. This is accentuated by the reduction in the role of the foreign minister of the Member State holding the Council Presidency, and by the previous decision to stop the European Council meeting in the Member State holding that Presidency. So there is a risk that while these changes enhanced the effectiveness of this institution, they decreased its legitimacy.

6.4 **Functioning**

The basic rule is that the European Council must act by 'consensus', which is not precisely defined, except where the Treaties provide otherwise.[169] In fact, the Treaties frequently provide otherwise, providing for a voting rule as regards the adoption of any formal decisions; for instance, unanimity is required for the adoption of Treaty amendments by a simplified procedure, QMV is required for appointments, and simple majority voting as regards the European Council's own rules of procedure. Meetings of the European Council are not public,[170] although they are often high-profile affairs attracting much press and public attention, and some of them have been significant turning points in the European integration process.

7 Transparency of the EU's political institutions

Intertwined with the concern about the democratic credentials of the EU institutions have been concerns about the openness and transparency of their decision-making. This was addressed first of all in the mid-1990s by the insertion of provisions on public meetings and access to documents in the rules of procedure of these three EU institutions. Subsequently, the Treaty of Amsterdam required general rules to be adopted, pursuant to the co-decision procedure (as it was then), regulating access to their documents (see now Article 15 TFEU).

This legislation, adopted in 2001,[171] has been the source of fertile litigation before the courts of the EU. Broadly speaking, that case law has followed the legislative/non-legislative

---

[169] Art 15(4) TEU.   [170] Art 4(3) European Council rules of procedure.
[171] Regulation 1049/2001 (OJ [2001] L145/43).

divide between the types of EU activity that the Treaty of Lisbon confirmed and elaborated upon. Therefore, where the Council and European Parliament are legislating, they are not simply obliged to meet in public (Article 15(2) TFEU). Given that, as previously described in sections 4 and 5, those institutions prepare their decisions at an earlier stage (particularly working groups, committees, and Coreper, for the Council), it is also necessary to ensure public access to the documents generated at an earlier stage, in order to ensure democratic accountability of the EU legislative process. So even though the 2001 legislation on access to documents provides for an exception related to the decision-making process, the Court of Justice has been unwilling to accept its application as regards any aspect of legislative activity, on the ground that the right of access to documents is linked to the democratic accountability of the EU institutions.[172]

On the other hand, as regards the non-legislative activity of the EU, the Court has been willing to accept a blanket presumption that whole categories of documents fall within the scope of one or more exceptions in the 2001 legislation, for instance, as regards infringement proceedings, merger control, and State aid investigations.[173] The assumption in these cases is rather that the efficiency of the decision-making procedure might be affected unduly by making it public.

8 Conclusion

As we have seen, the application of the principle of representative democracy to the EU is complex. Even though the 'lower house' of the EU's two-chamber legislature, the European Parliament, has been elected directly by the public since 1979, this has not alleviated a public perception that the EU is undemocratic, despite the significant growth in powers for this elected body. This has manifested itself in steadily lower turnouts to elections, and probably has many different causes: indifference or hostility to the EU in general; the lack of representation by population; a perception that the Parliament still has no real powers; a lack of understanding of the EU political system, that is, the practical impact of casting a vote in these elections; the costs and remoteness of the Parliament; and reduced interest in politics in general.

On the other hand, the Union's legislative 'upper house', the Council, has (like the European Council) a direct connection back to national democratic politics. But this is not perceived to solve the democratic problem either. This may be because of (again) a lack of understanding of the EU political system (there is a widespread belief that the *Commission* adopts legislation), or conversely because of the public's objection to the possibility that each Member State's democratically elected government might be outvoted on many issues. On this point, the trade-off between efficiency and (national) democratic accountability is self-evident, since the EU's interest in achieving its objectives will take priority over the view of the democratically elected government of one or more Member States.

Interestingly, by keeping the number of members in the Commission equal to the number of Member States, the EU has instead chosen to prioritize legitimacy over efficiency. This is consistent with a long-term trend that has seen the profile and authority of the EU's most efficient institution reduced in favour of the other political institutions, each of which

---

[172] See particularly Joined Cases C-39/05 P and C-52/05 P *Turco v Council* [2008] ECR I-4273, and more recently Case C-280/11 *Access Info Europe v Council*, judgment of 17 October 2013.

[173] See the recent recapitulation of the case law in Joined Cases C-514/11 P and C-605/11 P *LPN v Commission*, judgment of 14 November 2013.

can claim a far stronger EU-wide or national democratic mandate, and whose power over the appointment and removal of Commissioners and whose powers to influence or control the Commission's actions has steadily increased. It will be interesting to see whether the planned shift towards a more recognizable form of parliamentary system – with the voting in European Parliament elections in effect deciding who will obtain the office of Commission President – will have a broader effect on the legitimacy and effectiveness of the EU's political system.

Further reading

A ARNULL AND D WILLCOTT (eds), *Accountability and Legitimacy in the European Union* (Oxford: Oxford University Press, 2003)

R CORBETT, F JACOBS, AND M SHACKLETON, *The European Parliament* (8th edn, London: John Harper, 2011)

H DE WAELE AND H BROEKSTEEG, 'The Semi-Permanent European Council Presidency: Some Reflections on the Law and Early Practice' (2012) 49 *Common Market Law Review* 1039

D NAURIN AND H WALLACE (eds), *Unveiling the Council of the European Union: Games Governments Play in Brussels* (Basingstoke: Palgrave Macmillan, 2010)

D SPENCE (ed), *The European Commission* (3rd edn, London: John Harper, 2006)

Chapter acknowledgements

My thanks to Kieran Bradley for his comments on a draft of this chapter. The usual disclaimer applies.

4

Constitutionalism and the European Union

Robert Schütze

1 Introduction: constitutionalism(s)

Constitutionalism is the set of ideas that defines what a constitution is or ought to be. Various conceptions of constitutionalism have developed in legal history. According to a 'descriptive' constitutionalism, a constitution is the factual description of the institutions and powers of government.[1] By contrast, normative constitutionalism insists that constitutions do not merely *describe* the existing governmental structures, but *prescribe* their composition and powers.[2] Standing above all ordinary laws, constitutional laws are identified with those norms that represent the highest laws within a society. This *formal* definition has in the last two

---

[1] This 'descriptive' sense of 'constitution' can be found in Aristotle, *Politics*, trans E Baker (Oxford: Oxford University Press, 1998), Book III, §§ 6 and 7. In this 'descriptive' sense, there is no distinction between the 'government' and the 'constitution' (cf E Zoller, *Droit Constitutionnel* (Paris: Presses Universitaires de France, 1998) 10).

[2] cf T Paine, 'Rights of Man' in *Political Writings* (Cambridge: Cambridge University Press, 1997) 89: 'A Constitution is a thing antecedent to a government, and a government is only the creature of a constitution.'

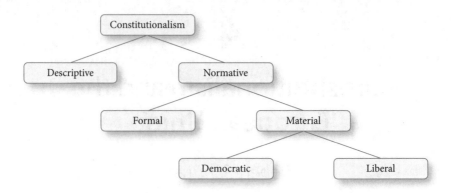

Fig 4.1 Concepts of constitutionalism

hundred years competed with a *material* understanding of what a constitution ought to be. This material constitutionalism links the – legal – concept of constitution with a particular *political* philosophy. According to a 'democratic' constitutionalism, a genuine constitution only exists where it is based on the idea of a 'government of the people, by the people, for the people'.[3] A 'liberal' constitutionalism, on the other hand, believes that a constitution is only a 'true' constitution if it sets limits to the powers of government,[4] and the two traditional constitutional limits here are the separation of powers and fundamental rights.[5]

Is there an EU constitution? This question has plagued EU law ever since its birth.[6] From a descriptive point of view, the EU has undoubtedly a constitution, since it has a set of institutions that engage in the business of government.[7] However, could the same be said from the perspective of normative constitutionalism? Does the EU have a formal constitution; and if so: what is the political philosophy that underpins that formal constitution? Section 2 explores the formal constitutionalist credentials of the Union legal order. We shall see there that the Union has claimed that the EU Treaties constitute the highest law in Europe. Sections 3 and 4 subsequently explore the constitutional nature of the Union from a 'democratic' perspective. Should the EU Treaties be denied their highest law status because they have not had a (national) democratic foundation, nor have they established a (national) system of representation? Sections 5 and 6 finally evaluate the Union legal order through the lens of liberal constitutionalism. This 'classic' constitutionalism assesses the constitutional nature of a document by insisting on a separation of powers and the existence of fundamental rights.

2 Formal constitutionalism: (contested) supremacy

Formal constitutionalism defines a constitution as the set of those norms that stand at the apex of the legal hierarchy. Constitutional norms are the highest norms within a legal order

---

[3] A Lincoln, 'Gettysburg Address, 1863' in HS Commager and M Cantor (eds), *Documents of American History*, vol I (Upper Saddle River, NJ: Prentice Hall, 1988) 429.

[4] cf CH McIlwain, *Constitutionalism: Ancient and Modern* (Ithaca, NY: Cornell University Press, 1947).

[5] cf 1789 Declaration of the Rights of Man and of the Citizen, Art 16 of which states: 'Toute Société dans laquelle la garantie des Droits n'est pas assurée, ni la séparation des Pouvoirs déterminée, n'a point de Constitution.'

[6] The EU legal order is not the only one suffering from this doubt. For the question of whether the UK has a legal constitution, see E Barendt, 'Is there a United Kingdom Constitution?' (1997) 12 *Oxford Journal of Legal Studies* 137.   [7] On the Union institutions and overall governmental system, see chapter 3.

and as such enjoy absolute – legal – 'supremacy' over all other norms. Standing on top of the hierarchical order, their validity cannot be legally derived from other norms but is *socially* 'postulated'.[8] Norms that are socially 'given' constitutional status can be produced in a variety of ways: they may be granted by a monarch,[9] they may be adopted by parliament,[10] or they may result from a treaty between States.[11] From a formal constitutionalist perspective, the material origin or content of a norm that is 'given' constitutional status is secondary. All that counts for a constitution is that it enjoys the *status* as the highest law of the land; and this legal status is not granted by another legal norm but is postulated by a social convention.

What are the highest norms in the EU legal order? It is generally accepted that the EU Treaties stand above Union legislation and all other forms of *EU* law.[12] However, what about the relationship between EU and national law? This question became relevant once the Union legal order insisted – and the Member States accepted – that EU law was directly applicable in the national legal orders.[13] For by integrating the EU legal order into the national legal orders, the question arose as to which legal norms would be 'supreme' in the case of a conflict. Modern federal states typically resolve conflicts between federal and state law in favour of the former: federal law is supreme law over state law.[14]

However, when the Union was born, the EU Treaties, did not expressly state the supremacy of EU law.[15] Did this mean that supremacy was a matter to be determined by the national legal orders (decentralized solution); or was there a Union doctrine of supremacy (centralized solution)? The difficulty has never been definitively resolved. Two competing perspectives thus

---

[8] H Kelsen, *General Theory of the State* (Piscataway, NJ: Transaction Publishers, 2005) 115–116:
If we ask why the constitution is valid, perhaps we come upon an older constitution. Ultimately we reach some constitution that is the first historically and that was laid down by an individual usurper or by some kind of assembly. The validity of this first construction is the last presupposition, the final postulate, upon which the validity of all the norms of our legal order depends.... This is the basic norm of the legal order under consideration.... The basic norm is not created in a legal procedure by a law-creating organ. It is not – as a positive legal norm is – valid because it is created in a certain way by a legal act, but it is valid because without this presupposition no human act could be interpreted as a legal, especially as a norm-creating act.

[9] For illustrations of monarchic constitutions, see the 1814 French Charte, as well as the 1820 Vienna Final Act: 'the entire authority of the state must, according to the basic concepts provided thereby, remain united within the head of state, and the sovereign can therefore only in the exercise of particular rights be constitutionally bound to the participation of the estates' (ibid, Art 57). On the 'monarchic' principle within nineteenth-century German constitutionalism, see ER Huber, *Deutsche Verfassungsgeschichte seit 1789 – Volume I* (Stuttgart: Kohlhammer, 1960) 653 *et seq*.

[10] On this (indirect) democratic creation, see section 3.1.

[11] On this form of constitutional creation, see section 3.2.

[12] cf Art 263 TFEU and Case 294/83 *Parti écologiste 'Les Verts' v European Parliament* [1986] ECR 1339.

[13] cf Case 26/62 *Van Gend en Loos v Netherlands Inland Revenue Administration* [1963] ECR 1. On the doctrines of direct applicability and direct effect, see R Schütze, *European Constitutional Law* (Cambridge: Cambridge University Press, 2012) 306 *et seq*, as well as chapter 6 later in this book.

[14] eg Art VI, cl 2 of the US Constitution states: 'This Constitution, and the Laws of the United States which shall be made in pursuance thereof; and all treaties made, or which shall be made, under the Authority of the United States, shall be the supreme Law of the Land.'

[15] The Constitutional Treaty would have added an express provision (Art I-6 CT): 'The Constitution and law adopted by the institutions of the Union in exercising competences conferred on it shall have primacy over the law of the Member States.' However, the provision was not taken over by the Lisbon Treaty. Yet the latter has added Declaration 17 which states: 'The Conference recalls that, in accordance with well settled case law of the Court of Justice of the European Union, the Treaties and the law adopted by the Union on the basis of the Treaties have primacy over the law of Member States, under the conditions laid down by the said case law.'

coexist within the EU: one European, one national. What does this mean for the 'constitutional' credentials of the EU Treaties? Let us look at both questions in turn.

2.1 Legal supremacy: two perspectives

Early on, the European Court of Justice tried to centralize the question of supremacy by turning it into a principle of EU law. In *Costa v ENEL*,[16] the EU judiciary had been asked whether national legislation adopted after 1958 could prevail over the EU Treaties. Italy had claimed that the EU Treaties – like ordinary international law – had been transposed into the Italian legal order by national legislation, which could therefore be derogated by subsequent national legislation. The Court rejected this presumption of the supremacy of national law by insisting on the supremacy of EU law:

> By contrast with ordinary international treaties, the E[U] Treaty has created its own legal system which, on the entry into force of the Treaty, became an integral part of the legal systems of the Member States and which their courts are bound to apply...[T]he law stemming from the Treaty, an independent source of law, could not, because of its special and original nature, be overridden by domestic legal provisions, however framed, without being deprived of its character as [European] law and without the legal basis of the [Union] itself being called into question.[17]

EU law should reign supreme over national law, since its 'executive force' must not vary from one State to another.

But how supreme was EU law? The fact that the EU Treaties prevailed over national legislation did not automatically imply that all EU law would prevail over all national law. Would the Court accept a 'nuanced' or 'relative' solution for a State's own highest (constitutional) norms? This issue was clarified in *Internationale Handelsgesellschaft*.[18] A German court had doubted that EU legislation could violate fundamental rights granted by the German Constitution and raised this very question with the European Court of Justice. Were the fundamental principles of national constitutions, including human rights, beyond the scope of EU supremacy? The Court disagreed. The validity of EU law could never be affected by national law – even by the most fundamental norms within the Member States. The Court's vision of the supremacy of EU law over national law was thus an absolute one: 'The whole of [EU] law prevails over the whole of national law.'[19] The European Treaties were thus constitutional treaties.[20]

This EU perspective is – unsurprisingly – not shared by the Member States. Thus, a competing national view coexists with an EU view. And this national perspective accepts the relative supremacy of EU law over some national law; yet this bounded supremacy is seen as granted and limited by national constitutional law (see further chapter 6). While accepting that the EU constitutes a 'new legal order' distinct from classic international law, many Member States indeed insist that its validity ultimately derives from the national decision to accede to the EU (see further chapter 7). This national perspective has traditionally

---

[16] Case 6/64 *Costa v ENEL* [1964] ECR 585.   [17] Ibid, 593–594.

[18] Case 11/70 *Internationale Handelsgesellschaft mbH v Einfuhr- und Vorratsstelle für Getreide und Futtermittel* [1970] ECR 1125.

[19] R Kovar, 'The Relationship between Community Law and National Law' in EC Commission (ed), *Thirty Years of Community Law* (EC Commission, 1981) 112–113. On the implications for the protection of human rights within EU law, see further chapter 9.

[20] Case 294/83 *Parti Ecologiste 'Les Verts' v Parliament* [1986] ECR 1339 at 1365, para 23: 'a [Union] based on the rule of law, inasmuch as neither its Member States nor its institutions can avoid a review of the question whether the measures adopted by them are in conformity with the basic constitutional charter, the Treaty'.

been expressed in two contexts. First, some Member States – in particular their supreme courts[21] – have fought a battle over fundamental rights within the Union legal order. It was claimed that EU law could not violate national fundamental rights. A similar constitutional contest arose in a second context: ultra vires control. This constitutional battleground became prominent in light of the expansive exercise of legislative and judicial competences by the Union. And again, while the Member States here generally accept the supremacy of EU law within limited fields, they contest that the EU can exclusively delimit these fields. In denying the Union a competence to interpret its own competences, Member States insist on the last word with regard to the competences of the Union.[22]

Case study 4.1: Constitutional conflicts and the German Federal Constitutional Court

A strong national view on the supremacy issue first crystallized around *Internationale Handelsgesellschaft*.[23] For after the European Court of Justice had espoused its absolute view on the supremacy of European law over national law, the case moved back to the German Federal Constitutional Court.[24] The Constitutional Court here clarified its per-spective on the supremacy question and famously replaced the European Court's vision with its counter-theory of relative supremacy. The reasoning of the German court was as follows: while the German Constitution expressly allowed for the transfer of sovereign powers to the EU, such a transfer was itself limited and controlled by national constitu-tional law. Did this mean that national law would prevail over EU law? The response of the German Federal Constitutional Court was the famous *So-Long* Doctrine.

> [I]n the hypothetical case of a conflict between [EU] law and a part of national constitu-tional law or, more precisely, of the guarantees of fundamental rights in the Constitution, there arises the question of which system of law takes precedence, that is, ousts the other. In this conflict of norms, the guarantee of *fundamental rights in the Constitution prevails so long as the competent organs of the [Union] have not removed the conflict of norms in accordance with the Treaty mechanism*.[25]

The Union legal order did indeed subsequently develop extensive human rights bill(s).[26] Yet with the constitutional conflict over fundamental rights settled, a second concern emerged: the ever-growing competences of the EU.

Who was to control and limit the scope of EU law? Was it enough to have the EU leg-islator be centrally controlled by the European Court of Justice? Or should the national constitutional courts be entitled to a decentralized ultra vires review? The EU view on this

---

[21] For an historical overview of the relationship between EU and national law, see A Oppenheimer, *The Relationship between European Community Law and National Law: The Cases* (Cambridge: Cambridge University Press, 1994). For more recent academic commentary, see W Sadurski, ' "Solange, Chapter 3": Constitutional Courts in Central Europe – Democracy – European Union' (2008) 14 *European Law Journal* 1; as well as R Mehdi, 'French Supreme Courts and European Union Law: Between Historical Compromise and Accepted Loyalty' (2011) 48 *Common Market Law Review* 439.

[22] On the (strange) German notion of 'competence-competence', see Schütze, *From Dual to Cooperative Federalism* (n 11) 34–36 and 151–156.

[23] Case 11/70 *Internationale Handelsgesellschaft mbH v Einfuhr- und Vorratsstelle für Getreide und Futtermittel* (n 18).

[24] BVerfGE 37, 271 (*Solange I (Re Internationale Handelsgesellschaft)*). For an English translation, see [1974] 2 CMLR 540.

[25] Ibid, 550–551 at paras 23 and 24 (emphasis added).   [26] On this point, see section 6.

problem is crystal clear: national courts cannot disapply – let alone invalidate – EU law.[27] A national vision on the ultra vires issue was, however, expressed by the German Federal Constitutional Court's *Maastricht* decision.[28] The court here held as follows:

> if European institutions or agencies were to treat or develop the Union Treaty in a way that was no longer covered by the Treaty in the form that is the basis for the Act of Accession, the resultant legislative instruments would not be legally binding within the sphere of German sovereignty. The German state organs would be prevented for constitutional reasons from applying them in Germany.[29]

The German Federal Constitutional Court thus threatened to disapply EU law that it considered to have been adopted ultra vires.

2.2 Contested hierarchies: federalism and constitutional pluralism

If *constitutional* law is the highest law within a legal order, will it not follow from the continued existence of *national* constitutional law that there cannot be any coexistent *European* constitutional law? Traditionally, classic constitutionalism indeed draws this conclusion: there can only be *one* 'supreme' constitution within a legal order – be it either a national or the EU constitution.

However, this 'unitary' or 'monistic' standard has never lived up to the constitutional practice of federal orders – like the US, where both the Union *and* the states were seen to have 'constitutional' claims.[30] Unlike the unitary constitutionalism within unitary States, where only a single level of government is generally recognized to have a 'constitutional' claim,[31] many federal unions have thus developed a federal or pluralist constitutionalism. Each of the two political bodies – the Union and its Member States – will have constitutional claims that may even sometimes come into conflict with each other.[32] Unlike unitary States in which the supremacy and sovereignty issue is settled, federal unions are characterized by a political equilibrium in which the locus of sovereignty remains 'suspended'.[33] Wherever the sovereignty question is – eventually – answered in favour of the Union, it

---

[27] Case 314/85 *Foto-Frost v Hauptzollamt Lübeck-Ost* [1987] ECR 4199. On the EU's judicial architecture, see further chapter 10.

[28] BVerfGE 89, 155 (*Maastricht* decision). For an English translation, see [1994] 1 CMLR 57.

[29] Ibid, 105.

[30] cf E Zoeller, 'Aspects internationaux du droit constitutionnel. Contribution à la théorie de la fédération d'états' (2002) 194 *Recueil des Cours de l'Académie de la Haye* 43. The same is true for Germany, where the 'Länder' have their own 'constitutions', see only the 'Saxonian Constitution' at http://www.freistaat.sachsen .de/538.htm.

[31] Traditional unitary States are France and the UK; and even if the latter has increasingly recognized a degree of administrative 'devolution', this devolution does not recognize the 'constitutional' autonomy of the decentralized regions.

[32] On the existence of constitutional conflicts in the US before and after the Civil War, see R Schütze, 'Federalism as Constitutional Pluralism: Letter from America' in M Avbelj and J Komárek, *Constitutional Pluralism in the European Union and Beyond* (Oxford: Hart Publishing, 2012).

[33] C Schmitt, *Verfassungslehre*, trans R Schütze (Berlin: Duncker & Humblot, 1993) 376–378. For that silence to remain, a homogeneity of interests must be fostered. This had already been pointed out by A de Tocqueville , *Democracy in America, Volume I*, trans H Reeve, P Bradley (ed) (New York, NY: Vintage 1954), 175–176: 'Since legislators cannot prevent such dangerous collisions as occur between the two sovereignties which coexist in the Federal system, their first object must be, not only to dissuade the confederate States from warfare, but to encourage such dispositions as lead to peace,… A certain uniformity of civilization is not less necessary to the durability of a confederation than a uniformity of interests in the States which compose it.'

continues to have a political existence, and the 'Union' is here transformed into a sovereign State. (This is what arguably happened to the US after the Civil War.[34]) Conversely, wherever the sovereignty question is – eventually – answered in favour of the Member States, the political existence of the federation disappears and the Union dissolves into an international organization. The normative ambivalence surrounding the location of sovereignty, and the consequent potential for constitutional conflicts, are indeed the core of all – real – federations.[35]

This fundamental insight into the pluralist nature of unions of states as 'multi-level' or 'federal' legal orders has recently been 'discovered' by an academic movement called 'constitutional pluralism'.[36] The central claim behind this 'new' school is this:

> EU law…poses the most pressing paradigm-challenging test to what we might call constitutional monism. Constitutional monism merely grants a label to the defining assumption of constitutionalism in the Westphalian age…, namely the idea that the sole centres or units of constitutional authorities are states. Constitutional pluralism, by contrast, recognizes that the European legal order inaugurated by the Treaty of Rome has developed beyond the traditional confines of inter-*national* law and now makes its own independent constitutional claims exist alongside the continuing claims of states.[37]

The idea of constitutional pluralism thus accepts – like constitutional federalism – the coexistence of multiple constitutional orders that are not hierarchically ordered but may interact in a *heterarchical* way.[38] However, the absence of an 'Archimedean point' from which all legal authority can be explained is – wrongly – hailed as a *sui generis* quality of the EU.[39] The theory of constitutional pluralism indeed speaks much federal prose without being aware of it. For unlike the unitary and hierarchical constitutionalism that was developed for the modern sovereign State, both federal constitutionalism and constitutional pluralism accept the existence of alternative and contradictory answers to the supremacy question and insist that sovereignty within a union of states is shared or suspended. And as we shall see in the next section, the distinction between State (unitary) constitutionalism and federal (pluralist) constitutionalism will also help us to analyse the democratic credentials of the EU.

---

[34] cf E Katz, 'The Development of American Federalism, 1763–1865' in A Bosco (ed), *The Federal Idea*, vol I (London: Lothian Foundation Press, 1992).

[35] Schmitt, *Verfassungslehre* (n 33) 378.

[36] The movement gained momentum in the aftermath of the *Maastricht* decision by the German Federal Constitutional Court (cf J Baquero-Cruz, 'The Legacy of the Maastricht-Urteil and the Pluralist Movement' (2008) 14 *European Law Journal* 389). One of the strongest proponents of this movement has claimed that 'Constitutional pluralism has been, perhaps, the most successful attempt at theorizing the nature of European constitutionalism' (MP Maduro, 'Three Claims of Constitutional Pluralism' in Avbelj and Komarek (n 32) 68). Personally, I share the more sceptical views of G Davies, 'Constitutional Disagreement in Europe and the Search of Pluralism' in ibid, 269: 'the investment in constitutional pluralism by scholars has not brought satisfactory returns'.

[37] cf N Walker, 'The Idea of Constitutional Pluralism' (2002) 65 *Modern Law Review* 317, 337.

[38] In the words of Maduro, 'Three Claims of Constitutional Pluralism' (n 36) 75: 'While the empirical thesis of constitutional pluralism limits itself to state that the question of final authority remains open, the normative claim is that the question of final authority ought to be left open. Heterarchy is superior to hierarchy as a normative ideal in circumstances of competing constitutional claims of final authority.'

[39] In particular Walker, 'The Idea of Constitutional Pluralism' (n 37) 338. His – 'Eurocentric' – views strikingly ignore the American experience, in which the Union and the states were seen to have 'constitutional' claims and in which the 'Union' was – traditionally – not(!) conceived in statist terms (cf E Zoeller, 'Aspects Internationaux du Droit Constitutionnel' (n 30) 43).

3 Democratic constitutionalism I: (popular) sovereignty

3.1 Unitary constitutionalism: 'We, the People'

Democratic constitutionalism insists that since 'the people' are sovereign, they must create the constitution. Popular sovereignty may thereby express itself either directly or indirectly. The former demands that the people directly adopt their constitution through a referendum.[40] The softer version of popular sovereignty allows this task to be delegated to an elected 'assembly',[41] which adopts the constitution 'on behalf' of the people.

What happens if we apply this unitary theory of popular sovereignty to the EU? Under this doctrine, only 'a people' can formally constitute itself into a legal sovereign. A constitution is thus regarded as a unilateral act of a democratic '*pouvoir constituant*':

> it is inherent in a constitution in the full sense of the term that it goes back to an act taken by or at least attributed to the people, in which they attribute political capacity to themselves. There is no such source for primary Union law. It goes back not to a European people but to the individual Member States, and remains dependent on them even after its entry into force. While nations give themselves a constitution, the European Union is given a constitution by third parties.[42]

In short, the EU would only have a constitution if the latter were adopted by 'the people'; and in the absence of an EU 'people' – or demos – the EU cannot have a European Constitution. A softer version of this argument has not denied that there 'is' a formal European Constitution but ultimately rejects the material legitimacy – the 'ought' to be – of that constitution:

> In federations, whether American or Australian, German or Canadian, the institutions of a federal state are situated in a constitutional framework which presupposes the existence of a 'constitutional demos', a single *pouvoir constituant* made of the citizens of the federation in whose sovereignty, as a constituent power, and by whose supreme authority the specific constitutional arrangement is rooted.... In Europe, that precondition does not exist. Simply put, *Europe's constitutional architecture has never been validated by a process of constitutional adoption by a European constitutional demos*... It is a constitution without some of the classic conditions of constitutionalism.[43]

---

[40] For advocates of this direct democratic source, see Paine, *Rights of Man* (n 2) 89: 'The constitution of a country is not the act of its government, but of the people constituting its government.' For the French expression of the same thought, see EJ Sieyes, 'What is the Third Estate' in *Political Writings* (Indianapolis, IN: Hackett Publishing, 2003).

[41] For illustrations of the indirect democratic source, see the 1791 French Constitution and the 1919 (Weimar) Constitution of Germany. The 1949 German Constitution was also originally adopted by the state parliaments.

[42] D Grimm, 'Does Europe Need a Constitution?' [1995] 1 *European Law Journal* 282 at 290. For a severe and brilliant early criticism of this view, see J Habermas, 'Remarks on Dieter Grimms's "Does Europe Need a Constitution?"' [1995] 1 *European Law Journal* 303.

[43] JHH Weiler, 'Federalism without Constitutionalism: Europe's Sonderweg' in K Nikolaidis and R Howse (eds), *The Federal Vision: Legitimacy and Levels of Governance in the United States and the European Union* (Oxford: Oxford University Press, 2001) 56–57 (emphasis added). In my opinion, Professor Weiler seriously mistakes the American case. For neither of the two Constitutions of the United States was ratified by a 'federal demos' in the form of 'the' American people. The Articles of Confederation were ratified by the state legislatures, while the 1787 Constitution was ratified by the state peoples.

But is this – unitary – standard for what counts as a democratic 'validation' of the EU 'constitution' the right standard for the EU? Unitary constitutionalism is based on the idea of indivisible sovereignty and thus insists on a unitary perspective: *one* people must form *one* State on the basis of *one* constitution. But what about federal or pluralist arrangements between peoples, States, and constitutions? Unitary constitutionalism is unable to envisage *two* peoples living in the same territory – yet, this is generally the case in federal unions.[44] It is unable to envisage two 'sovereigns' operating in the same territory – yet, this is generally the case in federal unions. It is unable to envisage *two* constitutional orders existing within the same territory – yet, this is generally the case in federal unions.[45] And, finally, it is unable to envisage a pluralist *pouvoir constituant* – yet, this is generally the case in federal unions.[46]

In sum, if unitary constitutionalism has not the right theoretical 'fit' for the non-unitary EU, let us see how a federal standard can explain the democratic credentials of the EU constitution.

3.2 Federal constitutionalism: 'We, the Peoples'

Who is the popular sovereign and who embodies the 'constituent power' within the federal or pluralist legal order? What are the historical and theoretical alternatives to the unitary focus on popular sovereignty?

We do find historical alternatives to unitary popular sovereignty in the constitutional history of the US. Believing that the framers of the 1787 US Constitution had 'split the atom of sovereignty',[47] early American constitutionalism was based on the idea that the constituent power underlying the American Union was exercised by a plurality of peoples. The 1787 Constitution had thus been ratified 'by the people, *not as individuals composing one entire nation*, but as composing the distinct and independent States to which they respectively belong'.[48] 'Each State, in ratifying the Constitution, [was] considered as a sovereign body, independent of all others, and only to be bound by its own voluntary act.' The 1787 Constitution was 'a[n] [international], and not a national act'.[49] Yet the American legal order had not been based on an ordinary international treaty. For instead of the ordinary state legislatures, the ratification of the 1787 US Constitution was achieved through state 'Conventions'.[50]

The famous phrase 'We, the People' must thus be read with two qualifications in mind. First, it did not refer to a popular referendum; and, secondly, it also did not refer to the

---

[44] cf O Beaud, 'The Question of Nationality within a Federation: A Neglected Issue in Nationality Law' in R Hansen and P Weil (eds), *Dual Nationality, Social Rights, and Federal Citizenship in the US and Europe* (Oxford: Berghahn Books, 2002). [45] On this point, see section 2.

[46] On this point, see section 3.2.

[47] *US Term Limits, Inc v Thornton*, 514 US 779 (1995), 838 (Justice Kennedy).

[48] J Madison, 'Federalist No 39' in J Madison et al, *The Federalist*, ed T Ball (Cambridge: Cambridge University Press, 2003) 184 (emphasis added). To bring the point home, Madison continues (ibid, 185):

> Were the people regarded in this transaction as forming one nation, the will of the majority of the whole people of the United States would bind the minority, in the same manner as the majority in each State must bind the minority; and the will of the majority must be determined either by a comparison of the individual votes, or by considering the will of the majority of the States as evidence of the will of a majority of the people of the United States. Neither of these rules have been adopted.

[49] Ibid, 185.

[50] On the novel (American) technique of constitutional 'Conventions', see G Wood, *The Creation of the American Republic: 1776–87* (Chapel Hill, NC: University of North Carolina Press, 1998) ch 8. These Conventions were composed of delegates who were elected to represent(!) their constituency. Unlike popular referenda, they operate as single-issue 'parliaments' that are solely called into being to decide whether the Constitution should be adopted.

'American people' but instead the peoples of the several states.[51] The (in)direct authority from the state peoples was nonetheless seen to give the US Constitution a normatively higher status than that of the Union and state *governments*. However, from a democratic perspective, the federal constitution enjoyed the same normative status as the various state constitutions.

The best theoretical generalization of the federal or pluralist conception or the constituent power has come from the pen of Carl Schmitt.[52] According to his federal theory, the normative foundation of every union of states is a 'federal treaty'. This 'federal treaty' is an international treaty of a constitutional nature.[53] 'Its conclusion is an act of the *pouvoir constituant*. Its content establishes the federal constitution and forms, at the same time, a part of the constitution of every member state.'[54] Each union of states is seen as a creature of international and national law.[55] Unlike unitary constitutionalism, a federal constitutional theory will thus not locate the constitution-making power in a unitary body: the people. A federal constitutional theory replaces the idea of a *single* sovereign subject with that of a pluralist constituent power. From the perspective of democratic constitutionalism, the constituent power behind a union of states will thus be the state *peoples* instead of a single 'demos'.

How should the democratic validation of a federal or pluralist constitution be expressed? The most direct expression would be a series of constitutional referenda in the member states. A less direct expression of popular sovereignty would be a ratification of the union constitution through state conventions. (This is what happened to the 1787 US Constitution, which was consequently seen as a 'constitutional' – and not a mere 'legislative' – text.) The least direct expression of popular sovereignty is to leave the ratification decision to the 'ordinary' state legislatures. And it is this third – parliamentary – version that is commonly used in the constitutional practice of the EU. Genetically, then, the EU Treaties are 'legislative' – not constitutional – treaties.[56] From a democratic point of view, they lack the 'higher' democratic status that theoretically legitimizes a constitution's normative position above ordinary (state) legislation.

The EU is not alone in this 'democratic deficit' with regard to the adoption of its constitution;[57] and in any event, before we come to the conclusion that the Union falls short of its

---

[51] The original 1787 draft preamble indeed read: 'We, the people of the States of New Hampshire, Massachusetts, Rhode-Island and Providence Plantations, Connecticut, New-York, New-Jersey, Pennsylvania, Delaware, Maryland, Virginia, North-Carolina, South-Carolina, and Georgia, do ordain, declare and establish the following constitution for the government of ourselves and our posterity.' However, due to the uncertainty about which of the 13 states would succeed in the ratification (according to Art VII of the Constitution-to-be, only nine states were required for the document to enter into force), the enumeration of the individual states was dropped by the 'Committee of Style' (cf M Farrand, *The Framing of the Constitution of the United States* (New Haven, CT: Yale University Press, 1913) 190–191).

[52] Schmitt, *Verfassungslehre* (n 33) esp Part IV.

[53] Ibid, 367 and 368 (all translations are by R Schütze).

[54] Ibid. This idea was subsequently taken up by I Pernice's concept of 'Verfassungsverbund' or 'multilevel constitutionalism' (cf 'Multilevel Constitutionalism and the Treaty of Amsterdam: European Constitution-Making Revisited?' (1999) 36 *Common Market Law Review* 703).   [55] Schmitt, *Verfassungslehre* (n 33) 379.

[56] It is difficult – if not impossible – to accept that 'the founding treaties as well as each amendment agreed upon by the governments appear as the *direct* expression of the common will of the [national] peoples of the Union' (Pernice, 'Multilevel Constitutionalism and the Treaty of Amsterdam' (n 54) 717 (emphasis added)). National ratifications are – with the exception of a few Member States – only indirect expressions of the common will of the national peoples of the union. National consent is typically expressed through national legislatures. It is equally difficult to agree that these national ratifications should be regarded 'as a *common* exercise of constitution-making power by the peoples of the participating State' (ibid, 717 (emphasis added)). This theory does not explain how each unilateral national act ultimately transforms itself into a collective act.

[57] On the adoption of the 1949 German Constitution by the state legislatures, see n 41.

constitutional aspirations when viewed in light of a democratic constitutionalism, we need to explore its second aspect: the democratic structure of its government.

4 Democratic constitutionalism II: (popular) representation

The foundational source of a constitution is only one aspect of democratic constitutionalism. For an undemocratically created constitution might still set up democratic institutions,[58] while a popular referendum might create an undemocratic regime.[59]

A governmental system is traditionally regarded as democratic when each governmental function can be legitimized by the will of the people. The modern 'translation' of this (ancient) republican ideal is representative democracy. 'Government is insulated from the people through the principle of representation'.[60] Within a representational government, democracy means that the legislature, or even the executive and the judiciary, should be *elected* by the people. In sum, modern democracy means that the constitution delegates power to elected officials, which exercise public power 'in the name of the people'.

Hardly any existing State constitution has created a completely democratic structure for all governmental powers. Not only is the judiciary often not elected, non-democratic elements can often be found even within the legislative branch.[61] However, the democratic credentials of a governmental system will typically be measured by means of the powers possessed by 'parliament'. Democratic constitutionalism here simply means 'parliamentarism', that is, a governmental regime in which parliament is the central and dominant actor. But what about the executive branch? Two constitutional models of democratic government have here developed: the parliamentary model and the presidential model. The parliamentary system is a model in which the (governing) executive – the prime minister and the cabinet – will be elected and controlled by parliament. By contrast, a presidential system will typically invest the – independent – executive with its own direct democratic legitimacy. This idea of a second democratic source took shape under the 1787 US Constitution.[62]

What are the democratic credentials of the Union's system of government? Article 10 TEU unambiguously demands: 'The functioning of the Union shall be founded on representative democracy.'[63] But how democratic or representative are its legislative and executive branches?

4.1 Democratic legitimacy and the Union legislature

Within a unitary State with one unitary people, parliamentary democracy demands that all legislative power should be placed in a parliament that is elected on the principle of 'one person, one vote'. The British 'Westminster system' has come to be identified with this unitary standard.

---

[58] The 1949 German Constitution is again a case in point.

[59] The 1852 Constitution of the Second French Empire was ratified by a plebiscite; and yet it established an undemocratic government.

[60] M Loughlin, *Foundations of Public Law* (Oxford: Oxford University Press, 2012) 284.

[61] eg in the UK, the second chamber (the House of Lords) is not elected.

[62] An illustration of a presidential (democratic) system is the (current) 1958 Constitution of the French Republic.   [63] Art 10(1) TEU.

But is this – unitary – standard the appropriate yardstick for a compound polity that is composed by a plurality of peoples? In a union of States, there will always be two democratic constituencies: each State will have its own 'demos', while the union will also have a 'demos' that is constructed out of the various State populations. Each of these democratic constituencies offers an independent source of democratic legitimacy; and a federal constitutionalism will have to take account of this dual democracy.

Within a union of States, one *institutional* expression of this dual democracy is the compound nature of the union legislator. It is typically made up of two chambers: a State chamber representing the State peoples is joined to a parliamentary chamber representing the union citizens as a whole.[64] Every union law is – ideally – legitimized by reference to two democratic sources: the consent of the State peoples and the consent of the union population as represented in the union parliament. As we have seen in chapter 3, the EU is based on this dual democratic legitimacy. Its legislative branch consists of two chambers: the European Parliament is formed through elections by the totality of the Union's citizens, whereas the Council indirectly represents the Member States' democratically organized peoples. When measured against a – federal – standard, the Union consequently does not suffer from a democratic deficit simply because one part of its legislative branch is not directly elected.[65]

But what about the democratic credentials of the European Parliament as such? How 'democratic' is its composition? Despite the insistence of the Treaties that the 'Citizens are directly represented at Union level in the European Parliament',[66] the distribution of seats within the European Parliament continues to be partly based on national 'quotas'. Instead of 'one person, one vote', the Union legal order has preferred a system that is according to Article 14 TEU 'degressively proportional'.[67] This means that the distribution of seats is proportionate to the size of the national populations; yet this proportionate system is qualified so as to allow smaller States' populations to have some representation within the European Parliament. Each State will have a minimum number of six European parliamentarians, while the maximum number of 'national' seats is limited to 96.[68] The European Council has offered the following definition of the Union's degressive proportionality system:

> In the application of the principle of degressive proportionality provided for in the first sub-paragraph of Article 14(2) of the Treaty on European Union, the following principles shall apply:
>
> – the allocation of seats in the European Parliament shall fully utilise the minimum and maximum numbers set by the Treaty on European Union in order to reflect as closely as possible the sizes of the respective populations of Member States;

---

[64] cf A Gerber, 'Les Notions de Représentation et de Participation des Régions dans les Etats Fédéraux', LLM thesis (European University Institute, 1993).

[65] In this sense also, see RA Dahl, 'Federalism and the Democratic Process' in JR Pennock and JW Chapman (eds), *Nomos XXV: Liberal Democracy* (New York: New York University Press, 1983) 107: 'although in federal systems no single body of citizens can exercise control over the agenda, federalism is not for this reason less capable than a unitary system of meeting the criteria of the democratic process'. The discussion here focuses on the constitutional aspect of the democratic deficit. It does not claim that there is no democratic deficit at the social level, such as the low degree of electoral participation or the quality of the public debate on Europe.   [66] Art 10(2) TEU.

[67] Art 14(2) TEU. See also Declaration (No 5) on the political agreement by the European Council concerning the draft Decision on the composition of the European Parliament; European Parliament, Resolution on the composition of the European Parliament (OJ [2008] C227/132); and now formally for the 2014–19 term, see European Council, Decision establishing the composition of the European Parliament (OJ [2013] L181/57).

[68] Art 14(2) TEU.

— the ratio between the population and the number of seats of each Member State before rounding to whole numbers shall vary in relation to their respective populations in such a way that each Member of the European Parliament from a more populous Member State represents more citizens than each Member from a less populous Member State and, conversely, that the larger the population of a Member State, the greater its entitlement to a large number of seats.[69]

While the idea of national 'quotas' for parliamentary seats is designed to protect smaller States, it distorts the democratic principle of 'one person, one vote'. The preference of a *degressively* proportionate system over a *purely* proportionate system therefore does constitute a – minor – democratic deficit of the Union. For since the EU Treaties charge the European Parliament to represent the Union citizens *directly*, its composition should not be mediated by the political existence of the Member States as States. This distortion in the democratic credentials has recently been subject to judicial scrutiny by the German Federal Constitutional Court. In its *Lisbon* decision,[70] the Court held that the composition of the European Parliament meant that it still represented the peoples of the Member States as opposed to the EU citizens as such.

Case study 4.2: The democratic deficit and the *Lisbon* decision of the Bundesverfassungsgericht

The German Federal Constitutional Court has 'reviewed' the democratic structures of the Union in a number of famous cases – the most important of which are its *Maastricht* and *Lisbon* judgments. In *Maastricht*,[71] the court explored how EU laws could be regarded as legitimized through national democracy. This exploration was continued in its *Lisbon* decision.[72] The court here held that in a Union with 'clear elements of executive and governmental cooperation' the primacy of national democratic legitimation could be justified; yet, were the Union to move towards a (federal) State, the national route would be blocked and a 'structural democratic deficit' would arise.[73]

Why would the Union fail the democratic standard in a (federal) State? The court answered this question by concentrating on the democratic principle of 'one person, one vote'; and held that the Union – even after Lisbon – 'lacks a political decision-making body created in equal elections by all citizens of the Union and with the ability to uniformly represent the will of the people.'[74] 'Even in the new wording of Article 14.2 Lisbon TEU, and contrary to the claim that Article 10.1 Lisbon TEU seems to make according to its wording, the European Parliament is not a representative body of a sovereign European people.'[75] In light of the degressively proportionate allocation of seats, 'the European Parliament factually remains a representation of the peoples of the Member States.'[76] Democratic representation within the Union was primarily *indirect* representation via the national States and peoples.[77]

Did this mean the court identified a democratic deficit within the Union? It did not. For the court admitted that it should not judge Union democracy by a State standard, but by a democratic standard 'commensurate with the status and the function of the

---

[69] European Council, Decision establishing the composition of the European Parliament (n 67) Art 1.

[70] BVerfGE 123, 267 (*Lisbon* decision). For an English translation, see http://www.bundesverfassungsgericht.de/entscheidungen/es20090630_2bve000208en.html

[71] BVerfGE 89, 155 (*Maastricht* decision). The following discussion refers to the English translation of the judgment: [1994] CMLR 57 (*Maastricht* decision).   [72] *Lisbon* decision (n 70).

[73] Ibid, para 264.   [74] Ibid, para 280.   [75] Ibid.   [76] Ibid, para 284.

[77] Ibid, para 286.

Union'.[78] And, 'In the present state of integration, it is therefore not required to democratically develop the system of the European institutions in analogy to that of a state.' This meant in particular that 'the composition of the European Parliament does not need to do justice to equality in such a way that differences in the weight of the votes of the citizens of the Union depending on the Member States' population figures are eliminated.'[79]

What about the governmental powers of the European Parliament? The TEU today defines the powers of the Parliament in Article 14 TEU as follows: 'The European Parliament shall, jointly with the Council, exercise legislative and budgetary functions. It shall exercise functions of political control and consultation as laid down in the Treaties. It shall elect the President of the Commission.'[80] This definition distinguishes between four types of powers: legislative and budgetary powers as well as supervisory and elective powers.

What are the legislative powers of parliament? Parliament may informally propose new legislation.[81] However, it is not – unlike national parliaments – formally entitled to propose bills. The task of making legislative proposals is, with minor exceptions, a constitutional prerogative of the Commission. Like other federal legal orders, the Union legal order thereby acknowledges a number of different legislative procedures (see further chapter 5). The Treaties now textually distinguish between the 'ordinary' legislative procedure and a number of 'special' legislative procedures.[82] The former is defined as 'the joint adoption by the European Parliament and the Council' on a proposal from the Commission.[83] This procedure reflects the federal idea of dual democracy with the European Parliament (more or less) *directly* representing the European people and the Council *indirectly* representing the national peoples. The structure of the ordinary legislative procedure thus fully satisfies the demands of democratic constitutionalism, while the same cannot be said about those 'special' legislative procedures in which the rights of Parliament are less than co-decision.

4.2 Democratic legitimacy and the Union executive

What are the democratic credentials of the Union's executive branch? Modern constitutionalism typically distinguishes between 'parliamentary' and 'presidential' systems. Within the former the executive is elected by parliament, whereas in the latter the executive is elected independently from parliament. The EU's governmental regime sits somewhere 'in between' both constitutional models. It has a dual executive composed of the European Council and the Commission.[84] The former is composed of the heads of State or government, which – as a body – is not dependent on any parliamentary election, yet whose members will have received direct or indirect *national* democratic legitimation. As regards the Commission as the second branch of the Union executive, it is the European Parliament that has increasingly come to

---

[78] *Lisbon* decision (n 70), para 266. In the words of para 271: 'Because and in so far as the European Union itself only exercises derived public authority, it need not fully comply with the requirements.'

[79] Ibid, para 278.   [80] Art 14(1) TEU.   [81] Art 225 TFEU.

[82] Special legislative procedures cover various degrees of parliamentary participation. Under the 'consent procedure', Parliament must give its consent before the Council can adopt EU legislation (cf Art 19 TEU). This is a cruder form of legislative participation that essentially grants a negative power. Under the 'consultation procedure', by contrast, Parliament is not even entitled to do that. It merely needs to be consulted – a role that is closer to a supervisory than to a legislative function (cf Art 22(1) TFEU).   [83] Art 289(1) TFEU.

[84] In the past, there was a third institution – the Council – that was heavily involved in the executive function. This has changed with the Lisbon Treaty (see further chapter 3), although the latter continues to contain elements of the former regime (cf the possibility of Council implementing acts, as set out in Art 291(2) TFEU; on this, see further chapter 5).

give *supranational* legitimacy to that body. Article 17 TEU describes the involvement of the European Parliament in the appointment of the Commission as follows:

> Taking into account the elections to the European Parliament and after having held the appropriate consultations, the European Council, acting by a qualified majority, shall propose to the European Parliament a candidate for President of the Commission. This candidate shall be elected by the European Parliament by a majority of its component members…The Council, by common accord with the President-elect, shall adopt the list of the other persons whom it proposes for appointment as members of the Commission. They shall be selected, on the basis of the suggestions made by Member States…The President, the High Representative of the Union for Foreign Affairs and Security Policy and the other members of the Commission shall be subject as a body to a vote of consent by the European Parliament. On the basis of this consent the Commission shall be appointed by the European Council, acting by a qualified majority.[85]

The appointment of the second branch of the EU executive is consequently built on a dual parliamentary consent. Parliament must – first – 'elect' the President of the Commission. And it must – secondly – confirm the Commission as a collective body.[86] Once appointed, the Commission will continue to remain 'responsible to the European Parliament'.[87] It must indeed enjoy the 'confidence' of the European Parliament; and where this parliamentary confidence is lost, Parliament may vote on a motion of censure. If this vote of mistrust is carried, the Commission must resign as a body. (The motion of collective censure thus mirrors Parliament's appointment power, which is also focused on the Commission as a collective body.[88]) In light of the European Parliament's elective and censuring power, one is therefore justified in characterizing the Union's governmental system as a '*semi*-parliamentary democracy'.[89]

What about the governmental functions exercised by the Union executive? The traditional task of the executive branch is to enforce legislation; and in discharging this task the executive will generally act *under* the Union legislature. Moreover, due to its more indirect democratic credentials, democratic constitutionalism has traditionally insisted that the executive should not be given – autonomous or delegated – law-making powers. However, with the advent and expansion of the 'administrative state' in the twentieth century, executive law-making has today become the norm in many legal orders and the Union legal order has followed this evolution. But like many other constitutional orders, it has imposed constitutional safeguards to control the delegation of legislative power to the executive.[90]

What are the constitutional or political safeguards of democracy imposed on delegated acts in the EU legal order? Constitutionally, the Union legislator is prohibited from delegating *essential* political choices to the executive.[91] Yet even for *non*-essential powers,

---

[85] Art 17(7) TEU.

[86] However, Parliament may request each nominated Commissioner to appear before Parliament and to 'present' his or her views. This practice thus comes close to 'confirmation hearings' (D Judge and D Earnshaw, *The European Parliament* (2nd edn, Basingstoke: Palgrave Macmillan, 2008) 5).   [87] Art 17(8) TEU.

[88] However, unlike the appointment power, Parliament has been able to sharpen its tools of censure significantly by concluding a political agreement with the Commission. Accordingly, if Parliament expresses lack of confidence in an individual member of the Commission, the President of the Commission 'shall either require the resignation of that Member' or, after 'serious' consideration, explain its refusal to do so before Parliament. On this point, see Framework Agreement on Relations between the European Parliament and the European Commission (OJ [2010] L304/47), para 5.

[89] P Dann, 'European Parliament and Executive Federalism: Approaching a Parliament in a Semi-Parliamentary Democracy' (2003) 9 *European Law Journal* 549 (emphasis added).

[90] B Schwartz, 'Delegated Legislation in America: Procedure and Safeguards' (1948) 11 *Modern Law Review* 449.

[91] On the constitutional limits imposed on a delegation of legislative power, see R Schütze, '"Delegated" Legislation in the (New) European Union: A Constitutional Analysis' (2011) 74 *Modern Law Review* 661 at 669 *et seq*. See further chapter 5.

the Union legislator has been unwilling to delegate power without political control. These political safeguards of democracy can now be found in the second paragraph of Article 290 TFEU. The provision allows the European Parliament or the Council to revoke the delegation or to veto the adoption of a specific delegated act. In establishing an alternative – as opposed to cumulative – veto power for the two branches of the Union legislator, the EU's constitutional safeguards for delegated legislation are democratically stronger than their equivalent in the US.[92] A less democratic system of executive law-making has been created for 'implementing acts'. However, the constitutional logic here is not to protect the powers of the EU legislator but rather to protect the Member States within the Union's system of executive federalism (ie the principle that, in accordance with Article 291 TFEU, the power to implement EU law in principle belongs to the Member States).[93]

5 Liberal constitutionalism I: separation of powers

5.1 The 'classic' separation of powers principle(s)

The central task of liberal constitutionalism is to establish limits to 'the [i]nconveniences of [a]bsolute power'.[94] It aims to protect freedom by establishing a 'government of laws, and not of men'.[95] For governmental power, even democratic governmental power is dangerous when used arbitrarily.[96] One of the oldest constitutional devices of limiting absolute power is to split it, therefore 'balance[ing] the [p]ower of [g]overnment, by placing several parts of it in different hands'.[97]

However, the central question behind the separation of powers doctrine is this: which governmental *parts* should be placed into which governmental *hands*? Liberal constitutionalism has here built on a tripartite division that was originally developed by a French aristocrat: Baron Charles de Montesquieu. When he published *The Spirit of Laws* in 1748,[98] three powers were famously identified:

> In every government there are three sorts of power: the legislative; the executive in respect to things dependent on the law of nations; and the executive in regard to matters that depend on the civil law. By virtue of the first, the prince or magistrate enacts temporary or perpetual laws, and amends or abrogates those that have been already enacted. By the second, he makes peace or war, sends or receives embassies, establishes the public security, and provides against invasions. By the third, he punishes criminals, or determines the disputes that arise between individuals. The latter we shall call the judiciary power.[99]

---

[92] Schütze, '"Delegated" Legislation' (n 91) 663 *et seq.*

[93] R. Schütze, 'From Rome to Lisbon: "Executive Federalism" in the (New) European Union' (2010) 47 *Common Market Law Review* 1385. On implementing acts, see further chapter 5.

[94] J Locke, *Two Treatises of Government* (Cambridge: Cambridge University Press, 2005) § 107 = 338.

[95] J Harrington as quoted in WB Gwyn, *The Meaning of the Separation of Powers* (Leiden: Martinus Nijhoff, 1965) 13.

[96] In the famous words of J Madison in 'Federalist No 51' (see n 48):

If men were angels, no government would be necessary. If angels were to govern men, neither external nor internal controls on government would be necessary. In framing a government which is to be administered by men over men, the great difficulty lies in this: you must first enable the government to control the governed; and in the next place oblige it to control itself. A dependence on the people is, no doubt, the primary control on the government; but experience has taught mankind the necessity of auxiliary precautions.

[97] Locke, *Two Treatises of Government* (n 94) § 107 = 338.

[98] Charles de Secondat, Baron de Montesquieu, *The Spirit of Laws*, trans and ed T Nugent, rev J Prichard (London: Bell, 1914), available at http://www.constitution.org/cm/sol.htm   [99] Ibid, Book XI, ch 6.

Having acknowledged three governmental 'powers' or functions, Montesquieu then moved on to advocate their 'distribution' between different institutions:

> When the legislative and executive powers are united in the same person, or in the same body of magistrates, there can be no liberty; because apprehensions may arise, lest the same monarch or senate should enact tyrannical laws, to execute them in a tyrannical manner. Again, there is no liberty, if the judicial power be not separated from the legislative and executive. Were it joined with the legislative, the life and liberty of the subject would be exposed to arbitrary control; for the judge would be then the legislator. Were it joined to the executive power, the judge might behave with violence and oppression.[100]

But did distribution here mean that each 'separate' power would need to be given to a 'separate' institution? Liberal constitutionalism has given two distinct answers to this question.

According to the *functional separation* version, each governmental institution must not be given more than one governmental function.[101] This reading appears – at first sight – to be chosen by the founding fathers of the US. For all legislative power seems exclusively vested in 'Congress',[102] the executive power solely vested in a 'President',[103] while the judicial power is reserved to the 'Supreme Court'.[104] The heart of this version of the separation of power is the distinction between law-creation and law-application. The separation between the making of laws and their (administrative or judicial) execution is designed to create a 'rule of law' in which the men who made the law would also be subject to it. This idea was subsequently expanded to define the – liberal – constitutional prohibition on the legislature not to pass 'individual laws', that is, laws that are tailored for a single individual or a limited group of individuals.[105] The insistence on the general nature of parliamentary laws was to prevent the legislative branch from overreaching into the executive domain. At the same time, the executive is – theoretically – not allowed to exercise any law-making power, as this is an exclusive prerogative of the legislature.

By contrast: according to the *institutional cooperation* version, each governmental function should be distributed over more than one institution. 'To form a moderate government, it is necessary to combine the several powers; to regulate, temper, and set them in motion; to give, as it were, ballast to one, in order to enable it to counterpoise the other.'[106] The exercise of the legislative function should thus ideally involve more than one institution: 'The legislative body being composed of two parts, they check one another by the mutual privilege of rejecting. They are both restrained by the executive power, as the executive is by the legislative.'[107] The idea behind this second conception is to create a system of

---

[100] Ibid.

[101] The theory of a functional separation of powers finds (almost) no matching constitutional practice. It has been said to contradict the British constitutional idea of parliamentary sovereignty: cf AV Dicey, *Introduction to the Study of the Law of the Constitution* (Indianapolis, IN: Liberty Fund, 1992) 3–10.

[102] Art I, Section 1 US Constitution: 'All legislative Powers herein granted shall be vested in a Congress of the United States, which shall consist of a Senate and House of Representatives.'

[103] Ibid, Art II, Section 1: 'The executive Power shall be vested in a President of the United States of America.'

[104] Ibid, Art III, Section 1: 'The judicial Power of the United States, shall be vested in one Supreme Court, and in such inferior Courts as the Congress may from time to time ordain and establish.'

[105] For the US Constitution, see Art I, Section 9: 'No Bill of Attainder or ex post facto Law shall be passed.' For C Schmitt, the prohibition for the legislature not to pass individual laws represents the cornerstone of the liberal State (*Verfassungslehre* (n 33) 146).

[106] De Montesquieu (n 98) Book V, ch 14. [107] Ibid.

checks and balances. And it is this – second – version of the separation of powers principle that truly informs the 1787 US Constitution.[108] American constitutionalism even
went beyond Montesquieu by introducing the idea of judicial 'checks' on the legislative
power. The US Supreme Court is thus entitled to check the 'constitutionality' of all governmental actions.[109]

What do the two versions of the separation of powers doctrine have in common? Both
versions require that there exist *distinct* governmental *institutions*; and in order to be distinct institutions, there must be a *personal* independence from one another. The simplest
expression of this principle is a constitutional prohibition that the same person(s) are part
of separate institutions.[110] Liberal constitutionalism may, however, go even further and
require the *political* independence of each institution from all the others:

> In order to lay a due foundation for that separate and distinct exercise of the different powers of
> government, which to a certain extent is admitted on all hands to be essential to the preserva-
> tion of liberty, *it is evident that each department should have a will of its own; and consequently
> should be so constituted that the members of each should have as little agency as possible in the
> appointment of the members of the others.*[111]

For liberal constitutionalism, as propagated by the founding fathers of the 1787 US Constitution (and Montesquieu),[112] the selection of the executive by parliament represents
a serious breach of the separation of powers doctrine. The modern English 'parliamentary system' would thus violate the separation of powers doctrine, since it is based on a
'fusion' – not a separation – of the legislative and executive branch.[113] A 'thick' liberal constitutionalism consequently recommends a 'presidential system', that is, a system in which
the executive branch is elected *independently*.

In light of this historical exegesis, what are the liberal constitutionalist credentials of the
EU Treaties? Is there a separation of powers doctrine; and, if so, which one?

5.2 Separating 'powers' in the EU

When born in 1958 with the genetic code of an international organization, the EU could
hardly be viewed in light of the classic *trias politica*.[114] For while it had executive and

---

[108] cf Madison, 'Federalist No 47' (n 48) 234 *et seq.*   [109] *Marbury v Madison*, 5 US 137 (1803).

[110] cf de Montesquieu (n 98): 'There would be an end of everything, were the same man or the same body,
whether of the nobles or of the people, to exercise those three powers, that of enacting laws, that of executing
the public resolutions, and of trying the causes of individuals.'

[111] Madison, 'Federalist No 51' (n 48) 251 (emphasis added).

[112] De Montesquieu (n 98): 'But if there were no monarch, and the executive power should be committed
to a certain number of persons selected from the legislative body, there would be an end then of liberty; by
reason the two powers would be united, as the same persons would sometimes possess, and would be always
able to possess, a share in both.'

[113] In the words of W Bagehot, *The English Constitution* (Oxford: Oxford University Press, 2001) 11:
The efficient secret of the English Constitution may be described as the close union, the nearly complete fusion, of the executive and legislative powers. According to the traditional theory, as it exists in
all the books, the goodness of our constitution consists in the entire separation of the legislative and
executive authorities, but in truth its merit consists in their singular approximation. The connecting
link is *the cabinet*. By that new word we mean a committee of the legislative body selected to be the
executive body.

[114] For the literature on the separation of powers in the Union legal order, see P Pescatore, 'L'executif communautaire: justification des traités de Paris et de Rome' (1978) 4 *Cahiers de droit européen* 387; W Hummer,
'Das institutionelle Gleichgewicht als Strukturdeterminante der Europäischen Gemeinschaften' in H Miehsler

judicial powers, its 'regulatory' competences were not immediately regarded as of a 'legislative' quality.[115] The subsequent ascendancy of the European Parliament changed this; and today the EU Treaties formally acknowledge 'legislative' procedure(s) in the EU legal order.[116] The legislative powers of the Union do, however, appear to allow for the adoption of legislative 'decisions',[117] and the Treaties certainly allow for the delegation of legislative power to the executive;[118] and in making these constitutional choices, the Union legal order seems to have rejected the functional version of the separation of powers doctrine.

Has the Union adopted the second version of the doctrine and, if so, how? The Union legal order has indeed followed the institutional cooperation version of the 'separation of powers' principle. The EU Treaties make this constitutional choice even clearer than the US Constitution. For while each Union institution also has 'its' article in the TEU, the latter expressly describes the various governmental functions in which each Union institution partakes.[119] The European Commission will, for example, be involved in the legislative,[120] executive,[121] and judicial process.[122] Institutional cooperation is consequently required in the exercise of most governmental functions. Under the ordinary legislative procedure, the Commission must thus formally propose the legislative bill, and the Parliament and the Council must co-decide on its adoption. The Treaties have indeed 'set up a system for distributing powers among different [Union] institutions, assigning to each institution its own role in the institutional structure of the [Union] and the accomplishment of the tasks entrusted to the [Union]'.[123]

---

et al (eds), *Ius Humanitatis: Festschrift zum 90. Geburtstag von Alfred Verdross* (Berlin: Duncker & Humblot, 1980); K Lenaerts, 'Some Reflections on the Separation of Powers in the European Community' (1991) 28 *Common Market Law Review* 11; P Huber, 'Das institutionelle Gleichgewicht zwischewn Rat und dem Europäischen Parlament in der künftigen Verfassung für Europa' (2003) *Europarecht* 574; JP Jacqué, 'The Principle of Institutional Balance' (2004) 41 *Common Market Law Review* 383; and G Conway, 'Recovering a Separation of Powers in the European Union' (2011) 17 *European Law Journal* 304.

[115] Early commentators therefore speak of the 'decision law' of the Community (see H Wagner, *Grundbegriffe des Beschlußrechts der Europäische Gemeinschaft* (Cologne: C Heymanns, 1965)). This argument has had a (partial) renaissance in the work of G Majone and his disciple P Lindseth (see *Power and Legitimacy: Reconciling Europe and the Nation-State* (Oxford: Oxford University Press, 2010). The (conceptual) error within these recent works appears to me to be the absence of any conceptualization of the notion of 'legislation' and 'legislative power'.   [116] Art 289 TFEU.

[117] According to Art 289(1) TFEU, the acts that can be adopted under the Union's legislative procedure(s) include the instrument of 'regulation, directive *or decision*' (emphasis added). This wording seems to suggest that the adoption of individual decisions by the Union legislature is possible. This would have been different under the (failed) Constitutional Treaty (CT); as its concept of a European (framework) law was confined to the instrumental matrix of old-style 'regulations' and 'directives' (see Art I-33 CT).

[118] On this point, see section 4.2.

[119] This is normally the first section of the TEU article dealing with the (respective) institution. See further chapter 3.

[120] Art 17(2) TEU: 'Union legislative acts may only be adopted on the basis of a Commission proposal, except where the Treaties provide otherwise.'

[121] Art 17(1) TEU: 'The Commission shall promote the general interest of the Union and take appropriate initiatives to that end. It shall ensure the application of the Treaties, and of measures adopted by the institutions pursuant to them. It shall oversee the application of Union law under the control of the Court of Justice of the European Union. It shall execute the budget and manage programmes. It shall exercise coordinating, executive and management functions, as laid down in the Treaties.'   [122] see Art 258 TFEU.

[123] Case C-70/88 *Parliament v Council (Chernobyl)* [1990] ECR I-2041, para 21.

This conception of the separation of powers principle informs Article 13(2) TEU. The provision is known as the principle of institutional balance and reads:

> Each institution shall act within the limits of the powers conferred on it in the Treaties, and in conformity with the procedures, conditions and objectives set out in them. The institutions shall practice mutual sincere cooperation.[124]

Article 13(2) TEU contains two constitutional commands. First, each institution must act within its powers as defined by the Treaties. This ultra vires doctrine is the horizontal expression of the vertical principle of conferral.[125] It is consequently not possible for an institution to extend its powers unilaterally through constitutional practice.[126] Nor may an institution transfer its powers to another institution – unless the Treaties expressly allow for such delegations of power. Secondly, 'Observance of the institutional balance means that each of the institutions must exercise its powers with due regard for the powers of the other institutions'.[127] This principle of 'mutual sincere cooperation' between the institutions in Article 13(2) TEU is the horizontal extension of the principle of sincere – vertical – cooperation in Article 4(3) TEU.[128]

Case study 4.3: European Parliament and judicial review

When the EU was born in 1958, the Treaty of Rome (the original treaty establishing the European Economic Community) only granted the European Parliament 'advisory and supervisory powers'.[129] Its advisory powers permitted Parliament to be consulted on Commission proposals before their adoption by the Council. The authors of the Treaty had felt that the right to be consulted was, however, not 'active' enough to justify giving Parliament a constitutional right to judicially challenge Union acts that had violated its prerogatives. The original provision on judicial review in the 1958 Treaty of Rome (ex Article 173 EEC) consequently only allowed two Union institutions – the Commission and the Council – to challenge the legality of Union acts before the European Court. This exclusion of the European Parliament remained in place even after the Single European Act (in force 1987) – despite the fact that the latter now provided Parliament in some instances with the active right to cooperate in the adoption of Union legislation.

Should the principle of institutional balance therefore entitle Parliament to bring an action before the Court? In *Parliament v Council (Comitology)*,[130] the Court at first rejected this idea. While recognizing the new role of the Parliament in the legislative sphere, the Court felt that the EEC Treaty had conferred 'specifically on the Commission the responsibility for ensuring that the Parliament's prerogatives are respected and for bringing for that purpose such actions for annulment as might prove to be necessary'.[131] This constitutional rationale assumed that the institutional interests of the Commission and the Parliament

---

[124] Art 13 (2) TEU.
[125] Jacqué, 'The Principle of Institutional Balance' (n 114) 383: 'From a legal point of view, the principle of institutional balance is one manifestation of the rule that the institutions have to act within the limits of their competences.' On the concept of conferral, see further chapter 5.
[126] Case 149/85 *Wybot v Faure* [1986] ECR 2391, esp para 23.
[127] Case C-70/88 *Parliament v Council (Chernobyl)* [1990] ECR I-2041, para 22.
[128] See generally chapter 5.   [129] Art 137 EEC.
[130] Case 302/87 *Parliament v Council (Comitology)* [1988] ECR 5615.   [131] Ibid, para 27.

were always aligned – an assumption that soon proved mistaken. In *Parliament v Council (Chernobyl)*,[132] the Court therefore changed its view and gave Parliament legal standing judicially to enforce its prerogatives.

According to the Court, the principle of institutional balance meant that each institution 'must exercise its powers with due regard for the powers of the other institutions', and this 'require[d] that it should be possible to penalize any breach of that rule which may occur'.[133] The principle of institutional balance mandated that 'Parliament's prerogatives, like those of the other institutions, cannot be breached without *it* having available a legal remedy'. The parliamentary prerogative to participate actively in the drafting of legislative measures would consequently imply the power to ask the Court to 'check' and 'control' the other institutions. This constitutional solution was subsequently codified in the Maastricht Treaty (in force 1993); and ever since the Treaty of Nice (in force 2003) Parliament is recognized as a fully privileged applicant under Article 263 TFEU.

Finally, what about the – personal and political – independence of the Union institutions? With regard to their 'personal' independence, this is indeed generally guaranteed by the Treaties; yet as regards their political independence this is not always the case. For some institutions are involved in the selection of another: Parliament, for example, is involved in the election of the President of the European Commission and also needs to consent to the appointment of the entire Commission.[134] The Commission's political dependence on another institution – Parliament – goes, as we saw previously, even beyond parliamentary approval, since the Commission continues to 'be responsible to the European Parliament'.[135] From a 'thick' liberal constitutionalist perspective, this constitutes a serious – albeit democratic – breach of the separation of powers principle.

6 Liberal constitutionalism II: fundamental rights

The idea of fundamental rights is an achievement of liberal constitutionalism. They are based on the discovery of the 'individual' – a discovery that ultimately led to the protection of an inviolable private sphere.[136] This philosophical idea was first minted into constitutional form in the aftermath of the American Revolutionary War. The 1776 Virginia Declaration of Rights stated: 'That all men are by nature equally free and independent and have certain inherent rights, of which, when they enter into a state of society, they cannot, by any compact, deprive or divest their posterity'.[137] This philosophy of inalienable rights was to inspire the adoption of the 'Bill of Rights' attached to the 1787 US Constitution; and it was subsequently expressed in the 1789 (French) Declaration of the Rights of Man and of the Citizen.[138] The declaration insisted on 'natural' rights that even bound the constitution-makers.[139] It soon became the symbol and stimulus for the liberal constitutionalism of the nineteenth century.

---

[132] *Parliament v Council (Chernobyl)* (n 127).   [133] Ibid, para 22.

[134] Art 17(7) TEU. For an analysis of this point, see earlier in the text.   [135] Art 17(8) TEU.

[136] E Wolgast, *Geschichte der Menschen- und Bürgerrechte* (Stuttgart: Kohlhammer, 2009) 33.

[137] 1776 Virginia Declaration of Rights, Art 1.

[138] For an analysis and historical interpretation of the declaration, see Wolgast, *Geschichte der Menschen- und Bürgerrechte* (n 136) ch 2.

[139] These rights were not 'founded' but simply 'declared' – hence the title: 'Declaration' – by the constitutional assembly.

Since the twentieth century, the protection of fundamental rights has become a central task of most constitutions.[140] Unlike the separation of powers that operates as a *political* safeguard of liberalism, the protection of human rights is typically conceived of as a *judicial* safeguard of liberalism that involves the judicial review of governmental action.[141] A thin liberal constitutionalism thereby restricts judicial review to actions of the executive.[142] A thick liberal constitutionalism, on the other hand, insists that even parliamentary legislation must be judicially reviewed in light of possible violations of fundamental rights.[143]

The EU follows this second constitutional tradition.[144] But what are the sources of fundamental rights in the Union legal order? Originally, there was no 'bill of rights' in the EU Treaties. Two *constitutional* sources for fundamental rights were, however, subsequently developed. The European Court of Justice at first began distilling fundamental rights from the general principles of EU law. This unwritten bill of rights was – despite the reference to 'general principles' – not grounded in a natural rights philosophy. For as we shall see later, the European Court identifies the source of these fundamental rights in the *constitutional* traditions of the *Member States*. With the Lisbon Treaty, a second constitutional source has been added: the Charter of Fundamental Rights of the European Union. Yet again, the Charter proclaims no 'inalienable' natural rights but – modestly – 'reaffirms' the fundamental rights as they result, inter alia, 'from the constitutional traditions and international obligations common to the Member States'.[145] EU fundamental rights are thus constitutional – not natural – rights.

6.1 Fundamental rights as 'general principles'

The birth of EU fundamental rights did not happen overnight. The Court had been invited – as long ago as 1958 – to review the constitutionality of an EU act in light of fundamental rights. In *Stork*,[146] the applicant had challenged a European Commission decision on the ground that the Commission had infringed German fundamental rights. In the absence of an EU bill of rights, this claim drew on the so-called 'mortgage theory'. According to this theory, the powers conferred on the EU were tied to a national human rights 'mortgage'. National fundamental rights would bind the EU, since the Member States could not have created an organization with more powers than themselves.[147] This argument was – correctly[148] – rejected by the Court. The task of the EU institutions was to apply EU laws 'without regard for their validity under national law'.[149] Thus, national fundamental rights could not be the direct source of EU human rights.

This position of the EU towards national fundamental rights has never changed. However, the Court's view evolved with regard to the existence of implied EU fundamental rights. Having originally found that EU law did '*not* contain any general principle, express or otherwise,

---

[140] On human rights as constitutional rights, see A. Sajó, *Limiting Government* (Budapest: Central European University Press, 1999) ch 8.

[141] See M Cappelletti, *Judicial Review in the Contemporary* World (Indianapolis, IN: Bobbs-Merrill, 1971). This 'legal constitutionalism' has recently been challenged by a school called 'political constitutionalism', see R Bellamy, *Political Constitutionalism: A Republican Defence of the Constitutionality of Democracy* (Cambridge: Cambridge University Press, 2007).   [142] Traditionally, this is the case for the UK.

[143] The classic example here is the US.

[144] On the power of constitutional/judicial review, see chapter 10.   [145] EU Charter, Preamble 5.

[146] Case 1/58 *Stork & Cie v High Authority of the European Coal and Steel Community* [1958] ECR English Special Edition 17.   [147] As the Latin legal proverb makes clear: 'Nemo dat quod non habet'.

[148] For a criticism of the 'mortgage theory', see R Schütze, 'EC Law and International Agreements of the Member States – An Ambivalent Relationship?' [2006–07] 9 *Cambridge Yearbook of European Legal Studies* 387 at 399–402.   [149] Case 1/58 *Stork v High Authority* (n 146) 26.

guaranteeing the maintenance of vested rights',[150] the Court subsequently discovered 'funda-mental human rights enshrined in the general principles of [EU] law'.[151] This new position was spelled out in *Internationale Handelsgesellschaft*.[152] The judgment confirmed the existence of an 'analogous guarantee inherent in [EU] law'.[153] And accordingly, 'respect for fundamental rights forms an integral part of the general principles of law protected by the Court of Justice'.[154]

Whence did the Court derive these fundamental rights? The famous answer here was that the Union's fundamental rights would be '*inspired* by the constitutional traditions common to the Member States'.[155] While thus not a direct source, national constitutional rights constituted an indirect source for the Union's fundamental rights. What was the nature of this indirect relationship between national rights and EU rights? How would the former influence the latter? A constitutional clarification was offered in *Nold*.[156] Drawing on its previous jurisprudence, the Court held:

> fundamental rights form an integral part of the general principles of law, the observance of which it ensures. In safeguarding these rights, the Court is bound to draw inspiration from con-stitutional traditions common to the Member States, and it cannot therefore uphold measures which are incompatible with fundamental rights recognised and protected by the constitutions of those States. Similarly, international treaties for the protection of human rights on which the Member States have collaborated or of which they are signatories, can supply guidelines which should be followed within the framework of [European] law.[157]

In searching for fundamental rights inside the general principles of EU law, the Court thus draws 'inspiration' from the common constitutional traditions of the Member States. The Court also uses international agreements of the Member States to identify EU fundamen-tal rights, and one such international agreement is the European Convention on Human Rights (ECHR). The Convention, indeed, soon assumed a 'particular significance' in iden-tifying fundamental rights for the EU.[158] The Lisbon Treaty goes even further and requires the EU itself to accede to the ECHR.[159] Once this happens, the Union will be directly bound by the Convention; yet this binding effect is not of a constitutional nature.[160]

6.2 The EU Charter of Fundamental Rights

The desire for a written bill of rights for the EU was first expressed in arguments favouring the Union's accession to the ECHR.[161] Yet an alternative strategy became prominent in the late twentieth century: the Union's own bill of rights.

---

[150] Ibid, 439 (emphasis added).   [151] Case 29/69 *Stauder v City of Ulm* [1969] ECR 419, para 7.
[152] Case 11/70 *Internationale Handelsgesellschaft mbH v Einfuhr- und Vorratsstelle für Getreide und Futtermittel* [1979] ECR 1125.
[153] Ibid, para 4.   [154] Ibid.   [155] Ibid (emphasis added).
[156] Case 4/73 *Nold v Commission* [1974] ECR 491.   [157] Ibid, para 13.
[158] See Joined Cases 46/87 and 227/88 *Höchst v Commission* [1989] ECR 2859, para 13:
The Court has consistently held that fundamental rights are an integral part of the general principles of law the observance of which the Court ensures, in accordance with constitutional traditions com-mon to the Member States, and the international treaties on which the Member States have collaborated or of which they are signatories. The European Convention for the Protection of Human Rights and Fundamental Freedoms of 4 November 1950 ... is of particular significance in that regard.
[159] Art 6(2) TEU states: 'The Union shall accede to the European Convention for the Protection of Human Rights and Fundamental Freedoms. Such accession shall not affect the Union's competences as defined in the Treaties.'   [160] On the status of international treaties concluded by the Union, see chapter 24.
[161] Commission, 'Memorandum on the Accession of the European Communities to the European Convention for the Protection of Human Rights and Fundamental Freedoms' [1979] *Bulletin of the European Communities*, Supplement 2/79, esp 11 *et seq*.

The initiative for a 'Charter of Fundamental Rights' came from the European Council, which transferred the drafting mandate to a 'European Convention'.[162] The idea behind an internal codification was to strengthen the protection of fundamental rights in Europe 'by making those rights more visible in a Charter'.[163] The Charter was proclaimed in 2000, but it was not at first legally binding. Its status (as regards the Union) was similar to the ECHR. It provided an informal inspiration but imposed no formal obligation on the EU institutions.[164] This ambivalent status was immediately perceived as a constitutional problem.[165] With the Lisbon Treaty, the Charter is today recognized as having 'the same legal value as the Treaties'. Article 6(1) TEU in effect 'appends' the – slightly amended original – Charter to the Treaties.

What fundamental rights are listed in the Charter? The Charter 'reaffirms' the rights that result 'in particular' from the constitutional traditions common to the Member States, the ECHR, and the general principles of EU law.[166] This formulation suggested two things. First, the Charter aims to codify existing fundamental rights and is not intended to create 'new' ones.[167] And, secondly, it codifies EU rights from various sources – and thus not solely the general principles found in the Treaties.

7 Conclusion

The EU's constitutional theory must be derived from its 'physical' constitutional choices – or else become a banal metaphysical formalism.[168] This chapter has tried to analyse the EU legal order, as established by the European Treaties, against three versions of constitutionalism: formal constitutionalism, democratic constitutionalism, and liberal constitutionalism. The liberal constitutional claim is the most easily satisfied: the Union has adopted a version of the separation of powers principle and also constitutionally protects fundamental rights. With regard to formal and democratic constitutionalism, on the other hand, the Union has had trouble in staking its constitutional claim. As we saw previously, this is, however, mainly due to the 'unitary' standard adopted by classic constitutionalism. When viewed in light of a 'federal' or 'pluralist' standard, this dramatically changes. For a federal standard is able to

---

[162] On the drafting process, see chapter 9, and further G de Búrca, 'The Drafting of the European Union Charter of Fundamental Rights' (2001) 26 *European Law Review* 126.

[163] EU Charter, Preamble 4. For a criticism of the idea of codification, see JHH Weiler, 'Does the European Union Truly Need a Charter of Rights' (2000) 6 *European Law Journal* 95.

[164] See Case C-540/03 *Parliament v Council* [2006] ECR I-5769, para 38: 'the Charter is not a legally binding instrument'.

[165] The Charter was announced at the Nice European Council in December 2000, and its status was one of the questions in the 2000 Nice Declaration on the Future of the Union.

[166] EU Charter, Preamble 5.

[167] See Protocol (No 30) on the application of the Charter of Fundamental Rights of the European Union to Poland and to the United Kingdom, Preamble 6: 'the Charter reaffirms the rights, freedoms and principles recognised in the Union and makes those rights more visible, but does not create new rights or principles'.

[168] The problem with much contemporary European 'constitutionalism' is that it has escaped into the realm of the metaphysical and mysterious. For the perfect example of this imperfect constitutional theory, see N Walker, 'Postnational Constitutionalism and the Problem of Translation' in JHH Weiler et al (eds), *European Constitutionalism Beyond the State* (Cambridge: Cambridge University Press, 2003). In the words of N Krisch, 'Europe's Constitutional Monstrosity' (2005) 25 *Oxford Journal of Legal Studies* 321 at 326: 'at [Walker's] level of generality, all the particular content of constitutionalism, all its connections to particular historical and social circumstances, are lost.'

recognize the existence of two constitutional claims – the national and the European claim – alongside one another; and it can also account for a pluralist version of popular sovereignty ('We, the Peoples') as well as the bicameral structure of the Union legislator. Table 4.1 provides a brief summary of the – respective – constitutionalist claims when read across a unitary and a federal standard.

Table 4.1 Unitary and federal constitutionalism: an overview

	Unitary standard	**Federal/pluralist standard**
Formal constitutionalism	There is *one* constitution in *one* polity, where the supremacy issue has *one* solution.	There are *two* or *more* constitutional levels in a *compound* polity, where the supremacy issue has *no* solution.
Democratic constitutionalism		
(a) Foundational origin	The Constitution is founded by *one* people ('We, the People').	The Constitution is founded on the basis of a *treaty* between multiple *peoples* ('We, the Peoples').
(b) Parliamentary structure	The legislator is (ideally) composed of *one* Parliament and represents *one* people.	The legislator is composed of *two* chambers, whereby the first represents the federal *people* and the second the State *peoples*.
Liberal constitutionalism		
(a) Separation of powers	There is *one* horizontal separation of powers.	There is a horizontal *and* a vertical separation of powers.
(b) Human rights	There is (typically) *one* Bill of Rights.	There is (typically) *one* federal and *one* State Bill of Rights.

Further reading

A von Bogdandy and J Bast, *Principles of European Constitutional Law* (Oxford: Hart Publishing, 2011)

P Craig, 'Constitutions, Constitutionalism, and the European Union' (2001) 7 *European Law Journal* 125

A Hamilton, et al, *The Federalist* (ed T Ball) (Cambridge: Cambridge University Press, 2003)

M Maduro, 'Contrapunctual Law: Europe's Constitutional Pluralism in Action' in N Walker (ed), *Sovereignty in Transition* (Oxford: Hart Publishing, 2003) 501

A Peters, *Elemente einer Theorie der Verfassung Europas* (Baden-Baden: Nomos, 2001)

C Schmitt, *Constitutional Theory* (Durham, NC: Duke University Press, 2008)

R Schütze, *European Constitutional Law* (Cambridge: Cambridge University Press, 2012)

JHH Weiler, *The Constitution of Europe* (Cambridge: Cambridge University Press, 1999)

5

Legislating in the European Union

Kieran St C Bradley

1 Introduction

The EU is not a State, though it exercises powers which are normally exercised by States. The Union does so through institutions of government and decision-making procedures whose design is modelled to a large extent on that of federal States, and which seek to balance the necessary freedom of action of the Union with the preservation of those powers the Member States have retained. The Union institutions enjoy a wide degree of functional autonomy and have been vested with extensive decision-making competences, which they can exercise independently of, and indeed against, the Member States. The exercise of these competences, as one might expect, is subject to various constraints, both procedural and substantive and, subject to one important exception,[1] is fully amenable to judicial review by the Court of Justice.

This chapter is about the procedures for the adoption of legislative and other normative[2] measures in the EU. It thus touches on a wide variety of subjects: forms of legal act, law-making competences and choice of procedure, the delegation of normative powers and the application of the constitutional principles of conferral, subsidiarity, and proportionality, as well as a number of more abstract matters, such as the hierarchy of norms and the 'democratic deficit'. While each subject is treated separately for the sake of a simpler presentation, it should be understood from the outset that these matters are closely related, both in legal theory and in the daily practice of the Union institutions.

The chapter thus describes the legal structures and the rules governing the allocation of powers between the Union and the Member States, and the distribution of powers between the different organs of Union government. It is political law of the highest order, in the sense that the principal parties concerned are the political actors of the Union (Member State governments[3] and the Union institutions), and the judgments of the Court of Justice regularly both involve an appreciation of politically sensitive matters and have major implications for the conduct of the political process. This area of law has evolved more significantly over time than many areas of material law;[4] all of the major Treaty revisions in the history of the Community, now Union,[5] have entailed reforms of the decision-making procedures. The Court is in effect engaged in a continuing dialogue with the Treaty authors; its interpretations of the relevant institutional provisions tend to influence the drafting of subsequent provisions, and are often incorporated in whole or in part into the Treaty.

Of particular note is the proliferation, or at least the reformulation and clarification, of rules seeking to constrain Union action which has accompanied the granting of new powers to the Union. This might give the impression that the powers of the Member States

---

[1] The Common Foreign and Security Policy (CFSP); see section 4.4.4.

[2] The term 'normative' is used to indicate 'setting a standard', and refers to measures of general application, as distinct from individual decisions.

[3] Member State parliaments also play a specific role in scrutinizing decision-making and Treaty reform: see respectively sections 5.2 and 10.

[4] See generally JHH Weiler, 'The Transformation of Europe' (1991) 100 *Yale Law Journal* 2403.

[5] For convenience, the term 'Union' will henceforth be used throughout, however anachronistic it may be in some contexts, unless it is necessary to distinguish between 'Union' and 'Community'.

are protected from Union encroachment essentially by legal rules and judicial process. Nothing could be further from the truth; the fact that ministers from the Member States make up one of the branches of the legislature, and also exercise many executive functions, such as appointments to office in certain of the Union institutions, always has been, and remains, the principal, and very effective, 'political safeguard of federalism', at least to the extent that the governments pursue this objective.

2 Forms of legal act (including 'soft law')

The main forms of normative act adopted by the institutions in implementing the Union's policy objectives are regulations and directives.[6] The institutions may also adopt rule-making decisions and international agreements, which are legally binding, and guidelines and recommendations, which have the legal effects attributed to them in their respective specific contexts.[7]

The Treaty prescribes the form of legal act for action in a small number of areas, such as regulations for common commercial policy, or directives to facilitate freedom of establishment and freedom to provide services.[8] Some provisions even restrict the content of the Union's action, for example by limiting its competence to 'incentive measures', which normally take the form of decisions.[9] For the most part, however, the institutions may choose the form of legal act they use to attain a particular objective; they must do so on a case-by-case basis and opt for the least intrusive form which will allow them to achieve their desired aim, in accordance with the principle of proportionality.[10] Secondary normative measures, that is, delegated and implementing acts,[11] also take the form of regulations, directives, or decisions, though their status as derived law is discernible from their title.

2.1 Regulations

Regulations are the most easily recognizable form of normative act at the disposal of the Union. A regulation 'shall have general application [and is] binding in its entirety and directly applicable in all Member States';[12] it is in effect the equivalent of a statute or law in a national legal order. Regulation 261/2004, for example, famously establishes a charter of the rights of air passengers in difficulty; some airlines even impose a 'Regulation 261' charge as part of the price of an air ticket, presumably with a view to covering compliance costs.[13] The Member States need not adopt any national measures to give effect to a regulation in national law, and indeed they may not do so, as this would disguise the Union character of the act, though they may be required to adopt national provisions to implement a regulation. Regulations are the legal instrument of choice for the implementation of the

---

[6] Art 288 TFEU provides the definition of the legal acts of the Union, though the list of such acts is incomplete.

[7] See eg Art 121(4) TFEU (broad guidelines on economic policy) or Art 126(7)–(9) TFEU (recommendations on the reduction of an excessive deficit).

[8] See respectively Art 207(2) TFEU and Arts 50(1) and 59(1) TFEU.

[9] For an example of an incentive measure, see Parliament and Council Decision No 1145/2002/EC of 10 June 2002 on Community incentive measures in the field of employment (OJ [2002] L170/1).

[10] Art 296, first para, TFEU; on proportionality, see section 6.   [11] See section 8.

[12] Art 288, second para, TFEU.

[13] OJ [2004] L46/1; the validity of the Regulation was vigorously but unsuccessfully contested by IATA and an association of low-cost airlines (Case C-344/04 *IATA and ELFAA* [2006] ECR I-403). For a case study of the Regulation, see chapter 23.

common policies, as distinct from, say, internal market measures, which usually take the form of directives, though there is no hard-and-fast rule in this regard.

2.2 Directives

Directives are normative acts addressed to the Member States, which are then required, within a specified deadline, to adopt the necessary national provisions to give effect to ('transpose') the policy objectives set out in the directive, and to notify the Commission of their transposition measures. A directive is therefore 'binding as to the result to be achieved' while 'leav[ing] to the national authorities the choice of form and methods';[14] the equivalent term in certain other languages translates back into English as 'guideline', though it is in effect a sort of framework law.[15] The instrument of the directive is said to reflect the principle of subsidiarity,[16] in that the Union is supposed to lay down only the rules and procedures which are strictly necessary to define and pursue its policy objectives, entrusting the Member States to adapt their national laws and procedures accordingly. Union policy is therefore applied through national legal forms, which are more familiar to both the citizen and the administrative authorities responsible for its concrete application. The directive is a particularly appropriate legal instrument for the pursuit of Union objectives in areas which are already subject to a developed legal framework in the Member States, such as national rules on the provision of services, to take a random example.[17]

The reality is somewhat different. In practice, directives often regulate a policy area in great detail, leaving the Member States precious little discretion, even as regards 'the form and methods', particularly where the matter being regulated is highly technical in character. While often attributed to a thirst for power on the part of 'Brussels', in reality the level of detail arguably reflects instead, at least in part, the limited extent to which the governments of the Member States trust each other faithfully to pursue the policy objectives they agreed on in signing the Treaty. The factual evidence would, moreover, tend to support the doubters: more or less all the Member States have been guilty, though not equally so, of failing properly to transpose, and/or to implement, Union directives.[18]

The Union's response to this state of affairs has been twofold. In the first place, the Court of Justice has recognized that, where a Member State has not implemented a directive by the deadline set, an individual may rely on those provisions of the directive which are unconditional and sufficiently precise in order to defeat the application of the conflicting national provisions. This direct effect of unimplemented provisions of directives is based on the idea that a Member State may not rely on its own turpitude to deny individuals rights deriving from Union law. It follows from this legal foundation that neither individuals nor public authorities may rely on such unimplemented provisions of directives in their dealings with (other) individuals.[19]

The second response came in the form of a special judicial procedure, introduced by the Maastricht Treaty in 1993,[20] under which the Court of Justice may impose financial penalties on a Member State which fails to comply with a previous Court judgment finding that the Member State has infringed Union law. In practice, a large proportion of the

---

[14] Art 288, third para, TFEU.   [15] eg in German 'directive' is 'Richtlinie' and in Dutch 'richtlijn'.
[16] See section 5.   [17] Parliament and Council Directive 2006/123/EC (OJ [2006] L376/36).
[18] See eg the Commission's annual reports on the monitoring of the application of EU law; the 2012 report was published as COM(2013) 726, 23 October 2013.
[19] On the legal effect of directives, see further chapter 6.
[20] Though formally known as the Treaty on European Union, this Treaty has been completely overhauled since; the 'Maastricht Treaty' therefore refers to the instrument as it came into force on 1 November 1993.

proceedings initiated under this heading have concerned failures to transpose and/or to apply directives properly. The Lisbon Treaty introduced a specific provision allowing the Court to impose a financial penalty on the Member State directly in infringement proceedings concerning its failure to notify the Commission of the national measures taken to transpose a directive adopted under a legislative procedure;[21] this has the advantage of allowing the Commission and the Court to concentrate on a single question of fact and law, and of course a Member State cannot notify transposition measures unless it has adopted them. Once the Commission has sight of the transposition measures, it can proceed with the more substantive task of verifying whether or not the measure implements the directive.

2.3 **'Rule-making decisions'**

The traditional Treaty definition of a 'decision' is an act which is 'binding in its entirety upon those to whom it is addressed'.[22] However, the Union institutions discovered long ago that certain policy measures, or measures laying down institutional arrangements, for example, could best be formulated in a decision rather than a regulation or directive, an instrument often referred to by the German term *Beschluß*, in contradistinction to the individual decision, the *Entscheidung*. As such a rule-making decision[23] was addressed to no one in particular, it was theoretically devoid of legal effect. This type of decision was nonetheless an important legal instrument; for example, the Erasmus programme on the mobility of students was set up by such a decision in 1987,[24] and prior to the Lisbon Treaty reforms, the arrangements by which the exercise by the Commission of its implementing powers was supervised had been laid down in decisions of 1987 and 1999 (amended in 2006).[25] It is for this reason that the Treaty now specifies that, while decisions are 'binding in [their] entirety', a 'decision which specifies those to whom it is addressed' is only binding on its addressees.[26]

2.4 **International agreements**

International agreements concluded by the Union are incorporated into its legal order by a Council decision, following a specific (non-legislative) procedure.[27] Such agreements are binding on the institutions of the Union and the Member States and therefore, subject to a few important exceptions, provide a criterion for the validity of Union acts.[28]

2.5 **Interinstitutional agreements**

In order to facilitate the smooth application of the institutional and budgetary provisions of the Treaties, over the years the political institutions have concluded a large number of so-called 'interinstitutional agreements'. While these might be considered more

---

[21] Art 260(3) TFEU.   [22] Art 249, fourth para, EC.
[23] There is, as yet, no single standard term to describe this form of legal instrument; K Lenaerts and P Van Nuffel refer to the *sui generis* decision (*European Union Law* (3rd edn, London: Sweet & Maxwell, 2011) para 22-096, p 916), and R Schütze calls it the 'non-addressed' decision (*European Constitutional Law* (Cambridge: Cambridge University Press, 2012) 322), though neither denomination clearly indicates the possible content of the measure.   [24] Council Decision 87/327/EEC (OJ [1987] L166/1).
[25] See section 8.2.   [26] Art 288, third para, TFEU.   [27] Art 218(2)–(8) and (10) TFEU.
[28] Arts 218 and 216(2) TFEU respectively; the General Agreement on Tariffs and Trade (GATT) and the World Trade Organization (WTO) Agreement comprise the most important exceptions. See chapter 24.

contractual than normative, they may nonetheless have important policy and even legal effects, and successive reforms have transformed the functional necessity to conclude agreements on specific matters into a Treaty obligation; one such is the multi-annual financial framework which, with the Lisbon Treaty, crossed over from agreement to regulation.[29] The Court has recognized that such agreements can be a useful supplement to the Treaty provisions themselves, and that certain delicate political questions can better be resolved by the application of an agreement between the main players than intervention by the judicial authority.[30] The Court will thus give legal effect to the substantive content of such an agreement, where the institutions intended to enter into a binding commitment in an area where there are under a duty to cooperate with each other, and accordingly annul an act adopted in contravention of the agreement.[31] Moreover, the Treaty now obliges the Parliament, the Council, and the Commission to 'consult with each other and by common agreement make arrangements for their cooperation'; the resulting interinstitutional agreements may be binding.[32]

2.6 **Recommendations, opinions, and other non-binding acts**

In principle, the essential characteristic of both recommendations and opinions is that they have 'no binding force'.[33] There are, however, important exceptions to this rule. In the specific area of economic and monetary policy, the lengthy and politically sensitive procedure for dealing with a Member State's excessive deficit requires the Council first to address recommendations to the Member State concerned; if the Member State does not put these into practice, the Council may in effect order it to take deficit-reduction measures, failing which the Council itself may adopt the necessary measures.[34] Even broad guidelines on economic policy may have some legal effects, in that non-compliance provides the basis for a Commission warning, followed by Council recommendations.[35]

While the content of the opinion of an institution or body which is consulted on a proposed normative act is not binding, respect of the consultation procedure is a substantive procedural requirement breach of which justifies the annulment of the act. The adopting institution(s) must therefore request and await the opinion of the body consulted.[36] Only the 'opinion' the Court of Justice may be asked to provide in the procedure for the conclusion of an international agreement, on the compatibility with Union law of the planned agreement, is wholly binding.[37] Though not a necessary part of the procedure by which such agreements are adopted, where one is provided, the opinion can have a decisive influence on the content of the agreement; a negative opinion requires in effect the renegotiation or abandonment of the agreement.

The institutions also adopt various forms of what is abusively called 'soft law'. Insofar as these do not have legal effects, they should not be called 'law' at all. This is notably the

---

[29] Compare Art 161, third para, EC with Art 312(2) TFEU.
[30] See in particular Case 34/86 *Council v Parliament* ('*1986 Budget*') [1986] ECR 2155, para 50.
[31] Case C-25/94 *Commission v Council* [1996] ECR I-1469, para 49.   [32] Art 295 TFEU.
[33] Art 288, fifth para, TFEU.   [34] Art 126(7)–(11) TFEU.
[35] Art 121(4) TFEU; see further chapter 19.
[36] See, as regards the consultation of the European Parliament, Case 138/79 *Roquette Frères v Council* ('*Isoglucose*') [1980] ECR 3333. The Court added a minor proviso to its *Isoglucose* ruling in Case C-65/93 *Parliament v Council* [1995] ECR I-643.
[37] Art 218(11) TFEU. The term 'opinion' is clearly a misnomer; under Art 103, third para, Euratom, the Court more correctly adopts a 'ruling'.

case of the 'open method of coordination', a substitute for, or addition to, normative Union action which has been applied in areas of regulation where traditional command and control mechanisms are considered inappropriate, or where the subject matter is deemed too sensitive or otherwise inappropriate for Union legislation, such as certain aspects of economic, social, and employment policies. Under this method, the Union sets guidelines which are to be implemented by national action plans; the fulfilment of these action plans is monitored through benchmarking and peer review. The process is intended to be participative; regional and local government, management and labour, and civil society are to be actively involved in the planning and review stages, and the private sector in its implementation.[38]

On the other hand, where a putative act of 'soft law', such as a Commission communication, has the effect of creating legal rights or obligations, it is not 'soft'; it is subject to judicial review and is likely to be annulled. Thus, for example, in *France v Commission*, the Commission had issued a communication which restated, ostensibly as its opinion, the substantive provisions of a proposal for a directive on pension funds which had not been adopted. The Court held that the communication created new obligations for the Member States and annulled it.[39] Moreover, where the European Parliament and the Council have been granted the power to adopt legislative acts, they may not adopt other, non-legislative, acts, such as declarations and recommendations.[40]

3 Hierarchy of norms

Within a national legal system, it is generally quite easy to identify the respective places of different legal instruments in the hierarchy of norms, particularly where the State in question operates under a written constitution. Thus, at its simplest, statutes are subordinate to the constitution, while statutory instruments must comply with the statute under which they are adopted. Moreover, the name of the particular legal act usually indicates its place in this hierarchy.

This has not always been the case in the EU, given that the denomination of an act as a 'regulation', 'directive', or 'decision' does not in itself determine its place in the hierarchy of norms. At the apex of the pyramid, so to speak, are the Treaties, including the Charter of Fundamental Rights, which has 'the same legal value as the Treaties',[41] and the fundamental principles of Union law developed in the case law of the Court, including the requirement to protect fundamental rights; collectively these may be termed 'primary law'. Acts which are based directly on the Treaty, including, in particular, Union legislation and similar normative measures, may be termed 'secondary law'. Under conditions laid down in the Treaty and/or secondary law, the Commission (and, in very limited cases, the Council) may adopt regulatory acts, which are based either on the Treaty or on enabling provisions in acts of secondary law.[42]

Obviously, the Court is not empowered to rule on the validity of provisions of the founding Treaties.[43] In *Pringle*, the Court nonetheless examined the question of whether

---

[38] See eg D Chalmers and M Lodge, 'The Open Method of Coordination and the European Welfare State' (2003) ESRC Centre for Analysis of Risk and Regulation.

[39] Case C-57/95 *France v Commission* [1997] ECR I-1627.

[40] Art 296, third para, TFEU; unless reflected in the text of the legal act, declarations by the legislature in any case had no legal effect even as a guide to interpretation of the act (Case C-292/89 *Antonissen* [1991] ECR I-745).

[41] Art 6(1), first subpara, TEU. See further chapter 9.   [42] See further sections 7.3 and 8.

[43] See Cases C-235/94 P *Roujansky v Council* [1995] ECR I-7 and C-167/94 *Grau Gomis* [1995] ECR I-1023.

an amendment to the Treaty had been validity adopted in accordance with one of the simplified revision procedures available since the Lisbon reforms, which allows the European Council to adopt amendments under certain procedural and substantive conditions.[44]

The hierarchical relationship between primary and secondary law is relatively simple. A normative act based directly on the Treaty must comply with the Treaty itself, the Charter, and the general principles of Union law. By the same token, a delegated or implementing act, which seeks to give effect to a measure of secondary law, must respect the conditions and limitations of the enabling provision of that measure, failing which the delegated or implementing act may be deemed ultra vires and annulled.[45] An enabling provision in an act of secondary law may itself be challenged for failing to respect the Treaty rules defining the conditions under which such delegations of power may be made, for example by delegating to the Commission the power to adopt essential elements of the matter being regulated, though this is rare in practice.[46]

The most problematic case arises in the event of an alleged clash between the two sources of primary law, such as the contention that a Treaty provision itself fails to ensure the protection of a fundamental right. In *Emesa Sugar*, the applicants in the main proceedings argued that the Treaty arrangements which prevented parties to Court of Justice proceedings from commenting on the Opinion of the Advocate General infringed their right to a fair hearing as defined in the case law of the European Court of Human Rights. In the result, the Court of Justice ruled that the role of the Advocate General was different from that of the various law officers who had been the subject of the case law of the Court of Human Rights, and that this case law therefore did not apply.[47] This view has been vindicated subsequently by the Strasbourg Court itself.[48] The planned accession of the Union to the European Convention on Human Rights[49] would provide a judicial avenue for the resolution of this particular type of dispute.

4 Competences and conferral

4.1 'Competence' as ability and 'competence' as power

The EU Treaties use the term 'competence' as a synonym for both 'legal authority' or 'power' and in its more quotidian meaning of 'personal ability'. The latter usage is to be found particularly in the provisions governing the qualifications for, and appointment to, office as a member of an institution or ancillary body; thus Commissioners are selected, inter alia, on grounds of their 'general competence', while 'jurisconsults of recognised competence' may be appointed to the Court of Justice.[50] It is, however, the former usage of the term which is relevant for the present chapter.

In its original English version, the EEC Treaty used 'competence' to mean power in only one, albeit highly relevant, provision; Article 173, second paragraph, EEC, identified 'lack

---

[44] Case C-370/12 *Pringle v Ireland*, judgment of 27 November 2012; see further section 10.

[45] See section 8.

[46] See Case C-359/92 *Germany v Council* ('*Product safety*') [1994] ECR I-3681.

[47] Case C-17/98 *Emesa Sugar v Aruba*, Order of 4 February 2000 [2000] ECR I-665, referring to the relevant case law of the European Court of Human Rights (ECtHR). On the role of the Advocate General, see chapter 10.

[48] *Kress v France* (Appl No 39594/98), ECtHR, judgment of 7 June 2001, and, as regards the EU system in particular, *Kokkelvisserij v Netherlands* (Appl No 13645/05), judgment of 20 January 2009.

[49] See chapter 9.

[50] See respectively Art 17(3), second subpara, TEU and Art 253, first para, TFEU.

of competence' as the first ground on which an act of the Council or the Commission could be annulled. The term was a direct translation of the word '*incompétence*', previously used in Article 33, first paragraph, of the 1951 Treaty of Paris establishing the European Coal and Steel Community (ECSC), which was only authentic in the French language.[51] The idea is equivalent to ultra vires in the administrative law terminology of the common law jurisdictions. The term 'power' was preferred in the remainder of the EEC Treaty, notably the injunction in Article 4(1) EEC that each institution 'act within the limits of the powers conferred on it'.

Both the Single European Act (1987) and the Maastricht Treaty (1993) used the term 'competence', in preference to 'power', at the same time as they significantly extended the formal powers of the Community, and established the Union and endowed it with extensive decision-making powers. The Treaty of Lisbon sought to classify the competences of the Union into three categories: exclusive, shared, and ancillary competences, incidentally providing a definition of 'competence' as being the power to 'legislate and adopt legally binding acts'.[52] Like the witches in *Macbeth* around their cauldron, the three principles of conferral, subsidiarity, and proportionality watch over the Union's competences on behalf of the Member States. Conferral determines what competences the Union enjoys, subsidiarity provides a test as to whether or not they should be exercised in a given case, and proportionality seeks to ensure the competences are exercised in such a manner as to encroach on the competences of the Member States, and the rights of individuals, as little as possible.[53]

4.2 Conferral

The principle underlying the division of competences between the Union and the Member States is set out in the first paragraph of Article 1 TEU, which states that 'the Member States confer competences [on the Union] to attain objectives they have in common'. As well as establishing the centrality of the principle of conferral (also referred to as the principle of 'attributed powers') in the first substantive provision of the Treaties, this paragraph identifies the *raison d'être* of the Union as being to attain certain common objectives of the Member States.

The principle of conferral is repeated insistently throughout the Union Treaties. Article 4(1) TEU thus declares that 'competences not conferred upon the Union in the Treaties remain with the Member States', Article 5(1) explains that '[the] limits of Union competences are governed by the principle of conferral', while Article 5(2) TEU provides that 'the Union shall act only within the limits of the competences conferred on it by the Member States in the Treaties to attain the objectives set out therein'. In addition, Article 13(2) TEU enjoins each of the institutions to act 'within the limits of the powers conferred on it in the Treaties'. The authors of the Lisbon Treaty did not, however, discover the moon, as they appear to believe; the same principle underlay all the previous Union and Community Treaties, right from the ECSC Treaty, which explicitly enjoined each of the institutions to act within the limits of its powers and vested the Court of Justice with jurisdiction to ensure they did so.[54]

---

[51] The ECSC Treaty was concluded for 50 years and expired in 2002; its provisions nonetheless occasionally provide useful insights into the 'original understanding' between the Member States on which the Union was first created.   [52] Art 2(1) TFEU.

[53] See respectively sections 4.2–4.4, 5, and 6.   [54] Arts 6, para 4, and 33, first para, ECSC.

4.3 Grants of legislative power ('legal bases')

The Treaties do not provide a list of areas of economic or policy activity in which the Union enjoys the plenitude of legislative power, and authorize the Union to act in those areas, in the same way as, for example, Article I, Section 8, of the Constitution of the United States empowers Congress to legislate in the domains listed in that provision. Instead, the Treaty grants the Union legislative competence in a number of discrete areas; though the Union's competences are often widely drawn, they are nonetheless hedged about in most cases by material restrictions and procedural requirements of different kinds, which are designed to protect the competences of the Member States. In two cases, the Union's legislative competence is phrased primarily in terms of pursuing objectives, those of establishing and ensuring the functioning of the internal market (Article 114 TFEU), and of attaining Union objectives where the necessary powers have not been provided elsewhere (Article 352 TFEU). The Court has regularly been called upon to ensure that the institutions do not exceed the boundaries of the former legal basis, while the requirement of a unanimous vote in the Council ensures that the legality of recourse to the latter arises only rarely.[55]

In accordance with the principle of conferral, every binding act the Union adopts must have a legal foundation either in the Treaties or in a valid pre-existing normative act; such foundation is known as the 'legal basis' of the act. This provision indicates who may adopt the act, what the act may contain, and what procedure must be followed to adopt it. Disputes on whether or not the Union has exceeded its competences tend to take the form of a challenge to the choice of legal basis for the particular act, rather than an allegation that the Union has no competence whatsoever; this is because Union competence to act on the particular matter may be available under another legal basis than the legal basis chosen, such as Article 352 TFEU, which, as noted above, under certain restrictive conditions, allows the Council to adopt measures to attain a Treaty objective where 'the Treaties have not [otherwise] provided the necessary powers'.[56]

Since the entry into force of the Single European Act in 1987, the Court has built up a large body of case law on the matter of the determination of the legal basis of Union acts.[57] Thus, in the *1986 GSP* case, the Court ruled that the legislature was obliged to identify the legal basis of binding acts and that this choice was amenable to judicial review.[58] In *Titanium dioxide*, it identified the aim and material content of the measures as the principal criteria for the determination of the legal basis, though, ironically, in this case the application of these criteria was not sufficient for the Court to find the correct legal basis of the contested directive.[59] The Court relied explicitly on the principle of conferral in striking down the first Tobacco Advertising Directive as being incorrectly classified as an internal market measure.[60]

Successful challenges to Union legislation on grounds of lack of competence are in practice very rare; even in the case of tobacco advertising, the validity of a second directive, carefully crafted to take account of the judgment of the Court in the first case, was

---

[55] Regarding the internal market, see *Tobacco advertising I* (n 60), *Biotechnological patents* (n 93), and
          and on Art 352 TFEU (then Art 235 EEC), see Opinion 2/94, *Accession to the ECHR* [1996]

    5/86 *Commission v Council* ('*1986 GSP*') [1987] ECR 1493 and Opinion 2/94 (n 55).
    duction to the subject, see K St C Bradley, 'Powers and Procedures in the EU Constitution: Legal
    ourt' in P Craig and G de Búrca (eds), *The Evolution of EU Law*, (2nd edn, Oxford: Oxford
    , 2011).   [58] *1986 GSP* (n 56).
)/89 *Commission v Council* ('*Titanium dioxide*') [1991] ECR I-2867.
    5/98 *Germany v Parliament and the Council* ('*Tobacco advertising I*') [2000] ECR I-8419.

subsequently upheld.[61] The grants of power to the Union are framed in terms of achieving certain objectives, which may lead it to adopt measures affecting areas of regulation which are in principle reserved to the Member States. This is particularly striking in the area of the internal market. Thus, for example, while the Member States may adopt their own rules on tobacco advertising in pursuit of public health objectives, the Union may harmonize these national provisions in order to ensure the proper functioning of the internal market in the relevant goods and services.[62]

4.4 Classification of competences

The TFEU classifies the various domains of activity of the Union into 'categories and areas of Union competence', each 'category' being comprised of a number of 'areas'. The different lists of categories of competence set out in Articles 2 to 6 TFEU complete and replace, in effect, the list of 'activities of the Community' formerly set out in Article 3 EC. There are three categories of competence: exclusive, shared, and ancillary; these are supplemented by two areas of competences which are excluded from these categories, because of the specific character of the matters concerned, that is, the power to adopt 'arrangements' for the coordination of the Member States' economic and employment policies, and the competence under the TEU to define and implement a common foreign and security policy.[63] Arguably, this categorization does not in any way affect the material scope of the competences themselves, which are regulated by the terms of the respective legal bases provided in the remainder of that Treaty and in the TEU. While it has been suggested that '[legal] consequences flow from [the] categorization' of competences,[64] the classification set out in Articles 2 to 6 TFEU does not represent a radical change from the pre-Lisbon situation as it arose from the case law of the Court of Justice.

4.4.1 Exclusive competence

The mark of an exclusive competence is that it is one which the Union is legally obliged to exercise, where Member State action would render Union action ineffective;[65] thus in such areas 'only the Union may legislate and adopt legally binding acts', though, of course, the Member States implement Union measures in such areas. The 'exclusive' character of a Union competence is not absolute, however; the Union may in turn authorize the Member States to adopt legislation and other measures.[66] Regulation 1219/2012, for example, allows Member States, under certain conditions, to conclude bilateral investment agreements which had been signed after 1 December 2009, when the Treaty of Lisbon brought foreign direct investment within the Union's exclusive competences, but not yet concluded when the regulation came into force, and even to negotiate and conclude new agreements.[67]

Prior to the Lisbon Treaty, the Court's case law had recognized that Member States may be authorized to adopt at the national level the necessary measures to avoid a legislative lacuna, where the Union has failed, for one reason or another, to exercise an exclusive competence, such as that of determining fishing quotas; in such circumstances, the Member States are acting as 'trustees of the common interest'.[68] Given the new provisions on the

---

[61] Case C-380/03 *Germany v Parliament and the Council* ('*Tobacco advertising II*') [2006] ECR I-11573.

[62] See also the Opinion of AG Poiares Maduro in Case C-58/08 *Vodafone v Secretary of State for Business, Enterprise and Regulatory Reform* [2010] ECR I-4999, para 1.

[63] On the latter, see section 4.4.4. On economic policy coordination, see chapter 19.

[64] P Craig and G de Búrca, *EU Law* (5th edn, Oxford: Oxford University Press, 2011), 73.

[65] JP Jacqué, *Droit institutionnel de l'Union européenne* (7th edn, Paris: Dalloz, 2012) para 23.

[66] Art 2(1) TFEU.   [67] OJ [2012] L351/40.

[68] Case 804/79 *Commission v UK* [1981] ECR 1045, para 30.

classification of competences, it is unlikely that the Court would accept that a Member State could benefit from an implicit authorization, as they might have in the past in certain circumstances.[69]

The list of exclusive competences provided in Article 3 TFEU is intended to be exhaustive: the customs union, 'competition rules necessary for the functioning of the internal market', monetary policy for the eurozone, 'the conservation of marine biological resources' (essentially the fixing of fishing quotas), the common commercial policy, and the adoption of international agreements to give effect to the Union's internal policies.[70] Most of these categories of competence had been identified as exclusive in the Court's case law, or are inherently exclusive. There are other matters within the area of the Union's shared competences which might at first blush be thought to be inherently exclusive, notably the power to harmonize national rules to ensure the establishment and functioning of the internal market.[71] The Court has not accepted this latter view, on the ground that even if only the Union may harmonize such provisions, the Member States may adopt measures in the substantive areas concerned until and unless the Union has completely occupied the field.[72]

4.4.2 Shared competences

The bulk of Union competences fall within the category described as 'shared'. This is a residual category, in that any competence not listed as being exclusive or ancillary is presumptively shared in character,[73] and the list provided is only that of the 'principal areas' of such competences: the internal market; the aspects of social policy identified in the Treaty; agriculture and fisheries (except measures on agricultural prices, levies, etc, and fishing quotas); environment and consumer protection; transport; trans-European networks; energy; the area of freedom, security, and justice; and common safety concerns in public health. In many of these areas, the Member States will already have in place a legal framework into which the Union rules may be integrated. Thus, for example, the 2010 and 2012 directives on the rights of accused persons to interpretation and translation and on information in criminal proceedings lay down Union-level rules in specific areas of criminal procedure, for which the Member States are otherwise fully responsible.[74]

The use of the term 'shared' is not obviously appropriate, in that it implies that the Member States remain competent to act in respect of matters which are already governed by Union legislation, whereas this is not the case. While the term 'concurrent' might have been more accurate, the choice of 'shared' was almost certainly deliberate and politically motivated. In these areas, Member States may 'exercise their competence to the extent the Union has not exercised its competence [or]...has decided to cease exercising its competence'; once the Union has adopted rules on a particular matter, Member State action is said to be pre-empted and they may no longer legislate.[75] Given the nature of Union

---

[69] See in particular Case 174/84 *Bulk Oil* [1986] ECR 559.

[70] On the Union's external competence, see chapter 24.

[71] Opinion of AG Fennelly in Case C-376/98 *Germany v Parliament and Council* ('*Tobacco advertising I*') [2000] ECR I-8419, para 136; see also section 5.3.

[72] Case C-491/01 *British American Tobacco* [2002] ECR I-11453, para 180; see also Art 114(4)–(8) and (10) TFEU, acknowledging and regulating the Member States' right to legislate in a particular area which has already been harmonized by internal market legislation.   [73] Art 4(1) TFEU.

[74] Respectively Directive 2010/64/EU (OJ [2010] L280/1) and Directive 2012/13/EU (OJ [2012] L142/1). See further chapter 25.

[75] Art 2(2) TFEU; the adoption of national measures would also fall foul of the Member State's general obligations not to jeopardize the attainment of the Union's objectives under Art 4(3), third para, TEU.

competences, however, pre-emption only concerns 'those elements of the Union action in question' and not the 'whole area' of the activity being regulated.[76]

In any case, to avoid pre-emption in the areas of research, technological development and space, and development cooperation and humanitarian aid, Article 4(3) and (4) TFEU provides explicitly that the exercise of Union competence does not have the effect of preventing the Member States exercising their competence in these areas. Furthermore, in a small number of areas, such as the harmonization of criminal procedure in order to facilitate mutual recognition of judgments of criminal courts, the definition of serious trans-border crimes, and social policy, the material scope of Union competence is also limited to setting minimum standards, thereby leaving the Member States free to adopt higher standards if they see fit.[77]

4.4.3 Ancillary (or 'complementary') competences

In certain areas, the Union may 'carry out actions to support, coordinate or supplement actions of the Member States'; its action is thus ancillary to that of the Member States, and takes the form of promoting cooperation between them, along with the adoption of Union-level incentive measures, including the provision of funding, to tackle particular problems. The exercise of an ancillary competence may not itself lead to the harmonization of national provisions; on the other hand, the fact that the Union has an ancillary competence in a given area does not preclude harmonization in the name of the internal market, where the conditions for recourse to the internal market legal basis are fulfilled.[78] The areas concerned are all matters of shared concern between the Member States, where the pursuit of national (or indeed local) policy objectives is inevitably affected by Union measures in areas of shared or exclusive competence, but where the matters regulated are too close to national or local interests, or even identity,[79] or are otherwise too politically sensitive, to grant the Union any more extensive influence: human health, industry, culture, tourism, education/vocational training/youth/sport, civil protection, and administrative cooperation. One of the most successful such ancillary actions is the Erasmus programme to encourage student mobility which was set up in 1987 and under which some three million students have completed periods of study in a Member State other than their home Member State.[80]

4.4.4 Common Foreign and Security Policy

The CFSP is given separate treatment from all other Union policies, less because of its location in the TEU rather than the TFEU, than because the decision-making procedures and legal instruments used in this policy area differ significantly from those which obtain under the general regime.[81] This is a legacy of the 'pillar' structure of the Union prior to the entry into force of the Lisbon Treaty. Legislation is expressly excluded, in preference to guidelines, decisions defining Union actions, positions, and implementing arrangements, and systematic cooperation between the Member States. The policy is defined and implemented by the European Council and the Council, and put into effect by the High Representative for

---

[76] Protocol No 25 on the exercise of shared competences.

[77] Arts 82(2), 83(1) and (2), and 153(2)(b) TFEU; the social policy measures may, moreover, only be implemented gradually. For more on these policies, see chapters 20 (social policy) and 25 (criminal law).

[78] See Case C-376/98 *Germany v Parliament and Council* ('*Tobacco advertising I*') [2000] ECR I-8410, paras 78 and 79.

[79] Art 4(2) TEU requires the Union to respect, inter alia, the national identities of the Member States.

[80] See now Parliament and Council Decision 1720/2006/EC (OJ [2006] L327/45).

[81] Art 24(1), second para, TEU.

Foreign Affairs and Security Policy, with the Parliament, the Commission, and the Court of Justice each playing correspondingly lesser, not to say rather marginal, roles. Though the provisions of the TEU on the fundamental constitutional and democratic principles apply to the CFSP, the rule of law as defined and defended in the general Union regime to a large extent does not.[82]

That said, the Court is given jurisdiction to review two categories of measure in the domain of foreign policy. The first is 'restrictive measures against natural or legal persons' adopted by the Council under the CFSP, including decisions to freeze the assets of individuals or associations in implementation of the positions of the sanctions committee of the United Nations Security Council, or to prohibit entry into the territory of the Union of persons considered undesirable for reasons of foreign policy. Such measures have direct and immediate effect on individuals, and its jurisdiction in this area allows the Court in particular to ensure that they enjoy due process and the protection of their fundamental rights, as illustrated most famously in the *Kadi* litigation.[83]

The second head of jurisdiction is designed to ensure that CFSP measures do not encroach on the competences conferred on the Union under the general regime and, conversely, to ensure that the exercise of competences under the general regime does not encroach on the CFSP.[84] In practical terms, it means that a measure adopted as a CFSP decision, for example, could be challenged on the grounds that the measure falls within the general regime instead. Given the extent of the Union's activity in external relations under both headings, and the wide variety of institutional actors and services involved in this domain,[85] there is a certain risk of overlap, or worse, contradiction. This is why the High Representative is expressly charged with ensuring the consistency of the Union's external action, and why the CFSP chapter starts by defining principles governing 'the Union's action on the international scene' which apply to both the CFSP and the general regime.[86] The interface between these two regimes proved highly controversial prior to the entry into force of the Lisbon Treaty, when the Court could only safeguard the integrity of Union policies, but not that of the CFSP, much to the chagrin of certain Member States.[87]

5 Subsidiarity

In its most general meaning, as a principle of constitutional design, subsidiarity requires that public power be attributed to the level of government (local, regional, national, etc) where it can most effectively be exercised. In the constitutional design of the Union, subsidiarity is intended to constitute a concrete manifestation of the Member States' aspiration that 'decisions [be] taken as closely as possible to the citizen'. That said, both the Union Treaties and the Court are rigorously neutral as regards the distribution of governmental powers within the Member States.[88]

---

[82] See generally Arts 23–46 TEU.

[83] See, in particular, Joint Cases C-402/05 P and C-415/05 P *Kadi v Council and Commission* [2008] ECR I-6351. For case studies of this judgment, see chapters 8 and 9.   [84] Art 40 TEU.

[85] At the institutional level, the European Council, the Council, the Commission, and the High Representative for Foreign and Security Policy each has autonomous powers in this field, while at the level of officials, the External Action Service, the Council, and the Commission all have a particular role to play, to say nothing of the foreign affairs departments of the Member States.

[86] Respectively Arts 18(4) and 21 TEU.

[87] Case C-95/05 *Commission v Council* ('*Small arms and light weapons*') [2008] ECR I-3651.

[88] See Case C-359/92 *Germany v Council* ('*Product safety*') [1994] ECR I-3681.

Instead, as formulated in Article 5(3) TEU, the principle of subsidiarity provides a test which is intended to act as a brake, under certain conditions, on the exercise of competence which has, indubitably, been conferred on the Union. It is for this reason that subsidiarity is sandwiched between the principles of conferral and proportionality. The primary function of the subsidiarity test is to provide a yardstick against which the political institutions are to evaluate whether or not the Union should exercise its competence in a particular area. The test is also intended to serve as a criterion of the validity of measures adopted, in the context of judicial review under Articles 263 and 267 TFEU.

From its first introduction into the Treaty as a modest qualification of the exercise of the then new Community competence in the field of environmental protection, the subsidiarity principle has been expanded, extended, and transformed into a principle of general application, of which each of the Union institutions is bound to ensure 'constant respect'.[89] The substantive Treaty principle has been supplemented by a Protocol which lays down procedural requirements to reinforce respect for subsidiarity, including provisions which allow the national parliaments to express their views on whether proposed legislation complies with this principle or not, the so-called 'early warning' mechanism.[90]

5.1 The subsidiarity test

The test does not apply to Union action in areas where it enjoys exclusive competence; while the interpretation of this notion, and hence the scope of application of the subsidiarity test, was a matter of some uncertainty before the Lisbon Treaty, the areas of exclusive competence are now listed in Article 3 TFEU.[91]

The first, negative, condition for Union action is that 'the objectives of the proposed action cannot be sufficiently achieved by the Member States, either at central level or at regional and local level' (the 'necessity test'). The objectives in question are Union objectives; otherwise the proposed action could not begin to be justified under the Treaty. The Union must assess the capacity of the Member States to achieve the particular objectives of the proposed action. In this context it is not obliged to rely solely on the assessment put forward by its usual interlocutors, the national governments; in the 'wide consultations' which the Commission carries out in preparing legislative proposals, it must 'take into account the regional and local dimension of the action envisaged'.[92] Within their respective institutions, both members of the European Parliament and ministers of sub-national governments, such as those of the German Länder, who participate in the work of the Council, have the opportunity to argue that the particular objectives can be better achieved at the Member State level. Where consulted, the Committee of the Regions will also be able to make a subsidiarity case against, or indeed for, Union action.

The second, positive, condition is that 'by reason of the scale or effects of the proposed action, [the Union objectives can] be better achieved at Union level'. It is difficult to see how this branch of the test would, in practice, operate as an autonomous impediment to Union action where the first branch of the test was satisfied. Where the 'scale or effects' of the action are shown to be too small or minor, then presumptively the objectives can be achieved by the Member States at some level of government. On the other hand, where under the necessity test the Member States cannot achieve the Union objectives, it follows

---

[89] Art 1, Protocol No 2.

[90] Protocol No 2 on the application of the principles of subsidiarity and proportionality.

[91] On uncertainty, see the judgments cited at section 5.4; the list of exclusive competences is set out at section 4.4.1.   [92] Art 2, Protocol No 2.

as night follows day that these can be 'better achieved at Union level', unless it is shown that the Union objectives can be better achieved at a different, third, level, such as by means of an international agreement.[93] In practice, such an agreement would necessarily require the participation of third States or an international organization, unless the opponent of Union action can show that an international agreement between the Member States would better achieve the Union's objectives. Moreover, the text of Article 5(3) TEU does not indicate whether the criterion 'can be better achieved' requires that the party challenging the Union action show that the objectives can theoretically be better achieved at the international level, or whether it must show that there is, in fact, a realistic prospect of such action, not-withstanding the necessary involvement of non-Union parties.

It is also difficult to imagine as a matter of law a Union action, or at least a legislative initiative, which would fully comply with the requirements of its legal basis, including the requirement (which is part of the proportionality test) that the action be suitable to achieve the aims of the measure, but fail because the scale or effects would be either so small or so large that the particular objectives cannot be better achieved at Union level. It has even been suggested that subsidiarity is inherently unfit for purpose, as it 'privileges [the] achievement [of Union objectives] absolutely', and is hence insensitive to the policy objectives and autonomy of the Member States.[94]

5.2 Protocol No 2: the 'early warning mechanism'

The so-called 'early warning mechanism', with its suggestion of impending hostilities, is ostensibly designed to allow national parliaments to ensure Union legislation complies with the subsidiarity test. In the first stage, the national parliaments receive draft legislative acts, whatever the originating institution or body,[95] as well as the subsequently amended drafts; the drafts must, moreover, be accompanied by a 'detailed statement making it possible to appraise compliance with the principles of subsidiarity and proportionality', including 'qualitative and wherever possible quantitative indicators', as well as certain other informa-tion, such as its financial impact and its repercussions for the law of the Member States.[96]

The national parliaments, or in the case of bicameral parliaments, their component chambers, then have an eight-week period in which to produce a 'reasoned opinion' on why the draft fails to comply with the subsidiarity principle, which is sent to the Presidents of the European Parliament, the Council, and the Commission. Given the close link between subsidiarity and competence, it is not surprising that some of the national parliamentary participants in the procedure succumb to the temptation to take a position on other mat-ters than subsidiarity strictly so called, such as the choice of legal basis or even the existence of a Union competence in the first place.[97] In such cases, the initiator will only be obliged to respond to the parliamentary opinions which deal with subsidiarity; equally, only these opinions will count in verifying which, if any, threshold has been attained.

---

[93] The Netherlands argued this point, unsuccessfully, in its challenge to the 1998 directive on biotechno-logical patents: Case C-377/98 *Netherlands v Parliament and Council* ('*Biotechnological patents*') [2001] ECR I-7079.

[94] G Davies, 'Subsidiarity: The Wrong Idea, in the Wrong Place, at the Wrong Time' (2006) 43 *Common Market Law Review* 63.

[95] As noted previously, both the ordinary and the special legislative procedures can be initiated in limited circumstances by institutions other than the Commission, or by a group of Member States.

[96] Art 5, Protocol No 2.

[97] See eg the variety of views expressed on the 'Monti II' proposal, which triggered the first collective opin-ion: section 3, Commission Annual Report 2012 on subsidiarity and proportionality, COM(2013) 566 final.

Reasoned opinions come in three varieties: the individual opinion, the collective opinion, and the special legislative opinion. The level of support for each type of opinion determines its formal impact on the legislative process. Each national parliament has two votes at its disposal, which are cast separately by the two chambers of a bicameral parliament or together by a unicameral parliament; in this context, the Luxembourg Chambre des députés and the Maltese Kamra tad-Deputati each wields double the voting power of the German Bundestag or the UK House of Commons.

5.2.1 Opinion of individual parliaments or chambers

The institutions are obliged to 'take account of' the reasoned opinions issued by an individual national parliament or chamber. In the absence of any indication to the contrary in the Treaty, however, they are not obliged to follow such opinion or take any further action.

5.2.2 Collective opinion

A collective opinion can only be adopted by at least one-third of the total votes (at present 19 out of 56); the threshold is lowered to a quarter of the votes (14) where the initiative falls within the area of freedom, security, and justice. In fact, the 'collective opinion' is not a single document but comprises the reasoned opinions of all the national parliamentary bodies which have concluded that the draft act does not comply with the subsidiarity test. Where the number of negative votes reaches the threshold, the draft legislation must be reviewed; however, after the review, the initiator of the draft act may maintain, amend, or withdraw it, and must provide reasons for doing so.

5.2.3 Special legislative opinion

The national parliaments may adopt a special legislative opinion only when they are examining a Commission proposal under the ordinary legislative procedure; the threshold for adopting such an opinion is a simple majority of the total votes available (29). As before, the Commission may choose to maintain, amend, or withdraw the proposal. Where it maintains the proposal, it must once again explain, this time in light of the national parliaments' contrary positions, how the proposal complies with the subsidiarity test; the Commission's position, confusingly also called a 'reasoned opinion', and those of the national parliaments (including, presumably, any positive opinions), are referred to the European Parliament and the Council. The two branches of the legislature are obliged to take 'particular account' – presumably something more than 'account' *simpliciter* – of the various opinions washing around; where a majority of the members of the European Parliament who take part in the vote or a 55 per cent majority of the members of the Council reject the proposal for reasons of subsidiarity compliance, it is dead in the water.

5.3 Scope of the early warning mechanism

While trumpeted in Article 12(b) TEU as allowing the national parliaments to 'see[ ] to it that the principle of subsidiarity is respected', the early warning mechanism is subject to a number of important limitations. In the first place, it only applies to legislation properly so called, excluding, in particular, measures adopted by an innominate non-legislative procedure, some of which are legislative in all but name, as well as delegated and implementing acts.[98] It is also limited to the initial proposal and amended versions of that proposal; it does not, therefore, allow the Member States' parliaments to examine, even briefly, the different

---

[98] These terms are explained at sections 7.3, 8.1, and 8.2 respectively.

preparatory acts which make their appearance later in the course of a legislative procedure. As noted elsewhere,[99] in the ordinary legislative procedure, the European Parliament and the Council no longer act on the basis of the Commission proposal after the Parliament adopts its first-reading position. Perhaps it is hoped that the legislature would nonetheless not ignore the views of the national parliaments during the remainder of the procedure. These limitations may be justified by the consideration that the application of the mechanism to other forms of normative measure, and preparatory acts subsequent to the Commission proposal, would have given rise to insuperable practical problems.

Even where it applies, however, the mechanism promises more than it delivers; at its strongest, the impact the community of national parliaments can make on a determined Union legislature is likely to be negligible. Under any scenario, the initiator can press on with its draft legislation; the requirement that it, and the legislature under the ordinary legislative procedure, provide reasons for doing so, or take account of a contrary position, or indeed 'particular account', does not appear to be a significant impediment to Union action, even where a large number of national parliaments oppose this on subsidiarity grounds. When faced with the first collective opinion in 2012, comprising 19 negative votes from 12 parliamentary assemblies, the Commission stuck to its view that the principle of subsidiarity had not been breached, but withdrew its proposal largely on the ground that this was 'unlikely to gather the necessary political support' in the legislature, particularly as the adoption of the proposed regulation would have required a unanimous vote in the Council.[100]

Moreover, the referral of the matter back to the legislature as a last resort may prove to be of little or no assistance to those who oppose the proposed measure. The provision that a majority of the votes cast in the European Parliament may kill off the proposal is to all intents and purposes the same rule as that which applies under the Parliament's first reading under the ordinary legislative procedure.[101] The voting requirement for the Council to block a proposal under the early warning mechanism is higher than the normal threshold; whereas the negative votes of 13 Member States are sufficient to block a legislative proposal under the ordinary legislative procedure, whatever the reasons for the minority's opposition, under Protocol No 2 fully 16 Member States (55 per cent) must object to the proposed measure in order to prevent its adoption on the ground of non-compliance with the subsidiarity principle.[102] In other words, if it were ever to be applied, the voting rule in the Council would actually make it more difficult for the Council to oppose a measure on subsidiarity grounds than for any other reason.

Bringing the national parliaments in on the act of adopting Union legislation might at first blush appear like a useful idea which strikes another blow for democratic decision-making. A slightly less charitable view would be that the prime utility of the early warning mechanism is to ensure that the national parliaments are at least informed about forthcoming Union legislation, to enable them to influence the position their own minister and her officials will be defending in Brussels. The question then arises as to why a set of Treaty provisions was required in order to regulate relations between the national governments and the national parliaments to which they are, at least according to Article 10(2) TEU,

---

[99] See section 7.1.1.

[100] Section 3, Commission Annual Report 2012 on subsidiarity and proportionality, COM(2013) 566 final. The subject matter of the proposal, the relationship in EU law between economic freedoms and the right to strike, was in any case highly controversial; see F Fabbrini and K Granat, 'Yellow Card But No Foul' (2013) 50 *Common Market Law Review* 115.   [101] See Arts 294(3) and 231 TFEU, and section 7.1.1.

[102] The figures refer to the Council voting rules which apply from 1 December 2014.

'democratically accountable'. Might not the objectives of this particular action have been better achieved by the Member States?

5.4 Judicial review of compliance with the subsidiarity test

By including a subsidiarity test in the Treaty as a general principle, the Member States clearly intended respect for this principle to be justiciable, despite the highly political character of the questions it raises, such as the respective capacity of the Union and the Member States (at different levels of government) to achieve defined policy objectives. Perhaps for this reason, some of the Member States which were amongst the keenest supporters of subsidiarity at the time of its incorporation into the Union legal order themselves hesitated to rely on a substantive breach of this principle when challenging legislation on which they had been outvoted; instead they preferred to plead that the legislature had failed to explain how the principle had been respected in the particular case, or that a particular legal basis should be interpreted in light of the requirements of subsidiarity.[103]

One of the most keenly argued questions has been whether, and if so how, the subsidiary test applies in the context of the adoption of internal market measures. In the *Working Time* case, the Court had held that once the legislature had found it was necessary to pursue a particular (here, social policy) objective, 'achievement of that objective...necessarily presupposes Community-wide action'.[104] This was interpreted in some quarters as indicating that the principle of subsidiarity did not apply to internal market measures, on the ground that 'the Member States simply cannot harmonise each other's laws, regulations or administrative action in fields which come within the scope of application of the Treaty'.[105] At first, the Court appeared to rally to this view, noting in the *Biotechnological Patent* case that harmonization in this area 'could not be achieved by action taken by the Member States alone'.[106]

However, in *British American Tobacco*, the Court clarified that, as the Union did not have exclusive competence to regulate economic activity on the internal market, the principle of subsidiarity did apply to measures in this area, before examining 'whether the objective of the proposed action could be better achieved at [Union] level'.[107] The Court noted that the objectives of the contested directive 'cannot be sufficiently achieved by the Member States individually' and that '[it] follows that...the objective of the proposed action could be better achieved at [Union] level'.[108] In *Vodafone*, on the other hand, the Court concluded that the objectives of the contested regulation 'could be best achieved at [Union] level', not because of the Member States' inability to achieve those objectives but 'by reason of the [Union-wide] effects of the...approach laid down in [the] Regulation'.[109] The Court therefore appears to favour a single test, 'better achievement at the Union level', though taking account of both the positive and the negative elements of the test as formulated in Article 5(3) TEU.

The setting up of the early warning mechanism described previously was accompanied by special provisions on judicial review at the suit of the national parliaments, restricted *ratione materiae* to alleged breaches of the subsidiarity principle. Such proceedings are

---

[103] Case C-426/93 *Germany v Parliament and Council* ('*Deposit guarantee scheme*') [1995] ECR I-3723; Case C-84/94 *UK v Council* ('*Working time*') [1996] ECR I-5755. [104] *Working time* (n 103).
[105] Opinion of AG Fennelly in *Tobacco advertising* (n 71) para 136.
[106] Judgment in *Biotechnological patents* (n 93) para 32.
[107] *British American Tobacco* (n 72) para 180. [108] Ibid, paras 182 and 183.
[109] Case C-58/08 *Vodafone v Secretary of State for Business, Enterprise and Regulatory Reform* [2010] ECR I-4999, para 78; see case study 5.1.

merely 'notified' by the national government on behalf of the parliament or chamber 'in accordance with their legal order'.[110] Some of the Member States allow a minority in the national parliament or chamber to initiate such actions; this is clearly consistent with the logic of the special provision, as a parliamentary majority would in any case be able to force the government to bring a normal annulment action act under Article 263 TFEU. Where the Committee of the Regions must be consulted on a particular proposal for legislation, it may also challenge the act adopted on subsidiarity grounds.

6 Proportionality

Though first formulated in the Treaty as a generally applicable principle at the same time as subsidiarity, the proportionality requirement had been recognized as a legal constraint on legislative and administrative action long before. The principle is currently formulated in Article 5(4) TEU as meaning that '[the] content and form of Union action shall not exceed what is necessary to achieve the objectives of the Treaties'.

   In effect, the Union Courts exercise only marginal review of respect for the proportionality principle in the context of legislation. In this area, the legislature enjoys wide discretion, as it must make political, economic, and social choices on the basis of complex assessments; the Court will only intervene if the action taken is manifestly inappropriate to the objective sought by the measure.[111] As a result, in order to show that the principle of proportionality has not been respected, a party would have to demonstrate either that the objective of the measure was not one the legislature could pursue under the Treaty, or that the same objective could be achieved by less intrusive means. The Court may thus be led to quite a concrete examination of other possible policy solutions, and an evaluation of whether the solutions chosen are appropriate to achieve the measure's objectives, and do not go beyond what is required to achieve those objectives. In *British American Tobacco*, for example, the Court had to rule on the validity of a ban on the manufacture within the Union of cigarettes for export to third States, where the cigarettes did not comply with the standards set by the legislation for sale within the Union.[112] The Court found that the legislature could validly take the view that the ban was a more efficient means to combat illegal trafficking in cigarettes than the mere reinforcement of import controls. In the *Spanish cotton subsidies* case, the Court found that by omitting to take account of labour costs in cotton production, the Council had not taken all the relevant factors into account as it was required to in order to achieve the objectives of the regulation, and had hence failed to comply with the principle of proportionality.[113]

   As with subsidiarity, each of the institutions is duty-bound to 'ensure constant respect' for the principle of proportionality, which respect must be justified in a 'detailed statement' accompanying draft legislative acts.[114] However, the principle of proportionality does not benefit from the same early warning mechanism or special provisions on judicial review as subsidiarity.

---

[110] The Dutch government led the way well before the Lisbon Treaty in the 'biotechnological patent' case, which it initiated at the behest of the lower house of parliament, rather than in pursuit of government policy: Case C-377/98 *Netherlands v Parliament and Council* ('*Biotechnological patents*') [2001] ECR I-07079.

[111] See *British American Tobacco* (n 72).   [112] Ibid, paras 122–141.

[113] Case C-310/04 *Spain v Council* ('*Spanish cotton subsidies*') [2006] ECR I-7285.

[114] Art 5, Protocol No 2.

Case study 5.1: *Vodafone*

The 2007 Roaming Regulation[115] brings down the prices paid by consumers for mobile phone calls made or received in a Member State other than their home Member State ('roaming'), by putting a cap on both wholesale prices, that is, those charged by the foreign host network operator to the customer's home provider, and retail prices, that is, those charged to the customer by his home provider for roaming calls. The regulation was challenged in the UK courts by a number of mobile phone operators, on the grounds that it was founded on an incorrect legal basis and that it breached the principles of subsidiarity and proportionality.[116]

The Court started by restating the fundamental tenets of its case law on recourse to the internal market legal basis:

- the object of the measure must be genuinely to improve the conditions for the establishment and functioning of the internal market;

- the legislature may only act where the differences in the national rules are such as to obstruct the fundamental freedoms and have a direct and appreciable effect on the functioning of the internal market in goods and services, or where such differences are likely to emerge;

- the legislature may amend existing internal market legislation to take account of a change in circumstances or the development of knowledge;

- the legislature enjoys a discretion, depending on the general context and the specific circumstances of the matter to be harmonized, as regards the method of approximation of national laws;

- provided that the conditions for using the internal market legal basis are fulfilled, the fact that other considerations (here consumer protection) may be decisive does not prevent the legislature relying on that legal basis.[117]

The Court noted the 'unique characteristics of the roaming markets', and in particular the fact that retail prices were excessive compared to the costs of providing the service, because of the high wholesale charges levied by the foreign host providers and the high retail mark-ups charged by the home provider. The individual national regulatory authorities had no means of controlling the wholesale prices of operators in other Member States, and in order to bring consumer prices down were likely to fix retail prices, which would lead to divergent national laws and distortions of the conditions of competition. In these circumstances, the adoption of a 'single coherent regulatory framework' was justified with a view to maintaining competition among operators of mobile networks.[118]

The Court's reasoning on recourse to the internal market legal basis largely dealt with the question of subsidiarity too. Given the interdependence between wholesale and retail charges, the Court found that 'reduc[ing] retail charges alone without affecting the level of costs for the wholesale supply of Community-wide roaming services would have been liable to disrupt the smooth functioning of the Community-wide roaming market'. 'Thus,' continued the Court, 'by reason of the effects of the common approach laid down by [the] Regulation...the objective pursued by that regulation could best be achieved at Community level.'[119]

---

[115] European Parliament and Council Regulation 717/2007 (OJ [2007] L171/32).
[116] *Vodafone* (n 109).   [117] Ibid, paras 32–36.
[118] Ibid, paras 42 and 38 respectively.   [119] Ibid, paras 77 and 78, judgment.

As to proportionality, the legislature's wide discretion means that the criterion of legality is not whether the measure adopted was the best possible measure but whether it is 'manifestly inappropriate having regard to the objective which the competent institution is seeking to pursue'. The legislature must nonetheless base its choice on objective criteria and evaluate 'whether the objectives pursued by the measure chosen are such as to justify even substantial negative economic consequences for certain operators'.[120]

The main issue as regards proportionality was whether consumer prices could have been brought down by imposing ceilings on wholesale charges only. The Court noted that the average retail charge for a roaming call was more than five times the cost of providing the wholesale service; setting a common ceiling on retail charges was obviously appropriate as a means of bringing these charges down. As to the necessity of capping retail as well as wholesale charges, the Court noted that in effect the only competition on retail prices took place in the form of complete retail packages, of which the rates of roaming charges were a minor element. This meant that there was no competitive pressure on operators to pass on to consumers any reduction in wholesale charges which would result from the setting of a ceiling on these charges alone; as a result, capping wholesale charges would not have had any effect on retail prices, which are those the consumer pays. In these circumstances, the legislature was entitled directly to set ceilings on retail prices as well, particularly as the system was limited in time and applied to a market which was subject to competition.

The *Vodafone* case is a textbook example of a substantive challenge to a controversial policy measure adopted by the Union legislature. Given the inherently cross-border character of the activity being regulated, and the practical impossibility for the national regulators to deal with the problem of high consumer prices without dividing up the market in roaming services into Member State blocks, the Court had little difficulty in finding that the regulation was correctly classified as an internal market measure and that it passed the subsidiarity test. Respect for proportionality did not detain the Court very long either, though it did check that the institutions had studied the existing market conditions thoroughly and had considered other possibilities of dealing with the problem, such as regulating wholesale prices only or retail prices only. The Court also noted the impact that the regulation could have on mobile phone operators. It is not surprising, however, that their interest in charging customers five times the actual cost of providing a roaming service did not weigh heavily in the balance.

7 Decision-making

Decision-making procedures are the means by which the Union exercises its competences. The procedure, which is dictated by the legal basis of the act,[121] determines precisely the degree of formal influence each institutional actor (institution or consultative body, Member State government or parliament) may bring on the outcome. Formal influence is, of course, not the full story, but other aspects of that story fall outside the compass of the present chapter.

Since the Lisbon Treaty entered into force, Union law makes an explicit distinction between 'legislation' and other forms of normative act, and between primary and secondary

---

[120] *Vodafone* (n 109) paras 52 and 53, judgment.   [121] See section 4.3.

normative measures. Legislation refers to any act adopted on the basis of a procedure iden-tified in the Treaty legal basis as being a legislative procedure, either 'ordinary' or 'special'; it is necessarily adopted in public.[122] The distinction is important in a number of respects, notably as regards the possibilities for individuals to challenge the measure in annulment proceedings, and the material scope of the 'early warning mechanism' for ensuring sub-sidiarity.[123] Moreover, under long-standing constitutional doctrine, the legislature must lay down the 'essential elements of the matter to be dealt with', and may not delegate the power to regulate these elements.[124] A certain number of normative acts are adopted directly on the basis of a Treaty provision by procedures not described as 'legislative', so-called 'innom-inate non-legislative procedures'.[125]

Normative measures which are based on enabling provisions contained in acts of sec-ondary law (adopted on the basis of legislative and assimilated procedures) take the form of delegated or implementing acts.[126]

7.1 Legislative and assimilated procedures

These are of three kinds: the ordinary legislative procedure (OLP), the special legislative procedures (SLPs), and the various innominate non-legislative procedures (INPs). Of these, the OLP is by far the most important in practical terms, as it applies for the adoption of the bulk of the Union's primary policy measures.

7.1.1 The ordinary legislative procedure

The details of the OLP are set out in Article 294 TFEU.[127] Two related Treaty rules are important in this context for the protection of the Commission's position: the requirements that the Council act by a qualified majority unless the Treaty provides otherwise, and that it may only amend a Commission proposal acting unanimously.[128] In essence, the adop-tion of a legislative act under the OLP requires the complete agreement of the European Parliament and the Council on a text, which agreement may be reached in a number of dif-ferent ways: Council approval of the Parliament's first reading position, mutual acceptance by the Parliament and the Council of each other's amendments on second reading, or the convening of a conciliation committee of equal numbers of each institution to hammer out a joint text which the two institutions approve on third reading.

Each of the institutions can prevent the adoption of the legislation proposed, at different stages of the procedure. A first reading rejection of the proposal by the Parliament, which only requires a majority of the members voting, could in turn be refused by the Council; in these circumstances, the Parliament would require a vote by a majority of its component members, rather than a simple majority, to prevent the adoption of the legislation, though in practice it would not be difficult to achieve this level of parliamentary support, for rea-sons of institutional pride as well as the merits of the proposal.

---

[122] Art 289(3) TFEU.

[123] See respectively sections 8 and 5.2. P Craig correctly argues that the distinction between legislative and non-legislative acts in this context is more formal than real, in the sense that both 'will lay down binding provisions of general application to govern a certain situation' (*The Lisbon Treaty* (Oxford: Oxford University Press, 2011) 58).   [124] Case 25/70 *Köster* [1970] ECR 1161; see also *Frontex*, case study 5.2.

[125] See section 7.3.   [126] See section 8.

[127] Both Parliament and the Council have published very helpful guides to the OLP on their respective web-sites, including in each case lists of the articles to which the OLP applies and diagrams on how the procedure operates: http://www.europarl.europa.eu/code/information/guide_en.pdf and http://www.consilium.europa .eu/uedocs/cms_data/librairie/PDF/QC3212175ENrevGPO2012.pdf

[128] Arts 16(3) TU and 293(1) TFEU: the latter is subject to limited and very specific exceptions.

In practice, a large proportion of such legislative acts are adopted in first reading, on the basis of a text negotiated between the parliamentary committee, represented by its rapporteur, and the Council formation responsible, represented by its president, in informal 'trialogue' meetings, with the Commission making up the threesome.[129]

Subject to a number of important, if limited, exceptions, the procedure may only be initiated by the Commission submitting a proposal;[130] the term 'proposal' is a term of art, which carries certain legal consequences for the position of the Commission.[131] Prior to submitting legislative proposals, the Commission is now legally obliged to 'carry out broad consultations with parties concerned in order to ensure that the Union's actions are coherent and transparent', under the 'democratic principles' which govern 'all its activities'.[132] More generally, in common with the other institutions, the Commission is also obliged to engage with citizens and representative associations, and 'maintain an open, transparent and regular dialogue with representative associations and civil society'. The Commission may be invited to submit legislative proposals by the European Parliament, by the Council, or by a million citizens from a minimum of a quarter of the Member States (7);[133] though not obliged to respond favourably, in each case the Commission must explain its reasons for not submitting a proposal.

Having initiated the OLP, the Commission may amend its proposal 'at any time during the procedure leading to the adoption of a Union act', as long as the Council has not acted;[134] this allows the Commission to modify its initial proposal to garner the support of a qualified majority which has emerged in the Council discussions.[135] The Commission's right to amend its proposal in effect disappears during the first reading, as the European Parliament and the Council no longer deliberate on the basis of the proposal once the Parliament has adopted its first reading position.[136] Though the Commission feigns to ignore this important aspect of the OLP, notably by presenting modified proposals after the Parliament's first reading, it is clear from the very wording of Article 294 TFEU that the Council's first reading is conducted on 'the European Parliament's position', rather than the Commission's proposal. Subsequent readings take as their subject matter 'the Council's position' (on first reading), the 'European Parliament's amendments' (on second reading), 'the positions of the European Parliament and the Council at second reading' (in conciliation), and 'the joint text' in third reading. Thus, in the OLP, the Commission may only 'alter its proposal ... during the procedures leading to the adoption of a Union act'[137] before the Parliament's first reading, though of course the rule is fully applicable for the adoption of Council acts under other procedures.

This does not mean that the Commission is excluded from the procedure after the Parliament's first reading; where the Council does not accept the Parliament's first reading position, the Commission makes known its position on the state of play, which allows it the opportunity to suggest a compromise which all three participants might accept, or at least a policy measure in line with its own thinking. Moreover, on second reading the Council

---

[129] See generally the Joint Declaration on practical arrangements for the co-decision procedure adopted by the European Parliament, the Council, and the Commission on 13 June 2007 (OJ [2007] C145/5).

[130] Art 17(2) TEU; the Commission may also take other forms of initiative (Art 17(1) TEU).

[131] The reference to a European Parliament 'proposal' in the English-language version of Art 223(1) TFEU is distinctly anomalous; the French version, eg correctly uses the term 'projet' (draft).

[132] Arts 11(3) and 9 TEU respectively; see also section 11.

[133] Respectively Arts 225 TFEU and 241 TFEU and Art 11(4) TEU.   [134] Art 293(2) TFEU.

[135] The operation in practice of this mechanism is described by AG Lenz in his Opinion in *1986 GSP* (n 56).

[136] Art 294(3) TFEU.   [137] See Art 293(2) TFEU.

must act unanimously, rather than by a qualified majority, if it wishes to adopt a European Parliament amendment on which the Commission has given a negative opinion. In any case, the Commission takes part in the proceedings of any conciliation committee convened to prepare for a third reading and, in practice, in any informal negotiations, where its expertise is often appreciated, particularly where it facilitates agreement between the principal parties.

Institutions and bodies other than the Commission may initiate the OLP, though only in areas of their special competence. The Court of Justice may propose amendments to its Statute, except regarding the status of its members and the Court's language regime which would require the application of a Treaty amendment procedure.[138] In March 2011, for example, the Court proposed amendments to improve the functioning of each of the three jurisdictions; these were adopted in August 2012, with the exception of the proposal to appoint extra judges to the General Court.[139] The Court shares its right of initiative with the Commission; where the Court initiates, the Commission is consulted, and vice versa. In practice, the Commission tends sagely to leave the Court to take such initiatives; indeed, even before it enjoyed a formal right of initiative, the Court was not shy of bringing its suggestions for reform to the political table, most notably proposing in late 1985 the creation of the Court of First Instance while the negotiations for the Single European Act were still in progress. The European Central Bank may submit recommendations for the amendment, under the OLP, of various provisions of the Statute of the European System of Central Banks and of the European Central Bank.[140]

Legislative measures in the field of judicial cooperation in criminal matters and police cooperation, for example, may be initiated by a quarter (7) of the Member States, as well as by the Commission. While this situation may appear somewhat anomalous, given the inclusion of this policy field within the general regime of Union decision-making, it still represents an important change from the previous position, where any single Member State, or all of them individually, could initiate such measures. The problem of parallel proposals from the Commission and the relevant number of Member States arose in a particularly acute form in respect of an initiative for what became the European Protection Order. While the Member States concerned placed their initiative in the domain of judicial cooperation in criminal matters, the Commission took the view that the proposed text included elements of judicial cooperation in civil matters. The different procedural arrangements under these two provisions precluded the possibility of combining them into a composite legal basis, while suggestions for recourse to other possible legal bases were all rejected.[141] The directive finally adopted clearly seeks to restrict its scope of application to criminal matters;[142] the institutional dispute, which was on occasion conducted in rather immoderate terms, is blamed for having delayed its adoption by several months.

---

[138] Art 281, second para, TFEU.

[139] While it was widely agreed that this measure was justified with a view to assisting the General Court to deal with its very considerable caseload, no agreement was reached on the means of distributing the new judicial posts amongst the Member States. On the Union's judicial system, see chapter 10.

[140] See Art 40(1) of that Statute; the rules on voting in the Bank's Governing Council may be amended, on a recommendation of the Bank, by the European Council, though the amendment is subject to national ratification (Art 40(2)).

[141] Of these, the most extraordinary was Art 3 TEU, which sets out the Union's objectives in the most general of terms and does not conform to any accepted definition of 'legal basis' in EU law.

[142] Directive 2011/99/EU (OJ [2011] L338/2); this was complemented by the adoption on 6 June 2013 of Regulation (EU) No 606/2013 on the mutual recognition of protection measures in civil matters (OJ [2013] L181/4).

Where the OLP is not initiated by the Commission, the Parliament's first reading takes place on the basis of an 'initiative' (of the Member States), a 'request' (from the Court of Justice), or a 'recommendation' (from the European Central Bank). The OLP is brought to a close by the signature of the legislative act by the presidents of the European Parliament and the Council.[143]

7.1.2 'Emergency brakes'

For the adoption of three categories of measure, a supplementary procedure grafted on the OLP allows a single Member State to call a 'time out' during the adoption procedure, and have the question referred to the European Council for a supplementary period for reflection. This so-called 'emergency brake' may only be applied if the Member State considers that the legislation being proposed would affect 'important' or 'fundamental' aspects of its existing national system. In the area of social security for those who have worked in other Member States, the European Council may block the adoption of the legislation either by taking no action or requesting the Commission to submit a new proposal.[144] The equivalent provisions in certain areas of criminal justice appear to be even more intrusive, in that the European Council may only refer the draft back to the Council for the OLP to continue 'in case of a consensus'; in such cases, however, it is possible for a group of at least nine Member States to go ahead with the proposal on the basis of enhanced cooperation.[145] To date, the emergency brake mechanism has not been used.

7.2 **Special legislative procedures**

There is no one special legislative procedure (SLP), but a wide variety of such procedures, which differ as regards who can initiate the procedure, who participates in the procedure, and what voting rules apply. While this plethora of procedural permutations certainly detracts from the legibility of the Treaty, each SLP is in fact restricted to a specific area of policy or institutional decision.

A large majority of SLPs are derogations from the application of the OLP in a particular area, to take account of national sensibilities of different kinds (notably political, budgetary, economic, and social). Thus, for example, provisions to facilitate the exercise of the right to free movement of citizens are adopted under the OLP, with the exception of those concerning social security and social protection, for which an SLP applies.[146] Similarly, while measures on judicial cooperation in civil matters are subject to the OLP, those concerning family law with cross-border implications are subject to an SLP.[147] In these 'derogation' cases, the SLP is initiated by a Commission proposal, the European Parliament is consulted, and the Council adopts the legislative act by unanimous vote.

In other areas, the European Parliament may be asked for its consent to a Council measure, for example, on Union action to combat discrimination on grounds other than nationality, or on certain decisions which have an impact on the Union's budget, such as measures implementing the own-resources decision, and the regulation establishing the multi-annual financial framework.[148] The Parliament may itself both initiate and adopt legislative measures on most matters concerning its own functioning (though not its seat or working places) or within its specific responsibility (the Statute of Ombudsman), with the Council

---

[143] Art 297(1), second para, TFEU.   [144] Art 48(2) TFEU.
[145] Arts 82(3) and 83(3) TFEU. On enhanced cooperation, see section 9.
[146] Art 21(2) and (3) TFEU.   [147] Art 81(2) and (3) TFEU.
[148] Arts 19(1), 311, fourth para, and 312(2) TFEU.

giving its consent and the Commission an opinion.[149] The Union budget is adopted under a very special legislative procedure[150] which, though complex, is a real improvement on its predecessor, where the scope of the Parliament's input depended largely on the elusive (and now abolished) distinction between compulsory and non-compulsory expenditure.[151] Similarly the European Investment Bank may initiate the procedure for the amendment of its own Statute, a right it shares with the Commission.[152]

7.3 Innominate non-legislative procedures

A number of normative measures are adopted directly on the basis of the Treaty by an INP. The procedural requirements tend to be minimal; in many cases the Council adopts the measure by a qualified majority on the basis of a Commission proposal, often without any participation of the European Parliament or at most after requesting its opinion. In some cases, the measures might arguably be considered executive rather than legislative in character, such as the fixing of agricultural prices and fishing quotas; in others, the exclusion of the OLP is more difficult to justify, such as the adoption of rules on private and public sector competition.[153] The latter example may reflect nothing more than an unwillingness to change an institutional arrangement which is as old as the Treaty itself. Certain emergency measures may be adopted by an INP, for example where a Member State is suffering from difficulties in obtaining oil supplies or from a sudden influx of third country nationals.[154]

An INP may be required by derogation from the OLP for the adoption of particularly sensitive measures in a 'normal' policy field, for example recommendations in some areas of ancillary competence,[155] as well as for the adoption of a small number of decisions in the area of economic and monetary union or decisions with a foreign policy aspect.[156] Thus, for example, the rules on personal data protection in the foreign policy domain are laid down by the Council, apparently acting without a Commission proposal or any participation of the European Parliament, whereas the general data protection provisions are adopted under an OLP.[157] An act adopted under an INP may even, in effect, allow for a minor amendment of the Treaty.[158]

The European Council, the Commission, and the European Central Bank also adopt measures directly on the basis of the Treaty in a small number of instances.[159]

7.4 Consultation and assimilated requirements

The consultation of different institutions and ancillary bodies, particularly the European Parliament, the Economic and Social Committee, and the Committee of the Regions, may be required in the context of an SLP or INP, or (obviously excluding the Parliament)

---

[149] eg Arts 223(2), 226, third para, and 228(4) TFEU.

[150] Art 314 TFEU; see also Case C-77/11 *Council v Parliament*, judgment of 17 September 2013.

[151] For an illustration of the difficulty of applying this notion and the relevant procedures, see *1986 Budget* (n 30).   [152] Art 308, third para, TFEU.

[153] Respectively Art 43(3) TFEU and Arts 103(1) and 109 TFEU (and in the field of transport, Art 95(3) TFEU).   [154] Respectively Arts 122(1) and 78(3) TFEU.

[155] See eg Arts 167(6) and 168(6) TFEU, on culture and public health respectively.

[156] Respectively Art 121(2) and (4) TFEU and Arts 26(2) and 29 TEU.

[157] See respectively Arts 39 TEU and 16 TFEU.

[158] See eg Art 83(1), third subpara, TFEU, authorizing the Council to add to the material scope of the Union's competences to define certain criminal offences and sanctions.

[159] See respectively Art 14(2), second para, TEU; Arts 45(3)(d), 105(3), 106(3), and 108(4) TFEU; and Art 132(1) TFEU.

in the first reading of the OLP. The content of the opinion provided does not bind the institution(s) participating in the decision-making procedure, but consultation is a substantive procedural requirement the breach of which justifies the annulment of the act.[160]

In a handful of areas within the general regime (as distinct from the CFSP), the European Parliament is merely informed of the adoption of Council measures;[161] this is a Treaty requirement which should, in principle, not only be respected but compliance with which is amenable to judicial review.[162] It is unclear, however, what the legal consequences of a breach of such a requirement would be, given that the 'information' could only take place after the adoption of the act, and the general principle that the validity of an act should be adjudged as of the time it was adopted.[163]

8 Derived normative acts: delegated and implementing measures

Derived normative acts are those which are based on an enabling provision in an act which is itself based directly on the Treaty, that is, legislation or an act adopted under an INP.[164] Such derived acts may no longer be described as 'secondary legislation', as the term 'legislation' is reserved, since the Lisbon Treaty entered into force, for normative measures adopted by either the OLP or an SLP.[165] The Lisbon Treaty, however, introduced the notion of 'regulatory act', which in principle covers all non-legislative normative acts adopted by the Union institutions, that is, those adopted under an INP, delegated acts, and implementing acts.[166] The current arrangements evolved from a system of delegation of implementing powers to the Commission, which was foreseen in the original EEC Treaty, under the supervision of committees of national civil servants, which was not. That system, which was seen in some quarters as interfering with the Treaty prerogatives of the Commission and, as regards supervision, the European Parliament, was known as 'comitology'.[167]

8.1 Delegated acts

'Delegated act' is now a term of art in EU law, designating the particular type of measure which the Commission adopts under Article 290 TFEU. Such measures lay down rules

---

[160] As regards consultation of the European Parliament, see *Isoglucose* (n 36).

[161] See in particular Art 215(1) TFEU, which concerns the adoption of economic or financial sanctions to give effect to a CFSP decision; the measures in question here are individual decisions rather than normative measures. Though the framework for adopting decisions freezing funds and similar measures as regards combating terrorism (where there is no necessary link to a CFSP decision) is adopted under an OLP (Art 75, first para, TFEU), Parliament is neither consulted on nor informed of Council measures implementing the framework.

[162] See the reasoning of the Court in Case C-70/88 *Parliament v Council* ('*Chernobyl – admissibility*') [1990] ECR I-2041.   [163] Case C-65/93 *Parliament v Council* ('*1993 GSP*') [1995] ECR I-643, para 29.

[164] See eg J Bast, 'New Categories of Acts after the Lisbon Reform: Dynamics of Parliamentarianism in EU Law' (2012) 49 *Common Market Law Review* 885.   [165] See section 7.

[166] Case T-18/10 *Inuit Tapiriit Kanatami v Parliament and Council* [2011] ECR II-5599, and Case C-583/11 P between the same parties, judgment of 3 October 2013.

[167] For a book-length treatment of the subject, see CF Bergström, *Comitology* (Oxford: Oxford University Press, 2005); for the legal situation immediately prior to the Lisbon Treaty's coming into force, see K St C Bradley, 'Halfway House: The 2006 Comitology Reforms and the European Parliament' (2008) 31 *Western European Politics* 837.

which the legislature could in principle have adopted itself but in respect of which it has chosen for different reasons – complexity of the subject matter, need for rapid updating to take account of changing conditions, etc – to delegate the power to adopt to the Commission. These are described in Article 290 TFEU as 'non-legislative acts of general application which supplement or amend non-essential aspects of the legislative act' or, in the jargon of the mid-2000s, 'quasi-legislative' measures. The wording of Article 290(1) TFEU is hardly a model of constitutional drafting; it is unnecessary to describe these as 'non-legislative acts', as they are not adopted under a legislative procedure as defined elsewhere in the Treaty. Equally, it was arguably unnecessary to specify that only non-essential elements may be supplemented or amended by derived measures, as the legal duty of the legislature to lay down the essential elements of legislation is a long-established canon of EU constitutional law.[168]

8.1.1 The Common Understanding

Article 290 TFEU is complete in itself and does not require any implementing measure in order to be applicable; all that is required is that the legislature determine in each individual case the objectives, content, scope, and duration of the delegation, and the supervisory mechanism(s) which apply to the exercise of delegated powers. It is therefore largely to pre-empt possible disputes on the application of this provision to legislation adopted under the OLP that the Parliament, the Council, and the Commission concluded a Common Understanding on the application of Article 290(1) TFEU.[169]

8.1.2 Forms of supervision

Article 290(1) TFEU provides for two forms of supervision: either branch of the legislature may revoke the delegation ('right of revocation') or, more intrusively, prevent the entry into force of individual delegated acts ('right of opposition'). The legislature may apply both supervisory mechanisms to the same delegation. The wording of Article 290(2) TFEU ('those [supervisory] conditions may be as follows') is strikingly ambiguous as to whether the legislature could resort to other types of supervisory mechanism than the two expressly mentioned, as the European Parliament has suggested; no other form of supervision is mentioned in the Common Understanding. The simplest explanation for this wording is that it would allow the Council, where it is acting under an SLP, to exclude Parliament from the supervision of the relevant delegated acts. That said, nothing in the Treaty would prevent the Parliament from supervising delegated acts adopted on the basis of a legislative measure adopted by the Council alone in accordance with an SLP, or vice versa. In adopting provisions on the procedure for elections to the European Parliament, for example, the Council acts under an SLP with the Parliament's consent. It would be consistent with this procedure, and with the wording of Article 290(2) TFEU (which refers to all 'legislative acts' without distinction), that the Parliament be entitled to supervise the exercise of any powers delegated to the Commission under such provisions, though this view is not universally shared.[170]

The Common Understanding provides that the revocation of a delegation does not affect the validity of any delegated acts already in force, though it will fall in the first place to the legislature, and ultimately to the Court, to determine the legal effects of a revocation. Under

---

[168] See *Köster* (n 124) and more recently Case C-355/10 *Parliament v Council* ('*Frontex*'), judgment of 5 September 2012, nyr, summarized as case study 5.2.

[169] See Council document no 8753 of 10 April 2011.

[170] See generally S Peers and M Costa, 'Accountability for Delegated and Implementing Acts after the Treaty of Lisbon' (2012) 18 *European Law Journal* 427.

the opposition procedure, the delegated act does not enter into force until the two-month objection period has expired. The Common Understanding lays down an 'urgency procedure', under which the delegated act may enter into force before the expiry of the objection period and be applied until either the Parliament or the Council lodges such an objection. While the delegation arrangements were intended to abandon comitology once and for all for the adoption of this category of third-level policy measure, the Member States insisted through the Council on specifying that in preparing delegated acts the Commission carry out consultations 'at the expert level', which some have seen as an attempt to reintroduce comitology by the back door.

8.1.3 Limitations on delegation and identification of delegated acts

It is entirely consistent with the concept of 'delegated act' as one the legislature could have adopted that such delegations may only be effected in legislative measures, and not in any other form of normative act; by contrast, implementing acts can be adopted on the basis of 'any legally binding Union act'.[171] As regards duration, while Article 290(1) TFEU leaves the legislature entirely free to delegate powers for a fixed term[172] or an indefinite duration, the institutions have agreed, essentially in the interests of efficiency, that where a fixed-term delegation is provided, the basic act 'should in principle provide for the delegation of powers to be tacitly extended for periods of an identical duration', unless either the Parliament or the Council objects in good time.

A delegated act may 'amend or supplement' a basic (legislative) act. The notion of 'amend' may be understood as referring to the formal amendment of a provision of, or annex to, the basic legislation, while 'supplement' means the addition of new (non-essential) elements. The modification of the framework or definitions laid down in the basic legislation would, on the other hand, be a bridge too far.[173] A 'delegated act' must be identified as such in its title.

8.2 Implementing acts

The arrangements for the adoption of implementing acts laid down in Article 291 TFEU are the second part of the comitology legacy. This provision starts by stating that, as implementation falls in principle within the responsibility of the Member States, the Union should only adopt implementing measures when 'uniform conditions for implementing legally binding Union acts are needed'. This restriction on the conferral of implementing powers is designed to safeguard the prerogatives of the Member States; at the same time, the Member States, rather than the Parliament or the Council, are charged with supervising the exercise of such powers. The exclusion of the Council from the supervisory arrangements may, however, prove illusory in practice, as the legal distinction between Member States' governments, which make up the Council, and national civil servants, who act on behalf of the Member States' governments, may have little real significance. Moreover, old habits die hard, and the Parliament and the Council have jointly insisted on some form of supervisory role, albeit rather modest, over the Commission's implementation of primary legal acts.

When such uniform conditions are required, the conferral of delegated powers on the Commission (and in exceptional cases, the Council) becomes obligatory, in accordance

---

[171] Art 291(2) TFEU; see section 8.2.

[172] The term used in the common understanding is 'determined', which has a quite different meaning in English; perhaps this is an example of a common misunderstanding.

[173] See case study 5.2 on *Frontex*, after section 8.3.

with Article 291(2) TFEU, and the Commission remains answerable to the European Parliament for its policy choices in this domain, notably by means of parliamentary questions and the (remote) possibility of a parliamentary motion of censure.[174] An 'implementing act' must be identified as such in its title.

8.2.1 Conferral of implementing powers and the Neo-Comitology Regulation

Article 291 TFEU does not specify which institution may confer implementing powers; such powers may be conferred in 'any legally binding Union act', including legislation. Outside the domain of the OLP, this power of conferral falls almost exclusively in practice to the Council, which adopts the vast majority of acts under both SLPs and INPs, though the Parliament adopts a limited number of legislative acts concerning its own functioning. Implementing powers 'in duly justified specific cases' may,[175] and in the area of the CFSP must, be conferred on the Council, which would therefore be conferring implementing powers on itself.[176]

The mechanisms for control by the Member States of the Commission's exercise of implementing powers are defined by the Parliament and Council Regulation 182/2011, the so-called 'Neo-Comitology Regulation'.[177] This provides for two principal supervisory mechanisms, the advisory procedure and the examination procedure; these have a number of common features, while the examination procedure has a large number of variants. In essence, however, the Commission is obliged to refer its draft implementing measure to a committee, which can, depending on the applicable procedure (or variant), require it to reconsider or amend its draft measure, or even prevent the Commission adopting the measure. Unlike the situation prior to the entry into force of the Lisbon Treaty, the new arrangements do not provide for any reversion of the power to decide, in the case of an unfavourable committee vote, to the Council.

8.2.2 Common features of the supervisory procedures

All of the committees which participate in the neo-comitology system are composed of 'representatives of the Member States'. The Member States are free to choose the level and professional background of their representatives in such committees: civil servant, academic expert, professional expert, member of professional association, and so forth. Each committee adopts its own rules of procedure on the basis of a model issued by the Commission.[178]

Under both advisory and examination procedures, the Commission submits a draft implementing measure; individual members of the committee may present amendments and the Commission is charged with 'find[ing] solutions which command the widest possible support within the committee', notably by presenting an amended draft. The Commission also fixes the timetable for consideration of its draft measures, subject to certain minimum deadlines and the possibility of applying a procedure for urgent consideration in 'duly justified cases'. The voting requirements of the committees are, naturally, modelled on those of the Council.

---

[174] See further chapter 3, section 3.2.5.

[175] This criterion was taken from the Court's judgment in Case 16/88 *Commission v Council* [1989] ECR 3457.

[176] For the legal situation prior to the Lisbon Treaty, see Case C-133/06 *Parliament v Council* [2008] ECR I-3189. [177] OJ [2011] L55/13.

[178] OJ [2011] C206/11; the appeal committee (see section 8.2.6) has its own rules of procedure, OJ [2011] C183/13.

8.2.3 Choice of supervisory procedure

Article 2 of the Regulation lays down a number of rather flexible guidelines regarding the choice of appropriate procedure for each category of implementing measure, a matter which the first comitology decision of 1987 had signally failed to tackle, and which remained controversial right up to the Lisbon Treaty reforms.[179] While the choice of procedure should take account of 'the nature [and] the impact of the implementing act', the examination procedure applies for acts of general scope and certain types of implementing act which may be sensitive in the Member States, such as those concerning 'programmes with substantial implications' (particularly budgetary), taxation, and certain policy areas where the Union enjoys very wide powers (agriculture and fisheries; protection of human, animal, and plant health and the environment; and the common commercial policy). The advisory procedure is therefore the default procedure, and the legislature may apply it to the 'sensitive' areas too, again 'in duly justified cases'.

8.2.4 The advisory procedure

The advisory procedure[180] is simple; the Commission submits a proposal, the committee gives its opinion (by consensus or by a simple majority vote of its component members), and the Commission proceeds, 'taking the utmost account of the conclusions drawn from the discussions...and the opinion'. In other words, the Commission is not bound by anything the committee says under this procedure; the 'utmost account' requirement is the so-called 'aerosol formula' invented in the 1960s as a sap to the Member States under a procedure which provided them with negligible powers. That said, the consultation of the committee is a substantial procedural requirement, non-compliance with which would justify the annulment of the implementing act;[181] moreover, given that the implementation in practice of Union measures is carried out by the national administrations in all but a handful of areas, it is in principle helpful for the Commission to know their views in advance.

8.2.5 The examination procedure

The examination procedure[182] is anything but simple, and is only presented here in its broad outlines. It provides that

- if the draft implementing act is supported by a qualified majority of the committee, the Commission may adopt it without more;
- a negative opinion prevents the Commission adopting that measure; it may either submit an amended version or refer the matter to the appeal committee.

Where the committee fails to adopt an opinion, the Commission may adopt the implementing measure, except in four cases: where the basic act provides it may not do so, or a simple majority of the component members of the committee oppose the draft measure, or in certain 'sensitive' policy areas, or finally where the measure lays down anti-dumping or countervailing duties (ie measures to respond to unfair trade measures of third countries) *and* a simple majority of the members of the committee oppose adoption. In the first three cases, the Commission may submit an amended version of the draft measure or refer the matter to the appeal committee; in the fourth case, the Commission is obliged to submit the matter to the appeal committee.

---

[179] Cases C-378/00 and C-122/04, both *Commission v Parliament and Council* [2003] ECR I-937 and [2006] ECR I-2001, respectively.   [180] Arts 2(3) and 4, Regulation 182/2011.

[181] See eg Case 30/88 *Greece v Commission* [1989] ECR 3711.

[182] Arts 2(2), 5, 6, and 7, Regulation 182/2011.

In 'exceptional cases', the Commission may override the opposition of an examination committee, where the adoption of the measure is required 'without delay', in order to 'avoid creating a significant disruption of the [agricultural] markets or a risk for the [Union's] financial interests'. The Commission must submit the measure immediately to the appeal committee, and repeal it immediately where the committee adopts a negative opinion; in other cases, the measure remains in force.

8.2.6 The appeal committee

In certain circumstances under the examination procedure, if the adoption of the draft measure is blocked by the committee, the draft must be submitted for consideration to an 'appeal committee'.[183] According to the preamble to the Regulation, the appeal committee 'should meet at the appropriate level', meaning in effect national representatives at a higher level than those who carry out the advisory or examination procedure. Whatever its personal composition, this would not be identical to that of the committee of permanent representatives of the Member State governments ('Coreper'), as the Commission may attend, but does not chair, meetings of Coreper.[184]

Under the appeal committee procedure, committee members may propose amendments to the draft implementing measure referred to it, in which case the Commission is enjoined to 'endeavour to find solutions which command the widest possible support', and to inform the committee how it has taken account of the suggested amendments or why it has rejected them. The committee acts by a qualified majority; a positive opinion means that the Commission must adopt the measure, no opinion means the Commission may do so, while a negative opinion means it may not adopt the measure.

8.2.7 'Immediately applicable implementing acts'

The basic act may also allow the Commission to adopt an implementing measure before this is submitted to the committee under the advisory or examination procedure, on 'duly justified imperative grounds of urgency'.[185] The measure is applied for up to six months (or longer if the basic act so provides). The Commission submits the measure to the relevant committee within 14 days of its adoption; a negative committee opinion obliges the Commission to repeal the measure immediately, otherwise it stays in force until the expiry date indicated.

8.2.8 Openness in committee governance

The Regulation seeks to ensure a certain degree of open government[186] in an area once characterized by systemic obscurity.[187] Thus the different committees are to publish their rules of procedure, their documents are subject to the Union rules on access to documents held by the institutions,[188] and the Commission is to keep a register of committee proceedings, to which Parliament and the Council may have access. The Parliament and the Council also receive, at the same time as the committees themselves, the meeting agendas and the draft implementing acts on which the committees are consulted, as well as the final draft of the implementing act following the delivery of the committee's opinion. This facilitates the exercise by each of the institutions concerned of their so-called 'right of scrutiny';

---

[183] Art 6, Regulation 182/2011.   [184] Art 240(1) TFEU; see further chapter 3, section 5.4.3.
[185] Art 8, Regulation 182/2011.   [186] Arts 10 and 11, Regulation 182/2011.
[187] For a brief history of the first 30 years, see K St C Bradley, 'Comitology and the Law: Through a Glass, Darkly' (1992) 29 *Common Market Law Review* 693.
[188] Regulation 1049/2001 (OJ [2001] L145/43); see also Case T-188/97 *Rothmans v Commission* [1999] ECR II-2463.

this is limited to expressing the opinion that the implementing act is ultra vires the basic act, in which case the Commission must review the draft act, and inform the two institutions whether it will maintain, amend, or withdraw the draft act. While the Commission has expressed the view that neither of these institutions should be involved in supervising the exercise of its implementing powers, the right of scrutiny imposes little appreciable restriction on the Commission's freedom of movement, and may even serve its interests in reducing the risk of subsequent legal proceedings.

As against this, there is no requirement in the Regulation for the publication of the names and/or professional affiliation of the members of the committees. Such information might in any case be considered personal data under the Union's data protection rules which also apply to the committees.[189]

8.3 Borderline between delegated and implementing provisions

The notions of 'delegated act' and 'implementing act' were both born out of the pre-Lisbon Treaty concept of implementing act[190] and despite (or perhaps because of) the efforts of the authors of the Lisbon Treaty, the borderline between these two types of act is not clear. Whereas the Treaty defines a 'delegated act' in terms of its content ('non-legislative acts of general application [which] supplement or amend certain non-essential elements of the legislative act'), it defines 'implementing act' in terms of its rationale, that is, the necessity to lay down 'uniform conditions for implementing legally binding Union acts'.[191] It is impossible to imagine a secondary measure which is a delegated act as to its content, but which is required in order to lay down uniform conditions for implementing legally binding Union acts. Moreover, the principal parties responsible for classifying such derived measures have diametrically opposing interests; being largely excluded from the supervision of implementing acts, the European Parliament has a natural preference for delegated acts, while the Council favours implementing acts, as the Member State officials who participate in the adoption procedures can in effect escape from parliamentary scrutiny of all kinds. In 2012, the Commission challenged before the Court the classification of certain of the measures it is charged with adopting under the Biocidal Products Regulation as 'implementing acts', on the ground that they should be considered 'delegating acts' instead.[192]

For a less controversial illustration of the articulation of these notions in practice, see the Commission delegated regulation amending Annex I to Regulation 211/2011 on the citizens' initiative[193] adjusting the minimum number of signatories per Member State to the modified composition of the European Parliament, and its implementing regulation laying down the technical specifications for the online collection of signatures.[194]

---

[189] Regulation 45/2001 (OJ [2001] L8/1); see also Case C-28/08 P *Bavarian Lager v Commission* [2010] ECR I-6055.

[190] Arts 202, third indent, and 211, fourth indent, EC referred to 'powers…for the implementation of [Council] rules'.

[191] T Christiansen and M Dobbels, 'Comitology and Delegated Acts after Lisbon: How the European Parliament Lost the Implementation Game' '(2012) 16, *European Integration online Papers* (EIoP), art 13, http://eiop.or.at/eiop/texte/2012-013a.htm, p 8.

[192] Case C-427/12 *Commission v Parliament and Council*, judgment of 18 March 14, concerning Regulation 528/2012 (OJ [2012] L167/25). Though deeply unhappy at the Council's insistence that certain secondary measures were considered implementing acts, the Parliament has nonetheless defended the validity of the Regulation with its customary vigour.   [193] OJ [2011] L65/1.

[194] Respectively Regulation 268/2012 (OJ [2012] L89/1) and Regulation 1179/2011 (OJ [2011] L301/3).

Case study 5.2: *Frontex*

In order to tackle the very troubling and recurring problem of irregular immigration by sea, particularly the Southern Mediterranean, the Commission proposed a set of rules governing sea-border operations carried out by the Member States and coordinated by Frontex, the agency responsible for the management of the Union's external borders; the draft measure was submitted in late 2009, with a view to its being in force in time for the following summer, when a new influx of immigrants was expected.[195] The rules were presented as a measure to implement the relevant provision of the regulation establishing the Schengen Borders Code, which laid down a few basic rules on border surveillance. The adoption of the new decision was subject to a comitology procedure left over from the pre-Lisbon Treaty era, the regulatory procedure with scrutiny. Under this procedure, where the committee did not give a positive opinion on the draft measure, the power to adopt the measure passed to the Council; at this stage the European Parliament was entitled, acting by a majority of its component members, to prevent the adoption of the measure, by citing one of a limited number of grounds, including the consideration that the measure proposed would exceed the implementing powers granted by the basic legislative act.

The comitology committee responsible did not approve the Commission's draft measure on the surveillance of the maritime borders, and the power to adopt it passed to the Council, which did so, in the absence of European Parliament opposition. At this point, however, Parliament had second thoughts, less on the merits of the measure than because of the procedure by which it had been adopted; on reflection, the Parliament took the view that the rules should have been adopted as a legislative act, rather than as an implementing measure, and challenged the Council decision as being ultra vires the Schengen Borders Code.[196]

The proceedings presented the Court with three main questions:

- Was the European Parliament entitled to challenge the validity of an act whose adoption it could have prevented?
- Is the legislature's determination that a particular provision constitutes an 'essential element' of the basic legislation open to judicial review?
- Did the contested decision exceed the implementing powers granted by the Schengen Borders Code?

On the first queston, the Court held that, in common with the other political actors of the Union, the Parliament did not need to demonstrate a subjective interest in the outcome of legal proceedings in order to be able to initiate an annulment action. Its right to do so was not conditional on any position it had taken during the course of the adoption process, such as its decision not to oppose the draft Council decision under the regulatory procedure with scrutiny. In particular, the Court firmly rejected the Council's somewhat surprising suggestion that the Parliament's scrutiny power could be considered in some way as a substitute for judicial review.

The Court also rejected the view, espoused by both the Council and the Commission, that the legislature enjoyed untrammelled freedom to decide whether a particular aspect of the basic legislative act constituted an 'essential element', which could only be modified in accordance with the legislative process, or a 'non-essential element' the power to modify

---

[195] For more on EU immigration control measures, see chapter 26.
[196] *Frontex* (n 168). On EU agencies, see chapter 8.

which could be delegated to the Commission (or, exceptionally, the Council). It noted that 'provisions [whose adoption] require[s] political choices falling within the responsibilities of the European Union legislature cannot be delegated'. Moreover, the Court continued, '[ascertaining] which elements of a matter must be categorised as essential is not...for the assessment of the European Union legislature alone, but must be based on objective factors amenable to judicial review'.

On the merits, the Court found that the adoption of rules conferring enforcement powers on border guards entailed political choices and constituted 'a major development in the [Schengen Border Code] system'. The Court was particularly concerned by the fact that the exercise of such powers 'mean[t] that the fundamental rights of the persons concerned may be interfered with to such an extent that the involvement of the European Union legislature is required'. The attempt by the Commission and the Council to hide the real nature of certain of the rules by dubbing them non-binding 'guidelines' also failed; in the context of Frontex operations, these particular guidelines 'must...be complied with [and] the rules...are intended to produce binding legal effects'.

The importance of the issues raised in this particular case, in which all the major political Union institutions, with the understandable exception of the European Council, as well as a dozen Member States, were involved, reaches well beyond the domains of external border policy and the comitology system. In the first place, by ruling the Parliament's action admissible, the Court sought to reconcile the fundamental desirability of judicial review with a healthy respect for the exercise of political discretion; the Court was presumably aware of the fact that, while the procedural requirements within the Parliament to decide to initiate legal proceedings are very light, opposition to a draft implementing act requires a vote of a majority of its component members.[197]

The European Parliament's decision not to prevent the adoption of the draft implementing act could, in the circumstances, be seen as a fully rational one, motivated by the desire to see a set of rules on border surveillance put in place by the summer, which would almost certainly not have been possible had the contested decision been blocked in spring 2010.[198] It was presumably for this reason that, exceptionally for an applicant party, the Parliament requested that the Court maintain the effects of the contested decision until this was replaced, which the Court accepted, adding that the replacement should be effected 'within a reasonable time'.

The institutions were also aware that, although the Council decision was adopted under a pre-Lisbon procedure, the Court's interpretation of the notion of 'essential elements' would be of fundamental importance for the application of Article 290 TFEU on delegated acts, which can only amend non-essential elements of basic legislation. The 2006 regulatory procedure with scrutiny was in effect a blueprint for the system of delegated acts adopted by the Lisbon Treaty. The Court rejected the Council's argument that the legislature could, for example, extend both the material and the territorial scope of 'surveillance', as laid down in the Schengen Borders Code, as well as the Commission's view that it be allowed to 'regulate new activities within the scope of the essential subject-matter and of the essential rules'. The finding that only the legislature could lay down provisions which may interfere substantially with the fundamental rights of the persons concerned is striking, especially as

[197] *Frontex* (n 168) para 39, judgment; some consider that, at the time it was adopted, this voting requirement was inconsistent with Art 198, first para, EC, according to which Parliament votes by a simple majority unless the Treaty itself provides otherwise (see now Art 231, first para, TFEU).
[198] Opinion of AG Mengozzi, *Frontex* (n 168) para 20 and fn 13.

the Court had refused to accept a similar argument – albeit in the context of a legal basis dispute — a matter of weeks previously.[199]

The most important aspect of the judgment is the role the Court has reserved for itself in this highly contentious area.[200] In holding that the assessment of whether a particular element 'must be based on objective factors amenable to judicial review', the Court applied the same test as it first adopted in 1987 to the matter of the choice of legal basis for legislation and other acts founded directly on the Treaty.[201] While the Court is, of course, prepared to allow the legislature a great deal of discretion in making political choices, it has shown willing strictly to enforce the rules determining which decisional procedure applies in each case.

9 Enhanced cooperation

The increasing heterogeneity of economic, social, and political conditions in the Member States making up the Union which results from successive enlargements has inevitably meant that certain Member States, while continuing to subscribe to the ideals and the values of the Union as a whole, are unwilling to participate in specific projects, even rather major ones. This has led to a variety of formal opt-outs from parts of the Treaties; some of these are permanent, subject to a possible abrogation of the relevant Protocol, such as the non-participation of Denmark and the UK in the euro, while others allow the non-participating Member State to opt back in to individual policy measures, such as Ireland and the UK in the area of freedom, security, and justice.[202] Conversely, where support for a particular measure, particularly one requiring unanimity in the Council, is insufficient for its adoption as a normal Union act, the Treaty allows a coalition of the willing to proceed with the measure and still use the forms, procedures, and institutions of the Union, adapting the calculation of voting majorities within the Council as required. This technique of policy-making is known as 'enhanced cooperation' and is available over the entire gamut of Union competences except the Union's exclusive competences; special rules apply for enhanced cooperation in CFSP. Such cooperation is 'enhanced' in the sense that, unlike other forms of Member State cooperation, it necessarily has a distinctly pro-Union flavour, and cannot be used as a means of avoiding the obligations of the Union method of policy-making.

Both recourse to enhanced cooperation and the conduct of such cooperation are subject to compliance with a large number of legal requirements.[203] The preliminary decision to authorize enhanced cooperation is taken by the Council 'as a last resort, when it has established that the objectives of such cooperation cannot be attained within a reasonable time by the Union as a whole'. The non-participating Member States may take part in

---

[199] Case C-130/10 *Parliament v Council* ('*Asset freezing*'), 19 July 2012; here the Court held that the Parliament could be excluded from the procedure for the adoption of a measure on asset freezing on the grounds that 'the duty to respect fundamental rights is imposed…on all the institutions and bodies of the Union' (para 83).

[200] In concentrating primarily on what the Court (allegedly) did not do, M Chamon completely overlooks this point: 'How the Concept of Essential Elements of a Legislative Act Continues to Elude the Court' (2013) 50 *Common Market Law Review* 849.   [201] See section 4.3.

[202] See further chapters 19, 25, and 26.   [203] Art 20 TEU and Arts 326–334 TFEU.

deliberations and the vote on authorizing enhanced cooperation, but only Member States intending to participate in such cooperation may vote upon and are bound by the resulting legal acts. The authorization decision is itself subject to judicial review.[204]

Enhanced cooperation must 'aim to further the objectives of the Union, protect its interests and reinforce the integration process'; it may not 'undermine the internal market or economic, social and territorial cohesion [or] constitute a barrier to, or discrimination in trade between Member States nor ... distort competition between them', and must respect the 'competences, rights and obligations' of non-participating Member States. While the coalition of the willing may be as few as nine Member States, such cooperation must be 'open at any time to all Member States'. Non-participating Member States may not impede the implementation of acts adopted under enhanced cooperation.

10 Treaty revision

The Treaties, including the Euratom Treaty, may now be amended under either the 'ordinary' revision procedure (which comes in two variants) or a simplified revision procedure, depending on the character and the extent of the modifications being undertaken.[205]

10.1 Simplified revision procedures

There are three 'simplified revision procedures' for amending the Treaties laid down in Article 48(6) TEU; Article 48(7), first subparagraph, TEU; and Article 48(7), second subparagraph, TEU, respectively and miscellaneous specific procedures.

10.1.1 Article 48(6) TEU procedure

The application of the Article 48(6) TEU procedure is subject to two material restrictions: it may not be used to increase the competences conferred on the Union, and it may only be used to amend Part Three of the TFEU, which contains all the policy provisions of the old EC Treaty (except those relating to external relations), along with those on the area of freedom, security, and justice formerly located in the TEU. Amendments may be proposed by a Member State, the European Parliament, or the Commission. The European Council decides, unanimously, on the amendments to the Treaties, after consulting the Parliament, the Commission, and, in the case of institutional changes in the monetary area, the European Central Bank. The amendments still need national ratification before they can come into force.[206]

10.1.2 Article 48(7) TEU procedures

The procedure laid down in Article 48(7), first subparagraph, TEU, allows the European Council, again acting unanimously, to replace a Treaty requirement for Council unanimity with a qualified majority voting rule, either for the adoption of a particular act or generally, except for decisions with defence or military implications. Similarly, the procedure under Article 48(7), second subparagraph, TEU, allows the European Council to replace a special

---

[204] Joined Cases C-274/11 and C-295/11, *Spain and Italy v Council*, judgment of 16 April 2013.

[205] For a truly comprehensive treatment of the subject, see S Peers, 'The Future of EU Treaty Amendments' (2012) 31 *Yearbook of European Law* 17.

[206] The first use of this procedure was challenged unsuccessfully in *Pringle v Ireland* (n 44).

legislative procedure in which the Council is the adopting institution with an ordinary legislative procedure, though a number of highly sensitive matters are excluded from the scope of this provision: decisions on the Union's budgetary resources and the multiannual financial framework, the application of the flexibility clause, and the suspension of a Member State's voting rights where it fails to respect the Union's fundamental values.[207]

In each case, these institutional reforms require the consent of the European Parliament, acting by a majority of its component members, and may be vetoed by any of the national parliaments within six months of the notification of the proposed amendment. In the absence of any contrary indication in the text, the two houses of any bicameral parliament would presumably have to agree on the exercise of such a veto. These procedures, known familiarly as 'passerelles',[208] do not allow the substitution of a more cumbersome decision-making procedure (unanimity or a special legislative procedure) where the Treaty already provides for the lighter procedure.

The Court has already ruled that it has jurisdiction to verify whether the Union was entitled to use the procedure under Article 48(6) TEU,[209] and by that token presumably has jurisdiction to review recourse to the other simplified revision procedures.

10.1.3 Miscellaneous specific revision procedures

Though not identified as such, other forms of specific simplified revision procedure are scattered throughout the Treaty. The Council may thus strengthen or add to the rights of Union citizens set out in Article 20(2) TFEU, for example, acting under a special legislative procedure, though in this case Member State approval is required before the modification enters into force. The Council may also amend the Treaty on certain matters without requiring such approval, for example, by substituting the ordinary legislative procedure for the special legislative procedure for the adoption of measures of judicial cooperation in the area of family law with cross-border implications (subject to a possible veto by a national parliament), or amending the Protocol on the excessive deficit procedure, while the Statute of the Court of Justice may be amended under an ordinary legislative procedure.[210] The European Council may also amend the Treaty by simple decision, for example extending the powers of the (possible future) European Public Prosecutor.[211] These may be considered specific provisions (leges speciales) which render inapplicable the general requirements of other procedures laid down in Article 48(6) and (7) TEU.

10.2 Ordinary revision procedures

The ordinary revision procedure, which is largely inspired by the procedure which produced the 'Constitution for Europe' in 2004, is unrestricted in material scope, and is hence available for any Treaty amendment, though it would presumably not be used where a less cumbersome procedure is available.[212] Amendments may be proposed by the Parliament, the Commission, or any Member State government, and are notified to the national parliaments. After consulting the European Parliament and the Commission and, where the amendments concern 'institutional changes in the monetary area' the European Central Bank, the European Council decides by a simple majority whether or not the procedure

[207] Respectively Art 311, third and fourth paras; Art 312(2), first subpara; Art 352; and Art 354 TFEU. The derogations from Art 48(7) TEU are set out in Art 353 TFEU. [208] From the French for 'footbridge'.
[209] Pringle v Ireland (n 44).
[210] Arts 81(3), second subpara, and 281, second para, TFEU. [211] Art 86(4) TFEU.
[212] Art 48(2)–(5) TEU.

should continue. If so, the President of the European Council convenes a convention comprising representatives of the national parliaments and the European Parliament, the heads of State or government of the Member States, and the Commission.

Acting 'by consensus', the convention may recommend Treaty amendments to a conference of the representatives of the Member States' governments ('intergovernmental conference' (IGC)), which adopts the amendments 'by common accord'. The matter does not end there, as the amendments still require ratification by the Member States; should this final stage of the procedure not be completed within two years of the adoption of the amendments, and providing four-fifths of the Member States (at present, 23) have ratified these, the question is referred to the European Council. While the Treaty is silent on what this last-gasp step may entail, the European Council has been quite successful in the past in coming up with astute, if legally obscure, solutions for the Member States unable to cross the finishing line (usually Ireland or, on one occasion, Denmark).

A variant of this procedure allows a simple majority of the European Council, with the consent of the European Parliament, to dispense with the convention stage entirely and move straight to the IGC, should none of the simplified procedures be available and should the scope of the proposed amendments not justify the convening of the convention. Once it consents to bypassing the convention stage, the European Parliament may not object to the content of the amendments adopted. On the other hand, the national parliaments may still register their disagreement with the procedure used, as well as the content of the amendment, at the ratification stage.

10.3 Accession and withdrawal

Specific rules cover the accession or withdrawal of a Member State.[213]

Accession to the Union is in principle available to '[any] European State which respects the [Union's] values and is committed to promoting them', under a two-stage procedure.[214] The decision on the application to accede is taken by the Council, unanimously, after informing the national parliaments, consulting the Commission, and obtaining the consent of the European Parliament acting by a majority of its component members. The conditions of accession, including any modifications of the Treaties, are then laid down in an agreement between the acceding State and the Member States (not the Union), which is in turn ratified by the Member States under their national procedures and by the acceding States. The Treaty does not define what the term 'European' designates.

Article 50 TEU provides a procedure for dealing with a request by a Member State to withdraw from the Union, by means of an agreement between the Union and that State. Should no such agreement be reached, the Member State will cease to be party to the Treaties two years after notifying the European Council of its intention to withdraw. With the exception of certain overseas countries and territories which have special relationships with Member States,[215] the Treaty does not make explicit provision for the withdrawal from the Union, or secession, of part of a Member State. In 1984, Greenland withdrew from the Communities in accordance with a special treaty, while remaining part of Denmark.[216]

---

[213] See Peers, 'The Future of EU Treaty Amendments' (n 205) section IV.   [214] Art 49 TEU.
[215] See Art 355(6) TFEU.
[216] Treaty amending, with regard to Greenland, the Treaties establishing the European Communities (OJ [1985] L29/1).

11 The 'democratic deficit'

11.1 Case law references

The Union's 'democratic deficit' refers to the lesser accountability of the Union institutions compared to the governments of the Member States. While it is hence more a political than a legal concept, traces of concern regarding the Union's democratic credentials may be found in the case law of the Court of Justice, going back at least as far as *Van Gend en Loos*.[217] There the Court relied, inter alia, on the fact that citizens participate in the functioning of the Community through the intermediary of the European Parliament in order to justify the autonomy of the Community's legal order and the direct effect of Treaty provisions. In proceedings which arose directly from the organization of the first direct elections to the Parliament in 1979, the Court again relied on the principle of democratic participation in Community decision-making both to interpret the scope of the right of the institutions to intervene in judicial proceedings and to evaluate the nature of the requirement that the European Parliament be consulted on draft legislation.[218] More controversially, in its *Titanium dioxide* ruling more than a decade later, the Court gave priority to the Community-level democratic participation in the legislative procedure of the European Parliament over the right of individual Member States to exercise a veto in the name of national democracy.[219] That said, the Court's recourse to the democratic principle as a determining, or even a relevant, factor in its judgments has been sparse and somewhat unpredictable.

11.2 Reform of decision-making procedures and principles

The Member States' shared concern with the democratic character of the Union manifested itself in successive rounds of Treaty reform which over time increased the formal powers of the European Parliament quite dramatically, first as regards the adoption and supervision of the Union budget, and subsequently both in policy-making generally and in institutional matters such as the appointment of the Commission. At the same time, the Member States made more explicit their understanding, which was always inherent in the structures of the Union, that the Union would be guided by principles such as conferral, subsidiarity, and proportionality, which seek to ensure that policy decisions are only taken by the Union where this is more appropriate than action at the national level. While the scope for national parliamentary supervision over the decisions of their ministers in Council meetings has been attenuated by qualified majority voting and the sharing of legislative power between the Council and the European Parliament, the national parliaments, indeed individual parliamentary chambers, have been given certain powers to supervise the adoption of Union legislation.

11.3 Treaty provisions on democratic principles

The insertion of the new 'provisions on democratic principles' into the TEU by the Lisbon Treaty should be seen in the context of this ongoing debate.[220] Having declared unreservedly that '[the] functioning of the Union shall be founded on representative democracy', the Treaty identifies the two components of that democracy: representation of the citizens at the Union level in the European Parliament, and representation of the Member States in the

---

[217] Case 26/62 [1963] ECR 1. [218] *Isoglucose* (n 36). [219] *Titanium dioxide* (n 59).
[220] See Arts 9–12 TEU.

European Council by heads of State/government, and in the Council by governments which are themselves democratically accountable. The 'right of [every citizen] to participate in the democratic life of the Union' is formally declared, along with the aspiration that decisions be 'taken as openly and as closely as possible to the citizen'. To give effect to the former, the Treaty lays down provisions on voting rights for (non-national) Union citizens in local and European Parliament elections in their Member State of residence, on open Union government and dialogue between the institutions and civil society, and on the citizens' initiative (which allows a million citizens from seven Member States to request the Commission to take a policy initiative), as well as recognizing the contribution of political parties at 'the European level'. Article 12 TEU also lists the different ways by which national parliaments 'contribute actively to the good functioning of the Union', though this is descriptive rather than prescriptive.

12 Conclusion

It is in the nature of constitutions to grant powers to institutions of government and at the same time create devices and rules to limit the exercise of those powers. In a federal-type entity, these devices and rules define and permit the policing of the boundaries both vertically, between the central government and the component States, and horizontally, between the different institutions or branches of government. While not formally a constitution, the EU Treaties clearly perform these functions by means of the rules on competence and on decision-making, both legislative and non-legislative, which they lay down.

It falls at first instance to the political institutions of the Union to ensure these boundaries are respected. This has always been so, owing to the design of these institutions, and in particular their composition and respective roles in Union governance. During the last quarter of a century, however, the Member States have dramatically increased the policy-making powers of the Union and at the same time established new legal rules and procedures which bring the Court of Justice more directly and more frequently onto the scene, as arbiter in boundary disputes between the institutional actors, but also as the court of last instance, in effect, for certain questions in new and very sensitive areas of litigation, such as custody disputes between couples, the legality of the detention of accused persons, and the protection of the rights of those suspected of harbouring terrorist sympathies whose assets have been frozen in pursuit of decisions taken outside the Union legal framework.

As a result, disputes on competence matters and the proper conduct of the decision-making procedures laid down in, or on the basis of, the Treaties become ever more fraught with political consequences. Time was when the principal issue of debate regarding competences was whether the Treaty, read as a whole, allowed the then European (Economic) Community to regulate a particular matter; now the Court is obliged to weigh up a variety of factors which are not obviously legal in character, such as the capacity of the Member States to deal with a particular matter, or the potential impact of Union action on private parties. This is not necessarily a negative development, but it has modified the role of the Court in the political life of the Union.

Likewise, as regards ensuring the proper conduct of decision-making, regarding which the early case law occasionally displayed a certain insouciance,[221] the Court has since the

---

[221] The 1973 judgments in Case 8/73 *Massey-Ferguson* [1973] ECR 897 and Case 5/73 *Balkan Import* [1973] ECR 1091, eg respectively allowed the Council to ignore the substantive requirements of Art 235 EEC (now Art 352 TFEU) and to bypass the requirement to consult the European Parliament on agricultural measures. Both judgments have subsequently been overruled on these points, albeit *sub silentio* in each case (see respectively sections 4.4 and 7.3).

early 1980s, and subject to a few blips, taken the institutional bull by the horns, and firmly established that this is an area which is fully subject to judicial review, rather than one which is left to the political institutions, or the most powerful amongst them, alone. The Court's admirably robust attitude is particularly evident, for example, in its case law on the choice of legal basis, the strict respect of procedural requirements in decision-making, and the delimitation between legislative and sub-legislative acts.

Despite being dragged into what might be considered essentially power struggles and turf wars between institutional actors, the Court has demonstrated an acute sense of the limitations on its own role. In so doing, it has managed to oversee a significant degree of judicialization of political decision-making, without embracing the politicization of judicial activity.[222]

Further reading

A BIONDI ET AL (eds), *EU Law after Lisbon* (Oxford: Oxford University Press, 2012) chs 2, 4, 5, 10, and 12

P CRAIG, *The Lisbon Treaty: Law, Politics, and Treaty Reform* (Oxford: Oxford University Press, 2010) chs 2, 5, 7, and 11

H HOFMANN, 'Legislation, Delegation and Implementation under the Treaty of Lisbon: Typology meets Reality' (2009) 15 *European Law Journal* 482

K LENAERTS AND JA GUTIÉRREZ-FONS, 'The Constitutional Allocation of Powers and General Principles of EU Law' (2010) 47 *Common Market Law Review* 1629

J-C PIRIS, *The Lisbon Treaty: A Legal and Political Analysis* (Cambridge: Cambridge University Press, 2012) chs 7, 8, 11, and 12

R SCHÜTZE, 'Subsidiarity after Lisbon: Reinforcing the Safeguards of Federalism?' (2009) 68 *Cambridge Law Journal* 525

Chapter acknowledgements

Kieran Bradley is a Judge at the EU Civil Service Tribunal. The views expressed are personal and may not be taken as representing those of any institution with which the author is or has been associated.

---

[222] See generally R Hirschl, 'The Judicialization of Politics' in K Whittington et al (eds), *The Oxford Handbook of Law and Politics* (Oxford: Oxford University Press, 2008).

6

The effects of EU law in the national legal systems

Michal Bobek

1 Introduction

EU law has many dimensions. There is the grand Brussels (Luxembourg/Strasbourg) world of EU institutions: policies, competences, types of legislative procedures, institutional balance, democratic deficit(s), Court of Justice, its composition, types of actions, and so on. Connected to this world are various multinational undertakings, transnational law firms, interest groups, and lobbyists. There is, however, also another dimension to EU law: the national one. At first sight perhaps less glamorous, sometimes even dull, this world of EU law is concerned more with the application of EU law in individual cases and to individual people: a pension claim of a migrant worker, the enforcement of a civil decision rendered in another Member State, a consumer protection dispute, a workplace discrimination case, to name just a few examples.

This chapter explains how these two worlds, Brussels and national, relate. It shows how EU law enters the national legal systems and how the provisions of the two normative legal systems interact. The chapter starts by explaining the default rules for the national application of EU law. It then focuses on three key principles: direct effect, indirect effect, and primacy. Further attention is paid to requirements formulated with respect to procedures for the national enforcement of EU law and State liability for breaches of EU law. The chapter closes with a case study, in which the interplay among the rules and principles introduced in this chapter is illustrated.

The principles discussed in this chapter represent the backbone of the entire legal system of the EU. Without them, the Union could hardly aspire to be more than (yet) another international organization. But still, in spite of their importance (or perhaps, later on, *because of* their importance), these principles are in fact nowhere written or enacted. There is no mention of primacy or direct effect in the Treaties. The principles discussed in this chapter are of judicial origin. They have been brought to life and upheld by the (established) case law of the Court of Justice of the European Union (the Court).

The fact that the key principles of national enforcement of EU law are almost entirely of judicial origin has its strengths and weaknesses. On the one hand, the system develops organically and incrementally, in constant interaction between the national courts and the Court. The Court can ensure effective enforcement of EU law and EU law-derived individual rights in the Member States in individual cases. On the other hand, as any case law-based system, a purely judicial world of remedies may suffer from lack of clarity, internal contradictions, and hidden reversals, which result in a perceived or real lack of predictability and foreseeability of the law. An ongoing tension between these two interests is the characteristic element of this entire area of law.

2 EU law in the Member States: institutions, procedures, principles

Imagine a passion: football, for example. Imagine a number of football clubs becoming increasingly unhappy with the state and quality of their common passion: low game quality, doping, rampant corruption in the game, etc. The clubs wish to join forces and do something about it. They have a number of options.

First, they could sign an agreement. They might call it the 'Fair Football Charter'. In the Charter, they would set out minimum requirements for each of the problems identified. These would be, however, just substantive rules. Their implementation and enforcement by and within the clubs would be left entirely to the individual clubs. Thus, some of the clubs might indeed faithfully implement the Charter, reflecting its provisions in the club's articles of association and rigorously enforcing it by all the club's organs. In other clubs, however, the Charter might just be put in a deep drawer in the president's office and scarcely looked at again.

Secondly, the clubs could be much more ambitious. They might wish not only to set some minimal rules, but also to provide for their enforcement. They might establish an organization and name it the 'Fair Football Federation'. The Federation would have a legal personality. It would be entitled to pass rules binding upon its members. Moreover, it would also supervise the enforcement of these rules. Within each of the clubs, representatives of the Federation would be stationed to enforce the Federation rules. The Federation representatives would act according to the Federation's own rules on administration and dispute settlement. Finally, a decision of a Federation representative on matters falling within the scope of the Federation powers would be final.

Today, EU law finds itself somewhere in the middle between these two scenarios. The first scenario represents the traditional way in which public international law obligations may be enforced within the States. The second scenario outlines a fully fledged federal structure, in which the federation lays down not only substantive rules, but also provides for their enforcement within its member units, both substantively and institutionally.

There are three important elements which need to be discussed in order to understand the nature of the current constitutional settlement within the EU and the issues raised in this chapter: *institutions, procedures, and principles*. In other words, *who* enforces EU law in the Member States, and *how*, following what procedures and guided by *what principles*.

On the *institutional* plane, EU law in the Member States is carried out by the existing national institutions. All the national institutions, be it the executive, the courts, or even the legislator, become de facto EU institutions when acting *within the scope of EU law*. The Union sets up no 'own' decentralized agencies, which would be present in the Member States and would enforce 'federal' EU law. For this purpose, the Union relies on the existing institutional structures of its Member States.

On the *procedural* plane, EU law is enforced according to existing national rules of procedure. Also here, the Union relies primarily on the procedures already extant in the Member States, to which it nonetheless attaches some further conditions, which will be explained later in this chapter.

National institutions thus become servants of two masters: the national States and the EU. It is the subject matter of the case or problem at hand which decides which master the national institution is serving at a given moment. Imagine, for instance, a civil servant deciding on social security claims in a national Social Security Administration in, say, the Netherlands. At one moment, she decides on a pension claim of person X, who has spent his entire life in the Netherlands. Applicable substantive law is Dutch, applicable procedure would be the Dutch law on administrative procedure. The ensuing decision is a purely national one. However, five minutes later, when deciding on the next pension claim submitted by person Y, who spent 25 years working in the Netherlands, but also seven years working in the UK and a further five years working in Belgium, the very same official suddenly becomes an EU official. She is applying EU law[1] to the case at hand. The overall procedure will still follow the Dutch law on administrative procedure. However, the decision issued by the same official sitting in the same office became a decision under EU law, rendered within the scope of EU law.

Thus, unless provided otherwise by EU law itself, the Member States put their national institutions and procedures at the disposal of the national enforcement of EU law. If the EU provides otherwise, the (default) national choice in this regard will be pre-empted by the Union. So far, the most significant pre-emption of Member States' autonomy occurred not on the level of procedures or institutions, but on the level of *principles*, which provide for the overall status of EU law in the Member States. Principles like direct effect, primacy, or indirect effect are the overall rules of engagement between the systems: EU law and the national law. They do not determine which particular institution shall implement EU law

---

[1] Regulation (EC) No 883/2004 of the European Parliament and of the Council of 29 April 2004 on the coordination of social security systems (OJ [2004] L166/1) and/or further implementing legislation.

or according to which procedure it shall be applied; they determine what happens in cases of divergence or even collisions between national law and EU law. The logic of the evolution of these principles is nonetheless the same as the one of 'mere' institutions and procedures according to which EU law is enforced in the Member States. In its key decision in *Van Gend en Loos*[2] and *Costa*,[3] the Court pre-empted the potential national choice and diversity with respect to the overall status of EU law in the Member States.

Thus, the current stage of the Union could be called a type of 'cooperative federalism'.[4] On the one hand, through progressive unification or harmonization, the Union has over the years clearly moved away from a public international model (the Fair Football Charter). Important principles of national application of EU law became unified. So did certain procedures and remedies, and institutional structures of the Member States. On the other hand, the Union is still quite far from a fully fledged federal structure (the Fair Football Federation), in which a complex federal institutional structure and procedures would be set up and, more importantly, the ultimate question of supremacy and final word resolved. Often, in facing difficulty in classifying the Union, the notional escape route taken at this stage is to call the Union either an international organization *sui generis* or a federation *sui generis*, depending on the ideological outlook of the observer and the yardstick chosen. There is, however, at least agreement that the Union is *sui generis*, that is, of its own kind, even if we may not be precisely sure what kind it is.

3 Direct effect

Direct effect means that an EU provision becomes the immediate source of law for the national court or administrator. No further implementing act is necessary for its application within the national legal order. EU provisions enlarge the pool of sources of law available to national authorities in deciding cases. Metaphorically speaking, directly effective EU law speaks for itself to the national judge or administrator in an unmediated way, without there being any need for its 'translation' by national law.

3.1 *Van Gend en Loos*

The principle of direct effect made its first appearance in 1963.[5] A company based in the Netherlands, *Van Gend en Loos*, imported a quantity of ureaformaldehyde from Germany. The company disagreed with the amount of duty charged by the Dutch Inland Revenue on this importation. It suggested that the Netherlands had in fact increased the amount of the duty by changing the tariff classification for ureaformaldehyde. Van Gend en Loos claimed that this was contrary to the then (now repealed) Article 12 EEC, which read:

> Member States shall refrain from introducing between themselves any new customs duties on import or exports or any charges having equivalent effect, and from increasing those which they already apply in their trade with each other.

---

[2] Case 26/62 *Van Gend en Loos* [1963] ECR English Special Edition 1.
[3] Case 6/64 *Costa* [1964] ECR English Special Edition 585.
[4] See further R Schütze, *From Dual to Cooperative Federalism: The Changing Structure of European* Law (Oxford: Oxford University Press, 2009) and the discussion in chapter 4 of this volume.
[5] *Van Gend en Loos* (n 2).

The question was soon raised whether such a standstill provision, which was contained in an international agreement (the then EEC Treaty) signed by States and binding between them, has any legal effects within those States. Can a private party invoke such provisions directly in the courts of a signatory party? To this question, the Court, in spite of the united opposition of all the Member States intervening (the Netherlands, Belgium, Germany), and against the Opinion of Advocate General Roemer issued in the case, answered a bold 'yes'. As famously put by the Court:

> The objective of the EEC Treaty, which is to establish a Common Market, the functioning of which is of direct concern to interested parties in the Community, implies that this Treaty is more than an agreement which merely creates mutual obligations between the contracting states....
>
> The conclusion to be drawn from this is that the Community constitutes a new legal order of international law for the benefit of which the states have limited their sovereign rights, albeit within limited fields, and the subjects of which comprise not only Member States but also their nationals. Independently of the legislation of Member States, Community law therefore not only imposes obligations on individuals but is also intended to confer upon them rights which become part of their legal heritage. These rights arise not only where they are expressly granted by the Treaty, but also by reason of obligations which the Treaty imposes in a clearly defined way upon individuals as well as upon the Member States and upon the institutions of the Community.[6]

Drawing on these general statements, the Court further held with respect to Article 12 EEC:

> The wording of Article 12 contains a clear and unconditional prohibition which is not a positive but a negative obligation. This obligation, moreover, is not qualified by any reservation on the part of states which would make its implementation conditional upon a positive legislative measure enacted under national law. The very nature of this prohibition makes it ideally adapted to produce direct effects in the legal relationship between Member States and their subjects.
>
> The implementation of Article 12 does not require any legislative intervention on the part of the states. The fact that under this Article it is the Member States who are made the subject of the negative obligation does not imply that their nationals cannot benefit from this obligation.[7]

In the view of the Court, a clear and unconditional prohibition such as Article 12 EEC, which does not necessitate any further implementation by the Member States, is capable of producing direct effect in the Member States' legal orders. What matters is the wording of the Treaty provision itself, not the original intent of its signatories. Thus, Treaty provisions could be directly effective even if the Member States did not intend it or, at best, were indifferent to such an idea when signing the Treaties. By opting for an *objective* test of direct effect, the Court cut the cord with traditional public international law, where the intent of the signatories is relevant for the later interpretation of a treaty.[8] Moreover, by stipulating that EU law is to be directly effective in all the Member States' legal systems irrespective of what their individual national constitutions state in relation to the domestic status of

---

[6] *Van Gend en Loos* (n 2) 12.   [7] Ibid, 13.

[8] cf Art 31 of the Vienna Convention on the Law of Treaties (1969), UN Treaty Series, vol 1155, p 331.

international law, the Court *pre-empted* national choices in that regard. By combining both of these points in one stroke, the Court indeed carved out *a new legal order*, independent of both international law as well as national constitutions.

3.2 **The conditions and the real test**

Focusing on later case law relating to the direct effect of EU law, the conditions set out in *Van Gend en Loos* soon became blurred. In *Van Gend en Loos*, the Court stated that a Treaty provision may produce direct effects in the Member States if it is

(a) clear;

(b) unconditional in the sense of not allowing for any reservations on the part of the Member States, and

(c) not dependent on any subsequent further implementation measures to be adopted by the Member States or the Community.

However, subsequent case law obscured these conditions in two ways. First, even Treaty articles which were conditional or dependent on further implementation measures were eventually deemed to be directly effective.[9] Secondly, direct effect was subsequently expanded to other sources of EU law: regulations, decisions, directives, as well as provisions of international agreements to which the EU is a party. The conditions for direct effect of these other sources, however, vary. Their application in practice, in particular with respect to potential direct effect of international agreements, is even more divergent. Thus, it is open to debate whether there is one 'direct effect' of EU law or rather a number of 'direct effects'.

The standard formula used by the Court for direct effect (of directives) today includes three conditions. A provision of a directive may be directly effective if it is

(a) unconditional,

(b) sufficiently precise,

(c) the Member State in question failed to implement the directive by the end of the period prescribed therein or failed to implement the directive correctly.[10]

The changing nature of the conditions for direct effect brings to the fore the true nature of the test. In spite of being labelled differently and sometimes even not labelled at all, the test has, in fact, always been the same: does the EU law provision in question contain an understandable and justiciable rule of behaviour, which can be applied by national authorities? It suffices if such a rule is recognizable and extractable from an EU provision. It does not need to be expressed verbatim in the provision itself. That is why EU provisions, which leave much to be desired in terms of clarity of their literal expression, can in fact be directly effective, as long as there is a clear rule of behaviour which can be extracted from such provisions.[11] Thus, in spite of the EU legal order since its very beginnings insisting on being

---

[9] See notably Case 2/74 *Reyners* [1974] ECR 631; Case 41/74 *Van Duyn* [1974] ECR 1337; Case 43/75 *Defrenne* [1976] ECR 455. It is quite telling that, eg in *Defrenne*, where the Court found that Art 119 EC (now Art 157 TFEU – equal pay for equal work) is directly effective, the conditions laid down in *Van Gend en Loos* for direct effect are neither discussed nor even cited.

[10] More recently, eg Case C-268/06 *Impact* [2008] ECR I-2483, para 57; Joined Cases C-152–154/07 *Arcor* [2008] ECR I-5959, para 40; Joined Cases C-397–403/01 *Pfeiffer* [2004] ECR I-8835, para 103; Case C-62/00 *Marks & Spencer* [2002] ECR I-6325, para 25.

[11] This rule of thumb is, however, applicable only to EU *internal* sources – Treaties and EU legislation. Direct effect of international agreements is a case apart. See n 25.

something more than 'mere' international law (see further chapter 7), direct effect remains a type of centrally imposed general 'self-execution' command for EU law in national legal orders in all but name.

To provide an example: Article 34 TFEU reads 'Quantitative restrictions on imports and all measures having equivalent effect shall be prohibited between Member States'. This provision is directly effective, in spite of containing two indeterminate legal notions ('quantitative restrictions' and 'measures having equivalent effect') which, as decades of the case law of the Court on the free movement of goods evidence, are in dire need of interpretation (see further chapter 12). However, the provision postulates a clear and unconditional prohibition, which can be applied judicially.

Equally, Article 157(1) TFEU provides that 'Each Member State shall ensure that the principle of equal pay for male and female workers for equal work or work of equal value is applied'. On the level of its literal expression, this article requires further implementation by the Member States. However, at the same time, a clear and unconditional prohibition can be extracted from it as well: there must be equal pay for equal work, irrespective of sex. In other words, the core requirement of the article, which is directly effective, is prohibition of discrimination in remuneration on the basis of sex (see further chapter 20).

EU law provisions which are not directly effective are those from which such an extraction exercise of an immediately applicable rule is impossible. These infrequent instances tend to be limited to provisions which are wholly incapable of judicial application. They include mere programme or aim-setting norms[12] or provisions which themselves were supposed to establish new legal constructs or institutions in the Member States, subject to considerable discretion to be exercised by the Member States in relation to choice and implementation.[13]

3.3 Direct effect in action

A directly effective provision of EU law may function in a number of ways. Two of them are frequent. First, a directly effective EU provision may *create a new rule* which did not previously exist in national law, and which will then be applied in the case at hand. Secondly, together with the principle of primacy of EU law, it may exclude the application of an *existing* but contrary national *rule*.

To illustrate the difference: imagine a hypothetical EU directive on judicial cooperation and judicial education. The aim of the directive is to facilitate judicial cooperation between the Member States in civil, commercial, and criminal matters. Apart from providing for systemic education of judges in EU law, it also grants all judges five days of additional paid leave annually for the purpose of further study. Member State A, we may call it Brutalia, did not implement this directive at all. Judges have a right to the same benefits as all other State employees. However, Brutalian State employees have no right to study leave in general. Member State B, which might be called Exceptia, has implemented the directive. However, it denied the five days' study leave to all national judges dealing with family cases. Exceptia stated that it suffers from a chronic shortage of family judges. Taking into account its constitutional as well as international human rights obligations

---

[12] See eg Joined Cases C-72/91 and C-73/91 *Sloman Neptun* [1993] ECR I-887 or Case 126/86 *Zaera* [1987] ECR 3697.

[13] eg setting up a new and quite complex mechanism for protection of employees in the event of the insolvency of their employer – see Joined Cases C-6/90 and C-9/90 *Francovich and Bonifaci* [1991] ECR I-5357.

to deal with family cases, especially those relating to minor children, in an expedient manner Exceptia simply cannot provide all family judges with five days of extra study leave every year.

Assume that the provision of the directive providing for the five extra days is directly effective. In Brutalia, judges invoking this provision against the State will ask the national court to apply it directly in the national legal order, thus *substituting* the directive for a non-existent (non-implemented) provision of national law. In Exceptia, family judges seeking to rely on the same provision will ask for the conflicting national rule which denies the five days' study leave to them to be *excluded* from the national legal order. Both of these examples are instances of direct effect, which can either substitute a national rule which is lacking, or exclude a conflicting one.[14]

There are two further important characteristics of the operation of the principle of direct effect which ought to be mentioned. First, the test for direct effect is carried out with respect to individual provisions of EU law. Thus, even a single section or indent of a Treaty article or a directive may be directly effective. Secondly, even EU provisions which do not grant any individual, subjective rights may be directly effective. Direct effect is concerned with objective justiciability of an EU provision. Granting individual rights is not a condition for direct effect. Subjective rights and their vindication might be the cause for an individual invoking EU law in the first place. Granting some individual rights will also be the logical consequence if the individual action was successful. Moreover, as we will see in the immediately following sections, in certain types of legal relationships, individual rights may bar an otherwise directly effective provision of a directive from being applied to the detriment of the individual. That said, however, granting of individual rights is in itself not one of the general conditions for direct effect.[15]

3.4 Differentiation I: types of legal acts

Subsequent case law of the Court expanded direct effect to other sources of EU law. However, as already mentioned, with this expansion also came differentiation between the various direct effects, their conditions, and their scope. The first type of differentiation relates to the type of source which may be directly effective. The second type of differentiation is based on the nature of the parties to a legal relationship for which the EU provision is supposed to be directly effective. The second differentiation makes the national application of EU law somewhat 'directional'. It distinguishes between vertical (an individual – ie physical or legal person – suing the State; also known as ascending vertical), reverse vertical (the State suing, or typically punishing, the individual; also known as descending vertical), and horizontal types of legal relationship (involving just private individuals – physical or legal persons – on both sides).

---

[14] The ongoing academic debate between the proponents of a narrow notion of direct effect (substitution only) or the broad notion of direct effect (substitution and exclusion) may be said to be resolved in favour of the latter by the Grand Chamber of the Court in *Pfeiffer* (n 10). But see notably K Lenaerts and T Courthaut, 'Of Birds and Hedges: The Role of Primacy in Invoking Norms of EU Law' (2006) 31 *European Law Review* 287. In any case, the debate is rather academic, as both sides recognize that EU law requires the exclusion of a conflicting national rule. They thus both arrive at the same outcome. They differ only in the argument whether the reason for exclusion is direct effect or, rather, the primacy of EU law.

[15] It is, however, as will be showed in section 6.3, one of the conditions for State liability for breaches of EU law. Naturally, however, direct effect and State liability are distinct remedies.

3.4.1 Treaty provisions

Van Gend en Loos and subsequent case law[16] established the direct effect of Treaty provisions. Over the years, the case law of the Court has confirmed the direct effect of the key Treaty provisions, such as the free movement of goods, persons, or capital provisions; competition law; State aid; and equal pay. Moreover, it would also appear that directly effective Treaty provisions can be invoked in any type of legal relationship: vertical, including reverse vertical, as well as horizontal.[17]

3.4.2 Regulations

Regulations were the optimal candidate for direct effect. From the very beginnings of the EEC, the Treaty stated that a regulation 'shall be binding in its entirety and directly applicable in all Member States'.[18] This original Treaty-based distinction between the effects of individual sources of EU law was, however, soon blurred by the Court's robust vision of direct effect. If also Treaty provisions and directives can produce direct effects in the Member States, what is then the difference between 'direct effect' and 'direct applicability' of regulations?

In earlier case law, the Court simply equated direct effect with direct applicability.[19] Later, however, this position became nuanced, separating the two categories again. *Direct applicability* means that unless expressly requested by the regulation itself,[20] no national implementing act is by default necessary. A regulation, once it has entered into force, will be immediately applicable in all the Member States. *Direct effect*, on the other hand, aims at the justiciability of a provision: can it be applied by a national authority directly?

The Court further stated that the direct effect of regulations is generally *presumed* and need not be specifically examined.[21] There might nonetheless be rare cases in which a provision of a directly applicable regulation is not directly effective.[22] Imagine a regulation which is so abstract and/or conditional upon a number of other further legislative acts, that it contains simply no 'executable' rules which could be applied judicially.

Finally, a regulation is applicable and directly effective in any type of legal relationship: vertical as well as horizontal. Equally, the enforcement of a regulation may naturally include sanctions imposed by a State against individuals. Competition law might provide examples in this respect. In this area of EU law, it frequently occurs that the Commission or the national authorities impose (considerable) sanctions on individual undertakings for violating their obligations provided for by EU regulations or Treaty articles.

3.4.3 Decisions

Decisions under Article 288 TFEU are of two kinds: addressed and non-addressed (see further chapter 5). An addressed decision is an individual act, stating its concrete addressee(s). A non-addressed decision amounts in practice to a legislative act in all but name. Although labelled a 'decision', it does not expressly name its addressees, but provides a set of abstract and general rules. This dual nature and use of decisions is also reflected with respect to their

---

[16] See nn 2 and 9.

[17] Already *Defrenne* (n 9) and Case 36/74 *Walrave and Koch* [1974] ECR 1405; later, eg Case C-281/98 *Angonese* [2000] ECR I-4139 or C-438/05 *Viking* [2007] ECR I-10779.   [18] Now Art 288 TFEU.

[19] Case 43/71 *Politi* [1971] ECR 1039, para 9.

[20] Recently, eg Case C-592/11 *Ketelä*, judgment of 25 October 2012, nyr, para 35 or Case C-316/10 *Danske Svineproducenter*, judgment of 21 December 2011, nyr, paras 39 and 40.

[21] Case C-367/09 *SGB Belgium* [2010] ECR I-10761, para 32; Case C-278/02 *Handlbauer* [2004] ECR I-6171, para 25. See also Case C-375/09 *Tele2 Polska* [2011] ECR I-3055, paras 31–35.

[22] Case C-403/98 *Monte Arcosu* [2001] ECR I-103.

potential direct effect. A decision addressed to concrete person(s) other than a Member State will be binding on those persons in its entirety. This is due, however, to the binding nature of an individual administrative decision. A decision addressed to a Member State or several Member States might produce direct effect with respect to individuals within those Member States in question, provided its provisions are sufficiently clear, precise, and unconditional.[23]

Direct effect of a decision is, however, limited to vertical situations, in which an individual is invoking a directly effective provision of a decision against the Member State to which it was addressed. The Court has refused to consider decisions as horizontally directly applicable. They cannot be invoked in a dispute between two individuals to whom the decision was addressed before the courts of their Member State.[24]

Finally, over the years the Court has examined and expanded direct effect to other sources of EU law, including international agreements to which the Union is party;[25] measures previously adopted under other 'pillars' (see chapter 2), and, most recently, to general principles of EU law.[26] Our attention in the ensuing section will, however, turn to the most complicated yet the most frequently used instance of direct effect: the case of directives.

3.5 Differentiation II: types of legal relationship

If it were not for directives, direct effect could have become a rather marginal topic of academic interest to EU constitutional lawyers. The default rule for a national judge would be directly to engage with EU law provided that its provisions are executable and justiciable. It was, however, the direct effect of directives and in particular the differentiation the Court introduced with respect to various types of legal relationship, followed by a number of exceptions to the exception itself, which made the case law difficult to comprehend.

As already mentioned in the previous section with respect to regulations and directly applicable Treaty provisions, their infusion into the national legal order is complete. They may be applied in any type of legal relationship: vertical, reverse vertical, as well as horizontal. On the other hand, for directives and, by extension also for decisions, the type of legal relationship, or rather the direction within, matters.

In *Van Duyn*,[27] the Court stated that directives may be vertically directly effective. The case involved a Dutch national, Mrs Van Duyn, who was refused leave to enter the UK to take up employment as a secretary with the Church of Scientology. The UK considered the activities of the said church to be socially harmful. Appealing the decision of the UK authorities, Mrs Van Duyn wished to rely, inter alia, on provisions of a directive.[28]

The Court stated that individuals may rely on a directive's provisions to vindicate their rights against the Member State. In order to do so, however, the provision of a directive

---

[23] Case C-18/08 *Foselev* [2008] ECR I-8745, para 11; Case C-156/91 *Hansa Fleisch Ernst Mundt* [1992] ECR I-5567, paras 12 and 13; Case 9/70 *Grad* [1970] ECR 825, para 5.

[24] Case C-80/06 *Carp* [2007] ECR I-4473, paras 19–22.

[25] For an introduction in this very complex area, see chapter 24. See also P Craig and G de Búrca, *EU Law: Text, Cases, and Materials* (5th edn, Oxford: Oxford University Press, 2011) 344 *et seq*. See further P Eeckhout, *EU External Relations Law* (2nd edn, Oxford: Oxford University Press, 2004) 324 *et seq* or M Mendez, 'The Legal Effects of Community Agreements: Maximalist Treaty Enforcement and Judicial Avoidance Techniques' (2010) 21 *European Journal of International Law* 83.

[26] Case C-144/04 *Mangold* [2005] ECR I-9981 and Case C-555/07 *Kücükdeveci* [2010] ECR I-365.

[27] Case 41/74 *Van Duyn* [1974] ECR 1337.

[28] Council Directive 64/221/EEC of 25 February 1964 on the co-ordination of special measures concerning the movement and residence of foreign nationals which are justified on grounds of public policy, public security or public health (OJ [1964] L56, English special edition: series I, vol 1963–4, p 117).

must be sufficiently clear and precise, unconditional, and the implementation period the Member State had for transposing the directive into the national legal order must have already passed.

There was no textual support in the Treaty for the conclusion reached by the Court. The Treaty stated[29] that directives are, in contrast to regulations, binding upon each Member State as to the results to be achieved, leaving to the national authorities the choice of form and method for their implementation. Thus, there was a strong argument suggesting that a directive is an obligation of result, binding the Member States but, in contrast to regulations, not directly applicable within their legal orders.

The strongest argument the Court offered for overriding the text of the Treaty was not in fact articulated in *Van Duyn* itself, but later.[30] It became known as the 'estoppel argument': a Member State that has failed to implement a directive cannot rely on that failure as a defence against an individual who is invoking the directive. In other words, direct effect may be seen as a certain type of 'sanction' against a defaulting Member State. If the Member State had implemented the directive on time and/or correctly, it could have exercised its choice as to how it wished to do so: how far it wanted to go and by what means. However, because it had failed to do so, it had forfeited that choice.

In spite of the estoppel rationale being contested,[31] it put the direct effect of directives on a more solid, albeit perhaps one-sided, footing. The argument that no one should be allowed to profit from their own wrong has a universal moral appeal. The same argument, however, also decisively framed the ensuing direction-based differentiation within the direct effect of directives. First, if a Member State cannot prevent an individual's reliance on a sufficiently clear and precise provision of a directive after the time for its implementation has elapsed, then that Member State is precluded from enforcing the non-implemented directive against its own nationals. Thus, reverse vertical direct effect of directives is excluded.[32] A Member State must first transpose the directive into its national law and only then can it enforce it against individuals.

Secondly, and more importantly, the State-centred rationale within the estoppel argument does not answer the question whether or not a directive can be directly effective in horizontal relationships between two private individuals. The Court addressed this question in *Marshall*.[33] Mrs Marshall challenged the compulsory retirement age for women in the UK, which was set at 62 at that time, as discriminatory. She wished to continue working, which would have been possible for a man, as the retirement age for men was set at 65. The question arose whether or not she could rely on the provisions of a directive prohibiting sex discrimination as against her employer. The Court stated that

> the binding nature of a directive, which constitutes the basis for the possibility of relying on the directive before a national court, exists only in relation to 'each Member State to which it is addressed'. It follows that a directive may not of itself impose obligations on an individual and that a provision of a directive may not be relied upon as such against such a person.[34]

---

[29] As it still does today in the third intent of Art 288 TFEU.

[30] Case 148/78 *Ratti* [1979] ECR 1629, para 22. See also Case 152/84 *Marshall* [1986] ECR 737, para 47.

[31] eg S Prechal, *Directives in EC Law* (2nd edn, Oxford: Oxford University Press, 2005) 223–226.

[32] Case 80/86 *Kolpinghuis Nijmegen* [1987] ECR 3969, paras 9 and 13; Case C-168/95 *Arcaro* [1996] ECR I-4705, paras 36 and 37; Joined Cases C-387/02, C-391/02 and C-403/02 *Berlusconi* [2005] ECR I-3565, paras 73 and 74.

[33] *Marshall* (n 30).   [34] Ibid, para 48.

In *Marshall*, as well as subsequent case law, a number of arguments were offered for not extending direct effect of directives to horizontal situations. One of the prominent arguments was that of legal certainty: individuals are not the addressees of directives. They are not obliged to follow directives in order to know their legal obligations. Therefore, directives cannot directly impose obligations upon them. Moreover, the key argument that served for the expansion of the principle of direct effect to directives in the first place, the estoppel argument, cannot be stretched so far as to justify the direct effect of directives in horizontal situations.[35]

3.6 No horizontal direct effect of directives: the rule and the exception

The choice made by the Court with respect to the horizontal direct effect of directives might be criticized. The greatest problem this area of case law has been facing is nonetheless not the choice the Court made in *Marshall*. The greatest problem is that the Court has not been ready to adhere to that choice *in substance*. In its ensuing case law, while verbally upholding the 'no-horizontal-direct-effect-of-directives' rule established in *Marshall*, the Court created a number of alternative avenues for reaching into horizontal relationships. These exceptions in fact undermined or even silently reversed the original position taken, without openly acknowledging that it was doing so.

The original rule is that EU law provisions generally are capable of direct effect. The exception to this rule is that in certain types of legal relationship, in particular in horizontal relationships, a directive or a decision is precluded from becoming directly effective. However, the subsequent case law of the Court has created further exceptions to the latter exception, thus silently reaffirming the original rule, in a number of ways:

(a) It has inflated the notion of the 'State' to encompass any organization or body which is subject to the authority or control of the State or has special powers beyond those which result from the normal rules applicable to relations between individuals. Therefore, all bodies or entities which are subject to the authority or control of a public authority or the State will, for the purpose of direct effect of directives, be considered to be part of the Member State.[36] This category includes, for instance, public hospitals, (fully) state-owned companies, or any private bodies which have been entrusted with the exercise of any aspect of a 'public authority'.

The Court has further held that even when a State is acting in a 'private capacity', for example as a normal employer, exercising no sovereign power or authority in a legal relationship, the relationship will, for the purpose of the direct effect of directives, still be deemed as vertical and not horizontal.[37] For instance, imagine staff employed by a State-run hospital or school. The staff (eg nurses, doctors, teachers) have normal, private law contracts of employment. They are not public officials. For the Court, however, even such, technically speaking, 'horizontal' and private law contractual relationships would be

---

[35] As the Court indicated in Case C-91/92 *Faccini Dori* [1994] ECR I-3325, paras 20–24. For further discussion, see P Craig, 'The Legal Effects of Directives: Policy, Rules and Exceptions' (2009) 34 *European Law Review* 349 or A Dashwood, 'From *Van Duyn* to *Mangold* via *Marshall*: Reducing Direct Effect to Absurdity' (2006–7) 9 *Cambridge Yearbook of European Legal Studies* 81.

[36] Case C-188/89 *Foster* [1990] ECR I-3313, paras 18 and 20; more recently, eg Case C-282/10 *Dominguez*, judgment of 24 January 2012, nyr, para 39 or Case C-6/05 *Medipac-Kazantzidis* [2007] ECR I-4557 para 43.

[37] *Marshall* (n 30) para 49; more recently, eg Joined Cases C-444/09 and C-456/09 *Gavieiro* [2010] I-14031, para 82 or Joined Cases C-250/09 and C-268/09 *Georgiev* [2010] ECR I-11869, para 70.

a type of ascending vertical relationship, as one of the parties is the State, even if acting as a normal 'private' employer. The employees could therefore rely on directly effective provisions of directives as against the employer.

(b) The Court has allowed very peculiar and unusual effects of Member States' failure to notify technical standards and regulations to spill over into private relationships, affecting individuals who were not only not to blame, but unlikely to even be aware of the failure of the Member State.[38] To give an example: imagine two Polish companies that conclude an otherwise perfectly valid contract for the delivery of several thousand plastic toys. At the time of delivery, the buyer refuses to accept the toys, claiming that although the products may be in compliance with all the applicable Polish legislation, a Polish statutory instrument adopted two years previously which lays down the maximum content of polymer additives for children's toys is a technical standard that should have been notified to the Commission. Because the Polish government failed to do so two years earlier, the private law contract concluded between the buyer and seller is invalid.

(c) The Court affirmed that (judicially created) general principles of law are applicable in horizontal relationships without any limitations.[39] Imagine an employment contract concluded between an individual and a private company (ie a company that does not fall into any of the exceptions already outlined in point (a) – that is, it is indeed a 'private-private' company). Suppose that the employer believes that in the employment contract there is a provision which constitutes discrimination on the basis of age: for instance, there is a different retirement age for men and women or there is an age-based differentiation in the amount of occupational pension premiums to be paid by the employer and employee respectively.[40] As both parties to the contract are private individuals, the direct effect of directives is excluded. However, no such limitation applies to the general principle of discrimination on the basis of age, the existence of which the Court has confirmed in the previously mentioned *Mangold* case. Such a general principle will then be applicable horizontally, with exactly the same (or, in fact, even broader) results as if the directive itself were horizontally directly applicable.[41]

(d) Perhaps most importantly, the Court has promoted a very robust vision of indirect effect/consistent interpretation (see the following section) as a way for directives to reach into horizontal relationships. Thus, the same result could often be achieved by consistent interpretation as would be achieved by directly applying a provision of EU law.

In sum, the original premise that directives have no horizontal direct effects and that unimplemented directives cannot impose obligations on individuals has over the years turned into a sort of hollow incantation. The combined effect of all the outlined exceptions to the rule of 'no-horizontal-direct-effect-of-directives' comes close to reversing the relationship

---

[38] The line of case law starting with Case C-194/94 *CIA Security International* [1996] ECR I-2201 and culminating, perhaps, in Case C-443/98 *Unilever Italia* [2000] ECR I-7535. However, in spite of still being subject to ardent academic discussion, subsequent case law has largely diminished the significance of this line of cases, with respect of its reach (see Joined Cases C-213/11, C-214/11, and C-217/11 *Fortuna*, judgment of 19 July 2012, nyr, but previously Case C-226/97 *Lemmens* [1998] ECR I-3711) as well as its impact on the validity of private contracts (Case C-159/00 *Sapod Audic* [2002] ECR I-5031).

[39] *Mangold* and *Kücükdeveci* (n 26). But see also Case C-13/05 *Chacón Navas* [2006] ECR I-6467 or Case C-101/08 *Audiolux* [2009] ECR I-9823.

[40] Most recently, eg Case C-476/11 *HK Danmark*, judgment of 26 September 2013, nyr.

[41] See also chapter 9.

between the rule and the exception. Unfortunately, as will be demonstrated in greater detail in case study 6.1, this silent reversal comes at a very high cost: the 'understandability' and the predictability of the law.

4 Indirect effect

The principle of indirect effect is also known as consistent interpretation, harmonious interpretation, or EU-consistent interpretation. It means the duty of all national bodies to interpret, as far as possible, all national law in light of and in conformity with EU law.

The requirement of consistent interpretation is certainly not a novel concept or a concept unique to EU law. It has been employed in a number of other legal orders for achieving consistency between independent sets of norms by the fiat of interpretation. Some municipal legal systems employ consistent interpretation as a way of implementing their international law obligations. A similar duty of constitutionally consistent interpretation has been imposed by a number of constitutional courts, thus expanding constitutional and human rights considerations into all types of legal relationship.[42]

In EU law, indirect effect became an important principle for the national application of EU law, both quantitatively and qualitatively. Although academic attention would typically focus on direct effect and in particular on hair-splitting taxonomic discussions of the direct effect of directives, the majority of EU law application at the national level in fact occurs under the heading of consistent interpretation.

4.1 The notion

The Court first articulated the principle of indirect effect in *Von Colson*.[43] Since then, and repeated in a number of other decisions, a more recent restatement of the principle can be found in *Pfeiffer*, where the Court held that

> the Member States' obligation arising from a directive to achieve the result envisaged by the directive and their duty under Article 10 EC to take all appropriate measures, whether general or particular, to ensure the fulfilment of that obligation is binding on all the authorities of Member States including, for matters within their jurisdiction, the courts…
>
> …when it applies domestic law, and in particular legislative provisions specifically adopted for the purpose of implementing the requirements of a directive, the national court is bound to interpret national law, so far as possible, in the light of the wording and the purpose of the directive concerned in order to achieve the result sought by the directive…
>
> Although the principle that national law must be interpreted in conformity with Community law concerns chiefly domestic provisions enacted in order to implement the directive in question, it does not entail an interpretation merely of those provisions but requires the national court to consider national law as a whole in order to assess to what extent it may be applied so as not to produce a result contrary to that sought by the directive.[44]

---

[42] A notable example is the case law of the German Federal Constitutional Court, which inspired a number of other constitutional courts around Europe. See BVerfGE 7, 198 (207) (*Lüth*); BVerfGE 30, 173 (187) (*Mephisto*); BVerfGE 34, 269 (280) (*Soraya*).

[43] Case 14/83 *Von Colson and Kamann* [1984] ECR 1891.

[44] *Pfeiffer* (n 10), paras 110–115.

The scope of indirect effect in the vision of the Court is very ambitious: *all* national law must be interpreted in accordance with *all* EU law by *all* national authorities. In contrast to direct effect, there are no source-based exceptions to this requirement, at least from the point of view of the Court. Even national law adopted prior to the EU legislation in question must be interpreted in conformity with the latter.[45] There is, however, no duty of consistent interpretation before the lapse of the implementation period in the case of directives.[46]

Indirect effect covers *all* EU law and *all* national law. Thus, although it is directives that are likely to be invoked most frequently for the purpose of consistent interpretation, Treaty provisions or regulations may also produce indirect effect. Consistent interpretation is not limited to EU law sources which cannot, for whatever reason, be directly effective. Also, directly effective sources, such as regulations or Treaty provisions, might be used only for consistent interpretation, if appropriate under the circumstances of the case. Moreover, even EU acts of a non-binding nature, such as recommendations, may produce indirect effect.[47] On the national side, *all national* law naturally covers not only national laws enacted specifically for the implementation of a directive or other EU act, but all national law of whatever legal force, including the national constitution, adopted prior or subsequently to the EU law source in question.

4.2 **The scope**

Given the breadth of the principle of indirect effect in the Court's case law, the real operation of the principle can hardly be put into one doctrinal box. It is rather a scale: a continuous scale of potential arguments of varying strength used in national adjudication and based on an EU law source. Thus, consistent interpretation may include, based on the particular strength of the argument drawn from EU law in the individual case:

(a) *Weak indirect effect*: an EU law provision is simply used as a confirming argument for a result which could safely be reached on the basis of national legal sources. The EU provision(s) provides an additional, subsidiary authority. The typical reasoning of a national court in such cases would be: the result we reach is X because national law says probably X, our constitutional case law requires X, moreover, X is a fair and equitable solution, and, *by the way*, X is also in conformity with EU directive Z, as interpreted by the Court in cases A and B.

(b) *Medium indirect effect*: an EU law provision typically determines the choice between several interpretative options, which are all plausible – the meaning of national statute X might be X_1, X_2, or even perhaps X_3. After consulting an EU law provision, typically a directive and its recitals, the national court decides that it is in fact X_2 that best reflects the aims and the purpose of the directive.

(c) *Strong indirect effect*: the wording of a *national* law provision starts to be twisted and bent in order to achieve conformity with an EU law provision. In similar cases, the

---

[45] Case C-106/89 *Marleasing* [1990] ECR I-4135, para 8.

[46] Case C-212/04 *Adeneler* [2006] ECR I-6057, para 115. However, even before the lapse of the implementation period, Member States must refrain from taking any measures liable seriously to compromise the attainment of the result prescribed by the directive. This so-called 'blocking effect' of directives was established in Case C-129/96 *Inter-Environnement Wallonie* [1997] ECR I-7411. See further Case C-157/02 *Rieser* [2004] ECR I-1477 or Case C-422/05 *Commission v Belgium* [2007] ECR I-4749.

[47] Case C-207/01 *Altair Chimica* [2003] ECR I-8875, para 41 or Joined Cases C-317–320/08 *Alassini* [2010] ECR I-2213, para 40.

national court typically steps outside the literal meaning of a provision and, relying more on systematic, purposive reasoning of national law in conjunction with EU law, begins to considerably modify the text or the established interpretation of a national provision.

The decision of the Czech Constitutional Court in the *European Arrest Warrant* (EAW) case[48] may provide an example of such a strong indirect effect. Article 14(4) of the Czech Constitution states that 'No citizen may be forced to leave his homeland'. In the view of the Constitutional Court, however, even such a categorical provision does not preclude Czech citizens from being surrendered on the basis of an EAW to other EU Member States. Naturally, this is likely to happen against the will of the citizen concerned. Thus, it is hard to argue that a Czech citizen would not be *forced to leave his homeland* if put on a plane in handcuffs and sent off to face trial in another Member State, unless of course one were to suggest that by now EU citizens consider the Union as their homeland, and that they are indifferent as to whether they will face trial in Luxembourg, Sweden, Greece, Bulgaria, or Italy. However, even in view of such constitutional text, the Constitutional Court 'interpreted' the Czech Constitution in conformity with EU law. In contrast, the German as well as Polish constitutional courts that faced similar constitutional provisions in their respective constitutions declared that the national constitutions were incompatible with the EU law requirement of extraditing their citizens. They stated that Germany and Poland respectively might participate in the EAW system but, in order to do so, the national legislation should first be amended.[49]

There is no clear borderline between instances of such strong consistent interpretation and direct effect. Arguments made on the basis of EU law represent a continuous line. On one side of the line are instances of weak indirect effect, in which the weight of an EU law argument borders on the irrelevant. On the other side, the strong interpretative bending of a national provision gradually slides into, in fact, directly applying EU law without openly acknowledging the fact.

With respect to the potential choice between direct effect and strong indirect effect, it is often the case that consistent interpretation can be better reconciled with the integrity of the national system. As we saw in the previous section, direct effect means the exclusion or substitution of a national rule. It requires an open acknowledgement on the part of the judge or administrator that she is disregarding otherwise perfectly binding national law, a statute, or even a constitution. Conversely, indirect effect is much less controversial. It superficially preserves the integrity of the national legal system, even if in substance the outcome of the case is the same.

4.3 Interpretation unbounded?

Seen from such a realist perspective, indirect effect offers quite a robust alternative to the previously discussed prohibition of the horizontal direct effect of directives. It might also reach into reverse vertical situations, in particular in administrative law but, as far as the interpretation of indeterminate legal notions is concerned, also in criminal law. The only thing needed is a national law provision that could reasonably be claimed to be interpreted in conformity with EU law. If there is such a provision, all the previously discussed

---

[48] Judgment of 3 May 2006, case no Pl ÚS 66/04, No 434/2006 Coll. An English translation of the decision is available at http://www.usoud.cz/en/decisions

[49] See also, eg J Komárek, 'European Constitutionalism and the European Arrest Warrant: In Search of the Limits of "Contrapunctual Principles"' (2007) 44 *Common Market Law Review* 9.

limitations, in particular those relating to the prohibition of horizontal direct effect of directives or decisions, fall away.

Imagine the following scenario: a Member State has incorrectly implemented the Unfair Terms in Consumer Contracts Directive.[50] Most importantly, it has not implemented the indicative list of prohibited terms contained in Annex 1 to the Directive. There is, however, in the national civil code, a general provision stating that consumers are the vulnerable party and as such are to be protected. Any provision in a contract between a consumer and a seller which creates a considerable imbalance in mutual obligations may be challenged by the weaker party.

A Mr X has concluded a consumer contract with a seller Y that provides, inter alia, that all disputes arising under the contract are to be settled exclusively by arbitration. Furthermore, the seat of the arbitrators is in the city where the seller has its main office. When the case comes to court, a national judge will declare this contractual term void, relying on the national general civil code provision interpreted in conformity with the Directive.[51]

Would such a case represent an instance of consistent interpretation of national law with a directive or an example of the prohibited horizontal direct effect of a directive? On the one hand, there is some textual basis in national law in the form of a type of general consumer protection clause. Thus, declaring unfair arbitration clauses void is a materialization of the general prohibition, for which EU law provided just inspiration. On the other hand, the seller might object stating that the rule which was in fact applied to his case and which just imposed an obligation on him came straight from a directive. It certainly has no textual foundation in national law.

This example illustrates the problem with doctrinal boxes. It also shows how indirect effect reaches into private horizontal relationships and imposes obligations on one party. Such an outcome ought to be prohibited, at least according to the standard dictum of the Court as regards direct effect which we examined in the previous section.

Finally, the same applies to the prohibition of reverse vertical direct effect. For the purposes of direct effect, the Member State cannot rely on a non-implemented or wrongly implemented directive to the detriment of the individual.[52] In other words, the directive cannot, *in itself and independently of a national law* adopted by a Member State for its implementation, impose obligations on an individual. But what if a Member State uses a provision of a directive for the purpose of consistent interpretation of national law, which in its outcome nonetheless disadvantages or even burdens the individual? For instance, imagine the interpretation of indeterminate legal notions in national tax law: who is a taxable person with respect to value added tax? What is a taxable activity? Suppose that a Member State wishes to respect the autonomous nature of EU law notions, as it ought to. Thus, in order to interpret the notions in EU tax law, it reaches into other areas of EU law, perhaps into another directive. By doing so and interpreting the notion in conformity, the Member State reaches the conclusion that person X is not subject to the tax, whereas person Y is. In consequence, one party has just been forced to pay a tax, which it would not have been obliged to pay if the Member State had not resorted to consistent interpretation. In this way, the Member State has applied EU law in a vertical situation to the detriment of an individual.[53]

---

[50] Council Directive 93/13/EEC of 5 April 1993 on unfair terms in consumer contracts (OJ [1993] L95/29). On the substance of this Directive, see further chapter 23.

[51] Point (q) of the annex to the Directive, which was, however, not implemented in national law.

[52] See n 32.

[53] See Case C-168/95 *Arcaro* [1996] ECR I-4705 or Case C-321/05 *Kofoed* [2007] ECR I-5759. Specifically in a criminal law context, see also Case C-105/03 *Pupino* [2005] ECR I-5285, para 45 or *Berlusconi* (n 32), para 74.

4.4 **Introducing some limits**

In reaction to the apparently boundless potential of indirect effect, the attention of the Court has turned to the question of its limits. The Court progressively formulated three limits to the originally vast duty of consistent interpretation. These are:[54]

(a) interpretative methods recognized by national law,

(b) general principles of law, and

(c) no interpretation *contra legem.*

The first limit may appear redundant. When interpreting national law, a national authority naturally limits itself to the interpretative methods recognized under national law. At the same time, however, such a condition may not be that odd if viewed in the broader context of the Court's case law. In the past, the Court has not hesitated strikingly to expand the powers of national authorities in the name of effective enforcement of EU law.[55] Thus, with respect to the scope of indirect effect, such a condition should perhaps be read as a soothing message: interpretation of law ought to remain interpretation, even in the face of the 'full effectiveness' of EU law.

The second limitation, general principles of law, particularly those of legal certainty, legitimate expectation, and non-retroactivity, might perhaps have more teeth. General principles put an equitable brake on far-reaching interpretative adventures in individual cases. They might be triggered if the interpretative outcome were to be to the detriment of the individual in both horizontal relationships (the other party could not have reasonably expected such an interpretation) as well as in cases of reverse vertical relationships (eg a national administrative authority suddenly changing its established administrative practice by relying on an EU law argument, without prior legislation to that effect in order that the results are foreseeable to those affected).

Thirdly, the prohibition of reaching an interpretative outcome *contra legem* comes from continental, in particular German, legal theory. There, a traditional distinction has been drawn between judicial decision-making within the law but outside its clear text (*praeter legem*) and decision-making against the law/statute (*contra legem*). In adjudication, the former might be possible, the latter is out of bounds.

What precisely might be reading of a provision *contra legem*? Does it mean only that a national authority cannot interpret a specific national provision as to amount to the textual denial of the original rule (an 'A' cannot become 'non-A' by the fiat of interpretation)? Or does it also mean that a national interpreter cannot start twisting and extensively modifying national law generally in order to reach 'an artificial or strained interpretation of national law'[56] only to achieve consistency with EU law?

From a recent decision in *Impact*,[57] it would appear that the Court had the latter, broader limit in mind. In that case, conformity of Irish law with EU law could be achieved by interpretation if retrospective effects of the national implementing Act were allowed. However, Irish law contains a general rule that precludes the retrospective application of legislation unless there is a clear and unambiguous indication to the contrary. The

---

[54] Case C-212/04 *Adeneler* [2006] ECR I-6057, paras 110 and 111. See also Case C-268/06 *Impact* [2008] ECR I-2483, paras 100 and 101; Joined Cases C-378–380/07 *Angelidaki* [2009] ECR I-3071, para 199; Case C-12/08 *Mono Car Styling* [2009] ECR I-6653, paras 61 and 63.

[55] Including, eg even the power of national administrators to set aside national law deemed incompatible with EU law, which is discussed in text accompanying nn 70 and 71.

[56] Opinion of AG Sharpston of 30 November 2006 in Case C-432/05 *Unibet* [2007] ECR I-2271, para 55.

[57] *Impact* (n 54).

national implementing Act contained, however, no such express provision. The Court concluded that:

> In the absence of such a provision, Community law – in particular the requirement for national law to be interpreted in conformity with Community law – cannot be interpreted as requiring the referring court to give [the relevant section of the national implementing Act] retrospective effect to the date by which [the Directive] should have been transposed, as the referring court would otherwise be constrained to interpret national law *contra legem.*[58]

In conclusion, indirect effect has been construed as a very robust duty incumbent upon all national authorities to ensure conformity with EU law in the process of interpretation. Originally perhaps construed as an alternative to direct effect, it soon became arguably more important than direct effect itself, and can reach into situations and relationships where direct effect cannot. In quantitative terms, consistent interpretation became the most important avenue for EU law penetration of the national legal orders in the process of adjudication. It is only in recent years that the Court has begun to set some boundaries to this originally limitless principle. These, however, remain yet to be properly explored.

5 Primacy

The principle of primacy of EU law means that in the case of conflict, EU law prevails over national law. In contrast to some aspects of direct effect, the principle of primacy poses more political than legal difficulties. In any type of large structure, in which the norms of multiple systems are supposed to coexist, sooner or later the question of their mutual hierarchy arises. What is striking with respect to the EU is the fact that even today questions of hierarchy, sovereignty, and the ultimate word remain unresolved. Both the Union and the Member States have different views on why and to what extent EU law is allowed to prevail over national law. Both of these views will be discussed in this section.

5.1 The Court's view

In *Van Gend en Loos,*[59] direct effect enabled the new legal order to penetrate independently into the national legal systems. The correlating question that had already surfaced in *Van Gend en Loos* was, however, with what legal force this occurs? Furthermore, what happens in the case of conflict between the directly effective Treaty provisions and national law?

5.1.1 Costa

The Court gave the answers to these questions a year later, in *Costa.*[60] The case concerned Italian legislation which was incompatible with the Treaty, but which was adopted after Italy joined the EEC. The question posed was whether such subsequent national legislation, encapsulating a clear expression of will of the national legislator, may unilaterally derogate from Treaty obligations.

---

[58] *Impact* (n 54) para 103.   [59] See n 2.
[60] Case 6/64 *Costa* [1964] ECR English Special Edition 585.

The resounding 'no' pronounced by the Court in reply to this question deserves to be repeated, as it also announces the ideological dimension of the European project:

> By contrast with ordinary international treaties, the EEC Treaty has created its own legal system which, on the entry into force of the Treaty, became an integral part of the legal systems of the Member States and which their courts are bound to apply.
>
> By creating a Community of unlimited duration, having its own institutions, its own personality, its own legal capacity and capacity of representation on the international plane and, more particularly, real powers stemming from a limitation of sovereignty or a transfer of powers from the States to the Community, the Member States have limited their sovereign rights, albeit within limited fields, and have thus created a body of law which binds both their nationals and themselves.
>
> The integration into the laws of each Member State of provisions which derive from the Community, and more generally the terms and the spirit of the Treaty, make it impossible for the States, as a corollary, to accord precedence to a unilateral and subsequent measure over a legal system accepted by them on a basis of reciprocity. Such a measure cannot therefore be inconsistent with that legal system. The executive force of Community law cannot vary from one State to another in deference to subsequent domestic laws, without jeopardizing the attainment of the objectives of the Treaty…
>
> It follows from all these observations that the law stemming from the Treaty, an independent source of law, could not, because of its special and original nature, be overridden by domestic legal provisions, however framed, without being deprived of its character as Community law and without the legal basis of the Community itself being called into question.
>
> The transfer by the States from their domestic legal system to the Community legal system of the rights and obligations arising under the Treaty carries with it a permanent limitation of their sovereign rights, against which a subsequent unilateral act incompatible with the concept of the Community cannot prevail.[61]

What the Court stated in *Costa* and further elaborated on in subsequent case law[62] is a claim for an unreserved, absolute EU law primacy: *all* EU law prevails over *all* national law. The basis for such a sweeping claim was, in the view of the Court, the *special and original nature* of the law stemming from the Treaty. Absent of any textual foundation to this effect in the Treaties themselves, the reasoning of the Court may appear somewhat circular: the special and original nature of the new Community requires the Community to have these special and original characteristics.

Primacy in combination with direct effect nonetheless provides for an efficient enforcement mechanism for EU law in national legal systems. The key to success is the *synergic effect* of both principles. One does not necessarily follow from the other but, together, they constitute a strong combination. This statement is best demonstrated by disassociating the two principles. Imagine: to have only primacy without direct effect would amount to something that is nominally supreme but in practice left outside the gates of the national legal order. To have direct effect without primacy would mean that the rank of EU law in the national legal systems would be left to the discretion of the individual national constitutions. Member State A could thus state that EU law takes precedence over national statutes

---

[61] Ibid, 593–594.

[62] Notably Case 11/70 *Internationale Handelsgesellschaft* [1970] ECR 1125; Case 106/77 *Simmenthal* [1978] ECR 629; Case C-213/89 *Factortame* [1990] ECR I-2433; Case C-119/05 *Lucchini* [2007] ECR I-6199; Case C-314/08 *Filipiak* [2009] ECR I-11049; Case C-409/06 *Winner Wetten* [2010] ECR I-8015; and, most recently, Case C-399/11 *Melloni*, judgment of 26 February 2013, nyr, with respect to the former 'third pillar' measures, notably, framework decisions.

but not the constitution, whereas Member State B might position EU law under the level of statutes, on the same level as derived legislation (statutory instruments).

To provide for both principles in almost one breath was a defining moment for EU law. Similarly to Christopher Columbus and his egg, the Court elegantly redefined the nature of the problem. It is said that when challenged that the discovery of the Americas was no great accomplishment, Columbus asked his critics to try to make an egg balance on its tip. After they had failed to do so, Columbus tapped the tip of the egg and made it stand on the crack. In a similar vein, instead of trying to explain to the Member States in future individual cases what is and what is not an effective enforcement of their international obligations, the Court pre-empted any national choice in this matter. It cracked national constitutional choices and gave EU law the same effects everywhere. Thus, in all the Member States, EU law is to have the same type of primacy over national law, irrespective of what the national constitution states with respect to the status of international law obligations in the national legal order. The choice made in *Costa* and *Van Gend en Loos* was perhaps not a legal revolution or a *coup d'état*,[63] but it was certainly a courageous choice which became *the* key element of the entire EU legal system.

The importance of this initial choice may be highlighted by contrasting the EU legal order with another advanced system of international cooperation, such as the European Convention on Human Rights. Absent any similar bold, original choice by the European Court of Human Rights that would have redefined the rules of the game, the status and effectiveness of domestic implementation and enforcement of the Convention is left to the constitutional systems of the signatory parties. This means that for some signatory parties, the Convention has the status of a national constitutional act, in others it is below the constitution but above statutory law, yet in others it is implemented by a simple statute. In the UK and Ireland, up until 1998 and 2003 respectively, the Convention was not domestically implemented at all.[64]

5.1.2 The scope and effect of primacy

There are three important aspects of the primacy principle which ought to be highlighted. First, primacy of EU law over national law means *primacy in application* in the individual case at hand. Primacy *does not affect the validity* of the national law provision in question. The principle of primacy of EU law requires only that the conflicting national provision is set aside. It shall be left non-applied in the individual case. The national provision, however, continues to be a valid part of the national legal order unless it is amended or repealed by the competent national authorities,[65] for example the legislator or the national constitutional court if the latter has such power under national law.

The underlying logic of primacy in application is one of two independent sets of norms: EU law and national law. Both sets influence each other, they interact, but neither of them is hierarchically supreme.[66] Norms of either set can be created or annulled exclusively by the institutions of that given set. National law can only be invalidated by the national institutions and EU law by the EU institutions.[67]

---

[63] See the discussion of *Costa* as the 'juridical coup d'état' by A Stone Sweet in M Poiares Maduro and L Azoulai, *The Past and Future of EU Law* (Oxford: Hart Publishing, 2010) 202.

[64] For further discussion of fundamental rights and the ECHR, see chapter 9.

[65] Joined Cases C-10–22/97 *IN.CO.GE* [1998] ECR I-6307, para 21; Case C-314/08 *Filipiak* [2009] ECR I-11049, para 83.

[66] That is also why this chapter uses the notion of 'primacy' and not 'supremacy'. Apart from the fact that the case law of the Court consistently refers to 'primacy' and not to 'supremacy' of EU law, the term primacy also better captures the nature of the principle, which is primacy in application, not hierarchical supremacy.

[67] With respect to judicial challenges to validity, only the Court can invalidate EU acts – Case 314/85 *Foto-Frost* [1987] ECR 4199. On the other hand, the Court can only declare a national rule incompatible with EU law. It cannot annul it.

Therefore, a national provision that was declared incompatible with EU law in a case falling within the scope of EU law and set aside by a national court or administrator can later be applied in purely national situations outside the scope of EU law. Until repealed, it remains a valid part of national law. Equally, in less fortunate scenarios, one court within one Member State may reach the conclusion that a provision of national law is incompatible with EU law and set it aside. Deciding in a parallel or even later case, a different court within the same legal system may decide that the same national law is compatible with EU law. Until there is a decision by a higher court within the national judicial hierarchy which binds both lower courts involved or a decision of the Court given on a preliminary ruling, neither of the lower courts is per se wrong.

Secondly, as already apparent from *Costa*, the primacy in application is, at least from the point of view of the Court, *unreserved and absolute*, certainly with respect to the *internal* acts of the Member States.[68] It is absolute in two dimensions: hierarchical and temporal. All EU law includes, indeed, all potential sources of EU law: primary law, including since the Lisbon Treaty also the Charter; general principles of EU law; and all sources of binding EU secondary law, such as directives. Any of these sources then prevails over all national law, including national constitutional provisions.[69] Furthermore, as was already apparent from *Costa*, from the point of view of the Court, EU law also prevails over subsequent national legislation.

Thirdly, the primacy of EU law empowers all national judges, from a court of first instance to the supreme jurisdiction, to set aside incompatible national laws. They can do so of their own motion, at whatever stage of procedure, and irrespective of what national law states in that regard.[70] They do not have to ask the Court before doing so.[71] However, what is perhaps more significant from a constitutional point of view is that the Court has extended the same powers to all bodies of the Member States, which means also to *national administrators*. National administrative authorities may also disregard national law in order to enforce directly effective provisions of EU law.[72]

The rise of 'omnipotent administrators' may cause concern. In the liberal rule of law tradition, the national administration/executive is the bound power. It is allowed to act only and exclusively on the basis and within the law, to which it is subordinate. From the point of view of the requirement of (strict) legality of all administrative action, there is something deeply perturbing about the idea that, for instance, every tax commissioner in every district town is entitled to disregard whenever she pleases (of her own motion) an act of parliament or even the national constitution, simply because she thinks that it is not compatible with a provision of the EU Value Added Tax Directive.

On the other hand, extending such powers to administrators is no doubt logical from the point of view of EU law. The Court proceeds from an international law holistic conception of a State: all Member State bodies are obliged to enforce EU law effectively within their respective competence. The fear that also extending the principles of primacy and direct effect to national administrations would amount to administration getting out of control is normatively as well as empirically unwarranted. Normatively, membership of the EU

---

[68] A specific exception to the unreserved primacy of EU law is provided by Art 351 TFEU with respect to international agreements concluded with third countries by a Member State before its accession to the EU. This traditional exception was, however, considerably narrowed by the Court in Joined Cases C-402/05 P and C-415/05 P *Kadi* [2008] ECR I-6351.   [69] Case C-285/98 *Kreil* [2000] ECR I-69.

[70] *Simmenthal* (n 62) para 21; *Lucchini* (n 62) para 61; *Filipiak* (n 62) para 81; *Winner Wetten* (n 62) para 56.   [71] Case C-555/07 *Kücükdeveci* [2010] ECR I-365, paras 53–55.

[72] Notably Case 103/88 *Costanzo* [1989] ECR 1839, para 31 or Case C-198/01 *CIF* [2003] ECR I-8055, paras 49–58.

means that 'national' legality became 'European' legality, as the pool of sources of law has enlarged. Empirically and pragmatically, even if applying EU law to its fullest and occasionally getting it wrong, national administrative authorities would hardly be doing anything other than that which occurs on a daily basis with respect to national law. Finally, in the same way as national law and its application, and also with respect to the administrative (mis)application of EU law, national administrations remain subject to full national judicial review, which naturally also includes questions of EU law.[73]

5.2 **The national views**

The story told so far was the Court's version, capturing the origins, justification, as well as effects of the principle of primacy of EU law through the case law of the Court. However, the nobility (or perhaps the plight, depending on the point of view) of the European project is the unresolved nature of the question of ultimate sovereignty: who has the last word within the Union? Is it the EU or the Member States?

This unresolved issue surfaces most clearly when views concerning the primacy of EU law and the therein-lurking question of sovereignty are articulated. On the one hand, is the robust vision of the Court postulating that EU law must have primacy owing to its special and original nature stemming directly from the Treaties. On the other hand, the approach of the Member States articulated in the decisions of their constitutional and/or supreme courts provides a considerably different narrative.

There is natural diversity in articulations of national responses to the Court's claims for absolute primacy of EU law. It reflects the richness of national constitutional traditions as well as nation-specific concerns. Still, the premises on which most of the national systems base their answers are, with the exception of distinctively monist systems such as the Netherlands or Estonia, remarkably similar.[74] This is perhaps not that surprising for two reasons. First, a national constitutional or supreme court is likely to perceive its role as the guardian of the integrity of the *national* constitutional system. Thus, responses given from such a position to claims for absolute primacy of EU law formulated by the Court are likely to start from similar assumptions and voice similar concerns. Secondly, a number of constitutional courts in 'old' as well as 'new' Europe have been under the distinct influence of the German Federal Constitutional Court[75] and its position vis-à-vis primacy of EU law articulated early in the 1970s.[76] The same ideas frequently 'migrate' horizontally around Europe, with national courts being well versed in the reservations expressed by others.

In a nutshell, the national responses to the Court's absolute primacy claim could be on the level of an ideal model formulated as follows:

(a) The basis for the system of EU law is not its 'special and original nature', but the Treaties signed by the Member States as an obligation under *international* law. The last

---

[73] See further, with a discussion of examples, M Bobek, 'Thou Shalt Have Two Masters: The Application of European Law by Administrative Authorities in the New Member States' [2008] 1 *Review of European Administrative Law* 62.

[74] See further, eg A-M Slaughter, A Stone Sweet, and JHH Weiler (eds), *The European Court of Justice and National Courts: Doctrine and Jurisprudence* (Oxford: Hart Publishing, 1998); for the new Member States, see eg A Łazowski (ed), *Brave New World: The Application of EU Law in the New Member States* (The Hague: TMC Asser Press, 2010).

[75] For detail, see M Bobek, *Comparative Reasoning in European Supreme Courts* (Oxford: Oxford University Press, 2013) 159, 255–257.

[76] In particular BVerfGE 37, 271 (*Solange I*) (in English [1974] CMLR 540). See also BVerfGE 73, 339 (*Solange II*) ([1987] 3 CMLR 225); BVerfGE 89, 155 (*Maastricht*) ([1994] 1 CMLR 57); BVerfGE 123, 267 (*Lisbon*) ([2010] 3 CMLR 276); and BVerfGE 126, 286 (*Honeywell*) ([2011] 1 CMLR 1067).

word in shaping the Union and its law rests with the Member States; so does the sovereignty. They remain, in the term coined by the German Federal Constitutional Court, the 'Masters of the Treaties'. The Member States simply decided to transfer the exercise of some competences to an advanced international organization. They have not given carte blanche to any irreversible 'Union of destiny'.

(b) *Internally*, within a given Member State, the reason for application of EU law on the national territory, including its primacy and direct effect, is the national constitutional mandate with which the constitution-maker expressed the wish to join the EU and/or is encapsulated in the respective 'Euro-article' of the national constitution. Therefore, in the eyes of the national constitution, EU law is hierarchically either *under* or *beyond* the national constitution, but not above it. The idea that EU law has primacy over the national constitution might be silently accepted as the outcome in an individual case, but hardly in normative and conceptual terms. Consequently, a clear constitutional wish to negate an obligation stemming from EU law or even a constitutional command to withdraw from the Union would take precedence over any EU law obligations.

(c) If it is the 'Euro-article' in the national constitution that opens the gates for domestic application of EU law, then a national guardian of constitutionality is entitled to check whether or not the Union remains within the powers conferred upon it by the national constitution. With such reasoning, most of the national constitutional courts would assume the power to review, for the purposes of the application of EU law on their territory, whether an EU act remained within the powers transferred to the Union (intra vires) or whether it went beyond (ultra vires). Assuming such power of review of EU acts in principle may not mean that it will be effectively exercised in individual cases. The national courts will frequently reserve such residual review for repetitive or manifest violations of the principle of conferral.

There are, of course, many national variations of these three rudimentary points that simply focus on the political ontology, constitutional hierarchy, and the question of control/review. The three points made were only intended to illustrate the starting assumptions for the position of national courts. Furthermore, around these three points, the themes have changed over the years. The motive for original reservations on the part of the Member States back in the 1970s was the lack of protection of fundamental rights by the then EEC. Later, in the 1990s, the main theme became finality of the integration process and the nature of the Union, especially after the Maastricht Treaty. With further expansion of the Union's competences after Maastricht and Amsterdam, the concerns voiced in the national constitutional jurisprudence moved on to setting limits to further integration. 'Hardcore' or 'unalterable' cores of national constitutions began to be emphasized, later to merge with concerns about the preservation of the national constitutional identity.

Most recently, the question of genuine protection of fundamental rights within the Union has surfaced again, this time in a somewhat different garb. It is primarily perhaps not the Union itself which would not be able to protect individuals against the EU institutions, but the multitude of mutual assistance and horizontal enforcement mechanisms in criminal, administrative, or civil matters introduced over the last decade. With the EU and the Court pushing for long-ranging horizontal mutual recognition in these areas, the individual and her fundamental rights protection may get lost in the cracks between the systems. Finally, the global 'fight against terrorism' since 2001, in which ends are put before means, also fuels the reappearance of effective fundamental rights protection as one of the key reservations to absolute primacy of EU law.

However, the beauty of the European constitutional project lies in its ability to function on the basis of mutual respect and voluntary compliance, not on blunt coercion. Although both the Court and national courts see primacy and sovereignty in quite different lights, both agree that EU law is to be given primacy in the individual case. Both thus arrive at the same outcome, however, following very different reasoning. As long as neither of the parties rocks the boat, that is, starts posing the wrong questions, such pragmatic balance can function very well.

6 National procedures for enforcing EU law rights in the Member States

As already explained in the opening section of this chapter, in the absence of relevant EU provisions on the matter, it is for each national legal system to choose and provide for institutions, procedures, and principles according to which EU law will be enforced at the national level. So far, this chapter has addressed three key principles of national enforcement of EU law: direct effect, consistent interpretation, and primacy. In this section, we turn to the requirements EU law has formulated with respect to procedures and remedies for enforcing EU law in the Member States in general terms.

In the words of the Court, the general rule is that

> in the absence of Community rules governing the matter, it is for the domestic legal system of each Member State to designate the courts and tribunals having jurisdiction and to lay down the detailed procedural rules governing actions for safeguarding rights which individuals derive from Community law...the detailed procedural rules governing actions for safeguarding an individual's rights under Community law must be no less favourable than those governing similar domestic actions (principle of equivalence) and must not render practically impossible or excessively difficult the exercise of rights conferred by Community law (principle of effectiveness).[77]

If transcribed into a more accessible form of successive steps, the Court is essentially saying:

(a) if the EU has its own procedural rules (of legislative or judicial origin), they take precedence over national rules;

(b) if there are no EU rules on the matter, it is the national procedural responsibility to enforce EU law following the general national rules and procedures;

(c) *but*, there are two qualifications to such full national procedural autonomy:

   (i) requirement of equivalence;

   (ii) requirement of effectiveness.

---

[77] *Impact* (n 57), paras 44–46. This is a more recent statement of the rule going back to Case 33/76 *Rewe-Zentralfinanz* [1976] ECR 1989, para 5 and Case 45/76 *Comet* [1976] ECR 2043, para 13; since then repeated in dozens of cases: more recently, eg Case C-432/05 *Unibet* [2007] ECR I-2271, para 39; *Impact* (n 54), paras 44 and 45; C-40/08 *Asturcom* [2009] ECR I-9579, para 41; Joined Cases C-317–320/08 *Alassini* [2010] ECR I-2213, paras 47–49; Case C-249/11 *Byankov*, judgment of 4 October 2012, nyr, para 69; Case C-93/12 *ET Agrokonsulting-04-Velko Stoyanov*, judgment of 27 June 2013, nyr, para 35.

The first step is hardly a surprise: the 'federal' choice, if exercised, pre-empts local choices. In contrast to the previously examined key principles of domestic application of EU law, which the case law of the Court essentially unified, a look at procedural rules for national enforcement of EU law offers a much more fragmented, mosaic-like picture. There is no European code of administrative, civil, or criminal procedure. The default procedures thus remain national, to which an EU 'brick' is sometimes and somewhat randomly added here or there.

The added bricks can be of *legislative* or *judicial* origin. EU legislation can either unify or harmonize certain questions or segments of national procedures. *Unification* of national procedures ensues by regulations which provide for a special regime in certain specific areas of procedure. Examples in this category include Regulation 44/2001 (Brussels I)[78] or Regulation 1346/2000.[79] Although limited in scope, such regulations attempt to cover the entire subject matter in question and exclude the parallel application of national laws in the same area. Thus, for instance, a German judge who is asked to enforce a final judgment issued by an Irish court in a commercial dispute ought to proceed by applying the relevant provisions of the Brussels I Regulation and not the general German provisions on the enforcement of foreign judgments.

Legislative *harmonization* in the area of national procedures for enforcement of EU law proceeds by directives. It seeks to approximate, but not to replace, national procedural rules.[80] Thus, for instance, a Czech administrative authority providing assistance and enforcing a (value added) tax decision for a Finnish administrative authority will proceed on the basis of the Czech code of tax procedure even if, in the background, both authorities are acting within the scope of application of the same directive.[81]

Finally, EU procedural rules can also be of judicial origin. Over the years, the case law of the Court has touched upon a number of elements of national procedural rules: access to court; standing; legal aid; time limits; interim relief, and injunctions in particular; *ex officio* application of EU law by national judges; evidence; finality of decisions (*res iudicata*); and many others. A notable example in this category, finding itself on the borderline between procedural and substantive law, is also the principle of State liability.

6.1 The not-so-autonomous national procedural autonomy

The fact that unless EU law provides otherwise, it is the national procedures which will govern the enforcement of EU law in the Member States, is often referred to as the principle of

---

[78] Council Regulation (EC) No 44/2001 of 22 December 2000 on jurisdiction and the recognition and enforcement of judgments in civil and commercial matters (OJ [2001] L12/1), which from 10 January 2015 will be replaced by Regulation (EU) No 1215/2012 of 12 December 2012 on jurisdiction and the recognition and enforcement of judgments in civil and commercial matters (OJ [2012] L351/1).

[79] Council Regulation (EC) No 1346/2000 of 29 May 2000 on insolvency proceedings (OJ [2000] L160/1).

[80] Examples include Council Directive 89/665/EEC of 21 December 1989 on the coordination of the laws, regulations and administrative provisions relating to the application of review procedures to the award of public supply and public works contracts (OJ [1989] L395/33) or Directive 2004/48/EC of 29 April 2004 on the enforcement of intellectual property rights (OJ [2004] L157/45). In recent years, a notable number of such harmonizing instruments have been adopted under the former third pillar (Justice and Home Affairs), eg Council Framework Decision 2002/584/JHA of 13 June 2002 on the European arrest warrant and the surrender procedures between Member States (OJ [2002] L190/1; see chapter 25) and EU legislation on asylum procedures (see chapter 26).

[81] Council Directive 2008/55/EC of 26 May 2008 on mutual assistance for the recovery of claims relating to certain levies, duties, taxes and other measures (OJ [2008] L150/28).

'national procedural autonomy'. The use of such a notion may be somewhat unfortunate: it implies freedom and choice for the Member States, which is in fact not present. When it comes to national enforcement of EU law, there is no 'autonomous' space free of EU law on the national level.

It is important to understand in this context that in contrast to the *legislative* unification or harmonization of national procedural rules, the *judicial* reach – that is, unification by the case law of the Court – is limitless. The exercise of EU legislative competence is governed by the principle of conferral. The Union can legislate only in specific areas attributed to it by the Treaties. Conversely, the case law of the Court can touch upon any aspect of national procedure, provided that the question relates to national enforcement of EU law-based rights and it has been submitted to the Court on a preliminary ruling. The logic of EU legislation is one of *area-specific, conferred* competence. In contrast, the logic of the Court's engagement with national enforcement of EU law is *functional and transversal*. It is not limited to any field or area of law.

All national procedural rules may therefore be subject to the dual requirement of equivalence and/or effectiveness, provided that EU law is involved in the individual case at hand. They may involve any part of the national judicial process: from rules on jurisdiction through access to court, fees, representation, to finality of judgments and their binding force. Seen from this perspective, it might be somewhat misplaced to refer to the original national procedural choice as 'national procedural autonomy', at least if we understand 'autonomy' in its dictionary sense as the ability to act and make decisions without being controlled by anyone else.[82]

6.2 From equivalence/effectiveness to the principle of effective judicial protection

The current form of national procedures for enforcing EU law on the national level is a somewhat odd mongrel. The default provisions will be the national procedural provisions. These might, however, be altered in specific sectors or in relation to specific questions by pieces of EU legislation or requirements formulated by the Court. Furthermore, the degree of unification/harmonization with respect to individual questions might also differ considerably: from full-scale unification to just a few accidental provisions relating to procedure hidden in a directive chiefly dealing with substantive issues. All this will remain interlinked with national provisions, without which national enforcement of EU law could not operate.

Most importantly, however, any other non-harmonized questions of national procedure are subject to the dual requirement of equivalence and/or effectiveness. *Equivalence* is in essence a prohibition of discrimination. EU law-based claims cannot be treated less favourably than 'purely national' claims. Thus, for instance, a national law cannot provide that the time limit for requesting the repayment of overpaid value added tax (which is an EU-harmonized tax) is six months, whereas the requests for the reimbursement of overpaid income tax (which is the competence of the Member States) can be made within two years following the end of the taxable period in question.

---

[82] See further M Bobek, 'Why There is No Principle of 'Procedural Autonomy' of the Member States' in H-W Micklitz and B de Witte (eds), *The European Court of Justice and the Autonomy of the Member States* (Antwerp: Intersentia, 2012).

Effectiveness is more difficult to capture. It requires not only that the enforcement of EU law-based claims cannot be rendered *practically impossible*, but also not *excessively difficult*. Impossible means impossible. It refers to situations where, for instance, an appropriate remedy would not be available at all. It would be equally unavailable for both EU law-based as well as purely national claims. Excessively difficult, on the other hand, relies more on subjective visions of the appropriate level of 'difficulty' claimants ought (not) to be facing when vindicating their rights under EU law. Moreover, 'excessively difficult' might mean something quite different to a multinational company with a dedicated litigation department than to a small high street business, even if both legal persons are making an identical claim.

The recent case law of the Court[83] has begun to discuss issues concerning national remedies more in terms of *effective judicial protection*. The dual requirement of equivalence and/or effectiveness is still present, but the rhetoric has shifted. This terminological move corresponds to the changes brought about by the Treaty of Lisbon. First, the Treaty of Lisbon inserted a new provision into Article 19(1) TFEU, which reads 'Member States shall provide remedies sufficient to ensure effective legal protection in the fields covered by Union law'. Secondly, Article 47 of the Charter of Fundamental Rights of the European Union, which became binding primary law, also guarantees the 'right to an effective remedy and to a fair trial'. Thus, not only with respect to judicial protection but also in other areas, the Charter has become the focal point of judicial discourse in the Court after Lisbon.

6.3 **State liability**

One of the examples of a more advanced judicial unification of a type of remedy is State liability for breaches of EU law. The principle made its first appearance in *Francovich*, where the Court stated that

> the principle of State liability for harm caused to individuals by breaches of Community law for which the State can be held responsible is inherent in the system of the Treaty.[84]

Since then, the conditions for State liability have been slightly reformulated by the Court. The current test, as articulated in *Brasserie du Pêcheur/Factortame*, reads:

> Community law confers a right to reparation where three conditions are met: the rule of law infringed must be intended to confer rights on individuals; the breach must be sufficiently serious; and there must be a direct causal link between the breach of the obligation resting on the State and the damage sustained by the injured parties.[85]

---

[83] eg *Impact* (n 54) paras 43–48; Case C-279/09 *DEB* [2010] ECR I-13880, paras 29–33; Case C-177/10 *Rosado Santana* [2011] ECR I-7907, paras 87–89; *Alassini* (n 77) paras 46–49; *ET Agrokonsulting-04-Velko Stoyanov* (n 77) para 59.

[84] *Francovich and Bonifaci* (n 13) para 35.

[85] Joined Cases C-46/93 and C-48/93 *Brasserie du Pêcheur/Factortame* [1996] ECR I-1029, para 51. More recently, eg C-278/05 *Robins* [2007] ECR I-1059, para 69; C-445/06 *Danske Slagterier* [2009] ECR I-2119, para 20; C-118/08 *Transportes Urbanos* [2010] ECR I-635, para 30; Case C-429/09 *Fuß* [2010] ECR I-12167, para 47; Case C-420/11 *Leth*, judgment of 14 March 2013, nyr, para 41.

Restating the test in a more accessible way reflecting the traditional categories of non-contractual (tortuous) liability, there are in fact five conditions in the test announced by the Court:

(a) a wrong (an act or an omission violating EU law)

   (i) of a legal provision which was intended to confer rights on individuals, and

   (ii) the wrong was sufficiently serious;

(b) damage;

(c) causal link between the wrong and the damage.

Conditions (a), (b), and (c) constitute the essence of any regime of tortious liability (non-contractual liability in civil law terms) of public authorities. The two EU-specific conditions are (i) and (ii). They represent qualifying factors with respect to the types of wrongs for which a State may incur liability. Not all violations of EU law committed by Member States will qualify, only those committed with respect to EU law provisions conferring rights on individuals and (cumulatively) those which are sufficiently serious.

Since *Francovich*, the case law of the Court has expressly confirmed that the Member State may be liable for violations of EU law committed by any branch of government (State organ). The fact that the administration may be liable for public wrongs was perhaps not that contentious.[86] The more contested scenarios, at least in some Member States, included the statement that a Member State may be liable for the acts or omissions attributable to the (sovereign) legislator.[87] The same applies to judicial violations of EU law, committed by lower courts as well as by national courts of last instance.[88] The Court proceeds from an international law holistic point of view: the duty correctly to implement and enforce EU law rests on the Member State as a unity. Equally, a potential violation of the primary duty may be committed by any body of the State.

Moreover, liability for breaches of EU law is not limited to the Member States. The Union may also incur non-contractual liability. The conditions are the same as those with respect to wrongs committed by the Member States.[89] Conversely, potential violations of EU law committed by individuals (private persons) are subject to general national regimes of non-contractual liability. The case law of the Court has so far been limited to mandating the Member States to allow for such type of liability, without, however, unifying its conditions.[90]

7 Connecting the dots: the interplay of the different principles

After having introduced the rules and the key principles for the application of EU law in the Member States, this section examines their interplay in greater detail. The following case study is based on *Audiolux*,[91] a 2009 decision of the Court. The facts of the original case have been modified for the purpose of this case study.

---

[86] See eg *Danske Slagterier* (n 85) or Case C-5/94 *Hedley Lomas* [1996] ECR I-2553.

[87] Typically for a failure to implement a directive or for implementing it incorrectly. See eg Case C-178/94 *Dillenkofer* [1996] ECR I-4845 or Case C-392/93 *British Telecommunications* [1996] ECR I-1631.

[88] Case C-224/01 *Köbler* [2003] ECR I-10239 or Case C-173/03 *Traghetti del Mediterraneo* [2006] ECR I-5177.   [89] Art 340 TFEU and Case C-352/98 P *Bergaderm* [2000] ECR I-5291, para 41.

[90] C-453/99 *Courage* [2001] ECR I-6297, paras 26–28; Joined Cases C-295–298/04 *Manfredi* [2006] ECR I-6619, paras 60–64; Case C-536/11 *Donau Chemie*, judgment of 6 June 2013, nyr, paras 22–25.

[91] *Audiolux* (n 39). For further background and insightful analysis, see also the Opinion of AG Trstenjak of 30 June 2009 in this case.

Case study 6.1: *Audiolux*

Audiolux was a minority shareholder in the RTL Group, a public limited company having its registered office in Luxembourg, whose shares are traded on the stock exchanges in Luxembourg, Brussels, and London. In the course of several stock market operations in 2001, the Bertelsmann company acquired most of the RTL shares. One of these operations included a shares swap, whereby the Groupe Bruxelles Lambert transferred its holding of 30 per cent of the RTL shares in exchange for 25 per cent of Bertelsmann shares. Later, Bertelsmann bought a further 22 per cent of RTL shares from the British group Pearson Television. Finally, once Bertelsmann had acquired control of RTL, it delisted RTL's securities from the London stock exchange, that is, it removed RTL shares from the London stock exchange, which meant that they could no longer be publicly traded. At the same time, Bertelsmann also decreased the basic capital of RTL.

Audiolux and other minority shareholders disagreed with the steps taken by Bertelsmann. They brought a number of actions in Luxembourg courts against Bertelsmann. In one of the actions, Audiolux asked the Luxembourg court to order Bertelsmann to offer Audiolux the opportunity to exchange its shares in RTL for shares in Bertelsmann under the same conditions as those offered to the Groupe Bruxelles Lambert. Audiolux suggested that when a major shareholder transfers its shares to another, minority shareholders are entitled to equal treatment by the majority shareholder. The key question which arose was thus, simply put, is there anything in EU law that would oblige Bertelsmann to treat all shareholders in the same way and offer them the same conditions?

The area of company law has been extensively harmonized by EU law. There are a number of binding as well as non-binding EU acts in this area,[92] which also regulate the question of trade in shares and the position of minority shareholders. Most importantly, Article 42 of Directive 77/91/EEC[93] provides that 'For the purposes of the implementation of this Directive, the laws of the Member States shall ensure equal treatment to all shareholders who are in the same position'. The fifth recital to the same Directive adds that:

> it is necessary…that the Member States' laws relating to the increase or reduction of capital ensure that the principles of equal treatment of shareholders in the same position and of protection of creditors whose claims exist prior to the decision on reduction are observed and harmonised.

Against such a factual and legal background, what would be the potential remedies open to Audiolux in the national legal system(s)?

First of all, Audiolux naturally needs to decide where and how to pursue its claim. In doing so, it will rely on existing national procedural rules in Luxembourg or elsewhere. However, as the claim is within the scope of EU law *ratione materiae*, any national procedures, judicial or administrative, will be subject to the EU requirement of *effective judicial protection* (the dual requirement of *equivalence and/or effectiveness*). Thus for instance, if the national legal system did not provide any type of remedy for the protection of minority shareholders, or made it subject to very onerous or impossible requirements relating to access to court, jurisdiction, standing, and so on, EU law would already be triggered.[94]

---

[92] For a more detailed overview, which is not necessary for the purposes of this case study, see the Opinion of AG Trstenjak at paras 3–16 and 75–83.

[93] Second Council Directive 77/91/EEC of 13 December 1976 on coordination of safeguards which, for the protection of the interests of members and others, are required by Member States of companies within the meaning of the second paragraph of Article 58 of the Treaty, in respect of the formation of public limited liability companies and the maintenance and alteration of their capital, with a view to making such safeguards equivalent (OJ [1977] L26/1). [94] See recently, eg *ET Agrokonsulting-04-Velko Stoyanov* (n 77).

Once in a court,[95] Audiolux might wish to rely directly on the provisions of the previously cited Directive 77/91/EC. It could suggest that Article 42 of the Directive is *directly effective*. Is Article 42 sufficiently clear, precise, and unconditional? With the implementation period for a directive from 1977 clearly passed, the question would turn on whether or not Article 42 contains a self-executing, justiciable rule of behaviour, which could be applied directly by a national court. Taking into account that Article 42 is a categorical, clear prohibition of discrimination between minority and majority shareholders, the answer would most likely be yes. Such a provision could produce direct effects.

There is, however, a different problem. Both Audiolux as well as Bertelsmann are private undertakings. Even on the very extensive notion of 'State' adopted by the Court, it is impossible to claim that Bertelsmann would be an emanation of the Member State.[96] Thus, Audiolux finds itself in a horizontal situation, in which it cannot rely on the direct effect of directives as against another individual,[97] Bertelsmann.

With direct effect excluded, how else could Audiolux try to bring Article 42 of the Directive and/or other provisions of EU law back into the game? First, there is *indirect effect*. For this purpose, Audiolux would have to find a provision in national law which could be interpreted in conformity with Article 42 of the Directive. Such national provision could be even a general one, a general prohibition of discrimination, even of a constitutional nature. As the lists of prohibited grounds of discrimination in national or European catalogues tend to be demonstrative only,[98] further grounds might be added judicially.

If Audiolux were able to convince a national judge to interpret a national provision in conformity with the Directive, then Bertelsmann might indeed face a judicially imposed obligation of treating Audiolux in the same way as Groupe Bruxelles Lambert. All that a national court would do is to apply its national constitution or statute *interpreted in conformity* with a provision of EU law. Bertelsmann might try to counter-suggest that such an interpretation violates legal certainty, thus reaching one of the limits introduced by the Court on indirect effect.[99] Such assessment would require a deeper immersion into previous national judicial and administrative practice in order to establish that such an interpretation would indeed be unexpected and unforeseeable. But, as there is no general ban on worsening an individual's position in horizontal relationships via consistent interpretation, indirect effect would be possible in a similar situation.

If a national judge were either unwilling or unable to interpret national law in conformity with EU law, Audiolux might try to claim that equal treatment of shareholders is a *general principle of EU law*. As such, it would transcend any material or temporal limits to its application expressed in the Directive. It would become horizontally applicable across EU law, or certainly within all EU company law. The beauty as well as the danger of general principles is that they know no bounds: temporal, material, or personal. As the Court does not 'create' them, but just 'discovers' them, they apply to any type of legal relationship irrespective of the temporal applicability of mere directives or regulations.

In its judgment in *Audiolux*, the Court was faced with this precise question. After having canvassed a number of EU law instruments issued over the course of three decades, the Court concluded that there is no general principle of equal treatment of shareholders in EU

---

[95] Or before an administrative authority, entrusted with supervision and regulation of a national securities market, as is the case in a number of Member States. However, as already previously discussed (text accompanying nn 70 and 71), the obligations of the national administrative authority would be largely the same.

[96] *Foster* (n 36).   [97] *Marshall* and *Faccini Dori* (nn 33 and 35).

[98] See eg Art 21(1) of the Charter or Art 14 ECHR – both lists are demonstrative only.

[99] See the text accompanying n 54.

law. Thus, relying on a general principle of EU law of equal treatment of shareholders would not be possible for Audiolux.

Finally, provided that Audiolux was not able to convince the national court in respect of any of the previous three grounds, it may try to claim damages from the Member State for its failure properly to implement Directive 77/91/EC. Assume that Luxembourg or any other Member State had indeed failed to implement Article 42 of the Directive. Could a claim for *State liability* succeed?

Examining the conditions for State liability,[100] Audiolux suffered actual and certain damage (calculated as the difference between the current value of its RTL shares and the price paid to the majority shareholder for the same shares). The damage is in causal link to the Luxembourg failure properly to implement the Directive (the wrong): if Article 42 of the Directive were transposed into national law, Audiolux should be treated the same. Thus, Article 42 of the Directive can be construed as conferring rights upon individuals (the guarantee of equal treatment).

The remaining and, in fact, hardly predictable question is whether or not the breach could be qualified as 'sufficiently serious'. The problem with this condition is its conceptual lack of clarity. In the practice of the Court, 'sufficiently serious breach' is a leftover category, which may include anything from subjective elements of liability (fault, contributory negligence, style of exercise of administrative discretion) to objective questions (clarity and precision of the EU provisions concerned). However, taking into account the categorical imperative of Article 42, which could even be construed as being directly effective, it could be suggested that the Member State had little discretion when implementing the Directive and that its failure to do so might indeed be sufficiently serious.

8 Conclusion

There is no doubt that the 'remedial landscape' in national cases involving EU law outlined in this chapter is rather complex. It will also be highly contextual, depending on national legislation and the approach of national judges. In some Member States, judges might be ready to set aside national rules or to twist them extensively in order to secure conformity with EU law. In other States, judges might perceive their role to be one of much more self-restraint. The highly valued unity and the often invoked effectiveness of EU law might frequently represent just a glowing idea, hovering over the surface of the dark waters of the real life of EU law in national courts.

One of the problems, perhaps *the* problem of a system of remedies construed in such a way, is the lack of foreseeability and predictability. Imagine that you were asked to provide legal counsel to a company or individual, for instance in the case study to either Audiolux or Bertelsmann. Would you be able to advise your client as to what the courts would decide? The tension between the requirement of effectiveness of national enforcement of EU law and the requirement of legal certainty and also in respect of national procedural choices, already introduced at the beginning of this chapter, clearly rises to the surface.

This is unfortunate and somewhat paradoxical. One of the reasons for which the Court refused to allow the horizontal direct effect of directives was the argument of legal certainty.

---

[100] *Brasserie du Pêcheur/Factortame* (n 85).

The simultaneous prohibition of the horizontal direct effect of directives and the massive building of alternative avenues for directives' reach into horizontal relationships, such as indirect effect or the general principles of law, hardly helped to safeguard legal certainty.

Finally, it is unlikely that there will be dramatic changes in the area examined in this chapter in the immediate future. There will naturally be new case law, both European and national, which will further develop and shape the effects of EU law in the Member States. However, the area is likely to remain a case law-defined and driven system. Large-scale legislative projects relating to national procedures and remedies which could be translated into binding legislation are unlikely to emerge in the near future. Furthermore, considering that the mood within the Union today, and in particular in the Member States, is scarcely supportive of judicial expansionism, 'system maintenance' might be a more appropriate policy for the immediate future.

Further reading

M AVBELJ AND J KOMÁREK (eds), *Constitutional Pluralism in the European Union and Beyond* (Oxford: Hart Publishing, 2012)

M BOBEK, 'Of Feasibility and Silent Elephants: The Legitimacy of the Court of Justice through the Eyes of National Courts' in M Adams et al (eds), *Judging Europe's Judges: The Legitimacy of the Case Law of the European Court of Justice Examined* (Oxford: Hart Publishing, 2013).

P CRAIG, 'The Legal Effects of Directives: Policy, Rules and Exceptions' (2009) 34 *European Law Review* 349

P CRAIG, 'The European Union Act 2011: Locks, Limits and Legality' (2011) 48 *Common Market Law Review* 1915

A DASHWOOD, 'From *Van Duyn* to *Mangold* via *Marshall*: Reducing Direct Effect to Absurdity' (2006–7) 9 *Cambridge Yearbook of European Legal Studies* 81

G DE BÚRCA AND JHH WEILER (eds), *The Worlds of European Constitutionalism* (Cambridge: Cambridge University Press, 2012)

B DE WITTE, 'Direct Effect, Supremacy and the Nature of the Legal Order' in P Craig and G de Búrca (eds), *The Evolution of EU Law* (2nd edn, Oxford: Oxford University Press, 2011)

M DOUGAN, *National Remedies before the Court of Justice* (Oxford: Hart Publishing, 2004)

M DOUGAN, 'When Worlds Collide! Competing Visions of the Relationship between Direct Effect and Supremacy' (2007) 44 *Common Market Law Review* 931

A ŁAZOWSKI (ed), *Brave New World: The Application of EU Law in the New Member States* (The Hague: TMC Asser Press, 2010)

K LENAERTS AND T COURTHAUT, 'Of Birds and Hedges: The Role of Primacy in Invoking Norms of EU Law' (2006) 31 *European Law Review* 287

T LOCK, 'Is Private Enforcement of EU Law through State Liability a Myth? – An Assessment 20 Years after *Francovich*' (2012) 49 *Common Market Law Review* 1675

H-W MICKLITZ AND B DE WITTE (eds), *The European Court of Justice and the Autonomy of the Member States* (Antwerp: Intersentia, 2012)

P PESCATORE, 'The Doctrine of "Direct Effect": An Infant Disease of Community Law' (1983) 8 *European Law Review* 155

M POIARES MADURO AND L AZOULAI, *The Past and Future of EU Law* (Oxford: Hart Publishing, 2010)

S Prechal, 'Community Law in National Court: The Lessons from *Van Schijndel*' (1998) 35 *Common Market Law Review* 681

S Prechal, *Directives in EC Law* (2nd edn, Oxford: Oxford University Press, 2005)

S Prechal, 'Direct Effect, Indirect Effect, Supremacy and the Evolving Constitution of the European Union' in C Barnard (ed), *The Fundamentals of EU Law Revisited: Assessing the Impact of the Constitutional Debate?* (Oxford: Oxford University Press, 2007)

A-M Slaughter, A Stone Sweet, and JHH Weiler (eds), *The European Court of Justice and National Courts: Doctrine and Jurisprudence* (Oxford: Hart Publishing, 1998)

W Van Gerven, 'On Rights, Remedies and Procedures' (2000) 37 *Common Market Law Review* 501

JHH Weiler, *The Constitution of Europe: 'Do the New Clothes Have an Emperor?' and Other Essays on European Integration* (Cambridge: Cambridge University Press, 1999)

7

EU law: is it international law?

Bruno de Witte

1 Introduction

The European Communities, and later the European Union, came into being as creatures of international law, as they were established by means of international treaties concluded by States. Today still, the TEU and the TFEU form the basic documents of the EU legal order. It logically follows from this that EU law is still part – albeit a very distinctive and advanced one – of international law. There are, however, also good reasons for thinking that the EU is now so different from any other international organization in the world that it has become 'something else', more like the central unit of a European federal State. This discussion on the proper 'legal nature' of the EU, and of EU law, has been going on for decades, and it is indeed a curious characteristic of EU law that its precise place within the legal universe is not firmly established. This is an illustration of how legal reality – in this case, the way in which European integration has been shaped in legal terms – puts pressure on the established categories of legal science. This chapter will present the terms of the discussion on the legal nature of EU law, so as to help the reader situate the 'place of EU law'[1] within the world of legal phenomena.

So, this chapter is not centrally concerned with another question which is sometimes dealt with under the same title of 'EU law and international law', namely the conditions

---

[1] N Walker, 'The Place of European Law' in G de Búrca and JHH Weiler (eds), *The Worlds of European Constitutionalism* (Cambridge: Cambridge University Press, 2012).

under which norms of international law that are binding on the EU (in most cases, because the EU has concluded a treaty with non-Member States) are applied within the EU legal order. That different, though related, question will be briefly considered in section 4. Before that, section 2 will present the 'straightforward' view that EU law is a part (or 'sub-system') of international law, and section 3 will discuss the 'alternative' view that EU law, although originating in international law, is now so distinctive that it should no longer be considered to be part of international law.

2 EU law as a sub-system of international law

2.1 The EU as an international organization?

There is no disputing the fact that 'the EU has successfully expanded its substantive mandate and institutional prerogatives to a level without parallel among international organizations',[2] and this raises the question whether it is still situated 'among international organizations' or has ceased to belong to that category. In fact, if one reads the scholarly literature of international law and of EU law, we find remarkably contrasting views on this question. A large part of the EU law literature takes the view that the EU, whilst certainly not yet a federal State, is also no longer an international organization, but rather a legal construct that is somewhere in between those two poles, in a category all of its own (this is often expressed by saying that the EU is a *sui generis* entity). If, however, one reads textbooks on international law or the law of international organizations, their authors unanimously agree that the EU is still an international organization and is still situated *within* international law. Similarly contrasting conceptions are implied by the legal education programmes of different European countries. In the UK, for example, the Law of the European Union is a mandatory core subject of the undergraduate law degree, whereas international law is typically considered as an altogether different subject, usually offered as an optional course for few students. In the Netherlands, by contrast, law students are usually confronted, in the mandatory part of their undergraduate degree, with a combined introduction course to international *and* European law, which highlights the close connection that is seen to exist between the two subjects.

There are two basic reasons why it makes sense – subject to later qualifications of this view – to view EU law as part of international law. The first reason is that EU law continues to find its origins in international treaties. The rule of recognition of EU law (ie the rule that allows us to decide whether a norm is part of EU law or not)[3] is whether a particular norm can be traced back, directly or indirectly, to the text of the TEU and the TFEU. We will highlight this continuing reliance on international law as the foundation of the EU legal order in the next subsections. The second reason is the extraordinary flexibility of international law. International law is mainly developed by means of treaties between States, but there are no legal limits to the kinds of cooperation that States can undertake by means of treaties;[4] indeed, the content of some treaties puts major limitations on the sovereign powers of the participating States. This is especially so when States create an international organization,

---

[2] A Moravcsik, 'The European Constitutional Settlement' in S Meunier and K McNamara (eds), *Making History: European Integration and Institutional Change at Fifty* (Oxford: Oxford University Press, 2007) 23.

[3] The notion of the 'rule of recognition' is a well-known element of the legal theory exposed by HLA Hart in his *The Concept of Law* (Oxford: Clarendon Press, 1972).

[4] Except for one, rather nebulous, limit, namely that States are not allowed to make treaties that would conflict with *jus cogens* norms; see Art 53 of the Vienna Convention on the Law of Treaties (1969).

that is, a permanent institutional structure for cooperation at the international level with its own organs possessing independent decision-making powers. There is a wide variety of such international organizations, ranging from the United Nations organization, of which almost all countries of the world are members and which deals with vital matters of peace and security, to the Office franco-allemand pour la jeunesse, a small bilateral organization created by France and Germany in order to stimulate youth exchanges between the two countries. Each such treaty creates a particular sub-system of international law with its own special rules. Although there is some controversy about the criteria to be used in deciding whether a legal entity can be called an international organization, there is no doubt that the European Communities first, and the European Union now, tick all the boxes: they were created by an international treaty between States and possess organs (which are called 'institutions' in EU law) with a will distinct from the will of the Member States.[5]

This said, the European Communities were, right from the start, a very special kind of international organization (section 2.2), and this peculiarity has become more evident with the passage of time (section 2.3). Yet, even today, the EU's pedigree in international law has not been cancelled and it reappears most forcefully when the Treaties on which the EU is based are being reformed, as they repeatedly have been in the past 30 years: those are major political events which take the legal form of Treaty amendments, that is, acts of international law (section 2.4).

2.2 The international origins of the European integration process

Between 1948 and 1951, three new international organizations were created in quick succession in Western Europe: the *Organisation for European Economic Co-operation* (OEEC; later named OECD) was established by a treaty signed in Paris on 16 April 1948 by 16 European States and the three Western Commanders-in-Chief of the German occupation zones; the *Council of Europe* was created by a statute (taking the legal form of a treaty) signed in London on 5 May 1949 by ten European States; and the *European Coal and Steel Community* (ECSC) was established by a treaty signed in Paris on 18 April 1951 by six European States. The creation of new international organizations was nothing unusual. Dozens of multilateral international organizations had been set up since the middle of the nineteenth century.[6] Most of them, though, had a universal remit, or at least an extra-European one, and the focus on creating ambitious multilateral entities responding to the 'need of a closer unity between all like-minded countries of Europe'[7] was a new development of the post-war period. All three organizations expressed, in their own way, the aspiration towards greater European unity, and they were often considered together in the legal scholarship of that period.[8]

In fact, during those immediate post-war years, active groups of European federalists had hoped to create a United Europe based on a federal constitution inspired by that of the US, and had sought to promote the adoption of federal solutions in the context of the various political initiatives taken in that period to reorganize the European political landscape.

---

[5] On the legal definition of an international organization, see J Klabbers, *An Introduction to International Institutional Law* (2nd edn, Cambridge: Cambridge University Press, 2009) 6–12.

[6] For a synthesis of this historical development, see A Peters and S Peter, 'International Organizations: Between Technocracy and Democracy' in B Fassbender and A Peters (eds), *The Oxford Handbook of the History of International Law* (Oxford: Oxford University Press, 2012).

[7] Statute of the Council of Europe, Preamble, para 4.

[8] In the English language literature, see eg AH Robertson, *European Institutions: Co-operation, Integration, Unification* (London: Stevens, 1959).

The European governments chose, instead, not to take the federal route and they rather shaped their new initiatives of European cooperation by using the age-old legal tool of the international treaty: the OEEC, the Council of Europe, and the ECSC were all created in the form of an international organization based on a treaty subject to ratification by the parliaments of their Member States. Both the OEEC and the Council of Europe were set up as rather old-fashioned and traditional international organizations, to the extent that their organs were kept under the close control of the Member State governments (the European Convention on Human Rights was a legal breakthrough within the Council of Europe, but it happened by means of a separate treaty which entered into force only later).[9] The ECSC Treaty, by contrast, was an innovative endeavour; it created a *different*, functionally and politically more effective, international organization.

Indeed, whereas the ECSC was based on what seemed like an ordinary international treaty, that treaty was far from ordinary in its content. A major, and at the time startling, innovation of the 'Schuman Plan',[10] contrasting with most pre-war and post-war cooperation projects, was that sovereign States should agree to transfer their powers to regulate the coal and steel industries to a common body, the High Authority. By signing the ECSC Treaty, as it emerged from the Schuman Plan through negotiations in 1950 and 1951, the governments of the six founding States agreed to relinquish national control over these two sectors of the economy and to allow the supranational High Authority to exercise State-like public authority in their stead.

The term *supranational*, itself, appeared only once in the ECSC Treaty, and not in a very prominent place, but it had been repeatedly used during the negotiations, and was rapidly adopted by political and legal commentators as the defining characteristic not only of the High Authority but also of the entire Community of which it was an organ. The supranational character of the ECSC Treaty did not spring so much from the substantive norms it contained, but from the way in which it distributed legal authority and organized the decision-making by its organs. The ECSC had three institutions composed of persons who were not government representatives (the High Authority, a parliamentary Assembly, and a Court of Justice); its institutions (particularly the independent High Authority) had the power to adopt binding acts, often by a majority vote; some of those decisions were directly applicable to private individuals and firms; and compliance by both the institutions and the Member States with their obligations was made subject to judicial enforcement. None of those features were entirely unprecedented in international law, so that the novelty of the ECSC did not reside in one or other of those specific characteristics but rather in their cumulative presence.[11]

When the EEC and the European Atomic Energy Community (EAEC) were created in 1957, as a further stage of the European integration process, they were equipped with an institutional regime that was as supranational as that of the ECSC. It is true that the Commission had a less prominent place in the decision-making system of the EEC than the High Authority had in the ECSC, but the Community's power to make directly applicable rules was now extended in its scope: broadly-based regulations could be adopted in a number of economic areas by the Council acting on a proposal by the Commission, in contrast

---

[9] On the extent to which the Statute of the Council of Europe, as agreed in 1949, constituted a dampener on the high hopes held by European federalists, see AJ Zurcher, *The Struggle to Unite Europe 1940–1958* (New York: New York University Press, 1958) ch 5.

[10] Thus named after the French minister of foreign affairs Robert Schuman who had launched the idea of the ECSC in a speech delivered in Paris on 9 May 1950.

[11] F Capotorti, 'Supranational Organizations' in *Encyclopedia of Public International Law*, vol 5 (Amsterdam: North-Holland, 1983) 263–264.

with the limited decisions, relating solely to the coal and steel industries, which the High Authority could adopt under ECSC law. All the other supranational characteristics of the earlier Treaty were fully maintained in the EEC, with the interesting addition of the preliminary reference procedure before the European Court of Justice whose supranational potential went, however, largely unnoticed in 1957.

2.3 The later evolution of the European Communities and the European Union

The 'treaty path' towards closer European integration, after having been confirmed when the EEC was established in 1957, was never abandoned during the later stages of the European integration process. Deliberate attempts to transform the European Communities into 'something else' (legally speaking) were made at several moments in the history of European integration, but none of those attempts resulted in a clear and explicit change of the legal nature of the organizations. And when the Maastricht Treaty, signed in February 1992, eventually created a new legal entity, called the European Union, alongside the European Communities, this was mostly seen as a *step back* in the European integration process. Indeed, the new legal entity was created, by the then 12 Member States, to host two new forms of interstate cooperation, in common foreign and security policy (CFSP) and justice and home affairs (JHA), which were marked by a *lesser* degree of supranationalism than the existing European Communities. So, the creation of the EU in the early 1990s was not a jump forward towards a federal Europe, but a partial return to more traditional forms of intergovernmental cooperation – despite the fact that, in other ways, the Maastricht Treaty did indeed deepen the integration process: it created the Economic and Monetary Union, it coined the co-decision procedure for EC law-making, it introduced the concept of European citizenship, etc.

The curious 'legal architecture' resulting from Maastricht, consisting of two separate treaties corresponding to two separate but interconnected organizations (the EC and the EU), has now been replaced – through the Lisbon Treaty – by a new architecture. We now still have (at least[12]) two separate and legally equivalent treaties (the TEU and the TFEU) but only a single organization, namely the European Union, which has now absorbed the European Community.[13] That single organization is still firmly rooted in international law. In fact, the first sentence of Article 1 TEU is couched in the traditional language of international law:

> By this Treaty, the HIGH CONTRACTING PARTIES establish among themselves a EUROPEAN UNION...on which the Member States confer competences to attain objectives they have in common.[14]

The evolution traced in the previous paragraphs would seem to lead to the logical conclusion that the EC, first, and the EU, now, remain creatures of international law, and therefore continue to belong to the legal category of international organizations. The European Treaties

---

[12] ie without counting the EAEC Treaty, which continues to have a separate legal existence and is not subordinated to the TEU and TFEU; but its political importance has dwindled over the years.

[13] See M Cremona, 'The Two (or Three) Treaty Solution: The New Treaty Structure of the EU' in A Biondi, P Eeckhout, and S Ripley (eds), *EU Law after Lisbon* (Oxford: Oxford University Press, 2012).

[14] The capitalized words in the main text are printed in capitals in the version published by the *Official Journal of the European Union* (OJ [2008] C115/16).

themselves do not contain express language to confirm this, but it may be noted that the EU Member States have accepted this qualification in the broader international arena. Indeed, there are many multilateral treaty provisions that use the terms 'international organization' or 'regional economic international organization' (REIO) where it is clear from the context that the (only) organization that is intended by that term is the EC or the EU.[15] The EU Member States participate in drawing up those multilateral international conventions and could therefore object to the qualification of the EC or the EU as international organizations, but they do not.

The EU (or, previously, the EC) is also viewed as an international organization under the constitutional law of many of its Member States. Today, some national constitutions contain clauses dealing with the transfer of powers to the EU (such clauses were introduced by some 'old' members usually at the time of the Maastricht Treaty, and by 'new' members at the time they acceded to the EU), but many countries continue to adopt a generic approach of allowing transfers of powers, or limitations of sovereignty, for the benefit of international organizations or international institutions without making special reference to the EU.[16] It is clear that those generic references to international organizations include the EU. Therefore, the prevalent view, from the perspective of national constitutional law, seems to be that the EU is indeed a creature of international law and therefore an international organization, and that State sovereignty has not been abandoned or shared, but rather is being 'exercised in common' within the framework of the Union.[17]

When we turn to the Court of Justice, which has been given the principal authority to interpret and apply EU law,[18] and therefore also the authority to declare what the legal nature of the EU is, we find no conclusive views on the matter. It is true that the Court of Justice has regularly stated that 'the EEC Treaty has created its own legal system,'[19] or similar language, but this, in itself, is nothing special: every other international organization has its own legal sub-system as defined by its founding treaty. The Court never added that this legal system was situated *outside* the scope of international law. In its famous early judgments *Van Gend en Loos* and *Costa*, the Court sought to differentiate the EEC Treaty from 'other' or 'ordinary' international treaties, but that otherness was not pushed to the conclusion that the EEC Treaty had created something other than an international organization.[20] Much has been made of the fact that the Court held, in its *Van Gend en Loos* judgment of 1963, that the EEC Treaty had created 'a new legal order of international law', whereas it dropped the last three words one year later

---

[15] See, among many other examples, the Energy Charter Treaty (1991), Art 1(2) and (3); the Convention on Biological Diversity (1992), Art 35; the UN Framework Convention on Climate Change (1992), Art 20; the UNESCO Convention on the Protection and Promotion of the Diversity of Cultural Expressions (2005), Art 27. See, on the practice of making these 'REIO' references, E Paasivirta and PJ Kuijper, 'Does One Size Fit All? The European Community and the Responsibility of International Organizations' (2005) 36 *Netherlands Yearbook of International Law* 169 at 206 *et seq*.

[16] See M Claes, 'Constitutionalising Europe at Its Source: The "European Clauses" in the National Constitutions: Evolution and Typology' (2005) 24 *Yearbook of European Law* 81.

[17] See, on this question of the continuing relevance of the notion of sovereignty in the context of European integration, N Walker, 'Late Sovereignty in the European Union' in N Walker (ed), *Sovereignty in Transition* (Oxford: Hart Publishing, 2003) and B de Witte, 'Sovereignty and European Integration: The Weight of Legal Tradition' in A-M Slaughter, A Stone Sweet, and JHH Weiler (eds), *The European Court and National Courts: Doctrine and Jurisprudence* (Oxford: Hart Publishing, 1998). [18] Art 19(1) TEU.

[19] eg in the European Court of Justice (ECJ), Joined Cases C-6/90 and C-9/90 *Francovich and Bonifaci v Italy* [1991] ECR I-5357, para 31.

[20] See, however, the Opinion of AG Poiares Maduro in the *Kadi* case who stated that the ECJ, in *Van Gend en Loos*, had considered the EEC Treaty to form a new legal order which was 'beholden to, but distinct from the existing legal order of public international law' (Opinion of 23 January 2008 in Joined Cases C-402/05 P and C-415/05 P *Kadi and Al Barakaat v Council and Commission*, para 21). The ECJ, in fact, did not quite use those words in its 1963 judgment, nor later.

in *Costa* when it simply spoke of 'a new legal order'. This has been interpreted, by a number of commentators, as a deliberate tearing away of Community law from its international legal moorings. Yet, the way in which the Court described the peculiar characteristics of the EEC Treaty was very similar in both those early judgments, so it would be very odd if that description had led, in 1963, to the conclusion that this was a special legal order *still of international law*, and only one year later to the opposite conclusion that it was a special legal order *no longer of international law*.

To conclude this discussion, it is worth nothing that the Court of Justice, in the many years since its *Costa* judgment, never sought to develop a doctrine affirming the specific *and* non-international nature of the EU. The Court often emphasized the autonomous nature of the Union legal order, but never stated in so many words that this autonomous legal order had ceased to be part of international law. In fact, there was no need for the Court to adopt the premise that the Community was 'something other' than an international organization in order to affirm and protect the advanced features of European law since, as we saw, international law is extraordinarily flexible as to the content of the cooperation between States. On the few occasions on which the Court gives an indication of the kind of legal entity the EU might be, it tends to use tautological categories, as in a recent judgment in which it described the EU as a '*union* based on the rule of law'.[21]

Case study 7.1: Revision Treaties

We have seen, in the preceding discussion, that the European Communities were founded, back in the 1950s, by means of international treaties concluded between their Member States. Since then, the *deepening* of the European integration process has taken place essentially by means of new Treaties between the Member States 'revising' (or 'amending', which has the same meaning) the existing Treaties. The *widening* of the European integration process took the form of a series of accession Treaties between the existing and the acceding States, organizing the way in which the new Member States could join the existing organizations. The main revision Treaties were the Single European Act, the Maastricht Treaty, the Treaty of Amsterdam, the Treaty of Nice, and most recently the Lisbon Treaty. Seven accession Treaties have been concluded so far: with the UK, Ireland, and Denmark; with Greece; with Spain and Portugal; with Austria, Finland, and Sweden; with nine Central and European countries and Cyprus; with Bulgaria and Romania; and most recently with Croatia. Revision Treaties are, legally speaking, more interesting than accession Treaties.

Whereas the latter tend to be based on the simple principle that the newcomers must accept the existing legal order with only little room for institutional accommodation and derogations, revision Treaties have led to major changes in the institutional set-up and policy scope of the European Communities and the EU.

---

[21] Case C-583/11 P *Inuit Tapiriit Kanatami v Parliament and Council*, judgment of 3 October 2013, para 91 (emphasis added). Note the shift from 'Union' (the *species*) to 'union' (the *genus*). The small-u term is left undefined, and should not be read as denying that EU law belongs to international law. Curiously, the concept of 'international union' was of common usage in the nineteenth and early part of the twentieth centuries to describe the early international regimes for technical cooperation, eg for post, telegraphy, and copyright (A Peters and S Peter, 'International Organizations: Between Technocracy and Democracy' in Fassbender and Peters, *The Oxford Handbook of the History of International Law* (n 6) 174–176).

It frequently happens, of course, that States may want to amend a treaty that they have previously concluded. The rules relating to such operations are set out in Articles 39 to 41 of the Vienna Convention on the Law of Treaties (1969). Article 39 contains the very simple default rule that a treaty may be amended by an agreement between all the parties, and that the normal rules on the conclusion of treaties apply to this amending agreement. This default rule may be set aside by the parties when concluding the original (to-be-amended) treaty.

The international legal regime of treaty amendment is, thus, one of utmost flexibility; the contracting parties[22] are free to arrange for the later amendment of 'their' treaty in the way they wish.[23] Indeed, a large and increasing number of multilateral treaties contain such a special amendment procedure, which is generally aimed at facilitating adaptation to changing circumstances, often by allowing for the amendment of a treaty without the agreement of all the States.[24] Article 48 EU, the amendment provision applying to changes of both the TEU and TFEU, is an example of a specific amendment clause but, contrary to most others, it does *not* provide more flexibility than the default rule of Article 39 Vienna Convention. It requires the agreement of *all* the parties (in this case, the Member States of the EU) for the valid adoption of the amendments and, *in addition*, it requires some involvement of the EU institutions in the preparatory phase and, in almost every case, the separate approval of the amendments by each State according to its own constitutional requirements.[25]

The EU's 'rule of change' is thus particularly rigid, not because this rigidity is prescribed by general rules of international law, but because its Member States have committed themselves to such a rigid mechanism. The original rule that the EC Treaties could only be revised with the agreement of all the Member States, which made perfect sense when the EC counted only six States, was left untouched on each later occasion, despite the fact that membership grew from six to 28, which has rendered the unanimity requirement an ever more cumbersome obstacle in the way of Treaty change.[26]

As to the *content* of the Treaty amendments, the Member States traditionally acted, to use a famous German expression, as the *Herren der Verträge* ('Masters of the Treaties'), bound by nothing else than the limits posed by their respective constitutions; they acted as 'independent and sovereign States having freely decided … to exercise in common some of their competences'.[27] The fact that the Member State governments acted as 'masters' of the Treaty text did not mean that they could also control what happened under the new Treaty once it had entered into force. The dynamic evolution of EU law in between Treaty revisions partly

---

[22] 'Contracting parties' is the expression used in the practice of international law to denote the States (or international organizations) that have accepted to be bound by a particular treaty.

[23] See A Aust, *Modern Treaty Law and Practice* (Cambridge: Cambridge University Press, 2000) 214: 'It is wrong to think that the Vienna Convention is a rigid structure which places obstacles in the way of treaty modification: rather, it allows states to include in treaties such amendment provisions as they wish.'

[24] For a survey of the wide variety of those special amendment procedures, see J Brunnée, 'Treaty Amendments' in DB Hollis (ed), *The Oxford Guide to Treaties* (Oxford: Oxford University Press, 2012).

[25] On the current, post-Lisbon, EU Treaty amendment regime, see chapter 5, and for an overview of the content of the major revision Treaties, see chapter 2. For further discussion, see S Peers, 'The Future of EU Treaty Amendments' (2012) 31 *Yearbook of European Law* 17; B de Witte, 'Treaty Revision Procedures after Lisbon' in Biondi, Eeckhout, and Ripley, *EU Law after Lisbon* (n 13).

[26] For an analysis of how, in particular, the requirement that each Treaty revision should be separately ratified by each State has placed obstacles in the way of Treaty change on many occasions, see C Closa, *The Politics of Ratification of EU Treaties* (Abingdon: Routledge, 2013).

[27] (This phrase was used by the Member State governments in the introductory part of the Decision on Denmark, adopted at the Edinburgh summit of 12 December 1992, but it referred back to their earlier adoption of the Maastricht Treaty).

escaped their control, and they could correct unwanted evolutions only on the occasion of a further Treaty revision and on the unlikely condition that they found a consensus to overrule, say, a particular interpretation of the Treaty text adopted by the Court of Justice.

The close control exercised by the Member State governments on the revision process has now been diluted somewhat. Compared to the previous revision clauses, the new rules enacted by the Lisbon Treaty for future revisions of the European Treaties innovate in two limited respects: they prescribe the use of the 'Convention method' for future revisions, and they provide for two so-called simplified revision procedures, in addition to the ordinary revision procedure.

The Convention method consists in the fact that all important Treaty revisions must, from now on, be preceded by a deliberative phase within a 'Convention' comprising representatives not only of the national governments but also of the national parliaments and of the EU institutions (especially the European Parliament). This new body is modelled on the Convention that was convened on an experimental basis, in 2002–3, to prepare the adoption of the Constitutional Treaty. The debate on the direction of future Treaty reforms is thus no longer confined to traditional diplomatic exchanges between national governments but is opened up to a wider constituency. Still, the Convention can only express an opinion or make proposals. The actual decision to amend the Treaties will still take the form of an agreement between Member State governments laid down in an international treaty.

As for the new simplified procedures, which apply for certain kinds of amendments mentioned in Article 48(6) and (7) EU, they allow for the text of the Treaties to be amended, not by another international treaty but by a unilateral decision of an organ of the EU itself (ie the European Council), on condition that the individual States, acting separately, 'approve' that decision. However, the articles thus amended will then take their place among the other articles of the TEU or TFEU, thereby sharing the international legal nature of those Treaties.[28]

What must be emphasized is that those innovations do not affect the fundamental rule of the game, namely that all Member States must give their unanimous consent to future amendments of the Treaties. The EU's rules of change thereby continue to be much more rigid than those applying to any national constitution, but also more rigid than those applying to the founding instruments of other, less integrated, international organizations.[29] They are a powerful confirmation of the fact that EU law is anchored in international law and that the Union's legal fate remains in the hands of the States that have created it, or joined it later on.

3 The specific features of EU law

Although the view that the EU is, and remains, a creature of international law may seem logical in view of the preceding discussion, it is in fact strongly contested in the legal literature. Many EU law scholars have argued, already since the 1960s, that the legal

---

[28] The possibility for a treaty establishing an international organization to be amended through a unilateral act of one of the organs of that organization is not unheard of in the practice of international law; see Brunnée, 'Treaty Amendments' (n 24) 362.

[29] For this comparison, see W Lehmann, 'Federal States and International Organisations: A Short Comparison of Their Amending Rules with the European Union', European Parliament note, December 2011, available at http://www.europarl.europa.eu/studies

characteristics of Community law (and now Union law) are so peculiar and far removed from what one normally observes in the world of international relations that it does not make good sense to consider it to be part and parcel of international law.[30] The EU is then no longer an international organization at all, but 'something else', a *sui generis* legal system that does not fit in the traditional dichotomy between (federal) States and international organizations. To continue to refer to it as an international organization would be 'to try to push the toothpaste back in the tube'.[31]

The legal features of EU law that could support this alternative view are manifold: the broad and flexible nature of EU competences which extend into all areas of law-making; the existence of a (partially) common currency and a common (though derivative) citizenship; the decision-making regime, marked by the involvement of institutions not controlled by the Member State governments and by recourse to majority voting in the State-controlled Council of Ministers; the relatively effective mechanism of State compliance; the habit of obedience by national courts to their duty to apply EU law.

This raises the question whether any of these legal features are incompatible with the notion of an international organization, thereby placing EU law as a whole outside the scope of international law. One could also argue that the incomparability of the EU results not from any one of those features but from their combination, which makes the EU a really unique phenomenon and makes it seem contrived to insist on the formal view of the EU as just another international organization. We will discuss these arguments in the following two subsections.

3.1 The incomparability of the EU's legal features

Advanced international organizations are being created year after year, and display one or several of the characteristic features of the EU, mentioned previously. Many international organizations have organs possessing the power to adopt operational decisions that are binding on States, and occasionally such decisions can even be adopted by a majority vote, that is, against the wishes of single Member States of the organization.[32] It is true, though, that those decisions seldom deal with very sensitive policy matters; they tend to be about technical issues.

In the EU, by contrast, there is a constant stream of new legislation in a broad range of policy areas, typically adopted nowadays through what the Lisbon Treaty has appropriately renamed the 'ordinary legislative procedure':[33] a procedure marked by the fact that the European Parliament and the Council must agree on the text, and that the Council can decide by a qualified majority of the represented Member States. Furthermore, in some crucial areas of EU law, such as competition law and monetary policy, decision-making powers

---

[30] Among those scholars figure also some prominent former members of the European Court of Justice who defended this view in an extra-judicial capacity: P Pescatore, 'International Law and Community Law – A Comparative Analysis' (1970) 7 *Common Market Law Review* 167; GF Mancini, 'Europe: The Case for Statehood' (1998) 4 *European Law Journal* 29. As mentioned in the previous section, the Court itself, in its judgments, never expressed a clear position on this controversy.

[31] JHH Weiler and UR Haltern, 'Constitutional or International? The Foundations of the Community Legal Order and the Question of Judicial Kompetenz-Kompetenz' in Slaughter, Stone Sweet, and Weiler, *The European Courts and National Courts* (n 17), 331 at 342.

[32] For a general view, see J von Bernstorff, 'Procedures of Decision-Making and the Role of Law in International Organizations' (2008) 9 *German Law Journal* 1939; ND White, 'Decision-Making' in J Klabbers and A Wallendahl (eds), *Research Handbook on the Law of International Organizations* (Cheltenham: Edward Elgar, 2011) 225; and J Wouters and P De Man, 'International Organizations as Law-Makers' in idem 190.

[33] Art 294 TFEU. See further chapter 5.

are almost entirely entrusted to supranational institutions (the European Commission and the European Central Bank, respectively) which are not controlled by the Member States. Democratic control of the European Commission, and democratic input in the law-making process, are exercised by the European Parliament, which is directly elected by the European citizenry – this is, of course, unknown to any other international law regime.

If we move from law-making to considering judicial enforcement of the law, also there we can find some examples of international organizations equipped with international courts having compulsory jurisdiction to settle disputes between States.[34] It is rare, though, for international courts to provide for direct access by individual plaintiffs. Apart from the case of the European Court of Human Rights, we mostly find this in the framework of regional integration organizations whose political and judicial institutions were, in fact, deliberately modelled on the EU.[35] Examples include the Caribbean Court of Justice, and the Andean Tribunal of Justice (an organ of the Andean Community), which is engaged in an active dialogue with national courts through a preliminary reference mechanism comparable to that existing in the EU.[36]

A feature of the EU's judicial enforcement regime which remains fairly unique is the power of the European Commission (an institution acting independently from the Member States) to sue the Member States before the Court of Justice for infringement of their EU law obligations. This mechanism has allowed the Court to state, very early on, that the general international rule allowing States to retaliate in the event of non-compliance by other parties to the same treaty (*inadimplenti non est adimplendum*)[37] did not apply in the context of Union law. This innovative characteristic was deduced by the Court from a specific feature of the EEC Treaty itself, namely this power of the Commission to bring infringement actions against non-complying States.[38] There is, thus, a specific system of State responsibility in EU law which does not allow States to adopt countermeasures in the event of a violation of EU obligations by the other States; yet, this specificity follows logically from choices made by the Member States themselves when they created the EEC and in particular from their decision to vest the Commission with an independent power to take incompliant Member States to court. It can therefore be seen as an example of the flexibility provided by international law: when creating an international organization, States can devise operational rules for their organization that derogate from (ie go further than) the general rules of international law.

---

[34] Y Shany, *The Competing Jurisdictions of International Courts and Tribunals* (Oxford: Oxford University Press, 2003) 3–7.

[35] KJ Alter, 'The Global Spread of European Style International Courts' (2012) 35 *West European Politics* 135.

[36] For an analysis of the actual functioning of the Andean preliminary reference system, which is successful but only in a specific area of the law and in relation to some national courts, see LR Helfer and KJ Alter, 'The Andean Tribunal of Justice and Its Interlocutors: Understanding Preliminary Reference Patterns in the Andean Community' (2009) 41 *New York University Journal of International Law and Politics* 871.

[37] See N White and A Abass, 'Countermeasures and Sanctions' in ME Evans (ed), *International Law* (3rd edn, Oxford: Oxford University Press, 2010).

[38] Joined Cases 90/63 and 91/63 *Commission v Luxembourg and Belgium* [1964] ECR English Special Edition 625:

> the [EEC] Treaty is not limited to creating reciprocal obligations between the different natural and legal persons to whom it is applicable, but establishes a new legal order which governs the powers, rights and obligations of the said persons, *as well as the necessary procedures for taking cognizance of and penalizing any breach of it*. Therefore...*the basic concept of the Treaty requires that the Member States shall not take the law in their own hands*. (emphasis added)

The same principle has been repeated by the Court many times since 1964; eg in Case C-111/03 *Commission v Sweden*, judgment of 20 October 2005, para 66.

As for the preliminary reference mechanism through which national courts engage in a dialogue with the Court when dealing with the application of EU law norms, this mechanism has been imitated elsewhere (see previously), but it has produced, in the EU legal system, some seemingly unique consequences, in particular the formulation of an obligation for national courts to recognize the *primacy* of EU law. Since this obligation is often cited as the most compelling evidence that EU law is no longer part of international law, it deserves to be looked at more closely in the next subsection.

3.2 The primacy of EU law, a federal characteristic?

The feature of Union law that is most widely mentioned as showing its remoteness from international law is its *primacy* within the national legal orders of its Member States. Indeed, whereas international treaties take precedence over national law, this precedence is situated at the international level rather than within the domestic legal orders. Already in 1930, the Permanent Court of International Justice held that it was 'a generally accepted principle of international law that in the relations between powers who are contracting parties to a treaty, the provisions of municipal law cannot prevail over those of the treaty.'[39] Yet, this statement is, in fact, limited to the 'relations between powers' on the international plane; it does not apply to the *internal* workings of the national legal systems, in respect of which international law does not seem to claim a priority of treaty norms over conflicting national norms. Indeed, the received view among international law scholars is the following:

> From the standpoint of international law states are generally free as to the manner in which, domestically, they put themselves in the position to meet their international obligations; the choice between the direct reception and application of international law, or its transformation into national law by way of statute, is a matter of indifference…These are matters for each state to determine for itself according to its own constitutional practice.[40]

One finds this view repeated in all contemporary international law textbooks.[41] In practice, though, we can observe a tendency towards greater recognition of the primacy of international law over national law in the text of national constitutions or in the case law of national constitutional and supreme courts.[42] It is also possible for a particular treaty to give specific guidance on the steps which States must take within their domestic legal order. This possibility was noted by the European Court of Justice in a judgment of 1999:

---

[39] Permanent Court of International Justice, *Greek and Bulgarian Communities*, PCIJ, Series B, No 17, p 32.

[40] RY Jennings and A Watts (eds), *Oppenheim's International Law*, vol I (9th edn, London: Longman, 1992) 82–83.

[41] For a more detailed treatment of the limited dictates of international law, and of divergent national constitutional practice, see M Mendez, *The Legal Effects of EU Agreements: Maximalist Treaty Enforcement and Judicial Avoidance Techniques* (Oxford: Oxford University Press, 2013) ch 1. See also E Denza, 'The Relationship between International and National Law' in ME Evans (ed), *International Law* (3rd edn, Oxford: Oxford University Press, 2010).

[42] See A Peters and UK Preuss, 'International Relations and International Law' in M Tushnet, F Fleiner, and C Saunders (eds), *Routledge Handbook of Constitutional Law* (Abingdon: Routledge, 2013) 36–40.

according to the general rules of international law there must be *bona fide* performance of every agreement. Although each contracting party is responsible for executing fully the commitments which it has undertaken it is nevertheless free to determine the legal means appropriate for attaining that end in its legal system, *unless the agreement, interpreted in the light of its subject-matter and purpose, itself specifies those means.*[43]

The TEU and TFEU (and their earlier pre-Lisbon versions) are agreements of the kind referred to in the sentence above. Their *wording* does not specify in any detail the means by which the Member States must comply with their commitments (except for the fact, recorded in what is now Article 267 TFEU, that they must allow their courts to refer preliminary questions to the Court on the interpretation of EU law), but, interpreting the Treaties in light of their *subject matter* and *purpose*, the Court came to the conclusion that some of their provisions should have direct effect in the domestic legal system (*Van Gend en Loos* and its progeny) and that all those norms that have direct effect should also have primacy over conflicting national law (*Costa* and its progeny).[44]

The principle that EU law prevails, or should prevail, over national law even before national courts is reminiscent of the supremacy of federal law over national law, which is entrenched in the constitutions of prominent federal States such as the US and Germany. It is not surprising, therefore, to find many EU law scholars who saw the primacy doctrine as a hallmark of the quasi-federal and non-international nature of European law. Writing very shortly after the foundational judgments *Van Gend en Loos* and *Costa*, Peter Hay devoted a chapter of his work on *Federalism and Supranational Organizations* to what he termed the 'Federal Relation of Community Law to National Law'.[45] In 1991, Joseph Weiler wrote, in his *Transformation of Europe*, that the doctrines of direct effect and primacy rendered the relationship between Community law and national law 'indistinguishable from analogous relationships in constitutions of federal states.'[46] Similar views have been expressed by many other authors until the present day.

On a closer look, though, the primacy of EU law is quite different from the supremacy of federal law in countries such as Germany, Switzerland, the US, or Canada. In all those countries, the supremacy of federal law is effectively guaranteed by the fact that its enforcement is largely in the hands of federal courts. In the EU legal order, the inconsistency of a national norm with an EU law norm can be directly examined by the Court of Justice only in the framework of an infringement action brought by the Commission under Article 258 EC, where the Court can make Union law prevail as a matter of course, just like any international court would give precedence to international law over the domestic laws of the States parties to an international dispute. Usually, however, inconsistencies between

---

[43] Case C-149/96 *Portugal v Council* [1999] ECR I-8395, para 35 (emphasis added). Of course, the agreement to which the ECJ refers in this extract is not the EC Treaty or EU Treaty but an external agreement concluded by the EC.

[44] On the legal effect of EU law in national legal systems, see generally chapter 6. For more on the development of the direct effect and primacy doctrines by the Court of Justice and their acceptance at the national level, see M Claes, *The National Courts' Mandate in the European Constitution* (Oxford: Hart Publishing, 2006) and, for a shorter synthesis, B de Witte, 'Direct Effect, Primacy, and the Nature of the Legal Order' in P Craig and G de Búrca (eds), *The Evolution of EU Law* (2nd edn, Oxford: Oxford University Press, 2011).

[45] P Hay, *Federalism and Supranational Organizations: Patterns for New Legal Structures* (Champaign, IL: University of Illinois Press, 1966).

[46] JHH Weiler, 'The Transformation of Europe' (1991) 100 *Yale Law Journal* 2403 at 2413. On the concept of federalism in EU law, see further chapter 4.

national law and EU law will come to light through litigation before national courts and will have to be solved by them, with the possible guidance of a preliminary ruling by the Court of Justice. In contrast with all federal States, there is no right of appeal to the Court of Justice against judgments of national courts that fail to recognize the primacy of EU law. Therefore, it is crucially important that the national courts should faithfully absorb and apply the primacy doctrine laid down by the Court of Justice, since it falls to them to make the doctrine a living reality.

This institutional factor has important consequences for the operation of the primacy doctrine. Since national courts conceive themselves to be organs of their State, they try to fit their 'European mandate' within the framework of the powers attributed to them by their national legal system. For those courts and, indeed, for most constitutional law scholars throughout Europe, the authority of EU law is rooted in their constitution, and subject to restrictions that may be imposed by the constitution.[47] This situation is in stark contrast with the position prevailing in federal States where the primacy of federal law is based on the federal constitution whose authority as the fundamental norm of the State is uncontested. In the EU legal order, on the contrary, the hierarchical relationship between EU law and national law needs to be more heavily emphasized by the Court of Justice and its supporters because the ultimate hierarchy of norms is not settled in favour of EU law.

It is not so clear, therefore, that the doctrines of primacy and direct effect count as features of EU law that distinguish it from international law. The doctrine of primacy, as presently formulated by the Court and accepted by the Member State courts, has, no doubt, a distinct federal flavour but it could also be described as a creative development of international law. The central rule of international treaty law is *pacta sunt servanda*: States are bound by their treaty obligations; and whenever a conflict between a treaty obligation and a norm of national law is brought before the International Court of Justice, or any other international court, the answer is clear: the treaty rule will prevail. The originality of the EEC Treaty, when it was concluded back in 1957, was to grant to the newly established Court, the ECJ, a jurisdictional competence which was then unique in the panorama of international law, namely that of guiding the activity of national courts while they are applying EU law by means of the preliminary rulings procedure. By means of this procedure, the ECJ had a 'window' through which it could intervene in pending national court cases and direct those national courts to respect the precedence of EU law.[48]

Seen from this angle, the direct effect and primacy doctrines do not so much signal a shift away from international law; they rather illustrate the dynamic potential of international law. The fact that, as a general rule, international law leaves to States a choice among various methods of domestic enforcement of international obligations does not prevent specific treaties or international decisions from imposing specific requirements in this respect. The TEU and TFEU may no longer be the only treaties that do this. Given appropriate circumstances, primacy within the domestic legal orders may be inscribed in other international treaties as well. It can, for example, be argued that the Agreement on the European Economic Area should also be considered as a treaty requiring primacy in

---

[47] For the evidence backing this statement, see the various 'national reports' in Slaughter, Stone Sweet, and Weiler, *The European Courts and National Courts* (n 17); and the comparative analysis by Claes, *The National Courts' Mandate in the European Constitution* (n 44).

[48] The importance of the preliminary rulings procedure in allowing for the emergence of the primacy doctrine was emphasized by D Wyatt, 'New Legal Order, or Old?' (1982) 7 *European Law Review* 147.

the domestic legal systems of its contracting parties.[49] The potential domestic impact of international law can, finally, also be illustrated by an entirely different, but quite radical, claim of supremacy. The UN Interim Administration in Kosovo (UNMIK), which was set up by Security Council Resolution 1244 of 1999, was given the power to adopt laws and regulations vested with direct effect and primacy over conflicting local (Serbian) laws. Thus, the separation between the international and municipal legal order entirely collapsed in pre-independence Kosovo, in a manner far more radical than anything experienced by EU Member States under EU law.[50]

3.3 Finding a name to describe the EU's specificity

The preceding discussion does not lead to an unambiguous conclusion. There are, in fact, two credible options for explaining the legal nature of the EU. The first option consists in saying that, in view of its basis in a set of international treaties, the EU is still an international organization and EU law is part of international law. This option must necessarily come with the recognition that the EU is an international organization unlike any other that has existed before, in view of the width and depth of the limitations that are put on the sovereignty of its Member States. But this option allows for other experiments of international cooperation to adopt some or all of the distinctive features of EU law in order to create similarly advanced organizations elsewhere in the world. This option is based, in other words, on a belief in the flexibility and dynamic potential of international law.[51]

The second option consists in arguing that, because of its particular legal features, the 'European legal order has...cut the umbilical cord with the international legal order'.[52] There is no entity that resembles the EU elsewhere in the world, and there is no realistic prospect for it to be created any time soon. As it is not a credible option to argue that the EU has become a federal State, the authors defending this view argue that the EU finds itself on a middle ground. It is more than an international regime and not (yet) a federal State, but it possesses features stemming from both sides.[53]

Under both these options, there is a strong urge to find new names and concepts to describe the specific nature of the EU. Under the first option, that denomination would serve to identify the sub-category of advanced international organizations of which the EU is the leading exemplar. Under the second option, the need for a new denomination is even more urgent. Since the proponents of that option argue that the EU is neither an international organization nor a federal State, they are hard pressed to find an appealing name for this intermediate category, beyond the rather feeble solution consisting in saying that the EU is simply *sui generis* (meaning: it is in a category all of its own).

---

[49] L Sevón and M Johansson, 'The Protection of the Rights of Individuals under the EEA Agreement' (1999) 24 *European Law Review* 373; the European Economic Area (EEA) Agreement (like the EU Treaties) does not expressly require the States parties to adopt the primacy rule, but the elements on which the ECJ based its primacy doctrine in *Costa v ENEL* would seem to be equally present in the EEA Agreement (at 382).

[50] See, among others, B Knoll, *The Legal Status of Territories Subject to Administration by International Organisations* (Cambridge: Cambridge University Press, 2008), who refers to the 'unmediated import of international law' (at 329).

[51] For a fuller articulation of this view, see B de Witte, 'The European Union as an International Legal Experiment' in de Búrca and Weiler, *The Worlds of European Constitutionalism* (n 1); and TC Hartley, 'International Law and the Law of the European Union' (2001) 72 *British Yearbook of International Law* 1.

[52] R Schütze, *European Constitutional Law* (Cambridge: Cambridge University Press, 2012) 66.

[53] Among the authors who have recently expressed this view, we can mention Schütze (see n 52), and M Avbelj, 'Theory of European Union' (2011) 36 *European Law Review* 818.

The term *supranational organization* served the name-giving purpose for many years, in the early decades of European integration, but it has now fallen into disuse, partly because of its now unfashionable hierarchical overtones, and partly because it failed to reflect the intergovernmental mode of integration that prevailed in the Second and Third Pillars of the EU after the Maastricht Treaty.[54] The term *confederation* is occasionally proposed, but it bears the stigma of weakness and instability that derives from the historical examples of confederations, and is therefore rather unusual as a denomination for the EU.[55] Alternative terminology should, in order to be attractive *and* true to reality, encapsulate both the international roots of the EU and its uniquely massive pooling of Member State powers and constitutional mode of operation.

No such alternative terminology has obtained Europe-wide currency so far, but influential descriptions in this vein have been proposed in Germany (the *Staatenverbund*) and in France (the *fédération d'Etats-nations*). The latter is a rather paradoxical denomination which is particularly popular among French authors.[56] It comes close to the German Staatenverbund, a term which was coined by Paul Kirchhof, and adopted in the Federal Constitutional Court judgment (the *Maastricht* judgment) which he helped to draft (as a member of that court) in 1993.[57] It was proposed as a deliberate neologism intended to occupy an intermediate space between the Bundesstaat (meaning: federal State) and the Staatenbund (meaning: confederation of States). According to Everling, a former German judge at the European Court of Justice, the term Staatenverbund 'stresses, *albeit in a fashion that is almost impossible to convey in other languages*, that the Member States are bound more tightly in the Union than in the traditional confederation of states.'[58] Other, very similar, terms proposed in the legal literature are those of a *federation of States*,[59] a *commonwealth*,[60] or a *constitutional order of States*.[61]

This terminological discussion is, perhaps, not of great practical importance. One does not need to find a consensus on the best categorical denomination for the EU in order to

[54] The term *supranational organization* is, however, still occasionally used to describe the nature of the EU, for lack of a better term. See eg K Lenaerts and P Van Nuffel, *European Union Law* (3rd edn, London: Sweet & Maxwell, 2011) 16–17.

[55] On the 'stigma of confederation', see M Burgess, *Federalism and European Union: The Building of Europe, 1950–2000* (Abingdon: Routledge, 2000) 259–260. Nevertheless, Burgess proposes rehabilitating and revitalizing the old concept as an adequate description of the EU (at 265–269).

[56] Among the French authors who have discussed or promoted the use of this concept in connection with the EU are: JL Quermonne, 'La "Fédération d'Etats nations": concept ou contradiction?' (2010) 84 *Revue française de droit constitutionnel* 677; V Constantinesco, 'Europe fédérale ou fédération d'Etats-nations' in R Dehousse (ed), *Une constitution pour l'Europe?* (Paris: Presses de Sciences Po, 2002); G Ricard-Nihoul, *Pour une Fédération européenne d'États-Nations: La vision de Jacques Delors revisitée* (Brussels: Larcier, 2012). J-C Piris (a former head of the EU Council's legal service) proposes the expression 'partially federal Union' (J-C Piris, 'The European Union: Towards a New Form of Federalism?' in J Fedtke and BS Markesinis (eds), *Patterns of Regionalism and Federalism: Lessons for the UK* (Oxford: Hart Publishing, 2006). For an elaborate legal historical study arguing that the federation has a long historical pedigree as a 'third model', in between the (federal) State and the international organization, see O Beaud, *Théorie de la fédération* (Paris: Presses universitaires de France, 2007).

[57] P Kirchhof later presented an updated version of his views, in English, in 'The Legal Structure of the European Union as a Union of States' in A von Bogdandy and J Bast (eds), *Principles of European Constitutional Law* (Oxford: Hart Publishing, 2005).

[58] U Everling, 'The European Union between Community and National Policies and Legal Orders' in von Bogdandy and Bast, *Principles of European Constitutional Law* (n 57) 719 (emphasis added).

[59] Schütze, *European Constitutional Law* (n 52) ch 2.

[60] N MacCormick, *Questioning Sovereignty: Law, State, and Nation in the European Commonwealth* (Oxford: Oxford University Press, 1999).

[61] A Dashwood, 'States in the European Union' (1998) 23 *European Law Review* 201.

study its law and its politics. But the underlying discussion on the true legal nature of the EU is interesting from the perspective of the self-understanding of legal science. Legal science has traditionally been based on two crucial distinctions which were used to 'organize the world' of normative phenomena: between State law and non-State law (ie legal norms developed by groups in society outside the State structures); and between national law and international law. The latter dichotomous distinction, which slowly emerged through centuries of scholarship, is called into question by the 'unruly' phenomenon constituted by EU law. The question is: can we still stick to the dichotomy (whereby EU law would be considered a sub-system within the category of international law); or do we need to recognize that the world of 'State law' should henceforth be divided in three: national law, international law, and EU law. But wouldn't this be a rather Eurocentric perspective?

3.4 The constitutional perspective on EU law

The controversy on the legal nature of the EU does not stand in the way of a widespread tendency, in the legal literature, to use constitutional terminology to describe and understand EU law. It is often claimed, also occasionally by the Court of Justice, that EU law forms a 'constitutional' legal order. Only a minority of scholars object to this usage, on the ground that constitutions are the basic legal instruments of sovereign States, and that constitutional terminology should therefore be reserved for States and not extended to non-State entities such as the EU.[62]

Around the turn of the century, the use of constitutional terminology to describe central features of the EU legal order had become commonplace in legal writing.[63] This approach was transferred from legal scholarship to practical politics in 2002–3, when the Convention on the Future of the Union set out to draft a new treaty text that would be called the Treaty establishing a Constitution for Europe. Most EU legal scholars applauded this project to formalize the EU's informal constitutional arrangements,[64] but it failed. During the so-called 'period of reflection' that followed the negative referenda in France and the Netherlands and the demise of the Constitutional Treaty, the Member State governments came to the conclusion that part of the Treaty's failure to take force was due to its overambitious constitutional design. In order to save most of the content of the reforms, they stated in June 2007 that 'the constitutional concept, which consisted in repealing all existing Treaties and replacing them by a single text called "Constitution" is abandoned.'[65] They also scrapped from the text of the Lisbon Treaty, which was subsequently agreed, some of the terminology used in the Constitutional Treaty that seemed too redolent of national constitutional texts, such as 'law' (instead of regulation or directive) or 'minister of foreign affairs' (instead of

---

[62] See eg D Grimm, 'Does Europe Need a Constitution?' (1995) 1 *European Law Journal* 282.

[63] Among the many writings of that period in which the terms constitution and constitutional were considered in relation to EU law, see JHH Weiler, *The Constitution of Europe* (Cambridge: Cambridge University Press, 1999); K Lenaerts, P Van Nuffel, and R Bray, *Constitutional Law of the European Union* (London: Sweet & Maxwell, 1999); J-C Piris, 'Does the European Union Have a Constitution? Does It Need One?' (1999) 24 *European Law Review* 557; P Craig, 'Constitutions, Constitutionalism, and the European Union' (2001) 7 *European Law Journal* 125; A Peters, *Elemente einer Theorie der Verfassung Europas* (Berlin: Duncker & Humblot, 2001).

[64] But see, for a critical voice, JHH Weiler, 'In Defence of the Status Quo: Europe's Constitutional *Sonderweg*' in JHH Weiler and M Wind (eds), *European Constitutionalism beyond the State* (Cambridge: Cambridge University Press, 2003).

[65] Those were the famous words used in the European Council's mandate for the intergovernmental conference that was to elaborate the Lisbon Treaty (Annex 1 to the European Council Conclusions of 21–22 June 2007, p 1).

High Representative of the European Union) and 'primacy of European Union law' (see generally chapter 2).

Still, the constitutional perspective on EU law continues to make sense even after the demise of the Constitutional Treaty,[66] and we find several textbooks on EU law that flaunt constitutional terms in their titles.[67] By using constitutional language, these authors seek to emphasize that the Treaties perform many of the same functions as a national constitution: they establish public authority, and allocate powers between different political institutions; they establish a division of competences between the EU and the Member States, in a way which is reminiscent of similar delimitations of competences in federal constitutions; they set out the basic values of the EU legal order, and the fundamental rights of persons; they organize a system of judicial review for the enforcement of EU law obligations and for the review of the validity of EU action. In other words, the usage of constitutional terminology seeks to underline the close similarity (or analogy) between some of the legal issues that arise under EU law and those that arise in the constitutional law of States (especially federal States).

Nor is this trend limited to EU law scholarship only. There is also a recent trend in the legal literature emphasizing that international law, more broadly speaking, has started to develop some constitution-like features[68] or, at least – taking a more normative perspective – that its constitutional features should be strengthened. This approach focuses naturally on international organizations,[69] which form an institutional reality whose constitutional features can be developed by such things as greater democratic accountability and effective judicial review of the organization's decisions. The institutional devices developed in the context of the EU can in fact serve as a source of inspiration for strengthening the rule of law and other constitutional principles in the legal regime of international organizations.[70]

4 The EU as object and subject of international law

In this final section, attention is drawn to the complex situation that arises from the fact that the EU, whilst being a treaty-based legal construct, can itself, in turn, conclude

---

[66] On the latter point there is a solid consensus in the EU law literature; see among others: G de Búrca, 'Reflections on the EU's Path from the Constitutional Treaty to the Lisbon Treaty, (2008) Jean Monnet Working Paper 03/08; N Walker, 'European Constitutionalism in the State Constitutional Tradition' (2006) 59 *Current Legal Problems* 51; L Besselink, 'The Notion and Nature of the European Constitution after the Lisbon Treaty' in J Wouters, L Verhey, and P Kiiver (eds), *European Constitutionalism beyond Lisbon* (Antwerp: Intersentia, 2009); S Griller, 'Is This a Constitution? Remarks on a Contested Concept' in S Griller and J Ziller (eds), *The Lisbon Treaty – EU Constitutionalism without a Constitutional Treaty?* (Vienna: Springer, 2008); K Lenaerts, 'De Rome à Lisbonne, la Constitution européenne en marche?' [2008] *Cahiers de droit européen* 229; L Pech, 'The Fabulous Destiny of the EC Treaty: From Treaty to Constitution to Treaty Again?' (2008) 15 *Irish Journal of European Law* 49.

[67] A Rosas and L Armati, *EU Constitutional Law – An Introduction* (2nd edn, Oxford: Hart Publishing, 2012); Schütze, *European Constitutional Law* (n 52); A von Bogdandy and J Bast, eds, *Principles of European Constitutional Law* (2nd edn, Oxford: Hart Pubishing, 2011). See also the discussion of constitutionalism and EU law in chapter 4.

[68] See eg J Klabbers, A Peters, and G Ulfstein (eds), *The Constitutionalisation of International Law* (Cambridge: Cambridge University Press, 2009).

[69] See A Peters, 'The Constitutionalisation of International Organisations' in N Walker, J Shaw, and S Tierney (eds), *Europe's Constitutional Mosaic* (Oxford: Hart Publishing, 2011).

[70] See A von Bogdandy. 'The European Lesson for International Democracy: The Significance of Articles 9–12 EU Treaty for International Organizations' (2012) 23 *European Journal of International Law* 315.

further treaties in order to advance its policy objectives (and see further chapter 24). In other words, the EU is both an *object* of international law made by others (its Member States) and a *subject* entitled to make new international law. This is, once again, not a unique feature of the EU: other international organizations have been given the capacity to conclude treaties;[71] indeed, some of them have concluded treaties with the EC or the EU.

The EU contributes to the development of international law in the same three main ways as States do: thorough its unilateral practice (which may contribute to the emergence of rules of customary international law);[72] through concluding treaties with non-EU States or international organizations; and through its activity as a member of some multilateral organizations, such as the World Trade Organization (WTO).[73] Of those three, treaty-making is particularly important. The EU has, in fact, replaced its Member States as an international actor in a number of policy fields, such as international trade or international fisheries regulation. The Member States have had to accept abandoning their power to conclude treaties in those areas that are within the EU's exclusive competence.[74] In other areas, such as environmental protection or immigration, the EU and the Member States share their treaty-making competence.

When an international agreement is concluded by the EU, then international law starts acting as a constraint on the EU. This constraint is simply expressed by the rule in the TFEU stating that EU agreements are binding on the institutions of the EU and also, as the case may be, on its Member States.[75] However, the legal force of the constraint is, in fact, very variable. Increasingly, the Union seeks to insert clauses into international agreements that guarantee the prevalence of existing or future EU law over the obligations contained in the agreement. The most blatant form of this 'reverse primacy' is the so-called disconnection clauses that the EU manages to insert into many Council of Europe conventions. According to these clauses, EU law dealing with subject matter covered in the Convention shall continue to apply between EU Member States, so that, on those matters, the Convention provisions will only apply to non-EU Member States.[76] Even in the absence of such conflict rules that preserve the integrity of the Union's own law, the prevalence of the international agreements may be limited by the fact that their self-executing nature is denied (as is notoriously the case with WTO law).[77] Finally, as highlighted in the *Kadi* judgment of 2008, the primacy of international agreements recognized by Article 216(2) TFEU relates to *secondary* EU law, but the application of international agreements within the EU legal order may be

[71] See Klabbers, *An Introduction to International Institutional Law* (n 5) ch 13.

[72] See, on this aspect of the interaction between EU law and general international law, F Hoffmeister, 'The Contribution of EU Practice to International Law' in M Cremona (ed), *Developments in EU External Relations Law* (Oxford: Oxford University Press, 2008) 54 *et seq.*

[73] For a recent collection of contributions on this theme, see B Van Vooren, S Blockmans, and J Wouters (eds), *The EU's Role in Global Governance: The Legal Dimension* (Oxford: Oxford University Press, 2013).

[74] This is perhaps the characteristic that is most unusual from the point of view of general international law; see discussion in B de Witte, 'The Emergence of a European System of Public International Law: The EU and Its Member States as Strange Subjects' in J Wouters, A Nollkaemper, and E de Wet (eds), *The Europeanisation of International Law* (The Hague: TMC Asser Press, 2008).   [75] Art 216, second para, TFEU.

[76] For a discussion of these disconnection clauses and similar devices aiming at preserving the integrity of pre-existing or future EU law against conflicting international obligations, see M Cremona, 'Disconnection Clauses in EC Law and Practice' in C Hillion and P Koutrakos (eds), *Mixed Agreements Revisited – The EU and Its Member States in the World* (Oxford: Hart Publishing, 2010).

[77] See, for a detailed discussion, M Mendez, *The Legal Effects of EU Agreements: Maximalist Treaty Enforcement and Judicial Avoidance Techniques* (Oxford: Oxford University Press, 2013).

denied if they conflict with the Treaties themselves or with the unwritten principles of primary EU law.[78]

The relationship between EU law and other forms of international law is seen by the Court of Justice as a relationship between distinct legal orders. Thus, in a recent case, the Court held that 'Security Council resolutions, on the one hand, and Council common positions and regulations, on the other hand, originate from distinct legal orders. Measures within the framework of the United Nations and the European Union are adopted by organs with autonomous powers, granted to them by their basic charters, that is to say, the treaties that created them.'[79]

The statement that the EU legal order is *autonomous* with regard to the surrounding international legal environment may, in fact, mean two rather different things: either that EU law, as a specialized international legal order, *deviates* from the general rules of international law on one or other point; or that the EU *fails to comply* with specific international obligations and gives priority instead to its own internal rules.

The *first meaning of autonomy*, namely the capacity to adopt special legal rules that deviate from the general rules of international law, is unproblematic. The general rules of international law are default rules which States can set aside and replace by more suitable rules in their mutual relations. This is particularly true for treaties establishing international organizations, in which the founding States are free to equip 'their' organization with institutional mechanisms and operational rules of their own liking with hardly any limits to their creativity. In an Advisory Opinion of 1996, the International Court of Justice affirmed that 'constituent instruments of international organizations are ... treaties of a particular type; their object is to create new subjects of law endowed with a certain *autonomy*, to which the parties entrust the task of realizing common goals.'[80]

A *second* and stronger *meaning of autonomy* is the capacity for a particular system to give priority to its own internal rules over and above external international obligations. This is a form of autonomy that is typical for those international organizations that are subjects of international law, and have used their capacity to conclude international agreements with States or other international organizations. When acting as subjects of international law, they may be led – just like States – to incur obligations under international law which may appear, at some point in time, to conflict with their own internal rules. In view of the multiplication of such external legal commitments of the EU, it is possible that they may occasionally enter into conflict with the EU's own domestic law.

In *Kadi*, the European Court of Justice thus refused the application of 'external' international obligations in order to preserve fundamental norms of the 'internal' legal order of the EU, namely the right of defence and the right to property. The wisdom of the Court's attitude has been very widely discussed in the literature.[81] But from the point of view that concerns us here, namely that of the relation between the EU legal order and the surrounding international legal environment, the judgment did not imply a major change. In particular, the Court did not call into question its traditional view that international

---

[78] Joined Cases C-402/05 P and C-415/05 P *Kadi and Al Barakaat v Council and Commission*, judgment of 3 September 2008. For further discussion of this judgment, see chapters 8 and 9.

[79] Case C-380/09 P *Melli Bank v Council*, judgment of 13 March 2012, para 54.

[80] ICJ, *Legality of the Use by a State of Nuclear Weapons in Armed Conflict*, Advisory Opinion of 8 July 1996, para 19.

[81] See, for some contrasting views (among many others): T Tridimas and JA Gutierrez-Fons, 'EU Law, International Law, and Economic Sanctions against Terrorism: The Judiciary in Distress' (2009) *Fordham International Law Journal* 660; and G de Búrca, 'The ECJ and the International Legal Order: A Re-Evaluation' in de Búrca and Weiler, *The Worlds of European Constitutionalism* (n 1).

agreements of the EU form part of the EU legal order upon their ratification and entry into force. The Court did, however, repeat the unsurprising view that international obligations concluded by the EU cannot prevail over the highest norms of the internal EU legal order. In defending that view, which is very similar to that adopted by national courts when confronted with a conflict between international and national constitutional law, the European Court of Justice appropriately highlighted the autonomy of the special legal order which the EU Member States have decided to carve out by using the instrument of...an international treaty.

5 Conclusion

The EU can be seen, as Wyatt and Dashwood aptly put it, as 'a developed form of international organization which displays characteristics of an embryonic federation'.[82] The various revision Treaties of the past decades (including the last one, the Lisbon Treaty) do not signal a change in this respect. They rather show that the Member State governments were not willing to contemplate a fundamental change of the EU's legal nature; on the contrary, they have actively experimented, in the Lisbon Treaty, with the toolkit of international treaty law, with generous use of Protocols, declarations, transition clauses, derogations, opt-outs, etc. But still, as we have seen, many EU law scholars disagree with this assessment and propose a different view of the EU as an unprecedented type of non-State entity.

The fact that, in this matter, legal scholars keep disagreeing has never stopped EU law from evolving through repeated Treaty revisions and through the institutional practice of its institutions and the legal interpretations by its Court of Justice. Indeed, there are hardly any practical consequences that derive from the choice of a given qualification. In particular, qualifying EU law as international law does not imply that the Treaties should be understood and interpreted from an intergovernmental perspective and that limitations of sovereignty should be narrowly construed. The Court has convincingly shown, since *Van Gend en Loos*, why the EC Treaty was a treaty that should be construed in a broader and purpose-oriented way, and other international courts have followed the same jurisprudential line in interpreting 'their' treaties. Still, it would seem that the recognition that EU law is an advanced *species* of the *genus* international law explains more easily some crucial characteristics of the EU legal order without hindering its autonomous development. It has the added advantage of making the 'European way of law'[83] a more amenable source of inspiration for other States, in other parts of the world, when they devise their own forms of international cooperation. The progressive development of international law would be weakened if its conceptual links with EU law were cut off.

Further reading

B DE WITTE, 'The European Union as an International Legal Experiment' in G de Búrca and JHH Weiler (eds), *The Worlds of European Constitutionalism* (Cambridge: Cambridge University Press, 2012)

---

[82] *Wyatt and Dashwood's European Union Law* (5th edn, London: Sweet & Maxwell, 2006) 132.

[83] A-M Slaughter and W Burke-White, 'The Future of International Law is Domestic (or, the European Way of Law)' (2006) 47 *Harvard Journal of International Law* 327.

TC HARTLEY, 'International Law and the Law of the European Union' (2001) 72 *British Yearbook of International Law* 1

J KLABBERS, *An Introduction to International Institutional Law* (2nd edn, Cambridge: Cambridge University Press, 2009)

A ROSAS AND L ARMATI, *EU Constitutional Law: An Introduction* (2nd edn, Oxford: Hart Publishing, 2012) chs 2 and 3

R SCHÜTZE, *European Constitutional Law* (Cambridge: Cambridge University Press, 2012) ch 2

N WALKER, 'The Place of European Law' in G de Búrca and JHH Weiler (eds), *The Worlds of European Constitutionalism* (Cambridge: Cambridge University Press, 2012)

8

General principles of EU law and EU administrative law

Herwig CH Hofmann

1 Introduction

Treaty provisions and Union legislation are only part of the story of how law can actually take effect in reality. A quite decisive factor is their implementation through administrative action. The basic themes of this chapter are, first, the steps which take place after legislation has been passed: who does what and by which means to make sure that political decisions made in a legislative act do not only remain 'law on the books'? The second theme is which rights exist in that context? How can they be protected? In other words, this chapter deals not only with the sub-legislative setting of rules and making of decisions, it also asks which principles and rules exist to ensure the legality and legitimacy of administrative action implementing EU law. Such principles of EU law are, of course, often relevant as criteria of legality of all forms of EU law. Where they are of special relevance to the matter discussed in this chapter they are addressed here. You will find them also discussed in other specific contexts, for example in chapters on legislation or on judicial review.

The legal issues addressed in this chapter influence questions as varied as one can imagine: will a medicine which one study finds to do more harm to a patient than good in combating the relevant disease be taken off the market in the entire EU? How much minimum capital should a bank maintain in order to be allowed to offer services? May a product labelled as 'organic' contain traces of genetically modified organisms? What level of training should the pilot of a commercial airliner maintain to be allowed to fly over and land at an airport in the EU? Can the bank account held by a citizen of the Union be frozen by order of the United Nations Security Council? Can I ask the administration in my home country to grant me access to the information that has been collected about me in another Member State of the Union? Is the permission to build an offshore wind-energy park legal when no previous study has been made to assess whether the flight patterns of migrating birds might thereby be disturbed?

Finding solutions to these questions will regularly require having a basic understanding of what are referred to in this chapter as general principles of EU law and of EU administrative law. Administrative law is part of public law enabling and constraining administrative conduct, that is, activity designed to implement EU law. The essence of EU administrative law is therefore the rules and principles governing the procedures for exercising administrative functions and the organization of the institutions and bodies exercising these functions. One word of caution, though, is necessary: the EU's legal order is particularly dynamic. This is due to the evolving nature of European integration and growing interdependencies between various levels of law and politics. The effect is that a combination of legal sources – international, EU, and national – are being used in most policy areas, adapting the needs of the policy area to the possibilities of a Union with limited conferral of powers, and often varying constellations of Member States taking part in specific policies.

In order to explain this area using a step-by-step approach, this chapter will give an overview of the key institutions and agencies of the EU and what they do (section 2). Then, it will move on to develop an understanding of the applicable law which is key to developing notions of accountability and the protection of rights in this field (section 3).

You are already familiar with some elements relevant in this chapter. You have, for example, read in chapter 5 (on decision-making and competences) about delegated and implementing acts under Articles 290 and 291 TFEU, and that the EU possesses only those powers conferred on it. In other contexts, you will have read about the separation of functions between the Member States and the EU – especially the principle of sincere cooperation between Member States and the Union. You will further have read about EU agencies (as regards some particular EU agencies, see chapters 25 and 26) and about the possibilities of delegation of powers to agencies. In view of the central themes of this chapter, these elements are brought together in this chapter to show how institutional, substantive, and procedural law resulting from rules and principles of EU law shape the legal reality.

2 Organizational levels and the distribution of powers in implementing EU law

In the EU's legal system, the exercise of the administrative function is undertaken by a diverse range of actors both at the EU level as well as at the Member State level. These are institutions and bodies of the Union as well as those of its Member States. The following discussion concentrates on some central principles of law governing this distribution and holding the actors on various levels to account.

2.1 Conferral of powers on the Union

Under the principle of conferral, not only is the Union barred from enacting legislation in cases where it is not authorized to do so by the Treaties, it is also barred from passing implementing acts if not authorized. This results from the principle of conferral under

Article 5(1) and (2) TEU and is explicitly restated in Article 291(1) TFEU, under which 'Member States shall adopt all measures of national law necessary to implement legally binding Union acts.'

Only where the Union is authorized to act, can it do so. When administrative functions are undertaken on the EU level, their exercise is organizationally fragmented. It is spread across the Commission (to a certain degree also the Council) and, increasingly, EU agencies. Comitology committees, made up of Member State experts, are designated to supervise and advise the Commission when undertaking implementing activity under Article 291 TFEU. These were already addressed and explained further in the context of chapter 5 on decision-making procedures.

Generally, where administrative powers are conferred on EU-level bodies, they are authorized to adopt acts with general content – so-called rule-making. Areas where Union bodies have also been conferred with powers to take single case decisions with binding force on individuals are increasingly frequent. Initially, it was the Commission which was given external decision-making powers in the area of competition law including antitrust under Articles 101 and 102 TFEU, merger control, and the control of State aid given by the Member States (see further chapters 17 and 18). More and more, EU agencies are also taking decisions addressing issues of EU-wide concern such as the granting of trademarks for the entire EU market, admitting chemical products as safe for use, and other such regulatory activity.

In most policy areas, however, even if legislation has been adopted by the EU and even if some common rules for the implementation of these rules have been adopted at the EU level, final decisions vis-à-vis individuals implementing EU policies are taken by Member State bodies. Examples of this approach are customs decisions. Despite the fact that customs law and tariffs are entirely governed by EU law, because the customs union and the common commercial (ie external trade) policy are 'exclusive competences' of the EU (see chapter 5), it is national customs officials who take the final decisions and enforce them. This is sometimes referred to as indirect administration of EU law.

2.2 Implementation of EU law by the Member States

In the absence of EU law provisions to the contrary, Member States not only have the right to implement EU law through their administrative apparatus, they are actually obliged to do so (see further chapter 6).

Member States, under the principle of 'sincere cooperation' in Article 4(3) TEU, are obliged to

> take any appropriate measure, general or particular, to ensure fulfillment of the obligations arising out of the Treaties or resulting from acts of the institutions of the Union.

They may do so by applying existing national legislation, but may also be obliged by EU law to pass specific national implementing legislation and to adopt associated administrative regulations in order to create the conditions necessary for implementation at the national level. Member States, under this model, enjoy only limited institutional or procedural autonomy to implement EU law.[1]

---

[1] Originally formulated in Case 33/76 *Rewe-Zentralfinanz EG v Landwirtschafts-Kammer für das Saarland* [1976] ECR 1989, para 5.

The limitations on the Member States' autonomy therefore arise from the fact that, in the fields of Union policy, Member States' substantive and procedural administrative law is to be applied within the framework of EU law. This framework consists of three basic concepts:

First, Member States have the right to set their own standards for substantive and procedural law only in the absence of any explicit requirements in Union law. Therefore, insofar as Union law itself makes provision as regards procedures, criteria, or organizational requirements, national administrations are obliged to act in conformity with these.[2]

Secondly, in the area of indirect administration, the legality of Member States' rules and procedures will be measured by their compliance with general principles of EU law and the EU's Charter of Fundamental Rights (see further chapter 9).

Thirdly, the application of national procedural rules in the implementation of Union law must be exercised in strict compliance with the principles of *equivalence* and *effectiveness*.[3]

2.2.1 'Equivalence' and 'effectiveness'

Under the principle of equivalence, in the absence of applicable EU law, Member States must grant at least equivalent protection for violation of EU law to that available against violation of national law.[4] Provisions used under national law may not be 'less favourable than those governing similar domestic actions (principle of equivalence)'.[5] A rule must therefore 'be applied without distinction', whether the infringement arises from Union law or national law.[6]

Where there is no equivalent national law, or where its application does not lead to the result of enforcing or protecting a right under EU law, the principle of equivalence will override the principle of effectiveness. National courts are obliged to set aside

> any provision of a national legal system and any legislative, administrative or judicial practice which might impair the effectiveness [of Union law].[7]

Even in cases where there is no equivalent form of protection of rights under national law, Member States, under the principle of effectiveness, may not make the exercise of rights conferred by Union law (even only temporarily) 'practically impossible or excessively difficult'.[8]

---

[2] National law might turn out to be inconsistent or even incompatible with EU provisions in the area. The EU's conflicts rules applicable to such situations are the principle of primacy and the possibility of direct effect of EU law. These interpretative principles oblige the Member States' bodies to set aside national law which is in conflict with EU law provisions; see eg case law since Case 106/77 *Amministrazione delle Finanze dello Stato v Simmenthal SpA ('Simmenthal II')* [1978] ECR 629 and the discussion in chapter 6.

[3] See Case C-261/95 *Palmisani v INPS* [1997] ECR I-4025, para 27. See also Case C-453/99 *Courage and Crehan* [2001] ECR I-6297, para 25.

[4] Joined Cases C-205–215/82 *Deutsche Milchkontor* [1983] ECR 2633, para 17; *Courage* (n 3) para 29.

[5] *Courage and Crehan* (n 3) para 29.

[6] Case C-231/96 *Edis* [1998] ECR I-4951, para 36; Joined Cases 66/79, 127/79 and 128/79 *Salumi* [1980] ECR 1237, para 21. Whether a situation under EU law is sufficiently similar to a situation regulated under national law is subject to detailed case-by-case analysis, the Court looking at the purpose and effect of a national measure in question – see Case C-326/96 *Levez* [1998] ECR I-7835, para 41.

[7] Case C-213/89 *Factortame* [1990] ECR I-2433, paras 19 and 20.

[8] *Courage* (n 3) para 29. This is a standard formula which can be found in many cases, eg Case C-128/93 *Fisscher* [1994] ECR I-4583, para 37; Joined Cases C-231–233/06 *Jonkman* [2007] ECR I-5149, para 28.

The obligations under the principles of equivalence and effectiveness apply not only to national courts but also directly to national administrations.[9] The latter are explicitly obliged under EU law to set aside national laws which are in conflict with directly effective EU law.[10]

2.2.2 Decision-making with 'trans-territorial' effect

In many cases, implementation of EU law by Member States requires the national bodies to take decisions which have an effect not only on the territory of that State but in the entire EU. This phenomenon can be well illustrated by looking at EU customs law. Once a toy from China has been imported into the EU, for example via a port in the Netherlands (eg Rotterdam), the toy can be sold throughout the Union without facing any further customs duties or controls; in other words, it can freely circulate in the Union. The Dutch customs officials classifying the product as a toy and assessing the customs tariff due to be paid, in that sense act as customs officials of the entire Union. They act on a mix of applicable law – they are agents of the Kingdom of the Netherlands and subject to the rules and procedures of their own hierarchic system – yet in the exercise of their duties as customs officials and in the classification of the goods, they act on the basis of EU law.

In order to mitigate this very common phenomenon of what might be referred to as decision-making with trans-territorial effect (some authors say trans-national effect), in most policy areas there is some form of common structure for the exchange of information and coordination of administrative action. These are sometimes referred to using the metaphor 'networks'. The objective of such structures of information exchange, which are established by EU legislation or international agreement between Member States, is to reduce potential problems arising from decentralized administration of a common legal space. An example of such a system is the so-called 'Schengen Information System',[11] basically a very large database on persons wanted by law-enforcement agencies who are to be denied entry to the Schengen zone, and stolen objects (see further chapters 25 and 26). Other such information networks exist, to name just a few examples, on food safety,[12] the environment,[13] external borders, fisheries,[14] maritime and ship safety,[15] customs, and

---

[9] S Prechal, *Directives in EC Law* (2nd edn, Oxford: Oxford University Press, 2005) 65–72.

[10] See Case 103/88 *Fratelli Costanzo v Comune di Milano* [1989] ECR 1839; Case C-224/97 *Ciola* [1999] ECR I-2517; Case C-118/00 *Larsy v Inasti* [2001] ECR I-5063; Case C-453/00 *Kühne & Heitz* [2004] ECR I-837. These cases, for the basis of that obligation, refer to the principle of sincere cooperation under Art 4(3) TEU (but the cases still refer to the old Art 10 EC). For a critique of this approach by the Court of Justice, see eg Prechal, *Directives in EC Law* (n 9) 65–72.

[11] Council Decision 2007/533/JHA of 12 June 2007 on the establishment, operation and use of the second generation Schengen Information System (SIS II) (OJ [2007] L205/63); Regulation (EC) No 1987/2006 of the European Parliament and of the Council of 20 December 2006 on the establishment, operation and use of the second generation Schengen Information System (SIS II) (OJ [2006] L381/4).

[12] Regulation (EC) No 178/2002 of the European Parliament and of the Council of 28 January 2002 laying down the general principles and requirements of food law, establishing the European Food Safety Authority and laying down procedures in matters of food safety (OJ [2002] L31/1); Commission Regulation (EU) No 16/2001 of 10 January 2011 laying down implementing measures for the rapid alert system for food and feed (OJ [2011] L6/7).

[13] Regulation (EC) No 401/2009 of the European Parliament and of the council of 23 April 2009 on the European Environment Agency and the European Environment Information and Observation Network (OJ [2009] L126/13).

[14] Council Regulation (EC) No 1005/2008 of 29 September 2008 establishing a Community system to prevent, deter and eliminate illegal, unreported and unregulated fishing, amending Regulation (EEC) No 2847/93, (EC) No 1936/2001 and (EC) No 601/2004 and repealing Regulation (EC) No 1093/94 and (EC) No 1447/1999 (OJ [2008] L286/1).

[15] Regulation (EC) No 1406/2002 of the European Parliament and of the Council of 27 June 2002 establishing a European Maritime Safety Agency (OJ [2002] L208/1).

value added tax.[16] These information exchanges are generally managed and maintained by EU agencies.

2.3 Delegation of powers within the Union

As discussed in chapter 3, delegation of powers from legislators to executive (in practice, administrative) bodies constitutes an inevitable aspect of modern legal systems. Reasons include the technical complexity of many areas of regulation, the limited effectiveness of hierarchical command structures, and the highly pluralistic societies which require knowledge and balancing of very diverse interests. At first glance, the principle of attributed powers under Articles 5(2) and 13(2) TEU provides a presumption against delegation. Under these provisions, powers should be exercised in the EU by those entrusted with them by the Treaties. However, delegation is not only a practical necessity but also a general phenomenon in the implementation of EU policies.

The Treaty provisions on delegation of powers, set out in Articles 290 and 291 TFEU, favour delegation to the Commission (see further chapter 5).[17] In this system, no reference is made to agencies as possible recipients of delegations – despite the express acknowledgement in the provisions on judicial review of acts (Article 263, paragraphs 1 and 5, TFEU) of EU agencies as potential decision-makers (see further chapter 10).[18] In the same vein, the 2011 Comitology Regulation (ie the general rules on the conferment upon the Commission of the power to adopt measures implementing EU acts, pursuant to Article 291 TFEU)[19] makes no mention of agencies and does not clarify the relation of decision-making with the help of comitology committees as opposed to agency decision-making.[20] Instead, it establishes for this delegation to the Commission two decision-making procedures only – the advisory and the examination procedures. Yet, some agencies have a legal basis directly in the Treaties.[21] Most, however, are created by legislative act despite lacking explicit empowerment in EU primary constitutional Treaty law to do so. Despite this, in the EU, agencies have been entrusted with pursuing different tasks,[22] ranging from the provision of

---

[16] See more generally on administrative cooperation in the field of taxation, Council Directive 2011/16/EU of 15 February 2011 on administrative cooperation in the field of taxation and repealing Directive 77/779/EC (OJ [2011] L64/1).

[17] Art 290 TFEU allows conferring upon the Commission the power to adopt quasi-legislative 'delegated' acts under the oversight of the European Parliament and the Council. Under Art 291, paras 2 and 3, TFEU, implementing powers shall be conferred on the Commission – exceptionally on the Council – 'where uniform conditions for implementing legally binding Union acts are needed'.

[18] Besides Art 263 TFEU, several other provisions in the TFEU directly take into consideration the importance and role played by agencies in the EU legal system. Among these, the most important are: Art 15 (transparency and access to documents), Art 16 (data protection), Art 228 (competence of the European Ombudsman), Art 265 (action for failure to act), Art 267 (reference for preliminary ruling), and Art 287 (jurisdiction of the European Court of Auditors). Also the EU's Charter of Fundamental Rights under Art 47 explicitly gives the right to an effective remedy, including against agencies. Agencies are further explicitly mentioned in Arts 41, 42, and 43 Charter.

[19] Regulation (EU) No 182/2011 of 16 February 2011, laying down the rules and general principles concerning mechanisms for control by Member States of the Commission's exercise of implementing powers (OJ [2011] L55/13), is the legislative act that under Art 291, para 3, TFEU lays down 'mechanisms for control by Member States of the Commission's exercise of implementing powers'.

[20] Instead it might actually be read to exclude the possibilities of delegating decision-making powers to independent EU agencies since it allows explicitly only for either the advisory or the examination procedure. Regulation 182/2011 (OJ [2011] L55/13).

[21] eg the European Police Office, Europol, Art 88 TFEU; the agency in charge of cooperation of judicial cooperation, Eurojust, Art 85 TFEU. On these bodies, see further chapter 25.

[22] The basis for this classification can be found in E Vos, 'Reforming the European Commission: What Role to Play for EU Agencies' (2000) 37 *Common Market Law Review* 1113 at 1120–1121. For a different

information, the provision of services as a basis for the adoption of implementing acts, and even the exercise of specific implementing powers.[23] Even though some agencies support the Commission only by collecting information or processing applications, other agencies have delegated powers to adopt individually binding decision-making, such as the Community Plant Variety Office (CPVO), the European Chemicals Agency (ECHA), and, in non-scientific fields, the Office of Harmonization for the Internal Market (OHIM). In these cases, agencies exert limited discretion, well qualified by the provisions of the relevant regulations.[24]

How, then, does an EU agency receive a mandate to exercise its powers, by whom, why, and within which limits? Delegation of powers in the EU is generally discussed in the context of the *Meroni* case from the very early days of European integration.[25] There the Court examined the question whether and to what extent the Commission (which was then called the High Authority) could delegate powers under Article 53 of the Treaty establishing the European Coal and Steel Community (ECSC) for the operation of the supply of ferrous scrap to two bodies it had set up on the basis of Belgian private law.[26] In *Meroni*, the Court explicitly allowed sub-delegation of Commission powers to private parties, despite the lack of explicit authorization in the ECSC Treaty. It, however, set some conditions for such sub-delegation: first, the Commission was authorized only to sub-delegate powers which it had previously been granted. Thereby, the Court reconfirmed the principle of conferral and prohibited actions ultra vires.[27] Secondly, the Commission had to control the exercise of the sub-delegated powers.[28] Thirdly, the Commission was barred from delegating powers to private parties which would allow them to adopt acts with quasi-legislative content because doing so would upset the 'institutional balance' of powers conferred on institutions in the ECSC Treaty.[29]

This reference to 'institutional balance' – a principle akin to the separation of powers – is the reason for also applying the standards set by *Meroni* today in the context of the EU.[30] Today, therefore, it is established that under EU law delegation of clearly defined powers, the exercise of which is subject to its supervision, is possible. Most EU agencies, which are established by EU legislative acts, are based on Treaty provisions permitting the adoption of 'measures' for the harmonization or approximation of national law such as, most importantly, Article 114 TFEU (the general legal base for the adoption of internal market measures), and subsidiarity, Article 352 TFEU (which gives residual power for the EU to act to attain one of its objectives, if the Treaties have not set out the necessary powers).

---

classification of agencies, see E Chiti, 'The Emergence of a Community Administration: The Case of European Agencies' (2000) 37 *Common Market Law Review* 309 at 315–317.

[23] Two examples of many: Art 42(5) of Council Regulation (EC) No 207/2009 of 26 February 2009 on the Community trade mark (codified version) (OJ [2009] L78/1); Art 62 of Council Regulation (EC) No 2100/94 of 22 July 1994 on Community plant variety rights (OJ [1994] L227/1), as amended.

[24] This was, eg in Case T-187/06 *Schräder v Community Plant Variety Office (CPVO)* [2008] ECR II-3151, confirmed on appeal in Case C-38/09 P *Schräder v Community Plant Variety Office (CPVO)* [2010] ECR I-3209.

[25] Joined Cases 9/56 and 10/56 *Meroni v ECSC High Authority* [1957–8] ECR English Special Edition 133.

[26] These were the 'Joint Bureau of Ferrous Scrap Consumers' and the 'Imported Ferrous Scrap Equalization Fund'.   [27] *Meroni* (n 25) para 150.

[28] *Meroni* (n 25) para 152.   [29] *Meroni* (n 25) para 152.

[30] See eg Case C-345/00 P *FNAB v Council* [2001] ECR I-3811, para 41 (on the relevance of the concept of institutional balance); Case C-301/02 P *Tralli v European Central Bank* [2005] ECR I-4071, paras 41–44; Case C-164/98 P *DIR Films International v Commission* [2000] ECR I-447, paras 52–55. On the limits to delegate by legislative act the right to amend an annex to such legislation by means of implementing acts (under the pre-Lisbon system), see Joined Cases C-154/04 and C-155/04 *Alliance for Natural Health* [2005] ECR I-6451, para 90.

Also, policy-specific powers exist allowing for the creation of structural 'measures' (ie agencies).[31]

3 Criteria for legality

In the day-to-day application of EU law, one of the most central questions which needs to be asked and answered concerns the legality of an act or action of an institution body or agency acting within a policy covered by EU law. In order to answer such a question, it is necessary to have a set of criteria in mind which can be used as mental guidance for analysing a case. Not all the principles listed here will give rise to rights of individuals or will be applicable in every case, but keeping them in mind as a checklist will be extremely helpful for structuring answers to a real-life problem.

General, overarching criteria for the legality of acts of the EU exist mostly in the form of general principles of law.[32] These general principles of EU law[33] have a constitutional status in that they bind Union institutions in the exercise of their legislative and administrative competences. Their function is to provide a guide to the interpretation of Union law, including the Treaties, to constitute grounds for the review of Union law, whether directly based on the Treaties themselves or subordinate acts, and to establish a basis for the non-contractual liability of the Union (Articles 268 and 340, second and third paragraphs, TFEU). In addition, such principles also have to be observed by the Member States when they implement Union law[34] and where they derogate from it,[35] that is, in all cases which 'fall within the scope of Community law'.[36]

In the following, I will first discuss proportionality (section 3.1), then various additional sub-elements of the rule of law including transparency, legality, and the protection of legitimate expectations (section 3.2). The discussion then turns to principles of good administration including the right to a fair hearing, to a reasoned act, and further rights of defence (section 3.3). This is followed by a discussion of the right to an effective judicial remedy (section 3.4) and information rights (section 3.5).

3.1 Proportionality

Article 5(4) TEU states that 'Under the principle of proportionality, the content and form of Union action, shall not exceed what is necessary to achieve the objectives of this Treaty.' The real content and relevance of the principle of proportionality, however, arises only from the interpretation given to it in the case law of the Court of Justice. Long before the

---

[31] See eg in the area of research, Arts 182, fifth para, and 187 TFEU; in the environmental field Art 192 TFEU (the legal basis for the European Environmental Agency (OJ [2009] L126/13)); in the air and maritime transport field Art 100, second para, TFEU; regarding border checks, asylum, and immigration in the context of the so-called 'Area of Freedom, Security and Justice', Arts 74 and 77(2)d) TFEU (the latter is the legal basis for the creation of the EU's external borders agency, Frontex (OJ [2004] L 349/1; see further chapters 5 and 26).

[32] The European Parliament has now called on the Commission to present a legislative proposal for a general act on administrative procedures to be followed by EU institutions and bodies when implementing EU law. So far, however, there is no standard EU 'administrative procedure act' or similar code or legal framework horizontally applicable throughout the policy areas touched by EU integration. The same is true at national level, as regards the national implementation of EU law: see chapter 6.

[33] General principles of law often include principles requiring standards of procedural justice in administrative procedures, eg the notions of proportionality, right of defence, and others.

[34] See Case 5/88 *Wachauf v Bundesamt für Ernährung und Forstwirtschaft* [1989] ECR 2609.

[35] Case C-260/89 *ERT v DEP* [1991] ECR I-2925.

[36] Ibid, para. 42. See also Case C-263/97 *First City Trading* [1998] ECR I-5537.

principle of proportionality was recognized in what is now Article 5(4) TEU, the Court had developed proportionality as a general principle of EU law. It might now be regarded as, directly or indirectly, the most widely used general principle of EU law. One of the reasons for this is that proportionality is a very versatile principle serving to review the legality of:

- acts of EU institutions and bodies when limiting or regulating the exercise of rights of individuals (eg the Commission adopts a decision fining a company for violation of EU antitrust law under Article 101 TFEU);[37]

- acts of EU institutions and bodies when limiting Member State powers by adopting EU acts (eg an EU directive of a legislative nature on the maximum working time of workers per week);[38]

- indirectly, in case of acts of Member State bodies when implementing EU law (eg the Dutch veterinary authorities confiscate Ms Jippes's pet sheep in order to comply with an EU regulation on the limitation of the outbreak of viral veterinary diseases);[39]

- acts of Member States when limiting or regulating in the context of rights or freedoms guaranteed by EU law (eg Greek authorities decide not to grant a broadcasting licence to a private TV station).[40]

The Court of Justice has developed the review of compliance with the principle of proportionality as a three-step test:

- Under the first level 'the principle of proportionality requires that measures adopted by European Union institutions do not exceed the limits of what is appropriate and necessary in order to attain the objectives legitimately pursued by the legislation in question.'[41]

- Secondly, 'when there is a choice between several appropriate measures recourse must be had to the least onerous'.[42] The notion of 'least onerous' therefore requires a clear definition of the rights in question.

- Thirdly, 'the disadvantages caused must not be disproportionate to the aims pursued',[43] that is, there must be an overall reasonable ratio between means and outcome.

Case study 8.1: Broadcasting of sports events in news programmes

The use of the proportionality test is best explained using a practical example such as the *Sky Österreich* case.[44] This case concerned the legality of a provision of an EU directive requiring companies which had acquired exclusive broadcasting licences for sports events also to allow limited reporting of those events by other, competing, channels. In review of the compliance of this requirement with the 'freedom to conduct a business', a right under Article 16 of the EU Charter of Fundamental Rights, the Court found that this right

---

[37] Joined Cases C-189, 202, 205–208 and 213/02 P *Dansk Rørindustri v Commission* [2005] ECR I-5425. On EU competition law, see further chapter 17.

[38] Case C-84/94 *UK v Council* ('*Working Time Directive*') [1996] ECR I-5755. On this legislation, see further chapter 20.   [39] Case C-189/01 *Jippes* [2001] ECR I-5689.

[40] Case C-260/89 *ERT v DEP* [1991] ECR I-2925.

[41] See eg Case C-343/09 *Afton Chemical* [2010] ECR I-7027, para 45, and Joined Cases C-581/10 and C-629/10 *Nelson*, judgment of 23 October 2012, nyr, para 71.

[42] See eg *Afton Chemical* (n 41) para 45, and *Nelson* (n 41) para 71.

[43] See eg *Afton Chemical* (n 41) para 45, and *Nelson* (n 41) para 71.

[44] Case C-283/11 *Sky Österreich*, judgment of 22 January 2013 (Grand Chamber), nyr.

needed to be balanced with the right to the freedom to receive information under Article 11(2) Charter. With regard to the first step of the proportionality test, the Court found that 'safeguarding of the freedoms protected under Article 11 of the Charter undoubtedly constitutes a legitimate aim in the general interest'.[45] The directive was also considered 'appropriate for the purpose of ensuring that the objective pursued is achieved' in that it allowed any broadcaster 'to be able to make short news reports and thus to inform the general public of events of high interest'.[46] In its analysis of the second leg of the proportionality test, the Court first explored which measures would have been conceivable which were capable of reaching the legitimate legislative goal but were at the same time less restrictive for the rights of the plaintiff. It considered, for example, the possibility of granting the rights holder the right partially to recover the costs of acquisition of the exclusive sports broadcasting rights. The Court, however, found that this less restrictive option would not achieve the objective pursued by the directive. It would effectively further restrict the access of the general public to the information.[47] The Court then turned to the third step of the proportionality test regarding the overall disproportionality of the directive. The Court found that the EU legislature had struck a fair 'balance between' the rights of the parties involved by limiting the broadcasting rights of the short news reports only to specific types of general news programmes and by requiring them to cite the source of the information.[48] Thereby, the disadvantages resulting for the rights holder were 'not disproportionate in the light of the aims' which the directive pursues and were 'such as to ensure a fair balance between the various rights and fundamental freedoms at issue in the case.'[49]

As noted, the principle of proportionality is applied in many different contexts. Within these different contexts, the degree of judicial review varies. In some cases, the Court (as described in chapter 5) will apply only marginal review and thereby only check for manifest errors of assessment in the different steps of application of the proportionality test.[50] This is especially the case where the institutions enjoy wide legislative discretion. The reason for the judicial self-restraint in these cases is that the Court is reluctant to replace the assessment of the legislature with its own assessment of the politically desirable outcome. Such restraint is therefore a question of respect for the separation of powers as expressed in Article 13(2) TEU. Increasingly, therefore, in the context of the review of legislative acts of the Union, the Court does not review the substance of an act but instead checks whether the institutions can prove that they themselves reviewed the proportionality of a measure before adopting it.[51]

---

[45] Ibid, para 52.   [46] Ibid, para 53.   [47] Ibid, paras 55–57.
[48] Ibid, paras 58–63.   [49] Ibid, paras 66 and 67.
[50] *Working Time Directive* (n 38), para 58:

As to judicial review of those conditions, however, the *Council must be allowed a wide discretion* in an area which, as here, involves the legislature in making social *political choices* and requires it to *carry out complex assessments*. Judicial review of the exercise of that discretion must therefore be limited to examining whether it has been *vitiated by manifest error of misuse of powers*, or whether the institution concerned has *manifestly exceeded the limits* of its discretion (emphasis added).

That means that although the Court reviews the different elements of discretion, it only reviews manifest errors in each of the steps.

[51] One way for the legislature to do just that is to prove that it has undertaken an impact assessment study weighing the effects of various policy alternatives and analysing the cost–benefit relation between a measure and its disadvantages to other rights and principles. eg Case C-58/08 *Vodafone* [2010] ECR I-4999, paras 51 *et seq*; Case C-176/09 *Luxembourg v European Parliament and Council* [2011] ECR I-3727, paras 56 *et seq*.

In areas other than the review of EU legislation, the Court tends to exercise less judicial self-restraint and will conduct a more full review of the proportionality of an act. Such cases include

- those where the institutions have no or only limited discretion – this is often the case in matters of administrative acts implementing legislation,[52]
- acts of Member States which limit EU fundamental rights or fundamental freedoms,[53]
- acts of the institutions which restrict the scope of applicability of a fundamental right or balance various rights and principles against each other.[54] This is now an explicit obligation under Article 52(1) Charter which reads: 'Subject to the principle of proportionality, limitations may be made only if they are necessary and genuinely meet objectives of general interest'. An example of this is the previously discussed *Sky Österreich* case in case study 8.1.

3.2 Rule of law: transparency, legality, legal certainty, legitimate expectations

The rule of law is, like the principle of democracy (see chapters 3 and 4), a foundational constitutional principle from which other principles and rules emanate. This chapter will not therefore present a comprehensive account of the rule of law's sub-elements but will focus on the relevant criteria for the review of the legality of acts for implementing EU policies.

The EU is established, as famously pronounced by the Court in *Les Verts*, as a 'Community based on the rule of law'.[55] Although there is a lively academic debate about what that actually means in practice, most people would agree that the rule of law is an 'umbrella principle' with some core content and numerous (sub-)principles, many of which can in themselves be regarded as having a certain independent existence.[56] In this understanding, the rule of law contains both elements which arise primarily as criteria for the legality of legislative acts and others which relate more directly to the exercise of administrative functions. The following is a selection of some of the main sub-elements of the rule of law within the EU's legal system.

3.2.1 Legality

One requirement of the rule of law is that actions of public bodies of the EU take place *under* and *within* the law. This means that, first, a legal basis is required (the principle of

---

[52] Case T-170/06 *Alrosa v Commission* [2007] ECR II-2601, paras 108–110; Case C-12/03 P *Commission v Tetra Laval* [2005] ECR I-987, paras 38–40.

[53] See eg Case C-200/02 *Catherine Chen v Secretary of State* [2004] ECR I-9925, para 32; Case C-413/99 *Baumbast* [2002] ECR I-7091, paras 90 and 91; Case C-41/02 *Commission v Netherlands* ('Vitamins drops') [2004] ECR I-11375, para 46:

> However, in exercising their discretion relating to the protection of public health, the Member States must comply with the principle of proportionality. The means which they choose must therefore be confined to what is actually necessary to ensure the safeguarding of public health; they must be proportional to the objective thus pursued, which could not have been attained by measures which are less restrictive of intra-Community trade.

[54] eg *Sky Österreich* (n 44) paras 47–66 and pre-entry into force of the Charter of Fundamental Rights: Case C-295/94 *Hüpeden* [1996] ECR I-3375 and Case C-296/94 *Pietsch* [1996] ECR I-3409.

[55] Case 294/83 *Les Verts v Parliament* [1986] ECR 1339, para 23.

[56] For many, see K Lenaerts, 'The Rule of Law and the Coherence of the Judicial System of the European Union' (2007) 44 *Common Market Law Review* 1625.

conferral under Article 5(2) TEU) which can be traced to primary law: 'Public authorities must have a legal basis and be justified on the grounds laid down by law'.[57] Secondly, the institutions and bodies must act within the limits of the powers so conferred on them. They may not, therefore, act ultra vires and have to comply with the procedural rules spelt out in their specific legal basis. In other words, the hierarchy of legal norms must be recognized and respected in that no act may violate higher level Union law,[58] including fundamental rights and other general principles in EU law.[59]

A further consequence of the rule of law is the requirement of the correct exercise of discretionary power, where such discretionary powers are conferred on the institution or body.[60] in particular, the institution or body must take into account all relevant factors for decision-making but is barred from acting on improper motives leading to misuse of its powers. As in any exercise of public powers, therefore, they must act in good faith and avoid any improper purpose.[61]

3.2.2 Legal and institutional transparency

Legal and institutional transparency is essential for the exercise of the rule of law and can be regarded as a precondition for establishing an accountable legal and political system.

Transparency, however, has multiple meanings and facts. In a narrow interpretation, it might be seen as referring to a minimal openness of process, access to documents, and publication of official measures. With respect to transparency in the sense of access to documents and freedom of information, a key Treaty provision is Article 15 TFEU, which, inter alia, expressly requires that the proceedings of all bodies are transparent (paragraph (3), third subparagraph), for example by publication of 'documents relating to the legislative procedures'.[62] Also, the legislature under Article 297 TFEU has the duty to publish all legislative measures and decisions. Access to documents is also restated in terms of an individual right in Article 42 Charter. Details are laid down by Regulation 1049/2001 on public access to documents.[63]

Case study 8.2: Tennis racquets on board planes?

Airport authorities at Vienna airport refused Mr Heinrich the right to board a plane because they found a tennis racquet in his cabin luggage. According to their information, tennis racquets were amongst the items prohibited from being carried on planes. Mr Heinrich, outraged about missing his flight, brought a case before the competent

---

[57] Joined Cases 46/87 and 227/88 *Hoechst v Commission* [1989] ECR 2859, summary point 3.

[58] Case 1/54 *France v High Authority* [1954] ECR 7, 23; Case 38/70 *Deutsche Tradax GmbH v Einfuhr- und Vorratsstelle für Getreide und Futtermittel* [1971] ECR 145, para 10.

[59] See eg Case 240/83 *Procureur de la République v ADBHU* [1985] ECR 531.

[60] Case 18/57 *Nold KG v ECSC High Authority* [1959] ECR 89.

[61] Art 263, second para, TFEU, dealing with actions for annulment before the Court of Justice, makes the application of these principles explicit in providing that actions against all EU institutions in respect of measures having legal effects may be based on the grounds of 'lack of competence, infringement of an essential procedural requirement, infringement of the Treaties or of any rule of law relating to their application, or misuse of powers' (see further chapter 10).

[62] Case C-345/06 *Heinrich* [2009] ECR I-1659, paras 41–47 and 64–66.

[63] Regulation (EC) No 1049/2001 of the European Parliament and the Council of 30 May 2001 regarding public access to European Parliament, Council and Commission documents (OJ [2001] L145/43). Replacement by a revised measure is currently being discussed among the institutions. See further chapter 3.

Austrian administrative court asking for a declaration that it was illegal for the authorities to refuse to allow him to board his plane with a racquet in his luggage.[64]

The Austrian court noted that the authorities were acting on the basis of an EU regulation
(622/2003) but, that it was impossible for individuals to comply with that regulation, since
the annex to the regulation listing prohibited items on planes had not been published in
the *Official Journal of the European Union*. Keeping secret the rules of conduct with which
individuals are required to comply constituted, in the view of the Austrian court, a severe
impairment of the most elementary principles of the rule of law. Such regulations should
therefore be declared by the Court of Justice as legally non-existent and hence non-binding.

The Court of Justice, in a preliminary ruling, adopted a slightly more differentiated position. It held that the annex to Regulation 622/2003 adapting the list of articles prohibited
on-board an aircraft, which was not published in the Official Journal, had no binding force
insofar as it seeks to impose obligations on individuals and therefore cannot be enforced
against individuals. Article 297(2) TFEU states clearly that EU law cannot take effect in law
unless it has been published in the Official Journal. The Court held that

> an act adopted by a Community institution cannot be enforced against natural and
> legal persons in a Member State before they have the opportunity to make themselves
> acquainted with it by its proper publication in the *Official Journal of the European Union*.
> In particular, the principle of legal certainly requires that Community rules enable those
> concerned to know precisely the extent of the obligations which are imposed on them.
> Individuals must be able to ascertain unequivocally what their rights and obligations are
> and take steps accordingly.

As a consequence, the Court declared that all the relevant implementing acts to the EU
Regulation could not be enforced against individuals. Until proper publication, tennis
racquets and other secretly listed items could be taken on-board. The Vienna authorities'
refusal to let Mr Heinrich board the plane with the racquet was therefore illegal.

In a broader sense, transparency is a structural principle for a legal system – something which might be lacking in the EU due to a certain lack of visibility as regards
the allocation of final responsibility for decisions made. This can be a consequence
of the complex multi-level structures of decision-making seeking to include various
interests. The complexity of the legal system is also a result of the evolution of EU law
through successive layers of Treaty amendments and of developments in institutional
practice, and the varying speed of integration through national 'opt-ins' and 'opt-outs'.
Transparency of a system is directly linked to the possibility of holding actors to account
and therefore interacts with certain other important precepts such as legal and institutional responsibility.[65]

3.2.3 Legal certainty and the protection of legitimate expectations

The principle of legal certainty and the principle of the protection of legitimate expect-
ations are both sub-concepts of the rule of law. They are consequently protected under
EU law and are criteria for the legality of acts adopted on the basis of or in the scope of
EU law.

---

[64] See Case C-345/06 *Gottfried Heinrich* [2009] ECR I-1659, paras 42–44 and 59–63.
[65] See Case T-188/97 *Rothmans International BV v Commission* [1999] ECR II-2463.

Legal certainty

Legal certainty is acknowledged as a general principle of EU law.[66] According to the Court of Justice the principle essentially requires two things:

- 'Legal rules be clear and precise, and aim to ensure that situations and legal relationships governed by Community law remain foreseeable'.[67]

- 'Individuals must be able to ascertain unequivocally what their rights and obligations are and take steps accordingly'.[68]

Practically speaking, this has a series of consequences, for example:

- EU institutions are barred from applying rules to individuals which are inconsistent or contradictory;[69]

- double jeopardy (also known as the principle of *ne bis in idem* in criminal law and embodied in Article 50 Charter in comparable terms) is prohibited;

- administrative proceedings must be conducted within a reasonable period of time;[70]

- there is a requirement of legal certainty with respect to legal charges and limitation periods;[71]

- retroactive effect of EU law is, in principle, prohibited.

The latter is, from a practical point of view, probably the most important consequence of the principle of legal certainty. Article 297(1) TFEU lays down that Union acts come into force only after publication, which implies that retroactive entry into force is in principle excluded.[72] Retroactive effect of Union law is exceptionally possible if such effect explicitly follows from Union law[73] and if the public interest in retroactive effect

---

[66] Case C 55/91 *Italien v Commission* [1993] ECR I-4813, para 66; Joined Cases T-55/93 and T-232/94, T-233/94 and T-234/94 *Industrias Pesqueras Campos v Commission* [1996] ECR II-247, paras 76, 116, and 119; Case 43/75 *Defrenne v SABENA* [1976] ECR 455, paras 69 *et seq*; Case C-143/93 *Gebroeders van Es Douane Agenten v Inspecteur der Invoerrechten en Accijnzen* [1996] ECR I-431, para 27; Joined Cases 205–215/82 *Deutsche Milchkontor v Germany* [1983] ECR 2633.

[67] Case C-199/03 *Ireland v Commission* [2005] ECR I-8027, para 69. See also Case C-29/08 *SKF* [2009] ECR I-10413, para 77.

[68] See eg Case C-158/06 *ROM-projecten* [2007] ECR I-5103, para 25 with further references.

[69] Case T-115/94 *Opel Austria v Council* [1997] ECR II-39, para 125; *Gebroeders van Es Douane Agenten* (n 66) para 27; there the Commission was held to be 'under an obligation to amend those regulations' which were detrimental to the principle of legal certainty, which requires that an individual will be able 'to ascertain unequivocally what his rights and obligations are and take steps accordingly'.

[70] Case T-347/03 *Branco v Commission* [2005] ECR II-2555, para 114; Case T-125/01 *José Martí Peix v Commission* [2003] ECR II-865, para 111; Joined Cases T-44/01, T-119/01 and T-126/01 *Vieira v Commission* [2003] ECR II-1209, para 167.

[71] Case T-240/02 *Koninklijke Coöperatie Cosun v Commission* [2004] ECR II-4237, paras 38, 44, 45, 58, 61, and 62; Case 41/69 *Chemiefarma v Commission* [1970] ECR 661, para 16; Case T-144/02 *Eagle v Commission* [2007] ECR II-2721, paras 64 and 65.

[72] Joined Cases T-64/01 and T-65/01 *Afrikanische Frucht-Compagnie v Council and Commission* [2004] ECR II-521, para 90; Case 98/78 *Racke v Hauptzollamt Mainz* [1979] ECR 69, para 20. This fundamental approach is also recognized within the legal systems of the Member States (see by comparison Case 63/83 *Regina Kirk* [1984] ECR 2689, para 22) and established with regard to criminal sanctions in Art 49(1) Charter and Art 7 ECHR.

[73] See Case T-357/02 *Freistaat Sachsen v Commission* [2007] ECR II-1261, para 98, where the Court stated that 'provisions of Community law have no retroactive effect unless, exceptionally, it clearly follows from their terms or general scheme that such was the intention of the legislature, that the purpose to be achieved so demands and that the legitimate expectations of those concerned are duly respected'.

overrides the private interest in the maintenance of the existing legal situation.[74] This indicates that balancing of interests in maintenance of different principles, for example that of the public in upholding the law and that of private parties in legal certainty, is necessary.[75] This requirement for balancing of the public interest in upholding the law and the private interest in maintaining a previously acquired legal position can be well illustrated when looking at questions of revocation of acts and recovery of monies. These are instances of application of the principle of legal certainty which relate to acts of individual application.

The case law with regard to revocation of acts of Union institutions, distinguishes *lawful* acts from those which have a legal defect (*unlawful* acts). It is important to recall that even unlawful acts, if not challenged and annulled (eg following an action for annulment before the Courts under Article 263 TFEU), are valid and have effect. This is one of the consequences of the principle of legal certainty.[76]

Lawful acts, in particular those creating rights for individuals or Member States, may not in principle be revoked since, generally, the interest of the individual in the continuous application of the act prevails over the public interest of revocation.[77]

On the other hand, the retroactive revocation of *unlawful* acts is

> permissible provided that the withdrawal occurs within a reasonable time and provided that the institution from which it emanates has had sufficient regard to how far the applicant might have been led to rely on the lawfulness of the measure.[78]

Similar concerns govern the question of recovery of monies. This is important, for example, in the area of subsidies which in EU law are called 'State aid'. National aid granted to companies is in principle subject to authorization by the Commission. The question arose in *Alcan*[79] as to whether such a recipient was individually affected by a determination of the Commission that the aid, which had already been advanced to the company by the national government, was unlawful. Could the principle of legal certainty be invoked by *Alcan* to avoid the sanction of repayment of the aid which was now declared unlawful?[80]

Legitimate expectations

The principle of the protection of legitimate expectations is a general legal principle of Union law, which has been recognized since the very early case law of the

---

[74] For the public interests recognized by the Court, see T Tridimas, *The General Principles of EU Law* (2nd edn, Oxford: Oxford University Press, 2006) 256–257.

[75] Joined Cases 42/59 and 49/59 *SNUPAT v High Authority* [1961] ECR English Special Edition 53.

[76] See also chapter 10.

[77] See Joined Cases 7/56 and 3–7/57 *Algera v Common Assembly* [1957–8] ECR 39. See also Case 159/82 *Verli-Wallace v Commission* [1983] ECR 2711, para 8; Case T-123/89 *Chomel v Commission* [1990] ECR II-131, para 34; Case T-197/99 *Gooch v Commission* [2000] ECR II-1247, para 52; Case T-251/00 *Lagardère and Canal+ v Commission* [2002] ECR II-4825, para 139.

[78] *Lagardère and Canal+* (n 77) para. 140. See also Case 14/81 *Alpha Steel v Commission* [1982] ECR 749; Case 15/85 *Consorzio Cooperative d'Abruzzo v Commission* [1987] ECR 1005; Case C-24/89 *Cargill v Commission* [1991] ECR I-2987; Case C-365/89 *Cargill v Produktschap voor Margarine, Vetten en Oliën* [1991] ECR I-3045; Case C-90/95 P *De Compte v Parliament* [1997] ECR I-1999; *Gooch* (n 77) para 53. See Case 15/60 *Simon v Court of Justice* [1961] ECR 239; Case 54/77 *Herpels v Commission* [1978] ECR 585.

[79] Case C-24/95 *Land Rheinland-Pfalz v Alcan Deutschland* [1993] ECR I-1591.

[80] The Court, in balancing the principles of legal certainty, on the one hand, against legality and effectiveness of EU law, on the other hand, requested repayment because otherwise Union law prohibiting State aid would be 'deprived of effectiveness' (see *Land Rheinland-Pfalz* (n 79) paras 36 and 37).

Court.[81] It is closely linked to that of legal certainty in that it gives individuals a right to rely on the validity of acts of Union institutions.[82] The issue of legitimate expectations arises particularly often where an administrative decision is cancelled or revoked. The entitlement to protection on the basis of legitimate expectations requires that three key elements are satisfied:

- The existence of justifiable reliance[83] (this can arise from a valid legislative act,[84] but can also arise from any act of a Union official conferring individual rights or benefits, for example by giving precise assurances, which can give rise to protected 'legitimate expectations'[85]).

- An affected interest[86] (expectations of the continuous existence of a future legal situation are not protected under Union law, if the beneficiary knew that the situation or assurance was illegal,[87] for example due to incorrect facts which the potential beneficiary had given.[88] Also, legitimate expectations cannot arise if the alleged assurance was made contrary to Union law, for example in the form of a promise not to apply or enforce the law[89]).

- Priority for the protection of expectations over the interest of the Union.

Case study 8.3: Tobacco farmers

Mr Crispoltoni was a tobacco farmer from Lerchi, in the region of Umbria in Italy. He belonged to a producers' association which processed leaf tobacco produced by its members and paid to its farmers an advance for the amount of leaf tobacco delivered by each farmer. The price was established by the association on the basis of a Council regulation on minimum pricing for agriculture markets for that year. During the season of 1988 – after the farmers had planted the tobacco in April, but before the harvest – the maximum quantity of tobacco which profited from the guaranteed minimum price was reduced by the Commission in an implementing regulation. The association therefore requested its farmers, including Mr Crispoltoni, to repay part of the advance they had received.

Mr Crispoltoni turned to the local court against the demand by the association. The local court in turn requested a preliminary reference from the Court of Justice expressing doubt as to the validity of the regulations on the ground that they could be contrary to the

---

[81] See Case 111/63 *Lemmerz-Werke* [1962] ECR English Special Edition 239, where the concept of protection of legitimate expectations was first explicitly enunciated. See also *Algera* (n 77), 118; *SNUPAT* (n 75) 103, 111, and 172 *et seq*; Case 14/61 *Hoogovens v ECSC High Authority* [1962] ECR 511, 511, and 548 (English Special Edition, 53).

[82] Cases C-177/99 and C-181/99 *Ampafrance und Sanofi* [2000] ECR I-7013, para 67, where the Court regarded the principle of legitimate expectations as a 'corollary of the principle of legal certainty'.

[83] Case T-176/01 *Ferriere Nord Spa v Commission* [2004] ECR II-3931.

[84] See Case 120/86 *Mulder v Minister van Landbouw en Visserij* [1988] ECR 2321; Case 170/86 *Van Deetzen v Hauptzollamt Hamburg-Jonas* [1988] ECR 2355.

[85] Case T-283/02 *EnBW* (n 85) para 89.

[86] Case 74/74 *CNTA v Commission* [1975] ECR 533, para 44.

[87] *EnBW* (n 85) para 113. See also Case T-13/99 *Pfizer Animal Health v Council* [2002] ECR II-3305, para 501.

[88] Case 228/84 *Pauvert v Court of Auditors* [1985] ECR 1973, para 14.

[89] See Joined Cases 303/81 and 312/81 *Klöckner v Commission* [1983] ECR 1507, para 34; Case 188/82 *Thyssen v Commission* [1983] ECR 3721, para 11; Case 162/84 *Vlachou v Court of Auditors* [1986] ECR 459, para 6.

principles of the protection of legitimate expectations, the non-retroactivity of legal rules, and legal certainty.

The Court found that the planting of the tobacco plants in April involved the greatest expense to the farmers. Since the Commission regulation was published only after the tobacco farmers had made their decisions on how much to plant that year, the regulation for all practical purposes 'had retroactive effect'. The Court found that

> although in general the principle of legal certainty precludes a Community measure from taking effect from a point in time before its publication, it may exceptionally be otherwise where the purpose to be achieved so demands and where the legitimate expectations of those concerned are duly respected. That case-law also applies where the retroactivity is not expressly laid down by the measure itself but is the result of its content.[90]

In this case, the Court held that the 'legitimate expectations of the operators concerned were not respected, in so far as the measures adopted, although foreseeable, were introduced at a time when they could no longer be taken into account' by the farmers since they were not 'notified in good time of any measures having effects on their investments'.[91]

The case nicely illustrates both the notion of protection of legitimate expectations and the difficulties which in reality exist when analysing the retroactive effect of a measure. These issues are staples of administrative litigation in the EU.

3.3 Good administration

The notion of good administration in the legal system of the EU is still evolving. It is perhaps best understood as an 'umbrella' concept containing rights, rules, and principles guiding administrative procedures.

3.3.1 General observations on good administration

The Court of Justice has referred to notions of 'good',[92] 'sound',[93] or 'proper'[94] administration since the very early case law.[95] Good administration[96] has now also been described as a 'principle',[97] as well as a 'general principle' of EU law.[98] It is thereby a right recognized as

---

[90] Case C-368/89 *Crispoltoni I* [1991] ECR I-3695, para 17.   [91] Ibid, para 20.

[92] Case 32/62 *Alvis* [1963] ECR 49, para 1A; Joined Cases 56/64 and 58/64 *Consten and Grundig v Commission* [1966] ECR 299.

[93] The first mention of the principle of *sound administration* was made in relation to the requirement to process an application within a *reasonable time* in the Joined Cases 1/57 and 14/57 *Société des usines à tubes de la Sarre* [1957] ECR 105, para 113.

[94] Case C-255/90 P *Burban* [1992] ECR I-2253, paras 7 and 12; Case T-167/94 *Nölle v Council and Commission* [1995] ECR II-2589, para 53.

[95] *Algera* (n 77); Case 64/82 *Tradax v Commission* [1984] ECR 1359.

[96] In several cases, the infringements protected under the notion of good administration were either not sufficient or did not bear on the outcome of decision-making and thus did not lead to the annulment of the decision of the Commission: Case T-62/98 *Volkswagen v Commission* [2000] ECR II-2707, paras 279–283; Case C-338/00 P *Volkswagen v Commission* [2003] ECR I-9189, paras 163–165; Case T-308/94 *Cascades SA v Commission* [1998] ECR II-925, para 61; Case C-476/08 P *Evropaïki Dynamiki v Commission* [2009] ECR I-207, paras 33–35.

[97] Case T-83/91 *Tetra Pak International v Commission* [1994] ECR II-755, paras 24–31.

[98] Joined Cases 33/79 and 75/79 *Kuhner v Commission* [1980] ECR 1677, para 25 (here, the Court explains that good administration is, by contrast to the more specific right of defence, 'only' a general principle of law); Case T-54/99 *max.mobil* [2002] ECR II-313, para 48. See also Case T-198/01 R *Technische Glaswerke Illmenau GmbH v Commission* [2002] ECR II-2153, para 85, and Case T-211/02 *Tideland Signal v Commission* [2002] ECR II-3781, para 37.

a general principle of EU law (Article 6(3) TEU). With the entry into force of the Charter under the Treaty of Lisbon, good administration is also recognized as a binding fundamental right under Article 41 Charter, pursuant to Article 6(1) TEU, which gives the Charter the 'same legal value' as the Treaties (see chapter 9).

Article 41 Charter reads:

1. Every person has the right to have his or her affairs handled impartially, fairly and within a reasonable time by the institutions, bodies, offices and agencies of the Union.

2. This right includes:

   a) the right of every person to be heard, before any individual measure which would affect him or her adversely is taken;

   b) the right of every person to have access to his or her file, while respecting the legitimate interests of confidentiality and of professional and business secrecy;

   c) the obligation of the administration to give reasons for its decisions.

3. Every person has the right to have the Union make good any damage caused by its institutions or by its servants in the performance of their duties, in accordance with the general principles common to the laws of the Member States.

4. Every person may write to the institutions of the Union in one of the languages of the Treaties and must have an answer in the same language.

Failure to comply with the principles of good administration may, in cases of sufficient seriousness of the breach, result in a manifest error of assessment and thus lead to an annulment of a decision due to its illegality,[99] with the possible consequence of rights to damages for violation of procedural principles.[100]

By comparison to the protection of the principle of good administration in the case law of the Court, the formulation of Article 41 Charter is significantly more limited in its material, institutional, and personal scope. Therefore whether good administration will be evoked to exist under Article 41 Charter, as opposed to granting the same right as a general principle of law under Article 6(3) TEU established in the case law of the EU Courts, has the potential to change the outcome of a case. This is why

- the wording of Article 41 Charter indicates that
  - the material scope of protection of good administration is predominantly intended to cover 'single case decision-making'. This arises specifically from the formulations in Article 41 Charter which cover an 'individual measure', access of a person to 'his or her' (specific) file, and the obligation to give reasons for administrative decisions – as opposed to the broader obligation of stating reasons in all 'legal acts' of the Union in Article 296, first paragraph, TFEU;[101]

---

[99] *Tideland Signal* (n 98) para 37.

[100] Case T-62/98 *Volkswagen* (n 96) para 607.

[101] J Ziller, 'Is a Law of Administrative Procedure for the Union Institutions Necessary?' (2011) 3 *Rivista italiana di diritto pubblico comunitario* 699 at 718, however, notes that 'nothing impedes applying art. 41 of the Charter on the right to good administration also to rule making, including to consultation procedures by the Commission'. For an opposite approach, see the Court of Justice in Case C-221/09 *AJD Tuna Ltd*, judgment of 17 March 2011, nyr, para 49, where the Court stated that Art 41 Charter does not cover the process of enacting measures of general application and the General Court in a recent line of civil service cases, eg Case T-135/05 *Crampoli v Commission* [2006] ECR II-A-2-1527, paras 149 and 150; Joined Cases T-98/92 and T-99/92 *Di Marzio and Lebedef v Commission* [1994] ECR II-541, para 58; Case T-65/92 *Arauxo-Dumay v Commission* [1993] ECR II-597, para 37; Case T-46/90 *Devillez v European Parliament* [1993] ECR II-699, para 37, in which

- the institutional scope of the right to good administration under Article 41(1) Charter is limited to 'institutions, bodies, offices and agencies of the Union';[102]

- the right to good administration as a general principle of EU law (Article 6(3) TEU), on the other hand, is also applicable

  - to general acts, for example, for the review of international (association) agreements,[103] as well as for non-legislative acts which, as the Court held, must be 'adopted by the Commission pursuant to the principle of sound administration and the duty of care';[104]

  - to Member State action in the scope of EU law in line with *ERT* and *Lisrestal* case law;[105]

  - under certain conditions to third parties if they have a qualified involvement in an administrative procedure.[106]

3.3.2 Sub-principles of good administration

In certain areas, Article 41 Charter merely defines minimum standards which thus also need to be understood in light of the case law of the Courts on the general principle of good administration.

The right to have his or her affairs handled impartially, fairly, and within a reasonable time: the duty of care

The central feature of the duty of care as such is the obligation of the administration impartially and carefully to establish and review the relevant factual and legal elements of a case, prior to making decisions or taking other steps.[107] In the context of the right to fair and impartial treatment, the duty of care requires a thorough establishment of facts prior to decisions and other measures. The decision must be taken 'carefully and impartially',[108] requiring the absence both of arbitrary action and of unjustified preferential treatment including personal interest. Most obviously this requires that there is no conflict of interest. At least for this reason, an interested party is entitled, as the General Court has held, to know the identity of persons conducting investigations and making decisions.[109]

---

it held that the Council when establishing acts of abstract general nature was not subject to the obligations equivalent to what is now protected in Art 41 Charter and that their violation could therefore not lead to the annulment of an act.

[102] Still more limited are the formulations regarding damages and language rights (Art 41(3) and (4) Charter) which speak of 'institutions' and 'servants in the performance of their duties' respectively.

[103] Opinion of AG Trstenjak in Case C-204/07 P *CAS SpA v Commission* [2008] ECR I-6135, para 146; Joined Cases T-186/97, T-187/97, T-190–192/97, T-210/97, T-211/97, T-216/97, T-217/97, T-218/97, T-279/97, T-280/97, T-293/97 and T-147/99 *Kaufring AG v Commission* [2001] ECR II-1337, para 257.

[104] Case C-248/99 P *Monsanto* [2002] ECR I-1, paras 91–93.

[105] In the latter case, the Court of Justice held that the applicants' right to be heard and their right to obtain an adequate statement of reasons had been infringed as a consequence of the interlocutor Member State's failure to keep them informed about the Commission's decision to reduce the economic assistance that the latter had initially granted them: Case T-450/93 *Lisrestal v Commission* [1994] ECR II-1177; *Kaufring* (n 103) paras 150–153.

[106] A good example of the analysis of this effect is Case T-260/94 *Air Inter SA v Commission* [1997] ECR II-997 with discussion by HP Nehl, *Principles of Administrative Procedure in EC Law* (Oxford: Hart Publishing, 1999) 91–94.

[107] See in that respect, AG Van Gerven in Case C-16/90 *Eugen Nölle v Hauptzollamt Bremen-Freihafen* [1991] ECR I-5163.

[108] Case C-269/90 *TU München v Hauptzollamt München Mitte* [1991] ECR I-5469, para 14.

[109] Case T-146/89 *Williams v Court of Auditors* [1991] ECR II-1293, para 40; Case T-305/94 *Limburgse Vinyl Maatschappij v Commission* [1999] ECR II-931, paras 317 *et seq.*

The notion of fairness in the wider sense is also relevant for the right to the treatment of an issue 'within a reasonable time'. After all, 'slow administration is bad administration'[110] and might be in violation of the concept of legal certainty. This concept is reflected in Article 265 TFEU (Article 232 EC), providing a remedy for undue delays in decision-making.

Hearing and access to one's file

Article 41(2)(a) and (b) Charter address the right to a fair hearing (*audi alteram partem* or *audiatur altera pars*) 'before any individual measure' which could affect a person 'adversely' is taken. Preparation of a hearing requires access to one's file.

Matters related to a fair hearing are

- the right to full information which may affect a person's position in an administrative procedure, especially where sanctions may be involved;[111]
- the right to be informed of
  - the administration's response to complaints or representations;[112]
  - the outcome of procedures and of decisions made;[113]
  - all matters necessary for their defence,[114] including rights of appeal.

The right to a fair hearing as a general principle of EU law must be observed 'in all proceedings initiated against a person which are liable to culminate in a measure adversely affecting that person'.[115] It is protected to the highest degree by the Court of Justice having stated that it 'cannot be excluded or restricted by any legislative provision'.[116] As a general principle of law, it thus supplements legislation which does not explicitly provide for its exercise.[117]

The right to a fair hearing requires that the party concerned

- must receive an exact and complete statement of the claims or objections raised,
- must also be given the opportunity to make its views known 'on the truth and relevance of the facts and circumstances alleged and on the documents used',[118]

[110] AG Jacobs in Case C-270/99 P *Z v Parliament* [2001] ECR I-9197, para 40, with reference to Art 41 Charter and claiming that this was 'a generally recognised principle'.

[111] Case 270/82 *Estel v Commission* [1984] ECR 1195, paras 13 *et seq*; Case 64/82 *Tradax v Commission* [1984] ECR 1359, paras 21 *et seq*; Case C-34/89 *Italy v Commission* [1990] ECR I-3603, paras 14 *et seq*; Case T-100/92 *La Pietra v Commission* [1994] ECR (civil service) I-A-83, II-275, paras 43 *et seq*; Case C-54/95 *Germany v Commission* [1999] ECR I-35, para 118.

[112] Case 179/82 *Lucchini Siderurgica v Commission* [1983] ECR 3083, para 27; Joined Cases 96–102, 104–106 and 110/82 *NV IAZ International Belgium v Commission* [1983] ECR 3369, paras 12 *et seq*.

[113] Case 120/73 *Lorenz v Germany* [1973] ECR 1471, para 5; Case 121/73 *Markmann v Germany* [1973] ECR 1495, para 5; Case 122/73 *Nordsee v Germany* [1973] ECR 1511, para 5; Case 141/73 *Lohrey v Germany* [1973] ECR 1527, para 5; see also R Bauer, *Das Recht auf eine gute Verwaltung im Europäischen Gemeinschaftsrecht* (Frankfurt am Main: Peter Lang, 2002) 64.

[114] Case 41/69 *Chemiefarma v Commission* [1970] ECR 661, para 27.

[115] Case T-306/01 *Yusuf and Al Barakaat International Foundation v Council and Commission* [2005] ECR II-3533, para 325.

[116] Case T-260/94 *Air Inter v Commission* [1997] ECR II-997, para 60; Case C-135/92 *Fiskano v Commission* [1994] ECR I-2885, para 39.

[117] Case 234/84 *Belgium v Commission* [1986] ECR 2263, para 27; Case 259/85 *France v Commission* [1987] ECR 4393, para 12.

[118] See eg Cases 100–103/80 *Musique Diffusion française v Commission* [1983] ECR 1835, para 10; Case 121/76 *Moli v Commission* [1977] ECR 1971, para 19; Case 322/81 *Michelin v Commission* [1983] ECR 3461, para 7; Case C-328/05 *SGL Carbon v Commission* [2007] ECR I-3921, para 71. In Joined Cases C-402/05 P and C-415/05 P *Kadi and Al Barakaat v Council and Commission* ('Kadi I') [2008] ECR I-6351, paras 338–352, the

- must be given right of access to documents and the file (which can be limited in the case of confidential information of third parties).

It is less clear when a right to a hearing might exist in situations where the proceedings lead to the adoption of an act of general application – such as a legislative act (Article 289 TFEU), a delegated act (Article 290 TFEU), or an implementing act with effect beyond a single case (Article 291 TFEU). Article 11(1) and (3) TEU requires Union institutions to hear views and opinions on Union measures and especially to enter into consultation procedures. This reinforces the view of the Court in *Denmark v Commission*[119] which had found that a right to a hearing is not excluded simply because the basic act is of general application. It is not clear, however, whether the hearing in these cases is a subjective right of individuals or just a factor for review of the act.

Reasoning of decisions

The obligation to give reasons for decisions which is also restated in Article 41(2)(c) Charter, in other words to provide grounds for the action taken, finds expression in the more general obligation under Article 296(2) TFEU to support all legal acts in the EU with reasons.[120] The extent of the obligation to state reasons under Article 296 TFEU comprises an indication of the legal basis of the act, the general situation which led to its adoption, and the general objectives which it intended to achieve:[121]

> the statement of reasons must disclose in a clear and unequivocal fashion the reasoning followed by the Community authority which adopted the measure in question in such a way as to make the persons concerned aware of the reasons for the measure and thus enable them to defend their rights and to enable the Court to exercise its supervisory jurisdiction.[122]

The lack of reasoning of an act is ground for its annulment.

Court held that overriding considerations of safety or the conduct of international relations might justify that certain matters may not be communicated to the persons concerned, but do not allow for evidence used against them to justify restrictive measures or for them not to be afforded the right to be informed of such evidence within a reasonable period after those measures were taken.

[119] Case C-3/00 *Denmark v Commission* [2003] ECR I-2643.

[120] In the laws of the Member States it can be observed that the duty to give reasons is limited to administrative acts of individual application. In France, the loi of 11 July 1979 provides that in certain cases, which were extended by the loi of 17 January 1986, the administration has to give reasons for individual decisions; see A de Laubadère, J-C Venezia, and G Yves, *Traité de Droit Administratif* (14th edn, Paris: LGDJ, 1996) Book 1, para 944; this statutory duty does, therefore, not apply to acts of general application, for which only in exceptional circumstances has a reasoning to be provided (ibid). See also J Schwarze, *European Administrative Law* (London: Sweet & Maxwell, 1992) 1386. Similarly, in Germany, § 39 of the Federal Law on Administrative Procedure (BVwVfG) only applies to administrative acts of individual application; see FO Kopp and U Ramsauer, *Verwaltungsverfahrensgesetz* (7th edn, Munich: Beck, 2000) § 39. Acts of general application adopted by the executive on the basis of a delegation must state their legal basis in accordance with Art 80(1), third sentence, of the Basic Law. This amounts, however, only to a limited form of reasoning; see Schwarze, *European Administrative Law* (loc cit), 1387. In English law, a duty to give reasons is recognized as a requirement of natural justice for administrative acts only in exceptional circumstances irrespective of whether the act is of individual or general application; see P Craig, *Administrative Law* (4th edn, London: Sweet & Maxwell, 1999) 377.

[121] Case 5/67 *Beus GmbH v Hauptzollamt München* [1968] ECR 83, 95 (English Special Edition, 83); see also *Pfizer Animal Health* (n 87) para 510; Case T-70/99 *Alpharma v Council* [2002] ECR II-3495, para 394; Case C-304/01 *Spain v Commission* [2004] ECR I-7655, para 51; Case C-184/02 *Spain and Finland v European Parliament and Council* [2004] ECR I-7789, para 79; Case C-342/03 *Spain v Council* [2005] ECR I-1975, para 55.

[122] *TU München* (n 108) paras 14 and 26.

Damages

The right to good administration in Article 41(3) Charter contains an explicit reference to the right to receive compensation for damage under Article 340 TFEU. Article 41 Charter therefore cannot limit the obligation to pay damages for violations of the principles listed in the provisions on good administration only. The right to damages is discussed in greater detail in chapter 10 on judicial review.

Language rights

The entitlement to 'write' to the institutions of the Union in one of the languages of the Treaties and to receive an answer in the same language simply repeats the existing right under Article 24(4) TFEU. Note, though, that Article 342 TFEU gives the Council the authority to establish the language regime for the institutions.[123] The right of free choice of the language is applicable to communication with 'institutions' of the EU. Agencies and other bodies may thus be subject to specific language regimes.[124]

3.4 Information-related rights: freedom of information and data protection

Any person, not only parties not subject to an individual measure, enjoys the general right of access to documents under Article 42 Charter and Article 15(3) TFEU.[125] Transparency of information can be regarded a precondition for both a fair and accountable administration and a functioning, participatory democracy in which citizens are able to engage in an informed debate and to exert influence on public decision-making. However, freedom of information, or more narrowly, the right of access to documents, has not always been regarded as a fundamental right or even a matter of priority in EU law.

In line with the administrative traditions of many European countries, public non-accessibility and secrecy were generally the norm in regard to information held by European authorities.[126] This approach changed gradually in light of the increasing recognition of the individual's right to information and as a shift in focus in the context of the 'Nordic' enlargement of 1995 which gave the Swedish and Finnish traditions in this area a strong influence in the EU.[127] The right of access to documents is now protected

---

[123] This was done by one of the first legal acts issued by the Council, Regulation 1/58 determining the languages used by the European Economic Community (OJ English Special Edition [1952–8] 59).

[124] See eg Case T-120/99 *Kik v OHIM* [2001] ECR II-2235, para 64.

[125] Art 15(3) TFEU, lays down that 'Any citizen of the Union and any natural or legal person residing or having its registered office in a Member State, shall have a right of access to documents of the Union institutions, bodies, offices and agencies, whatever their medium, subject to the principles and the conditions to be defined in accordance with this paragraph.'

[126] See eg Case C-170/89 *BEUC v Commission* [1991] ECR I-5709, in which the consumer protection NGO BEUC was denied access to non-confidential elements of Commission files in an anti-dumping case.

[127] See eg Section 12 of the Finnish Constitution of 1999 which expressly links freedom of expression and the right of access to information: 'Everyone has the freedom of expression....Documents and recordings in the possession of the authorities are public, unless their publication has for compelling reasons been specifically restricted by an Act. Everyone has the right of access to public documents and recordings.' See the unofficial translation of the Finnish Constitution of 1999 on the finlex website (http://www.finlex.fi). This provision has been described as having a lineage dating back to the eighteenth-century Swedish legislation at the time applicable in Finland. See for further references, P Leino, 'Comment Case C-353/99 P' (2002) 39 *Common Market Law Review* 621. See for an historic analysis of the development of the right to access to information, eg D Curtin, 'Citizens' Fundamental Right to Access to EU Information: An Evolving Digital Passepartout?' (2000) 37 *Common Market Law Review* 7 at 7–11; P Dyrberg, 'Accountability and Legitimacy: What is the Contribution of Transparency?' in A Arnull and D Wincott (eds), *Accountability and Legitimacy in the European*

both as a general principle of Union law and through provisions of primary law. The right of access to documents has, over the years, also been an element of several generations of regulation in secondary law.[128] Currently, Regulation 1049/2001 issued on the basis of what is now Article 15 TFEU is the general legislation on access to documents.[129] Further reaching rights are established in the field of environmental law, which profits from a more open approach through the specific implementation of the Aarhus Convention.[130] Limitations to the right of freedom of information result not least in data protection rights of individuals.[131]

Union law governing information contains not only rules on access to information but also on the protection of personal information data. Under Article 8 Charter, protection of personal information constitutes an individual right against the potential misuse of information both by governments and non-governmental actors. Limitations on privacy rights to the extent 'necessary in a democratic society' are, for example, explicitly recognized in Article 8 of the European Convention on Human Rights (ECHR). Legal persons are protected with respect to their professional or business secrets. This is recognized, for example, in Article 339 TFEU and in secondary legislation.[132]

Union (Oxford: Oxford University Press, 2002) 86–92; D Curtin, 'Citizens' Fundamental Right to Access to EU Information: An Evolving Digital Passepartout?' (2000) 37 *Common Market Law Review* 7 at 7–11; I Österdahl, 'Openness v Secrecy: Public Access to Documents in Sweden and the European Union' (1998) 37 *European Law Review* 336; all with further references.

[128] Initially, the institutions had adopted internal guidelines. Original decisions of the institutions (Council Decision 93/731 (OJ [1993] L340/43); Commission Decision 94/90 (OJ [1994] L46/58); European Parliament Decision 97/632 (OJ [1997] L263/27)) were based on the right to self-organization.

[129] Regulation (EC) No 1049/2001 of the European Parliament and of the Council of 30 May 2001 regarding public access to European Parliament, Council and Commission documents (OJ [2001] L145/43).

[130] Regulation (EC) No 1367/2006 of the European Parliament and of the Council of 6 September 2006 on the application of the provisions of the Aarhus Convention on Access to Information, Public Participation in Decision-making and Access to Justice in Environmental Matters to Community institutions and bodies (OJ [2006] L264/13).

[131] See esp Case C-28/08 P *Commission v Bavarian Lager* [2010] ECR I-6055 and Joined Cases C-92/09 and C-93/09 *Schecke* [2010] ECR I-11063, para 85:

It is necessary to bear in mind that the institutions are obliged to balance, before disclosing information relating to a natural person, the EU's interest in guaranteeing the transparency of its actions and the infringement of the rights recognised by Articles 7 and 8 of the Charter. No automatic priority can be conferred on the objective of transparency over the right to protection of personal data, even if important economic interests are at stake.

[132] See eg Art 16 of Commission Regulation (EC) No 773/2004 of 7 April 2004 relating to the conduct of proceedings by the Commission pursuant to Articles 81 and 82 of the EC Treaty (OJ [2004] L123/18); Art 28 of Council Regulation (EC) No 1/2003 of 16 December 2002 on the implementation of the rules on competition laid down in Articles 81 and 82 of the Treaty (OJ [2003] L1/1); Art 8 of Regulation (EC) No 1073/1999 of the European Parliament and of the Council of 25 May 1999 concerning investigations conducted by the European Anti-Fraud Office (OLAF) (OJ [1999] L136/1); Art 8(1) of Council Regulation (Euratom, EC) No 2185/96 of 11 November 1996 concerning on-the-spot checks and inspections carried out by the Commission in order to protect the European Communities' financial interests against fraud and other irregularities (OJ [1996] L292/2) of Regulation 1/2003 on antitrust enforcement. Art 28 of Regulation 1/2003 protects professional secrecy insofar as it provides that this information may only be used for purposes for which it was gathered by the Commission and within the competition network and that such information shall not be disclosed.

3.5 The right to an effective judicial remedy and additional rights of defence

The rule of law would be practically meaningless if persons affected by measures of the Union or the Member States acting under Union law were not able to object to or challenge actions affecting their interests.[133]

3.5.1 Right to an effective remedy

The existence of a right is linked to the existence of a remedy under the principle known as *ubi ius ibi remedium*, which in Union terms might read: where there is a right under Union law, there is a remedy to ensure its enforcement. Accordingly, the 'right to obtain an effective remedy in a competent court' is protected as a fundamental general principle of EU law,[134] and is also enshrined in Article 47 Charter and Articles 6 and 13 ECHR.

Article 47, first paragraph, Charter, largely following the language of the Convention, grants a 'right to an effective remedy before a tribunal', where rights and freedoms under Union law are violated. Since judicial protection of rights under EU law must be in first line offered by courts and tribunals of the Member States, certain provisions refer to the notion of courts such as Article 47, second paragraph, Charter clarifying that a tribunal be 'independent and impartial',[135] that hearings be 'fair and public', and that everyone 'ha[s] the possibility of being advised, defended and represented'.

A remedy under EU law, by analogy with Article 13 ECHR, 'must be "effective" both in law and in practice.'[136] The right to an effective judicial remedy under EU law is therefore also linked with the principle of effectiveness (flowing from Article 4(3) TEU as discussed previously). Under the *Factortame* formula, the right to an effective remedy offers protection against 'any provision of a national legal system and any legislative, administrative or judicial practice which might impair the effectiveness' of Union law.[137] That means that Member States

- may 'not render virtually *impossible or excessively difficult* the exercise of rights'[138] conferred by EU law,
- are obliged to 'guarantee real and effective judicial protection',[139]
- are barred from applying any rule or applying any procedure which 'might prevent, even temporarily, Community rules from having full force and effect'.[140]

---

[133] HCH Hofmann, GC Rowe, and A Türk, *Administrative Law and Policy of the European Union* (Oxford: Oxford University Press, 2011) 204.

[134] Case 85/76 *Hoffmann-La Roche v Commission* [1979] ECR 461, para 9; Case 222/84 *Johnston* [1986] ECR 1651, para 19.   [135] Case C-506/04 *Wilson* [2006] ECR I-8613, paras 60–62.

[136] *Kudla v Poland* (Appl No 30210/96) ECHR 2000-XI (Grand Chamber) para 157. Art 13 ECHR is, however, more limited than the right to effective judicial review under EU law. Art 13 ECHR protects only rights arising from the Convention – therefore only fundamental rights and freedoms. The general principle of EU law, by contrast, protects all rights arising from EU law in both a vertical and a horizontal level. For further explanation, see section 3.5.1.   [137] Case C-213/89 *Factortame* [1990] ECR I-2433, paras 19 and 20.

[138] See eg Case C-128/93 *Fisscher* [1994] ECR I-4583, para 37; Case C-261/95 *Palmisani* [1997] ECR I-4025, para 27; *Courage* (n 3) para 29; Case C-78/98 *Preston* [2000] ECR I-3201, para 39; Case C-187/00 *Kutz-Bauer* [2003] ECR I-2741, para 57; Case C-30/02 *Recheio-Cash & Carry* [2004] ECR I-6051, paras 17 and 18; Case C-212/04 *Adeneler* [2006] ECR I-6057, para 95; Joined Cases C-231–233/06 *Jonkman* [2007] ECR I-5149, para 28 (emphasis added).

[139] Case 14/83 *Van Colson* [1984] ECR 1891, para 23.

[140] *Factortame* (n 137) paras 19 and 20.

For a practical illustration of this, we turn to *Factortame*. The right to an effective judicial remedy resulted there in the obligation of the English High Court to offer interim relief measures to protect the plaintiff's interests under EU law, even though such measures were not available to that court under English law at the time.

Compliance with the right to an effective remedy, therefore, depends both on

- the *procedural* aspect – whether the Member State offers procedural rules granting fair possibilities of bringing a case and that admissibility criteria allow actual access to a court,

- and the more *substantive* issue – whether success on the grounds of the claim of violation of a right under EU law would lead to a remedy which is capable of addressing the violation of the right.[141]

3.5.2 Additional rights of defence

A guarantee of the respect for 'the rights of the defence of anyone who has been charged' is provided in Article 48 Charter. But more broadly, under EU law the rights of defence must be ensured not only in procedures before a court, but also in administrative procedures conducted by EU institutions and bodies or by Member State bodies implementing EU law. They are enforced even 'where there is no specific legislation and also where legislation exists which does not itself take account of that principle'.[142] The Court of Justice held that

> Respect for the rights of the defence constitutes a fundamental principle and must therefore be ensured not only in administrative procedures which may lead to the imposition of penalties but also during preliminary inquiry procedures such as investigations.[143]

Some of the rights of the defence in administrative proceedings, such as the right to be heard and the right to access to one's file, have been enshrined in Article 41(2) Charter and were discussed previously. Generally speaking, rights of defence include

- a limited right of legal professional privilege,[144] concerning the right to confidentiality of communications with an external lawyer;[145]

- a limited right against self-incrimination[146] – this, for example, prohibits the Commission, in a request for information in competition proceedings, to require the

---

[141] Correctly, the European Court of Human Rights has pointed out that with respect to Art 13 ECHR (in *MSS v Belgium and Greece* (Appl No 30696/09) [2011] ECHR 108 (Grand Chamber) paras 289 and 290) that 'the "effectiveness" of a "remedy" within the meaning of Article 13 does not depend on the certainty of a favourable outcome for the applicant.' Also, even if a single remedy does not by itself entirely satisfy the requirements of Art 13, the aggregate of remedies provided for under domestic law may do so.

[142] Case 222/84 *Johnston v Chief Constabulary* [1986] ECR 1651. See also Case C-32/95 P *Commission v Lisrestal* [1996] ECR I-5373, para 30.

[143] *Hoechst* (n 57) summary point 1.

[144] See Case 155/79 *AM&S* [1982] ECR 1575, paras 23–26; Case T-30/89 *Hilti v Commission* [1990] ECR II-163, para 18; Joined Cases T-125/03 and T-253/03 *Akzo Nobel Chemicals and Akcros Chemicals* [2007] ECR II-3523, paras 117 and 123, and Case C-550/07 P *Akzo* [2010] ECR I-8301.   [145] *Hilti* (n 144).

[146] See *Hoechst* (n 57); Case 374/87 *Orkem v Commission* [1989] ECR 3283. See also Case 27/88 *Solvay v Commission* [1989] ECR 3355; Case T-34/93 *Société Générale v Commission* [1995] ECR II-545, paras 72–74; Case C-407/04 P *Dalmine v Commission* [2007] ECR I-829, para 34.

undertaking 'to provide it with answers which might involve an admission on its part of the existence of an infringement'.[147]

Case study 8.4: Terrorism and rights

Following the September 2001 terrorist attacks on targets in the US, the United Nations introduced what it called 'smart sanctions'. The UN Security Council was authorized to establish lists of persons and entities which were accused by UN Security Council members of being in some way or another associated with terrorist organizations such as al-Qaeda. UN Member States were then required to freeze personal funds and economic resources including access to bank accounts and other assets of these listed persons and entities.

The EU, not a member of the UN but acting within its competencies, implemented these decisions of the UN Security Council by various legal acts. As a result, Mr Yusuf and Mr Kadi, Swedish citizens, woke up one morning to find that they could no longer withdraw money from their bank accounts. They brought cases before the General Court against the EU legal acts listing them amongst the persons and entities whose assets should be frozen.[148] The *Kadi* case was decided by the Court of Justice on appeal. Sanctions against Mr Yusuf were withdrawn after several years, apparently because he was struck from the list due to an error in transcription of his name from Arabic to other languages.

Some of the central legal questions arising in these cases were, aside from the jurisdiction of EU Courts and the degree of review of EU legal acts implementing UN Security Council decisions (on which, see chapter 9, case study 9.1), whether the rights of defence and the right to an effective judicial review were violated by the EU legal acts. The Court of Justice in the *Kadi I* and *Kadi II* cases, dismissed the notion of Union acts as capable of having some form of 'immunity' from judicial review.[149] It then went on also to address the issues of rights of defence and the right to an effective judicial review.

The General Court in *Yusuf* had already recalled that the right to a fair hearing required an individual to be able to 'learn about the accusations held against them, to be able to understand the evidence gathered against them and to be able to defend themselves against such accusations'.[150] The right to a fair hearing must be observed 'in all proceedings initiated against a person which are liable to culminate in a measure adversely affecting that person'.[151] Although 'the right to be heard cannot be extended to the context of a Community legislative process culminating in the enactment of legislation' applying generally, the right exists even if a legislative act also targets individuals.[152] However, according to the General Court, this standard under EU law was not applicable to the case. Rather, the impugned EU legal act implementing a UN Security Council decision was only to be reviewed against compliance with standards of *jus cogens* arising from public international law.

On appeal in *Kadi I*, the Court of Justice set aside the General Court's decision and held that 'the rights of the defence, in particular the right to be heard, and the right to effective judicial review of those rights, were patently not respected' when the EU simply

---

[147] Case C-407/04 P *Dalmine v Commission* [2007] ECR I-829, para 35. The Court made it clear in Case C-60/92 *Otto v Postbank* [1993] ECR I-5683, paras 15–17, that this limitation does not apply to civil proceedings in national courts.

[148] *Yusuf and Al Barakaat* (n 115); Case T-315/01 *Kadi v Council and Commission* [2005] ECR II-3649.

[149] *Kadi I* (n 118), esp paras 325–327.   [150] *Kadi I* (n 118) paras 325–327.

[151] *Yusuf and Al Barakaat* (n 115), para 325.   [152] Ibid, para 327.

implemented the UN Security Council resolution without following a procedure allowing for compliance with fundamental rights.[153] Therefore, it annulled the regulation freezing Mr Kadi's assets. The Court held

> that the Courts of the European Union must ensure the review, in principle the full review, of the lawfulness of all European Union acts in the light of fundamental rights, including where such acts are designed to implement Security Council resolutions, and that the General Court's reasoning was consequently vitiated by an error of law.[154]

The 'effectiveness of judicial review means that the competent European Union authority is bound to communicate the grounds for the contested listing decision to the person concerned and to provide that person with the opportunity to be heard in that regard.' The Court stated that, 'as regards a decision that a person's name should be listed for the first time, for reasons connected with the effectiveness of the restrictive measures at issue and with the objective of the regulation concerned, it was necessary that that disclosure and that hearing should occur not prior to the adoption of that decision but when that decision was adopted or as swiftly as possible thereafter.'[155] 'Since Mr Kadi had not been in a position effectively to make known his point of view in that regard, with the consequence that the rights of defence and the right to effective judicial review had been infringed.'[156]

The *Kadi II* case, decided by the Court of Justice in 2013,[157] arose from the UN Security Council's Sanctions Committee's attempts to remedy the situation by transferring a summary narrative of reasons for the listing of Mr Kadi (referred to as Mr Qadi) to him and publishing it on the UN website. Mr Kadi sent his statements to the Commission, requested the production of the evidence in support of the claims and assertions made in the UN's summary of reasons, and asked that he be allowed to submit comments on that evidence. Irrespective of these demands, the Commission adopted a new regulation continuing the freezing of Mr Kadi's assets without further commenting on the statements made by Mr Kadi in response to the allegations of the UN.

Again, Mr Kadi brought an action for annulment against this act before the General Court alleging, inter alia, breach of the right of the defence and of the right to effective judicial protection. The Court, in view of *Kadi I*, had found that it was to ensure 'in principle the full review' of the lawfulness of the contested regulation in light of the fundamental rights guaranteed by the EU. This meant that

> the Courts of the European Union must review the assessment made by the institution concerned of the facts and circumstances relied on in support of the restrictive measures at issue and determine whether the information and evidence on which that assessment is based is accurate, reliable and consistent.[158]

The Court found that there was a breach of Mr Kadi's rights of defence because

> those rights had been respected only in a purely formal and superficial sense, since the Commission considered itself strictly bound by the findings of the Sanctions Committee

---

[153] *Kadi I* (n 118) followed the AG. It upheld the Community standards of fundamental rights protection in paras 281 *et seq*.   [154] *Kadi I* (n 118), esp paras 326 and 327.

[155] *Kadi I* (n 118), esp paras 336–342 in the summary given by Joined Cases C-584/10 P, C-593/10 P C-595/10 P *Commission and UK v Kadi*, judgment of 18 July 2013 (Grand Chamber), nyr, para 24.

[156] *Kadi I* (n 118) paras 345–349 in the summary given by *Commission and UK v Kadi* (n 155) para 25.

[157] *Commission and UK v Kadi* (n 155).   [158] *Commission and UK v Kadi* (n 155) paras 39–41.

and at no time envisaged calling them into question in the light of Mr Kadi's comments or making any real effort to refute the exculpatory evidence adduced by Mr Kadi.

(a) No access to the evidence against him

Mr Kadi was refused access by the Commission to the evidence against him despite his express request, whilst no balance was struck between his interests and the need to protect the confidentiality of the information in question.

(b) Vague and insufficient allegations

The few pieces of information and the vague allegations in the summary of reasons relating to the listing of Mr Kadi…for example, that Mr Kadi was a shareholder in a Bosnian bank in which planning sessions for an attack on a United States facility in Saudi Arabia 'may have' taken place, were clearly insufficient to enable Mr Kadi to mount an effective [defence against allegations].[159]

The General Court also found 'that the principle of effective judicial protection had been infringed' on the grounds that neither was Mr Kadi afforded proper access to the information and evidence used against him,' nor had he been able to 'defend his rights with regard to that information and evidence in satisfactory conditions.' Further, no evidence of that kind or any indication of the evidence relied on against Mr Kadi had been disclosed to the Court.[160]

On appeal, the Court of Justice in its *Kadi II* judgment confirmed the General Court's interpretation of the violation of the right of defence and of an effective judicial review.[161] The right of defence arises from both the general principles of EU law affirmed, inter alia, by Articles 42(2) and 47 Charter. However, limitations to the exercise of the right is possible and conditions are stated in Article 52(1) Charter. This requires that limitations respect the essence of the right in question and are proportionate. It also requires analysis of the specific circumstances of the particular case, including the nature of the act at issue, the context of its adoption, and the legal rules governing the matter in question.[162]

One of the obligations which arises in the context of the right to good administration and is also related to the right of defence is the obligation of the Union administration regarding the 'duty of care'. In the words of the Court of Justice, when 'comments are made by the individual concerned on the summary of reasons, the competent European Union authority is under an obligation to examine, carefully and impartially, whether the alleged reasons are well founded, in the light of those comments and any exculpatory evidence provided with those comments.'[163]

The duty to state reasons for a decision arising from Article 296 TFEU and the right to an effective judicial review 'entails in all circumstances', 'that that statement of reasons identifies the individual, specific and concrete reasons why the competent authorities consider that the individual concerned must be subject to restrictive measures.'[164] The reason for

---

[159] Case T-85/09 *Kadi v Commission ('Kadi II')* [2010] ECR II-5177 (General Court) paras 171–180 as cited by *Commission and UK v Kadi* (n 155) para 43.

[160] *Kadi II* (n 159) paras 181–184 as cited by *Commission and UK v Kadi* (n 155) para 44.

[161] *Commission and UK v Kadi* (n 155) paras 97–134.

[162] Ibid, para 102.

[163] Ibid, para 114 with references to Case C-269/90 *Technische Universität München* [1991] ECR I-5469, para 14; Case C-525/04 P *Spain v Lenzing* [2007] ECR I-9947, para 58.

[164] *Commission and UK v Kadi* (n 155) para 116 with references to Joined Cases C-539/10 P and C-550/10 P *Al-Aqsa v Council and Netherlands v Al-Aqsa*, judgment of 15 November 2012, nyr, paras 140 and 142, and Case C-417/11 P *Council v Bamba*, judgment of 15 November 2012, nyr, paras 49–53.

this is that effective judicial review requires verification of the allegations and a review of whether 'those reasons, or, at the very least, one of those reasons, deemed sufficient in itself to support that decision, is substantiated'.[165] In the absence of sufficient reasoning of the act, the Courts will base their review 'solely on the material which has been disclosed to them' and if 'that material is insufficient to allow a finding that a reason is well founded, the Courts of the European Union shall disregard that reason'.[166] The reason behind this is that 'the essence of effective judicial protection must be that it should enable the person concerned to obtain...annulment' of the contested measure.[167]

The Court of Justice therefore concluded that

> follows from the criteria analysed above that, for the rights of the defence and the right to effective judicial protection to be respected first, the competent European Union authority must (i) disclose to the person concerned the summary of reasons provided by the Sanctions Committee which is the basis for listing or maintaining the listing of that person's name in Annex I to Regulation No 881/2002, (ii) enable him effectively to make known his observations on that subject and (iii) examine, carefully and impartially, whether the reasons alleged are well founded, in the light of the observations presented by that person and any exculpatory evidence that may be produced by him.[168]

The *Kadi* and *Al Barakaat* cases, as well as the *Ahmed Ali Yusuf* case, have become central reference points for several central issues of EU law. They address not only the relation between EU law and public international law obligations of the Member States in general, but they also clarify that it is inconceivable that any exercise of public authority by the EU could fail to comply with fundamental rights and EU general principles protecting both substantive and procedural rights of individuals. Procedural rights, especially regarding the rights of defence and of good administration including the right to a fair hearing, the right to access to one's file, and many other rule of law-related principles, were enforced by the Court of Justice in a highly publicized case.

4 Conclusion

In summary, with entry into force of the Charter of Fundamental Rights of the European Union under the Treaty of Lisbon (Article 6(1) TEU) many of the rights and principles which were initially established under the case law of the Court of Justice only, are now also restated in positive law. This adds to the prominence of principles which might initially not have been known to the wider public, such as the right to good administration in Article 41 Charter. Importantly, however, this has not led to the discarding of the 'old' approach of case law-led developments of rights as general principles. To the contrary, under Article 6(3) TEU, rights are also protected as general principles of EU law. There is no hierarchy between the different sources of Article 6(1) TEU versus Article 6(3) TEU. This contributes to the dynamism of the EU legal system, which continues to be capable of adapting to new challenges arising from policy areas increasingly becoming subject to 'Europeanization' and new influences, such as the drive towards more transparency of

---

[165] *Commission and UK v Kadi* (n 155), para 119.
[166] Ibid, para 123.   [167] Ibid, para 134.   [168] Ibid, para 135.

the legal system which took on board some of the more 'Nordic' legal traditions of the EU. One of the topics which was not addressed in this chapter but which is arising as a big challenge to EU administrative law is the possibility and, arguably, the need for a general administrative procedure act for the EU. This might clarify to a much greater degree than Article 41 Charter was capable of doing, the rights of individuals and obligations of administrations implementing EU law. Especially in the context of a highly integrated system of implementation of EU law in which Member State and EU institutions and bodies are involved, such clarification of applicable procedural provisions would add much to the transparency of the system, compliance with principles under the rule of law, and good administration in general.

Further reading

There is much literature on general principles of EU law, less so on EU administrative law. As always, it is important to study EU law by taking into account contributions from the different language groups which often discuss EU law from varying experiences and with a focus sometimes different from that chosen by authors of another.

J-B Auby and J Dutheil de la Rochère (eds), *Droit Administratif Européen* (Brussels: Bruylant, 2007)

M Chiti (ed), *Diritto amministrativo europeo* (Milan: Guiffrè Editore, 2013)

P Craig, *EU Administrative Law* (2nd edn, Oxford: Oxford University Press, 2012)

HCH Hofmann, GC Rowe, and AH Türk, *Administrative Law and Policy of the European Union* (Oxford: Oxford University Press, 2011)

JE Soriano García (ed), *Procedimiento Administrativo Europeo* (Navarra: Thomson Reuters, 2012)

JP Terhechte (ed), *Verwaltungsrecht der Europäischen Union* (Baden-Baden: Nomos, 2011)

T Tridimas, *The General Principles of EU Law* (2nd edn, Oxford: Oxford University Press, 2006)

9

Fundamental rights in the European Union

Eleanor Spaventa

1 Introduction

In this chapter we are going to look at fundamental rights in the EU. As we shall see, the original Treaties did not contain any specific reference to fundamental rights. For this reason it fell upon the Court of Justice to develop a fundamental rights jurisprudence to ensure that individuals would be adequately protected. Eventually this gap was remedied and the EU 'proclaimed' its own catalogue of rights, the Charter of Fundamental Rights of the European Union, which became 'legally binding' following the entry into force of the Lisbon Treaty. The Lisbon Treaty also provided for competence for the EU to accede to the European Convention on Human Rights (ECHR), a fundamental rights document adopted in the context of the Council of Europe (which is a separate organization from the EU). Accession negotiations have been concluded and the EU shall, once all the legal and political obstacles have been removed, become a party to the Convention so as to ensure that its fundamental rights record is open to external scrutiny by the European Court of Human Rights (ECtHR) established by that Convention, in the same way as that of the EU's Member States.

The protection of fundamental rights in the EU is a rich, and at times contested, area of EU law and it has become increasingly important with the expansion of the powers of the EU, especially in the field of criminal law. However, when reflecting on the debate on fundamental rights you should bear in mind the bigger picture: the more extensive the jurisdiction of the Court, the more enthusiastic its protection of individuals, the more pronounced the intrusion in national law.[1] Here, consider that once the Court of Justice has asserted jurisdiction, the national courts must relinquish it – if the Court decides that it is for itself to assess whether, for example, a national immigration rule falling within the scope of EU law is compatible with fundamental rights, it will then be only for the Court to balance the competing interests (ie the desire to curtail immigration vis-à-vis the rights of the migrant). Those incursions in what is felt to be the national jurisdiction might lead to problems, especially when national courts disagree with the level of protection afforded by the Court. Moreover, further judicial review of national legislation might be perceived as an unwelcome intrusion into the sovereignty of national parliaments.

This chapter will start by analysing the historical background and the development of the case law on fundamental rights since, despite the introduction of the Charter, an understanding of the previous case law is vital to appreciate when and how fundamental rights apply in the EU. We will then analyse the main Treaty provisions relating to fundamental rights protection, before turning to the Charter of Fundamental Rights of the EU. In the last section we will look at the relationship between the EU and the ECHR, including the extent to which the ECtHR agrees to scrutinize EU acts. We will also analyse the draft agreement on the EU's accession to the ECHR.

2 Historical background and development of the case law

We have seen in chapter 2 how in the aftermath of the Second World War there was a drive towards international cooperation, which also laid the roots for the creation and development of the European Communities. Not surprisingly, the atrocities committed during the war provoked a reaction aimed at ensuring that the past could not repeat itself and, as a result, the codification and protection of fundamental rights became of paramount importance both at international[2] and national level.[3] In particular, in the European context, State parties created a new international instrument, the ECHR.[4] The Convention is a catalogue of civil and political fundamental rights and States parties accepted not only to be bound by its rules but also to establish a supervisory mechanism

---

[1] In some instances, national courts are concerned about the fact that the standard of protection guaranteed by the Court of Justice is insufficient; see eg *Internationale Handelsgesellschaft* ('*Solange I*') [1974] 2 CMLR 540; the 'bananas saga' triggered by the ruling in C-280/93 *Germany v Council* [1994] ECR I-4973, N Reich 'Judge-Made "Europe à la carte": Some Remarks on Recent Conflicts between European and German Constitutional Law Provoked by the Banana Litigation' (1996) *European Journal of International Law* 103–111; and more recently, and in the context of the Charter, see Case C-399/11 *Melloni v Ministerio Fiscal*, judgment of 26 February 2013, discussed further in section 4.4.2. In relation to the problems raised by differing standards of protection in the context of the European Arrest Warrant, see also decision of Higher Regional Court in Stuttgart, translated and noted by J Vogel and J Spencer, 'Proportionality and the European Arrest Warrant' [2010] *Criminal Law Review* 474.

[2] Universal Declaration of Human Rights 1948; and ECHR, see n 4.

[3] See eg the German and Italian Constitutions.

[4] The ECHR was completed on 4 November 1950 and entered into force on 3 September 1953. The UK was the first State to ratify it, but it did not incorporate it into national law until 1998, with the Human Rights Act.

through the European Commission of Human Rights and the ECtHR;[5] this would ensure that good intentions would not remain unfulfilled ideals. Given this background, it might come as a surprise that fundamental rights were largely absent from the founding European Treaties;[6] the reason for such a gap is that, according to the original plans, European cooperation was to be part of a much broader political project which also comprised a European Defence Community Treaty and a European Political Community Treaty. The latter, provided as its first aim 'to contribute towards the protection of human rights and fundamental freedoms in the Member States'.[7] Furthermore, it incorporated the rights and freedoms contained in the ECHR (ie Part I),[8] and it limited accession to the Political Community to those European States that guaranteed fundamental rights as provided in the ECHR.[9] However (and as seen in chapter 2), both the Defence and the Political Community Treaties were abandoned in 1954 as the French national assembly would not ratify the former. As a result, fundamental rights remained largely absent from the founding Treaties establishing the three Communities.[10]

2.1 The development of the case law of the Court of Justice

This fundamental rights gap became all too apparent at a very early stage in the life of the Communities: in particular, national courts feared that Member States could use the Communities in order to circumvent the fundamental rights guarantees that had been at the centre of the post-war constitutionalizing effort. If the Communities had been given regulatory powers which could directly affect individuals, and those powers were not curtailed by fundamental rights, then individuals might see their fundamental rights limited beyond what was permissible under their own constitutional arrangements.

In an initial stage, individuals sought to enforce domestic fundamental rights against the (then) Communities' institutions.[11] However, those attempts failed since EU law (and previously EEC/EC law) can only be measured according to its own constitutional principles, otherwise the principle of supremacy would be compromised and the application of EU law would vary from one country to the other. The problem then was a serious one: national courts were not willing to allow executive action, even if exercised through international cooperation, to go unchecked, rather declaring that ultimately they would exercise jurisdiction to assess compatibility with (domestic) fundamental rights.[12] In this

---

[5] Until 1998 the European Commission of Human Rights acted as gatekeeper and decided on the admissibility of cases. Following the entry into force of Protocol 11 ECHR, the Commission has been abolished. The system was further restructured following the entry into force of Protocol 14 ECHR in 2010; this Protocol also provides for the possibility for the EU to join the Convention, subject (according to the explanatory report to the Convention) to the negotiation of a separate treaty to this effect (on which, see section 5.2).

[6] With the exception of the right not to be discriminated against on grounds of sex in relation to pay which was included from the start.

[7] See Information and Official Documents of the Constitutional Committee of the Ad Hoc Assembly (Paris 1953) 53 *et seq* (Art 2).

[8] See ibid, 53 *et seq* (Art 3).   [9] Ibid, (Art 116).

[10] See G de Búrca, 'The Evolution of EU Human Rights Law' in P Craig and G de Búrca, *The Evolution of EU Law* (2nd edn, Oxford: Oxford University Press, 2011.

[11] Case 1/58 *Stork v High Authority* [1959] ECR 17; Case 36-40/59 *Geitling v High Authority* [1960] ECR 425; Case 40/64 *Sgarlata v Commission* [1965] ECR 215.

[12] *Solange I* (n 1); see also *Steinike und Weinling* [1980] 2 CMLR 531; and cf also the Italian Constitutional Court rulings Sentenza 7/3/64, no 14 (in F Sorrentino, *Profili Costituzionali dell'Integrazione Comunitaria* (2nd edn, Turin: Giappichelli Editore, 1996) 61 *et seq*) and *Società Acciaierie San Michele v High Authority* (27 December 1965, no 98) [1967] CMLR 160.

way, one of the very foundations of the emerging European building – the principle of supremacy of EU law – was at risk of being compromised.[13] It did not take long for the Court of Justice to find that fundamental rights were part of the 'general principles of Community law' which the Court would protect (on the broader context of the general principles, see chapter 8).

In the case of *Stauder*,[14] Mr Stauder attacked a Commission decision which made the distribution of butter at reduced prices conditional upon the identification of the recipient; he claimed that having to be identified by name breached his right to dignity as protected by the German Constitution. The German court referred a question to the Court of Justice to assess the validity of the Commission's decision. However, this time the national court did not enquire as to the compatibility of a Community act with its own national constitutional fundamental rights; rather, it enquired whether the regime provided by the decision was 'compatible with the *general principles* of Community law in force'.[15] Having examined different language versions of the Commission's decision, the Court of Justice found that identification by name was not required by the Community act. It then continued:

> Interpreted in this way the provision at issue contains nothing capable of *prejudicing the fundamental human rights enshrined in the general principles of Community law* and protected by the Court.[16]

In this way, the Court made clear that

- it considered fundamental rights unwritten general principles applicable to the acts of the Communities' Institutions;

- it would protect such rights, so that an act of the Communities adopted in breach of fundamental rights would be declared void; and

- if more than one interpretation of a legal instrument was possible, that which did not infringe fundamental rights would have to be adopted.

In subsequent case law the Court clarified that in deciding which fundamental rights formed part of the general principles of Community law it would draw inspiration from constitutional traditions common to the Member States[17] and from international Treaties for the protection of human rights to which Member States were signatory or had collaborated;[18] of those, the most significant is without doubt the ECHR.[19]

As mentioned previously, the gap-filling function of general principles was of paramount importance not only to ensure that the Communities would be a constitutionally complete system, but also to assuage the fears of national courts in relation to fundamental rights protection. Whilst at first, some national courts, and especially the German

---

[13] Some authors (eg P Craig and G de Búrca, *EU Law: Text, Cases, and Materials* (5th edn, Oxford: Oxford University Press, 2011) 364) believe that the recognition of fundamental rights as general principles was due primarily to pressure from national courts; however, it should be pointed out that it is unlikely that experienced judges and jurists coming from countries with a strong constitutional ethos would be insensitive to such a major constitutional gap.   [14] Case 29/69 *Stauder* [1969] ECR 419.

[15] Ibid, para 1 (emphasis added).   [16] Ibid, para 7 (emphasis added).

[17] Case 11/70 *Internationale Handelsgesellschaft* [1970] ECR 1125, para 4.

[18] Case 4/73 *Nold* [1974] ECR 491, para 13.

[19] See eg Case 222/84 *Johnston v Royal Ulster Constabulary* [1986] ECR 1651; Case C-260/89 *Elliniki Radiophonia Tiléorassi AE (ERT) v Dimotiki Etairia Pliroforissis* [1991] ECR I-2925; Opinion 2/94 [1996] ECR I-1783; Case C-299/95 *Kremzow v Austria* [1997] ECR I-2629.

Federal Constitutional Court, were cautious in relinquishing jurisdiction,[20] with time it was accepted that the standard of protection afforded by the Court of Justice could be considered equivalent (never identical) to that afforded by domestic courts, so that the latter could entrust the review of the validity of Community/Union acts to the judgment of the Court of Justice.[21] This approach was therefore compatible with the *Foto-Frost* ruling,[22] where the Court made clear that it had sole jurisdiction to declare an act of the EU invalid.

2.2 The scope of application of fundamental rights as general principles

2.2.1 Fundamental rights as a limit to the acts of Union institutions

Fundamental rights as general principles of Union law (and now also those enshrined in the Charter) apply first and foremost as a limit to the acts of the Union institutions. Therefore, respect for fundamental rights is a precondition for the legality of any act of the Union, whether administrative or legislative. An example of such review can be seen in case study 9.1 on the momentous decision in *Kadi*. You have already seen in the first case study of this judgment (in chapter 8, case study 8.4) that this case developed the Court's case law on the right to be heard as a general principle of EU law; in this chapter we examine the importance of the *Kadi* judgment for the EU system of human rights protection.

Case study 9.1: Terrorism, fundamental rights, and the ruling in *Kadi I*

The background to *Kadi I*[23] follows from the terrorist attacks perpetrated against the US on 11 September 2001 after which there was a surge in international action aimed at combating terrorism. In this context, the UN adopted Resolution 1390(2002), which requires States to freeze the assets of those entities and individuals identified by the UN Sanctions Committee as being connected with Osama bin Laden, al-Qaeda, or the Taliban.[24] Those identified at UN level did not have any right to judicial review through the UN; rather, any request to be delisted was to be made to the State of nationality or residence, which would then make

---

[20] *Solange I* (n 1); see also *Steinike und Weinling* [1980] 2 CMLR 531; see also the Italian Constitutional Court rulings Sentenza 7/3/64, no 14 (in Sorrentino, *Profili Costituzionali dell'Integrazione Comunitaria* (n 12) 61 *et seq*) and *Societá Acciaierie San Michele* (n 12). On the *Solange* decision, see chapter 4, case study 4.1.

[21] *Wünsche Handelsgesellschaft* ('*Solange II*') [1987] 3 CMLR 225; this said the relationship between national supreme courts and the Court of Justice in relation to fundamental rights protection is a complex one; see eg *Maastricht* decision (*Brunner v EU Treaty* [1994] 1 CMLR 57); German Federal Constitutional Court, decision 7 June 2000 [2000] *Human Rights Law Journal* 251; and *Treaty of Lisbon* decision [2010] 3 CMLR 13; French Conseil Constitutionnel, Decision No 2004-496 (10 June 2004); Decision No 2004-497 (1 July 2004); the Polish Constitutional Court ruling in *Trybunal Konstytucyjny, arrêt du 27.04.05, P 1/05, Dziennik Ustaw 2005.77.680*, as reported by *Réflets-Informations rapides sur les développements juridiques présentant un intérêt communautaire*, no 2/2005, p 16, also available at http://curia.europa.eu/jcms/jcms/Jo2_9951/?hlText=reflets. See A Pliakos and G Anagnostaras, 'Who is the Ultimate Arbiter? The Battle over Judicial Supremacy in the EU' (2011) 26 *European Law Review* 109.

[22] Case 314/85 *Foto-Frost* [1987] ECR 4199, and see chapter 10.

[23] Joined Cases C-402/05 P and C-415/05 P *Kadi and Al Barakaat v Council* ('*Kadi I*') [2008] ECR I-6351, reversing the General Court's decisions in Case T-315/01 *Kadi v Council and Commission* [2005] ECR II-3649; Case T-306/01 *Yusuf and Al Barakaaat International Foundation v Council and Commission* [2005] ECR II-3533.

[24] This is also referred to as the 1267 Committee as it was created pursuant to UN Resolution 1267(1999).

representations to the Sanctions Committee.[25] The UN system was therefore highly unsatisfactory (and open to abuse) in that it deprived individuals of any possibility of defending themselves; furthermore, the reasons for inclusion in the list were not disclosed to those concerned.

Resolution 1390(2002) was implemented directly by the EU on the grounds that the existence of the free movement rights, and especially of free movement of capital, would render national implementation unsatisfactory.[26] As a result, individuals listed by the UN would have, almost automatically, their assets frozen in the EU. As the identification of those subject to the sanctions was carried out directly at UN level, there was no possibility for those individuals to know the reasons which led to such a step and consequently to defend themselves. Mr Kadi, a rich Saudi businessman,[27] challenged the freezing of his assets in front of the EU Courts. In particular, he relied on two grounds: first of all, he argued that there was no competence for the EU to adopt those measures.[28] Secondly, he argued that those measures breached his fundamental rights, and in particular his right of defence and his right to property. Both the General Court and the Court of Justice found that the EU had competence to adopt the contested measures. However, they differed on whether it was possible to carry out a fundamental rights review.

The General Court found that since the Union measures were giving effect to a UN Security Council resolution they could not be scrutinized in relation to fundamental rights as general principles of Union law. To do this, the Court argued, would amount to an indirect review of the UN resolutions, something that the Court felt unable to do. It therefore limited itself to reviewing the Union measures vis-à-vis the less stringent *jus cogens* requirements (general principles of international law). It then found that those had not been violated by the Union measures at issue. Following the ruling of the General Court, the application of EU fundamental rights to the acts of the Union institutions was not universal: when the Council was implementing a UN resolution, it would be sheltered from the application of EU fundamental rights.

The Court of Justice rejected this approach: it restated the autonomy of the Union legal system and the centrality of fundamental rights as general principles of Union law in this system. It then held:

> The obligations imposed by an international agreement cannot have the effect of prejudicing the constitutional principles of the EC Treaty, which include the principle that all Community acts must respect fundamental rights, that respect constituting a condition of their lawfulness which it is for the Court to review in the framework of the complete system of legal remedies established by the Treaty.[29]

---

[25] The system has then been amended, not least to address the concerns expressed by the Court of Justice in *Kadi*. See generally, E Spaventa, 'Counter-Terrorism and Fundamental Rights: Judicial Challenges and Legislative Changes after the Rulings in *Kadi* and *PMOI*' in A Antoniadis, R Schütze, and E Spaventa, *The EU and Global Emergencies* (Oxford: Hart Publishing, 2010).

[26] Common Position 2002/402/CFSP concerning restrictive measures against Usama bin Laden, members of the Al-Qaida organization and the Taliban and other individuals, groups, undertakings and entities associated with them (OJ [2002] L169/4; implemented by Regulation (EC) No 881/2002 imposing certain specific restrictive measures directed against certain persons and entities associated with Usama bin Laden, the Al-Qaida network and the Taliban (OJ [2002] L139/9), modified by Regulation 1286/2009 (OJ [2009] L346/42).

[27] See interview in *New York Times*, web edition, 13 December 2008, http://www.nytimes.com/2008/12/13/world/middleeast/13kadi.html?fta=y&_r=1&

[28] Express competence was only introduced with the Lisbon Treaty, see Art 215 TFEU.

[29] *Kadi I* (n 23) para 285.

It further rejected the reasoning of the General Court: the judicial review would have at its object only the Union implementing measures and not the UN Resolution. It therefore stated in the strongest possible terms that the European institutions cannot escape their fundamental rights obligations, even in those cases, such as the one at issue, where a finding of a breach might put the Union in breach of international law.[30]

The Court then found that the rights of the applicant had been violated: of paramount importance in this respect was the fact that Mr Kadi was never informed of the reasons that led to his inclusion in the list. Unaware of the evidence against him, he could not attempt to explain it or challenge it. Furthermore, the absence of any statement of reasons made it impossible for the Court to review whether inclusion in the list was justified (at least prima facie). Mr Kadi's right to defence had therefore been breached as he was in no position to defend himself or make his reasons heard.

Secondly, the Court had to assess whether the freezing measures constituted a disproportionate interference with Mr Kadi's right to property as guaranteed by the EU fundamental rights, and Protocol 1 to the ECHR. It found that while, in principle, those types of sanctions can be justified, in practice the absence of any procedural guarantee entailed a violation of his right to property. The Regulation was therefore annulled insofar as Mr Kadi was concerned.

2.2.2 Fundamental rights as a limit upon the acts of Member States

EU fundamental rights also apply, somehow more controversially, to the acts of the Member States when they are implementing EU law, or when they act within its scope. The basic principle behind this interpretation is that when Member States implement Union law,[31] or act within its scope by limiting one of the rights granted by the Treaties, they have to comply with all of the constitutional principles of the EU, including fundamental rights protection. Thus, if a Member State is implementing a regulation or a directive it has to exercise its discretion in a manner that is consistent with EU fundamental rights[32] (as well as with national fundamental rights where this is appropriate).

In NS,[33] the case related to the application of Regulation 343/2003,[34] which provides the criteria for allocating the Member State responsible to examine asylum claims: usually this would be the country where the asylum seeker first entered the territory of the Union. However, the Regulation also contains the so-called sovereignty clause according to which

---

[30] See also the rulings in Case T-85/09 *Kadi II* [2010] ECR II-5177, and Joined Cases C-584/10, C-593/10 and C-595/10 P *Commission and UK v Kadi*, judgment of 18 July 2013, nyr; Mr Kadi was eventually also delisted at UN level, see UN Security Council Press Release, 5 October 2012 (SC/10785), http://www.un.org/News/Press/docs//2012/sc10785.doc.htm

[31] The concept of implementation has been given a broad interpretation; see eg Case C-617/10 *Åklagaren v Hans Åkerberg Fransson*, judgment of 26 February 2013, nyr, examined in more detail in section 4.4.1.

[32] This obligation is very broad, also encompassing the possibility for a horizontal application of the general principles; see eg Case C-144/04 *Mangold* [2005] ECR I-9981; Case C-555/07 *Kücükdeveci v Swedex* [2010] ECR I-365; see generally E Spaventa, 'The Horizontal Application of Fundamental Rights as General Principles of EU Law' and M Dougan, 'In Defence of *Mangold*?' both in A Arnull, C Barnard, M Dougan, and E Spaventa, *A Constitutional Order of States? Essays in EU Law in Honour of Alan Dashwood* (Oxford: Hart Publishing 2011).

[33] Joined Cases C-411/10 and C-493/10 *NS v Secretary of State for the Home Department*, judgment of 21 December 2011.

[34] Council Regulation (EC) No 343/2003 establishing the criteria and mechanisms for determining the Member State responsible for examining an asylum application lodged in one of the Member States by a third-country national (OJ [2003] L50/1). On EU asylum law, see further chapter 26.

Member States retain the discretion to examine claims even when such examination is not their responsibility pursuant to the Regulation. In the *NS* case the claimants were challenging their deportation from the UK, the country where they were present, to Greece, which was responsible for their application (being the first port of entry). In particular, they argued that given the conditions under which asylum applications were dealt with in Greece, deportation would entail a breach of their right not to be subjected to degrading treatment as protected by Article 4 of the Charter and Article 3 ECHR.[35] The issue was then whether the discretion of the Member State should be subjected to review pursuant to EU fundamental rights: the Court found that the exercise of discretion still constituted implementation of EU law and that therefore EU fundamental rights were (at least to a certain extent) applicable. The UK could not therefore deport the applicants if it could not be unaware of the systemic deficiencies of the asylum system in the country of destination (Greece). As mentioned previously, this case law applies in the same way when Member States are acting 'within the scope' of EU law, that is to say when they are seeking to limit a right conferred on individuals directly by the Treaty. Thus, for instance, in *Familiapress* the Court held that when limiting the free movement of goods the Member States are bound to respect freedom of expression as guaranteed (then) by Article 10 ECHR.[36] This can also be seen in case study 9.2 on the decision in *Carpenter*.

Case study 9.2: Immigration, sovereignty, and fundamental rights: the case of Mr and Mrs Carpenter

Mrs Carpenter was a national of the Philippines living in the UK; she married Mr Carpenter, who was a British citizen also living in the UK, and applied for a residence permit as the spouse of a British national.[37] Her application was denied on the grounds that she had overstayed her visa and she was asked to leave the country and apply for a new visa from the Philippines. The immigration authorities accepted that the marriage of Mr and Mrs Carpenter was genuine, that is, it was not a sham entered into only to avoid the application of immigration rules. The refusal of leave to remain therefore constituted an interference with Mr and Mrs Carpenter's right to family life, as protected by both the ECHR and the general principles of EU law. The issue was then whether the interference was legitimate, in that it constituted a proportionate interference with the right to family life justified by the policy aim of curtailing illegal immigration by discouraging overstays on visas. The most obvious route would have been to invoke the Human Rights Act 1998,[38] which incorporates the ECHR in British law. However, according to a consistent body of case law, immigration policy, as long as it is applied proportionately, constitutes a legitimate ground to limit the right to family life; the claim was therefore unlikely to succeed by invoking the Human Rights Act.

Counsel for Mr and Mrs Carpenter therefore chose a different strategy: he sought to transform the case into an EU law case so that EU fundamental rights could be invoked.

---

[35] The ECtHR had examined a similar issue in *MSS v Belgium and Greece* (Appl No 30696/09), judgment of 21 January 2011, esp paras 358, 360, and 367, and found that, as a matter of ECHR law, Member States could not deport asylum seekers to the Member State responsible under the EU rules when they knew that the country of destination would not examine the application properly, and that the asylum seeker would be exposed to living conditions that amounted to degrading treatment.

[36] Case C-368/95 *Familiapress* [1997] ECR I-3689, esp para 24; see also Case C-36/02 *Omega Spielhallen-und Automatenaufstellungs-GmbH v Oberbürgermeisterin der Bundesstadt Bonn* [2004] ECR I-9609.

[37] Case C-60/00 *Carpenter* [2002] ECR I-6279.

[38] This could have been invoked as the UK government lifted the non-retroactivity clause.

This strategy had two advantages: first of all, if EU law was applicable, the Court of Justice would have jurisdiction to assess the case. Since Convention rights are a minimum standard (the Court of Justice will not fall below the protection granted by the Convention), he was hoping that the Court would be willing to grant more extensive protection to the right to family life. Secondly, if EU law could be invoked then in balancing the right to family life with the immigration policy of the Member State, the Court of Justice (and the national court) would also take into account the right to move granted by the Treaty. As a result, the balance might be tilted in favour of the claimants. But how did counsel manage to establish a sufficient link with EU law? After all, all the elements of the case were linked exclusively to the UK: Mr Carpenter was British; his wife had overstayed the visa granted by British authorities; neither party had moved to, or was returning from, another Member State. From an EU law perspective the case seemed prima facie purely internal. As a result, as you will see in chapter 13, the EU rules on the free movement of persons would not apply, and so the UK would be free to apply its own restrictions on immigration.

Counsel argued that Mr Carpenter, who ran a business selling advertising space, provided services to clients in other EU States; he also occasionally had to travel to France on business. He was therefore a service provider covered by Article 56 TFEU. Further, he argued that when he was travelling on business his wife would take care of his children; her deportation would therefore constitute a hindrance to his ability to travel to provide services. In order to assess whether this hindrance was justified, due recourse should be had to his family rights. Counsel thus suggested that deportation was a disproportionate interference with the Carpenters' family life and therefore an unjustified restriction on Mr Carpenter's right to provide services in the EU as protected (now) by the TFEU. The Court, broadly speaking and with marginal differences, accepted this reasoning. Regardless of the subtleties of the free movement issues, it should be noted that by linking the case to EU law, and by ensuring that EU fundamental rights were applicable, Mr and Mrs Carpenter obtained what they would have been denied had they relied solely on UK immigration rules and the Human Rights Act: Mrs Carpenter obtained leave to remain without having to return to the Philippines and apply from there.

As you will see in chapters 13 and 20, a more delicate situation arises when Treaty freedoms clash with fundamental rights so that the enjoyment of the former results in the limitation of another claimant's fundamental right.[39]

3 The response of the political institutions: from the 1977 Declaration to the Lisbon Treaty

It was mentioned previously that the gap in the Treaties concerning fundamental rights protection was largely coincidental; it is not surprising then that the developments in the case law of the Court met with the approval of the political institutions. In 1977, just eight years after the ruling in *Stauder* and once the case law was 'settled', the European Parliament, the Council, and the Commission issued a joint declaration to the effect that they considered themselves bound by fundamental rights as general principles of (then)

---

[39] See Case C-112/00 *Schmidberger* [2003] ECR I-5659; Case C-438/05 *International Transport Workers' Federation and Finnish Seamen's Union v Viking Line* [2007] ECR I-10779; Case C-341/05 *Laval un Partneri* [2007] ECR I-11767.

Community law.[40] After that, every Treaty revision strengthened the protection of funda-mental rights in the EU.[41] In particular, following the expansion of Union competences in the field of asylum, immigration, and criminal law, the protection of fundamental rights in the EU became of paramount importance for many of the Member States. The pro-cess of codification of the Court's case law, and the ongoing attention to fundamental rights, culminated in 2000 with the drafting of the Charter of Fundamental Rights of the European Union.[42] Whilst at first the Charter was 'merely' proclaimed by the three polit-ical institutions, almost mirroring the 1977 Declaration, the Lisbon Treaty subsequently gave it the same legal value as the Treaties themselves (Article 6(1) TEU). Furthermore, and as we shall see in more detail later, the debate as to whether the Union should become a party to the ECHR has finally received a positive answer and Article 6(2) TEU provides not only the competence for accession but also a legal obligation to do so.

Article 6 TEU also recognizes the continued relevance of the case law preceding the Charter; Article 6(3) TEU provides that

> Fundamental rights, as guaranteed by the European Convention for the Protection of Human Rights and Fundamental Freedoms and as they result from the constitutional traditions com-mon to the Member States, shall constitute general principles of the Union's law.

Thus, even after the incorporation of the Charter in the primary law of the EU, the Treaty restates the centrality of fundamental rights, the ECHR, and the common constitutional traditions, as general principles of Union law.[43] Article 6(3) therefore allows the Court of Justice to go beyond the rights contained in the Charter, should the need ever arise.

Besides Article 6 TEU, the Lisbon Treaty further enhanced the protection of fundamen-tal rights in several fields. Thus, for instance, it provides for (almost) full jurisdiction of the Court of Justice in the field of cooperation in criminal law;[44] for the Court's jurisdiction to review Common Foreign and Security Policy (CFSP) decisions that provide for measures against natural or legal persons;[45] and for slightly relaxed conditions for standing before the Union Courts.[46]

---

[40] OJ [1977] C103/1. Note that the declaration was referred to by the German Federal Constitutional Court in the ruling in *Solange II* (n 21) as one of the indications that the fundamental rights protection in the EEC had reached a satisfactory level and that they would as a result cease, for the time being, to exercise their power of scrutiny over EEC law. That power has, to a certain extent, been reinvoked in later case law; see n 21.

[41] See Preamble to the Single European Act; Art F(2) TEU (Maastricht version); Articles 7, 46, and 49 TEU as modified and renumbered by the Treaty of Amsterdam; and the modification to Art 7 TEU introduced by the Treaty of Nice.

[42] Charter of Fundamental Rights (OJ [2000] C364/1); other initiatives in the field of fundamental rights include the establishment of an EU Fundamental Rights Agency, Regulation (EC) No 168/2007 establishing a European Union Agency for Fundamental Rights (OJ [2007] L53/1); see generally P Alston and O de Schutter (eds), *Monitoring Fundamental Rights in the EU* (Oxford: Hart Publishing, 2005).

[43] On the 'multiple' sources of fundamental rights, see HCH Hofmann and BC Mihaescu, 'The Relation between the Charter's Fundamental Rights and the Unwritten General Principles of EU Law: Good Administration as the Test Case' (2013) 9 *European Constitutional Law Review* 73; on the post-Lisbon fundamental rights landscape, see S Morano-Foadi and S Andreadakis, 'Reflections on the Architecture of the EU after the Treaty of Lisbon: The European Judicial Approach to Fundamental Rights' (2011) 17 *European Law Journal* 595.

[44] See chapter 25. However, Art 276 TFEU excludes jurisdiction for the Court of Justice to review the valid-ity and proportionality of police and law enforcement operations of a Member State, or the exercise of Member States' responsibilities as regards law and order and internal security.   [45] Art 275(2) TFEU.

[46] See chapter 10; Art 263(4) TFEU provides that individuals can challenge regulatory acts which are of direct concern to them and which do not entail implementing measures, hence removing in those cases the need to prove individual concern. On the concept of 'regulatory act', see eg Case C-583/11 P *Inuit Tapiriit Kanatami v European Parliament and Council*, judgment of 3 October 2013.

Finally, respect for fundamental rights, as well as the other values listed in Article 2 TEU, is a precondition for accession to the EU,[47] and relevant for participation in the EU. For this reason, Article 7 TEU provides for a procedure to police and react to the risk of serious breaches of those values. In the case in which the Council determines that the breach is serious and persistent, it can suspend certain rights, including voting rights, of the Member State in question.

4 The Charter of Fundamental Rights

The adoption of the EU's Charter of Fundamental Rights is one of the most significant constitutional steps in the history of the EU.[48] This is particularly so for two reasons: first of all, the Charter was drafted using a new (and some might say revolutionary) procedure which involved not only representatives of national governments but also representatives of national and European parliaments.

Secondly, the fact that Member States felt the need to adopt a fundamental rights document (even though there is no general fundamental rights competence for the EU), is a further step in the long process of the constitutional evolution of the EU. We will first analyse the way the Charter was drafted and explain, in broad terms, its content, before turning to its scope of application.

4.1 The drafting of the Charter

In 1999 the Cologne European Council held in its conclusions that

> at the present stage of development of the European Union, the fundamental rights applicable at Union level *should be consolidated in a Charter and thereby made more evident.*[49]

According to the mandate contained in the Cologne Conclusions, the Charter should contain

- the rights and procedural guarantees contained in the ECHR and those derived by the common constitutional traditions, as general principles of European law;
- the rights pertaining to Union citizens (eg right to move and reside in Member States); and
- account was to be taken of the social rights contained in the European Social Charter and the Community Charter of the Fundamental Social Rights of Workers.

The Cologne European Council also identified the composition of the body that should be entrusted with the drafting of the Charter: it should be composed of the representatives of the heads of State and government (ie representatives of national executives), the President of the Commission, representatives of national parliaments, and members of the European Parliament.

---

[47] Art 49 TEU.

[48] For a detailed article-by-article analysis of the Charter, see S Peers, T Hervey, J Kenner, and A Ward (eds), *The EU Charter of Fundamental Rights: A Commentary* (Oxford: Hart Publishing, 2014).

[49] Cologne European Council, 3 and 4 June 1999, Presidency Conclusions, 150/99 REV 1, para 44 (emphasis added); see also Annex IV to the Conclusions.

The inclusion of representatives from both the European and national parliaments was a true novelty in the context of the EU (and international relations more broadly) since normally international treaties are drafted and negotiated by representatives of national governments and are then presented to national parliaments for ratification on a 'take it or leave it' basis. In this way, parliaments are less able to influence the outcome of negotiations. This time, however, given the fundamental importance of the document to be drafted, the Member States decided to include in the discussions representatives of directly elected parliaments hence enhancing the democratic credentials of the drafting body (called somewhat confusingly the 'Convention'). The final composition of the Convention was decided at the subsequent Tampere European Council[50] and included

- 15 representatives of the heads of State or government of the Member States,
- 1 representative of the Commission,
- 16 representatives of the European Parliament,
- 30 representatives of the national parliaments (two for each Member State).

The number of representatives of the European Parliament was set so as to counterbalance the number of representatives of the (then) Community executive (15 + 1); whilst the number of representatives of national parliaments was set at two for each Member State in order to ensure that those Member States which have a bicameral system could have a representative from each chamber. The Convention was then dominated by parliamentarians, rather than the executive: furthermore, in order to enhance its democratic legitimacy, all documents were made public and placed on the internet, and the Convention also accepted representations from acceding Member States as well as non-governmental organizations (NGOs). The mode of drafting of the Charter was considered a crucial step in the constitution building of the Union – so much so that, as you have seen in chapter 2, the same process was followed in the drafting of the Constitution for Europe; however, the latter failed, and the States reverted to intergovernmentalism (ie negotiation among Member States' governments only) for the Lisbon Treaty.

The Convention took just over ten months to draft the Charter of Fundamental Rights, which was then 'proclaimed' by the European Parliament, the European Commission, and the Council at Nice on 7 December 2000.[51] Following its proclamation, there was some uncertainty as to its legal value since, on the one hand, it had not been given official legal status but, on the other hand, it codified *existing* rights, hence making issues about its legal value if not redundant at least less crucial than would have otherwise been the case.[52] The issue has now been settled following the entry into force of the Lisbon Treaty: Article 6(1) TFEU expressly provides that the Charter has the same legal value as the Treaties.

4.2 The structure of the Charter

We have seen earlier that the mode of drafting the Charter was novel, being if anything more reminiscent of national constitution drafting than of international treaty-making; equally

---

[50] Tampere European Council, 15 and 16 October 1999, Annex to the Presidency Conclusions, available at http://ue.eu.int/ueDocs/cms_Data/docs/pressData/en/ec/00200-r1.en9.htm

[51] Charter of Fundamental Rights (OJ [2000] C364/1); the text of the Charter was modified by the Constitutional Treaty and it is this latter version that has been incorporated by the Lisbon Treaty.

[52] Advocates General referred to the Charter from the very beginning, see eg AG Alber in Case C-340/99 *TNT Traco Spa* [2001] ECR I-4109; the then Court of First Instance also referred to it in several cases, see eg Case T-177/01 *Jégo-Quéré* [2002] ECR II-2365.

novel was the choice made by the Convention to depart from the traditional dichotomy of civil and political rights/economic and social rights, instead approaching fundamental rights as an indivisible whole, hence placing all rights, at least theoretically, on the same level.[53] The Charter is thus divided into titles according to six fundamental values: dignity, freedom, equality, solidarity, citizens' rights, and justice. The substantive provisions are then complemented by the Preamble and by the so-called horizontal provisions (Articles 51 to 54), which are general provisions that set out the scope of application of the Charter, the legitimate grounds of limits on, and derogations from, Charter rights, as well as the relationship with the ECHR, national constitutions, and international human rights treaties. As we shall see later, the scope of application of the Charter mirrors that of the general principles so that the Charter applies to the Union institutions as well as to the Member States when they implement or act within the scope of Union law. The Charter is also complemented by 'explanations' which clarify the scope and, most importantly, the source of each of the Charter rights/provisions.[54] The identification of the 'origin' of Charter rights is of paramount importance for understanding their scope, since the Charter incorporates rights contained in other documents and in particular in the ECHR and in the TEU/TFEU. The Convention-derived rights must be interpreted to give *at least* the same protection granted by the Convention (Article 52(3)), whilst Treaty-derived rights must be given the same scope as their Treaty counterparts (Article 52(2)).

4.3 The substantive provisions of the Charter

Title I *Dignity* (Articles 1 to 5)

Title I contains those rights which are essential to the enjoyment of any other right: the right to human dignity;[55] the right to life; the right to the integrity of the person, which contains new generation rights such as the principle of informed consent in relation to medical intervention and the prohibition of eugenic practices; the prohibition of torture and inhuman and degrading treatment; and the prohibition of slavery and forced labour. As we have seen previously, in the *NS* case the prohibition of torture and inhuman treatment was relied upon to curtail the discretion of the UK and prevent it from deporting the asylum seekers to Greece.[56]

---

[53] The dichotomy between civil and political rights on the one hand, and social and economic rights on the other, is reflected at European level in the ECHR, which only protected civil and political rights. There is a long-standing debate, also between Western and non-Western countries, as to the respective strengths of different rights (eg is any right meaningful without the right to true democratic participation; or is any political right of any significance if individuals are not put in the condition to survive). The Charter seeks then to go beyond this debate and stress the indivisibility of fundamental rights. Furthermore, the structure and breadth of the Charter seeks to go beyond the traditional market-centrism which characterized the earlier stages of European integration.

[54] The original explanations can be found on the Council documents website (http://www.europa.eu), or as an official publication of the European Communities (*Charter of Fundamental Rights of the European Union: Explanations Relating to the Complete Text of the Charter* (Luxembourg: Council of the EU, 2001)); the amended explanations can be found in Explanations relating to the Charter of Fundamental Rights (OJ [2007] C303/02). Art 52(7) Charter provides that the explanations must be given 'due regard' by the courts of the Union and of the Member States; Art 6(1), third subpara, TEU provides that the Charter must be interpreted having due regard to the explanations.

[55] Case C-377/98 *Netherlands v Council* ('*Biotechnology Directive*') [2001] ECR I-7079; see also Case C-36/02 *Omega* [2004] ECR I-9609, esp para 34. Even though it is not expressly mentioned in the Convention, the right to dignity informs the interpretation of all Convention rights; eg *Tyrer v UK* (Appl No 5856/72) (1979–80) 2 EHRR 1.

[56] *NS* (n 33). See section 2.2.2.

Title II *Freedom* (Articles 6 to 19)

This heading contains some of the traditional civil and political rights, such as the right to liberty; the right to private life; the right to freedom of expression; the right to property; some new generation rights, such as the right to the protection of personal data; as well as some socio-economic rights, such as the right to work and the right to education. It is interesting to note that despite the Charter's ambitions to reflect a more contemporary take on rights, the right to freedom of thought and religion was not broadened explicitly to include the right not to hold a religious belief,[57] as suggested by many NGOs.[58] As we have seen in case study 9.1 in the *Kadi* case, the Court held that whilst the freezing of Mr Kadi's assets could in principle have been justified, in the case at issue it violated his right to property because it did not provide for sufficient procedural guarantees.

Title III *Equality* (Articles 20 to 26)

Title III contains traditional equality rights (non-discrimination on grounds of sex, race, sexual orientation, religion, belief, etc), together with the right not to be discriminated against on grounds of nationality within the scope of application of the Treaty and the rights of more vulnerable members of society such as children, the elderly, and disabled people. For more on the application of these rights in EU law, see chapter 20.

Title IV *Solidarity* (Articles 27 to 38)

Title IV is, at least in the UK,[59] the most contested part of the Charter in that it contains traditional social rights and 'principles', such as the right to collective bargaining and action, including the right to strike and protection against unjustified dismissal; the right to fair working conditions as well as protection for children and young people at work, and protection for the family, including protection against dismissal linked to maternity. It also includes 'recognition' of social security and social assistance; access to services of general economic interests; and the 'right' to health care, as well as the obligation for the Union to ensure a high level of environmental and consumer protection in its policies. It should be noted that some of these rights are entirely dependent on national laws and practices; whilst others are 'principles', that is, not self-standing rights, rather instructions that establish the principles the Union legislature must respect.[60] For more on the application of these rights in EU law, see again chapter 20.

Title V *Citizens' rights* (Articles 39 to 46)

Title V reproduces rights contained in the TFEU and mainly benefits only Union citizens. It includes the right to vote and stand for elections in the European Parliament and in municipal elections in the Member State of residence, the right to move and reside freely in the territory of the Member States, and the right to consular and diplomatic protection, all limited to Union citizens. The 'administrative rights' in this title, such as the right to good administration, the right to access documents, the right to complain to the Ombudsman, and the right to petition, are also available to non-EU citizens resident in or, in the case

---

[57] This is especially disappointing since the ECtHR has found that the right not to hold a religious belief is inherent in the correspondent ECHR right (Art 9): *Buscarini v San Marino* (Appl No 24645/95) (2000) 30 EHRR 208.

[58] cf Amnesty International Comments on the Draft Charter, CHARTE 4446/00, CONTRIB 300.

[59] For the position of UK and Poland on Title IV, see discussion in section 4.5 on Protocol No 30.

[60] On the distinction between principles and rights, see also discussion on Art 52(5) in section 4.4.2.

of legal persons, to companies having their registered office in, the EU. As an example of how the rights in Title V apply in practice, see chapter 13 regarding the free movement of persons.

Title VI *Justice* (Articles 47 to 50)

Title VI is concerned with the administration of justice and draws mainly on the ECHR and on the common constitutional traditions to the Member States. It includes the right to an effective remedy and a fair trial; the right to be presumed innocent and the right of defence; the principle of legality and proportionality of criminal offences and penalties; and the principle of *ne bis in idem*, which is to say the right not to be tried or punished twice for the same offence. These rights were relevant, for instance, in the *Kadi* and *Fransson* cases discussed in this chapter.

4.4 **The horizontal provisions**

As mentioned previously, Articles 51 to 54 set out the scope of application of the Charter, clarifying its field of application (Article 51), the scope and interpretation of rights and principles (Article 52),[61] the level of protection (Article 53), and the prohibition of abuse of rights (Article 54). Those are, without doubt, the most complex and difficult provisions of the Charter since they reflect anxieties and divisions amongst Member States in relation not only to what the Charter should achieve, but also in relation to the direction of the EU. In particular, some Member States fear that fundamental rights might become a vehicle for further intrusion into national sovereignty, even in those fields which Member States have reserved to themselves; that the Charter might eventually have the effect of granting the Court of Justice broad and general fundamental rights jurisdiction; and that the Charter is a further step towards a more integrated, and federal, EU. We shall now consider some of these issues.

4.4.1 **The scope of application of the Charter**

As we have seen, the Charter codifies existing case law making rights more visible to the citizen. Its primary addressee, then, is the EU. However, the Member States are also bound by EU fundamental rights when they exercise a discretion which has either been conferred by Union law (ie when they implement a Union law instrument) or when they bring themselves within the scope of EU law by limiting or derogating from one of the rights conferred by the Treaties. Article 51(1) therefore states that the provisions of the Charter are addressed to the EU institutions, agencies, and bodies and to the Member States 'only' when they implement Union law.[62] It should be noted, however, that the interpretation of what constitutes 'implementation' for the purposes of Article 51(1) is very broad. It covers cases in which the Member State is implementing or giving effect to a directive, regulation, or decision, as well as cases where the Member State is limiting one of the rights granted by the Treaty. More controversially it also

---

[61] See generally K Lenaerts, 'Exploring the Limits of the EU Charter of Fundamental Rights' (2012) 8 *European Constitutional Law Review* 375.

[62] To start with there was some confusion about the fact that whilst fundamental rights as general principles apply when the Member States implement EU law or *act within its scope* (see previously), Art 51 only referred to the former. However, the explanations to the Charter refer to Member States acting within the scope of EU law, and the Court, rightly, has adopted an integrated reading so that the reference to 'implement' in Art 51 also includes Member States acting within the scope of EU law; see eg Case C-256/11 *Dereci* [2011] ECR I-11315, para 72.

covers cases in which the Member States exercise a power that was 'reserved' to them in a piece of secondary legislation;[63] as well as cases where the subject matter is only partially related to EU law.

For instance, in *Åkerberg Fransson*,[64] the issue concerned whether the principle of *ne bis in idem* provided for in Article 50 Charter, applied to proceedings brought against Mr Åkerberg Fransson on charges of serious tax offences, including providing false information in relation to VAT. Several intervening Member States, together with the Commission, argued that the Charter was not applicable since the legislation which formed the basis for the proceedings was not implementing EU law. The Court disagreed: it found that the tax penalties and the criminal proceedings to which Mr Åkerberg Fransson was subjected were in part connected to his obligations to declare VAT. The Court then found that it followed from Directive 2006/112,[65] as well as from the principle of loyal cooperation, that Member States have an obligation to take 'all legislative and administrative measures' to ensure collection of VAT due on their territory. Furthermore, since part of the VAT revenue is destined to the EU's own resources, a lacuna in collection of the tax would also determine a reduction in the revenues of the EU. Since Article 325 TFEU obliges Member States to counter illegal activities affecting the financial interests of the EU, the tax penalties at issue also constituted implementation of that provision of the Treaty. For these reasons, and even though the proceedings also related to the collection of income tax, which is not harmonized at EU level, the Court found that the tax penalties and the criminal proceedings constituted 'implementation' of EU law and therefore fell within the scope of application of the Charter.[66]

Article 51(1) also states that institutions and Member States apply the Charter 'in accordance with their respective powers and respecting the limits of the powers of the Union as conferred in the Treaties', hence reinforcing the separation between Union and national competences. This is further restated in Article 51(2), which clarifies that

> The Charter does not extend the field of application of Union law beyond the powers of the Union or establish any new power or task for the Union, or modify powers and tasks as defined in the Treaties.

---

[63] See *NS* (n 33), also discussed previously.

[64] Case C-617/10 *Åklagaren v Hans Åkerberg Fransson*, judgment of 26 February 2013, nyr; noted in E Hancox, 'The Meaning of "Implementing" EU Law under Article 51(1) of the Charter: *Åkerberg Fransson*' (2013) 50 *Common Market Law Review* 1411; on this case and the reaction it provoked in the German Federal Constitutional Court, see F Fontanelli, '*Hic Sunt Nationes*: The Elusive Limits of the EU Charter and the German Constitutional Watchdog' (2013) 9 *European Constitutional Law Review* 315; and 'Ultra Vires – Has the Bundesverfassungsgericht Shown Its Teeth?', editorial (2013) 50 *Common Market Law Review* 925; D Sarmiento, 'Who is Afraid of the Charter? The Court of Justice, National Courts and the New Framework of Fundamental Rights Protection in the EU' (2013) 50 *Common Market Law Review* 1267.

[65] Directive 2006/112 on the common system of value added tax (OJ [2006] L347/1).

[66] In Case C-40/11 *Iida v Stadt Ulm*, judgment of 8 November 2012, nyr, the Court stated that in order to determine whether the Member State is implementing EU law,

> it must be ascertained among other things whether the national legislation at issue is intended to implement a provision of European Union law, what the character of that legislation is, and whether it pursues objectives other than those covered by European Union law, even if it is capable of indirectly affecting that law, and also whether there are specific rules of European Union law on the matter or capable of affecting it. (para 79)

See also Case C-87/12 *Ymeraga v Ministre du Travail, de l'Emploi et de l'Immigration*, judgment of 8 May 2013.

As we mentioned previously, Article 51 reflects a certain anxiety on behalf of the Member States that the Charter might become a vehicle to establish general fundamental rights jurisdiction for the Court of Justice.[67] These fears were duly taken into account by the Court in the ruling in *McB*.[68]

In *McB* the issue related to Irish rules on custody rights according to which, whilst the mother obtains automatic custody of her children, the unmarried father, lacking an agreement, must apply to a court to see his right recognized. When the McB couple separated, Mr McB applied for custody to the Irish courts; the mother, however, removed the children from the jurisdiction of the Irish courts before custody had been granted. Pursuant to Regulation 2201/2003 on the recognition of judgments in matters of parental responsibility, if children are wrongfully removed from their country of residence the jurisdiction is maintained by the latter's courts.[69] However, the Irish court denied jurisdiction on the ground that when the removal took place the father had not yet acquired custody rights. The Irish Supreme Court then referred a question to enquire whether the Regulation, read in light of the Charter, precluded the national rule that, in the case of unmarried fathers, subordinated custody rights to agreement between the parents or to judicial pronouncement. Mr McB argued that the Irish rules were inconsistent with his right to private and family life as guaranteed by Article 7 Charter, and Article 8 ECHR.

The question was very sensitive: family law is, broadly speaking, reserved to the Member States. As a result, Regulation 2201/2003, which merely coordinates national rules and does not harmonize them, refers to the law of the Member States to determine when removal of the child has been wrongful, thereby resulting in abduction. However, Mr McB was seeking through the medium of EU law a review of the national rules on custody: in this way a matter reserved to the Member State would become open to scrutiny by the Union judicature. The Court relied on Article 51 to limit the effects of the Charter, and it held:

> 52. It follows that, in the context of this case, the Charter should be taken into consideration solely for the purposes of interpreting Regulation No 2201/2003, and there *should be no assessment of national law as such*.[70]

The Court then performed an indirect review of national law by focusing on its own interpretation of the Regulation. In this way it sought to respect the letter and the spirit of Article 51 Charter and to balance the need to respect the competencies of the Member States, with the need to ensure that the rights of individuals are protected.

4.4.2 The scope and interpretation of the Charter

Very few fundamental rights are absolute; the vast majority of fundamental rights can be limited in order to protect the rights of others and/or to ensure that public policy objectives can be carried out. Take, for instance, the right to liberty on the one hand, and the need to impose custodial sentences for given crimes on the other; or the need to respect other people's property when enjoying one's own. In order to ensure that a balance can be struck between competing private or public interests, fundamental rights documents often

---

[67] On the duty of national courts in relation to the Charter, see again *Åklagaren v Hans Åkerberg Fransson* (n 64).   [68] Case C-400/10 PPU *McB* [2010] ECR I-8965.
[69] OJ [2003] L338/1.   [70] Emphasis added.

contain derogation and limitation clauses:[71] thus, for instance, the ECHR contains the permissible grounds of limitation in each of the relevant right-granting articles, and a general power to derogate from most of the Convention in emergencies (Article 15). By contrast, the Charter provides for just one general derogation and limitation clause. Article 52(1) states that limitations on the exercise of Charter rights must

- be provided by law,
- respect the essence of those rights,
- respect the principle of proportionality, and
- be necessary to meet the objectives of 'general interest recognised by the Union or the need to protect the rights and freedoms of others'.

Furthermore, in order to ensure consistency, Article 52(2) clarifies that Treaty-derived rights are to be exercised according to the conditions and limits defined by the Treaties (eg Union citizenship rights can be legitimately detailed/limited in Directive 2004/38; see further chapter 16). More importantly, in order to ensure adequate protection, paragraph 3 of the same article provides that insofar as Charter rights correspond to ECHR rights, their meaning and scope must be the same as those laid down by the Convention, even though it is open to the Union to afford more generous protection (eg in immigration cases the Union might legitimately give a more generous interpretation of the right to family life; see case study 9.2 on the *Carpenter* judgment). Article 52(4) provides that rights resulting from common constitutional traditions must be interpreted in harmony with those traditions.

These latter provisions are complemented by Article 53, which ensures that the protection afforded by the Charter cannot fall below that afforded by international law and international agreements to which the EU or all of the Member States are parties, including the ECHR, and by the Member States' constitutions.[72] The reference to national constitutions proved somewhat confusing: in particular, it was unclear whether Article 53 would amend the status quo according to which in relation to EU legislation the only fundamental rights standard which is relevant is that set by the EU constitutional order. In *Melloni*,[73] the Court of Justice clarified that Article 53 cannot be used to apply national fundamental rights (even when more protective than the Charter) to EU law which complies with the Charter. In that case, the issue related to the execution of a European Arrest Warrant;[74] this is an instrument pursuant to which Member States can request another Member State to surrender a suspect for the purposes of criminal prosecution; or to surrender a convicted person in order to execute a custodial sentence. Unlike extradition, the execution of a European Arrest Warrant is, besides a few listed exceptions, automatic. Mr Melloni had been convicted *in absentia* (ie he was not present at the trial); even though he was not physically

---

[71] In those cases in which derogations are not expressly provided, the courts will interpret the content of the rights to reflect the need to balance them against conflicting legitimate interests. For an example of how the Court of Justice applies the limitation clause, see the judgment of 17 October 2013 in Case C-291/12 *Schwarz*, in which the Court ruled that fingerprinting passport holders was a justified interference with the right to private life.

[72] On the interpretation of the Charter, see G de Búrca, 'After the EU Charter of Fundamental Rights: The Court of Justice as a Human Rights Adjudicator?' (2013) 20 *Maastricht Journal of European and Comparative Law* 168; P Popelier, C Van de Heyning, and P Van Nuffel (eds), *Human Rights Protection in the European Legal Order: The Interaction between the European and the National Courts* (Cambridge: Intersentia, 2011).

[73] Case C-399/11 *Melloni v Ministerio Fiscal*, judgment of 26 February 2013, noted in N de Boer (2013) 50 *Common Market Law Review* 1083.

[74] Council Framework Decision 2002/584/JHA on the European Arrest Warrant and the surrender procedures between Member States (OJ [2002] L190/1), consolidated version 28 March 2009.

present during the trials, because he had fled, he was legally represented by lawyers of his choosing. Once the conviction was final, the Italian authorities issued a European Arrest Warrant for the execution of the sentence. Mr Melloni was then arrested by the Spanish authorities. In an attempt to resist surrender to the Italian authorities, Mr Melloni argued, inter alia, that his conviction *in absentia* breached his right to a fair trial inasmuch as Italian procedural law did not allow appeal against (final) sentences imposed *in absentia*. He therefore argued that his surrender should be made conditional upon the possibility to appeal the Italian judgment. Otherwise, his rights as guaranteed by the Spanish Constitution would be violated.

The national court made a reference to the Court of Justice enquiring, amongst other things, whether Article 53 Charter allowed a Member State to make surrender conditional upon further review of the conviction *in absentia*, therefore providing protection of the right to fair trail and defence more generous than that afforded by the Charter but in line with its own national constitutional standard. In other words, the national court was enquiring whether, if the standard of protection afforded by the national constitution is higher than that afforded by the Charter, national courts can enforce the former. Whilst this is not a new question, having been discussed in cases such as *Internationale Handelsgesellschaft*,[75] it acquired a new poignancy given that Article 53 Charter provides that nothing therein can be interpreted as restricting or adversely affecting human rights as guaranteed by national constitutions. An affirmative answer would possibly maximize protection of human rights in the EU, always allowing the highest standard to prevail; however, it would jeopardize the principle of supremacy since the application of EU law would differ from country to country according to national fundamental rights standards. The Court of Justice, not surprisingly, held that

> It is settled case law that, by virtue of the principle of primacy of EU law, which is an essential feature of the EU legal order…, rules of national law, even of a constitutional order, cannot be allowed to undermine the effectiveness of EU law on the territory of that State…
>
> It is true that Article 53 of the Charter confirms that, where an EU legal act calls for national implementing measures, national authorities and courts remain free to apply national standards of protection of fundamental rights, *provided* that the level of protection provided for by the Charter, as interpreted by the Court, and the *primacy*, *unity* and *effectiveness* of EU law are not thereby compromised.[76]

As a result, national courts are prevented from imposing their own constitutional standards in those cases in which to do so would affect the uniform application of EU law, that is, when EU law leaves no discretion to Member States. On the other hand, and in the same way as was the case before the Charter, when EU law leaves space for the exercise of discretion by national authorities, the Charter only provides Member States with a floor of rights leaving national authorities (and national courts) the freedom to apply their own (higher or differing) constitutional standards.[77]

Article 52(5) introduces a distinction between rights and principles: the latter are judicially cognizable only in the interpretation of legislative and executive acts and in the

---

[75] Case 11/70 *Internationale Handelsgesellschaft* [1970] ECR 1125, and discussion in section 2.1; cf also, eg *Biotechnology Directive* (n 55).
[76] *Melloni* (n 73) paras 59 and 60.
[77] On this point, see also *Åklagaren v Hans Åkerberg Fransson* (n 64) para 29.

assessment of their validity. This basically means that programmatic provisions, such as Article 37, which provides that a high level of environmental protection must be integrated into Union policies, do not grant a free-standing right. An individual would therefore not be able to rely on Article 37 Charter in order to uphold a right to live in a pollution-free environment. Rather, the Court would be able to use Article 37 to interpret existing legislation as well as annul acts of the Union which clearly disregard the principles enshrined in that article.

Article 52(6) restates that full account must be taken of national law and practices specified in the Charter, whilst Article 52(7) instructs the courts to have due regard to the Charter explanations when interpreting the Charter.

Finally Article 54 provides a prohibition on abuse of rights, and it is almost identical to Article 17 ECHR. It is aimed at ensuring that the Charter rights cannot be used in order to deprive individuals of rights conferred therein.[78]

Very few people would take Articles 51, 52, and 53 Charter as examples of clear and unambiguous drafting; rather, those provisions reflect the tensions and anxieties pertaining to EU fundamental rights. Be that as it may, the Charter is a remarkable document – it took over 30 years following the *Stauder* judgment to provide Union citizens with a proper catalogue of rights in order to ensure, at least theoretically, better awareness and therefore increased protection of fundamental rights.

4.5 Protocol No 30 on the application of the Charter to Poland and the UK[79]

We mentioned earlier that the UK (and Poland) has a less than serene attitude towards EU fundamental rights – and as we have seen in case study 9.2 on *Carpenter*, the reasons for this scepticism lie not with reservations as to the need to hold the EU institutions to account; rather, they stem from a deep unease towards the possibility that national acts be subjected to (yet) another layer of fundamental rights scrutiny.[80] It is against this background, then, that Protocol No 30 should be understood: as a clarification (and possibly a reassurance to the British public) rather than a 'derogation' (or 'opt-out'?) proper.[81]

The Protocol is composed of a long Preamble followed by just two articles. Article 1(1) is tautological: it states that the 'Charter does not *extend* the ability' of the Court of Justice or any of the courts of Poland or the UK to find that the laws, regulations, administrative provisions, practices, or actions of Poland or the UK are inconsistent with the Charter.

---

[78] See in the ECHR context, eg *Lawless v Ireland (No 3)* (1979–80) 1 EHRR 15.

[79] In November 2009, the European Council promised to add the Czech Republic to Protocol No 30, in return for the Czech President ratifying the Lisbon Treaty (which he then did). A draft Protocol to the Treaties to this end was then drawn up, but the Czech Senate voted against being added to Protocol No 30, and the European Parliament expressed a negative opinion on such extension. It remains to be seen whether the Protocol extending Protocol No 30 to the Czech Republic will ever be signed or ratified. For the relevant documents, see http://www.europarl.europa.eu/oeil/popups/ficheprocedure.do?reference=2011/0817%28 NLE%29

[80] A cursory internet search provides many interesting, if wholly inaccurate, reports; see eg http://www .dailymail.co.uk/debate/columnists/article-181289/The-New-Soviet-Union-Europe-us.html#. On the UK and European (Convention) fundamental rights, see eg C Grayling (Lord Chancellor and Secretary of State for Justice) and T May (Home Secretary) speeches at the Conservative Party Conference 2013 (http://www.con servativepartyconference.org.uk/Speeches/2013_Chris_Grayling.aspx; http://www.conservativepartyconfer ence.org.uk/Speeches/2013_Theresa_May.aspx).

[81] On this point, see also the European Parliament Resolution on the Czech inclusion in Protocol No 30 in n 79.

As clarified by the Court, Article 1(1) is of no legal significance since the Charter codifies existing rights, rather than creating new ones. It is clear then that, also having regard to the horizontal provisions examined previously, the Charter cannot *extend* the jurisdiction of any court, whether in the UK, Poland, or in any other country in the EU.[82]

Article 1(2) is more confused: it states that Title IV (Solidarity), which contains social rights, does not create 'justiciable rights' applicable in Poland or in the UK, except insofar as 'Poland or the UK has provided for such rights in national law'. The legal relevance of this provision is further confused by the fact that it is in relation to Title IV that the distinction between rights and principles had been introduced (at the insistence of the UK). It is open to doubt whether there is any right in Title IV which is not already provided for in Union law and therefore also in the laws of the UK and Poland.[83] Article 2 also restates the obvious: if the Charter refers to national laws and practices, it shall apply to the UK and Poland only to the extent to which those two countries recognize in their laws and practices the rights and principles therein. For instance, the right to health care provided for in Article 35 Charter is entirely dependent upon national laws and practices, not least since the EU has very limited competence in this field.

5 The EU and the ECHR

The Lisbon Treaty introduced a new Article 6(2) TEU, which provides:

> The Union shall accede to the European Convention for the Protection of Human Rights and Fundamental Freedoms. Such accession shall not affect the Union's competences as defined in the Treaties.

Negotiations for accession started in June 2010 and ended (at least pending the Opinion of the Court of Justice) in April 2013; we will first look at the background to accession and then analyse the draft accession agreement.

5.1 Background to accession

The ECHR is a charter of rights adopted in the aftermath of the Second World War by the Council of Europe, a body distinct from, and of much wider composition than, the EU. In order to ensure that the Convention would have 'teeth', the contracting parties set up an international court, the ECtHR, entrusted with interpreting the ECHR and holding the contracting parties to account.[84] Uniquely for the time, cases before the ECtHR can be brought by individual parties; however, since the Convention is a 'safety net', setting only the minimum standard of fundamental rights for participatory Member States, individuals must have exhausted domestic remedies before being able to bring a case before the ECtHR.

---

[82] See *NS* (n 33) paras 116 *et seq*; see also the Opinion of AG Trstenjak in *NS* (n 33); and the Opinion of AG Kokott in *Bonda*, 15 December 2011, nyr.

[83] For a slightly different view, see C Barnard, 'The Opt-Out for the UK and Poland from the Charter of Fundamental Rights: Triumph of Rhetoric over Reality?' in S Griller and J Ziller (eds), *The Lisbon Treaty: EU Constitutionalism without a Constitutional Treaty?* (Vienna: Springer, 2008) 276–281.

[84] The ECtHR is based in Strasbourg and for this reason is at times referred to as the Strasbourg Court; the Court of Justice is instead at times referred as the Luxembourg Court.

It has been mentioned previously that, from the very first cases concerning human rights protection in the (then) EEC, the Court of Justice stated that it would draw inspiration also from the ECHR, and that this document had special importance for the EU. Furthermore, in interpreting fundamental rights, the Court of Justice looks at the jurisprudence of the ECtHR and whilst discrepancies in the interpretation given by the two courts have occurred, those have not been intentional.[85] And, starting with the Maastricht Treaty, the centrality of the ECHR in the system of fundamental rights protection in the EU has also been restated at Treaty level.[86]

In many respects, then, the ECHR is already part of EU public law: it is mentioned in the Treaties and it is applied through the case law of the Court of Justice. Yet, the fact that the EU is not a party to the Convention raises very serious legal and political issues, and especially:

- it excludes the jurisdiction of the ECtHR over the EU;

- it introduces an idiosyncrasy as regards the EU Member States, in that respect for human rights is a precondition for joining the EU and yet the EU does not subject itself to any external scrutiny of its fundamental rights compliance; and

- it leads to accusations of double standards as regards non-EU States, since the EU often imposes human rights conditionality clauses in international treaties.

For these reasons, discussions as to whether the EU should accede to the Convention have been long-running and in 1994 the Court of Justice was asked for an Opinion (2/94) on whether accession would be legally possible. The Court declared that, as the Treaties stood at the time, there was no competence for the Union to accede to the ECHR.[87] This eventually led to the adoption of Article 6(2) TEU.

5.1.1 The case law of the European Court of Human Rights: the doctrine of equivalent protection

The problems arising from the fact that the EU is not a party to the Convention became more pressing in the 1990s. In *M & Co*, the claimant attacked the acts of German authorities which were enforcing a European Commission decision taken within the field of competition law. The company argued that the ECHR was applicable, and the ECtHR had jurisdiction, since the obligations imposed by the ECHR on the German authorities did not cease just because the authorities were giving effect to a decision of the European Commission. Otherwise, it was argued, it would be all too easy for contracting parties to evade their obligations by acting through the medium of Union law rather than national law. The European Commission of Human Rights (then in charge of deciding on the admissibility of the case before the ECtHR), partially rejected such reasoning. It first noted that according to Article 1 ECHR, Member States are responsible for *any* violation of the Convention, whether it is a consequence of domestic or international law. However, it also found that the EU system both secured and controlled compliance with fundamental rights. To require the Member State to check whether the Convention rights had been respected in each individual case

---

[85] See eg Joined Cases 46/87 and 227/88 *Hoechst AG v Commission* [1989] ECR 2859 and cf *Niemietz v Germany* (1993) Series A, Vol 251, 16 EHRR 97; note that the European Court of Justice ruling predates the ECtHR interpretation; this divergence was corrected at the earliest possible opportunity, see Case C-94/00 *Roquette Frères SA v Directeur général de la concurrence, de la consommation et de la répression des fraudes* [2002] ECR I-9011. On the relationship between the Court and ECtHR, see generally C Timmermans, 'The Relationship between the European Court of Justice and the European Court of Human Rights' in Arnull, Barnard, Dougan, and Spaventa, *A Constitutional Order of States?* (n 32) ch 8.

[86] Art F(2) TEU, Maastricht Treaty; and now Art 6(3) TEU.

[87] Opinion 2/94 (n 19).

would be contrary to the very idea of transferring powers to an international organization.[88] This non-interventionist stance was successfully challenged in the case of *Matthews*.[89]

Ms Matthews, a resident of Gibraltar, was denied the possibility of voting in the European Parliament elections on the ground that franchise for such elections was reserved to British nationals resident in the UK. Residents in Gibraltar were therefore excluded, even though most of EU law applies to that territory. Ms Matthews then complained that her disenfranchisement was a violation of Article 3 Protocol 1 of the Convention, which guarantees the right to free elections. The issue was therefore a thorny one: at stake was the very foundation of the democratic process, the principle of democratic representation. However, the case related to the elections to the European Parliament, which, in this matter, were regulated by the 1976 Act on direct elections, a measure having the same value as the Treaties.[90] For this reason, the UK argued that the ECtHR did not have jurisdiction; and that the UK could not be held responsible for a potential violation arising from a collective act of the (then) 15 Member States, since it was unable to amend that act unilaterally.

The ECtHR found that acts of the (then) European Community were not subject to its scrutiny since the EC was not a contracting party to the Convention, and the latter did not exclude transfer of competences to international organizations provided Convention rights continued to be 'secured'. However, in the case of EC primary legislation, where the Court of Justice has no jurisdiction to assess compliance with fundamental rights, the UK, together with the other EC Member States would be responsible for violations of the Convention.

Matthews is a seminal case in that it lays the foundations for the subsequent evolution of the case law of the ECtHR on the relationship between the Convention and EU law. In particular, it makes clear that gaps in fundamental rights protection cannot be tolerated, so that when the Court of Justice is unable to protect those rights then the ECtHR is willing to step in and hold the Member States collectively responsible for upholding/violating Convention rights. In the case of *Bosphorus*,[91] the ECtHR further clarified that, even when the Court of Justice has jurisdiction, the review of the ECtHR is not altogether excluded. Rather, the ECtHR will refrain from exercising its jurisdiction over the act of an international institution (eg the EU) as implemented by a Member State (ie the contracting party to the Convention) only to the extent to which it deems that

> the relevant organisation is considered to protect fundamental rights, as regards both the substantive guarantees offered and the mechanisms controlling their observance, in a manner which can be considered at least *equivalent* to that for which the Convention provides…
>
> …
>
> 156. If such equivalent protection is considered to be provided by the organisation, the presumption will be that a State has not departed from the requirements of the Convention when it does no more than implement legal obligations flowing from its membership of the organisation.

---

[88] *M & Co v Germany*, decision of the European Commission of Human Rights, 9 February 1990 (1990) 64 ECmHRR 138; see also *Pafitis v Greece*, decision of the ECtHR, 26 February 1998; in *Cantoni v France* ECHR 1996-V 1614, the ECtHR held that the fact that a piece of national legislation reproduced word by word the provision of a Community directive did not subtract it from the scope of application of the Convention.

[89] *Matthews v UK* (Appl No 24833/94), ECtHR 1999-I.

[90] Act concerning the election of the representatives of the European Parliament by direct universal suffrage, annexed to Decision 76/787/ECSC, EEC, Euratom. This was later amended partly as a result of the ruling in *Matthews* (ibid), see Council Decision 2002/772/EC Euratom (OJ [2002] L283/1); the UK then changed its rules and faced a challenge before the Court of Justice in Case C-145/04 *Spain v UK* [2006] ECR I-7917.

[91] *Bosphorus v Ireland* (Appl No 45036/98), ECtHR 2005-VI, noted in [2005] *European Human Rights Law Review* 649.

> However, any such presumption can be rebutted if, in the circumstances of a particular case, it is considered that the protection of Convention rights was *manifestly deficient*. In such cases, the interest of international cooperation would be outweighed by the Convention's role as a 'constitutional instrument of European public order' in the field of human rights.

The ruling in *Bosphorus* then ensures that the safety net provided by the Convention remains in place even when the contested act can be ascribed to the EU rather than to its Member State; however, *Bosphorus* only provides protection against significant gaps in the safety net, since

- it establishes a presumption of equivalent protection of EU law with the ECHR,
- it is for the claimant to prove that such equivalent protection is not only lacking but manifestly deficient.

That said, in *Michaud v France*[92] the ECtHR clarified that the presumption of equivalent protection applies only when the control mechanism provided for by EU law has been fully brought into play. This is not the case where a national court refuses to make a reference on the compatibility between EU law and fundamental rights.[93] Furthermore, in cases where Member States are exercising discretion (eg normally when implementing directives but also when they implement regulations), the ECtHR will exercise full jurisdiction on the (discretionary) act of the Member States, since the latter are parties to the Convention.[94] (See Figure 9.1 at the end of this chapter.)

5.2 **EU accession to the ECHR**

As we have seen in the previous section, even though the EU is not yet party to the ECHR, the ECtHR has accepted, in limited cases, to exercise jurisdiction in order to ensure that membership of the EU does not deprive individuals of protection at least equivalent to that provided by the Convention. This state of affairs is not, however, completely satisfactory since, lacking accession,

- the jurisdiction of the ECtHR is limited to those cases where the claimant can rebut the presumption of equivalent protection; this means that overall it is more difficult for individuals to seize the ECtHR in cases relating to EU law than it is in domestic cases;
- the EU is not party to the proceedings so that it is the Member States collectively that incur responsibility, and the EU is not bound by the ECtHR ruling.

It is for these reasons, together with the political considerations mentioned previously, that accession to the ECHR has been deemed desirable. That said, accession of an international organization to a Convention which was aimed at States is not without its challenges. In this respect, consider: that the EU is also the sum of its Member States; that in most cases, an EU act would also involve an act of national authorities (even in cases in which a regulation is at issue, since it is usually for national authorities to police compliance, seize goods, etc); and that, crucially, in the EU there is already a

---

[92] *Michaud v France* (Appl No 12323/11), judgment of 6 December 2012, paras 114 *et seq.*

[93] For an interesting ruling concerning the duty of national courts of last instance to make a reference to the Court of Justice pursuant to Art 267 TFEU, see *Ullens de Shooten and Rezabek v Belgium* (Appl Nos 3989/07 and 38353/07), judgment of 20 September 2011.

[94] eg *MSS v Belgium and Greece* (n 35) esp para 338; this ruling had important effects in relation to the European asylum system framework, see *NS* (n 33), discussed at section 2.2.1.

supranational court, the Court of Justice, which is the only court entrusted with the interpretation and assessment of validity of Union law.[95] The relationship between the ECtHR and the Court of Justice was then one of the points that needed clarification in the accession negotiations; furthermore, also complex is the interaction between the Member States and the EU especially in those cases where responsibility might be more difficult to ascertain. To address these issues, the draft accession agreement provides for a co-respondent mechanism (see the following subsection) and for the possibility of 'delaying' proceedings to allow the Court of Justice to assess the compatibility with the Convention of the EU legislation if it did not have the possibility to do so before the case reached the ECtHR.[96]

5.2.1 Co-respondent mechanism

Article 3(2) draft agreement provides that, when an application is directed against a Member State of the EU, the EU may become a co-respondent if 'it appears' that the compatibility of EU law with the Convention is called into question. This provision will allow the EU to become a full party to the proceedings (at present the EU can only submit third party interventions), which also means it will become bound by the ruling of the ECtHR. Take, for instance, a case like NS[97] where deportation of asylum seekers to another EU Member State is made possible by an EU regulation, although Member States take the final (discretionary) decision as to whether they want to assess the asylum application themselves. If the individual brings the case against her Member State,[98] it seems reasonable that the EU might choose to become a co-respondent as there would be some uncertainty as to whether the potential breach has been caused by the EU legislation or by the implementing national act.

The reverse is also possible: in cases concerning a provision of the TEU or TFEU or another piece of EU primary law, Member States can become co-respondents in a case directed against the EU since, should a violation be found, they would have to act collectively to modify the Treaties or primary legislation. So, for instance, in a case like Matthews[99] where the complaint related to EU primary law (in that case the failure to extend the franchise for the European Parliament to EU citizens resident in Gibraltar), the case would be directed against the EU as the body primarily responsible for the adoption of the contested act. However, Member States have a direct interest in a case like this, since it is they who are in charge of amending EU primary law: it therefore seems reasonable that should they so wish, they can become co-respondents.

In order to ensure full protection for the individual, a new paragraph will be added to Article 36 Convention so that the admissibility of an application is decided without 'regard to the participation of a co-respondent in the proceedings'. As a result, the individual will not be penalized for not having correctly identified the potential responsibility of the EU in the alleged breach.

5.2.2 The role of the Court of Justice

As mentioned previously, in those cases in which the EU is co-respondent, that is, where EU law might conflict with the Convention, there is the possibility to delay proceedings to allow

---

[95] Case 314/85 *Foto-Frost* [1987] ECR 4199, and see chapter 10.

[96] Fifth negotiation meeting between the CDDH ad hoc negotiation group and the European Commission on the Accession of the European Union to the European Convention on Human Rights, *Final Report to the CDDH*, doc 47+1(2013)008rev2, available at http://www.coe.int/t/dghl/standardsetting/hrpolicy/Accession/Meeting_reports_en.asp; see P Gragl, *The Accession of the European Union to the European Convention on Human Rights* (Oxford: Hart Publishing, 2013).

[97] *NS* (n 33), see section 2.2.2.

[98] This would in fact be the case in *MSS v Belgium and Greece* (n 35).

[99] *Matthews v UK* (n 89), see section 5.1.1.

the Court of Justice to assess for itself whether the rule is compatible with the Convention. For instance, take the case of *Stauder* where Mr Stauder complained that identification by name of those eligible for discounted butter constituted a breach of his right to private life.[100] In a case such as this, lacking a prior ruling by the Court of Justice, the ECtHR would be able to delay proceedings to allow the Court of Justice to examine the matter, possibly suggesting an interpretation which would make the measure compatible with fundamental rights (as was the case in *Stauder,* where the Court of Justice was able to provide an alternative interpretation of the (then) Community instrument that did not breach the applicant's right).

The reasons for this procedure are clear: in the case of national rules, an individual must have exhausted domestic remedies before being able to bring a complaint before the ECtHR. This ensures that fundamental rights protection is primarily the responsibility of national courts; it is only when something was overlooked or went wrong in that forum that the ECtHR will intervene. The ECtHR is not a further court of appeal; rather, it ensures that a minimum standard of protection is applied throughout the territories of the contracting parties.

In the case of the EU, matters are more complex because, mostly, cases reach the Court of Justice through the preliminary ruling mechanism: conditions for direct access (standing) to the EU Courts to challenge the validity of EU law are strict. Since in most cases there is also a national enforcement element to the case, issues are more often examined by national courts which then decide whether a reference to the Court of Justice is appropriate.[101] In those cases, however, the parties have no control over whether the reference is made; and on what questions are asked of the Court of Justice. For this reason, it would have been unwise to include prior scrutiny by the Court of Justice as a prerequisite for the 'exhaustion' of domestic remedies under the Convention. Since the individual has no power to decide whether a preliminary reference is sought, she should not be penalized if the national court failed to refer the question to the Court of Justice. On the other hand, it was felt that in those cases it would be beneficial for the Court of Justice to have a 'first shot' at the correct interpretation of EU law and its compatibility with the Convention (and the Charter), not least since the matter might be resolved without the need for further investigation by the ECtHR. For this reason, when the EU is a co-respondent, and the Court of Justice has not yet assessed the Convention compatibility of the rules at issue, proceedings are delayed to allow the Court of Justice to examine the matter.

How well this system will work in practice remains to be seen;[102] on the one hand, in straightforward cases where the national court of last instance refused to request a preliminary ruling, thereby going against the wording and the spirit of Article 267(3) TFEU, the procedure provided in the Accession Treaty will allow for 'a fix', by allowing the Court of Justice to rule on the matter despite the absence of a preliminary reference. However, it could be questioned whether such a 'fix' should not be provided in the context of the EU itself rather than through an external mechanism.

In other cases, it might be more difficult to ascertain whether the Court of Justice has already ruled on the issue: take, for instance, the ruling in *Kaba II*,[103] where the Court of Justice was also asked to assess the compatibility of EU law, and in particular the role of the Advocate General, with fundamental rights. The Court reversed the order of the questions so as to avoid examining the fundamental rights issue.[104] It is open to debate whether in those cases the ECtHR

---

[100] Case 29/69 *Stauder* [1969] ECR 419, see section 2.1.   [101] See generally chapter 10.

[102] For a (more) positive assessment, see R Baratta, 'Accession of the EU to the ECHR: The Rationale for the ECJ's Prior Involvement' (2013) 50 *Common Market Law Review* 1305.

[103] Case C-466/00 *Kaba v Secretary of State for the Home Department* ('*Kaba II*') [2003] ECR I-2219.

[104] See also the case of *Michaud* (n 92), discussed in section 5.1, where the applicant complained about the relevant EU law breaching Art 8 ECHR. In Case C-305/05 *Order des barreaux francophones et germanophone v*

could delay the proceedings to allow the Court of Justice to have another say. Furthermore, the function of gatekeeper allocated by the TFEU to national courts might well be compromised if individuals can then seize the Court of Justice through the ECtHR. After all, the fact that it is for the national court to decide what questions to refer, and when, is aimed at ensuring that the Court of Justice is not flooded by unmeritorious and spurious claims.

Another slight oddity is that, when the Member State is a co-respondent, the special delaying procedure is not available. Member States can be co-respondent when the issue relates to the compatibility of a piece of primary law with the Convention. The most likely reason the Court of Justice does not need to be involved in those cases is that it has no jurisdiction to declare EU primary law invalid. However, it could be argued that the compatibility of primary (hence, more general) rules with fundamental rights might depend very much on the interpretation given to such rules, an interpretation which is for the Court of Justice to provide.

That said, there is no doubt that accession to the ECHR will be a positive step and will ensure that the EU is bound by the same rules that bind its Member States and its international partners. For an overview, see Figures 9.1, 9.2, and 9.3 at the end of this chapter.

6 Conclusion

The field of fundamental rights is that which has evolved more markedly with the evolution of the EU – it arose from a constitutionally limp Community, it was followed by institutional acknowledgement and progressive legislative recognition, to result eventually in full codification. Given its inextricable link with the process of deeper integration, it is not surprising that it is a field which is not only complex but also, at times, deeply contested. Some Member States would like to see more and better protection of fundamental rights in the EU, whilst others are deeply cautious, if not altogether sceptical, of giving the Court of Justice yet another weapon in its already powerful armoury. In particular, the fear is that fundamental rights jurisprudence will have an excessive impact on national rules and further blur the boundaries between EU and national sovereignty.

And yet, to most citizens those issues matter little: what is of value is that with every Treaty revision the rights of individuals against the EU legislature and executive (including where EU rules have been implemented by Member States) have been strengthened. Institutions that have the power deeply to affect the lives of many should be held to account: the Court, the Charter, and the Convention seek to do exactly that.

Conseil des Ministres [2007] ECR I-5305, the Court of Justice examined the compatibility of the same piece of legislation (Directive 91/308 on prevention of the use of the financial system for the purpose of money laundering (OJ [1991] L166/77), as amended by Directive 2001/97 (OJ [2001] L344/76), only with the right to fair trial as guaranteed by Art 6 ECHR (and Arts 47 and 48 Charter).

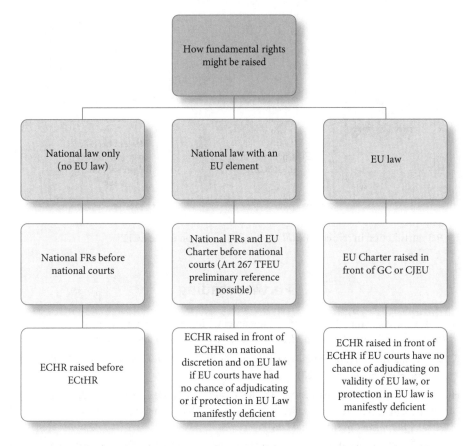

Fig 9.1 Fundamental rights protection in the EU before the EU's accession to the ECHR

Fig 9.2 Jurisdiction in respect of *national law* with an EU element post-EU accession to the ECHR

Fig 9.3 Jurisdiction in respect of *EU law* post-EU accession to the ECHR

Further reading

G DE BÚRCA, 'After the EU Charter of Fundamental Rights: The Court of Justice as a Human Rights Adjudicator?' (2013) 20 *Maastricht Journal of European and Comparative Law* 168

P GRAGL, *The Accession of the European Union to the European Convention on Human Rights* (Oxford, Hart Publishing, 2013)

HCH HOFMANN AND BC MIHAESCU, 'The Relation between the Charter's Fundamental Rights and the Unwritten General Principles of EU Law: Good Administration as the Test Case' (2013) 9 *European Constitutional Law Review* 73

K LENAERTS, 'Exploring the Limits of the EU Charter of Fundamental Rights' (2012) 8 *European Constitutional Law Review* 375

S PEERS, T HERVEY, J KENNER, AND A WARD (eds), *The Charter of Fundamental Rights: A Commentary* (Oxford: Hart Publishing, 2014)

A PLIAKOS AND G ANAGNOSTARAS, 'Who is the Ultimate Arbiter? The Battle over Judicial Supremacy in the EU' (2011) 26 *European Law Review* 109

D SARMIENTO, 'Who is Afraid of the Charter? The Court of Justice, National Courts and the New Framework of Fundamental Rights Protection in the EU' (2013) 50 *Common Market Law Review* 1267

10

Judicial protection before the Court of Justice of the European Union

Albertina Albors-Llorens

1 Introduction

Imagine a Union citizen who discovers that all his assets have been frozen in accordance with the provisions of an EU regulation because he is considered a suspected terrorist. He will want to take action against the EU and avail himself of the system of judicial protection set out by the Treaties. At the epicentre of this system is the Court of Justice of the European Union, which is the judicial organ of the Union and entrusted with the task of upholding the rule of law.[1] In the performance of this mandate, the Court reviews, in particular, the legality of the acts and omissions of Member States and EU institutions and interprets EU law at the request of the national courts. Following the entry into force of the Lisbon

---

[1] See Art 19(1) TEU.

Treaty, the Court of Justice of the European Union comprises three judicial bodies: the Court of Justice (generally referred to as the Court of Justice but in some quarters still as the European Court of Justice), the General Court (previously the Court of First Instance), and the Civil Service Tribunal.[2]

This chapter will provide an overview of the various procedural avenues to the Court and will use as a template the division between two main sets of proceedings: direct actions and preliminary references (see Figure 10.1).[3] The former are brought directly either before the Court of Justice, the General Court, or the Civil Service Tribunal and they are dealt with in their entirety by these courts. By contrast, the latter proceedings begin before a national court. When this court encounters a question on the interpretation or the validity of EU law, it may (or sometimes must) make a preliminary reference on this particular point to the Court of Justice. Once the Court delivers a preliminary ruling on the specific issue of EU law, the national court will apply the ruling to the facts of the case and will decide on the dispute between the parties. Therefore, the intervention of the Court of Justice is incidental – even if, as we shall see, the impact of this intervention has proved crucial to the formation and evolution of EU law as well as to the solution of disputes by national courts. This chapter will explore the structure of these two different sets of proceedings, will show how they interact, and will consider some key issues, such as whether they really ensure a complete system of judicial protection.[4]

2 The structure and jurisdiction of the Court of Justice of the European Union at a glance

The Court of Justice currently consists of 28 judges (one judge from each Member State[5]) and nine Advocates General[6] who deliver impartial and independent Opinions in cases that raise new points of law.[7] The Advocates General are members of the Court but their Opinions reflect their personal views on how a case should be decided and the freedom that they enjoy stands in contrast with the constraints to achieve consensus under which the judges operate. While the Opinions are not legally binding on the Court, they provide invaluable assistance in the analysis of cases and have been extremely influential in the development of EU law.[8]

---

[2] See Art 19(1) TEU. This provision allows for the establishment of specialized courts (see further Art 257 TFEU) but so far only one of these, the Civil Service Tribunal, has been created (see Council Decision 2004/752 (OJ [2004] L333/7)). The Civil Service Tribunal has jurisdiction to hear disputes involving the EU civil service (see Art 1 of Decision 2004/752) and its decisions may be subject to appeal on points of law before the General Court (see Art 11 Statute of the Court). For the exceptional possibility of the review of decisions of the General Court by the Court of Justice in this area, see Art 256(2) TFEU.

[3] This chapter focuses on the main procedural avenues to the Court in the context of challenges to the compatibility of the actions of Member States and of EU institutions with EU law. For the constitutional role of the Court in EU law, see chapter 3, and for its role in the context of international law, see chapter 7.

[4] See Case 294/83 Parti écologiste 'Les Verts' v European Parliament [1986] ECR 1339, para 23 and more recently, Case C-583/11 P Inuit Tapiriit Kanatami v European Parliament and Council, judgment of 3 October 2013, nyr, para 92.   [5] Art 19(2) TEU.

[6] Art 252 TFEU. Council Decision 2013/336 (OJ [2013] L179/92) increased the number of Advocates General from eight to nine, with effect from 1 July 2013 and to 11, with effect from 7 October 2015.

[7] See Art 20 Statute of the Court.

[8] On the significance of Opinions, see further A Dashwood, 'The Advocate General in the Court of Justice of the European Communities' (1982) 2 Legal Studies 202; K Mortelmans, 'The Court under the Influence of Its Advocates General: An Analysis of the Case Law on the Functioning of the Internal Market' (2007) 24 Yearbook of European Law 127; and T Tridimas, 'The Role of the Advocate General in the Development of Community Law: Some Reflections' (1997) 34 Common Market Law Review 1349.

The Court generally sits in chambers of three or five judges,[9] but may sit in a Grand Chamber of 15 judges when a Member State or an institution of the Union that is party to the proceedings so requests[10] or depending on the importance or difficulty of a case.[11] More unusually, it may sit as a Full Court in a number of cases provided in the Treaties[12] and where it considers that a case is of exceptional importance.[13] According to the Treaty, the General Court should be made up of at least one judge from each Member State with the exact number laid down by the Statute of the Court[14] – and currently set at 28 judges.[15] There are no Advocates General attached to the General Court but members of this Court may be called upon to perform the role of Advocate General,[16] a possibility that has been rarely used to date. The General Court normally sits in chambers of three or five judges but may also exceptionally sit as a Grand Chamber, as a Full Court, or even be constituted by a single judge.[17]

As explained earlier, in this chapter we will examine the main procedural routes to the Union judicature, taking as a starting point the basic division between direct actions and preliminary references. On the one hand, there are four main types of direct actions: infringement (or enforcement) proceedings (Articles 258 to 260 TFEU), the action for annulment (Articles 263 and 264 TFEU), the action for failure to act (Articles 265 and 266 TFEU), and the action for damages (Articles 268 and 340(2) and (3) TFEU). The plea of illegality (Article 277 TFEU) is brought directly before the Court but is used to plead the illegality of an EU act in an *incidental* way, that is, in the course of proceedings pending before the Court under another provision – generally, but not always, annulment proceedings under Article 263 TFEU.[18] Consequently, it cannot be brought independently but is always attached to a direct action and, therefore, it will be considered in this chapter within the same framework as the direct actions. In connection with any of these direct actions, the Court may also grant interim relief, which is also provided in the Treaty (Articles 278 and 279 TFEU). The objectives of these actions could be summarized as follows. Enforcement proceedings are brought by the Commission or a Member State against a Member State that has failed to comply with its obligations under EU law. The action for annulment and the action for a failure to act are used, respectively, to challenge illegal acts and omissions of the institutions, bodies, and agencies of the EU. Finally, the action for damages is used to obtain compensation for damage or loss suffered as a result of an unlawful Union act. Therefore, while enforcement proceedings aim to ensure the compliance of *Member States* with EU law, the other direct actions and the plea of illegality aim to provide protection against illegal acts and omissions of the *EU institutions*. On the other hand, there are two types of preliminary references provided in Article 267 TFEU: on the interpretation and on the validity of EU law. A representation of this structure can be found in Figure 10.1.

Direct actions and preliminary rulings are naturally imbued with a different philosophy in terms of the role played by the Court. In direct actions, the Court adjudicates on the dispute between the parties, whereas in preliminary rulings it simply gives advice

---

[9] Arts 251 TFEU and 16(1) Statute of the Court.   [10] Art 16(2) and (3) Statute of the Court.
[11] See Art 60 Rules of Procedure of the Court (OJ [2012] L 265/1).
[12] See Art 16(4) Statute of the Court and Arts 228(2), 245(2), 247, and 286(6) TFEU. These provisions concern the power of the Court to dismiss the Ombudsman, or compulsorily to retire members of the Commission or of the Court of Auditors in the event of misconduct or failure to fulfil the obligations arising from their offices.
[13] For a recent example, see Case C-370/12 *Pringle v Ireland*, judgment of 27 November 2012, nyr, on the legality of the European Stability Mechanism Treaty.   [14] Arts 19(2) and 254(1) TFEU.
[15] Art 48 Statute of the Court.   [16] Art 49 Statute of the Court.
[17] Art 50 Statute of the Court.
[18] Technically, the plea of illegality could also be attached to an action for a failure to act or to an action for damages but this would be rare.

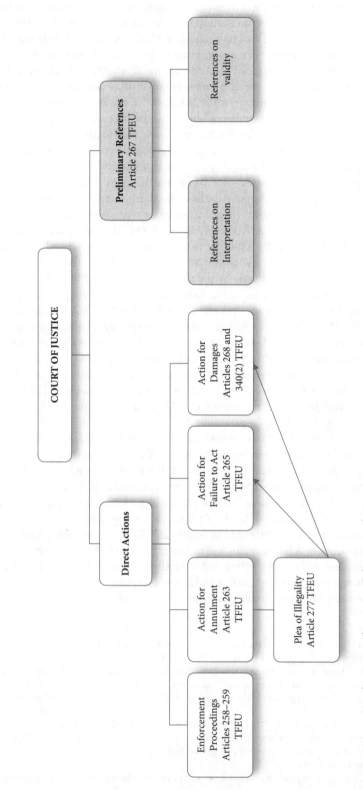

Fig 10.1 Avenues to the Court of Justice and the General Court

on a specific point of EU law, leaving the final resolution of the dispute to the national court. However, there are areas of interaction between them. It is therefore important to see the system of judicial protection provided in the Treaty as an integrated whole in order to understand how it really operates. A prominent example of this is the relationship between the action for annulment, the plea of illegality, and preliminary rulings on validity,[19] which will be considered in more detail later in this chapter.[20] Thus, a private applicant may bring annulment proceedings or a plea of illegality to challenge the legality of a Union act *directly* before the Union judicature but, as we shall see, stringent standing conditions attached to the action for annulment have meant that these have so far been unpromising options for private parties in large areas of the case law. However, it might be possible to challenge a national act implementing a Union act before a national court, which may then make a preliminary reference on the validity of the Union act on which the national one is based. If available,[21] this second avenue will provide a similar result to the one that a successful action for annulment or plea of illegality would have produced. While the Treaty of Lisbon has introduced some important changes to the standing conditions that apply to private parties wishing to bring an action for annulment, important questions still remain as to whether the combination offered by these remedies guarantees *complete* judicial protection for natural and legal persons against illegal acts of the institutions,[22] in the sense mandated by Article 47 of the Charter of Fundamental Rights of the European Union.[23]

Turning to the jurisdiction of the Court of Justice, it might be helpful to examine first the *areas* of EU law over which the Court has jurisdiction and then to consider the *functional division* of jurisdiction between the Court and the General Court. The Court of Justice now has full jurisdiction in most matters covered by EU law, including on the provisions in the area of freedom, security, and justice but with the restrictions imposed by Article 276 TFEU and Article 10(1) of Protocol 36 on Transitional Provisions.[24] However, the Court has no jurisdiction in common foreign and security policy matters, with the two exceptions provided in Article 275 TFEU.[25] Some restrictions also apply to the jurisdiction of the Court to review acts of the European Council or the Council determining that a Member State has committed a serious and persistent breach of the fundamental values of the Union set out in Article 2 TEU.[26]

Turning to the division of functions between the Court and the General Court, the latter has jurisdiction principally to hear, in the first instance, direct actions brought by private applicants, direct actions brought by Member States against the Commission,[27]

---

[19] See *Les Verts* (n 4) para 23.   [20] See section 6, case study 10.1.

[21] As explained later, this avenue is frequently, but not always, available. See section 3.2.4, The general standing test: direct and individual concern.

[22] See section 4.2.1.   [23] See chapters 8 and 9.

[24] According to Art 276 TFEU, the Court shall have no jurisdiction to review the validity or proportionality of operations carried out by the police or other law enforcement services of a Member State or the exercise of Member States' responsibilities regarding the maintenance of law and order and the safeguarding of internal security. Furthermore, Art 10(1) of Protocol No 36 provides temporary limitations to the Court's jurisdiction in relation to acts adopted under the ex Third Pillar before the entry into force of the Lisbon Treaty.

[25] Under Art 275(2) TFEU, the Court shall have jurisdiction to monitor compliance with Art 40 TEU and to rule on annulment proceedings brought against Council decisions providing for restrictive measures against private parties in the field of the common foreign and security policy.

[26] See Art 269 TFEU and Art 7 TEU.

[27] This is with the narrow exception of challenges against acts or omissions of the Commission in the context of providing authorization for enhanced cooperation under Art 331 TFEU (see Art 51 Statute of the Court). From the residual approach taken in Art 51 Statute of the Court – in combination with Art 256(1) TFEU – it follows that the General Court also has jurisdiction to hear actions based on Arts 263 and 265 TFEU brought by a Member State against acts and omissions of the European Central Bank.

and direct actions brought by Member States against certain acts of the Council.[28] All other direct actions – which are mainly infringement proceedings, those dealing with interinstitutional disputes, and actions brought by Member States against EU legislative acts[29] – together with all preliminary references, come before the Court of Justice.[30] Although Article 256(3) TFEU allows for jurisdiction to hear preliminary references in certain areas to be transferred to the General Court, this has not happened so far. Finally, there is an appeal on points of law from decisions of the General Court before the Court of Justice.[31]

3 Direct actions

In this section we will examine the main categories of direct actions before the Court. Thus, we will consider infringement proceedings, the action for annulment, the action for failure to act, and the action for damages. Additionally, we will also consider the plea or objection of illegality – which, as we saw previously, is always attached to a 'main' direct action. The first three actions and the plea of illegality mainly aim to obtain a decision from the Court that either a Member State (in the case of infringement proceedings) or a Union institution (in the case of the action for annulment, the action for a failure to act, and the plea of illegality) has *breached* EU law.[32] By contrast, the action for damages is a *compensatory* action which seeks to make good the harmful consequences that an EU measure or conduct or omission by an EU institution has on an applicant.

3.1 Infringement proceedings

3.1.1 Overview

Infringement proceedings address the situation where a *Member State* has breached EU law (eg by failing to implement a directive on time or enacting legislation that is contrary to EU law). The main applicant in these proceedings is the Commission and the key provision

---

[28] This applies (following Art 256(1) TFEU and Art 51 Statute of the Court) to acts of the Council where this exercises implementing powers under Art 291 TFEU and in certain instances in the fields of State aid (Art 108(2) TFEU) and anti-dumping proceedings (Art 207 TFEU). Additionally, the General Court has jurisdiction in actions based in contracts concluded by the Union which give jurisdiction to the Court (Art 272 TFEU) and in some actions concerning Community trademarks (see recital 14 to the Preamble and Art 65 of Regulation 207/2009 on the Community Trade Mark (OJ [2009] L78/1)).

[29] Legislative acts are those adopted by legislative procedure: either the ordinary legislative procedure or one of the special legislative procedures (see Art 289(3) TFEU and chapter 5).

[30] See also Art 218(11) TFEU, which allows a Member State, the European Parliament, the Council, and the Commission to request an opinion of the Court of Justice as to whether an international agreement envisaged by the EU is compatible with the Treaties. This provision has great constitutional significance particularly because if the Opinion is adverse, the agreement in question cannot enter into force unless it is amended or the Treaties are revised. For an example of where the Court gave an adverse Opinion, see Opinion 2/94, *Re Accession by the Community to the European Convention for the Protection of Human Rights and Fundamental Freedoms* [1996] ECR I-1783, where it concluded that the Union (then Community) had no competence to accede to the ECHR. The post-Lisbon version of Art 6(2) TEU now expressly provides for the accession of the Union to the ECHR (see further chapter 9).   [31] Art 256(1), second subpara 2, TFEU.

[32] In the case of infringement proceedings under Art 258 TFEU, this decision will take the form of a declaration that a Member State has failed to fulfil its obligations under EU law, whereas in the case of the action for annulment the Court not only might declare that an EU act is incompatible with EU law but will then go on to annul the act in question.

is Article 258 TFEU. Article 259 TFEU also allows a Member State to bring infringement proceedings but this provision has rarely been used.[33]

It is important to note that private parties *cannot* bring an infringement action before the Court.[34] This does not mean, however, that they cannot challenge illegal actions of the Member States, just that the vehicle for their challenge is a different one, namely starting an action before the national courts instead. Thus, as the Court emphasized in its seminal judgment in *Van Gend en Loos*, private parties can rely on the direct effect of EU law[35] – or, as the case may be, request that the national court makes a preliminary reference on the interpretation of EU law[36] – before their *national courts* to argue that Member States have effectively infringed EU law. Remedies are then provided at national level, subject to compliance with the principles of equality and effectiveness[37] and, following the establishment of the *Francovich* doctrine, private parties can, moreover, and as a matter of EU law, sue Member States in damages before the national courts.[38] Viewed together, all these avenues have the common aim of securing the protection of EU rights against possible infringements by Member States and national authorities.

Infringement proceedings have an administrative phase, where the Commission effectively gives a Member State an opportunity to remedy an infringement of EU law and to submit observations before resorting to litigation, and a judicial phase before the Court of Justice. A judgment of the Court finding that a Member State has failed to fulfil its obligations under EU law is binding on the Member State. If the Member State does not comply, then pecuniary sanctions may be imposed on it by the Court in a subsequent action under Article 260 TFEU.

3.1.2 The elements in Article 258 TFEU

The Commission can start infringement proceedings if it considers that 'a Member State has failed to fulfil an obligation under the Treaties'. We need therefore to ascertain what constitutes a 'Member State' in this context and what it means to 'fail to fulfil a Treaty obligation'. In the absence of specific Treaty guidance, these terms have been given meaning in the case law of the Court.

Consistent with the expansive interpretation of the notion of 'State' followed in other areas of EU law,[39] the Court held early on in the case law that a *Member State* may incur liability under Article 258 TFEU 'whatever the agency of the State whose action or inaction is the cause of the failure to fulfil its obligations, even in the case of a constitutionally independent institution.'[40] This has been developed to mean that not only the

---

[33] For an early example, see Case 141/78 *France v UK* [1979] ECR 2923 but see for a more recent and high-profile one, Case C-364/10 *Hungary v Slovakia*, judgment of 16 October 2012, nyr.

[34] They can complain to the Commission and their complaints play an important role in alerting this institution to potential infringements of EU law but the Commission ultimately has discretion in deciding whether or not to initiate an Art 258 TFEU action (Case T-247/04 *Aseprofar and Edifa v Commission* [2005] ECR II-3449, para 40).

[35] Case 26/62 *Van Gend en Loos v Netherlands Inland Revenue Administration* [1963] ECR 1, 13.

[36] See eg Case C-213/89 *The Queen v Secretary of State for Transport, ex p Factortame* ('*Factortame I*') [1990] ECR I-2433. Preliminary rulings on interpretation, while technically delivered in abstract terms, have effectively provided a much used vehicle to test the compatibility of national measures with EU law (see section 4.2).

[37] See chapter 6.

[38] Joined Cases C-6/90 and C-9/90 *Francovich v Italy* [1991] ECR I-5357, paras 33–37. See further chapter 6.

[39] See eg the broad interpretation of the notion of 'State' in the context of the case law on direct effect of directives (Case C-188/89 *Foster v British Gas* [1990] ECR I-3313, para 20).

[40] Case 77/69 *Commission v Belgium* [1970] ECR 237, para 15.

legislative,[41] executive,[42] and judicial[43] branches of the State are covered by this umbrella but also any other public bodies, such as territorial authorities in a federated State, in a region,[44] a locality,[45] or in an autonomous community and even private entities when controlled by the State.[46] In this context, the decisive point is whether the activities or omissions leading to the potential infringement of EU law can be *attributable* to the State and thus a substantive rather than a formalistic approach has prevailed when assessing the quality of the defendant in infringement proceedings.[47] However, and irrespective of the entity which is ultimately responsible for the breach under the internal constitutional arrangements of a Member State, the defendant in an action under Article 258 TFEU is the State itself and the action is formally brought against the government of the Member State in question.[48]

The next question is what constitutes a 'failure to fulfil a Treaty obligation'. This expression has been understood to refer both to positive acts and omissions, and not only to obligations imposed by the Treaties themselves but also those imposed by secondary legislation, international agreements,[49] and by the general principles of law.[50] Classic examples of positive acts attracting infringement proceedings would be the enactment of national legislation[51] or the pursuance of sustained administrative practices[52] that are contrary to EU law. However, the net of Article 258 TFEU has also been cast widely to cover omissions by Member States. A high-profile example of this is *Commission v France* ('*Strawberries*').[53] There, the Commission brought proceedings against the French government after the French authorities stood by and did nothing to prevent the continuous and systematic destruction of Spanish and Belgian agricultural produce by French farmers for a period of over ten years. While the disruption to the free movement of goods was, in reality, attributable to private parties, the failure of the French government to take any kind of action against such a sustained and grave violation of EU law amounted to a failure of the State to fulfil its Treaty obligations contrary to Article 34 TFEU[54] and Article 4(3) TEU.

3.1.3 Procedure

As explained earlier, there is an administrative phase and a judicial phase in infringement proceedings, both of which are reflected in the letter of Article 258 TFEU. It is important to understand, at the outset, that the Commission is an institution that acts in

---

[41] See Case 178/84 *Commission v Germany* [1987] ECR 1227, where proceedings were brought by the Commission against German laws intended to protect the purity of beer but which were contrary to Art 34 TFEU.

[42] See *Commission v UK* [1982] ECR 2793, where the UK government imposed restrictions on the importation of poultry products.

[43] Case C-129/00 *Commission v Italy* [2003] ECR I-14637, paras 29–41.

[44] Case C-2/90 *Commission v Belgium* [1992] ECR I-4431, where the measure contrary to EU law was a decree issued by the regional council of Wallonia.

[45] See Case 45/87 *Commission v Ireland* [1988] ECR 4929, where Dundalk Urban District Council was responsible for an infringement of EU law.

[46] Case C-325/00 *Commission v Germany* [2002] ECR I-9977, paras 17–21.

[47] See Case 249/81 *Commission v Ireland* ('*Buy Irish*') [1982] ECR 4005, paras 10–15.

[48] See Case C-95/97 *Région Wallonne v Commission* [1997] ECR I-1787, para 7.

[49] See Case C-61/94 *Commission v Germany* [1996] ECR I-3989, para 15.

[50] See eg the principle of equal treatment in Case 61/81 *Commission v UK* [1982] ECR 2601, para 14.

[51] See eg *Commission v Germany* (n 41).

[52] See eg Case 21/84 *Commission v France* [1985] ECR 1355, where the French authorities refused, without adequate justification, to approve postal franking machines from other Member States, thus contravening Art 34 TFEU.   [53] Case C-265/95 [1997] ECR I-6959. See also chapter 12.

[54] Further discussion of Art 34 TFEU can be found in chapter 12.

the public interest. A reflection of this is the discretion that it enjoys to decide whether and when to initiate both the administrative and the judicial phase in the proceedings.[55] Inevitably, this means that it will rank its priorities when deciding to pursue infringements of EU law and that it will not take up many of the complaints that it receives. Naturally, concerns soon arose about the lack of scrutiny over the Commission's exercise of its discretion in the context of Article 258 TFEU proceedings. In more recent times, some initiatives have sought to address a number of the deficiencies of this process. In particular, the 2002 Commission Communication to the European Parliament and the Council on relations with complainants in infringement proceedings[56] – which arose in response to criticisms from the Ombudsman when the Commission shelved a private complaint against the violation of public procurement rules by the Greek authorities[57] – aimed to increase the transparency and accountability of the Commission's decision-making process when dealing with complaints. This Communication has now been revised and updated by a 2012 Communication.[58] However, substantially – and despite these procedural safeguards – the broad discretion of the Commission remains uncontested.

The first formal step in the administrative – or pre-litigation – phase of the proceedings is the letter of formal notice, whereby the Commission defines the subject matter of the dispute and provides the basis for the Member State in question to submit observations. The Member State is given a reasonable period to respond and, following the submission of observations, the Commission may deliver a reasoned opinion describing the infringement of EU law and will then give the Member State a reasonable time limit – in practice, generally two months – to comply with the opinion. While the reasoned opinion may develop in more detail the points set out in the normally concise letter of formal notice, it cannot change the subject matter of the Commission's original complaint against the Member State or enlarge its scope.[59] If the Member State fails to comply with the opinion, the Commission may then decide to bring the matter before the Court of Justice, thus triggering the initiation of the judicial phase and the subject matter of its application must be the same or narrower than the subject matter of the reasoned opinion. The judgment of the Court will be a declaratory one, namely stating whether the Member State has breached EU law. During the course of the judicial proceedings, the Court may also decide to grant interim measures.[60]

Member States have deployed a variety of defences to explain their failures. The case law on this point shows clearly that the Court has given short shrift to these arguments and that, with very limited exceptions (eg *force majeure*[61]) the Court will concentrate on the objective existence of a violation of EU law and remain unmoved by any explanations from the Member States as to the reasons why they failed to comply with EU law. Just

---

[55] See Case 247/87 *Star Fruit Co SA v Commission* [1989] ECR 291, paras 11 and 12.

[56] OJ [2002] C244/5.

[57] Decision of the European Ombudsman on complaint 995/98/OV against the European Commission, available at http://www.ombudsman.europa.eu/decision/en/980995.htm

[58] COM(2012) 154 final.   [59] See Case 51/83 *Commission v Italy* [1984] ECR 2796, paras 6–8.

[60] See eg Cases 31/77 and 53/77 R *Commission v UK* [1977] ECR 921, where the UK had granted temporary aid to pig producers which was prima facie contrary to EU law and where the Commission applied and obtained a decision from the Court ordering this Member State to cease the application of the aid with immediate effect.

[61] See Case 101/84 *Commission v Italy* [1985] ECR 2629, where the Italian government argued that their failure to compile certain statistical information required under an EU directive was due to a bomb attack on their data processing centre. While the Court accepted that *force majeure* could be a valid defence, it made it clear that it would interpret it restrictively (para 16).

to mention a few of these unsuccessful defences: arguments that internal or practical difficulties stood in the way of their compliance with EU law,[62] that Union institutions or other Member States had also acted in breach of EU law,[63] or that unlawful legislation was in fact obsolete and not applied by the Member State.[64]

3.1.4 Sanctions

The Maastricht Treaty amended the TFEU (then the EEC Treaty) to enable the Court to impose sanctions on Member States that fail to comply with a judgment of the Court under Articles 258 and 259 TFEU finding them in breach of EU law. This involved a repetition of the whole procedure, comprising both the administrative and judicial phase, coupled with an application from the Commission to the Court for the imposition of a penalty and/or a lump sum.[65] Following the entry into force of the Lisbon Treaty, Article 260 TFEU has been amended with the aim of expediting the application of pecuniary sanctions. Essentially, the Lisbon changes are, as follows.

First, as provided in Article 260(2) TFEU, the pre-litigation procedure has been simplified in all cases where a Member State does not comply with the judgment of the Court. Thus, the Commission no longer needs to issue a second reasoned opinion but just a letter of formal notice – which will constitute the basis for the Member State to submit observations. Guidance on the determination of the penalties is provided in a 2005 Communication from the Commission.[66] This takes into account the seriousness of the infringement, its duration, and the deterrent effect of a sanction as well as the Member State's ability to pay. These sanctions may run to many thousands of euros.

Secondly, for the *specific* case where a Member State has failed to notify measures transposing a *legislative* directive[67] on time, special arrangements set out in Article 260(3) TFEU will apply. In particular, the Commission may, even at the stage of the *original* infringement proceedings, suggest that the Court imposes a penalty on the defaulting Member State in the same judgment delivered at the end of the Article 258 TFEU proceedings. In other words, the need for a second set of proceedings is obviated. Clearly, and as the Commission acknowledged in a 2010 Communication on the implementation of Article 260(3) TFEU, the purpose of this provision is to give yet another powerful incentive to Member States to implement directives on time and to protect individual rights against such a clear and generally indefensible violation of EU law.[68] The 2010 Communication also provides specific guidance as to the calculation of penalties in this particular situation but this is very similar to the mode of calculation used in Article 260(2) TFEU cases.

---

[62] Case 254/83 *Commission v Italy* [1984] ECR 3395.

[63] Joined Cases 90/63 and 91/63 *Commission v Luxembourg and Belgium* [1964] ECR 625, 631, and Case 232/78 *Commission v France* [1979] ECR 2729, para 9, respectively.

[64] See Case 167/73 *Commission v France* [1974] ECR 359.

[65] There have been cases where *both* a lump sum and a periodic penalty payment have been imposed (eg Case C-304/02 *Commission v France* [2005] ECR I-6263). For a more recent decision where a lump sum payment of €20,000,000 and a penalty of €50.000 per day (until the Member State in question complied with the judgment of the Court) were imposed, see Case C-610/10 *Commission v Spain*, judgment of 11 December 2012, nyr. See also Case C-270/11 *Commission v Sweden*, judgment of 30 May 2013, nyr.

[66] SEC(2005) 1658.

[67] The special arrangements provided in Art 260(3) TFEU do not apply to cases where the directive in question has not been adopted by legislative procedure. There, the general provisions in Art 260(2) TFEU apply.

[68] SEC(2010) 1371, para 7. This approach is in harmony with the vigorous stance that the Court has taken in other areas, such as in the development of the doctrines of direct effect of directives and State liability in damages, which created effective deterrents to prevent Member States from failing to implement directives on time (see chapter 6).

3.2 **The action for annulment**

3.2.1 Overview

The action for annulment and the action for a failure to act represent two dimensions of the same remedy, namely one that addresses the situation where an EU institution has either adopted an illegal act (eg enacting a directive that breaches a general principle of law) or has failed to act when it had an obligation to act under EU law (eg the Commission does not respond at all when an undertaking complains of a violation of the Treaty competition rules). Both avenues aim to obtain a decision from the Court that an act or that the failure to act of an institution, respectively, contravene EU law.

Article 263 TFEU sets out the principles and structure underlining annulment proceedings. Essentially, there are four pivotal points that the Court will examine when an action for annulment is brought. These are:

(a) compliance with the time limit for bringing the action;

(b) the reviewability of the act;

(c) the standing of the applicant – where the applicable rules vary significantly depending on whether the applicant is classified as 'privileged', 'semi-privileged', or 'non-privileged';

(d) the existence of possible grounds for the annulment of the act.

The first three refer to the *admissibility* of the action whereas the last one refers to the *substantive* challenge to the act. In the text that follows we will explore the action for annulment using as a basic structure the four key issues outlined above.

3.2.2 Time limit

The time limit for bringing an action for annulment provided in Article 263(6) TFEU is two months. This is deliberately very short to ensure that the legality of EU measures is uncertain for only a limited period. This time limit begins to run from the date of publication of the measure or of its notification to the applicant or, in the absence thereof, of the day on which it comes to the knowledge of the applicant. Even though this requirement is found in the final paragraph of Article 263 TFEU, it is of great practical importance and, logically, the first to be examined when proceedings are brought. Annulment actions brought outside the time limit are automatically inadmissible.

3.2.3 Reviewable acts

It follows from the first paragraph of Article 263 TFEU that the essential quality for an act to be reviewable is that it should be *legally binding*. This is demonstrated by the fact that this provision covers the review of acts of the institutions and of the offices or agencies of the Union intended to produce legal effects – and that it explicitly excludes recommendations and opinions.

In the post-Lisbon classification found in Articles 289 to 291 TFEU, both legislative acts (ie those adopted by legislative procedure) and non-legislative acts (by default those not adopted by legislative procedure, such as decisions adopted directly on the basis of the Treaties, delegated and implementing acts) that produce legal effects,[69] are reviewable. Most frequently, actions for annulment will be brought against regulations, directives, and decisions – which are the three types of binding legal acts listed in Article 288 TFEU. In these cases, therefore, the requirement for reviewability will be automatically fulfilled. Howe

---

[69] See chapter 5.

the Court has taken a non-formalistic approach when deciding the binding nature of EU acts. Thus, where acts have not been formally identified as belonging to one of the Article 288 TFEU categories, it has looked at the substance of the act and the intention of those who drafted it and has concluded that an act will be reviewable, irrespective of the form it takes or the title it receives, as long as it is capable of affecting an applicant by bringing about a distinct change in its legal position.[70]

A frequently cited example that reflects the spirit of this line of case law is the decision of the Court in *IBM v Commission*,[71] a competition case. The Commission is the enforcer at EU level of the main competition provisions in the Treaty, Articles 101 and 102 TFEU,[72] and the procedural steps that it takes when it decides to pursue an investigation about a possible breach of these provisions are now set out in Regulation 1/2003,[73] which entered into force in 2004. Its predecessor was Regulation 17/62, which applied for over 40 years, and which was in force when the *IBM* case was decided. Despite the existence of very important differences between these two instruments, they have in common that one of the stages in the Commission's enforcement procedure is the provision of a statement of objections, where the Commission – generally following a fact-finding phase and on the basis of the available evidence – delivers its *preliminary* findings as to the existence of an infringement of Articles 101 and/or 102 TFEU. The purpose of this statement is to give an opportunity to the parties to prepare their defence against the objections raised by the Commission before it reaches a final decision. In *IBM*, the undertaking addressee of the statement of objections sought to challenge the statement before the Court. Given that the statement was not formally classified as a 'decision' in the Treaty terminology, the Court examined whether in substance it produced legal effects. The Court concluded that the statement did not *in itself* produce legal effects but merely paved the way for the final decision of the Commission that would – if the Commission concluded, after hearing the observations of the parties, that an infringement had taken place – produce such effects.[74]

However, and in line with the non-formalistic view taken by the Court, each measure will always be scrutinized individually to see whether it produces legal effects, even when it is part of a series of procedural stages leading to a final decision. For example, if the Commission decides not to afford confidentiality to certain documents in the course of a competition investigation and to disclose them to third parties, the undertakings under investigation can challenge such a measure because it creates an immediate change in their legal position that has independent consequences which cannot be reversed by challenging the final decision of the Commission.[75] In this case, such a decision can be challenged.

In addition to the requirement that the act should be legally binding, Article 263(1) TFEU also provides that it should emanate from one of the bodies subject to review. This includes the institutions of the Union – with the exception of the Court of Justice of the EU and the Court of Auditors – and the agencies, offices, and bodies of the Union. Since Article 263 TFEU concerns the actions of the EU institutions, Member States can never be defendants in these proceedings.

---

[70] For an early example, see Joined Cases 8–11/66 *Société anonyme Cimenteries CBR Cementsbedrijven NV v Commission* [1967] ECR 75, 91 and for a clear statement from the Court of the prevalence of substance over form when deciding the binding nature of an act, see Case 60/81 *IBM v Commission* [1981] ECR 2639, para 9. For a more recent example of this consistent line of case law, see Case C-362/08 P *Internationaler Hilfsfonds v Commission* [2010] ECR I-669, para 52.   [71] Case 60/81 (n 70).

[72] See chapter 17.   [73] OJ [2003] L1/1.   [74] *IBM* (n 70) paras 10–12.

[75] See Case 53/85 *AKZO Chemie BV and AKZO Chemie UK Ltd v Commission* [1986] ECR 1965, paras 17–21.

3.2.4 Standing

We can classify applicants for judicial review into three main categories depending on the standing requirements that they must satisfy in order to bring annulment proceedings:

- privileged,
- semi-privileged, and
- non-privileged.

These will be examined in turn. The standing of the applicants classified in the first two categories is straightforward but the strict standing conditions imposed on non-privileged applicants have generated one of the most intricate and controversial bodies of case law emanating from the Court.

Privileged and semi-privileged applicants

According to Article 263(2) TFEU, the *privileged* applicants are the Member States,[76] the Parliament, the Commission, and the Council. They are privileged because they have an automatic right to bring proceedings and therefore they do not have to satisfy any *locus standi* conditions.[77] While the Parliament is today a fully fledged privileged applicant, it is noteworthy that – unlike the other privileged applicants – it only acquired this status fairly recently, at the time of the Treaty of Nice.[78] Both the limited role that the Parliament played in the legislative procedure until the introduction of what is today the ordinary legislative procedure and its historical lack of standing to challenge acts of the other institutions were among the arguments traditionally deployed to argue that a democratic deficit existed in the EU.

Post-Lisbon, the *semi-privileged* applicants are the Court of Auditors, the European Central Bank, and the Committee of the Regions. Unlike privileged applicants, semi-privileged applicants do not have an automatic right of action and can only bring proceedings when their prerogatives are at stake (eg they have not been consulted in a particular procedure).[79]

Non-privileged applicants

Natural and legal persons are commonly referred to as non-privileged applicants in the context of annulment proceedings. This is because Article 263(4) TFEU imposes strict standing conditions on them when they wish to challenge a potentially unlawful EU act, which means that their chances of securing access to the action for annulment are limited. Following the Lisbon amendments, there are three situations when natural or legal persons will have *locus standi* to bring an Article 263 TFEU action. These are:

- if they are the *addressees* of the act in question, they will have *automatic standing*;
- if they are *not the addressees* of the act, they will have to show that they are *directly and individually* concerned by it (*general test of standing*); *but*

---

[76] In this context, the notion of Member State refers to the *central* government authorities. Thus, autonomous communities and local and regional authorities do not enjoy the status of privileged applicants but are generally classified as legal persons that have to satisfy the standing requirements that apply to non-privileged applicants (see eg Case C-180/97 *Regione Toscana v Commission* [1997] ECR I-5245, paras 6–10 and Case T-238 *Comunidad Autónoma de Cantabria v Council* [1998] ECR II-2271, paras 42 and 43).

[77] See Case 45/86 *Commission v Council* [1987] ECR 1493, para 3.

[78] The Parliament had first no status at all as an applicant until the seminal judgment of the Court in Case C-70/88 *European Parliament v Council* ('*Chernobyl*') [1990] ECR I-2041, where the Court treated it as a semi-privileged applicant, a finding that was later incorporated in Art 263 TFEU (then Art 173 EEC) by the Maastricht Treaty.   [79] Art 263(3) TFEU.

- if they are *non-addressees* and wish to challenge a *regulatory act that does not entail implementing measures*, they will have to show only that they are *directly concerned* by it (*special standing test* or *Lisbon test*).

The first scenario is straightforward. If a private applicant is the addressee of an EU act (eg the addressee of a Commission decision withdrawing an agricultural aid previously awarded to the applicant), then it can automatically challenge it, as long as the action is brought within the time limit set out in Article 263(6) TFEU.

The second and third situations, which apply to non-addressees are, however, more problematic. The main reason for this is that the Treaty does not define the notions of 'direct and individual concern', of 'regulatory act', or of 'implementing measures' in this particular context. Therefore, the unenviable task of giving meaning to these important concepts, the application of which ultimately decides the fate of private parties in annulment proceedings, fell to the Court of Justice. This entailed, among other things, striking a balance between securing direct access to justice for private parties, whose rights and interests had been affected by EU measures, and the more practical, but important, consideration of preventing an opening of the floodgates of litigation. The result has been a complex body of case law, where the requirement of individual concern, in particular, has been very narrowly – and not always consistently – applied, rendering many actions brought by private parties inadmissible.

In the text that follows, we will grapple with the development of the case law interpreting these difficult notions. To this end, we will consider first the general standing test (direct and individual concern) and then the special or Lisbon test that applies to the challenge of regulatory acts that do not entail implementing measures. Logically it would seem that, post-Lisbon, an applicant would always try to satisfy the special or Lisbon test first because this is more lenient – crucially, there is no need to show individual concern. Only if the Lisbon test is inapplicable, would a non-addressee resort to fulfilling the general standing test which now applies residually to all other situations not covered by the Lisbon test – and these are still numerous. The general and special standing tests are represented in Figure 10.2. Historically, however, the general standing test was the original standing test

Fig 10.2 *Locus standi* of private applicants after Lisbon: Article 263(4) TFEU

and we will examine it first because it provides the necessary backdrop for tackling the fresh issues that are raised by the new Lisbon test.

The general standing test: direct and individual concern

'Acts'

According to Article 260(4) TFEU, a non-addressee can challenge an 'act' which is of 'direct and individual concern' to the applicant. The pre-Lisbon version of this provision referred specifically to *decisions* as the only acts that could be challenged by private parties and there was a long-drawn-out debate – in the face of somewhat unclear case law – as to whether non-privileged applicants could challenge general acts, such as regulations and directives, as well as decisions.[80] The Lisbon Treaty has now settled this point and the current wording of Article 263(4) TFEU uses the all-embracing term of 'acts', which encompasses both general and individual acts (whether or not listed in Article 288 TFEU) as long as they produce legal effects. In other words, non-privileged applicants can now clearly challenge not only decisions but also regulations and directives.

Individual concern

This leads us to the notions of individual and direct concern. The Court had a first opportunity to interpret 'individual concern' in the seminal *Plaumann* case.[81] There, Plaumann, a German company that imported clementines from countries outside the EU (then the EEC), challenged a decision of the Commission addressed to Germany refusing authorization partially to suspend the application of a customs duty set out in the Common Customs Tariff in relation to this fruit. Naturally, Plaumann's economic interests were affected by the Commission decision but since the company was not an addressee of the decision, it had to demonstrate individual and direct concern. The Court began its analysis by pointing out that the right of interested parties to bring an action should 'not be interpreted restrictively'.[82] Paradoxically, however, it went on to construe the test very narrowly by stating that non-addressees would be individually concerned if an act affects them 'by reason of certain attributes that are peculiar to them or by reason of circumstances in which they are *differentiated from all other persons* and by virtue of these factors distinguishes them individually *just as in the case of the person addressed*'.[83] The degree of individualization required to satisfy this test was therefore very high because an applicant effectively had to demonstrate that it was a de facto addressee.

In *Plaumann*, the Court gave a practical template to assess this degree of individualization. Thus, it held that Plaumann was not individually concerned because he was affected by the decision 'by reason of a commercial activity which may, at any time, be practised

---

[80] In some cases, the Court had applied a triple admissibility test when private applicants brought annulment proceedings against regulations or directives. This included, as well as the tests of direct and individual concern, the application of the *abstract terminology test* to decide that the contested act was not really a regulation but a decision in substance (see eg Joined Cases 789/79 and 790/79 *Calpak v Commission* [1980] ECR 797. In these cases, the application of this practically insurmountable test meant that most actions were dismissed as inadmissible. In other cases, the Court simply applied the tests of direct and individual concern, thus implicitly acknowledging that regulations could, in principle, be challenged by private parties (see eg Case C-152/88 *Sofrimport v Commission* [1990] ECR I-2477). The decision of the Court in *Codorníu v Council* (Case C-309/89 [1994] ECR I-1853) settled this divergence and from then onwards the Court acknowledged that true regulations could be challenged by private parties as long as these satisfied the general standing test.

[81] Case 25/62 *Plaumann v Commission* [1962] ECR 95.   [82] Ibid, 107.

[83] Ibid (emphasis added).

by any person'.[84] In other words, Plaumann was a member of an 'open category' of people because anyone could at any time (at least in theory) become an importer of clementines. Consequently, the fulfilment of the test of individual concern would seem to necessitate that the applicant is a member of a 'closed category' of people, that is, a category the membership of which is already formally fixed and ascertained *when the act in question enters into force*. This approach was soon reiterated in subsequent cases[85] and today still constitutes the main criterion to demonstrate individual concern[86] – but as we shall see, not the only one.

The *Plaumann* construction means, therefore, that carrying out a particular economic activity affected by the measure does not suffice to satisfy the test of individual concern. This is so even where the applicant is gravely affected by the measure[87] or when, at the time the measure was enacted, the applicant was effectively one of very few – or even the only one – carrying out that activity, as long as others could decide to undertake that activity *in the future* (ie after the date of the adoption of the act).[88] The Court's interpretation is, therefore, intensely formalistic not only because it seems dependent on demonstrating the existence of circumstances that have happened *before* the act in question was adopted, but also because it is detached from the actual effect that a measure has on an applicant and hence from economic reality. While those belonging to the closed category will generally suffer an adverse economic effect as a result of the measure, others outside the closed class may also experience such an effect and will nonetheless be deprived of standing.[89] A representation of the *Plaumann* test can be found in Figure 10.3.

Moreover, a number of issues have arisen in the application of the *Plaumann* test. First, it became necessary to illustrate what circumstances would actually propel an applicant into the 'magic circle' of a closed category. Looking at the case law, examples of applicants that satisfied the closed category test include those who – *before* the measure was adopted – had pursued an individual course of action such as applying for licences[90] or export refunds[91] or having pending contracts[92] or goods in transit.[93]

Secondly, while the closed category test is the main indicator of individual concern, the case law has provided, on a case-by-case basis, a number of exceptions which have

---

[84] *Plaumann* (n 81) 107.

[85] See eg Joined Cases 106/63 and 107/63 *Toepfer and Getreide-Import Gesellschaft v Commission* [1965] ECR 405, 411 and Case 62/70 *Bock v Commission* [1971] ECR 897, para 10.

[86] For more recent examples, see Case T-585/93 *Stichting Greenpeace Council (Greenpeace International) v Commission* [1995] ECR II-2205, paras 53–55; Case T-16/04 *Arcelor v Parliament and Council* [2010] ECR II-211, paras 106–115; and Cases C-71/09 P, C-73/09 P and C-76/09 *Comitato 'Venezia vuole vivere' v Commission* [2011] ECR I-4727, para 52.

[87] Case T-173/98 *Unión de Pequeños Agricultores v Council* [1999] ECR II-3357, para 50.

[88] See eg Case 1/64 *Glucoseries réunies v Commission* [1964] ECR 413, 417 and Case C-209/94 P *Buralux v Council* [1996] ECR I-615, paras 28 and 29.

[89] See eg Case 11/82 *Piraiki-Patraiki v Commission* [1985] ECR 207, where a Commission measure imposing quotas on the importation of Greek cotton yarn into France was challenged by two groups of Greek exporters. On the one hand, it was challenged by Greek traders, who had pending contracts *at the time the measure was adopted* and, on the other, by Greek traders who normally exported cotton to France but who had no pending contracts at the time. While the first group was accorded standing, (partly) on the basis that the traders were members of a closed class, the second group of exporters were denied standing, despite the fact that the measure clearly had an adverse effect on their economic interests.

[90] See eg *Toepfer and Getreide-Import Gesellschaft* (n 85). But, for those who applied for licences *after* the measure was adopted, individual concern was not found (see Case 38/64 *Getreide-Import Gesellschaft v Commission* [1965] ECR 203, 208).   [91] Case 100/74 *CAM v Commission* [1975] ECR 1393, paras 15–17.

[92] See eg *Piraiki-Patraiki* (n 89) para 19.

[93] *Sofrimport* (n 80) para 11.

Closed Category:
individual concern

Interested Parties:
no individual
concern

General Public:
no individual
concern

Fig 10.3 The *Plaumann* test for individual concern

unavoidably brought uncertainty to the application of the test. The majority of them refer to special cases where the Court obviously found compelling reasons why the individuals should be granted *locus standi* – even if these reasons were not always fully articulated.

For example, in *Codorníu v Council*,[94] a leading Spanish manufacturer of sparkling wine, which had held a trademark including the term 'crémant' since 1924, challenged a Council regulation that reserved the use of this term for certain sparkling wines manufactured in France and Luxembourg. The Court did not specifically refer to the closed category test but explained instead that the regulation effectively prevented Codorníu from using its trademark,[95] a circumstance that later case law has construed as meaning that the applicant had a 'specific right' acquired before the measure entered into effect that had been affected by it[96] and which the Court considered as a separate basis for individual concern alongside the closed category test. While applicants have repeatedly tried to demonstrate individual concern on the basis of the *Codorníu* test, they have hardly ever been successful.[97]

Another example was the well-known decision in *Les Verts v European Parliament*,[98] where members of a new political party challenged a decision of the European Parliament allocating funds to prepare for elections to parties *already* present in the Parliament. The

---

[94] Case C-309/89 (n 80).

[95] Ibid, para 21. On the impact of *Codorníu*, see further A Arnull, 'Private Applicants and the Action for Annulment since *Codorníu*' (2001) 38 *Common Market Law Review* 7.

[96] See Case C-87/95 P *Cassa Nazionale di Previdenza ed Assistenza a favore degli avvocati e dei Procuratori v Council* [1996] ECR I-2003, para 36 and Case T-99/94 *Asociación Española de Empresas de la Carne v Council* [1994] ECR II-871, para 20.

[97] For an example where parallels can be drawn with the approach in *Codorníu*, see Case T-33/01 *Infront v Commission* [2005] ECR II-5897, paras 158–169 and confirmed on appeal in Case C-125/06 P *Commission v Infront* [2008] ECR I-1451. In this case the applicants were found to be individually concerned because the decision in question had the specific purpose of altering the broadcasting rights acquired by the applicants before the measure had been enacted. [98] Case 294/83 (n 4).

applicants were clearly not part of a closed class as new political parties could be constituted in the future, but the Court effectively set aside this test to give standing to the applicants as any other situation would give rise 'to inequality in the protection afforded by the Court to the various groups competing in the same elections.'[99] This judgment seemed, therefore, a rare case of triumph of substance over form.

Furthermore, there have been specific areas of the case law, notably in competition,[100] State aid, and anti-dumping and anti-subsidy proceedings,[101] where the Court has taken not only a more flexible but also a more consistent approach to individual concern. These areas have in common the fact that basic procedural or enforcement regulations[102] set out in detail the rights of participation of interested parties in the administrative procedure leading to the adoption of an EU measure, which is generally a Commission decision (in the case of competition and State aid) or Council and Commission regulations (eg in the field of anti-dumping). There, the Court has consistently found applicants individually concerned when these have participated in the proceedings – for example, by submitting a complaint to the Commission that triggered the investigation[103] or by providing observations[104] during the procedure leading to the adoption of the contested measure or even in some case where they simply *had the right* to participate but they did not do so.[105]

In some isolated cases, the Court went even further and, exceptionally, found applicants individually concerned not on the basis of their procedural involvement but because of the substantial adverse economic effect that a particular measure had on them. The leading decision is *Extramet v Council*,[106] where the largest importer of calcium metal into the EU challenged a Council regulation imposing anti-dumping duties on the importation of that product. The applicant was found to be individually concerned because of its position as the leading importer of calcium metal into the EU and because its economic activity had been seriously affected by the contested regulation. These were arguments which, as we saw previously, had been consistently rejected in the mainstream case law on individual

[99] *Les Verts* (n 4) para 36.   [100] See chapter 17.

[101] EU anti-dumping policy addresses the situation where undertakings outside the EU export products to the EU at prices below the normal value of those products on their domestic market – or, in other words, 'dump' the products in the EU market causing injury to the market. The EU anti-dumping regulation (currently Regulation 1225/2009 (OJ [2009] L343/5)) sets out the procedure that applies to the imposition of anti-dumping measures. This Regulation works alongside EU anti-subsidy measures – see Regulation 597/2009 (OJ [2009] L188/93), which sets out the procedure for countervailing any direct or indirect subsidies granted by a government for the manufacture or export of a product originating outside the EU but intended for release in the EU.

[102] See eg in the context of competition proceedings, Regulation 1/2003 (OJ [2003] L1/1); in the context of State aid, Council Regulation 659/1999 (OJ [1999] L83/1) – most recently amended by Regulation 734/2013 (OJ [2013] L204/15) – and in the context of anti-dumping and anti-subsidy proceedings, see Regulation 1225/2009 and Regulation 597/2009 (n 101).

[103] See, in competition proceedings, Case 26/76 *Metro SB-Großmärkte GmbH & Co KG v Commission* ('*Metro I*') [1977] ECR 1875, para 13, where a competitor of an undertaking to whom a Commission decision was addressed had complained to the Commission. For an example in the field of anti-dumping, see Case 264/82 *Timex Corporation v Council and Commission* [1985] ECR 849, paras 13 and 14, and for an example in the field of State aids, see Case 169/84 *Compagnie française de l'azote (Cofaz) SA v Commission* [1986] ECR 391, para 25.

[104] See, in competition proceedings, Case 75/84 *Metro SB-Großmärkte GmbH & Co KG v Commission* ('*Metro II*') [1986] ECR 3021, paras 21–23. Here, the applicant had not complained to the Commission but had submitted observations during the procedure leading to the adoption of the Commission decision.

[105] See eg in the field of mergers, Case T-12/93 *Comité Central d'Entreprise de la Société Anonyme Vittel and Comité d'Etablissement de Pierval and Fédération Générale Agroalimentaire v Commission* [1995] ECR II-1247, paras 23 and 24.   [106] Case C- 358/89 [1991] ECR I-2501, para 17.

concern[107] and it is therefore unsurprising that some applicants tried thereafter to extrapolate the *Extramet* findings in order to prove their *locus standi*. However, the Court justified its approach in *Extramet* by referring to the 'exceptional circumstances' applying in that case and has been unwilling to extend it to other cases.[108]

Finally, there have been a small number of cases where the Court has based its assessment of individual concern on a *cumulative* test, seemingly requiring the applicants not only to be members of a closed category but also to show that the institution enacting the measure had a duty imposed by higher ranking rules of EU law to take into account the situation of the applicants which it had failed to observe. This can be seen in *Sofrimport*.[109] There, Sofrimport, an importer of Chilean apples into the EU, brought annulment proceedings against three Commission *implementing* regulations that suspended the issue of import licences for dessert apples with immediate effect. A *parent* – or basic – Council regulation[110] setting out the conditions and the framework within which the Commission could apply protective measures for fruit and vegetables included a provision that obliged the Commission to take into account the position of traders with goods in transit when adopting these measures. The Commission, however, failed to do so in this instance. At the time the regulations were adopted, Sofrimport had applied for an import licence and had a consignment of apples in transit to the EU. On arrival at the port of Marseilles, the French authorities refused to issue an import licence to Sofrimport.

The Court held that Sofrimport was individually concerned, first, because it was a member of a closed class[111] – it had applied for a licence and had goods in transit when the measures were adopted – and, secondly, because the Commission had failed to observe the duty imposed by the higher ranking EU rule.[112] An illustration of the factual background in *Sofrimport* can be found in Figure 10.4.[113] The obvious observation here is that if the applicant is a member of a closed class, it seems unnecessary to have to prove *additionally* the existence of a duty on the part of the institution. However, there is evidence in the case law that in those cases where the Court decides to apply the cumulative *Sofrimport* approach, it has required the fulfilment of *both* elements, thus suggesting that membership of a closed class was not enough in itself.[114] When the Court has been criticized for its restrictive approach, its response has always been that applicants can still bring proceedings in the national court and seek a preliminary reference from the Court of Justice under Article 267 TFEU (considered in section 4.2).

In many cases where private applicants did not satisfy the *Plaumann* test, the Court referred to the alternative possibility of indirectly challenging EU measures by bringing proceedings before the national courts in the hope that a preliminary reference on validity would be made to the Court of Justice.[115] Given the difficulties and the unpredictability associated with the application of the test of individual concern, it is unsurprising that repeated calls for a reformulation of the test were made. The most high-profile call for reform came

---

[107] It could be argued that although the decision in *Codorníu* (n 80) was crafted in later case law in terms of the existence of a 'specific right', some parallels can be drawn with the ruling in *Extramet* because both in *Codorníu* (implicitly) and in *Extramet* (explicitly), the Court alluded to the grave effect that the measures in question would have on the economic interests of the applicants.

[108] See eg Case T-598/97 *British Shoe Corporation v Council* [2002] ECR II-1155, paras 48–50.

[109] Case C-152/88 (n 80). See also section 6, case study 10.2. For another, earlier example, see *Piraiki-Patraiki* (n 89).

[110] This Regulation, post-Lisbon, would be classified as a legislative measure.

[111] *Sofrimport* (n 80) para 11.   [112] Ibid, paras 12 and 13.

[113] See also section 6, case study 10.2.

[114] See Case T-489/93 *Unifruit Hellas v Commission* [1994] ECR II-1201, para 25 and Case C-451/98 *Antillean Rice Mills v Council* [2001] ECR I-8949, paras 61 and 62.   [115] See further section 4.2.

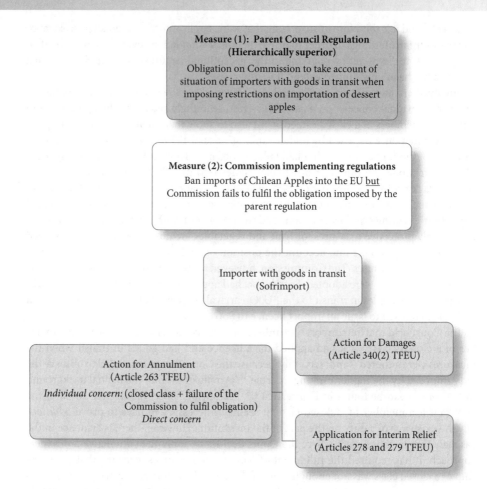

Measure (1): Parent Council Regulation (Hierarchically superior)

Obligation on Commission to take account of situation of importers with goods in transit when imposing restrictions on importation of dessert apples

Measure (2): Commission implementing regulations

Ban imports of Chilean Apples into the EU but Commission fails to fulfil the obligation imposed by the parent regulation

Importer with goods in transit (Sofrimport)

Action for Damages (Article 340(2) TFEU)

Action for Annulment (Article 263 TFEU)

Individual concern: (closed class + failure of the Commission to fulfil obligation)
Direct concern

Application for Interim Relief (Articles 278 and 279 TFEU)

Fig 10.4 *The Sofrimport* litigation

from the Opinion of Advocate General Jacobs in *Unión de Pequeños Agricultores (UPA) v Council*,[116] where a Spanish trade association representing small agricultural producers challenged a Council regulation that discontinued certain types of agricultural aid for small producers. Under the *Plaumann* test, the applicants were not individually concerned given that they were members of an open category of people. However, Advocate General Jacobs proposed a test that would render an applicant individually concerned where an EU measure 'has or is liable to have, a substantial adverse effect on his interests'.[117] In other words, he shifted the focus from a formalistic test to one based on the economic impact of an EU measure.

At the core of Advocate General Jacobs's submissions was the argument that it is not *automatic* that a private applicant who does not have standing to bring annulment proceedings can *always* obtain a remedy by bringing an action before the national court and hope that it will make a reference on validity to the Court of Justice.[118] This was his platform to argue for a relaxation of the test of individual concern because it effectively demonstrated

---

[116] Case C-50/00 P [2002] ECR I-6677.
[117] *UPA* (n 116) paras 60 and 103 of the AG's Opinion.
[118] Ibid, paras 36–49 of the Opinion.

that maintenance of the status quo could lead to situations of denial of justice,[119] a result at variance with the idea that the Treaty provides a *complete* system of judicial protection. *UPA* was a prime example of that kind of scenario, because the absence of implementing measures at national level – that is, the aid schemes were automatically discontinued as a result of the regulation without the need for any national intervention – meant that the applicants could not bring proceedings before the national court and therefore that the alternative of a preliminary ruling on validity was simply unavailable.

A couple of months later, the General Court in *Jégo-Quéré v Commission*[120] also followed Advocate General Jacobs and took the unprecedented step of further proposing a relaxation of the *Plaumann* test. The facts of this case showed a slightly different angle than in *UPA* in terms of the availability of national proceedings. A fishing company challenged a Commission regulation that imposed minimum mesh sizes for different net-fishing techniques. The measure required no implementation at national level. The right of action before the national court – and hence the possibility of a preliminary reference on validity – could be exercised there but *only* if the applicant infringed the requirements of the Commission regulation or, in other words, only if it breached the EU measure. This was not only a risky strategy (why does an applicant have to break the law to get a remedy?) but also one that is inconsistent with the principles of judicial protection. Therefore, both the proceedings in *UPA* and in *Jégo-Quéré* demonstrated the weakness of the argument that the route through the national courts *always* offers a satisfactory alternative to private applicants when these are not able to satisfy the standing conditions in Article 263(4) TFEU.[121] However, the Court of Justice in *UPA* did not follow these leads and confirmed the traditional construction of individual concern;[122] a position which it takes to this day.[123]

Direct concern

By contrast, the test of direct concern has been much less problematic. Essentially, this test has been construed as satisfied when there is a direct causal relationship between the act in question and the effect that it has on the applicant.[124] In practical terms, the Court has taken the view that the main situation when this causal link could be interrupted would be where the addressee of the measure had discretion as to how to implement the measure – and thus the ability to change the course of its application. In this case, the effect on the applicant would be caused by the measure adopted by the addressee rather than by the EU measure. Thus, in *Les Verts v European Parliament*,[125] the Court explained that the European Parliament's decision was of direct concern to the applicants because the decision constituted 'a complete set of rules which are sufficient in themselves and which require no implementing provisions since the calculation of the share of the appropriations to be granted to each of the political groupings concerned is automatic and leaves no room

---

[119] Ibid, paras 38–44.
[120] Case T-177/01 [2002] ECR II-2365, paras 49–51. The test proposed by the General Court in this case was slightly more restrictive than the one suggested by the AG in *UPA* but still more lenient than the closed category test. In particular, the Court suggested that an applicant would be individually concerned where 'the measure in question affects his legal position, in a manner which is both definite and immediate, by restricting his rights or by imposing obligations on him' (para 51).
[121] See further section 4.2 on the limitations of the system of preliminary rulings on validity.
[122] *UPA* (n 116) paras 44–45.
[123] For a recent example, see Case T-18/10 *Inuit Tapiriit Kanatami v European Parliament and Council* ('*Inuit I*') [2011] ECR II- 5599, paras 88–94.
[124] Joined Cases 41–44/70 *International Fruit Co v Commission* [1971] ECR 411, paras 23–28.
[125] Case 294/83 (nn 4, 98, and 99 and accompanying text, which includes a brief description of the facts).

for any discretion.'[126] Therefore, an applicant would be directly concerned where the act requires no implementation or, even if it does, the addressee of an act has no discretion as to how to implement it.

In interpreting the existence of discretion for the purposes of the application of the test of direct concern, the Court has taken the view that *even* if some discretion is left to the addressee, the measure can still be of direct concern to a non-addressee where the use of the discretion is 'entirely theoretical'. This is because there is no doubt as to the intention of the addressee to implement the EU measure in a particular way. For example, if a Commission decision *authorizes* a Member State to impose import restrictions, theoretically the Member State could decide not to use the authorization. However, if the Member State actually applied to the Commission for authorization to impose the restrictions, there is little doubt that they intend to use it.[127]

Conclusion

This section has shown the difficulties inherent in the application of the general standing test. In *UPA*,[128] the Court made it clear that it would not broaden the test of individual concern and that any changes should come through political agreement between the Member States in the form of an amendment of Article 263(4) TFEU.[129] It therefore came as no surprise that the Lisbon Treaty introduced a new standing test for private parties that would coexist with the general standing test with a view to making it easier for non-privileged applicants to secure standing under Article 263(4) TFEU. The question is whether this new test has resolved all the problems created by the general standing test.

The Lisbon test

Following the Lisbon amendments, Article 263(4) TFEU allows a non-privileged applicant to challenge a 'regulatory act which is of direct concern to the applicant and does not entail implementing measures.' Given that no requirement of individual concern needs to be satisfied, this test seems to have significantly improved the ability of private parties to challenge EU acts. However, the implications of the test could not be fully appraised until three issues were resolved. First, the notion of 'regulatory act' needed to be clarified. Secondly, it was necessary to elucidate, in this context, what it meant that the act in question 'does not entail implementing measures'. Finally, would the concept of direct concern in the Lisbon test be construed in the same way as in the established case law on the general standing test?

After much speculation, the first issue was addressed by the General Court in *Inuit I*[130], where it defined a 'regulatory act' as an act 'of general application apart from legislative acts'.[131] Therefore, and by default, it follows that the term would be applicable to general *non-legislative* acts, for example – but not exclusively – general implementing and delegated acts adopted under Articles 290 and 291 TFEU. By contrast, *legislative* regulations and directives – for example, those adopted under the ordinary or special legislative procedures – would not come under this definition and would be subjected to the general standing test and therefore to the rigours of the *Plaumann* test of individual concern as well as to the test of direct concern.[132] Since the act under review in *Inuit I* was a legislative regulation, the Lisbon test was inapplicable and the general test applied instead, with the result that the applicants were denied standing, mainly due to their failure to satisfy the test

---

[126] *Les Verts* (n 4) para 31.   [127] See eg *Piraiki-Patraiki* (n 89) paras 7–9.

[128] Case C-50/00 P (n 116).   [129] Ibid, para 45.

[130] Case T-18/10 (n 123). For a discussion of the *Inuit* litigation, see section 6, case study 10.1.

[131] Ibid, para 56.   [132] Ibid.

of individual concern. The General Court's decision in *Inuit I* was unsuccessfully appealed to the Court of Justice which confirmed the interpretation of 'regulatory act' given by the General Court.[133]

Only a few weeks after its decision in *Inuit I*, the General Court delivered judgment in a second key case: *Microban v Commission*.[134] This was the first time the Lisbon test was fully satisfied in a set of circumstances where the applicant probably would not have satisfied the general test of standing due to lack of individual concern. There, an American manufacturer of antibacterial additives challenged a Commission decision addressed to the Member States removing triclosan, a chemical substance, from the list of additives that could be used in the manufacture of plastics intended to be used with foodstuffs which had been drawn up by a previous Commission directive. The Commission decision was an implementing act. This time, the General Court found that the Commission decision was (a) a regulatory act because it was a non-legislative act of general application. It also held that the Commission decision was (b) of direct concern to the applicant because no discretion over its implementation was left to the Member States and (c) that the Commission decision clearly did not entail implementing measures since it imposed a direct prohibition on the use of triclosan. In *Microban*, the Court specifically addressed the third issue by confirming that the interpretation of direct concern would not be stricter in the context of the Lisbon test than in the context of the general standing test.[135]

Of course, the *Microban* decision showed the enhanced possibilities that the Lisbon test offered to private parties but it did not solve all the concerns generated by the long-standing case law in this area. In particular, the *Microban* decision did not entirely clarify the meaning to be given to the expression that the regulatory act must 'not entail implementing measures' – and the degree of differentiation between this limb of the test and the satisfaction of the test of direct concern.

Two recent judgments have now addressed these remaining issues. First, in *Palirria Souliotis v Commission*,[136] the General Court explained that the test of direct concern – which, as established in the case law, refers to the absence of 'real' or 'substantive' discretion on the part of the addressee – is different from the requirement that the act should not entail implementing measures.[137] Secondly, in *Telefónica v Commission*,[138] the Court of Justice adopted a narrow interpretation of the latter condition. Thus, it clarified that the absence of implementing measures means the absence of *any* measure to be taken by the addressee of the measure – that is, a Member State – to put the regulatory act into operation or, in other words, the absence of any measure that generates 'specific consequences' for the applicant.[139] The rationale behind this approach seems clear. If any measure is required at national level, theoretically there should be an opportunity to challenge it before a national court and hence the possibility of a preliminary ruling on validity. This interpretation raises further issues. For example, prima facie it might exclude non-legislative directives – for example a Commission directive that amends or implements a Parliament and Council directive[140] – from the ambit

[133] *Inuit Tapiriit Kanatami* (n 4) paras 50–61.   [134] Case T-262/10 [2011] ECR II-7697.
[135] *Inuit I* (n 123) paras 27–32. In fact, and although the Court applied the same parameters to decide direct concern in the general standing test, the form of words used by the Court at para 32 of the judgment leaves scope for a more relaxed interpretation of the test of direct concern in the framework of the Lisbon test.
[136] Case T-380/11, judgment of 12 September 2013, nyr.   [137] Ibid, para 44.
[138] Case C-274/12P, judgment of 19 December 2013, nyr.   [139] Ibid, paras 35 and 36.
[140] For a recent example of a non-legislative directive, see Commission Directive 2012/47/EU (OJ [2013] L31/43) amending Parliament and Council Directive 2009/43/EC on the terms and conditions of transfers of defence-related products within the Union (OJ [2009] L146/1).

of the Lisbon test. Thus, while it is possible for directives to leave little or no *discretion* to the Member States in their implementation (thus, the test for direct concern would be satisfied), they generally require *implementing* measures (thus, the test for 'not entail[ing] implementing measures' would not be satisfied). The challenge to these directives would therefore be subject to the general test on standing (which is unlikely to be satisfied due to the difficulties in showing the existence of individual concern). In practice, a challenge to these acts would always have to be made indirectly via the national route and then a preliminary reference on invalidity.

It follows from *Inuit I*, *Microban*, *Parrila Souliotis*, and *Telefónica* that the Lisbon test is simply a partial gap-plugging mechanism. In other words, it is designed to apply only where the national route for judicial review is unavailable due to the lack of national implementing measures and, as we shall see, it may not always be satisfied in that situation. Crucially, the interpretation followed by the General Court in *Inuit I* and *Microban* on the notion of regulatory acts excludes legislative acts from the Lisbon test, a position which has now been endorsed by the Court of Justice on appeal in *Inuit I*.[141] This means that, in relation to these acts, the general test still applies and hence that situations of denial of justice could still arise if the preliminary ruling avenue is not available (see section 4.2). In other words, a *UPA*-type situation could still arise today and the Lisbon test would not act as a gap-plugging mechanism.[142] In *UPA*, the Court had indicated that it could not alter the wording of the Treaty and that it was the responsibility of the Member States to ensure the existence of national avenues for bringing proceedings before the national court, where a preliminary reference on validity could be made; a finding that is now strengthened by the wording of Article 19(1) TFEU.[143] This shift of responsibility towards the national legal systems has strongly resurfaced in the recent judgment of the Court of Justice in *Inuit I*.[144] However, this non-interventionist approach of the Court still stands in stark contrast with its approach in other contexts, such as its development of the doctrine of direct effect and the principle of State liability in damages, where the Court, guided by the need to guarantee legal protection against action contrary to EU law, created a remedy to be invoked against Member States that applies *as a matter of EU law*.

The standing of associations and interest groups

The case law on Article 263(4) TFEU offers several examples of actions brought by associations created for the promotion of collective interests (eg trade associations[145]) or interest groups (eg environmental associations[146]). So far, the prospects for associations having standing have been rather bleak. In *Federolio*,[147] a case brought by a trade association,

---

[141] Case C-583/11 P (n 4) paras 50–61.

[142] In its decision in *Inuit Tapiriit Kanatami* (n 4) the Court of Justice dismissed the argument that the exclusion of legislative acts from the Lisbon test created a gap in the system of judicial protection contrary to Art 47 Charter and held that 'Article 47 of the Charter does not require that an individual should have an unconditional entitlement to bring an action for annulment of European Union legislative acts directly before the Courts of the European Union' (para 105).

[143] For a very interesting study of the concerns that arise as a result of the Court's strategy of devolving responsibility for providing judicial review to the national courts, see A Arnull, 'Judicial Review in the European Union' in A Arnull and D Chalmers (eds), *The Oxford Handbook of European Union Law* (Oxford: Oxford University Press, 2014, forthcoming).   [144] Case C-583/11 P (n 4) paras 98–107.

[145] Case T-122/96 *Federolio v Commission* [1997] ECR II-1559.

[146] Case T-585/93 *Greenpeace v Commission* [1995] ECR II-2205.

[147] Case T-122/96 (n 145).

the General Court identified the three alternative situations when these actions would be admissible:

(a) where a legal provision grants the association a series of procedural rights;

(b) where their members are themselves directly and individually concerned; and

(c) where the own interests of the association are affected, and in particular its position as negotiator is affected by the EU act in question.[148]

These conditions are notably difficult to satisfy, especially because outside the specific fields of competition, State aid, and anti-dumping proceedings it is rare for the procedural rights of associations to be laid down by legislation[149] or for associations to be active negotiators (in the sense of interlocutors of the EU institutions)[150] in the adoption of EU measures. Most actions for annulment refer to EU measures taken in the context of the common agricultural policy, where it is infrequent that trade associations are formally granted any procedural rights in the process leading to the adoption of legislative and non-legislative acts.[151]

Similar parameters applied to applications brought by interest groups. Thus, in the *Greenpeace* litigation,[152] where three environmental associations and several private individuals challenged a number of Commission decisions authorizing the granting of aid for the construction of two power stations in the Canary Islands, the General Court and the Court of Justice applied very similar criteria to those in *Federolio* with the result that the actions were dismissed as inadmissible. This result was particularly controversial at the time because of the obvious difficulties that arise for individual applicants when trying to fulfil the closed category test in the context of an environmental measure and the uncertain possibilities of an indirect challenge before the national courts. However, the effects of the *Greenpeace* line of case law have been somewhat mitigated today following the Union's signature of the UN Economic Commission for Europe (UNECE) Convention on Access to Information, Public Participation in Decision-Making and Access to Justice in Environmental Matters (the Aarhus Convention) in 1998 and the adoption of Directive 2003/4/EC on public access to environmental information,[153] which have enhanced the standing of environmental associations before national courts.[154]

In the aftermath of the Lisbon reforms, it remains to be seen whether the new standing test will have an impact on the formulation of the standing conditions applicable to associations. In particular, and in relation to the second situation set out in *Federolio* – where the association has standing if all the members individually have standing – it may be more plausible that an association or interest group might be able to challenge regulatory acts that require no implementation since individual concern is not a requirement under the Lisbon test.

---

[148] See *Federolio* (n 145) para 61. There have been some instances where the standing of associations has been eased further on the basis of the effect of the decision on their own interests *or those of its members*. See Case C-319/07 P *3F v Commission* [2009] ECR I-5963, for an interesting decision in the field of State aid, where a trade union was given standing to challenge a Commission decision finding that an aid scheme was prima facie compatible with EU law under the preliminary review procedure set out in Art 108(3) TFEU.

[149] For an example in anti-dumping proceedings, see Case 191/82 *Fediol v Commission* [1983] ECR 2913, paras 28–30.

[150] For an example in the field of State aids, see Case C-313/90 *CIRFS v Commission* [1993] ECR I-1125, paras 28–30.   [151] See eg Case *Federolio* (n 145) para 63.

[152] Stichting *Greenpeace* (n 86) and (on appeal) Case C-321/95 P *Stichting Greenpeace Council (Greenpeace International) v Commission* [1998] ECR I-1651.

[153] OJ [2003] L41/26.

[154] See also Arts 10–12 Council Regulation 1367/2007 (OJ [2006] L264/13).

3.2.5 Grounds for annulment and effects of a successful action for annulment

Once an applicant has managed to prove standing it is furthermore necessary to show that there is a suitable ground to challenge the legality of an EU act. Article 263(2) TFEU lists four grounds of annulment, which will be briefly examined in turn.

The first ground is lack of competence. The EU institutions are subject to the principle of conferral,[155] that is, they are only empowered to act in the specific areas provided by the Treaties. As a result, if an EU institution lacked the power to adopt an act – that is, there was no appropriate legal basis under the Treaty for its action – the act might be annulled by the Court due to lack of competence.[156] This ground will also be applicable where there has been an excessive delegation of power to an EU agency or institution[157] or where an institution implementing an EU act has not respected the limits of its powers or has gone beyond the mere implementation of a legislative act.[158]

The second ground is infringement of an essential procedural requirement. It applies whenever an EU institution has not complied with a rule of procedure in the adoption of the contested act. This would include, for example, failure to consult the European Parliament before adopting a measure where consultation is mandated by the Treaty,[159] failure to provide adequate reasons for the adoption of an act,[160] or infringement of the rights of the defence of the addressees of a Union act or of interested parties.[161]

The third ground for review is infringement of the Treaty or of any rule of law relating to its application. This has been understood to encompass a breach of the primary sources of EU law. Thus, it mainly includes Treaty provisions, international law provisions binding on the EU,[162] provisions contained in a measure of secondary legislation which is hierarchically superior to the contested act,[163] and general principles of law.[164] Infringement of general principles of law – which are understood in the broadest sense of the expression[165] and naturally include the rights provided in the EU Charter of Fundamental Rights – is a frequently argued ground in the context of the action of annulment.

Finally, the fourth ground is misuse of powers, which, although frequently argued, has rarely been successful because the required standard of proof is very difficult to meet. In particular, the applicant needs to show that the institution in question had the intention to use its powers for a purpose other than that for which the powers were conferred.[166]

If an action for annulment is well founded, the Court will annul the act in question[167] and such a declaration will have an *erga omnes* and *ex tunc* effect unless the Court decides otherwise. In other words, the act will be treated as if it had never existed.[168]

---

[155] Art 5(2) TEU.

[156] See Case C-376/98 *Germany v Parliament and Council* ('*Tobacco Advertising*') [2000] ECR I-8419. See further chapter 5.   [157] Case 9/56 *Meroni v High Authority* [1957–8] ECR 133, 150–152.

[158] Case 22/88 *Industrie- en Handelsonderneming Vreugdenhil BV v Minister van Landbouw en Visserij* [1989] ECR 2049, paras 16–26.   [159] Case 138/79 *Roquette Frères v Council* [1980] ECR 3333.

[160] See Case 18/57 *Nold v High Authority* [1959] ECR 41, 51–53.

[161] See Case C-291/89 *Interhotel v Commission* [1991] ECR I-2257.

[162] Joined Cases 21–24/72 *International Fruit Co NV v Produktschap voor Groenten en Fruit* [1972] ECR 1219.

[163] See eg Joined Cases 113–118/77 *NTN Toyo Bearing Co Ltd v Council* [1979] ECR 1185.

[164] See eg *Cornorníu* (n 80).   [165] See chapters 8 and 9.

[166] See eg Case 8/55 *Fédération Charbonnière de Belgique v High Authority* [1954–6] ECR 92, 303 and for a more recent example, see Case C-442/04 *Commission v Spain* [2008] ECR I-3517, paras 46–51. For a rare successful challenge in a case dealing with actions brought by civil servants of the EU, see Case 105/75 *Giuffrida v Council* [1976] ECR 1395.   [167] Art 264(1) TFEU.

[168] But see Art 264(2) TFEU, which allows for certain limitations to this principle.

3.3 **The action for failure to act**

The action for failure to act – set out in Articles 265 and 266 TFEU – represents the natural complement to the action for annulment. It is applicable where an institution, instead of acting illegally, failed to act when it had an obligation to do so. Given that the two actions represent two sides of effectively the same remedy, they share some important characteristics. However, there are also some special issues relating to the action for failure to act that should be considered separately. Of these, the most significant is an admissibility requirement, namely that *before* an action for a failure to act can be brought before the Court, the institution in question must have been called upon to act. Only if it has then failed to define its position within two months can an action be brought.[169] This is therefore an essential *pre*-litigation requirement.

Furthermore, three key issues need to be examined in connection with this means of redress. First, the time limit for bringing an action under Article 265 TFEU is two months, which starts to run after the end of the pre-litigation procedure.[170] Secondly, an action can be brought against the failure of an institution or of a body, office, or agency of the Union to adopt an act. While it is clear from the wording of Article 265(3) TFEU that such an act would have had to be a legally binding one when the action is brought by private parties, such a requirement is not specifically laid down in Article 265(1) TFEU when this action is brought by a Member State or a Union institution.[171]

Thirdly, post-Lisbon, Article 265 TFEU recognizes two categories of applicants: privileged and non-privileged. The first category encompasses the Member States and the EU institutions. The second refers to private parties. Again, and as with Article 263 TFEU, the conditions are exacting. A natural and legal person can only bring an action where an institution, body, office, or agency of the Union has 'failed to *address* to that person an act other than a recommendation or an opinion'. In fact, this is even more restrictive wording than that in Article 263(4) TFEU on three counts. It does not cover either the situation where the act in question would have been a general one or where it would have been addressed to a third party but would have been of direct and individual concern to the applicant, and it does not create a mirror image of the new Lisbon test in Article 263(4) TFEU applicable to the action for failure to act. Given that the Court has recognized that the action for annulment and the action for failure to act effectively represent two sides of the same remedy, it follows that the same requirements of standing should apply to private parties.[172] Therefore, it is somewhat surprising that the drafters of the Lisbon Treaty did not take the opportunity to align Articles 263 and 265 TFEU on this particular point.

3.4 **The plea of illegality**

The remedy of the plea of illegality is provided in Article 277 TFEU and although it is brought directly before the Court, it constitutes an incidental mechanism of review attached to a 'main' direct action. Thus, it allows an applicant who has brought a direct action before the Court – most frequently under Article 263 TFEU[173] – to plead the illegality of a general

---

[169] Art 265(2) TFEU.   [170] Ibid.

[171] On this point, see the observations by K Lenaerts, D Arts, and I Maselis, *Procedural Law of the EU* (2nd edn, London: Sweet & Maxwell, 2006) 332, who give as an example an action by the Parliament against the Commission when the latter has failed to submit a legislative proposal.

[172] See Case C-68/95 *T.Port v Commission* [1996] ECR I-6065, para 59.

[173] For a recent example, see Case T-526/10 *Inuit Tapiriit Kanatami v Commission* ('*Inuit II*'), judgment of 25 April 2013, nyr. See section 6, case study 10.1, and Figure 10.7.

EU act (ie a regulation or a directive or a general decision) that constitutes the basis of the act the annulment of which is sought in the main action pending before the Court.[174] A typical example would be a case where a Commission implementing regulation is being challenged before the Court by means of Article 263 TFEU proceedings. In the course of these proceedings, the applicants may wish to bring a plea of illegality against the parent legislative regulation (ie a Parliament and Council regulation) that constituted the basis of the implementing Commission regulation.[175]

There are therefore two important limitations to the use of Article 277 TFEU proceedings: they can only be brought against an *act of general application* and they are dependent on the existence of another action pending before the Court.[176] According to the literal wording of Article 277 TFEU, *any* party may bring a plea of illegality[177] but historically it was brought mostly by private parties attempting to escape the stringent standing conditions that applied to the direct challenge of general acts in the context of Article 263(4) TFEU.[178] As we have seen, their chances of success were very limited, particularly because the application of the tests of direct and individual concern frequently acted as a barrier to the admissibility of the main action of annulment – without which the plea of illegality could not prosper. In this sense, the Lisbon reforms to Article 263(4) TFEU offer an interesting new dimension to the use of the plea of illegality, because in those cases where the Lisbon test now applies, the use of the Article 277 TFEU action might be much more viable. Case study 10.1 shows precisely this in the context of the *Inuit* litigation.[179]

Finally, the grounds for the annulment of the act of general application are the same as those that apply in the context of the action for annulment.

3.5 **The action for damages**

The action for damages is set out in Articles 268 TFEU and 340(2) TFEU. It covers the situation where an applicant has suffered damage or loss as a result of illegal action by a Union institution or by its civil servants. It is an independent action[180] and its aim is to obtain an award in damages.[181] Therefore, unlike the other direct actions that we have considered so far, it is not a declaratory action.[182] In theory, any party may bring an action for damages but in practice, all actions have been brought by natural and legal persons. No standing conditions are attached to the action and the Statute of the Court provides a time limit of five years from the occurrence of the event giving rise to liability.[183] Despite these

---

[174] See in this respect, the observations of the Court in Case 92/78 *Simmenthal v Commission* [1979] ECR 777, para 36.

[175] For an illustration on how this mechanism operates, see Figure 10.6, which describes the *Inuit* litigation.

[176] See eg Joined Cases 87/77, 130/77, 22/83, 9/84 and 10/84 *Salerno v Commission and Council* [1985] ECR 2523, para 36.

[177] For an example of where an institution has brought a plea of illegality, see Case C-11/00 *Commission v European Central Bank* [2003] ECR I-7147, paras 76–78. See further M Vogt, 'Indirect Judicial Protection in EC Law: The Case of the Plea of Illegality' (2006) 31 *European Law Review* 364, 369–370.

[178] See *Simmenthal* (n 174) para 41.   [179] See section 6, case study 10.1.

[180] Case 4/69 *Lütticke v Commission* [1971] ECR 325, para 6.

[181] In practice, and notwithstanding the independence of the action for damages, applicants frequently bring together an action for annulment and an action for damages. See section 6, case study 10.2.

[182] As AG Sharpston pointed out in her Opinion in Case C-131/03 *RJ Reynolds Tobacco Holdings* [2006] ECR I-7795 referring to the Court's case law: 'A remedy for damages does not fall within the system of judicial review. Rather, it is an autonomous form of action, with a particular purpose to fulfil within the system of legal remedies.... An action for damages depends on a measure or on unlawful conduct having adverse material consequences for the applicant, whereas an action for annulment depends on its having legal consequences' (para 74).   [183] Art 46 Statute of the Court.

apparently generous conditions, private applicants have had limited success when bringing this action, mainly as a result of a restrictive interpretation of the requirements necessary to show liability on the part of the EU institutions.

In *Lütticke*,[184] the Court laid down three conditions to establish liability. These are:

(a) the existence of an unlawful act or conduct on the part of the institution;

(b) actual damage suffered by the applicant; and

(c) a causal link between the illegality of the act and the damage suffered by the applicant.

While these basic conditions have remained essentially unaltered since they were first introduced, an important case law evolution has taken place in the interpretation of the first one. Thus, and in the specific context of actions for damages brought against illegal Union acts,[185] the Court has shifted the parameters for the assessment of the nature and degree of that illegality.

Initially, a formalistic and very narrow approach prevailed in the early decision of the Court in *Aktien-Zuckerfabrik Schöppenstedt v Council*,[186] where the Court held that where the illegality stemmed from a *legislative* act 'involving measures of economic policy', the institutions would not incur liability unless 'a sufficiently flagrant violation of a superior rule of law for the protection of the individual has occurred'. [187] Suffice to say, this formula was extremely difficult to satisfy[188] and the case law on actions for damages arising from EU regulations and directives at the time showed that only in the most extreme of circumstances would private applicants manage to reach this formidable threshold of illegality.[189] In the case of individual acts, such as decisions, this enhanced ceiling of illegality did not apply.

A turning point in the case law, however, was the decision of the Court in *Bergaderm*,[190] where a private applicant sought compensation for damage arising from the restrictions on the use of certain ingredients in cosmetic products introduced by an EU directive and which had the effect of preventing the sale of one of the applicant's products. Although the applicant was unsuccessful, the ruling of the Court was highly relevant. First and foremost, it aligned the requirements of liability that apply, as a matter of EU law, when a Member State has infringed EU law and which were introduced by the *Francovich* line of case law[191] with those that apply where the liability emanates from an unlawful EU act.[192] This means that liability for unlawful acts under Articles 268 and 340(2) TFEU now arises where the rule of law infringed by the act was intended to confer rights on individuals, the breach is sufficiently serious, and there is a causal link between the breach attributable to the institution and the damage suffered by the applicant.

Furthermore, in the interpretation of the second condition – in parallel with cases on State liability – the Court drew a distinction depending *not* on the form of the act (eg general or individual)[193] but on a substantive criterion, namely whether the enacting

---

[184] Case 4/69 (n 180) para 10.

[185] While this section focuses on liability arising from illegal binding Union acts, see for an example of an action for damages against illegal *conduct* of the institutions, the sadly famous *Adams* case (Case 145/83 [1985] ECR 3539).   [186] Case 5/71 [1971] ECR 975.   [187] Ibid, para 11.

[188] See eg Case C-143/77 *Koninklijke Scholten-Honig v Council and Commission* [1979] ECR 3583.

[189] See, for rare, successful examples, section 6, case study 10.2 and case study 10.3.

[190] Case C-352/98 P *Laboratoires pharmaceutiques Bergaderm SA and Jean-Jacques Goupil v Commission* [2000] ECR I-5291. See further T Tridimas, 'Liability for Breach of Community Law: Growing Up and Mellowing Down?' (2001) 38 *Common Market Law Review* 301.

[191] See, in particular, Joined Cases C-46/93 and C-48/93 *Brasserie du Pêcheur and Factortame* [1996] ECR I-1029, considered in chapter 6.

[192] *Laboratoires pharmaceutiques Bergaderm SA* (n 190) paras 41 and 42.   [193] Ibid, paras 46 and 47.

institution enjoys discretion in the adoption of the measure. If the institution has discretion, that condition is fulfilled only if the institution in question has 'manifestly and gravely disregarded the limits of its discretion'.[194] However, where the institution has reduced or no discretion in the adoption of the act, the mere infringement of EU law suffices to establish liability.[195]

While the requirements to establish liability arising from discretionary acts are still demanding, *Bergaderm* has the merit of adopting a substantive rather than a formalistic approach in the determination of liability arising from EU acts and of introducing consistency in the tests for suing the Member States and the Union institutions in damages. While there have been suggestions in other areas of EU law that the Court tends to be more deferential towards the EU institutions than towards the Member States – for example when appraising the legality of their actions in light of the principle of proportionality[196] – the ruling in *Bergardem* sends a message of coherence and equality in the assessment of the parameters of liability arising from illegal acts.

4 Preliminary references

As explained previously, the preliminary reference procedure is a very different judicial avenue from direct actions. The parties in the case bring their action before the national court, rather than before the Court of Justice. At some stage in these proceedings, the national court makes a reference to the Court of Justice on a point of either the interpretation or the validity of EU law that is relevant to the case. The Court of Justice delivers a preliminary ruling, which is then applied to the facts of the case by the national court. From the standpoint of the Court of Justice, this is therefore (unlike the direct actions) a non-contentious procedure, where the parties in the main action have no right of initiative and are merely invited to be heard.[197] The preliminary reference mechanism is seen by the Court as the ultimate manifestation of the relationship of cooperation between the national courts and the Court of Justice[198] and as a reflection of their role as equal partners in the development of EU law. As a result, the Court has repeatedly construed the system of preliminary references as based not on the hierarchically infused relationship existing between a court of first instance and a court of appeal but on a separation of tasks between the national courts and the Court of Justice. While the role of the Court is to interpret or decide on the validity of EU law, that of the national court is to take cognizance of the facts of the case and of the applicable national law, to decide on the need and grounds for a reference and to apply the ruling of the Court to the case in hand.[199] However, as we shall see later, the development of the case law has occasionally cast some doubt on this outwardly neat division of responsibilities.

In the words of the Court, the essential function of Article 267 TFEU is to ensure that EU law is applied uniformly by the national courts.[200] This objective extends both to situations

---

[194] *Laboratoires pharmaceutiques Bergaderm SA* (n 190) para 43.   [195] Ibid, para 44.
[196] See chapter 8.   [197] Case 44/65 *Hessische Knappschaft v Maison Singer* [1965] ECR 965, 971.
[198] See Case 283/81 *CILFIT and Lanificio di Gavardo SpA v Ministry of Health* [1982] ECR 3415, para 7.
[199] Case 6/64 *Flaminio Costa v ENEL* [1964] ECR 585, 593 and Case 35/76 *Simmenthal SpA v Ministero delle
:liano* [1976] ECR 1871, para 4. On this separation of functions, see further the Recommendations
| courts and tribunals in relation to the initiation of preliminary ruling proceedings (OJ [2012]
ιras 7–10.
66/80 *International Chemical Corporation v Amministrazione delle finanze dello Stato* [1981] ECR
11. See also Case 166/73 *Rheinmühlen-Düsseldorf v Einfuhr- und Vorratsstelle für Getreide und
/* [1974] ECR 33, para 2.

where a national court is confronted with the application of EU law[201] and to those where it is faced with disputes as to the validity of EU acts[202] – which generate, respectively, preliminary references on interpretation and preliminary references on validity. Additionally, the preliminary reference procedure performs other related functions stemming from this primary goal. Thus, it contributes to the coherent development of EU law[203] and it acts as an indirect mechanism for the review of the legality of EU acts.[204]

The procedure is set out in Article 267 TFEU. Post-Lisbon, that provision is divided into four paragraphs, which delineate the key features of the system of preliminary references. Thus, Article 267(1) TFEU determines the existence of two kinds of preliminary references: on the interpretation and on the validity of EU law. The second and third paragraphs establish a difference between two types of national courts: those which have the discretion to refer and those which have an obligation to refer. Thus, whereas any national court or tribunal *may* make a reference to the Court, only those against whose decisions there is no judicial remedy *must* make a reference to the Court if a relevant question of EU law needs to be decided in order to give their judgment. Finally, the Lisbon Treaty added a fourth paragraph to the text of Article 267 in order to reflect the urgent preliminary ruling procedure[205] (PPU, as an acronym for the French denomination of this procedure), for cases where a reference is made for a person in custody.[206] We will consider these issues in turn.

4.1 What constitutes a 'court or tribunal of a Member State'?

The entire system of preliminary references rests on the entitlement or the obligation (as the case may be) of *national courts and tribunals* to ask questions on the interpretation or on the validity of EU law to the Court of Justice. The initiative to request a preliminary reference belongs exclusively to a national court or tribunal and it is therefore essential to ascertain which national bodies fit this specification. The Treaty did not define what constitutes a national court or tribunal for these purposes but a rich body of case law now gives us the characteristics that must be present, as a matter of EU law, for a national referring body to be classified as such. For example, in *Syfait I*[207] the Court provided a helpful summary of the main *cumulative* factors that determine this classification. Thus, the body must be

(a) established by law,

(b) have a permanent existence,

---

[201] See eg *Van Gend en Loos* (n 35).

[202] Case 314/85 *Foto-Frost v Hauptzollamt Lübeck-Ost* [1987] ECR 4199, para 15.

[203] Thus, some of the fundamental principles and doctrines in EU law, such as direct effect; supremacy; vertical direct effect of directives; State liability in damages; or procedural autonomy, equivalence, and effectiveness have all been developed through preliminary rulings.

[204] See eg Case C-263/02 P *Commission v Jégo-Quéré* [2004] ECR I-3425, para 30.

[205] See further C Barnard, 'The PPU: Is It Worth the Candle? An Early Assessment' (2009) 34 *European Law Review* 281.

[206] The Court has interpreted the wording in Art 267(4) TFEU broadly to include other cases, ie the wrongful removal of a child. See eg Case C-403/09 PPU *Detiček* [2009] ECR I-12193.

[207] See Case C-53/03 *Synetairismos Farmakopoion Aitolias & Akarnanias (Syfait) v GlaxoSmithKline plc and GlaxoSmithKline AEVE* ('*Syfait I*') [2005] ECR I-4609, para 29. On the requirement of independence and that the referring body is one acting as a third party in relation to the authority which adopted the decision under appeal, see Case C-24/92 *Corbiau v Administration des contributions* [1993] ECR I-1277, concerning a reference made by a tax authority, para 15 and *Syfait I*, above, involving a reference made by the Greek competition authority, paras 21–38. In both cases, the Court declined to give a reference because the referring bodies were not courts or tribunals within the meaning of Art 267 TFEU.

(c) exercise binding jurisdiction,

(d) its procedure must be *inter partes*,

(e) must apply the rule of law, and

(f) be independent.

Additionally, a national court may refer a question to the Court only if

(a) there is a case pending before it, and

(b) it is called upon to give judgment in proceedings intended to lead to a decision of a judicial nature.[208]

In many cases, it will be obvious that a national body fulfils these characteristics but there have been some instances where the particular features of a national referring body have provided interesting opportunities for the Court to assess whether they were national courts or tribunals within the meaning of Article 267 TFEU.[209]

4.2 Types of preliminary references: references on the interpretation and references on the validity of EU law

According to the first paragraph of Article 267 TFEU, there are two types of preliminary rulings: interpretative rulings and rulings on the validity of EU law. Preliminary references on the *interpretation* of EU law can request the interpretation of Treaty provisions;[210] general principles of law; or of acts of the institutions, bodies, or agencies of the Union. The latter encompass not only legally binding acts such as regulations, directives, and decisions but also non-legally binding acts such as recommendations and opinions[211] or even judgments of the Court.[212] According to the principle of separation of functions that permeates the preliminary reference procedure,[213] the Court of Justice can only interpret EU law but not decide on the legality of national law.[214] This is true inasmuch as questions on the interpretation of EU law are formulated in abstract terms and the Court will never directly conclude that a specific national measure is illegal. However, in practice, most interpretative questions are about the compatibility of national measures with EU law and, in many of these cases, the application of preliminary rulings on interpretation will leave the national courts with no alternative other than to declare that a national measure or principle is contrary to EU law.[215]

Preliminary references on *validity* can *only* concern legally binding acts of the institutions, bodies, or agencies of the Union. One fundamental aspect of this type of reference – which is, surprisingly, not reflected in the Treaty – was developed by the Court of Justice in its seminal decision in *Foto-Frost v Hauptzollamt Lübeck-Ost*.[216] There, one of the questions

---

[208] See *Syfait I* (n 207) para 29.

[209] See eg the case law on the position of national arbitral tribunals, ie Case 102/81 *Nordsee Deutsche Hochseefischerei GmbH v Reederei Mond Hochseefischerei Nordstern* [1982] ECR 1095, where an arbitrator appointed privately by the parties which did not fulfil *all* of these criteria, was not considered a court or tribunal for Art 267 TFEU purposes.   [210] See eg *Van Gend en Loos* (n 35).

[211] Case C-322/88 *Grimaldi v Fonds des maladies professionnelles* [1989] ECR I-4407.

[212] Case 135/77 *Bosch GmbH v Hauptzollamt Hildesheim* [1978] ECR 859.   [213] See section 4.

[214] Case C-373/89 *Caisse d'assurances sociales pour travailleurs indépendants 'Integrity' v Rouvroy* [1990] ECR I-4243, para 9.

[215] See, for some high-profile examples, Case C-271/91 *Marshall v Southampton and South-West Hampshire Area Health Authority* [1993] ECR I-4367 or *Factortame I* (n 36).

[216] Case 314/85 (n 202).

referred to the Court was whether a national court could review the legality of an EU meas-ure. The Court developed its reasoning on the basis that the essential purpose of the Article 267 TFEU procedure is to ensure a uniform application of EU law, which is of course indis-pensable for the functioning and survival of the Union legal order. If national courts could declare the invalidity of EU acts, this uniformity would be immediately lost. Therefore, the Court concluded that, while national courts could always *confirm the validity* of EU acts and not make a reference to the Court – as this would not jeopardize the unity of the Union legal system – *only the Court of Justice has the power to declare an EU act invalid*. Hence, a preliminary reference on validity is *always* mandatory where a national court has some doubts about the legality of a Union measure.[217] The finding of the Court in that case was further supported by the need to ensure a coherent system of judicial protection. Thus, given that the Court has exclusive jurisdiction to declare EU acts void under Article 263 TFEU, the power to annul EU acts must also be reserved to the Court of Justice.[218]

4.2.1 The relationship between annulment proceedings and preliminary references on validity

Preliminary rulings on validity offer private parties wishing to challenge the legality of EU acts an attractive alternative to the rigours of the standing tests imposed by Article 263 TFEU, as the Court itself has frequently pointed out.[219] A representation of the relation-ship between these two avenues can be found in Figure 10.5. However, the preliminary reference avenue does not *always* guarantee a remedy for private parties unable to sat-isfy the Article 263 TFEU conditions. Thus, in his Opinion in *UPA*[220] Advocate General Jacobs persuasively argued the insufficient value of this mechanism as an alternative to a direct challenge of an EU act under annulment proceedings. Apart from pointing out some procedural disadvantages and the fact that the decision on whether to refer and on the appropriate grounds of invalidity rest with the national court, he referred to cases where it would be less than straightforward for national proceedings – in the context of which a reference could be made – to be triggered. These would include cases where the EU meas-ure in question did not require implementing measures at national level (the facts of *UPA* itself), cases where an applicant would have to break the law first in order to challenge sanctions and thus set off proceedings (as would have been the case with *Jégo-Quéré*)[221] or cases where national law requirements would make it difficult or impossible to challenge national measures implementing EU law.[222]

While the introduction of the Lisbon test in Article 263(4) TFEU has somewhat miti-gated these objections, it is argued that a watertight system between these two remedies has not yet been fully achieved because, as we saw previously, the Lisbon test does not apply to legislative measures.[223] Thus, in the case of a legislative measure that does not require implementation (eg a Council and Parliament regulation imposing a direct pro-hibition on the use of a particular substance), it is still conceivable that neither a direct challenge nor a preliminary reference on validity might be available to a private applicant. The compatibility of this result with Articles 47 and 51 of the EU Charter of Fundamental Rights seems doubtful. Nevertheless, in its recent decision in *Inuit I*, the Court of Justice has intimated that the burden is on the national legal systems to ensure that an avenue to

---

[217] Ibid, paras 14–16.   [218] Ibid, para 17.

[219] See eg *Stichting Greenpeace Council* (n 152) para 33.

[220] Case C-50/00 P (n 116). See further nn 116–120 and accompanying text.

[221] Ibid, para 102 of the Opinion.

[222] See eg Case C-432/05 *Unibet (London) Ltd and Unibet (International) Ltd v Justitiekanslern* [2007] ECR I-2271 and A Arnull, 'The Principle of Effective Judicial Protection in EU Law: An Unruly Horse?' (2011) 36 *European Law Review* 51.   [223] See section 3.2.4.4, The Lisbon test.

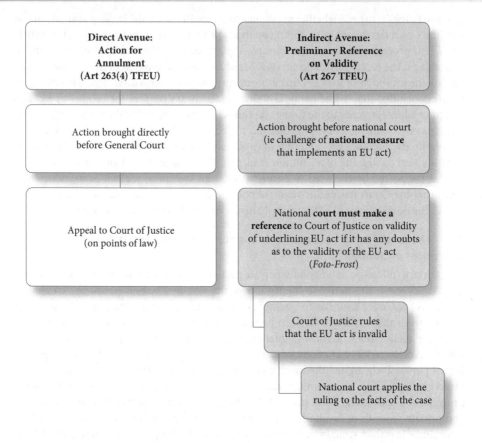

Fig 10.5 Private parties and the challenge of EU acts: the relationship between annulment proceedings and preliminary rulings on validity

make a preliminary reference to the Court of Justice *is* available under national law.[224] Future case law is necessary to elaborate how this approach might apply in cases involving the challenge of EU legislative measures that do not require any kind of implementation at national level.

An interesting aspect of the relationship between the action for annulment and preliminary rulings on validity was developed by the Court in *TWD Textilwerke Deggendorf GmbH v Bundesrepublik Deutschland*.[225] There, the Court provided a rule to prevent the evasion of time limits when an applicant had a clear possibility of bringing an action for annulment. Essentially, if an applicant would *clearly* have had standing to bring a direct action for annulment under Article 263 TFEU but did not do so within the time limit, the Court will not entertain a reference on validity if the applicant subsequently brings proceedings before the national court. In fact, the practical application of this rule is rather limited. First, and with the exceptions of where an applicant was the addressee of an act and a few other (rare) instances where consistent lines of case law indicate that an applicant would have certainly had standing to bring annulment proceedings,[226] it will normally

---

[224] See *Inuit Tapiriit Kanatami* (n 4) paras 100–104.   [225] Case C-188/92 [1994] ECR I-833.
[226] This could be the case, eg in competition, State aid, and anti-dumping proceedings. The *TWD* case concerned the challenge of a decision in the field of State aid.

be uncertain that an applicant would have had standing.[227] Depending on how the Court interprets the Lisbon text, this qualification may well change if clear case law emerges on the standing of private parties to challenge regulatory acts. Secondly, nothing prevents an applicant from bringing simultaneous proceedings before the Court of Justice – within the time limit set out in Article 263(6) TFEU – and before the national court, with the hope that a preliminary reference on validity will be made to the Court.

4.3 Discretion to refer and limits to this discretion

According to Article 267(2) TFEU, *any* national court or tribunal *may* make a reference to the Court when a case is actively pending before it if it considers that a decision on a question of EU law is necessary to enable it to give judgment. Thus any national court, however low in the judicial echelons of a Member State, has the broadest discretion to make a reference to the Court.[228] The separation of functions that underlines the preliminary reference procedure determines that only the national court can make these decisions and that the Court of Justice should not interfere in the exercise of this discretion.

However, as the caseload of the Court increased dramatically, the Court began to set what prima facie could be construed as limitations on this unfettered discretion by declaring the inadmissibility of some references from national courts that did not comply with certain criteria. Thus, there are broadly four main categories of cases where references have been rejected on this basis.[229]

First, the Court held in *Foglia v Novello*[230] that it would not entertain a reference where there is evidence that the parties before the national court have no genuine dispute and have contrived proceedings with the exclusive purpose of triggering a reference on a particular point of EU law. In that case, it appeared that the motive of the parties was to obtain a ruling from the Court that could then be applied to find the incompatibility of a French tax with Article 110 TFEU. Clearly, the function of the Court under Article 267 TFEU is to deliver rulings that will be applicable to a real dispute between the parties in national proceedings rather than provide advisory opinions. However, the controversial aspect of this decision rests in the conclusion that the Court of Justice should effectively have the power to question the *appropriateness* of the decision to refer – when the national court alone had direct knowledge of the facts and still decided to make a reference.[231]

Secondly, the Court has declined to give a reference in cases where it has found that the question referred was irrelevant, namely that it bore no relation to the actual case or to the subject matter of the action,[232] and, thirdly, where questions submitted were judged to

---

[227] See eg Case C-241/95 *The Queen v Intervention Board for Agricultural Produce, ex p Accrington Beef* [1996] ECR I-6699.

[228] *Rheinmühlen-Düsseldorf* (n 200) para 4.

[229] See C Barnard and E Sharpston, 'The Changing Face of Article 177 References' (1997) 34 *Common Market Law Review* 1113.   [230] Case 104/79 [1980] ECR 745.

[231] See further G Bebr, 'The Existence of a Genuine Dispute: An Indispensable Precondition for the Jurisdiction of the Court under Article 177 EEC Treaty [now Art 267 TFEU]' (1980) 17 *Common Market Law Review* 525. While the *Foglia* approach has not been broadly applied by the Court, in more recent years, the decision in Case C-318/00 *Bacardi-Martini SAS and Cellier des Dauphins v Newcastle United Football Co* [2003] ECR I-905 shows some similarities with that decision. The reference was also dismissed as inadmissible. However, there has also been support for the approach of the Court in *Foglia*, see D Wyatt, '*Foglia* (No 2): The Court Denies It has Jurisdiction to Give Advisory Opinions' (1982) 7 *European Law Review* 186.

[232] Case 126/80 *Salonia v Poidomani and Giglio* [1981] ECR 1563, para 6 and Case C-343/90 *Lourenço Dias v Director da Alfândega do Porto* [1992] ECR I-04673, para 18.

be hypothetical.[233] Considering the constraints under which the Court operates, it makes sense to avoid a proliferation of references which technically do not satisfy the terms of Article 267 TFEU because they are not really necessary to give judgment. On the one hand, it could be argued that only the national court can decide that a reference is not necessary. By virtue of the Court taking on this role instead, an erosion of the principle of separation of functions between the national courts and the Court and interference on the discretion of the national court under Article 267(2) TFEU could be said to have occurred. On the other, the approach of the Court in these cases could simply be seen as a question of jurisdiction. Thus, it could be argued that if the question referred is not necessary for solving the dispute, the Court simply has no jurisdiction under the terms of Article 267 TFEU and that the Court is simply verifying in these cases whether it has jurisdiction or not.

Fourthly, and much less controversially because there is no real interference on the discretion of the national court, the Court may declare references inadmissible where the national court has not articulated the questions properly[234] or has failed to submit sufficient information on the factual and legal background to the case.[235] If the Court is to give a helpful ruling, it needs the national courts to provide the necessary platform to do so. The main formal requirements that national courts should follow when formulating references are set out in Article 94 of the new Rules of Procedure of the Court of Justice.[236] These include setting out clearly the factual and legal background to the main proceedings, the relevant provisions of national law, and a statement of the reasons that prompted the national court to make a reference.

4.4 The duty to refer and the exceptions to this duty

Article 267(3) TFEU imposes an obligation to refer on national courts 'against whose decisions there is no judicial remedy' when a question on the validity or interpretation of EU law which is necessary to give judgment arises before them. These courts, as the Court has clarified,[237] include not only the highest courts in the judicial system of a Member State, such as the Supreme Court in the United Kingdom, but also those courts against whose decision there is no remedy *in the particular case*. This is relevant, for example, where small sums of money are involved and hence there is no possibility of appeal against the decision of a lower court[238] or in the case of appellate courts. The case law has established that if the decisions of an appellate court can be challenged before a supreme court, then the appellate court will not be a court of last resort in the sense of Article 267(3) TFEU.[239] However, if the appellate court has the power to prevent a further appeal, then it will be classified as a court of last resort and must make a reference.

The duty to refer relevant questions[240] imposed on courts of last resort seems to be an absolute one under the terms of Article 267(3) TFEU. However, the Court has created two main exceptions to this duty. The first is where the question referred is materially identical

---

[233] Case C-83/91 *Meilicke v ADV/ORGA FA Meyer AG* [1992] ECR I-4871, para 30, where a lengthy set of questions concerning the interpretation of an EU company law directive were held to be hypothetical.

[234] Ibid.

[235] Joined Cases C-320–322/90 *Telemarsicabruzzo v Circostel* [1993] ECR I-393.   [236] See n 11.

[237] *Flaminio Costa* (n 199) 592.   [238] Ibid.

[239] Case C-99/00 *Criminal proceedings against Kenny Roland Lyckeskog* [2002] ECR I-4839, para 16.

[240] The national court does not have an obligation to refer questions that are not necessary to give judgment (Case 283/81 *CILFIT and Lanificio di Gavardo SpA v Ministry of Health* [1982] ECR 3415, para 10). This stems from the letter of Art 267(2) and (3) TFEU.

to a question that has already been answered in a preliminary ruling[241] or where the points of law have already been dealt with by the Court in a previous ruling.[242] While the national court can still seek a ruling in this case, the Court has held that it has no obligation to do so.[243]

The second exception is more controversial and was laid down in the Court's landmark judgment in *CILFIT*.[244] There, the Court held that a national court of last resort does not have an obligation to seek a ruling from the Court 'where the correct application of Union law may be so obvious as to leave no scope for any reasonable doubt as to the manner in which the question raised is to be resolved'.[245] This is known as the *acte clair* doctrine. The reason why this exception is controversial is because it could be technically open to abuse and national courts of last resort might not make a reference by arguing that the interpretation of EU law is clear beyond doubt in circumstances where a reference is actually necessary.

On the one hand, this argument can be countered by the fact that in *CILFIT* the Court imposed draconian requirements on national courts before they can decide that a reference is not necessary. Thus, they have to compare all the different language versions of the provision of EU law at stake, take account of the peculiar EU law terminology and of the different meaning of legal concepts in EU law and in the national legal systems, and place every provision of EU law in its context and interpret it in light of EU law as a whole and of its particular state of evolution.[246] A rigorous application of these conditions therefore acts as a very reliable safeguard against the misuse of this exception and prevents an incorrect interpretation of EU law by the national courts. On the other hand, however, it could also be argued that it is difficult to monitor the proper application of these conditions by the national courts and hence that a careless use of *CILFIT* could ultimately result in a flawed application of EU law at the national level.[247] Furthermore, the decision in *CILFIT* ultimately dilutes the mandatory character of references under Article 267(3) TFEU. The application of the doctrine of State liability in damages, which the case law has extended to breaches of EU law by national courts of last resort,[248] appears as the only – but rather uncertain – mechanism available to parties before a national court of last resort to prevent an abuse of the *CILFIT* doctrine.[249]

4.5 Effects of a preliminary ruling

A preliminary ruling on interpretation delivered by the Court of Justice is binding on the national referring court[250] but other national courts and public authorities should treat the ruling as authoritative.[251] A preliminary ruling on validity, while technically only addressed to the referring court, gives ground for any other national court to regard the act as void

---

[241] Joined Cases 28–30/62 *Da Costa v Nederlandse Belastingadministratie* [1963] ECR 31, 38.
[242] *CILFIT* (n 240) para 14. [243] Ibid, para 15. [244] Ibid. [245] Ibid, para 16.
[246] Ibid, paras 17–20.
[247] The *CILFIT* decision attracted a great deal of attention in the academic literature and different views were formed as to its value and implications. See, among others, A Arnull, 'The Use and Abuse of Article 177 EEC [now 267 TFEU]' (1989) 52 *Modern Law Review* 622 and H Rasmussen, 'The European Court's *Acte Clair* Strategy in *CILFIT*' (1984) 9 *European Law Review* 242.
[248] See Case C-224/01 *Köbler v Republik Österreich* [2003] ECR I-10329.
[249] In theory, the Commission or another Member State could also bring infringement proceedings under Arts 258 and 259 TFEU. [250] Case 52/76 *Benedetti v Munari* [1977] ECR 163, para 26.
[251] *Da Costa* (n 241).

for the purposes of any judgment they are supposed to give.[252] Thus, effectively, there is little difference between the outcome of a successful action for annulment and that of a preliminary ruling on validity.

5 Interim relief

In the previous sections we considered the basic division between direct actions and preliminary references and we examined their characteristics and mode of application. One very important aspect to both sets of proceedings is how to protect the interests of parties affected while the main actions are pending before the Court of Justice and the national court respectively. This raises the question of the regulation of interim measures. Three main types of scenarios can be distinguished.

First, in relation to *direct actions*, interlocutory relief is provided in the Treaty itself. Thus, Articles 278 and 279 TFEU allow for the application for negative and positive interim relief in connection with a main direct action pending before the Court. The conditions for interim relief are set out in the Rules of Procedure of the Court of Justice[253] and include the existence of urgency – which is normally appraised considering whether there is a threat of serious and irreparable damage to the applicant – and of a prima facie case.

Secondly, in the case of *preliminary references on interpretation*, and particularly when the compatibility of national measures with EU law is at stake before the national court, interim relief will be granted according to the rules of national law while a reference is pending as long as these rules are both effective and non-discriminatory. For instance, in *Factortame I*[254] national principles on the application of interim relief were contested before the Court of Justice, while the main substantive reference on the interpretation of EU law – which, in practice, sought to ascertain the compatibility of UK legislation with EU law – was pending before the Court.[255]

Finally, where a *preliminary reference on validity* is pending before the Court, interim relief is not provided in the Treaty but common principles were developed by the Court of Justice as a natural consequence of the *Foto-Frost*[256] decision. Thus, in *Zuckerfabrik*[257] the Court held that a national court could suspend the enforcement of a *national measure* based on an EU measure the validity of which is being questioned before the Court of Justice (negative interim relief) and in *Atlanta*[258] that a national court could grant interim measures pending the ruling on validity from the Court of Justice (positive interim relief). While this is still *national* interim relief from a procedural point of view, binding conditions for granting interlocutory relief were developed in these judgments as a matter of EU law. These conditions are that a reference on validity must have been made to the Court, that there is urgency or the threat of serious and irreparable damage to the applicant, and that the national court takes account of the EU's interests.[259]

---

[252] *International Chemical Corporation* (n 200) para 13.

[253] See Art 160 Rules of Procedure of the Court of Justice and section 6, case study 10.1 and case study 10.2.

[254] See *Factortame I* (n 36).

[255] Case C-221/89 *Factortame II* [1991] ECR I-3905.   [256] Case 314/85 (n 202).

[257] Case C-143/88 *Zuckerfabrik Süderdithmarschen AG v Hauptzollamt Itzehoe* [1991] ECR I-415.

[258] Case C-465/93 *Atlanta Fruchthandelsgesellschaft mbH v Bundesamt für Ernährung und Forstwirtschaft* [1995] ECR I-3761.   [259] *Zuckerfabrik* (n 257) para 33.

6 The relationship between the Treaty remedies

As explained at the beginning of this chapter, it is important to understand how the system of remedies provided in the Treaty operates as an integrated whole. In this section, we will use three brief examples to illustrate how they interact in concrete cases.

Case study 10.1: Seal products, animal welfare, and hunting for subsistence: the *Inuit* litigation

Following concerns expressed by the European Parliament and by citizens and consumers in the EU on the application of cruel methods for the hunting of seals, several initiatives were taken at Union level to restrict the importation of seal products into the EU. In 2009, the Council and the European Parliament adopted Regulation 1007/2009[260] – under what is, post-Lisbon, the ordinary legislative procedure[261] – based on Article 114 TFEU with the aim of harmonizing national rules across the EU concerning the commercialization of seal products in the EU. According to the Preamble, the main aim of the Regulation was to eliminate the fragmentation of the internal market caused by different national rules and to take into account animal welfare considerations.[262] Essentially, the Regulation only allowed the placing in the Union market of seal products where these were the result of traditional methods of hunting by Inuit communities and contributed to their subsistence.[263]

The litigation originated by this Regulation provides an interesting example of the interplay between the action for annulment, the plea of illegality, and the application for interim relief (connected with the direct actions provided in the TFEU) (see Figure 10.6). In *Inuit I*,[264] several applicants including associations representing the Inuit people, seal hunters, trappers, and companies involved in the processing of seal products brought annulment proceedings against the Regulation under Article 263 TFEU. While the main action was pending, the applicants also applied for negative interim relief under Article 278 TFEU,[265] asking for the suspension of the Regulation. The application for interim relief was rejected by the General Court because the existence of urgency, one of the conditions for the grant of interim relief, was not present. In September 2011, the General Court issued its Order in *Inuit I*, where it concluded that the special Lisbon standing test was inapplicable given that Regulation 1007/2009 was a genuine legislative act and hence not within the meaning given to the notion of 'regulatory act' by the Court in that same case.[266] As a result, the General Court went on to apply the general standing test, found that the applicants were not individually concerned, and dismissed the action for annulment as inadmissible. The Court of Justice subsequently upheld the General Court's interpretation on appeal in *Inuit Tapiriit Kanatami*.[267]

---

[260] OJ [2009] L286/6.   [261] Then Art 251 EC and post-Lisbon Art 294 TFEU.

[262] See recitals 1–10 in the Preamble to the Regulation.

[263] See Art 3(1) Regulation 1007/2009 and the additional limited exceptions in Art 3(2).

[264] Case T-18/10 (n 123). See also sections 3.2 and 3.4.

[265] Case T-18/10 R *Inuit Tapiriit Kanatami v European Parliament and Council* [2010] ECR II-75. A second application for interim relief, also dismissed, was brought in Case T-18/10 R II [2010] ECR II-235.

[266] See section 3.2.4.4, The Lisbon test.   [267] Case C-583/11 P (n 4) and section 3.2.4.4, The Lisbon test.

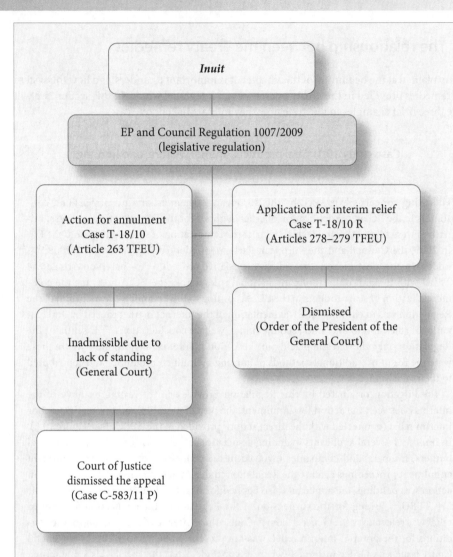

Fig 10.6 The Inuit litigation ('*Inuit I*') (Case T-18/10)

In August 2010, the Commission – which had been given implementing powers by Regulation 1007/2009 (the 'parent regulation')[268] – adopted Regulation 737/2010[269] (the 'implementing regulation') laying down detailed rules for the implementation of the parent regulation. Undoubtedly aware of the possible standing difficulties that they might encounter in the direct challenge of the parent regulation in *Inuit I* – which was pending at the time – several of the applicants who had brought the annulment action in *Inuit I*, brought a second action for annulment before the General Court in *Inuit II*.[270] This time, they directly challenged the Commission implementing regulation and simultaneously raised a plea of illegality against the parent regulation (see Figure 10.7). This case offered a good opportunity for the General Court to reaffirm its construction of the Lisbon standing test – especially since the Commission regulation could, in all likelihood, be classified as a 'regulatory

---

[268] OJ [2009] L286/36.   [269] OJ [2010] L216/1.
[270] Case T-526/10 (n 173).

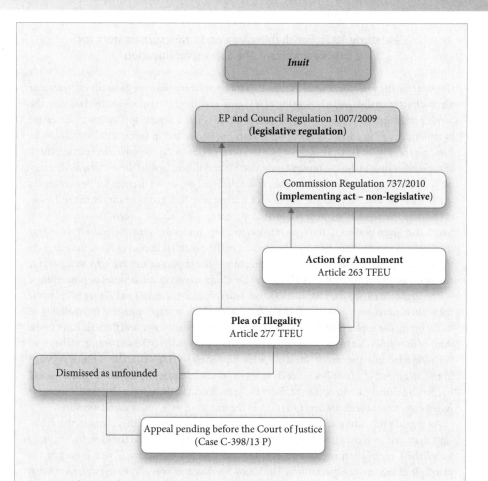

Fig 10.7 The Inuit litigation ('*Inuit II*') (Case T-526/10)

act'[271] – and perhaps even to elucidate the meaning of 'implementing measures' in that test which still remained uncertain even after *Microban*.[272]

Unfortunately, however, the General Court skipped the question of admissibility in its judgment in *Inuit II*[273] and instead considered directly the substantive grounds put forward to claim the illegality of both the parent and implementing regulations. All grounds put forward by the applicant – which included lack of legal basis, infringement of proportionality, and protection of fundamental human rights and misuse of powers – were dismissed as unfounded. While *Inuit II* shows the enhanced possibilities offered by the plea of illegality[274] after Lisbon – used there to mount a challenge against the parent regulation which had proved so elusive in *Inuit I* – it is disappointing that no more guidance on the application of the Article 263(4) TFEU conditions in relation to the direct annulment action was forthcoming from the Court. The decision in *Inuit II* is currently subject to appeal before the Court of Justice.

---

[271] See section 3.2.4.4, The Lisbon test.   [272] Case T-262/10 (n 134).

[273] Case T-526/10 (n 173) paras 18–21.

[274] Pre-Lisbon, it is very unlikely that the applicants would have satisfied the test of individual concern either in the challenge of the parent regulation or in the challenge of the implementing regulation. Therefore the use of the plea of illegality to challenge incidentally the former regulation in the context of a direct challenge to the latter would not have been possible.

Case study 10.2: Perishable cargo and a rare success story for a private applicant: the *Sofrimport* litigation

Considering the well-documented difficulties that private parties have generally encountered when directly challenging the legality of EU acts and the EU institutions in damages, the *Sofrimport* litigation[275] offers a rare glimpse of a case where a private applicant was successful in annulment proceedings, in securing interim measures and in suing the Commission in damages (see Figure 10.4). There, a French importer of Chilean apples who had a consignment of apples in transit to the EU, brought an action for annulment against three Commission regulations that suspended with immediate effect the issue of import licences for dessert apples without taking into account the position of traders who had goods in transit to the Union at the time the regulations were adopted. A parent or basic Council regulation in this area, which had given powers to the Commission to adopt protective measures, had imposed on the Commission an obligation to take account of the potential impact of these measures on traders with goods in transit before adopting them. The applicant also brought an action for damages under Article 340(2) TFEU against the Commission in the same set of proceedings.

The applicant also applied for interlocutory relief under Articles 278 and 279 TFEU[276] while the main actions were pending, citing, inter alia, the high storage costs, the impossibility of transporting the apples elsewhere without incurring very high costs, and the reduction in the value of the apples due to their loss of freshness. The Court ordered the suspension of the regulations in relation to the consignment of apples shipped by Sofrimport, and at the time stored in transit at the port of Marseilles, since there was a prima facie case and the threat of serious and irreparable damage to the applicant. Essentially, on the facts, there was a risk that Sofrimport might even have to cease trading as a result of the impact of the Commission's measures.

As regards the action for annulment, and as we saw earlier in this chapter, the applicant managed to secure standing under Article 263(4) TFEU[277] and the Court went on to annul the Commission regulations on the basis that the Commission had breached the principle of legitimate expectations. The action for damages was also successful. Given that *Sofrimport* was decided before the ruling in *Bergaderm*, and since the regulations were acts of general application that involved choices of economic policy, the *Aktien-Zuckerfabrik Schöppenstedt*[278] formula was applied by the Court. Thus, the Court considered whether a 'sufficiently serious breach of a superior rule of law for the protection of the individual' had occurred. Even though this formula has proved to be notably difficult to satisfy in many cases, the Court found that liability did arise in this case. It identified the breach of the principle of legitimate expectations of the applicants as the superior rule of law and found that the Commission's total disregard of its obligation to take account of the position of traders with goods in transit amounted to a sufficiently serious breach and that the damage suffered by the applicant went beyond the limits of the economic risks inherent in their business. The EU was therefore ordered to compensate Sofrimport for its losses.

Case study 10.3: Milk quotas and legitimate expectations: the *Mulder* litigation

In response to the chronic oversupply of milk products in the EU, the Council introduced a number of measures in the 1970s and 1980s in the context of the Common Agricultural

---

[275] *Sofrimport* (n 80).   [276] Case C-152/88 R *Sofrimport v Commission* [1988] ECR 2931.
[277] See section 3.2.4, The general standing test: direct and individual concern.   [278] See section 3.5.

Policy. Thus, a first Council regulation enacted in 1977 introduced a system of premiums that would be given to farmers who undertook not to market milk products for a five-year period and a second Council regulation imposed a levy on the treating or processing of milk products. Mr Mulder, a Dutch farmer, agreed not to deliver milk or dairy products for a period of five years from 1 October 1979. In 1984, the Council and the Commission adopted two further regulations designed to counteract the ever-present surplus of milk and introduced a system of quotas for the production of milk, whereby farmers had to apply to the relevant national authorities for reference quantities for the production of milk on the basis of which additional levies would be calculated. In particular, these measures provided that those reference quantities would be calculated on the basis of the quantities of milk produced in a particular year, which in the Netherlands was 1983. Mr Mulder had, of course, not produced any milk in the year 1983 following the undertaking that he gave as a result of the 1977 Council regulation. When he applied to the relevant national authority for a reference quantity of milk in 1984, his application was rejected on the basis that he had not produced any milk in 1983.

This set of facts indicated a fairly clear breach of the principle of legitimate expectations. When Mr Mulder agreed not to produce any milk between 1979 and 1984, following the provisions of the 1977 Council regulation, there was no indication that this would later prevent him from resuming his normal activity and the 1984 Council and Commission measures did not make any provisions for those who had not produced milk in the reference year of 1983. However, given that Mr Mulder was a private party, it was important to ascertain which avenue he would use to challenge the legality of the 1984 Council and Commission regulations.

In theory, the applicant had two options. The first would have been to bring a direct action for annulment under Article 263 TFEU before the Court. Had he decided to do this, Mr Mulder would have had to overcome the standing barrier in Article 263 TFEU. At the time, it was not even clear whether true regulations could be challenged by private parties and in some cases the Court still added the abstract terminology test[279] to the already formidable tests of individual and direct concern. This meant that the prospects of securing standing in the challenge of general measures under Article 263 TFEU were still rather bleak. The second option, which was the one chosen by the applicant, was to challenge before the national court the decision of the national authority rejecting Mr Mulder's application for a reference quantity of milk on the basis of the 1984 regulations. In the course of these national proceedings, the national court made a preliminary reference on the validity of the 1984 regulations to the Court of Justice under Article 267 TFEU, which led to the decision in *Mulder v Minister van Landbouw en Visserij* ('*Mulder I*').[280] There, the Court gave a preliminary ruling holding these regulations invalid on the ground of breach of legitimate expectations because they did not provide for the allocation of reference quantities to farmers in Mr Mulder's position.

This case therefore shows the possibilities that a preliminary reference on validity might offer as an alternative to a direct action for annulment. A few years later, and armed with the declaration of invalidity of the 1984 measures in *Mulder I*, the applicant and others in a similar position brought a direct action for damages before the Court under Article 340(2) TFEU against the Council and Commission for the losses that they sustained as a result of those measures. This led to the decision in *Mulder v Council and Commission* ('*Mulder II*'),[281] where the Court found the conditions for liability to be satisfied and awarded compensation to the applicants.

---

[279] See n 80.   [280] Case 120/86 [1988] ECR 2321.
[281] Joined Cases C-104/89 and C-37/90 [1992] ECR I-3061.

7 Conclusion

This chapter has viewed the composite of judicial avenues to the Court of Justice as a set of remedies that interact with a twofold purpose: to provide a system of protection against illegal action of the Member States and Union institutions and to secure a uniform and consistent interpretation and application of EU law at the national level. It has considered the main proceedings that come before the Court, both those that start and finish before the Court (direct actions) and those that start and finish before the national court but where the Court intervenes to address a question on the validity or interpretation of EU law (preliminary references). In other words, it has focused on what we could term the 'centralized' system of protection provided in the Treaty that has at its apex the Court of Justice. Of course, in order to appreciate the full extent and depth of the judicial protection offered by the Treaties, it is necessary to remember that this centralized system constitutes only one dimension of the remedial system.

A second and essential tier is the role performed by the national courts, which became a reality from the moment that the Court laid down the principles of direct effect and supremacy. This is a 'decentralized' dimension because the task of applying EU law falls on the national judiciaries. Thus, when national courts apply EU law by virtue of the doctrine of direct effect and use national remedies (subject to the principles of equality and effectiveness) and/or apply the doctrine of State liability in damages, they also protect natural and legal persons against violations of EU law by public authorities and/or private parties.[282]

We have seen in this chapter that within the centralized system of remedies available before the Court, there are aspects of horizontal interaction – that is, between some of the direct actions like annulment proceedings, the plea of illegality, or the action for damages. There are also elements of vertical (though not in a hierarchical sense) interaction – that is, between the national courts and the Court of Justice where the former raise preliminary references on interpretation to question the compatibility of national legislation with EU law or where preliminary references on validity are made to attain the same result as annulment proceedings. Likewise, there are synergies between the centralized and decentralized tiers mentioned previously. For example, the enforcement of EU law before the national courts through the principles of direct effect and supremacy often has a similar goal as enforcement proceedings before the Court. This second, decentralized aspect of judicial protection, is covered elsewhere in this book[283] but a panoramic view of judicial protection in EU law is only acquired when these two tiers are considered together and examined in light of their objectives.

In this chapter, one of the key themes was whether the Treaty system of remedies at EU level is truly a complete one. In relation to the protection afforded to private parties against potentially illegal measures adopted by the EU institutions – where only the Court has jurisdiction to annul or declare them invalid – it can be argued that while the Lisbon reforms have certainly narrowed the existing gaps, particularly by introducing the new special standing test that applies to the challenge of regulatory acts, it is far from clear that *all* the gaps have been plugged.

---

[282] See chapter 6.   [283] Ibid.

Further reading

A ALBORS-LLORENS, 'Remedies against the EU Institutions after Lisbon: An Era of Opportunity?' (2012) 71 *Cambridge Law Journal* 507

A ARNULL, 'Judicial Architecture or Judicial Folly? The Challenge Facing the European Union' (1999) 24 *European Law Review* 516

S BALTHASAR, '*Locus Standi* Rules for Challenges to Regulatory Acts by Private Applicants: The New Article 263(4) TFEU' (2010) 35 *European Law Review* 542

N BURROWS AND R GREAVES, *The Advocate General and EC Law* (Oxford: Oxford University Press, 2007)

M DOUGAN, 'The Treaty of Lisbon 2007: Winning Minds, Not Hearts' (2008) 45 *Common Market Law Review* 617

C HILSON, 'The Role of Discretion in EC Law on Non-Contractual Liability' (2005) 42 *Common Market Law Review* 677

J KOMAREK, 'In the Court(s) We Trust? On the Need for Hierarchy and Differentiation in the Preliminary Ruling Procedure' (2007) 32 *European Law Review* 467

K LENAERTS AND T CORTHAUT, 'Judicial Review as a Contribution to the Development of European Constitutionalism' (2003) 22 *Yearbook of European Law* 1

L PRETE AND B SMULDERS, 'The Coming of Age of Infringement Proceedings' (2010) 47 *Common Market Law Review* 9

T TRIDIMAS, 'Knocking on Heaven's Door: Fragmentation, Efficiency and Defiance in the Preliminary Reference Procedure' (2003) 40 *Common Market Law Review* 9

J USHER, 'Direct and Individual Concern: An Effective Remedy or a Conventional Solution?' (2003) 28 *European Law Review* 575

S WEATHERILL, *Cases and Materials on EU Law* (11th edn, Oxford: Oxford University Press, 2014) chs 7 and 8

Chapter acknowledgements

I am grateful to Anthony Arnull, Catherine Barnard, Alexander Kornezov, and the anonymous referees for their invaluable comments on previous drafts of this chapter. Any errors remain entirely my own.

11

The internal market and the philosophies of market integration

Jukka Snell

1 Introduction

The building of a European market has been at the heart of the European integration project from the very beginning. In fact, 'common market' was for a long time used as a synonym for what is now the EU; when the British voted in a referendum on European Economic Community membership in 1975, they voted on whether they wanted to be a part of a 'common market'. Today, when another referendum in the UK is a distinct possibility, access to the 'single market' is usually mentioned as the most pressing reason for continued EU membership. What is unclear is the exact nature of the European market, which the Treaties today call the 'internal market'. It is the aim of the present chapter to examine this question, as well as analyse the tools that the Treaties have created for the achievement of the internal market.

The main theme of the chapter is that the nature of the internal market is contested, lacks clarity, and has varied from time to time. This may at first glance appear surprising. After all, we have now had more than 50 years to work out what the internal market means, and in fact the internal market is one of the very few concepts the Treaties actually define. According to Article 26(2) TFEU 'the internal market shall comprise an area without internal frontiers in which the free movement of goods, persons, services and capital is ensured'. Unfortunately, the definition is somewhat circular.[1] In order to understand it, we need to understand the free movement of goods, persons, and so on. Yet when we seek to explore the meaning of the four freedoms, we quickly discover that they need to be understood against the background of the internal market. In other words, to understand the internal market, the four freedoms have to be understood, and vice versa.

The present chapter begins by setting out three possible ways an internal market could be arranged. Those models are host country control, the harmonized model, and home country control. Each represents a very different approach to, or philosophy of, economic integration. They entail differing consequences for the division of power between the EU and its Member States, and between courts and legislatures. They are also likely to result in different balances being struck between economic and non-economic interests; in other words, one may benefit trade while potentially undermining social or environmental protection, while another may do the opposite.

The chapter continues by examining how the nature of European market integration has changed in the course of the history of the EU. It will argue that the original common market paradigm set out in the Spaak Report[2] and incorporated into the Treaty of Rome gradually gave way to the single market paradigm first initiated by the European Court of Justice and subsequently embraced by the political institutions. Further, it will be argued that we may now be moving towards yet another paradigm change, where the internal market is influenced by the need to create a true economic union.

Finally, in sections 4 and 5 the chapter moves to investigate the principal tool the Treaty has created for the achievement of the internal market, namely Article 114 TFEU. First, the extent of the power that this provision puts in the hands of the EU legislature is analysed, partly through the use of a case study. Secondly, the use of this power is explored, with focus on two techniques of approximation of the laws of the Member States: minimum and total harmonization.

A word of caution: the present chapter is only able to offer a partial picture of the internal market. To obtain a fuller view, the chapters on the four freedoms need to be consulted.[3] Here, I will seek to set out the broad context and to examine the power of the EU political institutions actively and positively to push for the creation or perfection of the internal market. Yet the ability of the Court to disapply national laws that violate the free movement of goods, persons, services, or capital is equally fundamental in the shaping of the internal market.

2 The nature of the internal market: three models

All markets need freedom. Suppliers of products and inputs need to be able to sell and buy. In the EU, the four freedoms of goods, services, persons, and capital provide this. However, all markets also need rules and the European internal market is no exception. Rules create the market in the first place: they establish property rights and contracts without which a market would not exist. They regulate what things can be sold and bought, and what things cannot.[4] Rules set out health and safety requirements that products must meet to be lawfully marketed, or qualifications that service providers must possess to

---

[1] See the chapter by S Weatherill in M Adams, J Meeusen, G Straetmans, and H de Waele (eds), *Judging Europe's Judges: The Legitimacy of the Case Law of the European Court of Justice Examined* (Oxford: Hart Publishing, 2013).

[2] Report of the Heads of Delegation to the Foreign Ministers at the Messina Conference, 21 April 1956.

[3] Chapters 12, 13, 14, and 15.   [4] eg sale of human body parts or sex.

trade legally. The fundamental question then is: who is to set the rules for the European internal market?

2.1 Three models of market integration

In theory, three different ideal models of organizing an internal market can be envisaged.[5] It is to be stressed that these are ideals; they help us to think about the issue, but do not exist in pure form anywhere. Each of the three models has different implications for the power structure of the EU, and for the balance between different interests.

The first possible model is *host country control*. This means that the rules of the country where the economic activity takes place apply. If a good is produced in country A but then sold in country B, it has to comply with the requirements of the latter State. If a worker from country C goes to work in country D, it is again the laws of the latter State that apply. Host State control is, of course, the normal situation when it comes to trade between independent countries. However, by committing to the internal market, the EU has decided to move further. This means that the host country control has to be tempered at least with a rule of non-discrimination. In other words, the rules of the host country apply, but those rules cannot discriminate against things or people from the other Member States.

The second possibility is a *harmonized model*. Here the conditions of a single unitary State are replicated at the EU level. For each issue, there is only one rule, which has been produced by the EU. All products and factors of production must comply with it, but can then be sold and bought freely in the territory of the entire Union.

The final model is *home country control*. This is the mirror image of host country control. The rule that applies to any given product or input is the rule of its country of origin, not the rule of the country where it is sold. For example, if a good is produced in country A and sold in country B, it is the rule of the first State that applies. If a worker from country C goes to country D, it is again the rules of the former State that regulate the activity. In other words, there is an EU rule of mutual recognition. For this kind of model to work, there has to be a significant level of trust between the countries.[6] Country B has to be confident that the goods produced in country A are safe. Country D has to trust that qualifications the worker obtained in country C render him competent to engage in the activity he is planning to undertake. In the real EU, such absolute trust does not exist. Instead, where mutual recognition does apply, it is tempered with exceptions that allow the host country to deny recognition in certain cases.

2.2 The implications of the different models

2.2.1 Consequences for sovereignty

The three models outlined in the previous section have different implications for the sovereignty of Member States.[7] The model of *host country control* is likely to impose the fewest constraints on the autonomy of each State to regulate its own affairs, although much will

---

[5] M Poiares Maduro, *We the Court* (Oxford: Hart Publishing, 1998), who uses the terms decentralized model, centralized model, and competitive model. KA Armstrong, 'Mutual Recognition' in C Barnard and J Scott (eds), *The Law of the Single European Market: Unpacking the Premises* (Oxford: Hart Publishing, 2002) employs the same terminology as the present chapter.

[6] See eg K Nicolaïdis, 'Trusting the Poles? Constructing Europe through Mutual Recognition' (2007) 14 *Journal of European Public Policy* 682.

[7] See generally eg J Snell, 'Who's Got the Power? Free Movement and Allocation of Competences in EC Law' (2003) 22 *Yearbook of European Law* 323.

depend on how the rule of non-discrimination is applied. The second, *harmonized model* entails a vertical transfer of power from the State level to the EU level. Member States lose their power to regulate their own affairs; instead the laws come from the EU. However, it needs to be remembered that Member States are well represented in the EU legislature; in particular they form the Council.[8] In other words, under the harmonized model the Member States to a degree are pooling their sovereignty: they exercise it jointly. The *home country control model* involves a reassignment of sovereignty between the Member States. Each State loses its power to control matters within its own territory in certain circumstances. At the same time, the rules of each country extend further than they did before and now apply to circumstances outside its borders.

2.2.2 Institutional consequences

The different models also have different institutional consequences.[9] The balance between the power of the legislature and the power of the judiciary may be struck differently. In the *host country control model* the (national) legislatures are likely to play a dominant role, although it has to be noted that courts may be highly influential as well, depending on how the rule of non-discrimination is applied. If only overt or direct discrimination[10] is caught, their influence is likely to be small. However, if a far-reaching standard that also outlaws indirect or covert discrimination is adopted, the judiciary may become a much more important actor. In extreme cases, the distinction between host and home country control may even evaporate under the glare of a non-discrimination rule: it can be argued that a failure of a host country to take into account the fact that a product or an input has already been the subject of regulation in its home State and now must comply with a second set of rules is itself a form of discrimination. After all, a product or an input of the host country has to deal with only one set of rules and can enter the market unchanged, while one coming from another Member State is subject to a double burden and needs to be altered to enter the new market.[11]

In the *harmonized model* it can be expected that the (EU) legislature is the dominant player, but again this is not necessarily so. Of course, the natural way of creating a harmonized set of rules is that they are promulgated by the central legislature. However, the judiciary can also engage in harmonization, in two ways. It can create a deregulated, liberal, laissez-faire market by striking down rules in the name of the four freedoms.[12] Alternatively, it can be more selective and target those national rules that differ markedly from a European consensus.[13] For example, if Member States A, B, and C have very similar laws, while the law of D is very different, the Court might advance harmonization by disapplying the rule of D, thus encouraging its legislature to fall into line.

In the third, *home country control model*, the role of the judiciary is likely to be pronounced. It will have to ensure that mutual recognition takes place. It may also have to set the reach of mutual recognition in two ways, if the legislature has not done so. First, which rules are subject to mutual recognition in the first place? For example, if a worker from country A moves to country B, his qualifications may be recognized. But what about the salary levels – are they also set by the legislation or collective agreements of the home

---

[8] See further chapter 4.   [9] Snell, 'Who's Got the Power?' (n 7).

[10] For definitions of direct and indirect discrimination, see chapter 13.

[11] For the classic account, see G Marenco, 'Pour une interpretation traditionelle de la notion de mesure d'effet equivalent a une restriction quantitative' (1984) 19 *Cahiers de Droit Européen* 291.

[12] See N Bernard, 'The Future of European Economic Law in the Light of the Principle of Subsidiarity' (1996) 33 *Common Market Law Review* 633, 637.

[13] Poiares Maduro, *We the Court* (n 5) 72–76 calls this 'majoritarian activism'.

country? Is he subject to the criminal law of the host country, or is this mutually recognized as well, and so on. Secondly, mutual recognition is typically subject to exceptions that allow the host country to insist on the application of its own rules,[14] for example in the name of public policy. For home country control to work, the use of these exceptions needs to be carefully monitored by a judicial institution.

2.2.3 Welfare considerations

Each model obviously aims at improving the welfare of our societies, that is, making citizens better off. However, they do so in very different ways, with different consequences. The *host country control model* allows trade to take place, and basic economic theory tells us that this makes all participants wealthier.[15] It also allows for the protection of other interests. For example, the host country is free to set whatever environmental or consumer protection standards it sees fit, as long as it avoids discrimination. Different countries are able to maintain different levels of protection. This is important if the preferences vary from country to country. The citizens of State A may place a high value on a clean environment, while citizens of B may place a higher value on material things. Under host country control, each State is able to set its level of protection accordingly.

The *harmonized model* brings with it significant economic benefits, too, in particular in terms of economies of scale. There is only one rule that economic actors need to comply with, in contrast with the patchwork of national rules that host country control allows. This reduces various compliance and transaction costs, and may allow companies to produce more efficiently. Often, it is cheaper per unit to produce a large number of products than a small number. For example, a large factory with a long assembly line may be able to churn out goods more cheaply than a smaller enterprise. If there is only one product standard for a company to worry about, rather than a multitude of different standards, these economies of scale can be achieved. In practice, this is an argument that has often been put forward in Europe, and in particular it has been claimed that without unification European companies will struggle to compete against companies from countries with large home markets,[16] such as the US or China.

Under the harmonized model, other interests such as the environment can also be protected by appropriate rules being adopted at the EU level. However, there are at least three problems. By necessity, an EU-wide rule cannot take diversity into account: one rule has to fit all countries, even if their preferences vary. The more diverse the Member States are, the less likely it is that a compromise satisfying all can be found. Secondly, it can be doubted whether the EU legislature would in practice be capable of producing rules in sufficient quantity and quality to afford non-economic interests, such as the environment, appropriate protection. Finally, rules adopted at the EU level may prove inflexible, rigid, and difficult to change. The EU legislative process tends to be lengthy, and involves numerous actors, veto points, and supermajority requirements. When a particular piece of EU law has been adopted, it may not be easy to amend if circumstances change or if it proves less than completely satisfactory.[17]

---

[14] It is not a coincidence that in Case 120/78 *Rewe v Bundesmonopolverwaltung für Branntwein* ('*Cassis de Dijon*') [1979] ECR 649 the Court both insisted on mutual recognition and created additional justifications for Member States.

[15] See in the EU context, eg W Molle, *The Economics of European Integration: Theory, Practice, Policy* (5th edn, Aldershot: Ashgate, 2006).

[16] See eg P Cecchini with M Catinat and A Jacquemin, *The European Challenge 1992: The Benefits of a Single Market* (Aldershot: Wildwood House, 1988).

[17] FW Scharpf, 'The Joint-Decision Trap: Lessons from German Federalism and European Integration' (1988) 66 *Public Administration* 239.

The welfare implications of *home country control* are the most difficult to assess. This is because they introduce a complex element of regulatory competition into the mix.[18] Regulatory competition means that in addition to the competition between firms that all models of internal market entail there is also competition between legislatures. Each country will try to attract valuable assets, for example by creating policies designed to encourage inward investment and prevent capital flight. They supply policies in the same manner as companies supply products. Economic actors then choose among the offerings of the competing countries. For example, consumers in country A may buy products produced in, and according to the standards of, country B. They vote with their purse. This will benefit the producers based in country B, and will be a matter of concern for producers and the government of country A. It may be inclined to amend the rules of country A to make products coming from country A more attractive and to counteract the risk of capital flight. As another example, country C may wish to attract capital by imposing low taxes on corporate profits and creating a favourable regulatory climate. This may increase the flows of international inward investments to country C as investors vote with their feet, potentially forcing country D to reconsider its fiscal policies.

Economists teach us that regulatory competition can have many beneficial effects.[19] First, it increases choice. A consumer can choose between products manufactured according to the specifications of many different jurisdictions. A worker can choose whether to live in a country of high salaries and relentless rat race, or lower income but good quality of life. Secondly, it creates a discovery mechanism.[20] Countries innovate to produce attractive rules and policies. They are tested in the marketplace for regulations. Some of these prove successful and are copied. Others fail to achieve the desired effect and are abandoned. This creates valuable information about which public policies actually work and which ones do not. In a way, each State acts as a laboratory of democracy.[21] Thirdly, regulatory competition may counteract the predatory tendencies of public officials. If they impose excessive taxes or oppressive rules, there is the option of exit. For example, an entrepreneur hit with a confiscatory tax may relocate to another jurisdiction to escape it. This possibility makes the imposition of such taxes less likely. Thus, regulatory competition may help to tame the leviathan.[22]

Unfortunately, regulatory competition can also prove detrimental.[23] This is uncontestable in situations where the costs and the benefits of a policy fall on different jurisdictions. For example, assume that prevailing winds carry emissions from country A to country B. The government of country A would have no incentive to adopt appropriate environmental standards – after all, the benefits of the industrial activity fall on country A while the costs fall on country B. In the language of economics, there are externalities, which render regulatory competition harmful. Further, it is sometimes supposed that regulatory competition leads more generally to an uncontrolled race to the bottom. The worry is that

---

[18] See eg W Kerber, 'Interjurisdictional Competition within the European Union' (2000) 23 *Fordham International Law Journal* 217.

[19] See already CM Tiebout, 'A Pure Theory of Local Expenditures' (1956) 64 *Journal of Political Economy* 416.

[20] This aspect of competition is emphasized in FA Hayek, 'Competition as a Discovery Procedure' (2002) 5 *Quarterly Journal of Austrian Economics* 9.

[21] The expression was coined by Justice Brandeis of the US Supreme Court in *New State Ice v Liebmann* 285 US 262 (1932).

[22] This is a prime concern of public choice theory. See eg G Brennan and JM Buchanan, *The Power to Tax: Analytic Foundations of a Fiscal Constitution* (Indianapolis, IN: Liberty Fund, 1980).

[23] See J-M Sun and J Pelkmans, 'Regulatory Competition in the Single Market' (1995) 33 *Journal of Common Market Studies* 67 for an attempt at cost–benefit analysis.

countries, in order to attract capital, will start competitively lowering their standards of labour or environmental protection (since people tend to be less mobile than capital) in a destructive cycle that leaves each with zero regulation. Emotive words such as social or environmental dumping are often used in this context. Whether a race to the bottom is a real danger associated with home country control is fiercely contested. There are arguments that such fears are unfounded or at least unlikely to materialize in practice. At any rate, empirical evidence is scarce.[24]

2.2.4 Democratic concerns

The previous paragraphs have considered the effects of different models of integration on the welfare of citizens as passive rule-takers. It is also important to consider the matter from the point of view of citizens as active rule-makers. In other words, do the different models have particular pitfalls from the perspective of democracy?

All three models have been subject to democratic criticism, from different perspectives. The argument against the *host country control model* has been that it is under-inclusive. Laws are formulated by the citizens of the host State, or their representatives. They do not take into account the interests of outsiders, such as companies or workers of other Member States, who do not have a voice in the political process of the host country. Yet the laws also affect these outsiders. Thus, it is argued, the host country control model suffers from the weakness that some affected interests are not represented at all.[25] The *harmonized model* is vulnerable to the entire gamut of democratic deficit criticism that the EU is regularly subjected to.[26] This is covered elsewhere in this book.[27] The *home country control model* is open to criticism as well. A particular worry is that it distorts national democracy by favouring capital over workers.[28] Under home country control, actors have the option of exit. A factory owner who does not like the regulatory climate of country A can relocate his production facility to country B, or at least threaten to do so. The same exit option is also available for workers, in theory. In practice, the different factors of production, capital, and labour, have differing levels of mobility. Liquid capital can be sent to another jurisdiction at the press of a button, while human beings with family ties and fluent in their native language only will find the prospect of relocation daunting. Thus, the threat of capital flight tends to be more credible than the threat of loss of skilled workers, forcing national legislatures to pay particular heed to the demands of capital. The result could be, for example, that the tax burden on the mobile factor, capital, is lowered, while the burden on the less mobile factor, labour, is increased.

Where does the discussion of the three models leave us? It shows that there are profoundly different philosophies of economic integration. The approaches have very different consequences for fundamental features of our societies, such as distribution of power, institutional balance, welfare of citizens, and democracy. The creation of the internal market is

---

[24] See on a global scale, DW Drezner, *All Politics is Global: Explaining International Regulatory Regimes* (Princeton, NJ: Princeton University Press, 2007) who argues at 15 that 'There are anecdotal examples that support the idea of a race to the bottom, but the bulk of the evidence strongly suggests that these assertions are flatly wrong.'

[25] See eg C Joerges, 'What is Left of the European Economic Constitution? A Melancholic Eulogy' (2005) 30 *European Law Review* 461, 488.

[26] See for discussion, eg J Snell, 'European Constitutional Settlement, and Ever Closer Union, and the Treaty of Lisbon: Democracy or Relevance' (2008) 33 *European Law Review* 619.

[27] See esp chapters 2 and 4.

[28] M Kumm, 'Constitutionalising Subsidiarity in Integrated Markets: The Case of Tobacco Regulation in the European Union' (2006) 12 *European Law Journal* 503.

not a value-neutral technical project that can be left to the experts to manage, but must be an object of wider debate and contestation. The next section will show that, as the theory predicts, in the real world the nature of the internal market has been fought over. It has not remained stable, but has fluctuated and continues to fluctuate, displaying features of all three models that have been outlined previously.

3 The nature of the internal market: the historical experience

This section explores the evolution of the internal market of the EU.[29] It argues that there have been different paradigms of market integration. The initial paradigm was the common market. As envisaged in the Spaak Report that prepared the ground for the Treaty of Rome and in the early years of integration, the European marketplace would combine freedom and fairness, and would largely be achieved by the legislative activity of the EU. The planned common market had some affinities with the harmonized model discussed earlier. The common market paradigm was replaced by the single market paradigm in the course of the 1970s and 1980s. Under this paradigm, the European Court of Justice became a more important actor, and the substance of the law shifted towards a more competitive model where home country control had a larger role to play. However, it will be argued, the single market paradigm suffered from instability and weaknesses. Instead, a new economic union paradigm may be emerging.

A note about terminology: the original Treaty of Rome used the term common market. The Single European Act of 1986 inserted the term internal market, which coexisted with common market in the language of the Treaty. In the political discussions, the term single market was often preferred. The Lisbon Treaty, which came into force in 2009, replaced all references to the common market with internal market. The Court has tended to use all three concepts interchangeably. For example, in *Gaston Schul* it stated that the common market 'involves the elimination of all obstacles to intra-Community trade in order to merge the national markets into a single market bringing about conditions as close as possible to those of a genuine internal market.'[30] However, legal scholars have insisted that the common market and the internal market were different concepts.[31]

3.1 The common market

The common market was at the heart of the Treaty of Rome of 1957 that established the European Economic Community. The EEC was a response to the failure of a more ambitious attempt to integrate Europe.[32] In 1952, treaties for the European Defence Community and the European Political Community of 'supranational character' had been put forward. They did not survive the national ratification process, and were killed off by the

---

[29] See also P Craig, 'The Evolution of the Single Market' in Barnard and Scott, *The Law of the Single European Market* (n 5); M Egan, 'Single Market' in E Jones, A Menon, and S Weatherill (eds), *The Oxford Handbook of the European Union* (Oxford: Oxford University Press, 2012); and LW Gormley, 'The Internal Market: History and Evolution' in N Nic Shuibhne (ed), *Regulating the Internal Market* (Cheltenham: Edward Elgar, 2006).

[30] Case 15/81 *Gaston Schul* [1982] ECR 1409, para 33.

[31] See eg LW Gormley, 'Competition and Free Movement: Is the Internal Market the Same as a Common Market?' [2002] *European Business Law Review* 517.

[32] For an excellent short summary of the developments, see D Dinian, *Europe Recast: A History of European Union* (Basingstoke: Palgrave Macmillan, 2004).

French Parliament in 'an atmosphere of riot'.[33] A more modest approach was called for, and a Benelux proposal for a common market was chosen as a vehicle to move integration forward despite the ratification crisis. The groundwork for the common market was laid down in the Spaak Report,[34] which was produced under the chairmanship of Paul-Henri Spaak, the Belgian foreign minister. He had also been the author of the European Political Community Treaty, but with the common market project he expunged supranationalism from his vocabulary and focused on producing a blueprint for a treaty that would be acceptable for all parties, in particular France.[35]

The Spaak Report argued for the merger of separate national markets into a common market to arrest and to reverse the perceived international decline of Europe. The key benefits were thought to be the increasing division of work that would lead to efficiencies, achievement of economies of scale, and greater competition. To achieve this, three sets of actions were proposed. First, national protections creating obstacles to trade had to be suppressed. This involved the abolition of customs duties and quotas as well as those national regulations that resulted in the practical elimination or control of foreign competition. At the same time, however, it was recognized that common European-level regulations would be needed in the public interest or due to the nature of production or particular markets. Secondly, distortions of competition needed to be dealt with, whether they resulted from business practices, State aids, or disparities between national legislations. Thirdly, conditions for common growth had to be ensured by helping underdeveloped regions, by assisting business in adjusting to competition and modern production methods, and by freeing the circulation of factors of production: labour and to a degree also capital. The practical realization of the common market required the creation of institutions that would apply competition law, ensure State compliance with Treaty obligations, coordinate national policies, and provide parliamentary or judicial control.

The EEC Treaty followed closely the blueprint set up by the Spaak Report. For goods, there were rules on elimination of customs duties and quotas, and also a new provision outlawing measures of equivalent effect that apparently followed from a query by a mid-ranking customs official.[36] For persons and services, tools and a process for liberalization were established. There were to be issue- or sector-specific initiatives, with the Commission proposing and the Council adopting common rules that would realize free movement. For capital, a more modest degree of liberalization was envisaged, again following legislative initiatives. A harmonization mechanism was also created for the purposes of eliminating distortions of competition, and the Commission was charged with applying competition law and policing State aids. There was some coordination of economic policies, and the European Social Fund and the European Investment Bank were established to shelter the workforce, to help underdeveloped regions, and to assist business modernization. Following French concerns that its higher social costs would undermine the competitiveness of French companies, social provisions were included declaring, inter alia, the need to improve and harmonize working conditions and standards of living for workers, as well as setting out the principle that men and women should receive equal pay for equal work. The Protocol on Certain Provisions Relating to France was also annexed

---

[33] Dinian, *Europe Recast: A History of European Union* (n 32), quoting J Lacouture, *Pierre Mendès-France* (New York: Holmes and Meier, 1984).

[34] See n 2.

[35] P-H Laurent, 'Paul-Henri Spaak and the Diplomatic Origins of the Common Market, 1955–1956' (1970) 85 *Political Science Quarterly* 373.

[36] A Moravcsik, *The Choice for Europe: Social Purpose and State Power from Messina to Maastricht* (London: UCL Press, 1999) 146.

to the Treaty, allowing it potentially to take protective measures if payments for overtime work put its industry in a disadvantageous position.

The common market was a carefully calibrated mix of freedom and fairness. On paper, it had affinities with the harmonized model discussed in section 2.1. Markets would be opened, but in a controlled fashion. There would be no creative destruction, but instead a managed process of adjustment, adaptation, and fair competition. All the key concerns of France were addressed. This proved a recipe for political success. The Treaty sailed through the French Parliament just three years after the death of the European Defence and Political Communities.

The early years of market integration proceeded successfully. Customs duties and quotas were indeed eliminated. However, the harmonization of national rules did not proceed as planned. The empty chair crisis and Luxembourg Accords of the mid-1960s had replaced the planned majority voting rules in the Council with the requirement of unanimity.[37] This made it difficult to engage in successful harmonization. Further, the task of creating a common market was probably greater than had been anticipated. Even for goods, non-tariff barriers proved prevalent. In the words of one observer, 'the lowering of tariffs has, in effect, been like draining a swamp. The lower water level has revealed all the snags and stumps of non-tariff barriers that still have to be cleared away.'[38] Further, technical and other developments meant that ever more issues needed to be dealt with and laws that actually had been successfully adopted at the EU level required frequent revision.

3.2 The single market

The paradigm began to change in the 1970s. The European Court of Justice stepped forward to take the lead. In the early 1970s, it found in a series of cases that the four freedoms, with the exception of capital, were directly effective. They could be applied even in the absence of the legislative activity that the Treaty had envisaged.[39] Starting in the late 1970s, it reinforced this by creating the principle of mutual recognition.[40] The Treaty freedoms went beyond simple non-discrimination rules and also required that the host country accepts goods, services, or economic actors that fulfil the requirements of the home country on its markets, unless the host State has a good reason to oppose such market access and does so in a proportionate fashion. In other words, the principle is that a product good enough for, say, French consumers, is also good enough for, say, German consumers, unless Germany can convincingly show otherwise. To use the language of section 2.1, the Court moved the European market towards the home country model. At the same time, institutionally, it occupied a key position in advancing economic integration.

The Commission sought to capitalize on the rulings of the Court. It issued a Communication setting out a far-reaching interpretation of the principle of mutual recognition.[41]

---

[37] See eg J Gillingham, *European Integration 1950–2003: Superstate or New Market Economy?* (Cambridge: Cambridge University Press, 2003) 68–72.

[38] R Baldwin, *Non-Tariff Distortions of International Trade* (Washington DC: Brookings Institution, 1970), quoted in MP Egan, *Constructing a European Market: Standards, Regulation, and Governance* (Oxford: Oxford University Press, 2001) 41.

[39] See eg PP Craig, 'Once upon a Time in the West: Direct Effect and the Federalization of EEC Law' (1992) 12 *Oxford Journal of Legal Studies* 453, 463–467.

[40] Case 120/78 *Rewe v Bundesmonopolverwaltung für Branntwein* [1979] ECR 649. See further chapter 12.

[41] Communication from the Commission concerning the consequences of the judgment given by the Court of Justice on 20 February 1979 in Case 120/78 ('Cassis de Dijon') (OJ [1980] C256/2). See generally KJ Alter and S Meunier-Aitsahalia, 'Judicial Politics in the European Community: European Integration and the Pathbreaking *Cassis de Dijon* Decision' (1994) 26 *Comparative Political Studies* 535.

The initial reaction of the Member States was hostile. However, over time they became more receptive.[42] A national experiment at socialism had failed in France, and the French government moved from autarkic policies to support internal market liberalization. The Britain of Margaret Thatcher was pushing forward a programme of liberalization, and the Christian Democrats had replaced the Social Democrats in government in Germany. European businesses were lobbying hard for more economic integration to strengthen their position against US and Japanese competitors. The result was a relaunch of integration under the banner of the single market.[43]

The most visible element of the single market was the adoption of a new Treaty to amend the Treaty of Rome, the Single European Act (SEA), which followed an important Commission White Paper on the completion of the internal market[44] and entered into force in 1987. This document set out the aim of achieving the internal market by the end of 1992. The internal market was defined as 'an area without internal frontiers in which the free movement of goods, persons, services and capital is ensured'. To allow the aim to be realized, the SEA brought forward a new rule that allowed internal market legislation to be passed by qualified majority voting, rather than by unanimity. The SEA was supported by innovations in the Commission's approach to harmonization. Under the so-called 'new approach', harmonization would be focused on those national rules that survived the direct application of the Treaty. In other words, if the host country had to recognize the product of the home country under the four freedoms anyway, there was no need for the EU to legislate. Only if the host country was able to oppose the importation, for example on grounds of health and safety, was there a need for the EU legislature to engage. Further, the type of legislation would be different. Instead of detailed harmonization of rules on narrow sectors, broader directives would be adopted that would seek to harmonize only the essential health, safety, environmental, and other requirements. The details would be left for the European standardization process undertaken by bodies such as CEN (the European Committee for Standardization) and CENELEC (the European Committee for Electrotechnical Standardization). Finally, an early warning system was established that required Member States to notify new technical regulations to the Commission, so that it could take preventative action.[45]

The single market paradigm had a number of advantages. It aligned the Treaty, harmonization, and standardization. It abandoned unachievable ambitions for complete harmonization. It left room for experimentation and local differences. Most importantly, it was realistic. The measures that needed to be adopted were by and large passed; the deadline of 1992 was for the most part met. The single market was created in a workable form, and further advances could be built on this success.

---

[42] See A Moravcsik, 'Negotiating the Single European Act: National Interests and Conventional Statecraft in the European Community' (1991) 45 *International Organization* 19 and W Sandholtz and J Zysman, '1992: Recasting the European Bargain' (1989) 42 *World Politics* 95 for two classic studies of the impetus behind the single market project.

[43] According to K Nicolaïdes, 'Kir Forever? The Journey of a Political Scientist in the Landscape of Recognition' in M Poiares Maduro and L Azoulai (eds), *The Past and Future of EU Law: The Classics of EU Law Revisited on the 50th Anniversary of the Rome Treaty* (Oxford: Hart Publishing, 2010) 448: 'When I recently asked Lord Cockfield, Commissioner for the internal market, what he considered the greatest achievement of his career, he answered without a beat: to have exported Cassis from the European Court of Justice and goods to the single market Europe 1992 programme.'

[44] Commission White Paper, 'Completing the internal market', COM(85) 310 final.

[45] See J Pelkmans, 'The New Approach to Technical Harmonization and Standardization' (1987) 25 *Journal of Common Market Studies* 249.

Unfortunately, the single market paradigm was never fully stable. Despite its theoretical attractiveness, it did not really satisfy many of the key stakeholders. First, from the business perspective the approach was less than perfect. While mutual recognition was fine in theory, in practice its application left a lot to be desired. National authorities were still left as guardians of market access, and could deny mutual recognition on the basis of the derogations written in the Treaty, such as the needs of public policy, or on the basis of exceptions developed in the case law, such as consumer or environmental protection. In other words, an attempt by a company to penetrate the market of another country was often frustrated by the insistence of host State officials that local rules be obeyed because the rules of the home country did not in their view sufficiently protect non-economic interests. Whether such a requirement was lawful depended on the proportionality of the host country rule. This was very difficult to predict in advance and could only be tested in costly and lengthy litigation. As a result, for a company it would often be easier just to follow the local rule than to rely on European rights.[46]

For national governments, the single market model created at least two types of difficulty. The national publics expect States to protect them from environmental degradation, substandard products, and so on. If there is a problem, for example a food scandal, the national government may get blamed. Yet those governments have now given up their ability fully to control products that are sold in their country. They might end up bearing the responsibility for things that they cannot affect. Further, the kind of competition the single market model entails may be branded unfair. National companies on the losing end might blame their lack of success on the various 'unfair' regulatory advantages that foreign competitors enjoy, such as lower standards or wages, and demand protection. Under European law such protection is likely to be illegal. This could leave the national decision-makers between the rock of domestic public opinion that expects the government to protect local companies and the hard place of EU rules that outlaw it.

For organized interest groups, such as trade unions or environmental groups, the principle of mutual recognition at the heart of the single market represented a threat. As discussed in section 2.2, the principle potentially allows regulatory competition to take place. This could undermine the labour or environmental standards that the groups were committed to. Even if fierce regulatory competition failed to start, the balance of power between organized interest groups and industry was altered. The industry was provided with the ability to threaten relocation in the absence of domestic reforms. In other words, the industry could tell the government or trade unions that without changes, such as greater labour market flexibility, future investment decisions would be directed at other parts of the EU.[47]

For the advocates of further integration, the single market was insufficient. It was a construct of logic and economic advantage. It lacked emotional pull; it did not instil Euro-patriotism in citizens. In the words of Jacques Delors, the President of the Commission during the single market project, 'It is difficult to fall in love with the single market.' In fact, quite the opposite: some of the most bitter resistance the European project has encountered has been due to attempts to extend the single market.

---

[46] J Pelkmans, 'Mutual Recognition in Goods: On Promises and Disillusions' (2007) 14 *Journal of European Public Policy* 699, 708–711. The EU has put forward various initiatives to improve the functioning of mutual recognition, in particular European Parliament and Council Regulation (EC) No 764/2008 laying down procedures relating to the application of certain national technical rules to products lawfully marketed in another Member State (OJ [2008] L218/21).

[47] See generally C Barnard, 'Social Dumping and the Race to the Bottom: Some Lessons for the European Union from Delaware?' (2000) 25 *European Law Review* 57.

In this context, the enlargement of the Union is a significant factor. The expansions of 2004 and thereafter brought into the EU a large number of countries that were at quite a different level of economic development from the existing Member States. This created political problems. An attempt to enhance the effectiveness of the single market in the services sector by the adoption of a directive with a country-of-origin principle met fierce resistance, and resulted in the watering down of the directive. Judgments of the Court of Justice on the kinds of actions trade unions could take to oppose competition from the new Member States[48] entered into political discussion, for example in the context of the Irish referenda on the Lisbon Treaty, just as the threat of Polish plumbers 'stealing' the jobs of French plumbers had been invoked in debates on the Constitutional Treaty in France. In the UK, the free movement of workers and services was called into question when local workers demonstrated against the use of labour from other Member States at the Lindsey oil refinery.[49] Behind these phenomena was the economic insecurity that heightened competition created, in particular when the labour-cost differences between some of the new and old Member States were very substantial. Further, the single market with its mutual recognition requires mutual trust, and with enlargement that trust was at least temporarily undermined.[50]

The pressures described previously have had an impact on legal developments. As mentioned, the attempt to liberalize services markets in one fell swoop using the country-of-origin principle was abandoned.[51] The Commission has in certain areas moved away from the idea of divergent but coordinated national systems and instead returned to an approach based on more complete harmonization of rules.[52] The Commission has also contributed to uniformity at the level of implementation by working quietly to shift away from directives that need to be transposed by Member States to regulations that do not.[53] There have been attempts to emphasize social Europe and non-economic issues to appease disgruntled citizens, rather than leaving the matters for regulatory competition. This was expressed forcefully in the report for the Commission on the relaunch of the single market by Professor Monti. He advocated the creation of a stronger single market but also noted the need to build consensus to support it as 'today the single market...is seen by many Europeans...with suspicion, fear and sometimes open hostility.'[54] It also finds an expression in the Lisbon Treaty, which commits the EU to the goal of a 'social market economy' and, in a gesture full of symbolism, relegates the EU's commitment to undistorted competition from the first articles of the Treaty to a

---

[48]   See further chapters 13 and 20.

[49]   C Barnard, ' "British Jobs for British Workers": The Lindsey Oil Refinery Dispute and the Future of Local Labour Clauses in an Integrated EU Market' (2009) 38 *Industrial Law Journal* 245.

[50]   For an empirical assessment, see J Delhey, 'Do Enlargements Make the European Union Less Cohesive? An Analysis of Mutual Trust between EU Nationalities' (2007) 45 *Journal of Common Market Studies* 253. For details of the cases referred to here, see chapter 13.

[51]   K Nicolaïdis and SK Schmidt, 'Mutual Recognition "On Trial": The Long Road to Services Liberalization' (2007) 14 *Journal of European Public Policy* 717.

[52]   European Commission Green Paper on the Review of the Consumer Acquis, COM(2006) 744 final. See generally S Weatherill, 'Maximum versus Minimum Harmonization: Choosing between Unity and Diversity in the Search for the Soul of the Internal Market' in N Nic Shuibhne and LW Gormley (eds), *From Single Market to Economic Union: Essays in Memory of John A Usher* (Oxford: Oxford University Press, 2012).

[53]   According to Internal Market Scoreboards, as of 1 October 2012, there were 1,420 single market directives and 1,769 regulations in force. This contrasts with 1,490 directives and only 275 regulations in 2001. See J Pelkmans and A Correia de Brito, *Enforcement in the EU Single Market* (Brussels: CEPS, 2012) 107.

[54]   M Monti, 'A New Strategy for the Single Market: At the Service of Europe's Economy and Society', May 2010.

Protocol. In other words, some of the single market paradigm's basic features have been checked or challenged.

3.3 Economic union?

It is possible that we are now witnessing another paradigm shift for the internal market. The weakened, unstable single market paradigm may be giving way to an economic union paradigm. The proximate cause for this is the need to ensure the success of the single currency, the euro, which has been battered by the financial crisis that begun in 2007.

The internal market and the economic and monetary union (EMU) complement each other, as was already recognized in the Commission's slogan 'one market, one money'. In fact, a single currency only makes sense in the context of an internal market. A decision to adopt a single currency is always an exercise in balancing its benefits against its costs, and a well-functioning internal market increases the former and reduces the latter. The benefits of a single currency in terms of lower transaction costs, greater transparency, and the elimination of exchange-rate risk are only felt if there is trade and investment, and a single currency can in turn be expected to provide a further boost for them. The problem with a single currency is that it reduces flexibility: an individual Member State can no longer respond to economic developments by changing interest rates or the value of its currency. However, a well-functioning internal market may reduce the need for independent action by Member States if it brings with it an alignment of business cycles.[55] If every Member State experiences booms and busts simultaneously, a centralized monetary policy will work well. Further, in the literature on optimum currency areas, labour mobility has been identified as one of the key factors for a successful currency union.[56] If one Member State is experiencing fast growth while another is suffering a slowdown, the workers may move from the latter to the former. This compensates for the loss of independence in interest and exchange-rate setting. The problem for Europe is that free movement of workers remains largely words on paper, with only a small percentage of EU nationals taking advantage of their right to move to another country for employment.[57] More broadly, a well-functioning internal market allows the real exchange-rate channel to work. What this means is that a country whose economy is overheating due to low real interest rates, which result from a centrally set nominal interest rate and a high level of inflation, is automatically cooled down. Due to the high inflation, its goods and services become more expensive so its export sector suffers. The weakening export sector stabilizes the system. By contrast, in a country that is experiencing a slowdown due to an excessively high real interest rate, which results from a centrally set nominal interest rate coupled with low inflation, the export sector is going to accelerate. The low inflation will make its goods and services cheaper, and its export performance will be boosted. This again stabilizes the system automatically. The problem for the EU is that weaknesses in the internal market which, for example, still covers services only partially, have meant that the real exchange-rate channel has not operated with sufficient force to counteract localized overheating and bubbles.[58] It

---

[55] JA Frankel and AK Rose, 'The Endogeneity of the Optimum Currency Area Criteria' (1998) 108 *The Economic Journal* 1009.

[56] RA Mundell, 'A Theory of Optimum Currency Areas' (1961) 51 *The American Economic Review* 657.

[57] See further chapter 13.

[58] The dominance of the real interest-rate channel over the real exchange-rate channel has been described well in H Enderlein et al, *Completing the Euro: A Road Map towards Fiscal Union in Europe – Report of the 'Tommaso Padoa-Schioppa Group'* (Paris: Notre Europe, 2012).

is no accident that serious proposals for dealing with the euro crisis tend to call for the strengthening of the internal market.[59]

Moreover, it can be questioned how well the basic idea of a competitive single market model, and the current EMU more broadly, where each Member State is responsible for its own economic policies and then competes with others, fits with the reality of the single currency. The crisis has shown that eurozone countries are highly interconnected. When a number of countries allowed their labour costs and other elements of competitiveness to deteriorate disastrously, this proved to be a problem for the entire eurozone; ultimately the stronger countries and the European institutions could not let the weaker ones drown but needed to come forward with various rescue mechanisms. Further, within the eurozone, problems of one country can rapidly infect other States. If there are question marks over the health of the banks of one country, markets quickly become worried about the financial institutions of the other countries as well; if the ability of one Member State to stay within the euro is questioned, the markets quickly start to worry about the other countries. In other words, it is in the interest of all euro States to ensure that every euro State is economically healthy. It is not simply a matter of each State looking after its own performance and competing with the others.[60]

Finally, the crisis has shown the need for profound changes in the field of financial services, one of the most important sectors of modern economies. First, the crisis has led to a re-fragmentation of the single financial market, as companies have repatriated some of their activities, often at the behest of national supervisors. This means that some of the most tangible gains of the internal market have been lost. It also means that the conditions of competition for non-financial firms have diverged, as the availability and cost of capital may vary dramatically between countries. Further, the monetary policy decisions of the European Central Bank have lost some of their effectiveness as, for example, the cutting of interest rates may not result in a lower cost of finance on the ground. More broadly, the financial crisis has exposed the unhealthy relationship between many Member States and their banks. When individual banks have run into trouble, their home States have had to rescue them. This has increased their national debt and made investors doubt the solvency of countries such as Ireland and Spain. This has further weakened national banks, which often have large holdings of their government's bonds. In other words, national banking and fiscal problems have fed into each other. In sum, the single market model where banks and financial service providers were largely regulated, supervised, and ultimately supported by their home countries but operated on a pan-European scale has proven unsustainable.[61]

The move away from the single market paradigm can be seen graphically precisely in the case of financial regulation. This was a sector where the principle of home country control at one time reigned supreme. Every Member State regulated its own financial institutions, which then traded in the whole EU using the single passport that the home country had provided them.[62] The new financial services and banking rules that have been adopted since the financial crisis have abandoned the idea of home country control and moved to a

---

[59] See eg H Van Rompuy et al, 'Towards a Genuine Economic and Monetary Union', available at http://www .consilium.europa.eu/uedocs/cms_data/docs/pressdata/en/ec/134069.pdf at 10.

[60] For a succinct review of the issues, see Communication from the Commission, A blueprint for a deep and genuine economic and monetary union: launching a European debate, COM(2012) 777 final.

[61] Ibid.   [62] See further chapter 14.

centralized approach with a single rulebook rather than a number of competing and mutu-ally recognized national rules.[63]

It is thus possible that through a process of spillback the 'remorseless logic' of mon-etary integration requires an internal market fit for an economic union[64] – a market that works better and is more uniform and centralized than the one contemplated under the single market paradigm. If so, an acute dilemma emerges. How to manage the relationship between those Member States who have signed up to the euro, and those that have not? Again, we have already got a small taste of this in the context of the planned EU bank-ing union. The UK, a country with an opt-out from the euro and not participating in the banking union, has been deeply concerned about the possibility that in practice the euro countries would impose their view on the future shape of the internal market on the whole EU. A solution for this concern was found in the shape of a complex new decision-making mechanism that seeks to safeguard the interests of the outs.[65] However, similar concerns are likely to emerge elsewhere.[66]

To sum up, the nature of market integration has changed in the course of the develop-ment of European integration. In the beginning, what was contemplated was a common market that would balance freedom and fairness, and where the political institutions would play the leading role in creating the common market through harmonization. This did not work. The institutions proved unequal to the task. Instead, the Court seized the initiative in cooperation with the Commission and with the eventual support of the Member States. The result was a single market that was based less on harmonization and a level playing field and more on home country control and competition. However, it may be that we are now once again witnessing a shift in the internal market paradigm. The tensions inherent in the single market and the need to support the EMU may be pushing economic integration in a new, more centralized direction.

4 The law of the internal market: the power to harmonize

In practice, the law needs to supply two things to establish the internal market. First, there need to be rules on free movement. These are the subject of other chapters in this book.[67] Secondly, there needs to be a rule that allows the EU to legislate for internal market pur-poses. In the actual EU of today, there are a number of such rules. The most important among them is Article 114 TFEU.[68] This is the topic of the present section. It will discuss the extent of the power Article 114 TFEU gives to the EU, and the exceptions the same provision contains.[69]

---

[63] For critical overviews, see M Andenas and IHY Chiu, 'Financial Stability and Legal Integration in Financial Regulation' (2013) 38 *European Law Review* 335 and N Moloney, 'EU Financial Market Regulation after the Global Financial Crisis: "More Europe" or More Risks?' (2010) 47 *Common Market Law Review* 1317.

[64] See further on the relationship between 'microeconomic and macroeconomic constitutions', K Tuori and K Tuori, *Eurozone Crisis: A Constitutional Analysis* (Cambridge: Cambridge University Press, 2014, forthcoming).

[65] A Barker, 'Eurozone agrees common bank supervisor', *Financial Times*, 13 December 2012.

[66] See generally on the limits of market integration in the context of different models of capitalism, J Snell, 'Varieties of Capitalism and the Limits of European Economic Integration' (2010–11) 13 *Cambridge Yearbook of European Legal Studies* 415.   [67] See especially chapters 12–15.

[68] According to Art 4(2) TFEU, the internal market is a shared competence between the EU and the Member States.

[69] See on the issue of the choice of legal basis in the context of Art 114 TFEU, C Barnard, *The Substantive Law of the EU: The Four Freedoms* (4th edn, Oxford: Oxford University Press, 2013) ch 16.

4.1 The power

The wording of Article 114(1) TFEU is as follows:

> Save where otherwise provided in the Treaties, the following provisions shall apply for the achievement of the objectives set out in Article 26. The European Parliament and the Council shall, acting in accordance with the ordinary legislative procedure and after consulting the Economic and Social Committee, adopt the measures for the approximation of the provisions laid down by law, regulation or administrative action in Member States which have as their object the establishment and functioning of the internal market.

There are a number of points that can be made about this. The first three can be taken quickly. First, Article 114 TFEU is a residual provision. It can only be used if other legal bases are not available.[70] For example, Article 50 TFEU contains a specific legal basis for the right of establishment. Secondly, the procedure under Article 114 is the ordinary legislative procedure, which means majority voting in the Council. This was the key innovation of the SEA. However, the second paragraph of the same provision states that this does 'not apply to fiscal provisions, to those relating to the free movement of persons nor to those relating to the rights and interests of employed persons.' These matters were considered too sensitive by the Member States. Thirdly, Article 114 allows the EU to adopt 'measures'. This means that the legislature has the discretion to choose the legal instrument most suitable for the issue in hand; it is not bound to employ only directives, as is the case under a number of other legal bases.

Fourthly, the measures adopted must have as their object the establishment and functioning of the internal market, as defined in Article 26 TFEU. The crucial question is how far this power reaches. After all, almost everything has some kind of impact on the market. The extent of the power is particularly salient given that it operates under majority voting. In effect, Article 114 TFEU represents a bargain among the Member States: they gave up their vetoes, but only in the specific area of the internal market.

By way of comparison, in the US the Commerce Clause of the Constitution, which gives the Congress the power 'to regulate commerce...among the several states' has been used as the basis of very broad legislation, including the New Deal that was the response to the Great Depression of the 1930s and the Civil Rights Act of 1964. This federal legislative activity has been at the expense of the powers of the states. Between 1937 and 1995 the Supreme Court accepted all measures put forward by the Congress under the Commerce Clause, but more recently it has begun to exercise some control over the power, for example striking down the Gun-Free School Zones Act that made it a federal criminal offence to carry a firearm near a school. The Congress had adopted the Act on the basis of the power to regulate interstate commerce, but the Court found the nexus between commerce and the possession of firearms near schools too tenuous.[71] In other words, the power to regulate commerce can be interpreted as an almost unlimited legislative power; it depends on the attitude of the judiciary whether this is sustainable.[72]

The reach of Article 114 TFEU was confronted in the case of *Tobacco Advertising*.[73] This case is considered in detail in the case study below. The key points bear repeating. Article 114

---

[70] See eg Case C-533/03 *Commission v Council* [2006] ECR I-1025 for a practical illustration.

[71] *United States v Lopez* 514 US 549 (1995).

[72] See EA Young, 'Protecting Member State Autonomy in the European Union: Some Cautionary Tales from American Federalism' (2002) 77 *New York Law Review* 1612 for an interesting comparison between the US and the EU.

[73] Case C-376/98 *Germany v European Parliament and Council* [2000] ECR I-8419.

does not provide a general power to regulate the economy. This would go against the very idea of the EU with limited powers. Instead, measures adopted under it must genuinely seek either to establish the internal market or to improve its functioning. This boils down to two things: either the measure must eliminate obstacles or it must deal with appreciable distortions of competition. As the Tobacco Advertising Directive on the facts did neither, the Court annulled it, following Advocate General Fennelly.

Tobacco Advertising sent an important signal. Article 114 TFEU was not without limits, and the Court was prepared to police them. However, it did not lead to a more general wave of successful litigation. The Court's attitude remains permissive to the EU institutions. Particularly instructive in this respect is the ruling in *Swedish Match*.[74] It concerned a Directive adopted under Article 114 that banned all tobacco for oral use, except tobacco for chewing or smoking. This ban included snus, a type of tobacco placed between lip and gum popular in Sweden. It was argued by Swedish Match that the Directive did not in fact contribute to the internal market: how could the ban of a product establish or improve the internal market? The Grand Chamber of the Court rejected the argument, following Advocate General Geelhoed. It ruled that national laws concerning tobacco for oral use were developing in different directions, which was creating obstacles to trade. This justified action by the EU legislature, which could, if appropriate, even prohibit the marketing of a product. One possible way of explaining the ruling is that the Court upheld the ban of a particular type of product to allow the circulation of others. A directive might, for example, prohibit dangerous widget types so that only safe widgets remain on the market and can be traded freely. On the facts, this does not seem a convincing explanation, however. All oral tobacco products were banned, apart from smoking or chewing tobacco. It is not easy to see how this improved trade. When *Swedish Match* is looked at together with other cases decided after *Tobacco Advertising*, it seems that the practical limits of Article 114 are very wide indeed.[75] In fact, in the context of Treaty reform, the remit of Article 114 was singled out as a key question,[76] although in the end the Lisbon Treaty did not amend it.

Case study 11.1: Tobacco advertising

Can the EU ban tobacco advertising in Member States in order to achieve or improve the internal market, or would this go beyond the remit of Article 114 TFEU? Behind this question are important issues of principle: is the EU competent to regulate all economic activity, even against the objections of an individual Member State, given the majority voting under the provision? How far can the EU go in the name of the internal market in matters related to human health and other non-economic issues, given that the Treaty sets strict limits on its powers to regulate, for example, public health as such?

The idea of regulating tobacco advertising at the level of the EU has been around since 1984. However, it was only in 1998 that the EU legislature produced a Directive to tackle the issue generally.[77] Essentially the Directive banned all tobacco advertising. The legal basis

---

[74] Case C-210/03 *Swedish Match* [2004] ECR I-11893.

[75] See D Wyatt, 'Community Competence to Regulate the Internal Market' in M Dougan and S Currie (eds), *50 Years of the European Treaties: Looking Back and Thinking Forward* (Oxford: Hart Publishing, 2009).

[76] See the Laeken Declaration on the Future of the European Union, adopted by the European Council on 15 December 2001.

[77] European Parliament and Council Directive 98/43/EC on the approximation of the laws, regulations and administrative provisions of the Member States relating to the advertising and sponsorship of tobacco products (OJ [1998] L213/9).

selected was Article 114 TFEU. This meant that Germany, which opposed the Directive, could not veto it, but was outvoted. Germany, after losing the political battle, began a legal battle and challenged the validity of the Directive on a number of grounds, including the ground that it could not be validly adopted under Article 114 at all. This was not a surprise. Already in the legislative process it had been suggested that Article 352 TFEU, which requires unanimity in the Council, would be the correct legal basis; reportedly this was also the view of the Council Legal Services.[78]

The first argument that the Court confronted was that the Directive was in reality a health protection measure, not an internal market one, and that the Treaty specifically excluded any harmonization for the protection of human health. The Court acknowledged that the ban on health harmonization should not be circumvented. However, this does not mean that an internal market measure could not have any effect on health. In fact, health requirements have to be taken into account in all EU policies, and Article 114(3) expressly requires that a high level of human health protection be ensured. In other words, the Court explicitly recognized that in the internal market economic and non-economic issues are inextricably intertwined. When the market is regulated, this always impacts on other concerns; yet it does not make market regulation health regulation.

While the Court accepted that health reasons could even be 'decisive'[79] in an internal market directive, it did not accept that Article 114 TFEU gave the EU legislature a general power to regulate the market. Such a finding, said the Court, would be incompatible with the principle of conferred powers, which today can be found in Article 5 TEU. This was important. In the past, no one had been particularly concerned about the exact limits of the EU's powers. This was because the legislative process had operated under unanimity. When only measures that all Member States supported could pass, the precise limitations of EU competences had seemed an insignificant issue, and certainly no Member State had a reason to bring an action. With the abolition of national vetoes this changed. Member States that could no longer exercise complete control over the EU's political process suddenly became much more conscious of the legal limits.[80] This was something national courts had also picked up on.[81] In its ruling the Court responded.

Instead of a general power to regulate the economy, the Court continued, Article 114 TFEU provided two specific powers. First is the competence to establish the internal market, in other words to eliminate obstacles to free movement. The second is the competence to improve the functioning of the internal market, in other words to eliminate distortions of competition. The question to decide was whether the Directive did either of these things.

Elimination of obstacles is a familiar concept in internal market law. What exactly is an obstacle to one of the four freedoms is the central issue of EU economic law and is discussed elsewhere in the book.[82] The key point to note here is that the Court created a direct linkage between Article 114 TFEU and provisions such as Article 34 TFEU on free movement of goods: the wider the reading of the notion of obstacle, the wider the power to harmonize. In *Tobacco Advertising*, the Court added a couple of further points. Article 114 can be used to prevent the emergence of future obstacles to trade that could arise if national laws developed in different directions. It is not only for the elimination of existing barriers. However, the mere finding of disparities between national laws and an abstract risk of obstacles is

---

[78] See para 17 of the Opinion of AG Fennelly in *Tobacco Advertising* (n 73).

[79] *Tobacco Advertising* (n 73) para 88.

[80] JHH Weiler, *The Constitution of Europe: 'Do the New Clothes Have an Emperor?' and Other Essays on European Integration* (Cambridge: Cambridge University Press, 1999) 39–74.

[81] *Brunner* [1994] 1 CMLR 57.   [82] See further chapters 13 and 15.

not sufficient to justify the use of Article 114, and if it is future obstacles that are targeted, their emergence must be likely. On the facts, there was indeed a danger that barriers could arise, for example for the free movement of magazines or newspapers. A newspaper including tobacco advertisements legal in one country could be denied access into the market of another country that banned such advertisements. However, the Directive went much further than this. It also banned things such as umbrellas or ashtrays containing the logo of a tobacco company, and advertisements in cinemas. This did not facilitate trade. The Directive also failed to provide that products complying with it could move freely. Instead, Member States remained free to ban even those few goods that did conform to it.

For distortions of competition, the Court emphasized that only the elimination of appreciable distortions could justify recourse to Article 114 TFEU. Otherwise, the powers of the EU legislature would in practice be unlimited. After all, any differences between national rules can be said to affect conditions of competition at least indirectly. The Court accepted that differences between the laws of Member States on tobacco advertising could in certain circumstances indeed distort competition appreciably. For example, the organizers of a car race might decide to move the event to a country where sponsorship by tobacco companies was legal. However, the Directive was not limited to these kinds of issues but went much further. In this context, the argument that advertising agencies established in countries with the fewest restrictions had a competitive advantage was rejected by the Court. While such companies might enjoy increased profits, the effects were remote and indirect, and could not be deemed appreciable.

The result was that the Tobacco Advertising Directive was annulled by the Court. For the first time, a general EU legislative measure was struck down for a lack of competence. This was not the end, however. A few years later, a new Directive was adopted.[83] It was much more closely tailored to the internal market concerns.[84] Again, Germany challenged it. This time the Grand Chamber of the Court, noting the more limited reach of the second Directive, allowed it to stand.[85] In other words, the EU can regulate those aspects of tobacco advertising that can have implications for free movement or lead to real distortions of competition, but it cannot just ban all tobacco advertising in the Member States in the name of the internal market.

The fifth point about Article 114(1) TFEU is that it only gives the power for 'the approximation of the provisions laid down by law, regulation or administrative action in Member States'. In other words, under the provision the EU can bring national laws closer to each other, to harmonize. It does not give the EU the competence to create something new that is unrelated to pre-existing[86] or anticipated[87] national laws. Thus, national trademark laws could be harmonized under Article 114, but a new EU-wide trademark could not be established using it.[88] While national company laws were approximated using internal market powers, a new European public limited company form, Societas Europaea, was based on Article 352 TFEU.[89]

[83] European Parliament and Council Directive 2003/33/EC on the approximation of the laws, regulations and administrative provisions of the Member States relating to the advertising and sponsorship of tobacco products (OJ [2003] L152/16).
[84] See generally S Weatherill, 'The Limits of Legislative Harmonization Ten Years after Tobacco Advertising: How the Court's Case Law has Become a "Drafting Guide"' (2011) 12 *German Law Journal* 827.
[85] Case C-380/03 *Germany v European Parliament and Council* [2006] ECR I-11573.
[86] Case C-436/03 *European Parliament v Council* [2006] ECR I-3733, para 44.
[87] Case C-58/08 *Vodafone* [2010] ECR I-4999, which adopts a particularly permissive approach in this respect. [88] Opinion 1/94 [1994] ECR I-5267, para 59.
[89] Council Regulation (EC) No 2157/2001 on the Statute for a European company (OJ [2001] L294/1).

The Court had to confront the precise limits of the requirement of approximation in *ENISA*.[90] The EU legislature had established ENISA, the European Network and Information Security Agency, under Article 114 TFEU. This followed a series of earlier directives that regulated electronic communication networks and services, and dealt with the security of networks and information. The role of the agency was to help the Commission and the Member States on network and information security matters, ensuring the smooth functioning of the internal market. Its tasks included the identification of risks, the development of common methodologies for the prevention of security issues, the promotion of the exchange of best practice, and generally enhancing cooperation in the area of network and information security. The UK argued that Article 114 only allowed the harmonization of national laws, not the creation of new EU bodies. The test in the view of the UK was whether the result of the measure could be achieved if all Member States produced identical laws. The UK argued that since the establishment of ENISA was beyond the capacity of individual Member States, it did not qualify as a harmonizing measure. The Grand Chamber of the Court, disagreeing with Advocate General Kokott, held that the regulation setting up the agency was valid. The Court reasoned that the legislature was entitled to set up a body to contribute to the harmonization process when the adoption of various supporting measures would help the uniform implementation and application of other harmonizing measures. However, the tasks of such a body had to be closely related to the previous EU internal market legislation. On the facts, the Court decided that the objectives and tasks of ENISA were closely linked to the previous directives and supported their implementation.

The ruling in *ENISA* is important. Without it, the creation of new agencies would have to be based on the cumbersome Article 352 TFEU, which requires unanimity. The EU legislature has taken advantage of the relatively permissive attitude of the Court.[91] In the context of the financial crisis that began in 2007, it has established a set of important new financial supervisory authorities to deal with banks, securities and markets, and insurers and occupational pension providers. While ENISA's tasks concerned advice and cooperation, the European supervisory authorities have much wider powers, including the power to impose binding decisions.[92]

4.2 **The exceptions**

So far this section has discussed the power that Article 114 TFEU gives the EU. We finally turn to the qualifications contained in the same article.[93] Essentially, these qualifications represent a compromise. The countries with high standards in matters such as health and safety or the environment were concerned that under majority voting Article 114 could result in the lowering of the level of protection. The price for the acceptance of majority voting was a commitment to high standards, incorporated into Article 114(3), and possibilities for derogation, now found in paragraphs 4 to 10.

---

[90] Case C-217/04 *UK v European Parliament and Council* [2006] ECR I-3789. See also eg Case C-66/04 *UK v European Parliament and Council* [2005] ECR I-10553 (smoke flavourings).

[91] For another example, see Commission Proposal for a Regulation of the European Parliament and of the Council on a Common European Sales Law, COM(2011) 635 final.

[92] See E Fahey, 'Does the Emperor have Financial Crisis Clothes? Reflections on the Legal Basis of the European Banking Authority' (2011) 74 *Modern Law Review* 581. The ECJ confirmed the permissive approach in Case C-270/12 *UK v European Parliament and Council*, judgment of 22 January 2014, nyr.

[93] See generally I Maletić, *The Law and Policy of Harmonisation in Europe's Internal Market* (Cheltenham: Edward Elgar, 2013).

Article 114(4) TFEU provides a derogation for pre-existing national rules. It allows a Member State to maintain a higher level of protection than envisaged in a harmonization measure. This is subject to two qualifications. Only major needs listed in Article 36 TFEU or the protection of the environment or the working environment can justify a derogation, and the Commission must be notified. Article 114(5) provides a derogation for new national rules that have been adopted after harmonization. Again, a number of conditions, which are cumulative, need to be fulfilled.[94] There needs to be new scientific evidence. The evidence must relate to the environment or the working environment. There must be a problem that is specific to the relevant Member State and that has arisen after harmonization. Again, the Commission must be notified. Article 114(6) sets out the procedure that the Commission must follow when it receives a notification. In most cases it will have six months to decide whether to approve or reject the national measure. The criterion is whether the national measure is a means of arbitrary discrimination or a disguised restriction on trade between Member States and whether it constitutes an obstacle to the functioning of the internal market. It is important to note that the national rule is unenforceable against an individual relying on the direct effect of an EU harmonizing measure until Commission approval has been gained.[95] In other words, the Commission decision has a constitutive effect. If recourse to a derogation proves justified, the Commission is under an obligation to consider whether the existing harmonization measures need to be adapted or new ones adopted. In this way, the experiences of individual Member States can serve to inform EU harmonization.

The introduction of derogations to Article 114 TFEU was originally met with grave concern.[96] The worry was that Member States would routinely turn to them, frustrating the whole objective of Article 114. These fears have not materialized.[97] It seems that the Member States have been committed to the internal market, the standards of protection have generally been sufficiently high, and the onerous conditions for the derogations have discouraged reliance on them.

To sum up, Article 114 TFEU gives the Union the crucial power to harmonize in the name of the internal market. Its use does not require unanimity. In practice, it has been utilized frequently. The power is a wide one, but not without limits. In particular, it does not give the EU legislature a general competence to regulate the economy, only the competence to deal with obstacles or appreciable distortions of competition. It is only available for approximation, not for the creation of things such as new EU intellectual property rights or company forms unrelated to national laws. It is also subject to tightly circumscribed derogations that made the majority voting palatable for high-standard countries.

5 The law of the internal market: the types of harmonization

The final issue to be addressed in this chapter concerns the types of harmonization employed by the EU, and their legal implications. What kinds of measures are adopted under Article 114 TFEU and under other internal market legal bases? Various typologies could be offered. The present section concentrates on total and minimum

---

[94] See eg Joined Cases C-439/05 and 454/05 P *Land Oberösterreich* [2007] ECR I-7141.

[95] Case C-319/97 *Kortas* [1999] ECR I-3143.

[96] See eg P Pescatore, 'Some Critical Remarks on the "Single European Act"' (1987) 24 *Common Market Law Review* 9.   [97] See eg Barnard, *The Substantive Law of the EU* (n 69) ch 16.

harmonization,[98] which form the two paradigm cases,[99] and which represent quite different approaches.

Total harmonization was the predominant method of approximation in the early years of the EU, and is still employed today. In fact, as discussed in section 3.2, in some areas it has enjoyed something of a renaissance.[100] Total harmonization takes place when an EU measure, such as a directive, regulates something exhaustively, not leaving any room for divergent rules of the Member States. For example, a directive on widgets could lay down all the features and characteristics that widgets must comply with. Given that it is a directive, Member States would have to transpose its contents into their national law. However, they would not be entitled to add further conditions for widgets to meet.[101] In other words, the directive has pre-empted Member State activity; it has occupied the field.

Total harmonization has another important legal consequence: a national rule that complies with an EU measure totally harmonizing something is no longer open to challenge on the basis of the four freedoms of the Treaty.[102] The Member State can defend its national law against such a challenge by simply saying that the law is fully in line with the EU measure. Any challenge would have to demonstrate that the law somehow fails to respect the relevant EU measure.

Nevertheless, an EU measure harmonizing an area totally is not immune to legal scrutiny. A challenge could be brought on the grounds that the EU measure itself violates some higher ranking rule or principle of EU law. However, the crucial difference is that the question would be whether the EU measure violates EU law, not whether a national measure violates EU law. In these kinds of circumstances, the Court of Justice has traditionally taken a hands-off attitude and only struck down EU measures if they manifestly infringe the Treaty.[103]

Minimum harmonization sets the floor below which no Member State may go, but leaves them free to adopt more demanding rules. In this way, it is respectful of the national diversity that total harmonization suppresses. For example, the widget directive could just specify the minimum safety features that every widget must at the very least meet, but give the Member States the option to impose more stringent requirements. Minimum harmonization has often been used in the context of issues such as the protection of the environment or consumers, where some Member States have wished to impose or maintain tougher rules than the others.

A national law that goes beyond the requirements of the minimum harmonization measure would not enjoy immunity from the Treaty. Rather, any national rule would be open to challenge on the ground that it violates a Treaty free movement provision.[104] In this way, the Treaty forms the ceiling above which the Members States are not permitted to go. The mere fact that, say, a directive has authorized Member States to adopt more stringent

---

[98] Similarly, M Dougan, 'Minimum Harmonization and the Internal Market' (2000) 37 *Common Market Law Review* 853.

[99] An analytically more precise typology would be to contrast total with partial harmonization, and maximum with minimum harmonization, based on a distinction between the coverage and the level of regulation. However, in practice, total and maximum harmonization entail similar legal consequences, as do partial and minimum harmonization.

[100] See also eg European Parliament and Council Directive 2011/83/EU on consumer rights (OJ [2011] L304/64).   [101] See eg Case 5/77 *Tedeschi* [1977] ECR 1555.

[102] See eg Case C-324/99 *DaimlerChrysler* [2001] ECR I-9897.

[103] See eg Case C-233/94 *Germany v European Parliament and Council* [1997] ECR I-2405.

[104] See eg Case C-382/87 *Buet* [1989] ECR 1235.

rules on widgets, does not mean that those rules acquire immunity from the four freedoms if they are applied in a cross-border context.

Unfortunately, it is not necessarily easy in practice to decide whether a particular EU act seeks to bring about total harmonization or to leave Member States free to adopt stricter rules or to rely on grounds not listed in the measure. For example, the Services Directive,[105] which is an important piece of EU legislation that was designed to improve the operation of the single market in services, lists a number of grounds that Member States may use to limit service provision. However, there was a debate about whether these are the only grounds Member States can still rely on, which would correspond with the idea of total harmonization, or whether they are still free to invoke other reasons as well.[106] Ultimately, these issues boil down to the interpretation of the relevant harmonization measure,[107] and this may not always be an easy task.

To sum up, the EU legislative process produces different types of measures; the two paradigm cases are total and minimum harmonization. The legal consequences of the different types of harmonization vary. Member State compliance with a measure of total harmonization means that it cannot be criticized on the basis of the four freedoms, while a Member State going beyond the requirements of minimum harmonization must ensure that its national law is in line with the Treaty free movement rules.

6 Conclusion

The internal market has been at the heart of the European integration project from the beginning. However, there is no consensus on its fundamental nature and it has changed over time. Three possible ideal models can be distinguished: host country control, harmonized model, and home country control, based on the allocation of legislative power. The models represent fundamentally different philosophies of market integration, and entail different consequences for sovereignty, the balance of legislative and judicial powers, the protection of public policy interests, and democracy. In the historical experience of the EU, no model has been adopted in a perfect form. Nevertheless, when the integration moved from the original common market model to single market it did take a step towards the home country model and away from the harmonized model. The single market paradigm has not proven stable. In practice, the ideas of mutual recognition and regulatory competition have encountered resistance and created only limited market integration. It is possible that the internal market is shifting towards an economic union paradigm.

Whatever the model or the paradigm of the internal market, legally two things are needed: there need to be rules on free movement and a conferral of legislative power to the EU. The latter was the subject of this chapter. The key provision is Article 114 TFEU that gives the EU the competence to harmonize in order to achieve or improve the internal market. This is a broad power but not without its limits. The Court of Justice has found that it allows the EU legislature to deal with obstacles to trade and with appreciable distortions of competition. Another limit is that the power is there for approximation of national rules, not for the creation of new free-standing EU rights or things unrelated to Member State laws. The exact contours of this are subject to an important debate. It

---

[105] European Parliament and Council Directive 2006/123/EC on services in the internal market (OJ [2006] L376/36).

[106] See eg C Barnard, 'Unravelling the Services Directive' (2008) 45 *Common Market Law Review* 323, 367.

[107] See eg Case 148/78 *Ratti* [1979] ECR 1629.

needs to be noted that the harmonization that the EU engages in can take different forms. Particularly important types are total and minimum harmonization, which entail different legal consequences.

Further reading

C Barnard, *The Substantive Law of the EU: The Four Freedoms* (4th edn, Oxford: Oxford University Press, 2013)

C Barnard and J Scott (eds), *The Law of the Single European Market: Unpacking the Premises* (Oxford: Hart Publishing, 2002)

M Dougan, 'Minimum Harmonization and the Internal Market' (2000) 37 *Common Market Law Review* 853

M Egan, 'Single Market' in E Jones, A Menon, and S Weatherill (eds), *The Oxford Handbook of the European Union* (Oxford: Oxford University Press, 2012)

I Maletić, *The Law and Policy of Harmonisation in Europe's Internal Market* (Cheltenham: Edward Elgar, 2013)

N Nic Shuibhne (ed), *Regulating the Internal Market* (Cheltenham: Edward Elgar, 2006)

M Poiares Maduro, *We the Court. The European Court of Justice and the European Economic Constitution: A Critical Reading of Article 30 of the EC Treaty* (Oxford: Hart Publishing, 1998)

J Snell, 'Who's Got the Power? Free Movement and Allocation of Competences in EC Law' (2003) 22 *Yearbook of European Law* 323

J Snell, 'Varieties of Capitalism and the Limits of European Economic Integration' (2010–11) 13 *Cambridge Yearbook of European Legal Studies* 415

S Weatherill, 'The Limits of Legislative Harmonization Ten Years after Tobacco Advertising: How the Court's Case Law has Become a "Drafting Guide"' (2011) 12 *German Law Journal* 827

S Weatherill, 'Maximum versus Minimum Harmonization: Choosing between Unity and Diversity in the Search for the Soul of the Internal Market' in N Nic Shuibhne and LW Gormley (eds), *From Single Market to Economic Union: Essays in Memory of John A Usher* (Oxford: Oxford University Press, 2012)

12

Free movement of goods

Peter Oliver and Martín Martínez Navarro

1 Introduction

The aim of the internal market is to enable European manufacturers to sell the same product in all the Member States, thereby achieving economies of scale similar to those in the

US and creating greater prosperity throughout the region. It is as well to remember that the internal market was fostered not only by Europeans, but also by the *American* initiative known as the Marshall Plan. This plan to revive and enhance the European economies following the Second World War was realized by the Economic Cooperation Act 1948, which contains the following Declaration of Policy:

> Mindful of the advantages which the United States has enjoyed through the existence of a large domestic market with no internal trade barriers, and believing that similar advantages can accrue to the countries of Europe, it is declared to be the policy of the people of the United States to encourage these countries through a joint organization to exert sustained common efforts…which will speedily achieve that economic cooperation in Europe which is essential for lasting peace and prosperity.[1]

The Treaty of Rome of 1957 established the 'common market'. In its seminal judgment in *Gaston Schul*, the Court held:

> The concept of a common market as defined by the Court in a consistent line of decisions involves the elimination of all obstacles to intra-Community trade in order to merge the national markets into a single market bringing about conditions as close as possible to those of a genuine internal market.[2]

In the current Treaties, the 'common market' has been replaced by the 'internal market', which probably has the same meaning.[3] Article 3(3) TEU provides: 'The Union shall establish an internal market'. The internal market is defined in Article 26(2) TFEU as follows:

> The internal market shall comprise an area without internal frontiers in which the free movement of goods, persons, services and capital is ensured in accordance with the provisions of the Treaties.

This provision was first introduced into the Treaties, albeit in a slightly different form, by the Single European Act which came into force in 1987.

As a result, the Court frequently rules national measures to be contrary to the TFEU, even though they have of course been enacted by democratically elected governments. By signing and ratifying the various successive Treaties, the Member States have given their blessing to this. Nevertheless, it can sometimes raise the hackles of Member States or public opinion – as where the Germans were told that their centuries-old Purity Law was unlawful so that the sale of drinks as 'beer' must be allowed even if they contained such hitherto proscribed ingredients as rice or maize, which are commonly used for making beer in other Member States.[4] Italian national pride suffered a similar blow when the Court ruled that their country's ban on the sale of pasta containing soft wheat was in breach of Article 34 TFEU.[5] The Member States tolerate such occasional upsets for the simple reason that they are outweighed by the benefits, namely allowing goods made in their own Member

---

[1] This plan led to the establishment of the Organisation for European Economic Co-operation, which subsequently became the Organisation for Economic Co-operation and Development (OECD).

[2] Case 15/81 *Gaston Schul* [1982] ECR 1409, para 33. See further chapter 11.

[3] See also chapter 11.   [4] Case178/84 *Commission v Germany* ('*Beer*') [1987] ECR 1227.

[5] Case 90/86 *Zoni* [1988] ECR 4285.

States free access to the markets in the 27 other Member States (30 including the European Economic Area (EEA) States).

This chapter will look at the EU provisions which ensure the free movement of goods: the so-called *non-fiscal* rules prohibiting quantitative restrictions on the free movement of goods, such as quotas, and measures having equivalent effect, like the national rules on the composition of beer and pasta, as well as the *fiscal* rules prohibiting customs duties, charges having equivalent effect, and discriminatory internal taxation. Together these rules form the basis of the EU's customs union.

2 The customs union

2.1 The concept of a customs union

By virtue of Article 28(1) TFEU, the EU constitutes a customs union covering all trade in goods. According to a widely received definition, a customs union, in contrast to a free trade area, does not merely involve liberalization of trade between the parties; it also entails the establishment of uniform rules for goods coming from third countries.[6] Consequently, a customs union has an *external* and an *internal* dimension.

The *external* dimension of the EU as a customs union is reflected in the adoption of uniform common rules which apply to products originating from third countries: a common customs tariff (Article 31 TFEU) and the common commercial policy in trade with third countries (Article 207 TFEU). These matters fall outside the scope of the present chapter, which focuses instead on the *internal* dimension of the customs union.

The establishment of the customs union has involved, and continues to involve, the abolition of internal barriers to trade in goods between Member States. Free movement of goods within the internal market is to be achieved through

(a) the prohibition of customs duties and charges of equivalent effect or CEEs (Article 30 TFEU),

(b) the prohibition of quantitative restrictions and measures of equivalent effect or MEEs (Articles 34 to 36 TFEU), and

(c) the prohibition of internal discriminatory taxation (Article 110 TFEU).

Although the latter provision is not part of the Title of the TFEU relating to the internal market, it has in practice become assimilated to it, as will be explained in section 7. All these provisions are directly effective.[7]

Articles 30 and 110 apply to fiscal rules or pecuniary measures (ie an obligation to pay a sum of money), Articles 34 to 36 apply to non-fiscal rules or non-pecuniary measures (ie an obligation to comply with other types of requirement).

The counterpart to these prohibitions is a vast body of EU legislation harmonizing national laws so as to enable goods to flow more freely between Member States. That

---

[6] Opinion of the Permanent Court of International Justice of 1931 in the 'customs system between Germany and Austria', Compendium of Consultative Decrees, Directives and Opinions, Series A–B, no 41, p 51, and Art XXIV(8)(A) of the GATT 1947. See also Case C-125/94 *Aprile* [1995] ECR I-2919, para 32 and Case C-126/94 *Cadi Surgelés* [1996] ECR I-5647, para 14.

[7] Case 33/76 *Rewe-Zentralfinanz* [1976] ECR 1989, para 5 (Art 30); Case 74/76 *Iannelli v Meroni* [1977] ECR 557 (Art 34 TFEU); Case 83/78 *Redmond* [1978] ECR 2347 (Arts 34 and 35); and Case 7/65 *Lütticke* [1966] ECR 293 (Art 110).

legislation falls outside the scope of this chapter, and will be considered in chapters 11, 21, and 23.

2.2 Goods originating in a Member State and goods in free circulation

By definition, the provisions on free movement apply to goods originating in any Member State. For good measure, this is stated explicitly in Article 28(2) TFEU. The same paragraph also establishes that those provisions extend to products coming from third countries which are in free circulation in Member States.[8] The same principle applies to Article 110 TFEU, although this is not spelt out anywhere in the Treaty.[9]

Pursuant to Article 29 TFEU, products originating in a third country are considered to be in free circulation if the import formalities have been complied with and any customs duties or CEEs due have been levied in a Member State, unless they have benefited from a total or partial drawback. In practice, this simply means that the goods must have been cleared through customs, whether or not customs duties have actually been paid.[10]

In *Donckerwolcke*, it was held that goods originating in third countries and placed in free circulation 'are definitively and wholly assimilated to products originating in Member States'.[11] Consequently, the free movement rules are applicable without distinction to goods originating in the EU and to those which have been put in free circulation in one Member State, irrespective of the actual origin of the goods.[12] Thus a consignment of widgets from the US which is cleared through customs in Antwerp (Belgium) is in free circulation in that Member State, and is assimilated to Belgian goods for the purposes of Articles 30, 34 to 36, and 110. These widgets can subsequently move freely to other Member States. A particularly clear illustration of this principle is to be found in *Commission v Ireland*, where it was held that the defendant State had infringed Article 34 TFEU by imposing an import licensing system for potatoes originating in Cyprus (which was then outside the EU) but in free circulation in the UK.[13]

3 The meanings of 'goods'

The Treaty rules on free movement apply to goods. The English version of the TFEU uses the terms 'goods' (eg Article 28(1)) and 'products' (eg Articles 28(2) and 29). Although several other language versions also employ two different words, they plainly bear the same meaning in this context. What is more, Articles 34 and 35 TFEU speak of 'imports' and 'exports' respectively without referring to 'goods' or products'; but there is no doubt whatever that imports and exports of *goods* are meant.

---

[8] In reality, Art 28(2) TFEU refers explicitly to Art 30 TFEU and to Chapter 2 of the same Title. However, Chapter 2 consists solely of Art 33 TFEU, which concerns customs cooperation. It is suggested that this is an unintended omission deriving from the fact that the provision equivalent to Art 28(2) in the EC Treaty referred also to Chapter 2, which at the time contained the provisions equivalent to Arts 34–36. It is inconceivable that under the TFEU goods in free circulation no longer benefit from the prohibition of quantitative restrictions and measures of equivalent effect.

[9] Case 193/85 *Co-Frutta* [1987] ECR 2085, paras 24–29.

[10] The customs authorities may allow payment of customs duties to be deferred: Arts 70, 72–78, 124, and 129 of Regulation 450/2008 on the Modernised Customs Code (OJ [2008] L145/1).

[11] Case 41/76 *Donckerwolcke* [1976] ECR 1921, para 17.   [12] Ibid, para 18.

[13] Case 288/83 *Commission v Ireland* [1985] ECR 1761; see also Case C-216/01 *Budejovický Budvar* [2003] ECR I-13617, para 95.

The *locus classicus* is *Commission v Italy*, where the Court defined 'goods' to mean 'products which can be valued in money and which are capable, as such, of forming the subject of commercial transactions'.[14] On this basis, it held that works of art constituted goods, rejecting Italy's contention that 'goods' meant only 'ordinary merchandise'. Had the Court accepted Italy's position, restrictions on trade in works of art would have fallen outside the Treaty altogether, which would have been unthinkable. In any case, as will be explained in this chapter, the principle of free movement of goods does not prevent Member States from imposing restrictions under certain limited conditions.

The definition in *Commission v Italy* is not exhaustive.[15] In any case, waste is to be regarded as goods, whether or not it has any intrinsic commercial value.[16] Anomalously, electricity has also been held to constitute goods, even though it is not tangible and cannot be stored.[17] Finally, human corpses and body parts no doubt fall within this concept as well.[18]

On the other hand, transactions covered by the other three fundamental freedoms are not goods. Thus broadcasting is a service, not a product,[19] as is the operation of a lottery.[20] The same applies to intangibles other than electricity.[21] Similarly, coins and banknotes do not constitute goods, provided that they are still legal tender somewhere in the world.[22]

4 Nationality and residence

The Treaty provisions considered in this chapter apply regardless of the nationality of the trader,[23] or the purchaser. Similarly, the residence of the legal and natural persons involved is irrelevant. The only relevant criteria are the origin of the goods and, if they originate in a third country, whether they have been put into free circulation in the EU. In this regard, the free movement of goods differs from the other fundamental freedoms for which nationality and/or residence are crucial factors.

5 Customs duties and charges of equivalent effect

The prohibition of custom duties is set out in Article 30 TFEU:

> Customs duties on imports and exports and charges having equivalent effect shall be prohibited between Member States. This prohibition shall also apply to customs duties of a fiscal nature.

---

[14] Case 7/68 *Commission v Italy* ('*Works of art*') [1968] ECR 423, 428.

[15] AG Fennelly in Case C-97/98 *Jägerskiöld* [1999] ECR I-7319, 7328.

[16] Case C-2/90 *Commission v Belgium* ('*Walloon waste*') [1992] ECR I-4431.

[17] Case C-393/92 *Almelo* [1994] ECR I-1477. See AG Fennelly's comment in *Jägerskiöld* (n 15) para 20: 'To my mind, electricity must be regarded as a specific case, perhaps justifiable by virtue of its function as an energy source and, therefore, in competition with gas and oil.'

[18] See generally Case C-203/99 *Veedfald* [2000] ECR I-3569.

[19] Case 155/73 *Sacchi* [1974] ECR 409 and Case 52/79 *Debauve* [1980] ECR 833. See further chapter 14.

[20] Case C-124/97 *Läärä* [1999] ECR I-6067.

[21] See *Jägerskiöld* (n 15) (concerning fishing rights and permits).

[22] Case 7/78 *Thompson* [1978] ECR 2247 (coins) and Case C-358/93 *Bordessa* [1995] ECR I-361 (banknotes). See further chapter 15.

[23] Case 2/69 *Sociaal Fonds voor de Diamantarbeiders* ('*Diamonds*') [1969] ECR 211, paras 24–26 (Art 30 TFEU); Case C-402/09 *Tatu* [2011] ECR I-2711, para 36 (Art 110 TFEU).

5.1 **Customs duties**

The abolition of customs duties between Member States was an essential element in the establishment of the internal market since they are amongst the most blatant obstacles to trade. Customs duties are charges levied on goods by reason of the fact that they cross a frontier between Member States. Probably unsurprisingly, the Court has not had the opportunity to consider customs duties on many occasions due to the clear and unambiguous prohibition established by the Treaty. *Van Gend en Loos*[24] – the celebrated case where the Court first laid down the principle of direct effect[25] – is one of the few cases concerning customs duties. In this case the Court took the opportunity to state that the prohibition of customs duties is an 'essential provision' and constitutes one of the foundations of the EU.

5.2 **Charges of equivalent effect**

Article 30 TFEU also prohibits CEEs, as otherwise it would be very easy for Member States to circumvent the prohibition on customs duties. The Treaty contains no definition of CEEs, so the task of defining this concept has been left to the Court.

The landmark ruling on the definition of CEEs is the *Diamonds* case, due to the specific features of the disputed tax.[26] Belgium had established a Social Fund for Diamond Workers, the purpose of which was to award social benefits to diamond workers. All imports of unworked diamonds were subject to a contribution intended to enable the fund to fulfil its tasks. The amount of the contribution was 0.33 per cent of the value of the unworked diamonds imported. The Court ruled:

> Consequently, any pecuniary charge, however small and whatever its designation and mode of application, which is imposed unilaterally on domestic or foreign goods by reason of the fact that they cross a frontier, and which is not a customs duty in the strict sense, constitutes a charge having equivalent effect within the meaning of Articles [28] and [30] of the Treaty, even if it is not imposed for the benefit of the State, is not discriminatory or protective in effect or if the product on which the charge is imposed is not in competition with any domestic product.[27]

The following aspects of this definition should be highlighted. First, a CEE is a *pecuniary charge*, in other words an obligation to pay a sum of money.

Secondly, the charge must be imposed on domestic or foreign goods by reason of the fact that they cross a frontier.

Thirdly, it is irrelevant that the amount of the charge is minimal, as was the case in the underlying dispute (0.33 per cent). As the Court indicated, the justification for this is based on the fact that any charge, however small, constitutes an obstacle to the free movement of such goods. As mentioned in section 6, Articles 34 and 35 TFEU are not subject to a *de minimis* rule either.

Fourthly, the designation and mode of application are also irrelevant. This means that it does not matter how the charge is designated or applied, as otherwise it would be very easy for Member States to circumvent the prohibition.

---

[24] Case 26/62 *Van Gend en Loos* [1963] ECR 1.   [25] See further chapter 6.
[26] *Diamonds* (n 23); see also Joined Cases 2/62 and 3/62 *Commission v Luxembourg and Belgium* [1962] ECR 813.   [27] *Diamonds* (n 26) paras 15–18.

Fifthly, the concept of CEEs is not confined to charges imposed for the benefit of the State (although this is probably the most frequent situation), but extends to those which finance another entity such as a social fund. Moreover, CEEs are prohibited independently of any consideration of the purpose for which they were introduced and the destination of the revenue obtained. Thus, it is of no consequence that the charges are intended to finance certain benefits for a specific category of workers.

Sixthly, charges may constitute CEEs even if they are not discriminatory or protective. This means that a charge imposed on both imports and exports can be a CEE. What is more, a charge may be caught by Article 30 TFEU even if there is no domestic production of the goods in question: although Antwerp is one of the world's major diamond trading centres, Belgium has no diamond mines of its own.

Finally, the Court has consistently held that the prohibition of customs duties and CEEs constitutes a fundamental rule which does not permit of any exceptions.[28] The *Works of art* case is particularly interesting in relation to this issue.[29] The Court declared that the elimination of all obstacles to the free movement of goods by the abolition of customs duties and CEEs is a fundamental principle; and that exceptions to this fundamental rule must be strictly construed. Article 30 TFEU was therefore not subject to the exception provided in Article 36 TFEU, in the absence of any wording in the latter provision to that effect. If a Member State wishes to protect its artistic treasures, it may do so by adopting *MEEs* on exports provided that they are compatible with Article 36 TFEU.[30]

5.3 Permissible charges

Despite the strict approach adopted by the Court to customs duties and CEEs, there are two situations which may escape the prohibition contained in Article 30 TFEU, namely (a) where the payment is consideration for a service rendered, or (b) where it relates to inspections required by EU law. These are not exceptions to the prohibition on CEEs: such charges are not CEEs at all. However, attempts to show that a charge falls within one of these two situations rarely succeed.

5.3.1 Services rendered

According to the case law, the service must confer a specific advantage on the importer or exporter and the charge must be proportionate to the benefit conferred.[31] In *Statistical levies*,[32] Italy had imposed a small charge on imports and exports of goods. Italy argued, inter alia, that the charge constituted consideration for a service rendered, namely the availability of accurate statistics on imports and exports. The Court rejected this argument on the ground that the statistical information was beneficial to the economy as a whole, but not to the individual importer or exporter.[33]

---

[28] eg *Diamonds* (n 26) paras 19–21.
[29] *Works of art* (n 14).
[30] Art 36 TFEU will be more fully considered in section 6.5.
[31] Case 132/82 *Commission v Belgium* [1983] ECR 1649, para 8.
[32] Case 24/68 *Commission v Italy* [1969] ECR 193.
[33] See also Case 87/75 *Bresciani* [1976] ECR 129.

5.3.2 Inspections required by EU law

Where health inspections are *required* by EU law, Member States are entitled to recover the costs, subject to certain conditions.[34] In *Commission v Germany*, the conditions were stated to be as follows:

(a) the charge must not exceed the actual cost of the inspection;

(b) the inspections in question must be obligatory and uniform for all products in the EU;

(c) the inspections must be required by EU law; and

(d) they promote the free movement of goods by eliminating obstacles which could arise from unilateral measures of inspection adopted by Member States in accordance with Article 36.[35] In contrast, where EU law merely *permits* Member States to carry out the inspections, this exception does not apply.[36]

5.4 Charges imposed at the internal boundaries of Member States

As already mentioned, the factor which triggers the imposition of a customs duty or CEE is crossing a border. According to the traditional approach, this meant a border *between* Member States.[37] That approach takes full account of what are now Articles 28(1) and 30 TFEU: both these provisions clearly state that customs duties and CEEs must be abolished only between Member States.

However, subsequent case law has made it clear that the imposition of a charge on the crossing of an internal border may also be regarded as a CEE. For instance, in *Lancry*[38] certain French overseas territories imposed charges on goods of whatever provenance, including the European part of France, by reason of their entry into the territory concerned. The Court held that a charge levied at a regional border undermines the unity of the customs union and creates an obstacle to free movement of goods at least as serious as a charge levied at a national border. The same thinking underpinned *Carbonati Apuani*,[39] where the local authorities of Carrara (Italy) imposed a charge on marble transported from the town towards any other part of Italy or the EU. The Court stated that the Treaty defines the internal market as an area without internal frontiers, without drawing any distinction between interstate frontiers and frontiers within a State.

Probably, it is no accident that *Lancry* was decided shortly after the end of 1992, the date set for the completion of the internal market under the Single European Act.[40] Nevertheless, the fact remains that *Lancry* and its progeny are very hard to reconcile with Articles 28(1) and 30 TFEU and the case law under Articles 45, 49, and 56 TFEU on the free movement of persons.[41]

5.5 Remedies

The consequence of breaching the prohibition is that the Member State concerned must eliminate the CEE. Furthermore, in the event that charges have been unlawfully

---

[34] Case 46/76 *Bauhuis* [1977] ECR 5. The inspections themselves are MEEs; see section 6.

[35] Case 18/87 *Commission v Germany* [1988] ECR 5427, para 8.

[36] Case 314/82 *Commission v Belgium* [1984] ECR 1543.   [37] See also section 6.4.

[38] Case C-363/93 *Lancry* [1994] ECR I-3957, paras 25 *et seq.*

[39] Case C-72/03 *Carbonati Apuani* [2004] ECR I-8027, para 23.

[40] See the Conclusion to this chapter.   [41] See further chapter 13.

levied, the persons concerned have a right to repayment from the Member State in question.[42] Repayment will be subject to the conditions and procedures established by domestic law, which cannot be less favourable than those relating to similar claims regarding national charges and cannot render it virtually impossible or excessively difficult to obtain repayment.[43] However, in order to ensure that traders are not unjustly enriched, repayment may be excluded when the unduly levied charges have been incorporated into the price of the goods and have been passed on to consumers.[44]

6 Quantitative restrictions and measures of equivalent effect

According to Article 34 TFEU, quantitative restrictions (QRs) and MEEs on imports between Member States are prohibited. Article 35 TFEU lays down a corresponding prohibition as regards QRs and MEEs on exports. Finally, Article 36 TFEU is an exception clause which provides that QRs or MEEs falling under Article 34 or 35 may be justified in certain circumstances as being for the public good. These provisions are intended to eliminate non-fiscal barriers to trade between Member States.

6.1 Quantitative restriction: imports and exports

The TFEU does not define the concept of QRs. However, the Court of Justice has held that 'the prohibition on quantitative restrictions covers measures which amount to a total or partial restraint of, according to the circumstances, imports, exports or goods in transit'.[45] A 'total restraint' in this context is an import or export ban (ie a total prohibition on importing or exporting widgets); a 'partial restraint' is a system of import or export quotas (eg a restriction on importing or exporting more than 10,000 widgets per year).

From this definition, it is plain that the concept of QRs is the same, whether imports or exports are at stake. In contrast, the definition of MEEs on imports is fundamentally different from that of MEEs on exports. These two concepts will now be considered in turn.

6.2 Measures of equivalent effect: imports

6.2.1 The definition

The definition of MEEs under Article 34 has caused a great deal of ink to flow and given rise to a considerable amount of case law over the years. The big question is: to what extent, if at all, does a measure have to *discriminate* against imports for this provision to be engaged? In other words, how far does the Treaty encroach on the decisions of the democratically elected governments of the Member States?[46] Article 34 uses the word 'restrictions' but does not mention discrimination at all.

---

[42] Case 199/82 *San Giorgio* [1983] ECR 3595, para 12. Art 30 TFEU is directly applicable; see n 7.
[43] *San Giorgio* (n 42).
[44] Ibid, para 13. This idea was further developed in Joined Cases C-192–218/95 *Comateb* [1997] ECR I-165.
[45] Case 2/73 *Geddo* [1973] ECR 865, 879.   [46] See the Introduction to this chapter.

The best way to examine the case law is chronologically, considering in turn each of the four principal cases: *Dassonville*[47] (1974), *Cassis de Dijon*[48] (1979), *Keck*[49] (1993), and finally *Commission v Italy* ('*Trailers*')[50] (2009).

Dassonville

The classic definition of MEEs is to be found in *Dassonville*, where the Court held:

> All trading rules enacted by Member States, which are capable of hindering, directly or indirectly, actually or potentially, intra-Community trade are to be considered as measures having an effect equivalent to quantitative restrictions.[51]

This definition has been repeated in nearly every subsequent case, albeit with certain variations.[52] In particular, the word 'trading' is usually omitted,[53] so no importance can be attached to this word.

On any view, the most striking feature of the *Dassonville* formula is its great breadth. Just how broad it is can be seen from the ruling in *Commission v France* ('*Foie gras*').[54] In that case, the Commission alleged that France had infringed Article 34 TFEU by laying down standards for goods sold under the trade description *foie gras*. The defendant argued that the infringement was purely hypothetical, since this product was only produced in very small quantities in other Member States, and products from those States generally complied with the French standards in any event. The Court dismissed this argument in the following terms:

> Article [34] applies...not only to the actual effects but also to the potential effects of legislation. It cannot be considered inapplicable simply because at the present time there are no actual cases with a connection to another Member State.[55]

Indeed, because the *Dassonville* formula involves an examination of the 'actual or potential, direct or indirect effect' of the measure in question, the Court considers the inherent nature of that measure without regard to any economic or statistical analysis.[56] This means that it is inappropriate to consider statistical evidence as to the volume of imports of products subject to the national measure in question. This is neatly illustrated by *Commission v Ireland* ('*Buy Irish*').[57] The defendant contended that the contested advertising campaign encouraging the public to buy domestic goods in preference to imports was not an MEE because imports had actually risen since the campaign began! The Court gave this argument short shrift, pointing out that imports might have increased more in

---

[47] Case 8/74 *Dassonville* [1974] ECR 837.

[48] Case 120/78 *REWE-Zentral* ('*Cassis de Dijon*') [1979] ECR 649.

[49] Joined Cases C-267/91 and 268/91 *Keck and Mithouard* [1993] ECR I-6097.

[50] Case C-110/05 *Commission v Italy* ('*Trailers*') [2009] ECR I-519.

[51] *Dassonville* (n 47) 852.

[52] eg the Court has been known to speak of 'a direct or indirect, real or potential hindrance to imports between Member States' (Case 4/75 *Rewe-Zentralfinanz* [1975] ECR 843, 858).

[53] Case C-368/95 *Familiapress* [1997] ECR I-3689, para 7 and Case C-67/97 *Bluhme* [1998] ECR I-8033, para 18.   [54] Case C-184/96 *Commission v France* ('*Foie gras*') [1998] ECR I-6197.

[55] Ibid, para 17.

[56] Price controls have always constituted an exception: Case 65/75 *Tasca* [1976] ECR 291 and Case 13/77 *GB-Inno* [1977] ECR 2115.   [57] Case 249/81 [1982] ECR 4005.

the absence of the campaign.[58] What is more, reliance on statistical data would lead to perverse results, as the legality of a measure might vary from year to year, or even from month to month.

Equally, it is inherent in the *Dassonville* formula that some measures do not constitute even potential or indirect hindrances to imports and therefore fall outside the *Dassonville* formula altogether. Thus, in a handful of cases the Court has held that measures fell outside Article 34 TFEU on the ground that the possibility of their affecting imports was too 'uncertain and indirect'.[59] In effect, this is a rule of remoteness.[60]

The first in this line of cases was *Krantz*.[61] The plaintiff in the main case was a German company which had sold a machine on instalment terms to a company established in the Netherlands. Before all the instalments had been paid, the purchaser went bankrupt. Under Dutch bankruptcy law, the seller's reservation of property pending the payment of the final instalment could not be invoked against the tax authorities of the Netherlands. The plaintiff claimed that the Dutch law infringed Article 34 TFEU, since it operated as a disincentive to traders in other Member States to sell goods by instalment to the Netherlands. The Court dismissed this argument on the ground that the effects of such a rule were 'too uncertain and indirect to warrant the conclusion' that it was 'liable to hinder trade between Member States'.[62]

Ever since its ruling in *van de Haar*,[63] the Court has steadfastly refused to apply a *de minimis* rule. A spectacular illustration of this principle can be seen in *Bluhme*, where a ban on keeping certain species of bee applicable to less than 1 per cent of Danish territory was held to fall under Article 34.[64] As mentioned in section 5, Article 30 TFEU is not subject to a *de minimis* rule either.

Another consequence of the breadth of the concept of MEEs on imports is that the Court has ruled that Article 34 TFEU 'covers in general all barriers to imports which are not already specifically covered by other Treaty provisions'.[65] In relation to those articles, each of which constitutes a *lex specialis*, Article 34 TFEU has been described as a *lex generalis*.[66] We shall revisit this issue in section 8.

A further obvious characteristic of the *Dassonville* formula is that it refers exclusively to the *effects* of a measure, not its purpose; and the overwhelming thrust of the subsequent

---

[58] Ibid, paras 22 and 25; see also Case C-405/98 *Gourmet International* [2001] ECR I-1795, para 22 and Case C-463/01 *Commission v Germany* ('*Mineral water*') [2004] ECR I-11705, para 65.

[59] Case C-379/92 *Peralta* [1994] ECR I-3453; Case C-96/94 *Centro Servizi Spediporto* [1995] ECR I-2883; Case C-140/94 *Bassano di Grappa* [1995] ECR I-3257; and Case C-134/94 *Esso Española* [1995] ECR I-4223. In all these cases, the facts were extreme (at least in the eyes of the Court).

[60] As AG Kokott pointed out, the criteria of 'uncertainty and indirectness' are 'difficult to clarify and thus do not contribute to legal certainty' (para 46 of her Opinion in Case C-142/05 *Mickelsson* [2009] ECR I-4273).

[61] Case C-69/88 *Krantz* [1990] ECR I-583.

[62] As Stuyck has pointed out ('Is *Keck* Still Alive and Kicking?' in L Gormley, P Nihoul, and E van Nieuwenhuyze (eds), 'What Standard after *Keck*?' [2012] *European Journal of Consumer Law* 343, 345), cases in which the Court has followed this approach have frequently related to private law. See also Case C-93/92 *CMC Motorradcenter* [1993] ECR I-500 and Case C-44/98 *BASF* [1999] ECR I-6269.

[63] Joined Cases 177/82 and 178/82 [1984] ECR 1797.

[64] Case C-67/97 *Bluhme* [1998] ECR I-8033. See also Case C-309/02 *Radlberger* [2004] ECR I-11763, para 68.   [65] Case 252/86 *Bergandi* [1988] ECR 1343, para 33.

[66] Opinion of AG Tesauro in Joined Cases C-78–83/90 *Compagnie Commerciale de l'Ouest* [1992] ECR I-1847, 1865.

case law confirms this. That is scarcely surprising: Article 34 TFEU speaks of 'measures of equivalent effect' to quantitative restrictions, not 'measures of equivalent purpose' to quantitative restrictions. Although the Court has referred to the aim of a national measure in several instances,[67] it is not easy to find a single case in which a measure has been held to fall within the scope of Article 34 solely for this reason.

Cassis de Dijon

What the Court did not do in *Dassonville* was to give any indication as to whether discrimination is a necessary ingredient of an MEE.

The early cases all concerned so-called 'distinctly applicable' measures (those which discriminate against imports on their face).[68] The Court first encountered indistinctly applicable measures in the celebrated case of *Cassis de Dijon*.[69] The plaintiffs, who sought to import the French blackcurrant-based drink of that name, contested the validity of a provision of an indistinctly applicable German law requiring spirits to have a minimum alcohol content. Cassis de Dijon, which in France had a content of between 15 and 20 per cent, fell into the category of products required to have 25 per cent alcohol under the German provisions. The Court ruled that this measure did constitute an MEE. That judgment was followed by a large number of similar rulings relating to indistinctly applicable measures.[70]

In all these cases, the measures in issue did not discriminate against imports on their face (ie they were indistinctly applicable); but a more subtle form of discrimination was at work. Thus the provision in issue in *Cassis de Dijon* reflected the long-standing characteristics of German products, whereas producers in other Member States wishing to export to Germany needed to manufacture specifically for the German market, with all the added costs this entails. This is sometimes referred to as discrimination in fact.

What about measures which do not discriminate against imports *at all*? This issue came to a head in *Torfaen v B&Q*,[71] a reference from a court in Wales concerning the legality of the then ban on Sunday trading. The restrictions on Sunday trading in that case did not involve any discrimination against imports in any shape or form; nor were they aimed at imports in any sense. Nevertheless, the Court held that Article 34 TFEU was engaged.[72] This was controversial, since B&Q's reliance on that provision could fairly be described as abusive. However, the Court's ruling was the consequence of the very broad definition of MEEs resulting from *Dassonville* and *Cassis de Dijon* and its desire to ensure the elimination of any barriers to the free movement of goods. But many commentators thought the Court had gone too far in *Torfaen*.

---

[67] *Keck and Mithouard* (n 49) paras 12 and 14; Case C-379/92 *Peralta* [1994] ECR I-3453, para 24; and *Trailers* (n 50) para 37.

[68] This widely used term is not employed by the Court itself.

[69] *Cassis de Dijon* (n 48).

[70] eg Case 788/79 *Gilli* [1980] ECR 2071 (ban on sale of cider vinegar); *Beer* (n 4) (ban on use of generic name 'beer' for drinks made with rice or maize); Case 216/84 *Commission v France* [1988] ECR 793 (ban on sale of substitute milk powder); and *Zoni* (n 5) (ban on sale of pasta containing soft wheat).

[71] Case 145/88 [1989] ECR 3831.

[72] See also Case C-312/89 *CGT v Conforama* [1991] ECR I-997; Case C-332/89 *Marchandise* [1991] ECR I-1027; and Case C-169/91 *Stoke-on-Trent v B&Q* [1992] ECR I-6635 – all Sunday trading cases.

Keck

Four years after *Torfaen*, the Court took a dramatic and unusual step. In *Keck*, it reversed the Sunday trading cases and laid down a new test. It divided measures into two types:

(a) so-called 'product-bound' measures (sometimes referred to as 'product require-ments'), which concern the inherent characteristics of a product such as desig-nation, form, size, weight, composition, presentation, and labelling;[73] and

(b) measures relating to 'certain selling arrangements'.[74]

As to the former category, the Court confirmed its earlier case law. With respect to the latter category, a major change was announced: only those measures which discriminated against imports in law or in fact were to be regarded as MEEs.[75]

The judgment itself lacked clarity, but it was clarified by subsequent case law. Thus the concept of measures relating to 'selling arrangements', which the Court did not define in *Keck* itself, has been held to cover the following categories of measure:

- restrictions on when goods may be sold,[76]
- restrictions on where or by whom goods may be sold,[77]
- advertising restrictions,[78] and
- price controls.[79]

When any doubt exists as to whether a measure is product-bound or relates to a selling arrangement, the Court inclines towards the former,[80] although this has never been for-mulated as a principle.

The rationale behind *Keck* is that, in the absence of discrimination, selling arrangements – such as the Sunday trading rules – are less restrictive of free trade than product-bound measures because they do not require traders in other Member States to produce goods to particular specifications just for the Member State in question.

Nevertheless, *Keck* has been widely criticized over the years both by Advocates General[81] and others, as it is said to create an artificial and largely unworkable distinction. For a long time, the Court remained impervious to such criticism except in one respect: the distinc-tion between 'selling arrangements' and 'product-bound measures' gradually mutated into a distinction between 'selling arrangements' and *all* other measures, so that only the former

---

[73] *Keck and Mithouard* (n 49) para 15. The term 'product-bound' is not used by the Court itself.

[74] Ibid, para 16. This term is used by the Court.

[75] As to the concept of discrimination 'in fact' in this context, see Case C-391/92 *Commission v Greece* [1995] ECR I-1621 and Case C-322/01 *DocMorris* [2003] ECR I-14887; and see n 77.

[76] Joined Cases C-401/92 and 402/92 *'t Heukske* [1994] ECR I-2199 and Case C-69/93 *Punto Casa* [1994] ECR I-2355. The earlier Sunday trading cases, like *Torfaen*, were thus reversed.

[77] *Commission v Greece* (n 75) (ban on selling processed milk for infants except in pharmacies) and *DocMorris* (n 75) (ban on selling pharmaceuticals on the internet). Case C-369/88 *Delattre* [1991] ECR I-1487 and Case C-60/89 *Monteil* [1991] ECR I-1547 were therefore reversed.

[78] Case C-292/92 *Hünermund* [1993] ECR I-6787; Case C-412/93 *Leclerc-Siplec* [1995] ECR I-179; Case C-34/95 *De Agostini* [1997] ECR I-3843; and Case C-405/98 *Gourmet International* [2001] ECR I-1795. In the latter case, an 'outright ban' on advertising was held to be discriminatory in fact.

[79] *Keck* itself related to a prohibition on selling goods at a loss, which is a form of price control. See also Case C-531/07 *LIBRO* [2009] ECR I-3717.

[80] Case C-470/93 *Mars* [1995] ECR I-1923 and *Familiapress* (n 53).

[81] Especially AG Jacobs in *Leclerc-Siplec* (n 78); AG Poiares Maduro in Case C-158/04 *Alfa Vita* [2006] ECR I-8135; and AG Bot in *Trailers* (n 50).

were subject to a discrimination test.[82] Measures which could not be categorized as either product-bound or as selling arrangements were therefore found to be MEEs whether they were discriminatory or not.

Trailers

In 2009, the Court finally succumbed to this criticism in *Trailers*,[83] but in an ambiguous way. It appeared to confirm the pre-existing law, but then added that 'any other measure which hinders access to the market' also constitutes an MEE[84] – language which broadly reflects the test proposed by many critics of *Keck*. Opinions vary as to the meaning and importance of this pronouncement,[85] but the fact is that, five years later, it does not seem possible to identify a single case in which the Court has reached a different result from that which it would have reached before *Trailers*. Conceivably, the Court will one day apply this new test to a measure relating to a selling arrangement which is non-discriminatory but nevertheless highly restrictive (eg a ban on selling widgets except on Christmas Day). But for the moment this judgment remains a mystery.

6.2.2 A brief comparison with US constitutional law

Several authors have compared Article 34 TFEU with its US equivalent.[86] The US Constitution contains no provision equivalent to Article 34, as this was simply not at the forefront of the minds of the fathers of that instrument: they had more pressing concerns, namely the establishment of a vibrant federal State capable of withstanding internal tension and attacks from foreign powers. In stark contrast, the common market, and in particular the free movement of goods, was the very cornerstone of the venture which became the Treaty of Rome.

Nevertheless, the US Supreme Court has read a so-called 'dormant commerce clause' (ie an implicit prohibition) into Article 1, section 8, clause 3 of the Constitution, which provides: 'The Congress shall have power … to regulate commerce … among the several States'. The Supreme Court is very robust in its review of discriminatory state measures, but non-discriminatory measures are deemed to be lawful unless the burden imposed on trade from other states is 'clearly excessive in relation to the putative local benefit'.[87]

To some, it may come as a surprise to learn that in this field the fetters on the several US states are no greater than those binding the Member States of the EU. Set against the historical background just described, this is wholly understandable.

---

[82] Case C-473/98 *Toolex* [2000] ECR I-5681 (restriction on use); Case C-390/99 *Canal Satélite Digital* [2002] ECR I-607; and Case C-244/06 *Dynamic Medien* [2008] ECR I-505 (market authorization requirements).

[83] Case C-110/05 (n 50); see also *Mickelsson* (n 60).   [84] *Trailers* (n 50) para 37.

[85] See C Barnard, *The Substantive Law of the EU: The Four Freedoms* (3rd edn, Oxford: Oxford University Press, 2010) 103–108; Gormley, Nihoul, and van Nieuwenhuyze, 'What Standard after *Keck*?' (n 62).

[86] See C Barnard, 'Restricting Restrictions: Lessons for the EU from the US?' (2009) 68 *Cambridge Law Journal* 575; G Haibach, 'The Interpretation of Article 30 of the EC Treaty and the "Dormant" Commerce Clause by the European Court of Justice and the US Supreme Court' (1999) 48 *International and Comparative Law Quarterly* 155; and D Kommers and M Waelbroeck, 'Legal Integration and the Free Movement of Goods: The American and European Experience' in M Cappelletti et al (eds), *Integration through Law*, vol I (Berlin: Walter De Gruyter, 1985).

[87] *Pike v Bruce Church Inc* 397 US 137, 142 (1970). See D Regan, 'The Supreme Court and State Protectionism: Making Sense of the Dormant Commerce Clause' (1986) 84 *Michigan Law Review* 1091 and L Tribe, *American Constitutional Law*, vol I (3rd edn, New York: Foundation Press, 2000) 1029 *et seq*.

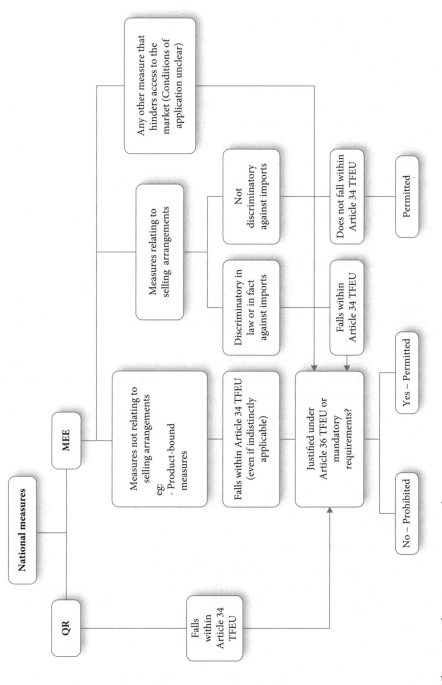

Fig 12.1 When national measures are permitted

6.2.3 Some examples of MEEs

At all events, MEEs come in a very wide variety of forms. We can only give a few examples here. In addition to those mentioned previously,[88] the following deserve a particular mention:[89]

- import licences, even if they are granted automatically;[90]
- inspections and controls;[91]
- the obligation to produce a certificate;[92]
- prohibition on the sale of goods of a certain description;[93]
- requirements as to the presentation[94] or labelling of products;[95]
- incitement to purchase domestic products in preference to imports;[96]
- restrictions on use;[97]
- restrictions on possession[98] or storage;[99] and
- restrictions on health-care coverage.[100]

The first category (import licences) is distinctly applicable by definition. The other categories of measure listed here constitute MEEs even if they are indistinctly applicable.

6.3 Measures of equivalent effect: exports

Export restrictions are rare, since Member States are usually motivated to promote exports: the Court has decided many hundreds of cases on Article 34 TFEU, but only a fraction of that number on Article 35 TFEU. However, there are several reasons why a State might take such a step:

- a desire to ensure supplies in times of shortage;[101]
- the protection of jobs in processing industries, in which case the export restriction will cover the raw material or component part, but not the finished product;[102]
- the prevention of parallel exports (so that manufacturers established in the Member State in question will be able to obtain higher profits on their export trade);

---

[88] See in particular nn 73 and 76–79 and the accompanying text.

[89] For a more thorough account, see P Oliver et al, *Oliver on Free Movement of Goods in the European Union* (5th edn, Oxford: Hart Publishing, 2010) ch 7.

[90] Case 51/71 *International Fruit Co* [1971] ECR 1107 and Case 41/76 *Donckerwolcke* [1976] ECR 1921.

[91] *Rewe-Zentralfinanz* (n 52) and Case 35/76 *Simmenthal* [1976] ECR 1871.

[92] Case 251/78 *Denkavit* [1979] ECR 3369 and Case C-205/89 *Commission v Greece* [1991] ECR I-1361.

[93] *Cassis de Dijon* (n 48); Case 788/79 *Gilli* [1980] ECR 2071; and *Commission v France* (n 70).

[94] Case 261/81 *Rau v De Smedt* [1982] ECR 3961 (requirement that margarine be sold in cubic packaging to distinguish it from butter) and C-366/04 *Schwarz* [2005] ECR I-10139 (prohibition on selling chewing gum from vending machines without a wrapper).

[95] Case 27/80 *Fietje* [1980] ECR 3839 (language requirement) and *Mars* (n 80).

[96] *Buy Irish* (n 57) and Case C-325/00 *Commission v Germany* ('*Quality label for domestic agricultural produce*') [2002] ECR I-9977.

[97] *Toolex* (n 82) and *Mickelsson* (n 60).

[98] Case C-293/94 *Brandsma* [1996] ECR I-3159 and Case C-400/96 *Harpegnies* [1998] ECR I-5121.

[99] Case 13/78 *Eggers* [1978] ECR 1935.　　[100] Case C-120/95 *Decker* [1998] ECR I-1831.

[101] As in Case 68/76 *Commission v France* ('*Export licences for potatoes*') [1977] ECR 515.

[102] Case C-203/96 *Chemische Afvalstoffen Dusseldorp* [1998] ECR I-4075 (restriction on exporting waste for reprocessing in another Member State).

- the maintenance of the quality or reputation of exports;[103] or
- the preservation of works of art for the nation.[104]

The definition of MEEs under Article 35 TFEU is radically different from that under Article 34 TFEU. The Court has consistently held that Article 35 TFEU only covers measures which discriminate against goods intended for export in favour of those destined for the domestic market.[105] The formulation of this definition is not consistent. The test which the Court actually applies is that set out in *Belgium v Spain* ('*Rioja*'), where Article 35 TFEU was held to apply to measures which have 'the effect of specifically restricting patterns of exports... and thereby of establishing a difference of treatment between trade within a Member State and its export trade'.[106] In *Groenveld*, the Court stated that it was necessary to show that the measure provided 'a particular advantage for national production or for the domestic market of the State in question at the expense of the production or of the trade of other Member States';[107] but in practice the Court does not require this condition to be fulfilled.

In at least two cases relating to restrictions on transit (which fall under both Articles 34 and 35 TFEU), the Court has applied the same test to both provisions;[108] but the measures in issue in those cases discriminated against goods intended for export in any event.

In this respect, the rules on the free movement of goods differ markedly from those governing the other fundamental freedoms, where a unitary approach is followed: 'import' restrictions (barriers to incoming transactions) and 'export' restrictions (barriers to outgoing transactions) are subject to the same test.[109] The rationale behind the Court's narrow interpretation of Article 35 TFEU appears to be that that provision should not be extended to cover restrictions on production (eg planning constraints on the construction of factories).[110] Nevertheless, it is widely considered that the test is too narrow, at least as regards marketing restrictions.[111]

This prompted Advocate General Trjstenjak in *Gysbrechts*[112] to advise the Court to transpose its case law on Article 34 in its entirety to Article 35 TFEU. The proceedings concerned a Belgian rule precluding vendors in a distance-selling contract from requesting the details of the purchaser's credit card before the expiry of the period during which the latter enjoyed a statutory right to withdraw from the contract (seven working days). In view of the obstacles to bringing legal proceedings in another Member State against defaulting consumers, this constituted de facto discrimination against goods intended for export. Despite the Advocate General's entreaties, the Court appears to have stood by its traditional

---

[103] Case 53/76 *Bouhelier* [1977] ECR 197 (obligation to supply quality certificates for exported watches only was in breach of Art 35 TFEU) and Case C-388/95 *Belgium v Spain* ('*Rioja*') [2000] ECR I-3123 (rule that wine could only be sold as 'Rioja' if it was produced and *bottled* in the eponymous region was an MEE).

[104] Measures adopted for the latter motive may well be justified under Art 36.

[105] eg Case 15/79 *Groenveld* [1979] ECR 3409 and Case 155/80 *Oebel* [1981] ECR 1993 (prohibition on baking at night not an MEE).

[106] *Rioja* (n 103) para 41.

[107] *Groenveld* (n 105) para 7.

[108] Case C-112/00 *Schmidberger* [2003] ECR I-5659 and Case C-320/03 *Commission v Austria* ('*Brenner*') [2005] ECR I-9871.

[109] Case C-415/93 *Bosman* [1995] ECR I-4921 and Case C-18/95 *Terhoeve* [1999] ECR I-345 (workers); and Case C-384/93 *Alpine Investments* [1995] ECR I-1141 (services).

[110] If planning laws discriminate against EU nationals based in Member States, they fall under Art 49 TFEU on the freedom of establishment; see chapter 14.

[111] AG Jacobs in *Alpine Investments* (n 109) 1157, and paras 42 *et seq* of the AG's Opinion in Case C-205/07 *Gysbrechts* [2008] ECR I-9947.

[112] *Gysbrechts* (n 111).

approach.[113] True, this ruling does at least make it plain that de facto discrimination will suffice to bring a measure under Article 35 TFEU, but that was never in doubt.[114]

Finally, with the current shortage of energy, we are likely to see Member States imposing export restrictions of gas, oil, and electricity – which could give rise to some interesting litigation.

6.4 **Purely national measures**

According to the traditional approach, the rules on the free movement of goods do not cover situations which are internal to a Member State.[115] By the same token, reverse discrimination (where a Member State treats its own domestic products less favourably than imports) was also thought to fall outside the scope of the Treaty. However, more recently, the Court has appeared to suggest that even traders in domestic products may rely on a breach of Article 34 TFEU.[116] This is very hard to square with the wording of Articles 28 and 34 TFEU, which specifically refer to restrictions *between* Member States.[117]

6.5 **Justification under Article 36 and the mandatory requirements**

6.5.1 Justifications under Article 36

Since exceptions to the rules on free movement are the subject of chapter 16, there is no need to attempt an exhaustive discussion of Article 36 TFEU in this chapter. However, a brief overview of some key issues is set out here.

Article 36 TFEU establishes the following:

> The provisions of Articles 34 and 35 shall not preclude prohibitions or restrictions on imports, exports or goods in transit justified on grounds of public morality, public policy or public security; the protection of health and life of humans, animals or plants; the protection of national treasures possessing artistic, historic or archaeological value; or the protection of industrial and commercial property. Such prohibitions or restrictions shall not, however, constitute a means of arbitrary discrimination or a disguised restriction on trade between Member States.

As its wording makes clear, Article 36 TFEU lays down exceptions to both Articles 34 and 35 TFEU. Article 36 does not constitute an exception to any other provisions of the Treaty.[118] Whether imports or exports are at stake, Article 36 applies in the same way. However, as an exception to a fundamental principle, Article 36 is to be construed narrowly.[119] One manifestation of this is that the party seeking to show that a measure is justified bears the burden of proof[120] – although inexplicably the Court departed from this well-established rule in *Trailers*.[121]

---

[113] For the view that the ruling in *Gysbrechts* did broaden the definition of MEEs on exports, see A Dawes, 'A Freedom Reborn? The New Yet Unclear Scope of Article 29 EC' (2009) 34 *European Law Review* 639.

[114] eg in Case C-350/97 *Monsees* [1999] ECR I-2921, a measure which discriminated de facto against goods intended for export had been held to fall foul of Art 35 TFEU.

[115] See Case 314/81 *Waterkeyn* [1982] ECR 4337; Case 286/81 *Oosthoek* [1982] ECR 4575; and Case 355/85 *Cognet* [1986] ECR 3231.

[116] Case C-321/94 *Pistre* [1997] ECR I-2343 and Case C-448/98 *Guimont* [2000] ECR I-10663.

[117] The same also applies to Art 35. Similarly, see section 6.3 and the discussion in chapter 13.

[118] *Works of art* (n 14).   [119] Ibid.

[120] *Denkavit* (n 92) and Case C-265/06 *Commission v Portugal* [2008] ECR I-2245, para 39 (plus literally hundreds of other cases).

[121] Case C-110/05 (n 50) paras 62 *et seq*.

6.5.2 The status of the mandatory requirements

The 'mandatory requirements' are grounds of justification not mentioned in Article 36 TFEU. They first made their appearance in _Cassis de Dijon_,[122] where the Court recognized three mandatory requirements: the prevention of tax evasion,[123] the prevention of unfair competition, and consumer protection.[124] Others followed, including environmental protection,[125] the improvement of working conditions,[126] and fundamental rights.[127] On any view, the creation of the mandatory requirements has been a piece of judicial activism.

The mandatory requirements recognized in _Cassis_ related to important policy concerns which were not relevant or prominent when the Treaty of Rome was drafted. So their introduction has not been the source of any controversy simply because it suits everyone. Nevertheless, it was in direct contradiction with the principle that Article 36 TFEU is to be construed narrowly. In an attempt to square this circle, the Court has traditionally held that only indistinctly applicable measures can be justified on the basis of the mandatory requirements.[128] However, this has led to various distortions.[129] In a number of recent cases, no doubt in response to various calls from the Advocates General,[130] the Court has therefore begun to treat the mandatory requirements in precisely the same way as the grounds of justification spelt out in Article 36 TFEU.[131] However, it has never formally renounced its traditional approach. The widespread view today is that the latter approach is clearly preferable:[132] the law should recognize that a measure may be objectively justified on (say) environmental grounds, even if it is distinctly applicable.[133]

Consequently, references in this chapter to Article 36 TFEU should be taken to include the mandatory requirements, unless otherwise indicated.

6.5.3 The general principles governing Article 36 TFEU

Proportionality

Article 36 TFEU is applied subject to the principle of proportionality.

Accordingly, the word 'justified' in the first sentence of Article 36 TFEU is understood to mean 'necessary':[134] measures are not justified if the same legitimate end could be achieved by less restrictive means.[135] Frequently, the Court identifies an alternative measure which

---

[122] Case 120/78 (n 48).

[123] See also _GB-Inno_ (n 56).

[124] See also _Gilli_ (n 70) and _Gysbrechts_ (n 111).

[125] Case 302/86 _Commission v Denmark_ ('_Returnable bottles_') [1988] ECR 4607; _Brenner_ (n 108); and Case C-28/09 _Commission v Austria_ ('_Brenner II_'), judgment of 21 December 2011.

[126] Case 155/80 _Oebel_ [1981] ECR 1993.   [127] _Schmidberger_ (n 108).

[128] Case 113/80 _Commission v Ireland_ [1982] ECR 1625 and Case C-1/90 _Aragonesa de Publicidad_ [1991] ECR I-4151, para 13.

[129] The most obvious example occurred in _Walloon waste_ (n 16).

[130] eg AG Jacobs in _Chemische Afvalstoffen Dusseldorp_ (n 102) paras 89–90 and Case C-379/98 _Preussen Elektra v Schleswag_ [2001] ECR I-2099, paras 225–226; AG Geelhoed in _Brenner_ (n 108) paras 104–107.

[131] _Brenner_ (n 108); Case C-54/05 _Commission v Finland_ [2007] ECR I-2473; and _Gysbrechts_ (n 111).

[132] This view has been expressed by two members of the Court: Judge Rosas, '_Dassonville_ and _Cassis de Dijon_' in M Poiares Maduro and L Azoulai (eds), _The Past and Future of EU Law: The Classics of EU Law Revisited on the 50th Anniversary of the Rome Treaty_ (Oxford: Hart Publishing, 2010) 444–445, Judge Timmermans, 'Creative Homogeneity' in N Wahl and U Bernitz (eds), _Liber Amicorum in Honour of Sven Norberg_ (Brussels: Bruylant, 2006) 472, 475 _et seq._ See also Oliver et al, _Oliver on Free Movement of Goods in the European Union_ (n 89) paras 8.04–8.16; and see chapter 16, section 3.1 of this book.

[133] That was the situation in _Walloon waste_ (n 16).

[134] _Eggers_ (n 99), para 30 and Case C-141/07 _Commission v Germany_ [2008] ECR I-6935, para 50.

[135] Case 104/75 _De Peijper_ [1976] ECR 613, paras 16–17.

would achieve the desired aim without affecting interstate trade to the same degree.[136] For instance, a requirement that products be adequately labelled has often been held to constitute a suitable substitute for a sales ban.[137]

To the extent that exhaustive guarantees are laid down in EU legislation for a particular matter (eg preventing the spread of a particular disease), reliance on Article 36 TFEU is no longer possible because national measures differing from that legislation are no longer necessary.[138] Had the Court decided otherwise, that would have defeated the purpose of the EU adopting the legislation.

A measure will not be regarded as proportionate unless it is appropriate and applies in a consistent and systematic manner. This rule is neatly illustrated by *Commission v Portugal*. The case concerned a ban on affixing tinted film to car windows, which the defendant claimed was justified for fighting crime and to enable the police to see whether seat belts were being worn. However, this argument was undermined when it emerged that there was no restriction in Portugal on marketing cars fitted with tinted windows from the outset.[139]

One aspect of proportionality is the principle of *mutual recognition*, which is also an application of the obligation of sincere cooperation under Article 4(3) TEU. Mutual recognition made its first appearance in the case law in *Cassis de Dijon*: it was held there that the sale of goods lawfully produced and marketed in one Member State may not be restricted in another Member State without good cause.[140] In practice, this test must not be read narrowly: it appears to suffice for the goods to have been lawfully produced *or* marketed in the first Member State;[141] and the principle almost certainly extends to goods produced outside the EU, at least if it is lawful to produce and market them in the Member State where they were first put into free circulation.[142] In short, the importing Member State cannot prohibit the sale of goods meeting equivalent standards to its own; and it cannot unnecessarily duplicate controls carried out in the other Member State.[143] Exceptionally, in *Dynamic Medien* the Court did not apply the principle: the case concerned the approval of DVDs for viewing by children of different ages; the Court saw no need for the German authorities to have any regard to the classification chosen for each film by the exporting Member State (the UK), no doubt because there is no possible yardstick for moral decisions of this kind.[144]

---

[136] eg Case C-387/99 *Commission v Germany* [2004] ECR I-3751, para 81.

[137] *Cassis de Dijon* (n 48) para 13 and *Gilli* (n 70) para 7.

[138] Case 148/78 *Ratti* [1979] ECR 1629 and *Toolex* (n 82) para 25.

[139] *Commission v Portugal* (n 120) para 43.

[140] *Cassis de Dijon* (n 48) para 14. See the Commission's Communications on mutual recognition, COM(1999) 299 and OJ [2003] C265/2. It has now become a general principle of Union law: M Möstl, 'Preconditions and Limits of Mutual Recognition' (2010) 47 *Common Market Law Review* 405.

[141] *Canal Satélite Digital* (n 82), para 37; AG La Pergola in *Foie Gras* (n 54) para 28.

[142] Surprisingly, there is no direct authority on this point, but this can be deduced from *Co-Frutta* (n 9) (see text accompanying n 9). Also, the opposite approach would no doubt be at variance with the law of the World Trade Organization. On putting goods into free circulation, see section 2.2.

[143] *Canal Satélite Digital* (n 82) paras 36 and 37.

[144] Case C-244/06 (n 82) para 44. See also, in relation to the freedom of establishment relating to gambling, Case C-316/07 *Stoss* [2010] ECR I-8069, paras 112 and 113.

Discrimination

Objective justification is much harder to prove when the measure is blatantly discriminatory; but it is not unknown.[145] So 'arbitrary discrimination' in the second sentence of Article 36 TFEU refers to disparate treatment which cannot be justified on an objective basis.[146]

6.5.4 Economic considerations

Purely economic considerations cannot justify restrictions falling under Article 34 or 35 TFEU:[147] objectives such as the promotion of employment or investment, curbing inflation, and controlling the balance of payments fall outside Article 36 TFEU. Otherwise, the internal market would be wholly undermined. However, some legitimate grounds of justification do contain an economic element. Examples include intellectual property (called 'industrial and commercial property' in Article 36 TFEU) and the preservation of the financial balance of social security and health-care systems (a mandatory requirement).[148]

Public (human) health deserves particular attention. As would be expected, it has been held to 'rank first among the ... interests protected by Article 36'.[149] It is also by far the most important ground of justification in terms of the number of cases decided by the Court.

Case study 12.1: How does the Court decide complex public health issues?

Many free movement cases before the Court raise complex public health issues. In infringement proceedings, the Court is required to decide these issues. In contrast, when delivering preliminary rulings, the Court is theoretically not meant to decide questions of fact, but in practice it frequently does so.[150]

Sometimes no assessment of scientific data is involved. For instance, *Commission v Germany* concerned a measure requiring each hospital to obtain all its supplies from the same pharmacy; since emergency supplies were included, it followed that the pharmacy had to be within a few kilometres of the hospital, thereby excluding pharmacies in other Member States and their products in nearly all cases.[151] Similarly, in *HumanPlasma* the Court was called upon to rule on whether Austrian legislation restricting the marketing of human blood was justified on public health grounds; under that legislation, blood could not be distributed in Austria if any money whatsoever had been paid to the donors, *even to cover their costs*.[152]

However, in many public health cases a profusion of scientific data is laid down before the Court. For example, in countless cases it has had to rule on the legality of measures restricting, or fixing maximum thresholds for, certain vitamins, minerals, or additives in specific foodstuffs.[153]

---

[145] *Rewe-Zentralfinanz* (n 52) and *Commission v Germany* (n 134). But this is still not completely settled as regards the mandatory requirements: section 6.5.1.

[146] For examples of arbitrary discrimination, see Case 121/85 *Conegate* [1986] ECR 1007 (imports) and *Bouhelier* (n 103) (exports).

[147] Case 7/61 *Commission v Italy* [1961] ECR 317, 329 and Case C-416/00 *Morellato (No 2)* [2003] ECR I-9343, paras 40–41.   [148] *Decker* (n 100).

[149] *De Peijper* (n 135); see also Case C-421/09 *HumanPlasma* [2010] ECR I-12869, para 32.

[150] On the difference between these types of proceedings, see chapter 10.

[151] *Commission v Germany* (n 134). This measure was held to be justified.

[152] *HumanPlasma* (n 149). On the basis of the factors discussed later, this measure was held not to be justified.

[153] eg Case C-192/01 *Commission v Denmark* [2003] ECR I-9693; Case C-95/01 *Greenham* [2004] ECR I-1333; and Case C-333/08 *Commission v France* [2010] ECR I-757.

Needless to say, the judges are lawyers who do not normally have any scientific train-ing.[154] These cases place them in a difficult position: on the one hand, as mentioned earlier, the Court attaches the utmost importance to public health; but, on the other hand, the Court has encountered a large number of dubious arguments based on public health over the years. Sometimes this is blatant. For instance, in *Cassis de Dijon* the Court can have had no difficulty in rejecting Germany's argument that the *minimum* alcohol requirement for certain drinks which was in issue there was justified so as to prevent a proliferation of low-alcohol drinks on the market, which would induce a tolerance to alcohol.[155] But usually the questionable nature of public health arguments will not be nearly so obvious.

Obviously, the Court will take full account of the results of scientific research,[156] but usu-ally each party will be in a position to submit such evidence in its support. So, to cope with these complex issues, the Court has developed some rules of thumb; these are essentially the same whether scientific data is in issue or not.

As mentioned earlier, the party seeking to show that a measure is justified on public health grounds bears the burden of proving this. However, if that party makes out a reason-ably convincing case on justification, then the burden shifts once again to the other party.[157]

Article 36 TFEU is purely permissive. Accordingly, it is up to Member States to decide how far they wish to go in protecting public health, as long as they remain within the limits of that provision.[158] It follows that a national measure may be justified even if no other Member State has adopted such a stringent rule.[159] Nevertheless, this circumstance may be an indication that the contested measure is disproportionate.[160]

The Court also attaches considerable importance to the position taken by other interna-tional organizations. For instance, in *Beer*,[161] the Court relied on recommendations of the World Health Organization as well as the UN's Food and Agriculture Organization; and in *HumanPlasma*, it did likewise with a recommendation of the Council of Europe.[162]

Finally, evidence of protectionist intent will of course weigh against a Member State claiming that its measure is justified on public health grounds. Thus, in *Commission v UK* the defendant had abruptly changed its policy on combating the poultry infection known as Newcastle disease and banned imports of poultry products from countries which had not adopted its new policy. This measure had clearly been timed to exclude imports of turkeys for the lucrative Christmas season, and the Court concluded that the measure was not justified.[163]

---

[154] The Court can commission an expert's report: Art 70 of its Rules of Procedure (see http://curia.europa.eu/jcms/upload/docs/application/pdf/2012-10/rp_en.pdf). But this procedure is very rarely used; and it would be unthinkable on a reference for a preliminary ruling where the Court is not *supposed* to rule on the facts anyway!

[155] *Cassis de Dijon* (n 48) paras 10 and 11. See also Case C-319/05 *Commission v Germany* [2007] ECR I-9811 where Germany had classified garlic capsules as medicinal products; this meant that a market authori-zation was required before they could be sold!

[156] *Greenham* (n 153) paras 40 and 42.

[157] eg *Beer* (n 4) and Case C-55/99 *Commission v France* [2000] ECR I-11499, paras 34–36.

[158] *Commission v Germany* (n 134) para 51 and *HumanPlasma* (n 149) para 39.   [159] Ibid.

[160] *Commission v France* (n 153) para 105 and *HumanPlasma* (n 149) para 41.

[161] eg Case C-178/84 (n 4) paras 44 and 52.

[162] *HumanPlasma* (n 149) para 44.

[163] eg Case 40/82 *Commission v UK* [1982] ECR 2793. This case concerned animal health, but the Court would certainly react in the same way if human health were in issue.

6.6 **Remedies**

As already mentioned, Articles 34 and 35 TFEU are directly effective.[164] Consequently, persons who suffer or have suffered damage by reason of a breach or a possible breach of one of those provisions are entitled to an effective remedy in the courts of the Member States. Occasionally, this has been spelt out in judgments relating to these provisions,[165] but in any case it follows from the general principle of effective judicial control, which is now enshrined in Article 19(1) TEU as well as Article 47 of the Charter of Fundamental Rights of the European Union.[166] In appropriate circumstances, the usual remedies should be available: annulment, injunctions (interim and final), as well as damages.

7 Internal taxation

The purpose of Article 110 TFEU is to prevent Member States from circumventing the prohibitions of Articles 30 and 34 to 36 TFEU by introducing internal taxes which are liable to discourage imports of goods from other Member States in favour of domestic products.[167] As we saw in section 2.2, the Court held in *Co-Frutta*[168] that this provision extends to goods originating in third countries but in free circulation in the Member States.

Article 110 TFEU refers to 'products from other Member States', which may suggest that it only prohibits discrimination against imported products. Nevertheless, it is now clear that discrimination against exports in favour of products intended for domestic consumption is also contrary to this provision.[169] This makes perfect sense, since the Treaty also prohibits customs duties, CEEs, QRs, and MEEs on exports.

If Article 110 TFEU were confined to taxes on goods themselves, then many types of discriminatory tax would fall outside the Treaties altogether, even though they constitute serious barriers to the internal market. Accordingly, the Court has consistently held that this provision 'must be interpreted widely so as to cover all taxation procedures which, directly or indirectly, conflict with the principle of equality of treatment of domestic products and imported products'.[170] Thus in *Bergandi*[171] the legality of a tax on the *use* of automatic gaming machines was assessed under this article. Similarly, discriminatory fees for health inspections[172] and port duties[173] were found to be in breach of Article 110 TFEU. Finally, in *Stadtgemeinde Frohnleiten* the same was held to apply to a discriminatory levy on the depositing of imported waste on a landfill site.[174]

Two separate prohibitions are in issue: a prohibition on internal discriminatory taxation in favour of similar domestic products (Article 110(1)); and a prohibition on internal taxation affording protection to other domestic products in competition with imported or exported products (Article 110(2)). In this respect, it should be noted that Article 110

---

[164] See n 7 and accompanying text.   [165] eg *Greenham* (n 153) para 35.
[166] OJ [2007] C303/1.   [167] *Tatu* (n 23) paras 52 and 53.
[168] Case 193/85 (n 9).
[169] Case 142/77 *Larsen* [1978] ECR 1543, paras 24–26. For the sake of simplicity, the remainder of this chapter will simply refer to imported products.
[170] *Bergandi* (n 65) para 25 and Case C-221/06 *Stadtgemeinde Frohnleiten* [2007] ECR I-2613, para 40.
[171] Case 252/86 (n 65).   [172] Case 29/87 *Dansk Denkavit* [1988] ECR 2965.
[173] Case C-90/94 *Haahr Petroleum* [1997] ECR I-4085.
[174] *Stadtgemeinde Frohnleiten* (n 170). Waste constitutes goods for the purposes of the Treaty: *Walloon waste* (n 16); see section 3.

TFEU is essentially permissive, unlike Articles 30, 34, and 35 TFEU which are prohibitive. Thus, Member States can impose taxes on products as long as they are not discriminatory or protective.[175]

7.1 Article 110(1) TFEU

The prohibition laid down in Article 110(1) applies if two cumulative conditions are met: first, the relevant imported product and the relevant domestic product must be similar; and, secondly, there must be discrimination (*unjustified* disparate treatment).

7.1.1 Similar products

In its early case law, the Court relied on a rather rudimentary criterion for determining whether products are similar, namely whether they were in the same fiscal, customs, or statistical classification.[176] However, probably due to the inherent limitations of this formalistic approach, the Court soon started to develop a test based on the products' characteristics and consumers' needs. According to the Court, a comparison must be made between products which, at the same stage of production, have similar characteristics and satisfy the same consumer needs.[177]

The Court followed this approach in the *Johnnie Walker* case, which concerned a Danish system of differential taxation which applied to Scotch whisky and fruit wine of the liqueur type.[178] The Court stated that, in order to establish whether two products are similar, it is necessary to begin by considering certain objective characteristics of the beverages, such as their origin, method of manufacture, organoleptic properties (taste, smell, etc), and alcohol content. Then it must be established whether the two beverages are capable of satisfying the same consumer needs. In the case at hand, it was held that the two beverages had manifestly different characteristics (eg different manufacturing methods, different alcoholic strengths) and therefore could not be regarded as 'similar products'.[179]

A further example of the interpretation of this concept may be found in *Commission v France* ('*Cigarettes*'), in which the Court held that light-tobacco cigarettes and dark-tobacco cigarettes should be regarded as similar.[180]

In conclusion, the concept of similarity has been broadly interpreted by the Court, but its precise boundaries remain somewhat unclear. Although it is usual to carry out a systematic and rigorous economic analysis to define the relevant product market in competition law,[181] there has been no attempt to draw inspiration from this for the purposes of Article 110 TFEU.

7.1.2 Discrimination

Article 110(1) does not oblige Member States to adopt any specific system of taxation, let alone to reduce or eliminate taxes. However, Member States must ensure that their taxation systems are 'neutral' between imported and domestic products and do not treat the latter more favourably.

---

[175] *Bergandi* (n 65) para 24.
[176] Case 27/67 *Fink-Frucht* [1968] ECR 223, 232.
[177] Case 45/75 *Rewe-Zentrale* [1976] ECR 181, para 12.
[178] Case 243/84 *John Walker & Sons* [1986] ECR 875.   [179] Ibid, paras 11–14.
[180] Case C-302/00 *Commission v France* ('*Cigarettes*') [2002] ECR I-2055.   [181] See chapter 17.

As is clear from its wording, Article 110(1) prohibits both direct and indirect discrimination.

Direct discrimination arises when the tax scheme differentiates explicitly on the basis of the origin of products. The most obvious examples are where only imports are subject to the tax,[182] where the tax burden imposed on imported products is heavier than that imposed on domestic products,[183] or where only domestic products may benefit from a reduction.[184] The same applies where domestic products are subject to a flat tax and imports to a progressive tax[185] – or vice versa[186] – if that leads, at least in some cases, to a higher rate being levied on imports. Direct discrimination also occurs where domestic producers are given longer time limits for the payment of the tax[187] or where the penalties applied for infringing the tax legislation are more severe for imported products than for domestic products.[188]

Indirect discrimination arises where the tax scheme does not explicitly differentiate by reason of the origin of the products but in fact imposes a heavier tax burden on imported products. An illustrative example is *Humblot*, where an individual challenged the French annual road tax on cars.[189] Under the scheme, France imposed a progressive tax rated at 16 CV (fiscal horsepower) or less. In contrast, cars with a higher fiscal horsepower were subject to a flat-rate tax, which was considerably higher. The Court noted that Member States were free to establish a progressive tax system which increased the rate depending on an objective factor such as horsepower. However, they must ensure that the system does not have any discriminatory effect. Although the scheme did not formally differentiate on the basis of the origin of the products, it was deemed to be manifestly discriminatory because only imported cars were subject to the higher flat-rate tax and all domestic cars were subject to the lower progressive tax. Moreover, the increase from the progressive tax to the flat-rate tax was much higher than any of the increases in the various steps existing within the progressive tax; indeed, the flat-rate tax was almost five times higher than the highest progressive tax rate.

In *Cigarettes*,[190] the Court examined the French excise duty on cigarettes. The system did not differentiate on the basis of the origin of the cigarettes. However, the tax on light-tobacco cigarettes was higher than that on dark-tobacco cigarettes. The Court noted that the system was designed in such a way that the products falling within the most favourable tax category (dark-tobacco cigarettes) came almost exclusively from domestic production whereas almost all imported products came within the least advantageous category (light-tobacco cigarettes). The scheme was therefore contrary to Article 110 TFEU. It was irrelevant that a very small fraction of imported cigarettes came within the most favourable category whereas conversely a certain proportion of domestic production came within the least favoured category.

---

[182] Case 57/65 *Lütticke* [1966] ECR 205.
[183] *Haahr Petroleum* (n 173).
[184] Case 148/77 *Hansen* [1978] ECR 1787 (tax reductions for certain fruit spirits and for spirits from small distilleries not available for imports) and Case 21/79 *Commission v Italy* ('*Regenerated oil*') [1980] ECR-1 (reduction to promote the recycling and regeneration of petroleum products not available for imports).
[185] Case 127/75 *Bobie* [1976] ECR 1079.   [186] Case C-213/96 *Outokumpu Oy* [1998] ECR I-1777.
[187] Case 55/79 *Commission v Ireland* [1980] ECR 481.   [188] Case 299/86 *Drexl* [1988] ECR 1213.
[189] Case 112/84 *Humblot* [1985] ECR 1367.
[190] Case C-302/00 (n 180).

Finally, in line with the traditional principle that the Treaty does not prohibit *reverse discrimination*,[191] Article 110(1) does not preclude Member States from imposing higher internal taxes on domestic products than on imported products.[192]

7.2 Article 110(2) TFEU: products in competition

The prohibition laid down in Article 110(2) TFEU applies if two cumulative conditions are met: first, the imported product and the domestic product must be in competition; secondly, the tax must protect the domestic product. Both conditions are more easily satisfied than those in Article 110(1) TFEU.

In *Fink-Frucht*, the Court briefly indicated that Article 110(2) does not require the imported product and the domestic product to be in *direct* competition. However, their competitive relationship cannot be merely fortuitous, but must be lasting and characteristic.[193]

The leading case in this area is the *Commission v UK* (*'Wine and beer'*) saga.[194] These proceedings, which concerned a differentiated tax scheme for beer (essentially a domestic product) and wine (all of which was imported), were brought by the Commission against the UK exclusively on the basis of Article 110(2). In its interlocutory judgment, the Court took the unusual decision, in view of the significant uncertainties as to whether beer and wine were in competition and whether the tax scheme had protective effects, to order the parties to re-examine the case and to submit reports on that examination by a fixed date.

In its final judgment, the Court emphasized that Article 110(2) applies to products which, without being 'similar', were in partial or potential competition. To a certain extent, wine and beer were capable of meeting identical consumer needs and thus there was a degree of mutual substitution. On the other hand, the Court acknowledged the substantial differences between their manufacturing processes and their natural properties. Ultimately, in view of the substantial differences in quality and price of wines, the Court considered that the products which should be regarded in competition were beer and the lightest and cheapest varieties of wine.[195]

Next, the Court considered whether the British tax scheme was protective of domestic beer. The parties disagreed as to the relevant method of comparison, namely the assessment of the tax burden by reference to (a) the volume of the beverage, (b) the alcoholic strength, and (c) the price of the products. The Court ruled that all criteria were useful and led to the conclusion that cheaper wines were subject to a considerably higher tax burden (up to several times higher depending on the criterion used) than domestic beer. Thus the British tax system had the effect of stamping wine with the hallmarks of a luxury product, which would not constitute a genuine alternative to domestic beer in the eyes of consumers.[196] Consequently, the UK had infringed Article 110(2) TFEU.

The outcome of the UK *Wine and beer* case stands in stark contrast to that in the much more recent Swedish case, which concerned the same products.[197] The Court stated that strong beers and intermediate wines were in competition. Although it recognized that the tax burden on wine by reference to alcoholic strength was between 20 and 50 per cent higher than that on beer, it went on to analyse whether this had the effect of reducing potential consumption of imported wine to the advantage of domestic beer. Taking into account that the relationship

---

[191] See section 6.4 and Case 35/82 *Morson* [1982] ECR 3723. For a detailed discussion on reverse discrimination, see Barnard, *The Substantive Law of the EU* (n 85) 88 and 89 (goods) and 230–232 (persons).

[192] Case 86/78 *Peureux* [1979] ECR 897, paras 32 and 33.   [193] *Fink-Frucht* (n 176).

[194] Case 170/78 *Commission v UK* [1980] ECR 417 (interlocutory judgment) and Case 170/78 *Commission v UK* (*'Wine and beer'*) [1983] ECR 2265 (final judgment).

[195] *Wine and beer* (n 194) final judgment, paras 7–12.

[196] Ibid, paras 13–28.   [197] Case C-167/05 *Commission v Sweden* (*'Wine and beer'*) [2008] ECR I-2127.

between the price of 1 litre of strong beer and that of 1 litre of competing wine was virtually the same before and after taxation (a ratio of 1:2), the Court concluded that the differential tax treatment was not likely to influence consumer behaviour in the long term and that Article 110(2) was not infringed.[198] It has been suggested that the diverging outcomes in the UK and Swedish *Wine and beer* cases are the result of the more sophisticated analysis carried out in the latter and the Commission's failure to prove actual or likely protective effects.[199]

7.3 The holistic approach to Article 110 TFEU

The determination as to whether two products are 'similar' within the meaning of Article 110(1) TFEU may often be difficult in practice since the precise boundaries of this concept remain blurred. Accordingly, in certain cases the Court has followed what might be called a 'holistic' approach to Article 110, namely an approach which does not distinguish between the first and the second paragraphs.

The holistic approach can be observed in the *Spirits* cases.[200] The French *Spirits* case concerned a tax scheme which differentiated between spirits obtained from wine or fruit (eg cognac, armagnac, and calvados) and those based on cereals (eg whisky, gin, and vodka). The former category was predominantly French, whereas spirits in the latter category were overwhelmingly imported. After indicating that it was necessary to interpret the concept of 'similar products' with sufficient flexibility, the Court emphasized that the relevant criterion should not be the strictly identical nature of the products but that of their 'similar and comparable use'. The Court noted that it was impossible to disregard the fact that all the relevant products had certain common features (eg they were distilled and contained alcohol), while at the same time they had their own characteristics (the raw materials used, flavourings, or manufacturing processes). It found that some spirits were 'similar' to one another within the meaning of Article 110(1) TFEU, although it might be difficult to decide this in specific cases. At all events, spirits had sufficiently common characteristics to consider that they were at least in partial competition for the purposes of Article 110(2) TFEU.[201] Accordingly, in view of the difficulties of establishing whether certain products should be regarded as 'similar', the Court found that France had infringed Article 110 taken as a whole.

It is submitted, however, that this approach can be problematic, due to the fact that Article 110(1) prohibits discrimination, while Article 110(2) prohibits protectionism. The consequence will be discussed in section 7.5. In any case, the Court has subsequently shown a more rigorous approach towards the separate application of Articles 110(1) and 110(2) TFEU.

7.4 Justification

Notwithstanding the foregoing, Article 110 TFEU does not oblige Member States to impose uniform taxes on products. Systems of differentiated taxation are common. Such systems will not be deemed contrary to Article 110 TFEU if they are justified by an objective and legitimate policy reason (eg environmental protection, social policy, or economic policy). A variety of cases illustrate this point of principle, although in many of them the scheme was found to have discriminatory or protective effects.[202]

---

[198] Ibid, paras 40 *et seq.*

[199] See P Craig and G de Búrca, *EU Law: Text, Cases, and Materials* (5th edn, Oxford: Oxford University Press, 2011) 64.

[200] Case 168/78 *Commission v France* [1980] ECR 347; Case 169/78 *Commission v Italy* [1980] ECR 385; and Case 171/68 *Commission v Denmark* [1980] ECR 447.

[201] *Commission v France* (n 200) paras 11–13.

[202] See *Hansen* (n 184) (tax differentiation to promote the use or certain raw materials, the production of spirits of high quality, or the continuance of certain classes of undertakings); *Regenerated oil* (n 184)

An interesting example is *Chemial Farmaceutici*, in which Italy had adopted a differentiated tax scheme applicable to ethyl alcohol obtained from fermentation (which derived from agricultural products) and to synthetic ethyl alcohol (which derived from oil).[203] In its judgment, the Court indicated that differentiated tax schemes may be permissible if three conditions are met. First, Member States may establish tax schemes which differentiate between products on the basis of objective criteria (eg the raw materials used or the production processes). Secondly, the differentiation must pursue legitimate economic objectives. Thirdly, the detailed rules must avoid any form of direct or indirect discrimination against imported products or any form of protection of competing domestic products.[204] The Court suggested that all three conditions were fulfilled in that case.

7.5 Remedies

The consequences of infringing Article 110(1) TFEU are different from the consequences of infringing Article 110(2) TFEU: in the case of a discriminatory tax (Article 110(1)) the Member State must equalize the taxes imposed on similar products; but with a protective tax (Article 110(2)) what is required is to eliminate the protectionist effect, without necessarily equalizing the tax on the imported product and that on the domestic competing product.[205]

Persons who have paid undue tax by reason of a breach of either paragraph of Article 110 may recover the sums concerned according to the same principles as those applying to infringements of Article 30.[206]

8 The boundary between the provisions on free movement of goods

In *Iannelli v Meroni*, the Court held: 'However wide the field of application of Article [34] may be, it nevertheless does not include obstacles to trade covered by other provisions of the Treaty.'[207] Consequently, it ruled in that case that Articles 30 and 34 TFEU are mutually exclusive.[208] For the same reason, Articles 34 and 110 TFEU are also mutually exclusive.[209] Beyond any doubt, Article 35 TFEU cannot be applied cumulatively with Article 30 or 110 TFEU either. Equally, a tax or charge can be caught either by Article 30 or 110 TFEU, but not both.[210]

The rationale behind these principles is spelt out in the following passage of Advocate General Jacobs's Opinion in *De Danske Bilimportører*:

> If a charge is caught by Article [30] it must be abolished, whereas if it is caught by Article [110] then only the discriminatory or protective element need be removed. A measure caught by Article [34] may be permitted if it pursues one or more justified aims in a manner proportionate

---

(tax scheme promoting environmental protection); and Case C-132/88 *Commission v Greece* [1990] ECR I-1567.

[203] Case 140/79 *Chemial Farmaceutici* [1981] ECR 1.   [204] Ibid, para 14.

[205] That is how the UK put an end to the infringement in *Wine and beer* (n 194).

[206] Case 68/79 *Hans Just* [1980] ECR 501; see section 5.5.

[207] Case 74/76 *Iannelli v Meroni* [1977] ECR 557, para 9. See also Case C-228/98 *Dounias* [2000] ECR I-577, para 39.

[208] See also Joined Cases C-78–93/90 *Compagnie Commerciale de l'Ouest* [1992] ECR I-1847 and Case C-383/01 *De Danske Bilimportorer* [2003] ECR I-6065, para 32.

[209] *Fink-Frucht* (n 176) and Case 74/76 *Iannelli v Meroni* [1977] ECR 557.

[210] Case C-234/99 *Nygård* [2002] ECR I-3657, para 17 and *De Danske Bilimportorer* (n 208) para 33.

to their achievement, whereas the scope for justification under Articles [30] or [110] is very much more limited. On the other hand, those two articles apply only in a limited set of circumstances, always involving a charge or tax, whereas Article [34] is capable of applying to a very wide variety of measures which may hinder trade.[211]

8.1 The two *Danish cars* judgments

In *Commission v Denmark* ('*Cars*'),[212] the Commission sought a ruling from the Court that Denmark had infringed Article 110 TFEU with its very high registration taxes for new vehicles. The Court ruled that Article 110 TFEU could not be infringed because there was no domestic production of new motor vehicles in Denmark. This provision, it was held, cannot be relied on to challenge the excessive level of national taxes unless they can be regarded as discriminatory or protective.[213] However, the Court further suggested that, although the Commission's action must fail because it was based exclusively on Article 110 TFEU, it might be possible to challenge the tax on the basis of Article 34 TFEU.[214]

A decade later, this rather unusual assertion led an association of importers of motor vehicles to contest the high registration tax imposed on new motor vehicles (frequently exceeding 200 per cent!) on the basis of Article 34 TFEU.[215] However, the Court found that the only relevant provision was Article 110 TFEU because the measure was of a fiscal nature and was part of a scheme of internal taxation. Nevertheless, it appeared to suggest that, if the tax was so high as to render imports of cars prohibitive, then it might be contrary to some other provision of the Treaty.

8.2 CEEs and discriminatory internal taxation

The dividing line between Articles 30 and 110 TFEU is that the former applies to charges imposed due to the fact that products cross a frontier, whereas the latter applies to taxes imposed within a Member State.[216] Thus, the chargeable event for taxes caught by Article 110 TFEU is an internal transaction, unconnected as such with the importation or exportation of the goods.

Two types of situation deserve to be briefly mentioned here: the cases in which the charge is imposed on goods which are not produced in the Member State in question; and the so-called 'parafiscal' charges.

As regards the cases in which there is no domestic production of the relevant goods, this fact is irrelevant for the characterization of the charge.[217] The charge may be a CEE[218] or an internal tax[219] depending on the chargeable event. If it is imposed by reason of the origin or destination of the product, it will be a CEE. In contrast, it will constitute internal taxation

---

[211] *De Danske Bilimportorer* (n 208) para 31 of the Opinion.

[212] Case C-47/88 [1990] ECR I-4509.   [213] Ibid, para 10.

[214] Ibid, paras 12 and 13.   [215] *De Danske Bilimportorer* (n 208).

[216] *Commission v Denmark* ('*Cars*') (n 211).

[217] This makes sense, as otherwise the same type of measure applied in two different Member States may be characterized differently, depending on whether there is domestic production of the goods in question. Moreover, the existence or otherwise of domestic production may change over time, which could create legal uncertainty.

[218] See *Diamonds* (n 23); see section 5.2.

[219] See *Co-Frutta* (n 9), in which Italy applied a tax on the consumption of bananas. Although the production of bananas was almost non-existent in Italy, the Court considered that the tax should be assessed under Art 110.

if it relates to a general system of internal dues applied systematically to categories of products in accordance with objective criteria irrespective of the origin of the products, even if there is no identical or similar domestic product.[220]

The phenomenon of 'parafiscal' charges relates to situations in which the proceeds are used to provide a benefit to the domestic industry. Usually, the charge is imposed both on imported and domestic products. Parafiscal charges may fall within the scope of Article 30 or 110 TFEU depending on whether the advantage granted to the domestic production wholly or partly offsets the burden of the charge. In the first case, the parafiscal charge will be regarded as a CEE, whereas the second case will be analysed from the perspective of internal discriminatory taxation.[221]

For instance, in *Koornstra*[222] the Dutch authorities imposed a charge on operators who transported shrimp in a Dutch fishing vessel. The charge was based on the quantities of shrimp landed. The revenue obtained from the charge was used to finance the purchase, installation, and maintenance of shrimp sieves and peelers. Koornstra was subject to the charge for shrimp landed in the Netherlands (which could benefit from the equipment in question) and also shrimp directly landed in other Member States (which could not benefit from the equipment). The Court held that, if the burden of the charge on shrimp landed in the Netherlands was fully offset by the advantage deriving from the use of the equipment, the charge should be regarded as a CEE on exports. In contrast, if the burden was only partially offset, then the charge should be regarded as internal taxation which discriminated against exported products.

8.3 What if there are two distinct, but closely linked measures?

Finally, there are situations in which two distinct measures may nevertheless be closely linked. This is clearly illustrated by the cases in which imports and/or exports are subject to health inspections, and a charge is imposed for those inspections. The inspections constitute MEEs (Articles 34 and 35 TFEU), while the charges are CEEs (Article 30 TFEU).[223]

9 Conclusion

As the reader will be aware, the Treaty of Rome which established the EEC came into force on 1 January 1958. All the provisions discussed in this chapter became effective by the end of 1969, but some had already done so before then.

In 1985, the Commission published a White Paper on 'Completing the internal market,'[224] which set as its goal the creation of a fully unified internal market – and not just for goods – by 1992. This created the political impetus for the adoption of the Single European Act of 1987, which amended the Treaties so as to attain that goal. As regards the free movement of goods, the objective set in the Single European Act was achieved to a very considerable extent, thanks to the adoption of a vast body of EU legislation. In particular, as from 1 January 1993, it became unlawful for a Member State to carry out systematic customs or

---

[220] *Co-Frutta* (n 9) para 10.

[221] Case 77/72 *Capolongo* [1973] ECR 611; Case 77/76 *Cucchi* [1977] ECR 987; *Compagnie Commerciale de l'Ouest* (n 66); Case C-28/96 *Fazenda Pública* [1997] ECR I-4939; *Nygård* (n 210); and Case C-517/04 *Koornstra* [2006] ECR I-5015.   [222] Case C-517/04 (n 221).

[223] *Bauhuis* [(n 34) paras 12 and 13.   [224] COM(85) 310.

other controls at its borders with the other Member States; it may only carry out such controls to the extent that it does so *within* its own territory.

Of course, that does not mean that the internal market for goods has been 100 per cent complete since the end of 1992. That is not even intended by the Treaties. Let us return to the quotation from the *Gaston Schul* judgment[225] set out at the very beginning of this chapter. To paraphrase that passage, the Court stated that the common market (now the internal market) involves the creation of a single market in conditions 'as close as possible' to those of a genuine internal market. In the same vein, Article 26(2) TFEU states that the internal market shall comprise an area without internal frontiers in which free movement is ensured 'in accordance with the provisions of the Treaties'. The Treaties include Article 36 TFEU (and its counterparts relating to the other fundamental freedoms). Thus the Treaties recognize that Member States can impose quantitative restrictions and MEEs for the public good in certain limited circumstances. That will always be the case, because it is not possible for the Union legislator to harmonize absolutely everything – even supposing that that is desirable!

So the internal market in goods will never be 100 per cent complete. But arguably it is now as nearly complete as it can ever be.

Further reading

C BARNARD, *The Substantive Law of the EU: The Four Freedoms* (3rd edn, Oxford: Oxford University Press, 2010) chs 2–6

L GORMLEY, *EU Law of Free Movement of Goods and Customs Union* (Oxford: Oxford University Press, 2009)

L GORMLEY, P NIHOUL, AND E VAN NIEUWENHUYZE (eds), 'What Standard after *Keck*?' [2012] *European Journal of Consumer Law* 193

P OLIVER ET AL, *Oliver on Free Movement of Goods in the European Union* (5th edn, Oxford: Hart Publishing, 2010)

J SNELL, 'Non-Discriminatory Tax Obstacles in Community Law' (2007) *International and Comparative Law Quarterly* 339

J SNELL, 'The Notion of Market Access: A Concept or a Slogan?' (2010) 47 *Common Market Law Review* 437

E SPAVENTA, 'Leaving *Keck* Behind? The Free Movement of Goods after the Rulings in *Commission v Italy* and *Mickelsson and Roos*' (2009) 34 *European Law Review* 914

Chapter acknowledgements

The authors write here in their personal capacity.

---

[225] *Gaston Schul* (n 2).

13

Free movement of natural persons

Catherine Barnard

1 Introduction

Any reader of this book is likely to have exercised rights of free movement within the EU: as a tourist on holiday in Italy, as a student studying on an Erasmus programme in Germany, as a chalet attendant working in the French Alps, as a ski instructor there, or as a recipient of services provided by Amazon in Luxembourg. All of these situations are covered by one of the following provisions of EU law:

- Article 45 TFEU on the free movement of workers, which allows EU nationals to work in another Member State in an employed capacity;
- Article 49 TFEU on freedom of establishment, which allows EU nationals to work in another Member State in a self-employed capacity;
- Articles 56 and 57 TFEU or the free movement of services, which allow EU nationals to provide or receive services in another Member State.

More generally, since the Maastricht Treaty in 1992, all EU nationals have become citizens of the Union (Article 20 TFEU), which, according to Article 21 TFEU, gives them certain rights to free movement, whether they are economically active or not.

The Treaty rights to free movement have been elaborated by the legislature, notably by Citizens' Rights Directive (CRD) 2004/38[1] and, for workers, by Regulation 492/11.[2] The advent of EU citizenship has produced some surprise twists in the direction of the case law[3] and has helped to shape the Court's interpretation of the secondary legislation.

The aim of this chapter is to give an overview of the EU rules on free movement of natural persons. It is a vast area of law, so this chapter is inevitably selective both in its choice of subject matter and the cases discussed. Four themes/questions will, however, be highlighted. First, is economic migration a good thing for the host State and its (non-migrant) citizens? If not, should States be able to control the number of economic migrants coming into their country? The original Treaty gave rights only to those migrants who were economically active (workers, self-employed, service providers). They were seen as contributing to the economy of the host State (ie the State in which they worked), through their labour and by paying taxes. They were thus seen as a benefit to the host State. However, inevitably these migrants compete with nationals in the host State for jobs and other limited resources (housing, maternity services, schooling). In some States this has prompted a rise in anti-migrant feeling and has led to the growing popularity of political parties hostile to immigration (eg the Dutch Party for Freedom and the Danish People's Party).

Secondly, judicial decisions, together with the CRD, have broadened the net of beneficiaries of free movement to include not just those who are economically active but also those who are not (so) economically active (work-seekers, students, persons of independent means – the 'semi-economically active') as well as the economically inactive (eg the homeless). Why should the non-economically active be able to migrate? Does a shared EU citizenship entitle them to move and if so enjoy social security benefits in the host State? Might this serve to undermine, rather than strengthen, any nascent solidarity upon which EU citizenship is based? At what price does this come to already over-burdened social welfare systems in the host States? And at what moment can Member States say that the

[1] OJ [2004] L8/17.
[2] OJ [2011] L141/1. See also Dir. to improve the enforcement of workers' rights (http://europa.eu/rapid/press-release_IP-14-421_en.htm)
[3] See eg Case C-138/02 *Collins v Secretary of State for Work and Pensions* [2004] ECR I-2703; Case C-184/99 *Grzelczyk* [2001] ECR I-6193; Case C-413/99 *Baumbast and R v Secretary of State for the Home Department* [2002] ECR I-7091.

question of who is admitted to their territory, and on what terms, is a matter for national law over which EU law has no say?

Thirdly, the extension of the rights of free movement to the semi- and non-economically active is an illustration of a broader dynamic witnessed elsewhere in EU law: an increasing reference to, and reliance on, human rights.[4] Migrants are no longer seen simply as factors of production but also as the bearers of human rights. This means that, in principle, they should enjoy a certain standard of living in the host State, as should their family members, irrespective of the nationality of those family members. The Court has used the advent of European citizenship to reinforce the link between migration and human rights – whether derived from the European Convention on Human Rights (ECHR) or from the EU Charter (see section 9).[5] What are the implications of this development? Does it mean that the right to free movement, itself a fundamental right in the Treaty and the Charter, applies not only to the young, fit, and well educated but also to groups viewed less favourably by society, including the Roma from Hungary and Romania[6] and travelling football fans?[7] Further, do third-country nationals (TCNs), also human beings but not EU citizens, benefit from these rights?

Fourthly, should a single set of rules apply across the free movement of persons provisions? At first sight, the answer to this question is yes: Articles 45, 49, 56, and 21 TFEU all concern natural persons who move from one EU State to another. Often it is difficult to police the boundaries between one provision and another (see section 4). It therefore makes sense to apply common principles. However, if this analysis is correct, why have separate Treaty provisions at all? This suggests that there are differences between the Treaty provisions, but, if so, what might they be?

While this chapter cannot hope to provide a definitive answer to these complex questions it will show how the EU judiciary and legislature have responded to some of the challenges raised by EU migration. The nature of that challenge is presented in the next section.

2 The context

2.1 The case for economic migration and the principle of equal treatment

While many people are (dimly) aware of their rights under EU law, they more often associate migration with an influx of labour coming into their own countries, threatening their jobs.[8] This fear was exacerbated by the 2004 and subsequent enlargements which brought countries into the EU whose wage costs were significantly lower than those in Northern European states. Headlines in the British press screamed 'East European surge blamed for 1m young Britons being on dole',[9] and that 'Eastern Europeans milk our

---

[4] See further chapter 9.

[5] C Barnard, 'Citizenship of the Union and the Area of Justice: (Almost) The Court's Moment of Glory' in A Rosas, E Levits, and Y Bot, *The Court of Justice and the Construction of Europe: Analyses and Perspectives on Sixty Years of Case Law* (The Hague: Asser Press, 2012).

[6] M Dawson and E Muir, 'Individual Institutional and Collective Vigilance in Protecting Fundamental Rights in the EU: Lessons from the Roma' (2011) 48 *Common Market Law Review* 751.

[7] *Gough and Smith v Chief Constable of Derbyshire* [2002] 2 CMLR 11 and E Deards, 'Human Rights for Football Hooligans?' (2002) 27 *European Law Review* 206.

[8] http://www.dailymail.co.uk/news/article-2307216/Britons-likely-job-East-European-migrants -Findings-contrast-countries-high-immigration.html (*Daily Mail*, 11 April 2013).

[9] *Daily Express*, 9 January 2012, http://www.express.co.uk/news/uk/294457/East-European-surge-blamed -for-1m-young-Britons-being-on-dole

benefits'.[10] Transitional arrangements were put in place by a number of countries to stop the sudden arrival of a large number of migrants from the Eastern European countries; these arrangements expired seven years after the enlargement.

On 1 January 2012 there were 13.6 million people living in an EU-27 Member State with citizenship of another EU-27 Member State (about 2.7 per cent of the EU's population). This compares with the figure for the EU-27 *foreign* population (people residing in an EU-27 Member State with citizenship of a non-EU-27 Member State) of 20.7 million, representing 4.1 per cent of the EU-27 population.[11] So inter-EU migration is significantly lower than non-EU immigration and considerably less than interstate migration in the US. Nevertheless some countries are more affected by migration than others: in absolute terms, the largest numbers of foreigners living in the EU on 1 January 2012 were found in Germany (7.4 million people), Spain (5.5 million), Italy (4.8 million), the UK (4.8 million), and France (3.8 million).[12] When an economy is growing, as it was in the UK in the mid-2000s, it proved possible to absorb and benefit from the skills of the million or so migrant workers, largely from Poland but also from the Czech Republic, Slovakia, and the Baltic States, who arrived in the UK in this period. But following the financial crisis, and the dramatic rise in unemployment, the picture changed. For politicians (but not necessarily employers – see case study 13.1), migrant workers were no longer seen as a benefit, providing the input of much needed skills, but as a burden on the economy and a threat to nationals getting jobs. Protectionist sentiments became a familiar part of the political discourse.[13]

And with the crisis came the concern that work-seekers from countries in an even worse situation would come to the Northern European States looking for work. In fact, Article 45 TFEU was included in the original Treaty to enable such movement to occur.[14] It continues to act as a safety valve: the number of Greeks and Spaniards moving to other EU countries has doubled since 2007, reaching 39,000 and 72,000 respectively. Germany saw a 73 per cent increase in Greek immigrants between 2011 and 2012, close to 50 per cent for Spanish and Portuguese nationals and 35 per cent for Italians.[15]

Under EU law these migrants enjoy equal treatment with nationals. This is morally justified – equality is, after all, a fundamental right.[16] It is also economically necessary. At a macro-level migrants offer a fresh pool of skilled labour – and the equality principle ensures that the migrants cannot undercut the terms and conditions of employment of local staff. At a micro-level the requirement of equal treatment (should) force employers to open their minds to the possibility

[10] http://www.express.co.uk/news/uk/7741/92-000-East-Europeans-milk-our-benefits (*Daily Express*, 23 May 2007). They even steal our fish: http://www.express.co.uk/news/uk/386379/British-rivers-stripped-of-fish-by-East-European-poachers (*Daily Express*, 23 March 2013); http://www.dailymail.co.uk/news/article-2306769/No-Eastern-Europeans-sign-placed-carp-fishing-lake-angry-landowner-claims-stolen-fish.html (*Daily Mail*, 10 April 2013).
[11] http://epp.eurostat.ec.europa.eu/statistics_explained/index.php/Migration_and_migrant_ population_ statistics (*Eurostat*, March 2013).   [12] Ibid.
[13] eg Gordon Brown, then British Prime Minister, famously declared that 'British jobs' should be for 'British workers', http://news.bbc.co.uk/1/hi/uk_politics/7010664.stm (*BBC News online*, 24 September 2007). See also the infamous encounter between Gordon Brown and Mrs Gillian Duffy in the 2010 election campaign , where he accused Mrs Duffy of being a 'bigot' for her comments about immigration. She said 'You can't say anything about the immigrants...but all these eastern European what are coming in, where are they flocking from?': http://www.guardian.co.uk/politics/2010/apr/28/gordon-brown-gillian-duffy-transcript (*The Guardian*, 28 April 2010).
[14] The Spaak Report, June 1956, http://aei.pitt.edu/995/1/Spaak_report.pdf
[15] http://www.oecd.org/els/mig/migrationpickingupbutrisingunemploymenthurtingimmigrants.htm (*OECD*, 13 June 2013). But not all of them stay: http://elpais.com/elpais/2013/09/16/inenglish/1379341141_472777.html (*El Pais: In English*, 16 September 2013), citing the OECD, reports that two-thirds of Spaniards who arrived in Germany in 2011 left within a year after failing to find a job.
[16] See further chapter 9.

of hiring non-local staff (see case study 13.1). Discrimination on the grounds of nationality artificially restricts employers' choice and denies employers the opportunity of recruiting the best person for the job, who might not be a national of that State, while at the same time thwarting the migrant's opportunities for economic improvement. But this is a hard message to sell at a time of unprecedentedly high levels of unemployment among the local population.

Case study 13.1: European staff help Ocado grow in Hatfield,
***Financial Times*, 14 March 2013**

The surge of eastern European workers arriving in the UK during the past decade may have caused consternation among some of the British public, but for the founders of online grocer Ocado, the influx was a rare opportunity.[17]

The upmarket food delivery business was forged as eight countries joined the EU in 2004, providing a welcome pool of labour for what was then a relatively unknown company undergoing rapid expansion.

Ocado's search for thousands of staff to pack shopping and deliver it to customers was matched by a supply of newly-mobile migrants from Poland, the Czech Republic, Slovakia, Lithuania and elsewhere, keen to secure jobs in more affluent western Europe.

Helped by intensive recruitment in cities including Krakow, as well as a bonus scheme for staff who recommend a friend or relative, about 40 per cent of the 2,000 employees at Ocado's distribution centre at Hatfield, a small town just north of London, are from Poland. They outnumber the 35 per cent who are white British, with the remaining jobs filled by staff from more than 40 nationalities.

In the warehouse aisle known as 'Ambient Zone Pick Bravo', Dariusz Karcz, 29, stands at a packing terminal surrounded by an apparently random assortment of groceries – apple juice, Fijian mineral water, paper towels, potatoes, and organic linguine. A conveyor belt snaking for 15 miles through the site shuttles each basket to his stand and the computer instructs Mr Karcz which goods to put inside.

For him, the move to Britain six years ago has proved a success. Interviewed and recruited in Poland, he earns £270 a week before bonuses, and shrugs off the suggestion that the labour is monotonous. 'This is a good job for people from eastern Europe,' he says. 'They can fulfil their needs, like buying a flat or a car or getting married. This job gives lots of opportunities to people like me.'

Reflecting that Mr Karcz and most of Ocado's other 'personal shoppers' are not native English speakers, the warehouse's health and safety signs are written in Polish and English. The packers' computer terminals run in several languages.

While the strategy of hiring abroad and catering to foreign staff may have looked smart when Britain's economy was booming, it is harder to justify now that growth is sluggish and youth unemployment is hovering under 1m.

Many employers surveyed anonymously by the Chartered Institute for Personnel and Development said in a report published on Wednesday that eastern European staff are still better qualified than British-born peers, have a better work ethic and are easier to retain.

Mark Watson, Ocado's director of planning and supply chain, is loath to criticise the local workforce. 'A lot of the folk that came over [from eastern Europe] are motivated to come and find employment, so that means [they] ... are generally quite good,' he says. 'But there are equally as many good folk around this area,' he adds.

---

[17] See also 'Employers turn to EU migrants to fill jobs', *Financial Times*, 13 March 2013, http://www.ft.com/cms/s/0/aeacadca-8c0c-11e2-b001-00144feabdc0.html#axzz2PFgH55qC

Hatfield itself has been transformed by the growth of the Ocado warehouse. It now has several Polish shops and such is its status as a magnet for Polish immigrants that Lech Walesa, Poland's former president, visited the town two years ago to speak to the Ocado workers. Mr Walesa, who was an electrician and shipyard worker before his political career, insisted on visiting the warehouse rather than head office, with employees cramming into two small meeting rooms to hear him speak.

An endorsement from the former president is undoubtedly a boost to those such as Mr Karcz, who has met British people he describes as 'not very friendly' to incomers from Poland.

When asked whether he and other eastern Europeans are guilty of taking British jobs, his answer is unequivocal.

'This, I cannot agree with,' Mr Karcz says, struggling to make himself heard above the whirr of conveyors. 'Some of the English people just don't like this job. For us it's perfect. In our country we would work so hard for a small amount of money.'

2.2 Benefit tourism?

So far we have talked about those migrants who are economically active (workers, the self-employed, and service providers/receivers) who move between EU States under Articles 45, 49, and 56 TFEU. But what about those who are not? Article 21 TFEU gives rights of free movement and residence to all EU citizens, economically active or not,[18] rights elaborated by the CRD.[19] For example, Article 6 CRD allows all EU citizens to move to another Member State for up to three months. They will enjoy equal treatment with nationals under Article 24 CRD but not in respect of social assistance (ie discretionary benefits intended to address need[20]) and student grants and loans (SG&L)) (see further section 6).

But what about social security more generally? Individuals insured in State A (ie covered by the benefits system in respect of, eg unemployment benefits and pensions as a result of contributions they have made) may be deterred from exercising their rights of free movement to State B if they lose their entitlement to benefits in State A. The Social Security Regulation, now Regulation 883/2004, was adopted to help address this problem.[21] It recognizes that determining the content of social security protection and the conditions under which it is granted is a matter for national law. However, the Regulation provides for the *coordination* (not harmonization) of national social security rules. It therefore lays down a number of common rules including

- equal treatment,
- aggregation (periods of insurance, residence, or employment in an EU country must be taken into account in all other Member States),

---

[18] *Baumbast* (n 3) para 83.

[19] OJ [2004] L158/77.

[20] The distinction between social security and social assistance has become blurred; first, because entitlement to social assistance has tended to become a matter of right rather than discretion and, secondly, because the burden of funding social insurance has resulted in moves to require a test of means even for some insurance-based benefits: R White, *EC Social Security Law* (Harlow: Longman, 1999) 6.

[21] OJ [2004] L166/1. It applies to all the traditional branches of social security: sickness, maternity, accidents at work, occupational diseases, invalidity benefits, unemployment benefits, family benefits, retirement and pre-retirement benefits, death grants.

- the single State rule (only one national system applies to the migrant at any one time, usually the State of employment), and
- exportability (allowing individuals to take benefits already accrued to another Member State).

As a result of the exportability principle, long-term benefits, such as pensions, must be paid by the Member State of origin, irrespective of where that person resides. This explains in part why so many retired Northern Europeans live in southern Spain: they can enjoy the sunshine while drawing their pensions from their own State. In the case of an individual who is unemployed but seeking employment in another Member State, he or she may be able to claim unemployment benefit for three months, payable by State B but at State A's rates. However, this payment is subject to strict conditions,[22] including registration with the home and host State authorities.

The discussion so far might play to fears expressed in some quarters that migrants are in fact benefit tourists and can simply turn up in a host State and demand benefits. The strict eligibility criteria under Social Security Regulation 883/2004, together with the total exclusion of social assistance for the first three months of residence for those who are not economically active under Directive 2004/38, makes benefit tourism difficult in practice. Furthermore, there is little evidence of it actually occurring. According to the *Financial Times*, in the UK at least, only a small minority of immigrants claim working age benefits – about 7 per cent versus 17 per cent for British-born nationals.[23] Further, Eastern European migrants have contributed more to the economy than nationals: they have made a net contribution to UK public finances every year between 2004, when their countries joined the EU, and 2009. In 2008–9 they paid 37 per cent more in direct or indirect taxes than they received in public goods and services – compared with Britons who contributed 20 per cent less than they received.[24] This research is now supported by an extensive report produced for the European Commission which shows that mobile EU citizens are less likely to receive disability and unemployment benefits in most countries studied.[25] Yet in a number of Member States this evidence remains contested or ignored.

2.3 The judicial response

So far we have considered some of the political debate surrounding the free movement of persons. What of the judicial response? This forms much of the subject matter for the rest of this chapter. The analysis that follows will be structured round seven questions which are considered in some form in most free movement of persons cases:

(a) Does EU law apply at all? If yes,

(b) Which provision of the Treaty/secondary legislation is/are engaged?

---

[22] The coordination of unemployment benefits are regulated by Title III, Chapter 6, Articles 61–65 of Regulation 883/2004 and Title III, Chapter V, Articles 54–57 of the Implementing Regulation 987/2009.

[23] 'Britain, the Balkans and benefit tourism', *Financial Times*, 25 March 2013, http://www.ft.com/cms/s/0/d0d832b0-9559-11e2-a151-00144feabdc0.html#axzz2PFgH55qC

[24] 'Most migrants pay their way', *Financial Times*, 25 March 2013, http://www.ft.com/cms/s/0/53 50c12a-9579-11e2-a4fa-00144feabdc0.html#axzz2PFgH55qC. For a detailed analytical study, see C Dustmann, T Frattini, and C Halls, 'Assessing the Fiscal Costs and Benefits of A8 Migration to the UK' (2010) 31 *Fiscal Studies* 1.

[25] See links on 'Impact of mobile EU citizens on national social security systems' (*European Commission*, 14 October 2013) http://ec.europa.eu/social/main.jsp?langId=en&catId=89&newsId=1980&furtherNews=yes. See also C Dustmann and T Frattini, 'The Fiscal Effect of Immigration to the UK' (2013) CREAM Discussion Paper Series no 22/13, http://www.cream-migration.org/publ_uploads/CDP_22_13.pdf

(c) Does EU law apply to this particular person? If yes,

(d) What rights do migrants enjoy under the secondary legislation?

(e) Has national law infringed EU law in any other way (the so-called restrictions approach)? If yes,

(f) Can that breach be justified? If yes,

(g) Is the breach compatible with human rights and proportionate?

We begin with the most fundamental question: does EU law apply at all?

3 Does EU law apply at all?

3.1 Introduction

Various attempts have been made by the parties to argue that their case falls outside the scope of EU law and so should be judged by the standards of national law only, which they consider to be more favourable. The leading case of *Viking* provides a good example of this.[26] Viking Line, the Finnish owners of a passenger ferry which plied the route between Helsinki in Finland and Tallinn in Estonia, wanted to reflag the vessel as Estonian. The Finnish Seamen's Union (FSU), fearing that Finnish seamen's jobs were at stake, threatened strike action, strike action which would have been lawful under Finnish law. The International Transport Federation (ITF) also told its members to black (ie not service) any Viking vessel. Viking Line argued that the action by FSU and ITF breached Article 49 TFEU.

The first question for the Court of Justice was whether EU law applied at all. The trade unions and some governments argued not. For example, the Danish government argued that the right of freedom of association, the right to strike, and the right to impose lock-outs fell outside the scope of the fundamental freedom laid down in Article 49 TFEU since, in accordance with Article 153(5) TFEU, the EU does not have competence to regulate those rights.

The Court disagreed:[27]

> even if, in the areas which fall outside the scope of the Union's competence, the Member States are still free, in principle, to lay down the conditions governing the existence and exercise of the rights in question, the fact remains that, when exercising that competence, the Member States must nevertheless comply with [Union] law (see, by analogy, in relation to social security (*Decker* and *Kohll*[28]); in relation to direct taxation (*Commission v France* and *Marks & Spencer*[29]).

In other words, even in areas such as social security, taxation, and strike action, where the EU has no – or highly circumscribed – competence to legislate (ie enact regulations or directives ('positive integration')), the negative Treaty provisions on the four freedoms will apply.

---

[26] Case C-438/05 *International Transport Workers' Union Federation et al v Viking Line ABP* [2007] ECR I-7779. See also chapter 20.   [27] *Viking Line* (n 26) para 40, case references put into footnotes.
[28] Case C-120/95 *Decker* [1998] ECR I-1831, paras 22 and 23 and Case C-158/96 *Kohll* [1998] ECR I-1931, paras 18 and 19.
[29] Case C-334/02 *Commission v France* [2004] ECR I-2229, para 21 and Case C-446/03 *Marks & Spencer v Halsey* [2005] ECR I-10837, para 29.

That said, there are three significant limitations on the application of the free movement provisions which the Court has, more or less consistently, upheld. The Treaty provisions apply only to those who

(a) hold the nationality of a Member State;

(b) have moved to another Member State; and

(c) (in the case of Articles 45, 49, and 56 TFEU) have been, or are, engaged in some economic activity in the Member State they have moved to.

If one of these conditions is not satisfied EU law will not apply. We shall consider these conditions in turn.

3.2 EU nationality

The free movement rights under Articles 45, 49, 56, and 21 TFEU apply to nationals of an EU Member State only; they do not apply to TCNs unless they are family members of the migrating EU national (see section 6.2.2). So who, then, is a national of a Member State? It had long been thought that this was a matter of national law.[30] However, the position has become muddied by the decision in *Rottmann*.[31] Rottmann, an Austrian national, was being investigated for serious fraud in Austria. During the investigations he moved to Germany where he acquired German nationality, with the result that, under Austrian law, he lost his Austrian nationality. When the German authorities discovered his past (which they had not known at the time of his naturalization) they tried to deprive him of his German citizenship.

At first sight EU law has nothing to say on this issue: not only did the case appear to concern a wholly internal situation to which EU law does not apply (see section 3.3), but it also raised questions about the determination of nationality, also an issue of national law. However, the Court of Justice took a different view. It said that even where a matter fell within the competence of the Member States, 'in situations covered by European Union law' the national rules concerned must have 'regard for EU law'.[32] Because the decision of the German authorities risked rendering him stateless, and thus depriving him of 'the status [of citizen of the Union] conferred by Article [20 TFEU][33] and the rights attaching thereto', the Court said that this situation did fall 'within the ambit of European Union law'.[34] EU law principles, including proportionality, therefore applied.[35]

So what does this mean in practice? The Court said that 'Having regard to the importance which primary law attaches to the status of citizen of the Union', when examining a decision withdrawing naturalization the national authorities had to take into account 'the consequences that the decision entails for the person concerned and, if relevant, for the members of his family with regard to the loss of the rights enjoyed by every citizen of the Union'. It added that it was also necessary to establish 'whether that loss is justified in relation to the gravity of the offence committed by that person, to the lapse of time between the naturalisation decision and the withdrawal decision and to whether it is possible for that person to recover his original nationality'.

---

[30] Case C-192/99 *R v Secretary of State, ex p Kaur* [2001] ECR I-1237, although cf Case C-369/90 *Micheletti v Delagación del Gobierno en Cantabria* [1992] ECR I-4239. See also Declaration No 2 on nationality of a Member State, annexed by the Member States to the final act of the Maastricht Treaty on European Union.
[31] Case C-135/08 *Rottmann v Freistaat Bayern* [2010] ECR I-1449.   [32] Ibid, para 41.
[33] Art 20 TFEU provides that 'Every person holding the nationality of a Member State shall be a citizen of the Union'.
[34] *Rottmann* (n 31) para 42.   [35] Ibid, para 55.

3.3 **The interstate element**

Not only must the individual be a national of a Member State but, according to the orthodoxy, he or she must have moved, be in the course of moving, or be likely to move between one Member State and another,[36] or returning to his or her State of origin after a period of time resident in a host State.[37] If there is no interstate element – the so-called wholly internal situation – then national law only applies.[38] This is more than a technicality. It is about division of competence: EU free movement law applies where there is an interstate element, national law applies otherwise.

Yet despite the solid constitutional foundations for the rule, it brings with it legal, political, and practical problems. First, the wholly internal rule can give rise to reverse discrimination. This means that EU citizens who migrate may be in a more favourable position than those who stay at home. So, for example, EU nationals who move from one Member State to another can invoke EU rights to, for example, bring their TCN spouse into the host State and reside with him there.[39] Those who do not exercise EU rights of free movement can rely only on national law and may find that national law denies admission to the TCN spouse.[40] This problem of reverse discrimination is particularly acute in States divided on federal or devolved lines. For example, in the UK higher education in Scotland is free for Scottish students domiciled in Scotland, and for EU students studying in Scotland, but not for students from England and Wales studying in Scotland. This has proved deeply divisive.[41]

Secondly, if the EU is about creating a single market, barriers created internally within a Member State should also be removed. This is the position that the Court took in respect of Article 30 TFEU on customs duties.[42] It also formed part of Advocate General Sharpston's reasoning in the *Walloon* case[43] that the wholly internal rules should be abolished, at least in respect of the devolved 'Scotland-type' situation. The Court firmly rejected her arguments and reiterated that the wholly internal rule continued to apply in the field of free movement of persons.

Thirdly, despite the Court's determination to uphold the wholly internal rule when, as in the *Walloon* case, it is pressed specifically on the point, the Court has been somewhat cavalier in maintaining the orthodoxy in individual cases. So, for example, in *Carpenter*[44] the Court said that EU law applied where a British man went – only occasionally – to another Member State to provide services (selling adverts in medical journals). This meant his wife, a Filipino national, was able to argue that her deportation (for overstaying her visa) would interfere with his free movement right, contrary to Article 56 TFEU, since without her there would be no one to look after his children from a previous marriage. *Carpenter* suggests that it takes very little movement for EU law to apply. This point was recognized by Advocate General Sharpston in *Ruiz Zambrano*.[45] The case concerned a failed Colombian asylum seeker living in Belgium. While his claim was being processed, he and his Colombian wife had two children (Diego and Jessica) who acquired Belgian nationality under Belgian law. When the Belgian authorities tried to deport him, he invoked EU

---

[36] See eg Art 3(1) CRD and Case C-434/09 *McCarthy v Secretary of State for the Home Department* [2011] ECR I-3375.　　　　　[37] See eg Case C-370/90 *Surinder Singh* [1992] ECR I-4265.

[38] See eg Case 175/78 *R v Saunders* [1979] ECR 1129. See eg A Tryfonidou, 'Reverse Discrimination in Purely Internal Situations: An Incongruity in a Citizens' Europe' (2008) 35 *Legal Issues of Economic Integration* 43.

[39] *Surinder Singh* (n 37).

[40] *McCarthy* (n 36).

[41] See eg http://www.dailymail.co.uk/news/article-2028531/Jennifer-Watts-19-leads-fees-apartheid-campaign-Scotlands-anti-English-bias.html (*Daily Mail*, 23 August 2011).

[42] Case C-72/03 *Carbonati Apuani Srl v Commune di Carrara* [2004] ECR I-8027. See further chapter 12.

[43] Case C-212/96 *Government of the French Community and Walloon Government v Flemish Government* [2008] ECR I-1683.　　　　　[44] Case C-60/00 [2002] ECR I-6279.

[45] Case C-34/09 [2011] ECR I-1177.

law to stop his deportation from the territory of the EU. His problem: he was a TCN and, in respect of Diego and Jessica, their situation was a wholly internal situation. Therefore, according to the orthodoxy, EU law should not apply.

On the question of the wholly internal rule, Advocate General Sharpston said:

> If one insists on the premiss that physical movement to a Member State other than the Member State of nationality is required before residence rights as a citizen of the Union can be invoked, the result risks being both strange and illogical. Suppose a friendly neighbour had taken Diego and Jessica on a visit or two to Parc Astérix in Paris, or to the seaside in Brittany. They would then have received services in another Member State. Were they to seek to claim rights arising from their 'movement' it could not be suggested that their situation was 'purely internal' to Belgium. Would one visit have sufficed? Two? Several? Would a day trip have been enough; or would they have had to stay over for a night or two in France?

In other words, the wholly internal rule, as interpreted by the Court in cases such as *Carpenter*, was flawed.

The Court did not consider the wholly internal rule. It adopted a different approach entirely. Following *Rottmann*, it said:[46]

> Article 20 TFEU precludes national measures which have the effect of depriving citizens of the Union of the genuine enjoyment of the substance of the rights conferred by virtue of their status as citizens of the Union.

It continued that a refusal to grant a Belgian right of residence to Mr Ruiz Zambrano, a TCN with dependent minor Belgian children, and also a refusal to grant him a work permit, had the effect of depriving the *children* of the genuine enjoyment of the substance of their EU rights. Mr Ruiz Zambrano was therefore able to stay in Belgium to look after his children, relying on rights derived from their citizen status.

This case is an example of the creative use of the citizenship provisions of the Treaty to deliver justice to the Ruiz Zambrano family. Inevitably, the decision precipitated a large number of claims brought by TCNs in various Member States to justify being allowed to stay in the EU. Subsequent references suggest that *Ruiz Zambrano* has come close to being confined to its unique facts (ie the removal from the territory of the EU as a whole, of dependent, young children who are EU citizens).[47]

To conclude, it would seem that the wholly internal rule is still good law where Articles 45, 49, 56, and 21 TFEU are at issue. However, as *Rottmann* and *Ruiz Zambrano* show, the requirement does not apply to cases decided under Article 20 TFEU.

3.4 Economic activity

Finally, in respect of the original Treaty provisions (Articles 45, 49, and 56 TFEU), the migrant workers, self-employed, and service providers must be engaged in economic activity. This, according to the Court in *Jundt*,[48] is 'the decisive factor' which brings an activity within the ambit of the provisions of the Treaty. In many cases the existence of economic

---

[46] *Ruiz Zambrano* (n 45) para 42.

[47] See eg *McCarthy* (n 36); Case C-256/11 *Dereci* [2011] ECR I-11315; Case C-40/11 *Iida v Stadt Ulm*, judgment of 8 November 2012, nyr; Joined Cases C-356/11 and 357/11 *O and S v Maahanmuuttovirasto*, judgment of 6 December 2012, nyr.

[48] Case C-281/06 *Jundt v Finanzamt Offenburg* [2007] ECR I-12231, para 32.

activity is assumed, particularly where the individual or company is being remunerated for the activity performed. However, it does become an issue with voluntary or semi-voluntary activities, especially those undertaken as part of a rehabilitation programme.[49] In *Jundt* the Court emphasized that 'the activity must not be provided for nothing' for Article 56 TFEU to apply, albeit that there is no need for the service provider 'to be seeking to make a profit'.[50]

The position is different under Article 21(1) TFEU. There, the link between free movement rights of the non-economically active and economic activity has been severed. The Court made this clear in *Baumbast*:[51]

> the Treaty does not require that citizens of the Union pursue a professional or trade activity, whether as an employed or self-employed person, in order to enjoy the rights provided in Part Two of the [TFEU] on citizenship of the Union.

Therefore, in the case of citizens wishing to exercise their rights under Article 21(1) TFEU, it is sufficient that they merely hold the nationality of one of the Member States; unlike individuals wishing to invoke Article 45, 49, or 56 TFEU, they need not be engaged in an economic activity.

4 Which Treaty provision is engaged?

Once it has been decided that EU law applies in principle, the next question is what Treaty provision is engaged: Article 45 TFEU on workers, Article 49 TFEU on establishment, Articles 56 and 57 TFEU on services, or Article 21 TFEU on citizenship? This question is not merely a semantic one of classification. While there are common principles underpinning all four articles there are, as we shall see, some important differences concerning which regulator (host or home State) controls the activity of the migrant, and the levels of justification required when a breach of the Treaty is established. These issues will be considered in section 8. First, we look at the elements which distinguish the different freedoms.

4.1 Free movement of workers

4.1.1 The definition of workers

Workers are essentially dependent labour. The Treaty has not defined the term but in *Lawrie-Blum*[52] the Court said that the essential feature of an employment relationship is that

> for a certain period of time a person performs services for and under the direction of another person in return for which he receives remuneration.

---

[49] Case 344/87 *Bettray v Staatssecretaris van Justitie* [1989] ECR 1621, para 17.

[50] *Jundt* (n 50) para 33.

[51] Case C-413/99 (n 3) para 83. See also the views of AG Jacobs in Case C-148/02 *Garcia Avello* [2003] ECR I-11613, para 61 and AG Cosmas's even grander claims in Case C-378/97 *Wijsenbeek* [1999] ECR I-6207, para 85:

Article [21 TFEU] does not simply enshrine in constitutional terms the *acquis communautaire* as it existed when it was inserted into the Treaty and complement it by broadening the category of persons entitled to freedom of movement to include other classes of person not pursuing economic activities. Article [21 TFEU] also enshrines a right of a different kind, a true right of movement, stemming from the status as a citizen of the Union, which is not subsidiary in relation to European unification, whether economic or not.

[52] Case 66/85 *Lawrie-Blum v Land Baden-Württemberg* [1986] ECR 2121.

Both the sphere of employment and the nature of the legal relationship between employer and employee, whether involving public law status or a private law contract, are immaterial. Therefore, on the facts of the case, the Court found that a trainee teacher had to be regarded as a worker for the purpose of Article 45(1) TFEU. In subsequent cases the Court has made clear that the individual must be engaged in a 'genuine and effective' economic activity which is not on such a small scale as to be 'purely marginal and ancillary'.[53] This is of particular relevance to part-time workers.[54]

4.1.2 The position of work-seekers

The term 'workers' also includes work-seekers who will enjoy the status of worker for a reasonable period.[55] The period allowed for the worker to remain in the host Member State looking for work depends on the rules of the particular Member State but the worker must be allowed a reasonable time in which to apprise themselves of offers of employment corresponding to their occupational qualifications and to take, where appropriate, the necessary steps in order to be engaged.[56] A declaration recorded in the Council minutes when two pieces of secondary legislation on free movement were adopted in the 1960s[57] talked about a three-month period but the Court rejected this document as an interpretative tool since no reference was made to it in the secondary legislation itself.[58] The Court also rejected the link with the three-month period under the Social Security Regulation 883/2004 in which the migrant can claim benefits while in the host State (see section 2.2). The Court therefore concluded that a period of six months, such as that laid down in the national legislation at issue, was sufficient but with the important caveat that if, after the expiry of that period, the person concerned produced evidence that he was continuing to seek employment and that he had genuine chances of being engaged, he could not be required to leave the territory of the host Member State.[59] This line of case law is now reflected in Article 14(4)(b) CRD.

4.1.3 Those deemed workers or self-employed

Finally, the CRD also provides that an individual retains worker (or self-employed) status in the host Member State in four prescribed situations:[60]

(a) He/she is temporarily unable to work as the result of an illness or accident.

(b) He/she is in duly recorded involuntary unemployment after having been employed for more than one year and has registered as a job-seeker with the relevant employment office.

(c) He/she is in duly recorded involuntary unemployment after completing a fixed-term employment contract of less than a year or after having become involuntarily unemployed during the first 12 months and has registered as a job-seeker with the relevant employment office. In this case, the status of worker shall be retained for no less than six months.

(d) He/she embarks on vocational training. Unless he/she is involuntarily unemployed, the retention of the status of worker shall require the training to be related to the previous employment.

---

[53] Case 53/81 *Levin* [1982] ECR 1035, para 17. The Court said that the rules relating to free movement of workers also applied to part-time workers, even where they earn less than the minimum wage of a particular Member State.

[54] Ibid.   [55] Case C-292/89 *R v IAT, ex p Antonissen* [1991] ECR I-745.

[56] Ibid, para 16.   [57] Official Journal, English Special Edition [1968] (II), p 485.   [58] *Levin* (n 53) para 18.

[59] Ibid, para 21.   [60] Art 17(3).

4.2 Establishment

While Article 45 TFEU concerns dependent labour, Article 49 TFEU concerns independent labour, namely the self-employed (and companies).[61] As the Court said in *Gebhard*:[62]

> the concept of establishment within the meaning of the Treaty is therefore a very broad one, allowing a [Union] national to participate, on a stable and continuous basis, in the economic life of a Member State other than his state of origin and to profit therefrom, so contributing to social and economic penetration within the [Union] in the sphere of activities as self-employed persons.

Many migrant self-employed people move to provide services in a professional or semi-professional capacity (eg lawyers, hairdressers, accountants). This may create confusion in respect of classification with service providers moving under Article 56 TFEU. The essence of the distinction between the two situations lies in the language of *Gebhard*: if the service provision is 'on a stable and continuous basis' Article 49 TFEU on freedom of establishment will apply. If the service provision is temporary then Article 56 TFEU on the free movement of services applies (see section 4.3). The distinction is important because it determines which State takes primary responsibility for regulating the activities of the service supplier: if it is a case of freedom of establishment then the *host* State is the principal regulator (this is also the case with migrant workers under Article 45 TFEU). If it is a case of service provision under Article 56 TFEU then it will be the *home* State which is the principal regulator, and any additional regulation by the host State will have to be carefully justified (see further section 8.2).

4.3 Services

4.3.1 Freedom to provide services

As we have seen, the distinguishing feature of Articles 56 and 57 TFEU on the free movement of services is that the service, which is 'normally provided for remuneration' (emphasizing the need for economic activity – see section 3.4), is temporary. Neither the Treaty nor the case law give any quantitative guidance as to what constitutes 'temporary'. However, in *Gebhard*[63] the Court said the temporary nature of the provision of services is to be determined in light of 'its duration, regularity, periodicity and continuity'. Providers of services may also equip themselves in the host Member State with the infrastructure necessary for the purposes of performing the service in question.[64]

While the early cases concerned lawyers seeking to provide services temporarily in other Member States,[65] a number of more recent cases have involved companies providing services and taking their own workforce with them to do the particular job.[66] These workers, described as posted workers, essentially bring their own labour law system with them. This means that they are employed under the terms and conditions of employment of the *home* State, not the host State where the work is performed. Where the service providers come from Eastern Europe and the work is performed in Northern Europe, the service providers enjoy a competitive advantage in terms of wage costs. To Northern European trade unions

---

[61] Case C-221/89 *R v Secretary of State for Transport, ex p Factortame* [1991] ECR I-3905, para 20. See further chapter 14.

[62] Case C-55/94 [1995] ECR I-4165.   [63] Ibid, para 39.

[64] Ibid. For additional guidance, see Art 3(2) of the proposed enforcement directive on posted workers: COM(2012) 131. This directive is intended to complement the Posted Workers Directive 96/71, which is discussed later.   [65] See eg Case 33/74 *Van Binsbergen* [1974] ECR 1299.

[66] Case C-341/05 *Laval* [2007] ECR I-987; Case C-346/06 *Dirk Rüffert v Land Niedersachsen* [2008] ECR I-1989. See further chapter 20.

this looks like social dumping and something to be prevented; to the Eastern Europeans it looks like taking advantage of their competitive position and something to be exploited.[67]

This tension between the two perspectives came to the fore in *Laval*.[68] The case concerned a Latvian company (Laval) which won a contract to refurbish a school in Sweden using its own Latvian workers who earned about 40 per cent less than comparable Swedish workers. The Swedish construction union wanted Laval to apply the Swedish collective agreement but Laval refused, in part because the collective agreement was unclear as to how much Laval would have to pay its workers. There followed serious industrial action against Laval which eventually led to its bankruptcy.

Laval successfully argued that this industrial action was contrary to *Union* law, in particular Article 56 TFEU on freedom to provide services, and the Posted Workers Directive 96/71. Directive 96/71 had been introduced – in part – to combat social dumping (ie States taking advantage of their low labour costs).[69] It required *host* States to impose some of their labour law rules on posted workers but only in the areas listed in Article 3(1) of the Directive, which includes minimum rates of pay and limits on working time. However, the Court said in effect that because Article 3(1) was an exception to the general rule that home State rules apply, it had to be interpreted narrowly and all of the detailed rules surrounding its operation had to be complied with. Because that was not the case on the facts, the Directive did not apply, and any industrial action taken to enforce the Directive was therefore also unlawful under Article 56 TFEU.

4.3.2 Other situations

So far we have talked about freedom to provide services. Although the Treaty talks only of the provision of services, the case law and the secondary legislation make clear that Article 56 TFEU also applies to EU nationals wishing to travel to receive services[70] and to provide services electronically.[71] In the case of natural persons the right to travel to receive a service has become particularly important in recent years: they can travel as tourists,[72] to receive medical treatment,[73] and education.[74] Service recipients enjoy protection not only under the Treaty but also under the Services Directive 2006/123.[75]

4.4 Citizenship of the Union

4.4.1 Economically, semi-economically, and non-economically active EU migrants

Article 21 provides 'Every citizen of the Union shall have the right to move and reside freely within the territory of the Member States, subject to the limitations and conditions laid down in the Treaties and by the measures adopted to give them effect.' As Figure 13.1

---

[67] This issue was expressly recognized in the Monti Report, 'A New Strategy for the Single Market', May 2010, http://ec.europa.eu/bepa/pdf/monti_report_final_10_05_2010_en.pdf, which said that the decisions in *Laval* (considered next) and its sister case *Viking* 'have exposed the fault lines that run between the single market and the social dimension…and that the cases [have] brought to the surface the strains to which the current regulatory framework for posting of workers is subject, in a context of divergent social and employment conditions among Member States and acute sensitivity about the perceived risks of social dumping and unfair competition.'   [68] Case C-341/05 (n 66).

[69] Speech of Vladimir Spidla, then EU Employment, Social Affairs and Equal Opportunities Commissioner, IP/06/423.   [70] Cases 286/82 and 26/83 *Luisi and Carbone* [1984] ECR 377.

[71] See by analogy Case 352/85 *Bond van Adverteerders v Netherlands* [1988] ECR 2085.

[72] *Luisi and Carbone* (n 72).

[73] Ibid. Case C-157/99 *Geraets Smits v Stichting Ziekenfonds* [2001] ECR I-5473. See further chapter 21.

[74] Case C-109/92 *Wirth v Landeshauptstadt Hannover* [1993] ECR I-6447.

[75] Arts 20 and 21 of Directive 2006/123 (OJ [2006] L376/76). See further chapter 14.

shows, not only are the *economically* active (workers, the self-employed, and service providers/recipients) citizens of the Union but so are the *semi-economically* active – students, and persons of independent means (PIMs) – whose position was first recognized by directives in the early 1990s: directives which have now been repealed and replaced by provisions in the CRD. Students and PIMs enjoy the right to free movement provided they have sufficient medical insurance and sufficient resources. The CRD (see section 6.2) also indicates that *non-economically* active citizens have the right of free movement, and the right to reside in the host State, at least for the first three months.

4.4.2 Non-migrant EU citizens

One final point, while this chapter concentrates on those EU citizens enjoying the rights to free movement under Articles 45, 49, 56, and 21 TFEU, it should not be forgotten that vast numbers of EU citizens have never exercised free movement rights (other than through tourism). Nevertheless, they enjoy certain rights (eg to equal pay for men and women, to consumer protection, to petition the European Parliament, and apply to the Ombudsman[76]) which are not contingent on their exercising their rights of free movement. As *Rottmann* and *Ruiz Zambrano* make clear, in exceptional cases they may also enjoy some rights under Article 20 TFEU (see section 3.2).

5 Does the EU measure apply to this particular defendant?

Once an assessment has been made as to the applicable Treaty provision (Article 45, 49, 56, or 21 TFEU), the next question is whether it can be invoked by the claimant against this particular defendant. The early case law made clear that the Treaty provisions on persons have vertical direct effect.[77] However, *Walrave and Koch*,[78] which said that 'the rule on non-discrimination applies in judging *all legal relationships*', suggested that the free movement of persons provisions had horizontal direct effect as well. Yet, subsequent cases

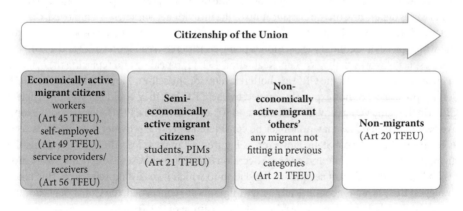

Citizenship of the Union			
Economically active migrant citizens workers (Art 45 TFEU), self-employed (Art 49 TFEU), service providers/ receivers (Art 56 TFEU)	Semi-economically active migrant citizens students, PIMs (Art 21 TFEU)	Non-economically active migrant 'others' any migrant not fitting in previous categories (Art 21 TFEU)	Non-migrants (Art 20 TFEU)

Fig 13.1 Coverage of Union citizenship

---

[76] Art 24.

[77] Art 45 TFEU – Case 167/73 *Commission v France* ('*French Merchant Seamen*') [1974] ECR 359 and confirmed in Case 2/74 *Van Duyn v Home Office* [1974] ECR 6311; Art 49 TFEU – Case 33/74 *Reyners* [1974] ECR 1299; Art 56 TFEU –*Van Binsbergen* (n 65); Art 21 TFEU –*Baumbast* (n 3). For a full discussion on direct effect, see chapter 6. For further details on remedies for migrant workers, see Dir. to improve the enforcement of workers' rights (http://europa.eu/rapid/press-release_IP-14-421_en.htm)   [78] Case 36/74 [1974] ECR 1405.

suggested a narrowing of this approach and, since they concerned action taken by public authorities[79] or professional regulatory bodies, such as the Bar Council,[80] this suggested an extended form of vertical direct effect only. Only in the context of Article 45 TFEU did the Court go further: in *Angonese*[81] it said that the prohibition of discrimination in Article 45 TFEU applied both to agreements intended to regulate paid labour collectively and to contracts between individuals[82] – in other words horizontal direct effect.

This raises the question whether the principle in *Angonese* extended to Articles 49 and 56 TFEU as well. The matter was considered in *Viking*[83] and *Laval*[84] where the Court said that Articles 49 and 56 TFEU applied to trade unions contemplating or taking strike action. Trade unions are, by definition, autonomous from the State. Does this mean that Articles 49 and 56 TFEU apply horizontally? Part of the judgment suggests yes.[85] For example, in *Viking* the Court said that 'obstacles to freedom of movement for persons and freedom to provide services would be compromised if the abolition of State barriers could be neutralised by obstacles resulting from the exercise, by associations or organisations not governed by public law, of their legal autonomy'. In reaching this conclusion, the Court cited the decisions in *Walrave and Koch* and *Angonese*.

However, other parts of the judgment suggest that the trade unions were liable only because of their collective power: the collective action taken by the Finnish Seamen's Union and the International Transport Federation was aimed at 'the conclusion of an agreement which is meant to regulate the work of Viking's employees collectively, and, that those two trade unions are organisations which are not public law entities but exercise the legal autonomy conferred on them, inter alia, by national law'. This suggests some form of extended vertical direct effect, thus putting trade unions in a similar bracket to other regulatory bodies, rather than full horizontal direct effect.

6 What rights do migrants enjoy?

6.1 Introduction

Once resident in a host State, migrants enjoy a wide range of rights. The precise nature of those rights varies depending on the classification of the individual (worker, self-employed, citizen, etc), the duration of residence (0 to 3 months, 3 months to 5 years, and 5 years and beyond), and which piece of secondary legislation is being considered (see Figures 13.2 and 13.3).

In respect of workers, the Workers Regulation 492/11, repealing and replacing the original Regulation 1612/68, and the CRD are both relevant; for the self-employed it is only the CRD. Service providers are not expressly covered by the CRD but they could fall within Article 6 CRD (in the same way as any EU national) and Article 7 CRD (as a PIM). For periods beyond five years the individual may no longer be considered a service provider but instead is seen as established in the host State. However, as Figure 13.2 makes clear, the Treaty remains the hierarchically superior rule and on some occasions the Court chooses to apply the Treaty provision but not the relevant secondary legislation to which it makes no reference. This tends to suggest that, as far as economically active migrants are concerned, the Court may view the secondary legislation as merely fleshing out the meaning of the Treaty.

For those who are not economically active and move to another Member State (students, PIMs, and others) their position is more heavily regulated by the CRD and, if the CRD does not apply, by the Treaty (see Figure 13.3). For those who do not move at all

---

[79] Case 41/74 *Van Duyn* [1975] ECR 1337.   [80] Case 71/76 *Thieffry* [1977] ECR 765.
[81] Case C-281/98 [2000] ECR I-4139.   [82] Ibid, para 34.
[83] Case C-438/05 (n 26).
[84] Case C-341/05 (n 66).   [85] Ibid, para 55; see also para 58.

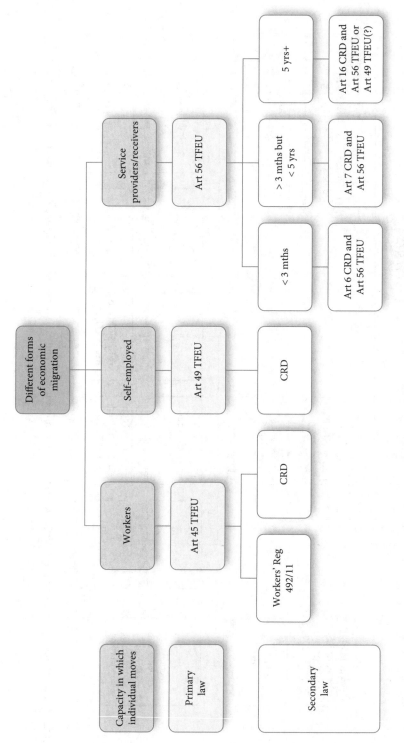

Fig 13.2 Summary of the primary provisions of the Treaty on free movement of economically active persons, together with the relevant secondary legislation

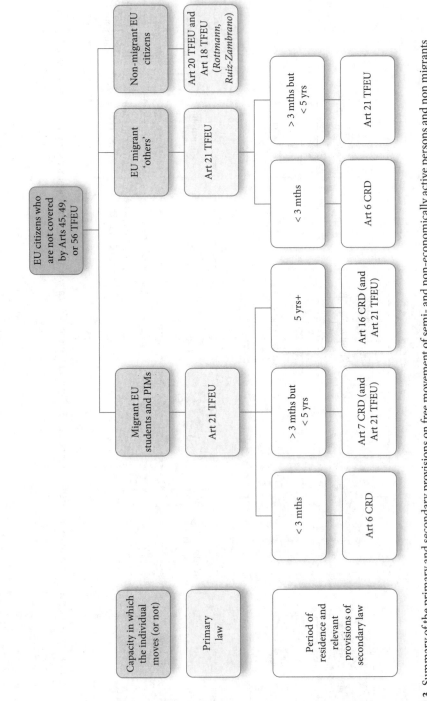

Fig 13.3 Summary of the primary and secondary provisions on free movement of semi- and non-economically active persons and non migrants

they may, as with *Rottmann* and *Ruiz Zambrano*, have recourse to Article 20 TFEU and the general principle of non-discrimination on the grounds of nationality in Article 18 TFEU.

This chapter cannot hope to be comprehensive about the rights enjoyed by migrants. It will therefore focus on certain key protections, in particular the right of residence and the principle of equal treatment.

6.2 The right of residence for EU migrants and their family members, and the principle of equal treatment

6.2.1 Periods of residence

The CRD adopts a tiered approach to legal rights: the longer a migrant is resident, the greater the rights he or she enjoys. It envisages three periods: up to three months, three months to five years, and five years and beyond. We shall examine the rights associated with each period in turn.

The right of residence for those entering for up to three months (Article 6)

Union citizens and their family members (see section 6.2.2), irrespective of the nationality of those family members, have the right of residence on the territory of another Member State for up to three months. In this period, the migrants are not subject to any conditions (eg as to resources, medical insurance) or formalities other than holding a valid identity card or passport (passport only in the case of TCN family members). In principle, all EU migrants and their family members enjoy equal treatment with nationals under Article 24(1) CRD from day one (but see *Collins*[86] below). However, for those who are not economically active (ie those are not workers[87] or the self-employed) and their family members, they are not entitled to equal treatment in respect of social assistance (SA) or student grants and loans (SG&L) (see Figure 13.4). This is a total exclusion from the equality principle (but only in respect of SA and SG&L – they will enjoy equal treatment in respect of other matters).

Even where the equality principle does apply, for example to the economically active, there is no guarantee that, say, an individual work-seeker will actually obtain the benefit from day one. As Mr Collins discovered, a number of Member States lay down residence conditions prior to permitting individuals to claim benefits (in order to prevent benefit tourism). Collins was an Irish national who claimed job-seeker's allowance within a week of his arrival in the UK. He was refused on the ground that he was not habitually resident in the UK. Requirements as to habitual residence are indirectly discriminatory. However, the Court found that such requirements could be objectively justified by the need to ensure that there was a genuine link between an applicant for an allowance and the geographic employment market in question; whether the habitual residence requirement was also proportionate was left to the national court (see Figure 13.5).[88]

---

[86] Case C-138/02 (n 3).

[87] There is a longer period of exclusion for work-seekers under Art 14(4)(b).

[88] Subsequently the national court found the rule to be proportionate, a view that other UK courts have followed in respect of challenges to other social security benefits which impose a residence requirement (eg *Patmalniece v Secretary of State for Work and Pensions* [2011] UKSC 11, where the Supreme Court held that this discrimination was justified because the Regulations were a proportionate response to the legitimate aim of protecting the public purse).

By allowing host States to justify the requirements that have to be fulfilled prior to obtaining a particular domestic benefit, but also ensuring that those requirements are proportionate, the Court struck a balance between (a) facilitating free movement (there might be an entitlement to a social welfare benefit in the future and any disproportionate restrictions should be removed straightaway) and (b) preventing the national welfare systems from being burdened by individuals like Mr Collins who had neither made contributions to the social welfare system in the UK nor had resided in the UK for a sufficient period to justify receiving benefits in the host State as part of the comfort blanket of national solidarity.[89] *Collins* does, however, make clear that the right to equal treatment is not absolute. It is subject to the rules set out in section 6.2.3 and summarized in Figure 13.5.

The 'right of residence' for those entering for three months to five years (Article 7)

Union citizens have a right to reside in the territory of another Member State for more than three months. They have a 'right of residence' if they

- are an employed person; or
- are a self-employed person; or
- have sufficient resources for themselves and their family members not to become a burden on the social assistance system in the host Member State during their stay and have comprehensive sickness insurance cover in the host Member State; or
- are enrolled at a private or public establishment, accredited or financed by the host State for the principal purpose of following a course of study, including vocational training, and they have comprehensive sickness insurance and assure the national authority (by means of a declaration) that they have sufficient resources for themselves and their family members not to become a burden on the social assistance system of the host State; or
- are family members (including TCNs) accompanying or joining a Union citizen who satisfies one of the above situations.[90]

Thus, those who are economically active and semi-economically active EU migrants, together with their family members, are entitled to a right of residence after three months in the host State. Those who are not economically active (EU migrant 'others' in Figures 13.3 and 13.4) are not entitled to a right of residence under the CRD. They can only hope for a liberal interpretation of the *Treaty* provisions on citizenship by the Court of Justice to allow them to stay in the host State or to get the benefit they seek.[91] If this does not happen, they can, in principle, be deported.[92]

Those with a right of residence under Article 7 CRD enjoy equal treatment with nationals (subject to the principles shown in Figure 13.5), provided they are workers, self-employed persons, persons who retain such status, and members of their families (see Figure 13.4).

---

[89] cf Case C-85/96 *Martinez Sala* [1998] ECR I-2691.

[90] There is a narrower list of family members who can join a migrant student: Art 7(4).

[91] cf *Martinez Sala* (n 89); Case C-456/02 *Trojani v CPAS* [2004] ECR I-7573 (considered in case study 13.2).   [92] Subject to the conditions in Art 15 CRD.

Those who are not fully economically active (migrant students and PIMs) will not enjoy a right of residence under Article 7 of the Directive unless they are financially and medically self-sufficient (subject to the decisions in *Grzelczyk* and *Baumbast* outlined later). These semi-economically active EU citizens also enjoy equal treatment with nationals, again subject to the principles shown in Figure 13.5, except in respect of maintenance aid for studies, including vocational training, consisting in SG&L, which are excluded from the scope of the equality principle (ie discrimination is permitted and SG&L can be confined to nationals only). Further, since students and PIMs are meant to be self-sufficient financially, they should not need access to the social assistance systems of the Member States. This requirement of self-sufficiency, combined with the exclusion of SG&L from the equality principle, means that for the semi-economically active access to social benefits is in practice curtailed for the first five years of their stay in the host State.

Those with a 'right of permanent residence' (Articles 16 and 17 CRD)

Those with permanent residence are in the most favourable situation. They are seen to be integrated into the host State and so they enjoy equal treatment with nationals without exception (ie no exceptions for social assistance or SG&L) (see Figure 13.4). The principles in Figure 13.5 continue to apply but given the directive is premised on the fact that those with five years residence are fully integrated, it is unlikely that a host State rule requiring more than five years residence in order to be entitled to a particular benefit would be either justifiable or proportionate.

There are two ways of acquiring permanent residence. First, Article 16 provides that those EU citizens residing in the host State for more than five years (workers, the self-employed, students, and PIMs, and their family members including those who are not nationals but who have resided with the Union citizen for five years) will have the right of permanent residence. None of the conditions applicable to students and PIMs concerning sufficient resources and medical insurance apply to those with permanent residence. However, students and PIMs must have satisfied the conditions laid down in Article 7 in order to accrue the five years of residence in the first place.[93]

Secondly, Article 17(1) provides that *workers and the self-employed* have the right to permanent residence in the host State in three additional situations:

(a) retirement at the pension age[94] or through early retirement, provided they have been employed in the host State for the preceding 12 months[95] and resided in the host State continuously for more than three years;

(b) incapacity, provided they have resided for more than two years in the host State[96] and have ceased to work due to some permanent incapacity;

---

[93] Joined Cases C-424/10 and C-425/10 *Ziolkowski v Land Berlin*, judgment of 21 December 2011, nyr. The Court of Appeal of England and Wales has confirmed that periods spent in prison do not count towards the five-year period: *C v Secretary of State for the Home Department* [2010] EWCA Civ 1406. For Court of Justice authority, see Case C-378/12 *Nnamdi Onuekwere v Secretary of State for the Home Department* and Case C-400/12 *MG*, both judgments of 16 Jan 2014, nyr.

[94] If the law of the host State does not grant the right to an old-age pension to certain categories of self-employed persons, the age condition is deemed to have been met once the person has reached the age of 60.

[95] Periods of involuntary unemployment duly recorded by the relevant employment office, periods not worked for reasons not of the person's own making, and absences from work or cessation of work due to illness or accident are to be regarded as periods of employment: Art 17(1), para 3.

[96] If the incapacity is due to an occupational accident or disease entitling the worker to a pension for which an institution of the State is entirely or partially responsible, then no condition to length of residence is imposed.

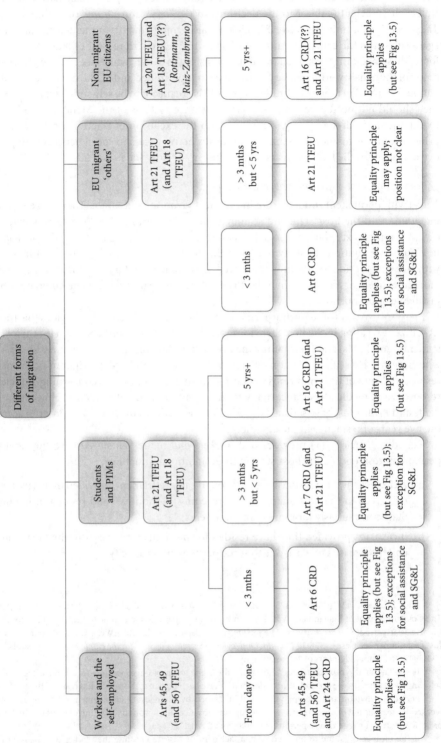

Fig 13.4 Summary of when the equality principle applies to migrants

(c) frontier workers, provided after three years of continuous employment and residence in host State A, they work in an employed or self-employed capacity in State B, while retaining their residence in State A to which they return each day or at least once a week.

The conditions as to length of residence and employment in (a) and (b) do not apply if the worker/self-employed person's spouse or partner[97] is a national of the host State or has lost the nationality of the host State through marriage to the worker/self-employed person.[98] Special provisions apply to the worker's family members.

6.2.2 Family members

As we have seen, EU migrants can migrate with their family members, including TCNs. Family members fall into two groups: (a) those who must be admitted[99] and (b) those whose entry and residence the host State must merely facilitate.[100] In respect of the first group, family member means[101]

(a) spouse;

(b) the partner with whom the Union citizen has contracted a registered partnership, on the basis of the legislation of a Member State, if the legislation of the host Member State treats registered partnerships as equivalent to marriage and in accordance with the conditions laid down in the relevant legislation of the host Member State;

(c) the direct descendants who are under the age of 21 or are dependants and those of the spouse or partner as defined in (b);

(d) the dependent direct relatives in the ascending line and those of the spouse or partner as defined in (b).

In respect of the second group (those whose admission must be facilitated), two sorts of family members fall into this category:[102]

(a) any other family members, not falling under Article 2(2) who, in the country from which they have come, are dependants or members of the household of the Union citizen having the primary right of residence, or where serious health grounds strictly require the personal care of the family member by the Union citizen;[103]

(b) the partner with whom the Union citizen has a durable relationship, duly attested.[104]

It had long been thought that the family provisions of the CRD, meant that TCN spouses could either accompany the migrant spouse when moving from State A to B, or join the migrant spouse in State B directly from a third country. *Akrich*[105] cast doubt on this orthodoxy. Mr Akrich was a Moroccan national who was convicted of theft in the UK and deported to Algeria. He returned clandestinely to the UK on various occasions. When he married a British national, she went to work in Ireland; and he was deported there.

---

[97] Partner as defined in Art 2(2)(b) CRD.   [98] Art 17(2).

[99] Art 3(1).   [100] Art 3(2).   [101] Art 2.

[102] Art 3(2) CRD. See also Case C-83/11 *Secretary of State for the Home Department v Rahman*, judgment of 5 September 2012, nyr.

[103] The fact that these conditions are satisfied must be proved by a document issued by the relevant authority in the country of origin or country from which they are arriving in the case of those seeking residence under Art 7: Arts 8(5)(e) and 10, for TCNs.

[104] By contrast, the fact that a 'durable relationship, duly attested' exists is satisfied merely by 'proof' for those seeking residence under Art 7: Arts 8(5)(f) and 10, for TCNs.

[105] Case C-109/01 *Secretary of State for the Home Department v Akrich* [2003] ECR I-9607.

Husband and wife subsequently wanted to return to the UK. Relying on the principles set out in section 3.3,[106] Mrs Akrich argued that her husband should be able to join her.

The Court said that Union law did not apply. At paragraphs 50 and 51 the Court said that in order to benefit from the rights under what is now Article 3(1) CRD, a TCN spouse (Mr Akrich) could move to another Member State with the migrant citizen (Mrs Akrich) only once the TCN spouse/registered partner had lawfully entered one EU State under national law (the first point of entry principle) and lawfully resided there (the prior lawful residence (PLR) principle). This suggested that Mr and Mrs Akrich could not return together to the UK. However, the Court added that where the marriage was genuine, the UK had to have regard to respect for Mrs Akrich's family life under Article 8 ECHR,[107] which suggested that the UK should admit husband and wife on human rights grounds. This is a further example of how the Court has used human rights to plug the gaps in legal protection provided by the Treaty and secondary legislation.

The decision, particularly in respect of the PLR principle, was subject to much criticism. Although based on the idea of separation of competence between Member States (deciding who could enter their territory) and the EU (guaranteeing movement between States after initial entry),[108] the PLR principle rested on shaky foundations, particularly in light of decisions such as *Carpenter*[109] (a TCN visa overstayer who subsequently married an EU citizen who was allowed to stay in the UK to enable the citizen to provide services). Eventually, in *Metock*[110] the Court expressly reversed the PLR principle, as laid down in paragraphs 50 and 51 in *Akrich* (but not the rest of the judgment, including the human rights point), following a careful textual analysis of the CRD.[111]

Metock concerned four TCNs who arrived in Ireland and unsuccessfully applied for asylum. While still resident in Ireland they married migrant EU citizens who were also resident in Ireland. None of the marriages was a marriage of convenience. The TCN spouses were all refused a residence card by the Irish authorities on the ground that they did not satisfy the PLR principle. Relying on the 'restrictions'/market access approach (see section 7.2), the Court said that 'if Union citizens were not allowed to lead a normal family life in the host Member State, the exercise of the freedoms they are guaranteed by the Treaty would be seriously obstructed.'[112] It continued that the Directive applied to all Union citizens who moved to, or resided in, a Member State other than that in which they were a national, and to their family members who accompanied *or* joined them in that Member State, regardless of whether the TCN has already been lawfully resident in another Member State.[113]

Thus, by giving a broad interpretation to the verb 'joined', the Court abandoned the PLR principle. Moreover, the Court went further than this: it gave rights not only to pre-existing couples (family reunification) but also to couples that meet in the host State (family formation).[114] The reason for this was that where the host State refused to grant TCN family members a right of residence this might discourage Union citizens from continuing to reside in the host State.[115] As Costello points out, in reaching this conclusion the Court rejects the usual conception of spousal dependency underpinning family reunification law, where the trailing spouse follows the worker to another Member State.[116] Instead, 'the Directive becomes an instrument for both family formation and

---

[106] *Surinder Singh* (n 37).   [107] Ibid, para 58.   [108] Ibid, para 49.
[109] Case C-60/00 (n 44).   [110] Case C-127/08 *Metock* [2008] ECR I-6241, para 58.
[111] Ibid, paras 49–55.   [112] Ibid, para 62.   [113] Ibid, para 70.   [114] Ibid, para 99.   [115] Ibid, para 92.
[116] C Costello, '*Metock*: Free Movement and "Normal Family Life" in the Union' (2009) 46 *Common Market Law Review* 587, 601.

family reunification, two modes of family migration that Member States often seek to differentiate', albeit that once in the host State, the family members are not in fact obliged to live with the migrant.[117]

Family members have the right, irrespective of their nationality, to engage in gainful activity[118] and, subject to the same limitations as for EU nationals, the right to equal treatment.[119] Children have the right to go to school.[120]

6.2.3 The meaning of equal treatment

As we have already seen, EU migrants enjoy equal treatment with nationals in certain situations (see Figure 13.4). Although the principle of equal treatment sounds positive in nature, in fact the law gives effect to it through the negative concept of non-discrimination. This means there shall be no direct or indirect discrimination. *Direct* discrimination arises where the migrant is, or may be, differently[121] and usually less favourably treated on the grounds of nationality. So in *Bosman*[122] the Court found that UEFA's so-called 3+2 rule,[123] approved by the Commission, that there could be no more than three foreign and two 'acclimatized' players (ie foreign players who had been in the host State for at least five years) in any football team breached Article 45 TFEU. According to the orthodoxy, directly discriminatory measures can be justified but only by reference to the express derogations (public policy, public security, and public health) laid down in Article 45(3) TFEU, Articles 52 and 62 TFEU, and Article 27 CRD (see further section 8.1), as well as any additional derogations found in the relevant secondary legislation such as language requirements for workers in Article 3(1) of Regulation 492/11, and the requirement to have sufficient resources and medical insurance in the case of students and PIMs under Article 7 CRD (see Figure 13.5).

An *indirectly discriminatory* measure focuses on the effect of the rule on the migrant. As *O'Flynn*[124] made clear, that effect can be actual or potential:

> 18. [C]onditions imposed by national law must be regarded as indirectly discriminatory where, although applicable irrespective of nationality, they affect essentially migrant workers or the great majority of those affected are migrant workers, where they are indistinctly applicable but can be more easily satisfied by national workers than by migrant workers or where there is a risk that they may operate to the particular detriment of migrant workers.

The Court continued:

> 19. It is otherwise only if those provisions are justified by objective considerations independent of the nationality of the workers concerned, and if they are proportionate to the legitimate aim pursued by national law.

Thus, an indirectly discriminatory rule – in this case a British requirement for the impecunious to be buried in the UK if the State is to pay for the funeral, a rule which was liable to disadvantage migrants who might want to be buried in their State of origin – can be saved by the State invoking not only the express derogations but also by the judicially developed 'objective justifications' (also referred to as public interest requirements).

---

[117] Case 267/83 *Diatta v Land Berlin* [1985] ECR 567.   [118] Art 23.   [119] Art 24(1).
[120] Art 10 of the Workers Regulation 492/11.   [121] Art 7(1) of the Workers Regulation 492/11.
[122] Case C-415/93 [1995] ECR I-4921.
[123] UEFA is the Union of European Football Associations, and the governing body of football in Europe.
[124] Case C-237/94 [1996] ECR I-2617.

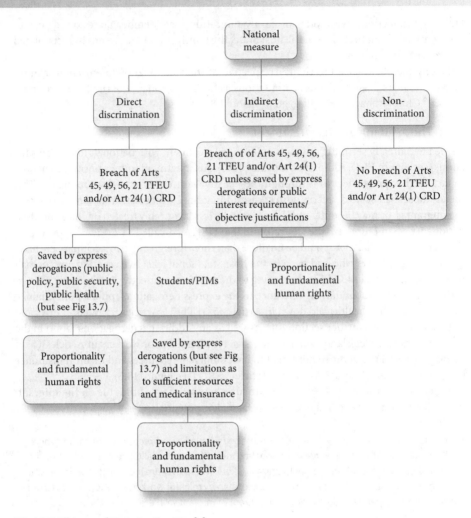

Fig 13.5 The non-discrimination model

These are State interests, considered to be valid under EU law, which take precedence over the free movement rights, provided the steps taken to achieve the objective are proportionate.

On the facts, the UK argued that its rule on the location of the burial was justified on the grounds of the prohibitive cost and practical difficulties of paying the allowance if the burial or cremation took place outside the UK. Surprisingly, the Court did not reject the justification on the basis that it was purely economic (see section 8.2) but on the facts: 'the expenses incurred within the United Kingdom by a migrant worker will be no different from those that would be incurred if burial or cremation were to take place within the United Kingdom'.[125] For good measure, the Court said that there was nothing to prevent the UK from limiting the allowance to a lump sum or reasonable amount fixed by reference to the normal cost of a burial or cremation within the UK.[126]

Rules considered to be indirectly discriminatory include residence requirements (see *Collins* discussed in section 6.2.1), length of service requirements, and registration rules.

---

[125] *O'Flynn* (n 124) para 28.   [126] Ibid, para 29.

Such rules all tend to favour the national to the detriment of the migrant. The Court does, however, allow such rules to be justified on the grounds of, for example, the need to show a genuine link with the territory of the host State (again, see *Collins*), or the protection of ethics of the profession,[127] or consumer protection[128] (these so-called public interest requirements are considered further in section 8.2).

Under the non-discrimination model, rules which do *not* discriminate are lawful. So a requirement that a tax applied to all those receiving the bulk of their income in State A, whether they are nationals of State A or migrants, would be lawful under the non-discrimination approach. However, as we shall see in section 7, the rise of the market access approach has cast doubt on this basic assumption. For now it is sufficient to note that where the Court decides cases under the CRD or the Workers Regulation 492/11 it tends to use the equal treatment approach as described in this section and illustrated in Figure 13.5.

6.2.4 Equal treatment and social advantages

While citizens in general enjoy the rights under the CRD, *workers* are in a more favourable position because they benefit from the rights in the Workers Regulation 492/11 as well. There is considerable overlap between the two measures; where there are differences it is likely that the worker will be able to rely on the most advantageous provision. This is particularly important in respect of receipt of *social advantages.* Workers, including work-seekers,[129] enjoy equal treatment in respect of social advantages under Article 7(2) of Regulation 492/11 from day one of their arrival in the host State (albeit that host States can impose proportionate, justified residence requirements for the migrant to establish a real link with the labour market of the host State[130]), which may, as in *Collins*, delay the worker from receiving the social advantage; non-economically active citizens can be denied *social assistance* for the first three months altogether. So how, then, do these terms differ?

The term 'social assistance', as used in the CRD, is not defined. However, in *Brey*[131] the Court said that the phrase social assistance means

> all assistance introduced by the public authorities, whether at national, regional or local level, that can be claimed by an individual who does not have resources sufficient to meet his own basic needs and the needs of his family and who, by reason of that fact, may become a burden on the public finances of the host Member State during his period of residence which could have consequences for the overall level of assistance which may be granted by that State.

This definition suggests that social assistance benefits are those intended to protect against destitution.

[127] Joined Cases 110/78 and 111/78 *Van Wesemael* [1979] ECR 35.
[128] Case C-180/89 *Commission v Italy* ('*Tourist guides*') [1991] ECR I-709.
[129] *Collins* (n 3).
[130] Joined Cases C-22/08 and 23/08 *Vatsouras* [2009] ECR I-4585, para 40.
[131] Case C-140/12 *Pensionsversicherungsanstalt v Brey*, judgment of 19 September 2013, nyr, para 61. In Case 578/08 *Chakroun v Minister van Buitenlandse Zaken* [2010] ECR I-1839 decided in the context of the Family Reunification Directive 2003/86, the Court said social assistance was assistance granted by public authorities which can be claimed by an individual not having stable and regular resources sufficient to maintain himself and his family. In Case C-160/02 *Skalka* [2004] ECR I-5613 the Court said a benefit constitutes social assistance 'in so far as it is intended to ensure a minimum means of subsistence for its recipient where his pension is insufficient, and entitlement is dependent on objective criteria defined by law'.

In *Even*[132] the Court defined social advantages broadly to include all benefits[133]

> which, whether or not linked to a contract of employment, are generally granted to national workers primarily because of their objective status as workers *or by virtue of the mere fact of their residence on the national territory* and the extension of which to workers who are nationals of other Member States therefore seems suitable to *facilitate their mobility* within the [Union].

The Court has interpreted the phrase to include benefits granted as of right[134] or on a discretionary basis,[135] and those granted after employment has terminated.[136] It also covers benefits not directly linked to employment, such as language rights,[137] death benefits,[138] and rights to be accompanied by unmarried companions.[139] This case law suggests that social advantages are used to facilitate migration – of workers and their family members – and to encourage integration into the labour market of the host State. In *Vatsouras*[140] the Court confirmed that 'Benefits of a financial nature which, independently of their status under national law, are intended to facilitate access to the labour market cannot be regarded as constituting "social assistance" within the meaning of Article 24(2) of Directive 2004/38.' They are therefore likely to be social advantages under the Workers Regulation. So it is in an individual's interests to argue that he or she is a worker and that the benefit concerns labour market integration and is thus a social advantage (to which the principle of equal treatment applies (see Figure 13.5)) and not social assistance (which is excluded from the scope of the equality principle for the first three months).

6.2.5 Other areas of equal treatment for the economically active and their family members

So far we have concentrated on the application of the equal treatment principle to social welfare benefits. However, the Workers Regulation 492/11 is quite expansive in the areas in which equal treatment is required. These include taxation;[141] any conditions of employment and work, in particular remuneration, dismissal, and, should the worker become unemployed, reinstatement or re-employment;[142] vocational training;[143] access to housing;[144] and trade union membership.[145] There is no reason why these rights to equal treatment across such a broad range of areas would not also apply to other economically active citizens under the general principle of equal treatment in the CRD and/or the Treaty. They could apply even to non-economically active citizens, albeit, as we have already seen, the principle of equal treatment may be subject to the integration test established in *Collins*.

---

[132] Case 207/78 *Criminal Proceedings against Even* [1979] ECR 2019.
[133] Ibid, para 22 (emphasis added).
[134] See eg Case C-111/91 *Commission v Luxembourg* [1993] ECR I-817; Case C-85/96 *Martínez Sala* [1998] ECR I-2691, para 28.
[135] Case 65/81 *Reina v Landeskreditbank Baden-Württemberg* [1982] ECR 33, para 17.
[136] See eg Case C-57/96 *Meints v Minister van Landbouw, Natuurbeheer en Visserij* [1997] ECR I-6689, para 36 (payment to agricultural workers whose employment contracts are terminated); Case C-35/97 *Commission v France* ('Supplementary retirement pension points') [1998] ECR I-5325; Case C-258/04 *Office national de l'empoli v Ioannidis* [2005] ECR I-8275, para 34.
[137] Case 137/84 *Criminal proceedings against Mutsch* [1985] ECR 2681, para 18 (criminal proceedings in the defendant's own language).
[138] *O'Flynn* (n 124) (social security payments to help to cover the cost of burying a family member).
[139] Case 59/85 *Netherlands v Reed* [1986] ECR 1283, para 28.
[140] Joined Cases C-22/08 and 23/08 (n 130), para 45.   [141] Art 7(2).
[142] Art 7(1).   [143] Art 7(3).   [144] Art 9.   [145] Art 8.

Originally, the principle of equal treatment also applied to qualifications.[146] However, this proved more of a hindrance than an asset. If a lawyer, who has spent six years qualifying in the UK, wanted to work in France but discovered that she can practice there only after requalifying as a French lawyer with a further six years of French study (ie equal treatment as regards the training which a French lawyer would have to undergo) this would be a considerable disincentive to her free movement. So the Court developed the principle of mutual recognition of qualifications, borrowing directly from the *Cassis de Dijon* line of case law.[147] In *Vlassopoulou*[148] the Court ruled that[149]

> national requirements concerning qualifications may have the effect of *hindering nationals of the other Member States in the exercise* of their right of establishment guaranteed to them by Article [49 TFEU]. That could be the case if the national rules in question took no account of the knowledge and qualifications already acquired by the person concerned in another Member State.

This meant that the host State had to compare a migrant's qualifications and abilities with those required by the national system to see whether the applicant had the appropriate skills to join the equivalent profession. If they were equivalent, then the host State was obliged to recognize the diploma. If they were not, then the host Member State could require the applicant to demonstrate that she had acquired the relevant knowledge and qualifications, which then had to be taken into account.[150] *Vlassopoulou* effectively pre-empted the 'diabolically complex and completely unnecessary'[151] directives adopted in the late 1980s and early 1990s, now repealed and replaced by Directive 2005/36.[152] Nevertheless, in respect of the occupations covered by the Directive, the Directive applies, not the case law.

6.3 Other rights specifically attached to EU citizens *qua* citizens

6.3.1 Overview of the rights

As Figure 13.1 shows, EU citizens can be migrant and non-migrant. Both groups can enjoy – as EU citizens *qua* citizens, not as workers, the self-employed, service providers, etc – certain rights under the Treaty which are found in Part Two TFEU specifically entitled 'Non-discrimination and citizenship of the Union'. These rights include the right to petition the European Parliament, to apply to the European Ombudsman, and to address the institutions and the advisory bodies of the Union in any of the Treaty languages and to obtain a reply in the same language. Further, as a result of Article 20(2) TFEU, which provides that 'Citizens of the Union shall enjoy the rights and be subject to the duties provided for in the Treaties', all citizens will enjoy the rights under the Charter, subject to the limits

---

[146] Case 11/77 *Patrick v Ministre des affaires culturelles* [1977] ECR 1199.

[147] See further chapter 12   [148] Case C-340/89 [1991] ECR I-2357.

[149] Ibid, para 15 (emphasis added). See also Case C-19/92 *Kraus v Land Baden-Württemberg* [1993] ECR I-1663, para 32.

[150] *Vlassopoulou* (n 148) paras 17–21. In Case C-345/08 *Krzystof Pesla* [2009] ECR I-11049 the Court said that EU law required the host State to carry out the examination of equivalence in light of the academic and professional training and experience as a whole before requiring a candidate to take an aptitude test. The knowledge to be taken as a reference point for the purposes of assessing whether a candidate can be admitted directly to a legal traineeship, was that attested by the qualification required in the host State.

[151] J Lonbay , 'Picking Over the Bones: The Rights of Establishment Reviewed' (1991) 16 *European Law Review* 507, 516.

[152] OJ [2005] L255/22. For full details, see 'Free Movement of Professionals' (*European Commission*), http://ec.europa.eu/internal_market/qualifications/index_en.htm. See further chapter 21. An amendment directive has now been adopted: Directive 2013/55 (OJ [2013] L354/132).

on the application of the Charter laid down in the horizontal clauses in Articles 51 and 52 Charter, as well as various other rights, including to equal pay for men and women under Article 157 TFEU.

In addition, migrant citizens enjoy the right to vote in local and European elections (Article 22 TFEU) and the right to diplomatic and consular protection from the authorities of any Member State in third countries (Article 23 TFEU). Most importantly, migrant citizens will enjoy the right to equal treatment in respect of social advantages, as the leading case of *Grzelczyk*[153] (considered in the following case study) makes clear. The right to equal treatment is derived from a combined reading of Articles 21, 20(2), and 18 TFEU (the latter being the non-discrimination provision). Prior to the adoption of the CRD, this was the only way for non-economically active citizens to gain access to the equality principle. Post the CRD, Article 24(1) CRD will cover much the same ground as the Treaty protection. However, as we have seen (see section 6.2.4 and Figure 13.4), there are significant limitations on the equality principle under Article 24(2) CRD in respect of social assistance and SG&L for the non-economically active (EU migrant 'others' in Figure 13.4), as well as for new and recent arrivals. For these individuals, as well as those non-economically active migrants who have resided in the host State for some time, the Treaty provisions, as interpreted by the Court in, inter alia, *Grzelczyk* remain relevant, since these individuals may not be covered by the CRD.

Case study 13.2: The *Grzelczyk* line of case law

Grzelczyk was a French student studying in Belgium. He worked during the first three years of his studies to help to support himself financially. He stopped working in his fourth and final year and applied to the Belgian authorities for the minimex, a minimum income guarantee. This does not count as student finance but it is a social advantage.[154] He was refused the benefit on the ground that he was not Belgian. Could EU law help him?

The Court said that, as a citizen of the Union lawfully resident in Belgium who has exercised his rights of free movement, he was entitled to equal treatment under Article 18 TFEU[155] because, as the Court famously said:

> Union citizenship is destined to be the fundamental status of nationals of the Member States, enabling those who find themselves in the same situation to enjoy the same treatment in law irrespective of their nationality, subject to such exceptions as are expressly provided for.[156]

Although equal treatment applied in principle to Grzelczyk, as we saw in section 6.2, it is not absolute. Article 21 TFEU is read subject to the express derogations and, in the case of students and PIMs, to the conditions concerning sufficient resources and sufficient medical insurance (see Figure 13.5).[157] The Belgian government argued that because Grzelczyk was asking for financial support, by definition he did not have sufficient resources, and so he could be denied equal treatment and removed from the territory.

---

[153] Case C-184/99 (n 3).

[154] Case 249/83 *Hoeckx* [1985] ECR 973. As the Court noted in *Grzelczyk*, student finance is excluded from the equality principle (now for the first five years) (see Figure 13.4) for students (and PIMs) but this case concerned social security benefits (*Grzelczyk* (n 153) para 39).   [155] *Grzelczyk* (n 153) para 36.

[156] Ibid, para 31.   [157] Ibid, para 37.

The Court disagreed. It said that students needed to declare only when they started their course that they had sufficient resources for themselves and their family.[158] If they ran out of money and sought financial help during their course, the State could withdraw a student's residence permit or not renew it, but 'in no case may such measures become the automatic consequence of a student who is a national of another Member State having recourse to the host Member State's social assistance system'.[159] For good measure, the Court then suggested that Grzelczyk should be entitled to some State support as long as he did not 'become an "unreasonable" burden on the public finances of the host Member State'.[160] This is because, in adopting the original 1990 residence directives on students and PIMs (now repealed and replaced by parts of the CRD), the States accepted 'a certain degree of financial solidarity between nationals of a host Member State and nationals of other Member States, particularly if the difficulties which a beneficiary of the right of residence encounters are temporary'.

In the subsequent case of *Baumbast*[161] the Court offered some more clarity in its reasoning. This time a German citizen, a PIM, did have sufficient resources (he worked in third countries) but did not have comprehensive medical insurance for himself and his family in the UK where he was living, including for emergency treatment, although he did have that insurance in Germany. Could the UK refuse to renew his residence permit? No, said the Court: he enjoyed a free-standing right to reside in the UK under Article 21(1) TFEU,[162] albeit subject to the limitations and conditions laid down by the TFEU and by the measures adopted to give it effect, namely (what is now) the CRD. However, the Court said that those 'limitations and conditions must be applied in compliance with the limits imposed by [Union] law and in accordance with the general principles of that law, in particular the principle of proportionality'.[163]

The Court then highlighted certain facts of Mr Baumbast's case: that he had sufficient resources, he had worked and therefore lawfully resided in the UK for several years, during that period his family also resided in the host Member State and remained there even after his activities as an employed and self-employed person in that State came to an end, neither Mr Baumbast nor the members of his family had become burdens on the public finances of the host Member State, and both Mr Baumbast and his family had comprehensive sickness insurance in another Member State of the Union. Under those circumstances, the Court concluded, 'to refuse to allow Mr Baumbast to exercise the right of residence which is conferred on him by Article [21(1) TFEU] by virtue of the application of the provisions of [the CRD] on the ground that his sickness insurance does not cover the emergency treatment given in the host Member State would amount to a disproportionate interference with the exercise of that right'.[164]

Extending the *Baumbast* reasoning to the facts of *Grzelczyk*, Grzelczyk had completed three out of four years of his degree. It would be disproportionate to interfere with his free movement rights by denying him access to the minimex. Conversely, extending the *Grzelczyk* reasoning to *Baumbast*, Baumbast was sufficiently integrated into UK society that there was a sufficient degree of solidarity between UK taxpayers and sick Germans and their families that Mr Baumbast and his family should be entitled to emergency medical treatment in the UK.

---

[158] Ibid, paras 41, 42, and 45.   [159] Ibid, para 43.   [160] Ibid, para 44.
[161] Case C-413/99 (n 3).
[162] Ibid, para 84.   [163] Ibid, para 91.   [164] Ibid, para 93.

The striking feature of these two cases is that the Court is using EU citizenship law to establish the right to equal treatment. It is also using EU citizenship rules to impose limits on the limits to equal treatment. Thus, it is now enough for students and PIMs to have sufficient medical insurance and resources, not comprehensive resources.[165]

Grzelczyk and *Baumbast* also establish that the concept of EU citizenship is a dynamic tool which can be used to achieve quite radical surgery on the secondary legislation. The Court has also used the Treaty provisions on citizenship to give certain protection to migrant EU citizens who are not economically active, including the homeless and others on the margins of soceity (EU migrant 'others' in Figure 13.3), as *Trojani*[166] shows. Trojani was a French national who arrived in Belgium and lived on various campsites for over a year before being given a place in a Salvation Army hostel where in return for board and lodging and some pocket money he did various jobs for about 30 hours a week as part of a personal socio-occupational reintegration programme. Like Grzelczyk, he was turned down for the minimex. Unlike Grzelczyk and Baumbast, he was not entitled to a right to reside in Belgium, due to his lack of sufficient resources. The denial of a right to reside, was, the Court found, proportionate. However, the Court did say that was another way of achieving EU rights. Because he was lawfully resident in Belgium for a certain period of time under *Belgian law*, with or without a residence permit,[167] he could therefore enjoy the right to equal treatment under Article 18 TFEU.

The principle of EU citizenship, and its interpretation by the Court, has served to be an effective source of rights for migrants. However, for Member States the effect of these cases is EU control over ever more of their decisions in areas, such as social security, still largely matters for national competence. This has contributed to making interior ministries of a number of Member States suspicious of the Court of Justice.

7 What rules/practices are prohibited by the Treaty?

7.1 Introduction

So far we have been talking about the principle of equal treatment which underpins the secondary legislation. However, a number of factual situations have arisen which fall outside the scope of the CRD and Regulation 492/11, and the Court has applied the Treaty to these cases instead. It is to this subject that we shall now turn.

The principle of non-discrimination underpins the Treaty provisions on free movement of persons. This is particularly clear in respect of Article 49 TFEU, which says that 'Freedom of establishment shall include the right to take up and pursue activities as self-employed persons and to set up and manage undertakings... *under the conditions laid down for its own nationals by the law of the country where such establishment is effected*'.[168] Discriminatory national rules will always breach the Treaty. However, according to the orthodoxy, non-discriminatory rules are lawful (see Figure 13.5).[169] Yet, as this section will show, non-discriminatory rules which nevertheless hinder market

---

[165] See also *Brey* (n 131).
[166] Case C-456/02 (n 91).   [167] Ibid, para 43.
[168] See also Art 57 TFEU, which says 'the person providing a service may, in order to do so, temporarily pursue his activity... under the same conditions as are imposed by that [host] State on its own nationals'.
[169] Case 221/85 *Commission v Belgium* [1987] ECR 719.

access have increasingly been considered 'restrictions' to free movement, using the language in Articles 49 and 56 TFEU, or 'obstacles' to free movement, using the language of the original Article 3 EEC. This language – of removing restrictions or obstacles – has become influential in shaping the Court's approach under the Treaty, particularly (but not exclusively[170]) in respect of Articles 49 and 56 TFEU, where the secondary legislation has been less influential. This approach has been used to remove barriers which are non-discriminatory on the grounds of nationality but which nevertheless hinder free movement. The 'restrictions' or 'obstacles' approach is also referred to as the 'market access' approach.

7.2 **The shift to market access**

The move away from the pure non-discrimination approach started in the 1990s. First, the Court became conscious, not only in the field of persons but also in goods, that the non-discrimination approach was not always sufficient to address a particular difficulty. The transfer rule at issue in *Bosman*[171] provides a good example of this problem. Under UEFA's rules, as they then stood, a football player out of contract could be transferred to another club on condition that the receiving club paid a transfer fee to the selling club. For players in the dusk of their career they might, like Mr Bosman, find that the fee was set too high and so the buying club could not or would not pay it, leaving the player without employment. As the Court noted, the rules were genuinely non-discriminatory: they applied not only to international transfers but also to transfers between clubs belonging to different national associations within the same Member State and were similar to the rules governing transfers between clubs belonging to the same national association. Under the discrimination approach, such rules would therefore have been lawful. However, this would have left Mr Bosman without a remedy. Recognizing this, the Court noted that the UEFA rules 'directly affect players' access to the employment market in other Member States and are thus capable of impeding freedom of movement for workers'. They thus breached Article 45 TFEU and needed to be justified (which was not possible on the facts).

In reaching this conclusion the Court confirmed the earlier decision in *Alpine Investments*,[172] where the Court said that the Dutch prohibition on cold-calling (ie unsolicited telephone calls to individuals) both in and out of the Netherlands by financial firms operating in the Netherlands breached Article 56 TFEU since the rule, while non-discriminatory, 'directly affects access to the markets in services in the other Member States and is thus capable of hindering intra-Union trade in services'.[173] The rule was, however, justified on the ground of protecting investor confidence in the Dutch financial markets.

In fact, in an earlier but, at the time, under-appreciated case, *Säger*,[174] the Court had already signalled its departure from the non-discrimination approach. The case concerned a German law which had the effect of prohibiting a company established in another Member State from providing to German holders of patents a monitoring and renewal service in respect of those patents in Germany. This was because the German law reserved such tasks exclusively to those possessing a particular professional qualification, such as that of patent agent. The Court said that Article 56 TFEU required[175]

---

[170] Case C-40/05 *Lyyski v Umeå universitet* [2007] ECR I-99 (on Art 45 TFEU); Case C-192/05 *Tas-Hagen v Raadskamer WUBO van de Pensioen- en Uitkeringsrad* [2006] ECR I-10451, paras 30–31 (on Art 21 TFEU).

[171] Case C-415/93 (n 122).

[172] Case C-384/93 *Alpine Investments v Minister van Financien* [1995] ECR I-1141.   [173] Ibid, para 38.

[174] Case C-76/90 *Säger* [1991] ECR I-4221, para 12.   [175] Ibid (emphasis added).

> *not only* the elimination of all discrimination against a person providing services on the ground of his nationality *but also* the abolition of any restriction, even if it applies without distinction to national providers of services and to those of other Member States, when *it is liable to prohibit or otherwise impede* the activities of a provider of services established in another Member State where he lawfully provides similar services.

The Court said that rules, such as the German one, which hinder market access or create a restriction on free movement breach Article 56 TFEU unless justified by reference to the public interest requirements or the express derogations. On the facts, the Court found that the rule could be justified on the ground of consumer protection but the law was not proportionate because the task of the service provider was essentially administrative (eg notifying patent agents when renewal fees had to be paid) and so did not require a qualified person to deliver it.

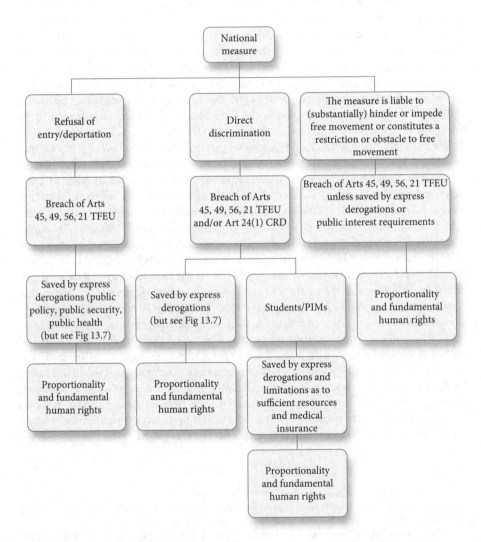

Fig 13.6 The restrictions model

Subsequent cases made clear that *Säger*, far from being an aberration, in fact marked a turning point.[176] For example, in *Gebhard*[177] the Court had to consider whether an Italian rule, requiring lawyers to be registered with the local Bar before they could use the title *avvocato*, breached Article 49 TFEU. The Court said:[178]

> national measures liable to hinder or make less attractive the exercise of fundamental freedoms guaranteed by the Treaty must fulfil four conditions: they must be applied in a non-discriminatory manner; they must be justified by imperative requirements in the general interest; they must be suitable for securing the attainment of the objective which they pursue; and they must not go beyond what is necessary to attain it.

It is striking that the Court talks of 'the exercise of fundamental freedoms' and not just Article 49 TFEU, thereby suggesting a generalization of the principle in *Säger* to Articles 45 and 49 TFEU as well as to Article 56 TFEU. The Court also changed the language from measures 'liable to prohibit or otherwise impede' in *Säger* to 'national measures liable to hinder or make less attractive the exercise of fundamental freedoms'. These terms are synonymous. The differences turn on quirks of translation and, sometimes, the context.

The formulae used in *Säger* and *Gebhard* tend to apply when the rules of the *host* State are at issue. When *home* State rules are at stake, the formula differs. This can be seen in *D'Hoop*,[179] which concerned a Belgian rule requiring students to have studied at a Belgian secondary school prior to receiving a 'tide-over allowance', a type of unemployment benefit. Ms D'Hoop, who was Belgian, having studied at a French high school before returning to Belgium was consequently denied the allowance. The Court said:[180]

> 30. [I]t would be incompatible with the right of freedom of movement were a citizen, in the Member State of which he is a national, to receive treatment less favourable than he would enjoy if he had not availed himself of the opportunities offered by the Treaty in relation to freedom of movement.
> 31. Those opportunities could not be fully effective if a national of a Member State could be deterred from availing himself of them by obstacles raised on his return to his country of origin by legislation penalising the fact that he has used them.

On the facts the Court found that since the tide-over allowance gave its recipients access to special employment programmes, and so aimed at facilitating the transition from education to the employment market, it was legitimate for the national legislature to ensure that there was a real link between the applicant for that allowance and the geographic employment market concerned.[181] However, the Court said that a single condition concerning the place where the diploma of completion of secondary education was obtained was 'too general and exclusive in nature' and that it unduly favoured an element which was not necessarily representative of the real and effective degree of connection between the applicant for the benefit and the geographic employment market. It was therefore disproportionate.[182]

In *Kranemann*,[183] another case concerning a home State rule, the Court adopted a different formula to the one in *D'Hoop*. The case concerned a German rule that trainees who

---

[176] See eg *Kraus* (n 149).
[177] Case C-55/94 (n 62) para 37.   [178] Ibid, para 39.
[179] Case C-224/98 *D'Hoop v Office National de l'emploi* [2002] ECR I-6191, para 31.   [180] Ibid.
[181] Ibid, para 38.   [182] Ibid, para 39.
[183] Case C-109/04 *Kranemann v Land Nordrhein-Westfalen* [2005] ECR I-2421, para 25.

did their practical legal training in Germany were entitled to reimbursement of all their travel expenses but not if they did their training in another Member State. The Court said:

> the Treaty provisions relating to freedom of movement for persons…preclude measures which might place [Union] nationals at a disadvantage when they wish to pursue an economic activity in the territory of another Member State.[184]

The Court continued that the German rule therefore constituted 'an obstacle' to the free movement of workers even if applied without regard to the nationality of the workers concerned.[185] Further, the rule could not be justified: aims of a purely economic nature could not constitute pressing reasons of public interest justifying a restriction on the fundamental freedom.[186]

7.3 The advantage of the market access approach

As *Kranemann* and *Säger* show, the Court concludes that the national rules are a 'restriction' or an 'obstacle' to free movement. In *Graf*,[187] considered in section 7.5, the Court expressly made the link between the obstacles approach and market access when it said that 'in order to be capable of constituting such an *obstacle*, [the provisions] must affect *access of workers to the labour market*'. This is why the *Säger* test is often referred to as the market access approach. The focus of the market access test is not on whether the migrant and national are being treated differently on the grounds of nationality but on whether there is a barrier – which may have nothing to do with nationality – which interferes with the ability of the migrant to get on to the market or, as the Court made clear in *Gebhard*, to exercise that freedom once on the market.[188]

The advantage of the market access approach is that it catches a multitude of national rules in its net, rules often built up over decades which may well have lost their original *raison d'être* but continue to interfere with the creation of a single market. Although the States have the possibility of justifying those rules, in many cases the justification may not be made out by the State (as in *Kranemann*) or the national rules may be disproportionate (as in *D'Hoop*). For this reason, the market access approach is perceived as deregulatory: it generates a bonfire of State regulation.

7.4 The disadvantage of the market access approach

7.4.1 Constitutional criticisms

But the market access approach has its critics. First, there are those who criticize it from a constitutional perspective: why is it legitimate for the EU to interfere with State rules adopted by democratically elected governments? The effect of the market access approach is to undermine the diversity of State rules and thus the essence of competitive federalism in the EU (where States compete with one another to attract the highest skilled migrants).[189]

---

[184] *Kranemann* (n 183) para 25. In the context of services the rule may be phrased rather differently: Case C-17/00 *De Coster v Collège des bourgmestre et échevins de Watermael-Boitsfort* [2001] ECR I-9445, para 30: 'Article [56 TFEU] precludes the application of any national rules which have the effect of making the provision of services between Member States more difficult than the provision of services purely within one Member State.'

[185] *Kranemann* (n 183) para 26.   [186] Ibid, para 34.

[187] Case C-190/98 *Graf v Filzmoser Maschinenbau GmbH* [2000] ECR I-493, para 23 (emphasis added).

[188] Ibid, paras 31 and 32.

[189] See further chapter 11. See also C Barnard, 'Restricting Restrictions: Lessons for the EU from the US?' (2009) 68 *Cambridge Law Journal* 575.

Even those who see the benefit of the market access approach fear it has reached – or has the potential to reach – too deeply into the national systems. For example, as we have already seen, in *Viking* and *Laval* the Court used the market access approach to declare strike action – taken in an area of domestic competence and which was lawful under national law – to breach Article 56 TFEU.

7.4.2 Legal and economic criticisms

The second criticism of the market access test is essentially legal/economic: the phrase 'market access/restriction' is 'inherently nebulous'.[190] Spaventa offers three possible interpretations.[191] The first, and narrowest, is that barriers to market access are those created by circumstances or legislation that make it more costly for individuals to enter a particular job or profession.[192] Such rules might include the need to register with the local Bar, as in *Gebhard*, when the individual is already registered in his or her home State. Such rules might be considered indirectly discriminatory and so would be caught under either the discrimination or the market access test.

The second, and much broader, approach to market access is that *any* regulation can be seen as a potential barrier to market access, since *any* regulation imposes and implies compliance costs. This approach was particularly evident in the field of taxation, where at times the Court came close to saying that the higher tax rate in another Member State constituted an obstacle to the free movement of persons.[193] Such a rule therefore breached the Treaty; and justification proved difficult because economic justifications are not permitted.

The third approach is what Spaventa describes as 'intuitive': rules which interfere with intra-Union trade are subject to judicial scrutiny while rules considered neutral as regards intra-Union trade should not. It is commonly thought that this is the test the Court is applying in practice. It can probably explain the decision in *Carpenter*.[194] It will be recalled that the UK wanted to deport Mrs Carpenter, the Filippino spouse of a UK national service provider, on the ground that she had overstayed her visa to remain in the UK. She argued that her deportation would interfere with her husband's ability to provide services since she looked after his children from a previous marriage while he was away. The Court said:[195]

> It is clear that the separation of Mr and Mrs Carpenter would be detrimental to their family life and, therefore, to the conditions under which Mr Carpenter exercises a fundamental freedom. That freedom could not be fully effective if Mr Carpenter were to be deterred from exercising it by obstacles raised in his country of origin to the entry and residence of his spouse.

Her deportation therefore breached Article 56 TFEU unless justified by public interest requirements (see sections 8 and 9).

---

[190] P Oliver and S Enchelmaier, 'Free Movement of Goods: Recent Developments in the Case Law' (2007) 44 *Common Market Law Review* 649, 674.

[191] 'From *Gebhard* to *Carpenter*: Towards a (Non-)Economic European Constitution' (2004) 41 *Common Market Law Review* 743, 757–758. See also C Barnard and S Deakin, 'Market Access and Regulatory Competition' in C Barnard and J Scott (eds), *The Legal Foundations of the Single Market: Unpacking the Premises* (Oxford: Hart Publishing, 2002).

[192] Citing FE Foldvary, *Dictionary of Free-Market Economics* (Cheltenham: Edward Elgar, 1998) 48.

[193] Case C-168/01 *Bosal v Staaatssecretaris van Financiën* [2003] ECR I-9409.

[194] Case C-60/00 (n 44).

[195] Ibid, para 45.

7.4.3 Linguistic criticisms

The third criticism of the 'market access' approach is linguistic. As *Gebhard* has shown, restrictions can occur not just at the stage of initial market access but also during the *exercise* of that freedom once on the market. Further, the language of market access sits increasingly uncomfortably in the world of free movement of natural persons. As the case law on citizenship shows, these are very human situations where individuals want to use EU law to ensure they can spend time with their families. They do not see themselves as gaining access to any market (especially if they are unemployed). It is perhaps for this reason that Advocate General Poiares Maduro experimented with other formulations than market access. For example, in *Marks & Spencer v Halsey* he said national policies 'must not result in less favourable treatment being accorded to transnational situations than to purely national situations'.[196] The Court has not gone as far but it does increasingly use the language of restrictions rather than market access in cases involving free movement of persons.[197]

7.5 The response to the criticisms

There are signs that the Court has paid some (inconsistent) heed to its critics. First, in the field of taxation there are indications that the Court has reverted to the discrimination approach. This can be seen in *Weigel*,[198] a case concerning a German husband and wife who transferred their residence to Austria where Mr Weigel had a job. They both brought their cars with them, which had to be reregistered in Austria, for which a hefty tax was charged. The Court rejected their arguments that this tax breached Article 45(2) TFEU, noting that the Austrian rule applied 'without regard to the nationality of the worker concerned to all those who registered a car in Austria and, accordingly, it is applicable without distinction'.[199] The Court then added that 'It is true that [the tax] is likely to have a negative bearing on the decision of migrant workers to exercise their right to freedom of movement.'[200] Under the *Säger* formula, this observation would have been enough for a finding of a breach of Article 45 TFEU, which the Member State would then have to justify.[201] However, in *Weigel* the Court resorted to the pure non-discrimination approach and said that, provided that nationals and migrants were treated in the same way, the fact that the tax regimes of the different Member States were different was compatible with Union law.[202]

Secondly, the Court has recognized that a threshold requirement may need to be added to the market access test to avoid the test from becoming all-embracing. For example, in the commercial context, *Commission v Italy* ('*Motor insurance*'),[203] the Court said that the obligation on an insurance company to provide third party cover to every potential customer constituted a 'substantial' interference in the operators' freedom to contract,[204] and that the obligation was likely to lead, in terms of organization and investment, to 'significant additional costs for such undertakings'.[205]

---

[196] *Marks & Spencer v Halsey* (n 29) para 37.
[197] Case C-224/02 *Pusa* [2004] ECR I-5763 and the AG's position in that case.
[198] Case C-387/01 *Weigel v Finanzlandesdirection für Vorarlberg* [2004] ECR I-4981.
[199] Ibid, para 52.   [200] Ibid, para 54.
[201] See, by analogy, the Art 56 TFEU case, Joined Cases C-430/99 and 431/99 *Sea-Land Service* [2002] ECR I-5235 considered in chapter 11.
[202] Ibid, para 55. The Court reached the same conclusion under Art 21 TFEU in Case C-365/02 *Lindfors* [2004] ECR I-7183.
[203] Case C-518/06 [2009] ECR I-3491. For parallels, see Case C-110/05 *Commission v Italy* ('*Trailers*') [2009] ECR I-519 discussed in chapter 12.
[204] *Motor insurance* (n 203) para 66.   [205] Ibid, para 68.

While *Motor Insurance* used an economic threshold, *Graf*[206] introduced a tortious one. Mr Graf, who worked in Austria, resigned to take up a job in Germany. By resigning he lost the chance of being dismissed and so could not claim a termination payment for his dismissal. He argued that the loss of a chance of being dismissed, and so being paid, interfered with his free movement rights. The Court disagreed. It noted that the entitlement to compensation on termination of employment was 'not dependent on the worker's choosing whether or not to stay with his current employer but on a future and hypothetical event, namely the subsequent termination of his contract without such termination being at his own initiative or attributable to him.' It continued:

> Such an event is *too uncertain and indirect* a possibility for legislation to be capable of being regarded as liable to hinder free movement for workers where it does not attach to termination of a contract of employment by the worker himself the same consequence as it attaches to termination which was not at his initiative or is not attributable to him.

While often not successful, States have increasingly relied on the 'too uncertain and indirect' formula to argue that EU law does not apply to the situation at issue.[207]

8 Derogations and justifications

As the net is cast ever wider through the market access approach, an increasing number of national rules are caught by EU law and so need justification. The general approach to derogations/justifications is discussed in detail in chapter 16. This chapter will therefore merely outline some of the issues that arise in respect of free movement of natural persons.

8.1 Express derogations

8.1.1 General express derogations

The basic rules

As Figure 13.6 shows, refusal of entry or deportation and any measures which are directly discriminatory can be justified only on one of the three express derogations in the Treaty: public policy, public security, and public health. These are listed in Article 45(3) TFEU (workers) and Articles 52 and 62 TFEU (establishment and services), and elaborated in the CRD. Common principles apply to these derogations as well as to the other derogations found in the Treaty. These are clearly established by the Court in the free movement of capital case *Église de Scientologie*:[208]

- Derogations from the fundamental principle of free movement have to be interpreted strictly, so that their scope cannot be determined unilaterally by each Member State without any control by the Union Institutions.

- Derogations cannot be misapplied so as, in fact, to serve purely economic ends.

---

[206] Case C-190/98 (n 187). For another way of avoiding the application of the four freedoms, see also Joined Cases C-51/96 and C-191/97 *Deliège v Ligue Francophone de Judo et Disciplines Associés* [2000] ECR I-2549, para 64 (rules which structure the market could not in themselves be regarded as constituting a restriction on the freedom to provide services prohibited by Art 56 TFEU).

[207] Joined Cases C-11/06 and C-12/06 *Morgan v Bezirksregierung Köln* [2007] ECR I-9161.

[208] Case C-54/99 [2000] ECR I-1335.

- Any person affected by a restrictive measure based on such a derogation has to have access to legal redress.
- Derogations are subject to the principle of proportionality.

However, overlaying these rules are the requirements laid down by the CRD which make it increasingly difficult for individuals to be refused entry/removed from a host State (see Figure 13.7).

Up to three months residence

For the first three months individuals can be refused entry/deported on any one of the three express grounds: public policy, public security, and public health. According to Article 27(2) CRD, 'Measures taken on grounds of public policy or public security shall comply with the principle of proportionality and shall be based exclusively on the personal conduct of the individual concerned. Previous criminal convictions shall not in themselves constitute grounds for taking such measures'. So the key issue for the public policy and public security derogations is personal conduct. Again Article 27(2) explains that 'The personal conduct of the individual concerned must represent a genuine, present and sufficiently serious threat affecting one of the fundamental interests of society. Justifications that are isolated from the particulars of the case or that rely on considerations of general prevention shall not be accepted.' This definition is derived from early decisions of the Court.[209]

As far as public health is concerned, Article 29(1) CRD provides 'The only diseases justifying measures restricting freedom of movement shall be the diseases with epidemic potential as defined by the relevant instruments of the World Health Organisation and other infectious diseases or contagious parasitic diseases if they are the subject of protection provisions applying to nationals of the host Member State.' There has been no case law on this derogation.

In respect of all three derogations the Member State must also consider whether the exclusion/deportation is proportionate and compatible with fundamental rights. This was an issue when Geert Wilders, the Dutch anti-Islamist politician, was refused permission to come to the UK between 12 February 2009 and 13 October 2009, where he was due to show his controversial film, *Fitna*, in a committee room in the House of Lords, the UK's second parliamentary chamber. The Home Office said his presence would be a 'threat to one of the fundamental interests of society'.[210] However, the ban was overturned after Wilders appealed to the Asylum and Immigration Tribunal (AIT).[211] The AIT recognized that 'As a Dutch national, the Appellant has an underlying right to come to the UK...He has that right unless he is validly prohibited from exercising it...His Article 10 [ECHR] rights [on freedom of expression], accordingly only supplement a prima facie right to enter'.[212] The tribunal also thought that the Home Secretary's decision would 'fail the test of proportionality, imposed generally by the European Union law and specifically'. This was due in part because he could be removed from the UK if he contravened public policy once here and in part because the police were 'well able to protect a right as fundamental

---

[209] Case 6/74 *Bonsignore v Obersdirektor of the City Cologne* [1975] ECR 297 (deportation order could not be made to make an example of the individual); *Van Duyn* (n 79) (scientology) (past association is irrelevant, present association is relevant; the activity does not have to be illegal in the host State); and Case 30/77 *Bouchereau* [1977] ECR 1999.

[210] http://www.geertwilders.nl/images/images/letter-denying-geert-wilders-entry-into-uk.pdf (*Geert Wilders Weblog*, 2009).

[211] *GW (EEA reg 21: 'fundamental interests') Netherlands* [2009] UKAIT 00050, available at http://www.refworld.org/pdfid/4b2620842.pdf   [212] Ibid, para 43.

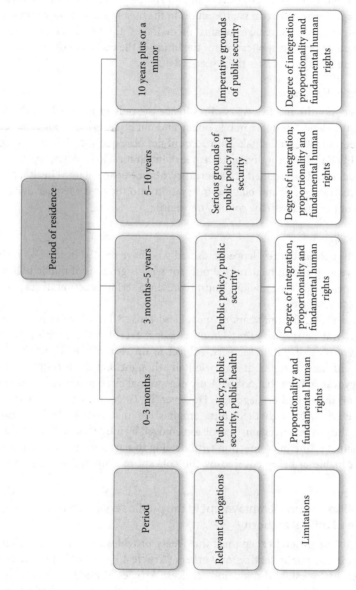

Fig 13.7 The public policy, public security, and public health derogations

in a democratic society as that of freedom of expression, and to prevent that right being exercised in a way which damages in fact, or threatens to damage any fundamental interest of our society.[213]

Finally, individuals refused entry/deported have the right at least to the minimum procedural protection provided by the Directive. This includes the right to receive notification of the reasons for the decision refusing them entry or deporting them,[214] generally a period of up to one month to leave,[215] and, according to Article 31, access to judicial and, where appropriate, administrative redress procedures in the host Member State to appeal against or seek review of any decision taken against them. If they are excluded from the State they have the right to submit an application for the lifting of the exclusion order after a reasonable period and in any event after three years.[216]

Three months to five years

Between three months and five years of residence the only grounds which the State can invoke to justify deportation are public policy and public security.[217] For those deported during this period, States must take into account not only questions of human rights and proportionality but also the individual's degree of integration into society (eg how long the individual concerned has resided on its territory, his or her age, state of health, family and economic situation, social and cultural integration into the host Member State, and the extent of his or her links with the country of origin).[218]

Five years and beyond

For those with permanent residence status and who have resided in the UK for between five and ten years they can be deported only for *serious* grounds of public policy (which presumably means that the individual must represent a seriously serious threat to a fundamental interest of society).[219]

For those resident for ten years or more, and those who are minors, an expulsion decision may not be taken against Union citizens, except if the decision is based on imperative grounds of public security, subject again to tests based on the degree of integration and human rights. It was originally thought that the threshold set for this final category was so high that only in truly exceptional circumstances (terrorism, murder) would an individual be deported. However, in *Tsakouridis*[220] the Court appeared to lower the bar. Although the Court emphasized that Article 28(3) 'considerably strengthens' the protection against expulsion enjoyed by individuals,[221] it concluded that 'the fight against crime in connection with dealing in narcotics as part of an organised group' was capable of being covered by the concept of 'imperative grounds of public security'.[222]

8.1.2 Specific exception: employment in the public service and the exercise of official authority

In addition to the general exceptions, the Treaty provides for a specific exception for employment in the public service for workers (Article 45(4) TFEU) and the exercise of official authority for establishment and services (Articles 51 and 62 TFEU). This allows States to reserve certain jobs which require a 'special relationship of allegiance to the

---

[213] *GW* (n 211) paras 54 and 55.   [214] Art 30(1).   [215] Art 30(3).
[216] Art 32.   [217] Art 29(2).   [218] Art 28(1).   [219] Art 28(2).
[220] Case C-145/09 *Tsakouridis* [2010] ECR I-11979, para 28.   [221] Ibid.   [222] Ibid, para 56.

state'[223] to be reserved to nationals only. Given that this provision allows States to discriminate directly, and thereby artificially reduce the pool from which they can select the best workers, the Court has taken a restrictive line on the scope of the derogation. For example, the Court adopts a functionalist rather than institutional (organic) approach. So it looks at the nature of the tasks performed by the individual rather than allowing entire sectors to be excluded.[224] The Court has also said that the derogation applies only at the moment of recruitment to the post, not to the terms and conditions of employment in that post.[225] Generally, the Court finds that most cases fall outside the scope of the derogation.[226]

8.2 Public interest justifications

In addition to the express derogations, the Court has recognized a range of public interest requirements to justify indirectly discriminatory rules and those which hinder market access. In *Gouda*,[227] as in *Cassis de Dijon* in the field of goods, the Court brought the public interest requirements together for the first time. It recognized the following 'imperative reasons in the public interest':

- professional rules intended to protect the recipients of a service;
- protection of intellectual property;
- protection of workers;
- consumer protection;
- conservation of the national historic and artistic heritage;
- turning to account the archaeological, historical, and artistic heritage of a country and the widest possible dissemination of knowledge of the artistic and cultural heritage of a country.

This rather eclectic list is not exhaustive: over 50 other justifications have since been recognized by the Court. What they have in common is that the State has identified an interest, which has also been recognized by the Court as worthy of protection, that should take precedence over the free movement of persons. As we have seen, purely economic justifications have not been recognized. However, this category has now been generally confined to cases where Member States are essentially advocating pure protectionism.

There is, however, one key difference in respect of the application of the justifications under Article 56 TFEU compared to those under Articles 45 and 49 TFEU. If a host State tries to invoke a justification to extend its law to the service provider, account must first be taken of the level of protection already provided by the home State. This reflects the idea, outlined in section 4.3, that the activities of service providers are primarily regulated by the home State. This is also referred to as the country of origin principle or the principle of home State control, which underpins the most controversial provisions of the Services Directive 2006/123.[228]

---

[223] Case 149/79 *Commission v Belgium* [1980] ECR 3881; and follow-up [1982] ECR 1845.

[224] Case 152/73 *Sotgiu* [1974] ECR 162.   [225] Ibid.

[226] eg teaching post in a State school (*Levin* (n 53); Case C-4/91 *Bleis* [1991] ECR I-5627), State nurse (Case 307/84 *Commission v France* [1986] ECR 1725), foreign language assistant in a university (Case 33/88 *Allue and Coonan v Universita degli studia di Venezia* [1989] ECR 1591).

[227] Case C-288/89 *Gouda* [1991] ECR I-4007.

[228] See further C Barnard, 'Unravelling the Services Directive' (2008) 45 *Common Market Law Review* 323.

9 Effect of fundamental rights and proportionality

Once (a) a breach of an EU rule has been established; (b) and a Member State has invoked an exception, derogation, or justification; (c) the exception, derogation, and justification must be read subject to the principles of fundamental human rights; and (d) proportionality (see Figures 13.6 and 13.7). The decision in _Carpenter_[229] provides a good example of how the Court's reasoning works in these free movement of persons cases. As noted previously, Mr Carpenter married Mrs Carpenter, a Filipino national who was living in the UK but who had overstayed her visa. When the UK authorities discovered this, they ordered her deportation. In her defence she successfully argued that if she were deported she would not be able to look after his children from a previous marriage and so her deportation would constitute an obstacle to Mr Carpenter's ability to provide services in other Member States under Article 56 TFEU. The Court agreed (a).[230]

However, the Court recognized the UK's right to 'invoke reasons of public interest to justify a national measure which is likely to obstruct the exercise of the freedom to provide services',[231] namely the need to ensure the respect for UK immigration law (b). However, that measure had to be 'compatible with the fundamental rights whose observance the Court ensures' (c). The Court continued that 'The decision to deport Mrs Carpenter constitutes an interference with the exercise by Mr Carpenter of his right to respect for his family life within the meaning of Article 8 [ECHR]'.

The Court then used the proportionality principle to strike a balance between the State's interest in the maintenance of its immigration laws and Mrs Carpenter's interest in her family life (d). It said a decision to deport Mrs Carpenter did 'not strike a fair balance between the competing interests, that is, on the one hand, the right of Mr Carpenter to respect for his family life, and, on the other hand, the maintenance of public order and public safety'.[232] It said that although Mrs Carpenter had infringed UK immigration laws, her conduct, since her arrival in the UK in September 1994, had not been 'the subject of any other complaint that could give cause to fear that she might in the future constitute a danger to public order or public safety'. Moreover, the Court added that 'it is clear that Mr and Mrs Carpenter's marriage, which was celebrated in the United Kingdom in 1996, is genuine and that Mrs Carpenter continues to lead a true family life there, in particular by looking after her husband's children from a previous marriage'. The Court therefore found that 'the decision to deport Mrs Carpenter constitutes an infringement which is not proportionate to the objective pursued.'[233]

10 Conclusion

The decision in _Carpenter_ illustrates, in microcosm, a number of the facets of free movement of natural persons highlighted by this chapter: the erosion of the requirement of an interstate element, how little it takes to establish an obstacle to free movement and thus a breach by the State of EU law, the need for the State to establish a justification in order to preserve State interests, but what the State can do to protect that interest is severely curtailed by the principles of human rights and proportionality. The generous reading of human rights in _Carpenter_, in particular the right to family life, also suggests that the Court

---

[229] Case C-60/00 (n 44).   [230] Ibid, para 39.   [231] Ibid, para 40.
[232] Ibid, para 43.   [233] Ibid, para 45.

views cases on the free movement of natural persons through a citizenship lens and thus is more willing to embrace a human rights dimension than it would be in cases on free movement of legal persons, which are considered in the next chapter.

The introduction of EU citizenship has also broken down the stark dichotomy found in the original Treaty of Rome between the economically active who could migrate and the economically inactive who could not. We now know that the economically semi-active (students, PIMs) and the economically inactive can migrate in the same way as the economically active. However, the basic divide is still visible in the politically and economically sensitive context of welfare benefits: those who are economically active and economically contributing (through paying taxes) enjoy equal treatment in all matters from day one (subject to the principles set out in Figure 13.5). The economically *inactive* are denied social assistance for the first three months and, in principle, cannot have recourse to social welfare benefits for the first five years, given the requirements of self-sufficiency. After five years, all migrants – economically active or not – are deemed to have sufficient ties to the host State that they enjoy full equal treatment with nationals. By introducing this sliding scale, the legislature has tried to strike a balance between the EU interests in free movement, on the one hand, and the preservation of national social security schemes, on the other.

But while the legal – and moral – position on immigration is clear, the Directive cannot address the problem of the hostility felt by locals fearing that migrants are taking 'our' jobs and housing. The only realistic response to this is prosperity: with greater economic prosperity comes the rising tide which lifts all of the (economically active and inactive) boats. Unfortunately, in the current economic climate those halcyon days seem a long way off. Reforms to the banking system, financial regulation, and economic governance more generally will put the eurozone on a firmer economic footing and thus may eventually lead to greater growth.[234] But there is little that the Court can do apart from sit on the sidelines and deal with the cases which come before it. Which it does, guided by the objectives laid down by the Treaty: to facilitate migration, ensuring that it is as easy to move between Poznan and Paris as it is between Rome and Rimini.

Further reading

M ADENAS AND W-H ROTH, *Services and Free Movement in EU Law* (Oxford: Oxford University Press, 2003)

C BARNARD, 'Unravelling the Services Directive' (2008) 45 *Common Market Law Review* 323

ACL DAVIES, 'One Step Forward, Two Steps Back, The *Viking* and *Laval* Cases in the ECJ' (2008) 37 *International Law Journal* 126

M DOUGAN, 'Cross-Border Educational Mobility and the Exportation of Student Financial Assistance' (2008) 33 *European Law Review* 723

E ELLIS, 'Social Advantages: A New Lease of Life' (2003) 40 *Common Market Law Review* 639

S ENCHELMAIER, 'Always at Your Service (within Limits): The ECJ's Case Law on Article 56 TFEU (2006–11)' (2011) 36 *European Law Review* 615

M EVERSON, 'The Legacy of the Market Citizen' in J Shaw and G More (eds), *New Legal Dynamics of the European Union* (Oxford: Clarendon Press, 1995)

E GUILD, S PEERS, AND J TOMKIN, *The Citizens' Rights Directive* (Oxford: Oxford University Press, 2014)

---

[234] See further chapters 11 and 19.

V Hatzopoulos, *Regulating Services in the European Union* (Oxford: Oxford University Press, 2012)

S Kingston, 'The Boundaries of Sovereignty: The ECJ's Controversial Role Applying the Internal Market Rules to Taxation' (2006–7) 9 *Cambridge Yearbook of European Legal Studies* 287

N Nic Shuibhne, 'The Resilience of EU Market Citizenship' (2010) 47 *Common Market Law Review* 1597

C O'Brien, 'Real Links, Abstract Rights and False Alarms: The Relationship between the ECJ's "Real Link" Case Law and National Solidarity' (2008) 33 *European Law Review* 643

E Spaventa, 'Seeing the Wood Despite the Trees? On the Scope of Union Citizenship and Its Constitutional Effects' (2008) 45 *Common Market Law Review* 13

14

Free movement of legal persons and the provision of services

Catherine Barnard with Jukka Snell

1 Introduction

Google Inc is a Californian firm with subsidiaries in various EU Member States. The search engine and all other services are run directly by Google Inc in the US. In the EU, they have a group of companies that are incorporated under local law and wholly owned by Google Ireland. Management for Europe is based in the UK subsidiary. Google Ireland has data centres at least in Belgium and Finland.[1] The US company Amazon, the world's biggest online retailer, has similarly complex arrangements. It has its European headquarters in Luxembourg; corporate offices in France, Germany, Italy, Slovakia, and the UK; development centres in Germany, Ireland, the Netherlands, Romania, and the UK; 'fulfilment centers' in France, Germany, Italy, Spain, and the UK which supply the goods; and customer services centres in Germany, Ireland, and the UK.[2] Although both Google and Amazon are secretive about the precise nature of their legal structure and what is done in each location,[3]

---

[1] See the AG's Opinion in Case C-131/12 *Google Spain SL, Google Inc v Agencia Española de Protección de Datos (AEPD), Mario Costeja González*, 25 June 2013, nyr, para 62.

[2] http://www.amazon.com/b?node=239366011.

[3] See the AG's Opinion in *Google Spain SL* (n 1) para 62.

the fact is that EU law is engaged whether, for example, Amazon Europe has subsidiaries (with separate legal personality) or branches (with no separate legal personality) or any other form of establishment in the other Member States.

The aim of this chapter is to consider the EU rules which apply to a legal person's establishment rights under Article 49 TFEU and its rights to provide services under Article 56 and 57 TFEU. The right of establishment, under Article 49 TFEU, implies the migrant company has a permanent link with the host Member State, while the freedom to provide services under Articles 56 and 57 TFEU envisages a much more temporary relationship between the provider/receiver and the host State. This distinction is reflected in the approach taken by the EU legislator and the Court of Justice: generally the host State controls the activities of the migrant person/company in the case of freedom of establishment, whereas the home State (country of origin) controls the activities of the migrant person/company in the case of free movement of services. But complications arise when a company wants to relocate from State A to B. To what extent can the home and the host State interfere with the corporate decision? This thorny question is considered in section 3 on the relationship between national company law and the EU rules on free movement.

Three themes run through this chapter. First, to what extent can and should legal persons be treated in the same way as natural persons? Although they are subject to common Treaty provisions are the policy issues different? For example, do companies benefit from human rights protection in the same way as natural persons? Does EU citizenship affect legal persons? Secondly, to what extent has the distinction between home State control (service providers) and host State control (establishment) actually been delivered on in the case law and the secondary legislation? Thirdly, has secondary legislation made a difference in this field or has the Treaty, as interpreted by the Court, been left to do the real work? If so, has the Court got the balance right between protecting State interest, on the one hand, and the interests of migrant companies, on the other?

This chapter is divided into three parts. First it discusses the Treaty provisions on freedom of establishment and free movement of services (section 2). These Treaty provisions are essentially negative: they prevent Member States from interfering with free movement, subject to the possibility of the State justifying its national rules for various public interest reasons. Secondly, the chapter considers some key pieces of secondary legislation adopted in the field of freedom of establishment and free movement of services: legislation intended to facilitate the operation of the freedoms in respect of legal persons (section 3). Some of the legislation, notably the Services Directive 2006/123, builds on the case law of the Court under Article 56 TFEU and requires Member States to remove national laws which interfere with the free movement of services and which cannot be justified. Other legislation requires Member States to adapt their rules to accommodate EU obligations. This legislation is harmonizing and is seen as imposing positive obligations on States. There is, for example, much harmonization in the field of company law and this is considered in section 3.4. There are, however, significant gaps in the EU's programme of corporate law harmonization, especially in respect of migrating companies, and it is here that the Treaty has been used to fill the holes.

2 The Treaty requirements

2.1 The relevant Treaty provisions

2.1.1 Freedom of establishment

Article 49 TFEU concerns the establishment of EU natural persons and companies, branches, and agencies in other Member States on a permanent or semi-permanent basis. It provides:

Within the framework of the provisions set out below, restrictions on the freedom of establishment of nationals of a Member State in the territory of another Member State shall be prohibited. Such prohibition shall also apply to restrictions on the setting-up of agencies, branches or subsidiaries by nationals of any Member State established in the territory of any Member State.

Freedom of establishment shall include the right to take up and pursue activities as self-employed persons and to set up and manage undertakings, in particular companies or firms within the meaning of the second paragraph of Article 54, under the conditions laid down for its own nationals by the law of the country where such establishment is effected, subject to the provisions of the Chapter relating to capital.

Article 54 TFEU talks specifically about companies:

Companies or firms formed in accordance with the law of a Member State and having their registered office, central administration or principal place of business within the Union shall, for the purposes of this Chapter, be treated in the same way as natural persons who are nationals of Member States.

'Companies or firms' means companies or firms constituted under civil or commercial law, including cooperative societies, and other legal persons governed by public or private law, save for those which are non-profit-making.

Article 55 TFEU adds:

Member States shall accord nationals of the other Member States the same treatment as their own nationals as regards participation in the capital of companies or firms within the meaning of Article 54, without prejudice to the application of the other provisions of the Treaties.

Thus Article 49 TFEU covers two situations. First, it covers the right for natural or legal persons to set up and manage undertakings, in particular companies and firms, in other Member States. This is known as primary establishment. In *Cadbury's Schweppes*[4] the Court said that Article 49 TFEU presupposes (a) actual establishment of the company in the host State (ie permanent presence), and (b) the pursuit of a genuine economic activity there. Both conditions need to be satisfied. This can be seen in *Stauffer*.[5] An Italian charitable foundation had commercial premises in Germany which it rented out, the letting being managed by a German property agent. The Court said that Article 49 TFEU did not apply because, while holding immovable property indicated permanent presence, there was no genuine economic activity because the property was not actively managed. The Court said that Article 63 TFEU on free movement of capital applied instead (see further section 2.2). In addition, case law has made clear that Article 49 TFEU also applies to individuals or companies from State A acquiring a majority shareholding in a company established in State B.[6]

---

[4] Case C-196/04 *Cadbury Schweppes v Commissioners of the Inland Revenue* [2006] ECR I-7995.

[5] Case C-386/04 *Centro di Musicologia Walter Stauffer* [2006] ECR I-8203, para 19.

[6] Case C-251/98 *Baars* [2000] ECR I-2787, paras 21 and 22, and Case C-208/00 *Überseering* [2002] ECR I-9919, para 77. Art 49 TFEU also applies to national rules which affect relations within a group of companies: Case C-446/04 *Test Claimants in the FII Group Litigation v Commissioners of Inland Revenue ('FII (No 1)')* [2006] ECR I-11753, para 118; Case C-231/05 *Oy AA* [2007] ECR I-6373, para 23.

Secondly, Article 49 TFEU provides the right for legal persons to set up agencies, branches, or subsidiaries in another Member State. This is known as secondary establishment. The Treaty does not define these terms but in *Somafer*,[7] a case on the interpretation of similar terms in the then Brussels Convention, the Court ruled:

> the concept of branch, agency or other establishment implies a place of business which has the appearance of permanency, such as the extension of a parent body, has a management and is materially equipped to negotiate business with third parties so that the latter, although knowing that there will if necessary be a legal link with the parent body, the head office of which is abroad, do not have to deal directly with such parent body but may transact business at the place of business constituting the extension.

It does not even matter if the establishment cannot be formally classed as a branch or agency, Article 49 will still apply to the entity. So in *Commission v Germany* ('*Insurance*'),[8] for example, the Court said that an insurance undertaking of another Member State which maintains a permanent presence in the host State comes within the scope of Article 49 TFEU even if that presence does not take the form of a branch or agency, but 'consists merely of an office managed by the undertaking's own staff or by a person who is independent but authorized to act on a permanent basis for the undertaking, as would be the case with an agency'.

The Court has been keen to ensure that the right to secondary establishment is effective. This can be seen in *Commission v Italy* ('*Foreign securities dealing*').[9] In order to set up as a securities dealer in Italy, Italian law required the dealer to be constituted in the form of a limited company with its registered office in Italy. The Commission successfully argued that this requirement prevented dealers from other Member States from making use of other forms of establishment, especially branches or agencies, and discriminated against them by obliging them to bear the expense of setting up a new company. The Court said that Article 49 TFEU expressly left traders free to choose the appropriate legal form in which to pursue their activities in another Member State[10] and so Italian law breached Article 49 TFEU. In seeking to justify the breach, the Italian authorities argued that the requirement to have a registered office in Italy was necessary for supervising and effectively sanctioning the dealer in question. The Court disagreed, reasoning that Italy had failed to show that this was the 'only means' of achieving the objective.

The fact that the Treaty encourages secondary establishment raises questions as to whether those wishing to form a company can take advantage of EU rules by incorporating a company in State A which has lenient incorporation rules and then, relying on Articles 49 and 54 TFEU, set up a branch or agency in State B, thereby avoiding State B's more onerous rules of incorporation. Early cases on services suggested that this tactic would fail since it is a well-established principle that EU law cannot be relied on for abusive or fraudulent ends.[11]

---

[7] Case 33/78 *Somafer SA v Saar-Ferngas AG* [1978] ECR 2183.

[8] Case 205/84 [1986] ECR 3755.

[9] Case C-101/94 *Commission v Italy* ('*Re Restrictions on Foreign Securities Dealing*') [1996] ECR I-2691. See also Case 270/83 *Commission v France* ('*Tax credits*') [1986] ECR 273; Case 79/85 *Segers v Bedrijfsvereniging voor Bank- en Verzekeringswegen, Groothandel en Vrije Beroepen* [1986] ECR 2375.

[10] *Tax credits* (ibid) para 22.

[11] See eg Case 33/74 *Van Binsbergen v Bedrijfsvereniging Metaalnijverheid* [1974] ECR 1299, para 13; Case C-23/93 *TV10 v Commissariaat voor de Media* [1994] ECR I-4795.

However, in *Centros*,[12] considered later in case study 14.1, the Court reached the opposite conclusion and said that relying on EU law rights does not constitute abuse.

Although the Treaty covers only the two situations of primary and secondary establishment, more recent case law shows that the Court is keen to use Articles 49 and 54 TFEU to achieve freedom of establishment more generally, without attempting to shoehorn the facts into either the primary or secondary establishment box. *SEVIC*[13] provides a good example. It concerned an inbound merger[14] by acquisition (the absorption of a Luxembourg company (SVC) by a German company (SEVIC)). However, German law on company transformations allowed for mergers only between companies established in Germany. While the Advocate General worked hard to show how an inbound merger could actually be viewed, from the German company's point of view, as the equivalent to setting up a secondary establishment in Luxembourg,[15] the Court did not bother with such analysis. Instead, it made the general observation:[16]

> the right of establishment covers all measures which permit or even merely facilitate access to another Member State and the pursuit of an economic activity in that State by allowing the persons concerned to participate in the economic life of the country effectively and under the same conditions as national operators.

The Court therefore said that cross-border mergers (making no express distinction between inbound and outbound mergers) constituted an exercise of the freedom of establishment. Since such mergers could not be registered in the German commercial register, this was likely to deter the exercise of freedom of establishment.[17] The Court recognized that while the national rules could be justified on the grounds of protecting the interests of creditors, minority shareholders, and employees, as well as protecting the effectiveness of fiscal supervision and the fairness of commercial transactions, the German law was nevertheless disproportionate because it involved a general refusal to register a merger between an in-State and out-of-State company, even where the protection of public interests, such as shareholder protection, was not threatened.[18]

SEVIC is therefore a good illustration of how the Court has used Article 49 TFEU to stop national rules interfering with corporate decisions to restructure in the way that they see fit to meet market conditions.[19] As it said in *SEVIC*:

> Cross-border merger operations, like other company transformation operations, respond to the needs for cooperation and consolidation between companies established in different Member States. They constitute particular methods of exercise of the freedom of establishment, important for the proper functioning of the internal market, and are therefore amongst those economic activities in respect of which Member States are required to comply with the freedom of establishment laid down by Article [49] TFEU.

---

[12] Case C-212/97 [1999] ECR I-1459.
[13] Case C-411/03 *SEVIC Systems* [2005] ECR I-10805. This case is considered in section 3.4.
[14] ie the acquisition of a foreign company by a domestic company.
[15] AG Tizzano in SEVIC (n 13) paras 35–37.
[16] SEVIC (n 13) para 18.   [17] Ibid, para 22.   [18] Ibid, para 30.
[19] See also Case C-438/05 *International Transport Workers' Federation and Finnish Seamen's Union v Viking Line ABP and OÜ Viking Line Eesti* [2007] ECR I-10779.

2.1.2 Free movement of services

The previous discussion shows that the concept of establishment is broad: it requires economic activity together with a degree of permanence by the individual/company in the host State.[20] As we shall see, the question of permanence distinguishes Article 49 TFEU from Article 56 TFEU on services.

The relevant Treaty provisions

Article 56(1) TFEU provides:

> Within the framework of the provisions set out below, restrictions on freedom to provide services within the Union shall be prohibited in respect of nationals of Member States who are established in a Member State other than that of the person for whom the services are intended.

Article 57 TFEU then gives a partial and negative definition of services:

> Services shall be considered to be 'services' within the meaning of this Treaty where they are normally provided for remuneration, in so far as they are not governed by the provisions relating to freedom of movement for goods, capital and persons.
>
> Services shall in particular include: (a) activities of an industrial character; (b) activities of a commercial character; (c) activities of craftsmen; (d) activities of the professions.
>
> Without prejudice to the provisions of the Chapter relating to the right of establishment, the person providing a service may, in order to do so, temporarily pursue his activity in the Member State where the service is provided, under the same conditions as are imposed by that State on its own nationals.

The principle of non-discrimination emphasized in Article 57(3) TFEU is repeated in Article 61 TFEU:

> As long as restrictions on freedom to provide services have not been abolished, each Member State shall apply such restrictions without distinction on grounds of nationality or residence to all persons providing services within the meaning of the first paragraph of Article 56.

Finally, Article 58 TFEU adds:

1. Freedom to provide services in the field of transport shall be governed by the provisions of the Title relating to transport.
2. The liberalisation of banking and insurance services connected with movements of capital shall be effected in step with the liberalisation of movement of capital.

From this it can be seen that for Articles 56 and 57 TFEU to be engaged three conditions must be satisfied. First, there must be a *service*. Article 57 TFEU (cited earlier) provides some examples of services; the case law has gone considerably beyond this traditional definition and has said that 'services' include

- the provision of people by an employment agency,[21]

---

[20] Case C-221/89 *R v Secretary of State for Transport, ex p Factortame* ('*Factortame II*') [1991] ECR I-3905, para 20.   [21] Case 279/80 *Webb* [1981] ECR 3305.

- medical services such as the termination of a pregnancy,[22]
- education,[23]
- business the provision of a television signal,[24]
- the transmission of programmes and advertisements from broadcasters in one Member State to cable networks in another,[25]
- lotteries,[26]
- building loans provided by banks,[27]
- judicial recovery of debts.[28]

Secondly, the service must *normally be provided for remuneration*, that is, it constitutes consideration for the service in question.[29] This excludes voluntary services from the scope of the Treaty.[30] The remuneration does not need to be paid directly by the recipient of the service. This can be seen in *Skandia*.[31] The case concerned contributions by an employer to a pension scheme on behalf of an employee. The Court said 'the premiums which Skandia pays are the consideration for the pension which will be paid to Mr Ramstedt when he retires. It is irrelevant that Mr Ramstedt does not pay the premiums himself, as Article [57 TFEU] does not require that the service be paid for by those for whom it is performed'. It continued, 'Moreover, the premiums unquestionably represent remuneration for the insurance companies which receive them'.[32] This case also shows that the remuneration and the service need not coincide in time: indeed they may be separated by years, even decades.

Thirdly, the services must be *temporary*, with the temporariness being assessed, according to *Schnitzer*,[33] 'in the light not only of the duration of the provision of the service but also of its regularity, periodical nature or continuity'. The Court added that service providers can equip themselves 'with some form of infrastructure in the host Member State (including an office, chambers, or consulting rooms) in so far as such infrastructure is necessary for the purposes of performing the services in question'.[34] It concluded:[35]

> Thus, 'services' within the meaning of the Treaty may cover services varying widely in nature, including services which are provided over an extended period, even over several years, where, for example, the services in question are supplied in connection with the construction of a large building. Services within the meaning of the Treaty may likewise be constituted by services which a business established in a Member State supplies with a greater or lesser degree of frequency or regularity, even over an extended period, to persons established in one or more other Member States, for example the giving of advice or information for remuneration.

---

[22] Case C-159/90 *SPUC v Grogan* [1991] ECR I-4685.

[23] Ibid.   [24] Case 62/79 *Coditel v Cine Vog Films* [1980] ECR 881.

[25] Case 352/85 *Bond van Adverteerders v Netherlands* [1988] ECR 2085; *TV10* (n 11).

[26] Case C-275/92 *Customs and Excise v Schindler* [1994] ECR I-1039.

[27] Case C-484/93 *Svensson and Gustafsson* [1995] ECR I-3955.

[28] Case C-3/95 *Reisebüro v Sandker* [1996] ECR I-6511.

[29] Case 263/86 *Belgian State v Humbel* [1988] ECR 5365, para 17.

[30] *SPUC v Grogan* (n 22).

[31] Case C-422/01 *Försäkringsaktiebolaget Skandia (publ) and Ola Ramstedt v Riksskatteverket* [2003] ECR I-6817.

[32] Ibid, para 24. The Court cited the health-care cases on this point, namely Case C-157/99 *Smits and Peerbooms* [2001] ECR I-5473, para 58, discussed in chapter 21.   [33] Case C-215/01 [2003] ECR I-14847.

[34] Ibid, para 28.   [35] Ibid, para 30.

Finally, despite the suggestion in Article 57 TFEU that services is a residual category, and only applies where the Treaty provisions on goods, capital, and persons do not, the Court roundly rejected this view in *Fidium Finanz*.[36]

The material scope of Articles 56 and 57 TFEU

Articles 56 and 57 TFEU apply in three situations. First, they apply to *the freedom to (travel to) provide services*. This was the situation envisaged by the Treaty.[37] Case law has also made clear that companies performing services can bring their own staff to perform the contract. These staff are referred to as posted workers and the rules governing the terms and conditions of employment are laid down in the Posted Workers Directive 96/71.[38]

Secondly, Articles 56 and 57 TFEU cover *the freedom to travel to receive services*. This situation was not envisaged by the Treaty but it was covered by early secondary legislation[39] and this has now been confirmed by the case law.[40]

Thirdly, Articles 56 and 57 TFEU cover the situation where *neither provider nor recipient travels*. This was also not expressly envisaged by the Treaty but since the Court has ruled that service provision includes electronic provision of services (where the service moves but not the provider or recipient), the Treaty applies here too.[41]

Finally, for the Treaty to apply the entity must be connected to a Member State (a question discussed in sections 2.4.2 and 3.4) and there must be some interstate element, albeit, as the case law has shown, this threshold is set fairly low: a potential interstate element will suffice.[42]

2.2 The relationship between Articles 49, 56, and 63 TFEU

2.2.1 Introduction

So far we have examined the different material scope of Articles 49 and 56 TFEU. An added complication arises when Article 63 TFEU on free movement of capital is added to the mix. The issue is important because the territorial scope of the provisions is different:

- Articles 49 and 56 TFEU apply only to movements of the self-employed and companies within the EU/EEA;
- Article 63 TFEU applies to movements of capital within the EU/EEA and between the EU/EEA *and* third countries.

Yet, the provisions on capital have, in particular, a close link with the free movement of services, a link recognized in Article 58(2) TFEU, which provides that the liberalization of banking and insurance services connected with movement of capital are to be effected in step with the liberalization of movement of capital. It has fallen to the Court to distinguish the material, and thus territorial, scope of the three fundamental freedoms but the guidance it has offered has not always been clear. In early decisions, the Court favoured, where

---

[36] Case C-452/04 *Fidium Finanz AG v Bundesanstalt für Finanzdienstleistungsaufsicht* [2006] ECR I-9521. See further chapter 15.   [37] *Van Binsbergen* (n 11).

[38] This Directive is discussed further in chapter 20.

[39] Art 1(b) of Directive 73/148 (OJ [1973] L172/14) required the abolition of restrictions on the movement and residence of 'nationals wishing to go to another Member State as recipients of services'.

[40] Joined Cases 286/82 and 26/83 *Luisi and Carbone* [1984] ECR 377 (Italians travelling to Germany to receive medical and tourism services); Case 186/87 *Cowan v Le Tresor Public* [1989] ECR 195 (Englishman mugged on French metro. As a recipient of a service he was entitled to receive criminal injuries compensation as a French man would). See also *Smits and Peerbooms* (n 32).

[41] See eg Case C-384/93 *Alpine Investments BV v Minister van Financien* [1995] ECR I-1141 (cold-calling by Dutch company offering financial services in other Member States).

[42] For issues connected with the interstate element, see chapter 13.

possible, deciding cases without reference to the capital provision.[43] In others, the Court considered the rule under two provisions.[44] This was fine as long as there was no third country element to the problem, since the free movement rules of the Treaty would apply in any event. But what if there is? In that case the free movement rules would apply only if capital movements were involved, but would not if establishment or services were at stake.

2.2.2 Services and capital

The Court was forced to address the services/capital divide in *Fidium Finanz,* where it was asked whether a company established in a non-Member State (Switzerland) could, in the context of granting credit on a commercial basis to residents of Germany, rely on the free movement of capital laid down in Article 63 TFEU, or whether the preparation, provision, and performance of such financial services were covered solely by the freedom to provide services laid down in Article 56 TFEU.

The Court recognized that the rules on granting credit on a commercial basis could equally involve service provision and capital movement. However, having looked at the context of the German rules (ie, they formed part of the German legislation on the supervision of undertakings which carried out banking transactions and offered financial services) the Court found that 'the predominant consideration is freedom to provide services rather than the free movement of capital'. Therefore a company in a non-Member State could not rely on Article 56 TFEU to challenge the detail of those rules, in particular the requirement to be authorized before trading in Germany.

2.2.3 Establishment and capital

The borderline between freedom of establishment and free movement of capital has also proved difficult. Generally, the Court looks at the object and purpose of the rule;[45] where that does not work, it will consider the facts of the case.[46] Generally, it has said:

- National legislation intended to apply only to those shareholdings which enable the holder to exert a definite influence on a company's decisions and to determine its activities (ie where the voting rights go beyond the 10 per cent threshold) falls within the scope of Article 49 TFEU on freedom of establishment.[47]

- National provisions which apply to shareholdings acquired solely with the intention of making a financial investment without any intention to influence the management and control of the undertaking (so-called portfolio investment) must be examined exclusively in light of the free movement of capital.[48]

The cases establishing these propositions generally concerned intra-EU movement. What about the situation where there is EU–third country movement? This was at issue in *FII*

---

[43] Case C-1/93 *Halliburton Services* [1994] ECR I-1137; Case C-410/96 *Criminal Proceedings against André Ambry* [1998] ECR I-7875, para 40; Case C-118/96 *Safir* [1998] ECR I-1897, para 35; Case C-200/98 *X and Y* [1999] ECR I-8261.

[44] See eg *Svensson and Gustafsson* (n 27) (capital and services).

[45] *Cadbury Schweppes* (n 4) paras 31–33; Case C-374/04 *Test Claimants in Class IV of the ACT Group Litigation* [2006] ECR I-11673, paras 37 and 38; Case C-524/04 *Test Claimants in the Thin Cap Group Litigation* [2007] ECR I-2107, paras 26–34.

[46] *FII (No 2)* (n 49) para 94.

[47] *FII (No 1)* (n 6) para 37; Case C-81/09 *Idrima Tipou* [2010] ECR I-10161, para 47.

[48] Joined Cases C-436/08 and 437/08 *Haribo Lakritzen Hans Riegel and Österreichische Salinen* [2011] ECR I-305, para 35.

(No 2).[49] The question was raised which of the Treaty provisions (Article 49 or 63 TFEU) applied to UK legislation on the tax treatment of dividends emanating from subsidiaries resident in third countries: subsidiaries in which the UK parent exerted a definite influence.

The Advocate General suggested two ways of dealing with the situation.[50] The first was to propose parallelism with intra-EU situations. In other words, when the influence in a company established in a third country was decisive, the assessment should be made in the framework of freedom of establishment. The application of the free movement of capital would thus be excluded. Because no right to freedom of establishment exists in third country relations, the situation would not be covered by the Treaty. This is what the Member States proposed.

The second option was to hold that the division between freedom of establishment and free movement of capital was only relevant to intra-EU situations. In third country relations no such distinction was necessary, or even required. Thus the provisions relating to free movement of capital would be applicable in third country relations not only for portfolio investments, but also for situations where there was decisive influence over the dividend-paying subsidiary in a third country. The Advocate General favoured the latter approach.

The Court seems to have followed the Advocate General. Emphasizing that the UK legislation did not apply exclusively to situations in which the UK parent exercised decisive influence over the third country subsidiary paying the dividends, it said the UK rules had to be assessed in light of Article 63 TFEU. It continued, 'A company resident in a Member State may therefore rely on that provision in order to call into question the legality of such rules, irrespective of the size of its shareholding in the company paying dividends established in a third country'.[51] However, the Court added an (opaque) caveat.[52] It said, obiter, that its ruling on Article 63(1) TFEU should not 'enable economic operators who do not fall within the limits of the territorial scope of freedom of establishment to profit from [Article 63(1) TFEU]'. In other words, its ruling in *FII (No 2)* should not allow third country operators to circumvent the territorial restrictions on Article 49 TFEU (and presumably Article 56 TFEU). This was not the case on the facts in *FII (No 2)* because UK law 'does not relate to the conditions for access of a company from that Member State to the market in a third country or of a company from a third country to the market in that Member State. It concerns only the tax treatment of dividends which derive from investments which their recipient has made in a company established in a third country'. This might suggest that the Court was trying to draw a distinction between a *Fidium*-style situation (which did concern a third country company trying to get access to the EU market), to which (the territorial limitations in) Article 49 or 56 TFEU would continue to apply, and tax cases such as *FII (No 2)* where a broader approach to Article 63 TFEU is applied. However, as we saw in chapter 13, the distinction between access to the market and exercise of the freedom once on the market, is a fine one and one the Court has not been able to maintain elsewhere.

2.3 To whom/what do Articles 49 and 56 TFEU apply?

Articles 49 and 56 TFEU have vertical direct effect. This means that they apply to the Member States[53] and also to regulatory bodies.[54] Less clear is the extent to which

---

[49] Case C-35/11 *Test Claimants in the FII Group Litigation v Commissioners of Inland Revenue ('FII (No 2)'),* 13 November 2012, nyr.

[50] Ibid, paras 111–113.   [51] Ibid, para 99.

[52] For criticism, see E Nijkeuter and MF de Wilde, '*FII 2* and the Applicable Freedoms of Movement in Third Country Situations' [2013] *EC Tax Review* 250.

[53] *Van Binsbergen*(n 11) paras 26 and 27.

[54] Case 36/74 *Walrave and Koch* [1974] ECR 1405, para 17. On the concept of direct effect, see further chapter 6.

these Treaty provisions apply to private bodies (in other words, whether they have horizontal direct effect). There are hints in *Viking*[55] that the rules do have horizontal application:

> 58. The Court has ruled, first, that the fact that certain provisions of the Treaty are formally addressed to the Member States does not prevent rights from being conferred at the same time on any individual who has an interest in compliance with the obligations thus laid down, and, second, that the prohibition on prejudicing a fundamental freedom laid down in a provision of the Treaty that is mandatory in nature, applies in particular to all agreements intended to regulate paid labour collectively (see, to that effect, Case 43/75 *Defrenne* [1976] ECR 455, paragraphs 31 and 39).
>
> 59. Such considerations must also apply to Article [49 TFEU] which lays down a fundamental freedom.

However, the Court then recognized that the problem in this case was not the behaviour of individuals but the collective power of the trade union (the Finnish trade union (FSU) which was threatening strike action when it learned that the Finnish shipping company was planning to reflag its vessel in Estonia):

> the collective action taken by FSU and ITF [International Transport Workers Federation] is aimed at the conclusion of an agreement which is meant to regulate the work of Viking's employees collectively, and, that those two trade unions are organisations which are not public law entities but exercise the legal autonomy conferred on them, inter alia, by national law.

This paragraph tends to locate the Court's decision – that Article 49 TFEU could be relied on by a private undertaking against a trade union or an association of trade unions – more firmly in the frame of an extended form of vertical direct effect. However, the question remains open.

2.4 **Establishing a breach**

2.4.1 Introduction

Once a claimant company has established that the national rule it wishes to challenge falls in the scope of Article 49 or 56 TFEU, it must then show that the rule breaches that Treaty provision. As we saw in chapter 13, at first the Court said that only discriminatory national rules breached the Treaty (chapter 13, section 7.2); subsequent cases suggested that the Court adopted a broader approach and prohibited any rule that interfered with free movement (chapter 13, section 7.2). The burden then shifted to the Member State to justify the rule and show that steps taken to achieve that objective were proportionate and, where appropriate, compatible with fundamental human rights (chapter 13, section 9).

2.4.2 Discrimination approach

In the early days, the Court, following the language of the Treaty, prohibited direct and indirect discrimination on the grounds of nationality (see Figure 13.5) both in respect

---

[55] Case C-438/05 (n 19).

of initial access to the market in the host State and to exercise of the activity once on that market.[56] In the case of a company, its 'nationality' equates with the location of its seat.[57]

Direct discrimination concerns less favourable treatment on the grounds of origin. According to the orthodox view, direct discrimination can be saved by the express derogations only (see section 2.5).[58]

Direct discrimination was at issue in *Factortame*.[59] Under the British Merchant Shipping Act 1988, a fishing vessel could be registered and thus entitled to fish in UK waters only if (a) the vessel was British-owned;[60] (b) the vessel was managed, and its operations directed and controlled from within the UK; and (c) any charterer, manager, or operator of the vessel was a qualified (British) person or company.[61] Inevitably the Court found that these rules breached Article 49 TFEU and could not be justified. This led to substantial claims for damages against the British State.

Indirect discrimination concerns a rule, such as a residence requirement of the corporate headquarters, which, on its face, applies to all companies but in fact disadvantages those with only a branch in the host State.[62] Such rules can, however, be objectively justified/justified on public interest grounds as well as saved by the express derogations (see section 2.5.2).[63]

In the context of the free movement of services, direct discrimination covers not only less favourable treatment on the grounds of nationality but also on the basis of establishment. This was confirmed by the Court in *Svensson and Gustafsson*, which concerned Swedish nationals resident in Luxembourg (at a time when Sweden was not yet an EU member) who were refused an interest rate subsidy on a building loan because they had borrowed the money from a (Belgian) institution which did not satisfy the requirement of being established in Luxembourg. The Court said:[64]

> the rule in question entails *discrimination based on the place of establishment*. Such discrimination can only be justified on the general interest grounds referred to in Article [46 TFEU], to which Article [62 TFEU] refers, and which do not include economic aims.

This decision has caused problems because a rule which concerns discrimination based on the place of establishment (direct discrimination) could equally be cast as a rule requiring residence in the host State which has been considered indirectly discriminatory and so can be objectively justified.

The corollary of the discrimination approach is that rules which do not discriminate do not breach the Treaty.

---

[56] Case 197/84 *Steinhauser v City of Biarritz* [1985] ECR 1819.

[57] *Tax credits* (n 9) para 18. However, sometimes it can equate with its fiscal residence: V Edwards, *EC Company Law* (Oxford: Oxford University Press, 1999).

[58] Case C-288/89 *Gouda* [1991] ECR I-4007, paras 10 and 11.

[59] Case C-246/89 *Commission v UK* ('*Factortame*') [1991] ECR I-3125; *Factortame II* (n 20).

[60] According to s 14(2), a fishing vessel was deemed to be British-owned if the legal title to the vessel was vested wholly in one or more qualified persons or companies and if the vessel was beneficially owned by one or more qualified companies or, as to not less than 75 per cent, by one or more qualified persons.

[61] According to s 14(7), 'qualified person' meant a person who was a British citizen resident and domiciled in the UK and 'qualified company' meant a company incorporated in the UK and having its principal place of business there, at least 75 per cent of its shares being owned by one or more qualified persons or companies and at least 75 per cent of its directors being qualified persons.

[62] *Tax credits* (n 9) Case C-330/91 *Ex p Commerzbank* [1993] ECR I-4017, para 15.

[63] *Gouda* (n 58) paras 12 and 13.

[64] *Svensson and Gustafsson* (n 27).

2.4.3 Restrictions/market access approach

The move to market access

But what about rules which are non-discriminatory but nevertheless hinder market access? This was at issue in *Alpine Investments*.[65] The case concerned a Dutch rule prohibiting cold-calling by the Dutch financial services industry both within and outside the Netherlands. It was argued that since this rule was non-discriminatory, EU law would not apply, following the principles laid down in *Keck*.[66] The Court disagreed: it said the Dutch rule breached Article 56 TFEU since although non-discriminatory,[67] it 'directly affects access to the markets in services in the other Member States and is thus capable of hindering intra-Union trade in services'.[68]

The decision in *Alpine Investments* presaged a broader shift towards the so-called market access/restrictions approach.[69] In fact, this change had already been signalled in the earlier case of *Säger*,[70] where the Court said that Article 56 TFEU required

> *not only* the elimination of all discrimination against a person providing services on the ground of his nationality *but also* the abolition of any *restriction*, even if it applies without distinction to national providers of services and to those of other Member States, when *it is liable to prohibit or otherwise impede* the activities of a provider of services established in another Member State where he lawfully provides similar services.

However, it was the decision in *Gebhard*,[71] a case on freedom of establishment, which made clear that the change was significant and applied across all the freedoms. The Court said:

> national measures liable to hinder or make less attractive *the exercise of fundamental freedoms guaranteed by the Treaty* must fulfil four conditions [to be compatible with the Treaty]: they must be applied in a non-discriminatory manner; they must be justified by imperative requirements in the general interest; they must be suitable for securing the attainment of the objective which they pursue; and they must not go beyond what is necessary in order to attain it.[72]

Thus national rules which are 'liable to prohibit or otherwise impede the activities of a provider of services' (*Säger*) or are 'liable to hinder or make less attractive the exercise of fundamental freedoms' (*Gebhard*) – terms which the Court uses interchangeably and are often referred to as the 'market access' approach for short – breach the Treaty unless they can be justified by the Member States and shown to be proportionate.

Sometimes the Court uses slightly different language for services, particularly when the rule being challenged is the home, not host State, rule. So, for example, in *Skandia*[73] the Court said:

> 26. In the perspective of a single market and in order to permit the attainment of the objectives thereof, Article [56 TFEU] precludes the application of any national legislation which has the effect of making the provision of services between Member States more difficult than the provision of services purely within one Member State.

---

[65] Case C-384/93 (n 41).
[66] Joined Cases C-267/91 and 268/91 *Keck and Mithouard* [1993] ECR 1-6097. See further chapter 12.
[67] *Alpine Investments* (n 41) para 35.   [68] *Alpine Investments* (n 41) para 38.
[69] For a discussion of the terminology, see further chapter 13.
[70] Case C-76/90 *Säger* [1991] ECR I-4221, para 12.   [71] Case C-55/94 [1995] ECR I-4165
[72] Ibid, para 37 (emphasis added).   [73] Case C-422/01 (n 31).

Thus, in the market access approach the Court looks at a particular rule from the perspective of the migrant service provider/company: is there a rule in the home or host State which is liable to interfere with its access to the market? The fact that the rule treats national service providers in just the same way is irrelevant: the question is the impact the rule has on the out-of-State provider.

In subsequent cases the Court simplified its language to reflect that of the Treaty: it says the Treaty prohibits 'obstacles' or 'restrictions' to free movement. This change of approach can be seen in *Viking*, where the Court said that proposed strike action to be taken by members of the Finnish Seamen's Union in protest at the Finnish company's decision to reflag its vessel as Estonian was a 'restriction' on freedom of establishment and so in principle contrary to Article 49 TFEU.

The Court has recognized a range of other rules as restrictions on freedom of establishment and free movement of services. These include

- authorization requirements;[74]
- rules restricting the number of establishments in a particular area;[75]
- residence requirements;[76]
- conditions relating to maximum/minimum staffing levels;[77]
- obligations to lodge guarantees with the relevant authorities;[78]
- rules setting compulsory minimum fees, or at least permitting control by the relevant authorities of the fees charged;[79]
- advertising restrictions.[80]

Whether the Court describes these rules as restrictions on free movement or hindrances to market access seems to make little difference. In the context of legal persons, at least, the Court seems to use the terms interchangeably. This can be seen in *Commission v Italy* ('*Motor insurance*'),[81] where the Court found that an Italian obligation to contract imposed on all insurance companies operating in the field of third party liability motor insurance and in relation to all vehicle owners, constituted a restriction on freedom of establishment and freedom to provide services. It said the imposition by a Member State of an obligation to contract 'constitutes a *substantial* interference in the freedom to contract which economic operators, in principle, enjoy'.[82] It continued that in a sector like insurance, 'such a measure affects the relevant operators' access to the market, in particular where it subjects insurance undertakings not only to an obligation to cover any risks which are proposed to them, but also to requirements to moderate premium rates'.[83] It concluded that 'Inasmuch as it obliges insurance undertakings which enter the Italian market to accept every potential customer, that obligation to contract is likely to lead, in terms of organisation and investment, to significant additional costs for such undertakings'.[84] The rules therefore beached

---

[74] Case C-189/03 *Commission v Netherlands* ('*Private security firms*') [2004] ECR I-9289, para 17; Case C-439/99 *Commission v Italy* ('*Trade fairs*') [2002] ECR I-305, para 39; Case C-169/07 *Hartlauer Handelsgesellschaft mbH v Wiener Landesregierung* [2009] ECR I-1721.

[75] Case C-134/05 *Commission v Italy* ('*Extra-judicial debt recovery*') [2007] ECR I-6251, para 64.

[76] *Ex p Commerzbank* (n 62).

[77] Case C-465/05 *Commission v Italy* ('*Private security activities*') [2007] ECR I-11091, para 105.

[78] Ibid, para 109.   [79] Ibid, para 127.

[80] Case C-405/98 *Gourmet* [2001] ECR I-1795, para 39; Case C-429/02 *Bacardi v Télévision Française 1 SA* [2004] ECR I-6613.   [81] Case C-518/06 [2009] ECR I-3491.

[82] Ibid, para 66 (emphasis added).   [83] Ibid, para 67.   [84] Ibid, para 68.

the Treaty but could be justified on the grounds of social protection for victims of road traffic accidents. The Court also said the rules were proportionate.

These cases demonstrate that while the restrictions approach is effective at challenging any national rules which interfere with free movement, it also reaches deeply into the national systems and challenges legitimate regulatory choices and policy decisions taken by democratically elected national governments. The Court is alert to this problem and has some tools to limit the reach of the restrictions approach, notably:

- that the effect of the national rule on free movement is too uncertain and indirect (ie a remoteness test);[85]
- some sort of *de minimis* test (ie an economic threshold) as was suggested in the *Motor insurance* case discussed previously, where the Court talked of a 'substantial interference in the freedom to contract'.[86]

However, the Court has not applied these tools consistently and generally the Court finds that most national rules do, in principle, interfere with free movement and so need to be justified by the State and shown to be proportionate (see Figure 13.6).

There are two exceptions to this general observation: rules concerning the exit of companies, which are considered in section 3.4, and national rules on taxation to which we now turn.

The special case of taxation
Introduction

Taxation is a necessary evil: without it there would be no public services. That said, companies like Amazon and Google employ armies of lawyers and accountants to establish complex corporate arrangements to reduce their tax liability. The restrictions approach appeared to add a new tool to the lawyers' armoury. It raised the spectre of challenges to all sorts of tax rules, including differential rates of taxation (eg where corporation tax rates are higher in State B than State A, companies in State A might argue that these higher rates are likely to deter them from establishing themselves in State B. State B's rules thus constituted a restriction on freedom of establishment).[87] The restrictions approach, combined with the Court's uncertain approach to justifications, made it almost impossible for finance ministries to draft any tax laws which could not, at least in principle, be challenged under EU law. Had a non-discrimination model been applied then State B's rules would not have breached Article 49 TFEU because they applied equally to all companies/subsidiaries established in State B or, if they did not, this was because the two situations (domestic and cross-border) were not in fact alike and so should have been treated differently. This would have resolved many problems. Yet the blanket application of the restrictions model in the early 2000s appeared to rule out space for a discrimination approach and led to the 'unplanned destruction' of national systems.[88]

---

[85] Case C-602/10 *SC Volksbank România v CJPC*, 12 July 2012, nyr, para 81, where the Court found that the effect of a national rule prohibiting credit institutions from levying certain bank charges was too indirect and uncertain to be regarded as liable to hinder intra-Union trade.

[86] *Motor insurance* (n 81). See also Case C-442/02 *CaixaBank France v Ministère de l'Économie, des Finances et de l'Industrie* [2004] ECR I-8961, especially the AG's Opinion.

[87] Although cf the early decision in Case C-336/96 *Gilly v Directeur des services Fiscaux du Bas-Rhein* [1998] ECR I-2793, para 34, where the Court appeared to reject such arguments.

[88] J Tiley and G Loutzenhiser, *Advanced Topics in Revenue Law* (Oxford: Hart Publishing, 2013) 11. See also chapter 21 for a good discussion of the issues raised by the case law of the Court of Justice in the tax field.

Furthermore, the Court's application of the restrictions model overlooked two key points. The first point is practical: by definition companies established in State A would never challenge tax rates in State B which were *lower* than those in State A.[89] So essentially the companies would cherry-pick the rules they wished to challenge and the Court, by accepting these challenges, disregarded the fact that tax policy is a package: some rates are higher (eg personal tax) and some are lower (eg corporation tax) and that the choice how to strike that balance is made by democratically elected governments. The restrictions model was being used to unpick those democratic choices and ultimately resulted in the unravelling of whole schemes of taxation.[90] This would not be so serious if the EU was in fact capable of reregulating in the field of taxation. While it has competence to legislate (eg under Article 113 TFEU), the unanimity requirement in the legal basis and the refusal by certain Member States to countenance EU-level tax legislation have resulted in the almost total absence of EU harmonization legislation. The restrictions approach adopted by the Court thus risked creating a legal vacuum.

The second point is that, again in the absence of any meaningful harmonization of tax rules at EU level, taxation policy is national but reflects internationally agreed norms on which, the Court recognized in the early case of *Gilly*,[91] it was reasonable for Member States to base their practice. The application of the restrictions approach thus risked undermining international standards without the EU having the realistic possibility of replacing those rules with standards of its own.

Overview of international rules on taxation

Under public international law of taxation Member States remain free to identify[92]

- the tax base (ie the nature and quantum of the receipts it wishes to tax and the identification of the entitlement to and nature of tax reliefs);
- the tax rate (ie the level(s) at which the tax would be set);
- how they wish to administer, assess, collect, and recover tax;
- the tax unit.

We shall focus on the question of the tax unit, that is those over whom States wish to assert legislative fiscal jurisdiction. Generally, this means that resident companies are taxed on their worldwide profits ('unlimited taxation'),[93] while non-resident companies

---

[89] See AG Geelhoed's Opinion in *FII (No 1)* (n 6) on this point.

[90] eg when the Court struck down the national rule in Case C-168/01 *Bosal Holding BV* [2003] ECR I-9409 it was estimated that the direct costs of the case amounted to €1.2 billion between 2003 and 2010. Even after changing its legislation it is estimated that the cost to the Netherlands was €0.55 billion a year to comply with the judgment: S Kingston, 'The Boundaries of Sovereignty: The Court's Controversial Role Applying the Internal Market Rules to Taxation' (2006–7) 9 *Cambridge Yearbook of European Legal Studies* 287.

[91] Case C-336/96 (n 87) paras 30 and 31.

[92] J Ghosh, *Principles of the Internal Market and Direct Taxation* (Oxford: Key Haven, 2007) 1–14. See also *Test Claimants in Class IV of the ACT Group Litigation* (n 45) para 50: 'It is for each Member State to organise, in compliance with Union law, its system of taxation of distributed profits and, in that context, to define the tax base as well at the tax rates which apply to the company making the distribution and/or the shareholder to whom the dividends are paid, in so far as they are liable to tax in that State.'

[93] See the UK: 'The UK has moved from a system of worldwide taxation for UK companies to a broadly territorial tax system, where the focus is on taxing profits earned in the UK. The key planks for this new approach are a dividend exemption, an elective branch exemption and a reformed Controlled Foreign Company (CFC) regime', 'A Guide to UK Taxation' (London: UKTI, 2013) 9, https://www.gov.uk/government/uploads/system/uploads/attachment_data/file/183408/A_guide_to_UK_taxation.pdf

are taxed only on profits arising from sources located in that taxing State ('limited taxation').[94] This is known as the principle of territoriality. The distinction between residents and non-residents, while suspect under general EU internal market law, is the bedrock of international tax law. Its operation can be seen in *Futura Participations*.[95] The case concerned a Luxembourg rule that while all income earned by resident taxpayers was taxable, irrespective of where it was earned, for non-resident taxpayers only profits and losses arising from activities in Luxembourg were taken into account when calculating tax payable in Luxembourg. The Court found that this rule was compatible with Article 49 TFEU because it conformed to the fiscal principle of territoriality.[96]

The corollary of the principle of territoriality is that generally the State of residence grants taxpayers tax advantages, for example tax relief (tax credits), because their financial interests are centred there and so the State of residence can best assess the taxpayers' ability to pay tax.[97] But one of the consequences of the principle of territoriality is that a company resident in State A but receiving profits in State B risks being taxed twice: once by the source State (State B) and then again in the home State (State A), where it is taxed on worldwide profits. To avoid this problem, a vast network of bilateral Double Taxation Conventions (DTCs), often based on the model OECD convention, have been drawn up between States agreeing on which State enjoys priority in cross-border situations.[98] International tax law lays down the general rule that priority of taxation lies with the source State, meaning that it is up to the home State (State A) to alleviate the double taxation. What if State A refuses to do so? While the early cases might have suggested this constituted a restriction on freedom of establishment, more recently the Court has realized that the risk of double taxation is the inevitable consequence of the parallel existence of 28 national systems and the Court has now recognized that the home State is not obliged to alleviate the double taxation.[99] This line of case law marked an important shift towards recognizing that the EU's restrictions case law should not trample over internationally agreed norms.

Return to a discrimination-based approach

At the same time as the Court was beginning to realize the significance of international rules on taxation, in two Grand Chamber decisions, *FII (No 1)*[100] and *ACT Group Litigation*,[101] the Court showed signs that it was rejecting a pure restrictions approach in favour of a discrimination model.

ACT concerned 'outgoing' dividends, that is, dividends paid by a UK subsidiary to a non-UK parent. Consistent with the principles of international tax law, the non-UK

---

[94] A point the Court recognized in Case C-446/03 *Marks & Spencer plc v Halsey (Her Majesty's Inspector of Taxes)* [2005] ECR I-10837, para 39.

[95] Case C-250/95 *Futura Participations SA and Singer v Administration des Contributions* [1997] ECR I-2471, para 22.

[96] For an endorsement of the principle of territoriality, albeit as a justification for the breach rather than, as in *Futura*, a conclusive reason to find no breach, see *Marks & Spencer v Halsey* (n 94) paras 39 and 43.

[97] Case C-279/93 *Finanzamt Köln-Altstadt v Schumacker* [1995] ECR I-225, para 32.

[98] S Kingston, 'A Light in the Darkness: Recent Developments in the ECJ's Direct Tax Jurisprudence' (2007) 44 *Common Market Law Review* 1321, 1331.

[99] Case C-194/06 *Orange European Smallcap Fund* [2008] ECR I-3747, paras 37–41.

[100] Case C-446/04 (n 6).

[101] Case C-374/04 (n 45). This section draws on C Barnard, *The Substantive Law of the EU: The Four Freedoms* (Oxford: Oxford University Press, 2013).

parent was not liable for UK tax on the dividends but nor was it entitled to a UK tax credit on those dividends. By contrast, UK parents receiving 'upstream' dividends from UK subsidiaries would have received a tax credit for the advance corporation tax paid by the UK subsidiary.

FII (No 1) concerned the reverse situation—'incoming' dividends payable by a non-UK subsidiary to a UK parent. The UK parent company was liable to UK corporation tax on the incoming dividends. It was granted tax relief for any foreign tax which the non-UK subsidiary had paid on the dividends abroad but was not otherwise entitled to a UK tax credit on them. By contrast, a UK parent receiving dividends from a UK subsidiary would not be liable to corporation tax on the dividends and would have received a tax credit for the advance corporation tax which the UK subsidiary had paid. In both *ACT* and *FII (No 1)* the claimants argued that the UK rules breached Article 49 TFEU.

In *ACT* the Court found that the UK rules were compatible with Article 49 TFEU. The Court said that the situation of a UK parent and a non-UK parent was not comparable because the non-UK parent was not subject to the tax charge while the UK parent was subject to the charge.[102] Therefore, the UK rules did 'not constitute discrimination prohibited by Article [49 TFEU]'.[103] By contrast, in *FII (No 1)* the Court found that the rules did breach Article 49 TFEU because in this case the two UK parent companies were in a comparable situation but the rules were discriminatory because the UK parent with the resident subsidiary got the tax credit, while the UK parent with the non-resident subsidiary did not. As the Court put it:[104]

> Article [49 TFEU] precludes a national measure which allows a resident company which has received dividends from another resident company to deduct the amount of ACT [advance corporation tax] paid by the latter company from the amount of ACT for which the former company is liable, whereas a resident company which has received dividends from a non-resident company is not entitled to make such a deduction in respect of the corporation tax which the last-mentioned company is obliged to pay in the State in which it is resident.

In *FII (No 2)* the Court expressly confirmed the discrimination approach:[105]

> It should be noted in this regard that, since European Union law, as it currently stands, does not lay down any general criteria for the attribution of areas of competence between the Member States in relation to the elimination of double taxation within the European Union..., each Member State remains free to organise its system for taxing distributed profits, provided, however, that the system in question does not entail discrimination prohibited by the FEU Treaty.

More recent case law has also adopted a more sophisticated and nuanced approach to justifications where discrimination was established.[106] It is to the subject of derogations and justifications more generally that we now turn.

---

[102] *ACT Group Litigation* (n 45), para 58. For a further example, see Case C-282/07 *Etat belge – SPF Finances v Truck Center SA* [2008] ECR I-10767, para 49.   [103] *ACT Group Litigation* (n 45), para 72.

[104] *FII (No 1)* (n 6), para 94. For a further example of discrimination between nationally sourced dividends and foreign sourced dividends, this time in the method used for calculating the tax, see FII (No 2) (n 49), para 65.   [105] *FII (No 2)* (n 49), para 40.

[106] See eg *Marks and Spencer v Halsey* (n 94); *Cadbury Schweppes* (n 4).

2.5 **Derogations and justifications**

Once a rule has been classified as a restriction or an obstacle to free movement, the question is whether Member States can justify those rules. The Treaty lays down an exhaustive list of derogations which apply across all four freedoms; the case law has supplemented those with judicially developed justifications.

2.5.1 **Express derogations**

General derogations

Articles 52(1) and 62 TFEU allow Member States to derogate from the the rules on freedom of establishment and the free movement of services on the grounds of public policy, public security, and public health. The general rules are set out in *Église de Scientologie*:[107]

- Derogations from the fundamental principle have to be interpreted strictly, so that their scope cannot be determined unilaterally by each Member State without any control by the Union institutions.

- Derogations cannot be misapplied so as, in fact, to serve purely economic ends.

- Any person affected by a restrictive measure based on such a derogation has to have access to legal redress.

- Derogations are subject to the principle of proportionality.

To this list we should also add that fundamental rights, where appropriate, need also to be taken into account.[108]

Exercise of official authority

There is a special exception from the free movement rules for the 'exercise of official authority' (Article 51(1) TFEU on establishment; Article 62 TFEU extends this to services). The nature of what constitutes official authority was considered in *Reyners*.[109] The Court said that Article 51 TFEU had to be narrowly construed: it applied only to those activities which had a 'direct and specific connection with official authority'.[110] In *Commission v Belgium* ('*Security guards*')[111] the Court said that the activities of private security firms, security-systems firms, and internal security services were not normally directly and specifically connected with the exercise of official authority.

Thus it seems that the derogations under Articles 51 and 62 TFEU must be restricted to activities which, in themselves, are directly and specifically connected with the exercise of official authority; functions that are merely auxiliary and preparatory, especially when carried out by a private body, which are supervised by an entity which effectively exercises official authority by taking the final decision, are excluded from the definition of the exercise of official authority.[112]

---

[107] Case C-54/99 *Église de Scientologie* [2000] ECR I-1335.

[108] See eg Case C-60/00 *Mary Carpenter v Secretary of State for the Home Department* [2002] ECR I-6279, paras 40 and 41. For full details, see chapters 9 and 16. For an example where a company has invoked fundamental rights in the context of a challenge to the national implementation of the Eleventh Company Law Directive (see n 194), see Case C-418/11 *Texdata Software GmbH*, 26 September 2013, nyr.

[109] Case 2/74 [1974] ECR 631.   [110] Ibid, para 45.

[111] Case C-355/98 *Commission v Belgium* [2000] ECR I-1221, para 26. See also Case C-283/99 *Commission v Italy* [2001] ECR I-4363, para 20; *Private security activities* (n 77), para 40.

[112] Case C-404/05 *Commission v Germany* ('*Inspection of organic production*') [2007] ECR I-10239, para 38; Case C-438/08 *Commission v Portugal* ('*Vehicle inspection*') [2009] ECR I-10219, para 37.

2.5.2 Public interest justifications

'Public interest' or objective justifications exist for indirectly discriminatory and non-discriminatory national measures which impede the activities of a provider of services and any other measure which hinders market access. Also known in the case law as 'imperative reasons in the public interest',[113] they have covered a wide range of public concerns such as

- the need to safeguard the reputation of the Dutch financial markets and to protect the investing public;[114]
- preventing gambling and avoiding the lottery from becoming the source of private profit;[115]
- avoiding the risk of crime or fraud;[116]
- avoiding the risk of incitement to spend, with damaging individual and social consequences;[117]
- maintenance of pluralism of the press;[118]
- fiscal cohesion;[119]
- combating money laundering;[120]
- protection of the interests of creditors, minority shareholders, and employees;[121]
- the effectiveness of fiscal supervision.[122]

Once a Member State has made out a justification it must then show that the steps taken to achieve that objective are proportionate (ie suitable and no more restrictive than necessary) and, where appropriate, are compatible with human rights. A case study on how these various requirements fit together can be seen in case study 14.1.

In the context of free movement of services, one extra factor needs to be taken into account: the extent to which the interest at stake in the host State is already protected in the home State. The Court made this clear in *Gouda*,[123] where it said that national restrictions came within the scope of Article 56 TFEU

> if the application of the national legislation to foreign persons providing services is not justified by overriding reasons relating to the public interest or if the requirements embodied in that legislation are already satisfied by the rules imposed on those persons in the Member State in which they are established.

This is a weak form of the country of origin principle (which is considered further in the discussion on the Services Directive in section 3.2).

However, the Court is prepared to override the country of origin principle where serious issues of public concern are at stake. This can be seen in *Jyske Gibralter*,[124] which concerned

---

[113] See also the ORRPI in the Services Directive 2006/123 (discussed in section 3) which serve an equivalent function in the context of the Directive.   [114] *Alpine Investments* (n 41).

[115] *Schindler* (n 26).   [116] Ibid.   [117] Ibid.

[118] *Gouda* (n 58), para 23.

[119] Case C-300/90 *Commission v Belgium* [1992] ECR I-305, para 14.

[120] Case C-212/11 *Jyske Bank Gibraltar Ltd v Administración del Estado*, 25 April 2013, nyr.

[121] *Überseering* (n 6), para 92.

[122] Case C-55/98 *Bent Vestergaard* [1999] ECR I-7641, para 23.

[123] Case C-288/89 (n 58), para 13.

[124] Case C-212/11 (n 120).

a Spanish rule requiring credit institutions providing services in its territory, without being established there, to forward directly to the Spanish financial intelligence unit (FIU) its reports on suspicious operations and any other information requested by the FIU. The Court found this rule was a restriction on the free movement of services. However, the Court said the breach could be justified, inter alia, on the grounds of combating money laundering and terrorist financing,[125] and the steps taken were proportionate. They were *suitable* because, since the Spanish authorities had exclusive jurisdiction with regard to the criminalization, detection, and eradication of offences committed on its territory, it was justified that information concerning suspicious transactions carried out in Spain be forwarded to the Spanish FIU.

The rules were also *no more restrictive than necessary* because, although there was provision in EU secondary law for the credit institution to provide information to the FIU of its home State which could then be shared with the FIU in the host State, there were deficiencies in the procedure. In particular, because disclosure relating to suspicious transactions was carried out to the home State FIU there was no obligation under the EU legislation for that information to be forwarded automatically to the host State FIU (Spain). This meant that the Spanish FIU might not have information corroborating the suspicions necessary so as to send a request for information to the FIU of the Member State of origin. Therefore, the Court said that even though disclosure to the Spanish FIU gave rise to additional expenses and administrative burdens on the part of service providers, those burdens were relatively limited given that the credit institutions already had to establish infrastructure necessary for information to be forwarded to the home State's FIU.

Case study 14.1: The application of the restriction/justification/proportionality approach

To see how these EU rules on restrictions/obstacle, justification, and proportionality fit together we shall consider the important decision of *Centros*[126] by way of example. Centros Ltd was a private company incorporated in the UK by two Danish citizens, Mr and Mrs Bryde, who were its sole shareholders. With a view to trading in Denmark, they applied to have a branch of the company registered in Denmark. At the time of the registration request, Centros had never traded in the UK, and for this reason the Danish registrar of companies refused to register the branch. He considered that the company was actually seeking to register its principal business establishment in Denmark and not just a branch, and that the Brydes were seeking to evade Danish law on minimum capital requirements. In Denmark companies had to have at least DKr 200,000 (approximately £20,000) when they were formed; the UK had no rules on minimum capital requirements.

The Court ruled that the registrar's refusal to grant the registration request constituted an *obstacle* to the freedom of establishment,[127] saying that it was 'immaterial' that the company was formed in the UK only for the purpose of establishing itself in Denmark where its main or entire business was to be conducted.[128] It also said that this was not a case of abuse because the national rules which the Brydes were trying to avoid were rules governing the formation of companies and not rules concerning the pursuit of certain trades, professions, or businesses.[129] In other words, they were not fraudulently taking advantage of the provisions of Union law[130] because they were doing what the Treaty expressly permits,

---

[125] Ibid, para 62.   [126] Case C-212/97 (n 12).   [127] Ibid, paras 29 and 30.
[128] Ibid, para 17, citing *Segers* (n 9).   [129] Centros (n 12) para 26.
[130] Ibid, para 24.

namely incorporating in one Member State and setting up a secondary establishment in another.[131]

The Danish government sought to *justify* the refusal to register on the ground of the need to maintain its rules on minimum capital requirements. It said that the rules served two purposes: first, to reinforce the financial soundness of companies in order to protect public creditors against the risk of seeing the debts owed to them become irrecoverable (since, unlike private creditors, they could not secure debts by means of guarantees); and, secondly, the law aimed at protecting all creditors from the risk of fraudulent bankruptcy due to the insolvency of companies whose initial capitalization was inadequate.

The Court ruled that the first justification offered was inadequate because it was inconsistent – the vital factor in the registrar's refusal to grant the registration request was the failure of the company to trade in the UK. This was immaterial to the protection of creditors since they would have been no better off had the company previously traded in the UK and been able to register its branch in Denmark.[132] Furthermore, EU company information disclosure directives put Danish creditors on notice that Centros Ltd was not a company governed by Danish law. The refusal to register was not only unjustifiable, it was also *disproportionate*. The Court said that the Danish authorities could have adopted less restrictive measures by, for example, making it possible in law for public creditors to obtain the necessary guarantees.

The Court did, however, recognize the validity of the second justification put forward by the Danish government about abuse. It said that its ruling did not prevent Denmark from adopting measures for preventing or penalizing fraud, either in relation to the company itself or to its members, where it had been established that the members were in fact attempting to evade their obligations towards private or public creditors by means of the formation of the company. However, the Court added that combating fraud did not justify a practice of refusing to register a branch of a company which had its registered office in another Member State[133] – but did not suggest what steps States could take to combat fraud which would be compatible with Union law.

2.5.3 The special case of gambling

All Member States impose significant controls on gambling: who can offer it, who can participate, what happens to the winnings. This is widely regarded as an area of great sensitivity for Member States and the Court has therefore applied a fairly relaxed level of scrutiny to national rules. Indeed, in the first major case which came before it, *Schindler*,[134] a reference from the UK, the Court so fell over itself to be accommodating to the UK (which was trying to defend its blanket ban on national lotteries despite the fact that the National Lotteries Bill was going through Parliament at the time) that it failed to consider the question of proportionality at all.

Since then, the cases have followed a more orthodox pattern, albeit still with a light touch review. So the Court tends to find that the rules imposing limitations on gambling are restrictions on free movement. This has been the case with the following rules:

- rules restricting the right to operate games of chance or gambling solely to casinos in permanent or temporary gaming areas,[135]

---

[131] *Centros* (n 12) para 27. See also *Cadbury Schweppes* (n 4), para 36.
[132] Ibid, para 35.   [133] Ibid, para 38.   [134] Case C-275/92 (n 26).
[135] Case C-6/01 *Anomar v Estado português* [2003] ECR I-8621, para 66.

- rules prohibiting the installation of computer games in venues other than casinos,[136]
- national rules restricting the provision of gambling activities to public and private monopolies,[137]
- rules confining off-course betting to a single company which was closely controlled by the State,[138]
- rule prohibiting – on pain of criminal penalties – the pursuit of activities in the betting or gaming sector without a licence or police authorization,[139]
- rules prohibiting Italian intermediaries from facilitating the provision of betting services on behalf of a British supplier.[140]

Having brought the rules within the purview of Article 49 or 56 TFEU, the Court then considers whether they can be justified on the grounds of various public interests outlined previously (eg preventing gambling and the incitement to spend).

The focus then shifts to proportionality. As we saw in *Centros*, the proportionality review is usually fairly rigorous. This has not been so with the gambling cases. As we saw in *Schindler*, the Court did not consider proportionality at all when upholding the national rule banning lotteries; in *Läärä*[141] it did examine proportionality but its approach was remarkably hands-off.[142] The case concerned a Finnish law granting exclusive rights to run the operation of slot machines to a public body, with the revenue raised going into the public purse. This rule had the effect of preventing a British company from operating its slot machines in Finland. The Court said the Finnish rules could be justified,[143] and the steps taken were proportionate.[144] The Court said that it was for the Member States to decide whether to prohibit the operation of such machines or only to restrict their use.

However, the Court has increasingly insisted that Member States at least be consistent in the application of their policies towards gambling. So where, as in *Carmen*, a Member State justified the restriction on free movement by reference to the need to prevent incitement to squander money on gambling and to combat gambling addiction, while at the same time encouraging the development of other games of chance which posed higher risks of addiction with a view to maximizing revenue, the Court said that the restriction was not suitable for attaining the objective in 'a consistent and systematic

---

[136] Case C-65/05 *Commission v Greece* [2006] ECR I-10341, para 56.

[137] Case C-46/08 *Carmen Media Group v Land Schleswig Holstein* [2010] ECR I-8149 and Case C-258/08 *Ladbrokes Betting & Gaming v Stichting de Nationale Sporttotalisator* [2010] ECR I-4757, respectively.

[138] Case C-212/08 *Zerturf Ltd v Premier Ministre* [2011] ECR I-5633. Rules prescribing the legal form and amount of share capital or the holder of a company may also constitute restrictions: Case C-347/09 *Dickinger* [2011] ECR I-8185; Case C-64/08 *Engelmann* [2011] ECR I-8219.

[139] Joined Cases C-338/04, C-359/04 and C-360/04 *Placanica* [2007] ECR I-1891, paras 42 and 44. See also Case C-433/04 *Commission v Belgium* ('*Tax fraud*') [2006] ECR I-10653, para 32.

[140] See also Joined Cases C-316/07 and C-358–360/07 *Stoß v Wetteraukreis* [2010] ECR I-8069.

[141] Case C-124/97 [1999] ECR I-6067.

[142] See also Case C-36/02 *Omega* [2004] ECR I-9609 and Joined Cases C-94/04 and C-202/04 *Cipolla v Fazari* [2006] ECR I-2049; Case C-250/06 *United Pan Europe Communications v Belgium* [2007] ECR I-11135.

[143] *Läärä* (n 141) para 33.

[144] Ibid, para 42. See also Case C-42/07 *Liga Portuguesa de Futebol Profissional (CA/LPFP) v Departamento de Jogos da Santa Casa da Misericórdia de Lisboa* [2009] ECR I-7633, where the Court found the Portuguese ban on operators established in other Member States from offering gambling over the internet was also proportionate to the objective of the fight against crime.

manner'.[145] Similarly, in *Lindman*[146] the Court ruled that a Finnish law, which taxed lottery winnings when the lottery took place in another Member State but not when they occurred in Finland, was not appropriate to achieve the objective of preventing wrongdoing and fraud, the reduction of social damage caused by gaming, the financing of activities in the public interest, and ensuring legal certainty. The Court said that the file transmitted by the referring court disclosed 'no statistical or other evidence which enables any conclusion as to the gravity of the risks connected to playing games of chance or, *a fortiori*, the existence of a particular causal relationship between such risks and participation by nationals . . . in lotteries organised in other Member States'.[147]

Generally, however, the Court will intervene only if the value judgements of the Member State appear manifestly unfounded. This might help to explain why, in *Gambelli*,[148] the Court indicated that an Italian law imposing criminal penalties, including imprisonment, on private individuals in Italy who collaborated over the web with a British bookmaker to collect bets – an activity normally reserved to the Italian State monopoly CONI – was disproportionate, although the Court said it was ultimately for the national court to decide bearing in mind that betting was encouraged in the context of games organized by licensed *national* bodies[149] and that the British supplier was already regulated in the UK.[150]

3 Secondary legislation in the field of freedom of establishment and the free movement of services

3.1 Introduction

So far we have considered the application of the Treaty provisions on freedom of establishment and free movement of services and how, outside the gambling sector, they are often used to strike down national laws which interfere with free movement. We turn now to consider some examples of how the EU has (re)regulated at EU level, laying down EU rules to facilitate freedom of establishment and free movement of services. We shall start with an examination of a piece of horizontal legislation, the Services Directive, which applies across all sectors, before looking at legislation in two specific sectors: first, financial services and, secondly, company law.

3.2 The Services Directive 2006/123

3.2.1 Introduction

The Services Directive[151] was intended to open up the market in services, which accounts for over two-thirds of Europe's gross domestic product (GDP). There were two main drafts of the directive: the controversial 'Bolkestein' draft of 2004,[152] and then the McCreevy draft of 2006 which reflected the significant changes introduced by the European Parliament. Chapter III of the Directive, which concerns the establishment of service providers,

---

[145] *Carmen* (n 137), para 71. However, controlled expansion may be consistent: *Zerturf* (n 138).
[146] Case C-42/02 *Lindman* [2003] ECR I-13519.   [147] Ibid, para 26.
[148] Case C-243/01 *Gambelli* [2003] ECR I-13031. See also *Placanica* (n 139), para 58. cf Case E-1/06 *EFTA Surveillance Authority v Norway* [2007] EFTA Ct Rep 8, para 51.
[149] *Gambelli* (n 148) para 72.   [150] Ibid, para 73.   [151] OJ [2006] L376/36.
[152] COM(2004) 2 final/3.

codifies much of the Court's case law. Chapter IV of the Directive specifically concerns the free movement of services and was subject to major revision in the McCreevy draft.

The Directive is built round four pillars:

- to ease freedom of establishment and the freedom of provision of services in the EU;
- administrative simplification (requiring States to simplify all the procedures used in creating and establishing a service activity. Formal requirements such as the obligation to submit original documents, certified translations, or certified copies must be removed, except for certain cases. From December 2009, undertakings and individuals must be able to carry out all the necessary formalities online using points of single contact) and administrative cooperation (requiring States to cooperate with each other);
- to strengthen rights of recipients of services as users (the rights here are fairly rudimentary, reiterating simply that consumers have the right to receive services and the right to information about those services);
- to promote the quality of services (this is the least-well-developed part of the Directive and focuses mainly on encouraging voluntary certification of activities or drawing up quality charters and European codes of conduct).

We shall focus on the first, and for the purposes of this chapter, most important, pillar of the Directive (see section 3.2.4). However, we begin by looking at the vexed question of the scope of the Directive and the exclusions from that scope.

3.2.2 Scope

According to Article 2(1), the Directive applies to 'services supplied by providers established in a Member State'. Services are defined in accordance with the General Agreement on Trade in Services (GATS): ' "Service" means any self-employed economic activity, normally provided for remuneration, as referred to in Article [57 TFEU]'.[153] The list of services found in Article 57 TFEU has been updated by the Directive to include

- business services such as management consultancy, certification, and testing; facilities management, including office maintenance; advertising; recruitment services; and the services of commercial agents;
- services provided both to businesses and to consumers, such as legal or fiscal advice; real estate services such as estate agencies; construction, including the services of architects; distributive trades; the organization of trade fairs; car rental; and travel agencies;
- consumer services such as those in the field of tourism, including tour guides; leisure services, sports centres, and amusement parks; and, to the extent that they are not excluded from the scope of application of the Directive, household support services, such as help for the elderly.[154]

The striking feature about this list is that the services identified are relatively uncontroversial and are often provided by small operators (SMEs). It is estimated that the Directive covers a wide group of service activities which represent around 40 per cent of the EU's GDP and employment.

---

[153] Art 4(1).   [154] Recital 33.

Assuming the activity is a service within the meaning of the Directive then the Directive can be used to challenge 'requirements which affect access to or the exercise of a service activity'.[155] The word 'requirement' is broadly construed by Article 4(7) of the Directive:

> any obligation, prohibition, condition or limit provided for in the laws, regulations or administrative provisions of the Member States or in consequence of case-law, administrative practice, the rules of professional bodies, or the collective rules of professional associations or other professional organisations, adopted in the exercise of their legal autonomy.

Thus, the Directive is underpinned by notions of market access rather than discrimination (see section 2.4).

3.2.3 Exclusions

Although the potential scope of the Directive is broad, in fact the effectiveness of the Directive is limited by the significant derogations. The principal exclusions can be found in Article 2(2) and (3). The list is long and broad, and includes important sectors such as health-care services,[156] financial services,[157] electronic communication services and networks,[158] temporary work agencies,[159] and private security services.[160] Further, services of general interest,[161] audiovisual services,[162] and gambling activities,[163] including lotteries, gambling in casinos, and betting transactions, are excluded from the scope of the Directive. In addition, Article 2(3) adds that 'This Directive shall not apply to the field of taxation.' Specific provision is also made in respect of social policy, including strike action, which is intended to fall outside the Directive. All these excluded sectors and activities remain subject to specific legislation, where it exists, or the Treaty rules.

3.2.4 Screening

Member States also had to screen existing legislation to remove legal and administrative barriers to the provision of services. This had to be done by December 2009. Different obligations apply depending on whether the rules concern establishment (Chapter III) or services (Chapter IV).

Establishment

The establishment chapter specifically deals with two groups of rules: (a) authorization schemes, and (b) 'other' requirements which are either prohibited or subject to evaluation.
    Authorization schemes are permitted provided that

- they do not discriminate (either directly or indirectly) against the provider in question,
- the scheme is justified by an overriding reason relating to the public interest (ORRPI),[164]

---

[155] Recital 9.   [156] Art 2(2)(f).   [157] Art 2(2)(b).   [158] Art 2(2)(c).
[159] Art 2(2)(e).   [160] Art 2(2)(k).   [161] Art 2(2)(a).   [162] Art 2(2)(g).
[163] Art 2(2)(h). See also recital 25 of the Preamble.
[164] Art 4(8) refers to ORRPIs recognized as such in the case law of the Court of Justice, including the following grounds: public policy (which includes issues relating to human dignity, the protection of minors and vulnerable adults, and animal welfare); public security; public safety; public health; preserving the financial equilibrium of the social security system; the protection of consumers, recipients of services, and workers; fairness of trade transactions; combating fraud; the protection of the environment and the urban environment; the health of animals; intellectual property; the conservation of the national historic and artistic heritage; social policy objectives and cultural policy objectives.

- the objective pursued cannot be attained by means of a less restrictive measure (eg monitoring the activities of the service provider or making a simple declaration).

Criteria for granting authorization must also satisfy these requirements, together with the obligations to be clear and unambiguous, objective, made public in advance, transparent, and accessible.[165]

The Directive concerns not only authorization schemes but also 'other requirements'. In respect of 'other requirements', the Directive distinguishes between (a) those which are prohibited, and (b) those which are 'suspect' and need to be evaluated. Article 14 lists eight requirements which are *prohibited*. This means that there are no ORRPI justifications or derogations available to Member States. The prohibited requirements include nationality requirements for the provider, its staff, individuals holding the share capital, or members of the provider's management or supervisory bodies;[166] or a rule forbidding a provider from having an establishment in more than one Member State.[167]

Article 15(2) identifies a further eight requirements, a number of which have already been considered 'restrictions' on freedom of establishment in the Court's case law, which are 'suspect'. These include quantitative or territorial restrictions, and an obligation on a provider to take a specific legal form. Unlike the prohibited requirements, the Directive requires Member States to evaluate whether these suspect requirements are compatible with the conditions laid down in Article 15(3) (ie non-discriminatory, necessary,[168] and proportionate). Only if they satisfy these tests will they be allowed to continue.

New legislation introduced in this area after 2009 has to be notified to the Commission.[169]

Services

The provisions on services proved to be the most controversial aspect of the Directive. The Bolkestein version of the Directive contained a strong country of origin principle ('Member States shall ensure that providers are subject only to the national provisions of their Member State of origin which fall within the coordinated field'). This meant that services should be regulated by the country in which the service provider was established and only exceptionally by the country in which the service was being provided (the host country), as provided by the derogations. For the Commission, the use of the country of origin principle in the Bolkestein version of the Services Directive was a logical extension of, for example, the Television Without Frontiers (TWF) Directive 89/552,[170] now the Audio Visual Media Services (AVMS) Directive 2010/13, and the E-commerce Directive 2000/31,[171] both of which had the country of origin principle at their core.

However, the Services Directive was considerably more ambitious than its sectoral forebears, since its horizontal approach meant that it covered all the sectors in its scope[172] not just specific sectors. Further, while the TWF/AVMS Directives contained a mix of deregulation (country of origin principle) and reregulation through minimum harmonization (eg rules on protection of minors, prohibition of racism), the Bolkestein proposal concerned only deregulation (country of origin principle) and very limited reregulation in the Chapter on quality; given the broad and unidentified nature of services covered, more extensive reregulation was not possible.

---

[165] Art 10(2).   [166] *Factortame II* (n 20).
[167] Case 96/85 *Commission v France* [1986] ECR 1475.
[168] Confusingly so-called when what is actually meant is objective justification, the language used in, eg Art 10(2)(b).   [169] Art 15(7).
[170] OJ [1989] L298/23.   [171] OJ [2000] L178/1.   [172] See eg COM(2004) 2, 8.

Such overt recognition of the country of origin principle proved to be too controversial for some Member States and the language of the McCreevy version of the Directive was changed and it was this version that made it into the final draft. Article 16 now provides:

> Member States shall respect the right of providers to provide services in a Member State other than that in which they are established.
> The Member State in which the service is provided shall ensure free access to and free exercise of a service activity within its territory.

This is followed by a list of seven particularly suspect requirements largely based on the Court's case law (including an obligation on the provider to have an establishment in the territory of the host State;[173] a ban on the provider setting up a certain form or type of infrastructure, including an office or chambers;[174] and the application of specific contractual arrangements between the provider and the recipient preventing or restricting service provision by the self-employed). These requirements, while frowned upon, can, however be saved by the express derogations in Article 17, the case-by-case derogations in Article 18,[175] and by a narrow list of public interest requirements provided for by the Directive.

But how great, in fact, is the difference between the country of origin principle and the freedom to provide services? Under the country of origin principle, the principal regulator would have been the home State; reinforced by the presumption that the host State could not impose any additional requirements unless there were very good reasons for this. The current approach appears to reverse this: it accepts that the host State can impose its own restrictions on the service provider, where there are good reasons for so doing, account being taken of the protection already provided in the home State.

The current approach therefore broadly reflects the case law of the Court where, as chapter 13, section 8.2 shows, the country of origin principle is not as firmly embedded in respect of services as it is in goods. It does exist, but not in terms of establishing the breach (as is the case for goods), but in terms of justifying the breach where the Court requires the host State to take into account requirements already imposed by the home State.[176] In practice, the difference may well be one of emphasis rather than substance: the country of origin principle raises a strong presumption of illegality of the host State measure; the current approach raises a weaker presumption of illegality. In practical terms, it means that service providers will continue to have to investigate the rules in each State in which they provide services.

After the 2009 deadline, Member States must inform the Commission of any changes in their requirements or any new requirements, together with the reasons for them (presumably based on Article 16(1) and (3), although this is not stated). The Commission must inform the other Member States but the Member States remain free to adopt the provisions in question. The Commission is then to provide annual 'analyses and orientations on the application of these provisions in the context of this Directive.'

---

[173] *Van Binsbergen* (n 11).   [174] *Gebhard* (n 71).

[175] This leads to the result that the physical safety of consumers can be protected under Art 18 but the economic interests of consumers cannot be protected under Art 16(1) or 16(3).

[176] See eg *Säger* (n 70), para 15: 'the freedom to provide services may be limited only by rules which are justified by imperative reasons relating to the public interest and which apply to all persons or undertakings pursuing an activity in the State of destination, *in so far as that interest is not protected by the rules to which the person providing the services is subject in the Member State in which he is established*' (emphasis added).

3.3 Financial services

3.3.1 Introduction

Financial services have for a long time been seen as a key sector for European economic integration.[177] There are at least two substantive reasons for this. First, financial services are a large and important sector where services can actually be traded across frontiers. The problem with many services, from hairdressing to care of the elderly, is that they do not travel well. They cannot be provided remotely and it is rare that either the provider or the recipient would wish to move to another country for the service activity. Partly as a result, the internal market in services is much less developed than that in goods. By contrast, in the field of financial services many services can be offered remotely, for example using the telephone or the internet. Further, companies operating in the field have often been eager to expand abroad, for example by establishing branches or subsidiaries. Thus, financial services are well suited for the creation of an internal market in services.

Secondly, through the free movement of financial services, a deep and liquid European capital market can be attained. This means easier access to capital for all European companies, as well as for individuals, who could access financial products such as loans from a wide variety of European providers. Financial service integration promises cheaper and more readily available capital, for the benefit of the entire EU economy.

Unfortunately, the financial services sector is as dangerous as it is beneficial. Again, two key issues should be highlighted. Economists would call these (a) information asymmetries and (b) externalities.[178] First, many financial products are complex: it is difficult for a buyer to understand all the features and risks involved. Financial advice may be of limited help; in practice, problems with the quality of advice have been common, sometimes due to conflicts of interests of the advisor. And the stakes are high: when something goes wrong, the consequences can be devastating for an individual – life savings can be lost, families ruined.

Secondly, there is the issue of financial stability[179] and in particular the various systemic externalities (contagion) relating to it. Banking has always been recognized as a particularly risky activity. Banks borrow short and lend long, meaning that they have to pay to depositors on demand but the loans they have issued will only be repaid gradually. This mismatch has resulted in bank runs when panicked depositors, fearing the bank's inability to pay them money they have on deposit, try to withdraw their funds from a bank, all at the same time, causing the bank to collapse (think of the scene in the film *Mary Poppins* where the little boy's demand for his 'tuppence' back led to a run on the bank where his father worked). States have tried to reduce such risks by various devices, including central banks as lenders of last resort, capital requirements, and deposit guarantees. A further complication is that many financial services providers are highly interconnected. They owe money to each other. If one collapses, others take a hit, which in turn may put their solvency in question – there is a danger of contagion. In such circumstances, States have often come to the rescue, spending taxpayers' money to bail out failing banks. Thus private debt becomes public debt and, in the case of Ireland and Spain, puts the State in a vulnerable position because its own lending costs become higher. And because there has been no EU pot of tax

---

[177] See eg already Commission White Paper, 'Completing the internal market', COM(85) 310 final, at 27–29.

[178] See further eg C Goodhart, 'How Should We Regulate Bank Capital and Financial Products? What Role for "Living Wills"?' in A Turner et al (eds), *The Future of Finance: The LSE Report* (London: London School of Economics and Political Science, 2010) 167–170.

[179] See on the connection between legal integration and financial stability, M Andenas and IHY Chiu, 'Financial Stability and Legal Integration in Financial Regulation' (2013) 38 *European Law Review* 335.

money that could be used to bail out the banks, it is the home State that has had to intervene, even if the bank's operations have been on a pan-European scale. This is sometimes called the 'international in life, national in death' – phenomenon.

3.3.2 The EU legislative framework

The unique desirability of financial service integration and the risks that it involves have resulted in a complex and evolving framework. It quickly became apparent that the freedoms that the Treaty set out were not sufficient for the creation of an internal market in this sector. In *Casati*[180] it was established that the free movement of capital lacked direct effect, and in a series of cases on insurance services it was found that Member States were entitled to restrict free movement on public interest grounds.[181] Due to the risks involved, they could place limitations, even though some harmonizing directives had been adopted.

The EU legislature responded by adopting a set of directives, such as the Investment Services Directive,[182] that were designed to create an internal market utilizing the device of mutual recognition.[183] The directives established the *minimum* standards that each country had to apply. The Member States could grant so-called passports to their financial services providers, which could then operate in the whole EU. The idea was home country control: companies based in State A were authorized and supervised there, and this was recognized by the other States.[184] As we have seen, this was consistent with the ideas underpinning Article 56 TFEU.

The system was overhauled following the creation of an ambitious Financial Services Action Plan at the end of the 1990s.[185] The directives went from minimum to full harmonization. They no longer sought to establish just the minimum standards, but attempted to regulate comprehensively. For example, the Investment Services Directive was replaced by MiFiD.[186] Each Member State still granted passports to its firms, but now using fully harmonized EU rather than national rules.[187]

The financial crisis that began in 2007 has ushered in a new phase.[188] In practice, the integrated financial market that had been created has re-fragmented, with many firms retreating from some of their overseas operations, often at the behest of their national supervisors. At the same time, the EU has adopted a new, more centralized, mode of regulation. Both the scope (ie the subject matter covered) and the intensity of its activities have grown. Examples of the former are the regulations on credit rating agencies and the Hedge Funds Directive.[189] An example of the latter is the EU's involvement not only in law-making but

---

[180] Case 203/80 *Casati* [1981] ECR 2595.

[181] See eg *Insurance* (n 8).

[182] Council Directive 93/22/EEC on investment services in the securities field (OJ [1993] L141/27).

[183] See further chapters 12 and 13.

[184] See eg E Lomnicka, 'Home Country Control Principle in the Financial Services Directives and the Case Law' in M Andenas and W-H Roth (eds), *Services and Free Movement in EU Law* (Oxford: Oxford University Press, 2002).

[185] Commission Communication, 'Implementing the framework for financial markets: action plan', COM(1999) 232. See on the evolution T Tridimas, 'EU Financial Regulation: Federalization, Crisis Management, and Law Reform' in P Craig and G de Búrca, *The Evolution of EU Law* (2nd edn, Oxford: Oxford University Press, 2011).

[186] European Parliament and Council Directive 2004/39/EC on markets in financial instruments (OJ [2004] L145/1), as amended.

[187] V Hatzopoulos, *Regulating Services in the European Union* (Oxford: Oxford University Press, 2012) 235–236.

[188] See N Moloney, 'EU Financial Market Regulation after the Global Financial Crisis: "More Europe" or More Risks?' (2010) 47 *Common Market Law Review* 1317.

[189] European Parliament and Council Regulation (EC) No 1060/2009 on credit rating agencies (OJ [2009] L302/1), as amended, and European Parliament and Council Directive 2011/61/EU on alternative investment fund managers (OJ [2011] L174/1).

also in supervision. New EU agencies have been established under the European System of Financial Supervisors, covering banking, securities markets, insurance, and occupational pensions. They have powerful roles in preparing the detailed rules of the 'single rulebook' that put into effect the more general EU legislation, they oversee the supervisory activities of national authorities, and they can, in certain circumstances, even impose binding decisions on individual companies.

Efforts are currently underway to go even further in the context of the eurozone and to establish a banking union.[190] The crisis has demonstrated dangerous negative loops between Member States and their banks. If a bank gets into trouble, its home country has typically had to rescue it. This can put a strain on its public finances. This in turn lowers the value of its bonds, which are often held by domestic banks. This may require further rescue operations, which further undermine government bonds, and so on. When this happens, other Member States may in the end have to come to the aid of the Member State itself. To break this negative loop, the European Central Bank (ECB) will become the direct supervisor for the most significant banks in the eurozone, and will participate in the single supervisory mechanism that covers all banks in the euro area.[191] It is thought that the ECB can adopt a more objective view of banks than national supervisors, which may get too close to their charges. To complement the system of supervision, a single resolution mechanism and a single resolution fund are planned.[192] The fund would be financed by payments from the banks themselves. It is hoped that this would allow failing banks to be resolved in an orderly manner, without the involvement of public money.[193] At the time of writing, the details of the system are being established. The UK looks set to stay outside the banking union, due to its non-participation in the single currency. In other words, while the general trend in EU legislation has been greater centralization, an important new fragmentation has also emerged.

3.4 EU company law

3.4.1 EU legislation

Harmonization directives

A chapter on free movement of legal persons would not be complete without some discussion of EU company law rules. Public and private limited companies are generally established under national law. The national law rules on the establishment of companies have now been subject to extensive harmonization by EU law. Article 50 TFEU, in particular Article 50(2)(g) TFEU, provides the main legal basis to adopt directives harmonizing EU company law. Company law directives have concerned

- disclosure requirements of companies and their branches,[194]

---

[190] See Communication from the Commission, 'A blueprint for a deep and genuine economic and monetary union: launching a European debate', COM(2012) 777 final. See also chapter 19.

[191] Council Regulation (EU) No 1024/2013 conferring specific tasks on the European Central Bank concerning policies relating to the prudential supervision of credit institutions (OJ [2013] L287/63).

[192] Commission proposal for a Regulation of the European Parliament and of the Council establishing uniform rules and uniform procedures for the resolution of credit institutions and certain investment firms in the framework of a Single Resolution Mechanism and a Single Bank Resolution Fund, COM(2013) 520 final; the Council agreement reached on 18 December 2013 (http://www.consilium.europa.eu/uedocs/cms_data/docs/pressdata/en/ecofin/140190.pdf); the Council and European Parliament still have to agree, and the goal is to do so by spring 2014.

[193] See the agreement on the Bank Recovery and Resolution Directive: http://europa.eu/rapid/press-release_MEMO-13-1140_en.htm?locale=en (EUROPA, 12 December 2013).

[194] See eg the Eleventh Company Law Directive 89/666/EEC (OJ [1989] L395/36).

- the maintenance and alteration of the capital of public limited liability companies,[195]
- the merger and divisions of public limited liability companies,[196]
- the single-member private limited liability companies,[197]
- take-over bids,[198]
- cross-border merger of companies,[199]
- certain rights of shareholders of listed companies,[200]
- companies' annual and consolidated accounts.[201]

The justification for the enactment of this legislation is firmly rooted in the need to attain the single market. As Edwards explains,[202] divergences in national company law rules on, for example, creditor and shareholder protection and company management may create a 'Delaware effect', encouraging the establishment of new companies in the Member State with the laxest laws, in the same way that US companies have long been attracted to incorporate in the small state of Delaware by company law rules that favour corporations' interests. In other words, corporate decisions to expand across frontiers which in a perfect internal market should be taken solely on economic grounds may in fact be 'significantly influenced by the relative burden of domestic regulation'. The adoption of EU legislation is intended to stop this from occurring.

Take, for example, what is now Directive 2012/30 on the coordination of safeguards for the protection of the interests of members and others in respect of the formation of public limited liability companies (eg PLCs in the UK, SAs in France), and the maintenance and alteration of their capital, with a view to making such safeguards equivalent. The Directive contains the following requirements:

- *Formation*: the Directive lays down a (very) minimum share capital (25,000 euros),[203] albeit that only one-quarter of the subscribed capital be paid up at the time of incorporation. It also prescribes rules on how that share capital may be formed. Further, the statutes or instruments of incorporation of a public company lay down the basic particulars of the company, including the exact composition of its capital.[204]

- *Maintenance of share capital*: the Directive provides that no distribution to shareholders must take the company's net assets below the company's subscribed capital.[205] It also imposes limits on the company's right to acquire its own shares.[206] Further, the Directive makes provision preventing public companies from using a subsidiary company (in which it holds a majority of the voting rights, or on which it can exercise a dominant influence) to make an acquisition of the parent company's own shares without complying with the relevant restrictions.[207]

- *Alteration of the share capital*: the Directive makes provision for situations where the share capital is increased[208] or decreased.[209]

---

[195] See eg Directive 2012/30/EU (OJ [2012] L315/74).
[196] See eg on mergers: Directive 2011/35/EU (OJ [2011] L110/1); on divisions: Sixth Company Law Directive 82/891/EEC (OJ [1982] L378/47).   [197] Directive 2009/102/EC (OJ [2009] L258/20).
[198] See Thirteenth Company Law Directive 2004/25/EC (OJ [2004] L142/12).
[199] The Tenth Company Law Directive 2005/56/EC (OJ [2005] L310/1).
[200] Directive 2012/30/EU (OJ [2012] L315/74).   [201] Directive 2013/34/EU (OJ [2013] L182/19).
[202] V Edwards, *EC Company Law* (Oxford: Oxford University Press, 1999) 3.   [203] Art 6.
[204] See especially Arts 2 and 3.   [205] Art 17.   [206] Arts 20–24.   [207] Art 28.
[208] Arts 29–33.   [209] Arts 34–43.

Thus, through a combination of minimum standards, coordination of national rules, and transparency requirements, the Directive is intended to guarantee minimum equivalent protection for shareholders and creditors of public limited companies.

All of this seems eminently sensible but some question whether there was ever a need for such EU legislation in the first place (most Member States already had such rules, and the market, particularly banks, may have imposed similar requirements anyway) and whether in fact EU company law more generally has made any real difference. Enriques is scathing in his criticism:[210]

> First, [EU] corporate law does not cover core corporate law areas such as fiduciary duties and shareholder remedies [and as we shall see below, exit of companies]. Second, [EU] corporate law rules are under enforced. Third, in the presence of very sporadic judicia[l] interpretation by the European Court of Justice, EU corporate law tends to be implemented and construed differently in each Member State, according to local legal culture and consistently with prior corporate law provisions. Fourth, when the EU has introduced new rules, it has done so with respect to issues on which Member States would have probably legislated even in the absence of an [EU] mandate. Last but not least, most [EU] corporate law rules can be categorized as optional, market-mimicking, unimportant, or avoidable.

There are, however, good reasons for why the EU has experienced such difficulties with harmonization of EU corporate law. These have much to do with the fundamental problem of an absence of agreement in the EU Member States over the function of company law. Is it, as the UK would have it, that company law is concerned with the relationship between shareholders and directors, or does it actually concern a wider range of constituencies including employees, as is the position in Germany?[211] The latter approach is reflected in the employee participation provisions found in the EU corporate forms (considered below) and the proposal, now at a fairly advanced stage on the disclosure by large companies of non-financial and diversity information (the corporate social responsibility proposal).[212]

EU corporate forms

In addition to harmonization legislation, EU company law has introduced its own EU company law forms, in particular SEs, SCEs, and EEIGs (see below). These instruments are referred to as the '29th regime' to the extent that they introduce new legal forms, in addition to the national forms, that do not harmonize, modify, or substitute the existing national legal forms, but provide an additional alternative legal form.

Of these new legal forms, the most important, established by Council Regulation 2157/2001,[213] is the Statute for a European company. Under this Regulation the EU has introduced its own type of EU public company, Societas Europea (SE), which can register in any Member State of the EU. There are over 2,000 such companies in existence.[214] The Regulation is complemented by an Employee Participation Directive 2001/86[215] that sets rules for participation by employees on the company's board of directors.

---

[210] L Enriques, 'EC Company Law Directives and Regulations: How Trivial are They?' (2006) 27 *University of Pennsylvania Journal of International Economic Law* 1, 2.

[211] J Borg-Barthet, 'Free at Last? Choice of Corporate Law in the EU Following the Judgment in *VALE*' (2013) 62 *International and Comparative Law Quarterly* 502.

[212] http://www.eu2013.lt/en/news/pressreleases/member-states-mandate-the-presidency-to-negotiate-on-directive-regarding-disclosure-of-non-financial-and-diversity-information (*eu2013.lt*, 14 December 2013).

[213] OJ [1985] L199/1.

[214] See 'European Company (SE) Database–ECDB' (ECDB), http://ecdb.worker-participation.eu/

[215] OJ [2001] L294/22.

There is also a statute allowing for European Cooperative Societies (Societas Cooperativa Europaea (SCEs)),[216] a European corporate form in the not-for-profit sector, also with accompanying employee participation requirements.[217] The SCE Regulation was adopted under Article 352 TFEU, and not under the general internal market legal basis Article 114 TFEU as the Commission and Parliament had advocated. This choice of legal basis was upheld by the Court[218] because, the Court said, the contested Regulation, 'which leaves unchanged the different national laws already in existence, cannot be regarded as aiming to approximate the laws of the Member States applicable to cooperative societies, but has as its purpose the creation of a new form of cooperative society in addition to the national forms.'

In addition, Council Regulation 2137/85[219] makes provision for a European Economic Interest Grouping (EEIG), also adopted under Article 352 TFEU. An EEIG is designed to 'facilitate or develop the economic activities of its members by a pooling of resources, activities or skills. It is not intended that the grouping should make profits for itself. If it does make any profits, they will be apportioned among the members and taxed accordingly. Its activities must be related to the economic activities of its members, but cannot replace them.'[220] It is not liable for corporation tax but its members have unlimited liability. Several thousand such EEIGs now exist, including the French–German TV channel ARTE.

More recently, there was a proposal for a Private Company Statute (Societas Privata Europaea (SPE)).[221] The aim of the proposal was to avoid private companies having to reincorporate in each Member State in which they operated. The proposal was withdrawn in 2013 because agreement could not be reached.

3.4.2 National company law and freedom of establishment

Introduction

As the previous discussion has indicated, there is now extensive secondary legislation in the field of company law. However, there are some significant holes in the EU legislation and it is in these areas where national law applies. This raises the question whether the application of the national law rules has the effect of interfering with Articles 49 and 54 TFEU. If the Treaty applies, it might be thought that there would be direct parallels in the case law and its application to natural and legal persons. In fact this is not quite the case.

There is a further problem. Different approaches can be found in the Member States to determine the seat of a company. The majority of Member States, including France and Germany, have adopted the *real seat theory* (*siège réel*), which says that a company is to be established under the law of the State in which its operational headquarters is situated, even though it might be formally incorporated in another Member State. A minority of Member States, including the UK, adopt the *incorporation theory*, which says that a company is governed by the law of the State in which it is formally incorporated, regardless of whether it is connected to that State in any other way (eg plant, premises, or staff). Borg-Barthet explains the different approaches in the following way:

> The rationale for the siège réel approach stems from the view that companies are concessions of the State and that the State with which they are most intimately connected should be able to prescribe their governance arrangements. It is an acknowledgment of the public function of companies. The 'real seat' theory is to be contrasted with the contractual incorporation theory,

[216] Regulation 1435/2003 (OJ [2003] L207/1).   [217] Directive 2003/72 (OJ [2003] L207/25).
[218] Case C-436/03 *Parliament v Council* [2006] ECR I-3733.   [219] OJ [1985] L199/1.
[220] 'European Economic Interest Grouping (EEIG)' (EUROPA), http://europa.eu/legislation_summaries/internal_market/businesses/company_law/l26015_en.htm   [221] COM(2008) 396.

which has long been adopted by the United Kingdom, among others. In keeping with contractarian theory, the incorporation theory favours party autonomy in choice of corporate law; it prescribes that a company should be governed by the law of the State in which it is incorporated. There is no need for the company to have its centre of administration in that territory, or indeed to operate in that territory at all.[222]

But what happens when the two systems conflict? Can a company incorporated in the UK, but with the bulk of its operations in Germany, demand that if Germany does not recognize its legal form, Germany is in breach of Articles 49 and 54 TFEU? This is considered below. First, we need to consider the seminal decision in *Daily Mail*[223] on the cross-border transfers of the corporate seat, a decision which provides the context for all subsequent case law developments.

The right of exit

Natural persons have a free right to leave their home State.[224] However, the Court has refused to recognize an unrestricted right of exit for companies. This was first seen in the early case of *Daily Mail*.[225] Having pointed to the wide variety of national laws on the factors providing a connection to the national territory and the absence of coordination directives, the Court concluded that neither Article 49 TFEU nor Article 54 TFEU conferred on companies incorporated in State A the right to transfer – without any restriction or impediment from State A – their central management, control, and administration to State B while at the same time retaining their status as companies in State A.[226] This judgment does not mean that companies cannot move their residence but that – at the present stage of development of Union law – restrictions, particularly those concerning taxation at issue in *Daily Mail*, can be imposed on emigrating companies by the home State.

With the development of the 'restrictions' case law (see section 2 and especially the decisions in *Centros* and *SEVIC*), some commentators wondered whether the position might now be different. However, in *Cartesio*[227] the Court essentially upheld its decision in *Daily Mail* but nuanced it. It drew a distinction between (a) where the seat of a company incorporated under the law of one Member State is transferred to another Member State with *no* change as regards the law which governs that company (the situation in *Daily Mail* and *Cartesio*), and (b) where a company governed by the law of one Member State moves to another Member State with an attendant change as regards the national law applicable (reincorporation).[228]

In respect of the first situation, the Court said the matter fell outside the scope of Union law because the company no longer satisfied the preconditions of being a company formed under national law. In the absence of harmonization, it was for *national law* to define the connecting factor (ie registered office only (for those States applying the incorporation theory) or registered office and real seat (for those States applying the *siège réel* theory)) required for a company to be regarded as incorporated under the law of that Member State.[229] The Court said:

---

[222] Borg-Barthet, 'Free at Last?' (n 211) 503.   [223] Case 81/87 [1988] ECR 5483.

[224] See eg Case C-10/90 *Masgio v Bundesknappschaft* [1991] ECR I-1119, paras 18 and 19; Case C-415/93 *Bosman* [1995] ECR I-4921, para 104.   [225] Case 81/87 (n 223).

[226] Ibid, para 24.   [227] Case C-210/06 *Cartesio Oktató és Szolgáltató bt* [2008] ECR I-9641.

[228] Ibid, para 111.   [229] Ibid, para 109.

Thus a Member State has the power to define both the connecting factor required of a company if it is to be regarded as incorporated under the law of that Member State and, as such, capable of enjoying the right of establishment, and that required if the company is to be able subsequently to maintain that status. That power includes the possibility for that Member State not to permit a company governed by its law to retain that status if the company intends to reorganise itself in another Member State by moving its seat to the territory of the latter, thereby breaking the connecting factor required under the national law of the Member State of incorporation.[230]

By contrast, in the second situation the Court said that the company is *converted* into a form of company which is governed by the law of the Member State to which it has moved. The Court said that the power of Member States to determine the connecting factor did not justify the Member State of incorporation (State A) preventing that company from converting itself into a company governed by the law of the new Member State (State B) to the extent that it was permitted by State B's law to do so, by requiring the company's winding-up or liquidation. The Court said that a barrier (eg the requirement by State A for the company to be wound up in State A and then reincorporated in State B) to the actual conversion of a company 'constitutes a restriction on the freedom of establishment of the company concerned which, unless it serves overriding requirements in the public interest, is prohibited under Article [49 TFEU]'.[231]

VALE[232] added an important gloss to this. The case concerned a cross-border conversion: an Italian company, VALE Costruzioni Srl, wanted to convert into a Hungarian company. It successfully applied to be removed from the Italian register of companies, but the Hungarian court refused the subsequent application for the new Hungarian company, VALE Epítési Kft to be registered as the 'successor in law' of VALE Costruzioni Srl. Under Hungarian law, conversion was possible for domestic companies. In other words, Hungarian law was interfering with VALE's freedom of establishment. While *Cartesio* suggested that it was for the host State to determine the rules for incorporation ('to the extent that it is permitted under [the new State's] law to do so'),[233] the Court said the new State's law must comply with the principles of Articles 49 and 54 TFEU, including the principle of equal treatment. Because Hungarian law allowed Hungarian companies to convert but not companies governed by the law of another Member State, there was a breach of the Treaty which could not be justified given the blanket nature of the rule.

Thus, while *Daily Mail* remains good law, the Court in *SEVIC* (on the right to cross-border mergers, considered in section 2) and *VALE* (on the right to cross-border conversions) seems keen to limit its scope. The enactment of EU legislation would obviously help: the adoption of the Cross-Border Mergers Directive 2005/56 was speeded up by the legislator in anticipation of the *SEVIC* ruling;[234] and the Commission is trying again to introduce a legislative framework on cross-border seat transfers/conversions.[235]

Recognition of companies established under a different legal regime

What about the situation, seen in *Centros*, where a company established in the UK but conducting all of its business in Denmark through a branch, wants to have that branch recognized in Denmark? English law permits companies to be incorporated in the UK but

---

[230] *Cartesio* (n 127) para 110.   [231] Ibid, para 113.

[232] Case C-378/10 *VALE Epítési kft*, 12 July 2012, nyr, noted in T Biermeyer (2013) 50 *Common Market Law Review* 571.   [233] Ibid, para 112.

[234] See the note by P Behrens (2006) 43 *Common Market Law Review* 1669.   [235] COM(2012) 740, 2.

with their residence or main operations in another Member State. This outcome would not be permitted by Member States which operate the *siège réel* doctrine. The Court, by ruling, as we saw earlier, that the Danish registrar's refusal to recognize the branch constituted an unjustified obstacle to the UK company's freedom of establishment, implicitly called into question the status of the *siège réel* doctrine under EU law and created if not a Delaware effect certainly a market for incorporations under EU law. Becht et al note that the UK experienced a 400 per cent increase in incorporations of companies that had their head-quarters in other Member States after *Centros*.[236]

A permutation on *Centros* arose in *Überseering*,[237] which raised the question whether a company incorporated under one legal regime (State A) but which then transferred its principal place of business to another (State B) could retain its legal status as a company in State A and have that status recognized in State B. Überseering, a Dutch company, sued a German company, NCC, for defective work carried out by NCC on Überseering's behalf in Germany. Prior to bringing the proceedings, all the shares in Überseering were acquired by two German nationals. The German court found that, since Überseering had trans-ferred its centre of administration to Germany, as a company incorporated under Dutch law it did not have legal capacity in Germany because it had not been formed according to German law and so could not bring proceedings.[238] German law thus refused to rec-ognize the legal personality which Überseering enjoyed under Dutch law (and continued to enjoy under Dutch law even after its centre of administration had been moved),[239] with the result that the German courts effectively denied the company access to justice in Germany.

The Court said that this case concerned an immigrating company and the recogni-tion (or rather lack of it) by one Member State (Germany) of a company incorporated under the law of another Member State (the Netherlands).[240] The Court said that because Überseering was a company validly incorporated under the law of the Netherlands, where its registered office was established, the company had no alternative under German law but to reincorporate in Germany if it wished to enforce its rights under a contract before a German court.[241] This contravened Articles 49 and 54 TFEU because 'The requirement of reincorporation of the same company in Germany is therefore tantamount to outright negation of freedom of establishment'.[242] The Court then considered whether the restric-tion on freedom of establishment could be justified. It said that while it was conceiv-able that overriding requirements relating to the general interest (eg the protection of the interests of creditors, minority shareholders, employees, and even the taxation author-ities) could – in certain circumstances and subject to certain conditions – justify restric-tions on freedom of establishment, they could not justify an outright negation of freedom of establishment.[243]

The effect of this judgment may be to erode the *siège réel* doctrine still further. It requires German courts to recognize companies validly formed under Dutch law, even though they would not be recognized under German law. Indeed, a company with its 'registered office, central administration or principal place of business within the [Union]' cannot be denied access to any other Member State. This does not necessarily mean that the Court is

---

[236] M Becht, C Mayer, and HF Wagner, 'Where do Firms Incorporate?' [2008] *Journal of Corporate Finance* 241, 242 cited in Borg-Barthet, 'Free at Last?' (n 211).

[237] Case C-208/00 (n 6).

[238] Ibid, para 9.   [239] Ibid, paras 63 and 71.   [240] Ibid, para 66.

[241] Ibid, para 79.   [242] Ibid, paras 80 and 81.   [243] Ibid, paras 92 and 93.

privileging the incorporation theory; rather that it is paying more attention to the State in which the company has been incorporated.

Together these cases show a powerful form of judicially induced harmonization taking place. However, as *Daily Mail* and *Cartesio* show, the process is taking place more carefully and slowly than advocates of a full-scale application of the market access approach might expect and this highlights one of the key distinctions between the case law on free movement of natural persons and that on free movement of legal persons.

4 Conclusion

The free movement of legal persons is firmly entrenched in the EU system. Companies like Amazon and Google make use of it without ever resorting to the courts. Some of this may be to do with the fact that Member States are keen to host such companies and the tax and employment opportunities they bring, without the stick of EU law. However, compliance with national corporate rules is onerous for smaller companies wishing to expand their operations to other Member States and here EU law has made some difference in harmonizing requirements. But there are big gaps in the provision and the Court, through its case law, has precipitated some important changes, most notably in forcing the recognition of companies established in other Member States. Here the driving force has not been developing the higher ideals of citizenship and human rights but the more hard-headed imperative of ensuring that companies can take full advantage of the opportunities that the single market has to offer.

The single market has been a powerful force in opening up national markets to competition from providers in other Member States. The EU legislative programme has obviously been of assistance here. However, the Services Directive has failed to live up to its potential in part because some Member States remain resistant to applying single market rules to the services sector.[244] Further, the services logic, based on home State control, applied in the 1990s to the financial services sector, proved insufficiently robust in the face of the crisis. And the crisis has forced a more general rethink as to the balance of interests between the Member States and private interests. This can be seen most acutely in *EFTA Surveillance Authority v Iceland*,[245] concerning the Icelandic government's failure to ensure (as required by Articles 7 and 10 of the then Directive 94/19 on deposit guarantees) payment of compensation to Icesave depositors holding deposits in branches in the UK and the Netherlands of Landsbanki, an Icelandic bank which went bust.[246] The EFTA Court said[247]

> that the Directive does not envisage that the defendant itself must ensure payments to depositors in the Icesave branches in the Netherlands and the United Kingdom, in accordance with Articles 7 and 10 of the Directive, in a systemic crisis of the magnitude experienced in Iceland.

Here it is the troubled State's interest that has prevailed. Pragmatism sometimes prevails over law.

---

[244] http://www.consilium.europa.eu/uedocs/cms_data/docs/pressdata/en/intm/119725.pdf (*Consilium*, 10 March 2011).

[245] Case E-16/11 *EFTA Surveillance Authority v Iceland*, 28 January 2013, nyr.

[246] OJ [1994] L135/5.   [247] *EFTA* (n 245) para 178.

However, the EU legislator, albeit playing catch-up, has intervened to try to prevent such systemic failures happening again: most importantly through the agreed revisions to the Deposit Guarantee Directive[248] and the Bank Failure Directive,[249] which, together with the Capital Requirements Directive IV package implementing the new global standards on bank capital and liquidity,[250] comprise 'key pillars of the single rulebook necessary for the stability and integrity of the EU's internal market in financial services', which in turn 'provides a common foundation which allows a move to the banking union without any risk of fragmenting the single market.'[251]

Further reading

M ANDENAS AND W-H ROTH (eds), *Services and Free Movement in EU Law* (Oxford: Oxford University Press, 2002)

C BARNARD, *The Substantive Law of the EU: The Four Freedoms* (4th edn, Oxford: Oxford University Press, 2013) chs 10 and 11

N BOEGER (ed), *Perspectives on Corporate Social Responsibility* (Cheltenham: Edward Elgar, 2008)

J BORG-BARTHET, *The Governing Law of Companies in EU Law* (Oxford: Hart Publishing, 2012)

V EDWARDS, *EC Company Law* (Oxford: Oxford University Press, 1999)

J GHOSH, *Principles of the Internal Market and Direct Taxation* (Oxford: Key Haven, 2007)

M GRAETZ AND A WARREN, 'Dividend Taxation in Europe: When the ECJ Makes Tax Policy' (2007) 44 *Common Market Law Review* 1577

V HATZOPOULOS, *Regulating Services in the European Union* (Oxford: Oxford University Press, 2012) 235–236

S KINGSTON, 'The Boundaries of Sovereignty: The ECJ's Controversial Role Applying the Internal Market Rules to Taxation' (2006–7) 9 *Cambridge Yearbook of European Legal Studies* 287

N MOLONEY, 'EU Financial Market Regulation after the Global Financial Crisis: "More Europe" or More Risks?' (2010) 47 *Common Market Law Review* 1317

N MOLONEY, 'Resetting the Location of Regulatory and Supervisory Control over the EU Financial Markets: Lessons from Five Years On' (2013) 62 *International and Comparative Law Quarterly* 955

J SNELL, 'Non-Discriminatory Tax Obstacles in Community Law' (2007) 56 *International and Comparative Law Quarterly* 339

---

[248] See Directive 2009/14/EC of the European Parliament and of the Council of 11 March 2009 amending Directive 94/19/EC on deposit-guarantee schemes as regards the coverage level and the payout delay (OJ [2009] L68/3) and, more importantly, the revisions to the Directive agreed at the end of 2013 (http://europa.eu/rapid/press-release_MEMO-13-1176_en.htm?locale=en (*EUROPA*, 17 December 2013)) which maintain the deposit guarantee of €100,000; but the new rules will better coordinate the way governments arrange for that insurance to be paid (http://www.ft.com/cms/s/0/ee398a08-67ad-11e3-8ada-00144feabdc0.html#axzz2oDZdn5ka (*ft.com*, 18 December 2013)).

[249] http://europa.eu/rapid/press-release_MEMO-13-1140_en.htm?locale=en (see n 193).

[250] Regulation (EU) No 575/2013 on prudential requirements for credit institutions and investment firms and amending Regulation (EU) No 648/2012 (OJ [2013] L176/1); and Directive 2013/36/EU on access to the activity of credit institutions and the prudential supervision of credit institutions and investment firms, amending Directive 2002/87/EC and repealing Directives 2006/48/EC and 2006/49/EC (OJ [2013] L176/338).

[251] European Commission, 'A Roadmap towards a Banking Union', COM(2012) 510 final, p 5, http://eur-lex.europa.eu/LexUriServ/LexUriServ.do?uri=COM:2012:0510:FIN:EN:PDF

J Tiley and G Loutzenhiser, *Advanced Topics in Revenue Law: Corporation Tax; International and European Tax; Savings; Charities* (Oxford: Hart Publishing, 2013)

T Tridimas, 'EU Financial Regulation: Federalization, Crisis Management, and Law Reform' in P Craig and G de Búrca, *The Evolution of EU Law* (2nd edn, Oxford: Oxford University Press, 2011)

Chapter acknowledgements

I am grateful to Julian Ghosh, Chris Kuner, Marios Koutsias, Steve Peers, and Vassilis Hatzopoulos for their advice. Jukka Snell kindly provided the section on financial services. Some sections of this chapter first appeared in the report for the UK government's balance of competence review on services.

15

Free movement of capital

Leo Flynn

1 Introduction

From the signature of the Treaty of Rome in 1957 until 31 December 1992, the focus of European integration was the common market, later known as the internal market. Since the signature of the Maastricht Treaty in 1992 and arguably for the foreseeable future, the focus of European integration has become the development of the eurozone, as the chief incarnation of economic and monetary union (EMU).[1] Free movement of capital is central to both market integration and to EMU. Without it, neither is possible.

EU law on the free movement of capital was, relative to the other internal market freedoms, comparatively underdeveloped until the end of the 1980s. Since then, however, there

---

[1] See more generally chapter 19.

has been a major shift in its role. The completion of the single market, targeted for 31 December 1992, involved a liberalization of the rules on capital movement. Shortly afterwards, with the entry into force of the Maastricht Treaty, those liberalized rules became a core element of a new step in European integration – the creation of the single currency and the institutions charged with managing EMU.

This chapter will first consider the development of the current rules on capital, focusing on their material scope, direct effect, and role in relation to third countries. It will then explain how the concept of restrictions, which is a feature of all internal market freedoms, operates in relation to capital. The chapter will next deal with the power of Member States to limit capital flows between different parts of the Union, as well as into and out of the Union. Finally, it will examine the effects of case law regarding capital movement in relation to philanthropic and charitable activities, in order to see how the free movement of capital affects the ability of Member States to design the instruments by which they organize the delivery of services they consider are in the public interest.

Two themes will be evident in this chapter. One of them is the extent of the role of free movement of capital in EMU and whether this gives rise to differences in regard to that particular free movement when compared with the other freedoms which only have a part to play in the creation of the internal market. The other, which is applicable to all of the freedoms underpinning the internal market, is the extent to which national conceptions of public interest must be recalibrated in order to take account of constraints which the free movement of capital places on the choices and priorities of the Member States. When national authorities view public interest objectives primarily in the framework of the national territory, does the case law on free movement of capital force them into either abandoning those goals or else 'Europeanizing' them?

2 The legal framework and its origins

2.1 The evolution of the original rules on capital

In relation to free movement of capital and EMU in EU law, it is important to bear in mind that many of the key developments in that field have economic as opposed to legal origins, most of which have their foundations in the international monetary system. In order to see why certain features of the law on free movement of capital take the form they do, it is worth surveying that evolution.

2.1.1 Bretton Woods and the post-Second World War international monetary environment

The original Treaty of Rome establishing the EEC included only minor provisions for monetary cooperation between its six founding Member States. They all participated in the Bretton Woods international monetary system set up in 1944. That system was based on the gold standard and established fixed exchange rates with a mechanism for adjustments when necessary. Since the Bretton Woods system was intended to create monetary stability in the world economy following the upheavals of the Great Depression and the Second World War, a parallel system in Europe seemed unnecessary.

2.1.2 The pre-Maastricht rules on capital

The rules in the EEC Treaty on capital and payments were in two separate parts of the Treaty. Capital was governed by Articles 67 to 73 EEC, while payments were dealt with in Article 104 EEC.

Article 67(1) EEC obliged Member States to 'progressively abolish between themselves all restrictions on the movement of capital belonging to persons resident in Member States and any discrimination based on nationality or on the place of residence of the parties or on the place where such capital is invested.' However, that obligation was a qualified one: Article 67(1) EEC laid down the duty of abolition 'to the extent necessary to ensure the proper functioning of the common market'. There was, moreover, no express standstill clause, prohibiting the introduction of new restrictions. Those limitations on the freedom were later pointed to by the Court when it ruled in *Casati* in 1981 that Article 67(1) EEC did not have direct effect, in contrast with its counterparts on goods, workers, establishment, and services.[2]

Article 69 EEC provided a legal base for directives for the progressive implementation of Article 67 EEC. There was significant legislative activity in the early 1960s:

- the First Capital Directive[3] was adopted in 1960, and
- the Second Capital Directive[4] was adopted in 1962.

Those Directives divided transactions involving capital into different categories, in the form of a Nomenclature divided into four lists. Transactions within List A were to be completely liberalized while national restrictions were permitted for those in the other parts, with the limitations varying in permissible intensity. In that early period, the trend was for the Capital Directives to introduce greater liberalization of capital movements.

2.1.3 The growth of monetary instability from the 1960s onwards and European responses

In the late 1960s, currency instability became an increasing feature in international monetary relations. As the Bretton Woods system began to show signs of weakness, which threatened monetary stability in Europe, pressure grew within the EEC for a new framework to provide greater currency stability at the European level. As a result, in December 1969, at the Hague Summit, the heads of State and government decided to make EMU an explicit goal of the Community and set up a high-level group to examine how to achieve it, chaired by Luxembourg's Prime Minister, Pierre Werner.

The resulting Werner Report, issued in October 1970, proposed a three-stage plan to create an economic and monetary union within a decade. The principal economic as well as monetary policy decisions would be taken at Community level and certain policy responsibilities would, therefore, be transferred from the national level. In addition to fixing currency conversion rates and the creation of a single currency and a single monetary policy, EMU would foster harmonization and ultimately unification of economic policies at Community level. It would include control over the essential features of Member States' national budgets, and involve the creation of corresponding Community institutions, including a Committee of Central Bank Governors and a body to take decisions regarding economic policy, politically responsible to a reformed European Parliament.

---

[2] Case 203/80 *Casati* [1981] ECR 2515.

[3] First Directive of 11 May 1960 for the implementation of Article 67 of the Treaty (OJ [1960] L9/21; English Special Edition, Series I, Chapter 1959–62, p 49).

[4] Second Council Directive 63/21/EEC of 18 December 1962 adding to and amending the First Directive for the implementation of Article 67 of the Treaty (OJ [1963] L9/62; English Special Edition, Series I, Chapter 1963–4, p 5).

In 1971, the Bretton Woods system effectively collapsed, ending the fixed exchange-rate regime and bringing about a wave of instability on foreign exchanges. The EMU project was temporarily abandoned. Instead, in April 1972, the six Member States set up a so-called 'snake in the tunnel' mechanism to narrow the fluctuation margins between the Community currencies (the snake) in relation to fluctuations against the US dollar (the tunnel).

Against the background of growing international monetary turmoil from the mid-1960s onwards, although the Commission attempted to bring about greater liberalization of capital movement, the Council could not agree on such measures. A draft Third Capital Directive was proposed in 1964, amended in 1967, and after almost a decade of stasis was withdrawn by the Commission in 1976. Indeed, in 1972 the Council adopted Directive 72/156, based on Articles 70 and 103 EEC, which allowed for *greater restrictions* to be introduced on capital movements.

2.1.4 The foundations of EMU: the SEA and the Delors Report

In 1978, following a Franco-German initiative, the Community decided to relaunch monetary integration at the Brussels European Council by creating a European Monetary System (EMS), with the objectives of stabilizing exchange rates, reducing inflation, and preparing for monetary integration. The EMS entered into force in March 1979.

As part of the drive to complete the internal market which began with the adoption of the 1985 White Paper, legislative moves to liberalize capital movement were relaunched. In 1988 the Third Capital Directive[5] was adopted, repealing the first two Directives of the 1960s. That Directive shared the structure of its predecessors, with a nomenclature annexed to the Directive which set out various transactions involving capital. However, it introduced full liberalization, along with a series of exceptions on specific grounds. The Court ruled in *Bordessa* that the prohibition on restrictions on capital movements in the Third Capital Directive was directly effective.[6]

With the adoption of the Single European Act (SEA) in 1986, monetary cooperation was included as a new area of Community competence. The establishment of the internal market brought a new stimulus to the idea of a single currency. At Hanover in June 1988 the European Council concluded that 'in adopting the Single Act, the Member States of the Community confirmed the objective of progressive realisation of economic and monetary union.' A committee was set up under the chairmanship of Commission President Jacques Delors with 'the task of studying and proposing concrete steps leading towards this union'.

The following year, in April 1989, the Delors Report set out a plan to introduce EMU over three stages, including an institutional framework to allow policy to be decided and executed at the Community level in economic areas of direct relevance for the functioning of EMU. It included the creation of a monetary institution, namely a European System of Central Banks (ESCB), which would become responsible for formulating and implementing monetary policy as well as managing external exchange-rate policy. Unlike the Werner Plan, the Delors Report envisaged that the coordination of economic policy could be carried out within the existing institutional framework.

Most of the ideas set out in the Delors Report later formed the basis for the EMU provisions agreed in the Maastricht Treaty. The Delors Report was adopted by the

---

[5] Third Capital Directive 88/361/EEC (OJ [1988] L178/5).
[6] Joined Cases C-358/93 and 416/93 *Bordessa* [1995] ECR I-361.

Madrid European Council, which decided to launch the first stage of EMU on 1 July 1990.[7]

When the EEC Treaty was amended by the Maastricht Treaty in order to allow for Stages Two and Three of EMU as envisaged by the Delors Report, the Treaty's authors took the provisions of the Third Capital Directive and rewrote them in the form of what are now Articles 63 to 66 TFEU. As a result, the Court continues to refer to the Third Capital Directive in litigation relating to those new provisions.

2.2 Overview of the current provisions

The provisions relating to free movement of capital are found in Title IV of the TFEU, in Articles 63 to 66 TFEU. Those provisions are significantly more liberal than their predecessors in the EEC Treaty, Articles 67 to 73 EEC, which were repealed by the Treaty of Amsterdam.

Article 63 TFEU prohibits all restrictions on the movement of capital, as well as on payments, between Member States and between Member States and third countries. By virtue of free movement of capital, individuals and companies can, for example, transport cash; open, make deposits into and withdrawals from, and close bank accounts; take out loans; register mortgages; buy and sell shares; receive dividends; or obtain and give gifts. They can invoke the free movement of capital to carry out any of those transactions across borders – and, unusually for the four freedoms, that border need not be the frontier between two Member States: it can be between a Member State and a third country.

Several limitations then follow the basic principle of free movement set out in Article 63 TFEU – a 'grandfather clause'[8] relating to third country-directed restrictions (Article 64 TFEU) and an exceptions clause (Article 65 TFEU).

Article 64(1) TFEU allows Member States and the Union to keep in place specific types of rules affecting free movement of capital to and from third countries that were already in place on a certain cut-off date (31 December 1993 for all Member States except Bulgaria, Estonia, and Hungary, for which the relevant date was 31 December 1999) even though those rules contravene Article 63 TFEU. For example, if Spain had legislation dating to 1980 that prevented foreigners from purchasing real estate in certain regions, it would be entitled to maintain those rules, but only in respect of third country nationals.

Article 64(1) TFEU provides that Article 63 TFEU

> shall be without prejudice to the application to third countries of any restrictions which existed on 31 December 1993 under national or Union law adopted in respect of the movement of capital to or from third countries involving direct investment – including in real estate – establishment, the provision of financial services or the admission of securities to capital markets. In the cases of Bulgaria, Estonia and Hungary, the relevant date is 31 December 1999.

Article 65 TFEU is similar to Articles 36, 45(3), and 52 TFEU. It sets out grounds for an express exception to the basic principle of free movement. Article 65(1)(a) TFEU allows the Member States to apply provisions of their tax law which distinguish between

---

[7] See further chapter 19.

[8] A grandfather clause is a provision in which an old rule continues to apply to some existing situations, while a new rule will apply to all future cases.

taxpayers who are not in the same situation with regard to their place of residence or with regard to the place where their capital is invested. Article 65(1)(b) TFEU permits Member States to, inter alia, take measures which are justified on grounds of public policy or public security.

Article 66 TFEU allows safeguard measures to be taken by the Council in order to deal with exceptional circumstances in which movements of capital to or from third countries cause, or threaten to cause, serious difficulties for the operation of EMU. Such measures with regard to third countries may last for up to six months and must be strictly necessary.

Prior to the entry into force of the Lisbon Treaty in 2009, the rules on capital set out powers relating to freezing of assets, within Article 60 EC. That provision is now to be found, as Article 75 TFEU, in the part of the TFEU concerning freedom, security, and justice.

3 Material scope of the capital rules

3.1 Defining capital

The TFEU contains almost no elements indicating what comes within the material scope of the free movement of capital, unlike, for example, the indications offered in Article 57 TFEU about services.[9]

Capital movements cover, in essence, those resources used for, or capable of, investment intended to generate revenue. That term covers, for example, cash, bonds and other debt instruments, and shares.

However, it not only covers resources in the form of money but also in kind, such as a gift of a washing machine[10] or the loan of a car.[11] The notion of capital is, in that context, opposed to that of 'current payments', which covers all financial dealings relating to trade in goods and services between the residents of a country and individuals residing in the rest of the world. The distinction between capital and current payments was accepted in *Luisi and Carbone*,[12] in which the Court referred to the existence of different Treaty provisions dealing with each of those notions.

The Court has given indications of what is meant by 'capital'. In some cases, it rules on the point without any particular reasoning being offered. However, the Court has more often invoked the provisions of the Third Capital Directive, together with the Nomenclature annexed to that Directive, to define what constitutes a capital movement.[13] Relying on the Third Capital Directive, the Court has classified the following situations as implicating the free movement of capital:

- investments in and transfers of immovable property,[14]

- acquisition of shares or securities in the capital markets,[15] and

- receipt of dividends.[16]

---

[9] See further chapters 13 and 14.   [10] Case C-318/07 *Persche* [2009] ECR I-359.
[11] Joined Cases C-578–580/10 *van Putten, Mook and Frank*, judgment of 26 April 2012, nyr.
[12] Case 286/82 [1984] ECR 377, paras 21 and 22.
[13] Case C-222/97 *Trummer and Mayer* [1999] ECR I-1661, paras 20 and 21.
[14] Case C-302/97 *Konle* [1999] ECR I-3099, para 22; Joined Cases C-519–524/99 and C-526–540/99 *Reisch* [2002] ECR I-2157, para 30.   [15] Case C-98/01 *Commission v UK* [2003] ECR I-4641, paras 39–41.
[16] Case C-35/98 *Verkooijen* [2000] ECR I-4071, paras 27–30; Case C-319/02 *Maninen* [2004] ECR I-7477.

Advocate General Colomer severely criticized that feature of the Court's reasoning in his joint Opinion on *UK Golden Shares* and *Spanish Golden Shares*, when he stated that

> in order to give substance to the terms 'movements of capital' and 'payments', the Court of Justice must turn to the hallowed techniques of interpretation. To my mind it is particularly inappropriate to use secondary legislation for the purposes of ascertaining the meaning of one of the fundamental freedoms laid down in the Treaty.

However, the Court did not let his admonition deflect it from maintaining its approach.[17]

3.2 Relationship with other Treaty freedoms

It can be difficult to establish a 'bright line' which separates free movement of capital and the other Treaty freedoms. However, the significance of such a division has diminished greatly with the development of case law on capital which is extremely similar to that of its counterparts, most notably through the market access/restrictions approach.[18] Even so, on at least two points, the division may be quite important:

- first, until it is clear whether the rules on capital are horizontally directly effective, in actions between private law persons, knowing whether the relevant EU rules are those on free movement of persons, for example, and not capital, could be crucial.

- secondly, because free movement of capital, unlike all other internal market freedoms, potentially applies to movements to and from third countries, it can again be vital to determine which Treaty freedom(s) can be invoked.

The Treaty does not exclude the concurrent application of free movement of capital and other Treaty freedoms. Indeed, Article 65(2) TFEU implicitly allows an overlap between the freedoms:

> The provisions of this chapter [on capital and payments] shall be without prejudice to the applicability of restrictions on the right of establishment which are compatible with the Treaty.

That overlap will be discussed in the next sections.

3.2.1 Capital and payments/goods

The relationship between free movement of goods and free movement of capital is relatively unexplored. As noted earlier, the Court has clarified that the tax treatment of charitable gifts is covered by free movement of capital, even if they are made in kind in the form of everyday consumer goods.[19] The Court had already analysed the tax treatment of gifts to third persons resident in another Member State in the context of inheritances and legacies,[20] ruling that the tax treatment of transferred assets, which can include both sums of money and

---

[17] See *Commission v UK* (n 15) para 39 and Case C-463/00 *Commission v Spain* [2003] ECR I-4581, para 52, where the Court indicated that the method of interpretation criticized by the AG was in line with 'settled case-law'.   [18] See the discussion on that point in chapter 13.

[19] *Persche* (n 10) paras 25 and 29.

[20] See Case C-364/01 *Barbier* [2003] ECR I-15013; Case C-513/03 *van Hilten-van der Heijden* [2006] ECR I-1957; Case C-11/07 *Eckelkamp* [2008] ECR I-6845; Case C-43/07 *Arens-Sikken* [2008] ECR I-6887; Case C-67/08 *Block* [2009] ECR I-883; Case C-35/08 *Grundstückgemeinschaft Busley v Ciprian* [2009] ECR I-9807; Case C-510/08 *Mattner* [2010] ECR I-3553; and Case C-132/10 *Halley* [2011] ECR I-8353.

movable and immovable property, comes within Article 63 TFEU. It therefore rejected the claim which the Greek government had advanced with particular strength in *Persche*, that a gift of consumer goods should be analysed in relation to free movement of goods.

The cleavage between goods and payments, on the other hand, has been well examined. In *Thompson*,[21] the Court ruled that 'means of payment are not to be regarded as goods falling within the provisions of Articles [34 to 37 TFEU]'. The same view was taken in *Bordessa*, where the Court ruled that banknotes do not constitute goods.

3.2.2 Capital and payments/persons

The relationship between free movement of capital and free movement of persons gives rise to discussion mainly in relation to freedom of establishment. However, issues relating to the free movement of workers can surface in a case on capital. For example, as a result of the Second Capital Directive, savings repatriated by migrant workers returning to their home Member State appeared in List A of the original Nomenclature.

In *Barbier*, dealing with an assessment of the value of a non-resident's estate for inheritance tax purposes, the Court, having analysed under the rubric of capital a rule limiting favourable treatment of the value of immovable property to residents, stated:

> It follows from the foregoing that it is not necessary to examine the questions referred for a preliminary ruling in so far as they concern freedom of movement for persons. Suffice it to point out in that regard that the tax consequences in respect of inheritance rights are among the considerations which a national of a Member State could reasonably take into account when deciding whether or not to make use of the freedom of movement provided for in the Treaty.[22]

3.2.3 Capital and payments/establishment and services

The freedoms to provide services (whether on a permanent basis, under Article 49 TFEU, or on a temporary basis, under Article 56 TFEU) and of capital movement are the hardest to separate of all the market freedoms.[23]

As to the *freedom of establishment*, the judgments of the Court are often ambiguous as to when the rules on capital, establishment, or both should be applied. There is an unusual degree of clarity in *Reisch*, where the Court stated that

> as is apparent from Article [50(2)(e) TFEU], the right to acquire, use or dispose of immovable property on the territory of another Member State, which is the corollary of freedom of establishment, … generates capital movements when it is exercised.[24]

However, in cases that do not involve immovable property, the Court's position has been less categorical.

The Court initially avoided addressing issues relating to free movement of capital in cases which also concerned freedom of establishment. Greater certainty seems to have emerged in the last decade on the question of how those freedoms are to be divided, to the extent that the Court has been able to deal with it by means of a reasoned order in one case.[25] In several rulings the Court has reiterated that national provisions fall within

---

[21] Case 7/78 *R v Thompson* [1978] ECR 2247, paras 25–27.

[22] *Barbier* (n 20) para 75.

[23] See Art 65(1)(a) and (2) TFEU, as well as the second sentence of Art 49 TFEU.

[24] *Reisch* (n 14) para 29.

[25] Case C-268/03 *De Baeck* [2004] ECR I-5961.

the material scope of the rules on establishment where they concern shareholdings which give rise to a certain influence on the decisions of the company and help to determine its activities. If such national rules have restrictive effects on the free movement of capital, such effects are to be considered as the inescapable consequence of the possible restriction on the freedom of establishment and so there is no need to examine those rules in light of Articles 63 to 65 TFEU.[26]

Holböck[27] and *Scheunemann*[28] provide examples of how the dividing line between capital movement and establishment is determined.

In *Holböck*, an Austrian taxpayer in receipt of dividends from a company in Switzerland objected to the taxation of those dividends in Austria at the full income tax rate when dividends distributed to natural persons by companies established in Austria were subject to tax at half the average rate. The Court noted that the Austrian legislation in question was not intended to apply only to those shareholdings which enable the holder to have a definite influence on a company's decisions and to determine its activities. Such legislation could, therefore, fall under free movement of capital or freedom of establishment.

That ruling can be contrasted with *Scheunemann* regarding a German taxpayer who had inherited her father's shares in a Canadian firm of which he was sole shareholder. She sought to benefit from exemptions on inheritance tax available if a legacy in the form of shares made up more than one-quarter of the total shares in a firm and if the legatee retained those shares for more than five years. She argued that the rule was intended to deal with capital movements (in the form of inheritances). The Court accepted the argument of the German government that the threshold of one-quarter of the shares in a firm was intended to ensure that only persons running a business obtained the tax exemption. Since it was decisive to have control over the firm, the freedom of establishment was relevant (which is not applicable to situations involving third countries).

As to the *freedom to provide and receive services*, there are extremely close links between the Treaty chapters on services and on capital and payments. For example, Article 58(2) TFEU provides that the liberalization of banking and insurance services connected with movement of capital shall be effected in step with liberalization of movement of capital. On the other hand, the personal scope differs between the Treaty provisions on services and on capital. Free movement of capital grants the same rights to EU citizens and third country nationals.[29] The freedom to provide services does not. Unlike the free movement of capital, the services rules can be relied on only by Union citizens.

In *Safir*, Advocate General Tesauro expressed concern that the cumulative application of provisions relating to two or more freedoms might undermine the framework for each one envisaged by the Treaty, as a result of the distinctions between them.[30] He proposed to the Court that it should resolve the problem by focusing on the monetary nature or otherwise of the restriction. Thus, if the measure at issue directly affected the transfer of capital, rendering it impossible or more difficult, the rules on capital would apply. In opposition, if the rule only indirectly restricted movement of capital and primarily

---

[26] See Case C-196/04 *Cadbury Schweppes and Cadbury Schweppes Overseas* [2006] ECR I-7995, para 33; Case C-524/04 *Test Claimants in the Thin Cap Group Litigation* [2007] ECR I-2107, para 34; and Case C-415/06 *Stahlwerk Ergste Westig* [2007] ECR I-151* Summ pub, para 16.

[27] Case C-157/05 *Holböck* [2007] ECR I-4051.

[28] Case C-31/11 *Scheunemann*, judgment of 19 July 2012, nyr.

[29] Case C-484/93 *Svensson and Gustavsson* [1995] ECR I-3955.

[30] Case C-118/96 *Safir* [1998] ECR I-1897, Opinion of AG Tesauro, points 9–19.

constituted a non-monetary restriction on the freedom to provide services, the rules on services would apply.[31]

The Court simultaneously applied the services and capital rules in *Italian recruitment agencies*,[32] where the Commission claimed that an obligation imposed on undertakings providing for temporary workers to lodge a guarantee with a bank having its seat or a branch in Italy violated both the capital and services rules. Having stated that the guarantee requirement was in itself a restriction on employment agencies' freedom to provide services, the Court ruled that the obligation to lodge the guarantee with a bank established in Italy was both a restriction on capital movement from the employment agency's perspective and discrimination, within the meaning of Article 56 TFEU, against banks established in other Member States. Thus, the same rule was, from the standpoint of the two different groups affected by it, a violation of both freedoms. That analysis dispels disquiet about the concurrent application of the two freedoms because they are applied to different aspects of the rule's material effects.[33]

In *Fidium Finanz*, the Court again had to examine the relationship between the two freedoms.[34] German legislation provided that any person carrying out banking activities in Germany had to obtain written authorization from the Bundesanstalt für Finanzdienstleistungsaufsicht (the BaFin). Such authorization was to be refused to companies that did not have their central administration or a branch in Germany. Fidium Finanz was a company incorporated under Swiss law with its registered office and central administration in Switzerland. It granted small loans over the internet to clients abroad, most of whom were in Germany. Fidium Finanz did not have the authorization required to carry on those activities in Germany. Consequently, the BaFin prohibited it from carrying on lending activities targeted at customers in Germany.

The Court held that such rules fall within the provisions on the freedom to provide services, not the free movement of capital. Companies established in non-member countries are not entitled to rely on the freedom to provide services. The Court acknowledged that the activity of granting credit on a commercial basis concerns, in principle, the rules on both services and capital. Consequently, it considered to what extent the German rules affected the exercise of those two freedoms. It held that the requirement of approval and the fact that it is impossible to get such approval if the company does not have its main administration or a branch in Germany effectively impeded access to the German financial market for companies established in non-member countries.

However, such rules affect primarily the freedom to provide services. It is certainly possible that by making financial services offered by companies established in non-member countries less accessible for clients established in Germany, there will be a reduction in cross-border financial traffic relating to those services. However, that restrictive effect on capital movements was merely an unavoidable consequence of the restriction imposed as regards the provision of services. Since Article 56 TFEU cannot be invoked by natural or legal persons from outside the Union, and since the freedom to provide services was the only relevant freedom for examining the German legislation, it was not necessary to examine the compatibility of the German rules with the free movement of capital.

---

[31] For an approach similar to that proposed by AG Tesauro, see Case C-356/08 *Commission v Austria* [2009] ECR I-108* Summ pub and Case C-602/10 *SC Volksbank România*, judgment of 12 July 2012, nyr.

[32] Case C-279/00 *Commission v Italy* [2002] ECR I-1425, paras 37 and 38.

[33] See also, for a similar approach, Case C-531/06 *Commission v Italy* ('*Italian pharmacists*') [2009] ECR I-4103 and Case C-233/09 *Dijkman and Dijkman-Levaleije* [2010] ECR I-6649.

[34] Case C-452/04 *Fidium Finanz* [2006] ECR I-9521.

4 Personal and geographical scope of the capital rules

4.1 Against whom can the capital rules be invoked?

As the prohibition contained in Article 63(1) TFEU is framed in a clear and imperative way, it obviously lends itself to creating direct effects. Indeed, it is clearer than its counterpart in the Third Capital Directive, Article 1, which was ruled by the Court in *Bordessa* to be capable of direct effect. The Court was, therefore, willing to hold that Article 63(1) TFEU had direct effect in relation to third country capital movements in *Sanz de Lera*.[35] In *Pension funds communication* the Court, in relation to the Treaty rules on capital, services, and establishment, stated that

> while those provisions, which have direct effect, prohibit imposing unjustified restrictions on the freedoms concerned, they are not sufficient in themselves to ensure the elimination of all obstacles to free movement of persons, services and capital.[36]

It is, therefore, clear that the free movement of capital is capable of vertical direct effect.

By contrast, the issue of horizontal direct effect of the capital rules has not been definitively addressed by the Court to date. Most case law on capital deals with legislative and administrative measures adopted by the Member States. The application of that freedom to acts of the Member States which are unrelated to their official authority has been raised in the case law but it has not been necessary for the Court to explore the issue. Clearly, the Member States can deal with assets that constitute capital in the same way as any private person would, as a promoter, borrower, lender, guarantor, or other non-regulatory participant on the security markets. The Belgian government argued the point in *Belgian Eurobonds*, claiming that a Eurobond issue, to which Belgian residents were prohibited from subscribing, was a market transaction in which it had acted as a private borrower, not as a public authority.[37] It argued that in limiting access to a Eurobond issue to investors who did not reside in Belgium, it had behaved in the same way as any borrower so as to maintain a standard feature of such issues, the waiver of withholding tax on interest. It claimed that there had, therefore, been no 'restriction'. The Court held that because the waiver of tax was provided for in a regulatory measure that only the State as a public authority could take, that claim was not made out.[38] Therefore, on the facts before it, the Court was dealing with a classic situation of vertical direct effect.

In *Federconsumatori*, the Court was asked about provisions in Italy's company law legislation which allowed public authorities holding shares in a company that had previously been publicly owned directly to appoint one or more members of the company's board.[39] Investors in a formerly publicly owned firm opposed a proposal by the municipality of Milan, which held shares in that firm, that it be entitled to name a proportion of the firm's directors based on the proportion of shares it held. That proposal was accepted by the firm's shareholders at its general meeting.

The Court, however, considered (based on the findings of the national court which had referred the issue to it) that the municipality's entitlement was a derogation from standard

---

[35] Joined Cases C-163/94, 165/94 and 250/94 *Sanz de Lera* [1995] ECR I-4821.
[36] Case C-64/95 *Commission v France* [1997] ECR I-627, para 20.
[37] Case C-478/98 *Commission v Belgium* [2000] ECR I-7587, paras 22–26.
[38] See also *Commission v UK* (n 15) paras 48 and 49.
[39] Joined Cases C-463/04 and C-464/04 *Federconsumatori* [2007] ECR I-10419.

company law, in that it could only be granted to the State or public bodies holding shares in a firm. It was not removed from the field of application of Article 63 TFEU merely because that entitlement had been placed by the national legislator in the company law code. Admittedly, the right of nomination was not conferred by statute directly on the public bodies in question since it depended on a decision of the shareholders in a general meeting. However, it was only by reason of the statutory provision that a public shareholder could, unlike a private shareholder, obtain the right to participate in the company's board with greater influence than its shareholding would ordinarily allow.[40] As a result, the Court again refused to accept that the national rule was only the result of private law.

The manner in which Article 63 TFEU applies to measures which are not dependent on public law powers has thus not been resolved, and the closely entwined issue of horizontal direct effect for Article 63 TFEU is also open.

4.2 When can an EU national invoke the capital rules against their own Member State?

To date, the Court has never applied free movement of capital to a fact situation which is entirely without a single Member State ('a wholly internal situation'). However, as with the other freedoms, once a cross-border element is in place, a national of a Member State is free to invoke the Treaty's provisions against their own national authorities. It can be seen in *Barbier*, where the Court examined the Treaty's impact on Dutch legislation on the assessment of tax due on the inheritance of immovable property.

In the Netherlands, the tax authorities were required to reduce inheritance tax where the deceased person holding legal title had been under an unconditional obligation to transfer the property to another person who had financial ownership of that property but only if, at the time of his death, the owner of the legal title resided in that Member State. As a result, the heirs of Mr Barbier, a Dutch national holding property in the Netherlands and resident in Belgium at the time of his death, were not entitled to carry out such a reduction. The cross-border element here was the investment in property in the Netherlands from Belgium and the Court stated that 'the rights... are not subject to the existence of other cross-border elements'.[41]

4.3 Third countries

The free movement of capital is applicable throughout the entire territory of the Union. The persons invoking it need not be nationals of a Member State, as can be seen from *Svensson and Gustaffson* and *Bordessa*, in both of which third country nationals invoked that freedom; nor is it necessary that the currencies be those of a Member State.

Article 63 TFEU is unique amongst the internal market freedoms in that it clearly covers third country transactions, treating capital movements into, out of, and within the Union in the same way. By contrast, goods originating outside the Member States cannot claim the benefit of free movement between Member States until they have cleared the Union's common customs frontier, workers must have the nationality of one of the Member States in order to benefit from Article 45 TFEU, and Articles 49 and 56 TFEU refer to 'nationals of a Member State' and 'nationals of Member States' exclusively when they create the freedoms of establishment and of provision and receipt of services.

---

[40] See also Case C-112/05 *Commission v Germany* [2007] ECR I-8995.
[41] *Barbier* (n 20) para 59.

Although the basic freedom enunciated in Article 63(1) TFEU deals with external capital movements in the same broad terms as are used for intra-Union capital movements, the existence of Articles 64 and 66 TFEU clearly creates a less liberalized framework. Even so, that limitation did not prevent the Court from ruling that ex Article 73B(1) EC was capable of direct effect with regard to third country capital movements in *Sanz de Lera*.

On the other hand, the Court seems careful not to venture views on third country currencies unnecessarily; for example, although in *Trummer and Mayer* the question referred by the national court was drafted in terms of 'foreign currencies', the Court transformed it to 'currency of another Member State'.[42] Such a re-characterization of the factual context at issue before the Court proved quite important in *Maninen*, where Member States argued that practical difficulties in obtaining information about the tax treatment of dividends issued in another country justified limiting a tax credit system designed to prevent double taxation of dividends issued by Finnish companies.[43] The Court responded that the case before it did not in any way concern the free movement of capital between Member States and non-member countries.

As we saw in section 3.2.3, the main arguments in *Fidium Finanz* turned on the fact that the free movement of capital provisions apply to third countries as well as to the Member States. When it challenged Germany's authorization requirement, the Swiss-established firm, Fidium Finanz, could only invoke the EU provisions governing the free movement of capital. Because the Court based its review of the German authorization requirement on the right to provide services and not on the right of free movement of capital, it denied any extension of free movement rights to the Swiss firm.

The Court returned to the issue in *A*, a reference on Sweden's tax treatment of dividends received in that country which originated from a company in Switzerland.[44] Dividends distributed in the form of shares in a subsidiary of the company making the dividend could be exempt from income tax in Sweden. Sweden only granted the exemption where the distributing company was established in a European Economic Area (EEA) country or a third country with which Sweden had concluded an information-exchange agreement. It did not have such an agreement with Switzerland. In the ensuing case before the Court it was argued that Article 63 TFEU only had direct effect as regards third countries in relation to categories of capital movement not covered by Article 64(1) TFEU.

The Court disagreed, holding that Article 64(1) TFEU did not affect the direct effect of the capital rules. It was also argued that the concept of restriction should be treated differently in relation to third countries than in relation to Member States. The Court did not accept the view that for movement between Member States, free movement of capital was linked to the completion of the internal market, while for movement to and from third countries it was related to economic and monetary union.

The same concept of 'restriction' therefore applies whether the movement is between Member States or between a Member State and a third country. However, the Court noted that whether a restriction is justified may vary depending on whether it applies to intra-Union capital movements or movements involving third countries. It went on to hold that since the award of the exemption was dependent on certain conditions being fulfilled and since third countries were not bound to provide information which would allow the national tax authorities to verify if the taxpayer met those conditions, it was justifiable to impose such a restriction on capital movements from Switzerland.

---

[42] *Trummer and Mayer* (n 13). See also Case C-367/98 *Commission v Portugal* [2002] ECR I-4731.
[43] *Maninen* (n 16).
[44] Case C-101/05 *A* [2007] ECR I-11531.

4.3.1 Defining a 'third country'

Finally, the question of what constitutes a 'third country' has also surfaced. In *Ospelt*, the Court was faced with the argument that Liechtenstein was a third country for the purpose of Article 64 TFEU so that legislation restricting free movement of capital as regards that country could be maintained insofar as it had been, in substance, in force on 31 December 1993.[45] The cases concerned a refusal to allow a Liechtenstein-resident owner of farmland in Austria to transfer her property to a foundation also established in Liechtenstein because the foundation would not farm the land itself. The Court ruled that since 1 May 1995, the date on which the EEA Agreement entered into force in respect of Liechtenstein, Member States could no longer invoke that provisions vis-à-vis that country because the provisions in that agreement on free movement of capital and discrimination are identical to those under Union law with regard to relations between the Member States. 'Third country', at least for those purposes, thus does not seem to cover Iceland, Liechtenstein, and Norway from the time when the EEA Agreement entered into force there.

On the other hand, in *Fokus Invest*, the Court held that a company formed under Swiss law could not, through a company established under Austrian law, claim an entitlement to purchase real estate in that Member State.[46] Article 64 TFEU allowed the Austrian authorities to retain a restriction on the acquisition of immovable property in the form of an authorization regime.

Lastly, the situation of overseas countries or territories (OCTs), was examined in *Prunus and Polonium* (in that case the British Virgin Islands). In line with previous internal market rulings, the Court confirmed that OCTs only benefit from provisions of EU law in the same manner as Member States when EU law expressly provides that they are to be treated in such a manner. As such, OCTs are treated by Article 64 TFEU as non-Member States.[47]

5 Restrictions

5.1 Equal treatment and non-discrimination

Article 63(1) TFEU prohibits 'restrictions' on the movement of capital and the related provisions on capital only refer to discrimination in Article 65(3) TFEU when limiting the scope of available exceptions. The long-standing debate on restrictions/discrimination which has been a feature in relation to the other Treaty fundamental freedoms[48] does not resonate here. Nevertheless, as will be seen, the case law can be broken down into a typology of measures which is familiar from the jurisprudence on other freedoms.

The Court was directly confronted with the discrimination/restriction distinction in the litigation relating to golden shares.[49] In *UK Golden Shares* the Court reiterated its ruling in *Portuguese Golden Shares*[50] and in *French Golden Shares*[51] that

> the prohibition laid down in Article [63 TFEU] goes beyond the mere elimination of unequal treatment, on grounds of nationality, as between operators on the financial market.[52]

---

[45] Case C-452/01 *Ospelt* [2003] ECR I-9743.   [46] Case C-541/08 *Fokus Invest* [2010] ECR I-1025.
[47] Case C-384/09 *Prunus and Polonium* [2011] ECR I-3319, para 37.   [48] See further chapter 13.
[49] 'Golden shares' refer to a series of control mechanisms used by public authorities in relation to firms which were previously State-owned after their privatization. The classic example would be a single share held by the minister which gives him or her special rights over decisions taken by the firm.
[50] *Commission v Portugal* (n 42) para 44.
[51] Case C-483/99 *Commission v France* [2002] ECR I-4781, para 40.
[52] *Commission v UK* (n 15) para 43.

Thus, the fact that a rule does not discriminate as regards nationals of other Member States and applies without distinction on grounds of nationality does not place it outside the scope of Article 63(1) TFEU.[53]

As a result, the Court has generally refrained from qualifying national measures as being either discriminatory (in relation to the persons involved) or distinctly applicable (in relation to currency in which the capital is denominated or the place where an investment is made). A 2011 ruling on a tax amnesty instituted by Portugal in 2005 illustrates the Court's reluctance to go beyond restriction in most cases.[54] Portugal sought to encourage taxpayers who had not declared their assets to regularize their tax situation, and established that an amnesty would apply for previously undeclared assets that were declared to the tax authorities. The declared assets would be subject to a one-off payment of 5 per cent of their value. However, a lower payment (2.5 per cent) would be imposed if those assets were Portuguese State securities or if the proceeds of the assets were repatriated to Portugal and invested in such State securities. By treating Portuguese bonds more favourably than the securities issued by other Member States, Portugal was found to be in breach of Article 63 TFEU. Limiting the preferential tax treatment to taxpayers holding public debt securities issued by Portugal was held by the Court to be a restriction on free movement of capital, without any comment on its discriminatory character.

5.2 **What constitutes a restriction?**

As already noted, the case law on capital restrictions categorizes measures in a manner familiar from the jurisprudence on other freedoms.

As with the other Treaty market freedoms, a *total ban* will constitute a restriction. In *Belgian Eurobonds*, the Court ruled that a prohibition on Belgian residents acquiring securities of a loan on the Eurobond market was a restriction on the movement of capital.[55]

A *prior authorization system* will also constitute a restriction, one which, moreover, will face difficulties in being considered compatible with the Treaty. In *Reisch*, when faced with a prior authorization regime for purchases of land, the Court stated bluntly that, 'those measures…restrict, by their very purpose, the free movement of capital'.[56] They remain restrictive even where authorization is deemed to have been granted if the transaction is not deferred by the public authorities within a relatively brief period or if failure to request authorization attracts no penalty.[57]

Moving away from specific examples, what features must a national measure have in order to be considered a restriction? In general, the Court's analysis of an alleged restriction turns on the effect of national provisions, notwithstanding the remarks in *Reisch* about purpose. In *Barbier*, the Court offered two independent reasons as to why measures constituted restrictions:

- They discouraged the purchase of immovable property situated in the Member State concerned and the transfer of financial ownership of such property to another person by a resident of another Member State.

---

[53] See also Case C-42/01 *Portugal v Commission* ('*Cimpor takeover*') [2004] ECR I-6079, para 44.
[54] Case C-20/09 *Commission v Portugal* [2011] ECR I-2637.
[55] *Commission v Belgium* (n 37) para 27.
[56] *Reisch* (n 14) para 32.
[57] Case C-54/99 *Église de Scientologie* [2000] ECR I-1335, para 15.

- They also had the effect of reducing the value of the estate of a resident of a Member State other than that in which the property is situated who is in the same position as Mr Barbier.[58]

The dissuasive effect or discouragement inherent in the rule has been the principal basis on which the Court has identified restrictions. In *Verkooijen*, the Court developed the practical application of the dissuasion test.[59] It examined Dutch legislation which refused to extend an exemption from tax to dividends received from shares held in foreign firms, looking at its effects on capital supply and demand. For the provider of the capital, the potential shareholder resident in the Netherlands, it

> has the effect of dissuading nationals of a Member State residing in The Netherlands from investing their capital in companies which have their seat in another Member State.

For the recipient of the capital, such a provision

> also has a restrictive effect...[I]t constitutes an obstacle to the raising of capital in The Netherlands because the dividends...receive less favourable tax treatment...so that their shares are less attractive to investors residing in The Netherlands than shares in companies which have their seat in that Member State.[60]

On the few occasions it has used the additional costs approach, the Court has expressly confirmed that no *de minimis* rule exists as regards free movement of capital.[61]

The central role of deterrence or discouragement can be seen in the infringement action brought by the Commission in respect of the 'VW law'.[62] Under German company law, each share in a public limited company carries one vote. However, the VW law provided that the voting rights of any individual shareholder in the Volkswagen firm were limited to 20 per cent irrespective of the number of shares actually held. The Commission claimed that the VW law constituted an unjustified restriction on the free movement of capital.

The Court accepted that capping shareholders' rights was a recognized instrument of company law. However, it pointed to the key difference between a cap decided on by shareholders themselves and one imposed by means of national legislation from which they could not derogate. Although the cap applied without distinction, it limited the possibility for other shareholders to participate in the company with a view to creating or maintaining lasting and direct economic links with it which would make possible direct participation in the management of the company or in its control. Because of its effects, the VW law was liable to deter investors from other Member States.[63]

---

[58] *Barbier* (n 20) para 62. See also *Trummer and Mayer* (n 13).

[59] *Verkooijen* (n 16).

[60] See also *Commission v Portugal* (n 42) para 45; *Maninen* (n 16) paras 22 and 23; Case C-242/03 *Weidert and Paulus* [2004] ECR I-7379, paras 13 and 14; and Case C-315/02 *Lenz* [2004] ECR I-7063, paras 21 and 22.

[61] *Dijkman and Dijkman-Levaleije* (n 33) para 42. See also Case C-251/98 *Baars* [2000] ECR I-2787, Opinion of AG Alber, point 47.

[62] *Commission v Germany* (n 40).

[63] For similar rulings, see Case C-212/09 *Commission v Portugal* ('*GALP*'), judgment of 10 November 2011, nyr. See also Case C-171/08 *Commission v Portugal* ('*Portugal Telecom*') [2010] ECR I-6813 and Case C-543/08 *Commission v Portugal* ('*EDP*') [2010] ECR I-11421.

6 Exceptions and justifications

6.1 Treaty-based limitations and exceptions

In common with the other internal market freedoms, the basic prohibition on restrictions on the free movement of capital is accompanied by exception clauses. All exceptions to the freedoms are to be interpreted in a narrow fashion and can only be used in a manner that respects the principle of proportionality. The grounds set out in the Treaty on which Member States may limit free movement are essentially common to all the freedoms. It is possible to transpose the reasoning of the Court in relation to those matters from one area to another.[64]

Article 65 TFEU allows action to be taken to limit the free movement of capital within the Union and in relation to third countries. It also covers freedom of payments.

6.1.1 Article 65(1)(a) TFEU: fiscal matters

Article 65(1)(a) TFEU deals with fiscal matters, stating that the provisions of Article 63 shall be without prejudice to the right of Member States to apply the relevant provisions of their tax law between taxpayers who are not in the same situation with regard to their place of residence or with regard to the place where their capital is invested. It must be read in light of Declaration No 7 on the Treaty of European Union in which the 1991 Intergovernmental Conference affirmed that the Member States would apply that exception only with respect to the relevant provisions of their tax law which existed at the end of 1993. However, that Declaration is itself limited to capital movements between the Member States and payments effected between Member States.

The exception has not been invoked very often, but Article 65(1)(a) TFEU was extensively argued in *Verkooijen*, where the Dutch government and the Member States intervening in its support argued that the limitation of a fiscal exemption to those dividends paid on shares in companies established in the Netherlands came within its scope. The Court excluded the applicability of that exception on the basis that the facts in the principal case arose prior to the entry into force of the Maastricht Treaty.[65] However, in an obiter observation, it went on at paragraph 43 to say:

> the possibility granted to the Member States by Article [63(1)(a) TFEU] of applying the relevant provisions of their tax legislation which distinguish between taxpayers according to their place of residence or the place where their capital is invested has already been upheld by the Court. According to that case-law, before the entry into force of Article [63(1)(a) TFEU], national tax provisions of the kind to which that article refers, insofar as they establish certain distinctions based, in particular, on the residence of taxpayers, could be compatible with [EU] law provided that they applied to situations which were not objectively comparable...or could be justified by overriding reasons in the general interest, in particular in relation to the cohesion of the tax system.

The Court, therefore, treats that clause in the way its drafters seem to have intended: as embodying such case law as *Bachmann*[66] and *Schumacker*.[67] *Verkooijen* confirms that the principle of proportionality would, in any event, apply whenever the clause is invoked. The

---

[64] See further chapters 13 and 16.   [65] *Verkooijen* (n 16) para 42.
[66] Case C-204/90 *Bachmann* [1992] ECR I-249. See also Case C-300/90 *Commission v Belgium* [1992] ECR I-305 relating to fiscal cohesion.   [67] Case C-279/93 *Schumacker* [1995] ECR I-225.

Court thereby dismissed the argument raised by some Member States in that case, that the terms of Article 65(3) TFEU – 'The measures and procedures referred to in paragraphs 1 and 2 shall not constitute a means of arbitrary discrimination or a disguised restriction on the free movement of capital' – make clear that the limitation does not apply to Article 65(1)(a), which speaks of 'provisions', rather than 'measures and procedures', of national tax law.

That analysis was further developed in *Maninen*, where the facts arose after Article 65(1)(a) TFEU became applicable. The Court pointed out that it is subject to a restrictive interpretation. It went on to draw a distinction between unequal treatment, which is permitted under Article 65(1)(a) TFEU, and arbitrary discrimination, which is prohibited under Article 65(3) TFEU. In order for unequal treatment of revenue from national dividends and revenue from foreign dividends to be lawful, the Court held that such treatment must concern situations which are not objectively comparable or be justified by overriding reasons in the general interest, with any justification being subject to a strict proportionality test.

In that respect, the situation of a Finnish taxpayer receiving dividends from a Finnish firm was the same as that of a Finnish taxpayer receiving dividends from a Swedish firm; both sources of income could be subject to double taxation because of the manner in which the two tax systems were structured. Moreover, while the principle of territoriality which had been accepted by the Court in relation to freedom of establishment[68] was not relevant in *Maninen*, the Court held that in any event that principle cannot justify different treatment of dividends distributed by Finnish firms and those paid by firms established in other Member States, if the categories of dividends concerned share the same objective situation. The Court went on to reject a justification based on cohesion of the national tax system, as well as to exclude the reduction of tax receipts as a basis for justifying unequal treatment which was not based on objective differences.

6.1.2 Article 65(1)(b) TFEU: general

Article 65(1)(b) TFEU allows Member States to take all requisite measures to prevent infringements of national law and regulations, in particular in the field of taxation and the prudential supervision of financial institutions. It also allows them to lay down procedures for the declaration of capital movements for purposes of administrative or statistical information. Finally, under that provision a Member State may take measures which are justified on grounds of public policy or public security. Article 65(1)(b) TFEU is, in effect, a combination of Article 4 of the Third Capital Directive and Articles 36 and 52 TFEU: the first two sets of exemption come from the Directive, while the final one, relating to public policy and public security, is inspired by the other Treaty provisions.

'[T]o prevent infringements of national law and regulations, in particular in the field of taxation and the prudential supervision of financial institutions'

Nothing similar to that formula is to be found in the other Treaty exception clauses; as such it underlines the very sensitive nature of the free movement of capital. The Member States' power to prevent infringement of national law is set out in a non-exhaustive fashion. In *Bordessa*, the Court, interpreting the equivalent term found in Article 4(1) of the Third Capital Directive, ruled that Member States could take measures necessary to combat illicit activities that are of comparable gravity to those in the fields of fiscal matters and the supervision of financial institutions, such as money-laundering, drug-trafficking, and terrorism.

---

[68] Case C-250/95 *Futura Participations and Singer* [1997] ECR I-2471.

It is open to question whether they would now be considered as falling under the final limb of Article 65(1)(b) TFEU, on public policy and public security.

If public policy and public security are the appropriate bases on which to uphold restrictive national measures outside the field of tax and banking supervision, then the Court might now take a narrower approach to the phrase 'to prevent infringements of national law and regulations' than it took in *Bordessa*. Irrespective of the scope of legislation covered by Article 65(1)(b) TFEU, it is clear from *Konle* that Member States' power to take 'requisite' measures to prevent infringement of laws limits permissible restrictions on capital to those necessary to achieve the goal pursued.

'[T]o lay down procedures for the declaration of capital movements for purposes of administrative or statistical information'

Another example of the relatively broad freedom given to Member States by Article 63(1)(b) TFEU is found in the fact that Member States are expressly authorized to have systematic controls in relation to capital for administrative and statistical purposes. For the other freedoms, no such leeway has been accorded under the Treaty.[69]

'[T]o take measures which are justified on grounds of public policy or public security'

Although the final limb of Article 65(1)(b) TFEU echoes the other exemption clauses in the Treaty, it contains a shorter list of grounds which may be invoked by the Member States. There are no references to public morality or public health, or to official authority. A basic problem that arises here is that the Court traditionally took the view that such provisions should be strictly interpreted and were confined to matters of a non-economic nature. However, many public interest grounds that might be relevant in relation to capital movements could involve economic concerns.

Église de Scientologie, in which a French court asked if a refusal to authorize proposed direct foreign investment in France by adherents of the Church of Scientology was compatible with the Treaty, provided an opportunity to clarify the scope of public policy.[70] Although the national court did not raise that specific point in its reference, the Court followed Advocate General Saggio, who considered it necessary to examine that question when identifying the conditions under which a system of prior authorization could permissibly restrict the free movement of capital. He considered that the jurisprudence developed around that concept in the fields of workers and goods could be transposed to that of capital. As a result, the term would be strictly interpreted, would exclude typically economic interests, and would be subject to control by the Union institutions and by the national courts.

As for public security, that ground arose in *Albore*,[71] in which an Italian court asked if legislation requiring nationals of other Member States to obtain authorization for the acquisition of buildings situated in zones declared to be of 'military importance' while its own nationals had no such obligation was compatible with the freedoms of establishment and capital. The Italian government did not raise public security in its arguments but the Court nevertheless examined the issue in its judgment. The Court, relying on case law related to free movement of goods, stated that public security extends to the external security of the Member State but noted that the concept was subject to the principle of

---

[69] Compare Case 42/82 *Commission v France* [1983] ECR 1013, para 64 (goods) and Case 321/87 *Commission v Belgium* [1989] ECR 997, para 15 (persons).

[70] *Association Église de Scientologie* (n 57).

[71] Case C-423/98 *Albore* [2000] ECR I-5965.

proportionality and could not, in any event, permit arbitrary discrimination. It went on to say that a mere reference to requirements of defence of the national territory could not suffice to bring a national rule that discriminates against nationals of other Member States in access to the property market in some or all of that Member State within the scope of Article 345 TFEU. The position would be different only if it were demonstrated, for each area to which the restriction applied, that non-discriminatory treatment of the nationals of all the Member States would expose the military interests of the Member State concerned to real, specific, and serious risks which could not be countered by less restrictive procedures. The Court left it to the national court to decide, in the case before it, whether there was sufficient justification for the contested restriction.

Public security also arose in *Belgian Golden Shares*.[72] The golden shares in question entitled Belgian authorities to oppose any transfer, use as security, or change in intended use of various strategic assets held by energy distribution firms, and to oppose certain management decisions which were contrary to guidelines on the country's energy policy. The Court held that the objective pursued by the national legislation, safeguarding energy supplies in the event of a crisis, fell within the ambit of a legitimate public interest and specifically within the public security justification in Article 65(1)(b) TFEU. It then went on to examine if the legislation properly responded to a genuine and sufficiently serious threat to a fundamental interest of society and found that, because no less restrictive measures could have been taken to attain the objective, it was justified.

The Court used the same analysis in *French Golden Shares*,[73] in relation to the safeguarding of petroleum supplies in the event of a crisis, the justification for the controls on the acquisition of holdings in the privatized Elf-Aquitaine. However, in that case, the French legislative provisions did not reflect the limited nature of the justification invoked, since neither the prior authorization regime nor the opposition procedure in the legislation was limited by reference to such circumstances. Unlike the Belgian legislation, it was not based on any precise, objective criteria and so went beyond what was necessary to achieve the goal.[74]

6.2 Justifying restrictions

Cassis and its equivalent rulings in relation to the other internal market freedoms introduced what was, in effect, a regulatory function for the Court of Justice. That regulatory role arises because the Court has been led to indicate when a restriction on internal market freedoms is justified in ruling on infringement actions against the Member States and, more controversially, in answering questions submitted to it by national courts for a preliminary ruling. Under that jurisprudence, national measures liable to hinder or make less attractive the exercise of fundamental freedoms guaranteed by the Treaty can be justified only if they fulfil four conditions:

- they must be applied in a non-discriminatory manner,
- they must be justified by overriding reasons based on the general interest,
- they must be suitable for securing the attainment of the objective which they pursue, and
- they must not go beyond what is necessary in order to attain that objective.

---

[72] Case C-383/98 *Commission v Belgium* [2002] ECR I-4809.
[73] Case C-483/98 *Commission v France* [2002] ECR I-4781.
[74] See also *Commission v Spain* (n 17).

Even in relation to Article 67 EEC, the Court had indicated in *Veronica Omroep* that the maintenance of pluralism within a Member State's television market could justify limits on investment in a channel operating under foreign law and so permit restrictions on free movement of capital.[75] It did not take long for the case law on that question to develop along similar lines to that followed for the other freedoms.

As regards the present provisions of the Treaty, the Court first considered the question in detail in *Trummer and Mayer*, where Finland argued that the rule at issue before the Austrian courts in that case was based on an 'overriding factor serving the public interest', namely ensuring the predictability and transparency of the mortgage system.[76] The Court accepted that such public interests could be legitimately pursued by means selected under the law of the State in which that objective was to be attained.

By the time it came to give judgment in *Reisch*, the Court was able to express its position in a clear fashion:

> restrictions may nevertheless be permitted if the national rules pursue, in a non-discriminatory way, an objective in the public interest and if they observe the principle of proportionality, that is if the same result could not be achieved by other less restrictive measures.[77]

6.2.1 Grounds of justification

As to the grounds that have been accepted as 'objectives in the public interest' or as 'overriding requirements of the general interest' in the context of free movement of capital, they are reminiscent of the other freedoms. They include

- protection of creditors (by means of the transparency of a mortgage registration system),[78]

- maintenance of a permanent population and stable economic activity in rural or mountainous regions,[79]

- protection of the environment,[80] and

- 'preserving agricultural communities, maintaining a distribution of land ownership which allows the development of viable farms and sympathetic management of green spaces and the countryside as well as encouraging a reasonable use of the available land by resisting pressure on land, and preventing natural disasters'.[81]

However, while the list of such grounds of justification is not closed, the Court requires more than a general reference to goals that are in the public interest. In consequence, in *Spanish Golden Shares* the Court made it clear that a generic reference to 'strategic imperatives and the need to ensure continuity in public services' was not a sufficient basis on which to invoke such overriding requirements of general interest. That Spanish legislation failed to establish how the undertakings involved (a tobacco producer and a group of commercial banks) took responsibility for a public service function.[82]

---

[75] Case C-148/91 *Veronica Omroep* [1993] ECR I-487, paras 13 and 14.

[76] *Trummer and Mayer* (n 13).

[77] *Reisch* (n 14) para 33.

[78] *Trummer and Mayer* (n 13) para 30.

[79] *Konle* (n 14) para 40.

[80] *Reisch* (n 14) para 35.

[81] *Ospelt* (n 45) para 39. See also Case C-256/06 *Jäger* [2008] ECR I-123, para 50 and Case C-370/05 *Festersen* [2007] ECR I-1135, para 28.

[82] *Commission v Spain* (n 17) para 70.

Against that background, we can look to see how the Court evaluates grounds of justification as legitimate or otherwise.

In *VW law*,[83] the German government argued that the VW law was justified by the protection of workers' interests and the protection of minority shareholders. The Court found that, as regards the protection of workers' interests, the national authorities had been unable to explain why, in order to protect that firm's employees, it was appropriate and necessary for the federal and regional authorities to hold a strengthened and immovable position in the capital of Volkswagen. As to the protection of minority shareholders, the Court repeated its scepticism and noted that in some instances the public authorities might use their enhanced powers to defend general interests which might be contrary to the economic interests of the company and so contrary to the interests of its other shareholders.

The protection of public health arose as a ground of justification in relation to capital and establishment (Articles 63 TFEU and 49 TFEU) in *Italian pharmacies*.[84] Italian legislation excluded non-pharmacists from owning and operating pharmacies – in the case of legal persons, only those which were controlled by a natural person qualified as a pharmacist could operate pharmacies. While it was a non-discriminatory restriction affecting the two freedoms equally, the Court accepted that public health could be used to justify that restriction, noting the importance of the objective of ensuring that the provision of medicinal products to the public is reliable and of good quality.

The fight against tax evasion was accepted by the Court in *Établissements Rimbaud*[85] as a ground which could properly be invoked. However, it stated that such a justification could be permissible only if it was targeted against purely artificial contrivances and that any general presumption of evasion was not permitted. Here, the Court confirmed that the legislation was appropriate to combat tax evasion because it was directed against practices the sole aim of which was to enable natural persons to avoid paying tax on capital in France.[86]

Finally, the 2011 ruling on a tax amnesty instituted by Portugal in 2005 emphatically confirms that purely economic grounds cannot be used to justify a restriction.[87] The Court rejected Portugal's attempt to save that restriction by claiming that payment of a lower amount by taxpayers holding Portuguese State bonds took account of the benefit to the State which did not exist where the taxpayer had invested in securities from other Member States. That argument was, it held, in reality an attempt to justify a measure restricting free movement of capital by pursuit of an objective that is economic in nature, namely offsetting the Member State's lost tax revenue.

Although only the Court can ultimately decide whether a ground of justification is legitimate, the Commission in its role as 'guardian of the Treaties' has sometimes to take a view on those matters. Its perspective can be particularly important where a new issue arises and there has not yet been time for a preliminary reference to be made to the Court. For example, in the early part of 2013, Cyprus imposed a series of capital controls to prevent the uncontrollable outflow of bank deposits, which could lead to the banks' collapse and the immediate risk of the failure of the country's financial system. The Commission took the view that the stability of financial markets and of the banking system in that Member State was 'a matter of overriding public interest and public policy justifying the imposition

[83] *Commission v Germany* (n 40).
[84] Case C-531/06 (n 33).
[85] Case C-72/09 *Établissements Rimbaud* [2010] ECR I-10659.
[86] See also Case C-451/05 *ELISA* [2007] ECR I-8251.
[87] *Commission v Portugal* (n 54).

of temporary restrictions on capital movements'.[88] That evaluation shows the potential breadth of grounds of justification, but it has yet to be examined by the Court.

6.2.2 Proportionality

The *Cassis de Dijon* case law allows traders and the Commission to attack national measures that do not discriminate but which could have a restrictive effective on trade. Under that Court-developed test, the national measure will be allowed to stand only if the restrictive effect on the internal market freedom is an inescapable side product of the pursuit, by proportionate means, of a public interest goal. In order for the contested measures to be considered proportionate, the rule must be suitable and necessary. However, the approach to necessity has been more nuanced than that bare description might suggest.

Moreover, difficult procedural questions arise in order to determine whether a given restriction is necessary. Adjudication on the acceptability of national rules when measured against the internal market freedoms raises the issue of how closely courts should review the evaluation of the decision-making which adopted the contested rules.

Suitability

Proportionality requires that the measures under scrutiny be suitable for securing the attainment of the objective that they pursue. In a few rather unusual cases the Court looks only to the suitability requirement because that test is not satisfied, so there is no need to see if less restrictive means are available. For example, in *Trummer and Mayer* the Court stated that even if creditor protection was at the heart of the national system at issue in the case, the rules in place were not suitable to achieve that goal. They required registration of all mortgages, with the value of the secured debt denominated either in the national currency or as an amount of gold. There was predictability for lower-ranking creditors, by fixing the value of debt secured against the mortgage. However, that benefit was gained at the price of lack of predictability for higher-ranking creditors whose secured debts had been given in foreign currencies. Moreover, some insecurity was inherent in the national legislation because it allowed for the value of the mortgage to be expressed in terms of the price of fine gold, a measure of value also subject to fluctuation in the same way as foreign currencies. While that legislative provision had fallen into disuse, it had not been formally repealed. Thus, the Court applied the criterion relating to the national rule's suitability to set aside creditor protection as a justification for those rules.

Absence of any less restrictive means

Suitability is a floor, a threshold control on the measure's status. The greater hurdle for national authorities is to show the absence of less restrictive means of achieving the legitimate goal that is the measure's object. That second requirement is at the heart of the proportionality principle.

The absence of less restrictive means can be well illustrated by the case law on prior authorization regimes that subject a proposed transaction to *ex ante* administrative review. Such regimes were at the heart of both *Bordessa* and *Sanz de Lera*, as regards controls on currency exports. In *Bordessa*, the Court took the view that a prior authorization procedure for the export of currency was incompatible with Article 4 of the Third Capital Directive, the predecessor to Article 63 TFEU. Such a procedure excessively limited the free movement of capital because it suspended the export of banknotes and submitted the free circulation of capital to the discretion of the national administration. In *Sanz de Lera*, the Court

---

[88] Commission Press Release IP/13/298, 28 March 2013.

indicated that a declaration procedure, setting out the transaction's nature and the identity of the parties to it, was sufficient to ensure the genuine use of currency exports to third countries without impermissibly hindering movement of capital.

However, prior authorization regimes in different contexts may have other purposes. Where they are intended to fulfil a preventive function, *ex ante* controls may respect the proportionality requirement. It is potentially the case as regards the prior authorization requirements for purchase of immovable property.

The Court stated in *Konle* that a Member State may justify its requirement of prior authorization for the purchase of building land by invoking an object of general interest where, inter alia, the same result cannot be achieved by other less restrictive procedures.[89] The need for a prior authorization procedure was not made out in *Konle*. A procedure simply involving a declaration would be sufficient where, as in that case, there would be adequate repressive measures if a breach of the agreed declaration was duly established after the property had been acquired. The restriction in question was not, therefore, 'essential'.[90]

By contrast, in *Ospelt* the Court took a more favourable view of such regimes in relation to agricultural land.[91] It accepted that the objective of maintaining viable agriculture required keeping land intended for agriculture in use and continuing to make use of it under appropriate conditions. Prior supervision is legitimate to ensure that transfer of such land does not lead to change of use which would be incompatible with long-term agricultural use. Moves to restore the *status quo ante* would not provide the same guarantee and would be inadequate to ensure that the land's suitability for such use is not irretrievably impaired. However, the Court indicated that one condition applied in that system was unnecessary to secure the objective invoked. There was no justification for the exclusion of transfers to persons who, although they will not farm the land themselves, will lease it to farmers. Such limitations cannot be justified because they are over-broad.

The status of a prior authorization regime as regards foreign direct investment is less clear. In *Église de Scientologie*, the Court followed Advocate General Saggio, who had taken the view that prior authorization was potentially licit in respect of direct foreign investment. In his view, there are forms of investment that would be difficult to dislodge in an expeditious fashion. Therefore, EU law should permit, he argued, resort to prior authorization. The Court agreed: a prior declaration system might be inadequate to counter the dangers of a genuine and sufficiently serious threat to public policy and public security.

Though the proportionality principle arose in the 'golden shares' cases, the measures' proportionality was not examined in most of them because the Court found that the systems were incapable of satisfying another criterion. Thus, in *Portuguese Golden Shares* there was no need to examine the proportionality of that system because the grounds of justification invoked (the State's financial interests) did not constitute an overriding requirement of general interest.[92] In *French Golden Shares*, the basis of the authorization system was insufficiently clear, as was part of the system in *Spanish Golden Shares*.

The fate of the rules at issue in *Belgian Golden Shares* shows that an opposition system is likely to be viewed more favourably than a prior authorization system. The Court upheld the compatibility of the Belgian regime with Article 63 TFEU. It took account of the *ex post facto* nature of the powers of intervention, the strict time limits within which they were to

---

[89] *Konle* (n 14).
[90] See also *Reisch* (n 14).
[91] *Ospelt* (n 45).
[92] *Commission v Portugal* (n 42).

be exercised, and the limited nature of the measures that could be taken (veto in respect of decisions concerning strategic assets and specific management decisions).

Italian pharmacies,[93] on Italian legislation which excluded non-pharmacists from own-ing and operating pharmacies, is of interest here as well. The Court accepted that the pro-tection of public health could be invoked to justify that legislation, which was a restriction both on free movement of capital and the freedom of establishment. In light of the risks to individuals' health from inappropriate medicinal products, and to the financial balance of social security systems which pay for drugs, the Court found that restricting who could own and operate a pharmacy was an appropriate means of achieving that goal. It considered that while both pharmacists and non-pharmacists providing that service were motivated by profit, the former group had a training and responsibility which the latter did not have and which moderated their conduct. A Member State was, therefore, entitled to find that such an exclusion rule was a suitable means of achieving that goal, even if other Member States did not find it necessary. The Court went on to find that the Commission had not demon-strated that there were less restrictive means of achieving the same goal.

Because the free movement of capital applies in principle to third countries as well as to intra-Union movements, the issue arises whether justifications will be accepted in the same manner for a restriction relating to a third country as to a Member State. That point came up in *Établissements Rimbaud*, where the Court held that the case law on intra-Union restrictions cannot be transposed in its entirety to movements of capital between Member States and third countries, because such movements take place in a different legal con-text.[94] While the Court had ruled previously regarding the French legislation in issue in *Établissements Rimbaud* that a taxpayer established in another Member State had to be able to present evidence showing that the company was not a screen behind which a natural person subject to capital tax in France was sheltering,[95] the same possibility did not have to be given to non-resident taxpayers established in Lichtenstein. As between Member States there is a Directive from 1977 which allows Member States to verify administrative information in relation to tax matters; there is no counterpart to that Directive as regards Lichtenstein. As such, France was not required to examine the situation of a taxpayer estab-lished in Lichtenstein on a case-by-case basis.

6.3 Procedural requirements applied to justifications and exceptions

In recent years, the Court has developed a set of procedural requirements relating to the justifications and exceptions invoked by national authorities. Some of the precursors of that development relate to the Treaty-based exceptions. However, for the most part that phenomenon has been seen in relation to the mandatory requirements and overrid-ing requirements of general interest. The national measure must allow traders, invest-ors, purchasers, or other persons invoking the freedom to be sure that any restriction will not be applied in a discriminatory manner, as well as being clear when a particular form of restriction will be applied. If those requirements are not satisfied, the Court has ruled that the Treaty precludes such a measure and may do so without examining its proportionality.

The clearest statement of the Member States' obligations in relation to the procedural aspect of justifying a restriction on a freedom can be found in *Église de Scientologie*. The

---

[93] Case C-531/06 (n 33).
[94] See also Case C-540/07 *Commission v Italy* [2009] ECR I-10983 and *A* (n 44).
[95] *ELISA* (n 86).

Court had confirmed that a prior authorization regime could be acceptable in relation to foreign investment, but then stated:

> 21. [T]he essence of the system in [the present case] is that prior authorisation is required for every direct foreign investment which is 'such as to represent a threat to public policy [and] public security', without any more detailed definition. Thus, the investors concerned are given no indication whatever as to the specific circumstances in which prior authorisation is required.
>
> 22. Such lack of precision does not enable individuals to be apprised of the extent of their rights and obligations deriving from Article [63 TFEU]. That being so, the system established is contrary to the principle of legal certainty.[96]

6.4 The limits of restrictions

In relation to free movement of capital, the broad scope of the dissuasion test articulated in the case law to date raises the question whether the interpretation of 'restriction' may catch too much. If so, that 'over-inclusion' could create pressure for a supple approach to justification. There would be an attendant risk that such flexibility would in turn generate problems when applied to 'hardcore' restrictions on free movement of capital. The issue surfaced in *UK Golden Shares*, where the UK government argued that the measures at issue, rules in a privatized company's articles of association which prevent any investor acquiring shares in that firm carrying the right to more than 15 per cent of the votes, did not restrict access to the market within the meaning of *Keck*.[97] The Court stated that the measures in issue were not comparable with rules concerning selling arrangements. It noted that although the relevant restrictions on investment operations applied without distinction to both residents and non-residents, they affected the position of a person acquiring a shareholding as such; they were liable to deter investors from other Member States from making such investments and thus affected access to the market. The analysis leaves free movement of capital in a position similar to the freedom to provide services in the wake of *Alpine Investments*, in which the Court refused to apply *Keck* to the rule before it, but did not exclude its potential applicability to that Treaty freedom.

Case study 15.1: Capital movements in the public interest

SOCIAL SERVICES OF GENERAL INTEREST AND NATIONAL IDENTITY

Social services such as health and long-term care, childcare, social housing, and the care and social inclusion of vulnerable groups are very important to individuals' and communities' feelings of identity – for example, if you consider the differing conceptions between countries in the Nordic, Central European, and Mediterranean regions (as well as between countries in those regions) as to what is the appropriate role of the individual, the family, the local community, and the State in relation to all those activities, you will see that such services are intimately connected with the sense of what makes a given society distinctive or gives it a particular character.[98]

Those services operate on the basis of the solidarity principle (or to put it another way, they are provided outside the logic of a market system), are intended to protect those

---

[96] On this point, also contrast *Commission v France* (n 73) and *Commission v Spain* (n 17) with *Commission v Belgium* (n 72).

[97] *Commission v UK* (n 15) para 43.

[98] See also chapter 18 on public services and EU law.

considered most vulnerable, are not for profit, and are strongly rooted in local cultural traditions. It has become apparent in recent years that the free movement of capital can have a significant impact on the mechanisms by which such services are delivered. This case study seeks to examine the impact of that freedom on the provision of social services in the Member States. In doing so, we will be looking at the impact of the legal issues considered in this chapter – at the material scope of 'capital', at the concept of 'restriction', at the scope of the exceptions laid down by the Treaty, at how grounds of justification can be developed, at the role of proportionality, and at differences between justification in relation to capital moving between Member States as opposed to between Member States and third countries. The main theme examined here can be summarized by the question: is there an emerging Union-level view of when capital movements are in the public interest?

THE *PERSCHE* RULING

If the Member State decides that in addition to (or instead of) direct provision of such a social service by public law bodies, private law operators will be made responsible (possibly only in part) for delivery of that service, it can use a wide variety of financing mechanisms. For example, it may seek to facilitate or encourage private financing by means of tax breaks; they could be given to persons who make donations to service providers. Such fiscal mechanisms raise issues regarding free movement of capital. The Court was first confronted with the issue of funding of those services and its connection with free movement of capital in *Persche*.[99] Mr Persche claimed as an exceptional tax-deductible expense his donation of bedlinen and towels, and also Zimmer frames and toy cars for children, to the Centro Popular de Lagoa (a retirement home to which a children's home had been added) in Portugal. The German authorities rejected his request because the recipient of the donation was not established in Germany.

The Court first clarified that the taxable treatment of such gifts came within the scope of the rules on capital, even if they were made in kind in the form of everyday consumer goods. It then noted that the inability in Germany to deduct gifts to bodies recognized as charitable if they were established in other Member States was likely to affect the willingness of German taxpayers to make gifts for the benefit of those bodies. As such, the German legislation restricted the free movement of capital. In order for the German legislation to be compatible with the Treaty, the difference in treatment would have to concern situations which are not objectively comparable or would have to be justified by an overriding reason in the public interest (and be proportionate in the pursuit of the legislation's objective).

Was there indeed an objective difference between donations to German charities and donations to Portuguese charities?

The Court started by recognizing that it was for each Member State to determine whether it would provide for tax advantages in favour of bodies which concerned themselves with activities that it recognized as being charitable and taxpayers who made gifts to those bodies. However, where a Member State decided to grant tax advantages to bodies pursuing certain charitable purposes, the Court held that it could not restrict the benefit of such advantages only to bodies established in that Member State.

There are, however, some counter-arguments to the idea that tax breaks for charitable gifts must extend to donations outside the Member State:

- A right for taxpayers to deduct the value of gifts from their tax bill decreases the Member State's tax revenues, and the Member State should have to allow that fall in

---

[99] Case C-318/07 (n 10).

its income only if there is also a reduction in its expenses by the taxpayer taking over a burden (eg providing for the elderly) that would otherwise fall on the State.

- Such tax advantages allow the Member State to discharge some of its duties, and those responsibilities do not exist beyond its borders since they are an expression of the bonds of solidarity within that society.

- Giving such tax advantages for charitable gifts outside the Member State cannot be effectively controlled to ensure that the taxpayer is genuinely giving to charity (as opposed to reducing her tax bill by bogus means).

The Court acknowledged that providing tax breaks for charitable donations could encourage charitable bodies to substitute themselves for the public authorities in assuming certain responsibilities, which was an aspect of the first counter-argument above. However, it went on to hold, in line with the case law examined on justification, that the need to prevent a reduction of tax revenues was neither amongst the objectives in Article 65 TFEU nor was it capable of constituting an overriding reason in the public interest.

As regards the second counter-argument, the Court accepted that there was no requirement in Union law for a Member State automatically to confer on foreign bodies recognized as having charitable status in their Member State of origin the same status in their own territory. Member States had discretion as to what goals or activities they wish to consider charitable. However, the Court did not uphold that counter-argument: Germany's freedom to define the interests of the general public it wished to promote did not allow it to refuse equal treatment to a body recognized as having charitable status in Portugal which satisfied the requirements imposed by German law and the object of which was to promote the very same interests of the general public. In other words, is it likely that body would be recognized as having charitable status in the Member State of the taxpayer? If the activities of the Centro Popular benefit children and old people, that element is decisive to establish if it is comparable with an identical body established in Germany. There is no relevance to the fact that those children and elderly persons are Portuguese or reside in Portugal.

The Court went on to dismiss the third counter-argument, based on a need to safeguard the effectiveness of fiscal supervision. As shown regarding grounds of justification, national authorities can require a taxpayer to provide such proof as they consider necessary to determine whether the conditions for deducting expenses had been met. However, the mere fact that the taxing authorities might be faced with administrative disadvantages could not justify a blanket refusal to grant taxpayers advantages which they could obtain in respect of gifts to national bodies of the same kind. The Court also held that Germany could not exclude the grant of tax advantages for gifts made to a body established and recognized as charitable in Portugal purely because, in relation to such bodies, the German tax authorities were unable to check, on the spot, compliance with requirements imposed by their tax legislation. Even in relation to national charitable bodies, an on-the-spot inspection was not usually required. Moreover, the provision of information in the framework of mutual assistance between tax administrations under Directive 2011/16 would normally suffice to check that the recipient body fulfilled the conditions imposed by German legislation.

On that final point, the Court distinguished the situation of charitable bodies in third countries, because non-member countries are not under any international obligation to provide information. It was therefore as a rule legitimate for the Member State of taxation to refuse to grant such a tax advantage to charitable bodies in a third country.[100]

---

[100] The Court has also explored the questions of tax breaks for private funding of charities and of activities in the public interest in other recent cases: compare the ruling in *Persche* with Case C-25/10 *Missionswerk*

THE *WONINGSTICHTING SINT SERVATIUS* RULING

In 2011, the Court moved on in *Woningstichting Sint Servatius*[101] to deal with the means by which a Member State organizes delivery of a social service. The Dutch Constitution requires the government to promote adequate housing. Dutch law creates a system of housing associations which are non-profit-making, must operate exclusively in the public housing sector and in a designated geographical area, and are answerable to the minister. The minister has the power to authorize housing associations to construct experimental projects which she believes to be in the interests of public housing, even where that would depart from the general regime governing such associations. Servatius was an approved association operating in the Maastricht area; it sought to build housing as part of a mixed-use development (commercial, rented dwellings, owner-occupied, parking) in Liège, some 30 km from the Dutch border, and was prepared to use some of the funds it had obtained at favourable rates because of its status as an approved association. Servatius sought the minister's permission to carry out that project. The minister refused to approve it on the basis of the project's location in Belgium. As a climax to litigation in the national courts challenging that refusal, the Dutch Council of State referred a series of questions regarding, inter alia, free movement of capital to the Court.

In light of its long-standing case law on prior authorization systems for the purchase of real estate, the Court found that the requirement for those institutions to obtain prior authorization from the competent minister before investing in immovable property in other Member States constituted a restriction on the free movement of capital.[102] The Dutch authorities had either to bring the national legislation within the scope of one of the Treaty's exceptions or to justify the measure.

As to the claim that the promotion of social housing is covered by the notion of 'public policy' in Article 65 TFEU, the Court was brisk and to the point: even if housing associations fail to comply with their statutes and divert the funds they receive for other purposes, that behaviour cannot amount to a genuine and sufficiently serious threat to a fundamental interest of society. On the other hand, the Court was quite willing to accept that requirements related to public housing policy in a Member State and to the financing of that policy could constitute overriding reasons in the public interest and therefore justify the restriction at issue.[103] Indeed, apart from the inherent importance of that policy for any Member State, specific features of the Dutch housing market reinforced the significance of the ground invoked, namely a structural shortage of accommodation and a particularly high population density.[104] As ever, once a legitimate ground of justification has been raised to defend a national rule that restricts free movement of capital, the decisive question is whether the measure is proportionate. The Court left that issue to the national court.[105]

Werner Heuchelbach [2011] ECR I-497 and Case C-10/10 *Commission* v *Austria* ('*University donations*') [2011] ECR I-5389.

[101] Case C-567/07 [2009] ECR I-9021.   [102] Ibid, paras 22–24.

[103] See also Joined Cases C-197/11 and C-203/11 *Libert*, judgment of 8 May 2013, nyr, para 52.

[104] *Woningstichting Sint Servatius* (n 101) para 30.

[105] A comparable approach was taken by the Court to a similar social service, the provision of pensions and severance payments, in *Polish OPFs* (see Case C-271/09 *Commission v Poland*, judgment of 21 December 2011, nyr, para 75) and *VBV – Vorsorgekasse* (see Case C-39/11, judgment of 7 June 2012, nyr, para 31). Member States argued that they were guaranteeing the stability and security of assets managed by the funds responsible for those payments by requiring them to invest only in their home Member State. In both cases the Court found the rule was a restriction on free movement of capital and was sceptical about the claims that it could be justified.

> **CONCLUSION**
>
> Free movement of capital rules can severely limit what Member States traditionally thought of as their freedom in an area of particular sensitivity for local, regional, and national identity. First, free movement of capital constrains the choices which Member States can make where the providers are of social services financed through the tax system, whether by relieving them of fiscal burdens imposed on other taxpayers or by inducing taxpayers to make contributions directly to them. Secondly, at the other end of the financial cycle, the power of Member States to direct providers of those services to offer a wider or narrower range of services is also affected by free movement of capital.

7 Conclusion

The development of free movement of capital since it joined the ranks of the other internal market freedoms, after the Maastricht Treaty came into force, has seen the Court align it closely with those other freedoms. There has also been a significant increase in the extent to which it is litigated: in the period from 2008 to 2013, there were some 91 cases before the Court in which that freedom was invoked, compared with 77 cases in the preceding decade. Moreover, because of its role in EMU, which involves a different and deeper level of integration amongst the Member States than the creation of the internal market, and because of its special role as regards non-member countries, the free movement of capital will always be particularly sensitive.

Further reading

L FLYNN, 'Coming of Age: The Free Movement of Capital Case Law 1993–2002' (2002) 39 *Common Market Law Review* 773

S GRUNDMANN AND F MÖSLEIN, 'Golden Shares – State Control in Privatised Companies: Comparative Law, European Law and Policy Aspects' [2004] 1 *Euredia* 623

S PEERS, 'Free Movement of Capital: Learning Lessons or Slipping on Spilt Milk?' in C Barnard and J Scott (eds), *The Law of the Single European Market: Unpacking the Premises* (Oxford: Hart Publishing, 2002)

J SNELL, 'Non-Discriminatory Tax Obstacles in Community Law' (2007) 56 *International and Comparative Law Quarterly* 339

J USHER, *The Law of Money and Financial Services in the European Community* (2nd edn, Oxford University Press, 2000)

Chapter acknowledgements

Leo Flynn is an Official of the European Commission. The views expressed in this text are personal.

16

Exceptions to the free movement rules

Niamh Nic Shuibhne

1 Introduction

The free movement rights conferred on natural and legal persons by EU law are at the heart of both Union citizenship and the achievement of the internal market. However, these rights are not absolute. The realization of free movement rights is a core Union objective, but it is also recognized that other interests and values should sometimes take precedence. This means that, in certain circumstances, free movement rights can be restricted in compliance with EU law if (a) for discriminatory or distinctly applicable restrictive measures, a derogation ground expressly provided for in the TFEU can be engaged; (b) for indirectly or non-discriminatory, that is, indistinctly applicable restrictive measures, an overriding requirement relating to the public interest that is capable of justifying a restriction of the fundamental freedoms established by the Treaty can be demonstrated; and (c) in both cases, the restriction also satisfies a proportionality test, that is, it is both appropriate and necessary for achieving the relevant public interest objective.

This chapter explores derogation, justification, and proportionality; and asks when Member States can lawfully displace the obligations placed on them by free movement law. The approach taken is to explain how the derogation and justification systems work by exploring the principles that underpin their application, rather than to outline the various relevant public interest grounds in a substantive sense.[1] The chapter also outlines the more specific rules that apply to derogations from the free movement of persons, which are underpinned by the rights attached to the status of Union citizenship and are codified in EU legislation.

The topic of exceptions to the Treaty's free movement rules reflects an important theme that shapes much of EU law: how to balance the acknowledged need for common internal market and citizenship standards that apply uniformly in all of the Member States with appropriate recognition of respect for national regulatory diversity and for the limits of Union competence. A secondary theme that emerges through the discussion is that while the frameworks applicable to derogation and justification can, at one level, be presented in a relatively systematic way, there is far more inconsistency with respect to their application through case law practice. A more explicit review and recalibration of the relevant rules would therefore be a welcome development.

2 The Treaty framework: derogations

Following a brief overview of the role and purpose of derogation in free movement law, and of the broader Treaty framework that increasingly affects the resolution of these questions, this section then outlines the explicit derogation grounds provided for in the Treaty.

2.1 The role of derogation and the broader legal framework

The EU Treaties establish a complex system in which many different objectives, interests, and values are accommodated, but also need to be balanced against each other. For example, Article 3(3) TEU provides that 'The Union shall establish an internal market'. But it goes on to list a series of other tasks and objectives that include sustainable development, balanced economic growth and price stability, a highly competitive social market economy, full employment, social progress, protection and improvement of the quality of the environment, equality between women and men, protection of the rights of the child, and respect for cultural and linguistic diversity. Article 4 TEU requires that 'competences not conferred upon the Union in the Treaties remain with the Member States' and that the Union 'shall respect the equality of Member States...as well as their national identities'. Article 4(2) TFEU confirms that the internal market is an area for which regulatory competence between the Union and the Member States is shared.

The fact that States can legitimately restrict free movement rights in certain circumstances – on the basis that another interest should take precedence over free movement

---

[1] For comprehensive discussion of the different grounds of public interest, see C Barnard, *The Substantive Law of the EU: The Four Freedoms* (4th edn, Oxford: Oxford University Press, 2013) chs 6 and 13.

objectives – is an important expression of the resulting regulatory balance.[2] An important challenge for the Court of Justice is thus to ensure the achievement of effective internal market integration while still allowing for more localized regulatory diversity that fits with the constitutional mandate of shared EU/Member State competence.[3]

To resolve disputes connected to EU free movement rights, the Court of Justice normally addresses three distinct questions:

(a) Does the challenged measure constitute a *restriction* of the free movement rights guaranteed by the Treaty?

(b) If it does, can the measure be *justified*?

(c) If it can, is the measure *proportionate*?

It has been shown in several of the other chapters of this book that it is not difficult to establish an actual or potential restriction of free movement rights within the meaning of the Treaty. For example, in *CaixaBank* the Court defined restrictions on freedom of establishment as 'All measures which prohibit, impede or render less attractive the exercise of that freedom'.[4] A national measure that falls within this definition will have to be set aside unless it can be shown that the measure is both justifiable and proportionate. It is important to remember, therefore, that even an overtly discriminatory restriction of free movement rights can be saved if a Member State can demonstrate that there is a good – that is, justifiable and proportionate within the limits of EU law – reason for it.

2.2 **Derogation and EU legislation**

Where EU legislative measures establish regulatory standards for a particular issue, no derogation is permitted unless expressly provided for by the relevant legislation. The basic rule here is that 'A national measure in a sphere which has been the subject of exhaustive harmonisation at [Union] level must be assessed in the light of the provisions of the harmonising measure and not those of the Treaty'.[5] This means that any permitted derogations will normally need to be accommodated within the legislation from the outset. EU legislation can provide for (a) a general derogation clause, establishing that the Commission will examine difficulties that a Member State might encounter when applying provisions of the measure on a case-by-case basis, and may decide to permit the Member State to derogate from the relevant obligation for a specified period; or (b) specific derogation clauses, establishing a specific exception for a Member State vis-à-vis part of the measure's requirements. Examples of both of these mechanisms can be found in Directive 2005/36/EC, which regulates the recognition of professional qualifications to facilitate freedom of establishment and the provision of cross-border professional services.[6] Article 114 TFEU, the legal basis used for most internal market harmonization measures, also establishes a post-adoption derogation procedure for the grounds specified in

---

[2] AG Bot expressed it in the following way in Case C-141/07 *Commission v Germany* [2008] ECR I-6935: 'The rules surrounding the exercise of [a Member State's] reserved powers mean that if its legislation causes a restriction of one of the fundamental freedoms of movement it must be in a position to provide a legitimate reason...to justify this' (para 83 of the Opinion). [3] See also chapter 11.

[4] Case C-442/02 *CaixaBank France v Ministère de l'Économie, des Finances et de l'Industrie* [2004] ECR I-8961, para 11.

[5] Case C-322/01 *Deutscher Apothekerverband eV v 0800 DocMorris NV and Jacques Waterval* [2003] ECR I-14887, para 64.

[6] Directive 2005/36/EC of 7 September 2005 on the recognition of professional qualifications (OJ [2005] L255/22); Art 61 of the Directive is the general derogation clause; for a specific derogation clause, see eg Art 33(a).

Article 36 TFEU (see section 2.3) or relating to the protection of the environment or the working environment.[7]

Where EU legislation provides for minimum harmonization, States remain free in principle to adopt more stringent standards to protect the public interest at national level. In the classic language of minimum harmonization, the standards prescribed by Union legislation constitute only the 'floor', that is, a threshold that any related national measures must implement and respect. However, following the judgment in the *Tobacco advertising* case,[8] EU minimum harmonization measures must also now include a free movement clause. For example, in the revised version of the Tobacco Advertising Directive[9] – adopted after the Court of Justice annulled the original measure – Article 8 provides that 'Member States shall not prohibit or restrict the free movement of products or services which comply with this Directive'. In such circumstances, national measures that go beyond the standards mandated by the Directive can still be tested against the derogation and justification framework established by the Treaty and related case law. Thus, while EU legislation marks the 'floor' for public interest protection, as noted previously, the Treaty represents a boundary or 'ceiling' for national regulatory discretion.

However, for most areas of free movement law, the question of derogation normally arises when there is no relevant Union legislation in the first place, that is, in the context of negative integration.[10] In such situations, national measures can be tested against the exceptions to, or limits of, the freedoms already provided for by the Treaty.

2.3 Overview of the Treaty-based derogation grounds

The derogation grounds specified in the Treaty can be used to defend State action taken for a variety of public interest reasons that are expressly articulated and protected as *Union* concerns, as Table 16.1 shows.

As these provisions demonstrate, the Treaty freedoms may be derogated from for reasons connected to, broadly speaking, concerns linked to public policy, public security, or public health. The protection of public health is the derogation raised most frequently in the case law on free movement restrictions, especially for restrictions on the free movement of goods. In fact, the Court considers that 'the health and life of humans rank foremost among the assets and interests protected by the Treaty'.[11] In recognition of that special position, the Court also acknowledges that

> it is for the Member States to determine the level of protection which they wish to afford to public health and the way in which that level is to be achieved. Since the level may vary from one Member State to another, Member States must be allowed discretion.[12]

---

[7] See Art 114(4) and (5) TFEU.

[8] Case C-376/98 *Germany v Parliament and Council* [2000] ECR I-8419.

[9] Directive 2003/33/EC of 26 May 2003 on the approximation of the laws, regulations, and administrative provisions of the Member States relating to the advertising and sponsorship of tobacco products (OJ [2003] L152/16).

[10] This point has been expressed by the Court as the precondition that 'there are no [Union] harmonising measures providing for measures necessary to ensure the protection of [the relevant] interests' (Case C-112/05 *Commission v Germany* [2007] ECR I-8995, para 72).

[11] Case C-171/07 *Apothekerkammer des Saarlandes* [2009] ECR I-4171, para 19. See further chapter 12.

[12] Ibid. For an example of public health concerns that potentially permitted a discriminatory restriction on free movement rights, see Case C-73/08 *Bressol and Chaverot v Gouvernement de la Communauté française* [2010] ECR I-2735.

Table 16.1 Summary of Treaty derogations available for the four freedoms

Treaty: rights	Treaty: derogation	Grounds
Article 21 TFEU *Citizenship*: movement/ residence rights	*Article 21 TFEU*	'limitations and conditions laid down in the Treaties and by the measures adopted to give them effect'
Articles 34 and 35 TFEU *Goods*: quantitative restrictions on imports/exports	*Article 36 TFEU*	'public morality, public policy or public security; the protection of health and life of humans, animals or plants; the protection of national treasures possessing artistic, historic or archaeological value; or the protection of industrial and commercial property'
Article 45 TFEU *Workers*	*Article 45(3) TFEU*	'limitations justified on grounds of public policy, public security or public health'
	Article 45(4) TFEU	'employment in the public service'
Article 49 TFEU *Establishment*	*Article 51 TFEU*	'exercise of official authority'
	Article 52 TFEU	'grounds of public policy, public security or public health'
Article 56 TFEU *Services*	*Article 62 TFEU*	Article 52 TFEU grounds ie 'public policy, public security or public health'
Article 63 TFEU *Capital*	*Article 65 TFEU*	'exercise of official authority'; 'public policy or public security' plus taxation and 'prudential supervision of financial institutions'

There is clearly some variation of approach to derogation across the freedoms, with a more extended list of grounds for Article 36 TFEU, for example, and also for the free movement of capital. Moreover, Article 36 TFEU requires that 'Such prohibitions or restrictions shall not... constitute a means of *arbitrary discrimination* or a *disguised restriction* on trade between Member States'.[13] This proviso means that a Member State's derogation arguments will not normally be accepted if the State has not placed comparable restrictions on goods produced domestically.[14] Although the proviso in Article 36 TFEU is not an express part of the derogation provisions for the other Treaty freedoms, the broader principle that it contains is more generally applicable.[15]

Article 30 TFEU provides that 'Customs duties on imports and exports and charges having equivalent effect shall be prohibited between Member States. This prohibition shall

[13] Emphasis added. See similarly, Art 65(3) TFEU for capital: 'The measures and procedures referred to in paras 1 and 2 shall not constitute a means of arbitrary discrimination or a disguised restriction on the free movement of capital and payments as defined in Article 63'.

[14] eg in the context of derogation arguments based on public morality, compare the circumstances of and decision in Case 121/85 *Conegate Ltd v HM Customs & Excise* [1986] ECR 1007, where a prohibition on certain imported goods was not matched by a prohibition on their domestic manufacture, with the earlier case of Case 34/79 *R v Henn and Darby* [1979] ECR 3795.

[15] For discussion of the absence of comparable restrictions placed on nationals in the sphere of freedom of establishment, see eg Case 115/81 *Adoui and Cornuaille v Belgian State and City of Liège* [1982] ECR 1665.

also apply to customs duties of a fiscal nature'. Exceptionally, however, no corresponding derogation grounds are provided for in the Treaty. A charge that is imposed purely because goods have crossed a frontier can fall outside the scope of the Treaty only in very limited circumstances that have been established through case law:

> such a charge escapes that classification if it relates to a general system of internal dues applied systematically and in accordance with the same criteria to domestic products and imported products alike, if it constitutes payment for a service in fact rendered to the economic operator of a sum in proportion to the service, or again, subject to certain conditions, if it attaches to inspections carried out to fulfil obligations imposed by [Union] law.[16]

The concept of public policy might be construed as a generic notion that offers considerable leeway to the Member States in principle. However, the Court of Justice has interpreted the scope of this derogation ground very strictly in practice.[17] This narrow approach was of particular importance before the Court had fully developed a broader justification framework (outlined in section 3) that is not confined to the public interest grounds listed in the Treaty. In that early case law, States sought recognition from the Court of emerging public interest concerns, such as protection of the environment or consumers, which were simply not recognized as important public interest premises by the Treaty's drafters in the 1950s. However, the Court declined to expand the concept of public policy to accommodate the evolution of public interest concerns in this way.[18]

It should also be noted that the way in which restrictions on the movement and residence rights of EU citizens may be limited is unusual, in the sense that such rights are subject not only to the derogation grounds listed elsewhere in the Treaty (ie public policy, public security, or public health) but also to 'measures adopted' to give effect to the Treaty, that is, limits established in secondary legislation. The way in which Article 21 TFEU is constructed thus marks an exception to the normal rule that secondary law cannot adjust primary law. This point becomes particularly important for the discussion in section 6, which focuses on the provisions of Directive 2004/38/EC on the free movement of Union citizens and their family members within the territory of the Member States that govern expulsion decisions.[19]

Finally, it should be noted that Article 45(4) TFEU provides that 'The provisions of this Article shall not apply to employment in the public service'. Similarly, for freedom of establishment (and also, through Article 62 TFEU, freedom to provide services), Article 51 TFEU states that 'The provisions of this Chapter shall not apply, so far as any given Member State is concerned, to activities which in that State are connected, even occasionally, with the exercise of official authority'. Again, however, the Court has curtailed the potential breadth of both of these exclusions. The scope of 'employment in the public service' has been interpreted to mean only

> posts which involve direct or indirect participation in the exercise of powers conferred by public law and duties designed to safeguard the general interests of the State or of other public authorities and thus presume on the part of those occupying them the existence of a special

---

[16] Case C-389/00 *Commission v Germany* [2003] ECR I-2001, para 23 (confirming Case 18/87 *Commission v Germany* [1988] ECR 5427, para 6); for further discussion of each of these three exceptions, see Barnard, *The Substantive Law of the EU* (n 1) 48–50.

[17] Case 231/83 *Cullet v Centre Leclerc* [1985] ECR 305, para 30.

[18] See eg Case 177/83 *Kohl KG v Ringelhan & Rennett SA and Ringelhan Einrichtungs GmbH* [1984] ECR 3651, on consumer protection.   [19] OJ [2004] L158/77.

relationship of allegiance to the State and reciprocity of rights and duties which form the foundation of the bond of nationality.[20]

Similarly, the 'exercise of official authority' as it relates to establishment and services 'must be restricted to activities which in themselves are *directly and specifically* connected with the exercise of official authority' and, conversely, 'does not extend to certain activities that are auxiliary or preparatory' in that context.[21]

The Court has rationalized its narrow interpretative approach to both of these provisions on the basis that they amount to exceptions to the 'fundamental character' of free movement rights and, as such, they 'cannot be given a scope which would exceed the objective' for which they were included in the Treaty in the first place.[22]

3 The justification framework: public interest requirements

As has been shown in previous chapters, restrictions on free movement rights can be (a) directly discriminatory on the grounds of nationality (ie discriminatory in law), (b) indirectly discriminatory (ie not discriminatory in law, but discriminatory in result or effect), or (c) non-discriminatory (ie not discriminatory in law or in effect, but still restrictive of free movement rights).

The basic rule for derogation from free movement rights is that directly discriminatory restrictions can be defended *only* by recourse to the grounds provided for expressly in the Treaty. However, to defend indirectly discriminatory and non-discriminatory – that is, indistinctly applicable – restrictions of free movement rights, States can raise virtually any public interest argument that they wish, without being confined to the policy objectives that are predetermined by the Treaty's limited derogation provisions. Their arguments may not be successful; but the key point to emphasize here is that there are few subject-matter limitations, in principle, on the kinds of public interest concerns that States can assert when they seek to justify the retention of national rules or practices that restrict EU free movement rights. This open-ended justification framework will now be outlined in more detail, followed by consideration of whether the formative distinction between discriminatory and other types of restriction still holds. The key limits imposed on the scope of State discretion by EU law – for example arguments based on economic rationales are normally not permitted – are then discussed further in section 4.

3.1 From 'mandatory requirements' to 'overriding requirements in the public interest'

To defend indistinctly applicable national measures, Member States can, in effect, submit justification arguments based on any public interest grounds that they consider to be relevant. This open-ended justification route could be glimpsed in early free movement case law.[23] However, it was first more substantively developed as the doctrine of

---

[20] Case C-405/01 *Colegio de Oficiales de la Marina Mercante Española v Administración del Estado* [2003] ECR I-10391, para 39 (confirming Case 149/79 *Commission v Belgium* [1980] ECR 3881, para 10).

[21] Case C-61/08 *Commission v Greece* [2011] ECR I-4399, paras 77 and 78 (emphasis added).

[22] Case 2/74 *Reyners v Belgian State* [1974] ECR 631, para 43.

[23] Case 33/74 *Van Binsbergen v Bestuur van de Bedrijfsvereniging voor de Metaalnijverheid* [1974] ECR 1299, para 12: 'specific requirements imposed on the person providing the service cannot be considered incompatible with the Treaty where they have as their purpose the application of professional rules *justified by the general good*' (emphasis added).

'mandatory requirements' for Article 34 TFEU in *Cassis de Dijon*.[24] In that case, the Court considered that

> Obstacles to movement within the [Union] resulting from disparities between the national laws relating to the marketing of the products in question must be accepted in so far as those provisions may be recognized as *being necessary in order to satisfy mandatory requirements* relating *in particular* to the effectiveness of fiscal supervision, the protection of public health, the fairness of commercial transactions and the defence of the consumer.[25]

In this way, the Court of Justice was able to accommodate genuine policy concerns that were not relevant or prominent when the Treaty of Rome was drafted, such as the protection of consumers (and, in subsequent cases, protection of the environment[26]); without the need for Treaty amendment of the express derogations, or the definitive resolution of broader debates about the relative value of either an updated but still fixed list of permissible public interest grounds or codification of a more open-ended approach across the board. Some examples of other justification grounds that the Court has recognized in principle include[27]

- combating drug tourism,[28]
- ensuring road safety,[29]
- maintaining press diversity,[30]
- preserving the cohesion of a tax system,[31]
- protecting national or regional socio-cultural characteristics,[32]
- protecting the recipients of a service through the application of professional rules,[33]
- protecting workers.[34]

The Court has also confirmed that national measures protecting fundamental rights can constitute valid justification grounds, as discussed in more detail in section 4.4.

The rather opaque language of 'mandatory requirements' is rarely used in the case law anymore. The Court now tends to use the more transparent, and helpful, language of public interest requirements. For example, addressing Article 21 TFEU, the Court has stated that 'indirect discrimination on grounds of nationality can be justified only if it is based on *objective considerations* independent of the nationality of the persons concerned'.[35] More

---

[24] Case 120/78 *Rewe-Zentrale AG v Bundesmonopolverwaltung für Branntwein* ('*Cassis de Dijon*') [1979] ECR 649.   [25] Ibid, para 8 (emphasis added).

[26] Case 302/86 *Commission v Denmark* [1985] ECR 4607.

[27] For a more extensive list of justification grounds, see C Barnard, 'Derogations, Justifications and the Four Freedoms: Is State Interest Really Protected?' in C Barnard and O Odudu (eds), *The Outer Limits of European Union Law* (Oxford: Hart Publishing, 2009).

[28] eg Case C-137/09 *Josemans v Burgemeester van Maastricht* [2010] ECR I-13019, para 82.

[29] eg Case C-55/93 *Criminal proceedings against van Schaik* [1994] ECR I-4837, para 19.

[30] Case C-368/95 *Vereinigte Familiapress Zeitungsverlags- und vertriebs GmbH v Heinrich Bauer Verlag* [1997] ECR I-3689, para 26.

[31] eg Case C-204/90 *Bachmann v Belgian State* [1992] ECR I-249, para 28.

[32] eg Case C-169/91 *Council of the City of Stoke-on-Trent and Norwich City Council v B&Q plc* [1992] ECR I-6635, para 11.

[33] eg Joined Cases 110/78 and 111/78 *Ministère public and 'Chambre syndicale des agents artistiques et impresarii de Belgique' ASBL v Van Wesemael* [1979] ECR 35, para 28.

[34] eg Case C-113/89 *Rush Portuguesa Ld v Office national d'immigration* [1990] ECR I-1417, para 18.

[35] Case C-75/11 *Commission v Austria*, judgment of 4 October 2012, nyr, para 52 (emphasis added), expressed later in the same paragraph as concerning a 'legitimate objective of the national provisions'.

generally, the Court has confirmed that national measures may be justified 'in order to meet imperative requirements'[36] or by 'overriding reasons in the public interest capable of justifying restrictions on the fundamental freedoms guaranteed by the Treaty.'[37]

More significantly, the open-ended justification framework that was developed originally for Article 34 TFEU now applies to measures that restrict any of the rights conferred by the Treaty freedoms. The decision in *Gebhard*, which mainly concerned the dividing lines between freedom of establishment and the provision of services, is widely considered to articulate a classic statement of the restriction/justification formula that operates across the different sectors of free movement law:

> national measures liable to hinder or make less attractive the exercise of fundamental freedoms guaranteed by the Treaty must fulfil four conditions: they must be applied in a non-discriminatory manner; they must be justified by imperative requirements in the general interest; they must be suitable for securing the attainment of the objective which they pursue; and they must not go beyond what is necessary in order to attain it.[38]

The justification framework is not premised on public interest concerns that are protected as Union interests in the same way as the Treaty-set grounds for derogation. Rather, the justification system has the potential to recognize more national or local understandings of, and concerns related to, the public interest. Through the logic of mandatory requirements, the Court has created, in other words, a genuinely merits-based system. This development means that national concerns can be examined on a case-by-case basis. The Court's assessment of the public interest can also evolve over time, in tune with how the premises of public interest evolve too.

The development of the justification framework is also, of course, a striking example of the Court's significant law-shaping powers in the field of free movement, since the Court has, in effect, recognized significantly more public interest arguments than the limited categories specified explicitly in the Treaty. On the other hand, the Member States have never stepped in to regain constitutional ownership of the issue post-*Cassis* – and so it is arguable that implicit (but nonetheless legitimizing) political acceptance can be attributed to the Court's approach for that reason.

At one level, the flexibility extended to the Member States through the combination of Treaty derogations and case law justifications is remarkable. It enables them to raise even the most singular, local, or esoteric, but nonetheless genuine, public interest arguments without the need to shoehorn their concerns artificially into the limited grounds available in the Treaty[39] – recalling, in particular, the Court's parallel insistence that the meaning of public policy must be interpreted very narrowly on its own terms. However, in a longitudinal study analysing the Court's judgments in 1984, 1994, and 2004, Barnard established that the case law 'show[s] a remarkable shift by the Court from considerable deference to Member States' regulatory freedom in 1984...to a greater willingness to review Member State justifications in 1994 ... [to] a more substantial review of the Member

[36] Case C-110/05 *Commission v Italy* ('*Trailers*') [2009] ECR I-519, para 59.
[37] Case C-384/08 *Attanasio Group Srl v Comune di Carbognano* [2010] ECR I-2055, para 50.
[38] Case C-55/94 *Gebhard v Consiglio dell'Ordine degli Avvocati e Procuratori di Milano* [1995] ECR I-4165, para 37.
[39] eg the Court has accepted the possibility that free movement restrictions could be justified in principle by 'the need to guarantee the stability and security of the assets administered by an undertaking for collective investment created by a severance fund' (Case C-39/11 *VBV – Vorsorgekasse AG v Finanzmarktaufsichtsbehörde* ('*FMA*'), judgment of 7 June 2012, nyr, para 31).

States' justifications in 2004, albeit combined with a recognition of a greater of number of justifications'.[40]

Barnard's assessment demonstrates that while States may raise a greater number of justification arguments in principle, that does not mean that they have had any greater success in restricting free movement rights in practice. The study also highlights the importance of both the function of the Court in making these determinations and the standard of proof that the Member States must reach when shaping their arguments. Both of these points will be picked up again in section 4.

3.2 Discriminatory and non-discriminatory restrictions

Formally, the distinction introduced in section 1 still stands, that is, directly discriminatory restrictions cannot be justified for any reasons other than the derogation grounds specified expressly in the Treaty. However, it has become increasingly difficult to sustain the veracity of that distinction by reference to case law practice. Initially, a particular point of strain emerged when States sought to justify directly discriminatory restrictions of free movement rights on the ground of environmental protection. In such cases, the Court at least endeavoured, if not altogether convincingly, to classify the national measure as non-discriminatory (or indistinctly applicable),[41] in order to enable the defendant State's arguments on environmental protection to be heard by the Court at least. Attention has been drawn to the confusing case law that has developed in consequence.[42] However, the Court has never openly confirmed that the justification framework can also be applied to save directly discriminatory measures or clarified the basis on which such a step might be taken. It has never, for example, reversed the narrow interpretation applied to the derogation grounds listed in the Treaty in a way that would enable protection of the environment to fit within the explicitly protected concept of public policy.

In more recent case law, the Court has seemed to circumvent the issue by sidestepping any classification of the nature of the restriction at issue and, in particular, avoiding the language of discrimination altogether. In *Commission v Austria* ('*Brenner II*'), for example, the Court was asked to review a ban that precluded vehicles weighing over 7.5 tonnes from carrying certain goods, affecting a motorway route with significant implications for transalpine traffic. Even though the Commission had argued that the measure was discriminatory, the judgment of the Grand Chamber stated very briefly that the contested national rule was a measure having equivalent effect to a quantitative restriction and was therefore precluded by Article 34 TFEU – with no discussion of what *kind* of restriction this actually was at all. However, the exclusion of local and regional traffic from the scope of the ban clearly underpinned the Commission's classification of the measure as discriminatory.

Importantly, there are also several examples of imperative public interest requirements, other than environmental protection, being considered in cases that involve

---

[40] Barnard, 'Derogations, Justifications and the Four Freedoms' (n 27) 295.

[41] See esp Case C-2/90 *Commission v Belgium* ('*Walloon waste*') [1992] ECR I-4431. In Case C-28/09 *Commission v Austria* ('*Brenner II*'), judgment of 21 December 2011, nyr, AG Trstenjak described the Court's approach in *Walloon waste* as 'work[ing] around' the rule on discriminatory restrictions and Treaty-based derogations (fn 34 of the Opinion).

[42] See AG Jacobs in Case C-379/98 *PreussenElektra AG v Schhleswag AG, in the presence of Windpark Reußenköge III GmbH and Land Schleswig-Holstein* [2001] ECR I-2099, paras 222–238 of the Opinion; AG Trstenjak in *Air quality* (n 41) paras 79–91 of the Opinion.

distinctly applicable restrictions of free movement rights. The issue is not, in other words, confined to the potentially worthy or special nature of environmental protection any longer. For example, in *Commission v Finland*,[43] the Court stated that 'it is clear from settled case-law that national legislation which constitutes a measure having equivalent effect to quantitative restrictions can be justified by one of the reasons of public interest laid down in Article [36 TFEU] *or by imperative requirements*'[44] – even though the contested procedural requirements were imposed on imported cars only. Similarly, in *Fachverband der Buch- und Medienwirtschaft*, concerning pricing restrictions imposed only on imported books, the Court first confirmed the narrow scope of 'protection of national treasures possessing artistic, historic or archaeological value' in Article 36 TFEU; but then stated that 'the protection of books as cultural objects can be considered as an overriding requirement in the public interest capable of justifying measures restricting the free movement of goods'.[45] Neither is the issue confined to the free movement of goods.[46]

In his Opinion in *PreussenElektra*, concerning restrictions on the free movement of goods, Advocate General Jacobs called direct attention to the weakening distinction between derogation grounds and the broader justification framework established by case law. He noted, first, that 'the Court has not formally abandoned the rule that imperative requirements cannot be invoked in connection with directly discriminatory measures' but also, secondly, that 'In view of the fundamental importance for the analysis of Article [36] of the Treaty of the question whether directly discriminatory measures can be justified by imperative requirements, the Court should, in my view, clarify its position in order to provide the necessary legal certainty'.[47] Weatherill has argued that 'There is strong normative appeal to a model whereby all types of justification are in principle available, but according to which the presence of discrimination would make the job of the regulator in showing that the chosen scheme is lawful particularly onerous'.[48] Similarly, in *Commission v Austria*, Advocate General Trstenjak supported 'in principle' the premise that protection of the environment (at least) should be available as an overriding reason in the public interest to justify discriminatory measures 'under any circumstances'.[49] She then suggested that 'the discriminatory character of a measure restricting the free movement of trade can be taken into account in a proportionality test in which the necessity and reasonableness of such measures in particular can be examined more closely'.[50] This aspect of proportionality review will be addressed in section 5.

If the Court were to reverse the convention that the justification of directly discriminatory measures is confined to the grounds spelled out in the Treaty – whether for protection of the environment only or, in line with its case law, more broadly for imperative

[43] Case C-54/05 [2007] ECR I-2473.   [44] Ibid, para 38 (emphasis added).
[45] Case C-531/07 *Fachverband der Buch- und Medienwirtschaft v LIBRO Handelsgesellschaft mbH* [2009] ECR I-3717, paras 32–34.
[46] eg outlining the varied approaches evident in case law on national restrictions placed on gambling, affecting the freedom to provide services, see AG Mengozzi in Case C-153/08 *Commission v Spain* [2009] ECR I-9735, paras 77–81 of the Opinion. In another example, relating to Arts 21 and 49 TFEU, the Court in Case C-524/06 *Huber v Bundesrepublik Deutschland* [2008] ECR I-9705, a case concerning aspects of a data processing system that applied only to nationals of other Member States, considered the objective of fighting crime as an element of protecting public order; but the Court did not discuss that objective in the Treaty-set language of public policy or public security.
[47] AG Jacobs in *PreussenElektra* (n 42) paras 228 and 229 of the Opinion.
[48] S Weatherill, 'Free Movement of Goods' (2012) 61 *International and Comparative Law Quarterly* 541, 544.
[49] AG Trstenjak in *Air quality* (n 41) paras 83 and 89 of the Opinion respectively.
[50] Ibid, para 90.

requirements to be considered on a case-by-case basis – it would enable the application of the merits-based justification framework across the board. This would, in turn, obviate the need for the Court to resolve questions about how to distinguish between *types* of discrimination, which is not always a straightforward exercise.[51] It cannot be ignored, however, that to collapse the distinction between derogation and justification so definitively would challenge the significance of having a limited pool of public interest grounds actually stipulated in the Treaty in the first place. It would also simply push many of the complexities that we encounter in free movement law to the third stage of analysis, that is, the determination of proportionality – a stage of review that is not free from complexity or controversy on its own terms, as outlined as section 5.

4 Application of the derogation and justification frameworks

A number of principles and questions that are relevant to the application of both the Treaty-based derogation framework and the case law-driven justification framework are outlined in this section. It addresses (a) the Court's general approach to, and role in, the determination of public interest; (b) the relevant burden and standard of proof; and (c) specific issues relating to the justification of free movement restrictions on the basis of arguments connected to the protection of fundamental rights.

4.1 General principles

4.1.1 The range of justifications

Derogation and justification arguments seek to establish an exception to the free movement rights guaranteed by the Treaty. In section 2, it was shown that the Court interprets those rights widely and thus defines any exceptions to them as narrowly as possible, having regard to the 'fundamental character' of the Treaty freedoms. On the other hand, however, we also saw in section 3 that the justification framework has evolved and expanded over time. Adjudication of the extent to which public interest arguments can supersede free movement rights constitutes a prime space within which debates about the character of the internal market, and indeed the EU polity more broadly, are aired and progressed.

The significance of this point becomes even more apparent when it is remembered that the Court rarely excludes issues from the scope of the Treaty at the stage of establishing a restriction of free movement rights on the grounds of the subject matter affected in isolation.[52] Instead, it navigates relevant moral and other complexities at the stages of justification and proportionality. For example, it is argued that the Court's softer approach to proportionality review in cases involving national restrictions on gambling is directly connected to the moral sensitivities associated with this activity, which clearly differ across

---

[51] On this point, see AG Sharpston in *Bressol and Chaverot* (n 12) paras 43–76.

[52] eg Case C-159/90 *Society for the Protection of Unborn Children Ireland Ltd (SPUC) v Stephan Grogan* [1991] ECR I-4685, para 21: 'medical termination of pregnancy, performed in accordance with the law of the State in which it is carried out, constitutes a service within the meaning of…the Treaty'; Case C-268/99 *Jany v Staatssecretaris van Justitie* [2001] ECR I-8615, para 49: 'prostitution is a provision of services for remuneration which…falls within the concept of economic activities'. For an exception, when the activity in question was unlawful in *all* of the Member States, see *Josemans v Burgemeester van Maastricht* (n 28), para 41.

the Member States.[53] This point is explained in more detail in section 5, in the context of proportionality review.

A similarly generous approach, emphasizing that discretion should be allocated to the Member States in determining the measures that need to be put in place to ensure the effective protection of overriding requirements of public interest, can be seen in the *Trailers* case on national rules regulating the use of goods. Here, the Court considered that the contested national rules were justified on the ground of road safety and proportionate to the achievement of that objective, against the views of two Advocates General.[54] In that case, however, the Court also widened the scope of Article 34 TFEU to catch non-discriminatory restrictions of the free movement of goods, leading to suggestions that the Court's 'margin of appreciation' approach to justification and proportionality was in fact compensating for the greater number of national measures that would actually now be caught by Article 34 TFEU in the first place. This example demonstrates the intricate connection between how restrictions are defined and how they are, in turn, defended.

The Court does not distinguish between or rank different public interest concerns in a formal or systematic way although, as noted previously in the context of the case law on gambling restrictions, nuanced differences in approach can nevertheless be detected in the case law. However, a more favourable approach to a Member State defence at the conceptual level does not mean that the Court will not thoroughly scrutinize the persuasiveness of the State's claims, as case study 16.1 on public health derogations suggests.

Case study 16.1: Derogating on grounds of public health

We saw in section 2.2 that, in its decision in *DocMorris*, addressing the compatibility of national restrictions on the operation of pharmacies with the Treaty provisions on establishment and services, the Court stated that 'the health and life of humans rank foremost among the assets and interests protected by the Treaty and that it is for the Member States to determine the level of protection which they wish to afford to public health and the way in which that level is to be achieved. Since the level may vary from one Member State to another, Member States must be allowed discretion.'[55] This statement would appear to suggest the existence of a devolved regulatory space within which the Member States may determine and implement their own responses to public health concerns. In reality, however, the requirements of EU law are much more prescriptive and public health defences rarely succeed before the Court.

First, a State must actually demonstrate that any alleged risks to public health are genuine.[56] Where scientific data is relied upon, it must be 'the results of international scientific research' and the 'latest scientific data available at the date of the adoption of [the national] decision' in order for the State's arguments to be persuasive enough to merit a restriction of free movement rights.[57] The Court has also confirmed that

> an assessment of the risk could reveal that scientific uncertainty persists as regards the existence or extent of real risks to human health. In such circumstances... a Member State

---

[53] See S Planzer, 'The ECJ on Gambling Addiction: Absence of an Evidence-Oriented Approach' [2010] 3 *European Journal of Risk Regulation* 289 and S van den Bogaert and A Cuyvers, 'Money for Nothing: The Case Law of the EU Court of Justice on the Regulation of Gambling' (2011) 48 *Common Market Law Review* 1175, esp 1206–1210.   [54] cf the decision in *Trailers* (n 36) with the Opinions of AG Léger and AG Bot.

[55] *Apothekerkammer des Saarlandes* (n 11) para 19.

[56] eg Case 90/86 *Criminal proceedings against Zoni* [1988] ECR 4285, para 13.

[57] Case C-95/01 *Criminal proceedings against Greenham and Abel* [2004] ECR I-1333, paras 40 and 42.

may, in accordance with the precautionary principle, take protective measures without having to wait until the existence and gravity of those risks are fully demonstrated.[58]

But the Court also emphasized that 'the risk assessment cannot be based on purely hypothetical considerations'.[59]

Secondly, for natural persons, and reflecting the particular implications of – and the level of protection that attaches to – the status of Union citizens, restrictions of freedom of movement on the grounds of public health are strictly delimited by the requirements of Directive 2004/38/EC, Article 29 of which provides as follows:

1. The only diseases justifying measures restricting freedom of movement shall be the diseases with epidemic potential as defined by the relevant instruments of the World Health Organisation and other infectious diseases or contagious parasitic diseases if they are the subject of protection provisions applying to nationals of the host Member State.

2. Diseases occurring after a three-month period from the date of arrival shall not constitute grounds for expulsion from the territory.

3. Where there are serious indications that it is necessary, Member States may, within three months of the date of arrival, require persons entitled to the right of residence to undergo, free of charge, a medical examination to certify that they are not suffering from any of the conditions referred to in paragraph 1. Such medical examinations may not be required as a matter of routine.

Finally, in the case law on access to health-care services, the Court has shown that it is also willing to review aspects of the structure of national health-care systems – even though these kinds of national policy choices are closely connected to models of social solidarity and to the controversial question of the allocation of resources, a point picked up again in section 4.1.2.[60] It is also important to recognize that the Member States are generally responsive to their obligations under EU law in such circumstances, notwithstanding the sensitive nature of the national policy change that may be required. For example, in its decision in *Watts*, the Court confirmed that the obligation on States to reimburse the cost of hospital treatment provided in another Member State also applies to a publicly funded national health service that provides such treatment free of charge, such as the National Health Service (NHS) in the UK.[61] The implications of that judgment were subsequently given effect in national law, providing a strong example of the financial as well as regulatory consequences of the primacy of EU law.[62]

4.1.2 Economic justifications

It is a standard premise of free movement law that 'aims of a purely economic nature cannot constitute an overriding reason in the general interest justifying a restriction of

---

[58] *Greenham and Abel* (n 57) para 43.   [59] Ibid.

[60] eg Case C-158/96 *Kohll v Union des caisses de maladie* [1998] ECR I-1931; Case C-368/98 *Vanbraekel v Alliance nationale des mutualités chrétiennes (ANMC)* [2001] ECR I-5363; Case C-372/04 *Watts v Bedford Primary Care Trust and Secretary of State for Health* [2006] ECR I-4325, paras 103 and 104; and Case C-173/09 *Elchinov v Natsionalna zdravnoosiguritelna kasa* [2010] ECR I-8889.

[61] *Watts* (n 60).

[62] See para 1 of the Explanatory Notes attached to the Health Care (Reimbursement of the Cost of EEA Services etc) Regulations (Northern Ireland) 2012 (SI 2012/167); National Health Service (Reimbursement of the Cost of EEA Treatment) (Scotland) Regulations 2010 (SI 2010/283); and National Health Service (Reimbursement of the Cost of EEA Treatment) Regulations 2010 (SI 2010/915).

a fundamental freedom guaranteed by the Treaty'.[63] This principle has clear roots in the ambitions as well as the logic of closer integration. Extending equal opportunities to the nationals of other Member States – for example, in the context of employment, or the provision of public goods and services – costs money. If States could plead financial concerns in order to defend restrictions placed on free movement rights, there is a risk that the whole purpose of the internal market could easily be negated.

However, a more ambiguous case law thread accepts that 'none the less... *interests of an economic nature*'[64] can provide a legitimate defence to free movement restrictions. This line of reasoning emerged initially in case law on access to medical services. In *Kohll*, the Court accepted that

> the objective of maintaining a balanced medical and hospital service open to all ... although *intrinsically linked* to the method of financing the social security system, may also fall within the derogations on grounds of public health... in so far as it contributes to the attainment of a high level of health protection.[65]

However, in *Vanbraekel* the economic premise seemed to stand more autonomously, with the statement that

> it cannot be excluded that the risk of seriously undermining the financial balance of a social security system might constitute an overriding reason in the general interest capable of justifying a barrier to the principle of freedom to provide services.[66]

This perforation of the economic objectives exclusion remains a consistent feature of case law on medical services,[67] and the dynamic has crept outwards into public spending issues more generally too – for example, in cases on the funding of education[68] and social benefits.[69]

In some cases, the apparently economic aim is arguably not of a *purely* economic nature. In *FKP Scorpio*, for example, an accepted justification argument based on 'the need to ensure the effective collection of income tax' can be seen to embody broader systemic or structural objectives too.[70] But the economic and other objectives discussed in many of the judgments that veer into economic territory – especially judgments on access to health-care services – cannot be distinguished in the same way. The manner in which the case law is evolving thus suggests, once again, an exception from the more established approach seen in the case law on derogations and justifications that has not been tackled explicitly and seems, in consequence, to be spreading further by stealth.

---

[63] Case C-35/98 *Staatssecretaris van Financiën v BGM Verkooijen* [2000] ECR I-4071, para 48.

[64] *Commission v Germany* (n 2) para 60 (emphasis added).

[65] *Kohll* (n 60) para 50 (emphasis added).   [66] *Vanbraekel* (n 60) para 47.

[67] See more recently, eg *Watts* (n 61) paras 103–104 and *Elchinov* (n 60) para 42.

[68] eg Joined Cases C-11/06 and 12/06 *Morgan and Bucher* [2007] ECR I-9161, para 36: 'There is no doubt that the objective of ensuring that students complete their courses in a short period of time, thus contributing in particular to the financial equilibrium of the education system of the Member State concerned, may constitute a legitimate aim in the context of the organisation of such a system'.

[69] eg Joined Cases C-396/05, C-419/05 and C-450/05 *Habelt, Möser and Wachter v Deutsche Rentenversicherung Bund* [2007] ECR I-11895, para 83: 'the Court has accepted that the risk of seriously undermining the financial balance of the social security system may justify a barrier of that kind'.

[70] Case C-290/04 *FKP Scorpio Konzertproduktionen GmbH v Finanzamt Hamburg-Eimsbüttel* [2006] ECR I-9461, para 35.

4.1.3 The horizontal scope of the Treaty

At the level of establishing a restriction of free movement rights, the Court of Justice has effected different levels of horizontality in the case law to date: (a) rules that regulate freedom of movement in a collective manner even if not adopted by a public body (seen in case law on establishment, services, and workers),[71] (b) assigning Member State responsibility for private actions that impede free movement (goods),[72] (c) rules adopted by a private law body that holds the power to regulate in reality (goods),[73] and (d) full horizontal reach (workers).[74] If the Treaty can, in certain circumstances, catch the actions of private bodies and even private individuals, it then becomes important to ask whether such bodies and individuals can also rely on the derogation and justification frameworks provided by the Treaty and developed in the case law respectively.

In *Fra.Bo*, Advocate General Trstenjak identified two approaches to this question in the case law to date.[75] First, she observed that 'in most judgments', the Court simply applies the usual justification standard – establishing an overriding reason in the public interest – to private bodies and individuals as well.[76] However, secondly, she also identified a limited case law thread on what she termed 'special grounds in the private interest'.[77] In the case law on the regulation of various sporting activities, for example, she noted that the Court has considered justification arguments based on grounds such as the recruitment and training of young players.

In general, the expansion of *legitimate* interest beyond *public* interest can be rationalized by the limited capacity of private actors either to affect or to influence the kinds of policy issues affected and influenced by State bodies. If the scope of the Treaty reaches into private market behaviour in the field of free movement, then it seems inevitable that the corresponding scope of relevant justification arguments has to be altered too.

4.2 The jurisdiction of the Court of Justice

The key point to emphasize here is that the function of the Court of Justice is necessarily different in direct actions and indirect actions. In infringement proceedings against a Member State, taken under Article 258 TFEU, the Court must decide directly on all aspects of the case – including the outcome of any justification and proportionality arguments that have been submitted. However, for preliminary rulings,

> It is one of the essential characteristics of the system of judicial cooperation established under Article [267 TFEU] that the Court replies in rather abstract and general terms to a question on the interpretation of [Union] law referred to it, while it is for the referring court to give a ruling in the dispute before it, taking into account the Court's reply.[78]

---

[71] Case 36/74 *Walrave and Koch v Association Union cycliste internationale, Koninklijke Nederlandsche Wielren Unie and Federación Española Ciclismo* [1974] ECR 1405 and Case C-415/93 *Union royale belge des sociétés de football association ASBL v Bosman* [1995] ECR I-4921.

[72] Case C-265/95 *Commission v France* ('*Spanish strawberries*') [1997] ECR I-6959.

[73] Case C-171/11 *Fra.bo SpA Deutsche Vereinigung des Gas- und Wasserfaches eV (DVGW) – Technisch-Wissenschaftlicher Verein*, judgment of 12 July 2012, nyr.

[74] Case C-281/98 *Angonese v Cassa di Risparmio di Bolzano SpA* [2000] ECR I-4139.

[75] AG Trstenjak in *Fra.Bo* (n 73) paras 38 and 39 of the Opinion.   [76] eg *Angonese* (n 74) para 42.

[77] Citing eg Case C-325/08 *Olympique Lyonnais SASP v Olivier Bernard and Newcastle UFC* [2010] ECR I-2177, para 38.

[78] Case C-162/06 *International Mail Spain SL v Administración del Estado and Correos* [2007] ECR I-9911, para 24. See further chapter 10.

In essence, this means that the Court of Justice resolves questions of law, but the referring court retains authority over questions of fact. In most cases, therefore, the final view on justification – and especially proportionality – should be left to the national court.[79]

In reality, however, the *extent* of the Court's review in preliminary rulings tends to vary. In particular, there are several examples in free movement case law where the Court exceeds the baseline of resolving the relevant questions of law and effectively decides the case – including the questions of fact – by itself. The very detailed 'guidance' provided for the referring Swedish court in the *Laval* case provides a useful, and controversial, example.[80] There, the Court concluded unambiguously that

> collective action such as that at issue in the main proceedings cannot be justified in the light of the [protection of workers] where the negotiations on pay, which that action seeks to require an undertaking established in another Member State to enter into, form part of a national context characterised by a lack of provisions, of any kind, which are sufficiently precise and accessible that they do not render it impossible or excessively difficult in practice for such an undertaking to determine the obligations with which it is required to comply as regards minimum pay.[81]

On one view, more definitive Luxembourg rulings are provoked by the Court's understandable wish to provide the referring court with a genuinely 'useful answer' to the dispute before it.[82] Very detailed responses are also likely to appeal to national courts for that reason. But not even the acknowledged virtues of procedural economy and judicial cooperation displace the fact that constitutional boundaries written into Article 267 are overridden when the Court of Justice delivers overly prescriptive judgments and makes definitive findings on all aspects of a referred case. Nor do these kinds of responses in preliminary rulings help to ensure that national courts assume the analysis of cases through an EU legal prism themselves – helping to embed EU law more seamlessly into national legal orders than seems to have happened to date.[83]

4.3 The burden and standard of proof

Whether a public interest argument is being made on derogation grounds or as an overriding public interest requirement, the *burden* of proof falls on the Member State seeking to establish that defence. The required *standard* of proof is more difficult to pin down, since the procedural rules relevant to proceedings before the Court of Justice – whether for direct or indirect actions – contain very little detail on the issues of evidence and proof.[84] Two general principles can, however, be extracted from guidance that the Court has provided in the case law.

---

[79] See further Case C-14/09 *Genc v Land Berlin* [2010] ECR I-931, para 32: 'The national court alone has direct knowledge of the facts giving rise to the dispute and is, consequently, best placed to make the necessary determinations'.

[80] Case C-341/05 *Laval un Partneri Ltd v Svenska Byggnadsarbetareförbundet, Svenska Byggnadsar betareförbundets avdelning 1, Byggettan and Svenska Elektrikerförbundet* [2007] ECR I-11767. See further chapters 13 and 20.   [81] *Laval* (n 80) para 110.

[82] Case C-142/05 *Åklagaren v Mickelsson and Roos* [2009] ECR I-4273, para 41.

[83] See further H van Harten, 'Proportionality in Decentralized Action: The Dutch Court Experience in Free Movement of Services and Freedom of Establishment Cases' (2008) 35 *Legal Issues of Economic Integration* 217; J Baquero Cruz, '*Francovich* and Imperfect Law' in M Poiares Maduro and L Azoulai (eds), *The Past and Future of EU Law: The Classics of EU Law Revisited on the 50th Anniversary of the Rome Treaty* (Oxford: Hart Publishing, 2010).

[84] The currently applicable Rules of Procedure of the Court of Justice are published at OJ [2012] L265/1.

First, it is not sufficient for States merely to assert the relevance of a public interest objective to defend a contested national measure. Relatedly, generalizations will not be enough to meet the required standard of proof. Instead, States must present evidence to support and demonstrate the veracity of their claims.[85] Secondly, that evidence must be sufficiently 'precise' in order to 'substantiate' the arguments submitted.[86] The Court has described the nature of 'precise' evidence in different ways – for example, 'specific evidence',[87] 'appropriate evidence',[88] 'conclusive evidence'[89] – but the common requirement is that the evidence presented must *substantiate* the Member State's arguments. The Court of Justice increasingly discusses the required standard of proof that Member States should meet in its free movement case law. Moreover, we can see examples of this just as much in preliminary rulings as in direct actions.[90]

4.4 Fundamental rights as limits to free movement

The role of the EU in protecting fundamental rights has long been a controversial issue. But two specific questions arise in the context of undertaking a balancing exercise between freedom of movement and fundamental rights when considering the principles that govern exceptions to free movement law: (a) whether it is appropriate or effective to treat arguments based on fundamental rights in the same way as 'normal' derogations or justifications in the first place; and (b) whether the Lisbon Treaty, and especially the resulting binding nature of the Charter of Fundamental Rights, alters the way, in a more general sense, in which free movement disputes should now be resolved by the Court when Member States seek to displace the obligations placed on them by EU free movement law.

4.4.1 Fundamental rights as derogations and justifications

In essence, and linking back to the discussion in section 3, this issue relates to the extent to which EU law circumscribes the ability of the Member States to invoke justification arguments or, at least, the discretion that they enjoy in that context. Fundamental rights are protected in EU law as both general principles of EU law, long established through case law, and through the Charter of Fundamental Rights, which now has 'the same legal value as the Treaties' (Article 6(1) TEU). As a general rule, the Court has made it clear that 'A Member State may invoke reasons of public interest to justify a national measure which is likely to obstruct the exercise of [free movement rights] only if that measure is compatible with the fundamental rights whose observance the Court ensures'.[91] The intensity of review that the Court can apply in these circumstances is considered in section 4.4.2.

In some cases, however, the Member States themselves seek to defend a restriction of free movement rights on the ground that the contested national measure exists in order to protect fundamental rights. Here, the sometimes different *levels* of protection provided within national systems, often required by national constitutions, can give rise to a persisting point

---

[85] Case C-333/08 *Commission v France* [2010] ECR I-757, para 97.

[86] Case C-161/07 *Commission v Austria* [2008] ECR I-10671, paras 36 and 37.

[87] Case C-147/03 *Commission v Austria* [2005] ECR I-5969, para 63.

[88] Case C-319/06 *Commission v Luxembourg* [2008] ECR I-4323, para 51.

[89] Case C-400/08 *Commission v Spain* ('*Shopping centres*') [2011] ECR I-1915, para 62.

[90] See eg the extensive discussion of proof with respect to both justification and proportionality arguments in *Bressol and Chaverot* (n 12).

[91] Case C-60/00 *Carpenter v Secretary of State for the Home Department* [2002] ECR I-6279, para 40.

of contention between the Union and its Member States, and especially between the Court of Justice and national constitutional courts.

The Court of Justice has confirmed that the protection of fundamental rights by a Member State can be a legitimate basis on which to restrict the free movement rights guaranteed by the Treaty. In *Omega*, a case involving restrictions on laser killing games in Germany on the basis of the degree of protection accorded to human dignity by the German Constitution, the Court stated that

> since both the [Union] and its Member States are required to respect fundamental rights, the protection of those rights is a legitimate interest which, in principle, justifies a restriction of the obligations imposed by [Union] law, even under a fundamental freedom guaranteed by the Treaty such as the freedom to provide services.[92]

It is important to note that the Court considered that ensuring respect for human dignity was a requirement of *Union* law, 'it being immaterial in that respect that, in Germany, the principle of respect for human dignity has a particular status as an independent fundamental right'.[93] However, the Court clearly had regard to the specific level of protection provided for under German law in its subsequent assessment of the proportionality of the restrictions. The use of proportionality to accommodate national differences in this way is returned to in section 5.

The earlier judgment in *Schmidberger* is widely considered to have offered a useful reading of how fundamental rights protection should be managed in free movement cases. There, a decision by an Austrian public authority to authorize an environmental protest – resulting in the closure of a major interstate motorway for just over 30 hours – was challenged as a restriction on the free movement of goods. In its judgment, the Court presented the nature of the decision that it needed to make as raising

> the question of the need to reconcile the requirements of the protection of fundamental rights in the [Union] with those arising from a fundamental freedom enshrined in the Treaty and, *more particularly*, the question of the respective scope of freedom of expression and freedom of assembly, guaranteed by Articles 10 and 11 of the ECHR, and of the free movement of goods, where the former are relied upon as justification for a restriction of the latter.[94]

Having established that freedom of expression and freedom of assembly are rights that can be limited in certain circumstances under the system of European Convention on Human Rights (ECHR) law, the Court concluded that 'the interests involved *must be weighed* having regard to all the circumstances of the case in order to determine *whether a fair balance was struck* between those interests'.[95] The Court added that

> The competent authorities enjoy a wide margin of discretion in that regard. Nevertheless, it is necessary to determine whether the restrictions placed upon intra-[Union] trade are proportionate in the light of the legitimate objective pursued, namely, in the present case, the protection of fundamental rights.[96]

---

[92] Case C-36/02 *Omega Spielhallen- und Automatenaufstellungs-GmbH v Oberbürgermeisterin der Bundes stadt Bonn* [2004] ECR I-9609, para 35.   [93] Ibid, para 34.
[94] Case C-112/00 *Schmidberger, Internationale Transporte und Planzüge v Republik Österreich* [2003] ECR I-5659, para 77 (emphasis added).
[95] Ibid, para 81 (emphasis added).   [96] Ibid, para 82.

The Court's approach to the balancing of the different interests involved in cases where free movement rights and fundamental rights need to be 'reconciled' was considered to have broken down, however, in the controversial decisions in *Viking Line*[97] and *Laval*. In these judgments, the Court of Justice confirmed, for the first time, that the right to take collective action is a fundamental social right protected by EU law, on the basis that the protection of workers constitutes a recognized overriding public interest requirement. But the outcomes in the cases, which privileged freedom of establishment and the free provision of services respectively, seemed to dilute the normative significance attached to fundamental rights in cases like *Omega* and *Schmidberger*. For example, Barnard has questioned whether the fundamental social rights invoked in these cases can ever have the capacity to displace free movement rights since 'The moment collective action is found to be a "restriction"…the "social" interests are on the back-foot, having to defend themselves from the economic'.[98]

Both the realization of free movement objectives and the protection of fundamental rights are provided for in the EU Treaties. In reality, it will fall to the Court of Justice to reconcile these interests in individual cases given that there are no clear signals about their relative normative weighting in the Treaty itself. Reflecting the language used in *Schmidberger* and *Omega*, Advocate General Trstenjak has argued against seeing fundamental freedoms and fundamental rights as being in a 'hierarchical relationship' – again emphasizing the role and potential of proportionality, and considering that 'a restriction on a fundamental freedom is justified, when that restriction arose in the exercise of a fundamental right and was appropriate, necessary and reasonable for the attainment of interests protected by that fundamental right'.[99]

However, it is clear that the protection of fundamental rights has been enhanced in many respects by the Lisbon Treaty, not only through the binding status conferred on the Charter but also, for example, by the requirement in Article 6(2) TEU that the EU must accede to the ECHR. Advocate General Mengozzi is among those who see these enhancements as also signalling a distinct legal effect:

> As a result of the entry into force of the Treaty of Lisbon, when working conditions constitute an overriding reason relating to the public interest justifying a derogation from the freedom to provide services, they must no longer be interpreted strictly. In so far as the protection of workers is a matter which warrants protection under the Treaties themselves, it is not a simple derogation from a freedom, still less an unwritten exception inferred from case-law. To the extent that the new primary law framework provides for a mandatory high level of social protection, it authorises the Member States, for the purpose of safeguarding a certain level of social protection, to restrict a freedom, and to do so without European Union law's regarding it as something exceptional and, therefore, as warranting a strict interpretation.[100]

It will be important to track the Court's response to this challenge in future case law.

---

[97] Case C-438/05 *International Transport Workers' Federation and Finnish Seamen's Union v Viking Line ABP and OÜ Viking Line Eesti* [2007] ECR I-10779.

[98] C Barnard, 'Social Dumping or Dumping Socialism' (2008) 67 *Cambridge Law Journal* 262, 264.

[99] AG Trstenjak in Case C-271/08 *Commission v Germany* [2010] ECR I-7091, paras 186 and 189 of the Opinion.

[100] AG Mengozzi in Case C-211/08 *Commission v Spain* [2010] ECR I-5267, para 53 of the Opinion. Similarly, the 2010 Monti Report drew attention to the 'new legal context' post-Lisbon in its specific comments on the judgments in *Viking Line* and *Laval* (M Monti, 'A New Strategy for the Single Market: At the Service of Europe's Economy and Society', May 2010, http://ec.europa.eu/bepa/pdf/monti_report_final_10_05_2010_en.pdf, p 70.

4.4.2 Review of national measures 'implementing' Union law

As noted in section 4.4.1, the extent to which Member State derogation and justification arguments on public interest grounds can themselves be scrutinized for their compatibility with EU standards of fundamental rights protection is an important question in EU law. It is also an issue that has become even more complicated following the binding effect conferred on the Charter by the Lisbon Treaty.

On one view, when a Member State is trying to extract itself from its obligations under free movement law, a credible argument can be made that the national measure should therefore be treated as, in effect, falling outside the scope of Union law altogether. However, in its decision in *ERT*, the Court held that

> where a Member State [seeks] to justify rules which are likely to obstruct the exercise of the freedom to provide services, such justification, provided for by [Union] law, must be interpreted in the light of the general principles of law *and in particular of fundamental rights*.[101]

On this understanding of exceptions to free movement law, the frameworks of derogation and justification are themselves part of Union law. Any national measures taken for that purpose also fall within the scope of EU law for the purposes of fundamental rights review.

Article 51 of the Charter seemed to indicate a deliberate retreat from the position established by *ERT*. It states that 'The provisions of this Charter are addressed ... to the Member States *only when they are implementing* Union law'.[102] This wording arguably conveys Member State action in a positive or active sense only, such as measures adopted to implement an EU directive. However, early signs in the post-Lisbon case law seem to indicate that the Court will continue to interpret the concept of 'implementing' Union law quite broadly – and, for present purposes, as still capturing Member State measures taken to derogate from or justify restrictions of free movement rights. For example, in *Åkerberg Fransson*, the Court referred to the explanations attached to the Charter,[103] which do not have binding effect but have clearly influenced the Court's interpretation of the Charter nonetheless, to rule that 'the fundamental rights guaranteed by the Charter must therefore be complied with where national legislation *falls within the scope of* European Union law'.[104] Interestingly, however, the referring national court afterwards signalled its intention to apply the Luxembourg Court's preliminary ruling more narrowly than might have been expected.[105] That decision suggests that the meaning – and limits – of 'implementing' Union law remains an unresolved controversy.

5 Proportionality

5.1 Overview of the proportionality test

Even if the Court of Justice accepts that a national measure may legitimately restrict free movement rights in principle, the proportionality test then becomes critical since 'a restriction on the fundamental freedoms enshrined in the Treaty may be justified only if the

---

[101] Case C-260/89 *Elliniki Radiophonia Tileorassi AE (ERT) v Dimotiki Etairia Pliroforissis* [1991] ECR I-2925, para 43 (emphasis added).   [102] Emphasis added.

[103] Published at OJ [2007] C303/17.

[104] Case C-617/10 *Åkerberg Fransson*, judgment of 26 February 2013, nyr, para 21 (emphasis added).

[105] BVerfGE, 24 April 2013, 1 BvR 1215/07, 2013 NJW, 1948; see further the Editorial Comments in (2013) 50 *Common Market Law Review* 925.

relevant measure is *appropriate* to ensuring the attainment of the objective in question and does not go beyond what is *necessary* to attain that objective'.[106] The first – appropriateness – test is also often expressed as an assessment of *suitability*.

It is more debated whether what is normally referred to as proportionality *stricto sensu* (ie the greater the impact on free movement, the greater the importance attached to satisfying the public interest objective on which the Member State relies) is a distinct third test or is absorbed by the test of necessity.[107] In general, however, the Court increasingly and consistently articulates proportionality as a two-step test appraising (a) the suitability and (b) the necessity of the relevant national measure.

The Court sends somewhat mixed messages on the need to submit empirical evidence to establish the proportionality of a national measure. For example, in *Stoß*, in the context of restrictions on gambling, the Court first noted that 'the referring courts are in doubt as to whether, in order to justify restrictive measures...the national authorities *must be able to produce a study* supporting the proportionality of those measures which was prior to their adoption'.[108] The Court then considered that

> if a Member State wishes to rely on an objective capable of justifying an obstacle to the freedom to provide services arising from a national restrictive measure, *it is under a duty* to supply the court called upon to rule on that question with *all the evidence of such a kind* as to enable the latter to be satisfied that the said measure does indeed fulfil the requirements arising from the principle of proportionality.[109]

But it was conceded that 'it cannot...be inferred...that a Member State is deprived of the possibility of establishing that an internal restrictive measure satisfies those requirements, *solely on the ground that that Member State is not able to produce studies* serving as the basis for [its] adoption'.[110] On balance, however, it is clear that States have a far greater chance of success if they do submit appropriate evidence to substantiate their proportionality claims.

Linking back to the points made in section 4.2 about the particular role of the Court of Justice within the preliminary rulings procedure, the task of that institution is to provide and reinforce a coherent guiding structure for the application of proportionality in cases with an EU legal dimension. Thus the determination of proportionality is properly part of the task of the referring court in these cases – since that is the judicial body closest to the dispute itself, to the detail and discussion of the evidence submitted, and to the nuances of the public interest conceptions at stake.[111] National courts also have distinct responsibilities in this regard: in their judgments, they should demonstrate through clear reasoning and engagement with relevant EU case law that they have reached their conclusions on proportionality in accordance with the legal guidance established by the Court of Justice, which they are required to follow even if different kinds of proportionality tests or criteria are more usually applicable under national law.

---

[106] *Attanasio Group* (n 37) para 51 (emphasis added).

[107] Se AG Poiares Maduro in Case C-434/04 *Criminal proceedings against Ahokainen and Leppik* [2006] ECR I-9171, para 26 of the Opinion.

[108] Joined Cases C-316/07, C-358–360/07, C-409/07 and C-410/07 *Stoß* [2010] ECR I-8069, para 70 (emphasis added).

[109] Ibid, para 71 (emphasis added), referring to Case C-227/06 *Commission v Belgium* [2008] ECR I-46, paras 62 and 63.   [110] *Stoß* (n 108) para 72 (emphasis added).

[111] For recognition of this by the Court, see eg Case C-405/98 *Konsumentombudsmannen (KO) v Gourmet International Products AB (GIP)* [2001] ECR I-1795, para 33.

In reality, however, the division of functions between national courts and the Court of Justice is more complex. For example, we saw both a prescriptive assessment of proportionality in *Laval*, alongside a more devolved 'margin of discretion' approach in *Omega* in section 4.4.1. The reticence of the Court to engage in a more extensive proportionality review was also noted in section 4.1.1 with respect to the *Trailers* case, even though Advocate General Bot, in the second Opinion on the case, argued persuasively that less restrictive measures could indeed be put in place to achieve the road safety public interest objective at stake.[112] We return to this point in section 5.4.

5.2 **Appropriateness**

Restrictive national measures taken in the public interest will be considered to be appropriate or suitable if 'the means which they employ are suitable for the purpose of attaining the desired objectives'.[113] This criterion has also been expressed as confirming that the national measure is 'appropriate to ensuring attainment of the objective pursued only if it genuinely reflects a concern to attain it in a consistent and systematic manner'.[114] This limb of the proportionality test, which is essentially a procedural review, is normally addressed very briefly in the case law, with the Court frequently simply stating that the measure 'is' (or is not[115]) appropriate, without providing detailed reasoning.[116]

5.3 **Necessity**

Assessment of the necessity of a national measure normally involves a more substantive consideration of whether alternative measures that can achieve the stated public interest objective but have *less restrictive* effects on EU trade can be conceived.[117] Assessing the proportionality of a national measure in this sense will thus involve consideration of whether alternative measures could be *equally* effective in terms of achieving the public interest objective that has been accepted as legitimate in principle, but *less* restrictive having regard to their effect on EU trade.[118]

The Court has also confirmed that 'the burden of proof cannot be so extensive as to require the Member State to prove, positively, that *no other conceivable measure* could enable that objective to be attained under the same conditions'.[119] At a general level, the Court requires that 'If a Member State has a choice between various measures to attain the same objective it should choose the means which least restricts [free movement]'.[120] Sometimes, it gauges the proportionality of national measures by engaging in a comparative review of solutions adopted in other States.[121] But it has also confirmed that 'the fact

---

[112] AG Bot in *Trailers* (n 36) paras 167–171 of the Opinion; cf the judgment of the Court at paras 65–67.

[113] Case C-463/01 *Commission v Germany* [2004] ECR I-11705, para 78.

[114] *Attanasio Group* (n 37) para 71.

[115] See eg Case 124/81 *Commission v UK* ('*UHT milk*') [1983] ECR 203, para 32: 'It has not been shown that public health in the United Kingdom has been affected in the slightest by such imports'.

[116] eg *Trailers* (n 36) para 64.

[117] eg Case C-443/10 *Bonnarde v Agence de Services et de Paiement* [2011] ECR I-9327, para 35: 'Whilst the requirement...does indeed appear to be...appropriate for the attainment of the objectives of protecting the environment and combating fraud, it must however be verified that it is necessary to attain those objectives and that there are no other less restrictive means of doing so'.

[118] eg Case C-205/07 *Gysbrechts and Santurel Inter BVBA* [2008] ECR I-9947, para 53.

[119] *Trailers* (n 36) para 66 (emphasis added).

[120] Case 261/81 *Walter Rau Lebensmittelwerke v De Smedt PVBA* [1982] ECR 3961, para 12.

[121] eg Case C-126/91 *Schutzverband gegen Unwesen in der Wirtschaft v Yves Rocher* [1993] ECR I-2361, para 18 and *Commission v France* (n 85) para 105.

that one Member State imposes less strict rules than another Member State does not mean that the latter's rules are disproportionate'.[122]

5.4 Proportionality as a tool for mediating public interest

Proportionality is a mechanism that can usefully be deployed to manage the complexities inherent in public interest concerns, which can often differ in degree across the Member States. Where it can be argued, using appropriate evidence, that a contested national measure is both suitable and necessary to achieve stated public interest objectives that the Court has deemed to be a legitimate aim for the State to pursue, the concomitant restrictions of free movement rights can be defended. When the Court of Justice delves into the detail of proportionality itself, States rarely succeed in persuading the Court that the measures under review satisfy the proportionality test. In free movement law, however, it is essential to study the judgments of national courts too – whether or not a preliminary reference was made – in order to understand the calibration of proportionality in EU law in a more complete and also realistic sense.

But it is also important to remember that assessments made on the basis of proportionality are at the fringes of law. They often require scientific or other expert, for example economic, evidence to be interrogated by legal practitioners and, sometimes, the outcome seems to amount more to a subjective value judgement than a more neutral legal assessment.[123]

The discussion in this chapter has also pointed to several examples of a varying *intensity* of proportionality review. In section 4, for example, it was noted that areas of particular sensitivity tend to attract a less intensive degree of review from the Court. This message is clearly apparent in the Court's instructions to referring courts where relevant (eg in the use of goods case law, which involved a potentially controversial widening of the scope of restrictions of Article 34 TFEU). These issues are explored in more detail in case study 16.2 on gambling restrictions.

Case study 16.2: Navigating public moralities through proportionality review

The value of a clear, coherent, and predictable body of case law is obvious when considered from the perspective of legal certainty. It is not, however, the only consideration that can be taken into account in the development of EU law.

It was shown in section 4.1 that the unlawfulness, or restricted lawfulness, of an activity within a Member State will not remove the subject matter from the material scope of the Treaty – or, therefore, from possible review by the Court of Justice if national regulatory measures are challenged as a restriction of EU free movement rights. The regulation of gambling activities provides a very good example of behaviour that is perceived and therefore regulated in different ways by different Member States, in order to reflect divergent underpinning national conceptions of the morality, or otherwise, of such activities. Things become especially interesting in this context when States have to confront the limits potentially imposed on their regulatory discretion by the demands of EU law and the internal

---

[122] *Pharmacies* (n 64) para 51; recalling eg Case C-384/93 *Alpine Investments BV v Minister van Financiën* [1995] ECR I-1141, para 51 and *Omega* (n 92) para 108.

[123] For discussion and illustration of these points, and related literature, in an applied context, see C Barnard, 'A Proportionate Response to Proportionality in the Field of Collective Action' (2012) 37 *European Law Review* 117.

market: can they continue to prohibit their own nationals and economic operators from participating in an activity that they seek to proscribe or restrict within their own national borders when it is lawfully and often more freely accessible in other States – moreover, at the mere click of a mouse in the online age?

In *Schindler*, which concerned advertising restrictions in the UK relating to a lottery organized in Germany, the Court was mindful of arguments about the social harm that gambling pursuits can create or exacerbate, but it declined to take an overtly paternalistic stance. Applying its standard approach, the Court held that 'Even if the morality of lotteries is at least questionable, it is not for the Court to substitute its assessment for that of the legislatures of the Member States where that activity is practised legally'.[124]

However, such restrictions will almost always be justifiable in principle for reasons connected to protecting the national public interest, especially where a State can show that it clearly takes a 'consistent and systematic' policy approach to the restriction of gambling.[125] In *Liga Portuguesa*, Advocate General Bot rationalized the Court's approach as follows:

> the national authorities must be allowed a sufficient margin of discretion to determine the requirements entailed by the protection of gamblers and, more generally, taking account of the social and cultural characteristics of each Member State, the preservation of public order, with regard to the organisational arrangements of gaming and betting and the amount of stakes, as well the use made of the profits to which they give rise. The Member States are therefore free to set the objectives of their policy on betting and gaming and, where appropriate, to define in detail the degree of protection sought.[126]

At this point, then, the intensity of the applicable level of proportionality review becomes critically important. And it is apparent that, in the gambling case law, there is consistent evidence of relatively light-touch assessment on the part of the Court of Justice. Advocate General Bot defended that level of scrutiny by referring again to the margin of discretion attributed to Member States in this context, arguing that proportionality review in the arena of gambling restrictions 'should consist in ascertaining that the State in question has not manifestly exceeded its margin of discretion in the context in which those measures were adopted and applied'.[127]

This deference to national discretion is typically described and discussed in the academic commentary as a more procedural than substantive assessment of the appropriateness and necessity of national measures.[128] It is also more likely that the Court will refrain from making a definitive pronouncement on proportionality itself in the cases that reach it through the Article 267 TFEU procedure.[129]

Regulation of gambling activities must reflect and accommodate moral sensitivities, but review of restrictions on access to the gambling market must also recognize the fact that it is a lucrative trade sector. On one view, the reticence of the Court to get involved more substantively in its review of national gambling restrictions makes it difficult to ascertain how, and the extent to which, the rights of citizens and economic actors who wish to participate

---

[124] Case C-275/92 *Her Majesty's Customs and Excise v Schindler* [1994] ECR I-1039, para 32.

[125] eg Case C-42/07 *Liga Portuguesa de Futebol Profissional and Bwin International Ltd v Departamento de Jogos da Santa Casa da Misericórdia de Lisboa* [2009] ECR I-7633, para 61.

[126] Ibid, para 67 of the Opinion.   [127] Ibid, para 258.

[128] See F de Witte, 'Sex, Drugs and EU Law: The Recognition of Moral, Ethical and Cultural Diversity in EU Law' (2013) 50 *Common Market Law Review* 1545 and van den Bogaert and Cuyvers, 'Money for Nothing' (n 53).

[129] See eg Case C-258/08 *Ladbrokes Betting & Gaming Ltd and Ladbrokes International Ltd v Stichting de Nationale Sporttotalisator* [2010] ECR I-4757, para 50.

in such activities are being restricted in different parts of the supposedly border-free EU market. The resulting space created for the meaningful regulatory diversity in a sensitive policy area showcases, on the other hand, how the elasticity inherent in proportionality review can be used to manage a spectrum of divergent, and genuinely held, moral and social views.

However, it should not be forgotten that the Court is itself, in a sense, making a moral and social decision here too. In prescribing the level of proportionality review that should be applied in case law according to the relevant subject matter, the Court is essentially communicating its own view as to when the primary free movement rights conferred by the Treaty should prevail over and above other interests and values, and when they should not. Choices made about the application of proportionality may, therefore, be merited and they may even prove to be effective when viewed in a wider social and even constitutional context; but they are not neutral.

6 Derogating from the free movement of persons

It was observed in section 2 that the free movement rights of natural persons holding Member State nationality – irrespective of the purpose for which they have moved, that is, whether they are exercising economic activity (eg working) or not (eg moving for the purpose of study or even more temporarily for holidays) – are connected to the status of EU citizenship. These rights are thus subject to restrictions laid down in secondary legislation as well as by the Treaty itself. The ethos of citizenship adds a distinct element to the issue of derogation too, since it bolsters the free movement rights conferred on Member State nationals in the first place. It is not surprising, therefore, that the Court has consistently asserted that Union citizenship is 'destined to be the fundamental status of nationals of the Member States, enabling those who find themselves in the same situation to enjoy the same treatment in law irrespective of their nationality, subject to such exceptions as are expressly provided for'.[130]

For this reason, Directive 2004/38 has tightly curtailed the extent to which Member States can lawfully deport EU citizens from their territories. The approach of, and rules codified by, the Directive capture and strengthen several principles developed in the case law over many years. Two different sets of rules will be outlined in this section: (a) the general provisions of the Directive that govern derogation from free movement rights in the form of expulsion orders against EU citizens, and (b) the specific issue of deportation based on economic grounds.

6.1 Deportation and Directive 2004/38: general principles

Member States may only restrict the movement and residence rights of EU citizens and their family members on the grounds of public policy, public security, or public health. The limited scope of the public health derogation has already been outlined in section 4.1.

Article 27(2) of the Directive requires that decisions based on public policy or public security 'shall comply with the principle of proportionality and shall be based exclusively on the personal conduct of the individual concerned'. This means that expulsion decisions taken in respect of groups of EU citizens, which are often preventive in motivation but taken

---

[130] Case C-184/99 *Grzelczyk v Centre public d'aide sociale d'Ottignies-Louvain-la-Neuve* [2001] ECR I-6193, para 31.

without due consideration of the circumstances or behaviour of each individual member of that group, are not permissible under EU law. The Directive also delimits the meaning of personal conduct as 'represent[ing] a genuine, present and sufficiently serious threat affecting one of the fundamental interests of society'.[131] In general, however, it is important to remember that the rights now codified by and expanded upon in the Directive retain their character as primary rights conferred by the Treaty, as interpreted by the case law of the Court. Legislation can shape the exercise of the primary free movement rights, but it cannot go as far as to undermine the very existence of those rights. In *Baumbast*, for example, the Court was clear on this point:

> the application of the limitations and conditions acknowledged in Article [21(1) TFEU] in respect of the exercise of that right of residence is subject to judicial review. Consequently, any limitations and conditions imposed on that right do not prevent the provisions of Article [21(1) TFEU] from conferring on individuals rights which are enforceable by them and which the national courts must protect.[132]

Other provisions of Directive 2004/38 establish a net of procedural protection for individuals subject to expulsion decisions: conditions that relate to the notification of decisions (Article 30); administrative and judicial review redress procedures, as appropriate (Article 31); the duration of exclusion orders, including the opportunity to submit an application for the lifting of such an order after a 'reasonable period' (Article 32); and limitation of expulsion as a 'penalty or legal consequence of custodial penalty' (Article 33).

Article 28 of the Directive enshrines a further series of safeguards that protect EU citizens from expulsion, which reflect the degree of connection established between the citizen and the host State (see Figure 13.7). Article 28(1) requires a Member State to take into account 'considerations such as how long the individual concerned has resided on its territory, his/her age, state of health, family and economic situations, social and cultural integration into the host Member State and the extent of his/her links with the country of origin'. In some respects, these criteria reflect the more general requirement of respect for family life, guaranteed by Article 8 ECHR and Article 7 Charter.

Article 28 of the Directive also fixes prescribed criteria regarding the nature of the public policy or public security issues that can be taken into account, depending on the length of time that the affected EU citizen has resided in the relevant host State. Where a Member State national and/or their family member(s) acquire the status of permanent residence in the territory of a host State, in accordance with the conditions set down in Articles 16 to 18 of the Directive, they can only be expelled on *serious* grounds of public policy or public security. According to Article 28(3), only *imperative* grounds of public security can justify an expulsion decision against a citizen who has either resided in the host State for the previous ten years or is a minor, unless expulsion can be shown in the latter case to be 'necessary for the best interests of the child'.

Through the levels of protection established by Article 28, the EU legislature clearly intended to strengthen the residence rights acquired by EU citizens in host States over time, noting the progression from 'serious' to 'imperative' grounds of public policy or public security. However, this distinction might be less meaningful in practice than may have been assumed, as case study 16.3 on the relevance of criminal convictions suggests.

---

[131] Reflecting pre-citizenship case law such as, eg Case 30/77 *R v Bouchereau* [1977] ECR 1999, para 35. A detailed discussion of relevant case law can be found in Joined Cases C-482/01 and C-493/01 *Orfanopoulos and Oliveri v Land Baden-Württemberg* [2004] ECR I-5257.

[132] Case C-413/99 *Baumbast and R v Secretary of State for the Home Department* [2002] ECR I-7091, para 86.

Case study 16.3: Deportation and criminal convictions

Article 27(2) of Directive 2004/38/EC reflects a principle that had emerged through the case law: 'Previous criminal convictions shall not in themselves constitute grounds for taking' expulsion decisions. The general principle that an individual must continue to represent 'a genuine, present and sufficiently serious threat affecting one of the fundamental interests of society' applies in this context too.

The judgment in *Calfa*, in which a lifelong ban from Greece imposed as a result of a conviction for a drugs-related offence (which attracted a three-month term of imprisonment) was successfully challenged on the basis of the prospective impact on the applicant's free movement rights, also demonstrates that the application of proportionality is relevant here since 'as the Court has repeatedly stated, the public policy exception, like all derogations from a fundamental principle of the Treaty, must be interpreted restrictively'.[133]

Expulsion can never be the *automatic* consequence of a criminal conviction; and neither can preventive expulsion decisions be taken following a criminal conviction unless a real risk of reoffending can be demonstrated. The Court has made it clear in the case law that 'the existence of a previous criminal conviction can justify an expulsion only in so far as the circumstances which gave rise to that conviction are evidence of personal conduct constituting a present threat to the requirements of public policy'.[134]Awareness of these EU legal obligations can also be seen in national case law reviewing the validity of expulsion decisions issued on the basis of criminal convictions.[135]

In *Tsakouridis*, the Court of Justice was asked to consider 'whether and to what extent criminal offences in connection with dealing in narcotics as part of an organised group' amounted to 'serious' or 'imperative' grounds of public security.[136] Ultimately, the Court of Justice left the decision to the referring court, but against a backdrop of the 'devastating effects' of dealing in narcotics and the 'serious evil for the individual' as well as 'social and economic danger to mankind' of drug addiction, the Court then provided detailed guidance on the scope of Article 28 and the other interests that national decision-makers needed to take into account:

> In the application of Directive 2004/38, a balance must be struck more particularly between the exceptional nature of the threat to public security as a result of the personal conduct of the person concerned...by reference in particular to the possible penalties and the sentences imposed, the degree of involvement in the criminal activity, and, if appropriate, the risk of reoffending...on the one hand, and, on the other hand, the risk of compromising the social rehabilitation of the Union citizen in the State in which he has become genuinely integrated...The sentence passed must be taken into account as one element in that complex of factors.[137]

The Court also emphasized the need for the referring court to take both the requirements of proportionality and the fundamental rights of the individual concerned into account, noting in particular the right to respect for family life.

Subsequent case law seems to indicate that the different standards codified within Article 28 of the Directive may be less meaningful in practice and less restrictive of Member State discretion than had been anticipated. In particular, in *PI*, it was argued that the gradation

[133] Case C-348/96 *Criminal proceedings against Calfa* [1999] ECR I-11, para 23.
[134] *Orfanopoulos and Oliveri* (n 131) para 67.
[135] eg *R (Chindamo) v Secretary of State for the Home Department* [2006] EWHC 3340 (Admin).
[136] Case C-145/09 *Land Baden-Württemberg v Panagiotis Tsakouridis* [2010] ECR I-11979, para 39.
[137] Ibid, paras 51 and 52.

between serious and imperative grounds became blurred. The applicant had been convicted and sentenced to a term of seven years' imprisonment for sexual assault offences committed over a period of 11 years, the victim of which was his former partner's daughter. While again reciting the case law on taking decisions on a case-by-case basis and ensuring adequate respect for fundamental rights and procedural safeguards, the Court indicated that

> it is open to the Member States to regard criminal offences…as constituting a particu-
> larly serious threat to one of the fundamental interests of society, which might pose a
> direct threat to the calm and physical security of the population and thus be covered
> by the concept of 'imperative grounds of public security', capable of justifying an expul-
> sion measure under Article 28(3), as long as the manner in which such offences were
> committed discloses particularly serious characteristics, which is a matter for the refer-
> ring court to determine on the basis of an individual examination of the specific case
> before it.[138]

While fully recognizing the grave nature of the offences and the gravity of the impact of the crimes committed for the victim, commentators have, however, questioned whether the legislative intention underpinning the notion of imperative grounds of public security should properly apply to a case of this kind, that is, in the absence of risk to the security of broader State society in more systemic terms.[139] The Opinion of Advocate General Bot per-haps gives an indication of the concern driving the decision, at paragraph 62: 'To acknow-ledge that Mr I. may derive from his criminal conduct the right to the enhanced protection provided for in Article 28(2) and (3) of that directive would, in my view, conflict with the values on which citizenship of the Union is based'.

6.2 Deportation on economic grounds

Article 27(1) of Directive 2004/38 states that the grounds of public policy, public security, or public health may not be invoked 'to serve economic ends'. However, the link between deportation and financial resources is more complex in reality. For residence rights in a host State beyond an initial (and largely unregulated) stay of three months, Article 7 estab-lishes the basic threshold conditions of 'sufficient resources…not to become a burden on the social assistance system of the host Member State' and 'comprehensive sickness insur-ance'. Recital 16 of the Directive's Preamble provides more nuance:

> As long as the beneficiaries of the right of residence do not become an *unreasonable* burden on
> the social assistance system of the host Member State they should not be expelled. Therefore,
> *an expulsion measure should not be the automatic consequence of recourse to the social assistance
> system*. The host Member State should examine whether it is a case of temporary difficulties
> and take into account the duration of residence, the *personal circumstances* and the amount of
> aid granted in order to consider whether the beneficiary has become an *unreasonable* burden
> on its social assistance system and to proceed to his expulsion. In no case should an expulsion
> measure be adopted against *workers, self-employed persons or job-seekers* as defined by the
> Court of Justice save on grounds of public policy or public security.[140]

---

[138] Case C-348/09 *PI v Oberbürgermeisterin der Stadt Remscheid*, judgment of 22 May 2012, nyr, para 33.

[139] For discussion, see G Anagnostaras, 'Enhanced Protection of EU Nationals against Expulsion and the Concept of Internal Public Security: Comment on the *PI* Case' (2012) 37 *European Law Review* 627.

[140] Emphasis added.

Article 14(3) of the Directive confirms that 'An expulsion measure shall not be the *automatic* consequence of a Union citizen's or his or her family member's recourse to the social assistance system of the host Member State'.[141] But the inverse of this position is that recourse to the host State's social assistance system *can*, therefore, be a *legitimate* factor in expulsion decisions in some cases – thus rationalizing economically grounded justification reasons in this strand of free movement law, even if only to a limited extent.[142] The irony of the fact that this exception to the general rule is found within the rights attached to the most 'fundamental status' that EU nationals can enjoy is self-evident. It is one of the starkest disconnects between the conceptual potential of Union citizenship and the legal constraints placed on its realization.

It is important to remember, however, that the general principles that shape the deportation of EU citizens apply here too: decisions must be taken on an individual, case-by-case basis, in line with the requirements of proportionality, and mindful of the procedural safeguards guaranteed to all EU citizens by the Directive.

7 Conclusion

This chapter has provided an overview of the Treaty-based derogation system and the broader justification framework that enable Member States lawfully to restrict free movement rights in certain circumstances. The general approach taken by the Court of Justice seeks to interpret the public interest concerns that underpin any such restrictions as narrowly as possible, mindful of the fact that the realization of primary Treaty rights is at stake. National measures taken in the public interest are thus also subject to a two-step proportionality review that interrogates both the suitability and necessity of the action taken. As Advocate General Bot pointed out in his Opinion for the *Trailers* case, 'It is . . . the review of proportionality which enables the Court to weigh the interests associated with attainment of the internal market against those relating to the legitimate interests of the Member States'.[143] Both the public interest and proportionality elements of a defendant State's public interest submissions must be properly supported with appropriate evidence.

Notwithstanding the strictness of the scrutiny applied to reviewing exceptions to free movement law in general, however, there are also clear examples of a more hands-off approach in certain sectors of the case law – normally, when sensitivities are involved vis-à-vis the substantive public interest concerned either in a general sense or specifically for the Member State in question. Several potential points of case law incoherence can be added to this factor, including (a) the inherently pliable nature of public interest and, especially, proportionality through the process of legal adjudication; (b) the dissolving distinction in the case law between Treaty-based derogations and broader public interest arguments; and (c) the changing shape of the EU legal context following the amendments brought about by the Lisbon Treaty. The search for the optimal balance between uniform EU free movement rights and respect for national and more local expressions of regulatory diversity clearly continues.

---

[141] Emphasis added.

[142] The lawfulness of this course of action, potentially at least, is confirmed in eg *Grzelczyk* (n 130) para 42: 'That interpretation does not, however, prevent a Member State from taking the view that a student who has recourse to social assistance no longer fulfils the conditions of his right of residence or from taking measures, within the limits imposed by Community law, either to withdraw his residence permit or not to renew it'.

[143] AG Bot in *Trailers* (n 36) para 101 of the Opinion.

Further reading

C BARNARD, 'Derogations, Justifications and the Four Freedoms: Is State Interest Really Protected?' in C Barnard and O Odudu (eds), *The Outer Limits of European Union Law* (Oxford: Hart Publishing, 2009)

J MORIJN, 'Balancing Fundamental Rights and the Common Market Freedoms in Union Law: *Schmidberger* and *Omega* in the Light of the European Constitution' (2006) 12 *European Law Journal* 15

N NIC SHUIBHNE and M MACI, 'Proving Public Interest: The Growing Impact of Evidence and Proof in Free Movement Case Law' (2013) 50 *Common Market Law Review* 965

W-H ROTH, 'Economic Justifications and the Internal Market' in M Bulterman, L Hancher, A McDonnell, and H Sevenster (eds), *Views of European Law from the Mountain: Liber Amicorum Piet Jan Slot* (Dordrecht: Kluwer, 2009)

17

Competition law

Alison Jones and Christopher Townley

1 Introduction

This chapter examines the two core TFEU competition rules governing anti-competitive agreements (Article 101) and abuse of a dominant position (Article 102). Despite several changes in the Treaties governing the EU, these provisions remain largely unchanged since the original Treaty of Rome 1957. That does not mean that the interpretation of these provisions has stood still, however. As the EU Treaties themselves have changed, from ones with largely economic goals, to a much more integrated social and economic system, a question which has arisen is whether the competition law rules should be read as part of this integrated web, or as isolated provisions. A growing view is that they should be competition law pure and simple and that they should pursue an economic objective: the maximization of consumer welfare. Simultaneously there has been a push to move away from the form-based interpretation of the rules frequently adopted in the past, towards a more effects-based economic approach. This chapter focuses on these two themes (the goals of EU competition law; and the importance of economic, effects-based analysis) when discussing Articles 101 and 102 and considering who these competition law rules apply to, when they apply, and to which types of conduct.

2 Overview of EU competition law

2.1 EU competition law

More than 125 jurisdictions around the world now have in place systems of competition law (or antitrust law as they are known in the US).[1] Such systems are, essentially, designed to protect the process of competition, and to deal with market imperfections arising, in a free market economy. Without competition law rules, firms may be free to act to distort the process of competition by, for example, colluding or merging with their competitors. Further, firms which win the competitive battle or 'natural' monopolies may be free to act without any competitive restraint being exercised over their behaviour.

The original EEC Treaty (the Treaty of Rome) incorporated competition laws. Indeed, the activities of the EEC included, amongst other things, not only the creation of an internal market but also 'a system ensuring that competition in the internal market is not distorted'.[2] This provision embedded the principle of undistorted competition in the fundamental provisions of the Treaty and provided the foundation for the specific competition rules set out therein, including

- an article prohibiting restrictive agreements between undertakings[3] (now Article 101 TFEU'):
  - Article 101(1) prohibits 'all agreements between undertakings, decisions by associations of undertakings and concerted practices which may affect trade between Member States and which have as their object or effect a prevention, restriction or distortion of competition within the common market';
  - such agreements are prohibited and restrictive provisions within them are void (see Article 101(2))[4] unless the agreement satisfies the four criteria for legal exception, or exemption, set out in Article 101(3) – broadly where specified benefits are passed on to consumers and offset the restrictive effects;
- an article prohibiting 'any abuse by one or more undertakings of a dominant position' held within a substantial part of the internal market 'in so far as it may affect trade between Member States' (now Article 102 TFEU);
- rules to prevent Member States maintaining in force measures contrary to these and other Treaty rules (now Article 106 TFEU);
- rules prohibiting Member States granting unlawful State aid to undertakings so as to distort competition (now Articles 107 to 109 TFEU).

---

[1] In contrast, 'Until the mid 20th century less than 10 competition regimes existed worldwide' (*UNCTAD*) http://unctad.org/en/Pages/DITC/CompetitionLaw/ResearchPartnership/Benchmarking-Competition. aspx.

[2] Art 3(f) later Art 3(1)(g) EC Treaty. Although following Lisbon this provision was amended and removed to Protocol 27 to the Treaties.   [3] See section 4.1.

[4] As interpreted by Case 56/65 *Société Technique Minière v Maschinenbau Ulm GmbH* [1966] ECR 235.

In addition, to ensure that the EU competition system is comprehensive and effective, merger control rules have been added by Council regulation to the competition law arsenal.[5]

This chapter focuses on Articles 101 and 102, the rules governing anti-competitive agreements and conduct. Although the original EEC Treaty has been amended, renamed, and renumbered on several occasions, the wording of these rules has essentially remained unaltered.

2.2 Objectives of EU competition law

A question which is fundamental to the interpretation and application of the competition law rules is what is their objective? The EU Treaties do not define the core concepts set out in the competition law rules, such as a restriction of competition or an abuse of a dominant position, or explain what the relevant goals are. It has therefore been for the EU Courts to put flesh on, and to interpret, these provisions. The case law makes it clear that Articles 101 and 102 both have the same goal(s).[6]

Several goals have been proposed. The main ones are Ordoliberalism, consumer welfare, and the single market. Ordoliberalism is a school of thought born of a group of economists and lawyers from Freiburg, Germany. According to this school the competition rules should protect 'individual economic freedom of action as a value in itself, or vice versa, the restraint of undue economic power.'[7] This freedom is viewed as a political (even human) right. It includes the freedom for firms to compete with others without powerful firms interfering to restrict them. This competition law system should therefore focus on eliminating cartels, the market power of single firms, and contracts creating unjustified limits on firms' competitive autonomy. 'Ordoliberals would prefer a state of inefficiency coupled with freedom rather than a totalitarian, but efficient, state.'[8] Although this objective appears to have influenced the development of the case law and decisional practice in the past, Ordoliberalism does not today have significant support from the European Commission, academics, or practitioners, even if apparent references to this goal can, arguably, still be gleaned from EU Court case law.[9] Indeed, the Commission received considerable criticism for following this type of approach in the early years of its application of Articles 101 and 102 and at the end of the 1990s it set about significantly 'modernizing' its interpretation and application of the EU competition law rules.

The current view of the Commission is that the appropriate goal for Articles 101 and 102 is 'to protect competition on the market as a means of enhancing consumer welfare and of ensuring an efficient allocation of resources.'[10] This stance is supported by many

---

[5] See now Regulation 139/2004 (OJ [2004] L1/1).

[6] Case 6/72 *Europemballage Corporation and Continental Can Company Inc v Commission* [1973] ECR 215, paras 24 and 25.

[7] W Möschel, 'The Proper Scope of Government Viewed from an Ordoliberal Perspective: The Example of Competition Policy' (2001) 157 *Journal of Institutional and Theoretical Economics* 4.

[8] L Lovdahl Gormsen, *A Principled Approach to Abuse of Dominance in European Competition Law* (Cambridge: Cambridge University Press, 2010) 43.

[9] Case C-1/12 *Ordem dos Técnicos Oficiais de Contas (OTOC) v Autoridade da Concorrência*, judgment of 28 February 2013, nyr, paras 92 and 93 (Art 101); Joined Cases 6/73 and 7/73 *Istituto Chemioterapico Italiano SpA and Commercial Solvents Corporation v Commission* [1974] ECR 223 (Art 102).

[10] Commission guidelines on the application of Article 81(3) [now Art 101(3)] of the Treaty (Art 101(3) Guidelines) (OJ [2004] C101/97) para 13.

academics and practitioners.[11] Under this approach, broadly, competition and the benefits of a competitive market (which generally delivers lower prices, greater choice, innovation, and efficiency) is undermined, when the conduct at issue allows or will allow the relevant undertaking or undertakings to exercise *market power*, that is,

> the ability to maintain prices above competitive levels for a significant period of time or to maintain output in terms of product quantities, product quality and variety or innovation below competitive levels for a significant period of time.[12]

Despite prevalent support for this view, and the important role that the Commission has played in the development of EU competition policy, the interpretation of the Treaties is a matter for the EU Courts and case law does not provide unambiguous support for a consumer welfare approach.[13] For example, the Court of Justice held that the function of Article 102 is precisely to prevent

> competition from being distorted to the detriment of the public interest, individual undertakings and consumers, thereby ensuring the well-being of the European Union.[14]

More recently, however, in *Post Danmark*,[15] the Grand Chamber of the Court gave a judgment which, although containing no express statement about the objectives of the law, did focus heavily on the effects of the conduct on consumers.

It will be seen from some of the cases discussed later that the rules have also been applied as a mechanism to ensure the functioning of the internal market – that is, to prohibit conduct which 'might tend to restore the national divisions in trade between Member States'[16] as this could frustrate the most fundamental objectives of the EU, the creation of an internal market. This goal is not pursued in most other competition laws around the world, but its importance is still reiterated by the EU Courts.[17]

An additional issue which arises is whether the competition law rules should pursue a sole goal or whether other public policy goals can also be taken into account when applying them. Again, although consensus is growing that the sole goal of the rules should be consumer welfare, instances can be found where anti-competitive arrangements or conduct pursuing certain public policy goals, such as environmental protection, administration of justice, and public health, have been held not to breach Article 101 and 102.[18] Even though Articles 101 and 102 do not in themselves refer to such public policy goals, the EU Courts have taken account of these factors,[19] perhaps because

---

[11] See eg O Odudu, *The Boundaries of EC Competition Law: The Scope of Article 81* (Oxford: Oxford University Press, 2006) ch 6.   [12] Art 101(3) Guidelines (n 10) para 25.

[13] C Townley, 'Which Goals Count in Article 101 TFEU? Public Policy and Its Discontents' (2011) 32 *European Competition Law Review* 441.

[14] Case C-52/09 *Konkurrensverket v TeliaSonera Sverige* [2011] ECR I-527, para 22.

[15] Case C-209/10 *Post Danmark v Konkurrencerådet*, judgment of 27 March 2012, nyr.

[16] Joined Cases 56/64 and 58/64 *Établissements Consten and Grundig-Verkaufs v Commission* [1966] ECR 299, 340.

[17] Joined Cases C-403/08 and 429/08 *Premier League Ltd v QC Leisure and Murphy v Media Protection Services Ltd*, judgment of 4 October 2011, nyr, para 139 (Art 101); Joined Cases C-468–478/06 *Sot Lélos kai Sia EE v GlaxoSmithKline AEVE Farmakeftikon Proïonton* [2008] ECR I-7139, paras 65 and 66 (Art 102).

[18] See C Townley, *Article 81 EC and Public Policy* (Oxford: Hart Publishing, 2009) ch 2.

[19] Case C-519/04 P *Meca Medina v Commission* [2006] ECR I-6991, para 45; Case C-309/99 *Wouters v Algemene Raad van de Nederlandse Orde van Advocaten* [2002] ECR I-1577, paras 97 *et seq*; and Case T-193/02 *Laurent Piau v Commission* [2005] ECR II-209, para 102; and references in nn 9 and 17.

of the importance they place upon teleological and contextual readings of the EU Treaties. For example, Article 11 TFEU states that 'Environmental protection requirements must be integrated into the definition and implementation of the Union's policies and activities, in particular with a view to promoting sustainable development.'[20]

3 Enforcement and consequences of infringement

Articles 101 and 102 are enforced

(a) publicly, by a network of competition authorities (the European Competition Network (ECN)), comprised of the Commission and the national competition authorities (NCAs) of the Member States; and

(b) privately, through civil litigation in the national courts.

3.1 Enforcement by the Commission and NCAs

Council Regulation 1/2003[21] confers significant powers on the Commission to enforce Articles 101 and 102, including the power to investigate in an administrative procedure violations of the provisions, to issue decisions, and to impose significant fines upon undertakings found to be in breach (fines of up to 10 per cent of their worldwide turnover). Although this enforcement structure confers considerable power on the Commission (which acts as integrated decision-maker investigating, prosecuting, and deciding an individual case), the case law of the European Court of Human Rights suggests that, as the Commission's decisions are subject to review by the EU Courts,[22] the structure is likely to be compatible with Article 6 of the European Convention on Human Rights (ECHR), and in particular satisfies the investigated undertaking's right 'In the determination of his civil rights and obligations or of any criminal charge against him' to a 'fair and public hearing within a reasonable time by an independent and impartial tribunal' (the 'right to a fair trial').[23] Because, however, Articles 101 and 102 proceedings may culminate in the imposition of punitive fines (criminal charges for the purposes of Article 6(1) ECHR), 'the presumption of innocence resulting in particular from Article 6(2) of the ECHR...applies to the procedures relating to infringements of the competition rules.'[24] The burden is therefore on the Commission, or other person, alleging an infringement of Article 101(1) or 102 to establish 'sufficiently precise and coherent proof'[25] of an infringement.[26]

Initially the Commission played the central role in the enforcement process. This was partly because, from 1962 to 2004, it had the exclusive right to rule on the compatibility of an individual agreement with Article 101(3) and so to exempt individually agreements from the Article 101(1) prohibition (following the notification of the agreement to the

---

[20] See nn 138 and 139 and accompanying text and also chapter 22.   [21] OJ [2003] L1/1.

[22] See Regulation 1/2003, recital 33 and Art 31; and Arts 261 and 263 TFEU.

[23] See esp *A Menarini Diagnostics SRL v Italy* (Appl No 43509/08), ECtHR, 27 September 2011.

[24] Case C-199/92 P *Hüls AG v Commission* [1999] ECR I-4287, paras 149 and 150.

[25] Joined Cases 29/83 and 30/83 *Compagnie Royale Asturienne des Mines SA and Rheinzink GmbH v Commission* [1984] ECR 1679. The standard of proof in private litigation is a matter for the national courts of the relevant Member State.

[26] Joined Cases C-89/85 etc *Re Wood Pulp Cartel: Ahlström Osakeyhtiö v Commission* ('*Wood Pulp II*') [1993] ECR I-1307, para 127.

Commission).[27] Although *block exemptions* (see section 6.3.5), granted by EU regulation, exempt certain categories of agreement from Article 101(1), this set-up meant that it was difficult for NCAs and national courts to play a meaningful role in the enforcement process. From 1 May 2004, however, Regulation 1/2003 removed the Commission's exclusive competence to apply Article 101(3)[28] and so purports to make both Articles 101 and 102 directly effective in their entirety. Regulation 1/2003 thus paved the way for greater enforcement of the rules at the national level and sets out provisions designed to ensure consistency in application and interpretation by the different decision-makers.[29]

Regulation 1/2003 also permits, and in some cases requires, NCAs to apply Articles 101 and 102 in addition to their national competition laws. Many NCAs have the power to fine undertakings in breach of Article 101 or 102 (and/or national equivalents) following an administrative procedure similar to that followed by the Commission. In some Member States, there is provision for even more severe sanctions – including for individuals as well as undertakings. In the UK, for example, directors of companies that have breached the rules may be disqualified from acting in that capacity for up to 15 years. Further, individuals who have caused their firm to make or to implement horizontal hardcore cartel agreements[30] may commit a criminal offence and may potentially be liable to imprisonment for a period of up to five years and/or an unlimited fine.[31]

3.2 Private enforcement through civil litigation in the national courts

A claimant that has been or is being injured by an agreement or conduct that infringes Article 101 or 102 may also bring private proceedings before a national court seeking a declaration of nullity, an injunction, and/or damages to compensate loss suffered as a consequence. EU law requires national courts to protect the rights which individuals derive from these directly effective provisions of EU law and, in certain circumstances, to award damages to those who have been injured by a breach.[32] Nonetheless, up until recently there has been relatively little 'antitrust litigation' brought by private individuals before national courts. Indeed, 'in only 25% of all antitrust infringement decisions the Commission took in the past seven years did victims seek to claim compensation.'[33]

Although private litigation is now beginning to grow in some Member States, it is clear that private litigation in several Member States has been, and is still being, deterred by a number of other obstacles. The Commission hopes to tackle some of these, and in June 2013 it made a proposal for a Directive designed to remove many practical difficulties confronted by victims of infringements of the EU antitrust rules when instigating damages claims.[34]

---

[27] Regulation 17 (OJ English Special Edition [1959–62] 87) Art 9(1).

[28] Regulation 1/2003, recitals 6–8 and Arts 5 and 6.

[29] But see C Townley, 'Co-ordinated Diversity: Revolutionary Suggestions for EU Competition Law (and for EU Law Too)' (2014) 33 *Yearbook of European Law*, forthcoming.

[30] Broadly, arrangements between competitors to fix prices, restrict output, share markets, or rig bids, see further section 6.3.2 and case study 17.1.   [31] Enterprise Act 2002, s 204 and Part 6.

[32] Case C-453/99 *Courage Ltd v Crehan* [2001] ECR I-6297. See also Joined Cases 295–298/04 *Manfredi v Lloyd Adriatico Assicurazioni SpA* [2006] ECR I-6619 and chapter 14.

[33] Commission Press Release IP/13/525, 'Commission proposes legislation to facilitate damages claims by victims of antitrust violations', 11 June 2013.

[34] Proposal for a directive of the European Parliament and of the Council on certain rules governing actions for damages under national law for infringements of the competition law provision of the Member States and the European Union, COM(2013) 404 final; see also Commission Press Release IP/13/205 (6 March 2013) and MEMO/13/531 (11 June 2013).

4 Who do Articles 101 and 102 TFEU apply to and when do they apply?

4.1 Undertakings

Articles 101 and 102 apply to 'undertakings'. Undertaking has been defined in the same way under both Articles 101 and 102.[35] The term is not defined in the EU Treaties but the case law has settled that 'the concept of an undertaking encompasses every entity engaged in an economic activity, regardless of the legal status of the entity and the way in which it is financed' (*Höfner*).[36]

4.1.1 Entities and single economic units

The concept of an *entity* has been interpreted expansively to cover natural persons (including sole traders), legal persons (companies, including Ltd, plc, GmbH, SA, etc, and cooperatives, including agricultural ones), and even States.

A single undertaking – or entity – is not, however, necessarily synonymous with natural or legal personality[37] but denotes an economic unit which may be comprised of one or more persons, natural or legal.[38] For example:

- For the duration of their employment relationship, where employees are incorporated into undertakings and form an economic unit with them, employees are not considered to be separate entities.[39] The cases do not therefore look behind the legal personality of the company but treat individuals working within it as constituent elements of it.

- Agents are not considered to be entities separate from their principal, but rather to form an integral part of the principal's undertaking,[40] where they bear no, or insignificant, financial and commercial risks on the contracts they conclude/negotiate. Risks might relate to the sale of the goods, such as who owns the goods in the 'agent's' possession. They might also be linked to investments specific to the market, which allow the agent to negotiate with third parties on its principal's behalf.[41]

- The single economic entity doctrine potentially expands the notion of entity to entire corporate groups. This means that Articles 101 and 102 do not interfere with the internal organization of such groups (agreements between members of the group are intra-undertaking and not between separate undertakings).[42] In the

---

[35] Case T-68/89 *Società Italiano Vetro* [1992] ECR II-1403, para 358.

[36] Case C-41/90 *Höfner and Elsner v Macrotron* [1991] ECR I-1979, para 21.

[37] Commission Decision, *Pre-insulated Pipe Cartel* (OJ [1999] L24/1) para 154.

[38] Case 170/83 *Hydrotherm Gerätebau GmbH v Compact de Dott Ing Mario Adredi & CSAS* [1984] ECR 2999, para 11 and Case C-97/08 P *Akzo Nobel v Commission* [2009] ECR I-8237, para 55.

[39] Case C-22/98 *Jean Claude Becu* [1999] ECR I-5682, para 26. Sometimes it is hard to patrol this boundary, see C Townley, 'The Concept of an "Undertaking": The Boundaries of the Corporation – A Discussion of Agency, Employees and Subsidiaries' in G Amato and C-D Ehlermann (eds), *EC Competition Law: A Critical Assessment* (Oxford: Hart Publishing, 2007).

[40] Case C-266/93 *Bundeskartellamt v Volkswagen and VAG Leasing GmbH* [1995] ECR I-3477, paras 18 and 19. See also eg Case C-279/06 *CEPSA Estaciones de Servicio SA v LV Tobar e Hojos SL* ('*CEPSA*') [2008] ECR I-6681, paras 33–44; Case C-217/05 *Confederación Española de Empresarios de Estaciones de Servicio (CEES) v Compañia Española de Petróleos SA* [2006] ECR I-11987, paras 38–63. Contrast, *Consten and Grundig* (n 16) 340.

[41] *CEES* (n 40) paras 46 and 51. See also Commission guidelines on Vertical Restraints (OJ [2010] C130/01) paras 12–21.   [42] *Consten and Grundig* (n 16) 340.

context of parent–subsidiary relationships the entities will constitute a single economic unit if the subsidiary 'enjoys no economic independence'[43] or if the entities 'form an economic unit within which the subsidiary has no real freedom to determine its course of action on the market'[44] but carries out the instructions issued by the parent company controlling it. The question of when exactly a parent is able to, and does actually, exercise decisive influence over the policy and direct the conduct of its subsidiary, so the latter does not enjoy real autonomy or independence in determining its course of action in the market[45] has proved controversial, especially as the doctrine is now frequently relied upon as a mechanism for attributing liability to a parent for the conduct of its subsidiary that has violated the rules.[46] The cases establish that where a parent holds a 100 per cent shareholding in a subsidiary, or an insignificant amount less,[47] a rebuttable presumption that the parent does in fact exercise decisive influence over the commercial policy and conduct of its subsidiary applies.[48] Further, that the ability to, and actual, exercise of decisive influence can be ascertained even where the parent holds only a majority or minority interest in a subsidiary[49] where the 'factual evidence, including, in particular, any management power exercised by the parent company or companies over their subsidiary'[50] supports such a finding.

4.1.2 Economic activity

The definition of undertaking set out in *Höfner* requires that the entity be engaged in *economic activity*, that is, the offering of goods and services on a market. In principle, such an offer could 'be carried on by a private undertaking in order to make a profit'.[51] As the notion of undertaking focuses on the nature of the activity carried out by the entity concerned, it is clear that 'a given entity might be regarded as an undertaking for one part of its activities while the rest fall outside the competition rules'.[52] Thus 'the fact that, for the exercise of part of its activities, an entity is vested with public powers does not, in itself, prevent it from being classified as an undertaking . . . in respect of the remainder of its economic activities'.[53]

---

[43] Case 22/71 *Béguelin Import Co v SAGL Import Export* [1971] ECR 949, para 8.

[44] Case 15/74 *Centrafarm BV and Adriaan De Peijper v Sterling Drug Inc* [1974] ECR 1183, para 41. See also *Hydrotherm* (n 38) para 11; Case T-11/89 *Shell v Commission* [1992] ECR II-757, para 311; and generally WPJ Wils, 'The Undertaking as Subject of EC Competition Law and the Imputation of Infringements to Natural or Legal Persons' (2000) 25 *European Law Review* 99.

[45] Case 48/69 *Imperial Chemical Industries v Commission* ('*Dyestuffs*') [1972] ECR 619, paras 125–146.

[46] See A Jones, 'The Boundaries of an Undertaking in EU Competition Law' (2012) 8(2) *European Competition Journal* 301.

[47] See eg Case T-299/08 *Elf Aquitaine v Commission* [2011] ECR II-2149 and Case C-508/11 *Eni SpA v Commission*, judgment of 8 May 2013, nyr.

[48] *Akzo Nobel* (n 38) para 60. It is for the parent to rebut the presumption. The Commission is obliged to consider the rebuttal evidence and if it fails to do so its decision will be overturned, see eg Case T-185/06 *L'Air liquide SA v Commission* [2011] ECR II-2809.

[49] Case T-141/89 *Tréfileurope Sales SARL v Commission* [1995] ECR II-791. See also *Commercial Solvents* (n 9) (parent and subsidiary in which the parent held a 51 per cent shareholding were to be treated as an economic unit).

[50] Case T-132/07 *Fuji Electric System Co Ltd v Commission* [2011] ECR II-4091, para 181.

[51] Case C-67/96 *Albany International v Stichting Bedrijfspensioenfonds Textielindustrie* [1999] ECR I-5751, AG Jacobs, para 311.

[52] Case C-475/99 *Firma Ambulanz Glöckner v Landkreis Südwestpfalz* [2001] ECR I-8089, AG Jacobs, para 72.

[53] Case C-49/07 *Motosykletistiki Omospondia Ellados NPID (MOTOE) v Elliniko Dimosio* [2008] ECR I-4863, para 25.

For example, activities which fall within a State's public powers (eg legislating[54]) are not considered to be of an economic nature; whereas, when States act outside these areas, such as when they provide employment procurement services (eg the Job Centre), this is economic activity.[55] Note too that the activity need not, in fact, be carried out for profit. It is enough if it could be.[56]

There are also other ways in which activity which may seem economic is not considered to be for the purposes of Articles 101 and 102. For example, it is not enough if a State is merely purchasing goods, 'the subsequent use of the purchased goods [must also] amount to an economic activity.'[57] Further, consumers consuming, that is, purchasing in a personal capacity, is not considered to be economic activity either.[58]

4.2 **May (appreciably) affect trade between Member States**

The Court of Justice has held that that 'in order to come within the prohibition imposed by Article [101(1)], the agreement must affect trade between Member States and the free play of competition to an appreciable extent.'[59] To fall within the scope of Articles 101 and 102, agreements or conduct must therefore have a minimum level of cross-border effects. This jurisdictional test sets out the external reach of the provisions and 'the boundary between the areas respectively covered by Community law and the law of the Member States.'[60] In addition, Regulation 1/2003 clarifies that when applying national competition laws to conduct which appreciably affects trade between Member States, NCAs and national courts must also apply Articles 101 and/or 102 and may not apply national rules governing agreements more strictly (they cannot prohibit an agreement infringing national competition law if it does not infringe Article 101).[61]

The Court has recently confirmed that for an arrangement or practice to be capable of affecting trade between Member States, it must be possible to foresee with a

> sufficient degree of probability, on the basis of a set of objective factors of law or of fact, that they have an influence, direct or indirect, actual or potential, on the pattern of trade between Member States in such a way as to cause concern that they might hinder the attainment of a single market between Member States…Moreover, that influence must not be insignificant.[62]

In making the required assessment the question is whether the arrangement or practice as a whole affects trade; it is not necessary that the anti-competitive elements affect trade or

---

[54] Case C-113/07 *SELEX Sistemi Integratei v Commission* [2009] ECR I-2207, para 70. Note that the question of what are 'public powers' is one of EU law: *Jean Claude Becu* (n 39) para 31.

[55] *Höfner and Elsner* (n 36) paras 22 and 23.

[56] eg in *Höfner and Elsner* (n 36), the German State did not charge for its service of helping people to find work. The fact that this could, in principle, be carried out for profit was sufficient to find that it was engaged in an economic activity.

[57] Case C-205/03 P *Federación Española de Empresas de Tecnología Sanitaria v Commission* [2006] ECR I-6295, para 26.   [58] Case C-180/98 *Pavel Pavlov* [2000] ECR I-6451, paras 76–82, by implication.

[59] *Béguelin Import* (n 43). The text of Art 101(1) does not explicitly require that the effect on competition or trade should be appreciable.

[60] Case C-238/05 *Asnef-Equifax v Asociación de Usuarios de Servicios Bancarios* [2006] ECR I-11125, para 33.

[61] Regulation 1/2003, recital 8 and Art 3(1). There are also limits on the result they can come to at national law, when Arts 101 and 102 are triggered, ibid, recital 8 and Art 3(2).

[62] *Asnef-Equifax* (n 60) para 34. Also Commission guidelines on the affect on trade concept contained in Articles 81 and 82 of the Treaty (OJ [2004] C101/81).

that trade is affected adversely. It could be sufficient therefore that the conduct increases the volume of trade.[63]

Despite the insertion of an appreciability element in the test, the affect on trade test has been construed very widely so that it is hard to find cases where agreements operating within the EU do not have an appreciable effect on trade.[64] Some arrangements, by their very nature, reinforce the partitioning of markets on a national basis, thus impeding the economic interpenetration that the EU Treaties aim to generate.[65] For example, where national arrangements concern undertakings from other Member States[66] or incorporate restraints on cross-border trade or where a dominant firm charges different prices in different Member States. This latter arrangement is likely to increase trade of the relevant product from the low-priced State to the high-priced one.[67]

Arrangements relating only to the marketing of products in a single Member State, may also affect trade between Member States.[68] For example, an agreement precluding a buyer from purchasing goods from a competing supplier may affect trade by prohibiting the buyer from contracting with competitors in other Member States.

There may even be an appreciable effect on trade between Member States where an undertaking, located outside the EU, agrees to distribute products in Russia and not to import them into the EU.[69]

4.3 Exclusions

Although Articles 101 and 102 do not contain any specific exclusions, in practice a number of exclusions exist from one or both of these provisions by virtue of, for example, express Treaty provisions, the EU Courts' case law, or EU regulation. These exclusions are normally justified on public policy grounds. Exclusion avoids a need to balance these objectives *within* the framework of Articles 101 and/or 102.[70] For example:

- Article 346(1)(b) TFEU provides that the provisions of the EU Treaties, including the competition rules, do not preclude a Member State from taking measures that it considers 'necessary for the protection of the essential interests of its security which are connected with the production of or trade in arms, munitions and war material.' Such measures shall not adversely affect the conditions of competition in the internal market regarding products which are not intended for specifically military purposes.

- In *Albany*[71] the Court excluded from the ambit of Article 101 certain agreements belonging to the realm of social policy. This case concerned an agreement between employers and labour which aimed to improve the conditions of work and employment in the Dutch textile industry. Although the arrangements potentially seemed to breach Article 101, they also appeared to be in accordance with EU social provisions,

---

[63] *Asnef-Equifax* (n 60) para 38.

[64] eg Joined Cases C-215/96 and 216/96 *Carlo Bagnasco v Banca Popolare di Novara soc coop arl and Cassa di Risparmio di Genova e Imperia SpA* [1999] ECR I-135 and Case 229/83 *Association des Centres distributeurs Édouard Leclerc and others v Sàrl 'Au blé vert' and others* [1985] ECR 1.

[65] *Asnef-Equifax* (n 60) para 37.

[66] Ibid, paras 35 and 66.   [67] See the cases cited at n 17.

[68] Commission guidelines on the affect on trade concept contained in Articles 81 and 82 of the Treaty (OJ [2004] C101/81) para 77.

[69] Case C-306/96 *Javico International and Javico v Yves Saint Laurent Parfums* [1998] ECR I-1983.

[70] See section 2.2.   [71] Case C-67/96 (n 51) para 59.

which encourage collective bargaining.[72] The Court, by reading the EU Treaties as a whole, permitted social policy objectives to trump the competition law ones and held that agreements adopted by management and labour to improve conditions of work and employment fell outside the scope of Article 101(1) altogether.

- Article 42 TFEU gives some precedence to the Common Agricultural Policy objectives (listed in Article 39 TFEU, such as ensuring a fair standard of living for the agricultural community) over the competition ones. By virtue of this provision, Regulation 1184/2006 states that certain agricultural arrangements fall outside Article 101 (but not Article 102): broadly, agreements concerning the production or sale of agricultural products or the use of joint facilities for the storage, treatment, or processing of agricultural products, and under which there is no obligation to charge identical prices, unless the Commission finds that competition is thereby excluded or that the objectives of Article 39 TFEU are jeopardized.[73]

Arguably, these express derogations support the view that public policy objectives should not be taken into account in the application of Articles 101 and 102: if 'it were legitimate to balance competing goals within' Article 101 these provisions would be redundant.[74] Another view, however, is that there is a difference between removing some considerations from the scope of the competition rules entirely and allowing public policy goals to be weighed against competition ones (balancing).[75] If, however, public policy goals can be readily considered within Articles 101 and 102, then it seems correct that there is less need for exclusions from the competition rules based on public policy concerns.

5 Identifying anti-competitive agreements and conduct

5.1 The use of economic analysis

It has been seen that although Ordoliberal ideas, the internal market project, and other public policy goals, have been influential to the development and interpretation of the EU competition law rules, the emerging view is that their goal should be to prohibit and prevent conduct which will harm consumer welfare and efficiency.

Even if it were to be agreed, however, that the sole goal of the competition law rules is or should be to enhance consumer welfare, that does not mean that this is an easy objective to achieve. On the contrary, the economic objective means that complex economic principles and tools must generally lie at the heart of providing a coherent framework for analysing whether conduct infringes the rules. These will not always establish a clear outcome for a case. For example, it has been seen that the applicability of the law frequently requires a determination of the question of whether or not a particular firm has market power.[76] The answer to this question leaves considerable scope for disagreement on a number of issues, such as:

- How can the existence of market power be identified? Can it be measured directly, or can it only be identified indirectly through use of proxies such as an analysis of market shares and other factors such as barriers to entry into the market? EU law has generally used indirect mechanisms for assessing market power, requiring the relevant

---

[72] See TFEU, Art 151 etc.
[73] Regulation 1184/2006 (OJ [2006] L214/7) recitals 2–4 and Art 2(1).
[74] Odudu, *The Boundaries of EC Competition Law* (n 11) 169.
[75] Townley, *Article 81 EC and Public Policy* (n 18) 101 and 102.　　　[76] See section 2.2.

market to be identified (from both a product and geographic perspective) and an assessment of the conditions of competition on that market.[77] There is a growing view, however, that, especially in merger analysis, other tools (eg pricing pressure indices) can substitute for traditional analysis based on market definition, market shares, and concentration measures.[78]

- What market (product, geographic, and temporal) does the undertaking(s) operate on?[79] Does a producer of sparkling water, for example, operate on a market for sparkling water, bottled water, fizzy drinks, soft drinks, or another product market and is the market local, national, or broader?

- Does the firm compete vigorously on the market or do barriers to entry exist[80] which prevent other undertakings from entering that market and challenging that firm's position on the market?

- What is the theory of harm raised in a given case (what are the consumer welfare implications of the practices), and, for example, how are short-term efficiencies to be weighed against efficiencies which might be achieved in the longer run?[81]

Clearly, in addition to being complex, such analysis is time-consuming, expensive, and difficult to apply in practice. Although therefore competition law should be guided by economics, it cannot always replicate economists' (frequently conflicting) views.[82]

5.2 **Form and effects: type 1 and type 2 errors**

Competition law systems have, therefore, to consider how to construct legal rules or standards to distinguish anti-competitive conduct which will harm consumer welfare from pro-competitive conduct (to separate the beneficial sheep from the antitrust goats[83]) in a way which will be both sufficiently

(a) clear – enabling firms to comply with them and courts or other decision-makers to administer them, and

(b) accurate – identifying and prohibiting anti-competitive conduct whilst permitting (and not deterring) that which may promote competition.

Although the view could be taken that, in order to ensure accuracy, anti-competitive effects should be identified and balanced against any pro-competitive benefits in every competition case, such an approach is likely to impose too high a burden on firms, competition agencies (and other claimants), and courts, creating a risk both that pro-competitive agreements will be deterred and too little enforcement/condemnation of harmful agreements will occur. In selecting the optimal approach for a given case, a trade-off may therefore need to be made between more complex standards, requiring detailed factual and economic analysis, which are more difficult and costly to apply, and simpler, clearer, bright-line rules,

---

[77] See especially section 7.2.

[78] See eg 'Special Issue: Louis Kaplow's *Why (Ever) Define Markets*' (2012) 57 *Antitrust Bulletin* and J Farrell and C Shapiro, 'Antitrust Evaluation of Horizontal Mergers: An Economic Alternative to Market Definition' (2010) 10 *The BE Journal of Theoretical Economics* 1.

[79] See section 7.2.   [80] Ibid.

[81] See eg the discussion of refusal to deal in section 7.3.3 – an obligation on a firm to supply a competitor may increase competition in the short run but may deter firms from innovating in the longer run if firms perceive that there is a risk that they will be forced to supply the fruits of their labour to competitors.

[82] See eg Justice Breyer's dissenting judgment in *Leegin Creative Leather Products Inc v PSKS, Inc, DBA Kay's Kloset* 551 US 877 (2007).   [83] Ibid.

which require less sophisticated analysis and less emphasis on expert economic evidence but which may, consequently, be less accurate (or even inaccurate) in some cases.

It may also be necessary to consider whether an approach which may sometimes condemn legitimate business practices (false positives or 'type 1' errors) and so potentially chill pro-competitive conduct is a lesser or greater evil than one which may sometimes allow anti-competitive practices to escape antitrust prohibitions (false negatives or 'type 2' errors).[84]

In seeking to set out accurate, administrable, consistent, objective, and transparent rules, most competition law systems accept that some sorting of agreements and other conduct into categories is required, distinguishing between and affording different treatment to, for example:

- conduct which is very likely to cause anti-competitive effects and unlikely to have offsetting benefits – where a *presumption* of incompatibility with the rules may be applied;
- conduct which is very unlikely to cause anti-competitive effects – in some systems, such conduct may benefit from a safe harbour or a presumption of compatibility with the rules; and
- conduct the effects of which are more ambiguous – which require closer individual scrutiny of anti-competitive and pro-competitive effects.

Where such categories exist, a controversial issue to be decided is what type of conduct should go into each category (and, in particular, when are presumptions of illegality and legality to be applied). It will be seen in the following discussion, that the EU competition laws are not drafted in themselves in a 'form-based' way (where a prohibitory approach is based on the form of that agreement or conduct),[85] but rather are 'effects-based' (focusing on agreements which restrict competition[86] and abuses of a dominant position). Nonetheless, the EU authorities have often been criticized for failing to take a sufficiently economically rigorous approach to the application of the laws and for relying too heavily on formalistic rules and presumptions that certain types of conduct will have anti-competitive effects and should be prohibited. Under the process of 'modernization',[87] the Commission has generally displayed a greater willingness to focus on effects. It now uses more rigorous economic analysis in its decision-making, spelling out convincing theories of harm and examining the actual or likely anti-competitive effects of the conduct at issue on the basis of the actual facts before it.

6 Article 101 TFEU

6.1 Introduction

It has been seen that Article 101 has two substantive parts. Article 101(1) contains the core prohibition of collusive arrangements between separate undertakings which restrict competition, whilst Article 101(3) provides a legal exception for agreements achieving offsetting

---

[84] See eg OECD, 'Policy Roundtables: Resale Price Maintenance (2008)', DAF/COMP(2008)37, http://www.oecd.org/daf/competition/43835526.pdf

[85] A clear example of such a system was that which existed in the UK under what, in its final form, was the Restrictive Trade Practices Act 1976.

[86] But see the discussion of agreements which restrict competition by object, section 6.3.2.

[87] See section 2.2.

benefits. It has been seen that the burden is on the Commission, or other person, alleging an infringement of Article 101(1), to establish sufficient proof of an infringement.[88] Only if established does the burden shift onto the undertakings claiming the benefit of exemption to establish that Article 101(3) is fulfilled.[89]

The concepts of undertaking and affect on trade have already been considered. This section consequently focuses on the question of what constitutes collusive conduct targeted by Article 101 and which agreements have restrictive effects on competition and are prohibited by it.

6.2 Agreements, concerted practices, and decisions

Article 101(1) prohibits joint, not individual, conduct. The reference to 'agreements between undertakings, decisions by associations of undertakings and concerted practices' thus requires some element of 'collusion' between independent undertakings. The different types of collusion referred to in Article 101(1) are distinguishable from each other only by their intensity and the forms in which they manifest themselves and must be understood in light of the concept inherent in the Treaties' competition rules that each economic operator must determine independently the policy which it intends to adopt on the market.[90]

In many Article 101 cases the existence of an agreement is not in doubt. There may be doubt, however, as to the precise terms of the agreement or as to whether the terms can be said to restrict competition. In other cases, frequently where it is suspected that a serious violation of the competition rules has been committed (eg horizontal price fixing), evidence that independent undertakings agreed or concerted to fix prices will, effectively, prove a violation of Article 101(1).[91] If detected, heavy sanctions may be imposed on the undertakings proved to have been party to the infringement. In such cases, the parties who have been 'colluding' are likely to do so in an amorphous way and to try to conceal any collusion rather than attempt to try to defend the legitimacy of the practices under Article 101(3). The challenge in such scenarios is to uncover and establish the existence of such covert operations and, where evidence is skimpy, to determine whether or not the behaviour on the market results from collusion, which is prohibited under Article 101, or independent behaviour, which is not.

6.2.1 Agreement

The term 'agreement' has been held to encompass situations where undertakings have 'expressed their joint intention to conduct themselves on the market in a specific way'[92] or where there is 'a concurrence of wills between economic operators on the implementation of a policy, the pursuit of an objective, or the adoption of a given line of conduct on the market'.[93] As long as there is a concurrence of wills, constituting the faithful expression of

---

[88] See section 3.1.

[89] See Regulation 1/2003, recital 5 and Art 2. In Cases C-204/00 P etc *Aalborg Portland A/S v Commission* ('*Cement*') [2004] ECR I-123, para 78.   [90] Case C-238/05 *Asnef-Equifax* (n 60).

[91] As the agreement has as its 'object' the restriction of competition and its anti-competitive 'effect' does not need to be demonstrated, see section 6.3.

[92] Case T-41/96 *Bayer AG v Commission* [2000] ECR II-3383, para 67, aff'd on appeal Cases C-2 and 3/01 P [2004] ECR I-23, relying on, eg, Case 41/69 *ACF Chemiefarma NV v Commission* ('*Quinine Cartel*') [1970] ECR 661, para 112. See also Case C-49/92 *Commission v Anic Partecipazioni* [1999] ECR I-4125, paras 79 and 122 and Case T-99/04 *AC-Treuhand AG v Commission* [2008] ECR II-1501, para 118.

[93] Case T-41/96, *Bayer AG*, ibid.

---

the parties' intention,[94] its form or nature is unimportant – it can catch agreements: whether horizontal (between competitors operating at the same level of the economy, eg two bicycle manufacturers) or vertical (between non-competitors operating at different levels of the economy, eg a bicycle manufacturer and a bicycle retailer),[95] whether or not they are intended to be legally binding, whether or not sanctions are provided for a breach, and whether they are written or oral.[96] An agreement may also be found where an offer to collude is accepted tacitly, for example where an undertaking participates in meetings at which anti-competitive agreements are concluded, without manifestly opposing them.[97]

6.2.2 Concerted practices

The term 'concerted practice' catches looser forms of collusion. It does not require an agreement or even a plan or a meeting of minds, but catches reciprocal coordination which 'knowingly substitutes practical co-operation' between the undertakings 'for the risks of competition',[98] so precluding 'any direct or indirect contact between such operators, the object or effect whereof is either to influence the conduct on the market of an actual or potential competitor or to disclose to such a competitor the course of conduct which they themselves have decided to adopt or contemplate adopting on the market'.[99] Where firms engage in conduct designed to remove strategic uncertainty about each other's future conduct on the market, for example through a direct, or even indirect,[100] exchange[101] or disclosure[102] of strategic information, they are not acting independently or unilaterally and so their conduct is subject to Article 101.

6.2.3 Decisions by associations of undertakings

The reference to decisions by associations of undertakings facilitates holding 'associations liable for the anti-competitive behaviour of their members'.[103] In *Wouters v Algemene Raad van de Nederlandse Orde van Advocaten*,[104] Advocate General Léger stated that the concept

> seeks to prevent undertakings from being able to evade the rules on competition on account simply of the form in which they coordinate their conduct on the market. To ensure that this principle is effective, Article [101(1)] covers not only direct methods of coordinating conduct between undertakings (agreements and concerted practices) but also institutionalised forms of cooperation, that is to say, situations in which economic operators act through a collective structure or a common body.[105]

---

[94] *Bayer AG* (n 92) para 69. See also Case T-62/98 *Volkswagen AG v Commission* [2000] ECR II-2707, aff'd Case C-338/00 P *Volkswagen AG v Commission* [2003] ECR I-9189.

[95] *Consten and Grundig* (n 16).

[96] See eg Case 28/77 *Tepea BV v Commission* [1978] ECR 1391.

[97] *Aalborg Portland A/S* (n 89) para 81.

[98] *ICI v Commission* (n 45) paras 64 and 65.

[99] Joined Cases 40/73 etc *Re the European Sugar Cartel: Coöperatieve Vereniging 'Suiker Unie' UA v Commission* [1975] ECR 1663, para 174.

[100] But see *Wood Pulp II* (n 26) (no collusion established where undertakings had announced their price increases in advance and the information had been rapidly transferred between both buyers and sellers by means of publication in the trade press).

[101] Case C-8/08 *T-Mobile Netherlands BV v Raad van bestuur van de Nederlandse Mededingingsautoriteit* [2009] ECR I-4529, paras 54–62.

[102] See eg *Re the European Sugar Cartel* (n 99); Joined Cases T-25/95 etc *Cimenteries CBR SA v Commission* [2000] ECR II-491; and Joined Cases T-202/98 etc *Tate & Lyle, Napier Brown and British Sugar* [2001] ECR II-2035, aff'd Case C-359/01 P *British Sugar* [2004] ECR I-4933.

[103] J Faull and A Nikpay (eds), *The EC Law of Competition* (2nd edn, Oxford: Oxford University Press, 2007) para 3.102.   [104] Case C-309/99 (n 19).

[105] *Wouters* (n 19) para 62, AG Léger.

This concept has thus been interpreted broadly to catch recommendations[106] and other schemes[107] designed to coordinate the members' behaviour on the market and/or to exclude competitors.

6.2.4 Unilateral conduct

In some cases the EU Courts have annulled a Commission decision for failing to provide adequate evidence of an agreement, decision, or concerted practice. For example, no agreement to restrict trade between Member States was found in the *Bayer/Adalat* case. Although the supplier had pursued a policy designed to try to stop French and Spanish wholesalers from selling products into the UK, the EU Courts found that the Commission had *not* shown that Bayer had sought to obtain agreement or acquiescence from its wholesalers to adhere to its policy or that the wholesalers had acquiesced explicitly, or implicitly, in it.[108] In addition, in *Wood Pulp II*,[109] the Court of Justice held that even if it can be established that all suppliers on a market have acted in parallel (eg by making identical transaction prices), parallel behaviour alone cannot be relied upon to furnish proof of a concerted practice between the suppliers to fix prices unless concertation is the only plausible explanation for the conduct.

6.3 Identifying which agreements infringe Article 101 TFEU

6.3.1 Categories of analysis

According to the General Court, in order to determine whether an agreement is prohibited by Article 101, a claimant must first identify the anti-competitive aspects of an agreement – it must establish a restriction of competition, whether by object or effect within the meaning of Article 101(1). Article 101(3) is then used to weigh pro-competitive effects against those restrictions identified. In distinguishing anti- from pro-competitive agreements, four broad categories of analysis are used in the EU (see Table 17.1).

6.3.2 Agreements which restrict competition by object

Certain agreements are considered to be very likely to harm the objectives pursued by the competition rules and are *presumed* to restrict competition – to be restrictive by object. The question whether or not an agreement is restrictive of competition by object thus has a critical impact on the likelihood of a violation being established and the burden of proof. Where it is shown that the object of an agreement is to restrict competition (and the other conditions of Article 101(1) are satisfied), there is no need to demonstrate anti-competitive effects – a violation of Article 101 is proved unless it can be demonstrated that the agreement satisfies the Article 101(3) criteria. Where the object of the agreement is not found to restrict competition, however, the burden of proving that this is its *effect* is on the person alleging the breach. This is a difficult burden to discharge. Only where this is established does the burden shift onto the party/parties seeking to defend it under Article 101(3).

The Court of Justice has held that in order to determine whether conduct is 'by its very nature' injurious to competition, 'regard must be had inter alia to the content of its

---

[106] See eg Commission Decision, *FENEX* (OJ [1996] L181/28).

[107] See eg *Stichting Certificatie Kraanverhuurbedrijf and Federatie van Nederlandse Kraanbedrijven* (OJ [1995] L312/79) and Joined Cases T-213/95 and T-18/96 *Stichting Certificatie Kraanverhuurbedrijf and Federatie van Nederlandse Kraanbedrijven v Commission* [1997] ECR II-1739.

[108] *Bayer AG* (n 92) paras 66–185.   [109] Joined Cases C-89/85 etc (n 26).

Table 17.1 Categories of analysis: distinguishing anti- from pro-competitive agreements

Presumption of illegality	Agreements which contain provisions which are restrictive of competition by object (see section 6.3.2) are presumed to infringe Article 101(1). The Commission's view is that they are also presumed not to satisfy the conditions of Article 101(3) (consequently, the safe harbour of a block exemption (see section 6.3.5) will not apply). Although these presumptions are rebuttable, in practice it is hard to do so.
Presumption of legality	Agreements which do not appreciably restrict competition fall outside the scope of Article 101(1) (see section 6.3.4): agreements between undertakings which have a weak position on the market are presumed to have an insignificant effect on competition and to be compatible with Article 101(1). Agreements benefiting from an EU block exemption are also presumed to be compatible with Article 101 (see section 6.3.5): it is assumed that agreements satisfying a block exemption will produce efficiencies which offset any anti-competitive effects. Such agreements benefit from an exemption from Article 101 (a safe harbour) which can only be withdrawn prospectively.[110]
Full economic analysis	It is only in cases where these presumptions do not apply that agreements have to be analysed individually to determine whether they have as their effect the restriction of competition (Article 101(1)) and, if so, whether the agreement is exempted from the prohibition as it satisfies the four conditions of Article 101(3) (see sections 6.3.3 and 6.3.5).

provisions, the objectives it seeks to ascertain and the economic and legal context of which it forms part.'[111]

Content

Although this statement makes it clear that the objectives and context of the agreement are important to the assessment in addition to its content, jurisprudence has, over the years, established that agreements containing the following restraints (see Table 17.2) are highly likely to be found, in principle, to be restrictive of competition by object.[112]

There is a fairly broad consensus that competition law systems should treat cartel activity as an automatic violation of the rules (see case study 17.1 on the *Marine Hoses* case). However, a controversy about this 'list' is that it also includes vertical restraints. Since vertical agreements are not made between competitors but between providers of complementary goods and services, they are less obviously anti-competitive than horizontal agreements and provide greater scope for efficiencies.

In *Consten and Grundig*, for example, the parties complained that the Commission has been wrong to find a restriction by object as the agreement had been essential to enable Grundig to penetrate the French market: Consten would not have proceeded without the territorial protection from other distributors which could otherwise have taken a

[110] Regulation 1/2003, Art 29(1) and (2).
[111] Case C-501/06 P *GlaxoSmithKline Services Unlimited v Commission* [2009] ECR I-9291, para 58.
[112] But see further eg, A Jones and B Sufrin, *EU Competition Law* (5th edn, Oxford: Oxford University Press, 2014) ch 4.

Table 17.2 Agreements highly likely to be found to restrict competition by object

Horizontal cartels – arrangements between competitors	Vertical arrangements
To eliminate competition between them by fixing prices (all sell at €X), limiting output (to only sell Y bicycles) or sharing markets (A sells bicycles in France and B sells them in Germany), see especially *European Night Services v Commission*.[113]	To fix or set the minimum prices at which retailers can sell the contract product (resale price maintenance).[114]
To reduce capacity (A, B, and C agree that C should close factories and leave the market), see *Competition Authority v Beef Industry Development Society Ltd (BIDS)*.[116] To exchange information designed, directly or indirectly, to fix purchase or selling prices (see *T-Mobile Netherlands BV v Raad van bestuur van de Nederlandse Mededingingsautoriteit*[118]).	To confer absolute territorial protection (ATP) on a distributor or otherwise partition national markets.[115] This principle has been embedded in EU law since the important case of *Consten and Grundig*.[117] In this case an agreement was concluded between Grundig, a German manufacturer of consumer electronics, and Consten, appointed as its exclusive distributor in France. In order to encourage Consten to promote its products in France, Grundig agreed not to sell the product in France itself and to prohibit all other distributors from seeking sales, actively or passively, within France. The Commission's decision finding that the agreement infringed Article 101 – it was restrictive of competition by object and did not meet the criteria for exemption under Article 101(3) – was affirmed by the Court of Justice. There seems little doubt that this approach is influenced by the single market objective.

'free ride' upon Consten's promotional and investment efforts. Even though, therefore, the agreement resulted in the existence of only one distributor of Grundig products in France (there was a restriction on competition between distributors of Grundig products – *intra-brand competition*), the agreement led to an increase in competition for consumer electronics products in France (there was an increase in *inter-brand competition* because the products had not been sold in France before). Although this approach gained support from Advocate General Roemer, the Court of Justice upheld the Commission's decision. The agreement, giving Consten the exclusive right of sale of Grundig products in France, had as its *object* the restriction of competition so that an assessment of its *effect* was unnecessary. The Court has reiterated this view, that vertical restraints may be restrictive by object, on several occasions – especially territorial

---

[113] Joined Cases T-374/94 etc [1998] ECR II-3141, para 136.
[114] See eg Case 243/83 *SA Binon & Cie v SA Agence et Messageries de la Presse* [1985] ECR 2015, para 44.
[115] See esp *GlaxoSmithKline* (n 111) para 61, and *Premier League Ltd and Murphy* (n 17).
[116] C-209/07 [2008] ECR I-8637   [117] Joined Cases 56/64 *and* 58/64 (n 16).
[118] Case C-8/08 (n 101) paras 36–43.

restraints eliminating any possibility of competition between distributors in different Member States.[119]

The objectives and context of the agreement

The objective and context of the agreement can be relied upon to expand or contract the category of object restraints. It is only in exceptional circumstances, however, that the objective or the context of an agreement can lead to a finding that an agreement containing restraints set out in the previous list is *not* restrictive by object. In *Wouters v Algemene Raad van de Nederlandse Orde van Advocaten*,[120] for example, the Court found that rules adopted in the Netherlands which prohibited members of the Bar practising in full partnership with accountants did not have as their object or effect the restriction of competition. Although the agreement restricted services that could be offered and reduced scope for efficiencies, the Court concluded that it was not unreasonable for the Bar Council to take the view that these restraints were necessary for the proper practice of the legal profession.[121] The Commission has also stated that severe restraints in vertical agreements 'may be objectively necessary to ensure that a public ban on selling dangerous substances to certain customers for reasons of safety or health is respected'[122] or to encourage substantial investments by a distributor in order to start up on a market and so fall outside of Article 101(1).[123] It appears, therefore, that an agreement containing severe restraints but designed to achieve public policy[124] or efficiency objectives may exceptionally escape being categorized as restrictive by object or even restrictive of competition at all.

6.3.3 Agreements which restrict competition by effect

Where it is not found that the object of the agreement is to restrict competition, the likely impact of the agreement on inter-brand competition or intra-brand competition must be determined before it can be decided whether it has restrictive effects. This requires proof that the agreement either (a) affects 'actual or potential competition to such an extent that on the relevant market negative effects on prices, output, innovation or the variety or quality of goods and services can be expected with a reasonable degree of probability',[125] or (b) restricts a supplier's distributors from competing with each other since potential competition that could have existed between the distributors absent the restraint is restricted.

In *Delimitis v Henninger Bräu*,[126] for example, the Court set out guidance for determining whether a beer supply agreement, incorporating a 'beer tie' (a commitment by the buyer to purchase beer exclusively from named suppliers – and so not from other beer suppliers) infringes Article 101(1). It held that as the purpose of the beer tie was to secure advantages (to guarantee both an outlet for the supplier and a supply of products to the retailer, to ensure that the retailer concentrates its sales efforts on the distribution of the contract goods and to ensure the ability of the retailer to gain access to the market on favourable terms) it could not be characterized as restrictive by object.

---

[119] See nn 114 and 117, and also, more generally, Case C-32/11 *Allianz Hungária Biztosító Zrt, Generali-Providencia Biztosító Zrt v Gazdasági Versenyhivatal*, judgment of 14 March 2013, nyr.

[120] Case C-309/99 (n 19).   [121] Contrast *OTOC* (n 9) 9.

[122] OJ [2010] C130/1, para 60.   [123] Ibid, para 61.

[124] See eg E Rousseva and M Marquis, 'Hell Freezes Over: A Climate Change for Assessing Exclusionary Conduct under Article 102 TEFU' [2012] *Journal of European Competition Law and Practice* 32.

[125] Art 101(3) Guidelines (n 10) para 24. This could be because the agreement restricts actual or potential competition between the parties or between any one of the parties and third parties that could have existed absent the agreement, ibid, paras 25 and 26.

[126] Case C-234/89 [1991] ECR I-935. See V Korah, 'The Judgment in *Delimitis*: A Milestone towards a Realistic Assessment of the Effects of an Agreement or a Damp Squib' (1992) 14 *European Intellectual Property Review* 167.

Whether or not the agreement had a restrictive effect depended on whether it would foreclose competitors from entering or expanding in the market. This was dependent on the relevant market, the number and size of producers operating on the market, the existence of networks of similar agreements, the saturation of the market, and brand loyalty, etc. Only if access could be said to be inhibited would it be necessary to assess whether the agreement in question (which is taken to mean the agreements of that particular producer or brewer) contributes appreciably to that situation. In effects cases therefore it is crucial to assess contractual restraints, not abstractly as restraints but in the context in which they operate, before their effect can be determined.

In *Société Technique Minière v Maschinenbau Ulm GmbH* ('*STM*'),[127] the Court held that an agreement appointing an exclusive distributor in France which, in contrast to that concerned in *Consten and Grundig*, did not confer ATP (or complete exclusivity over the right to distribute in France) on the distributor did not have as its object a restriction of competition. Rather, accepting similar arguments to those raised by the parties in *Consten and Grundig* (two weeks later), it indicated that an exclusive distribution agreement would not restrict competition if the appointment of an exclusive distributor was necessary in order to enable a manufacturer to penetrate a new market. Before it could be determined whether the agreement restricted competition, the agreement should be examined in light of the competition which would occur *if the agreement in question were not or had not been made*. In this case it seemed that the economic justifications for the agreement might outweigh the territorial restrictions inherent in the agreement.

6.3.4 Agreements of minor importance

It has been seen that EU law is not concerned with agreements which have an 'insignificant effect on the market, taking into account the weak position which the persons concerned have on the market of the product in question'.[128] 'Thus an exclusive dealing agreement, even with absolute territorial protection, may, having regard to the weak position of the persons concerned on the market in the products in question in the area covered by the absolute protection, escape the prohibition laid down in Article [101(1)]' (*Völk*).[129]

Because of the huge practical importance of the concept of appreciability, the Commission has provided clarification, by Notice,[130] of when, in its view, an agreement is likely to be of minor importance: essentially where the parties' market shares do not exceed 10 per cent (where the agreement is between competitors (actual or potential)) or 15 per cent (where it is between non-competitors). The question of when an agreement found to be restrictive by object can fall outside Article 101(1) on *de minimis* grounds is controversial, however. The current Commission Notice – which is under review – is explicitly stated not to apply to agreements incorporating such restraints (which it describes as hardcore).[131]

The assumption had always been that such agreements could, nonetheless, as held by the Court in *Völk*, be of minor importance if the parties' market shares were considerably lower than those set out in the Notice (the more serious the restraint, the less likely it is to be insignificant).[132] In a recent case, however, the Court held, in a somewhat ambiguous judgment, that an agreement which is restrictive of competition by object is so injurious

---

[127] Case 56/65 (n 4).   [128] See section 4.2.
[129] Case 5/69 *Völk v Vervaecke* [1969] ECR 295, 302.
[130] Commission Notice on agreements of minor importance which do not appreciably restrict competition under Article 81(1) (*De Minimis* Notice) (OJ [2001] C368/13).   [131] Ibid, para 11.
[132] See Faull and Nikpay, *The EC Law of Competition* (n 103) para 3.164.

to competition that it always constitutes an appreciable restriction of competition.[133] The Commission states in its press release announcing its review of the *De Minimis* Notice, that, in its view, this judgment reflects a change of policy, clarifying that the *de minimis* doctrine does *not* apply to agreements which have as their object the restriction of competition.[134] Nonetheless, the Commission's draft Notice does not go this far. Rather, it again states only that the market share thresholds set out in the Notice do not apply to agreements which have as their object the restriction of competition or characterized as hardcore restrictions in any current or future block exemption (which it generally considers to constitute restrictions by object).[135]

6.3.5 Article 101(3) TFEU

Any agreement which infringes Article 101(1) may in principle benefit from Article 101(3) (including agreements containing object restraints).[136] In practice, however, it is a significant burden to establish that its four cumulative criteria are met. To do so, it must be established that

- the agreement leads to an improvement in the production or distribution of goods or the promotion of technical or economic progress: the Commission's view is that this criterion requires the parties to establish that, despite the fact that the agreement restricts competition, efficiency gains, cost efficiencies, and/or qualitative efficiencies, creating value in the form of new or improved products (dynamic efficiencies), will result from the economic activity that forms the object of the agreement (there must be a causal link between the agreement and the claimed efficiencies).[137]

  A controversial issue is whether Article 101(3) also permits the parties to rely on broader public policy benefits (eg environmental benefits) achieved by the agreement. Although a sole consumer-welfare objective would suggest that such considerations should not be assessed, the teleological interpretation adopted by EU authorities in the past at least has suggested that Article 101(3) can be interpreted broadly against the backdrop of the wider EU aims and objectives[138] so that its application does not produce results inconsistent with other EU policies;[139]

- the agreement allows consumers a fair share of the benefit: by showing that there is a pass-on of the cost and quality efficiencies to consumers;[140]

- the agreement only contains restrictions which are indispensable to the achievement of the benefits shown to result from the agreement. This criterion is often difficult to establish, particularly where object restrictions are incorporated within the agreement. The Commission takes the view that restrictions will not be indispensable if the efficiencies specific to the agreement can be achieved by other practicable and less restrictive means, or if individual restrictions are not reasonably necessary to produce the efficiencies;

---

[133] Case C-226/11 *Expedia Inc v Autorité de la Concurrence*, judgment of 13 December 2012, nyr, para 38.

[134] See Commission's new draft Notice on agreements of minor importance, 11 July 2013, http://ec.europa.eu/competition/consultations/2013_de_minimis_notice/de_minimis_notice_en.pdf

[135] See ibid, para 12.

[136] Case T-17/93 *Matra Hachette SA v Commission* [1994] ECR II-595, para 85.

[137] Art 101(3) Guidelines (n 10) paras 45 and 64–72.

[138] Art 101(3) could therefore be construed to permit authorization of agreements which provide benefits, eg from a regional, social, environmental, cultural, and/or industrial perspective, see G Monti, 'Article 81 EC and Public Policy' (2002) 39 *Common Market Law Review* 1057.

[139] See, Townley, *Article 81 EC and Public Policy* (n 18) and Odudu, *The Boundaries of EC Competition Law* (n 11) 161.   [140] Art 101(3) Guidelines (n 10) paras 83–104.

- the agreement as a whole must not afford the parties the possibility of eliminating competition: as 'Ultimately the protection of rivalry and the competitive process is given priority over potentially pro-competitive efficiency gains which could result from restrictive agreements'.[141]

Parties will be spared the difficult task of determining whether these criteria apply to their agreement individually if it meets the conditions, and so falls within the 'safe harbour', of one of the block exemptions set out in an EU regulation. These regulations grant 'exemption' from Article 101(1) to categories of agreements that satisfy their conditions and their benefit can only be withdrawn prospectively. Some pertain to specific sectors (eg insurance). Others apply more generally, for example, to vertical (Regulation 330/2010[142]), horizontal cooperation (Regulations 1217/2010[143] and 1218/2010[144]), or technology transfer (Regulation 772/2004[145] (under review)) agreements. As the block exemptions are directly applicable,[146] agreements falling within their ambit benefit from the legal certainty that they are automatically exempt from the Article 101(1) prohibition. Most of the block exemptions now contain market-share thresholds and a list of 'hardcore restraints' which, if included within the agreement, preclude the application of the block exemption. The list of hardcore restraints mirrors closely the object restraints discussed previously and reflect the Commission's view that agreements containing such restraints are presumed to violate Article 101 and so cannot benefit from a block exemption. For example, the Vertical Block Exemption Regulation 330/2010, applies only where

- the supplier's and buyer's market shares do not exceed 30 per cent of the relevant market; and

- the agreement does not incorporate any hardcore restraints – which include, for example:

  - provisions fixing or setting minimum selling prices to be adhered to by the buyer;

  - incorporation (with some exceptions) of restrictions on the territory into which, or of the customers to whom, the buyer may sell the contract goods or services; and

  - the restriction of active or passive sales to end-users by members of a selective distribution system.

Case study 17.1: Cartels and the *Marine Hose* cartel

Parties to cartels – essentially anti-competitive arrangements between competitors to fix prices, make rigged bids (collusive tenders), establish output restrictions or quotas, or share or divide markets[147] – deliberately set out to interfere with free competition and to act instead to protect the prosperity of the participants as a whole. Such cartels 'diminish social welfare, create allocative inefficiency and transfer wealth from consumers to the participants in the cartel'.[148] The formation and successful operation of a cartel is easier for firms operating in an oligopolistic market – a market in which there are only a few players – where it is easier to coordinate conduct and where each firm's profits are strongly dependent upon the course of action chosen by its competitors.

---

[141] Art 101(3) Guidelines (n 10) para 105.   [142] OJ [2010] L102/1.   [143] OJ [2010] L335/36.
[144] OJ [2010] L335/43.   [145] OJ [2004] L123/11.   [146] Art 288 TFEU.
[147] 'Recommendation of the Council Concerning Effective Action against Hard Core Cartels', OECD Publication C(98)35/FINAL, 25 March 1998, available on the OECD's website.
[148] Commission, XXXIInd Report on Competition Policy (2002), part 26.

There is a fairly general consensus that as cartel activity poses a serious threat to economies and consumers it constitutes 'the supreme evil of antitrust'[149] and 'the most egregious'[150] violation of competition law and requires clear competition law rules against them. Debate is now focused on the question of how best to reflect the seriousness of the offence and to ensure that cartel activity is detected, deterred, and punished. The *Marine Hoses*[151] cartel illustrates both the way in which business people may go about rigging the market, and interfering with the free play of competition on it, and the different views as to how such conduct should be detected, deterred, and punished. In both the US and the UK criminal proceedings were pursued. In the EU, the Commission imposed hefty sanctions on the undertakings involved for violation of Article 101.

The case concerned a number of companies involved in the manufacture and sale on a global basis of marine hoses – used principally for the transportation of oil from remote places offshore. These manufacturers operated a bid-rigging, price-fixing, and market-sharing allocation agreement designed to suppress and eliminate competition between them. The cartel was managed and facilitated by Peter Whittle, who essentially designated a champion or winner for each job on which the conspirators 'bid' and provided others with instructions on how to bid on the job with the objective of ensuring that the designated champion would win it. Cartel members went to great lengths to conceal its existence, meeting clandestinely in locations around the world and using code names.

In 2006, however, one of the conspirators, the Yokohama Rubber Co Ltd, disclosed details of the cartel to the US, EU, and Japanese competition authorities. When the cartel members next met in Houston, the meetings were monitored and the individuals involved were arrested. The US competition agency cooperated with some of its counterparts in the EU (including the Commission and UK competition agency[152]) and at the same time as the arrests were occurring in the US, surprise unannounced inspections were made both at the conspirators' premises and the homes of an individual in Europe. Each competition authority thus investigated the activities of the cartel insofar as the cartel had effects in its jurisdiction. The operation of the cartel in the end proved costly to the companies and individuals involved:

- plea agreements and criminal convictions were made in the US under criminal antitrust laws;

- class actions for damages were launched in the US;

- under the US plea agreements, three British nationals (Peter Whittle, Bryan Allison, and David Brammer), were returned to the UK, pleaded guilty to committing a criminal (cartel) offence in the UK, and were sentenced to prison;[153]

---

[149] *Verizon Communications v Law Offices of Curtis v Trinko* 540 US 398, 408 (2004). See eg 'Fighting Hard Core Cartels: Recent Progress and Challenges Ahead' (OECD, 2003), and M Monti, 'Fighting Cartels Why and How? Why Should We be Concerned with Cartels and Collusive Behaviour?', 3rd Nordic Competition Policy Conference, Stockholm, 11–12 September 2000.

[150] OECD Publication C(98)35/FINAL (n 147).

[151] Commission Press Release IP/09/137, 'Commission fines marine hose producers €131 million for market sharing and price-fixing cartel' (*EUROPA*, 28 January 2009) http://europa.eu/rapid/press-release_IP-09-137_en.htm?locale=en

[152] See speeches by SD Hammond, 'Recent Developments, Trends, and Milestones in the Antitrust Division's Criminal Enforcement Program', Department of Justice, 56th Annual Spring Meeting, Washington, DC, 26 March 2008 and A Nikpay, 'Cartel Enforcement: Past, Present and Future', Law Society Anti-Trust Section, London, 11 December 2012.

[153] *R v Whittle, Brammar and Allison* [2008] EWCA Crim 2560.

- the European Commission imposed fines of €131,510,000 on five groups of companies involved in the cartel for entering into a single and continuous agreement which had as its object the restriction of competition (one fine was reduced on appeal);[154] and

- Japanese and Australian competition authorities also found violations of their competition law rules.

In an interview, Mr Allison subsequently stated: 'I would never ever do it again, and I wouldn't recommend to anyone that they do it. The loss to you in terms of your life is too great'.

Case study 17.2: Selective distribution and *Pierre Fabre v Président de l'Autorité de la concurrence*

Selective distribution systems are distribution systems 'where the supplier undertakes to sell the contract goods or services, either directly or indirectly, only to distributors selected on the basis of specified criteria and where these distributors undertake not to sell such goods or services to unauthorised distributors.'[155] Many selective distribution systems in the EU do not infringe Article 101, either because they meet the conditions, and so benefit from the safe harbour of the EU block exemption applicable to vertical agreements (Regulation 330/2010) or because they do not have as their object or effect the restriction of competition. In particular, they will not infringe Article 101(1) where the selective distribution system is necessary to maintain a specialist trade capable of providing suitable services for high-quality and/or technically complex products and where resellers are chosen on the basis of objective and qualitative criteria applied in a non-discriminatory way.

Pierre Fabre[156] concerned a selective distribution system operated by Pierre Fabre for the distribution of its cosmetics and personal care products in France. The agreements stipulated that sales of these products had to be made in a physical space, meeting specified requirements, and that a qualified pharmacist had to be present. The French competition authority found that the agreement was not compatible with the competition law rules. Rather, this agreement violated Article 101 (and the French code de commerce) as the obligation for a pharmacist to be physically present at sale operated as a de facto ban on internet selling. Consequently, the ability of the distributor to sell the contractual products outside its contractual territory was considerably reduced.

Following an appeal, the French cour d'appel de Paris made a reference to the Court of Justice which subsequently held that

(a) as the de facto ban eliminated cross-border trade, the restraint at issue was 'liable to restrict competition'.[157] It was restrictive of competition by object as the restriction was not a proportionate means of pursuing a legitimate aim – individual advice from a pharmacist was not necessary in the context of non-prescription medicines or to maintain Pierre Fabre's prestigious brand image;

(b) because the agreement incorporated a 'hardcore' restraint – it precluded (through incorporation of the de facto ban on internet selling) active or passive sales to end-users by the retailers within the selective distribution system – the block

---

[154] Commission Press Release IP/09/137 (n 151); Case T-146/09 *Parker ITR Srl v Commission*, 17 May 2013.
[155] Regulation 330/2010, Art 1(e).   [156] Case C-439/09 [2011] ECR I-9419.
[157] Ibid, para 38.

exemption did not apply. It was not necessary to adopt a broad interpretation of the block exemption provisions as undertakings have the option of asserting that Article 101(3) applies on an individual basis to their agreement (see section 6.3.5, agreements can individually satisfy the conditions of Article 101(3) even if they do not satisfy the conditions of a block exemption regulation);

(c) it did not have sufficient information before it to provide guidance to the referring court on the question of whether the agreement individually satisfied the criteria of Article 101(3).

When the matter reverted to the French court, applying the guidance set out by the Court, it upheld the fine that had been imposed on Pierre Fabre by the French competition authority.

7 Article 102 TFEU

7.1 Introduction

It has been seen that Article 102 prohibits any abuse by one or more undertakings of a dominant position. The article relies on several concepts that are utilized in Article 101, such as undertaking and appreciable effect on trade between Member States. This section consequently focuses on dominance and abuse. The dominant position must be in the internal market, or in a substantial part of it. Once again, in interpreting these concepts, the question whether Article 102 pursues an Ordoliberal, consumer-welfare, and/or market-integration goal is highly important. Although it has been seen that the trend is to embrace a sole consumer-welfare goal, it is not clear that the EU Courts are following that trend.[158]

7.2 Dominance

Article 102 only applies where an undertaking[159] holds a dominant position. Arguably, the concept of dominance should relate to the adverse consequences which result when an undertaking has market power rather than simply having commercial power.[160] In *Hoffmann-La Roche* the Court of Justice held that a dominant position relates to a position of economic strength enjoyed by an undertaking

> which enables it to prevent effective competition being maintained on the relevant market by affording it the power to behave to an appreciable extent independently of its competitors, its customers and ultimately of the consumers. Such a position does not preclude some competition.[161]

---

[158] But see eg *Post Danmark* (n 15), especially the section on objective justification, paras 41–43 and the Commission Guidance on the Commission's enforcement priorities in applying Article 82 of the EC Treaty to abusive exclusionary conduct by dominant undertakings (Guidance Paper) (OJ [2009] C45/7) paras 28–31.

[159] The Court has confirmed that Art 102 also applies where two or more undertakings are collectively dominant on a market, see eg Jones and Sufrin, *EU Competition Law* (n 112) ch 5. Only single dominance is discussed in this chapter.

[160] G Monti, *EC Competition Law* (Cambridge: Cambridge University Press, 2007) 124–130.

[161] Case 85/76 *Hoffmann-La Roche v Commission* [1979] ECR 461, paras 38 and 39.

Although this definition focuses on the concept of independence, rather than the power of the firm to exercise market power and maintain supra-competitive prices (as many economists might prefer),[162] the General Court in *AstraZeneca* explicitly equated this notion of 'independence' with the market power of a dominant firm and its ability to maintain high prices.[163]

It has been seen that market power is ordinarily identified indirectly in EU competition law. Indeed, the Court has defined two steps in assessing dominance. First, the relevant market must be identified (from both a product and geographic perspective). Secondly, it must be determined whether the undertaking is dominant on the relevant market. This is done by looking at market shares and other factors indicating dominance.

Where market shares are very large and have been held for some time, the Court of Justice has accepted that they are generally, and, *save in exceptional circumstances*, a good proxy for market power or dominance.[164] In *Akzo* it established a presumption of dominance for firms with a market share of 50 per cent or more:

> With regard to market shares the Court has held that very large shares are in themselves, and save in exceptional circumstances, evidence of the existence of a dominant position...That is the situation where there is a market share of 50%.[165]

Although dominance may also be found where market shares are below 50 per cent,[166] in practice a finding of dominance is unlikely if the undertaking's market share is below 40 per cent.[167] When assessing dominance, however, it is important not to look exclusively at market shares, as although they provide a snapshot of how the market is at that time, they do not indicate why the undertaking has these market shares, for example, whether it is because it produces the best products more efficiently or because it is not vulnerable to new entry into its market by competitors. In addition to considering market shares, therefore, it is also important

- to compare the undertaking's market share with those of its rivals[168] – an undertaking with a market share of 40 per cent is less likely to be found dominant when its nearest rival has a share of 40 per cent, than when its nearest rival has a share of 5 per cent;
- to consider how the firm's market shares have changed over time – falling shares hint at declining market power;[169]
- to consider the dynamics of competition on the market – competition today and how the market might develop in the future (especially in high tech markets);
- to consider whether or not there are barriers to entry or expansion into the market; and
- to consider buyer power.[170]

In particular, the question whether there are barriers to entry or expansion is crucially important. If there are no or low barriers to entry/expansion into a market, an undertaking will be deterred from increasing prices (and so be unable to exercise market power). This is

---

[162] See eg L Ortiz Blanco, *Market Power in EU Antitrust Law* (Oxford: Hart Publishing, 2012) 47.

[163] Case T-321/05 *AstraZeneca v Commission* [2010] ECR II-2805, para 267, aff'd Case C-457/10 P *AstraZeneca v Commission*, judgment of 6 December 2012, nyr, paras 177–181.

[164] *Hoffmann-La Roche* (n 161) para 41.

[165] Case C-62/86 *AKZO Chemie v Commission* [1991] ECR I-3359, para 60.

[166] eg Case 27/76 *United Brands v Commission* [1978] ECR 207, paras 108–129 (40–45 per cent) and Case T-219/99 *British Airways v Commission* [2003] ECR II-5917, paras 189–225 (39.7 per cent).

[167] Guidance Paper (n 158) para 14.   [168] *Hoffmann-La Roche* (n 161) para 48.

[169] M Motta, *Competition Policy: Theory and Practice* (Cambridge: Cambridge University Press, 2004) 120.

[170] See Guidance Paper (n 158) para 18 and Motta, *Competition Policy* (n 169) 121–123.

because if the undertaking raises prices then others outside the market might see potential to make profits and enter the market. Consequently, even a firm with a 100 per cent market share, may not have market power, in the sense that it will be able to sustain supra-competitive prices.[171] In contrast, where barriers to entry/expansion are high, even a significant price increase by a (dominant) firm will not attract new entrants to compete with it.

An essential question is therefore what constitutes a barrier to entry or expansion? Economists have differing views about this issue. According to Stigler, in the absence of statutory regulation and where raw materials are available, barriers exist only when a new entrant faces higher costs than those firms already in the marketplace face, or had to face.[172] By way of contrast, Bain defines barriers to entry more widely, as anything that makes entry more costly.[173]

The EU Courts, and the Commission, have taken a relatively broad approach when identifying barriers to entry and 'other factors indicating dominance'.[174] This approach has led to criticism being levied on the EU Courts and Commission.[175] If too great an emphasis is placed on market shares and an over-expansive definition of barriers to entry is adopted, an exaggerated picture of an undertaking's market power may be created. This, in turn, may deter firms from engaging in conduct which is pro-competitive or at least neutral from a competition perspective for fear of contravening Article 102 (type 1 errors).

The Commission has now pledged in its 'Guidance on the Commission's Enforcement Priorities in Applying Article 82 [102 TFEU] to Abusive Exclusionary Conduct by Dominant Undertakings'[176] to adopt a more economic approach, based on a consumer welfare objective. Not only does this Notice downplay the relevance of market shares in assessing dominance, which it acknowledges only give a first indication of market structure,[177] but it stresses the importance of examining constraints imposed on an undertaking by 'credible threats of future entry or expansion' – where entry/expansion is 'likely, timely and significant'.[178] The Guidance Paper states that barriers to expansion or entry can take various forms:

> They may be legal barriers, such as tariffs or quotas, or they may take the form of advantages specifically enjoyed by the dominant undertaking, such as economies of scale and scope, privileged access to essential inputs or natural resources, important technologies…or an established distribution and sales network…The dominant undertaking's own conduct may also create barriers to entry, for example where it has made significant investments which entrants or competitors would have to match…or where it has concluded long-term contracts with its customers that have appreciable foreclosing effects.[179]

---

[171] W Baumol, J Panzar, and R Willig, *Contestable Markets and the Theory of Industry Structure* (revised edn, New York: Harcourt Brace Jovanovich, 1988); cf Motta, *Competition Policy* (n 169) 73–75.

[172] G Stigler, *The Organisation of Industry* (Homewood, IL: Richard D Irwin, 1968).

[173] J Bain, *Barriers to New Competition: Their Character and Consequences in Manufacturing Industries* (Cambridge, MA: Harvard University Press, 1956). Monti explains the differences in the following way: if newly devised planning laws prevent the construction of a factory necessary for the competitor's entry, this is an entry barrier under both definitions. On the other hand, the fact that the incumbent has an efficient distribution network is not an entry barrier under Stigler's definition because if such a network is key to market success, it is an investment which both incumbent and new entrant have to make to participate in the market. It can, however, constitute an entry barrier under Bain's definition because it is an extra cost which makes entry more risky (G Monti, 'The Concept of Dominance in Article 82' (2006) 2 *European Competition Journal* (Special edn) 31, 5, available at https://www.lse.ac.uk/collections/law/staff%20publications%20full%20text/monti/ECJdominancepaper.pdf

[174] 'Other' meaning factors other than market share. The Commission now uses the term 'barriers to entry': see eg Commission Guidelines on the assessment of horizontal mergers under the Council Regulation on the control of concentrations between undertakings (OJ [2004] C31/5) and the Guidance Paper (n 158).

[175] And suggests a more Ordoliberal approach, Monti, *EC Competition Law* (n 160) 144–148.

[176] Guidance Paper (n 158).   [177] Ibid.   [178] Ibid, para 16.   [179] Ibid, para 17.

The Guidance Paper is not, however, intended to constitute a statement of the law and, in some respects, it clearly diverges from the approach set out in the case law of the EU Courts.

7.3 Identifying conduct which infringes Article 102

Article 102 makes it clear that it is not an offence for a firm to hold a dominant position: an abuse of that dominant position must be committed. The EU Courts have consistently stressed, however, that although a finding of dominance is not a recrimination, a dominant firm does have a special responsibility 'not to allow its conduct to impair genuine undistorted competition'.[180]

7.3.1 Abuse

Article 102 itself sets out an illustrative, but not exhaustive, list of abuses, including 'directly or indirectly imposing unfair purchase or selling prices or other unfair trading conditions' (Article 102(a)), 'limiting production, markets or technical development to the prejudice of consumers' (Article 102(b)), and 'applying dissimilar conditions to equivalent transactions with other trading parties, thereby placing them at a competitive disadvantage' (Article 102(c)).

Although the provisions make it clear that Article 102 applies to 'exploitative' abuses (where a dominant undertaking takes advantage of its market power and exploits it) and certain price discrimination (see section 7.3.4), the main concern in the application of Article 102 has, since *Continental Can*,[181] been with exclusionary abuses – 'practices that cause consumers harm through their impact on competition',[182] for example, predatory pricing (see case study 17.3), exclusive dealing obligations (where a buyer is obliged to purchase all of its requirements from the dominant supplier), or refusal to supply/deal. In *Continental Can* the Court of Justice, in an extremely important judgment, clarified that the object of Article 102 is not just to protect consumers directly from the exploitation of market power, but also to protect them from conduct which through its impact on the structure of competition is detrimental to them indirectly – in that case an undertaking sought to strengthen its position and eliminate competition by taking over a competitor. Conduct may also constitute an abuse where the conduct is inimical to the single market, so parallel trade is prejudiced.

The Court has set out general statements about the nature of the concept of an (exclusionary) abuse. In particular, it has held that it

> is an objective concept relating to the behaviour of an undertaking in a dominant position which is such as to influence the structure of a market where, as a result of the very presence of the undertaking in question, the degree of competition is weakened and which, through recourse to methods different from that which condition normal competition in products or services on the basis of the transactions of commercial operators, has the effect of hindering the maintenance of the degree of competition still existing in the market or the growth of that competition.[183]

---

[180] Case 322/81 *NV Nederlandsche Vanden-Industri Michelin v Commission* ('*Michelin I*') [1983] ECR 3461, para 57.   [181] Case 6/72 (n 6).

[182] *Post Danmark* (n 15) para 20. The categories of exclusionary and exploitative abuse are not mutually exclusive, however, see Jones and Sufrin, *European Competition Law* (n 112) ch 7.

[183] *Hoffmann-La Roche* (n 161) para 91.

The emphasis on the objective nature of the concept indicates that it is not essential that fault or subjective intent to exclude competitors or weaken competition is established. The clear presence of an anti-competitive objective/intent may, however, reinforce a finding that there is an abuse of a dominant position.[184]

7.3.2 Exploitative abuses

The view could be taken that there is nothing wrong with charging supra-competitive prices which 'at least for a short period—is what attracts "business acumen" in the first place; it induces risk taking that produces innovation and economic growth'.[185] However, it has been seen that Article 102 specifically targets exploitative behaviour, including charging customers more than the competitive price, or through providing an inferior service.

Most competition authorities are cautious about tackling exploitative abuses, especially high pricing. Not only may they be reluctant to engage in price regulation – the antithesis of the free market – but unfairly high prices are difficult to identify (how can a *fair* selling price be determined?) and, even if identified, are hard to remedy. Such conduct may therefore be better dealt with by regulatory agencies specialized in dealing with natural or legal monopolies (such as OFWAT for water in the UK[186]), through contract or consumer protection laws, or by acting decisively against exclusionary conduct designed to perpetuate a position of dominance.[187]

In its *1998 Football World Cup* decision,[188] however, the Commission looked at the distribution and sale arrangements for entry tickets to the 1998 Football World Cup which were operated by Comité français d'organisation de la Coupe du monde de football 1998 (CFO). Essentially, customers could only purchase tickets from CFO if they provided a postal address in France. Consequently, 'only by entering into wholly arbitrary, impractical and exceptional arrangements...could most of the general public resident outside France have obtained tickets direct from CFO.' The conduct was exploitative in the sense that it 'had the effect of imposing unfair trading conditions on residents outside France which resulted in a limitation of the market to the prejudice of those consumers'. By discriminating against customers on the grounds of nationality, the behaviour was also inimical to the internal market objective.

7.3.3 Exclusionary abuses

The Court of Justice's definition of abuse (set out in section 7.3.1) requires a difficult line to be drawn between unlawful exclusionary behaviour and competition on the basis of performance or competition on the merits (normal competition). For example, in the area of 'pricing' it is frequently hard to distinguish unlawful exclusionary pricing practices from hard-line price competition (see case study 17.3).

It has often been complained that the EU competition law rules developed to identify abusive behaviour are excessively broad and so chill aggressive competition and low-cost pricing, arguably 'the very conduct the antitrust laws are designed to protect'.[189] Further, that they place too great an emphasis on the form of the conduct, and insufficient on its effects. For example, the incorporation of an exclusive dealing obligation (a duty only to sell the dominant undertaking's products) has been treated almost automatically as an

---

[184] *AstraZeneca v Commission* (n 163) para 359.
[185] *Verizon Communications* (n 149) para 2 (Scalia J).
[186] http://www.ofwat.gov.uk/
[187] XXIVth Report on Competition Policy (Commission, 1994) part 207.
[188] Commission Decision, *1998 Football World Cup* (OJ [2000] L5/55).
[189] *Matsushita Electric Industrial Co v Zenith Radio Corp* 475 US 574, 594 (1986).

abuse.[190] In other cases, the Commission and the Court of Justice have also, arguably, been too willing *to presume* anti-competitive effects when a competitor is excluded from the market. For example, in *Commercial Solvents* it was held that CSC, dominant in the supply of a raw material, aminobutanol, had abused its dominant position when it ceased selling aminobutanol to Zoja, which used it to make an anti-tuberculosis drug. CSC had decided to start making this drug itself and wanted to stop supplying Zoja. The Court held that

> an undertaking which has a dominant position in the market in raw materials and which, with the object of reserving such raw material for manufacturing its own derivatives, refuses to supply a customer, which is itself a manufacturer of these derivatives, and there-fore risks eliminating all competition on the part of this customer, is abusing its dominant position.[191]

The Court did not clarify, however, why it considered this conduct to be abusive. In par-ticular, whether it simply sought to constrain CSC's economic power, especially because of its impact on Zoja's freedom to compete on the market (a seemingly Ordoliberal goal), or whether it was concerned about the impact of the elimination of Zoja on competition downstream (and consumer welfare).[192] If the latter, the Court simply seemed to assume the harm to competition downstream from the exclusion of Zoja without actually assessing the actual impact on it.[193]

Although in some areas (including refusal to supply, ie cases like *Commercial Solvents*) the law has now evolved somewhat,[194] complaints about this type of approach triggered a vigorous debate about the nature of an abuse of a dominant position which eventually resulted, in 2009, in the Commission publishing its Guidance Paper.[195] During the debate, core issues were Article 102's objectives, the trade-off between rules and standards, and how any such tests should be constructed. In the Guidance Paper the Commission states that it will more closely analyse the effects of conduct and focus its resources only on cases where the exclusionary conduct of the dominant firm impairs effective competition by 'foreclosing their competitors in an anticompetitive way, thus having an adverse impact on consumer welfare'.[196]

It has been noted that the Commission's approach set out in the Guidance Paper is not always completely consistent with that of the EU Courts. In the context of some abuses, however, the case law adopts a more effects-based and less formalistic approach. In the area of refusal to supply, for example, the Court of Justice has become more cautious than it appeared in *Commercial Solvents* about declaring such conduct to be abusive. It now appears to recognize that although requiring access to an upstream product or facility may facilitate competition downstream, an obligation to deal interferes with

---

[190] See *Hoffmann-La Roche* (n 161).   [191] *Commercial Solvents* (n 9) para 25.

[192] R Whish and D Bailey, *Competition Law* (7th edn, Oxford: Oxford University Press, 2012) 196 and 197. Cf Monti, *EC Competition Law* (n 160) 162–169.

[193] More recent cases are equally ambiguous, eg for the abuse of margin squeeze see *TeliaSonera* (n 14) paras 22–37.

[194] Case C-7/97 *Oscar Bronner v Mediaprint Zeitungs- und Zeitschriftenverlag* [1998] ECR I-7791, para 41.

[195] Guidance Paper (n 158). This guidance states that it is not an expression of the law, merely an explan-ation of when the Commission will prioritize its scarce resources for investigating Art 102 issues. However, it reads like substantive guidance and consequently there is a risk that it will be treated as such: see L Lovdahl Gormsen, 'Why the European Commission's Enforcement Priorities on Article 82 EC Should Be Withdrawn' [2010] 2 *European Competition Law Review* 49.   [196] Guidance Paper (n 158) para 19.

the dominant firm's right to choose its trading partner and risks discouraging investment and innovation both by the dominant firm (which has developed the asset its rival wants access to[197]) and the rival downstream. It risks 'discouraging similar investments elsewhere, as the prospect of being expropriated of their investments discourages firms from introducing new inputs and facilities in the first place.'[198] The case law now establishes that a refusal to deal by a vertically integrated dominant firm (as in *Commercial Solvents*, eg where the dominant firm supplied a raw material upstream used for the manufacture of a drug downstream) to a downstream rival will only constitute an abuse where[199]

(a) access to its product, service, or facility is 'indispensable' for the rival to compete (there are no actual or potential substitutes for it).[200] When demonstrating that no actual or potential substitutes exist upstream and that access to the existing product or system is therefore indispensable, it is not sufficient simply to demonstrate that it is not economically viable for the rival to compete without access to the product or facility (eg the raw material). To be indispensable, it is necessary at the very least to show that it is not economically viable to create a competing scheme even if it had similar economies of scale to the dominant undertaking;[201]

(b) the refusal is likely to eliminate all competition on the secondary market (even if not imminent).[202]

7.3.4 Price discrimination: Article 102(c) TFEU

Article 102 not only prevents dominant firms from impairing the competitive position of competitors through exclusionary price-cutting tactics (primary line injury), but it condemns price discrimination which may distort competition between downstream buyers (secondary line injury). The expansive interpretation given to Article 102(c) by the EU Courts has led to concern that less efficient buyers may be protected by Article 102 from their more efficient rivals with the result that customers may have to pay higher prices. The presence of this explicit provision, once again, forces us to ask questions about Article 102's goal(s). Price discrimination can often be consumer-welfare enhancing, for example where it allows a supplier to expand output by extracting from each consumer the maximum that they are willing to pay.[203] Does this explicit reference to discrimination demand the consideration of goals other than consumer welfare?

7.3.5 Objective necessity and efficiencies

Although not set out in the wording of Article 102, the EU Courts have consistently held that a dominant undertaking may provide objective justification for behaviour that is otherwise liable to be caught by the prohibition under Article 102. Broadly, it may do this either by showing that its conduct is objectively necessary or that the abusive conduct is counterbalanced, outweighed even, by objective economic justifications – advantages in terms of efficiency that also benefit consumers.[204]

---

[197] Arguably, there should be less concern about this issue where the firm has not developed the asset itself, but the government has developed an 'asset' and then privatized it: *Post Danmark* (n 15) para 23.

[198] Motta, *Competition Policy* (n 169) 68.

[199] See esp Cases C-241/91 P etc *RTE and ITP v Commission* [1995] ECR 1-743 and *Oscar Bronner* (n 194).

[200] *Oscar Bronner* (n 194) para 41.   [201] Ibid, paras 45 and 46.

[202] The EU Courts have been willing to assume that such conduct will harm the competitive structure and, possibly, consumers through the elimination of rivals on the downstream market.

[203] Motta, *Competition Policy* (n 169) 23.

[204] *Post Danmark* (n 15) para 41.

It appears that objective necessity relates to factors external to the dominant undertaking,[205] justifying conduct on technical or commercial grounds,[206] for example the conduct was required for health and safety reasons or because the buyer was a bad debtor, or has a bad credit rating. The Commission states that such justification must be proportionate and that it is normally for public authorities to set and enforce public health and safety standards.[207]

In terms of efficiencies, the dominant undertaking must show that the gains likely to result from its conduct counteract any likely negative effects on competition in the affected markets, that those gains have been, or are likely to be, brought about as a result of that conduct, that such conduct is necessary for the achievement of those gains in efficiency and that it does not eliminate effective competition, by removing all or most existing sources of actual or potential competition. This assessment must be made on the basis of the whole circumstances of the case.[208] Furthermore, as it is an objective assessment, it does not matter that generating efficiencies was not an explicit motivation for the dominant undertaking's actions.[209] The Court of Justice has thus written into Article 102 a defence virtually identical to Article 101(3).

Case study 17.3: Predatory pricing and *AKZO Chemie v Commission*

Predatory pricing occurs where a firm with market power lowers its price with the purpose of eliminating or disciplining its competitors. The lower prices may be applied across the board or targeted at certain customers. The practice harms consumer welfare as, although prices are lowered in the short term, the dominant firm invests in a strategy which allows it to exclude its competitors and, following the predatory siege, to hurt consumers by raising prices and charging supra-competitive prices. A particular problem for competition law is how a rule or standard can be crafted to identify predatory pricing and to distinguish it from hard-nosed price competition. An overly broad rule might deter low-cost pricing and encourage complaints by less efficient rivals losing out in the competitive battle.

In 1975, in an influential article, Areeda and Turner[210] proposed a cost-based test for identifying predatory behaviour. They suggested a rule that where a firm charges prices below its average variable costs (AVC – variable costs are those that vary with output, eg fuel, materials, and labour, and are distinct from fixed costs (eg management overheads and rent) which do not vary with output/how much of a good or service the firm sells) it should be held to be engaged in unlawful predatory behaviour, but that a firm pricing at or above AVC should be conclusively presumed to have acted lawfully. Although there has been considerable concern expressed about the accuracy and appropriateness of this test, and in particular whether it screens out too many legitimate predatory-pricing claims, most competition systems now adopt some form of price–cost test for identifying low-cost pricing which is likely to be predatory and to exclude equally efficient competitors from the market. How any such test is constructed is likely to determine whether the rule is likely to

---

[205] Case COMP/39.525 *Telekomunikacja Polska*, 22 June 2011, para 874, on appeal Case T-486/11, judgment pending.

[206] Case 311/84 *Centre belge d'études de marché – Télémarketing v Compagnie luxembourgeoise de télédiffusion* [1985] ECR 3261, paras 26 and 27.   [207] Guidance Paper (n 158) para 29.

[208] Case C-95/04 P *British Airways v Commission* [2007] ECR I-2331, para 86.

[209] *Post Danmark* (n 15) paras 42 and 43.

[210] P Areeda and DF Turner, 'Predatory Pricing and Related Practices under Section 2 of the Sherman Act' (1975) 88 *Harvard Law Review* 697.

be over- or under-inclusive (leading to type 1 or type 2 errors). In the US, for example, the Supreme Court has held that, in addition to showing that a defendant has predated below a certain measure of costs, a claimant must show that the defendant has a dangerous probability of recouping its investment in below-cost pricing. The Supreme Court thus favours a test which will, if anything, be under-inclusive and will not deter firms, even dominant ones, from engaging in aggressive low-cost pricing. This approach prefers the risk of type 2 to type 1 errors. In the EU, in contrast, the Court of Justice has held that a presumption of predation applies where a dominant firm prices below AVC and that 'demonstrating that it is possible to recoup losses is not a necessary pre-condition for a finding of predatory pricing'.[211] Further, predatory pricing may also be demonstrated even where pricing is above AVC, if it is below average total costs (ATC – fixed and variable) and forms part of a strategy designed to eliminate a competitor from the market. These rules were established in a line of cases commencing with *AKZO*.[212]

This case concerned the conduct of AKZO Chemie BV's UK subsidiary, which produced organic peroxides – speciality chemicals used in the plastics industry and as bleaching agents for flour. Two other suppliers (ECS and Diaflex) also offered a range of flour additives in the UK. When, however, ECS decided to start supplying organic peroxides for plastics application, AKZO found out and ordered ECS to stop and threatened to harm ECS's organic peroxides sales to the flour industry if it refused. ECS did not comply, so AKZO offered organic peroxides to ECS's biggest customers in the flour industry at low prices (which were significantly lower than those charged by AKZO to its own customers). AKZO had superior financial resources to ECS and could withstand such a strategy for longer.

The Commission found that AKZO had violated Article 102 and imposed fines of €10 million and ordered it to terminate the infringement. The Court upheld the Commission's finding that AKZO was dominant. It affirmed

- the finding that the relevant market was that of organic peroxides (and rejected the wider market definition proposed by AKZO); and
- the Commission's finding that AKZO was dominant on the market. The Commission had noted that: AKZO's market share was large in itself (50 per cent), and equivalent to that of all the remaining producers combined; its market share had remained steady from 1979 to 1982; and AKZO was even able to raise its profit margins in periods of economic downturn. The Court confirmed the Commission's findings adding 'very large shares are in themselves, and save in exceptional circumstances, evidence of the existence of a dominant position…That is the situation where there is a market share of 50% such as that found to exist in this case.'

The Court then affirmed the Commission's finding that AKZO had abused its dominant position. It held that a dominant firm must not eliminate a competitor and thereby strengthen its own position other than by using methods which come within the scope of competition on the basis of quality. Not all competition on price can be regarded as legitimate. Rather, the Court held that

- 'Prices below average variable costs by means of which a dominant undertaking seeks to eliminate a competitor must be regarded as abusive. A dominant undertaking has no interest in applying such prices except that of eliminating competitors so as to

---

[211] Case C-202/07 P *France Télécom SA v Commission* [2009] ECR I-2369, para 113.
[212] Case C-62/86 (n 165).

enable it subsequently to raise its prices by taking advantage of its monopolistic position, since each sale generates a loss, namely the total amount of the fixed costs . . . and, at least, part of the variable costs relating to the unit produced';

- 'prices below average total costs, that is to say fixed costs plus variable costs, but below average variable costs, must be regarded as abusive if they are determined as part of a plan for eliminating a competitor. Such prices can drive from the market undertakings which are as efficient as the dominant undertaking but which, because of their smaller financial resources, are incapable of withstanding the competition waged against them.'

In this case, AKZO had been selling below its ATC over a prolonged period of time with the intention of selectively targeting the customers of ECS to force ECS either to abandon them or to match a loss-making price in order to retain them. Both the Commission and the Court also rejected, on the facts, AKZO's justification that it had acted not to discipline ECS but to sell off surplus stock. Although the Court held that AKZO's behaviour was particularly serious, it reduced the Commission's fine by 25 per cent because this was the first time that the Court had clarified the law in this area.

In a later case, *Post Danmark A/S v Konkurrencerådet*,[213] the Court confirmed that prices above average total costs are not predatory: Article 102 does not 'seek to ensure that competitors less efficient than the undertaking with the dominant position should remain on the market' and so precludes only pricing practices 'that have an exclusionary effect on competitors considered to be as efficient as it is itself'.[214]

Arguably, the emphasis placed in this line of cases on the need for the conduct to be able to drive from the market undertakings which are as efficient as the dominant firm, suggests that the rules in this area are not simply designed to protect smaller, even perhaps if they are less-efficient, competitors (as an Ordoliberal goal might do) but are designed to protect customers from price rises once the rivals have been disciplined (to prevent conduct which will harm consumer welfare). A presumption is applied, however, that where the test is met, the dominant firm, having disciplined or excluded its competitor(s) will be able to raise prices, recoup losses made during the predatory siege, and harm consumers. The risk of consumer harm from the predatory strategy is thus assumed: in contrast to the position in the US, actual proof that the strategy is likely to be successful is not required.

8 Conclusion

Articles 101 and 102 prohibit anti-competitive agreements between entities engaged in economic activity and the unilateral conduct of entities which hold a dominant position in the EU or a substantial part of it. The provisions apply insofar as the agreement or conduct at issue affects trade between Member States. As severe consequences may flow for undertakings which violate either rule (including fines and exposure to damages claims), it is essential that they understand what conduct is prohibited by the rules and why.

Over the last ten years, the Commission has set out its view that the objective of Articles 101 and 102 should be to prohibit conduct which harms consumer welfare. This is

---

[213] Case C-209/10 (n 15) para 36, but see eg the exceptional facts of Joined Cases C-395 and 396/96 P *Compagnie Maritime Belge v Commission* [2000] ECR-1365.
[214] *Post Danmark* (n 15) paras 21 and 25.

supported by many academics and practitioners; the EU Courts have not, however, clearly supported this approach. Even if such an approach is accepted, a core difficulty in applying Articles 101 and 102 is how to distinguish anti-competitive agreements and conduct from conduct which is neutral or pro-competitive in a way which (a) provides undertakings and decision-takers with sufficient certainty, whilst at the same time (b) ensuring that a coherent and accurate antitrust system is maintained. Although in the past the EU authorities have been criticized for adopting too formalistic an approach to this issue, relying on over-inclusive rules, in recent years the Commission has taken significant strides towards modernizing the interpretation and application of Articles 101 and 102 and to ensure that an effects-based approach is adopted where feasible, focusing on the effects of the conduct in a greater number of cases.

Further reading

A Jones and B Sufrin, *EU Competition Law* (5th edn, Oxford: Oxford University Press, 2014)

L Lovdahl Gormsen, *A Principled Approach to Abuse of Dominance in European Competition Law* (Cambridge: Cambridge University Press, 2010)

M Monti, *EC Competition Law* (Cambridge: Cambridge University Press, 2007)

M Motta, *Competition Policy* (Cambridge: Cambridge University Press, 2004)

O Odudu, *The Boundaries of EC Competition Law: The Scope of Article 81* (Oxford: Oxford University Press, 2006)

C Townley, *Article 81 EC and Public Policy* (Oxford: Hart Publishing, 2009)

R Whish and D Bailey, *Competition Law* (7th edn, Oxford: Oxford University Press, 2012)

18

Public services and EU law

Leigh Hancher and Wolf Sauter

1 Introduction

Everyone uses public services (eg transport and education) every day of their lives, and some people are totally reliant upon such services (eg long-term care or social housing). Public services also have a major economic impact; for example, health care alone typically accounts for 10 per cent (and rising) of gross domestic product (GDP) in the EU Member States, while the price of energy services has a multiplier effect on the economy as a whole. EU law must therefore attempt to balance social objectives and public service obligations (largely defined at national level) with the need to maintain the internal market and free competition. This has proved difficult because it raises fundamental questions of competence (who has the power to decide what services are to be provided in a State, at what level, and for how much?) and legitimacy (should the EU be interfering in these areas at all?).

Given the economic impact of public services it was inevitable that the Court would eventually consider that EU law would apply. But what EU law? Consider, for example, the provision of social care for the elderly in a remote part of State A. If State A decides that the care should be provided by a private contractor, what process will be used to select that contractor? This is already regulated by EU law: the EU public procurement rules may apply.[1] What if the

---

[1] See eg Directive 2004/18. This is not considered further in this chapter.

State is concerned that no private contractor will make a bid because of the costs involved in travelling to remote parts of the territory? So the State offers inducements: exclusivity on the contract for ten years, preferred bidder status for subsequent more lucrative contracts in more populous parts of State A, or a more favourable tax regime to the successful contractor. This raises issues under the competition rules (Articles 101 and 102 TFEU), State aid rules (Article 107 TFEU), and the obscure but important exception in Article 106 TFEU (see Figure 18.1). It is a discussion of these provisions and their interaction which forms the major part of this chapter. However, first we begin by considering the meaning of the term 'public services' and the related term used by the EU, 'services of general economic interest' (SGEIs).

2 Public services and SGEIs

2.1 What are public services?

Services in general in EU law are defined in Article 57 TFEU both positively, as being provided for remuneration, and negatively, as not covered by the TFEU provisions on goods, capital, or persons.[2] However, *public* services are not as such defined in EU law. Opinions on what qualifies as a public service vary between (as well as within) the Member States.[3]

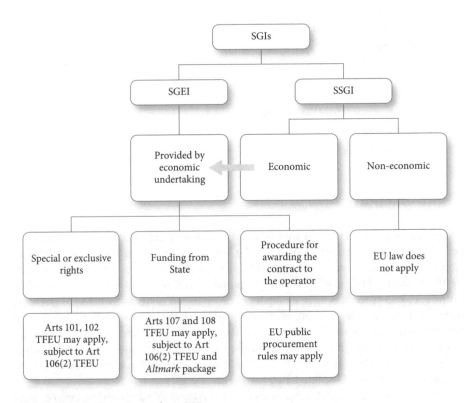

Fig 18.1 How EU law may apply to SGIs

---

[2] See further chapter 13.

[3] The need for further clarification and simplification of the application of the Treaty State aid regime to the financing of SGEIs was, however, acknowledged. In 2006 the Commission published a paper on Social Services of General Interest (COM(2006) 177, 26 April 2006). In 2007 it published yet another Communication on

They are generally understood as services that supply some public good, that is, a good the consumption of which is in the general interest, which would be undersupplied or would not be supplied at all if purely left to market forces. Examples include health care, employment services, sanitation, or transport services. Governments typically perform these themselves or fund their performance by others. Where the State does not perform the public service itself, it usually defines the characteristics of the service (quality, availability, and price), sometimes called public service obligations (PSOs) or universal service obligations, which must be provided by others.

Further, what counts as a public service varies over time. For example, at one time the limited set of analogue telephone services (known as POTS (Plain Old Telephony Services)) were provided as a public service in all Member States by national monopolists (whose networks were deemed to be 'natural monopolies', eg British Telecom in the UK and France Telecom in France). POTS have now been replaced by a constantly expanding range of competing digital services and service providers. By way of another example, some Member States rely on a national health service (NHS), other States provide health care using private suppliers, while others have parallel or mixed regimes.[4] In all of these cases a public service is likely to be involved to some extent, although clearly the scope of the publicly defined service will differ from State to State.

Although there is no formal definition of public services in the EU or a formal categorization of public services in EU law, primary EU law does recognize the concept of SGEIs in Articles 14 and 106 TFEU, Protocol No 26 to the TEU and TFEU, and Article 36 of the Charter of Fundamental Rights of the European Union. Conceptually, SGEIs are a subset of the overarching category of services of general interest (SGIs), alongside another partially overlapping subset which are *social* services of general interest (SSGIs) (see Figure 18.2). SSGIs raise issues of EU law where they are provided for remuneration and thus are also SGEIs because they are economic in nature: the overlapping segment in Figure 18.2. This could be, for example, undertakings providing publicly defined long-term care services (eg house cleaning and laundry, personal care, and supervision of medication at home) to elderly citizens in exchange for remuneration at regulated rates. In all instances, qualifying as a genuine SGEI requires, at a minimum, that the services involved are provided by

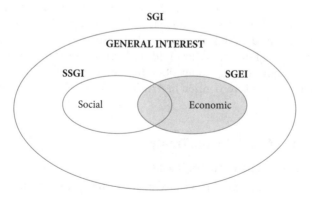

Fig 18.2 Categorizing public services

Source: European Commission, COM(2011) 146 final.

Services of General Interest including social services of general interest (COM(2007) 725, 20 November 2007). Finally, the Commission recently published a 'FAQ' on this subject (SWD(2013) 53 final/2, 29 April 2013).

⁴ See further chapter 21.

undertakings in markets (in principle in exchange for remuneration), as would be the case with the example of long-term care for the elderly in State A discussed in section 1.

Using external contractors to provide public services via SGEIs is attractive to governments because contractors are often more efficient and less costly than public provision. SGEIs may engage EU law due to the fact they involve economic activity. However, they may benefit from a proportionate exception to the general free movement and competition rules due to Article 106(2) TFEU, which provides that undertakings entrusted with the operation of SGEIs will be subject to the rules contained in the Treaties 'in so far as the application of such rules does not obstruct the performance, in law or in fact, of the particular tasks assigned to them'. Article 106(2) TFEU is considered in more detail in section 2.2.2.

So far we have talked about SGEIs being provided by private operators. SGEIs may, however, be provided by the State itself. The extent to which the State will be subject to EU law in the provision of public services is far from clear due to the Court's inconsistent approach to drawing the line between 'economic' and 'non-economic' services (see Figure 18.1). A number of cases take an objective and 'maximalist' approach, holding that any activity consisting in the offering of goods and services on a market is an economic activity, even if the activity is carried out by the public sector or under PSOs. However, other cases have carved out a 'solidarity' exception via the definition of 'undertaking', or have used the definition of 'services' at Article 57 TFEU to exclude services organized by the State, such as public higher education from the ambit of the Treaty rules on State aid and competition.[5] This type of delineation is a useful way to avoid ruling on controversial issues.

Where the State decides that the public service is to be provided by a private operator it may grant the operators certain special or exclusive rights. An *exclusive* right would be, for example, the monopoly right granted to the private operator of a ferry service to a remote island with year-round access, enabling quieter periods to be subsidized by seasonal tourist traffic. Exclusive rights therefore serve as one way to allow internalization of cross-subsidies and thereby funding for non-profitable public services. *Special* rights serve a similar beneficial function. For example, a State may grant a limited set of licences to deliver fourth-generation mobile communications services. This may be needed to ensure spectrum usage is efficiently allocated (because of physical scarcity), to meet minimum standards of service provision, to guarantee investment (providers will know the number of their competitors in advance), and may also generate funds for the public purse (if such rights are auctioned). While the grant of both exclusive and special rights serve to promote the provision of the service involved at a level perceived to be in the public interest, it has the effect of restricting competition from other providers. The need to balance these competing interests is recognized in Article 106(2) TFEU. This article is considered in section 2.2.2.

2.2 Recognition of SGEIs by the Treaty

2.2.1 Article 14 TFEU and Protocol No 26

Article 14 TFEU, and Protocol No 26 added by the Lisbon Treaty, contain provisions that are highly relevant to the scope and organization of public services, and were intended by the Member States to limit the Commission's powers with respect to SGEIs. The Member States possess wide discretion to define what an SGEI is on the basis of their specific social needs and their cultural and political traditions. This has been reaffirmed in the Lisbon

---

[5] Case 263/86 *Humbel* [1988] ECR 5365.

Treaty in, for example, Article 1 of Protocol No 26. The Protocol concerns the common values that are the subject of SGEIs and those other SGIs which, not being economic in nature, remain outside the scope of the Treaties.[6]

Article 14 TFEU provides:

> Without prejudice to Article 4 of the Treaty on European Union or to Articles 93, 106 and 107 of this Treaty, and given the place occupied by services of general economic interest in the shared values of the Union as well as their role in promoting social and territorial cohesion, the Union and the Member States, each within their respective powers and within the scope of application of the Treaties, shall take care that such services operate on the basis of principles and conditions, particularly economic and financial conditions, which enable them to fulfil their missions. The European Parliament and the Council, acting by means of regulations in accordance with the ordinary legislative procedure, shall establish these principles and set these conditions without prejudice to the competence of Member States, in compliance with the Treaties, to provide, to commission and to fund such services.

Thus Article 14 TFEU, as amended by the Lisbon Treaty, confers a legislative competence on the European Parliament and the Council (without prejudice to Articles 106 and 107 TFEU considered later) to establish principles and conditions enabling SGEIs to fulfil their mission. This power has so far not been used. It is important to note that the final text of Article 14 TFEU expressly recognizes the continued competences of the Member States to provide and finance such services, albeit without prejudice to the State aid rules.

Protocol No 26 on SGIs – which has equal legal status to the Treaty itself – consists of two Articles. The first recognizes

> the essential role and the wide discretion of national, regional and local authorities in providing, commissioning and organising services of general economic interest as closely as possible to the needs of the users; the diversity between various services of general economic interest and the differences in the needs and preferences of users that may result from different geographical, social or cultural situations; a high level of quality, safety and affordability, equal treatment and the promotion of universal access and of user rights.

According to Article 2 of the Protocol: 'The provisions of the Treaties do not affect in any way the competence of Member States to provide, commission and organise non-economic services of general interest'.

2.2.2 Article 106 TFEU

The main substantive Treaty provision with regard to SGEIs is Article 106 TFEU:

> 1. In the case of public undertakings and undertakings to which Member States grant special or exclusive rights, Member States shall neither enact nor maintain in force any measure contrary to the rules contained in the Treaties, in particular to those rules provided for in Article 18 and Articles 101 to 109.
>
> 2. Undertakings entrusted with the operation of services of general economic interest or having the character of a revenue-producing monopoly shall be subject to the rules contained in the Treaties, in particular to the rules on competition, in so far as the application

---

[6] Apart from the essential role and wide discretion of public authorities in organizing and delivering these services close to the users, the relevant values include geographical, social, or cultural diversity; a high level of quality, safety and affordability; equal treatment; and the promotion of universal access and of user rights.

of such rules does not obstruct the performance, in law or in fact, of the particular tasks assigned to them. The development of trade must not be affected to such an extent as would be contrary to the interests of the Union.

3. The Commission shall ensure the application of the provisions of this Article and shall, where necessary, address appropriate directives or decisions to Member States.

Thus, Article 106(1) TFEU states that special and exclusive rights (eg monopoly operating licences for ferry services or a limited set of fourth-generation mobile communications networks) may not breach the provisions of the Treaty, which is to be understood as referring especially to the rules on competition and free movement. Article 106(2) TFEU states that an exception for SGEIs is warranted with regard to the Treaty rules, in particular on competition, to the extent that this is proportional to the public interest pursued. This is to say the measures must be

- suitable to reach their goal; and
- necessary in the sense of employing the least restrictive effective means. This means that while there must be a balance between the interest promoted and the interest infringed, the interest promoted must gain more than is lost in terms of the competing interest that would be sacrificed.

In theory this could lead to a restricted application of the exemption, and could in turn interfere with the competence of Member States to define SGEIs, as recognized by the Treaty (Article 14 TFEU). In practice the two are compatible provided strict criteria are satisfied. In section 4, we shall consider how the test in Article 106(2) TFEU has been balanced by the Court, and then the Commission, with the EU rules on State aid.

2.3 Conclusion

It follows that the concept of SGEIs occupies an uneasy place in EU law, since it is an EU concept, subject to the powers of interpretation and monitoring of the EU institutions, with a view to ensuring a uniform application throughout the EU, but at the same time it falls within the express province of Member States to decide which services are classed as SGEIs.[7] The Commission (as well as the Courts) has sought to square this circle by professing to exert only marginal control on the way Member States organize SGEIs; on a closer look at the Commission decision practice,[8] however, one can argue that the control is more than just marginal. For the purpose of this chapter, this control takes the form of using, inter alia,[9]

- Article 37 TFEU to examine the situation where the State itself provides a service (eg alcohol, electricity) through a commercial monopoly,
- Article 107 TFEU to consider how the provision of public services is funded.

We shall consider the application of these Treaty provisions in turn.

---

[7] See the TFEU Protocol No 26 on Services of General Interest (OJ [2010] C83/310), as well as Art 36 of the Charter of Fundamental Rights of the European Union.

[8] See eg in public service broadcasting – where the position of Member States is further bolstered by TFEU Protocol No 29 on the system of public broadcasting in the Member States (OJ [2010] C83/312) – where under the guise of marginal control, the Commission reviews the scope of the public mission of public broadcasters in great detail: Commission Communication on the application of State aid rules to public service broadcasting (OJ [2010] C257/1) paras 43–49 and for a good illustration, Case E-3/05 *Financing of public broadcasting in Germany* (OJ [2007] C185/1) 237–242.

[9] For other examples of control, see chapters 15 and 17.

3 Commercial monopolies

The rules on commercial monopolies are set out in Article 37 TFEU, a rather neglected provision of the Treaty. Member States have different traditions with regard to their reliance on commercial monopolies: some Nordic States have State monopolies on alcohol production and distribution whereas some Mediterranean States have monopolized the distribution (and formerly the production) of tobacco (and even matches). Most Member States at one time monopolized the production of electricity and gas. Article 37 TFEU is located with the Treaty rules prohibiting quantitative restrictions and measures of equivalent effect (MEEs) between Member States[10] and aims to bar discrimination based on nationality.[11]

Article 37 TFEU states:

1. Member States shall adjust any State monopolies of a commercial character so as to ensure that no discrimination regarding the conditions under which goods are procured and marketed exists between nationals of Member States.

   The provisions of this Article shall apply to any body through which a Member State, in law or in fact, either directly or indirectly supervises, determines or appreciably influences imports or exports between Member States. These provisions shall likewise apply to monopolies delegated by the State to others.

2. Member States shall refrain from introducing any new measure which is contrary to the principles laid down in paragraph 1 or which restricts the scope of the articles dealing with the prohibition of customs duties and quantitative restrictions between Member States.

3. If a State monopoly of a commercial character has rules which are designed to make it easier to dispose of agricultural products or obtain for them the best return, steps should be taken in applying the rules contained in this Article to ensure equivalent safeguards for the employment and standard of living of the producers concerned.

State monopolies of a commercial character and the principle of free movement of goods are rather awkward companions, but the key point is that unlike the prohibition on quantitative restrictions and MEEs in Articles 34 to 36 TFEU, monopolies are not prohibited by Article 37 TFEU. Rather, they need to be adjusted to ensure the abolition of discrimination.

In the *Swedish pharmacy* case of 2005[12] the Court of Justice ruled that it was necessary to consider whether the way in which the State monopoly in question was organized and operated was liable to place medicinal preparations from other Member States at a disadvantage or whether that monopoly did in practice place such medicinal preparations at a disadvantage. Thus, it held that to rule out a risk of discrimination, first, the selection system of a sales monopoly had to be based on criteria that were independent of the origin of the products and had to be transparent by providing both for an obligation to state reasons for decisions and for an independent monitoring procedure. Secondly, the retail network of such a monopoly had to be organized in such a way that the number of sales outlets was not limited to the point of compromising consumers' procurement of supplies. Finally,

---

[10] See further chapter 12.

[11] eg in a preliminary ruling the Court of Justice found (Case C-438/02 *Krister Hanner* ('*Swedish pharmacy*') [2005] ECR I-4551) that the way in which the Swedish State monopoly, Apoteket, is organized and operates, and more particularly its system of selecting medicinal preparations, is liable to place trade in medicinal preparations from other Member States at a disadvantage as compared with trade in Swedish medicinal preparations. Thus, that State monopoly is not arranged in such a way as to exclude any discrimination against medicinal preparations from other Member States, so it infringed Art 37(1).   [12] Ibid.

such a monopoly's marketing and advertising measures had to be impartial and independent of the origin of the products and had to endeavour to make known new products to consumers.

Further, it held that Article 106(2) TFEU could not be relied upon by Sweden because a sales regime of the kind at issue could not be justified under Article 106(2) TFEU in the absence of a selection system that excludes any discrimination against medicinal preparations from other Member States.

In the earlier 1997 'Electricity cases', the Court, however, held that several Member States were entitled to justify their State monopolies for the import/export and supply of electricity (and gas) even if contrary to Article 37 TFEU, on the basis of Article 106(2) TFEU.[13] Energy supply was viewed as an essential service which could only be guaranteed on the basis of these types of exclusive rights. At the relevant time, secondary legislation opening up these markets had not been adopted and the Court seemed reluctant to deny the Member States the right to determine their own energy policies.

4 State aid

4.1 Introduction

It is clear that in order to exist and/or to ensure affordable access for citizens, public services must be funded – but by whom? For *non*-public services the norm is that they are paid directly by users (eg a subscription to a newspaper). *Public* services can be paid either directly by the State (and therefore indirectly by the taxpayer) or, where feasible, through cross-subsidization from profitable to less profitable or non-commercial activities, in which case there will be direct payments or co-payments contributed by users which may be dependent on the users' level of income or use. This affordable access can be achieved by private or public means, or by a mixed regime. The rules on State aid in Articles 107 and 108 TFEU serve to counteract the distortions of competition in the internal market that ensure that certain undertakings, but not others, are favoured financially by public authorities. The State aid rules thus serve to prevent overcompensation of public service provision, as a possible source of funding for activities under competition, and hence to maintain a level playing field between undertakings that are active in the same market.

The conditions that must be met for a State aid to exist in any sector, as required by Article 107(1) TFEU, and the exceptions to the general rule that bars the grant of State aid unless the Commission has approved it, will be spelled out below. It is important, however, to state at the outset that in addition to the general Treaty rules on State aids, again Article 106 TFEU may be of particular significance to SGEIs. As we shall see, if public services qualify as SGEIs then they may be entirely exempt from the standard State aid regime.

4.2 The State aid regime

4.2.1 The basic criteria

The Treaty State aid rules are set out in Articles 107 and 108 TFEU. Article 107(1) TFEU states that, in principle, aid is prohibited in any form if granted

(a) to an undertaking,

(b) by the State or through State resources,

[13] See eg Case C-154/97 *Netherlands v Commission* [1997] ECR I-5699.

(c) the aid is selective (ie limited to certain undertakings),

(d) the aid constitutes an economic advantage on the beneficiary,

(e) the aid distorts or threatens to distort competition in the internal market,

(f) the granting of the aid must affect trade between the Member States.

Exceptions are possible (Article 107(2) and (3) TFEU) but an application needs to be made to the Commission, which has exclusive competence to grant those exemptions (Article 108(2) TFEU) (see Figure 18.3),[14] unless the Council has empowered it to exempt certain types of aid by means of a block exemption.[15] In order to seek an individual exemption the Member State wishing to grant the aid must notify the Commission and, in respect of a standstill obligation, the aid may not be granted until cleared by the Commission.[16]

For the purposes of this chapter, the first and fourth criteria of the six outlined above are of particular importance. The aid must be granted to *undertakings*. This is part of the definition of what it means to give a State aid, and therefore support given to other types of entities (eg government departments) does not constitute State aid under EU law. The category of 'undertaking' is functional in nature: national legal classifications are not relevant, but the actual activities performed by the entity concerned are. Generally speaking, undertakings are active in markets where they provide goods and/or services in competition, and in exchange for remuneration. Using these criteria the Court has, for instance, found that medical doctors are undertakings in *Pavlov* (2000) but air traffic security authorities (*Eurocontrol*, 2009) are not.[17]

In respect of the criteria of conferring an *economic advantage on the beneficiary* the Court has ruled that this need not mean only the grant of a direct financial contribution but can be in terms of a preferential assignment of property rights to real estate, below market interest rates on financing (loans), or selective tax breaks, which would allow the beneficiary to receive a benefit that it would not otherwise enjoy under normal market conditions. Conferring an advantage does require distinguishing the recipient from other market parties: a general tax rebate does not constitute an advantage – the core of State aid control relates to selectivity, that is, one or more market parties or sectors getting better treatment than everyone else.

But what if, in the context of the provision of public services, the State pays the private contractor? Does that constitute an economic advantage and so engage the State aid rules (the State aid approach) or does it not (the compensation approach), in which case the State aid rules do not apply? This issue was considered in the seminal decision in *Altmark*.[18]

4.2.2 The *Altmark* case

The decision in *Altmark* is of key importance in settling the long-standing debate on the merits of the 'State aid approach' versus the 'compensation approach'.[19] Advocates of the former claimed that even if the financial transfers only amounted to compensation for

---

[14] cf the position under Arts 101 and 102 discussed in chapter 17.

[15] For a detailed analysis, see L Hancher, T Ottervanger, and PJ Slot, *EU State Aids* (4th edn, London: Sweet & Maxwell, 2012).

[16] For a discussion of the procedural rules in Art 108 TFEU, see C Quigley, *European State Aid Law and Policy* (2nd edn, Oxford: Hart Publishing, 2009) Pt III.

[17] Joined Cases C-180–184/98 *Pavel Pavlov v Stichting Pensioenfonds Medische Specialisten* [2000] ECR I-6451 and Case C-113/07 P *SELEX Sistemi Integrati SpA v Commission and Organisation européenne pour la sécurité de la navigation aérienne ('Eurocontrol')* [2009] ECR I-2207.

[18] Case C-280/00 [2003] ECR I-7747.

[19] A compensation approach was first found in Case 240/83 *Procureur de la République v Association de défense des brûleurs d'huiles usagées (ADBHU)* [1985] ECR 531.

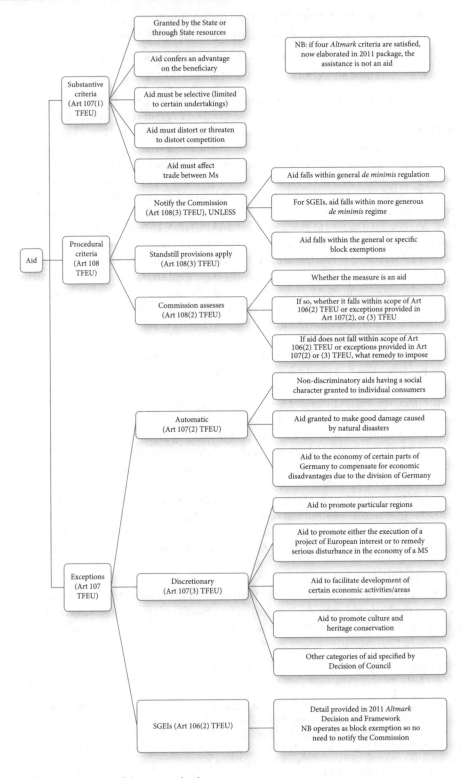

Fig 18.3 A summary of the State aid rules

the performance of the public services, they should still be notified to the Commission for clearance. However, the proponents of the compensation approach argued that the notification was unnecessary and would lead to an unwelcome caseload for the Commission as well as legal uncertainty. Prior to the *Altmark* ruling, the Court of Justice and the General Court had taken different approaches, culminating in the *Ferring* case in 2001, where the Court of Justice appeared to opt for the 'compensation' approach.[20] The procedure in *Altmark* was unusual too because the Court allowed for two separate opinions from Advocate General Léger, which both opposed the solution chosen by the Court. In its ruling, the Court opted for a compromise between the two competing approaches but one which focused on procedural conditions.

The case itself concerned the conditions for the award of a regional transport licence in Germany.[21] The licence had been awarded to Altmark Trans but not its competitors, which complained, inter alia, that State aid had been granted because, in addition to its licence, Altmark Trans had been granted subsidies to operate its service (or to cover its losses as its competitors claimed). The Court ruled that if the undertaking concerned was entrusted with a PSO in exchange for its financing there could be no case of State aid because instead of enjoying an economic advantage, the compensation was a quid pro quo for a service provided. However, in order for the State aid rules not to apply, the following four '*Altmark* conditions' need to be satisfied:

(a) The recipient undertaking is actually required to discharge PSOs and those obligations have been clearly defined.

(b) The parameters on the basis of which the compensation is calculated have been established beforehand in an objective and transparent manner.

(c) The compensation does not exceed what is necessary to cover all or part of the costs incurred in discharging the PSOs, taking into account the relevant receipts and a reasonable profit for discharging those obligations.

(d) Where the undertaking which is to discharge PSOs is not chosen in a public procurement procedure,[22] the level of compensation needed has been determined on the basis of an analysis of the costs which a typical undertaking, well run and adequately provided with the relevant means so as to be able to meet the necessary public service requirements, would have incurred in discharging those obligations, taking into account the relevant receipts and a reasonable profit for discharging the obligations.

While *Altmark* did offer some clarification on the question of the funding of public services and whether that funding constituted State aid, the decision also created new difficulties, not least because the Court held subsequently that the scope of its ruling was not limited in time, but also applied retroactively.[23] Obviously this generated further confusion, as many types of SGEIs had been entrusted prior to *Altmark* without reference to any type of procurement or tender procedure which had now become the preferred requirement of the fourth *Altmark* condition.

Furthermore, the alternative test in the fourth condition, the so-called efficiency test (ie that the 'benchmark of a well-run and well-resourced firm' should be used) raised difficulties in practice. For example, in its first decision after *Altmark*, in *BBC Digital*

---

[20] Case C-53/00 *Ferring SA v Agence centrale des organismes de sécurité sociale (ACOSS)* [2001] ECR I-9067.

[21] See n 18.

[22] Public procurement is a desirable condition to set because it requires 'competition for the market', which is a useful proxy for efficiency in those cases where the scope for 'competition on the market' is limited.

[23] Case T-289/03 *British United Provident Association Ltd (BUPA) v Commission* [2008] ECR II-81.

Curriculum,[24] the Commission held that the fourth criterion had not been met as there had been no public procurement procedure and the UK authorities had failed to provide the Commission with any information which would have allowed it to determine whether those costs could be considered as corresponding to those of a 'typical' undertaking. However, the Commission then went on to apply Article 106(2) TFEU to rule on the compatibility of the State aid measure with EU law. This seemed to imply that it was possible for an undertaking to receive aid that exceeded the costs of an ideal, efficient undertaking, without this resulting in overcompensation, as long as the examination was carried out under Article 106(2) TFEU. Indeed, this approach has been confirmed in subsequent cases (see eg *Bpost* (2012) and section 5).[25]

4.2.3 The *Altmark* package

Thus, where not all four *Altmark* conditions are met (as we have seen, generally the fourth condition is problematic), then the payment may be a State aid. However, that aid may still be declared compatible with the internal market based on the SGEI exception in Article 106(2) TFEU, following notification to the Commission. In order to clarify its policy with regard to the application of Article 106(2) TFEU to such aid, the Commission adopted its 2005 *Altmark* package, the body of which consisted of a formal exemption Decision and a 'soft law' Framework.[26] This package was revamped in 2011 following extensive consultation.[27] The 2011 Decision and Framework are now accompanied by an interpretative Communication as well as a *de minimis* Regulation that sets out a cut-off point for the level of aid below which undertakings carrying out SGEIs are not subject to the State aid regime.[28] In essence, the Communication and the *de minimis* Regulation relate to the conditions under which a measure escapes the qualification of State aid under Article 107 TFEU (and therefore escapes the application of State aid rules altogether). The Decision and the Framework define the conditions under which a measure, qualified as State aid, is deemed to be or can be found compatible with the internal market on the basis of Article 106(2) TFEU (see Figure 18.3).

The Communication

The Communication is intended to provide clearer guidance to Member States and in particular decentralized bodies, such as local authorities, on the law and on Commission policy. It provides some guidance on the different concepts of SGIs, SSGIs, and SGEIs (see section 2 for more discussion of these terms) but with respect to these various categories of public services, different checklists of criteria are used without reference to a hard core

---

[24] Case N-37/03 (OJ [2003] C271/47).

[25] See Commission MEMO/12/38, 25 January 2012, http://europa.eu/rapid/press-release_MEMO-12-38_en.htm?locale=en

[26] Commission Decision on the application of Article 86(2) of the EC Treaty to State aid in the form of public service compensation granted to certain undertakings entrusted with the operation of services of general economic interest (OJ [2005] L312/67); Community framework for State aid in the form of public service compensation (OJ [2005] C297/4).

[27] Commission Decision on the application of Article 106(2) of the Treaty on the Functioning of the European Union to State aid in the form of public service compensation granted to certain undertakings entrusted with the operation of services of general economic interest (OJ [2012] L7/3); Communication of the Commission, European Union framework for State aid in the form of public service compensation (OJ [2012] C8/15).

[28] Communication from the Commission on the application of the European Union State aid rules to compensation granted for the provision of services of general economic interest (OJ [2012] C8/4); Commission Regulation on the application of Articles 107 and 108 of the Treaty on the Functioning of the European Union to *de minimis* aid granted to undertakings providing services of general economic interest (OJ [2012] L114/8).

of common criteria in order to determine whether an activity is economic in nature or whether solidarity or public authority prevails. In the latter case then the public service should be an SSGI and in the former case it should be an SGEI. We will go into more detail on this issue later, especially when discussing the scope for social services.

In order to be classified as SGEIs services must be 'addressed to citizens or be in the interest of society as a whole'.[29] The Commission will only check national designations for a manifest error – in order to establish whether a service can be provided on the same terms by the market. The Framework (see section 4.2.3, The Framework) specifies that this is usually the case unless provisions of Union law provide a stricter standard.[30]

The Communication places particular emphasis on the first part of the fourth *Altmark* condition with regard to the use of public procurement procedures. In those cases where the public procurement rules have not been applied to select the SGEI provider, the amount of compensation must be based on generally accepted market remuneration or, in the absence of such a standard, the amount of compensation must be based on the analysis of the costs of a typical undertaking that is well run and adequately provided with material means, taking into account a reasonable profit. The Communication indicates a clear preference for Member States to use procurement rules.

The Decision

The 2011 Commission Decision, which takes Article 106(3) TFEU as its legal basis, is in practice a block exemption that has created a safe harbour for aid to undertakings below a particular threshold, as well as for particular economic sectors, and exempts them from the notification and standstill obligations of Article 108(3) TFEU.[31] Provided certain conditions (that are discussed later) are met, the relevant aid is considered to be compatible with the internal market on the basis of the final sentence of Article 106(2) TFEU.[32] In order to benefit from the exemption, the undertaking concerned must be entrusted with the operation of a SGEI by means of one or more official acts (the form of which may be determined by the Member State). Importantly, these acts – whatever form they might take – have to specify at least

- the nature and the duration of the PSOs;
- the undertaking and territory concerned;
- the nature of any exclusive or special rights assigned to the undertaking;
- the parameters for calculating, controlling, and reviewing the compensation;
- the arrangements for avoiding and repaying any overcompensation.

Moreover, the Decision contains detailed requirements with respect to the calculation of the compensation involved. Particular attention is paid to cases where the undertaking

---

[29] Commission Communication (n 28) para 50.

[30] Member States cannot attach specific public service obligations to services that are already provided or can be provided satisfactorily and under conditions, such as price, objective quality characteristics, continuity and access to the service, consistent with the public interest, as defined by the State, by undertakings operating under normal market conditions. As for the question of whether a service can be provided by the market, the Commission's assessment is limited to checking whether the Member State's definition is vitiated by a manifest error, unless provisions of Union law provide a stricter standard (ibid, para 13).

[31] Commission Decision (2005) (n 26); Commission Decision (2011) (n 27).

[32] The Commission is entrusted by virtue of a Council Regulation to adopt block exemption regulations pertaining to various forms of sectoral aid. These measures do not, however, relate to Art 106(2) but to Art 108(3). The Council has recently adopted amendments to the enabling Council Regulation.

entrusted with operating an SGEI is also engaged in other economic activities, such as operating a universal service on certain loss-making public transport routes while also engaged in parallel profitable public transport provision. Overcompensation to the SGEI must be clawed back. The Decision is applied primarily to the social services, inter alia, because there is relatively little cross-border activity in these sectors.

The Framework

The Framework is perhaps the most contentious document in the package. In line with the Commission's policy of having a proportionate approach, the Framework presents the principles guiding the standard assessment, but also includes provisions for a simplified assessment of aid normally covered by the Decision, and provisions for in-depth assessment of cases involving serious distortions to competition and trade. The compatibility test under the 2011 Decision and Framework can be summarized as checking the existence of an entrustment act and the absence of overcompensation.

However, for certain cases, namely large undertakings performing SGEIs that can be found in the utilities sectors such as transport, electronic communications, post, energy, water, and waste disposal, the Framework provides for a more far-reaching test.

States cannot claim the safe harbour provided by the block exemption in the Decision. In this context the Framework provides guidance which makes the outcome of individual State aid and SGEI cases more predictable. For these sectors, compliance with Union public procurement rules, where applicable, is a condition for compatibility.

The reason why the Commission has singled out utilities for a potentially stricter assessment than other sectors is understandable as a device: it enables the Commission to concentrate its limited resources on the most serious cases, which may well raise important policy choices.

The Regulation

The Regulation applies a *de minimis* regime to aid that amounts to less than €500,000 over any period of three fiscal years. This threshold is more generous than the general State aid '*de minimis*' Regulation[33] to which it constitutes a *lex specialis* exception and reflects the Commission's desire to create a safe harbour for small, localized public services. In other words, there is a block exemption regardless of the amount of aid granted concerning specific (social) sectors set out in the Framework, and a general threshold of €500,000 over three years for aid considered so minimal that it does not warrant scrutiny. Above this threshold and beyond the scope of the block exemption, individual clearance decisions are made based on the Framework.

Figure 18.4 provides a flow chart that illustrates the working of the package.

5 Case studies

In the following sections, we will look in greater detail at the various public services. For this purpose we have made a basic distinction between (a) the utilities, which are network-based, and (b) social services, which aim at providing various types of care to individuals. Utilities are economically more significant from an internal market perspective than social services where there is much less cross-border provision and investment. Three case studies are presented from the utilities sectors, and three from health care as examples of the application of the rules to the social services sector.

---

[33] Regulation 1998/2006 (OJ [2006] L379/5).

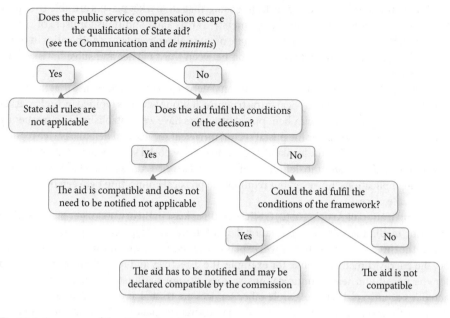

Fig 18.4 Summary of the *Altmark* package

Source: Pesaresi et al [2012] *Competition Policy Newsletter* 1.

5.1 **The utilities sectors**

In contrast to social services, the provision of which is largely left unharmonized, the markets for post, energy, information communication technology (ICT) services, and transport have been gradually liberalized – that is, opened up to competition – by a series of EU legislative packages. The successive packages have broadly required the removal of exclusive or special rights, including the rights to produce and supply as well as import and export the goods or services in question, while harmonizing the regulation of the remaining 'natural monopoly' elements – usually the transmission or infrastructural network which is difficult if not impossible to replicate. In addition, the legislation often allows Member States to impose universal service obligations (USOs) on all providers active in the sector in question. Various forms of compensation for the provision of these USOs are possible, as explained later. In addition, it may still be possible to designate certain services, outside the USO, as SGEIs. In this case the 2011 package, discussed previously, applies in full, with the exception of the transport and broadcasting sectors. These two sectors are governed by separate Treaty provisions as well as sectoral legislation in the case of certain forms of transport, whereas the broadcasting sector is governed by a Protocol.[34]

The modern approach to *ex ante* regulation of network industries such as energy, telecommunications, and transport relies on the notion of essential facilities or monopoly bottlenecks (eg an electricity or gas transmission system or a railway network, which are very costly to build and so cannot be duplicated by competitors) and the idea that competition should be allowed wherever it leads to efficient market allocations. Hence, some form of regulation is required to allow new market entrants to use these essential facilities. National regulatory authorities are required to supervise conditions of access, including

---

[34] Protocol No 29, appended by the Treaty of Amsterdam, on the system of public broadcasting in the Member States (OJ [2010] C257/1). See also Quigley, *European State Aid Law and Policy* (n 16) 319–322.

pricing, to the monopolistic networks to ensure that all market players are able to supply their services downstream to final customers.[35] Tariffs and conditions for users of energy networks, for example, are regulated *ex ante* by specialized regulatory authorities in order to avoid high prices and/or discrimination between third parties and subsidiaries of the network owner.

Although the postal sector is not a traditional network sector, in the sense that the postal delivery network is a fixed physical infrastructure, it is one which is typified by high market entry barriers, given that incumbent postal providers have well-established and frequently very high market shares. For the postal sector, universal service and default service regulation is aimed at ensuring the availability of good quality postal services at affordable prices. For telecommunications, the definition of universal services does not include explicit services and applications, however, but requires the physical connection between households at affordable prices.

The application of Article 106(2) TFEU should at least in theory no longer play the same buffer or mediating role between national and European competences in these sectors.[36] Yet, as the three short case studies will explain, the picture is by no means clear. In particular, the energy directives, unlike for example, the directives and related measures adopted for the postal and telecommunications sectors, do not designate particular services or activities as universal services, while other services are treated as competitive services. Nor do any of these sector-specific rules provide any concrete guidance on financing of the universal services in question. This means that any State support to ensure their provision must be examined under the State aid rules.

In the next section we will consider three different utility (or network) sectors and we will examine to what extent the scope for Member States to impose an SGEI or a PSO, and finance the provision of it, is limited by the degree of market liberalization required by secondary sector-specific liberalization.

Case study 18.1: Broadband

The ICT sector is fully liberalized and ICT services are provided by the market. As such, the sector mainly benefits from State aid, if at all, for broadband network infrastructure development. The market for the services provided over electronic networks is fully liberalized and operators also compete to roll out new networks. The relevant legislation does not, however, mandate that network provision is a USO or PSO: this is essentially left to the market. According to the Universal Service Directive in the electronic communications sector, Member States are not obliged to impose USOs, for example if market forces would suffice to ensure that a service meeting the requirements of the definition of universal service is provided. If States determine that USOs must be imposed, then the addressee of the obligations must be selected in an open, transparent, and non-discriminatory procedure (eg an auction). Financial compensation for the addressee, if any, is limited to the net costs of providing universal service, and then only if that obligation represents an unfair burden on the addressee (taking into account, eg the intangible benefits arising from providing universal service and the administrative costs of running

---

[35] See further L Hancher and P Larouche, 'The Coming of Age of EU Regulation of Network Industries and Services of General Economic Interest' in P Craig and G de Búrca (eds), *The Evolution of EU Law* (2nd edn, Oxford: Oxford University Press, 2011).

[36] It has been held by the Court of Justice that a Member State is now excluded from designating a service which was not defined as a universal service in the Postal Directive 97/67 (OJ [1998] L15/14) as part of the USO.

a compensation mechanism). The financial compensation mechanism itself must be transparent and minimize distortion to the market.[37]

It is only if the market does not provide the network investment that Member States can intervene. If they do so in the form of financial support, then they are subject to the 2012 Commission Guidelines on broadband aid, and to the strict conditions set out in those Guidelines.

In relation to the SGEI definition in the broadband sector, the Commission restates in its most recent Guidelines,[38] that 'Member States cannot attach specific PSOs to services that are already provided or can be provided satisfactorily and under conditions, such as price, objective quality characteristics, continuity and access to the service, consistent with the public interest, as defined by the State, by undertakings operating under normal market conditions'.[39]

In areas where private investors have already invested in a broadband network infrastructure (or are further expanding the network) and are already providing competitive broadband services with an adequate broadband coverage, setting up a parallel competitive and publicly funded broadband infrastructure cannot be considered as an SGEI within the meaning of Article 106(2) TFEU.[40]

However, where it can be demonstrated that private investors are not in a position to provide in the near future (ie within three years) adequate broadband coverage to all citizens or users, thus leaving a significant part of the population unconnected, a public service compensation may be granted to an undertaking entrusted with the operation of an SGEI, provided the conditions of the 2011 SGEI Communication are fulfilled.[41]

It should also be emphasized that the deployment and the operation of a broadband infrastructure can qualify as an SGEI only if such infrastructure provides all users in a given area with universal connectivity, residential and business users alike. Support for connecting businesses only would not be sufficient.[42]

The Commission also ensures that the objectives of its liberalization packages are still adhered to and therefore insists that the compulsory nature of the SGEI mission also means that the network operator can no longer refuse wholesale access to the infrastructure on a discretionary and/or discriminatory basis (because, eg it may not be commercially profitable to provide access services to a given area). Hence, competitors will have access to the network.

The Commission has also stressed that as the market for electronic communications is fully liberalized, it follows that an SGEI mission for broadband deployment cannot be based on the award of an exclusive or special right to the provider of the SGEI within the meaning of Article 106(1) TFEU.

---

[37] Directive 2002/22/EC (Universal Service Directive) (OJ [2002] L108/51).

[38] Broadband Guidelines (OJ [2013] C25/1).

[39] See more generally point 48 of the Commission Communication on the application of the EU State aid rules to compensation granted for the provision of services of general economic interest (OJ [2012] C8/4) and point 13 of the Commission Communication on a European Union framework for State aid in the form of public service compensation (OJ [2012] C8/15).

[40] In order to be considered compatible State aid, the aid in question would have to be assessed under Art 107(3)(c) TFEU and in the context of the remaining, somewhat complex, 'balancing test' provided in the remainder of these detailed Guidelines.

[41] See para 49 of the Commission Communication on the application of the EU State aid rules to compensation granted for the provision of services of general economic interest (OJ [2012] C8/4).

[42] See also Commission Decision N 284/05 – *Ireland, Regional broadband Programme: Metropolitan Area Networks (MANs), phases II and III* and Commission Decision N 890/06–*France, Aide du Sicoval pour un réseau de très haut débit*.

CALCULATION OF THE COMPENSATION AND CLAWBACK

For the calculation of the SGEI compensation, the principles of the 2011 *Altmark* package fully apply. However, the Guidelines add a clarification for SGEIs intended to cover unconnected neighbourhoods or districts (so-called 'white spots') within a broader area in which some operators have already deployed their own network infrastructure or may plan to do so in the near future.

If the area for which the SGEI is entrusted is not limited just to the white spots, because of their size or location, the SGEI provider may need to deploy a network infrastructure in the profitable areas already covered by commercial operators as well. In such situations, any compensation granted should only cover the costs of rolling out an infrastructure in the unprofitable white spots, taking into account relevant revenue and a reasonable profit.[43]

Case study 18.2: Post

The EU law on postal services consists of three postal directives: Directive 97/67/EC of 1997, as amended by Directive 2002/39 and Directive 2008/6/EC.[44] This law gradually liberalized postal services. It also guaranteed citizens that postal services would remain accessible everywhere and to everyone under the same conditions (ie the universal postal service). The general aim is that customers can benefit from new forms of services, higher quality, and lower prices, provided by both the incumbents and alternative postal operators. At the same time, universal service will be maintained. To that end, universal service providers can be compensated for the net cost of providing the universal service when this net cost represents an unfair burden for the operator.[45]

The Commission seems determined to continue scrutinizing the sector, underlining that it must ensure that competition in terms of quality and price is not distorted by undue public support to the incumbents, especially through overcompensation for 'legacy costs'. 'Only in this way the liberalization of postal services across the EU will create the scope for new operators and innovative services to appear.'[46]

Indeed the postal sector liberalization has highlighted a variety of complex issues, and generated a large body of case law, including the funding of these so-called 'legacy costs'. Legacy costs can, for instance, relate to the personnel that such providers may have inherited from the old monopoly period when a single national postal authority (often part of the State) had an exclusive right to provide most forms of post and parcel services. State aid

---

[43] Any profit in excess of a reasonable profit, ie profits beyond the average industry return on capital for deploying a given broadband infrastructure, could be assigned to the financing of the SGEI in the non-profitable areas while the remaining profits could be part of the financial compensation granted. See Commission Decision in Case N 331/08–*France, THD Hauts de Seine*.

[44] Under the third Postal Directive, 16 Member States had to open their postal markets fully by 31 December 2010. The remaining 11 completed liberalization by the end of 2012. Postal Directive 97/67 (OJ [1998] L15/14), amended by Directive 2002/39 (OJ [2002] L176/21) and Directive 2008/6/EC (OJ [2008] L52/3).

[45] Art 7(3) of the Postal Directive provides that 'Where a Member State determines that the universal service obligations . . . entail a net cost . . . and represent an unfair financial burden on the universal service provider(s), it may introduce: (a) a mechanism to compensate the undertaking(s) concerned from public funds; or (b) a mechanism for the sharing of the net cost of the universal service obligations between providers of services and/or users'.   [46] See Commission SPEECH/12/37 of 25 January 2012.

to cover such legacy costs is unlikely to be deemed to be part of the USO, and therefore has to be assessed under Article 107(3)(c) TFEU, especially in order to ensure that the sums involved would not be used to finance the provision of various services which have been opened up to competition – for example, parcel or courier postal services. However, it has always been accepted that USOs constitute an SGEI.[47]

Even after liberalization, an adequate level of postal service may also require that a network of post offices is still in place. The provision of post offices with a 'territorial presence mission' does not fall within the USO definition, as this relates to products such as letters, but it may qualify as an SGEI. The application of these principles is illustrated in several recent Commission decisions.

First, in the Belgian *Bpost* case the Commission concluded that it could not find any reference in Belgian law to an additional mission requiring the postal incumbent to operate a larger network of offices beyond the territorial coverage imposed by the USO to meet objectives of territorial cohesion or development. However, the Commission approved a pension relief of €3.8 billion from which De Post-La Poste (now Bpost) benefited through the Belgian pension reform of 1997, aligning the social contributions paid by Bpost for its statutory personnel with the private sector. At the same time, the Commission ordered Belgium to recover €417 million of incompatible aid from Bpost, since the yearly compensations received in the period 1992–2010 for public service missions resulted in some overcompensation.[48]

In the UK *POL* case, the Commission authorized public assistance in the form of a 'network SGEI subsidy' to the UK Post Office Ltd (POL), for the funding of its network of post offices. The UK authorities had argued that the post office network performs an important social and economic role which extends beyond the specific postal and government services offered over the post office counter, and as such act as focal points for the communities they serve, and are used as sources of information and advice for citizens. The Commission reasoned that as the 'fourth *Altmark* criterion' was not met in this case it had to be assessed under the Framework of 2011. It concluded that the aid is compatible with EU rules because it does not overcompensate the net costs of the important public service tasks entrusted to POL and thus does not give POL any unfair competitive advantage.[49]

In the *La Poste* and *POL* decisions, the Commission examined the question to what extent the maintenance of a retail network by postal operators constitutes an SGEI. In both Decisions, the Commission examined cases of retail networks which went beyond the access requirements of the Postal Directive, related to the USO. In the *POL* decision it concluded that such a 'territorial presence mission' could be considered as a genuine SGEI. By contrast, in the *La Poste* Decision, the Commission refused to identify a separate retail network SGEI, because it could not find any reference to an additional mission requiring the postal incumbent to operate a larger network of offices beyond the territorial coverage imposed by the USO to meet objectives of territorial cohesion or development.

---

[47] See eg Commission Decision 2002/782/EC *Poste Italiane* (OJ [2002] L282/29).

[48] See Commission MEMO/12/38 (n 25).

[49] See Commission Decision *UK – Post Office Ltd* SA.33054 (2012/N) (OJ [2012] C121/55) and also the earlier SA.31156 (N508/2010) (OJ [2011] C147/54).

Case study 18.3: Energy – regulated tariffs as SGEIs

In sectors such as energy, the liberalization directives recognize that Member States may continue to impose PSOs on energy companies, in order to ensure the various objectives listed in Article 3(2) of the current Directive 2009/73 on the internal market for gas and Directive 2009/72 on the internal market for electricity.[50] This right is without prejudice to the application of the State aid rules, so that if a Member state chooses to provide compensation to an energy supplier in order, for example, to provide services to 'vulnerable customers', then the compensation will be assessed under the *Altmark* package. In practice, many Member States continue to impose regulated retail tariffs to ensure that domestic consumers (as opposed to industrial consumers) are not exposed to high or fluctuating prices. In other words, energy policy includes social objectives and hence Member States avoid having to finance these objectives directly from public funds but can achieve the same objective by controlling retail prices.

Federutility[51] is an interesting test case where the Court of Justice balanced consumer protection and energy market liberalization objectives. The case came by way of reference from Italy and concerns the powers of public authorities to continue to set prices for the supply of gas in the absence of competition. An Italian law granted the Italian Gas and Electricity Authority the power to fix 'reference prices' for the sale of gas to certain customers. Such reference prices were to appear in the offer made by a supplier to a customer in the context of its USOs. This was challenged by the gas suppliers in question before the Italian administrative courts, which in turn referred several questions for a preliminary ruling to the Court of Justice.

The Court confirmed that – irrespective of harmonization – Member States were entitled to define the scope of their 'public service obligations' and to take account of their own national policy objectives and national circumstances. At the same time, the Court imposed a number of strict conditions in order to ensure that the national measure was also proportional. In particular, it could only be temporary and had to be reviewed at regular intervals. This case, although not directly concerned with the application of the Treaty State aid rules, is important because it seems to suggest that even after the adoption of a series of harmonizing measures, Member States could still take their own national policy interests into account when imposing a PSO on an energy company – for example, a nuclear generator or a renewable energy producer, and compensate it by means of subsidies for performing those tasks, providing that the terms of that compensation comply with the Framework discussed at section 4. As noted at section 4, the Framework requires a detailed assessment of the compensation involved for the utility sectors.

These three short case studies drawn from the utility sectors confirm that although Member States can still have some discretion to assign SGEIs, the conditions under which they do so are now more strictly controlled by the Commission and the Courts. The scope of the SGEI is subject to close review, especially if the sector has been subject to harmonization in secondary legislation or soft law guidelines and the impact of the measure in question on competition is assessed in greater detail than tends to be the case where no secondary legislation or equivalent forms of liberalization have been adopted. In this regard, the Commission will only declare the aid to be compatible with the internal market if the

---

[50] Directive 2009/72 (OJ [2009] L211/55) and Directive 2009/73 (OJ [2009] L211/94).
[51] Case C-265/08 [2010] ECR I-3377.

recipient adheres to certain conditions, for example upholding non-discriminatory access to broadband infrastructure.

Further, these short case studies also show that there is still some scope left for national policies, but there is a heavy burden on the national authorities to make out their case and to demonstrate that the aid is proportionate. If it is not, substantial amounts of aid can be deemed illegal and the Commission orders its recovery. This is in contrast to the social services sectors considered in section 5.2. If the service is to be recognized as a genuine SGEI then the public tasks must be clearly defined in rules or regulations, and any restrictions on competition must be clearly demonstrated to be necessary and the costs involved may not exceed the public benefits achieved.

5.2 Social services

The 2011 Communication on SGEIs goes into greater detail on three types of social services: social security (including pensions), health care, and education. Somewhat confusingly a separate list of criteria is given for each of these categories as regards the question whether they should be regarded as (a) non-economic, not provided by an undertaking, and therefore not caught by the rules on State aid; or (b) as economic, provided by an undertaking, and therefore potentially an SGEI (provided there is an act of assignment and proportional compensation).

5.2.1 Social security

There are two sets of criteria that determine whether a social service is economic in nature and therefore potentially an SGEI or whether it is primarily solidarity-based. The first, which focuses on a positive identification of the solidarity aspect, sets out the characteristics that would be incompatible with identifying a social service as an SGEI. It asks whether the service is compulsory, whether it pursues an exclusively social purpose, and whether it is non-profit. In addition, it asks whether the benefits are independent of the contributions made and are not necessarily proportionate to the earnings of the person insured and whether the scheme is supervised by the State.

The second set of criteria used to identify social services as SGEIs takes the reverse approach and focuses more on the characteristics of economic schemes and is therefore negative with regard to solidarity – that is to say, it sets out the characteristics that are incompatible with a solidarity-based form of social security. These are optional membership; dependency of entitlements on (a) contributions paid and/or (b) the financial results of the scheme; for-profit status; and the provision of entitlements which are supplementary to those under a basic scheme, such as supplementary industry-specific schemes which may involve agreements between the social partners (employers and unions).

5.2.2 Health care

In general there are two types of health-care systems to be found in the Member States: the so-called Beveridge systems that are national health services (NHS), publicly provided, tax funded, and free at point of use; and Bismarck systems that are (public or private) insurance-based. In both systems, health-care providers can be public or private.[52]

NHS services are so far assumed to be solidarity-based and not to involve undertakings. This is even the case where they engage in activities that are in themselves potentially of an economic nature, such as buying goods or services, as long as they do so for the ultimate

---

[52] See further chapter 21.

purpose of offering a non-economic service.[53] Conversely, where health-care providers are in competition, the fact that a hospital is public does not affect the classification of its activities as market-based and economic. As has been mentioned previously, even individual medical practitioners (or for that matter, pharmacies) who meet these criteria can be regarded as undertakings for the purposes of the competition and State aid rules. This means that, broadly, providers of health care and health-care insurers are subject to the State aid rules but NHS-type purchasers are not.

5.2.3 Education

Public education that is part of the national educational system and as such funded and supervised by the Member States is regarded as non-economic. This view is not affected by the fact that parents or pupils may pay tuition or enrolment fees that defray part of the cost of education. Because these fees cover only a fraction of the costs of the service, these payments cannot be regarded as remuneration, nor do the Member States engage in establishing and maintaining the services concerned with the objective of obtaining remuneration. Instead they aim to fulfil a public task of a social, cultural, and educational character.

Educational services that are financed predominantly by the market, on the other hand, must be regarded as economic, as their aim is to offer a service for remuneration: the essential feature of a provision of services for remuneration consists in the payment by the pupil or a third party of school fees covering a major part of the costs of the education.[54]

Finally, the European Commission has stated that the primary activities of research organizations – notably universities – fall outside the scope of the State aid rules because they are non-economic activities.[55] This includes education, the conduct of independent (non-contract) research and development, and the dissemination of research results.[56]

5.3 Health care

In this section we will discuss three leading cases regarding health care and SGEIs.[57] Two of these regard health insurance, in both cases voluntary supplementary, rather than basic compulsory, insurance. The third case concerns hospital services. There is no harmonized sectoral regime for health care, although there has long been EU regulation of health-care goods (pharmaceuticals and medical devices) and there is some regulation regarding establishment (mutual recognition of professional qualifications).[58] More recently a directive on patients' rights for cross-border health-care services has been adopted (see further chapter 21).[59] Our focus here, however, will be on SGEIs. In this case study we will look at the way in which the EU Courts apply the *Altmark* criteria in the health-care sector and to what extent sector-specific factors play a role.

---

[53] Case C-205/03 P *Federación Española de Empresas de Tecnología Sanitaria (FENIN) v Commission* [2006] ECR I-6295.
[54] Case C-109/92 *Stephan Max Wirth v Landeshaupstadt Hannover* [1993] ECR I-6447.
[55] Community framework for State aid for research and development and innovation (OJ [2006] C323/1).
[56] cf B von Wendland, 'State Aid and Public Funding for Universities and Other Research Organisations' [2010] *Competition Policy Newsletter* 54; A Gideon, 'Higher Education Institutions and EU Competition Law' [2012] *Competition Law Review* 169.
[57] This section draws on L Hancher and W Sauter, *The EU Competition and Internal Market Law in the Healthcare Sector* (Oxford: Oxford University Press, 2012).
[58] Also general rules such as the EU rules limiting working time apply to health care (but not the Services Directive, which contains an exception for health care, as well as for SGEIs). See also chapter 21.
[59] Directive 2011/24/EU of the European Parliament and of the Council of 9 March 2011 on the application of patients' rights in cross-border healthcare (OJ [2011] L88/45).

Case study 18.4: Irish risk equalization – the *BUPA* case

Our first example is the 2008 judgment of the General Court in the case that was started by BUPA against a 2003 Commission State aid Decision clearing the Irish system of risk equalization between private providers of supplementary health-care insurance.[60] Risk equalization is a mutual compensation mechanism between health insurers for those among them that carry above-average risks due to the make-up of their insured population. One insurer may, for instance, have a greater relative share of elderly people or of persons suffering from a chronic disease. Alongside community rating (no price discrimination) and open enrolment (all customers must be accepted) it serves to ensure that insurers compete on the merits – better services and more effective purchasing – instead of on selecting healthy customers. It is thus a way to combat what is known in economics as the adverse selection effect by which insurers wish to insure only healthy people who in turn do not want insurance because they do not need it, leaving the insurance market dysfunctional and the mass of consumers uninsured.

BUPA was a private health insurer that entered the Irish market for voluntary supplementary private health insurance. The voluntary market covered some 50 per cent of the population and was dominated by VHI, a former monopolist. Although BUPA was much smaller than VHI, the risk-equalization system that the Commission had approved in its 2003 Decision on the Irish scheme was triggered to the advantage of VHI. Consequently BUPA challenged the Commission's Decision before the General Court as well as appealing the relevant Irish decisions before the Irish courts. The Commission Decision was upheld by the General Court based on a double approach. First, it applied the *Altmark* criteria that at the time of the Commission Decision did not yet exist but the applicability of which had not been limited in time by the Court of Justice (so they could be applied retroactively). Second it also based its ruling on the SGEI criteria: entrustment with a PSO, necessity, and proportionality. Not much later the Irish Supreme Court found the risk-equalization system unconstitutional under Irish law. BUPA, however, was not much aided by this finding as it had meanwhile withdrawn from the Irish market.

As regards the *Altmark* criteria, it is noteworthy that the General Court in relation to the first criterion (the existence of an SGEI) did not demand that the service concerned was available to the entire population of the Member State concerned: instead the obligation to deal with all-comers at standard conditions (open enrolment) was considered sufficient to find the existence of a universal service. The fact that different services with price differentiation were concerned did not mitigate this consideration, nor did the fact that not all consumers (in fact almost half of the population) either could or would pay for these services.

The second *Altmark* criterion requires clearly defined parameters for compensation and this was not contested. The necessity and proportionality of the compensation were more difficult to establish in the absence of a direct link between the universal service and the need for compensation. Here the General Court accepted that the arrangement was 'consistent with the purpose and the spirit of the third *Altmark* condition in so far as the compensation is calculated on the basis of elements, which are specific, clearly identifiable and capable of being controlled'.[61] This meant applying almost the exact same test as under the second *Altmark* criterion. Likewise with respect to the fourth *Altmark* condition the General Court formulated an alternative version because it would not be possible to

---

[60] *BUPA* (n 23).
[61] Ibid, para 237.

determine in advance which insurer had a right to compensation and therefore to compare its costs with those of an efficient competitor. Because compensation was based on the average costs in the market (and not on those of the individual competitor) an incentive towards efficiency would be retained. It follows that it is not sufficient to avoid notification for a Member State merely to assert that the costs of the undertakings concerned are less than the costs of providing the service in question.

In this manner the General Court substantially amended the relatively recently minted *Altmark* criteria in the first important case where they were applied – by broadening their scope. By contrast, several other aspects of the case, such as the scope for market entry and the undesirable effects of *ex post* compensation, were not addressed. In any event, by moderating the fourth *Altmark* condition, the General Court put pressure on the approach of the Commission adopted in its health-care decisions discussed previously. In these decisions the Commission started from a strict reading of the criterion of the costs of a well-run company in order to determine whether notification was required. It is for the Member State to satisfy this test and if the compensation is not awarded by tender, then the Member State must provide evidence that the company is well run.

As long as the Court of Justice has not shed any light on this matter, at least in the health-care sector, it remains unsolved whether the fourth condition should be applied in a strict or lenient manner. If the approach adopted by the General Court is upheld by the Court of Justice, the Member States will enjoy more regulatory freedom than the Commission was prepared to allow them in its decisions discussed previously. Although it may take a strict approach to enforcing the *Altmark* criteria in relation to notification issues, the Commission is nonetheless prepared to declare the State measures as compatible with Article 106(2) TFEU on the basis of a cursory examination of the economics of the measure or its effect on competition.

Case study 18.5: Brussels hospitals and SGEI – *CBI v Commission*

Our second case concerns an appeal by the private hospitals association in Brussels against a Commission Decision finding that the State funding of the public hospitals in Brussels (the IRIS-H) did not warrant a full-scale State aid investigation.[62] The Commission had accepted that the IRIS-H were charged with providing an SGEI, derived from the regulatory context. This included, inter alia, an obligation to accept all patients (not just those coming in for emergency treatment, but for all wards) and to offer bilingual services (both French and Dutch being official languages in the Brussels region). The Commission had carried out only a so-called preliminary investigation, finding that there was no serious risk of distortions of competition on the internal market. At the same time the Commission had invested a lot of time and effort coming to this conclusion. The General Court held that this in itself demonstrated that serious difficulties could be shown, warranting a second-phase investigation.

In its Decision the Commission had tested only the first (entrustment) and the fourth (efficiency) *Altmark* criteria, deriving the entrustment from the context of the applicable regulatory regime but concluding that the efficiency test had not been met as it could not

---

[62] Case T-137/10 *Coordination bruxelloise d'institutions sociales et de santé (CBI) v Commission*, judgment of 7 November 2012, nyr.

be established that the IRIS-H met the standard of an average well-run undertaking. Next it applied the SGEI exemption, which consists only of entrustment, necessity, and proportionality, in the context of the 2005 *Altmark* package. The main substantive difference between the SGEI test in Article 106(2) TFEU as elaborated in the 2005 Decision and the *Altmark* criteria is that the fourth *Altmark* criterion (tender or efficiency test) is not included in the criteria of the SGEI package. In addition there is an important procedural difference: the SGEI package and its more detailed substantive assessment criteria that elaborate on Article 106(2) TFEU applied only from the end of 2005 when it was adopted, whereas the *Altmark* case applies to past situations without limitation.

The findings of the General Court were as follows:

- It held that the Commission had not sufficiently investigated the contents of the alleged act of entrustment of the IRIS-H.

- In its Decision the Commission was satisfied that clear cost parameters had been specified in advance and adhered to, allowing 100 per cent of costs plus a reasonable rate of return, with adequate measures in place to correct overcompensation. The General Court, however, was less easily satisfied and rejected the conclusion that the requirement of clear anterior parameters had been respected.

- Finally, it rejected the conclusion that overcompensation would be effectively prevented.

Consequently the Commission's decision was quashed and the Commission was charged with carrying out a second-phase investigation. The General Court thus appears to be tightening its approach compared to the *BUPA* case.

Case study 18.6: Supplementary insurance for bakery workers – *AG2R Prévoyance*

In *AG2R Prévoyance* the Court of Justice addressed the applicability of the competition rules and abuse of dominance in relation to an exclusive right in the context of an SGEI. Here the Court held that the provident society that was charged with the task of managing a supplementary health-care scheme set up by employers and unions in the traditional bakery sector in France, was on the one hand an undertaking, so the competition rules applied, but on the other hand should be regarded as being entrusted with carrying out an SGEI in the sense of Article 106(2) TFEU.[63] Compulsory affiliation to this managing body was justified due to this SGEI as it would ensure that universal cover was provided and that the undertaking entrusted with the task of providing supplementary insurance for all persons insured would not end up with an increasing share of bad risks. Hence, the compulsory affiliation guaranteed that the managing body concerned was able to carry out its SGEI task under economically acceptable circumstances. The concept of SGEI led the Court to accommodate health-care-specific concerns in its reasoning.

However, it is noteworthy that in *AG2R Prévoyance* the Court did not assign any value to the act of entrustment of the imputed SGEI. It merely derived the relevant task from the fact that the supplementary health-care scheme at issue was characterized by a high degree

---

[63] Case C-437/09 *AG2R Prévoyance v Beaudout Père et Fils SARL* [2011] ECR I-973. cf JW van de Gronden and W Sauter, 'Taking the Temperature: EU Competition Law and Healthcare' [2011] *Legal Issues of European Integration* 213.

of solidarity with contributions not proportionate to the risks insured and fixed at uniform rates, partly paid by the employer and partly by the employee, without any role for factors such as age or health. Furthermore, the Court pointed to the constraints imposed on AG2R that were related to the continuity of the cover granted to the persons insured. This approach is a striking departure from earlier cases where the Union Courts have gone to some trouble in order to identify the legal context from which the existence of SGEIs could be derived.

In *AG2R* it seems that in the view of the Court the mere existence of obligations (related to a general interest) imposed upon a managing body suffices to assume this body is engaged in providing an SGEI. Moreover, in this particular case the entities, which decided on the designation of the management of the scheme concerned, were social partners, that is to say the employers and trade unions representing employees in the traditional bakery sector. Although French legislation provides that collective bargaining agreements may be imposed by law on an entire sector, French law does not oblige the social partners to arrange for supplementary health-care schemes. Hence, the mission to provide these insurance services originated with the private entities concerned and not from the State. This is in line with the *Albany* (1999) case law where the Court seems to have accepted that an SGEI mission may be designated by social partners. At issue in these cases were supplementary pension schemes and the provision of such schemes by private pension funds was found to constitute an SGEI.[64]

5.4 Lessons from the case studies

These three recent court cases in the health sector demonstrate, on the one hand, an increasing application of the State aid rules to health care and, on the other hand, the use of a formalized regime of exceptions that benefit health-care systems which are designed to pursue public goals in a proportionate manner. A degree of flexibility is allowed by the Commission and General Court that yet remains to be corrected or confirmed by the Court of Justice itself. Public services and State aid are in principle compatible but may require a further rationalization of means and ends. In this context, the SGEI exception is the main relevant instrument of EU law.

6 Conclusion

Public services are an open category of services that can be added to by the Member States. If a public service is provided by undertakings, that is, at least partially or potentially in competition, then competition and State aid rules usually apply. In such cases public entrustment of particular tasks and public funding remain possible provided the rules for compensation for SGEIs are respected. This means essentially that public tasks must be clearly defined and any restrictions on competition must be necessary and the costs involved to other parties may not exceed the public benefits achieved. Thus a balance can be achieved between the social objectives of the Member States and the internal market

---

[64] Case C-67/96 *Albany International BV v Stichting Bedrijfspensioenfonds Textielindustrie* [1999] ECR I-5751; Joined Cases C-115/97, C-116/97 and C-117/97 *Brentjens' Handelsonderneming BV v Stichting Bedrijfspensioenfonds voor de Handel in Bouwmaterialen* [1999] ECR I-6025; and Case C-219/97 *Maatschappij Drijvende Bokken BV v Stichting Pensioenfonds voor de Vervoer- en Havenbedrijven* [1999] ECR I-6121.

objectives of the EU. Service providers from other Member States can and do compete to provide social and utility services and to obtain a steady stream of compensation for doing so.

The rules on SGEIs and public funding have been spelled out in secondary legislation and soft law instruments. As we have explained, the Commission is continuing to tighten controls on economically significant utility services, so that Member States have less freedom to determine both the organization and financing of these types of SGEI. This has been compared with the more relaxed regime on the politically sensitive sectors of social services and health care, where there is little applicable secondary legislation and, furthermore, the Commission justifies leaving more scope to Member States on the ground that there is less cross-border activity in these sectors. We have also noted that for SGEIs in the utility sector, there is also a recurring tandem between the State aid rules for SGEIs and the public procurement rules – an area where further developments may well be expected.

The scope for national policies towards social services and health care is in general restricted if they seek (even partially) market-based solutions to the problems that public services are intended to address – such as universality and affordability. The purpose of the limits imposed by European law is to allow competition to work effectively in a market insofar as compatible with the proportionate restraints needed to operate SGEIs. The efficiency-enhancing effects of markets are, after all, among the main reasons to entrust undertakings with SGEIs in the first place (as opposed to reserving provision to public authorities). At the same time, the EU regime not only sets boundaries to national policies but it also promotes their rationalization and justification, thereby enhancing the legitimacy of both national and EU-level intervention.

Sectoral harmonization and liberalization are neither preconditions for, nor the necessary results of, the use of the SGEI legal framework for public services in the EU. However, as is illustrated by the utilities sector, in the course of harmonization the scope of PSOs may well be defined at EU level, even if only as a minimum level of service provision which may be supplemented according to national preferences. Within the overall framework of SGEIs, the EU regime for public services, provided certain basic rules are met, is context-specific and so differs from sector to sector. This à la carte or flexible approach appears appropriate given the wide range of activities and national preferences involved, even if flexibility comes at the price of legal certainty.

Further reading

CH Bovis, 'Financing Services of General Interest in the EU' [2005] *European Law Journal* 79

JL Buendia Sierra, *State Intervention and EU Competition Law* (Oxford: Oxford University Press, 2014)

G de Búrca (ed), *EU Law and the Welfare State: In Search of Solidarity* (Oxford: Oxford University Press, 2005)

B Cantillon, H Verschuren, and P Ploscar (eds), *Social Inclusion and Social Protection in the EU: Interaction between Law and Policy* (Antwerp: Intersentia, 2012)

M Cremona (ed), *Market Integration and Public Services in the European Union* (Oxford: Oxford University Press, 2011)

M Dougan and E Spaventa (eds), *Social Welfare and EU Law: Essays in European Law* (Oxford: Hart Publishing, 2005)

M Freedland and S Sciarra (eds), *Public Services and Citizenship in European Law: Public and Labour Law Perspectives* (Oxford: Oxford University Press, 1998)

D Géradin, 'The New Package of Services of General Economic Interest' [2012] *Journal of European Competition Law and Practice* 1

JW van de Gronden and W Sauter, 'Taking the Temperature: EU Competition Law and Healthcare' [2011] *Legal Issues of European Integration* 213

L Gyselen, 'Public Service and EU Competition Law' [2011] *Journal of European Competition Law and Practice* 572

L Hancher and P Larouche, 'The Coming of Age of EU Regulation of Network Industries and Services of General Economic Interest' in P Craig and G de Búrca (eds), *The Evolution of EU Law* (2nd edn, Oxford: Oxford University Press, 2011)

L Hancher and W Sauter, *The EU Competition and Internal Market Iaw in the Healthcare Sector* (Oxford: Oxford University Press, 2012)

A Héritier, 'Market Integration and Social Cohesion' [2001] *Journal of European Public Policy* 825

M Krajewski, U Neergaard, and J van de Gronden (eds), *The Changing Framework for Services of General Interest in Europe: Between Competition and Solidarity* (The Hague: TMC Asser Press, 2009)

L Nistor, *Public Services and the EU* (The Hague: TMC Asser Press, 2011)

T Prosser, 'EU Competition Law and Public Services' in E Mossialos et al (eds), *Health Systems Governance in Europe: The Role of European Union Law and Policy* (Cambridge: Cambridge University Press, 2010)

M Ross and Y Borgmann-Prebil (eds), *Promoting Solidarity in the European Union* (Oxford: Oxford University Press, 2010)

W Sauter, 'The *Altmark* Package Mark II: New Rules for State Aid and the Compensation of Services of General Economic Interest' [2012] *European Competition Law Review* 307

FW Scharpf, 'The European Social Model' [2002] *Journal of Common Market Studies* 645

E Szyszczak and JW van de Gronden (eds), *Financing Services of General Economic Interest: Reform and Modernization* (The Hague: TMC Asser Press, 2013)

19

Economic and monetary union

Alicia Hinarejos

1 Introduction

The Economic and Monetary Union (EMU) is one of the most important and best-known aspects of EU integration; it is also one of the most controversial. It envisages a single monetary policy, conducted by a single monetary authority; a single currency, the euro; and coordination of national economic policies. Not all Member States of the EU participate in all phases of EMU: as of 2013, 17 Member States have entered the last stage of EMU and adopted the euro as their currency; these countries constitute the 'eurozone' or 'euro area'.[1]

Centralized monetary policy for the euro area is conducted by an EU institution, the European Central Bank (ECB), assisted by the national central banks; all together they form the European System of Central Banks (ESCB). At the same time, economic policy remains in the hands of Member States, within certain limits. There is thus an underlying tension within EMU between a centralized monetary policy and essentially decentralized economic and fiscal policy. Ultimately, this asymmetric design of EMU proved to have certain flaws that contributed to the current euro area government debt crisis and have made it more difficult to address said crisis. This chapter will explain how EMU was set up, and the flaws within the system. It will also give a brief overview of the euro crisis and

---

[1] An eighteenth Member State, Latvia, is due to join EMU in January 2014.

its relationship to, and consequences for, EMU. Finally, the chapter will look to the current debate on the future of EMU and the EU.[2]

2 History and design of EMU

States normally control their monetary policy (matters such as the production of currency and interest rates) alongside their fiscal policy (the acquisition of public funds through, eg taxation or debt, as well as the allocation of those funds through public spending or the creation of a social insurance system). Monetary and fiscal policies are traditionally considered two sides of the same coin. The term 'economic policy' is potentially broader than these two policies taken together – as it may also cover all instances of intervention in the economy through the use of regulation (eg concerning wages or other aspects of labour law).

The EMU was part of the project of European integration dating back to the early 1970s.[3] Its formal legal origins lie with the Treaty on European Union, adopted in 1991, which granted the (then) European Community the competence to establish an economic and monetary policy which would include the fixing of exchange rates leading to the introduction of a common currency, a central monetary and exchange rate policy conducted with a view to maintaining price stability, and limited coordination of national economic policies. After exchange rates were indeed fixed in 1998,[4] a new common currency, the euro, was introduced in 1999.[5] Euro banknotes and coins were introduced in 2002. As noted previously, as of 2014, 18 Member States have entered the last stage of EMU and adopted the euro as their currency; these countries constitute the 'eurozone' or 'euro area'.[6] The remaining Member States, apart from Denmark and the UK,[7] are committed to adopting the euro when their economies satisfy a set of pre-established requirements, or convergence criteria, set out in the Treaty and a Protocol.[8] These criteria seek to limit inflation, annual public deficit, and total accumulated public debt. Countries are also required to have maintained stable exchange rates and long-term interest rates for a certain period of time before joining EMU. There are no express provisions in the Treaty on terminating EMU as a whole, or on a Member State leaving EMU, voluntarily or otherwise – presumably unless the Member State decides to leave the EU altogether, pursuant to Article 50 TEU.

The creation of an economic and monetary union was considered the next logical step of economic integration, after the establishment of the internal market.[9] What is most

---

[2] Certain sections of this chapter draw on material included in A Hinarejos, 'The Euro Area Crisis and Constitutional Limits to Fiscal Integration' (2011–12) 14 *Cambridge Yearbook of European Legal Studies* 243.

[3] For an overview of its historical origins prior to the TEU, see F Snyder, 'EMU – Integration and Differentiation: Metaphor for European Union' in P Craig and G de Búrca, *The Evolution of EU Law* (2nd edn, Oxford: Oxford University Press, 2011).

[4] Council Regulation (EC) No 2866/98 on the conversion rates between the euro and the currencies of the Member States adopting the euro (OJ [1998] L359/1).

[5] Council Regulation (EC) No 974/98 on the introduction of the euro (OJ [1998] L139/1).

[6] These countries are: Austria, Belgium, Cyprus, Estonia, Finland, France, Germany, Greece, Ireland, Italy, Latvia, Luxembourg, Malta, the Netherlands, Portugal, Slovakia, Slovenia, and Spain.

[7] The Danish and UK opt-outs are set out in Protocols attached to the Treaties: Protocol No 15 on certain provisions relating to the United Kingdom of Great Britain and Northern Ireland and Protocol No 16 on certain provisions relating to Denmark.

[8] Based on what is now Art 140 TFEU and Protocol No 13 on the convergence criteria.

[9] Economists have traditionally distinguished the following progressive stages: Free Trade Area, Customs Union, Common Market, Monetary Union, Economic Union, Political or Full Union. B Balassa, *The Theory of Economic Integration* (London: Allen and Unwin, 1961). See also C Barnard, *The Substantive Law of the EU: The Four Freedoms* (3rd edn, Oxford: Oxford University Press, 2010) 8 *et seq*; P Verloren van Themaat,

significant about this area of Union competence is its asymmetry, or the fact that monetary policy has been separated from fiscal policy (and from the broader national economic policy):[10] EMU includes a full monetary union, defined and conducted at the EU level, while economic/fiscal policies are still conducted at the national level.

Indeed, the EU has exclusive competence in monetary policy for the Member States whose currency is the euro, according to the Treaties.[11] Monetary policy is defined and implemented for the whole eurozone by the ESCB: this system includes the national central banks (eg the Deutsche Bundesbank, De Nederlandsche Bank), and has the ECB at its helm.[12] The ESCB and all its components are supposed to be independent and free from political influence.[13]

But EMU does not include a full fiscal or economic policy conducted at the EU level. Instead, Member States remain in control of their own fiscal policies, and of their broader economic policies, within certain limits that will be discussed later. So far, EMU has merely given Member States a framework to coordinate these policies to a certain degree:[14] Article 2(3) TFEU marks economic policy as an area where the EU's competence is a coordinating one; that is, where the Union is merely supposed to provide arrangements to facilitate coordination of policies that remain national in nature.[15] Coordinating competences were introduced in the Lisbon Treaty (in force 1 December 2009) and, although they seem to hover somewhere between shared and supporting competences, their constitutional character is not fully defined yet.[16] It seems safe to say, nevertheless, that the Union has no proper legislative competence at the moment to generate an independent economic or fiscal policy.

The design of EMU, then, gives great predominance to the monetary component, while integration of economic policies lags much further behind. This final design was the result of a debate in the 1960s and 1970s between 'monetarists' and 'economists': the first ones believed that the starting point of EMU should be fixing exchange rates or the introduction of a common currency, and that coordination of economic policies would then follow. On the contrary, the 'economists' believed that coordination of economic

---

'Some Preliminary Observations on the IGC: The Relations between the Concepts of a Common Market, a Monetary Union, an Economic Union, a Political Union and Sovereignty' (1991) 28 *Common Market Law Review* 291.

[10] The issue of economic governance within an asymmetric EMU has been discussed for many years. For a review of the literature, see N Jabko, *Which Economic Governance? Facing up to the Problem of Divided Sovereignty*, (SIEPS Report 2011:2 (Stockholm: SIEPS, 2011). For an historical analysis of the Franco-German debate concerning the appropriate EMU architecture, see J Pisani-Ferry, 'Only One Bed for Two Dreams: A Critical Retrospective on the Debate over the Economic Governance of the Euro Area' (2006) 44 *Journal of Common Market Studies* 823; see also W Schelkle, 'The Theory and Practice of Economic Governance in EMU Revisited: What Have We Learnt about Commitment and Credibility?' (2006) 44 *Journal of Common Market Studies* 669.

[11] Art 3(1)(c) TFEU. On the concept of exclusive EU competences, see further chapter 5.

[12] On the design of the ESCB and ESM, see R Smits, *The European Central Bank: Institutional Aspects* (The Hague: Kluwer, 1997); F Antembrink, *The Democratic Accountability of Central Banks: A Comparative Study of the European Central Bank* (Oxford: Hart Publishing, 1999). [13] Art 130 TFEU.

[14] On economic coordination, see eg I Harden, 'The Fiscal Constitution of EMU' in P Beaumont and N Walker (eds), *The Legal Framework of the Single European Currency* (Oxford: Hart Publishing, 1999); D Hodson and I Maher, 'The Open Method as a New Mode of Governance: The Case of Soft Economic Policy Co-ordination' (2001) 39 *Journal of Common Market Studies* 719; F Amtenbrink and J de Haan, 'Economic Governance in the European Union' (2003) 40 *Common Market Law Review* 1075; JV Louis, 'The Economic and Monetary Union: Law and Institutions' (2004) 41 *Common Market Law Review* 575; I Maher, 'Economic Governance: Hybridity, Accountability and Control' (2007) 1 *Colombia Journal of European Law* 679.

[15] Art 2(3) TFEU: 'The Member States shall coordinate their economic and employment policies within arrangements as determined by this Treaty, which the Union shall have competence to provide.'

[16] For more on the concept of coordinating competences, see chapter 5.

policies should happen prior to the introduction of a common currency. Needless to say, the 'monetarists' prevailed;[17] as a result, while all members of the euro area are bound to each other through a common currency, each of them is free to conduct their own fiscal and economic policies, within certain limits. The next section will turn to the nature and effectiveness of these limits.

3 The Stability and Growth Pact and measures of coordination before the crisis

The limits imposed on national fiscal policies were initially laid down in the Treaties and in the Stability and Growth Pact, based on Articles 121 and 126 TFEU.[18] Member States agreed to keep their annual deficit and debt below a certain percentage of their gross domestic product (GDP), or the value of all goods and services produced within their national borders in a year. Imagine, for example, a country with a GDP of €100 billion; if it borrows €5 billion in one year, the country has a 5 per cent annual deficit for that year. If the same country has borrowed €80 billion over the years, it has 80 per cent debt. With the Stability and Growth Pact, States agreed to keep their annual deficit below 3 per cent of their GDP, and their debt below 60 per cent of their GDP. This was the 'preventive arm' of the Pact; there was also a 'corrective arm', or excessive deficit procedure, allowing the Council, on a recommendation from the Commission, to penalize and even impose fines on euro area Member States that did not abide by the rules.

In practice, however, the need for political agreement within the Council in order to impose sanctions meant that the corrective arm of the Pact lacked effectiveness. In 2002 and 2003, the Commission initiated excessive deficit procedures against Germany and France, respectively. These countries adopted measures to address the situation, but the Commission did not consider them effective enough. Accordingly, the Commission urged the Council to pursue more forceful action.[19] In both cases, the Council voted and decided not to follow the Commission's recommendations. The Commission then challenged the legality of the resulting Council measures before the Court of Justice.[20] The judgment was complex; what is most relevant for the current discussion is that the Court rejected the Commission's claim that the Council's failure to adopt the Commission's recommendation was in itself a decision, and one that should be annulled.[21] Ultimately, the Commission could not require the Council to pursue further action against France, Germany, or any other country that breached the Pact. Recurring breaches without significant consequences

---

[17] See the historical overview literature in n 10.

[18] The origins of the Stability and Growth Pact lie in a resolution from 1997 (Resolution of the European Council on the Stability and Growth Pact, 17 June 1997). This spawned two Regulations (preventive and corrective arm, respectively): Council Regulation (EC) No 1466/97 on the strengthening of the surveillance of budgetary positions and the surveillance and coordination of economic policies (OJ [1997] L209/1) and Council Regulation (EC) No 1467/97 on speeding up and clarifying the implementation of the excessive deficit procedure (OJ [1997] L209/6). The excessive deficit procedure is further detailed in Protocol No 12 attached to the Treaties.

[19] The Commission recommended to the Council that deadlines be set, that specific measures be imposed on France and Germany, and that the Council's recommendations be made public.

[20] Case C-27/04 *Commission v Council* [2004] ECR I-6649.

[21] For more information on this and other aspects of the judgment, see F Snyder, 'EMU Integration and Differentiation: Metaphor for European Union' in P Craig and G de Búrca, *The Evolution of EU Law* (2nd edn, Oxford: Oxford University Press, 2011); I Maher 'Economic Policy Coordination and the European Court: Excessive Deficits and ECOFIN Discretion' (2004) 29 *European Law Review* 831.

were likely to diminish the credibility of the Pact further. As a consequence, it was considered preferable to reform the Pact in 2005: its rules were made more flexible, allowing for even greater discretion.[22] In general, the Pact appeared to have lost its teeth.

Aside from the Pact, Member States were also supposed to follow the Broad Guidelines on Economic Policy, issued by the Council every three years with a view to coordinating national economic policies (and affecting fiscal policy, but also regulation of the economy more broadly).[23] The Guidelines are not legally binding: States make certain commitments in order to comply with these recommendations,[24] and then they report annually on their progress. Due to the lack of a credible sanctioning mechanism, it is not clear how effective the Guidelines have been in the past.[25] Additionally, members of the eurozone also seek to coordinate their policies within the Eurogroup, an informal gathering of the finance ministers of all euro countries, together with the Commission Vice-President for Economic and Monetary Affairs, and the President of the ECB.[26]

To sum up: the assumption at the heart of EMU was always that a central monetary policy and a single currency necessitate effective coordination of economic and fiscal policies, yet this coordination may have turned out to be more difficult than anticipated. This imbalance between the different sides of EMU is related to the current euro area crisis, which the next section will discuss.

4 The euro area crisis and its relationship to EMU

The effects of the financial crisis that erupted in 2007 were felt globally. In the EU, these effects were amplified by certain flaws in the design of the EMU: in 2010, it became clear that the economies of several euro area members were in serious trouble, and that the euro area had a government debt crisis (also called sovereign debt crisis) on its hands.[27] Although the most obvious symptoms of the crisis affected specific countries, the crisis has a much broader scope. From a political or constitutional perspective, the crisis has not only cast doubt on the viability of a mechanism of integration such as the one envisaged in EMU, but also on the future of the EU as a political project in the face of citizens' growing disaffection.

What is a sovereign debt crisis, and how does it start? Countries continuously refinance their public or sovereign debt, which means that they pay debts that have matured by borrowing new money from the markets. To this end, a country sells financial instruments (eg bonds) that yield interest; this interest compensates investors for the time during which they are not able to use their money, as well as for the risk they take in lending it. Prior to the outbreak of the crisis, the cost of funding for most euro area economies was similar, with Greece paying a small risk premium compared to Germany. The crisis changed this: once the markets

---

[22] Council Regulation (EC) No 1055/2005 amending Regulation (EC) No 1466/97 (OJ [2005] L174/1); Council Regulation (EC) No 1056/2005 amending Regulation (EC) No 1467/97 (OJ [2005] L174/5).

[23] On the basis of Art 121 TFEU.

[24] eg the 2010 guidelines included the following recommendation: 'Member States and the Union should put measures in place to promote the decoupling of economic growth from resource use, turning environmental challenges into growth opportunities and making more efficient use of their natural resources, which also assists in preventing environmental degradation and ensuring biodiversity' (Council Recommendation 2010/410/EU (OJ [2010] L191/28) 33).

[25] On the Guidelines and their effect, see D Hodson, *Governing the Euro Area in Good Times and Bad* (Oxford: Oxford University Press, 2011) ch 5 ('Why the BEPGs Failed to Bite').

[26] Art 137 TFEU and Protocol No 14 on the Euro Group.

[27] For an overview of the crisis, see House of Lords (EU Select Committee), 'The Euro Area Crisis', 25th Report of Session 2010–12, HL Paper 260.

paid more attention to the specifics of each euro economy, they started to have doubts as to specific countries' credibility as debtors. Typically, this lack of confidence leads to rising costs of borrowing and refinancing, since a country in this situation needs to compensate investors with a higher risk premium. As its borrowing costs rise inexorably, the troubled country risks being shut out of private markets; as a result of this vicious circle, State default – the situation where a State is not able to repay its debts – becomes a more likely possibility.[28]

In the case of the euro area, markets started to doubt the ability of some euro countries (Ireland, Portugal, and Greece, initially) to repay their debt, for different reasons. All three countries received financial assistance after committing to the implementation of strict austerity measures. These 'bail-outs' – which are, strictly speaking, loans – came from the International Monetary Fund (IMF)[29] and from two different European emergency mechanisms.[30] While the bail-outs seemed to ameliorate the situation in Ireland and Portugal, the Greek problem was of a much greater scale; the country was revealed to have long misrepresented the volume of its debt and, in general, the state of its finances, in order, at least at first, to be able to join the euro.[31] Market fears spread to other countries as well, especially Spain and Italy, which meant that these countries too saw their economy threatened by the rising cost of borrowing money under the worsening conditions offered by a wary market.

The imbalance between EU monetary policy, on the one hand, and national fiscal/economic policies, on the other, was relevant to the crisis in several respects. First, some economists believe that different national economic policies fostered competitive asymmetries between the euro area members;[32] when left unchecked, these asymmetries put certain members in a position that was more vulnerable to the global economic crisis.[33] Secondly, the monetary union (and the strong euro)[34] meant that, initially, certain eurozone members were able to borrow money from the markets much more cheaply than they should have, creating a certain incentive for running up national debt. Thirdly, individual euro countries were not able to use the tools of monetary policy, by now out of their hands; for example, they were not able to produce more money (quantitative easing) in order to alleviate their debt, or alternatively to devalue their currency, so as to make their exports cheaper and foster economic growth. Fourthly, the perception that some euro countries may default affected the value of the common currency and thus the economies of all members of the euro area; more specifically, there was a risk of contagion as the risk of default in one State made investors wary of the same happening in others. And, finally, independent

---

[28] Rather, a default on private debt is inevitable in the absence of official sector financing.

[29] The IMF is an international organization. Its members (188 countries to date) contribute money to a fund which can be used to make conditional loans to struggling economies.

[30] The European Financial Stability Mechanism, a small loan facility within the EU system, and the European Financial Stability Fund, a much bigger, temporary vehicle created on an intergovernmental basis. There was also an ad hoc loan agreement for Greece. See further section 5.1.2.

[31] For an overview of the Greek situation and the EU's response, see Editorial Comments, 'The Greek Sovereign Debt Tragedy: Approaching the Final Act?' (2011) 48 *Common Market Law Review* 1769; H Hofmeister, 'To Bail Out Or Not to Bail Out? – Legal Aspects of the Greek Crisis' (2010–11) 13 *Cambridge Yearbook of European Legal Studies* 113.

[32] This means that different members within the currency area will have different economic structures (eg some are manufacture- and export-driven, while others rely on the provision of services) and will not be equally competitive. Sub-optimal labour and capital mobility add to this problem.

[33] For a brief overview, see eg S Micossi, 'Misguided Policies Risk Breaking Up the Eurozone and the EU' (2011) CEPS Policy Brief No 260, 4, http://papers.ssrn.com/sol3/papers.cfm?abstract_id=1996457

[34] More specifically, it was the perception (in retrospect proved to be partly correct because of the extraordinary level of official sector financing provided) that other euro area economies would provide financial support if one member threatened to default.

fiscal policies meant that better-off members of the euro area were (justifiably) reticent to bail out members in risk of default, since the latter might not alter their behaviour in the absence of an incentive for fiscal responsibility. For the same reason, better-off euro countries are equally reluctant to pool their public debt in the future, for example by having the whole euro area issuing bonds jointly.[35] In short, the asymmetry at the heart of the EMU has arguably contributed to the fiscal problems of some euro countries, or at least allowed them to happen; it has exposed all euro area members to the problems of a few; and it has made it difficult to address these problems at the EU level.[36]

Against this background, it seemed that, while a bail-out or the creation of a rescue mechanism could temporarily preserve financial stability in the euro area as a whole, it was also necessary, in the longer term, to address the imbalance between the strong monetary union and the weak economic coordination between the members of the euro area. The next two sections will discuss the bail-out mechanisms, as well as the reforms undertaken to improve economic coordination since the beginning of the crisis.

Case study 19.1: Dealing with the euro crisis

Countries A, B, and C are all members of the euro area.

Before the global financial crisis, country A's banks bought a great deal of 'toxic' financial products, which means that it is now in trouble and likely to default. Rather than facing a meltdown of its economy, country A decides to bail out its banks. As a result, country A now has a very large volume of public debt and faces problems of liquidity.

Country B also faces problems of liquidity, for other reasons. It already had a problem with public debt, and it is now finding that, because of the financial crisis, it has become more difficult to borrow money in the markets, either by borrowing directly from banks or by selling bonds to private investors. When its struggles become public, private investors panic and no one wants to buy country B bonds, because they are considered 'junk bonds' (ie not likely to be repaid when they mature). To make up for the level of risk, country B has to offer an ever-increasing interest rate. Very soon it will be so expensive for it to borrow money through the issuing of bonds (ie it will have to offer such high interest rates in return) that it will be effectively shut out from the market, and thus unable to borrow the necessary money to refinance ('roll over') its debt. A default looks more and more likely.

When faced with this situation, all members of the euro area decide that it makes sense to bail out countries A and B (ie lend them money on advantageous conditions). Investors are already worrying about the creditworthiness of other members of the euro area, which makes it more likely that these other countries, too, will face escalating costs when borrowing money from the markets. The economies of all euro area countries are also intertwined in other ways: country C's banks, for example, own a great deal of country B's debt; so

---

[35] There is also a question whether joint bonds (sometimes called 'Eurobonds') would violate the no-bail-out clause in the Treaty, Art 125 TFEU (discussed in section 5.1.2). See J Delpla and J von Weizsäcker, 'The Blue Bond Proposal' (2010) Bruegel Policy Brief 2010/03; J Delpla and J von Weizsäcker, 'Eurobonds: The Blue Bond Concept and Its Implications' (2011) Bruegel Policy Contribution 2011/02. For a concise overview of the discussion on Eurobonds, see House of Lords (EU Select Committee), 'The Future of Economic Governance in the EU', 12th Report of Session 2010–11, HL Paper 124-I, pp 58 et seq. On the legality of Eurobonds within the current Treaties, see P Athanassiou, 'Of Past Measures and Future Plans for Europe's Exit from the Sovereign Debt Crisis: What is Legally Possible (and What is Not)' (2011) 36 *European Law Review* 558, 571 et seq.

[36] This does not mean that EMU is the root of all fiscal problems; after all, some non-eurozone States, like the UK, have run up enormous deficits.

much, that country C's economy would suffer a severe blow if country B were unable to pay country C's banks.

Of course, the citizens of different countries see a potential bail-out in a very different light: the residents of country C are not happy about sending their tax money to country A or B. They think that they should not be paying for countries that chose to spend too much, instead of being responsible like they were. They also worry that, once country B receives a bail-out, its government will just go back to spending too much, safe in the belief that the country will be saved again if necessary.

On the other hand, citizens in countries A and B hope for solidarity from the rest of the euro area. They start to wonder whether the Union is only a 'proper' union as long as the economy is going well. They also argue that the richer countries in the euro area (and, chief among them, country C) have benefited from the internal market and EMU for many years; in fact, they argue that these countries have benefited far more than anyone else, because of the way their industries work (they have a competitive manufacture- and export-based industry). Accordingly, they think, these rich countries should now be willing to share some of the wealth.

In the end, the bail-outs take place, and countries A and B need to comply with very strict conditions in order to receive the money. They have to make quite dramatic economic reforms and implement cutbacks across the board. The citizens of these countries perceive these conditions as draconian and unfair. People feel let down and tensions grow; the media start a campaign against the government and citizens of country C, who do not understand the backlash and feel like everyone else in the Union is taking advantage of them.

In order to keep this sort of thing from happening again, there is a consensus that the way in which EMU works needs to change.

First, country A's troubles could have been avoided if the behaviour of banks had been better regulated; accordingly, the EU decides to work towards a better, more harmonized approach to regulation in this area.

Secondly, it is agreed that no member of the euro area should be allowed to get in a situation as bad as that of country B before the bail-out. In principle, the Stability and Growth Pact should have stopped country B from accumulating such volume of debt, but the Pact has never been properly enforced and everyone knows it. Accordingly, the Member States want to give teeth to the Pact, and to do so they adopt new measures to make sure that sanctions are applied whenever a euro country goes above the level of debt or deficit set out in the Pact. Further, there is a feeling that more detailed and substantive measures are needed; after all, the problem is not only the level of spending, but the fact that some economies in the euro area are less competitive than others.

A set of measures designed to improve surveillance are adopted: this means that, every year, members of the euro area have to send reports on the state of their economy, as well as their draft budgets for the next year, to the Commission. The Commission produces a report for each country with specific recommendations (eg 'you should reform your pension system', or 'you need to cut salaries in the public sector'). If a country is perceived to be in serious trouble, either because of its excessive deficit or because of imbalances in its economy, it will be placed under special monitoring and, if it fails to address the situation, sanctions may be imposed.

Certain governments start voicing their discontent with what they perceive as undemocratic interference from the Commission, and citizens grumble about Brussels. On the other hand, other members of the euro area, together with the Commission, reason that this sort of control has been proven necessary by the crisis, and that EMU and the euro have no future without it.

5 Addressing the crisis

It is never easy to address an economic crisis. In the case of the euro area, several factors have made it even more difficult. As you will remember from section 2, there is an imbalance at the heart of EMU: the powers of the EU vary widely between monetary policy, where it has an exclusive competence for the euro area, and economic policy, where it merely has a coordinating competence and where policy decisions are made at a national level. This was one of the causes of the crisis, and it is also one of the factors that make it difficult to address. The EU has been trying to drive the euro area out of the crisis while staying within its limited powers – this is not easy, and the danger is that the EU can be perceived to be either overstepping into very delicate national matters, on the one hand, or simply ineffective, on the other. In addition, Member States have also tried to address the crisis by acting collectively outside the legal framework of the EU.

It was discussed earlier that the design of EMU followed the 'monetarist' line of economic argument, according to which, once monetary policy had been centralized, sufficient economic coordination would follow – an assumption that has not been borne out by facts. There are further reasons why economic and fiscal policy was left to the Member States: these are very sensitive areas, and the feeling, to date, was that they were most appropriately discussed and conducted within the national political process. These areas have to do with the allocation of limited resources in our societies, our understanding of the role of the State, and the role and boundaries of solidarity between citizens; decisions taken here concern, for example, tax rates, public sector salaries, or the level of pensions. Understandably, the idea of a growing role for the EU in these areas is typically met with concern; one of the arguments most often put forward is that the Union does not (yet?) have the necessary democratic legitimacy to decide on matters such as taxation, pensions, or the boundaries of the welfare state.[37] These concerns have not only been expressed in the political discussion; in fact, several national constitutional courts believe that there are necessary limits to European integration. In particular, the German Federal Constitutional Court has been quite vocal in its position that a full economic and fiscal policy would be beyond those limits.[38]

Because of all this, the EU is limited in what it can do in this area, and it has to be very careful in negotiating its actions. With this in mind, we will now discuss the measures adopted to address the crisis.

The EU's response to the crisis has been multi-faceted.[39] First, we have seen that a quick intervention was necessary in order to stabilize the situation of euro countries (section 5.1). To this end, several loan facilities were created, and the ECB also played an important role in calming down the markets. Secondly, several measures have been adopted in order to improve budgetary surveillance and economic coordination (section 5.2). Thirdly, the EU has undertaken, and is still in the process of undertaking, important reforms aimed at the creation of a stronger financial framework, and a so-called 'banking union' for the euro area (section 5.3). This is because, as we have seen, the euro area crisis is connected to the global financial crisis that started in 2007, and which had inadequate financial regulation as one of its causes.

---

[37] On the democratic legitimacy of the EU, see further chapters 3 and 4.

[38] Decision of 30 June 2009, BVerfGE 123, 267 (*Lisbon* decision) esp paras 175–252.

[39] The distinction between the three following aspects of EU action comes from C Barnard, 'The Financial Crisis and the Euro Plus Pact: A Labour Lawyer's Perspective' (2012) 41 *International Law Journal* 98.

5.1 Stabilization: the ECB and bail-outs

As we have seen, several euro countries have been in acute financial trouble and in need of assistance. This assistance has come mainly from two sources: from the ECB, and from loan facilities created for this purpose.

5.1.1 The evolving role of the ECB

The ESCB is tasked with conducting the Union's monetary policy, with the primary objective of maintaining price stability (Article 127(1) TFEU). The ECB is able to work towards its primary objective through a series of measures that include the setting of interest rates and the supply of liquidity to the banking system (ie to banks and credit institutions) against appropriate collateral. What it is not able to do, according to the Treaties, is to provide liquidity directly to the EU or to the Member States: the Treaties were worded in such a way as to preclude the possibility of the ECB becoming a direct lender of last resort to any Member State, or to the EU institutions.[40] This is another manifestation of the tension within EMU highlighted previously: while there is a central monetary policy and an institution such as the ECB, decentralization in the areas of economic and fiscal policy means that Member States are supposed to remain responsible for their own debts.

Nevertheless, the ECB has had to adjust its role due to the crisis:[41] it has intervened in the markets in order to assist euro countries in trouble, stopping short of buying their bonds directly, which is prohibited in the Treaty. It has typically acted in the secondary markets, that is, buying sovereign bonds from investors who had bought them from the countries in trouble: in May 2010, it purchased €40 billion of Greek government bonds in this way. It has also adopted other measures to make these bonds more attractive to investors. Most recently, in September 2012, the ECB established its Outright Monetary Transactions Scheme: if a Member State is having liquidity problems and private investors are not buying its bonds, the ECB will step in and buy these bonds in the secondary market, provided the Member State complies with certain conditions. As the role of the ECB continues to evolve and expand to address the crisis, concerns also arise as to the legality of its actions.[42]

5.1.2 The bail-outs

In 2010, specific emergency mechanisms were created in order to provide financial support to struggling euro area economies: the European Financial Stability Mechanism (EFSM), a relatively small loan facility within the EU system, and the European Financial Stability Fund (EFSF), a bigger, temporary loan vehicle created on an intergovernmental basis – that is, by members of the euro area acting collectively, but outside the legal framework of the EU. After detailed negotiations, countries in specific crisis situations were able to receive funds from both mechanisms, as well as from the IMF.[43]

This, however, was not sufficient to reassure the markets. Both the EFSF and the EFSM were temporary in nature, and had limited lending power. There were also doubts as to the

---

[40] Art 123(1) TFEU: 'Overdraft facilities or any other type of credit facility with the European Central Bank or with the central banks of the Member States in favour of Union institutions...central governments, regional, local or other public authorities...shall be prohibited, as shall the purchase directly from them by the European Central Bank or national central banks of debt instruments.'

[41] D Wilsher, 'Ready to Do Whatever It Takes? The Legal Mandate of the European Central Bank and the Economic Crisis' (2012–13) 15 *Cambridge Yearbook of European Legal Studies* 503.

[42] At the time of writing, there is a challenge pending before the German Federal Constitutional Court concerning the legality of the ECB's Outright Monetary Transactions Scheme: Pending case, Bundesverfassungsgericht, 2 BvR 1390/12; 2 BvR 1421/12; 2 BvR 1438/12; 2 BvR 1439/12; 2 BvR 1440/12; 2 BvR 1824/12; 2 BvE 6/12.   [43] See n 29.

legality of these facilities. The EFSM, in particular, was created on the basis of Article 122 TFEU, which states that the EU may help a State in 'extraordinary circumstances'; some interpreted this provision to exclude circumstances brought about by a country's own behaviour (eg through flawed fiscal or economic policies). More generally, it was questionable whether both emergency mechanisms were compatible with the 'no-bail-out clause' set out in Article 125 TFEU, which states that a Member State's debt shall not be assumed by either the Union or other Member States. Some interpreted this clause as a ban on any form of financial assistance, including the creation of loan facilities. In short, a Treaty amendment was considered necessary.[44]

In March 2011, the European Council amended Article 136 TFEU using a simplified amendment procedure, introducing a new paragraph (3) that affirmed the Member States' power to create a permanent crisis mechanism to safeguard the stability of the euro.[45] Even before this amendment was ratified, the members of the euro area had already signed an international agreement creating the European Stability Mechanism (ESM). This is a permanent and more powerful intergovernmental mechanism, established outside the framework of the EU Treaties, which may grant financial assistance to countries in difficulties, subject to stringent conditions. Several challenges at the national level delayed the entry into force of the ESM Treaty until 27 September 2012 for 16 signatories to the Treaty, and a few days later for Estonia.

The intergovernmental nature of the ESM is a manifestation of a wider trend since the beginning of the crisis: that of Member States attempting to address different aspects of the sovereign debt crisis through intergovernmental means, at times completely outside the EU legal order, yet still using the EU institutions.[46] This is the case with the ESM Treaty, but also with the Treaty on Stability, Coordination, and Governance (sometimes called the 'fiscal compact'), which will be discussed in the next section. The rise of this brand of intergovernmentalism has spurred very different concerns. On the one hand, acting in this way could be ineffectual due to the lack of effective enforcement,[47] in which case precious time would be wasted that should be used to address the crisis. On the other hand, if it does indeed turn out to be effective, we should perhaps worry about the lack of transparency, judicial control, and democratic legitimacy, since, typically, negotiations in an intergovernmental setting are conducted behind closed doors, and involving only national executives. In fact, the concern that Member States were trying to avoid using EU mechanisms in order to circumvent control was at the heart of the challenge to the legality of the ESM brought before the Irish courts and the Court of Justice in *Pringle*.

---

[44] On the legality of the rescue packages, see JV Louis, 'Guest Editorial: The No-Bailout Clause and Rescue Packages' (2010) 47 *Common Market Law Review* 971; on the legality of these and other measures, see Athanassiou, 'Of Past Measures and Future Plans for Europe's Exit from the Sovereign Debt Crisis' (n 35).

[45] European Council Decision 2011/199/EU amending Article 136 of the TFEU with regard to a stability mechanism for Member States whose currency is the euro (OJ [2011] L91/1). The amendment entered into force in May 2013. It was based on Art 48(6) TEU, which provides for a simplified Treaty amendment procedure, which could be used because the amendment did not enlarge the competence of the EU (since the resulting intergovernmental mechanism is not part of the EU structure). For an overview of the mechanism and the resulting changes, see B de Witte, 'The European Treaty Amendment for the Creation of a Financial Stability Mechanism' (2011) 6 *SIEPS European Policy Analysis* 1; House of Lords EU Select Committee, 'Amending Article 136 of the TFEU', 10th Report of Session 2010–12, HL Paper 110. On Treaty amendment procedures, see further chapter 5.

[46] S Peers, 'Towards a New Form of EU Law? The Use of EU Institutions outside the EU Legal Framework' (2013) 9 *European Constitutional Law Review* 37.

[47] See further chapter 5 on decision-making and chapter 6 on the nature of EU law.

Case study 19.2: The ESM and the *Pringle* Decision

One of the challenges to the legality of the ESM Treaty before the national courts was brought by Mr Pringle, a member of the Irish Parliament.[48] Mr Pringle argued, among other things, that the simplified procedure should not have been used to amend the TFEU, and that the ESM Treaty itself was contrary to several provisions of the EU Treaties, mostly concerning EMU. The Irish Supreme Court decided to make a reference for a preliminary ruling to the Court of Justice. In the unsurprising but momentous *Pringle* decision, the Court sitting in a Full Court of all 27 judges – which is exceedingly rare – rejected all challenges and confirmed the legality of the ESM Treaty.[49] The decision is significant for various reasons. First, it clarified, to a degree, the relationship between an intergovernmental mechanism such as the ESM and the EU Treaties. Secondly, it shed light on whether the Member States can allocate tasks to the EU institutions outside the EU framework. Finally, it provided a purposive and dynamic interpretation of the EMU provisions; most importantly, of the no-bail-out clause.

The first question posed to the Court of Justice in *Pringle* concerned the use of the simplified procedure to amend the TFEU. This procedure can only be used to amend Part Three of the Treaty, and the Court had to consider whether the amendment, formally of a provision within Part Three, nevertheless affected in substance the nature and scope of the Union's competence in monetary and economic policy (set out in Part One of the Treaty). The Court decided that the ESM fell outside the EU's exclusive monetary policy competence because of its different aim and instruments. The ESM seeks to safeguard the stability of the euro area, whereas the objective of the eurozone's monetary policy is price stability. Moreover, the ESM would operate through the granting of financial assistance, which is not an instrument of monetary, but economic, policy.

Having decided that the ESM was an instrument of economic policy, the Court went on to find that this mechanism complemented the EU's competence in economic policy without encroaching on it. This is because the Union only has a coordinating competence in the area, and it would lack the power to establish a permanent emergency mechanism like the ESM. Member States, however, are able to create such a mechanism themselves, as long as they comply with EU law in doing so. The Court was satisfied that this compliance with EU law is ensured by the fact that financial assistance from the ESM will only be granted following compliance with strict conditions by the relevant Member States. The Court concluded that the TFEU amendment did not grant any new powers to the EU – something that could not have been done through the simplified procedure either. In the Court's view, Article 136(3) TFEU simply clarified a pre-existing competence of the Member States.

Next, the Court had to deal with a series of questions concerning the compatibility of the ESM Treaty itself with several provisions of the EU Treaties. The Court reaffirmed its position that the ESM would not subvert the EU's coordinating competence in economic policy. It considered the ESM a financial mechanism, not a mechanism for the coordination of economic policies; and that the aim of the conditionality attached to ESM assistance is not to coordinate national economic policies, but to ensure compliance with EU

---

[48] This section draws on material included in A Hinarejos, 'The Court of Justice of the EU and the Legality of the European Stability Mechanism' (2013) 72 *Cambridge Law Journal* 237.

[49] Case C-370/12 *Pringle v Ireland*, judgment of 27 November 2012, nyr.

law – more specifically, with the EU's coordinating economic measures, and with the EU Treaties' no-bail-out clause.

This brings us to one of the most difficult questions facing the Court in *Pringle*: whether the no-bail-out clause in the TFEU precluded the creation of a mechanism of financial assistance such as the ESM. The Court adopted a purposive reading of the no-bail-out clause. This provision, according to the Court, has two aims: the first one is to encourage prudent budgetary policy in the Member States by ensuring that they remain responsible to their creditors, thus submitting Member States to market discipline. The second, more general aim is to safeguard the financial stability of the euro area.

The Court inferred from this that the no-bail-out clause does not cover all forms of financial assistance; more specifically, it does not preclude a mechanism such as the ESM as long as it is only activated when necessary to safeguard the financial stability of the euro area as a whole, the Member State that receives assistance remains responsible to its creditors, and the assistance is subject to conditions that prompt the Member State to implement a prudent budgetary policy.

The Court also had to consider the legality of the allocation of tasks to the EU institutions outside the framework of the EU, particularly as the ESM Treaty allocated tasks to the ECB, the Commission, and the Court itself. The Court concluded that this allocation was not problematic, as long as it was not done in an area of exclusive EU competence and it did not alter the essential character of the institutions' powers under the EU Treaties. Interestingly, the Court did not mention the consent of all Member States as a requirement for this use of the institutions; although consent had been given in this particular case, clarification of this point may have been useful in the future. Furthermore, it had been argued that Member States should only be allowed to task EU institutions when using the enhanced cooperation mechanism set out in the EU Treaties (ie the procedure which allows a group of Member States to go ahead and adopt EU law measures without some other Member States).[50] The Court rejected this argument, at least as regards cases such as the present one, where enhanced cooperation cannot be used because the EU does not have the prerequisite competence to act. This leaves open the question of whether it is possible to confer powers to the EU institutions outside the context of enhanced cooperation in an area of (non-exclusive) EU competence.

In addition, it had been argued that placing the ESM outside the EU framework breached the right to legal protection, guaranteed in Article 47 of the Charter of Fundamental Rights of the European Union. The Court's response was that, when creating the ESM, the Member States were not implementing EU law, which meant that they were acting outside the scope of the Charter. Accordingly, the Member States do not have to comply with the Charter when acting pursuant to the ESM Treaty; questions remain, though, concerning the application of the Charter to EU institutions when they are acting in the context of the ESM Treaty.[51] This is significant because of the conditionality attached to ESM aid, which typically requires the receiving Member State to effect cutbacks that impact citizens' social rights. The legality of similar conditions, normally set out in a 'memorandum of understanding', has been

---

[50] For more on enhanced cooperation, see chapter 5.

[51] The AG appeared to assume that EU institutions are bound by the Charter even when acting outside the scope of EU law (para 176 of her Opinion); the Court did not mention the issue, perhaps because it assumed that the institutions could not adopt binding acts pursuant to the ESM Treaty: see S Peers, 'Towards a New Form of EU Law?' (n 46) 51 *et seq*.

questioned before the Court of Justice on several occasions; the Court has so far declined jurisdiction, claiming the lack of a link to EU law.[52]

Finally, the Irish court asked whether the failure of the Member States to wait until the amendment of the TFEU entered into force before signing and ratifying the ESM Treaty affected the legality of the latter. The Court of Justice answered in the negative, because Member States had always had the power to create a mechanism such as the ESM. Accordingly, the new paragraph added to Article 136 TFEU simply clarified the existence of such power, but did not give rise to it.

Overall, the *Pringle* judgment brought few surprises. Some of the measures intended to address the euro area crisis may have been adopted in a legal grey area, but few would argue that they were unnecessary. While the ESM may not be perfect, few expected the Court of Justice to stand in the way of an emergency mechanism that had political support, and the demise of which would probably have sent the euro area back into the acute phase of the crisis. The degree of deference shown by the Court to the political process in *Pringle* is not surprising, and it is arguably justified in such exceptional circumstances. The EMU provisions in the Treaties were designed to prevent a crisis, but not to manage one; as such, they needed to be interpreted in a purposive and dynamic manner to ensure that the EU's legal framework does not become obsolete and that the eurozone is capable of dealing effectively with this crisis of confidence. Questions, of course, remain: the relationship between a mechanism such as the ESM and the EU Treaties, as well as the future role of the Court of Justice in controlling certain aspects of ESM activity – however unlikely this may seem at the moment – will need to be further clarified in the future.

5.2 Budgetary and economic coordination measures

Bail-outs, while essential, are only one factor in addressing the euro area crisis. In the longer term, it is necessary to address the imbalance between the strong monetary union and the weak economic coordination between the members of the euro area. This is what the Member States have tried to do through the adoption of several measures or packs of measures since the beginning of the crisis. Some of these measures are EU instruments; these generally focus on strengthening budgetary and economic surveillance at the EU level. On other occasions, Member States have adopted instruments that are formally outside the EU legal order. This section will first consider EU legislation (the so-called Six-Pack and the Two-Pack), followed by EU 'soft law' (the Euro Plus Pact) and measures adopted by Member States outside the EU framework (the Treaty on Stability, Coordination and Governance, also known as the 'fiscal compact').

5.2.1 EU legislation: the Six-Pack and the Two-Pack

Since the beginning of the crisis, the EU has legislated in order to enhance different aspects of economic and budgetary surveillance. Very broadly speaking, Member States have

---

[52] Case C-434/11 *Corpul Naţional al Poliţiştilor*, order of 14 December 2011, nyr; Case C-134/12 *Corpul Naţional al Poliţiştilor*, order of 10 May 2012, nyr; Case C-369/12 *Corpul Naţional al Poliţiştilor*, order of 15 November 2012, nyr; and Case C-128/12 *Sindicato dos Bancários do Norte*, order of 7 March 2013, nyr. See also pending Case C-264/12 *Sindicato Nacional dos Profissionais de Seguros e Afins*. These cases concern EFSF, EFSM, and BoP assistance. The Court has claimed the lack of a link to EU law despite the implementation of the conditions into a Council decision. See C Barnard, 'The Charter, the Court – and the Crisis' (2013) University of Cambridge Faculty of Law Research Paper No 18/2013.

to share a great deal of information regarding their budget and their economy with the Commission, which analyses countries' reports and gives them specific recommendations. The Commission is supposed to ensure, among other things, that Member States comply with a strengthened Stability and Growth Pact. If a Member State runs an excessive deficit, it will be under special obligations to report and follow recommendations; the Council may impose sanctions on euro countries. The Commission will also ensure that Member States' economies do not suffer macroeconomic or competitiveness imbalances (eg concerning liabilities of the financial sector, level of unemployment, or house prices)[53] – if that is the case, the euro country in trouble will, again, have special obligations, and sanctions may be imposed. In general, the EU has legislated to regulate the different aspects of EU surveillance and correction of the budgetary and economic policies of all Member States, and especially of eurozone members.

The first measures adopted by the EU in this regard constitute the Six-Pack: this is a package of measures (five regulations and one directive) adopted in November 2011,[54] with a view to improving the framework for surveillance of budgetary positions and economic policies. These measures create an annual cycle of policy coordination called the 'European Semester' and a procedure for the prevention and correction of macroeconomic imbalances; the measures also strengthen the enforcement of the Stability and Growth Pact by, among other things, creating an enhanced system of sanctions for members of the euro area.[55] Although these sanctions stop short of being automatic, a system of reverse qualified majority voting has been introduced whereby a qualified majority in the Council would be necessary to avoid the imposition of a sanction, rather than in order to impose it.

In May 2013, the so-called Two-Pack was adopted in order to further strengthen surveillance of euro countries. It consists of two regulations: the first one creates an enhanced surveillance mechanism of draft budgetary plans, building on the preventive arm of the Stability and Growth Pact. The second regulation creates a system of enhanced surveillance for euro area countries that face financial difficulties, of automatic application to those countries that receive certain types of financial assistance (including from the ESM).[56]

---

[53] There is a scoreboard containing 11 indicators (including the three mentioned here) that are used to determine the existence of an imbalance; for the 2012 scoreboard, see http://ec.europa.eu/economy_finance/indicators/economic_reforms/eip/

[54] Regulation (EU) No 1173/2011 on the effective enforcement of budgetary surveillance in the euro area (OJ [2011] L306/1); Regulation (EU) No 1174/2011 on enforcement measures to correct excessive macroeconomic imbalances in the euro area (OJ [2011] L306/8); Regulation (EU) No 1175/2011 on the strengthening of the surveillance of budgetary positions and the surveillance and coordination of economic policies (OJ [2011] L306/12); Regulation (EU) No 1176/2011 on the prevention and correction of macroeconomic imbalances (OJ [2011] L306/25); Council Regulation (EU) No 1177/2011 on speeding up and clarifying the implementation of the excessive deficit procedure (OJ [2011] L306/33); Council Directive 2011/85/EU on requirements for budgetary frameworks of the Member States (OJ [2011] L306/41).

[55] Regulation 1173/2011 (see n 54) creates gradual financial sanctions for euro area countries; this covers both the preventive and the corrective arm of the Stability and Growth Pact. Regulation 1174/2011 (n 54) foresees the imposition of enforcement measures to correct excessive macroeconomic imbalances in the euro area.

[56] Based on Arts 136 and 121 TFEU, and of application to euro countries. Regulation (EU) No 473/2013 on common provisions for monitoring and assessing draft budgetary plans and ensuring the correction of excessive deficit of the Member States in the euro area (OJ [2013] L140/11); Regulation (EU) No 472/2013 on the strengthening of economic and budgetary surveillance of Member States in the euro area experiencing or threatened with serious difficulties with respect to their financial stability (OJ [2013] L140/1).

5.2.2 The Euro Plus Pact

At the European Council Meeting of 24–25 March 2011,[57] the heads of State or government of the euro area, plus six other Member States,[58] agreed to adopt a 'Euro Plus Pact' in order to 'achieve a new quality of economic policy coordination'.[59]

The Pact focuses on four areas: competitiveness, public finance, employment, and financial stability. It does not impose enforceable legal obligations on the Member States which signed it: the latter 'undertake' to enhance economic coordination in areas that remain firmly within national competence. While agreeing on economic objectives, 'participating Member States will pursue these objectives with their own policy-mix'.[60] The document sets out a series of reforms that shall be given special consideration in order to achieve each aim.[61] Member States report on their commitments and progress within the framework of the European Semester, but no sanctions can be imposed.

5.2.3 The Treaty on Stability, Coordination and Governance

In December 2011, the European Council agreed on the need for a new fiscal treaty or fiscal compact that would foster budgetary discipline further and that would allow the members of the euro area to 'move towards a stronger economic union',[62] and to 'work towards a common economic policy'.[63] The first intention was to adopt such a treaty within the framework of the EU. Ultimately, the UK's refusal thwarted this plan, and it was agreed that the new treaty would be a purely intergovernmental instrument adopted outside the EU framework, albeit with institutional ties to it.[64] After several drafts of the treaty were made public, an agreement was reached on the final text at the European Council meeting of 30 January 2012; the resulting 'Treaty on Stability, Coordination and Governance in the EMU' (hereafter TSCG) was signed on 2 March 2012 by all Member States apart from the UK, the Czech Republic, and Croatia, which joined the EU subsequently. The Treaty entered into force on 1 January 2013 for the 16 Member States that had ratified it prior to this date.[65]

The TSCG has two clearly distinguishable parts: one dealing with budgetary discipline, and one concerning economic convergence and cooperation.[66]

---

[57] European Council, 'Conclusions – 24/25 March 2011', EUCO 10/1/11 REV 1, http://www.consilium.europa.eu/uedocs/cms_data/docs/pressdata/en/ec/120296.pdf

[58] Bulgaria, Denmark, Latvia, Lithuania, Poland, Romania. The Pact remains open to the remaining Member States if they wish to join.

[59] EUCO 10/1/11 REV 1 (n 57) 5.   [60] Ibid, Annex 1, 14.

[61] In the case of employment, eg the reforms to be given consideration include 'flexicurity', life-long learning, and tax reforms.

[62] Statement by the euro area heads of State or government, 9 December 2011, 1.

[63] Ibid, 5. This commitment to a 'common economic policy' was also mentioned in the earlier drafts of the TSCG, but it was removed later on and it is not present in the final signed version.

[64] As a general observation, the intergovernmental nature of the TSCG and its place outside the institutional structure of the EU is reflected in the fact that, while there is a certain involvement of the EU institutions, this has been kept to a minimum. Indeed, while the use of the EU institutions may lend more credibility to the commitments set out in a treaty of this kind, it is problematic to square this use with the EU Treaties, and to make it politically palatable. On the relationship with the EU Treaties and the legal problems arising from the use of EU institutions, see House of Lords EU Select Committee, 'The Euro Area Crisis' (n 27) 28 et seq. For a thorough but concise legal analysis, see Editorial Comments, 'Some Thoughts concerning the Draft Treaty on a Reinforced Economic Union' (2012) 49 *Common Market Law Review* 1; S Peers, 'The Stability Treaty: Permanent Austerity or Gesture Politics?' (2012) 8 *European Constitutional Law Review* 404.

[65] For subsequent ratifiers, the Treaty entered into force on the first day of the month following their ratification. As of March 2014, the Treaty had been ratified by 24 out of 25 signatories (Belgium was in the process of completing ratification).

[66] The Treaty also deals with governance of the euro (concerning, eg regular meetings of the euro area and their organization); this part will not be discussed here.

As regards budgetary discipline, the Treaty sets out certain balance rules on fiscal stance that Member States shall implement at the national level, and it imposes limits on the size of public debt and structural deficit, covering similar ground to previous instruments such as the Stability and Growth Pact and the Six-Pack.[67] The most important addition in this respect is the obligation to implement rules on budgetary discipline into national law.[68] Whereas a previous draft made it obligatory to implement these rules into the national constitution, the final Treaty does not go as far – merely stating that implementation at the constitutional level is 'preferable'. If not of constitutional rank, the rules should be, at least, 'otherwise guaranteed to be fully respected and adhered to throughout the national budgetary processes' (Article 3(2) TSCG). This will allow several signatories to avoid a referendum – which would have been required, were it necessary to amend the national constitution. Finally, although the TSCG is not part of the legal system of the EU, its signatories agreed to give jurisdiction to the Court of Justice to monitor compliance with the duty to implement the rules on budgetary discipline into national law.[69]

The second front of the TSCG is economic convergence: Member States undertake 'to work jointly towards an economic policy that fosters the proper functioning of the economic and monetary union', through 'enhanced convergence'.[70] As to the specific tools to be used, on the one hand, Article 9 TSCG states that the contracting parties will take 'the necessary actions and measures in all the areas which are essential to the proper functioning of the euro area',[71] an undertaking which could be interpreted quite broadly. An earlier draft of the Treaty referred in this provision to the Euro Plus Pact. It would seem that the drafters were thinking, here, of the sort of soft law initiative that the Euro Plus Pact exemplifies: political commitments that are enforced through soft law mechanisms rather than sanctions.

On the other hand, the contracting parties shall also seek to use EU law 'whenever appropriate and necessary' (Article 10 TSCG). To that end, they undertake to make use of the competence contained in Article 136 TFEU (which allows the Council to adopt measures aimed at strengthening budgetary surveillance within the euro area, and broad economic policy guidelines for the same countries)[72] and of the enhanced cooperation mechanism (mentioned already, in the *Pringle* case study) set out in Article 20 TEU and Articles 326 to 334 TFEU.

All in all, it seems fair to conclude that the legal significance of the Treaty is limited – political significance being, of course, a different matter.[73] The Treaty does not add much that is 'new' in terms of economic or fiscal integration, apart from the judicially enforceable duty on the contracting parties to introduce the budget disciplinary rules into national

---

[67] National budgets must be in balance or surplus; this requirement would be met if the annual structural government deficit does not exceed 0.5 per cent of GDP at market prices.

[68] This is for the first time a legally binding obligation, but the Euro Plus Pact already contained the same commitment. For an analysis, see Editorial, 'The Fiscal Compact and the European Constitutions: "Europe Speaking German"' (2012) 8 *European Constitutional Law Review* 1; F Fabbrini, 'The Fiscal Compact, the "Golden Rule", and the Paradox of European Federalism' (2013) 36 *Boston College International and Comparative Law Review* 1.

[69] This is made possible by the TFEU itself, Art 273.   [70] Art 9 TSCG.

[71] Art 9 TSCG continues: 'in pursuit of the objectives of fostering competitiveness, promoting employment, contributing further to the sustainability of public finances and reinforcing financial stability.'

[72] Art 136 TFEU allows the Council to use the procedures in Arts 121 and 126 TFEU (which concern the issuing of Broad Economic Policy Guidelines and the excessive deficit procedure) to adopt measures that affect only euro area members. As a result of this power, eg part of the Six-Pack (concerning enforcement), and all of the Two-Pack, are applicable only to euro area members.

[73] From that point of view, the Treaty may be considered an attempt to show leadership and appease investors, as well as an attempt to make bail-outs more palatable to (paying) domestic electorates.

law.[74] Of course, much will depend on how some of its provisions are interpreted by the signatories in the future.

More generally, though, the TSCG is another manifestation of a trend that has been discussed already in this chapter: the rise of intergovernmentalism in dealing with the eurozone crisis, and the willingness to act formally outside the EU legal order when necessary, while still using or allocating tasks to some of the EU institutions. The Court of Justice considered this use of the EU to be in accordance with EU law in *Pringle*; however, in that case, all Member States had given their consent to the use of EU institutions within the ESM Treaty, albeit that the Court did not mention this as a requirement. On the contrary, the UK did not give its consent to the allocation of tasks to EU institutions in the TSCG; at the time of writing, however, the UK had not challenged the legality of this allocation before the Court.[75]

5.3 Financial regulation and banking union

The global financial crisis that started in 2007 was the precursor to the euro area sovereign debt crisis: in some cases, euro countries amassed unmanageable debt because they had to bail out their banks. More generally, the financial crisis worsened the economic problems of certain euro countries, and made it more difficult for them to borrow money. So it is natural that part of the EU's response to the crisis has been to seek better regulation of the financial markets, in order to avoid a similar financial crisis in the future.[76] Some of these reforms apply to the whole EU financial sector, not just within the euro area. These reforms include setting up a new framework of financial supervision with a new European Banking Authority,[77] as well as the progressive building of a 'single rulebook', a single set of common rules that would apply to all financial institutions operating in the EU. At the moment, the single rulebook comprises, inter alia, stricter rules on capital requirements for financial institutions,[78] and revised harmonizing rules on national deposit-guarantee schemes;[79] other proposals include common rules on recovery and resolution tools, with a

---

[74] As well as certain obligations to support the Commission when it comes to applying the excessive deficit procedure (Art 7 TSCG). This means that the contracting parties commit not to vote in Council against sanctions proposed by the Commission, although this obligation cannot be legally enforced.

[75] S Peers, 'Towards a New Form of EU Law?' (n 46) 53–55.

[76] N Moloney, 'EU Financial Market Regulation after the Global Financial Crisis: "More Europe" or More Risks?' (2010) 47 *Common Market Law Review* 1317; E Ferran, 'Crisis-Driven Regulatory Reform: Where in the World is the EU Going?' in E Ferran, N Moloney, JA Hill, and JC Coffee (eds), *The Regulatory Aftermath of the Financial Crisis* (Cambridge: Cambridge University Press, 2012).

[77] Together with a European Insurance and Occupational Pensions Authority, a European Securities and Markets Authority, and a European Systemic Risk Board. Regulation (EU) No 1093/2010 establishing a European Supervisory Authority (European Banking Authority) (OJ [2010] L331/12); Regulation (EU) No 1094/2010 establishing a European Supervisory Authority (European Insurance and Occupational Pensions Authority) (OJ [2010] L331/48); Regulation (EU) No 1095/2010 establishing a European Supervisory Authority (European Securities and Markets Authority) (OJ [2010] L331/84); Regulation (EU) No 1092/2010 on European Union macro-prudential oversight of the financial system and establishing a European Systemic Risk Board (OJ [2010] L331/1).

[78] Directive 2009/111/EC on banks affiliated to central institutions, certain own funds items, large exposures, supervisory arrangements, and crisis management (OJ [2009] L302/97); Directive 2010/76/EU on capital requirements for the trading book and for re-securitisations, and the supervisory review of remuneration policies (OJ [2010] L329/3); and the more recent and stronger prudential requirements for banks adopted in 2013: Regulation (EU) No 575/2013 of the European Parliament and of the Council of 26 June 2013 on prudential requirements for credit institutions and investment firms (OJ [2013] L176/1) and Directive 2013/36/EU of the European Parliament and of the Council of 26 June 2013 on access to the activity of credit institutions and the prudential supervision of credit institutions and investment firms (OJ [2009] L176/338).

[79] See Directive 2009/14/EC on deposit-guarantee schemes (OJ [2009] L68/3) and the more comprehensive reform of the rules in this area proposed by the Commission in July 2010 (negotiations are still

view to helping national authorities intervene to manage banks in difficulty.[80] Finally, the EU has also adopted stricter measures regulating credit-rating agencies.[81]

Other reforms would apply in principle to the euro area, although they are open to other Member States wishing to join: the intention is to create a so-called 'banking union',[82] which starts with a single supervisory mechanism for banks, led by the ECB,[83] and which would also comprise a single resolution mechanism, in order to deal with the failure of banks within the euro area in a centralized manner.[84] The ESM, discussed earlier in this chapter, will be able to recapitalize banks directly once a single supervisory mechanism for all euro area banks is in effect.

6 The future of EMU

So what next for EMU? The intention behind the post-crisis measures adopted by the EU and the Member States was, one, to bring the euro area out of the acute phase of the crisis, and two, to foster confidence by improving the way in which economic coordination happens in the future. At the time of writing, the measures seem to have achieved the first objective; only time will tell how effective they are in achieving the second one.

The crisis, however, has also prompted a more general discussion as to the future of EMU, and even as to the future of the EU as a political project. Do we want more than just economic coordination? Do we think that it is the 'destiny' of EMU to lead to a full economic union – and, if so, does this presuppose a full political union too?

If the EMU were to venture beyond economic coordination (ie towards a full economic or fiscal union), it could do so by either granting the EU the competence to conduct its own fiscal policy – which would mean that the EU would raise taxes and would thus have its own independent budget – and its own broader economic policy. Alternatively, the EU could be given more and more powers over the fiscal and economic policies of the Member States; so, while the EU would not have its own resources, it would gain power over how Member States raise revenues, and what they do with them. Incidentally, some might argue that the EU is already attempting to gain this sort of control, if through primarily soft law mechanisms (as we saw in section 5.2, the Commission makes specific recommendations to Member States in its country reports). Regardless, taking either of these paths to their natural conclusion would substantially change the nature of the EU, as well as of the

ongoing at the time of writing): Commission Proposal for a Directive on Deposit Guarantee Schemes (recast), COM(2010) 369.

[80] At the time of writing, finance ministers of the Member States had reached an agreement on the proposal for a Bank Recovery and Resolution Directive (ECOFIN Council of 27 June 2013): 11148/1/13 REV 1.

[81] Regulation (EU) No 462/2013 on credit rating agencies (OJ [2009] L146/1) and Directive 2013/14/EC (OJ [2013] L145/1).

[82] Conclusions from the European Council of 27–28 June 2013, EUCO 104/2/13; Communication from the Commission to the European Parliament and the Council: a Roadmap towards a Banking Union, COM(2012) 510 final.

[83] Council Regulation (EU) No 1024/2013 conferring specific tasks on the ECB concerning policies relating to the prudential supervision of credit institutions; Regulation (EU) No 1022/2013 of the European Parliament and of the Council amending Regulation (EU) No 1093/2010 establishing a European Supervisory Authority (EBA) as regards the conferral of specific tasks on the ECB pursuant to Council Regulation (EU) No 1024/2013.

[84] At the time of writing, there was still no agreement on the SRM package: Commission Proposal for a Regulation establishing uniform rules and a uniform procedure for the resolution of credit institutions and certain investment firms in the framework of a Single Resolution Mechanism and a Single Bank Resolution Fund, COM(2013) 520 final.

relationship between the EU and the Member States; these changes may require substantial political reforms.[85]

It is possible to think of further steps towards integration within EMU that are more limited in nature: it is the case, for example, of the proposed 'Eurobonds',[86] a mechanism for the mutualization of debt among euro area countries. These bonds would be issued by either a single euro country or the whole eurozone (there are different versions of the proposal); all members of the eurozone would be liable for the debt. These proposals have not been successful so far: in the absence of more effective coordination of national fiscal and economic policies, some members of the euro area are reluctant to mutualize or be jointly responsible for debt in this way.

There are powerful reasons why it is difficult to push EMU further than what it is now without corresponding reforms in the political realm. We have already discussed some of them briefly in section 5; now we will focus on the problem of democratic legitimacy and the fears of national constitutional courts.

6.1 **Democratic legitimacy**

A significant obstacle to a full-fledged EU economic and fiscal policy is democratic legitimacy: the question is to what extent an overarching capacity to determine the amount and provenance of public resources and its uses (thus including taxation, but also, eg social insurance mechanisms) can be decoupled from national politics, in the absence of a comparable degree of democratic legitimacy at the EU level. This problem seems much more acute when considering the direct redistribution of wealth that comes with fiscal policy than when considering purely regulatory policies, such as the single market. In the latter, the previously mentioned decoupling from national politics has already occurred, to a certain degree.[87]

The debate concerning the democratic deficit of the EU has been going on for years; it is a nuanced, varied debate to which this chapter can only nod briefly. One of the generally accepted premises of the debate is that, although the role of the European Parliament has grown over the years, the EU cannot claim to have the degree of representative democracy that States have. Where opinions diverge is to what extent this is a fatal flaw. Some argue that because only limited competences have been delegated to the EU the Union needs less democratic legitimacy than a State, and that it derives enough indirect legitimacy from national politics.[88] Many argue that the EU is able to generate democratic legitimacy of

---

[85] For the Commission's take on the future of EMU, see its 'Blueprint for a deep and genuine economic and monetary union: launching a European debate', COM(2012) 777 final, as well as the Commission's Communications to the European Parliament and Council, 'Towards a deep and genuine Economic and Monetary Union: Ex ante coordination of plans for major economic policy reforms', COM(2013) 166 final, and 'Towards a Deep and Genuine Economic and Monetary Union: The introduction of a Convergence and Competitiveness Instrument', COM(2013) 165 final.   [86] See n 35.

[87] See eg C Joerges, 'The Market without the State? The "Economic Constitution" of the European Community and the Rebirth of Regulatory Politics' (1997) 1 *European Integration online Papers*, art 19. More generally, on 'disembedded' market and politics, K Polanyi, *The Great Transformation: The Political and Economic Origins of Our Time* (Boston, MA: Beacon Press, 2011); C Joerges and J Falke (eds), *Karl Polanyi, Globalisation and the Potential of Law in Transnational Markets* (Oxford: Hart Publishing, 2011).

[88] Either through the involvement of national executives in law-making, or because of the original consent given to the Treaties, or a combination of both. See A Moravcsik, 'In Defence of the "Democratic Deficit": Reassessing Legitimacy in the EU' (2002) 40 *Journal of Common Market Studies* 603; A Moravcsik, 'Preferences and Power in the European Community: A Liberal Intergovernmental Approach' (1993) 31 *Journal of Common Market Studies* 473; G Majone, *Regulating Europe* (London: Routledge, 1996); G Majone, 'Europe's "Democratic Deficit": The Question of Standards' (1998) 4 *European Law Journal* 5; G Majone,

its own through mechanisms that are different from the ones typically found within the national framework, such as deliberative democracy, and through the protection of outsiders whose interests are not represented within – but affected by – national politics.[89]

Convincing as these arguments may be, it is still arguable that a fiscal policy, encompassing matters such as the redistribution of wealth through taxation and the organization of the welfare system, for example, would require a higher degree of democratic legitimacy than the establishing and functioning of the internal market does, even with all the latter's ramifications. Fiscal measures, with taxation as the paramount example, speak very directly to the link between the citizen and the State. The power to impose the positive obligation on citizens to contribute taxes (as well as the general power to determine how this wealth is going to be distributed)[90] seems to necessitate a degree of political contestation and of connection between the citizen and the State that is currently lacking at the EU level, either through representative or deliberative democracy. Equally, a full fiscal policy would be too essential and wide-ranging to be characterized as part of a limited delegation of powers to the Union, with sufficient indirect legitimacy being derived from national politics.[91]

6.2 'Reserved domains' and the disappearing State

A connected concern is the extent to which taking steps towards a full economic/fiscal union would threaten essential aspects of the Member States' identity as States. While this question may seem primarily theoretical, it has an important practical side: it is unlikely that national constitutional courts would allow integration to proceed to a stage that threatens or does away with an important aspect of their State's constitutional identity, however defined. 'Constitutional identity' is the term used by the German Federal Constitutional Court, but several national constitutional courts have made largely similar remarks to the effect that there must be limits to European integration – imposed by the national constitutions that they enforce – because certain areas are too integral to the sovereignty or the identity of the Sate.[92]

Dilemmas of European Integration (Oxford: Oxford University Press, 2005); and P Lindseth, *Power and Legitimacy: Reconciling Europe and the Nation-State* (Oxford: Oxford University Press, 2010). On different intellectual approaches to democratic legitimacy in the EU, see AJ Menéndez, 'The European Democratic Challenge: The Forging of a Supranational Volonté Générale' (2009) 15 *European Law Journal* 277.

[89] See eg Menéndez, 'The European Democratic Challenge' (n 88) 15; D Curtin, 'Framing Public Deliberation and Democratic Legitimacy in the European Union' in S Besson et al (eds), *Deliberative Democracy and Its Discontents* (Aldershot: Ashgate, 2006); and D Halberstam, 'The Bride of Messina: Constitutionalism and Democracy in Europe' (2005) 30 *European Law Review* 775. On the EU as a corrector of national political processes, see also M Maduro, *We, the Court* (Oxford: Hart Publishing, 1998) 168 *et seq*; M Poiares Maduro, 'Europe and the Constitution: What if This is as Good as It Gets?' (2000) Webpapers on Constitutionalism & Governance beyond the State, No 5, 11. Maduro further argues that giving a voice to foreign actors may even raise the voice of some domestic actors in cases where the national political process has been captured by a national interest group: ibid, 18–19. More generally, see D Held, *Democracy and the Global Order* (Cambridge: Polity Press, 1995).

[90] While the law of the single market may have a bearing on some of these decisions, what is discussed here is a general power to adopt these decisions even when there is no connection to the internal market; there is a crucial difference of degree.

[91] Moravscik's argument is based on the fact that the EU is limited to a 'modest subset of the substantive activities pursued by modern states'. He explicitly excludes taxation and the setting of fiscal priorities, among other essential areas: Moravcsik, 'In Defence of the "Democratic Deficit"' (n 88) 607.

[92] See eg Case K32/09 *Treaty of Lisbon*, judgment of Polish Constitutional Tribunal of 24 November 2010; *Re Constitutionality of Framework Decision on the European Arrest Warrant* (Czech Constitutional Court) [2007] 3 CMLR 24. For an overview, see D Chalmers 'Democratic Self-Government in Europe' (2013) Policy Network Paper, 15 May 2013.

The German Federal Constitutional Court has been most vocal on the question of limits to integration, which it addressed explicitly in its decision on the Lisbon Treaty.[93] The German Court went on to ground the existence of these limits to European integration on the need for democratic legitimacy (which takes us back to the previous section). It stated that the 'constitutional identity' of Germany required legitimate democratic government. Building on its seminal *Maastricht* decision,[94] the German court then drew a link between certain areas of competence, real democratic legitimacy, and the State.[95] It contended that, in order to regulate or govern these areas legitimately, democratic representation of the kind that is found only in a State is necessary. The court concluded that, unless things changed dramatically in the future (ie unless the Member States were willing to change the current constitutional settlement and, one assumes, create a federal State at the EU level that would have the representative democratic legitimacy of a State),[96] there would always be certain areas of competence that needed to remain the purview of national democracy. Transferring these competences in the current circumstances would go against the 'constitutional identity' of Germany: neither the German Constitution nor the German court would allow this. Crucially for our discussion here, these special competences, or 'reserved domains', highlighted in the *Lisbon* judgment include 'fundamental fiscal decisions on public revenue and expenditure, [and] decisions on the shaping of the social state'.[97]

The German court's later decisions on the constitutionality of the Greek bail-out and Germany's guarantees to the EFSF,[98] which insisted on the need for parliamentary approval in every individual instance, refer once more to budgetary powers (the exercise of which is legitimized through representative democracy) as part of the constitutional identity of Germany. When considering the legality of the ESM Treaty, the German court considered again that national parliamentary approval was necessary for any increase in Germany's contribution to the fund.[99] It seems that a transfer of power to the EU to create its own fiscal policy would inevitably tread into some of the domains identified by the German court, and it seems safe to assume that other national constitutional courts would be equally troubled by these developments.[100] As mentioned previously, several other constitutional

---

[93] Decision of 30 June 2009, BVerfGE 123, 267. For comments on this case, see D Thym, 'In the Name of Sovereign Statehood: A Critical Introduction to the Lisbon Judgment of the German Constitutional Court' (2009) 46 *Common Market Law Review* 1795; M Payandeh, 'Constitutional Review of EU Law after *Honeywell*: Contextualising the Relationship between the German Constitutional Court and the EU Court of Justice' (2011) 48 *Common Market Law Review* 9.   [94] Decision of 12 October 1993, BVerfGE 89, 155.

[95] Decision of 30 June 2009 (n 93) para 175.

[96] In its decision, the German court equates democratic legitimacy with the legitimacy that emanates from representative democracy, without considering other concepts of democracy that have been put forward as being more adequate for the EU and also potentially capable of legitimizing government (see n 94).

[97] Decision of 30 June 2009 (n 93) para 252: 'decisions on substantive and procedural criminal law, on the disposition of the monopoly on the use of force by the police and by the military, fundamental fiscal decisions on public revenue and expenditure, decisions on the shaping of the social state and of particular cultural importance, for example on family law, the school and education system and on dealing with religious communities.'

[98] Decision of 7 September 2011, BVerfGE, 2 BvR 987/10; 2 BvR 1485/10; 2 BvR 1099/10. On the German court's judgment and its relationship to the EU response to the euro crisis, see Editorial, 'The Euro Crisis: Storm, meet Structure' (2011) 7 *European Constitutional Law Review* 349. Several months later, the German court rejected that a parliamentary committee consisting of nine members could give the necessary parliamentary approval: decision of 28 February 2012, BVerfGE, 2 BveE 8/11.

[99] Decision of 12 September 2012, BVerfGE, 2 BvR 1390/12; 2 BvR 1421/12; 2 BvR 1438/12; 2 BvR 1439/12; 2 BvR 1440/12; 2 BvE 6/12. This concerned the legality of both the ESM Treaty and the TSCG.

[100] The Court of Justice, for its part, acknowledged a Member State's 'constitutional identity' as a limit to EU law in Case C-208/09 *Ilonka Sayn-Wittgenstein v Landeshauptmann von Wien* [2010] ECR I-13693. For a comment of this aspect of the case, see LFM Besselink, 'Respecting Constitutional Identity in the European

courts have also referred to a list of similarly 'reserved domains'; some of them have also grounded their reasoning on the need for democratic legitimacy explicitly,[101] while others have just argued that certain areas are part of the core of a State's sovereignty.[102]

Of course, we do not know how the German Federal Constitutional Court will apply its 'constitutional identity' doctrine in this area in the future; the same goes for other national constitutional courts that have expressed similar concerns. It is likely that this vague limit would preclude rather extreme developments, but it has not, for the time being, precluded ratification of the treaties creating the EFSF and ESM, or of the TSCG.[103]

7 Conclusion

The elements of EMU include a centrally conducted monetary policy, a common currency for those countries within the euro area, and coordination of fiscal and economic policies that remain national in nature. This chapter has provided an introduction to the historical origins and set-up of EMU, and it has shown that there is an imbalance between the more centralized part of this Union (monetary policy) and the decentralized part (fiscal and economic policy). This tension has been a constant of EMU since its inception, and it is connected to the sovereign debt crisis in the euro area.

EMU has evolved in recent years due to the need to address the immediate effects of the euro area crisis and to avoid future ones. This chapter has distinguished between three different approaches taken by the EU and its Member States in this regard: (a) stabilization through the evolving role of the ECB and the creation of bail-out mechanisms, (b) the creation of further budgetary and economic coordination measures, and (c) further financial regulation for the whole of the EU and steps towards an eventual banking union in the euro area.

While the measures adopted by the EU and the Member States seem to have brought the euro area out of the acute phase of the crisis, it remains to be seen how successful they will be in improving economic coordination in the future and addressing the tension at the heart of EMU. More generally, the crisis has also prompted a general debate on the future of EMU and of the EU as a political project. The question is whether EMU should move beyond economic coordination and towards a full economic union; and, crucially, whether – or to what degree – this move would require turning the EU into a full political union.

Economic and fiscal policy are very sensitive areas, where important decisions are taken concerning the allocation of resources in society. These decisions touch upon our understanding of social justice, solidarity, and the role of the State. Accordingly, many still feel that these policies are most appropriately debated and conducted within the national political process. The idea of a growing role for the EU in these areas is often met with concern, and the argument that the EU does not have, at this moment, the necessary democratic

Union: An Essay on ECJ (Second Chamber), Case C-208/09, 22 December 2010, *Ilonka Sayn-Wittgenstein v. Landeshauptmann von Wien*' (2012) 49 *Common Market Law Review* 671. See further Case C-51/08 *Commission v Luxembourg* [2011] ECR I-4231.

[101] See eg *Treaty of Lisbon* (n 92) *Re Constitutionality of Framework Decision on the European Arrest Warrant* (n 92).

[102] See eg *Ratification of the Lisbon Treaty* (French Constitutional Council) Case 2007-560 [2010] 2 CMLR 26.

[103] At the time of writing, the German Federal Constitutional Court is still to decide on the legality of the ECB's Outright Monetary Transactions Scheme, see n 42.

legitimacy to decide on matters such as taxation or the size and features of the welfare state. So while it may seem necessary for EMU to evolve, the euro area countries and the institutions of the EU find themselves in uncharted, and extremely uncertain, waters.

Further reading

C BARNARD, 'The Charter, the Court – and the Crisis' (2013) University of Cambridge Faculty of Law Research Paper No 18/2013

B DE WITTE AND T BEULKERS, 'The Court of Justice Approves the Creation of the European Stability Mechanism outside the EU Legal Order: *Pringle*' (2013) 50 *Common Market Law Review* 805

M MADURO, 'A New Governance for the European Union and the Euro: Democracy and Justice' (2012) RSCAS Policy Paper 2012/11

AJ MENENDEZ, 'The Existential Crisis of the European Union' (2013) 14 *German Law Journal* 453

S PEERS, 'The Stability Treaty: Permanent Austerity or Gesture Politics?' (2012) 8 *European Constitutional Law Review* 404

S PEERS, 'Towards a New Form of EU Law? The Use of EU Institutions outside the EU Legal Framework' (2013) 9 *European Constitutional Law Review* 37

K TUORI 'The European Financial Crisis: Constitutional Aspects and Implications' (2012) EUI Working Papers, Law 2012/28

20

Labour and equality law

Mia Rönnmar

1 Introduction

Labour and equality law is central to the functioning of society and economy – but also to the everyday life of individuals. Labour law regulates the individual employment relationship and employment rights, as well as the labour market more generally, and the relations between the State, employers and employees, and their representatives – the social partners. Equality law nowadays is a central part of labour law, but also extends its reach beyond working life. Both the development and content of EU labour and equality law throughout the years – and still today – reflect a tension between the EU and national sovereignty, economic and social integration, and market and human rights discourses.

Labour and equality law is regulated by a complex mix of Treaty provisions, fundamental rights, and general principles of EU law, secondary law, collective agreements at EU level, case law from the Court of Justice, and soft law measures. To this we can add regulation at national level. A selection of key labour and equality law issues are discussed in this chapter, such as restructuring of enterprises; information, consultation, and worker participation;

fundamental Treaty freedoms and national collective labour law; flexible work and working conditions; the EU and national labour law in times of economic crisis; and gender equality, comprehensive equality, and protection against discrimination on other grounds.

Section 2 presents the legal framework and evolution of EU labour and equality law. Section 3 provides a discussion on some central issues in EU labour law. Section 4 continues with a similar discussion on EU equality law. Section 5 contains some concluding remarks.

2 The legal framework and evolution of EU labour and equality law

2.1 The evolution of EU labour and equality law and Treaty developments

Social policy is often understood to include areas connected to the welfare state, such as social security, social assistance, health care, and housing. At EU level most of the (hard law) regulation in the area of social policy refers to EU labour and equality law.[1] Together they form part of the EU social model, an often-used, but rather vague, concept. Values such as democracy, individual rights, collective bargaining, the market economy, equality of opportunity, and flexicurity (ie combining flexibility for employers and security for employees) are said to be central to the European social model, a model which is recognized by all EU institutions.[2] Despite a (common) European social model there is still great variety among the Member States' labour law and industrial relations systems, as regards, for example, the importance of constitutional principles, the balance between legislation and collective bargaining, the degree of State intervention or voluntarism, the role of the courts and case law, and the degree of trade union organization and forms of workers' representation. Traditionally reference has been made to the Romano-Germanic system, the Anglo-Irish system, and the Nordic system of industrial relations. In the Romano-Germanic system the State plays a central and active role in industrial relations, and an emphasis is put on constitutional and statutory regulation of employment rights. In several countries belonging to this system, collective agreements can be extended to all employees and employers. Within the Romano-Germanic system the southern Mediterranean States display some specific characteristics, as do the countries which joined the EU as part of the enlargement since 2004. The Anglo-Irish system, in line with voluntarism or collective laissez-faire, provides a limited role for the State. Collective agreements are not legally binding, and there is no extensive statutory regulation, although there is a trend towards increasing legislative activity. Similarly, the Nordic system builds on voluntarism and statutory non-intervention. Collective agreements are an important legal source, and set wages

---

[1] In principle, the substantive content of social security is a matter for the Member States and national legislation. However, the coordination of social security in the EU and between the Member States was implemented early on as a way to facilitate the free movement of workers, see now Regulation 883/2004 (OJ [2004] L166/1). Through soft law and the open method of coordination not only employment policy, but also aspects linked to social security, such as old-age pensions, social inclusion, and social protection, have been further developed. Social security aspects, such as the coordination of social security will, in principle, not be discussed here, see eg F Pennings, *European Social Security Law* (5th edn, Antwerp: Intersentia, 2010). Aspects on free movement of workers, discrimination on grounds of nationality, and EU citizenship are also excluded here, see chapter 13.

[2] The concept of the 'social dimension of the EU' refers – in contrast to the economic dimension – to the part of EU politics and legal regulations connected to the citizen's social needs, social protection, and social integration. The labour market, social security, and families are central areas of regulation in the social dimension, see A Numhauser-Henning and M Rönnmar (eds), *Normative Patterns and the Legal Development of the Social Dimension of the EU* (Oxford: Hart Publishing, 2013).

and working conditions. The trade union organization rates are high, as well as the collective bargaining coverage rate. However, today there is also quite extensive statutory regulation, often providing for derogations by way of collective agreements.[3]

EU labour and equality law aims for a partial harmonization of the different labour law and industrial relations systems in the Member States. This partial harmonization is reflected in the fact that the personal scope of most EU labour and equality law directives is defined in relation to the different notions of an employee, developed and existing in each of the Member States. However, in the area of free movement of workers, EU law contains a separate, autonomous, and far-reaching notion of an employee. This uniform notion of an employee has recently seemed to 'spread' into other areas of labour and equality law, such as equal pay and working time.[4]

There is no comprehensive coverage of EU labour and equality law, nor does it replicate national labour law in this area. Furthermore, EU labour law emphasizes and regulates issues of a cross-border nature and the intersection between the internal market and fundamental freedoms and national labour law.[5]

The legal framework for the adoption of EU rules on labour and equality law has changed a number of times, and Treaty competence has gradually expanded (from the single provision on equal pay in the Treaty of Rome,[6] where labour law was seen mainly as a domestic issue and the focus was on economic integration and free movement, to the current elaborate Treaty support, through important revisions in, for example, the Maastricht, Amsterdam, and Lisbon Treaties).[7] Secondary law is now well developed, and a large number of directives have been adopted in this area. The development has not been linear, however. There have been phases of activity, such as in the 1970s, when a number of directives, for example, in the area of equality law and restructuring of enterprises, were adopted with reference to the 1974 Social Action Programme, and the Court of Justice delivered a number of important judgments. On the other hand, we have also witnessed phases of inactivity or stagnation, such as at the beginning of the 1980s.

EU labour and equality law is an area of shared competence, and the principles of subsidiarity and proportionality are thus important.[8] Article 3(3) TEU states that:

> The Union shall establish an internal market. It shall work for the sustainable development of Europe based on balanced economic growth and price stability, a highly competitive social market economy, aiming at full employment and social progress, and a high level of protection and improvement of the quality of the environment....It shall combat social exclusion and discrimination, and shall promote social justice and protection, equality between women and men, solidarity between generations and protection of the rights of the child.

---

[3] See eg C Barnard, *EU Employment Law* (4th edn, Oxford: Oxford University Press, 2012) 58 *et seq* and B Hepple and B Veneziani (eds), *The Transformation of Labour Law in Europe: A Comparative Study of 15 Countries 1945–2004* (Oxford: Hart Publishing, 2009).

[4] See Case C-66/85 *Lawrie-Blum v Land Baden-Württemberg* [1986] ECR 2121 and Case C-53/81 *Levin v Secretary of State for Justice* [1982] ECR 1035. cf also Case C-428/09 *Union syndicale Solidaires Isère* [2010] ECR I-9961. See M Freedland and N Kountouris, *The Legal Construction of Personal Work Relations* (Oxford: Oxford University Press, 2011) for a comparative and theoretical discussion on the legal construction of the employment relationship.

[5] See eg A Davies, *EU Labour Law* (Cheltenham: Edward Elgar, 2012) 3 *et seq* and B Bercusson, *European Labour Law* (2nd edn, Cambridge: Cambridge University Press, 2009). [6] Art 119.

[7] See the chapters by Barnard, More, and Bell in P Craig and G de Búrca (eds), *Evolution of EU Law* (1st and 5th edns, Oxford: Oxford University Press, 1999 and 2011) on the evolution of EU labour and equality law and a close examination of the Treaty developments in this area.

[8] After the Lisbon Treaty expressly stated in Art 4(2)(6)TFEU.

The Lisbon Treaty thus introduced *social market economy* as one of the main aims of the EU, which implies an integration of economic and social integration within the EU and confirms the EU's economic *and* social objectives.[9]

The centrality of the attainment of equality is also emphasized by the Treaty: according to Articles 8 and 10 TFEU the EU must adopt a *mainstreaming* approach in relation to equality and non-discrimination. This means that in *all* its activities and policies (not just those in the social field) it must aim to eliminate inequalities, to promote equality between men and women, and to combat discrimination. In the social field more particularly, Article 151 TFEU provides that the Union and the Member States, having in mind fundamental social rights,[10] shall have as their objective

> the promotion of employment, improved living and working conditions, so as to make possible their harmonisation while the improvement is being maintained, proper social protection, dialogue between management and labour, the development of human resources with a view to lasting high employment and the combating of exclusion.

However, even though the competence of the EU covers labour and equality law areas such as non-discrimination;[11] equality between men and women;[12] flexible work and working conditions, including working time and health and safety; employment protection; and information, consultation, and worker participation,[13] the competence of the EU is still limited.[14] Central aspects of national labour law and industrial relations systems, such as pay, the right of association, the right to strike, and the right to impose lock-outs, are excluded from the EU's competence to adopt directives[15] – though not from the scope of EU law, a question to which we will return later in the discussion of *Viking* and *Laval* and the right to collective action (section 3.2.2).

2.2 Law-making and legal sources in EU labour and equality law

The traditional 'Community method', whereby the Commission proposes legislative measures and the Council and European Parliament adopt them, is important in EU labour and equality law. The main body of EU labour and equality law is made up of directives, which provide flexibility and adaptability in relation to the variety of national labour law and industrial relations systems in the EU.[16] Directives must be implemented in the Member States by legislation or by the social partners (employers' organizations and trade unions) and collective bargaining; however, in the latter case it remains the responsibility of the

---

[9] For a discussion on social market economy and the previous 'decoupling' of economic and social integration, see eg F Scharpf, 'The European Social Model: Coping with the Challenges of Diversity' (2002) 40 *Journal of Common Market Studies* 645.

[10] Set out in international human rights sources such as the Council of Europe's European Social Charter and the EU's Community Charter of the Fundamental Social Rights of Workers.   [11] Art 19 TFEU.

[12] Arts 157 and 153(1)(i) TFEU.

[13] Art 153(1) TFEU. The predecessors to Art 153 TFEU were Art 137 EC and Art 118a EEC.

[14] To adopt directives on the basis of Arts 19 and 153(1)(c), (d), (f), and (g) unanimity is required, while to adopt directives on the basis of Art 157 TFEU and the other parts of Art 153 qualified majority is required.

[15] Art 153(5) TFEU.

[16] Barnard points to the flexibility provided for by three different forms of directives in EU labour and equality law, framework directives, directives aimed at partial harmonization, and directives setting minimum standards which the Member States can improve upon, see Barnard, *EU Employment Law* (n 3) 61 *et seq.*

Member States to guarantee that individuals are afforded the rights and full protection provided by the directive.[17]

In national labour law and industrial relations systems, the social partners are often consulted and involved in the legislative process, and collective agreements regulate working conditions and other labour law issues. The Maastricht Treaty, and the Social Policy Agreement (signed by all Member States except the UK), subsequently integrated into the Treaty through the Treaty of Amsterdam (and thus now applies to the UK), incorporated a similar process at EU level: the *European social dialogue* and collective route to legislation at Union level.[18] The Commission is charged with the task of promoting the consultation of management and labour at Union level. Before submitting proposals in the social policy field, the Commission must consult the European social partners on the possible direction of Union action (the first consultation). If, after such consultation, the Commission considers Union action advisable, it must consult the European social partners regarding the content of the envisaged proposal (the second consultation).[19] They may then inform the Commission of their wish to initiate the process provided for in Article 155 TFEU, possibly resulting in contractual relations and European collective agreements (also called framework agreements).

Social dialogue takes place at both cross-industry and sectoral levels. The actors at the general cross-industry level include the European Trade Union Confederation (ETUC), representing employees, and BusinessEurope (formerly UNICE) and the European Centre of Employers and Enterprises Providing Public Services (CEEP), representing employers.[20] A number of agreements have been reached at cross-industry level, for example agreements on parental leave, part-time work, and fixed-term work. These agreements can be implemented either through a decision by the Council and a directive, or by the social partners themselves.[21] There is no substantive role for the European Parliament in this process. In recent years, however, the European social dialogue at cross-industry level seems to have stagnated.

Soft law measures are increasingly important in EU labour and equality law – both as a complement and alternative to hard law regulation. The insertion of the Employment Title into the Treaty of Amsterdam and the development of the European Employment Strategy (EES) has been called a 'shift of paradigm' for EU labour law. Labour law is now seen as an integrated part of employment policy, which in turn is now subject to the Integrated Guidelines and the Europe 2020 Strategy (which replaced the Lisbon Strategy in 2010), which puts forward three mutually reinforcing priorities: smart growth, sustainable growth, and inclusive growth. The EES integrates the flexicurity strategy where national systems are supposed to combine workforce flexibility with employment security. Employment policies in the Member States are coordinated through the so-called *open method of coordination* and the European Semester, using guidelines, benchmarking, targets, National Reform Programmes, and recommendations.

Finally, the Court of Justice has played a central role in EU labour and equality law, and case law has contributed greatly to the development of this area of law. The principles and

---

[17] cf Art 155 TFEU. See Case C-187/98 *Commission v Greece* [1999] ECR I-7713 and Case 143/83 *Commission v Denmark* [1985] ECR 427.

[18] See C Welz, *The European Social Dialogue under Articles 138 and 139 of the EC Treaty* (Dordrecht: Kluwer Law International, 2008). Art 152 TFEU now also states that the EU recognizes and promotes the role of the European social partners, and shall facilitate dialogue between the social partners.

[19] Art 154 TFEU.

[20] cf Case T-135/96 *UEAPME* [1998] ECR II-2335. At sectoral level, sectoral dialogue committees have been established.   [21] Art 155(2) TFEU.

rules developed by the Court in case law have often – not least in equality law – been codified later in secondary law and directives. The Court has frequently strengthened the protection of individual employees, but when faced with a conflict between economic integration (the free movement rules) and employment rights, it has favoured free movement (section 3.2.2).

In recent years, not least after the enlargement of the EU, it has been increasingly difficult to reach political agreement on hard law solutions. Instead, there has been a continued emphasis on European social dialogue, the open method of coordination, and soft law mechanisms, and an increased importance of the Court of Justice and the case law.

2.3 The Charter of Fundamental Rights of the European Union and the constitutionalization of EU labour and equality law

At an early stage, respect for fundamental rights and freedoms became part of EU law, and the jurisprudence of the Court of Justice on fundamental rights and general principles of EU law developed with reference to constitutional traditions common to the Member States and from international conventions, most especially the European Convention on Human Rights (ECHR).[22] The Lisbon Treaty implies a new emphasis on fundamental rights, and a further *constitutionalization* of EU labour and equality law. According to Article 6 TEU, the Charter of Fundamental Rights of the European Union is made legally binding and part of primary law, and the EU is to accede to the ECHR.[23] One aspect of a future accession relates to the relationship between the Court of Justice and the European Court of Human Rights (ECtHR) and the possible conflicts between case law from these two courts. This is of particular relevance following the decisions in *Viking* and *Laval* considered later. The Charter encompasses rights, freedoms, and principles of great relevance to EU labour and equality law, such as respect for private and family life (Article 7), freedom of expression (Article 11), freedom of assembly and of association (Article 12), equality before the law (Article 20), non-discrimination (Article 21), equality between men and women (Article 23), right to information and consultation within the undertaking (Article 27), right of collective bargaining and collective action (Article 28), protection in the event of unjustified dismissal (Article 30), and fair and just working conditions (Article 31).[24]

At present, as the case law of the Court of Justice on the Charter of Fundamental Rights develops, attention is drawn to the content and meaning of specific articles, as well as to the general scope, application, and interpretation of the Charter. The provisions of the Charter are 'addressed to the institutions, bodies and offices and agencies of the Union with due regard for the principle of subsidiarity and to the Member States only when they are implementing Union law'.[25] According to the explanations to the Charter, the requirement to respect fundamental rights is binding on the Member States when they act within the scope of Union law. According to settled case law of the Court, general principles of EU law, including fundamental rights, apply when Member States implement, derogate from,

---

[22] See further chapter 9.

[23] The Treaty of Amsterdam had also highlighted fundamental rights. The protection of fundamental social rights in working life was strengthened, eg through express reference in the Treaty to the European Social Charter from 1961 and the 1989 Community Charter of Fundamental Social Rights of Workers, cf Art 136 EC.

[24] According to Art 52 a distinction is to be made between *rights* and *principles* when it comes to interpretation and application (where principles, eg will not be directly effective in the national courts). This in turn relates to the traditional distinction between civil and political rights and economic and social rights, respectively. However, the Court has not always adhered strictly to this distinction; see eg *Viking* and *Laval*, considered in section 3.2.2. See further Barnard, *EU Employment Law* (n 3) 28 *et seq* and M Mikkola, *Social Human Rights of Europe* (Helsinki: Karelactio, 2010). See also the AG's Opinion in Case C-176/12 *Association de mediation sociale*, opinion of 18 July 2013, nyr.   [25] Art 51 Charter.

and act within the scope of EU law.[26] The Charter does not extend the field of application of EU law beyond the powers of the Union or establish any new power or task for the EU.[27] We will return to the Charter throughout this chapter, for example, in relation to collective action, working time, and equality law.

3 Labour law

3.1 Restructuring of enterprises and information, consultation, and worker participation

We now turn to a substantive discussion on some key labour law issues. The discussion starts with transfers of undertakings, collective redundancies, and employer insolvency (the three areas outside sex equality first regulated by the EU), and continues with a consideration of information, consultation, and worker participation, which has in recent years been seen as a key component of the flexicurity agenda.

3.1.1 Transfers of undertakings, collective redundancies, and employer insolvency

Transfer of undertakings

The Transfers of Undertakings Directive,[28] the Collective Redundancies Directive,[29] and the Employer Insolvency Directive[30] – often referred to as the 'Restructuring Directives' – were adopted as part of the 1974 Social Action Programme. The Directives address social consequences of restructuring and economic change, and aim to increase the protection of employees and to promote industrial democracy and worker participation.

The Transfers of Undertakings Directive 2001/23 aims at safeguarding the rights of employees when a business is transferred, and to provide rights to information and consultation for workers' representatives. The Directive applies to 'any transfer of an undertaking, business, or part of an undertaking or business to another employer as a result of a legal transfer or merger'. The extensive case law of the Court of Justice on the crucial concept of a transfer of an undertaking has been codified in the Directive, and Article 1(1)(b) now contains the following definition:

> a transfer of an economic entity which retains its identity, meaning an organised grouping of resources which has the objective of pursuing an economic activity, whether or not that activity is central or ancillary.[31]

---

[26] See Case C-5/88 *Wachauf* [1989] ECR 2609; Case C-260/89 *ERT* [1991] ECR I-2925; and Case C-309/96 *Annibaldi* [1997] ECR I-7493. cf also Case C-617/10 *Åklagaren v Hans Åkerberg Fransson*, order of the Court of 7 May 2013, nyr. See also Barnard, *EU Employment Law* (n 3) 28 *et seq.*

[27] Art 51(2). Art 52(1) clarifies that limitations on the exercise of Charter rights and freedoms must be provided for by law and respect the essence of those rights and freedoms. The principle of proportionality also applies. In addition, Art 52(3) states that as far as the Charter contains rights which correspond to rights guaranteed in the ECHR, the meaning and scope of those rights shall be the same as those laid down in the ECHR.

[28] Directive 2001/23/EC (OJ [2001] L82/16), first adopted as Directive 77/187/EEC (OJ [1977] L61/126).

[29] Directive 98/59/EC (OJ [1998] L225/16), first adopted as Directive 75/129/EEC (OJ [1975] L48/29).

[30] Directive 2008/94/EC, first adopted as Directive 80/987/EEC (OJ [1980] L283/23).

[31] See eg Case 24/85 *Spijkers v Benedik* [1986] ECR 1119; Case 287/86 *Ny Mølle Kro* [1987] ECR 5465; Case C-392/92 *Schmidt v Spar und Leihkase* [1994] ECR I-1311; Case C-13/95 *Süzen v Zehnacker Gebäudereinigung GmbH Krankenhausservice* [1997] ECR I-1259; and Case C-101/10 *Scattolon v Ministero dell'Istruzione, dell'Universita et della ricerca* [2011] ECR I-5951.

This definition of a transfer of an undertaking in principle includes contracting out. In the case of *Rask*,[32] Philips and ISS had made an agreement according to which ISS would assume full responsibility for the running of Philips's canteens, including menu planning, preparation of food, and recruitment and training of staff. For this Philips agreed to pay ISS a fixed monthly sum and authorized ISS to use, free of charge, Philips's premises. The Court clarified that the Directive applied to a situation in which the owner of an undertaking by contract assigns to the owner of another undertaking the responsibility for running a facility for staff, previously operated directly, in return for a fee and various other benefits determined by the agreement between them. The significance of this decision cannot be overstated: at a time when all governments are engaged in the process of contracting out public services,[33] account must be taken of protecting employees' rights in accordance with Directive 2001/23.

The Directive provides that the employment relationship and the transferor's rights and obligations arising from a contract of employment (or an employment relationship) are automatically transferred on the date of the transfer to the transferee.[34] The transferee must continue to observe the terms and conditions agreed in any collective agreement on the same terms applicable to the transferor under that agreement, until the date of expiry of the collective agreement or application of another collective agreement.[35] The Directive also provides some employment protection. The transfer of the undertaking does not in itself constitute grounds for dismissal by the transferor or the transferee. However, this does not stand in the way of dismissals due to economic, technical, or organizational reasons, entailing changes in the workforce.[36]

The Employer Insolvency Directive

The Employer Insolvency Directive applies to employees' claims from employment contracts or employment relationships against employers which are in a state of insolvency.[37] The Member States are required to put in place an institution which guarantees employees the payment of their outstanding claims for remuneration for a specific period.

Information and consultation provisions of the Transfers of Undertakings and Collective Redundancies Directives

As well as an obligation to notify the competent public authority of large-scale redundancies,[38] the Collective Redundancies Directive contains an obligation to inform and consult workers' representatives. This emphasis on information and consultation can also be found in the Transfers of Undertakings Directives. Today EU labour law clearly emphasizes worker participation, and aims for a partial harmonization of provisions regarding information, consultation, and worker participation which is also afforded protection by Article 27 of the Charter of Fundamental Rights.[39] When employers are contemplating collective redundancies – a larger number of dismissals for one or more reasons not related to the individual workers concerned – they must begin consultations with the workers' representatives in good time with a view to reaching agreement.[40] These consultations must, at least, cover ways and means of avoiding collective redundancies or reducing the number of workers affected, and of mitigating the consequences. To enable workers' representatives to

---

[32] See Case C-209/91 *Rask and Christensen v ISS Kantineservice A/S* [1992] ECR I-5755.

[33] See further chapter 18.   [34] Art 3(1).

[35] Art 3(3). The Member States may limit the period for observing such terms and conditions, but not less than one year.   [36] Art 4.

[37] Art 1. See Art 2(1) for a definition of insolvency.   [38] Arts 2 and 3, respectively.

[39] cf Bercusson, *European Labour Law* (n 5).   [40] Art 2.

make constructive proposals, the employer must, in good time during the course of the consultations, supply workers' representatives with all relevant information, and notify them in writing of pertinent information, for example, the reasons for the projected dismissals and the criteria proposed for the selection of workers to be made redundant.[41] However, the Directive is not always applied as intended. In a high-profile and much debated case in 1997 Renault unexpectedly announced – while totally ignoring the obligations to inform and consult the workers' representatives – the closure of its plant in Vilvoorde in Belgium, with a resultant loss of 3,000 jobs.

The Transfers of Undertakings Directive also provides that both the transferor and the transferee are required to inform the representatives of affected employees of certain matters, for example, the date and reasons of the transfer and the legal, economic, and social implications of the transfer. Where the transferor or the transferee envisages measures in relation to the employees, it must consult the workers' representatives with a view to reaching an agreement.[42]

3.1.2 European Works Councils and a general framework for information and consultation

The Transfers of Undertakings and Collective Redundancies Directives made provision for information and consultation in the specific contexts of a transfer or collective redundancies. What about a more general duty to inform and consult workers? Within the EU, the national systems of information, consultation, and worker participation display clear differences. The legal basis varies, and there are differences in the ways in which worker participation is delivered. In *single-channel systems* worker participation is channelled only through trade unions, while in *dual-channel systems* worker participation is channelled both through trade unions and work councils. EU law in this area has developed chronologically starting with worker participation relating to specific questions (transfers of undertaking and collective redundancies (considered in section 3.1.1)), then to worker participation in transnational companies (European Works Councils), and finally to a general framework for information and consultation at workplace level (Directive 2002/14).[43] The subject matter of information and consultation varies, and the degree of involvement varies from simple information, to consultation, and, most intense of all, consultation with a view to reaching an agreement (as with the Transfers of Undertakings and Collective Redundancies Directives).

In respect of transnational companies, several attempts to establish procedures for transnational information and consultation in the EU were made prior to the adoption of the European Works Council Directive in 1994.[44] The Preamble to the European Works

---

[41] See for discussions on the timing of information and consultation in the case law from the Court, Case C-44/08 *Akavan Erityisalojen Keskusliitto AEK ry v Fujitsu Siemens Computers Oy* [2009] ECR I-8163 and Case C-12/08 *Mono Car Styling SA, in liquidation v Dervis Odemis* [2009] ECR I-6653. See also Joined Cases C-235–239/10 *Claes v Landsbanki Luxembourg* [2011] ECR I-1113 on the links between collective redundancies and employer insolvency.

[42] A critical issue is the definition of workers' representatives. This was considered by the Court in two landmark decisions brought forward by the Commission against the UK, see Case C-382/92 [1994] ECR I-2435 and Case C-383/92 [1994] ECR I-2497.

[43] There are also further Directives in the area of information, consultation, and worker participation, such as Directive 2001/86/EC supplementing the Statute for a European company with regard to the involvement of employees; Directive 2003/72/EC supplementing the Statute for a European Cooperative Society with regard to the involvement of employees; and Directive 2005/56/EC on cross-border mergers of limited liability companies.

[44] Directive 2009/38/EC (Recast), first adopted as Directive 1994/45/EC.

Council Directive emphasizes that procedures for informing and consulting employees, regulated at national level, often are not geared to the transnational structure of the entity which makes the decisions affecting those employees. The purpose of the Directive is thus to improve the right to information and consultation of employees in Union-scale undertakings and Union-scale groups of undertakings. To that end, a European Works Council or a procedure for informing and consulting employees must be established. The Directive set up a two-stage procedure for establishing a European Works Council: first, voluntary negotiation and, secondly, mandatory (subsidiary) provisions.[45] Central management must negotiate in a spirit of cooperation with employee representatives with a view to reaching an agreement on the detailed arrangements for information and consultation of employees.

The European Works Council Directive was revised in 2009 in order, for example, to modernize the legislation, to increase the number of European Works Councils established, and to remedy the lack of legal certainty resulting from some of its provisions or the absence of certain provisions.

In respect of a general framework for information and consultation, after much discussion and political compromise the Council of Ministers finally adopted the Information and Consultation Directive in 2002.[46] The purpose of the Directive is to establish a general framework which sets out minimum requirements for the right to information and consultation of employees in undertakings or establishments within the Union. The practical arrangements for information and consultation must be defined and implemented in accordance with national law and industrial relations practices in individual Member States. Furthermore, the social partners in the Member States may, at the appropriate level, negotiate agreements, thereby 'customizing' these arrangements. The employer and employees' representatives must work in a spirit of cooperation, and the Directive provides different rules on information and consultation, such as an obligation to consult with a view to reaching an agreement on decisions likely to lead to substantial changes in work organization or contractual relations.

3.2 Freedom to provide services, freedom of establishment, and national collective labour law

Cross-border issues are central to EU labour law. We will now explore the important relationship – and as it turns out, conflict – between the internal market and fundamental freedoms and national collective labour law.

3.2.1 Freedom to provide services and posting of workers

The free movement of services is one of the fundamental Treaty freedoms,[47] and Article 56 TFEU states that

> restrictions on freedom to provide services within the Union shall be prohibited in respect of nationals of Member States who are established in a Member State other than that of the person for whom the services are intended.

Posting of workers – the transnational provision of services whereby a company sends ('posts') workers from one Member State (the home State) to another Member State (the

---

[45] This subsidiary provision clarifies the composition and operating methods of the European Works Council and requires that an annual information and consultation shall be held.
[46] Directive 2002/14/EC.   [47] See further chapters 13 and 14.

host State) to fulfil a contract – raises the question of what wages and working conditions are to be applied to posted workers.[48] Should they be governed by the laws of the host State or the State of origin (home State)? If home State laws apply, then this puts services providers from a State with lower labour costs (eg one of the new Member States) at an advantage over contractors established in the host State which must pay higher labour costs. If host State laws apply to the posted worker this competitive advantage is lost. Famously the Court suggested in *Rush Portuguesa* that host State law would apply:

> [Union] law does not preclude Member States from extending their legislation, or collective labour agreements entered into by both sides of industry, to any person who is in employment, even temporarily, within their territory, no matter in which country the employer is established; nor does [Union] law prohibit Member States from enforcing those rules by appropriate means.[49]

However, some argued that the application of the entire body of host State law to posted workers would constitute a restriction of the free movement of services. According to the *Säger*[50] market-access line of case law, such a restriction may be accepted only if justified by overriding reasons of public interest, and if proportional – that is, if the measure is suitable for securing the attainment of the objective pursued and does not go beyond what is necessary in order to attain it.

Article 56 TFEU is supplemented by the Posted Workers Directive 96/71,[51] adopted on a free movement Treaty base.[52] It has a twofold (and conflicting) aim: to enable the free movement of persons and services, and to provide protection for workers in the case of the posting of workers and the transnational provision of services.[53] When it comes to the protection of workers, the focus is on posted workers and their terms and conditions of employment, and not on workers in the host State and their protection against social dumping.[54]

Article 3 of the Posted Workers Directive lays down the nucleus of mandatory rules for minimum protection, which the host Member State must ensure (regardless of the law applicable to the employment relationship) that the undertakings guarantee to workers posted to their territory. The terms and conditions in question can be laid down by law, regulation, or administrative provision, and/or by collective agreements or arbitration awards declared universally applicable within the meaning of Article 3(8). The nucleus of mandatory rules covers, for example, maximum work periods and minimum rest periods; minimum paid annual holidays; the minimum rates of pay; health, safety, and hygiene at work; and equality of treatment between men and women and other provisions on non-discrimination. Article 3(7) states that the Directive will not prevent the application of terms and conditions of employment which are more favourable to workers. Lastly, according to Article 3(10), the Directive allows Member States, in compliance with the Treaty,

---

[48] A posted worker is a worker who 'for a limited period, carries out his work in the territory of a Member State other than the State in which he normally works', Art 2.

[49] Case C-113/89 *Rush Portuguesa* [1990] ECR I-1417.

[50] cf Case C-76/90 *Säger* [1991] ECR I-4221, para 12 and Case C-55/94 *Gebhard* [1995] ECR I-4165. See also C Barnard, '*Viking* and *Laval*: An Introduction' (2007–08) 10 *Cambridge Yearbook of European Legal Studies* 463.   [51] Directive 96/71/EC (OJ [1997] L18/1).

[52] Arts 57(2) and 66 EC.   [53] Preamble, recitals 1, 2, and 5.

[54] The concept of social dumping refers to practices and behaviour aimed at providing a competitive advantage to companies due to lower labour standards, such as wages. See further, eg B Hepple, *Labour Laws and Global Trade* (Oxford: Hart Publishing, 2005).

to apply terms and conditions of employment on matters other than those covered by the nucleus of mandatory rules for minimum protection in the case of public policy provisions, on a basis of equality of treatment.

The recent controversial case law developments in this area, such as *Laval*,[55] *Rüffert*,[56] and *Commission v Luxembourg*,[57] and the debate they have caused, display a tension and difference of perspective between the old and new Member States, and Member States which are receiving and sending posted workers, respectively. This case law clarifies that the Posted Workers Directive establishes only a minimum protection of a nucleus of mandatory rules, and does not provide for equal treatment of domestic and foreign employers, as a means of combating social dumping. In other words, the host State can apply its labour law rules to posted workers but only in the area listed in Article 3(1); in all other areas home State law applies. The position in *Rush Portuguesa* is therefore no longer good law. Further, the cases show that despite the suggestions in Article 3(7) and (10), the Directive is a *maximum* Directive, establishing a 'ceiling' for the terms and conditions of employment that a trade union or a State may require foreign service providers to apply to employees.[58]

3.2.2 The right to collective action

Increasing European integration, enlargement, and cross-border activity highlight free movement and economic freedoms – as well as the need for social protection and the need to protect against social dumping. Important case law from the Court of Justice – *Viking* and *Laval* – addresses these issues. They concern, on the one hand, the EU fundamental Treaty freedoms, free movement of services, and freedom of establishment and, on the other hand, national collective labour law and fundamental trade union rights, such as the right to collective action, freedom of association, and right to collective bargaining.

Case study 20.1: *Viking* and *Laval*

The *Viking* case[59] was referred by the Court of Appeal in the UK to the Court of Justice for a preliminary ruling. It concerned a dispute between the International Transport Workers' Federation (ITF) and the Finnish Seamen's Union (FSU) on the one hand, and Viking, a ferry operator, and its subsidiary (Viking Eesti), on the other. Viking wanted to reflag one of its vessels, the *Rosella*, from the Finnish flag to the Estonian flag, in order to reduce wage costs. As long as *Rosella* was under the Finnish flag, Viking was obliged under Finnish law and the terms of a collective agreement to pay the crew wages at the same level as those applicable in Finland. Estonian wages for crew were lower than Finnish wages. Reflagging the vessel to Estonia would enable Viking to enter into a new collective agreement. Since the

---

[55] Case C-341/05 *Laval* [2007] ECR I-11767.   [56] Case C-346/06 *Rüffert* [2008] ECR I-1989.

[57] Case C-319/06 *Commission v Luxembourg* [2008] ECR I-4323. cf also Case C-271/08 *Commission v Germany* [2010] ECR I-7091, dealing with the implementation of public procurement rules for pension services based on collective agreement.

[58] In the field of free movement of services, the Services Directive – Directive 2006/123/EC (OJ [2006] L376/36) – and its relationship to labour law and fundamental trade union rights caused intensive discussions, both before and after adoption of the Directive. Art 1(7) of the Services Directive now states that 'This Directive does not affect the exercise of fundamental rights as recognised in the Member States and by [Union] law. Nor does it affect the right to negotiate, conclude and enforce collective agreements and to take industrial action in accordance with national law and practices which respect [Union] law'.

[59] Case C-438/05 *Viking* [2007] ECR I-10779.

ITF was running a campaign opposing such 'flags of convenience',[60] it sent out a circular to its affiliates asking them, in the name of solidarity, to refrain from entering into negotiations with Viking. The FSU gave Viking notice of a strike.

The *Laval* case[61] was referred by the Swedish Labour Court to the Court of Justice for a preliminary ruling. In May 2004, Laval, a Latvian company, posted workers from Latvia to work on Swedish building sites. The work was undertaken by a subsidiary company, and included the renovation and extension of school premises. In June 2004, Laval and the Swedish Building Workers' Union started negotiations with a view to concluding a collective agreement.[62] Laval later signed collective agreements with a *Latvian* trade union, regulating the work at the site. Consequently, no agreement was reached between Laval and the *Swedish* Building Workers' Union. In November, the Swedish Building Workers' Union started collective action in the form of a blockade at all Laval building sites, and another Swedish trade union took sympathy action. After work on the site had been interrupted for some time, the subsidiary company became bankrupt. The Latvian workers posted by Laval returned to Latvia.

Viking addresses questions on the compatibility of the right to take collective action with the freedom of establishment (Article 49 TFEU), while *Laval* addresses questions on the free movement of services (Article 56 TFEU), the right to take collective action, and the Swedish implementation of the Posted Workers Directive. Here, we leave aside the issue of the Posted Workers Directive which was considered in section 3.2.1.

In both *Viking* and *Laval* the Court declared that collective action fell within the scope of the Treaty, and that Articles 56 and 49 TFEU could be invoked against trade unions (even though the right to strike is excluded from the EU's competence to adopt directives according to Article 153(5) TFEU).[63] The Court, with reference to Article 28 of the Charter, also recognized the right to take collective action as a fundamental right which forms an integral part of the general principles of Union law. However, the exercise of the right to collective action could be restricted, as on the facts of these cases.

The Court then considered in *Viking* whether the collective action at issue constituted a restriction of the freedom of establishment, and in *Laval* whether the collective action constituted a restriction on the free movement of services.

Although in both cases the Court emphasized that the Union not only has an economic but also a social purpose, it concluded in *Laval* that the collective action constituted a restriction on the free movement of services. It said that such a restriction was warranted only if it pursued a legitimate objective compatible with the Treaty, and is justified by overriding reasons of public interest. If that is the case, the restriction must be suitable for securing the attainment of the objective which it pursues and must not go beyond what is necessary in order to attain this objective (the *Säger* market-access approach). The Court declared that the right to take collective action for the protection of the workers of the host State against social dumping could constitute an overriding reason of public interest. However, the specific obligations linked to the signing of the collective agreement in the building sector in

---

[60] The term 'flag of convenience' refers to the practice of registering a ship in a State different from that of the ship owner's, in order to reduce operating costs and avoid the regulation (labour law etc) of the State of the ship owner. [61] Case C-341/05 (n 55).

[62] A so-called 'application' agreement to the collective agreement for the building sector.

[63] The Court also dismissed the 'Albany argument', see Case C-67/96 *Albany International v Stichting Bedrijfspensioenfonds Textielindustrie* [1999] ECR I-5751, ie that the right to collective action would be immune against fundamental Treaty freedoms, as the right to collective bargaining had been immune against competition law provisions.

Laval (which also went beyond the nucleus of mandatory rules for minimum protection in Article 3(1) of the Directive) could not be justified as necessary to attain such an objective.

Similarly, in *Viking* the Court found that the collective action constituted a restriction on the freedom of establishment. When it came to justification and proportionality, the Court left the assessment to the national court. However, it provided some guidance, requiring the national court to consider whether the jobs and conditions of employment of the trade union members on board the *Rosella* were jeopardized or under serious threat and, if so, whether, under the national rules and collective agreements, the trade union had other means at its disposal which were less restrictive on freedom of establishment. Only if these conditions were satisfied would the strike action be justified and proportionate.

Due to the application of the *Säger* market-access approach, both *Viking* and *Laval* have been interpreted as putting fundamental Treaty freedoms and economic integration first, and trade union rights and social integration, second.[64] The cases prompted huge and critical debate. Proposals have been put forward for the need to revise the Posted Workers Directive or to revise the Treaty. Some Member States, such as Sweden and Denmark, have also had to reform their laws on collective action and posted work, especially those building on autonomous collective bargaining.[65]

At EU level, it was thought that the Lisbon Treaty and the new emphasis on 'social market economy' might have changed the landscape. In 2012 the Commission put forward two proposals, a Monti II Regulation on the exercise of the right to take collective action in the context of freedom of establishment and the freedom to provide services, and a Directive on the enforcement of the Posted Workers Directive.[66] The Monti II Regulation was withdrawn by the Commission following serious opposition from the trade unions and by many Member States' parliaments on grounds of subsidiarity.

Another important development post-*Laval* and *Viking* has been the reorientation of the ECtHR case law regarding freedom of association, and the resulting, possibly conflicting, case law of the Court of Justice and the ECtHR; this is crucial considering the mandate from the Lisbon Treaty for the EU to accede to the ECHR. In two landmark decisions from 2008 and 2009 respectively – the case of *Demir and Baykara v Turkey* and the case of *Enerji Yapi-Yol Sen v Turkey*[67] – the ECtHR aligned its case law with the International Labour Organization (ILO) Conventions No 87 on freedom of association and protection of the right to organize, and No 98 on the right to organize and collective bargaining, as well as the Council of Europe's European Social Charter. The freedom of association, as protected by Article 11 ECHR, is now said to comprise the right to bargain collectively *and* the right to industrial action.

The ILO Committee of Experts, in response to a complaint by the trade union in the *BALPA* case (a British industrial dispute which showed how trade unions can face the threat of employer claims for massive damages if they go on strike without complying with

---

[64] See eg A Davies, 'One Step Forward Two Steps Back? The *Viking* and *Laval* Cases in the ECJ' (2008) 38 *Industrial Law Journal* 126 and J Malmberg and T Sigeman, 'Industrial Action and EU Economic Freedoms – The Autonomous Collective Bargaining Model Curtailed by the European Court of Justice' (2008) 45 *Common Market Law Review* 1115.

[65] On the legal implications of *Viking* and *Laval* in different national contexts, see eg A Swiatkowski (guest ed), 'The *Laval* and *Viking* Cases: Freedom of Services and Establishment v Industrial Conflict in the European Economic Area and Russia' (2009) 69 *Bulletin of Comparative Labour Relations* and E Ales and T Novitz (eds), *Collective Action and Fundamental Freedoms in Europe: Striking the Balance* (Antwerp: Intersentia, 2010).

[66] COM(2012) 130 and COM(2012) 131.

[67] Judgment of 12 November 2008 and judgment of April 2009. See eg KD Ewing and J Hendy, 'The Dramatic Implications of *Demir and Baykara*' (2010) 39 *Industrial Law Journal* 2.

the ruling in *Viking* and *Laval* to the letter), observed with '*serious concern* the practical limitations on the effective exercise of the right to strike of the BALPA workers in this context' and declared that 'the doctrine that is being articulated in these judgements is likely to have a significant restrictive effect on the exercise of the right to strike in practice in a manner contrary to the Convention'.[68]

These different developments at the international level prompt the important question: are *Viking* and *Laval* and EU law compatible with international labour law, such as ILO Conventions, the ECHR, and the European Social Charter?[69]

3.3 Flexible work and working conditions

EU labour law also regulates important issues which affect the individual employment relationship. We now turn to a discussion of the regulation of flexible work and working conditions, such as health and safety and working time.

3.3.1 Part-time, fixed-term, and temporary agency work

The process of flexibilization of the labour market has led to an increase in flexible work, such as fixed-term work, temporary agency work, and self-employment. In recent years EU labour law and employment policy have been greatly influenced by a *flexicurity* agenda (inspired, eg by the practice in the Netherlands and Denmark). Flexicurity is about combining flexibility for employers and security for employees, and aims at reducing labour market segmentation and increasing economic growth.[70] Flexicurity is partly about deregulation of employment protection combined with equal treatment of various forms of flexible employment, but it is also about effective active labour market policies, reliable and adaptable systems for lifelong learning, and modern social security systems. The Council has adopted Common Principles of Flexicurity and these have been integrated into the EES and the Europe 2020 Strategy, principles which have been criticized for focusing predominately on labour market flexibility and deregulation rather than employment security.

The Part-Time Work Directive,[71] Fixed-Term Work Directive,[72] and Temporary Agency Work Directive[73] form part of this flexicurity agenda. The Part-Time Work and Fixed-Term Work Directives result from the European Social Dialogue (considered in section 2.2). The aims of the Directives differ in part. The purpose of the Part-Time Work Directive is to provide for the removal of discrimination against part-time workers and to improve the quality of part-time work, while facilitating the development of part-time work on a voluntary basis and contributing to the flexible organization of working time in a manner which considers the needs of employers and workers.[74] The purpose of the Temporary Agency Work Directive

---

[68] cf also in 2013, the similar opinion of the ILO Committee of Experts in relation to the Swedish post-*Viking* and *Laval* legislation and the final judgment by the Swedish Labour Court in the *Laval* case, stating damage liability for the trade unions (approximately €55,000). See further M Rönnmar, 'Laval Returns to Sweden: The Final Judgment of the Swedish Labour Court and Swedish Legislative Reforms' (2010) 39 *Industrial Law Journal* 280.

[69] See also the decision of ESCR to Complaint No 85/2012 *Swedish Trade Union Confederation (LO) and Swedish Confederation of Professional Employees (TCO) v Sweden*, Decision on admissibility and merits, 3 July 2013, public on 20 November 2013, discussed by C Barnard, 'Posting Matters' (2014) *Norwegian Journal of Labour Law* forthcoming.

[70] See COM(2007) 359 final. See also S Fredman, 'Women at Work: The Broken Promise of Flexicurity' (2004) 33 *Industrial Law Journal* 299 and M Rönnmar, 'Flexicurity: The Notion of Equal Treatment and Labour Law' in M Rönnmar (ed), *Swedish Studies in European Law: Labour Law and Social Security Law*, vol 4 (Oxford: Hart Publishing, 2011) 153.

[71] Directive 97/81/EC (OJ [1998] L14/9). [72] Directive 99/70/EC (OJ [1999] L175/43).

[73] Directive 2008/104/EC (OJ [2008] L327/9). [74] Cl 1.

is to ensure protection of temporary agency workers and to improve the quality of temporary agency work, while also taking into account the need to establish a suitable framework for use of temporary agency work with a view to contributing effectively to the creation of jobs and to the development of flexible forms for working.[75] The Fixed-Term Work Directive is more restrictive as regards flexibility, and its purpose is to improve the quality of fixed-term work by ensuring the application of the principle of non-discrimination, and to establish a framework to prevent abuse arising from the use of successive fixed-term employment contracts or relationships.[76] Thus, the first two Directives want to encourage this type of flexible work, while the third Directive has an emphasis on the protection of these flexible workers.

The principle of non-discrimination and equal treatment has not been given a coherent design in the Directives. In the Part-Time Work Directive and the Fixed-Term Work Directive there is a *principle of non-discrimination*, which states that in respect of employment conditions, part-time/fixed-term workers must not be treated in a less favourable manner than comparable full-time/permanent workers solely because they work part-time/have a fixed-term contract or relation, unless that different treatment is justified on objective grounds.[77] In these two Directives the principle of non-discrimination is limited in that it requires that any unfavourable treatment of the part-time worker or fixed-term worker is to relate *solely* to the part-time work or fixed-term employment contract. It also enables the employer to justify such unfavourable treatment with objective grounds.[78] By contrast, in the Temporary Agency Work Directive the principle of equal treatment states that for the duration of their assignment at a user undertaking, the basic working and employment conditions of temporary agency workers (not all terms and conditions of employment) must be at least those which would apply if the workers had been recruited directly by that undertaking to occupy the same job.[79] There is no possibility of justifying different treatment but there are some important exceptions to the rule, including allowing States the possibility of not applying the principle of equal treatment for a certain period.

Employment protection is only partly regulated in these Directives.[80] For example, the Fixed-Term Work Directive prevents abuse arising from the use of successive fixed-term employment contracts or relationships. The Member States must introduce one or more of the following measures, in a manner which takes account of the needs of specific sectors and/or categories of workers:

- objective reasons justifying the renewal of such contracts or relationships,
- the maximum total duration of successive fixed-term employment contracts or relationships,
- the number of renewals of such contracts or relationships.[81]

---

[75] Art 2. A temporary agency worker is a worker with a contract of employment or an employment relationship with a temporary-work agency with a view to being assigned to a user undertaking to work temporarily under its supervision and direction, Art 3(1)(c).

[76] Cl 1.   [77] Cl 4 in both Directives.

[78] The case of *Wippel* is central, and discusses, eg the question of comparability, see Case C-313/02 *Nicole Wippel v Peek & Cloppenburg GmbH & Co KGK* [2004] ECR I-9483.

[79] Art 5. The Directive provides for certain exemptions from the principle of equal treatment. These exemptions constitute adjustments to specific national contexts, and Art 5(3) provides, eg for exemptions in collective bargaining as long as the overall protection of temporary agency workers is respected.

[80] See eg Art 30 Charter, the Fixed-Term Work Directive, and the Transfers of Undertakings and Collective Redundancies Directives, as well as different Equality Directives, which ban discriminatory dismissals.

[81] Cl 5. The Court has developed a substantial case law in relation to this provision, see eg Case C-212/04 *Adeneler* [2006] ECR I-6057; Joined Cases C-378–380/07 *Angelidaki* [2009] ECR I-3071; and Case C-596/10 *Kücük*, judgment of 8 March 2012, nyr. Note, however, that the Directive does not introduce any requirement for objective reasons for the parties' first entry into a fixed-term employment contract.

3.3.2 Working time and health and safety

Working conditions – and their improvement – is an important aspect of EU labour law, and the area of health and safety has a long-standing tradition. Two types of directives are relevant here: directives related to the harmonization of Member State regulation in the area of free movement of goods and the character and control of different products to ensure the goods are safe (so-called Product Directives); and directives related to health and safety and the working environment in the workplace (so-called Workplace Directives). The Framework Directive on Health and Safety[82] aims at introducing measures to encourage improvements in the health and safety of workers at work, and lays down minimum standards in this area.[83] It stipulates general principles on the prevention of occupational risks, the protection of health and safety, the elimination of risk and accident factors, and consultation of workers and their representatives. The employer has a duty to ensure the safety and health of workers in every aspect related to work.[84]

In addition to the general health and safety directives, the EU has adopted one directive as a health and safety measure which has proved highly controversial: the Working Time Directive.[85] The aim of the Directive is to lay down minimum health and safety requirements for the organization of working time. The Directive contains provisions on, for example, daily rest, breaks, weekly rest periods, maximum weekly working time, annual leave, and night work. The Directive also provides for adaptations through the use of collective agreements, as well as an 'opt-out' for Member States in relation to Article 6 and the maximum 48-hour week.[86]

According to Article 7 every worker is entitled to paid annual leave of at least four weeks, in accordance with the conditions for entitlement to, and granting of, such leave laid down by national legislation and practice. This minimum period of paid annual leave may not be replaced by an allowance in lieu, except where the employment relationship is terminated. Article 31 of the Charter on fair and just working conditions also states every worker's right to an annual period of paid leave. In recent years the Court of Justice has delivered a series of judgments in relation to paid annual leave, for example in relation to sick leave. The Court has emphasized that 'the entitlement of every worker to paid annual leave must be regarded as a particularly important principle of European union social law from which there can be no derogations'.[87]

The Working Time Directive is controversial, and has been difficult to align with the demands of certain sectors, particularly health care. The Court's highly controversial rulings on the definition of working time – which includes on-call time where that time is spent on the employer's premises – has increased the pressure to reform the Directive.[88] Several attempts have been made to revise the Working Time Directive in recent years, but so far they have proved unsuccessful.

---

[82] Directive 89/391/EEC (OJ [1989] L183/1).

[83] On the basis of the Framework Directive a number of more specific 'daughter Directives' have been adopted, cf Art 16(1).

[84] See further E Ales (ed), *Health and Safety at Work: European and Comparative Perspectives* (Dordrecht: Kluwer Law International, 2013).

[85] Directive 2003/88/EC (OJ [2003] L299/9). The UK unsuccessfully challenged the legal basis of the Directive (Art 118a EEC), see further Case C-84/94 *UK v Council* [1996] ECR I-5755.

[86] Art 22(1).

[87] See eg Case C-173/99 *BECTU* [2001] ECR I-4881; Joined Cases C-350/06 and C-520/06 *Schultz-Hoff* [2009] ECR I-179; and Case C-282/10 *Dominguez*, judgment of 24 January 2012, nyr.

[88] See eg Case C-303/98 *Simap* [2000] ECR I-7963; Case C-241/99 *CIG v Sergas* [2001] ECR I-5139; and Case C-151/02 *Jaeger* [2003] ECR I-8389.

3.4 **EU and national labour law in times of economic crisis**

The current economic crisis – and the EU's and the Member States' responses – have had important implications for European labour markets and for labour law. Resultant high unemployment, especially youth unemployment, has had devastating effects in many countries and has led to social protest and unrest, and put into question the EU's legitimacy and highlighted its 'democratic deficit'. The responses to the crisis have varied among the Member States, and have come in different stages. In 2008/9 many Member States first put crisis-related measures in place, such as internal flexibility, short-time working arrangements, and wage concessions. The subsequent 'eurozone' and sovereign debt crisis in 2010, caused in part by governments' attempts to 'bail out' banks in financial difficulty, led to fundamental financial and governance reforms at EU level.[89]

Since devaluation of the currency is not an option within the eurozone, focus has instead been on far-reaching austerity measures (so-called internal devaluation) and deregulatory labour law reforms in many Member States.[90] These measures have targeted employment protection regulation, collective bargaining, and wage-setting – at the heart of national labour law and industrial relations systems – and crucially areas which largely fall outside EU competence. The Member States that have been given so-called 'bail-out' packages (by the 'Troika' (the European Commission, the European Central Bank, and the IMF)) – Greece, Portugal, and Ireland – have been particularly affected. The Memoranda of Understanding accompanying the 'bail-out' packages and signed by these Member States specify which labour law and labour market reforms are to be considered and introduced. In several Member States these reforms were also introduced hastily, without recourse to democratic and participatory procedures. Furthermore, there are signs that some governments may be using the crisis as a 'cover' for introducing further deregulation. Deregulatory reforms have been introduced in many Member States, including Greece, Portugal, Spain, Italy, the UK, Hungary, and Poland.

These developments have been harshly criticized by the ILO, trade unions, and labour law scholars, and deep concerns have been expressed, for example, as regards the disrespect for fundamental rights, the strong move towards labour market flexibilization, and the neglect of notions such as decent work and high-quality employment. These reforms have also been legally challenged at several levels – in national constitutional courts, in the Court of Justice, and before international human rights bodies, such as the ILO and the Council of Europe. Greece has particularly been in the spotlight in this regard.

A number of preliminary references have also been made to the Court related to national measures introduced as part of 'bail-out' packages. In *Sindicato dos Bancários do Norte*,[91] for example, the Portuguese legislation introducing salary reductions for certain public sector workers was questioned from the perspective of the Charter of Fundamental Rights and the principles of equality and non-discrimination, and the right to fair and

---

[89] See chapter 19, discussing the EMU and the financial governance reforms, and C Barnard, 'The Financial Crisis and the Euro Plus Pact: A Labour Lawyer's Perspective' (2012) 41 *Industrial Law Journal* 98. In addition, the Commission's proposals for recommendations to the Member States regarding their national reform programmes within the context of the European Semester for policy coordination and the European Employment Strategy have, following the economic crisis, contained deregulatory elements targeted at wage setting and employment protection, and caused controversy and opposition.

[90] See eg S Clauwaert and I Schömann, 'The Crisis and National Labour Law Reforms: A Mapping Exercise' (2012) ETUI Working Paper 2012.04 and S Laulom et al, 'How has the Crisis Affected Social Legislation in Europe?' (2012) ETUI Policy Brief No 2/2012.

[91] Case C-128/12 *Sindicato dos Bancários do Norte*, opinion of 26 September 2013, nyr.

just working conditions. The Court, without any real explanation, found that it lacked jurisdiction.[92]

Thus, so far the Court has refused to apply the Charter to these cases.[93] By contrast, the European Committee of Social Rights, in relation to a number of collective complaints, has found, for example, recent Greek reforms to be in violation of the right to a fair remuneration and the right to social security.[94] In 2011 the ILO sent a specific High Level Mission to Greece and the ILO Committee of Experts, in its General Report on the Application on Conventions and Recommendations, has expressed deep concern about the Greek developments in relation to Conventions No 87 and No 98 and the freedom of association and right to collective bargaining,[95] and has stated that the reforms of collective bargaining and negotiations structures are 'likely to have a significant – and potentially devastating – impact on the industrial relations system in the country'. The Committee also deeply regretted that these reforms were introduced without full and thorough discussions with all the social partners.

4 Equality law

4.1 Introduction to equality law

So far we have concentrated on matters traditionally in the field of labour law. We now turn to the area where the EU has played a particularly important role, that is equality law, which has been the EU's flagship contribution to social policy. Equality law is a central and well-developed part of EU labour law – and has gradually extended its reach beyond working life.[96] Equality law has a clear human rights basis – but also a market and economic basis. The inclusion of the equal pay provision in Article 119 EEC in the Treaty of Rome (now Article 157 TFEU) was based on an economic rationale and the concern that some Member States could gain a competitive advantage through the use of cheap female labour. In time, the human rights and social basis of equality law was strengthened. In *Defrenne (No 2)* the Court recognized for the first time the economic *and* social aim of the Treaty provision on equal pay,[97] and in *Defrenne (No 3)* the general principle of equal treatment and non-discrimination was recognized.[98]

EU equality law first contained protection against discrimination on grounds of nationality and gender; until 1999 these were the only protected grounds. The principle of

---

[92] cf also the *Pringle* case, where the European Stability Mechanism was challenged, but found lawful by the Court, Case C-370/12 *Pringle*, judgment of 27 November 2012, nyr; see further P Craig (guest ed), 'Pringle: Legal Reasoning, Text, Purpose and Teleology' (2013) 20 *Maastricht Journal of European and Comparative Law* 3 and chapter 19 of this book.

[93] See, further, C Barnard, 'The Charter, the Court – and the Crisis' (2013), University of Cambridge Faculty of Law Research Paper No 18/2013.

[94] See eg the European Committee of Social Rights decisions in relation to Complaint No 65/2011 and Complaint Nos 77–80/2012,

[95] Even though the Committee also acknowledges the 'very difficult, challenging and exceptional circumstances, which the country has had to face over the last few years'.

[96] For a detailed discussion on EU equality law, see eg E Ellis and P Watson, *EU Anti-Discrimination Law* (2nd edn, Oxford: Oxford University Press, 2012).

[97] Case 43/75 *Defrenne (No 2) v Sabena* [1976] ECR 455.

[98] Case 149/77 *Defrenne (No 3) v Sabena* [1978] ECR 1365. cf also Case C-144/04 *Werner Mangold v Rudiger Helm* [2005] ECR I-9981 and Case C-555/07 *Seda Kücükdevici v Swedex GmBH & Co* [2010] ECR I-365. The three seminal *Defrenne* cases all concerned a female air hostess, Ms Defrenne, employed by Sabena Airlines.

non-discrimination on the basis of nationality has been essential to European integration and the EU. EU equality law in general builds on the development and content of gender equality.[99] In 1999, through the Treaty of Amsterdam, the EU's competence in the equality field widened significantly through the inclusion of Article 13 EC (now Article 19 TFEU), which enables the EU to take appropriate action to combat discrimination based on sex, racial or ethnic origin, religion or belief, disability, age, or sexual orientation. In 2000 two important directives were adopted on the basis of Article 13 EC: the Race Directive[100] and the Employment Equality Directive,[101] covering discrimination on grounds of religion or belief, disability, age, and sexual orientation. This development is often described as a move towards comprehensive equality, which entails the protection of more and broader discrimination grounds, both within and outside working life. The Charter of Fundamental Rights provides for equality before the law and equality between men and women. Article 21 contains an 'open list' of discrimination grounds and provides that

> Any discrimination based on any ground such as sex, race, colour, ethnic or social origin, genetic features, language, religion or belief, political or any other opinion, membership of a national minority, property, birth, disability, age or sexual orientation shall be prohibited.

When it comes to the development of secondary law in the area of gender equality, little happened until the 1970s, when three directives were adopted in the framework of the 1974 Social Action Programme: the Equal Pay Directive,[102] the Equal Treatment Directive,[103] and the Equal Treatment in Social Security Directive.[104] Subsequent directives included directives on occupational schemes[105] and on the self-employed.[106] All but the Equal Treatment in Social Security Directive have now been replaced by new directives: the Equal Pay, the Equal Treatment, and the Occupational Schemes Directives have all been replaced by the Recast Directive;[107] and the Self-Employed Directive has been replaced by Directive 2010/41/EU.[108] Following the Maastricht Treaty, another set of directives was adopted: the Directive on Pregnant Workers,[109] the Directive on Parental Leave,[110] and the Burden of Proof Directive.[111] The Parental Leave Directive is the result of the European social dialogue, and has now been renegotiated and replaced by Directive 2010/18/EU.[112] The other two Directives have also been replaced or are pending amendment.[113] In addition, in 2004 a Directive on Gender Equality in Goods and Services[114] was adopted.

From a more general perspective, Hepple has described and analysed the development of equality law in Europe since 1945 as a process from legal recognition of the right to equality in international legal instruments, to formal equality, to substantive equality, to the dawn of comprehensive and transformative equality. This development is closely

---

[99] Later on a more complex interplay between regulation on different grounds, and different Directives, has evolved, as well as a discussion on a hierarchy of grounds, where the ban on race discrimination is the most far-reaching, while the ban on gender discrimination has firmer Treaty support and is expressed in 'stronger' legal language, see eg M Bell, 'The Principle of Equal Treatment: Widening and Deepening' in P Craig and G de Búrca (eds), *The Evolution of EU Law* (2nd edn, Oxford: Oxford University Press, 2011).

[100] Directive 2000/43/EC.   [101] Directive 2000/78/EC.   [102] Directive 75/117/EEC.

[103] Directive 76/207/EC.   [104] Directive 79/7/EEC.

[105] Directive 96/97/EC, amending Directive 86/378/EEC (OJ [1997] L46/20).

[106] Directive 86/61/EEC (OJ [1986] L359/5).

[107] Directive 2006/54/EC (OJ [2006] L204/23).   [108] Directive 2010/41/EU (OJ [2010] L180/1).

[109] Directive 92/85/EEC (OJ [1992] L348/1).   [110] Directive 96/34/EC (OJ [1996] L145/4).

[111] Directive 97/80/EC (OJ [1998] L14/6).   [112] Directive 2010/18/EU (OJ [2010] L68/13).

[113] Directive 97/80/EC is thus now covered by the Recast Directive whereas the Directive on Pregnant Workers is in the process of being changed, see COM(2008) 637 final.   [114] Directive 2004/113/EC.

connected to the protection of human rights and the value of human dignity – but also to the influence of EU law and the interventions by the Court of Justice. This development has also been intertwined with social, political, and economic developments, such as increased labour market participation for women, increased migration, a shift from standard to flexible employment, an ageing population, and restructuring and globalization.[115]

The Equality Directives are generally based on a human rights model: the prohibition against discrimination is designed as an individual right and enforced through complaints to the courts. Traditionally discrimination law was based on *formal equality*, and linked to the liberal tradition and the Aristotelian thesis of 'what is alike shall be treated alike'. Yet EU law has recognized a role for *substantive equality* (ie equality as regards outcome and results) as well, for example, by bans on indirect discrimination, rules on a reversed burden of proof, and provisions on positive action. A proactive mainstreaming approach – to aim to eliminate inequalities, to promote equality between men and women, and to combat discrimination – has also been developed and enforced, and now enjoys Treaty support.[116] The role of soft law has also been important, often paving the way for hard law measures.

Today, the Equality and Non-Discrimination Directives are aligned to a great extent and contain protection, for example, by way of the prohibition on direct and indirect discrimination, harassment, and instructions to discriminate, with scope for positive action, and the reversed burden of proof. Discrimination based on gender is prohibited in employment, vocational training, occupational social security benefits, social security, and access to and supply of goods and services, while discrimination based on religion or belief, disability, age, and sexual orientation is prohibited in employment and vocational training only. The protection against race discrimination is the most far-reaching, and applies to employment, vocational training, social protection, including social security and health care, as well as social advantages, education, and access to and supply of goods and services.

4.2 Gender equality

The Treaty provision on equal pay, now Article 157 TFEU, forms the starting point for EU gender equality law. Article 157 TFEU is both horizontally and vertically directly effective, and thus applies not only to the Member States but also to private employers. Article 157(3) TFEU, introduced at Amsterdam, gives the European Parliament and the Council the power to adopt measures to 'ensure the application of the principle of equal opportunities and equal treatment of men and women in matters of employment and occupation, including the principle of equal pay for equal work or work of equal value'.

Seven of the sex equality Directives were recast and consolidated in the Recast Directive.[117] Sex is broadly construed: in *P v S and Cornwall County Council*[118] the Court of Justice interpreted the concept of sex to include transsexuality and gender reassignment (though not sexual orientation). The Recast Directive sought to bring about simplification, modernization, and improvement of EU law in this area, and the aim of the Directive is to 'ensure the implementation of the principle of equal opportunities and equal treatment of men and women in matters of employment and occupation'.[119] It applies to access

---

[115] See B Hepple, 'Equality Law' in Hepple and Veneziani, *The Transformation of Labour Law in Europe* (n 3). Bell, in turn, has discussed this development in terms of widening and deepening, see M Bell, 'The Principle of Equal Treatment: Widening and Deepening' in Craig and de Búrca, *The Evolution of EU Law* (n 99).

[116] Art 3(3) TEU and Arts 8 and 10 TFEU.

[117] Which was adopted under Art 141(3) EC, now Art 157(3) TFEU.

[118] Case C-13/94 *P v S* [1996] ECR I-2143.   [119] Art 1.

to employment, including promotion, and to vocational training, to working conditions, including pay, and to occupational social security schemes.

The Directive bans direct and indirect discrimination, and discrimination here includes harassment, sexual harassment, instruction to discriminate, and any less favourable treatment of women related to pregnancy or maternity leave within the meaning of Directive 92/85/EEC (see section 4.2.4).[120] Member States may maintain or adopt positive-action measures within the meaning of Article 157(4) TFEU, with a view to ensuring full equality in practice between men and women in working life, that is, *substantive equality. Direct discrimination*, closely related to formal equality, refers to the situation 'where one person is treated less favourably on grounds of sex than another is, has been or would be treated in a comparable situation'.[121] Direct discrimination requires no motive or intention to discriminate. It is enough if the less favourable treatment is grounded upon or caused by, in this case, gender. However, in principle, there is a need to identify an actual or hypothetical comparator.[122]

As a basic premise, direct discrimination cannot be justified. However, there are some exemptions from the equal treatment principle, such as provisions for the protection of women, especially as regards pregnancy and maternity, and as regards employment where 'by reason of the nature of the particular occupational activities concerned or the context in which they are carried out such a characteristic (eg gender) constitutes a genuine and determining occupational requirement' (GOR). So a requirement for a woman to play Juliet and a man Romeo is likely to satisfy the GOR test, provided the objective is legitimate and the requirement proportional.[123] Added to this is the scope for positive discrimination (eg allowing employers to appoint a woman to a job where she is equally qualified with a man but women are underrepresented).[124]

The ban on *indirect* discrimination, a step towards the realization of substantive equality, was first developed by the Court of Justice, and inspired by the concept of disparate impact in US law. The ban on indirect discrimination targets measures which are discriminatory in effect. Today, *indirect discrimination* refers to the situation

> where an apparently neutral provision, criterion or practice would put persons of one sex at a particular disadvantage compared with persons of the other sex, unless that provision, criterion or practice is objectively justified by a legitimate aim, and the means of achieving that aim are appropriate and necessary.[125]

4.2.1 Pay

The early cases of indirect discrimination, such as *Jenkins* and *Bilka-Kaufhaus*,[126] related to unfavourable working conditions for part-time workers, usually women. This situation is

---

[120] Art 2.   [121] Art 2(1)(a).

[122] This is, however, not the case in regard to direct discrimination of pregnant women, see section 4.2.4.

[123] Art 14(2).

[124] Art 3. In Case C-158/97 *Badeck* [2000] ECR I-1875, the Court clarified that positive action is compatible with EU law 'if it does not automatically and unconditionally give priority to women when women and men are equally qualified, and the candidatures are the subject of an objective assessment which takes account of the specific personal situations of all candidates'. cf also Case C-450/94 *Kalanke* [1995] ECR I-3051 and Case C-409/95 *Marshall* [1997] ECR I-6363.   [125] Art 2(1)(b).

[126] Case C-96/80 *Jenkins* [1981] ECR 911 and Case C-170/84 *Bilka-Kaufhaus* [1986] ECR 1607. cf also Case C-167/97 *R v Secretary of State for Employment, ex p Nicole Seymore-Smith and Laura Perez* [1999] ECR I-623, which concerned the coverage of employment protection.

now largely covered by the Part-Time Work Directive 97/81 discussed earlier. Article 4 of the Recast Directive contains the principle of equal pay and provides that

> for the same work or for work to which equal value is attributed direct and indirect discrimination on grounds of sex with regard to all aspects and conditions of remuneration shall be eliminated. In particular where a job classification system is used for determining pay, it shall be based on the same criteria for both men and women and so drawn up as to exclude any discrimination on grounds of sex.

The concept of pay is broad and refers to the 'ordinary basic or minimum wage or salary and any other consideration, whether in cash or in kind, which the worker receives directly or indirectly in respect of his/her employment from his/her employer'.[127]

4.2.2 Harassment

Harassment is defined as unwanted conduct related to the sex of a person with the purpose or effect of violating the dignity of a person, and of creating an intimidating, hostile, degrading, humiliating, or offensive environment,[128] while *sexual harassment* is defined as 'where any form of unwanted verbal, non-verbal or physical conduct of a sexual nature occurs, with the purpose or effect of violating the dignity of a person, in particular when creating an intimidating, hostile, degrading, humiliating or offensive environment'.[129] This is per se discriminatory.

4.2.3 The reversed burden of proof and remedies

The protection and efficiency of equality law has been increased by the reversed burden of proof, developed by the Court, and subsequently codified in secondary law (first in the Burden of Proof Directive, now in the Recast Directive). When 'persons who consider themselves wronged because the principle of equal treatment has not been applied to them establish before a court or other competent authority, facts from which it may be presumed that there has been direct or indirect discrimination, it shall be for the respondent to prove that there has been no breach of the principle of equal treatment'.[130]

The Directive also contains provisions on victimization, sanctions and remedies, procedures, and the need for Member States to take adequate measures to promote social dialogue between the social partners, with a view to fostering equal treatment.[131] The Treaty-based mainstreaming approach directed at the EU is complemented here by a similar obligation for the Member States to take equality between men and women into account when formulating and implementing law, regulations, and administrative provisions, as well as policies and activities in the areas referred to in the Directive.[132]

---

[127] Art 2(1)(e). See also eg Case C-427/11 *Kenny*, judgement of 28 February 2013, nyr. See further Barnard, *EU Employment Law* (n 3) 298 *et seq* on, eg the scope for objective justification and the concept of pay. [128] Art 2(1)(c).
[129] For a further discussion of sexual harassment and harassment on grounds of gender, and the challenges associated with the current framework, see A Numhauser-Henning and S Laulom, *Harassment Related to Sex and Sexual Harassment Law in 33 European Countries: Discrimination versus Dignity* (European Network of Legal Experts in the Field of Gender Equality, 2012). [130] Art 19.
[131] The EU has put in place institutional support for the realization of gender equality, eg the establishment of the European Institute for Gender Equality in Vilnius. [132] Art 29.

4.2.4 Pregnancy, maternity, and parental leave

While most of the EU gender equality law is premised on the idea that men and women should be treated equally, for obvious reasons this does not work in the case of pregnancy and maternity.[133] The Court first clarified in *Dekker*[134] that discrimination on grounds of pregnancy constitutes direct discrimination on grounds of sex, as pregnancy is intrinsically linked to the female sex. In these cases there is no need for a comparator. This is now codified in the Recast Directive, according to which gender discrimination includes 'any less favourable treatment of a women related to pregnancy'.[135] In case law the Court has applied this principle, for example in cases of appointment, dismissal and employment, and working conditions.[136] According to the Recast Directive 'a woman on maternity leave shall be entitled after the end of her period of maternity leave, to return to her job or to an equivalent post on terms and conditions which are no less favourable to her and to benefit from any improvement in working conditions to which she would have been entitled during her absence'.[137]

In 1992 the Directive on Pregnant Workers was adopted, with the purpose of implementing measures to encourage improvements in the safety and health at work of pregnant workers, and workers who have recently given birth or who are breastfeeding. This Directive applies to 'workers' as defined by EU law in the areas of free movement of workers and equal pay. The Directive obliges the employer to assess health and safety risks and to take necessary measures to avoid situations where workers are exposed to such risks. If it is not possible to adjust the working situation, the employee has a right to leave with pay and benefits intact. In addition, workers are entitled to three specific forms of protection: first, to time off, without loss of pay, in order to attend antenatal examinations; secondly, to a continuous period of at least 14 weeks' maternity leave, of which at least two mandatory weeks must be allocated before and/or after confinement (compensation is to be provided at least at a level equivalent to sick pay);[138] and, thirdly, protection against dismissal during the period from the beginning of their pregnancy to the end of their maternity leave, save in exceptional cases not connected with their conditions which are permitted under national law and practice.[139] Furthermore, any less favourable treatment of a woman related to maternity leave within the meaning of Directive 92/85/

---

[133] The first Equal Treatment Directive (76/207/EEC) contained no specific provisions for rights for pregnant workers. It allowed, as does Art 28(1) of the Recast Directive, for employers to make special provisions, derogating from the principles of equal treatment, to protect pregnant workers and women on maternity leave.

[134] Case C-177/88 *Dekker v Stichting Vormingscentrum voor Junge Volwassen Plus* [1990] ECR I-3941.

[135] Art 2(2)(c).

[136] See also eg Case C-506/06 *Sabine Mayr v Bäckerei und Konditorei Gerhard Flöckner OHG* [2008] ECR I-1017 as regards *in vitro* fertilization; cf also Case C-207/98 *Mahlburg* [2000] ECR I-549 and Case C-109/00 *Tele Danmark* [2001] ECR I-6993. As regards questions of remuneration in cases of pregnancy and maternity leave, the developments have been less straightforward and the protection is in some cases weaker, see further Case C-342/93 *Gillespie v Northern Health and Social Services Boards* [1996] ECR I-475 and P Foubert, *The Legal Protection of the Pregnant Worker in the European Market* (Dordrecht: Kluwer Law International, 2002).

[137] Art 15. The Member States maintain the right to recognize distinct rights to paternity and/or adoption leave. However, if the Member State recognizes such rights it must take the necessary measures to protect working men and women against dismissal due to the exercise of such rights and to ensure that they are entitled to return to their jobs after such leave, Art 16.

[138] Arts 8 and 11.

[139] Art 10. See *Tele Danmark* (n 136), where the Court stated that the prohibition of dismissal applies both to employment contracts of an indefinite duration and to fixed-term contracts, and Case C-438/99 *Melgar (Jiménez) v Ayuntamiento de Los Barrios* [2001] ECR I-6915, where the Court recognized the direct effect of Art 10.

EEC also constitutes gender discrimination according to the Recast Directive.[140] In 2009 the Commission put forward a proposal to revise the Pregnant Workers' Directive, for example to extend the period of maternity leave to 18 weeks, but the proposal was rejected by the Council.

In 1996 the European social partners at cross-industry level concluded, as a result of the European Social Dialogue, their first Framework Agreement on Parental Leave, which was later adopted as the Parental Leave Directive. In 2010 this Directive was repealed and replaced by a new Directive. The aim of the Parental Leave Directive is to lay down minimum requirements designed to facilitate the reconciliation of parental and professional responsibilities for working parents, taking into account diversified family structures and national law and practices.[141] Men and women are entitled to an individual right to parental leave on the grounds of the birth or adoption of a child to take care of that child until a given age up to eight years, to be defined by Member States and/or social partners. The parental leave must be granted for at least a period of four months, and in order to promote equal opportunities and equal treatment between men and women, in principle it should be provided on a non-transferable basis.[142] The more specific conditions on access and detailed rules for applying parental leave are to be defined by law and/or collective agreements in the Member States. The Member States decide whether parental leave should be paid and, if so, at what level. At the end of the parental leave the workers have the right to return to the same job, or if that is not possible, to an equivalent or similar job consistent with their employment contract or employment relationship.[143] The Member States and/or social partners must also take the necessary measures to protect workers against less favourable treatment or dismissal on the grounds of an application for or the taking of parental leave.[144]

To conclude, EU law does not provide much actual protection for employees when it comes to reconciling parenthood and family life. Many crucial issues are left to the Member States to regulate. The case law of the Court in this area has without doubt provided protection for women, but at the same time underlined perceived differences between men and women in their capacity as parents.

4.2.5 Gender equality beyond the workplace

When it comes to gender equality beyond working life, the Equal Treatment in Social Security Directive 79/7, adopted in the 1970s, aims at the progressive implementation of the principle of equal treatment for men and women in matters of social security and social protection. The ban on direct and indirect discrimination applies to the working population, including self-employed persons, and to statutory social security schemes in relation to sickness, invalidity, old age, accidents at work and occupational diseases, and unemployment (and social assistance, insofar as it is intended to supplement or replace these schemes).[145] Since the Directive aims only at the progressive implementation of the equality principle it does allow States to maintain discriminatory State pension ages.

---

[140] Art 2(2)(c).   [141] Cl 1.   [142] Cl 2.   [143] Cl 5.

[144] Cl 5(4). From the mid-1980s onwards a number of soft law measures in the area of gender equality have been adopted, eg as regards equal opportunities and work–family balance, see eg OJ [1986] L203/2 and OJ [2000] C218/5.

[145] The Self-Employed Directive complements the Recast Directive and the Equal Treatment in Social Security Directive and lays down a framework for putting into effect in the Member States the principle of equal treatment between men and women engaged in an activity in a self-employed capacity, or contributing to the pursuit of such an activity.

The Directive on Gender Equality in Goods and Services adopted in 2004 on the basis of Article 13 EC, extends the scope of gender equality law to the access to and supply of goods and services. The aim of the Directive is

> to lay down a framework for combating discrimination based on sex in access to and supply of goods and services with a view to putting into effect in the Member States the principle of equal treatment between men and women.

As with the Recast Directive, direct and indirect discrimination, harassment and sexual harassment, and instruction to discriminate are all prohibited, and these bans apply to goods and services which are available to the public in both public and private sectors, as long as they are offered outside the area of private and family life.[146] Most notable in this Directive is Article 5(1), which provides that Member States must ensure in all new contracts that the use of sex as a factor in the calculation of premiums and benefits in insurance and related financial services will not result in differences in an individual's premiums and benefits. In *Test-Achats*[147] the Court used Articles 21 and 23 of the Charter of Fundamental Rights and the general principle of equal treatment for men and women to invalidate Article 5(2), which allowed for an exemption from the main rule and a possibility for the Member States to permit proportionate differences in an individual's premium and benefits in these cases (eg the UK relied on Article 5(2) to justify allowing the insurance industry to charge higher insurance premiums to young male drivers than to young female drivers). The Court argued that

> this provision, which enables the Member States in question to maintain without temporal limitation an exemption from the rule of unisex premiums and benefits, works against the achievement of the objective of equal treatment between men and women, which is the purpose of Directive 2004/113, and is incompatible with Articles 21 and 23 of the Charter.

In 2012 the Commission put forward a proposal for a Directive on the basis of Article 157(3) TFEU for the improvement of the gender balance among non-executive directors of companies listed on stock exchanges.[148] The purpose of the proposal is to increase substantially the number of women on corporate boards and to promote gender equality in economic decision-making. The proposal is interesting, as it provides for unusual flexibility for the Member States as regards the realization of the Directive's aims, while at the same time it is clearly inspired by the Court's case law as regards positive action in employment.

4.3 Comprehensive equality and protection against discrimination on other grounds

4.3.1 Discrimination on grounds of racial or ethnic origin

The Race Directive 2000/43 aims at combating discrimination on grounds of racial or ethnic origin.[149] The Directive applies in employment, vocational training, social protection,

---

[146] Art 3. However, the Directive does not apply to the content of media, advertising, and education.

[147] Case C-236/09 *Association Belge des Consommateurs Test-Achats ASBL v Conseil des ministres* [2011] ECR I-773.   [148] See COM(2012) 614 final.

[149] Art 1. The concept of racial or ethnic origin is not defined in the Directive, however, differences of treatment based on nationality is not covered. Compare also the Preamble that states that the 'European Union rejects theories which attempt to determine the existence of separate human races. The use of the term "racial origin" in this Directive does not imply an acceptance of such theories'.

including social security and health care, social advantages, education, and access to and
supply of goods and services, and contains protection against direct and indirect discrimination, harassment, and instructions to discriminate as well as the rule on a reversed burden of proof. The Directive provides scope for positive action, as well as an exemption for
genuine and determining occupational requirements.

Article 2(2)(a) of the Race Directive states that direct discrimination requires *one person*
to have been treated less favourably than another. Despite this, the Court found in *Firma
Feryn*[150] that a public statement by an employer that he would not recruit employees of a
certain ethnic or racial origin constituted direct discrimination, even though there was no
identified victim. This has been called *discrimination by declaration*.[151]

4.3.2 Discrimination on other grounds

The Employment Equality Directive lays down a general framework for combating discrimination on the grounds of religion or belief, disability, age, or sexual orientation, as regards
employment and occupation. Like the Race Directive, this Directive contains protection
against direct and indirect discrimination, harassment, and instructions to discriminate,
as well as a rule on a reversed burden of proof. The Directive provides a scope for positive
action, as well as an exemption for genuine and determining occupational requirements.

Disability

In relation to *disability*, Article 5 regulates the issue of reasonable accommodation and
states that 'employers shall take appropriate measures, where needed in a particular case,
to enable a person with a disability to have access to, participate in, or advance in employment, or to undergo training, unless such measures would impose a disproportionate burden on the employer'.[152] In *Coleman*[153] a woman was found to have suffered discrimination
when she was treated less favourably and harassed because of her son's disability, so-called
'*transferred*' or '*associated discrimination*'. The Court held that the applicability of the ban
on discrimination was not dependent on 'a particular category of persons' but by reference
to the grounds protected by the Directive.[154]

The EU Member States and the EU have signed the United Nations Convention on the
Rights of Persons with Disabilities. In *HK Danmark*[155] the Court aligned its interpretation of the concept of disability with that of the UN Convention and declared that the
Convention formed an integral part of the EU legal order, wherefore the Directive had to 'as
far as possible, be interpreted in a manner consistent with that Convention'. The Court also
clarified that a reduction in working hours may constitute one of the reasonable accommodation measures referred to in Article 5.[156]

---

[150] C-54/07 [2008] ECR I-5187.

[151] *Firma Feryn* has now been confirmed in Case C-81/12 *ACCEPT*, judgement of 25 April 2013, nyr, in
relation to sexual orientation. In relation to sexual orientation, see also Case C-267/06 *Maruko* [2008] ECR
I-1757, where the Court held that a survivor's benefit granted under an occupational pension scheme fell
within the scope of Directive 2000/78/EC, and that Arts 1 and 2 precluded legislation under 'which, after the
death of his life partner, the surviving partner does not receive a survivor's benefit equivalent to that granted
to a surviving spouse, even though, under national law, life partnership places persons of the same sex in a
situation comparable to that of spouses so far as concerns that survivor's benefit'.

[152] cf also the European Disability Strategy 2010–2020.

[153] Case C-303/06 [2008] ECR I-5603.   [154] Ibid, para 50.

[155] Joined Cases C-335/11 and C-337/11 *HK Danmark*, judgment of 11 April 2013, nyr. cf also Case
C-152/11 *Odar*, judgment of 6 December 2012, nyr.

[156] On the issue of illness, the Court stated that 'if a curable or incurable illness entails a limitation which
results in particular from physical, mental or physiological impairments which in interaction with various
barriers may hinder the full and effective participation of the person concerned in professional life on an

Age

Age, as grounds for discrimination, and the legal regulation of age discrimination, stand out in some respects. The protection against age discrimination covers all chronological ages; thus, both old people and young people are protected. Discrimination on grounds of age – even direct discrimination – can be justified to a greater extent than discrimination on other grounds.[157] This is related to the traditional role age is assigned in the labour market and in labour law. Article 6 states that Member States 'may provide that differences of treatment on grounds of age shall not constitute discrimination, if, in the context of national law, they are objectively and reasonably justified by a legitimate aim, including legitimate employment policy, labour market and vocational training objectives, and if the means of achieving that aim are appropriate and necessary'. In recent years, much of the case law from the Court in the equality and non-discrimination field has evolved around age discrimination, and particularly (old-age) discrimination. The first case was *Mangold* in 2005, which created a lot of attention and debate.[158] In this case the Court unexpectedly declared that not only was age discrimination covered by the Employment Equality Directive, but also that EU law encompassed an (independent) general principle of non-discrimination on grounds of age which might have some form of horizontal application.[159] This was reaffirmed in 2010 in *Kücükdevici*.[160]

Many of the cases have dealt with mandatory retirement rules, and whether these are acceptable, despite the ban on age discrimination. Mandatory retirement is covered by the Employment Equality Directive, and the Court basically deems rules on mandatory retirement to be age discriminatory but can nevertheless be justifiable.[161] The Member States have been given a large margin of appreciation, and when applying Article 6 the Court has found the differences of treatment on grounds of age to be objectively and reasonably justified by legitimate aims, such as intergenerational fairness in terms of access to employment, prevention of humiliating forms of termination of employment, and a reasonable balance between labour market and budgetary concerns. In addition, the means for achieving these aims have frequently been found appropriate and necessary, especially where the individual is entitled to a pension on retirement.[162]

Remedies and reform

Both the Race Directive and the Employment Equality Directive contain provisions on victimization, sanctions and remedies, and procedures.

In 2008 the Commission put forward a proposal, on the basis of Article 19 TFEU, for a Directive aimed at extending the protection against discrimination on grounds of religion or belief, disability, age, or sexual orientation beyond working life to the areas of social protection, including social security and health care, social advantages, education, and access

---

equal basis with other workers, and the limitation is a long-term one, such an illness can be covered by the concept of "disability" within the meaning of Directive 2000/78' (*HK Danmark* (n 155) para 41). The Court, however, also, with reference to its earlier case *Chacón Navas* (Case C-13/05 [2006] ECR I-6488), held that 'Illness as such cannot be regarded as a ground in addition to those in relation to which Directive 2000/78 prohibits discrimination' (*HK Danmark* (n 155), para 42).

[157] See, however, also section 4.3.2, Comparison with the other Equality Directives in relation to flexible work.
[158] *Werner Mangold v Rudiger Helm* (n 98).
[159] See further chapter 6.
[160] Case C-555/07 (n 98).
[161] eg in *Palacios de la Villa, Age Concern England, Rosenbladt, Georgiev, Fuchs and Köhler*, and *Hörnfeldt*.
[162] See further A Numhauser-Henning, 'The EU Ban on Age Discrimination: Potentials and Pitfalls' (2013) 29 *International Journal of Comparative Labour Law and Industrial Relations* 391.

to and supply of goods and services in parallel with the Race Directive.[163] So far, the negotiations have been unsuccessful (due to the difficulty in reaching unanimous agreement as required by Article 19 TFEU).

Comparison with the other Equality Directives

The Equality Directives just discussed are all premised on the principle of equal treatment. They thus have in common with the atypical work directives — Part-Time Work, Fixed-Term Work, and Temporary Agency Work Directives – the use of the principles of non-discrimination and equal treatment as a way to protect employees and improve the quality of flexible work (section 3.3.1). However, neither of these principles is phrased expressly in terms of prohibitions on direct and indirect discrimination or harassment and instruction to discriminate in the atypical work directives, which would put them in line with the Recast, Race, or Employment Equality Directives. In addition, these principles of non-discrimination and equal treatment display a basic difference with regard to traditional equality law. Here, equal treatment is not based on the personal characteristics of the employee (such as race, age, or sexual orientation), but instead on the employment contract and its form and content. This problem is reflected in the *Wippel* case, where full-time workers who were working under a contract which fixed a working week of 38.5 hours were found not to be comparable to Ms Wippel, who was working on a 'work-on-demand' contract.[164]

5 Conclusion

Today, EU labour and equality law enjoy elaborate Treaty support and encompass a large body of secondary law, mainly comprising directives. The Court has developed a rich case law in these areas. This chapter has dealt with many different – though not all – issues of labour and equality law, such as restructuring of enterprises; information, consultation, and worker participation; fundamental Treaty freedoms and national collective labour law; flexible work and working conditions; the EU and national labour law in times of economic crisis; and gender equality, comprehensive equality, and protection against discrimination on other grounds.

We have witnessed an increasing constitutionalization of EU labour and equality law, and the new Treaty aim of a social market economy is likely to influence future developments. Equality law has continuously expanded its scope beyond working life, and in recent years the Court has strengthened the protection against discrimination in some ways, for example through the creation of concepts such as transferred discrimination and discrimination by declaration. At the same time, the *Viking* and *Laval* cases and the development following the economic crisis have fundamentally challenged not only national labour law and freedom of association and rights to collective action and collective bargaining, but have also given rise to a crisis as regards the EU and Social Europe. The *Viking* and *Laval* litigation raises further questions as to whether EU law, and national legal responses to EU law, are really in line with international law.

---

[163] See COM(2008) 426 final. See also COM(2008) 412 final. See further L Waddington, 'Future Prospects for EU Equality Law: Lessons to be Learnt from the Proposed Equal Treatment Directive' (2011) 36 *European Law Review* 163.

[164] *Nicole Wippel v Peek & Cloppenburg GmbH & Co KGK* (n 78).

Thus, EU labour and equality law will continue to face important societal and economic challenges. The challenges also relate to enlargement and continuing variety in Member States' labour law and industrial relations systems, increasingly segmented labour markets and vulnerable groups of workers, an ageing population, and high youth unemployment. A key question will be how to find the appropriate balance between competing interests, as well as between competing rights.

Further reading

C Barnard, 'EU "Social" Policy: From Employment Law to Labour Market Reform' in P Craig and G de Búrca (eds), *The Evolution of EU Law* (2nd edn, Oxford: Oxford University Press, 2011)

C Barnard, *EU Employment Law* (4th edn, Oxford: Oxford University Press, 2012)

M Bell, 'The Principle of Equal Treatment: Widening and Deepening' in P Craig and G de Búrca (eds), *The Evolution of EU Law* (2nd edn, Oxford: Oxford University Press, 2011)

B Bercusson, *European Labour Law* (2nd edn, Cambridge: Cambridge University Press, 2009)

ACL Davies, *EU Labour Law* (Cheltenham: Edward Elgar, 2012)

E Ellis and P Watson, *EU Anti-Discrimination Law* (2nd edn, Oxford: Oxford University Press, 2012)

B Hepple and B Veneziani (eds), *The Transformation of Labour Law in Europe: A Comparative Study of 15 Countries 1945–2004* (Oxford: Hart Publishing, 2009)

J Kenner, *EU Employment Law: From Rome to Amsterdam and Beyond* (Oxford: Hart Publishing, 2003)

R Nielsen, *EU Labour Law* (Copenhagen: DJØF Publishing, 2013)

21

EU health law

Tamara Hervey

1 Introduction

EU health law is the 'new kid on the block'.

The EU's involvement in human health has only relatively recently begun to be recognized as a distinct area of EU law. Before the EU legislature was granted formal competence to adopt health measures, it relied on implied competence, based on the objectives in Article 2 EEC, particularly 'raising of the standard of living'. Explicit competence to adopt public health measures was given to the EU legislature by the Maastricht Treaty. But much of the

EU's health law is based on other competence provisions, in particular those on creating and sustaining the internal market. When the EU legislature adopts measures in other fields that affect health, it is obliged to 'take into account' 'requirements linked to . . . the protection of human health'. This 'mainstreaming' obligation is found in Articles 9 and 168(1) TFEU.

EU health law has also unfolded through many of the 'directly effective' provisions of the TFEU, especially those on free movement of the factors of production, and on free and fair competition, and on the legislation that supports those measures. The Court of Justice has found that EU law on free movement of goods, services, workers, and freedom of establishment, as well as on anti-competitive agreements, and abuse of a dominant position, applies in health contexts. This means that EU health law has been developed through litigation, as well as through Treaty reform and EU legislation.

Hence, EU health law has a 'transversal' nature, cutting across different areas of EU law. It is found in what may seem to be surprising places, to EU lawyers, and especially to health lawyers and those in the health policy community. As we will see in this chapter, EU health law is an excellent case study illustrating many important questions for EU lawyers. What is an appropriate balance in EU law between the 'economic' (free trade, fair competition) and the 'social' (protecting human health, making provision for health care through a national welfare system)? Does EU law push health-care systems towards an 'individual services' model, based on patient choice, and away from a 'welfare system' model, based on equitable care, and maximizing efficiency from public resources, through providing cost-effective care using public services? Where should these questions be determined? Is it appropriate that they are decided by the Court of Justice and national courts, through preliminary references, or should legislation be involved? Where legislative or administrative decisions affect human health, which interests should be represented in those decision-making processes, and how should they be represented? If legislation or administrative action is to be involved, should it be taken at the regional, national, EU, or even global level? What, if anything, does EU law mean for global (health) equality?

This chapter will examine how key provisions of EU law examined earlier in this book interact with health. We start with probably the best-known area of EU health law: the free movement of patients.

2 Patient mobility

Three main aspects of EU law secure patient mobility: EU legislation covering migrant workers and their families, Treaty law on free movement of services, and EU legislation on 'patients' rights'. We consider each in turn.

2.1 Migrant workers: coordination of health-care systems

EU legislation seeks to remove restrictions on free movement of workers that would arise from uncoordinated social security systems. There is, of course, no EU-level social security or health-care system.[1] Each Member State determines its own social security and health-care entitlements. However, if no EU-level law covered this situation, potential migrant workers might be reluctant to take up employment in another Member State because, if they did, they and their families might lose access to health care and medical treatment in the event of illness. The EU legislature's response to this restriction on free

---

[1] See also chapter 13.

movement of workers was to adopt legislation which requires the *coordination* of the separate national social security systems, including their health-care systems. In the relevant EU law, migrant patients are not patients as such, they are migrant workers.

EU law on migrant patients as migrant workers is covered by legislation that dates from the 1970s. Now replaced by Regulation 883/2004,[2] this legislation supports migrant workers, and their families, in the event of them needing to rely on the social security or national health-care system of the host Member State, for instance in the event of an illness or disability that means they are no longer able to work. Regulation 883/2004 essentially covers mobility of patients in three situations:

- emergency medical treatment (relying on the European Health Insurance Card (EHIC; the old E111),

- authorized medical treatment (treatment authorized by the home State, 'home State control'),

- exceptional medical treatment (where the treatment is covered under the patient's home legislation and the treatment is not available for that patient within the time regarded as medically justifiable for obtaining that treatment in their home Member State).

First, there is an entitlement to emergency medical treatment that becomes necessary during a stay in the territory of another Member State.[3] So this would cover, for example, a tourist who suffers appendicitis or a broken limb while on holiday in another EU State. Emergency medical treatment is administered through the EHIC. Secondly, there is a system whereby Member States may authorize individual treatment in another (host) Member State.[4] The home Member State pays for the treatment, and retains responsibility and control over whether to authorize it. Some Member States, particularly smaller States such as Luxembourg and Malta, are frequent users of this provision, partly through tradition and partly because medical expertise and equipment is felt to be superior in other countries. Other Member States, such as the UK, use it rarely.

The third situation was added to the legislation following some litigation involving experimental treatment, where medical opinion was divided on the value of a therapy (in this case, hydrotherapy, a form of physiotherapy or pain management involving hot, cold, or mineral-rich water) and the patient wanted to have the treatment in another Member State.[5] Article 20(2) now requires Member States to grant authorization where the treatment (a) is covered by the health (insurance) system in the home Member State; and (b) cannot be given to the patient within a 'time limit which is medically justifiable' in the home Member State, taking into account the patient's 'current state of health and the probable course of his/her illness'. By implication, then, a patient (who may or may not be a migrant worker) may, exceptionally, rely on Article 20(2).

The key feature of Regulation 883/2004 is thus that, although Member States must adjust their health-care systems so as to allow access of migrant workers, and in exceptional circumstances under Article 20(2) others, Member States essentially keep control over their national health systems. The numbers of migrant workers are relatively small. In any event, virtually all patients accessing medical care under the Regulation are already contributing to the national economy of the host State. They are thus contributing to the national health

---

[2] OJ [2004] L166/1. For a corrected version of the text, see OJ [2004] L200/1. This replaced Regulation 1408/71/EEC (OJ [1971] L149/2; English Special Edition, Series I, Chapter 1971 (II), p 416) and entered into force on 1 May 2010.

[3] Regulation 883/2004/EC, Art 19.   [4] Regulation 883/2004/EC, Art 20.

[5] Case 117/77 *Pierek (No 1)* [1978] ECR 825 and Case 182/78 *Pierek (No 2)* [1979] ECR 1977.

system in the same way as nationals (either through taxation or through 'social insurance', the two main ways in which European health-care systems are financed). Although the emergency and exceptional medical treatment rules constitute an exception to that general position, they do not constitute a major incursion into the power of the Member States to determine entitlements under their national health systems, and arrange them as they see fit. However, a second aspect of EU health law on patient mobility, based on Article 56 TFEU, has disturbed that equilibrium.

2.2 Freedom to receive health-care services

Article 56 TFEU provides that 'restrictions on freedom to provide services within the Union shall be prohibited'. The Court of Justice has held that Article 56 TFEU implies an entitlement of a service *recipient* to go to another Member State to receive services.[6] 'Services' in this context must be provided for remuneration. The Court recognized as early as 1984 that private medical services fall within the scope of Article 56 TFEU.[7] The remuneration for the service need not come directly from the recipient of the services.[8] So health-care services paid for by a sickness insurance fund could fall within the TFEU's concept of services. This is so even though sickness insurance funds are a common means by which Member States finance their national health-care systems. Table 21.1 outlines the key differences between the two models[9] of health-care system found in the EU: Bismarck and Beveridge.

The Court confirmed this principle in the *Kohll* case in 1998.[10] *Kohll* concerned a patient (Mr Kohll's daughter) receiving non-hospital care (orthodontic treatment) in a situation where the home Member State (Luxembourg) operated a system of reimbursement, whereby patients pay for their treatment and are subsequently refunded by their sickness insurance fund. Ms Kohll's doctor recommended treatment by an orthodontist established in Trier, Germany, just over the border. But the Luxembourg social security medical supervisors refused to authorize payment for the treatment from the social security fund. Only one orthodontist established in Luxembourg would have been able to give the treatment, hence Ms Kohll would have had a much longer wait if she had not crossed the border. Kohll challenged the refusal to authorize payment, and the national court referred to the Court under Article 267 TFEU as to whether this refusal was consistent with EU law.

The Court held that 'the special nature of certain services does not remove them from the ambit of the fundamental principle of freedom of movement'.[11] Luxembourg's defence to non-payment included the need to guarantee the quality of medical services, and the need to control health expenditure. The Court was not impressed. It pointed out that health professional qualifications had been harmonized by EU legislation since the 1970s. Hence, the Court claimed, the quality of medical services across the EU was guaranteed. Mr Kohll was seeking reimbursement only for the rate that would have been reimbursed had the treatment taken place in Luxembourg. So no threat to the financial stability of the national

---

[6] Joined Cases 286/82 and 26/83 *Luisi and Carbone* [1984] ECR 377 and Case 186/87 *Cowan* [1989] ECR 195.

[7] *Luisi and Carbone* (n 6) para 16 and Case C-159/90 *Society for the Protection of Unborn Children Ireland v Grogan* [1991] ECR I-4685, para 18.

[8] Case 352/85 *Bond van Adverteerders* [1988] ECR 2124.

[9] This is a *model*. No country adheres to either type in its pure form. All countries have a mix of different funding types, and variations on each type are found across the EU.

[10] Case C-158/96 *Kohll* [1998] ECR I-1931.   [11] Ibid, para 20.

Table 21.1 Model of types of organization of national health-care systems in the EU

Type	Bismarck	Beveridge
Underlying basis	Social insurance	Taxation
Funding source	Compulsory insurance – paid for by employers and employees	General taxation – paid for by tax-paying population: human beings and legal entities
Coverage	Originally only employees (by sector) and their families. Extended to whole population	Whole population
Funding administered by	Sickness insurance funds (public or private entities, which hold insurance on behalf of patients)	Health ministry (national, or sometimes regional, government)
Health care provided by	Hospitals, clinics, which may be public or private entities	Publicly owned hospitals and clinics
Access determined by	Sickness insurance fund's contract with providers, from among which patients can choose, subject to health-care professional opinion	Health-care professionals, traditionally no patient choice
Patient experience, re funding	May be 'benefits in kind' system, where patient receives health care without awareness of funding arrangements; or may be 'reimbursement' system, where patient pays for care and is reimbursed by insurance	Patients receive benefits in kind, and are not involved in the funding arrangements

health system was present. In the face of Member States which seem reluctant to accept the logic of this reasoning, the Court has repeated it in numerous cases, including as recently as 2011.[12]

Kohll left many questions open. Does the decision apply to health-care systems that operate on a 'benefits in kind' basis? Does it apply to health-care systems funded through public taxation, rather than social insurance? Does it apply to hospital care? Does it apply where the two Member States concerned are at very different stages of economic development, with consequent significant differences in what the national health systems can afford? What if the medical treatment is cheaper in the host Member State: could a patient make a profit from their home national health system? What about if a treatment is forbidden or restricted in the home Member State, on ethical grounds, such as IVF for women over 40 years old – would that Member State be forced to pay for it if it were undertaken in another Member State, where it is permitted? Does it apply to services ancillary to the medical treatment itself? What about travel and accommodation for an accompanying family member? What is the *Kohll* ruling's relationship with Regulation 883/2004? What 'objective public interest' justifications would be successful, and under what circumstances?

It was not a surprise that further litigation followed, clarifying many of these questions.

[12] Case C-255/09 *Commission v Portugal* ('*Non-hospital medical care*') [2011] ECR I-10547.

Case study 21.1: Mrs Watts' hip replacement

Mrs Watts, a wheelchair user, was told in September 2002 that she needed a double hip replacement, and that she would have to wait for around a year before she could have the treatment, under the care of Bedford Primary Care Trust (PCT), England. Her daughter, a journalist, knew of the *Kohll* ruling, and asked the PCT to authorize treatment abroad. The PCT refused, saying that surgery would be available in England for Mrs Watts within a reasonable time, taking account of her consultant's assessment of her medical need. In March 2003, her condition worsened. Even though her NHS waiting time had also shortened, Mrs Watts decided to have the surgery in Abbeville, France. She paid the French hospital for her treatment in advance. She then asked the PCT for reimbursement of the cost, and was again refused.

Mrs Watts sought judicial review of that decision first in the High Court, which upheld the PCT's decision, and then on appeal before the Court of Appeal, which referred the case to the Court of Justice. The Court held that the *Kohll* ruling applied to the English NHS, even though hospital treatment is provided to patients who need it in England free of charge, and paid for by taxation. Although it is acceptable for cross-border hospital care to be subject to prior authorization, it was not acceptable that that prior authorization was based on a system that paid no attention to the individual patient concerned. Prior authorization could not be refused just because of hospital waiting times, where these were used as a general instrument for planning and managing hospital resources, on the basis of predetermined general clinical priorities. What was required is an individual objective assessment of the patient's medical situation, including her pain and disability at the time the authorization was sought.

The case settled before the Court of Appeal gave its final ruling. Mrs Watts was represented by Richard Stein, a well-known judicial review and human rights solicitor. For him, the case was a victory not only for Mrs Watts, but also because of the changes it forced on the NHS at the time. Rather than risk increasing numbers of patients going abroad, the NHS reduced waiting times for elective procedures such as hip replacements, by allowing PCTs to contract with private hospitals in England with unused capacity. It also meant that decisions about undue waiting times were individual medical decisions, not general administrative decisions.

But others have criticized the ruling, pointing out that Mrs Watts, and patients like her, are relatively healthy, and relatively wealthy. The case moves the NHS towards a more consumerist basis, with a strong emphasis on individual patient choice. In the context of an NHS with limited resources, it may be that increased choice for some patients means worse treatment for others, who are less able to exercise such choice.

The principles in *Kohll* apply to all types of national health-care system.[13] This must be correct. Although it is common to distinguish between 'Bismarckian' social insurance health-care systems and 'Beveridge' taxation systems, in reality these categories represent only ideal types (see Table 21.1). Every health-care system across the EU relies on a mix of funding sources, including user charges; compulsory, social, voluntary, or private insurance; as well as public taxation. Given the budgetary constraints that all Member States

---

[13] Case C-157/99 *Geraets-Smits and Peerbooms* [2001] ECR I-5473; Case C-372/04 *Watts* [2006] ECR I-4325; and Case C-444/05 *Stamatelaki* [2007] ECR I-3185.

face, it would be wrong of the Court of Justice to prevent policy experimentation that might lead to more efficient funding of national health-care systems. Given that all the Member States use taxation to some extent in their health-care systems, there is no good reason to distinguish between 'Beveridge' and 'Bismarck' systems in terms of the scope of application of Article 56 TFEU. It is also right that the Court does not distinguish between hospital and non-hospital care, in terms of the scope of Article 56 TFEU.[14] Good medical practice can mean treating patients outside hospitals where possible, and many Member States have health-care systems that are based on polyclinics and other health institutions that do not involve patients staying overnight. It would be wrong if the application of Article 56 TFEU inadvertently encouraged Member States to bring as much health care as possible into hospitals.

Although *Kohll* applies in principle whichever two Member States are concerned, Article 56 TFEU does not require Member States to extend the 'basket of care' that is reimbursable under their health system.[15] This presumably applies both to innovative treatments, which tend to be expensive, and also to treatments that have been excluded from coverage on ethical grounds in a particular Member State. No litigation that has reached the Court of Justice has attempted to extend *Kohll* in such a way as to undermine such ethics-based settlements involving national health systems. The pre-*Kohll* case of *Grogan*[16] involved privately remunerated abortions; the *Diane Blood* case,[17] involving posthumous use of gametes without written consent, was confined in its reach, because subsequent changes to the practices of the Human Fertilisation and Embryology Authority meant that its fact-pattern could not arise again. In any event, it was not referred to the Court of Justice by the national court. Moreover, a patient may not make a profit through relying on their rights to cross-border health care under Article 56 TFEU.[18] However, expenditure on the patient's board and lodging, while receiving cross-border health care, can be regarded as an integral part of the treatment itself.[19]

Where free movement of patients is concerned, the most significant aspect of the *Kohll* ruling is the exceptionally broad definition given to the term 'restriction' in that context.[20] As the Court has put it:

> Article [56 TFEU] precludes the application of any national rules which have the effect of making the provision of services between Member States more difficult than the provision of services purely within a Member State.[21]

In terms of the relationship between Article 56 and Regulation 883/2004, the Court has held that the rules in the Regulation on authorization must be interpreted consistently with the Treaty. The consequence is that, if national rules on prior authorization make it more difficult to have the treatment in another Member State, then those rules (even though permitted by the EU legislature) are 'restrictions' in the sense of Article 56 TFEU, and are prohibited unless justified.[22] Given that national health systems are organized on a national territorial basis, the effect is that all sorts of perfectly logical rules from the point of view

---

[14] Case C-368/98 *Vanbraekel* [2001] ECR I-5363.
[15] Case C-173/09 *Elchinov* [2010] ECR I-8889.
[16] Case C-159/90 (n 7).
[17] *R v Human Fertilisation and Embryology Authority, ex p Blood* [1997] 2 All ER 687.
[18] *Vanbraekel* (n 14).   [19] Case C-8/02 *Leichtle* [2004] ECR I-2641.
[20] For a more detailed discussion on this point, see chapter 13.
[21] *Stamatelaki* (n 13) para 25. See also chapter 13.
[22] Case C-56/01 *Inizan* [2003] ECR I-12403 and *Leichtle* (n 19).

of running an efficient health system, with scarce public resources, potentially fall foul of Article 56 TFEU.

Fortunately, the Court's jurisprudence has taken this into account. The Court has long recognized that the social protection provided by national social security systems can be an 'objective public interest' justifying restrictions on the free movement of services.[23] To begin with, in the context of free movement of patients, the Court allowed restrictions on hospital care, referring to the distinct characteristics of the hospital sector, in particular the planning of the number of hospitals, their geographical distribution, the way in which they are organized, the equipment with which they are provided, and the nature of the health services they are able to offer. By 2010, the Court had recognized that a restriction on free movement of patients could be justified outside a hospital setting where treatment involved the use of major medical equipment, such as PET (positron emission tomography) scanners, MRI (magnetic resonance imaging) scanners, hyperbaric chambers, and cyclotrons, outside hospital infrastructures, again on the basis of the planning necessary to ensure a balanced range of high-quality treatment, and at the same time control costs by avoiding wastage of resources.[24] This brings the case law into line with the legislative position in Article 8(1) of Directive 2011/24, which is discussed in the following section.

2.3 The Patients' Rights Directive

Where the Court of Justice creates significant uncertainties for relevant actors, the governments of the Member States, acting within Council, may have a stronger incentive to adopt EU-level legislation, to clarify matters, or indeed to seek to persuade the Court to modify its approach. This was the case for the case law on free movement of patients. The governments of the Member States called on the Commission in 2006 to bring forward a specific legislative proposal responding to *Kohll*. This followed the adoption of the general Directive 2006/123/EC on services in the internal market, which does not apply to

> healthcare services whether or not they are provided via healthcare facilities, and regardless of the ways in which they are organised and financed at national level or whether they are public or private.[25]

A lengthy legislative process ensued, resulting in the adoption of Directive 2011/24/EU on Patients' Rights in Cross-Border Healthcare.[26] The Commission's stated aims of the proposal[27] were as follows:

- to help patients exercise their rights to reimbursement for health treatment in any EU country (cross-border health care),
- to provide assurance about the safety and quality of cross-border health care,
- to foster cooperation between health systems to improve health care for all.

These aims, along with the title of the Directive, make the Directive sound highly patient-focused, bolstering patient choice and autonomy, as well as promoting high-quality,

---

[23] Case C-272/94 *Guiot and Climatec* [1996] ECR I-1905. See further chapters 13 and 16.

[24] Case C-512/08 *Commission v France* ('*Major medical equipment*') [2010] ECR I-8833.

[25] Directive 2006/123/EC, Art 2(2)(f).

[26] Directive 2011/24/EU of the European Parliament and of the Council on the application of patients' rights in cross-border healthcare (OJ [2011] L88/45).   [27] COM(2008) 414 final.

and efficiently provided, health care. Actually, once analysed, the terms of the Directive are rather more about ensuring enhanced national control over cross-border health care.

Directive 2011/24/EU articulates the 'general principle' that the home Member State must reimburse the costs of patients receiving cross-border health care.[28] But this rule is subject to three important exceptions:

- the 'basket of care' provision;
- Regulation 883/2004;
- Directive 2011/24/EU, Articles 8 and 9.

We shall examine these exceptions in turn. First, the rule that cross-border patients are to be reimbursed by their home Member State applies *only* if the treatment concerned is among the benefits to which that patient is entitled in the home Member State.[29] Thus the home Member State controls the 'basket' of health-care entitlements. There is no independent right of a patient to receive any health care they might wish to receive, if that treatment is not available at home.

Secondly, the rule on reimbursement by the home State is subject to Regulation 883/2004. Article 22(2) of the Regulation requires national authorities to consider whether a treatment method available in another Member State 'corresponds to benefits provided for' by the legislation of the home Member State. If it does, then prior authorization rules that refuse to reimburse a treatment carried out in another Member State, may breach EU law.[30] But if we turn this reasoning to its logical reverse, if the treatment sought does *not* correspond to benefits provided under the home system, it follows that there is no obligation to authorize treatment in another Member State under the Regulation. Hence, there is no obligation to pay for such treatment under the Patients' Rights Directive either.

Thirdly, the reimbursement rule is subject to Articles 8 and 9 of the Patients' Rights Directive. Article 8 permits Member States to provide for a system of prior authorization for reimbursement of the costs of cross-border health care, listing the types of health care that may be subject to such prior authorization. The list goes much further than the Court's jurisprudence:[31]

(a) health care that is 'made subject to planning requirements relating to the object of ensuring sufficient and permanent access to a balanced range of high-quality treatment in the Member State concerned or to the wish to control costs and avoid, as far as possible, any waste of financial, technical and human resources and:

    (i) involves overnight hospital accommodation of the patient in question for at least one night; or

    (ii) requires use of highly specialised and cost-intensive medical infrastructure or medical equipment';[32]

(b) health care that 'involves treatments presenting a particular risk for the patient or the population'; or

(c) health care that is 'provided by a healthcare provider that, on a case-by-case basis, could give rise to serious and specific concerns relating to the quality or safety of the

---

[28] Directive 2011/24/EU, Art 7(1).   [29] Ibid.
[30] *Elchinov* (n 15) para 62.
[31] See eg *Geraets-Smits and Peerbooms* (n 31) and Case C-385/99 *Müller-Fauré/Van Riet* [2003] ECR I-4509.
[32] See also *Major medical equipment* (n 24).

care, with the exception of healthcare which is subject to Union legislation ensuring a minimum level of safety and quality throughout the Union'.

Member States may therefore refuse to authorize reimbursement of cross-border health care under the terms of the Directive. Although in theory the Court could assert the entitlements of patients under the constitutionally superior Article 56 TFEU, in practice the Court has, since around 2010, been bringing its Article 56 TFEU jurisprudence into line with the Directive.[33] Nevertheless, there are circumstances in which Member States *must* authorize cross-border treatment. These are outlined in Article 8(5):

> when the patient is entitled to the healthcare in question in accordance with Article 7, and when this healthcare cannot be provided on its territory within a time-limit which is medically justifiable, based on an objective medical assessment of the patient's medical condition, the history and probable course of the patient's illness, the degree of the patient's pain and/or the nature of the patient's disability at the time when the request for authorisation was made or renewed.

As already noted, the provision is consistent with the system under Regulation 883/2004, in that it leaves the control over the 'basket' of health-care entitlements with the home Member State. Moreover, the Patients' Rights Directive contains a further protection for the national health systems of home Member States, under Article 8(6). Authorization need not be granted where

(a) the patient will, according to a clinical evaluation, be exposed with reasonable certainty to a patient-safety risk that cannot be regarded as acceptable, taking into account the potential benefit for the patient of the sought cross-border healthcare;

(b) the general public will be exposed with reasonable certainty to a substantial safety hazard as a result of the cross-border healthcare in question;

(c) this healthcare is to be provided by a healthcare provider that raises serious and specific concerns relating to the respect of standards and guidelines on quality of care and patient safety, including provisions on supervision, whether these standards and guidelines are laid down by laws and regulations or through accreditation systems established by the Member State of treatment;

(d) this healthcare can be provided on its territory within a time-limit which is medically justifiable, taking into account the current state of health and the probable course of the illness of each patient concerned.

So we see that, in spite of its name, the arrangements under the Patients' Rights Directive give significant control to the national health authorities in the home (paying) Member State. If health care can be given in the home Member State, within a time limit that is 'medically justifiable', then the patient has no rights under the Directive to cross-border health care. The Directive has thus significantly tightened national control over the litigation processes begun by the *Kohll* case. Nonetheless, Member States that had in the past given very little information to patients about their options to seek health care in other Member States have now been obliged to make matters much clearer to such patients. This is probably the most significant aspect of the legislation.

---

[33] See V Hatzopoulos and T Hervey, 'Coming into Line: The EU's Court Softens on Cross Border Healthcare' (2013) 8 *Health Economics Policy and Law* 1.

3 Health-care professionals

EU health law also covers health-care professionals. The relevant law seeks to secure free movement of self-employed persons establishing themselves in another Member State, workers, and service providers, through mutual recognition of professional qualifications (a key component of general EU law on free movement of persons). Originally, EU legislation on mutual recognition of professional qualifications took two broad approaches: a 'sectoral' approach that covers specific professions (eg dentist or midwife), and a 'general' approach that applies to other professional qualifications. The two approaches were brought together into one legislative instrument in 2005.[34] A range of problems with the relevant EU law have led to proposals for reform.

3.1 The 'sectoral' approach

The law on professional mobility in the EU has been covered by internal market legislation since the 1970s. Some of the first professions to be regulated by the EU were the medical and nursing professions: doctors, dentists, pharmacists, midwives, general care nurses. The EU legislature originally adopted a 'sectoral' approach to mutual recognition of professional qualifications, so as to enable freedom of movement. The essential aim of its original directives was to enable the automatic recognition in all Member States of a licence to practise a profession in one Member State. Each sector was covered by two directives. One defined at EU level the minimum educational requirements for access to the profession. Member States were required, where necessary, to adjust their national degree programmes in order to meet these requirements. The other directive simply listed, by official title, all diplomas which satisfy the requirements. Host Member States were allowed to ensure that health professionals had sufficient language skills to communicate with their patients.[35] But otherwise, the beauty of the sectoral system was its simplicity: it allowed for recognition of qualifications without the need for assessing the qualifications of each migrant professional on an individual basis.

That was the idea in theory. In practice, however, in many Member States non-national health professionals were not universally accepted or trusted, and the minimum training requirements were seen as inadequate, as they did not cover the specific content of training, or dictate the level of competence that a professional must reach. For instance, comparisons between the number of patients that trainee doctors were required to treat before qualifying showed significant differences – one study from the 1990s showed that UK trainee doctors had to see around 210 patients with trauma before qualifying, whereas the equivalent figure in Sweden, Finland, the Netherlands, and France was around 30 patients. Worse, the need for full EU legislative agreement meant it was difficult to change educational requirements to reflect changes in scientific understanding or good practice in medical education. Moreover, the sectoral system worked only for professions where there was a general consensus across the Member States about the scope and meaning of a particular professional title. This is not the case for many health professions, such as psychologists, chiropractors, osteopaths, or opticians.

---

[34] Directive 2005/36/EC (OJ [2005] L255/22).
[35] Confirmed in Case C-424/97 *Haim II* [2000] ECR I-5123.

3.2 **The 'general' approach**

In the late 1980s, the EU moved to a system of 'general' directives on mutual recognition of qualifications, covering all other professions. The two systems (general and sectoral) were consolidated in Directive 2005/36/EC,[36] which is the current applicable legislation. Many of its key principles were established through the Court's case law.[37] Under the general system, the basic logic is the idea of 'mutual recognition'. Member States are required to consider, on a case-by-case basis, whether a qualification from another Member State is equivalent to its own qualification. Host Member States must take into account professional qualifications, and experience of practice in another Member State, and compare the knowledge and abilities certified by the professional qualification, and experience, with those required by national rules.[38] If the qualification is not equivalent, then the Member State must decide what 'compensating measures' must be taken by a health-care professional seeking to establish herself in the host Member State. 'Compensating measures' can take the form of an aptitude test, or a period of adaptation. Health-care professions differ quite significantly across the EU, so Member States consider compensating measures to be justified in the vast majority of health professions covered by the 'general' system.

In general, 'compensating measures' apply only to the exercise of freedom of *establishment*. Host Member States may not restrict provision of *services* for any reason relating to professional qualifications. If the service provider is lawfully established in one Member State, they must be allowed to provide services in any other.[39] The distinction between establishment and services here is about permanence or temporary activity.[40] However, what is important here is that this general rule does *not* apply to health services. Directive 2005/36/EC explicitly allows Member States to check the professional qualifications of the health service provider prior to the first provision of services.[41]

Nevertheless, this ability to check qualifications of health professionals who provide cross-border services has not always been effectively used. Various Member States have used the EU service mobility rules to bring in locums (temporary staff) from other Member States so as to fill gaps in national capacity, and provide continuity of care, particular at unpopular times, such as weekends. The case of David Gray, a patient who was killed by a German locum, Daniel Ubani, on his first UK shift, is an illustration of how differences in professional practice between different Member States can have tragic consequences. Ubani had administered a lethal dose of diamorphine, and later admitted that he was not familiar with the drug as used in British contexts. He was convicted of manslaughter and gross negligence, and struck off the UK register of GPs, although apparently was able to continue to practise in his home Member State. After Ubani's conviction, the British Medical Association, General Medical Council, and the House of Commons Health Committee called for reform of EU law on mutual recognition of health professionals' qualifications, and this reform is now underway, as part of a general revision of the relevant EU legislation.

3.3 **Concerns about EU law on health professionals**

Several problems with EU law on health professionals have been identified:

- no provision for continuous professional development,

---

[36] OJ [2005] L255/22.   [37] See further chapter 13.   [38] Directive 2005/36/EC, Art 14.
[39] Ibid, Art 5(1). This rule is also reflected implicitly in Directive 2006/123/EC (OJ [2006] L376/36), Art 16.
[40] Directive 2005/36/EC, Art 5(2); Case C-55/94 *Gebhard* [1995] ECR I-4165. See also chapter 13.
[41] Directive 2005/36/EC, Art 7(4).

- lack of transparency on professional misconduct,
- 'regime shopping',
- they do not concern quality of care.

The EU rules operate on the assumption that initial training of a health professional, at the start of her career, is an adequate guarantor of fitness to practise across a whole career. Yet medical training must keep up with developments in medicine, and continuous professional development is necessary for all health-care practitioners. Moreover, in order to protect patients, systems of peer review, external evaluation, audit, and inspection have been instituted across EU Member States. Some Member States, such as Germany and the Netherlands, require formal revalidation every five years. But there is a very wide range of diversity in systems between, and even within, Member States. Nothing in EU law supports such professional development, or tackles the diversity with its obvious problems for a notional internal market in health-care services. The European Accreditation Council for Continuing Medical Education provides a 'soft law' approach to bringing together best practice in continuing medical education and continuing professional development. But it is not the same as mandatory EU-level legislation.

One of the major concerns about free-moving health-care professionals within the EU is the extent to which 'rogue' health professionals might rely on their free movement rights to evade being barred from practice. Member States are required by Directive 2005/36/EC, Article 33, to exchange information, 'directly relevant to . . . competence or professional reliability' on 'disciplinary or administrative actions or criminal sanctions and decisions concerning insolvency or bankruptcy involving fraud taken by their competent authorities'. Information exchange is subject to national privacy and data protection law. The obligation applies only where another Member State's health system requests the information. A consortium of regulatory bodies was set up in 2005 and its 'Edinburgh Agreement' established a template for a European Certificate of Current Professional Status. A subsequent 'memorandum of understanding' covers agreement to share pertinent information both reactively (when a host Member State requests it) and, in some circumstances, proactively. Again, this is not the same as enshrining such duties in EU legislation. For instance, significant differences in the way that national legislation on data protection is interpreted may impede sharing of information, and possibly lead a host Member State to conclude that a professional is fit to practise when they have been deemed unfit in their home Member State. Moreover, there are significant differences between Member States in terms of perceptions of professional misconduct, and the standard of proof that authorities are required to demonstrate.

A third problem concerns the very different qualification standards that must be met in order to access different health-care professions across the EU. There are two aspects to this problem. First, aspiring health professionals might 'shop around' for the Member State in which they can qualify the most quickly, or cheaply, and subsequently work in another Member State, where the road to qualification for that profession is normally longer. Of course, under the general approach compensation measures may well be applied in such a case, but they could not be so under the sectoral approach, so there is some fear that health professionals covered under that approach might take advantage of any differences in practice between Member States' training requirements (even though in theory they are meant to be the same under the sectoral approach).

Secondly, many Member States, seeking to plan capacity and avoid an over-production of qualified professionals, restrict the numbers of students who can access medical training of various types. Some of these rules have been challenged before the Court of Justice as breaching EU law on non-discrimination on grounds of nationality.[42] The Court has found that indirect discrimination may be justified by the objective of 'maintaining a balanced high-quality medical service',[43] as long as a national court is satisfied that there is a real link between that need and the specific arrangements made for training of future health professionals. The Court has accepted that a Member State need not wait until a capacity shortage arises before taking action, and that forward planning may constitute an objective public interest justification. However, in providing evidence justifying the policy, the Member State must take into account migration patterns of health professionals across the EU.

Fundamentally, the problem with EU law on health professionals is that it is not the aim of the EU provisions to protect patients or to ensure high-quality, cost-effective care. Rather, EU law seeks to promote the free movement of service providers and freedom of establishment of professionals. The relevant EU directives do not grant individual rights to patients, and thus could not be enforced by a patient who received sub-standard care from a professional moving between Member States in reliance upon the Directive.

3.4 **Proposed reform**

The European Commission has proposed revisions to its general professional mobility rules, principally in order to further liberalize services markets across the EU, promote growth through exploiting economies of scale, and make it easier for professionals to relocate and set up in another Member State, hence creating more jobs and tackling workforce skills shortages in some Member States.[44] The proposal builds on the existing legislation and administrative arrangements, including the 'Internal Market Information System' (an online system for local, regional, and national administrative authorities to share and access information about professional qualifications and services provision). It proposes a 'European Professional Card', which is supposed to facilitate the procedure for recognizing professional qualifications. There is certainly evidence that the current procedures for recognition do not work effectively. The UK Department for Business, Innovation and Skills reported evidence of a UK physiotherapist seeking professional recognition in another Member State. He waited four months before receiving a reply, which asked for more information. He supplied that information, but seven months later was asked for the same information, in a different form. A further six months later, he still had not received a decision.[45]

The proposals have raised concerns among health professionals:

- patient safety and quality of professional competence should be paramount, not administrative simplification or European competitiveness;
- the host Member State should remain competent to recognize health professionals;
- Member States must retain competence over training requirements;

---

[42] Case C-147/03 *Commission v Austria* [2005] ECR I-7963 and Case C-73/08 *Bressol* [2010] ECR I-2735.

[43] *Bressol* (n 42) para 62.

[44] Proposal for a Directive of the European Parliament and of the Council amending Directive 2005/36/EC on the recognition of professional qualifications and Regulation on administrative cooperation through the Internal Market Information System, COM(2011) 883 final.

[45] https://www.gov.uk/government/uploads/system/uploads/attachment_data/file/32276/11-794-uk-government-response-mutual-recognition-professional-qualifications.pdf (*gov.uk*, March 2011).

- the idea of 'partial access', where a professional may carry out some of the activity during an adaptation period, is not acceptable for health professions;
- 'backdoor' temporary mobility remains a significant concern.

Some of these concerns have been met with specific aspects of the proposal. It seeks to clarify safeguards for patients, with language competency controls in the host Member State, although it is not clear whether employers could also apply such controls, if regulatory authorities were already doing so. It proposes an alert mechanism if a health professional is prohibited, even temporarily, from practising. However, this applies only to professionals covered by the 'sectoral' approach, rather than imposing a proactive alert obligation applicable to *all* health professionals. The proposal envisages a greater use of technology to screen and share information. Required theoretical and practical hours of medical training and training of nurses are further specified.

4 Health-care institutions

EU health law also applies to health-care institutions. The Court has established that there is nothing special about these bodies that removes them from the scope of EU free movement or competition law. The organization of health systems is a matter for each Member State but, when exercising that power, the Member States must comply with EU law. Some, such as Chris Newdick, have claimed that EU health law therefore implies a threat to European health systems, moving them away from their historical roots based on 'solidarity' (the act of supporting the less well off in a society, through distribution of resources) between citizens within a welfare state, and towards a market-based system, based on individual choice. This section considers such claims, looking first at freedom of establishment and freedom to provide services; then turning to some aspects of EU competition law.

4.1 Freedom of establishment/freedom to provide services

EU law on freedom of establishment and freedom to provide services applies to health-care institutions where they provide services for remuneration, including where remuneration comes from a third party, such as a social insurance fund. The scope of the provisions covers a very wide range of possible 'restrictions' on free movement.[46] Hence, many national rules concerning the organization of national health systems are subject to scrutiny for their compliance with EU law. Some examples include

- single-practice rules, prohibiting health professionals from being registered or practising in more than one Member State;[47]
- registration rules, requiring formal registration and authorization to provide certain health services;[48]
- territorial or capacity-planning rules, restricting the numbers of health-care professionals operating in a geographical area, or the system as a whole;[49]

---

[46] See further chapter 14.
[47] Case C-96/85 *Commission v France* [1986] ECR I-1475 and Case C-351/90 *Commission v Luxembourg* [1992] ECR I-3945.
[48] Case C-108/96 *Mac Quen* [2001] ECR I-837 and Case C-294/00 *Deutsche Paracelsus Schulen v Gräbner* [2002] ECR I-6515.   [49] Case C-456/05 *Commission v Germany* [2007] ECR I-10517.

- limitations on the choice of legal form (eg where a company is established, who may be a partner or company director, who may own a company);[50]
- rules prohibiting profit-making suppliers of long-term care.[51]

Merely stating that a regulatory arrangement is part of the structure and ethos of the national health system is inadequate as a defence in these cases. Member States are required to show that the policy is justified by an objective public interest (eg patient safety, timely access to care, professional ethics, or financial stability of the health-care system), and that the proportionality test is met.[52] The applicable test here requires a Member State to show that the measure constitutes the least restrictive means of protecting the objective public interest, and that no other imaginable measure could achieve that objective with a lesser detrimental effect on free movement. Member States have not been particularly successful in meeting this test. This may be because Member States have been reluctant to accept that free movement law could apply to public health services at all, and so have not always offered an explicit justification. However, it is also because the strong version of the proportionality test is very difficult to meet. Where a particular policy or practice forms part of a public health system, it is not always easy to show that revision of that *specific individual* policy or practice, to enhance free movement, will really jeopardize the financial viability of the *entire system*.

4.2 Competition law

The basic aims of EU competition law are to prevent anti-competitive behaviour and to punish it where it takes place.[53] The three main areas of EU competition law are its anti-cartel rules, its monopolies rules, and its rules regulating mergers. Enforcement is now largely undertaken by national competition authorities, although formal enforcement by individuals through courts is also possible.[54] However, often the effects of the application of competition law in the health sector come from pressure to comply, rather than formal legal sanctions. For example, in October 2011 the Italian Antitrust Authority announced that, in response to its investigation, six foreign companies offering parents storage of umbilical cord blood had agreed to change their marketing material to better inform potential consumers about current scientific developments in the field.[55] The companies had targeted parents in Italy, where cryopreservation of umbilical cord blood for personal use (as opposed to as part of a public blood bank) is prohibited. The unfair commercial practices were targeted as anti-competitive collusive behaviour, which is contrary to competition law.

EU competition law applies to 'undertakings', and prohibits anti-competitive agreements[56] and abusive monopolies.[57] A special exemption applies to 'public undertakings and undertakings to which Member States grant special or exclusive rights'.[58] If such

---

[50] Case 221/85 *Commission v Belgium* ('*Clinical biology laboratories*') [1987] ECR 719; Case C-196/01 *Commission v France* ('*Biomedical laboratories*') [2004] ECR I-2351; Joined Cases C-171/07 and 172/07 *Apothekerkammer des Saarlandes* [2009] ECR I-4171; and Case C-531/06 *Commission v Italy* ('*Pharmacies*') [2009] ECR I-4103.

[51] Case C-70/95 *Sodemare* [1997] ECR I-3395.   [52] See also chapter 16.

[53] G Monti, *EC Competition Law* (Oxford: Oxford University Press, 2007). See further chapter 17.

[54] Case C-453/99 *Courage v Crehan* [2001] ECR I-6297 and Joined Cases C-295–298/04 *Manfredi* [2006] ECR I-6619.

[55] See http://www.agcm.it/en/newsroom/press-releases/1968-umbilical-cord-preservation-antitrust-intervenes-to-change-the-advertising-messages-of-six-companies.html (*AGCM*, 24 October 2011).

[56] Art 101(1) TFEU. An exemption is available under Art 101(3) TFEU.   [57] Art 102 TFEU.

[58] Art 106 TFEU.

undertakings are 'entrusted with the operation of services of general economic interest', they are only subject to the Treaty rules, including those on competition, 'insofar as the application of such rules does not obstruct the performance, in law or in fact, of the particular tasks assigned to them'.[59] The ways in which EU competition law applies to health institutions are illustrated by two high-profile cases concerning health services: *BetterCare Ltd v Director of Fair Trading*,[60] a decision of the British Competition Appeal Tribunal and *Ambulanz Glöckner*, a decision of the Court of Justice.[61]

4.2.1 *BetterCare*

In the *BetterCare* case, a Northern Irish local authority had purchased nursing and social care services, in BetterCare's residential homes, under a standard contract. The local authority itself also provided such residential nursing and social care services, in the same market. In BetterCare's view, the contract for the care services offered unreasonably low prices and unfair contract terms, and was thus abuse of a dominant position. The original complaint was dismissed on the basis that the local authority was not acting as an 'undertaking', because it was purchasing nursing and social care in an 'act of solidarity', for people who lacked the means of their own to pay.

That decision was overturned. The definition of 'undertaking' concerns whether a body is engaged in an 'economic activity', that is, the offering of goods and services in a market,[62] and the extent to which it is subject to State control.[63] Although some acts of the local authority (eg refusing to register a home as licensed to contract with the authority to provide residential care) would not be 'economic' acts, acts such as contracting-out provision of care to the private sector are 'economic' because, when the local authority acquired places in BetterCare's residential care homes on this basis, it was entering into contracts for services in a market.[64] The tribunal went on to decide that the prohibition on 'abuse of a dominant position' applies to unfair purchase prices or unfair trading conditions imposed by a dominant buyer. Likewise, the potential abuse of applying dissimilar conditions to equivalent transactions with other trading parties, also applies to buyers. The tribunal also found that the local authority was a seller of services on the relevant market.[65]

4.2.2 *Ambulanz Glöckner*

Ambulanz Glöckner[66] involved emergency and non-emergency ambulance services. The public authorities of a German *Land* (similar to a state) had entrusted the German Red Cross and the Maltese Aid Service to provide the *Land*'s public ambulance service. This exclusive licence was challenged by a private firm seeking to enter the market, on the basis that the licence was an abuse of a dominant position. The Court of Justice held that the

---

[59] Art 106(2) TFEU. See also chapter 15.   [60] [2002] CAT 7.

[61] Case C-475/99 *Ambulanz Glöckner* [2001] ECR I-8089.

[62] Regardless of the legal status of the body or the manner in which its activities are financed, see Case C-41/90 *Höfner and Elser* [1991] ECR I-1979; Case 118/85 *Commission v Italy* [1987] ECR 2599, para 7; Case C-35/96 *Commission v Italy* [1998] ECR I-3851, para 36; Joined Cases C-180–184/98 *Pavlov* [2000] ECR I-6451, para 75; *Ambulanz Glöckner* (n 61) para 19; and Case C-205/03 P *FENIN* [2006] ECR I-6295.

[63] Case C-350/07 *Kattner Stahlbau* [2009] ECR I-1513 and Case C-113/07 P *SELEX Sistemi Integrati* [2009] ECR I-2207, paras 70–72, 76–77, 79, 92, 96, 102, and 114.   [64] *BetterCare* (n 60) paras 168–171.

[65] Ibid, paras 200 and 201. The case was remitted to the Office of Fair Trading, which decided that no abuse had taken place after all, therefore there was no need to decide whether the local authority was an undertaking, see R Whish and D Bailey, *Competition Law* (7th edn, Oxford: Oxford University Press, 2012) 337.

[66] Case C-475/99 (n 61).

medical aid organizations were 'undertakings', reasoning that because the activity of providing emergency transport services and patient transport services has not always been, and is not necessarily, carried on by public authorities, this was a service, for remuneration from users, on a market, and hence the activity was an economic activity. There was an abuse of a dominant position because the *Land* was required to consult with the medical aid organizations before granting any further licences.

The Court then considered the question whether the grant of exclusive rights to the Red Cross and Maltese Aid was justified as the operation of a 'service of general economic interest'.[67] The Court held that it would be justified, if the exclusive rights were necessary to ensure that those organizations could perform the tasks entrusted to them. The revenue from non-emergency transport offset the costs of providing emergency transport, and that was what made the service economically viable. If private operators were to be allowed to enter the market, and take the more profitable elements of it, this would affect how much that cross-subsidization could continue, and ultimately jeopardize the quality and reliability of the public service.

This 'no cream-skimming' argument is found in several earlier cases, to the effect that Article 106(2) TFEU protects the 'economic equilibrium' of public service provision, which would be upset if further private operators were permitted to enter the market and take the more profitable elements of it, undermining the solidarity-based cross-subsidization that the grant of special or exclusive rights permits.[68] Essentially, the Court applies a proportionality test in its reasoning here: the objective public interest justifying the monopoly or anti-competitive practice is balanced against the restriction on competition. Member States may create undertakings, within their health systems, that operate in ways that breach EU competition law *only* where this is justified by a legitimate national objective, such as providing a health service to all, and where the consequent restriction of competition is limited to what is *necessary* to achieve this objective.

4.3 Assessment

Where a Member State operates its health system on a 'social solidarity' footing, then health-care institutions will not be covered by EU law. National health systems remain within national competence. If, however, a Member State makes changes to its health system, which involve the State acting as an 'economic operator', perhaps seeking to increase management efficiency therein, then EU law will apply. For instance, changes to the ways in which the English NHS operates, with greater use of contracting-out, will lead to increased application of EU competition law in this area. Countries such as the Netherlands, Hungary, and Germany, which have moved in this direction, have already seen competition law being applied to many health institutions. For instance, EU law has been used to scrutinize hospital mergers, including the controversial Zeeland hospitals merger in the Netherlands. Zeeland is located on a relatively isolated peninsula, and the increase in patient travelling time expected after the proposed merger resulted in intense lobbying in opposition to the proposals. It was claimed that, were the merger to go ahead, there would be a significant risk of abuse of a dominant position, as the merged entity would have over 80 per cent of the relevant market. The Competition Authority allowed the merger, subject to some behavioural conditions

---

[67] See further chapter 18.   [68] See eg Case C-320/91 *Corbeau* [1993] ECR I-2523.

(a price cap, quality improvements, and enhancing the bargaining power of the hospitals' consultants).[69]

EU law has also been applied to social insurance bodies (the main way in which health systems are financed across the EU as a whole),[70] hospitals, pharmacies, laboratories, blood and tissue banks, and dentists, as well as health professional organizations. On the one hand, this seems entirely appropriate. It is consistent with the general approach to the balance of competences between the EU and its Member States. As Advocate General Maduro put it in *FENIN*:[71]

> the power of the State which is exercised in the political sphere is subject to democratic control. A different type of control is imposed on economic actors acting on a market: their conduct is governed by competition law. But there is no justification when the State is acting as an economic operator, for relieving its actions of all control.

On the other hand, this approach assumes that the roles and concepts of 'market' and 'State solidarity' are entirely distinct. But in practice they are not. Different types of market involve different levels of competition, and so a more subtly differentiated application of EU law would be more responsive to changing policy contexts within the Member States. Member States are being encouraged to experiment with market models, responding to the challenges of fiscal prudence, ageing populations, and increased demand for ever more expensive medical treatments. Where they do so, they are unlikely to seek to move from a totally solidarity-based provision to one that is totally based on free competition within a market. Instead, they may phase in competitive elements, perhaps only within one part of the system, in order to protect the stability of the health-care system as a whole, and to allow for a period of adjustment. And yet, the ways in which EU competition and free movement law are applied involve considering not health *systems*, but a set of *individual services*, which may or may not be categorized as services of general interest. The structure and approach of EU health law is therefore not conducive to an effective transformation of health services to meet contemporary challenges.

5 Medical devices and pharmaceuticals

The EU has regulated health-care products since the 1960s. Its legislation and administrative rules cover the entire 'life cycle' of such products, from the research and bringing to the market phase, through manufacture, authority to sell, 'pharmacovigilance' (ensuring products on the market are safe, and acting on information that comes to light that suggests they might not be), liability for harm, price controls, and advertising or information. Figure 21.1 illustrates the life cycle of such health-care products.

The EU has also used competition and free movement law to seek to open up markets in these products, and enhance the global competitiveness of the European pharmaceuticals and medical devices industries, while at the same time protecting patients, and those parts

---

[69] See M Canoy and W Sauter, 'Hospital Mergers and the Public Interest: Recent Developments in the Netherlands', available at http://papers.ssrn.com/sol3/papers.cfm?abstract_id=1470695.

[70] Case T-289/03 *BUPA v Commission* [2008] ECR II-81 and Case C-437/09 *AG2R Prévoyance v Beaudout Père et Fils SARL* [2011] ECR I-973; though contrast Joined Cases C-264/01, C-306/01, C-354/01 and C-355/01 *AOK Bundesverband* [2004] ECR I-2493, and see also Case C-185/11 *Commission v Slovenia* ('*Non-life Insurance*'), judgment of 26 January 2012, nyr.   [71] Para 26.

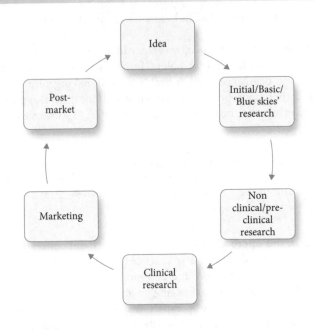

Fig 21.1 The cycle of health technology innovation

Source: G Bache, M Flear, and T Hervey, 'The Defining Features of the European Union's Approach to Regulating New Health Technologies' in M Flear, T Hervey, A-M Farrell, and T Murphy (eds), *European Law and New Health Technologies* (Oxford: Oxford University Press, 2013).

of the industry that pursue innovation and rely on intellectual property law to protect the fruits of their inventions. These competing objectives are not easily reconciled.

5.1 Medical devices

At present, EU law treats pharmaceuticals and medical devices quite separately. The medical devices legislation[72] creates a special, sector-specific version of the system of 'CE' product safety certification, a process governed in general in the EU by the General Product Safety Directive.[73] Product safety is determined by 'certification bodies', which are private companies. Comparison with other countries, such as the US, has shown that many medical devices are permitted within the EU, but not elsewhere, which has raised concerns about the appropriateness of this process for medical devices.

The best-known example is the Poly Implant Prothèse breast implants, manufactured in France and approved by a private German certification body, TÜV-Rheinland. The products duly carried a CE marking, to warranty their safety for the European market, although the manufacturer fraudulently substituted an industrial-grade silicone which caused a much higher rupture rate. The EU's medical devices legislation is currently under review.[74]

---

[72] Directive 98/79/EC (OJ [1998] L331/1), as amended; Directive 90/385/EEC (OJ [1990] L189/17), as amended.   [73] Directive 2001/95/EC (OJ [2002] L11/4). See also chapter 23.

[74] European Commission, Proposal for a Regulation on medical devices, COM(2012) 542 final; European Commission, Proposal for a Regulation on *in vitro* diagnostic medical devices, COM(2012) 541 final.

5.2 **Pharmaceuticals**

Pharmaceuticals (defined by 'presentation'[75] and by 'function'[76]) must have an advance marketing authorization before being sold anywhere in the EU. Marketing authorization can be from a national regulatory body, such as the UK's Medicines and Healthcare Products Regulatory Agency, or from the EU's European Medicines Agency (EMA). Authorization from the EMA is required for pharmaceuticals developed using biotechnology or other high technology processes.[77] Other 'novel' pharmaceuticals, for example those derived from human plasma, may use the EMA procedures. In practice, this covers virtually all truly new pharmaceuticals.

The EMA operates through its scientific committees, made up of national representatives. It assesses marketing authorization applications, which must be made accompanied by a dossier of specified evidence from clinical trials, designed to demonstrate quality, safety, and efficacy. The test is whether the new pharmaceutical works better than a placebo – there is no obligation to show that it is better than existing treatments. Because such existing treatments are likely to be cheaper (not least because they are likely to be off-patent), this requirement is controversial. There are also significant concerns about whether the EMA's procedures are sufficiently robust to deal with the powerful pharmaceutical industry, whose practices have been criticized for being insufficiently attentive to patient safety, as well as presenting significant burdens to national health systems which must pay for expensive new treatments that are brought to market, if they are authorized within the system.

Criticisms have also been made of the lack of transparency of the EMA, and lack of legal oversight of its work. A good example is the Nordic Cochrane Centre's attempts, described in detail by Ben Goldacre[78] and others, to gain access to data on which the EMA relied to make its decisions on two weight-loss drugs, orlistat and rimonabant. Orlistat is currently approved for long-term use by the EMA and US and Canadian authorities; rimonabant is not, due to safety concerns. After a lengthy process, during which the EMA maintained that it could not release the data it held because of the commercial interests of the companies concerned, or because individual patient data could not be removed from the files, the European Ombudsman recommended that the EMA release the documents.[79] The EMA agreed to do so, and the information was finally released some three years and seven months after the original request.[80] The role of the EMA is considered further in case study 21.2.

---

[75] 'Any substance or combination of substances presented for treating or preventing disease in human beings' – Directive 2001/83/EC on the 'Community Code relating to medicinal products for human use' (OJ [2001] L311/67), Art 1(2), as amended.

[76] 'Any substance or combination of substances which may be used in or administered to human beings either with a view to restoring, correcting or modifying physiological functions by exerting a pharmacological, immunological or metabolic action, or to making a medical diagnosis' (ibid).

[77] Regulation (EEC) No 2309/93 of 22 July 1993 laying down Community procedures for the authorization and supervision of medicinal products for human and veterinary use and establishing a European Agency for the Evaluation of Medicinal Products (OJ [1993] L214/1), as amended, Annex A.

[78] B Goldacre, *Bad Pharma* (London: Fourth Estate, 2012) 70–79.

[79] http://www.ombudsman.europa.eu/en/cases/decision.faces/en/5459/html.bookmark (*European Ombudsman*, November 2010).

[80] PC Gøtzsche and AW Jørgensen, 'Opening Up Data at the European Medicines Agency' [2011] *British Medical Journal* 342:d2686.

Case study 21.2: Nancy Fern Olivieri and the deferiprone trials

In the early 1990s, a Canadian scientist working within the University of Toronto, Dr Olivieri, signed a contract with Apotex to support a randomized clinical trial on deferiprone, a promising new treatment for thalassaemia (a blood disorder). The contract included standard confidentiality clauses, which required her to keep all trial data secret for a number of years, unless disclosure was authorized by the company. Olivieri had previously approached the Canadian Medical Research Council, which had declined to sponsor such trials itself, but had suggested that she apply under its 'university-industry' programme. The involvement of private industry in university research is absolutely standard practice in Canada and indeed in Europe.

Initial trial data was positive, and Olivieri published a paper to that effect in 1995. However, later that year she became concerned that, while the results overall looked promising, for a small subgroup of patients, outcomes were much worse. She asked Apotex if she could conduct a separate trial to investigate this, and explained that she had an ethical obligation to inform those patients, and also the University's Research Ethics Board. Apotex reviewed her data, told her that they did not agree with her interpretation of it, terminated her contract, and reminded her of the obligations under the confidentiality clauses. Academics John Abraham and Courtney Davis say that Olivieri had broken an 'unspoken code' of loyalty to the company. The company vice-president is reported as explaining, 'we had problems with her'.

Deferiprone was not granted marketing authorization from Canadian or US authorities. However, undaunted, Apotex turned to the global market. In 1998, it applied to the EMA for a marketing authorization, using Olivieri's trial data, but without her signature. EMA's scientific committee reviewed the data, and recommended that the EMA grant an authorization. Before the European Commission took a formal decision, Olivieri wrote to the committee members, and to the EMA, setting out her concerns. EMA reinvestigated, but granted authorization.

Olivieri sought judicial review of the Commission's decision. The General Court held that the case was inadmissible. It took the view that Olivieri had not established an interest in bringing proceedings in order to protect public health or in order to defend her professional reputation. That decision, to decide the case on the basis of lack of *locus standi* (see chapter 10) and therefore not to review its substance, is highly unfortunate. There are obvious differences in opinion as to how to interpret the relevant scientific information. We might legitimately expect EU law, and the scrutiny of courts, to support processes of making scientific disagreement more visible to policy-making processes and indeed to the public. And yet the Court's decision meant that in this instance it failed to take the opportunity of increasing transparency and accountability. Deferiprone is still on the EU market.

6 Blood, organs, and human tissue

The EU also regulates blood, organs, and human tissue. It does so in two main ways: by requiring Member States to set up institutions and processes of quality control to ensure patient safety; and through intellectual property law. We consider each in turn.

6.1 Patient safety

In the 1990s, the EU adopted various measures of soft law concerning blood safety, responding to the global AIDS epidemic, and the fact that the EU was reliant on blood from developing and transitional economies, especially in the global South. These soft law measures set out non-binding principles for blood donation in the EU, and recommended that the Member States should 'encourage the voluntary and unpaid donation of blood or plasma,'[81] on the basis that this is the safest source of human blood. Now Article 168(4) TFEU gives the EU competence to adopt 'measures setting high standards of quality and safety of organs and substances of human origin, blood or blood derivatives'. The EU has done so, following a standard model in its legislation,[82] which requires Member States to establish 'competent authorities', the task of which is to ensure that quality assurance procedures are followed. The competent authorities manage risk in the collection, testing, processing, storage, and distribution of human materials, and collect and share information on safety.

Anne-Maree Farrell has criticized the EU's blood safety laws for failing to acknowledge sufficiently the reality of the EU market for human blood and plasma products.[83] The underlying approach stresses voluntary donation and an ethic of altruism. There is, however, some scope for out-of-pocket payments, in all of the relevant legislation.[84] The Organs Directive goes further, in that it recognizes that living organ donors might need to be compensated for loss of income.[85]

As well as EU legislation on blood and organ safety, there is Court of Justice case law. The Court has held that Austrian legislation prohibiting importation of blood products where payment had been made for the donation of the blood breaches EU law on free movement of goods, and is not justified by the need to protect public health.[86] Its reasons include the provisions in the Blood Safety Directive which permit reimbursement of donors' expenses and other small tokens of payment. Implicitly, therefore, the Court has accepted that EU law does not require that the donation of human material in health contexts be completely separated from the internal market. This example has important implications for the balance between the interests of EU-wide economic development, expressed through the permissive position of internal market law, and the interests of individuals in safe health care, expressed through policies of precaution.

6.2 Intellectual property

The purpose of a patent is to grant the inventor of a novel product or process exclusive rights over its invention for a period of time, in exchange for full disclosure of the invention. The idea is to reward innovation, by allowing inventors to safeguard the fruits of their labours and investment. Patents can therefore be used as a way of *indirectly* regulating behaviour, because in practice, without the safeguard of a patent right, inventors may either be discouraged from seeking new discoveries, or may seek to keep their inventions secret, thus inhibiting the benefits of those inventions being known more widely.

Where a novel product or process involves human material, either in the product itself or in the process by which the product is created, questions of ethics arise. The EU has

---

[81] Recommendation 98/463/EC, para 14.

[82] Blood Safety Directive 2002/98/EC (OJ [2003] L33/30); Tissues and Cells Directive 2004/23/EC (OJ [2004] L102/48); Organs Directive 2010/53/EU (OJ [2010] L207/14).

[83] See A-M Farrell, *The Politics of Blood* (Cambridge: Cambridge University Press, 2012).

[84] Directive 2002/98/EC, Art 20; Directive 2004/23/EC, Art 12; Directive 2010/53/EU, Art 13(2); see Case C-421/09 *Humanplasma* [2010] ECR I-12869, para 44.   [85] Directive 2010/53/EU, Art 13(2).

[86] *Humanplasma* (n 84).

become involved in these questions, including through the EU law that applies to new health technologies.[87] Directive 98/44/EC on the legal protection of biotechnological inventions requires Member States to recognize biotechnology patents, including for products or processes that contain human material.[88] But the Directive excludes patentability of certain products or processes, including where commercial exploitation would be contrary to *ordre public*, or morality.[89] In particular, the Directive provides that 'uses of human embryos for industrial or commercial purposes' shall be considered unpatentable.[90] The scope of this exclusion is not entirely clear from the text of the Directive.

In *Brüstle*,[91] the Court was asked to clarify what is patentable under the Directive. The science is complex here, and consequently so are its legal and ethical implications. The litigation, brought by the campaigning group Greenpeace, arose in the context of a patent for 'isolated and purified neural precursor cells, processes for their production from embryonic stem cells, and the use of neural precursor cells for the treatment of neural defects'.[92] Neural precursor cells are specialized, immature cells, which have the capacity to develop into various parts of the mature human body, in particular to do with the nervous system. In the very early stages of fertilization, they are found in the blastocyst, the pre-embryonic entity that has developed 5 to 6 days after the ovum (egg) is fertilized. Brüstle's neural cell product and process involve obtaining these neural precursor cells from human embryonic stem cells. The process of doing so involves destroying the blastocyst. The product and the process of transplanting these neural precursor cells into the nervous system are used in the treatment of neural disorders, such as Parkinson's disease, for which there is currently no cure. The question before the Court was the meaning of the term 'the human embryo' in Article 6(2)(c) of the Directive. Does it mean all stages of human life, from the moment of fertilization of the ovum? Does it include the blastocyst? Does it include ova fertilized by transplantation of a nucleus from a mature human cell (sometimes called 'therapeutic cloning'), or by stimulating an unfertilized ovum to grow through cell division by parthenogenesis (a form of asexual reproduction where growth occurs without fertilization)?

The Court adopted a purposive approach to its interpretation of the Directive, pointing to the Directive's aim both to 'promote investment in the field of biotechnology' and to protect human dignity.[93] Hence, 'the human embryo' must be interpreted in its widest sense. It includes any fertilized human ovum, including ova fertilized through 'therapeutic cloning', and non-fertilized ova where growth and development has been stimulated through parthenogenesis. The Court's reasoning is that such ova are 'capable of commencing the process of development of a human being'.[94] By the same token, a product the creation of which involves the destruction of a human embryo, by removing the stem cells from the embryo at the blastocyst stage, is also unpatentable.[95]

The Court of Justice left to the national court the question whether embryonic stem cells derived from a blastocyst are capable of commencing the process of development into a human being, in light of scientific developments.[96] The German Federal Court held that they were not, reasoning that *in vitro* stem cells could not develop without significant intervention. Thus stem cells derived from a blastocyst are patentable in the EU (or at least in Germany). The German Federal Court accepted that, although this was not the case when Brüstle filed for the patent, scientific techniques do now exist whereby human embryonic

---

[87] See further M Flear, A-M Farrell, T Hervey, and T Murphy (eds), *European Law and New Health Technologies* (Oxford: Oxford University Press, 2013); T Hervey and H Black, 'The European Union and the Governance of Stem Cell Research' (2005) 12 *Maastricht Journal of European and Comparative Law* 11.

[88] OJ [1998] L213/13, Art 1(1).   [89] Ibid, Arts 4, 5, and 6.   [90] Ibid, Art 6(2)(c).

[91] Case C-34/10 *Brüstle v Greenpeace* [2011] ECR I-9821.   [92] Ibid, para 15.   [93] Ibid, para 32.

[94] Ibid, para 36.   [95] Ibid, paras 47–52.   [96] Ibid, para 37.

stem cells can be obtained without destroying a human embryo. Therefore, products deriving from a line of stem cells that did not involve the destruction of a blastocyst are also patentable.

The case illustrates well the interactions between national and EU-level judicial decision-making on matters of ethical sensitivity. The Court articulates a strong ethic of human dignity, drawing on Europe's long human rights tradition. Although the legal basis of the Directive is to create the internal market, the needs of market actors appear secondary in the Court's reasoning. Yet, in practice, the significant discretion left to the national court allows for patenting of inventions involving human material, at least in those Member States where national courts are willing to exercise the discretion left to them by the preliminary reference procedure accordingly. Hence, some of the more extreme predictions from the commentary surrounding the Court's *Brüstle* decision (eg that the biotechnology industry would cease to invest in the EU) turned out to be unwarranted.

7 Public health

As we have already seen, the EU has explicit competence to adopt public health legislation. But internal market law also has important effects on public health, where it concerns trade in products that impact on health, in particular, food, alcohol, and tobacco. For example, when Finland joined the EU, it was required to dismantle its State monopoly on alcohol sales. Following the accession of Estonia in 2004, Finland had to reduce its domestic prices in the face of cheap imports from just 'over the water'. The consequence was a steep rise in deaths from alcohol-related problems. Scotland's Alcohol (Minimum Pricing) Act 2012 is being challenged for its consistency with EU law, by various private parties, including the Scotch Whisky Association. The Scottish Court of Session, noting 'overwhelming evidence of grave health, social, economic and public order consequences caused in Scotland as a result of excessive alcohol consumption', has found the rules justified.[97] France, Spain, Italy, Portugal, and Bulgaria (all major wine-producing countries) have indicated their opposition to the rules.[98] In a separate case, the Court has held that EU law prohibits promoting wine on the basis of health claims.[99]

In principle, the EU has considerable legal powers which could be deployed to address obesity, which has become a major European health problem since the 1990s: the Common Agricultural Policy above all, but also food regulation within the internal market. In practice, however, the food industry's links with powerful national governments have kept EU food legislation relatively low key. For example, the proposed 'traffic light' system on 'guideline daily amounts' (the proportion of an average adult recommended amount of protein, fat, sugars, salt, and so on present in a food) did not survive in the text that was finally adopted in the 2011 EU Food Information Regulation.[100]

The EU's public health law concerning tobacco began with its 'Europe against Cancer' programme, established in 1987.[101] By the late 1980s, the EU legislature was able to use new qualified majority voting procedures to overcome opposition in Council from some Member States to legislative measures. Several directives, covering tobacco products and their labelling,

---

[97] *Scotch Whisky Association* [2013] CSOH 70.
[98] http://www.bbc.co.uk/news/uk-scotland-scotland-politics-22182607 (*BBC News online*, 25 July 2013).
[99] Case C-544/10 *Deutsches Weintor eG*, judgment of 6 September 2012, nyr.
[100] Regulation (EU) No 1169/2011 on the provision of food information to consumers (OJ [2011] L304/18).
[101] Resolution of Council and the Representatives of the Governments of the Member States on a programme of action of the European Communities against cancer (OJ [1986] C184/19).

as well as taxation, had been adopted by 1992.[102] These cover matters such as permitted tar, carbon monoxide and nicotine levels, and health warnings. The health warnings provisions were considerably tightened in 2001[103] to include an obligation to list ingredients and additives, and a ban on misleading product descriptions, such as 'light' and 'mild'. The European Commission has proposed new legislation on tobacco additives, labelling, and packaging, as well as on new products, in particular 'e-cigarettes' (electronic devices which release vapour, some of which contain nicotine, designed to look like cigarettes and for users to mimic the action of smoking), which have appeared on the EU market since 2001.[104] The global tobacco industry has been persistent in its opposition to EU health law in this area. Nothing better exemplifies this opposition than the tobacco advertising example.[105]

Case study 21.3: Tobacco advertising

Although the tobacco industry claims that its advertising is aimed at encouraging existing smokers to switch brands, banning tobacco advertising has been proven to reduce smoking. The EU's control of tobacco advertising began with a ban on all TV advertising of tobacco, in Directive 89/552/EEC on cross-border TV services. Eventually, after years of opposition to proposals, Directive 98/43/EC introduced a more comprehensive ban on tobacco advertising across the EU.

This Directive was immediately challenged by Germany, as well as several tobacco companies, as unlawful. The argument was that its 'legal basis' (the Treaty provision giving competence to the EU institutions to adopt the law) was insufficient. The legal basis was for internal market legislation; this was, in reality, a public health measure. Hence, to rely on internal market competence was a misuse of power. The Court of Justice rejected this particular reasoning, but it did hold that the Directive was invalid. It pointed out that prohibiting tobacco advertising on items such as posters, parasols, ashtrays, and so on, which do not cross borders, or in advertising slots in cinemas, in no way facilitates trade within the internal market in those products.

Following the ruling, the Commission regrouped and proposed a revised Directive, which was duly adopted. Subsequent challenges to that Directive were unsuccessful.

Why is Germany so opposed to tobacco advertising regulation? This was a bit of a puzzle. Production of tobacco in Europe, such as it is, is mainly concentrated in the south of Europe. Only around 3,000 hectares are devoted to growing tobacco in Germany; compare the figure for Italy, for instance, which is some 30,000. Information that has come to light, in part through orders made by US courts requiring access to documents, sheds some light on lobbying processes. It seems that the significant German technical industry producing machinery and machine parts for production of cigarettes, not the tobacco-growing industry itself, explains the German opposition to tobacco regulation, and also why the tobacco industry targeted Germany as a key component of its opposition to EU regulation.

---

[102] Directive 89/622/EEC on labelling (OJ [1989] L359/1); Directive 90/239/EEC on tar yield (OJ [1990] L137/36); Directive 92/41/EEC on smokeless tobacco (OJ [1992] L158/30); Directive 92/80/EEC on taxes on manufactured tobacco other than cigarettes (OJ [1992] L 316/10); Directive 92/78/EEC on taxes other than turnover taxes (OJ [1992] L316/1); Directive 92/41/EEC amending labelling Directive 89/622/EEC (OJ [1992] L158/30).   [103] Directive 2001/37/EC on manufacture, presentation and sale (OJ [2001] L194/26).
[104] European Commission, Proposal for a Directive of the European Parliament and of the Council on the approximation of the laws, regulations and administrative provisions of the Member States concerning the manufacture, presentation and sale of tobacco and related products, COM(2012) 788 final.
[105] See also chapter 11.

8 Global contexts

Health is a global concern. Patients seeking medical treatment outside their home country do not confine themselves to the EU – global medical tourism is on the increase. An increasingly mobile world, with cheaper and more frequent air travel, and a global food industry (food is an important disease vector, eg salmonella in eggs and pork, e-coli in beef, BSE in beef, campylobacter in poultry) mean that tackling communicable diseases must happen on a global level. EU and national regulation of food, alcohol, and tobacco, to protect health, must fit within global trade rules for goods, governed by the World Trade Organization (WTO). The pharmaceuticals and medical devices industries are global. Pharmaceutical companies, in particular, are influential global actors, often operating through international organizations, such as the International Conference on Harmonisation of Technical Requirements for Registration of Pharmaceuticals for Human Use (ICH). The ICH agrees technical requirements for demonstrating the quality, safety, and efficacy of new medicines. Although formally non-binding, the ICH guidelines have a 'hard' effect in practice, because, under national or EU law, compliance is necessary for clinical trials or marketing authorization. The EMA's 'Guidance Notes' are based on ICH standards. The World Bank has considered the opportunities and challenges arising from the creation of global health service markets. How does EU health law contribute to global health?

The EU was explicitly given external Treaty competence in health fields for the first time in 1992. The Lisbon Treaty has now consolidated and reconfirmed EU external competence rules: 'The Union and the Member States shall foster cooperation with third countries and the competent international organisations in the sphere of public health'.[106] In 2003, the EU signed the World Health Organization (WHO) Framework Convention on Tobacco Control, the WHO's first binding international treaty on global health concerns.

8.1 Health through the common commercial policy

There is, overall, relatively little formal EU external relations law in health fields. But the EU's 'common commercial policy' and its development cooperation policy (discussed at section 8.2) form a central platform for those aspects of its external health law that are more developed. EU health policy concerning the safety of food (and feed), covered by the WTO Agreement on Sanitary and Phytosanitary Measures (SPS),[107] falls within the fields of trade in goods and agriculture, both of which are within the EU's competences. Competence is shared with the Member States, so both the EU and the Member States have ratified the SPS Agreement. Specific public health scares, such as the BSE/vCJD ('mad cow') crisis or dioxins in pork, have prompted international agreements with countries such as the US,[108] Australia, and New Zealand, in which the EU agreed very detailed rules on animal slaughter, sterilization, inspection, and so on. The EU is associated with a more precautionary approach to risks to human health than the US.

---

[106] Art 168(3) TFEU.

[107] WTO Agreement on the Application of Sanitary and Phytosanitary Measures 1995 (OJ [1994] L336/40).

[108] Agreement between the EC and the USA with regard to the bovine and porcine fresh meat trade (OJ [1993] L68/1); Agreements between the EC and the USA on sanitary measures to protect public and animal health in trade in live animals and animal products (OJ [1998] L118/3 and OJ [2003] L316/21); Agreement between the EC and New Zealand on sanitary measures applicable to trade in live animals and animal products (OJ [2003] L214/38).

8.2 Health through development cooperation

The EU's development cooperation policy affects health in several ways – through the EU's contribution to the Millennium Development Goals,[109] which, for instance, include public health concerns and global health inequalities; through infrastructure and capacity building, including human resource development; and through specific project-based work, for instance combating HIV/AIDS, malaria, and tuberculosis. An important element of the EU's development policy concerns access to essential medicines.

The concept of 'essential medicines' dates from work done by the WHO in the 1970s. 'Essential medicines' are those needed for the priority health needs of a population. The WHO 'essential medicines' list provides a check for governments, particularly in least developed countries. The idea is that access to these 'essential medicines', should be available, irrespective of class, race, religion, sexuality, and other 'forbidden grounds', and at a price affordable to individuals and the community.[110] Millennium Development Goal 8E states that developed countries, in collaboration with the pharmaceutical industry, shall provide access to affordable essential medicines in developing countries.[111] Yet it is reported that there has been no progress overall towards this Goal since 2007. Many patients in least developed and developing countries do not have access to essential medicines.

The EU has been criticized for supporting a global intellectual property regime that contributes to this global health inequality. Operating through the WTO's Agreement on Trade-Related Aspects of Intellectual Property Rights (TRIPS), the EU has recognized a global 20-year patent for novel pharmaceuticals. During that time, generic equivalents to those pharmaceuticals may not enter the marketplace. These generics are much cheaper to produce than on-patent pharmaceuticals, because they are 'reverse engineered' from the on-patent product. The entry into force of TRIPS in 1995 put an end to the practice in many developing countries, particularly India, of making such generics both for home markets and for markets in other developing and least developed countries. However, in 2001 a group of 80 developing and least developed countries successfully proposed the Doha Declaration, which

> reaffirms the right of WTO members to use, to the full, the provisions in the TRIPS Agreement which provide flexibility...to protect public health and, in particular, to promote access to medicines for all.[112]

One possibility for increasing global equal access to essential medicines is to encourage developing and least developed countries to take advantage of these TRIPS flexibilities. Some have suggested that the EU has done quite the opposite. On the other hand, EU technical assistance to developing countries in intellectual property matters puts more emphasis on incorporating TRIPS flexibilities in national law, including those flexibilities concerning public health, than technical assistance from other developed countries.

Pharmaceuticals are an example of a product that is particularly easy to trade. Pharmaceuticals are not perishable, are relatively light and lacking bulk, and they attract high prices. Offering cheaper pharmaceuticals to the world's least developed countries thus

---

[109] The Millennium Development Goals are a series of time-bound targets (with a deadline of 2015) towards ending extreme poverty, agreed at the UN in 2000.

[110] http://www.who.int/topics/essential_medicines/en/ (*WHO*).

[111] http://www.un.org/millenniumgoals/global.shtml (*UN*).

[112] The Doha Declaration on the TRIPS Agreement and Public Health, adopted by the WTO Ministerial Conference, 14 November 2001, WT/MIN(01)/DEC/2.

runs the risk that the products are simply re-exported to the global North, where they will attract greater profits. The EU has sought to enable differential pricing schemes for essential medicines to be supplied to some of the world's poorest countries. Regulation 953/2003 to avoid trade diversion into the EU of certain key medicines[113] sets up a scheme whereby manufacturers or exporters of medicines used to treat HIV/AIDS, tuberculosis, or malaria may apply for 'tiered pricing' for sales into one of 76 named countries.[114] The Regulation makes it illegal to import tiered-priced products into the EU, or to release them for free circulation or place them in a free trade zone or a free warehouse.[115] The system has been used to authorize some nine products.[116] However, the numbers of products sold are declining, suggesting that this approach is not particularly effective compared, for instance, to encouraging generics production, in securing access to essential medicines.[117]

Assessing the contribution of EU health law to overall global health is not easy. Some aspects of EU health law – such as its approach to health risks arising from trade in food – suggest a positive contribution. Equally, EU law on 'tiered pricing' of pharmaceuticals suggests a commitment to at least attempt to redress significant global inequalities embedded in patterns of trade and the structure of the global pharmaceutical industry. Yet even the very selective examples covered in this section are enough to show that EU law may actually have *negative* effects on global health through, for instance, supporting the TRIPS system.

9 Conclusion

EU health law cuts across the taxonomy accepted by EU lawyers[118] as establishing the categories of EU law.[119] In order to understand EU health law, we need to look at the health implications of many areas of EU law, including free movement law, competition law, and external relations law.

EU health law illustrates many of the key tensions of EU law in general. How should EU law balance the 'economic', such as benefits from free trade and fair competition, and the 'social', such as arrangements within welfare systems? How should EU law balance individual choice, such as patients choosing where to have medical treatment, and community solidarity, such as protecting cash-strapped national health systems from individual claims on resources? Who should decide: courts or the legislature? Which courts: national courts or the Court of Justice? Is it justifiable for a court, for the Court of Justice, to undermine a legislative settlement, for instance on coordination of national health systems for migrant patients? Where should decisions about risks to health be made: at regional, national, EU, or global level? Who should be 'at the table' to ensure such decisions are legitimate? How do we ensure sufficient transparency, and judicial scrutiny, to support decisional accountability? How, if at all, should EU law tackle global inequality? These questions will continue

---

[113] OJ [2003] L135/1, as amended.   [114] Regulation 953/2003, Annex II.

[115] Ibid, Art 2.

[116] Listed in Regulation 953/2003, as amended, Annex I, see also European Commission Annual Report (2009) on the application of Council Regulation (EC) No 953/2003 of 26 May 2003 to avoid trade diversion into the European Union of certain key medicines, COM(2010) 652. All of the authorizations are held by GlaxoSmithKline.   [117] European Commission, COM(2010) 652, p 9.

[118] Represented, eg in the main chapter headings in textbooks on EU law, in the way in which the TEU and TFEU are organized into different parts and chapters, each covering different legal topics, and in the taxonomy according to which the EU institutions, particularly the European Commission, organize EU law.

[119] T Hervey and JV McHale, *EU Health Law* (Cambridge: Cambridge University Press, 2004) 're-reads' the places where EU law and health law interact, through the categories of health law, rather than those of EU law.

to be resolved through litigation and legislation, involving the EU institutions, and in interactions with national and global actors.

Further reading

J Abraham and C Davis, 'Science, Law, and the Medical-Industrial Complex in EU Pharmaceutical Regulation: The Deferiprone Controversy' in M Flear, A-M Farrell, T Hervey, and T Murphy (eds), *European Law and New Health Technologies* (Oxford: Oxford University Press, 2013)

A Den Exter and T Hervey (eds), *European Union Health Legislation* (Antwerp: Maklu, 2012)

S Greer, T Hervey, M McKee, and J Mackenbach, 'Health Law and Policy of the European Union' (2013) 381 *The Lancet* 1135

L Hancher and W Sauter, *EU Competition and Internal Market Law in the Health Care Sector* (Oxford: Oxford University Press, 2012)

T Hervey, 'If Only It Were So Simple: Public Health Services and EU Law' in M Cremona (ed), *Market Integration and Public Services in the EU* (Oxford: Oxford University Press, 2011)

C Newdick, 'Citizenship, Free Movement and Health Care: Cementing Individual Rights by Corroding Social Solidarity' (2006) 43 *Common Market Law Review* 1645

J Van de Gronden, E Szyszczak, U Neergaard, and M Krajewski (eds), *Health Care and EU Law* (New York: Springer, 2011)

22

Environmental law

Elisa Morgera

1 Introduction

Environmental protection is as an essential component of any policy aimed at improving human well-being: clean air and water, healthy lands and seas are essential to human life and health, adequate nutrition, and cultural and recreational activities. Environmental protection may also contribute to ensuring the long-term maintenance of economic activities that are based on the use of natural resources (the agricultural, fishing, and logging industry) or depend on well-preserved natural features (the tourism industry). While traditionally environmental regulation tended to protect the environment from degradation arising from economic activities, more recently it has attempted to protect the environment and encourage economic growth at the same time. Thus, one of the key themes that will be explored in this chapter is how and to what extent EU environmental law has attempted to reconcile these apparently conflicting objectives, either by trying to strike a balance between competing environmental and economic objectives or by integrating environmental and economic objectives through market-based mechanisms and other innovative regulatory approaches. As environmental protection is a dynamic and ever-expanding area of international law, the other key theme explored in this chapter is the influence of international environmental law over EU environmental law, and attempts by the EU to influence the further development of international environmental law.

In about 35 years the EU has developed over 200 secondary legislative instruments covering a wide array of environmental issues, ranging from the conservation of nature to water, air pollution, climate change, noise, dangerous substances, genetically modified organisms, waste, and nuclear safety. This legislative activity has been highly influential on Member States, where 70–80 per cent of national environmental law is of EU origin.[1] In addition, EU environmental law has been very pervasive in 'greening' other areas of EU law, such as the Common Agricultural, Transport, and Fisheries Policies. Environmental law is also an area where the EU has experimented with new concepts and approaches that have progressively become part of general EU law.[2] This is the case of the subsidiarity principle, which calls for Union action only if and insofar as the objectives to be achieved cannot be sufficiently achieved by the Member States but can be better achieved at EU level by reason of the scale or effects of the proposed action.[3] It is also demonstrated by the use of financial penalties against Member States infringing EU law, which has been progressively refined in environmental cases.[4]

This chapter will first introduce the legal framework of EU environmental policy, by explaining its historic evolution, as well as its current objectives and principles. It will then explore three representative areas of EU environmental law: nature conservation, water, and climate change, with a view to highlighting two trends of broader relevance to the understanding of EU environmental law as a whole: the interaction between environmental protection and economic development, and the interaction between EU and international environmental law.

2 The legal framework

2.1 Evolution of EU environmental law

Given the abundance and pervasiveness of EU environmental law today, it may be surprising that initially the EEC, when it was established by the original Treaty of Rome in 1957, had no mandate to address issues related to environmental protection. It has only been over time, through successive Treaty revisions, that the EU environmental policy that we know today has emerged. The evolution of the Treaty provisions on the environment thus provides key indications as to the Union's changing approach to environmental regulation, which has to a significant extent also been shaped by concurrent developments in international environmental law.[5]

---

[1] L Kramer, 'Regional Economic International Organizations: The European Union as an Example' in D Bodansky et al (eds), *The Oxford Handbook of International Environmental Law* (Oxford: Oxford University Press, 2007).

[2] J Jans, 'Environmental Spill-Overs into General Community Law' (2008) 31 *Fordham International Law Journal* 1360.   [3] Art 5(3) TEU; see further chapter 5.

[4] Case C-387/97 *Commission v Greece* [2000] ECR I-5047; Case C-278/01 *Commission v Spain* [2003] ECR I-14141; Case C-304/02 *Commission v France* [2005] ECR I-6263; and Cae C-494/01 *Commission v Ireland* [2005] ECR I-3331.

[5] E Morgera, 'European Environmental Law' in Alam et al (eds), *Routledge Handbook of International Environmental Law* (Abingdon: Routledge, 2012) and I von Homeyer, 'The Evolution of EU Environmental Governance' in J Scott (ed), *Environmental Protection: European Law and Governance* (Oxford: Oxford University Press, 2009).

Table 22.1 Summary table of the evolution of EU environmental law

	Treaty changes	Evolution of EU environmental law	Enlargements	International environmental law developments
First Phase (1958–72)	• European Coal and Steel Community (1952–2002) • **Treaty of Rome (1958)** - Birth of the EEC (common market) • EURATOM Treaty (1958)	• Lack of reference to the environment in the Treaty of Rome • Incidental environmental action: eg Directive 67/548 on classification, packaging and labelling of dangerous preparations[6]	• Founding members: Belgium, Germany, France, Italy, Luxembourg, and the Netherlands	• Sporadic initiatives for the protection of natural resources at the international level
Second Phase (1973–86)		• First Environmental Action Programme (1973–76) • Case 240/83 *ADBHU*: environmental protection as an 'essential objective' • 1979: Wild Birds Directive[7]	• 1973: UK, Ireland, and Denmark • 1981: Greece • 1986: Spain and Portugal	• 1972: Stockholm Conference on Human Environment • EC becomes party to Barcelona Convention for the protection of the Mediterranean Sea against Pollution (1978), Berne Convention on the Conservation of European Wildlife and Natural Habitats and Convention on the Conservation of the marine fauna and flora of the Antarctic (1982), Convention on the Conservation of Migratory Species and Convention on Long-range Transboundary Air Pollution (1983)
Third Phase (1987–92)	• **Single European Act (1987)** - Elimination of remaining barriers to single market	• explicit legal basis for environmental policy • unanimous decision-making • 1992: Habitats Directive[8]		• EC becomes party to Convention for the Protection of the Ozone Layer and its Montreal Protocol (1989)

(Continued)

[6] OJ [1967] 196/1.   [7] See n 93; discussed in section 3.1.   [8] See n 94; discussed in section 3.2.

Table 22.1 (*Continued*)

	Treaty changes	Evolution of EU environmental law	Enlargements	International environmental law developments

Fourth Phase (1993–97)	• **Maastricht Treaty (1993)**
	  – EC & EU
	  – Economic and monetary union
	  – Cooperation in foreign and security policy
		• introduced 'environment' into overarching Treaty provisions
		• precautionary principle and objective of promoting measures to deal with regional and worldwide environmental problems
		• reference to 'sustainable growth'
		• qualified majority voting (with exceptions)
		• 1996 Directive on Integrated Pollution Prevention and Control[9]
			• 1995: Austria, Finland, and Sweden	• 1992: Rio Conference on the Environment and Development
				• EC becomes a party to UN Framework Convention on Climate Change (UNFCCC), the Convention on Biological Diversity (CBD) and Basel Convention on the Control of Transboundary Movements of Hazardous Wastes and their Disposal (1994)

Fifth Phase (1999–2008)	• **Treaty of Amsterdam (1999)**
	  – Fundamental rights and principles of democracy, liberty, and rule of law
	  – Area of Freedom, Security and Justice
		• Sustainable development and high level of environmental protection among the overarching provisions of EC law
		• Environmental integration as general principles of EU law (Article 11 TFEU)
		• Co-decision (ordinary legislative procedure)
			• 2004 ('big-bang enlargement'): Cyprus, Czech Republic, Estonia, Hungary, Latvia, Lithuania, Malta, Poland, Slovakia, and Slovenia
			
			Envt'l policy becomes formally an area to be
				• 2002: World Summit on Sustainable Development
				• EC becomes a party to the UN Convention on the Law of the Sea, UN Convention to Combat Desertification (1998); Kyoto Protocol to the UNFCCC and Cartagena Protocol on Biosafety to the CBD (2003); Stockholm Convention on Persistent Organic Pollutants
				(*Continued*)

[9] Directive 2008/1/EC of the European Parliament and of the Council of 15 January 2008 concerning integrated pollution prevention and control (codified version) (OJ [2008] L24/8).

Table 22.1 (*Continued*)

	Treaty changes	Evolution of EU environmental law	Enlargements	International environmental law developments
		• 2000: Water Framework Directive[10]	specifically addressed in pre-accession negotiations	and Rotterdam Convention on the Prior Informed Consent Procedure for Certain Hazardous Chemicals and Pesticides in International Trade (2004); Aarhus Convention on Access to Information, Public Participation in Decision-Making and Access to Justice in Environmental Matters (2005)
			• 2007: Romania and Bulgaria	
The present (2009–…)	• **Lisbon Treaty (2009)**	• Explicit reference to climate change (Article 191(1) TFEU)	• 2013: Croatia	2009: UN Climate Change Conference in Copenhagen
	• EU with legal personality (merged with EC)	• new legal basis on energy policy (Article 194 TFEU)	[Candidate countries: Turkey, Serbia, Montenegro Iceland, and Macedonia	2012: Rio+20 UN Summit
	• Institutional amendments	• Environmental component of new unified legal basis for external action (Articles 3(5) TEU and 21(2) TEU)		
	• EU Charter with the same legal value as Treaties (Article 6 TEU)		Potential candidate countries: Albania, Bosnia and Herzegovina, and Kosovo]	
	• General integration/ coherence clause (Article 7 TFEU)	• 2009: Climate and Energy Package[11]		

Source: based on J Jans and H Vedder, *European Environmental Law* (Groningen: Europa Law Publishing, 2012) ch 1; K Inglis, 'Enlargement and the Environment *Acquis*' (2004) 13 *RECIEL* 135; and Morgera, 'European Environmental Law' (n 5). The year of entry into force of Treaties is provided (and in the case of multilateral environmental agreements, the date of entry into force of that agreement for the EU is indicated).

---

[10] See n 127; discussed in section 4.1.

[11] See nn 175, 181–183, and 186–188; discussed in section 5.1.1.

If we consider parallel international developments, it is not so surprising that the Treaty of Rome did not contain any reference to the environment: environmental issues were generally not a policy concern in the 1950s. It was only with the convening of the first global summit on environmental protection in 1972 (the Stockholm Conference on the Human Environment) that the international community (and the EEC) recognized the urgent need for environmental protection.[12] The Stockholm Conference is traditionally seen as the birth of modern international environmental law. The same year, a summit of heads of State of the EEC Member States declared that economic expansion was not an end in itself, and that European integration was ultimately to help to attenuate disparities in living conditions, including by protecting 'non-material' values such as environmental protection. The origin of EU environmental law was thus linked to human well-being, as also being a necessary goal for economic growth. On that understanding, European leaders called for an action programme to launch an EEC environmental policy.[13] The following year the First Environmental Action Programme was adopted[14] and in its aftermath EEC law was enacted to tackle differences in Member States' environmental legislation that were considered to have a (potential) detrimental effect on intra-Community trade and competition.[15] This practice permitted the adoption of EEC legislation on aquatic pollution, air pollution, industrial hazards, and toxic waste, albeit only to the extent permitted by economic considerations, in the absence of a legal basis in the Treaties for the Community to adopt measures which solely concerned the environment. EU environmental law was therefore initially aimed to develop environmental protection legislation that would also contribute to economic integration.

In 1985, however, the Court of Justice affirmed that environmental protection had become one of the Community's 'essential objectives', and that environmental protection measures, being of general interest, could justify certain restrictions to the free movement of goods as long as they were non-discriminatory and did not go beyond the inevitable restrictions justified by the pursuit of the objective of environmental protection.[16] The Court, therefore, addressed possible conflicts between environmental protection and economic objectives by sanctioning the possibility of an autonomous environmental policy of the EEC independent of the establishment of the common market.[17]

It was then the Single European Act (in force 1987) that introduced an explicit legal basis for an autonomous EEC environmental policy, setting the objectives, principles, and criteria to guide environmental law-making at EEC level.[18] Accordingly, in the field of the environment the EEC was to take legislative action to preserve and improve the quality of the environment, contribute towards the protection of human health, and ensure a prudent and rational utilization of natural resources. These powers were subject to unanimous decision-making by the Council in consultation with the Parliament. In addition, with Spain and Portugal joining the EEC in 1986, Germany and Denmark – countries with traditionally higher environmental standards – insisted on introducing in the Treaty a provision allowing Member States to maintain or introduce more stringent environmental protection measures than might be pursued at EEC level.[19]

---

[12] Declaration of the United Nations Conference on the Human Environment, UN Doc A/Conf.48/14/rev.1 (16 June 1972).

[13] Bulletin EC 1972, No 10.

[14] Declaration of the Council of the European Communities and of the representatives of the Governments of the Member States meeting in the Council of 22 November 1973 on the programme of action for the European Communities on the environment (OJ [1973] C112/1).

[15] On the basis of Art 100 EEC, later Art 94 EC (now Art 115 TFEU); see also Case 92/79 *Commission v Italy* [1980] ECR 1115.   [16] Case 240/83 *ADBHU* [1983] ECR 531.

[17] M Lee, *EU Environmental Law: Challenges, Change and Decision-Making* (Oxford: Hart Publishing, 2005) 16.

[18] Post-SEA, Art 130r EEC.   [19] This Treaty rule is still in force today (Art 193 TFEU).

Following the convening of another major global summit, the 1992 United Nations Conference on Environment and Development in Rio de Janeiro, environmental law also gained more prominence at European level. The Maastricht Treaty (in force 1993) elevated environmental protection to being one the objectives of the EC.[20] The Treaty also significantly amended the legal basis on environmental policy, by adding a reference to the precautionary principle (discussed later[21]) and the objective of promoting *international* measures to deal with regional or worldwide environmental problems.[22] In addition, the Maastricht Treaty established that the general rule for decision-making on environmental policy would be qualified majority in the Council (ie the Member States' environment ministers), thereby facilitating the adoption of new environmental law at EC level. Only certain matters remained subject to unanimity.

The Treaty of Amsterdam (in force 1999) fine-tuned the inclusion of environmental protection in the general clauses of the EC Treaty. It included the 'harmonious, balanced and sustainable development of economic activities' and a 'high level of protection and improvement of the quality of the environment' among the objectives of the EC.[23] It also upgraded a pre-existing requirement for environmental mainstreaming in other policy areas of the EU ('environmental integration') to a general principle of EU law.[24] Finally, the Treaty of Amsterdam established that co-decision was the normal decision-making procedure for environmental policy, thus ensuring a veto power for the European Parliament.[25] This procedure has remained relevant for present environmental policy (renamed the 'ordinary legislative procedure' by the Lisbon Treaty).[26] And starting with the so-called 'big-bang' enlargement of 2004 (ie the admission of ten new Member States), environmental policy formally became an area to be specifically addressed in pre-accession negotiations, given the need for 'upward pressure' to align the environmental protection policy of new Member States with that of the EU.[27]

With the latest Treaty amendments,[28] the Lisbon Treaty (in force 2009) singled out climate change as one of the global environmental issues in which the EU is expected to play a significant role at the international level,[29] thereby reflecting the political priority attached to this specific environmental problem by the EU since the early 2000s.[30] The Lisbon Treaty also added two new provisions further supporting environmental integration: one requires integrating animal welfare requirements in certain policy areas,[31] and the other has regard to the need to preserve and improve the environment in the context of EU energy policy, by promoting energy efficiency, energy saving, and the development of renewable forms of energy.[32]

Possibly the most significant environmental feature of the Lisbon Treaty, from an environmental perspective, is the emphasis placed on the international dimension of the EU environmental policy. The Treaty introduces an express link between sustainable development and EU external relations, by clarifying that 'in its relations with the wider world, the Union shall…contribute to…the sustainable development of the Earth.'[33] Furthermore, the new legal basis on EU external action provides that the EU shall define and pursue common

---

[20] Post-Maastricht, Arts 2 and 3(k) EC.   [21] Section 2.3.2.
[22] Post-Maastricht, Art 130r(1) EC.   [23] Post-Amsterdam, Art 2 EC.
[24] Post-Amsterdam, Art 6 EC (now Art 11 TFEU).   [25] Post-Amsterdam, Art 175 EC.
[26] Art 294 TFEU. For more details on this procedure, see chapter 5.
[27] M Soveroski, 'EC Enlargement and the Development of European Environmental Policy: Parallel Histories, Divergent Paths?' (2004) 13 *RECIEL* 127, 129.
[28] M Lee, 'The Environmental Implications of the Lisbon Treaty' (2008) 10 *Environmental Law Review* 131 and H Vedder, 'The Treaty of Lisbon and European Environmental Policy' (2010) 22 *Journal of Environmental Law* 285.   [29] Art 191(1) TFEU.
[30] E Morgera and G Marín Durán, 'The UN 2005 World Summit, the Environment and the EU: Priorities, Promises and Prospects' (2006) 15 *RECIEL* 11.
[31] ie in the areas of agriculture, fisheries, transport, internal market, research and technological development, and space policies (Art 14 TFEU).
[32] Art 194(1) TFEU.   [33] Art 3(5) TEU.

policies and actions, and work for a high degree of cooperation in all fields of international relations, with the specific objective of fostering the sustainable environmental development of developing countries, in order to eradicate poverty; and help to develop international measures to preserve and improve the quality of the environment and the sustainable management of global natural resources, in order to ensure sustainable development.[34]

2.2 Objectives of EU environmental policy

The objectives of EU environmental policy are very broadly defined as

- preserving, protecting, and improving the quality of the environment;
- protecting human health;
- ensuring the prudent and rational utilization of natural resources; and
- promoting measures at international level to deal with regional or worldwide environmental problems, and in particular combating climate change.[35]

Basically, it is almost impossible to define clearly on this basis the boundaries of EU environmental policy. There is sufficient flexibility for the EU to tackle, through its environmental policy, new and emerging environmental issues. In addition, this provision permits wide discretion in the choice of environmental measures to be adopted at EU level: these may include conservation, restoration, repression, precaution, prevention, and eminently procedural environmental measures.[36]

2.2.1 Competence and scope of EU legislation

While there are no clear substantive limits to the exercise of EU environmental competence, this is shared with the Member States[37] and is therefore subject to the principle of subsidiarity: the EU will take action if the objectives of the proposed environmental action cannot be sufficiently achieved by the Member States and if by reason of the scale or effects of the proposed action, these objectives are better achieved at the EU level.[38] Furthermore, environmental competence is exercised under the decision-making procedures set out by the Treaty: generally it is subject to agreement between the Council (acting by qualified majority voting) and the European Parliament (under the ordinary legislative procedure). In certain specific areas, however, the Treaty requires unanimous decision-making by the Council in consultation with the European Parliament (ie a special legislative procedure), namely

- provisions primarily of a fiscal nature;
- measures affecting town and country planning, quantitative management of water resources or affecting, directly or indirectly, the availability of those resources, and land use with the exception of waste management; and
- measures significantly affecting a Member State's choice between different energy sources and the general structure of its energy supply.[39]

These are areas in which Member States wish to retain a higher degree of control because of their politically sensitive nature or concerns about the preservation of national sovereignty.

---

[34] Art 21(2)(d) and (f) TEU.   [35] Art 191(1) TFEU.

[36] J Jans and H Vedder, *European Environmental Law* (4th edn, Groningen: Europa Law, 2012) 26–35.

[37] Art 4(2)(e) TFEU. For more on the concept of shared competence, see chapter 5. Note that EU measures adopted on the environment legal basis 'shall not prevent any Member State from maintaining or introducing more stringent protective measures'. Such measures must be compatible with the Treaties. They shall be notified to the Commission (Art 193 TFEU).   [38] Art 5(3) TEU. For more on the concept of subsidiarity, see chapter 5.

[39] Art 192 TFEU. For more on special legislative procedures, see chapter 5.

As to the territorial scope of EU environmental competence, reference to worldwide and regional environmental problems in the Treaty clarifies that the EU can also take unilateral and multilateral measures targeting the environment beyond its borders, in the same way as can its Member States, within the limits imposed by international law.[40] An example, discussed in more detail later, is the regulation of the greenhouse gas emissions of international airlines.[41]

As the environmental competence of the EU is shared with the Member States, Member States can exercise their competence only as long as the EU has not exercised its competence, or has decided to cease to exercise it.[42] In this respect, it should be emphasized that the scope of EU competence vis-à-vis that of the Member States is difficult to determine, as EU environmental policy is subject to continuous evolution.[43] This has important implications on the international scene where environmental law-making is constantly taking place. If the EU adopted environmental measures internally, Member States would no longer have competence to undertake international obligations that would affect those EU rules. This is not the case, however, if the EU measures allow (as is often the case) Member States to adopt more stringent measures,[44] including in principle the possibility of undertaking more stringent international obligations. However, this flexibility for Member States is constrained by the duty of sincere cooperation enshrined in Article 4(3) TEU, according to which:

> Pursuant to the principle of sincere cooperation, the Union and the Member States shall, in full mutual respect, assist each other in carrying out tasks which flow from the Treaties.
>
> The Member States shall take any appropriate measure, general or particular, to ensure fulfilment of the obligations arising out of the Treaties or resulting from the acts of the institutions of the Union.
>
> The Member States shall facilitate the achievement of the Union's tasks and refrain from any measure which could jeopardise the attainment of the Union's objectives.

The Court has interpreted the duty as entailing enforceable substantive and procedural obligations upon Member States with a view to protecting unity in the international representation of the EU.[45]

Finally, with reference to international treaties on environmental matters, in the vast majority of cases both the EU and its Member States negotiate and conclude multilateral environmental agreements together (so-called 'mixed agreements'[46]), which entail significant internal efforts to ensure proper coordination at all stages, including that of implementation.

2.3 Principles of EU environmental policy

The Treaty also identifies the principles that should guide EU environmental policy, both as a guide for law-making and for interpretation. These principles are a high level of environmental protection; the precautionary principle; as well as the principles that preventive action should be taken, that environmental damage should as a priority be rectified at source, and that the polluter should pay.[47] Environmental principles also include environmental integration and sustainable development. These principles, as will be discussed in

---

[40] Jans and Vedder, *European Environmental Law* (n 36) 31–36.
[41] See case study 22.3 in section 5.2.   [42] Art 2(2) TFEU.
[43] Jans and Vedder, *European Environmental Law* (n 36) 61–64.   [44] Art 191(4) TFEU.
[45] Case C-266/03 *Commission v Luxembourg* ('*Inland Waterways Agreement*') [2005] ECR I-4805, para 60; Case C-433/03 *Commission v Germany* ('*Inland Waterways Agreement*') [2005] ECR I-6985, para 66; and Case C-246/07 *Commission v Sweden* ('*POPs Convention*') [2010] ECR I-3317, para 104.
[46] For more on the concept of mixed agreements, including a case study of their use in the area of environmental law, see chapter 24.   [47] Art 191(2) TFEU.

the following subsections, may play a key role in ensuring an appropriate balance between environmental protection and economic growth in the EU, in some instances.

The EU legislator, however, has a significant margin of discretion in implementing the principles. Only in exceptional cases could an EU measure be annulled for insufficient regard to these principles, in cases of manifest error of appraisal by the EU legislature. The Court clarified this in a preliminary reference involving EU legislation on the protection of the ozone layer (further discussed later),[48] emphasizing that the protection of the environment necessarily presupposes complex assessments weighing the respective merits and drawbacks of any given action, taking account of a series of parameters, in particular available scientific and technical data.[49] The underlying reason for such judicial restraint is the need to strike a balance between environmental principles and other policy priorities of the EU, as well as the need to allow ample room for manoeuvre in tackling the complexity of environmental challenges. Nonetheless, the environmental principles have proven very important shaping factors in EU environmental law and assist in better understanding the various pieces of secondary EU environmental legislation, as will be shown in the following sections.

2.3.1 'A high level of environmental protection'

The principle of a high level of environmental protection is included among the general objectives of the EU,[50] although it is made subject to consideration of the 'diversity of situations in the various regions of the Union'.[51] While the principle prevents the EU from adopting the lowest common denominator among the Member States' environmental protection measures,[52] the Court of Justice clarified that it does not necessarily call for the highest standard that is technically possible.[53] The case involved a preliminary reference on an EU provision prohibiting the use, importation, release for free circulation, or marketing of hydrochlorofluorocarbons (a substance that depletes the ozone layer).[54] At the national level, a company using the prohibited substance in fire-fighting products raised the question whether the prohibition could be justified only if it allocated absolute priority to the highest possible level of environmental protection.[55] The Court concluded that the legal basis for environmental policy does not necessarily aim to ensure absolute, immediate, and global protection of the environment and therefore allows the EU legislator to pursue a level of environmental protection that is not the highest possible. Consequently, the provision at stake was considered consistent with the Treaty because it still aimed at improving appreciably the protection of the environment.[56]

Overall, the principle of a high level of environmental protection reflects a moving target – the idea of continuous improvement of environmental protection standards across the Member States.[57]

2.3.2 'The precautionary principle'

The precautionary principle, also a principle of international environmental law,[58] provides guidance in situations of scientific uncertainty. It has been interpreted by the Commission

[48] See section 2.3.1.

[49] Case C-284/95 *Safety Hi-Tech Srl v S & T Srl* [1998] ECR I-4301, paras 71–73.

[50] Art 3(3) TEU.   [51] Art 191(2) TFEU.

[52] L Kramer, *EU Environmental Law* (7th edn, London: Sweet & Maxwell, 2011) 12–13.

[53] *Safety Hi-Tech Srl v S & T Srl* (n 49).

[54] Art 5 of Council Regulation (EC) No 3093/94 on substances that deplete the ozone layer of 15 December 1994 (OJ [1994] L333/1).   [55] *Safety Hi-Tec* (n 53) para 58.

[56] Ibid, paras 76–78.   [57] Kramer, *EU Environmental Law* (n 52) 12.

[58] Rio Declaration on Environment and Development, UN Doc A/CONF.151/26 (1992), vol I, principle 15.

as a risk-management tool comprising a risk assessment leading to the establishment of precautionary measures that are

> proportional to the chosen level of protection, non-discriminatory in their application, consistent with similar measures already taken, based on an examination of the potential benefits and costs of action or lack of action, and subject to review in the light of new scientific data.[59]

The trigger of the precautionary principle is a situation where

> preliminary objective scientific evaluation, indicates that there are reasonable grounds for concern that the potentially dangerous effects on the *environment, human, animal or plant health* may be inconsistent with the high level of protection chosen for the [EU].[60]

2.3.3 'The prevention principle'

The 'prevention' principle, also an international environmental principle,[61] calls for taking action to protect the environment at an early stage, with a view to preventing damage from occurring rather than repairing it.[62] The main difference with the precautionary principle lies in the availability of data on the existence of a risk, although such distinction may be difficult to draw in practice. The Court of Justice, for instance, relied on the prevention principle, as well as that of a high level of protection, to review an export ban on British beef adopted in the context of the Common Agricultural Policy because of a possible – rather than certain – risk related to mad cow disease.[63] Guidance on the application of the prevention principle in EU law stresses the need to improve information for decision-makers and the public (eg through monitoring and surveying requirements), introduces procedures supporting prompt and informed decision-making on the environment such as the environmental impact assessment, and monitors implementation of adopted measures to ensure their adaptation in light of new circumstances or knowledge.[64]

2.3.4 'Rectification at source'

The 'rectification at source' principle means that environmental damage should as a priority be rectified at its source, and has had particular resonance in the area of waste management. The Court of Justice held that according to this principle local authorities must take measures necessary to ensure the reception, processing, and removal of their own waste, so that this waste can be disposed of as close as possible to its place of production. This interpretation allowed the Court to justify measures that discriminated against waste produced in different areas.[65] The case, therefore, represents a derogation from the normal approach to free trade in goods in EU law,[66] which is necessary in the case of irreconcilable conflict between environmental protection and economic growth.

---

[59] Commission, Guidelines on the Precautionary Principle, COM(2000) 1, para 6.
[60] Ibid, para 3 (emphasis added).   [61] Rio Declaration, principle 2.
[62] Jans and Vedder, *European Environmental Law* (n 36) 40–42.
[63] Case C-157/96 *National Farmers Union* [1998] ECR I-2211, para 64.
[64] Resolution of the Council of the European Communities and of the Representatives of the Governments of the Member States, meeting within the Council, on the continuation and implementation of a European Community policy and action programme on the environment (1982–1986) (OJ [1983] C46/1), (Third Environmental Action Programme) 6–7.   [65] Case C-2/90 *Commission v Belgium* [1992] ECR I-4431.
[66] See discussion of the usual approach to free movement of goods in chapter 12.

2.3.5 'Polluter pays' principle

The 'polluter pays' principle, also an international environmental principle,[67] posits that the costs of the measure to deal with pollution should be borne by those causing the pollution, through the imposition of environmental charges, environmental standards, or environmental liability. In addition, the principle has been interpreted in the EU context so that environmental protection should not in principle depend on the granting of State aid or policies placing the burden on society, and that requirements should not target persons or undertakings for the elimination of pollution that they did not contribute to producing. Accordingly, the Court of Justice indicated that farmers are not obliged to bear all the costs of pollution by nitrates, but only those caused by their own agricultural activities. So it is up to authorities to take account of other sources of pollution and, having regard to the circumstances, avoid imposing on farmers unnecessary costs of eliminating pollution.[68]

2.4 Environmental integration

The principle of environmental integration – also a principle of international environmental law[69] – is included among the general principles of EU law. It is framed in clearly mandatory wording and acts as a mechanism for the operationalization of sustainable development.[70] It reads:

> Environmental protection requirements must be integrated into the definition and implementation of the Union policies and activities, in particular with a view to promoting sustainable development.

It aims to prevent progress in environmental protection from being undermined by developments in other policy fields that disregard environmental concerns. Environmental issues should be integrated into all policies of the EU, internal and external, both at the stage of the framing of these policies and at the stage of their implementation. Environmental integration therefore requires that other EU policy areas must 'pursue' the EU environmental objectives, and 'aim at' or 'be based on' the EU environmental principles.[71] Thus, it has resulted in the application of the precautionary principle outside the environmental sphere, in the area of the protection of public health[72] and of the prevention and high level of protection principles in the area of agriculture.[73]

Nonetheless, the environmental integration principle does not assign priority to environmental concerns over other objectives of the EU, including economic objectives. Rather, it imposes a general obligation on EU institutions to reach an integrated and balanced assessment of all the relevant environmental aspects, and that the resulting decision respects the principle of proportionality – that the policy or action does not go beyond what is strictly necessary for the protection of the environment.[74] The environmental integration principle also entails that EU environmental law itself is interpreted broadly, in light of the

[67] Rio Declaration, principle 16.   [68] Case C-293/97 *Standley* [1999] ECR I-2603, paras 46–52.

[69] Rio Declaration, principle 4.   [70] Art 11 TFEU.

[71] N Dhondt, *Integration of Environmental Protection into Other EC Policies: Legal Theory and Practice* (Groningen: Europa Law, 2003) 84.

[72] Jans and Vedder, *European Environmental Law* (n 36) 21, on the basis of Joined Cases T-74, 76, 83, 85, 132, 137 and 141/00 *Artegodan GmbH ao v Commission* [2002] ECR II-4954.

[73] *National Farmers Union* (n 63).

[74] Jans and Vedder, *European Environmental Law* (n 36) 17–18.

environmental objectives, principles, and criteria of Article 191 TFEU, even when they are not explicitly incorporated in the specific secondary legislation at issue.[75]

Environmental integration has indeed resulted in significant legislative developments, both in terms of 'greening' other areas of EU law, as well as in recourse to an 'integrationist' approach in the development of EU environmental law (relying, for instance, on environmental impact assessments,[76] strategic environmental assessments,[77] and integrated pollution prevention and control[78]).

2.5 Sustainable development

The principle of sustainable development is among the 'objectives' of the EU both in its internal and external actions.[79] In addition, sustainable development is specifically referred to as a 'principle' in the Preamble to the TEU,[80] but notably is not mentioned as the legal basis for the environmental policy of the EU.[81] The principle of sustainable development is notoriously the product of international environmental law,[82] where it is traditionally (but not exclusively) seen as 'development that meets the need of present without compromising the ability of future generations to meet their own needs'[83] and generally operationalized as a balancing exercise between 'three pillars' – environmental, social, and economic development.[84] In EU law, however, the connection between sustainable development and environmental regulation is unclear and somewhat controversial. Some authors argue that sustainable development provides an opportunity to give preference to short-term economic interests and may therefore work against environmental protection.[85] In actual fact, the Court of Justice has not engaged in defining the legal implications of sustainable development,[86] and it is usually left to EU policy documents to provide guidance on sustainable development. This is notably the case of the 'Europe 2020' strategy for smart, sustainable, and inclusive growth[87] – the high-level road map for growth in the EU in the current decade. It therefore remains to be verified in the details of EU environmental law

---

[75] Dhondt, *Integration of Environmental Protection into Other EC Policies* (n 71) 179, on the basis of Joined Cases C-175/98 and C-177/98 *Lirussi and Bizzaro* [1999] ECR I-6881; Joined Cases C-418/97 and C-419/97 *ARCO Chemie Nederland* [2000] ECR I-4475; and Case C-318/98 *Fornasar* [2000] ECR I-4785, where the Court adopted broad interpretations of EU waste legislation.

[76] Directive 2011/92/EU on the assessment of the effects of certain public and private projects on the environment (OJ [2012] L26/1).

[77] Directive 2001/42/EC on the assessment of the effects of certain plans and programmes on the environment (OJ [2001] L197/30).

[78] Directive 2010/75/EU on industrial emissions (integrated pollution prevention and control – recast) (OJ [2010] L334/17).

[79] Arts 3(3) and (5) and 21(2)(f) TEU.   [80] TEU, recital 9.

[81] L Kramer, 'Sustainable Development in the EC' in H Bugge and C Voigt (eds), *Sustainable Development in International and National Law* (Groningen: Europa Law, 2008) 378–379.

[82] Rio Declaration, principles 3–4.

[83] World Commission on Environment and Development, *Our Common Future* (Oxford: Oxford University Press, 1987) ch 2, para 1; which was quoted in Commission, Towards Sustainability: A European Programme of policy and action in relation to the environment and sustainable development (OJ [1993] C138/5).

[84] Political Declaration of the World Summit on Sustainable Development, UN Doc A/CONF.199/20 (4 September 2002), resolution 1 (WSSD Declaration), para 5.

[85] Kramer, 'Sustainable Development in the EC' (n 81) 391–393; A Ross-Robertson, 'Is the Environment Getting Squeezed Out of Sustainable Development?' [2003] *Public Law* 249.

[86] Even if it had an opportunity to do so: Case C-142/95 P *Associazione degli Agricoltori della provincia di Rovigo v Commission* [1996] ECR I-6669 and Case C-371/98 R *v Secretary of State for Environment, Transport and the Regions, ex p First Corporate Shipping* [2000] ECR-I 9235.

[87] Commission, Europe 2020: A European Strategy for Smart, Sustainable and Inclusive, Growth, COM(2010) 2020; European Council conclusions, 17 June 2010.

and its implementation how sustainable development operates in practice – as we will see in the next section.

3 Nature protection

EU law on nature protection remains mainly focused on traditional conservation measures (protected areas and species[88]) that emerged in the late 1970s and early 1990s. It has developed in a 'patchy' manner, resulting in a system that is complex and ambiguous, and the components of which in part overlap.[89] Nonetheless, it is considered 'highly influential…[in] affecting for the first time Member States' use of land'[90] and equipped to accommodate modern challenges, such as adaptation to climate change.[91] Notwithstanding its long-standing place in EU environmental law, full and effective implementation of nature protection legislation in the EU remains a challenge.[92] In most cases, the challenge is due to conflicts with economic development projects that are resolved without sufficient attention to nature protection.

The cornerstones of EU nature protection law are two directives: the Wild Birds Directive,[93] initially adopted in 1979, and the subsequent and complementary Habitats Directive.[94]

3.1 The Wild Birds Directive

The Wild Birds Directive has a narrow scope: it aims to protect the species of wild birds naturally occurring in the European territory of the Member States (that are mainly migratory species), because they constitute a common heritage and their effective protection is typically a trans-frontier environmental problem entailing common responsibilities.[95] The Directive aimed to implement relevant international obligations under the Ramsar Convention on Wetlands of International Importance, which protects key habitats for migratory birds.[96] The Directive, on the one hand, includes provisions on the protection of habitats of wild birds, including through the designation of Special Protection Areas for birds in danger of extinction;[97] and, on the other hand, it provides for the direct protection of wild bird species, including by prohibiting or regulating their deliberate killing and capture.[98]

---

[88] Although the EU has also regulated on plant health and animal welfare.

[89] N de Sadeleer, 'EC Law and Biodiversity' in R Macrory (ed), *Reflections on 30 Years of EU Environmental Law: A High Level Protection?* (Groningen: Europa Law, 2005) 368–369.

[90] J Holder and M Lee, *Environmental Protection, Law and Policy* (Cambridge: Cambridge University Press, 2007) 627.

[91] A Trouwborst, 'Conserving European Biodiversity in a Changing Climate: The Bern Convention, the European Union Birds and Habitats Directives and the Adaptation of Nature to Climate Change' (2011) 20 *RECIEL* 62.

[92] European Parliament, Resolution on the implementation of EU legislation aiming at the conservation of biodiversity (2009/2108(INI), 21 September 2010, http://www.europarl.europa.eu/oeil/popups/ficheprocedure.do?lang=en&reference=2009/2108%28INI%29

[93] Directive 2009/147/EC on the conservation of wild birds (OJ [2010] L20/7) (codified version including subsequent amendments to the original 1979 Wild Birds Directive).

[94] Directive 92/43/EEC on the conservation of natural habitats and of wild fauna and flora (OJ [1992] L206/7).   [95] Ibid, Preamble.

[96] Ramsar Convention on Wetlands of International Importance, 2 February 1971, 996 UNTS 245.

[97] Wild Birds Directive, Arts 3 and 4.   [98] Ibid, Arts 5–9.

Importantly for understanding how sustainable development operates in practice, the Wild Bird Directive contains a general obligation to maintain the population of the wild bird species at a level which corresponds in particular to ecological, scientific, and cultural requirements, *while taking account* of economic and recreational requirements, or to adapt the population of these species to that level.[99] However, in a series of decisions the Court of Justice emphasized that the obligation to designate Special Protection Areas must be *solely* based on objective, environmental (ornithological) criteria on the basis of Article 4 of the Directive, without consideration of economic or recreational requirements that are mentioned in Article 2 of the Directive.[100] The Court, therefore, maintained that while the Wild Birds Directive contained a general provision that could have justified a balancing of different interests, it mostly aimed at an absolute protection of nature without the need to balance scientific (ornithological) criteria with other (economic) interests.[101] This is therefore one of the rare cases in which the balance struck clearly favours environmental protection over economic development objectives.

3.2 The Habitats Directive

The Habitats Directive was originally adopted in 1992. While it employs the same legal technique as the Wild Birds Directive (protection of listed species and protection of habitats through the designation of protected areas), it has a markedly different approach, explicitly espousing sustainable development:

> the main aim of this Directive being to promote the maintenance of biodiversity, taking account of economic, social, cultural and regional requirements, this Directive makes a contribution to the general objective of sustainable development; . . . the maintenance of such biodiversity may in certain cases require the maintenance, or indeed the encouragement, of human activities.[102]

It also has a much broader scope than the Wild Birds Directive. This can be explained by intervening international obligations under the Convention on Biological Diversity, which aims to protect all life on earth rather than singling out a group of species, and also focuses on their sustainable use.[103] As a result, the Habitats Directive has a more ambitious and holistic approach than the Wild Birds Directive, by aiming to protect fauna and flora and their habitats and also by creating a *coherent ecological network* of protected areas – called 'Natura 2000' – that includes areas already protected under the Wild Birds Directive.[104] The Habitats Directive thus aims to maintain or restore the natural habitats and the populations of species of wild fauna and flora in the European territory at a favourable status[105] – that is, a situation that ensures their long-term maintenance and that is likely to continue to exist for the foreseeable future.[106]

Similar to the Wild Birds Directive, the Habitats Directive contains both provisions on species protection and on habitat protection. As to the former, it calls upon Member States to monitor the conservation status of all habitats and species, and to provide

---

[99] Ibid, Art 2.

[100] Case C-355/90 *Santoña Marshes* [1993] ECR I-4221; Case C-44/95 *Lappel Bank* [1996] ECR I-3805; and Case C-3/96 *Commission v Netherlands* [1998] ECR I-3031.

[101] Holder and Lee, *Environmental Protection, Law and Policy* (n 90) 634.

[102] Habitats Directive, Preamble.

[103] Ibid, Arts 2(1) and 1. Convention on Biological Diversity, 5 June 1992, 1760 UNTS 79, entered into force for the EU on 29 December 1993.   [104] Ibid, Art 3(1).

[105] Ibid, Art 2.   [106] In approximation: ibid, para 1(e).

different degrees of protection to species and plants listed in its Annexes by prohibiting certain activities depending on the conservation status of the species.[107] As to the latter, the Habitats Directive provides for the designation of Special Areas of Conservation comprising sites hosting the natural habitat types listed in Annex I and habitats of the species listed in Annex II, with a view to enabling the natural habitat types and the species' habitats concerned to be maintained or, where appropriate, restored at a favourable conservation status in their natural range.[108]

On the other hand, however, the Habitats Directive offers a compromise between comprehensive nature protection and the protection of economic interests that can be damaged by limiting human activities and development opportunities in certain areas. As opposed to the Wild Birds Directive, therefore, the Habitats Directive makes it explicit that protective measures '*shall take account of* economic, social and cultural requirements and regional and local characteristics.'[109] In addition, the Habitats Directive introduces sustainable development-based provisions for the management of designated protected areas. Ordinarily, the protection regime for a designated Special Area of Conservation may be overridden on social and economic grounds. Even for priority areas, the conservation regime may be overridden, but only on the more restrictive grounds of public health, public safety, or for certain environmental reasons following an Opinion by the European Commission and subject to the adoption of compensatory measures.[110] This system of derogation from the protection of sites in the Natura 2000 network is also applicable to areas designated under the Wild Birds Directive.[111]

These provisions clearly show that the more sustainable development-focused approach of the Habitats Directive departs from the absolute preference for conservation and environmental criteria under the Wild Birds Directive. But it is only in the phase of implementation that this difference becomes significant and that it is possible to assess whether sustainable development really achieves a pragmatic and constructive approach to balancing nature conservation and economic development concerns, or whether it mostly serves as an opportunity to give more prominence to economic interests. A closer look at the application of EU nature protection law in practice, therefore, can tell us to what extent EU law has succeeded in reconciling conflicting economic and environmental objectives.

Case study 22.1: Sustainable development in the implementation of the Habitats Directive

The actual role of sustainable development in the context of implementation of the Habitats Directive can be ascertained at two points in time: first, that of designation of protected areas and, secondly, that of possible exceptions to the conservation regime of these areas.

As to the former, in the *First Corporate Shipping* case, a private landowner challenged a proposal to designate an area under Bristol Port Authority's jurisdiction in the west of England as a Special Area of Conservation under the Habitats Directive. An important part of that area had already been classified as a Special Protection Area under the Wild Birds Directive. The Court eventually ruled out the consideration of economic and social issues at the initial (Member State-level) stage of designation of protected areas under the Habitats Directive, fearing that this would prevent the European Commission from obtaining a complete picture of the variability of habitats across Europe and their connections.

---

[107] Convention on Biological Diversity, Arts 12–16.   [108] Ibid, Arts 3–11.
[109] Ibid, Art 2(3) (emphasis added).   [110] Ibid, Art 6(4).   [111] Ibid, Art 7.

These are both seen as necessary elements to ensure the creation of an effective and representative EU ecological network such as Natura 2000.[112]

What the Court did not rule out, however, was consideration of economic and other concerns at later stages of the selection process. And, indeed, the Opinion of Advocate General Léger suggested that the Habitats Directive precludes a Member State, during the first stage, from excluding sites eligible for designation as a protected area on the basis of economic considerations. In the second stage, at the time of concertation between the Member States and the Commission, areas that appear of important economic and social interest may not be selected and designated as Special Areas of Conservation because of economic and social requirements. This determination follows on an assessment of whether or not the maintenance of human activities in the area concerned may be reconciled with the objective of conservation or restoration of natural habitats and wild fauna and flora.[113] Advocate General Léger further argued in his Opinion that sustainable development does not imply that environmental interests should 'prevail necessarily and systematically' over other interests protected by other EU policies, but rather underlines the need for a balancing between various interests that may possibly clash with each other but must be reconciled.[114] The implementation of the Habitats Directive, therefore, allows for balancing environmental and economic interests, and provides opportunities for the latter to prevail in the case of conflict.

Secondly, in order to evaluate the actual prevalence of economic interests over the environmental protection objectives of the Habitats Directive, academic studies[115] have examined the practice of the European Commission in assessing deviation from the conservation regimes of priority sites in the Natura 2000 network. And it appears that such practice is disappointing in two respects. First, the Commission has generally approved development projects in Natura 2000 sites on the basis of low standards and unconvincing reasoning from the Member States.[116] For instance, projects have been approved in the absence of the required assessment of alternative locations[117] and, even where such an assessment has been carried out, the Member State had not been able to prove that there was no alternative to the suggested project.[118] In addition, the Commission appears to be quite lenient in assessing the adequacy of compensation proposed by Member States to offset the negative impacts of proposed developments on Natura 2000 sites, when there are no alternatives and there exist imperative reasons of overriding public interest.[119] The Commission has never issued a negative opinion on the groups of deficiency of proposed compensation measures.[120] It also appears that economic considerations (related to the existence of imperative reasons of overriding public interest) further 'contaminate' the assessment by the Commission of the

---

[112] *First Corporate Shipping* (n 86) paras 22–25.

[113] Ibid, Opinion of AG Leger, 7 March 2000, paras 50, 51, and 58.

[114] Ibid, paras 54–57.

[115] L Kramer, 'The European Commission's Opinions under Article 6(4) of the Habitats Directive' (2009) 21 *Journal of Environmental Law* 59 and D McGillivray, 'Compensating Biodiversity Loss: The EU Commission's Approach to Compensation under Article 6 of the Habitats Directive' (2012) 1 *Journal of Environmental Law* 417.

[116] Kramer, 'The European Commission's Opinions under Article 6(4) of the Habitats Directive' (n 115) 84.

[117] Habitats Directive, Art 6(4); see discussion by Kramer (n 115) 61–64.

[118] Kramer, 'The European Commission's Opinions under Article 6(4) of the Habitats Directive' (n 115) 77–78.

[119] Habitats Directive, Art 6(3). McGillivray, 'Compensating Biodiversity Loss' (n 115) 431–434. See also the discussion by Kramer, 'The European Commission's Opinions under Article 6(4) of the Habitats Directive' (n 115) 65–66 and 81–84.   [120] McGillivray, 'Compensating Biodiversity Loss' (n 115) 440.

separate question of ecological compensation.[121] In addition, Member States rarely provide monitoring reports of the implementation of compensation measures,[122] making it difficult, if not impossible, to assess whether the environmental objectives of the Directive are achieved.

A more ecologically minded approach would instead see the Commission thoroughly reviewing the adequacy of compensation and initiating infringement procedures against Member States that do not take obligations under the Habitats Directive seriously.[123] It has also been remarked that, as 'the environment has no voice of its own',[124] whereas economic interests are usually well represented by directly concerned entrepreneurs, it is necessary to increase guarantees of transparency and public participation. This could allow environmental protection organizations and interested citizens to make a case for the environment and thus counterbalance lobbyism from developers, or expose instances of lax enforcement and possibly corruption.[125]

4 Water

While EU nature protection law remains fragmented and overlapping, EU water law is an area where the EU has not only engaged in significant rationalization and integration, but also pursued an ambitious and participatory approach to ensure more effective implementation. EU water law initially developed in a piecemeal fashion, first focusing on narrow pieces of legislation on different types of water use or water pollution (eg surface water use, quality of drinking water, discharge of dangerous substances into the water, quality of fishing water) in the 1970s and then focusing more on implementation challenges and subsidiarity issues in the early 1990s. All these instruments were criticized for being out of date, contradictory, and 'ill-equipped to accommodate subsequent advancements in scientific expertise.'[126] They have now in large part been substituted by the 2000 Water Framework Directive (WFD),[127] which aims to ensure the implementation of several international agreements containing obligations on the protection of freshwater, as well as on the protection of marine waters from land-based pollution.[128]

4.1 The Water Framework Directive

The WFD is notable for many innovative features. First of all, it attempts to regulate water management by taking into account the ecological reality of freshwater: it therefore focuses

---

[121] McGillivray, 'Compensating Biodiversity Loss' (n 115) 447.   [122] Ibid, 446.

[123] A Nollkaemper, 'Habitat Protection in EC Law: Evolving Conceptions of a Balance of Interest' (1997) 9 *Journal of Environmental Law* 271.

[124] Kramer, 'The European Commission's Opinions under Article 6(4) of the Habitats Directive' (n 115) 76–77 and 85.

[125] Ibid, 85. Transparency issues are also raised by McGillivray, 'Compensating Biodiversity Loss' (n 115) 448–449. The role of public participation in balancing exercises is further discussed in case study 22.2 on the Water Framework Directive: see section 4.

[126] D Matthews, 'The Framework Directive on Community Water Policy: A New Approach for EC Environmental Law' (1997) 17 *Yearbook of European Law* 191, 198. On the poor record of implementation of earlier EU water law, see A Jordan, 'European Community Water Policy Standards: Locked in or Watered Down?' (1999) 37 *Journal of Common Market Studies* 13, 13.

[127] Directive 2000/60/EC establishing a framework for Community action in the field of water policy (OJ [2000] L327/1) Art 22.   [128] WFD, Preamble.

on the 'river basin'[129] – the ecological water unit – to determine the government structure for water management. This implies that water management needs to be based on the integrated nature of the water cycle, its links with land use, and the needs of water-dependent organisms beyond humans, thus 'framing regulation around hydrological complexities rather than administrative convenience.'[130] In addition, the WFD seeks to regulate freshwater in a comprehensive manner, integrating quality and quantity aspects of water management and covering management of all freshwater resources (surface and groundwater).[131] Furthermore, the Directive drafters sought to learn from past mistakes by combining different regulatory techniques. Namely, it combines regulatory approaches to identifiable sources of water pollution (eg industrial waste pipes entering freshwater courses) and to diffuse sources of pollution (eg the cumulative effect of fertilizer run-offs).[132] The WFD also attempts to implement an economic approach to environmental protection by promoting water pricing as a specific means to favour sustainable water use. It does not, however, go as far as requiring full cost recovery.[133]

This nonetheless ambitious approach is pursued by the WFD through 'proceduralization' – a combination of flexibility and decentralization which, however, is constrained by procedural requirements and accountability mechanisms. Flexibility and decentralization aim to allow better accommodation of different national and regional conditions across the EU, such as ecological and economic conditions, as well as administrative capacities and traditions. As a result, the WFD does not specifically prescribe how to manage and protect water resources, and instead leaves this determination to the implementation phase in the various Member States. The WFD, consequently, contains few clear-cut obligations and rather focuses on a series of quite demanding and in many respects unprecedented procedural steps to be mainly taken by national competent authorities in balancing environmental and economic factors. This is, for instance, the case of the several information-gathering requirements that are in place to ensure well-informed and adaptive action: water authorities are to carry out an analysis of the characteristics of each river basin district, review the environmental impacts of human activities, and undertake an economic analysis of water use in accordance with technical specifications set at the EU level and subject to review and update.[134] Secondly, water authorities are to establish programmes for monitoring water status with a view to providing a coherent and comprehensive overview of water status in each river basin district.[135] Thirdly, national authorities are to develop programmes of measures and management plans[136] for each river basin, which are subject, once again, to regular review and update including of permits and authorizations issued in accordance with the programme of measures.[137] Reviews and updates are meant to provide systematic opportunities for Member States to reconsider previous decisions striking a balance between environmental and economic conditions and to factor in new ecological information and technology developments.

The WFD procedural requirements thus aim to ensure that the discretion left to Member States is used wisely and with a view to achieving the environmental objectives established by the Directive,[138] and ultimately a 'good water status by 2015'.[139] Through information-gathering, planning, and review Member States are expected to reflect on how continuously to improve their water management. In addition, the role of the European

---

[129] Ibid, Art 2(13).

[130] M Lee, 'Law and Governance of Water Protection Policy' in Scott, *Environmental Protection* (n 5) 29.

[131] WFD, Art 1.   [132] Ibid, Art 10.   [133] Ibid, Art 9.

[134] Ibid, Art 5.   [135] Ibid, Art 8.   [136] Ibid, Arts 11 and 13.

[137] Ibid, Art 11(5).   [138] Ibid, Arts 3(4) and 4.   [139] Ibid, Art 5.

Commission is significant: it reviews management plans, analyses and monitors programmes elaborated at the Member State level, and reports on progress in implementing planned programmes of measures.[140] It can also provide recommendations for the resolution of issues having an impact on water management reported to it by any Member States.[141] In addition, the Commission can make suggestions for the improvement of future water basin management plans in its periodic reports on the implementation of the Directive.[142] Furthermore, the Directive aims to rely on the key stakeholders to check the appropriate use of flexibility by national authorities, through guarantees for participatory decision-making in water management.[143] In that regard, national water authorities have specific public information and consultation duties, in particular at the stage of the elaboration and review of the management plans.[144] To ensure accountability in the use of discretion at the national level, the WFD also includes several procedural obligations for national authorities to back up their decisions with explanations and justifications.[145] This means that water authorities are to make reasoned public commitments in relation to their interpretation and implementation choices vis-à-vis the WFD, thereby allowing public scrutiny of the approach taken for each river basin district,[146] including their balancing of environmental and economic factors.

4.2 The Common Implementation Strategy

As a result of its flexible and innovative approach, the WFD involves different levels of government and a variety of actors in its implementation. While the text of the Directive mainly details the institutional roles and responsibilities for water management at Member State level, other dimensions of multi-level water governance at EU level have surfaced from practice, most notably through the implementation of the WFD in the context of the Common Implementation Strategy (CIS).

The CIS was not foreseen in the text of the Directive, but emerged as an idea from a meeting of Member States' water authorities involved in the implementation of the WFD in October 2000.[147] Basically the CIS aimed to facilitate information-sharing and capacity-building among Member States coming to grips with the novelties of the Directive. To some extent, the CIS contributes to bringing forward regulation of water management in situations in which certain information 'simply does not exist yet'.[148] Its focus is creating a common understanding of methodological questions related to the technical and scientific implications of the WFD.[149] From another angle, the strategy may facilitate monitoring of progress in implementation by promoting an exchange of experiences in applying the open-ended provisions of the Directive and complying with the 'factors to be taken into account' to that end.[150] The strategy thereby allows the 'testing and validation of different approaches to the Directive', pooling good practice and information from different sources at different levels of government and from non-governmental sources, as well as building on shared technical and human resources for the benefit of less economically advanced Member States.[151]

---

[140] WFD, Art 15.   [141] Ibid, Art 12.   [142] Ibid, Art 18(2)c.

[143] Lee, 'Law and Governance of Water Protection Policy' (n 130) 43–45; and W Howarth, 'Aspirations and Realities under the Water Framework Directive: Proceduralization, Participation and Practicalities' (2009) 21 *Journal of Environmental* Law 391, 395.   [144] WFD, Art 14.

[145] Ibid, Art 4.   [146] Lee, 'Law and Governance of Water Protection Policy' (n 130) 37.

[147] Common Implementation Strategy for the Water Framework Directive: Strategic Document, as agreed by the Water Directors under the Swedish Presidency (2001).

[148] Lee, 'Law and Governance of Water Protection Policy' (n 130) 35.

[149] CIS Strategic Document (n 147) 2.

[150] Lee, 'Law and Governance of Water Protection Policy' (n 130) 36.   [151] Ibid, 47.

It also aimed to involve the public in the WFD implementation and develop formal guiding and supporting documents on key aspects of the WFD.[152] Stakeholder involvement is foreseen as both observers and participants in the specific working groups with a view to facilitating an exchange of 'views and concerns' for discussion between all parties directly responsible for the WFD implementation and those who are interested in or will be affected by it.[153] Participation and peer review through the CIS may thus provide opportunities for accountability of national water authorities at the supranational level – that is, before the European Commission and other Member States, as well as non-governmental experts from across the EU.[154] Ultimately, however, the CIS is a highly technical exercise that produces documentation which, although made publicly available, is not easily accessible to non-expert audiences.[155] There are therefore doubts as to whether it can truly provide an additional layer of transparency and checks on the subsidiarity-based implementation of the WFD or whether it will exclude the broader public from vital decisions regarding an essential natural resource such as water.[156]

In relation to the second theme of this chapter, it can finally be observed that both the WFD and its CIS support cooperation between Member States and international organizations. According to the WFD, Member States have the possibility of using international treaty bodies, such as international river commissions, to coordinate their implementation activities and may also designate such bodies as competent authorities.[157] And beyond the letter of the Directive, the CIS has influenced the ways in which Member States participate in certain international river commissions, particularly in terms of interinstitutional coordination and public participation in these fora.[158] In addition, the interaction between Member States and international river commissions has also led to direct cooperation between these international law bodies and local water authorities.[159]

Case study 22.2: Implementation of EU water regulation and sustainable development – the diversion of the Greek River Acheloos

The River Acheloos is one of the most important natural water systems in Greece and constitutes a particularly important fluvial ecosystem. For more than 20 years, Greek authorities have been trying to divert the River Acheloos, through a major project intended to serve not only irrigation purposes but also electricity production and water supply to urban centres. However, the Greek Council of State had repeatedly annulled on environmental protection grounds a series of administrative decisions permitting successive versions of that project. As Greek authorities eventually tried to authorize the project through a legislative – rather than an administrative – act, a preliminary reference was submitted to the Court of Justice as to the compatibility of the legislative act with the WFD. Among the various questions posed to the Court, those related to the balancing of the environmental

---

[152] Ibid, 2–3.   [153] Ibid, 14–15.   [154] Ibid.

[155] Which were acknowledged at Carrying Forward the Common Implementation Strategy for the Water Framework Directive – Progress and Work Programme for 2003 and 2004, as agreed by the Water Directors (2003) 8.

[156] Lee, 'Law and Governance of Water Protection Policy' (n 130) 51; Howarth, 'Aspirations and Realities under the Water Framework Directive' (n 143) 415.   [157] WFD, Art 3(4) and (6).

[158] E Hey, 'Multi-Dimensional Public Governance Arrangements for the Protection of the Transboundary Aquatic Environment in the European Union: The Changing Interplay between European and Public International Law' (2009) 6 *International Organizations Law Review* 191, 207.

[159] Ibid, 219–221.

protection objectives of the WFD and economic interests provide further illustrations of the main theme of this chapter.

The Court was asked whether the diversion of water from one river to another is permitted under the Directive and, if so, whether it can only be justified to meet drinking water supply needs or also other economic objectives (irrigation and power generation). Advocate General Kokott addressed this question in detail. She opined that while there is no absolute prohibition on the diversion of water in the WFD, such diversion may still significantly affect the environment and could therefore be incompatible with the Directive's environmental objectives.[160] Advocate General Kokott further noted that derogations from the WFD environmental objectives may be allowed under certain conditions. In particular, the balancing of environmental and economic interests under the WFD must ensure that the reasons for water diversion are of overriding public interest and/or that the benefits for the environment and society must be outweighed by the benefits of the diversion to human health, human safety, or sustainable development. She thus considered that drinking water supply is generally of great importance for human health; and power generation and irrigation may also be seen as legitimate public interests. However, the latter two interests are less important than drinking water supply, and are primarily economic in nature. Consequently, the contribution made by those measures to achieving economic objectives must outweigh the adverse effect on the environmental objectives.[161]

Following this line of reasoning,[162] the Court held that the WFD must be interpreted as meaning that

- a water diversion must not be such as to jeopardize seriously the realization of the WFD environmental objectives;
- to the extent that the water diversion is liable to have such adverse effects, consent may be given if the conditions set out in the WFD are satisfied;[163] and
- the fact that it is impossible for the receiving river basin to meet from its own water resources its needs in terms of drinking water, electricity production, or irrigation is not an essential condition for a water diversion to be compatible with the WFD, even if the conditions are satisfied.[164]

To ensure transparency and fairness in the balancing exercise, the WFD provisions on public participation are also relevant. In the Acheloos case, therefore, another question was raised as to whether the fact that the legislative act approving the water diversion had been adopted without public consultation was compatible with the Directive, and in particular its Article 14(1) which reads:

Member States shall encourage the active involvement of all interested parties in the implementation of this Directive, *in particular* in the production, review and updating of the river basin management plans. Member States shall ensure that, for each river basin district, they publish and make available for comments to the public, including users.[165]

Regrettably the Court of Justice quickly disposed of this issue, by considering that a national parliament-level act approving management plans for river basins where no procedure

[160] Opinion of AG Kokott in Case C-43/10 *Nomarchiaki Aftodiokisi Aitoloakarnanias*, opinion of 13 October 2011, nyr, paras 66 and 67.   [161] Ibid, paras 83–91.
[162] Case C-43/10 *Nomarchiaki Aftodioikisi Aitoloakarnanias*, judgment of 11 September 2012, nyr, para 49.   [163] ie WFD, Art 4(7)(a)–(d).
[164] *Nomarchiaki* (n 162) para 69.   [165] Emphasis added.

for public information, consultation, or participation had been implemented, did not fall within the scope of Article 14(1) of the WFD.[166] The conclusion notably differs from that of Advocate General Kokott, who had instead considered that the lack of consultation could infringe Article 14 where individuals and interested parties have a right[167] to be actively involved in the implementation of the WFD in general, not just in the production, review, and updating of the river basin management plans. She noted that there is no exception for legislative measures under the WFD, and therefore public authorities *should* integrate public participation procedures into the relevant legislative process or its preparatory stages.[168] A more environmentally-minded interpretation by the Court would have rather tended to maximize opportunities for members of the public to keep a check on national authorities' balancing of environmental and economic interests.

5 Climate change

Climate change is a priority for EU environmental policy and is inextricably linked to international law. This has become quite evident from the explicit mention of it in the Lisbon Treaty:

> The Union policy on the environment shall contribute to the pursuit of the following objectives:...promoting measures at [the] international level to deal with regional or worldwide environmental problems, and *in particular combating climate change.*[169]

The EU has harboured leadership ambitions in the fight against climate change since the early years of international climate change cooperation in the 1990s. Various generations of EU climate laws have succeeded each other since then, in an effort not only to ensure prompt implementation of international law (as seen in the context of nature protection and water management), but also to *influence its development.*[170]

5.1 An overview of the 2009 Climate and Energy Package

The 2009 Climate and Energy Package is the most recent example of such legislative waves: it is a comprehensive set of legal acts aimed at responding to European *and* global climate change and energy challenges, and integrating climate change considerations into a range of sectors and policies. It therefore implements in different ways the environmental integration principle.[171] The very fact that the EU decided to adopt a 'package' of legislative measures that jointly address climate change and energy points towards a highly integrated approach. In addition, in many respects the Package includes innovative legal measures that support not only climate change mainstreaming in other policy areas, but also the environmental sustainability of proposed climate change measures

---

[166] *Nomarchiaki* (n 162) paras 74–75.

[167] As already established by the Court in Case C-32/05 *Commission v Luxembourg* [2006] ECR I-11323, paras 80–81.   [168] Opinion of AG Kokott in *Nomarchiaki* (n 160) paras 122–129.

[169] Art 191(1) TFEU, fourth indent (emphasis added).

[170] K Kulovesi, 'Climate Change in EU External Relations: Please Follow My Example (or I Might Force You To)' in E Morgera (ed), *The External Environmental Policy of the European Union: EU and International Law Perspectives* (Cambridge: Cambridge University Press, 2012) 115.   [171] See section 2.3.1.

vis-à-vis other areas of EU environmental law (eg to avoid negative impacts on nature protection).[172]

The package is explicitly related to the EU's efforts to play a global leadership role in the battle against climate change, and was adopted at a time when the future of international climate change cooperation under the multilateral climate change regime remains unclear. The package was in fact adopted in the lead-up to the 2009 UN Climate Change Conference in Copenhagen, which was expected to reach agreement on a new and more ambitious multilateral treaty on greenhouse gas reductions but failed to bring conclusive results.[173] In the face of continued inability to agree at the multilateral level, the EU volunteered to increase its mid-term emission reduction target to 30 per cent, which would be more compatible with the requirements of climate science, but made this proposal conditional on the adoption of a comprehensive international climate treaty.[174] While this proposal has not yet been taken up by other countries, the EU has reflected this possibility in its own climate regulation.[175]

The sustainable development dimension of the package is quite significant: EU climate change law offers further opportunities to explore the use of economic instruments to support environmental protection. One of its underlying objectives is 'to make the European economy a model for sustainable development in the 21st century' by transforming it into a low-carbon, high energy-efficiency economy under the assumption that climate change objectives can be achieved while continuing to pursue economic prosperity and job creation within the EU.[176] The same vision can be found in the Europe 2020 strategy, which reiterates the so-called '20-20-20' climate change target: a 20 per cent reduction in EU greenhouse gas emissions from 1990 levels, raising the share of EU energy consumption produced from renewable resources to 20 per cent, and a 20 per cent improvement in the EU's energy efficiency.[177] Against this background, the package in fact responds to multiple economic concerns including energy security, long-term competitiveness, trade, and development cooperation.[178]

5.2 Components of the package

As to its specific components, the package first contains a Directive extending and revising the EU Emission Trading Scheme (ETS) from 2013 onwards. The ETS is a market-based mechanism capping greenhouse gas emissions from energy-intensive industrial sectors and currently covering approximately 40 per cent of the EU's total greenhouse gas emissions. The use of a market-based mechanism is considered useful

---

[172] K Kulovesi, E Morgera, and M Munoz, 'Environmental Integration and the Multi-Faceted International Dimensions of EU Law: Unpacking the EU's 2009 Climate and Energy Package' (2011) 48 *Common Market Law Review* 829.

[173] Commission, Towards a comprehensive climate change agreement in Copenhagen, COM(2009) 39 final.

[174] Council, Conclusion on the preparation for the 16th session of the Conference of the Parties to the UN Framework Convention on Climate Change, 29 November–10 December 2010, 3036th Environment Council Meeting, Luxembourg, 14 October 2010.

[175] Directive 2009/29/EC amending Directive 2003/87/EC so as to improve and extend the greenhouse gas emission allowance trading scheme of the Community (OJ [2009] L140/63) (the ETS Directive), Preamble and Art 1(1).

[176] Commission, 20 20 by 2020. Europe's climate change opportunity, COM(2008) 30 final, pp 2–3.

[177] Europe 2020 (n 87) 4.

[178] LG van Schaik, 'The Sustainability of the EU's Model for Climate Diplomacy' in S Oberthür and M Pallemaerts (eds), *The New Climate Policies of the European Union: Internal Legislation and Climate Diplomacy* (Brussels: VUB Press, 2010) 264 and 266.

to allow private operators to find the most cost-effective way to comply with the EU greenhouse gas emission reduction obligations, with the understanding that 'placing a price on carbon' will send an unequivocal signal to the private sector. In this case, therefore, the EU is trying to integrate environmental protection and economic development. The ETS, however, is far from being free from difficulties and setbacks: for once, the carbon price has effectively remained too low to promote low-carbon investment and innovation.[179] In addition, the ETS has been revealed to be vulnerable to fraud and cybercrime.[180] On these and other accounts, the ETS thus remains a learning-by-doing regulatory experiment.

The ETS Directive is complemented by the Effort-Sharing Decision, which introduces binding emission targets for each Member State for 2013–20 in sectors not included under the ETS, such as transport, buildings, agriculture, and waste.[181] The package also comprises a Directive regulating for the first time the controversial climate change mitigation technology of carbon capture and storage (CCS) in geological formations, and creates incentives for pilot activities.[182]

The package further includes the Renewable Energy Directive, which, also for the first time, addresses jointly all forms of renewable energy. It aims to increase the share of renewable energy to 20 per cent of the EU's overall consumption and to 10 per cent of transport petrol and diesel consumption by the year 2020.[183] The Renewables Directive, in addition, includes unprecedented sustainability criteria for biofuels.[184] That is, the EU has set the first supranational standards supporting the sustainable production of fuels of renewable and biological origin that may help to supplant fossil fuels and therefore help the fight against climate change. In doing so, the EU has tried to tackle concerns associated with the alleged negative impacts of biofuel production on the environment (particularly in terms of habitat destruction and deforestation), indigenous and local communities, and small-hold farmers.[185] The Renewables Directive is linked to the Fuel Specification Directive, which was amended as part of the package with a view to facilitating the more widespread blending of biofuels into petrol and diesel.[186]

Another element in the package targets energy efficiency: this is the Passenger Car Regulation, which aims to reduce greenhouse gas emissions from transport by setting the first legally binding fleet standards for carbon dioxide emissions from new passenger

[179] E Morgera and K Kulovesi, 'The Role of the EU in Promoting International Climate Change Standards' in I Govaere and S Poli (eds), *EU Governance of Global Emergencies* (Leiden: Brill, forthcoming 2014).

[180] See Europol, press release, 'Carbon Credit Fraud Causes More than 5 Billion Euros Damage for European Taxpayers', 9 December 2009, https://www.europol.europa.eu/content/press/carbon-credit-fraud-causes-more-5-billion-euros-damage-european-taxpayer-1265; and more recently, European Voice, 'ETS still vulnerable to fraud', 7 August 2013, http://www.europeanvoice.com/article/2013/august/ets-still-vulnerable-to-fraud-report/78033.aspx

[181] Decision No 406/2009/EC on the effort of Member States to reduce their greenhouse gas emissions to meet the Community's greenhouse gas emission reduction commitments up to 2020 (OJ [2009] L140/136).

[182] Directive 2009/31/EC on the geological storage of carbon dioxide (OJ [2009] L140/114) (the CCS Directive).

[183] Directive 2009/28/EC on the promotion of the use of energy from renewable sources (OJ [2009] L140/16) (the Renewables Directive), Art 3(4). [184] Ibid, Arts 17 and 18.

[185] CBD Subsidiary Body on Scientific, Technical and Technological Advice, 'New and emerging issues relating to the conservation and sustainable use of biodiversity: biodiversity and liquid biofuel production', UN Doc UNEP/CBD/SBSTTA/12/9 (2007).

[186] Directive 2009/30/EC amending Directive 98/70/EC as regards the specification of petrol, diesel and gas-oil and introducing a mechanism to monitor and reduce greenhouse gas emissions (OJ [2009] L140/88).

cars.[187] Energy efficiency is then addressed by a separate Directive adopted in 2012.[188] In addition, the package complements amended guidelines on State aid for environmental measures, which were adopted by the Commission in 2008.[189]

5.3 International reach of the package

Overall, the package contains various provisions linked to the EU's *international* agenda on climate change. Notably, the new ETS Directive aims to support the establishment of carbon trading schemes in other regions with a view to expanding the global carbon market first in very advanced countries, and later in emerging economies.[190] In addition, the ETS is an example of EU legislation aiming to generate climate finance for developing countries: it recommends that at least 50 per cent of the revenues generated from the ETS should be used for adaptation, technology transfer, as well as afforestation and reforestation activities in developing countries.[191]

Furthermore, the Renewables Directive provides for joint renewable energy projects between EU Member States and third countries.[192] Its biofuel sustainability criteria also apply to biofuels produced in third countries and imported into the EU, and are explicitly motivated by the concern that biofuel production in third countries might not respect minimum environmental or social requirements.[193] The criteria are expressly based on international reference documents.[194] Hoping to inspire domestic action beyond its borders and possibly even similar developments in international law, the EU has systematically referred to its sustainability criteria in multilateral fora and in the context of its bilateral relations with third countries.[195] In the latter regard, it should be noted that the Renewables Directive indicates that the EU will endeavour to conclude bilateral or multilateral agreements with third countries containing provisions on the sustainability criteria.[196] Similarly, the CCS Directive has been portrayed by the EU as a source of inspiration for the further development of the international climate change framework.[197] To support its position at the multilateral level, the EU has made available to developing countries capacity-building and collaborative research and development opportunities,[198] which are explicitly reflected in the CCS Directive.[199] The latter also points to the possibility of extending a network of CCS demonstration projects in key third countries.[200] Whether third countries are willing to cooperate with the EU in the implementation of these measures, however, remains to be seen on a case-by-case basis.

---

[187] Regulation (EC) No 443/2009 setting emission performance standards for new passenger cars as part of the Community's integrated approach to reduce carbon dioxide emissions from light-duty vehicles (OJ [2009] L140/1).   [188] Directive 2012/27/EU on energy efficiency (OJ [2012] L315/1).

[189] Commission, Community guidelines on State aid for environmental protection, (Notice) 2008/C 82/01 (OJ [2008] C82/1).

[190] ETS Directive, Art 25(1)(a).   [191] Ibid, Art 10(3).   [192] Renewables Directive, Art 9(1).

[193] Ibid, preambular para 74. J Scott, 'The Multi-Level Governance of Climate Change' [2011] 4 *Carbon and Climate Law Review* 25.   [194] Renewables Directive, recitals 69, 73, and 77.

[195] E Morgera, 'Ambition, Complexity and Legitimacy of Pursuing Mutual Supportiveness through the EU's External Environmental Action' in B Van Vooren, S Blockmans, and J Wouters (eds), *The EU's Role in Global Governance: The Legal Dimension* (Oxford: Oxford University Press, 2013).

[196] Renewables Directive, Art 18(4).

[197] See EU submission to the UNFCCC Subsidiary Body for Scientific and Technological Advice, in UNFCCC, 'Views related to carbon dioxide capture and storage in geological formations as a possible mitigation technology: Submissions from Parties', UN Doc FCCC/SBSTA/2010/MISC.2 (2010), 31–42.

[198] Ibid, 41–42.   [199] CCS Directive, recital 7.   [200] Ibid, Art 38(2).

Case study 22.3: Influencing environmental multilateralism through EU climate regulation – international aviation emissions

In the area of climate change it is quite evident that the EU uses its internal regulation not only to implement international environmental law, but also to try to influence ongoing multilateral environmental processes. These attempts, however, do not necessarily go unchallenged by third countries. A glaring example is the EU's unilateral action to include aviation activities in the ETS.[201] From 1 January 2012, all airlines, including those from third countries, were expected to participate in the ETS for their flights departing from and arriving at European airports. This EU initiative needs to be understood in the context of a long-standing international impasse on whether and under which international forum (the international climate change regime or the International Civil Aviation Organization) to take action on emissions from international aviation.

US and Canadian airlines and airline associations contested the measures transposing the relevant EU Directive in the UK. A preliminary reference was then submitted to the Court of Justice to clarify whether, among other things, the Directive violated international law. The Court concluded that the Directive did not violate international law, in particular its principles of territoriality and sovereignty of third States, as the scheme was applicable only to aircraft that were physically present in the territory of the Member States (ie flying into and out of EU airports) and therefore under the jurisdiction of the EU. In addition, the Court noted that the EU was allowed to comply with the international climate change obligations in the manner and at the speed upon which it had agreed.[202] Interestingly, Advocate General Kokott noted that the EU 'could not reasonably be required to give ... [multilateral] bodies unlimited time in which to develop a multilateral solution.'[203] Thus, the Court of Justice found that the EU can take bold climate change measures with a view to anticipating and possibly influencing legal developments at the international level, as long as it ensures a link to its territory and has provided sufficient opportunities for other countries to reach an agreement in the context of relevant international organizations.

The Court's decision, however, did not pacify the concerns of third countries. A coalition including Brazil, China, India, Russia, South Africa, and the US continued to oppose the inclusion of international aviation emissions within the EU ETS.[204] Faced with these external pressures, in November 2012 the European Commission indicated that the EU had decided to 'stop the clock' for one year on the implementation of the inclusion of non-EU flights under the ETS.[205] The Commission motivated the decision by reference to intervening positive developments at the International Civil Aviation Organization and a desire to create a positive atmosphere for international negotiations.[206] It remains to be seen whether

---

[201] Directive 2008/101/EC of the European Parliament and of the European Council amending Directive 2003/87 so as to include aviation activities in the scheme for greenhouse gas emission allowance trading within the Community (OJ [2009] L8/3). On the ETS, see section 5.5.1.

[202] Case C-366/10 *Air Transport Association of America*, judgment of 21 December 2011, nyr (Grand Chamber).

[203] Ibid, opinion of 6 October 2011, paras 185 and 186.

[204] International Centre for Trade and Sustainable Development, 'Opponents of EU Aviation Carbon Law Agree on Possible Countermeasures', *Bridges Weekly Trade News Digest*, 22 February 2012, http://ictsd.org/i/news/bridgesweekly/126278/

[205] Stopping the clock of ETS and aviation emissions following last week's International Civil Aviation Organisation (ICAO) Council, MEMO/12/854, 12 November 2012.   [206] Ibid.

the EU is recalibrating its arms with a view to effectively and constructively influencing multilateral environmental decision-making,[207] or whether it has been subject to pressure from Member States over the economic implications of the scheme.[208]

6 Conclusion

The EU as an environmental regulator has set for itself very broad and ambitious object-ives. It has used its law-making powers abundantly to address a variety of environmen-tal challenges and in many respects has improved its environmental regulation in a gradual fashion, learning from past mistakes and engaging in significant innovation. Nonetheless, different areas of the EU environmental *acquis* appear at different stages of development: some, like nature protection, continue to rely mostly on traditional approaches such as listing species threatened by extinction and establishing protected areas; others, such as water and climate change, have instead adopted cutting-edge regu-latory approaches, such as proceduralization, multi-level environmental management, and market-based instruments. In all these areas, however, implementation challenges remain significant and a difficulty persists in appropriately balancing environmen-tal protection with continued economic and social development – a taxing aim that is embodied in the principle of sustainable development. It remains to be seen whether the concept of green growth may provide new impetus in EU law to identify and pursue opportunities for business development, job creation, and public sector savings arising from environmental protection.[209] This concept is central to the Europa 2020 strategy[210] and EU climate change policy, and corresponds to the idea of a 'green economy'[211] that the EU championed at the international level during the Rio+20 Summit on Sustainable Development.

This chapter also demonstrates that the study of EU environmental law would not be complete without an understanding of the role of the EU as a global environmental actor, proactively engaged in the development and implementation of international environ-mental law. To a significant extent, EU environmental law aims to fulfil the international environmental obligations of the Union and/or its Member States. In addition, as seen in the specific area of climate change, the EU increasingly develops its internal environ-mental regulation to anticipate or even influence the making of international environ-mental law.[212]

---

[207] Morgera and Kulovesi, 'The Role of the EU in Promoting International Climate Change Standards' (n 179).

[208] B Lewis and V Volcovici, 'US, China turned EU powers against airline pollution law' (*Reuters*, 10 December 2012) http://www.reuters.com/article/2012/12/10/us-eu-airlines-climate-idUSBRE8B801H20121210

[209] E Morgera and A Savaresi, 'A Conceptual and Legal Perspective on the Green Economy' (2012) 21 *RECIEL* 14.

[210] Europe 2020 (n 87). The commitment to green growth is complemented by the 'smart growth' pillar on developing an economy based on knowledge and innovation; and the 'inclusive growth' pillar, which concerns fostering a high-employment economy in delivering social and territorial cohesion.

[211] 'The Future We Want', UN Doc A/RES/66/288 (11 September 2012) Annex, paras 56 and 62.

[212] H Vedder, 'Diplomacy by Directive: An Analysis of the International Context of the Emissions Trading Directive' in M Evans and P Koutrakos (eds), *Beyond the Established Legal Orders* (Oxford: Hart Publishing, 2011) 105.

Further reading

J Jans and H Vedder, *European Environmental Law* (4th edn, Groningen: Europa Law, 2012)

L Kramer, *EU Environmental Law* (7th edn, London: Sweet and Maxwell, 2011)

M Lee, *EU Environmental Law: Challenges, Change and Decision-Making* (Oxford: Hart Publishing, 2005; second edition forthcoming 2014)

R Macrory, *Reflections on 30 Years of EU Environmental Law* (Groningen: Europa Law, 2006)

G Marín Durán and E Morgera, *Environmental Integration in the EU's External Relations: Beyond Multilateral Dimensions* (Oxford: Hart Publishing, 2012)

E Morgera (ed), *The External Environmental Policy of the European Union: EU and International Law Perspectives* (Cambridge: Cambridge University Press, 2012)

J Scott (ed), *Environmental Protection: European Law and Governance* (Oxford: Oxford University Press, 2009)

P Wenneras, *The Enforcement of EC Environmental Law* (Oxford: Oxford University Press, 2007)

23

European consumer law

Geraint Howells

1 Introduction

Few areas of national law have been influenced as heavily by EU law as consumer protection. This impact at first remained contained within the specialism, but with the adoption
of the Unfair Terms in Consumer Contracts Directive,[1] which introduced minimum controls on unfair terms in consumer contracts, and especially the Consumer Sales Directive,[2]
which set minimum quality standards for goods, the reach of the legislation spread out to
irritate[3] core areas of private law and in particular sales law, which is the cornerstone of
national commercial law regimes. In particular, the modern approach of the EU legislator
is being strongly influenced by a new breed of European private lawyers. Many of these are
from Germany and see European contract law inspired by the ethic of consumer welfare
values as a means of releasing their national law from the shackles of the Bismarckian
era German Civil Code. However, the prospect of a European private law developing has
support beyond Germany with the enthusiasm of some transcending mere consumer law
or even contract law and encompassing a broader desire to reform private law across the
whole EU. Some even favour the development of a European Civil Code;[4] though others
are more modest in their goals.[5] Nevertheless, the notion of a common European sales
law has found political support from those within the European Commission, who see
the increase in cross-border trade as a goal in its own right.[6] However, consumer critics of
current policy sometimes argue that the European Commission is becoming more interested in consumer law harmonization as a means of promoting trade rather than protecting
consumers.

One impact of the EU has been to remove national rules that claimed to protect consumers but acted as unjustified barriers to trade. This is considered in section 2. The rest of
the chapter is about the EU's positive harmonization agenda, which is needed not only to
give the EU a social face, but also because many national consumer protection measures
are justified and a harmonized approach is the only way to promote the free circulation of
goods and services. Section 3 provides general commentary on the EU's approach. A distinctive feature of EU consumer law is an emphasis on empowering consumers to make
the right decisions. Information duties (including the duty to not mislead) and the right
of withdrawal are key instruments in this approach and are reflected on in sections 4 and
5. Such decision-based rules are favoured as they promote autonomy more than substantive rules and interfere less in national private law legal systems. However, the EU also
provides for substantive consumer law issues, which are considered in sections 5 to 10,
with details being provided on product safety, product liability, unfair contract terms, and

---

[1] Directive 1993/13 (OJ [1993] L95/29).   [2] Directive 1999/44 (OJ [1999] L171/12).

[3] To borrow the language from the well-known article on good faith as a legal irritant by G Teubner, 'Legal
Irritants: Good Faith in British Law or How Unifying Law Ends Up in New Divergences' (1998) 61 *Modern
Law Review* 11.

[4] A Hartkamp et al (eds), *Towards a European Civil Code* (4th edn, Alphen aan den Rijn: Kluwer Law
International, 2010); H Collins, *The European Civil Code: The Way Forward* (Cambridge: Cambridge University
Press, 2008). cf P Legrand, 'Against a European Civil Code' (1997) 60 *Modern Law Review* 44.

[5] H Beale, 'The Future of the Common Frame of Reference' (2007) 3 *European Review of Contract Law* 257;
C von Bar, 'Coverage and Structure of the Academic Common Frame of Reference' (2007) 3 *European Review
of Contract Law* 350. cf H Eidenmüller et al, 'The Common Frame of Reference for European Private Law –
Policy Choices and Codification Problems' (2008) 28 *Oxford Journal of Legal Studies* 659.

[6] COM(2011) 635 final, 11 October 2011, 2–4. The Common European Sales Law is intended as an optional
sales law for cross-border contracts. It is currently undergoing political scrutiny by the European Parliament.
For more detail see section 11.6.

sale of goods law. The last topic, considered in section 12, is enforcement and redress which is a current priority for the EU. Having created a set of EU consumer protection rules it is clear that for these to be effective there must be enforcement measures in place. Given the small scale of many individual consumer disputes this poses challenges even in the most efficient national legal systems. Across the EU there are different blends of public and private enforcement and different levels of practical enforcement depending on the resources available and the efficiency of court services and regulators.

2 The negative impact of EU law on national consumer protection rules

The bulk of this chapter is concerned with the positive consumer protection rules introduced by the EU that now pervade national consumer law. However, there is another important contribution of EU law in removing redundant national laws. EU law might be compared to a glacier removing all national consumer protection rules that impede the development of the internal market without having any real consumer protection purpose, or at least any purpose that could not be achieved by any less restrictive means. Thus unjustified rules limiting the ingredients could not be used to exclude imports from other EU Member States – the German Beer Purity Law limiting ingredients of beer to water, barley, and hops[7] and Italian rules requiring pasta to be made from durum wheat[8] were successfully challenged, as was a German ban on the importation of 'Cassis de Dijon' because it did not have a high enough alcohol content to satisfy requirements of German law.[9] Many advertising rules, especially under the German Unfair Competition Law, were successfully challenged because whilst claiming to protect consumers they were in reality placing unfair limits on competition.[10] An illustrative example was the need for the Court of Justice to find the cosmetic name 'Clinique' should not be banned because of the risk of confusing German consumers that the product had medicinal properties. Out of this line of cases came the EU image of the average consumer being 'reasonably well-informed and reasonably observant and circumspect, taking into account social, cultural and linguistic factors'.[11] This was a reaction to some overprotective national regimes which really did not serve the consumer well as they unduly restricted competition. The Court has, however, shown itself to be sensitive to genuine consumer needs. The ambition of a level playing field was achieved in large part by using (old) Article 30 EC (now Article 34 TFEU) with an expansive definition of 'measures having effects equivalent to quantitative restrictions'[12] and applying the concept of mutual recognition.[13]

Not all national consumer law rules could be removed in this way for the very good reason that some had legitimate consumer protection goals. Indeed, the Court was alert to genuine consumer protection needs and would refuse challenges where a genuine consumer protection concern was at stake. For instance, it upheld a French ban on the

---

[7] Case C-178/84 *Commission v Germany* [1987] ECR 1227.
[8] Case 202/82 *Commission v France* [1984] ECR 933 and Case 90/86 *Zoni* [1988] ECR 4285.
[9] Case C-120/78 *Cassis de Dijon* [1979] ECR 649.
[10] Case C-315/92 *Clinique* [1994] ECR I-317; Case C-470/93 *Mars* [1995] ECR I-1923; Case C-210/96 *Gut Springenheide* [1998] ECR I-4657; C-303/97 *Kessler* [1999] ECR I-513; and Case C-220/98 *Estée Lauder* [2000] ECR I-117.   [11] Directive 2005/29 (OJ [2005] L149/22) recital 18.
[12] Case C-8/74 *Dassonville* [1974] ECR 837.   [13] *Cassis de Dijon* [1979] (n 9).

marketing of educational materials on the doorstep.[14] These national rules might be justi-fied on the basis of a Treaty provision[15] or the Court-established mandatory requirements which in *Cassis De Dijon* were said to include consumer protection as a justification for national laws that would otherwise be obstacles to movement.[16] To take the glacier analogy one step further, these areas of legitimate consumer protection might be compared to the mounds left behind after the glacier has done its work. EU law then gets to work on these issues by positively harmonizing the rules that are needed for consumer protection in a way that promotes the internal market.

3 Consumer protection and the internal market

3.1 Legal basis

In the early days the only legal basis for introducing EU consumer rules was the internal market provisions. Indeed Article 114 TFEU, which provides for the adoption of 'measures for the approximation of the provisions laid down by law, regulation or administrative action in Member States which have as their object the establishment and functioning of the internal market' is still the basis for most EU consumer laws. Article 114(3) requires such measures to take as a base a high level of consumer protection.

Article 169 TFEU provides for a specific consumer protection provision which provides that 'In order to promote the interests of consumers and to ensure a high level of con-sumer protection, the Union shall contribute to protecting the health, safety and economic interests of consumers, as well as to promoting their right to information, education and to organise themselves in order to safeguard their interests.' However, when it comes to the legislative means to achieve these aims, it is content to cross-reference to Article 114 TFEU or otherwise limit the scope to 'measures which support, supplement and monitor the policy pursued by the Member States.' As a result, few EU provisions rely on Article 169 TFEU as a legal base. Consumer protection also features in Article 38 of the Charter of Fundamental Rights.

The legal basis for EU activity in consumer law being based for the most part on Article 114 TFEU might explain the dominance of the internal market perspective in the European Commission's consumer policy. It was not always so. There is indeed a certain irony in that the European Commission was the most fervent advocate of consumer protection at a time when its powers in this field were limited. It had to justify intervention solely on the ground that harmonized rules were needed to promote the functioning and establishment of the internal market.[17] Once intervention was justified the European Commission had the free-dom to choose the appropriate level and consumer protection objectives could come into play. Indeed, the primacy of consumer protection as the motivating force is evident in one of the first legislative measures being the Doorstep Selling Directive, which provided a can-cellation for sales and services contracts signed in the consumer's home.[18] Whilst a case can be made out for such legislation promoting the internal market – there are a few companies

---

[14] Case C-382/87 *Buet* [1989] ECR 1235. In Case C-286/81 *Oosthoek* [1982] ECR 4575 a Dutch ban on the use of free gifts to promote sales was upheld; nowadays such national bans are likely to fall foul of the Unfair Commercial Practices Directive (on which see later).   [15] Art 36 TFEU.
[16] *Cassis de Dijon* (n 9).
[17] eg Directive 85/577 gave particular regard to Art 100 EEC. For a detailed overview of the development of EU competence for consumer protection, see S Weatherill, *EU Consumer Law and Policy* (Cheltenham: Edward Elgar, 2005) 1–23. On the relationship between consumer protection and the internal market, see further chapters 11 and 12.   [18] Directive 85/577 (OJ [1985] L371/31).

that operate doorstep selling on a pan-European basis – it is evident that the motivation for the law was the vulnerability of people buying in their homes, normally from local businesses operating high-pressure sales techniques.

Despite consumer protection featuring more prominently in recent Treaty amendments there has been in fact a noticeable change in tone with the emphasis being placed on the internal market impact of divergent consumer laws. Whilst consumer law has risen up the EU's agenda and been more mainstreamed, it is possible to argue that the protection element has become less important. The internal market needs harmonized rules, not the best consumer protection rules. Those defending the EU policy would argue that they fulfil the obligation to adopt a high base of protection, but there is scope to debate what that means and certainly it is not necessarily the same as the highest level found in some Member States.

3.2 EU consumer law as a driver for greater cross-border trade

It should be recognized that the present Treaty still does not see consumer legislation as an end in itself. Any such laws have to be internal market-related or support and supplement national law.[19] The major motivations are to promote active cross-border consumerism as well as encouraging businesses to seek consumers in other Member States to make markets within the EU more competitive. The European Commission is frustrated at the lack of growth in cross-border trade.[20] This is very evident when we come to see its attempts to introduce maximal harmonization in the Consumer Rights Directive[21] and subsequently (when that was unsuccessful for unfair terms and sale of goods, which were removed from the initial proposal[22]) by the attempt to try to adopt an alternative optional regime for cross-border sales in the proposed Regulation on a Consumer European Sales Law. The Commission has few levers to increase cross-border trade besides making the law more harmonized. This has driven the change in emphasis in EU consumer policy. The objective of European consumer law is no longer to provide a platform of minimum rights so that consumers could be confident in buying anywhere in the Union. Rather, it is increasingly the policy (though this has been resisted in some areas[23]) to make the EU rules the sole source of consumer protection (maximal harmonization, ie a uniform EU law that does not permit Member States to apply lower *or* higher standards) to give traders the confidence to trade across borders. Such an approach results from a change of focus to one that prioritises inspiring businesses with the confidence to trade across borders without the risk of being surprised by unfamiliar national laws.[24]

---

[19] Arts 2(5) and 114(1) TFEU.

[20] eg business attitudes towards cross-border sales and consumer protection showed a decrease in businesses conducting cross-border transactions (29 per cent in 2006, 21 per cent in 2008), see 'Business Attitudes towards Cross-Border Sales and Consumer Protection' (2006) Commission Eurobarometer, Flash EB Series #186, http://ec.europa.eu/consumers/topics/flash_eb_186_ann_report_en.pdf

[21] Directive 2011/83 (OJ [2011] L304/64).   [22] COM(2008) 614 final, 8 October 2008.

[23] eg in addition to doorstep selling and distance selling contracts the initial proposal for a Consumer Rights Directive also sought the full harmonization of unfair contract terms and consumer sales: COM(2008) 614 final, 8 October 2008. The final version of the Consumer Rights Directive, adopted in 2011 after intense legislative discussion, does not include the areas of unfair contract terms and consumer sales (Directive 2011/83 (OJ [2011] L304/64)).

[24] Though the argument is sometimes invoked that consumers may be made more active in the internal market if only the EU law applies as the rules are more certain. However, it is hard to understand how the possibility that national laws might provide for better than the minimal rights can be a deterrent to cross-border shopping.

The message from the European Commission is clear: consumers have more to gain from increased competition between traders who are emboldened to supply consumers in other States than they risk from any marginal reduction in consumer protection at the national level. This is controversial and the European Commission has not managed the soft politics of this process well, with consumer organizations remaining nervous about such developments.[25] The extent to which changes in the law really will impact on cross-border trade is unclear[26] with other factors such as language, delivery costs, and access to redress should things go wrong also being important factors.[27] Equally, the extent to which maximal harmonization can fulfil the Commission's ambitions is limited by the scope of harmonizing measures (for Member States retain competence in areas not harmonized, subject to EU free movement law, as discussed later) and the discretion within the laws themselves for national differences to emerge in implementation, application, and enforcement.[28] What is also missing from this debate is any consideration of what is the optimum amount of cross-border shopping. More seems impliedly viewed as better, but sending consumers travelling around Europe or having traders delivering goods long distances conflicts with another important EU policy of environmental protection.[29]

3.3 Legislative approach

Traditionally EU legislation in the consumer protection field used directives and applied to cross-border trade and domestic trade alike. There are increased signs that both these approaches are being eroded. Regulations are being preferred as the legislative instrument, as evidenced by recent proposals for a Regulation on a Consumer European Sales Law[30] and Product Safety.[31] This may be appropriate if in fact EU law gives little discretion in implementation and especially if EU law is to become the sole source of law due to the use of maximal harmonization. This may be beneficial to consumers as regulations become directly applicable and so immediately available for use by consumers. Consumers struggle to obtain rights under directives that are not implemented or not properly implemented as most of their transactions are with private parties and not emanations of the State, and directives lack 'horizontal direct effect' against private parties.[32] However, in one famous case German consumers, relying upon the principle of Member States' damages liability for their breach of EU law, did recover from the German State for losses caused by the failure to set up a compensation fund for package travel holiday insolvencies as required by EU legislation.[33]

In many areas the traditional approach of national law sitting alongside EU rules will continue. In such areas there are advantages to the use of directives as they provide the

---

[25] U Pachl, 'Common European Sales Law – Have the Right Choices Been Made: A Consumer Policy Perspective' (2012) 19 *Maastricht Journal of European and Comparative* Law 180, 189.

[26] eg the results of a 2010 study show that 57 per cent of traders consider that harmonization of the law would not impact on their cross-border sales: 'Retailers' Attitudes towards Cross-Border Trade and Consumer Protection' (2011), Commission Eurobarometer, Flash EB Series #300. See also BEUC, 'European Contract Law 28th regime – BEUC'S 10 Reservations' (2011) BEUC Position Paper, X/2011/118; Pachl, 'Common European Sales Law' (n 25) 185.

[27] SEC(2011) 1409 final, 29 November 2011, 3.

[28] See also discussion of open-textured norms at section 10.2.

[29] On the substance of environmental policy, see chapter 22.   [30] COM(2011) 635 final.

[31] COM(2013) 78 final.

[32] Case C-91/92 *Paola Faccini Dori v Recreb Srl* [1994] ECR I-3325. For more on the nature and legal effect of directives and regulations, see chapters 5 and 6.

[33] Joined Cases C-178/94, C-179/94, C-188/94, C-189/94 and C-190/94 *Dillenkofer v Bundesrepublik Deutschland* [1996] ECR I-4845.

flexibility to create a coherent national framework. There is, however, also a tendency, started in the area of access to justice, where national procedural law autonomy is fiercely protected, for EU law only to apply where there is a cross-border trade dimension. The arguments here are nuanced and need to be considered on a case-by-case basis. Whilst some contexts may justify such a parallel regime being established, there is a danger in making the law too complex if multiple or overlapping regimes emerge. This is likely to be one of the debating points surrounding the proposed optional Common European Sales Law.[34]

4 Information policy

Information has been a prized technique of consumer protection by the EU. Many of the national consumer protection rules that were found to be incompatible with Article 30 EC (now Article 34 TFEU) could be so held because informing the consumer about the goods or services was seen as a more proportionate way of achieving the desired consumer protection objective.[35] Also national rules restricting the provision of information in advertising have been successfully challenged.[36] Rules permitting explicit or implicit comparisons with competitors and their products ('comparative advertising') which comply with key principles is also evidence of the desire to promote competition by better informing consumers.[37]

In its positive harmonization agenda the EU has also favoured information provision rules. This is partly out of an ideological belief in promoting consumer autonomy by rectifying the lower amount of information the consumer has in relation to the seller (so-called 'information asymmetry').[38] If consumers are provided with more information it is hoped they will make better decisions. It also has the practical advantage of being easier to achieve in a multi-State context than changing substantive practices or legal standards. The relevant rules cover both information in advertising and marketing and the information that has to be supplied pre-contractually, in the contractual documentation and post-contractually.

4.1 Information obligations

Some of the earliest EU consumer law measures were concerned with the provision of misleading information.[39] These are now found in the Unfair Commercial Practices Directive.[40] As well as containing a general clause controlling unfair practices, the Directive also contains 'mini-general clauses' which prohibit misleading and aggressive practices. There is also an annex containing practices that are always to be considered unfair. The Directive was also innovative by including an obligation to promote the provision of relevant information through the rules on misleading omissions; thus introducing a positive duty on traders to provide material information.[41] The bulk of EU rules concern positive obligations to provide

---

[34] See section 11.6.

[35] eg in *Commission v Germany* (n 7) and *Cassis de Dijon* (n 9).

[36] Case C-362/88 *GB-INNO-BM* [1990] ECR I-667; Case C-44/01 *PippigAugenoptik* [2003] ECR I-3095; S Weatherill, 'The Rôle of the Informed Consumer in EC Law and Policy' (1994) 2 *Consumer Law Journal* 49.

[37] Directive 97/55 (OJ [1997] L290/18) recital 2, now Directive 2006/114 (OJ [2006] L376/21) recital 6; Weatherill, 'The Rôle of the Informed Consumer in EC Law and Policy' (n 36) 178.

[38] S Grundmann, W Kerber, and S Weatherill (eds), *Party Autonomy and the Role of Information in the Internal Market* (Berlin: De Gruyter, 2001); G Howells, A Janssen, and R Schulze (eds), *Information Rights and Obligations: A Challenge for Party Autonomy and Transactional Fairness* (Aldershot: Ashgate, 2005).

[39] Directive 84/450 (OJ [1984] L250/17).   [40] See section 11.5.

[41] Directive 2005/29, Art 7; G Howells, H Micklitz, and T Wilhelmsson, *European Fair Trading Law* (Aldershot: Ashgate, 2006) 147–158.

specific information pre-contractually and in the contractual documentation. This has gradually become a more and more prevalent form of regulation as can be seen by contrasting the very early Doorstep Selling Directive, in which the only information obligation was to inform the consumer of the right of cancellation,[42] with the far more extensive rules in the Distance Selling[43] and Distance Marketing of Financial Services Directives.[44] The information obligations in the latter Directive totalled more than 30 and resulted from a need to satisfy all States in order to have agreement on a maximal harmonization list. The Consumer Rights Directive[45] now has substantial information rules that extend to all consumer contracts, but has specific detailed rules under which off-premises and distance contracts are treated similarly. It replaces the earlier directives on doorstep and distance selling.

4.2 Information and behavioural economics

The extensive rules on information may be helpful to provide the consumer with a full record of what was agreed, but if the aim is to improve consumer decision-making more attention is needed to the lessons of behavioural economics and in particular the limited processing powers of consumers.[46] This branch of research uses the insights of psychology as to how consumers actually behave to challenge traditional formal economic models that assume consumers will always act rationally when provided with information. This allows more realistic appraisals of the impact of not just contractual information obligations, but also the rules concerning advertisements and the role of warnings, for example, in relation to product safety. It is not just the amount of information that is important, but also how it is presented and the account taken of the likely reaction by consumers to the information. Behavioural economics has been used to inform tobacco policy, for example, to draft the warnings about the risks of smoking to make them relate to consumer concerns, to give them authority, and to inform their placement and rotation.[47] Currently pictorial warnings are allowed, but the proposal to make them compulsory is an example of how evidence of their impact on smoking reduction can help to inform policy.[48] In the consumer credit field more might be done to take account of how consumers budget since even very high interest rates as indicated by the APRs (annual percentage rate charges) may not impact significantly on consumers' decisions if they focus more on how much has to be repaid each month. There might be scope to personalize information, for example to inform consumers about how they have actually used their bank accounts or gym membership.[49] The EU is showing an awareness of the impact of behavioural economics on consumer policy and has held several conferences on this theme, but it takes time to apply this to rules where the natural tendency is to play safe and appease Member States by allowing them all to keep their national preferences.

[42] Directive 85/577, Art 4.   [43] Directive 97/7 (OJ [1997] L144/19) Art 4.
[44] Directive 2002/65 (OJ [2002] L271/16) Art 3.   [45] Directive 2011/83 (OJ [2011] L304/64).
[46] G Miller, 'The Magical Number Seven, Plus or Minus Two: Some Limits on Our Capacity for Processing Information' (1956) 63 *Psychological Review* 81; G Howells, 'The Potential and Limits of Consumer Empowerment by Information' (2005) 32 *Journal of Law and Society* 349; Better Regulation Executive and National Consumer Council, 'Warning: Too Much Information Can Harm' (2007) http://www.berr.gov.uk/files/file44367.pdf. There are other ways in which the EU uses behavioural insights, eg by requiring that there be positive consent to any add-ons to prices, rather than pre-ticked boxes (eg when purchasing holiday insurance): see Consumer Rights Directive, Art 22.
[47] G Howells, *The Tobacco Challenge* (Aldershot: Ashgate, 2011) 272–275.
[48] COM(2012) 788 final, 19 December 2012.
[49] O Bar-Gill and F Ferrari, 'Informing Consumers about Themselves' (2010) 3 *Erasmus Law Review* 93.

5 Right of withdrawal

5.1 Justification

The EU has also promoted the right of withdrawal for particular contracts as a consumer protection technique. This shares some of the objectives of the information strategy insofar as it does not seek to challenge the substance of the deal, but rather seeks to promote more informed consumer choices. Sometimes it does this by giving the consumer further information about the product by being able to handle it in person before becoming irrevocably bound to the contract, in other cases it serves as a safety valve ensuring that consumers are not bounced into a decision when, for example, accosted on their doorstep or by a telephone call without proper time to reflect on whether the goods or services truly meet their needs.

5.2 Harmonization

This right, which has been given various names such as cancellation or withdrawal, first appeared in 1985 in the Doorstep Selling Directive.[50] It has since been extended to distance selling[51] and to particular contracts where the risks of high-pressure selling are prevalent, such as timeshare,[52] or where the consequences for consumers of a rash decision are serious, for example, life assurance[53] and credit contracts.[54] These rights grew up piecemeal and there were different lengths of the withdrawal periods, different times from which that withdrawal period began to run, different rules on how withdrawal could be affected and the consequences once the right was invoked (though often these were left to national law), and different rules about the effect on the withdrawal period if information obligations were not complied with.[55] As part of a broader programme of consolidation of EU contract law there have been proposals to develop a more harmonized approach to the right of withdrawal, notably by the Acquis Group.[56] This has yet to be put into practice, but the Consumer Rights Directive has at least standardized the procedure for distance and off-premises contracts with a 14-day right of withdrawal period.[57]

5.3 Effective consumer protection?

The right of withdrawal is undoubtedly a helpful consumer protection technique.[58] It gives consumers encouragement to use certain distribution channels such as the internet with

---

[50] Directive 85/577, Art 5; on the variety of terminology, see B Pozzo, 'Harmonisation of European Contract Law and the Need of Creating a Uniform Terminology' (2003) 6 *European Review of Private Law* 754, 764.

[51] Directive 97/7, Art 6; Directive 2002/65, Art 6.

[52] Directive 2002/122 (OJ [2008] L33/10) Art 6.

[53] Directive 2002/83 (OJ [2002] L345/1) Art 35.

[54] Directive 2008/44 (OJ [2008] L133/66) Art 14.

[55] Case C-91/02 *FacciniDori* [1994] ECR I-3325; Case C-481/99 *Heininger* [2001] ECR I-9945; Case C-336/03 *easyCar* [2005] ECR I-1947; Case C-350/03 *Schulte* [2005] ECR I-9215; Case C-412/06 *Hamilton* [2008] ECR I-2383; Case C-205/07 *Gysbrechts* [2008] ECR I-9947; Case C-489/07 *Messner* [2009] ECR I-7315; Case C-227/08 *MartínMartín* [2009] ECR I1939; and Case C-511/08 *HeinrichHeine* [2010] ECR I-3047.

[56] Research Group on the Existing EC Contract Law (Acquis Group), *Contract I – Pre-Contractual Obligations, Conclusion of Contract, Unfair Terms* (Munich: Sellier, 2007); *Contract II* (Munich: Sellier, 2009); *Contract III* (Munich: Sellier, forthcoming 2014).   [57] Directive 2011/83, Art 9.

[58] P Rekaiti and R Van den Bergh, 'Cooling-Off Periods in the Consumer Laws of the EC Member States: A Comparative Law and Economics Approach' (2000) 23 *Journal of Consumer Policy* 371.

the confidence that they can return goods that do not meet their expectations without having to give a reason. It is a protection against over-forceful salesmen in some contexts where consumers may be especially vulnerable, such as in their homes.[59] It is particularly useful as it is a self-help technique consumers can use without having to invoke a formal procedure. They simply have to withdraw to escape from their contractual obligations. However, if they have paid money over and the trader does not follow his legal obligations a claim may be needed to recover the amounts due. There are nevertheless limitations on its effectiveness.[60] Consumer behaviour indicates both that consumers are reluctant to admit they made poor choices and that they will be reluctant to take the initiative to withdraw from the contract. Traders are entitled to require consumers to pay the cost of returning goods and this may be a practical disincentive, particularly in a cross-border situation.[61] Also in some instances it may not be possible for consumers to determine whether they have made a good choice during the time allowed for withdrawal. This is true of many financial services products. In these cases a better solution may be to provide consumers with fair exit routes during the course of the contract.

6 Rules establishing consumer expectations

The rules on information provision and the right of withdrawal, though fettering the complete freedom of traders as to how they do business,[62] essentially build on the freedom of contract model. Indeed they can be seen as reinforcing that model by ensuring the consumer enters into an agreement with full knowledge and consent. It is where the consumer is given substantive non-excludable rights[63] that the extent of freedom of contract is less and potentially ceases to be the main underlying concept. In EU law these non-excludable rights are backed up by provisions both within the Directives[64] and in EU private international law[65] that prevent consumers losing core rights granted by EU law by choosing the law of a non-Member State. Some have even claimed that such a regime should be viewed more like a tort law or regulatory regime; namely, a regime imposed by the law rather than a contractual regime where the premise is that the obligations are derived from the parties' mutual agreement.[66] However, many substantive rules in practice leave some margin for traders to affect the expectations of consumers by the way they market and present the products.

---

[59] G Howells, 'The Right of Withdrawal in European Consumer Law' in H Schulte-Nölke and R Schulze (eds), *European Contract Law in Community Law* (Cologne: Bundesanzeiger, 2002) 230–232; M Loos, 'Rights of Withdrawal' in G Howells and R Schulze (eds), *Modernising and Harmonising Consumer Contract Law* (Munich: Sellier, 2009); H Eidenmüller, 'Why Withdrawal Rights?' (2011) 7 *European Review of Contract Law* 1, 7–18.   [60] Howells, 'The Right of Withdrawal in European Consumer Law' (n 59) 233.

[61] eg the inclusion of the potential cost of return by the consumer would have to be taken into account when calculating the total cost, see G Borges and B Irlenbusch, 'Fairness Crowded Out by Law: An Experimental Study on Withdrawal Rights' (2007) 163 *Journal of Institutional and Theoretical Economics* 84, 100.

[62] Howells, Janssen, and Schulze, *Information Rights and Obligations* (n 38).

[63] eg the right of withdrawal in Directive 85/577, Art 6; Directive 97/7, Art 12(1); and Directive 2008/122, Art 12(1). Later a number of substantive rights affecting the core obligations towards consumers are considered.

[64] eg Directive 93/13, Art 6(2); Directive 97/7, Art 12(2); and Directive 1999/44, Art 7(2).

[65] These are the rules which govern which law and jurisdiction apply, see Regulation 593/2008 on the law applicable to contractual obligations (Rome I), Art 6(2).

[66] R Brownsword, 'Regulating Transactions: Good Faith and Fair Dealing' in Howells and Schulze, *Modernising and Harmonising Consumer Contract Law* (n 59).

Some of the laws we shall consider can be seen as specialist consumer rules with limited impact on the general law – product safety, product liability, and to some extent unfair commercial practices law might be viewed in this light. By contrast the directives on unfair contract terms and, particularly, sale of goods law strike more into the heartland of private law. Whilst they could be viewed as creating specialist regimes for consumer contracts, the Consumer Sales Directive in particular in many countries became a model for a broader reform of sales law. This was particularly the case in Germany, where reform of the sales provisions in the German Civil Code had long been recognized as essential but had stalled under political inertia. The Consumer Sales Directive gave fresh momentum to a more general modernization of German sales law not restricted to consumer contracts.[67] Out of this grew a brand of 'European private law' scholarship that sought to modernize European contract law more generally. However, some also see this as a threat to consumer protection as the European private lawyers prioritize harmonization over consumer protection and therefore will sacrifice some more protective national rules to achieve their broader ambition of a modern common European contract law.[68] The substantive rights will now be outlined, before some general reflections on them are made.

7 Product safety

7.1 Public law control and consumer protection

Although most of the rules setting minimum standards are private law in nature, it should not be overlooked that there are significant public law controls aimed at protecting the consumer, for instance in the field of product safety. The EU's involvement in product safety grew out of its work on technical harmonization and the realization that many standards needed a consumer safety element. The new approach to technical harmonization[69] saw a suite of directives being adopted (eg on personal protective equipment,[70] machinery,[71] and toy safety[72]) that set down general expectations of safety, backed up by an annex laying out essential safety requirements. These were then operationalized by the development of European (CEN) standards by privatized standards bodies. Traders could choose either to meet the Directive's standards in their own way or adopt the CEN standard (as transformed into a national standard) and benefit from safe harbour provisions. Compliance with standards was indicated by use of the CE marking, which indicates conformity with standards and should not be (but often is) confused with a safety mark.

7.2 General Product Safety Directive

The EU realized that some consumer products were not covered by new approach directives and in 1992 adopted a General Product Safety Directive[73] that set a general safety

---

[67] C Herresthal, '10 Years after the Reform of the Law of Obligations in Germany – The Position of the Law of Obligations in German Law' in R Schulze and F Zoll (eds), *The Law of Obligations in Europe* (Munich: Sellier, 2013) 186 *et seq.*

[68] H-W Micklitz, 'The Targeted Full Harmonisation Approach: Looking behind the Curtain' in Howells and Schulze, *Modernising and Harmonising Consumer Contract Law* (n 59) 75–83.

[69] Council Resolution of 7 May 1985 on a new approach to technical harmonization and standards (OJ [1985] C136/1).   [70] Directive 89/686 (OJ [1986] L399/18).

[71] Directive 2006/42 (OJ [2006] L157/24), amending Directive 95/16 (OJ [1995] L213/1).

[72] Directive 2009/48 (OJ [2009] L170/1), replacing Directive 88/378 (OJ [1988] L187/1).

[73] Directive 92/59 (OJ [1992] L228/24).

requirement for all consumer products that applied where there were no specific EU rules.[74] It also set out powers the Member States had to have to react to product safety concerns,[75] introduced reporting obligations to the EU on the part of Member States about product safety incidents[76] as well as an emergency procedure to allow the EU to adopt decisions on serious and immediate risks where Member States have taken different positions.[77] This Directive was subsequently amended[78] to clarify a number of issues, but also to place an obligation on producers to report product safety issues and to provide an express recall obligation.[79] Additional amendments have recently been proposed to further clarify concepts, make clear the relationship with vertical directives, integrate even more the standardization approach, and significantly enhance enforcement. It is also proposed that the new rules should be set out in regulations, one dealing with the substantive rules, the other with the enforcement mechanisms.[80] An important outcome of this Directive has been to ensure at least every Member State has an authority responsible for product safety.

8 Product liability

Product safety laws put standards in place to ensure products are safe and provide measures to remove any unsafe products that do reach the market. The Product Liability Directive,[81] on the other hand, seeks to compensate those injured by defective products. It is something of an outlier in the consumer *acquis*, partly due to its origins in the directorate concerned with internal market affairs (DG MARKT) rather than consumer protection (DG SANCO).[82] Its adoption was in large measure due to the personal tenacity of Dr Taschner, a Commission official, who was convinced of the need to introduce strict product liability in response to the thalidomide disaster in the 1960s in which many children suffered deformities as a result of their mothers taking a morning sickness preventative drug. It was hard to establish fault liability as the effects of drugs on children *in utero* were unexpected. This Directive shows the value of being able to adopt a common European approach, as Member States' legal systems were struggling with the limitations of contract (due to privity) and tort (due to fault requirement) to address product liability claims, but each feared being the first to introduce strict liability that did not require fault in case it imported a US-style litigation explosion. The 1970s had seen a product liability insurance crisis in the US with the liability risks making it hard or impossible for some producers to obtain insurance. The Directive seeks in the words of the recital to provide 'liability without fault on the part of the producer' as this was viewed 'as the sole means of adequately solving the problem, peculiar to our age of increasing technicality, of a fair apportionment of the risks inherent in modern technological production.'[83] Instead of fault, liability would be based on defectiveness that is found when a product 'does not provide the safety which a person is entitled to expect.'[84] However, this standard is open-textured, in the sense that it requires a general assessment. The extent to which

---

[74] Directive 92/59, Arts 3 and 4.   [75] Ibid, Arts 5 and 6.

[76] Ibid, Arts 7 and 8.   [77] Ibid, Art 9.

[78] Directive 2001/95 (OJ [2001] L11/4).

[79] See D Fairgrieve and G Howells, 'General Product Safety – A Revolution through Reform?' (2006) 69 *Modern Law Review* 59.   [80] COM(2013) 78 final, 13 February 2013.

[81] Directive 85/374 (OJ [1985] L210/29).

[82] For more on the structure of the European Commission, see chapter 3.

[83] Directive 85/374, recital 2.   [84] Ibid, Art 6(1).

such assessment is based on consumer expectations or if there is a role for risk-utility analysis is moot. Equally the strictness of the liability regime will depend upon how the defences are interpreted and in this respect the inclusion of the (optional)[85] development risks defence is significant. This seeks to protect producers where there was no way they could have known of the defect and risks thereby returning the debate to a negligence-style analysis where what is important is the conduct of the producer rather than the condition of the product. The Court of Justice, on the one hand, interpreted the defence narrowly as being lost by the most advanced knowledge even if that did not at the time form part of the scientific consensus. Thus as long as one researcher has identified the risk, the defence is lost as producers would be expected to invest in further research or insurance. On the other hand, the judgment tended towards a negligence-style analysis by requiring the knowledge to have been reasonably accessible; Advocate General Tesauro famously gave the example of research only published in Manchurian, which European producers might not be expected to know about.[86] Whether this accessibility requirement is justified is a moot point.[87]

9 Unfair terms

The Unfair Terms in Consumer Contracts Directive[88] was inspired by German law and is therefore restricted to non-individually negotiated terms: in effect standard form contracts.[89] This controls terms which are unfair because contrary to the requirement of good faith, they cause a significant imbalance in the parties' rights and obligations arising under the contract, to the detriment of the consumer.[90] The reference to good faith was symbolically important to many continental States where good faith had been an important means of controlling unfairness. However, as it is not the sole criteria of unfairness, but has to be combined with a significant imbalance, it might in fact be considered a limiter on controls by requiring procedural as well as substantive unfairness.[91]

However, it is likely that the use of flagrantly unfair terms (eg the exclusion of liability for negligently caused death and personal injury) will be viewed as a breach of good faith per se. There is no black list of terms that are automatically unfair, but rather an annex with a non-exhaustive list of terms that are indicatively unfair. The assessment cannot, however, cover 'the definition of the main subject matter of the contract nor to the adequacy of the price and remuneration ... in so far as these terms are in plain intelligible language.'[92] This exemption from control has been broadly construed by the UK's Supreme Court in a case where bank charges were unsuccessfully challenged.[93] Many bank accounts in the UK work on the basis that the service is free of charge as long as the account is in credit, but there are heavy charges incurred if the user goes overdrawn without permission. These charges were held not to be subject to review (and also could not be controlled as penalty clauses as they were provided for in contract rather than resulting from a breach). However, this core term

---

[85] The development risks defence is excluded in Finland and Luxembourg, whereas there are limitations on the defence in France, Germany, and Spain.

[86] Case C-300/95 *Commission v UK* [1997] ECR I-2649.

[87] M Mildred and G Howells, 'Comment on "Development Risks: Unanswered Questions"'(1996) 61 *Modern Law Review* 570   [88] Directive 93/13 (OJ [1993] L95/29).

[89] Directive 93/13, Art 3(2).   [90] Ibid, Art 3(1).

[91] R Brownsword and G Howells, 'The Implementation of the EC Directive on Unfair Terms in Consumer Contracts – Some Unresolved Questions' [1995] *Journal of Business Law* 243.

[92] Directive 93/13, Art 4(2).   [93] *OFT v Abbey National plc* [2009] UKSC 6.

exemption runs counter to the Nordic tradition of allowing fairness of the core terms and those States' desire to retain this stronger control is an impediment to agreeing maximal harmonization in this area.

Individual consumers can challenge unfair terms, which if found to be unfair will be non-binding. The contract will continue in existence if it is possible to sever the offending terms. However, few consumers will in practice have sufficient incentive to challenge unfair terms and indeed it is important to ensure they are not included in contracts as consumers may be unaware that the terms are unfair and therefore not binding and simply follow the contract terms. Therefore preventative controls allowing for injunctions against unfair terms were included. The Unfair Terms in Consumer Contracts Directive is an early example of the EU favouring injunctions brought by public authorities or consumer groups.[94]

10 Sale of goods

The basic principle behind the Consumer Sales Directive[95] is that goods should be in conformity with the contract, by which it is understood that they should

- comply with any description,
- possess the qualities of any model or sample,
- be fit for any particular purpose known to and accepted by the seller,
- be fit for the purposes goods of the same type are normally used, and
- show the normal quality and performance the consumer can reasonably expect.[96]

In assessing this last criterion the Directive was innovative in, subject to certain conditions, taking into account public statements made not only by the seller but also the producer or his representative, for example, on the labelling or in advertisements.

The remedies regime has been the most controversial element. The remedies provided by the Directive include repair, replacement, rescission (which broadly equates with termination of the contract), or price reduction.[97] Controversially a hierarchy of remedies was introduced with the consumer first having to seek repair or replacement. The right to reject non-conforming goods is a prized remedy by consumers in several States and potential loss of the right to invoke this without having first to allow the seller the opportunity to cure is one reason why there has been resistance to moving to maximal harmonization is this field. In UK law the domestic remedies of rejection and/or claims for damages run in parallel with the EU-inspired remedies.

There are also rules on guarantees that are voluntarily provided, but these do not control their content as much as ensure that they are treated as legally binding, set out the terms in plain and intelligible language (covering issues such as duration, territorial scope, and name and address of guarantor), and make it clear to consumers that they have rights under national law that are not affected.[98]

---

[94] The outcome in Case C-153/13 *Pohotovosť, sro v JánSoroka* will determine whether the Unfair Terms in Consumer Contracts Directive precludes legislation of a Member State which does not allow a legal person whose purpose is the protection of consumers' rights to intervene in court enforcement proceedings.

[95] Directive 1999/44 (OJ [1999] L171/12).   [96] Ibid, Art 2.

[97] Ibid, Art 3.   [98] Ibid, Art 6.

11 General comments on substantive rights

11.1 Goods and services

Whilst unfair terms legislation applies to any consumer contract, most of the EU legislation providing general substantive rights focuses on goods. Only recently has the EU turned its attention to digital goods.[99] Less has been done in the services field. The attempt to legislate for service liability is one of the few examples of the European Commission abandoning a legislative initiative.[100] Of course there are examples of EU intervention into particular services and it has been active in the field of services of general interest[101] and financial services.[102] The EU has also adopted a Services Directive,[103] which does contain some consumer protection measures on information provision, dispute resolution, and promoting voluntary measures to improve quality, but is mainly concerned with the freedom to provide services across borders. Nevertheless, as in most national systems, the wide variety of services and the difficulty in determining expected outcomes have made it harder to legislate in this field.

11.2 General standards

The general standards adopted are also by their very nature open-textured standards that do not provide concrete answers but require a complex assessment of the facts against the norms set out in general terms. Open standards are inevitable when setting such general norms, but create a severe risk of different interpretations emerging and in the EU context this includes national legal systems reading their traditional approach to the rules. The discretion can be structured by use of relevant guiding factors being included in the legislation. An increasingly common practice now is for guidance to be issued by the European Commission.[104] Court decisions are also a way of concretising the norms' meaning through experience. Despite one initial brave attempt to determine whether a term was unfair[105] the Court of Justice has since backed off and made it clear that the application of the unfairness

---

[99] For the recent attention paid to digital products, see Directive 2011/83 and COM(2011) 635 final, 11 October 2011. For the development in the UK, in particular with respect to remedies, see the 2012 BIS Consultation on the supply of goods, services and digital content. See also N Helberger et al, 'Digital Content Contracts for Consumers' (2013) 36, *Journal of Consumer Policy* 37.

[100] COM(90) 482 final, 20 December 1990.

[101] eg electricity services under Directive 96/92 (OJ [1996] L27/20), now Directive 2003/54 (OJ [2003] L176/37); postal services under Directive 97/67 (OJ [1997] L15/14), now Directive 2008/6 (OJ [2008] L52/3); conditional access services (ie where pre-authorization is needed to access, eg television and internet services) under Directive 98/84 (OJ [1998] L320/54); and particular aspects of information society services under Directive 2000/31 (OJ [2000] L178/1).

[102] eg Directive 2002/65 (OJ [2002] L271/16) on the distance marketing of consumer financial services and Directive 2007/64 (OJ [2007] L319/1) on payment services.

[103] Directive 2006/123 (OJ [2006] L376/36).

[104] Guidance document on the relationship between the General Product Safety Directive (GPSD) and Certain Sector Directives with Provisions on Product Safety; Guidance on the Implementation/Application of Directive 2005/29/EC on Unfair Commercial Practices, SEC(2009) 1666, 3 December 2009. In the financial services field there is the very complex Lamfalussy procedure that allows regulators from across Europe to come together to develop rules in a consistent manner. This was named after the chairman of the committee that proposed the scheme: see 'Final Report of Committee of Wise Men on the Regulation of European Securities Markets', 15 February 2001, http://ec.europa.eu/internal_market/securities/docs/lamfalussy/wisemen/final-report-wise-men_en.pdf   [105] Joined Cases C-240–244/98 *Océano* [2000] ECR I-4941.

test to consumer contract terms is a matter for national courts.[106] Indeed it is rare for Court of Justice cases to give very helpful guidance on the content of the rules. The split roles, between the Court as interpreter of EU law and national courts which apply it, means that Court of Justice judgments can be rather abstract and the true impact only revealed by seeing how the judgment was received and applied in the national system, which can be difficult for lawyers from other Member States to discover. National decisions, even those not subject to a reference, can assist, but there is a need for the development of databases that allow learning to be shared and a common knowledge developed. Furthermore, there is a need to go beyond mere provision of information and provide for synthesis of the rules. Projects such the *ius commune* textbook[107] might have an educative role to play, but the development of guidance based on experience might be a helpful way forward in practical terms. Such soft law risks circumventing the European Parliament and so any such guidance should ideally be explicitly provided for in legislation.[108]

11.3 Channelling of liability

Obligations in EU law are imposed on several actors, including the seller, producer, and importer. Sales law traditionally focuses on the seller and the Consumer Sales Directive follows this pattern save for the provisions of voluntary guarantees where the producer may well be the guarantor. The General Product Safety Directive places obligations on both suppliers and producers, but those on producers are normally more onerous. The Product Liability Directive channels liability to the producer, with suppliers only having a secondary liability when they cannot disclose the identity of the producer or their supplier. The Directive does, however, impose liability on some own-branders and importers into the EU. Importer liability is in practice important if EU consumers are to be given effective protection, however, there may be problems if the importer itself is based outside the EU. As it is the importer into the EU and not into the consumer's State it may still involve complex litigation requiring consumers to sue in other Member States. The General Product Safety Directive by contrast focuses attention on those distributors which are responsible for the first stage of distribution on the national market. This is more helpful in practical enforcement terms than looking to the importer into the EU.

11.4 Minimum content

Safety requirements, product liability, unfair terms, and sales law are all seen as representing minimum non-excludable rights. However, how high the minimum content is might be debatable since, as Mr Justice Burton noted in the product liability context, there is a tension between the non-excludability of the rights and the freedom to prevent liability arising through warnings.[109] Equally, in sales law, defects that are drawn to the buyer's attention do not give rise to liability.[110] As no unfair terms are automatically unfair it is moot as to the extent to which even those terms which on their face are unfair can be rendered fair by transparency, though one suspects that good faith places a limit on the extent to which transparency can make good an imbalance. Our case study of passenger rights (see below)

---

[106] Case C-237/02 *Freiburger Kommunalbauten* [2004] ECR I-3403.

[107] H-W Micklitz, J Stuyck, and E Terryn (eds), *Consumer Law: Ius Commune Casebooks for a Common Law of Europe* (Oxford: Hart Publishing, 2010).

[108] In the product liability context, see D Fairgrieve, G Howells, and M Pilgerstorfer, 'The Product Liability Directive: Time to get Soft?' [2013] 4 *Journal of European Tort Law* 1.

[109] *A v National Blood Authority* [2001] 3 All ER 289.   [110] Directive 1999/44, Art 2(3).

is one area where EU law does provide minimum rights that cannot be deviated from. The advantage of such rights is that they form a minimum set of expectations on which consumers can rely. The downside is that they constrain the offerings on the market and impose minimum obligations and with them costs which all market participants have to bear and this can increase the minimum cost of products.

Case study 23.1: Air passenger rights

On 15 April 2010 I sat in Zurich Airport at six o'clock in the morning when I heard that my Swiss Air flight to Manchester had been cancelled due to an ash cloud from the volcano Eyjafjallajökull in Iceland. Although Switzerland is outside the EU, due to a bilateral agreement I was covered by Regulation 261/2004[111] that governs air passenger rights and placed an obligation on the airline to look after me until my journey could be completed. If I had been in, say, Dubai and not using a European carrier I would most likely have been left without assistance even if I had bought a return ticket from Manchester.[112] Although the International Montreal Convention[113] provides an international scheme of passenger rights, it is less protective than the EU Regulation as it excuses airlines that took all measures that could have been reasonably required to avoid the damage or where it was impossible to take such measures. This would seem to cover air traffic control grounding flights due to volcanic ash.

The EU Regulation provisions apply in all circumstances except that the duty to pay financial compensation is not applicable in 'extraordinary circumstances which could not have been avoided even if all reasonable measures had been taken.'[114] This exemption does not affect the obligation to provide assistance. Fortunately, my airline immediately agreed to my request for a train ticket and, despite the travel agent claiming trains could only be booked to London, I arrived home in Manchester in the early hours of the next day, tired but having made some new friends en route. Others were less fortunate and spent several days waiting to return home. European airlines had the duty to care for them, which included accommodating them and providing meals and refreshments. This burden was not shared by non-European carriers flying from outside the EU or other transport sectors within the EU. At the time there was a regulation on passenger rights for rail[115] and subsequently rules for ferries[116] and coaches[117] came into force. The rail sector might have been affected, but obviously the volcano did not impact on trains in the same way or else I would not have managed to get home so quickly! With respect to the rules on coaches and ferries, there are limitations on the extent of the obligation to provide accommodation, which carriers can cap at €80 per day for a maximum of two days for coaches[118] and three for ferries.[119]

The duty to pay compensation to airline passengers does not vary according to the price of the ticket. The same obligations flow from the delay and cancellation of a 1p ticket bought from a low-cost carrier as arise with regard to a business class seat with a scheduled airline. The low-cost carriers also complained that any compensation payable is at a fixed rate ranging between €125–600 depending on distance of flight and duration of delay; whereas for rail and ferry it is a reimbursement of 25–50 per cent of the ticket price and for coach 50

---

[111] OJ [2004] L46/1.   [112] Case C-173/07 *Emirates Airlines v DietherSchenkel* [2008] ECR I-5237.
[113] Convention for the Unification of Certain Rules for International Carriage by Air, done at Montreal, 28 May 1999. The Convention has been concluded by the EU (OJ [2001] L194/38).
[114] Regulation 261/2004, Art 5(3).   [115] Regulation 1371/2007 (OJ [2007] L315/14).
[116] Regulation 1177/2010 (OJ [2010] L334/1).   [117] Regulation 181/2011 (OJ [2011] L55/1).
[118] Ibid, Arts 8 and 21.   [119] Regulation 1177/2010, Art 17(2).

per cent of the ticket price. This differential treatment was litigated before the Court, which found that the harm suffered was the same regardless of the price paid, but then justified the different treatment of airlines as compared to other modes of transport by some rather tendentious arguments based on the distance of airports from urban centres and the procedures for checking and reclaiming baggage.[120]

However, the Commission consulted on revising passenger rights[121] in light of the volcano episode and some court decisions that were quite strict against airline carriers. *Sturgeon v Condor Flugdienst GmbH* treated a three-hour delay as equivalent to cancellation for the purposes of compensation[122] and *Wallentin-Hermann v Alitalia* made clear the narrow circumstances in which technical fault could be classed as an extraordinary circumstance in order to justify not paying compensation.[123]

There is now a proposed regulation in this field which will clarify various points.[124] Concerning the previous discussion, it includes a definition of extraordinary circumstances in line with that of the Court of Justice decision in *Wallentin-Hermann v Alitali*.[125] An annex sets out circumstances which will and will not be treated as extraordinary. Regular maintenance issues and unavailability of crew (unless on strike) are treated as not being extraordinary. Natural disasters rendering safe operation of the flight impossible, such as volcano ash, would be extraordinary. It also follows the *Sturgeon* decision in treating a long delay as equivalent to cancellation as regards compensation, but increases the threshold to five hours for intra-community flights or journeys of less than 3,500 km and to nine or 12 hours depending on length for longer flights to third countries. Also in cases of extraordinary circumstances it would allow carriers to limit accommodation costs to a maximum of €100 per passenger for a maximum of three nights. However, this limitation cannot be applied to certain vulnerable groups. This loss of passenger rights is attempted to be mitigated by better rerouting rights, including on planes of other carriers; and carriers, airports, and other actors have to set up contingency plans to optimize the care and assistance of stranded passengers.

Guaranteeing non-excludable passenger rights is a classic example of minimum consumer rights potentially affecting the market choices available. Low-cost airlines may – though the impact of such costs might in fact be rather small – have to put up their fares to provide this basic cover. In effect the rules say that if you choose to operate a business flying people around Europe you need to be responsible for their welfare if they become delayed or stranded due to cancellations. The airlines become the insurer of their consumers and the EU obliges all market operators to guarantee a minimum level of customer services as the price for being allowed to be part of the marketplace. This cannot be waived in return for lower fares. This may restrict contractual freedom, but one might prefer this to the alternative of lots of people being stranded with no means of shelter and basic nourishment. This is one of the few true examples of collectivization of consumer risks and the current debate is an important test of how well that will be maintained. The solution on the table at the moment continues the principle that the harm caused should be compensated irrespective of price, but places limits on the amounts recoverable. It still leaves the dilemma that if

---

[120] Case C-344/04 R (*International Air Transport Association and European Low Fares Airline Association*) v *Department for Transport* [2006] ECR I-403.

[121] See Public consultation on the possible revision of Regulation (EC) No 261/2004 on air passenger rights, at http://ec.europa.eu/transport/themes/passengers/consultations/doc/2012-03-11-apr-public-consultation.pdf

[122] Case C-402/07 *Sturgeon v Condor Flugdienst GmbH* [2009] ECR I-10923.

[123] Case C-549/07 *Wallentin-Hermann v Alitalia* [2008] ECR I-11061.

[124] COM(2013) 130 final, 13 March 2013.

[125] See also Case C-12/11 *McDonagh v Ryanair Ltd*, judgment of 31 January 2013, nyr.

another volcano ash disaster occurs, significant numbers may be stranded for more than three days without assistance. Is this a risk that can be left to the individual? Or should the State/EU step in to assist with such emergencies? Or is there a role for private insurance, with the lessons of behavioural economics being used to nudge[126] consumers to obtain such cover?

11.5 Extent of harmonization

The Court of Justice determined that the Product Liability Directive was a maximal harmonization directive, meaning that Member States cannot introduce rules that go beyond the scope of the Directive.[127] The Court avoids the use of the phrase 'maximal' and the Commission prefers the terms 'full' or 'total'. However, maximal seems the better contrast with minimal harmonization where Member States retain the discretion to be more protective. 'Full' and 'total' seem misleading as even in areas where EU law allows no discretion for Member States to retain or introduce more protective rules it is common that it does not cover the whole field and areas outside the scope remain within the competence of Member States. Thus, for example, whilst the Unfair Commercial Practices Directive is well known for adopting a maximal harmonization approach, the issues of taste and decency remain outside its scope. The General Product Safety Directive is also widely assumed to also be maximal in character. By contrast the Unfair Terms and Consumer Sales Directives are expressly stated to be minimal in character.[128] Indeed it was the attempt to make rules in these areas maximal when the Consumer Rights Directive was first proposed that caused that Directive to be the most debated Directive in EU history.[129] The contentious issues were, for different Member States, the potential loss of the right to reject in sales law and loss of freedom to control core terms by national law.

11.6 Cross-border-only rules

For a long time it was assumed that the EU consumer rules should apply to all supplies whether domestic or cross-border. In the next section, it is shown that as regards redress a different approach was often taken with the rules being crafted to deal only with cross-border situations. As regards the substantive law, a significant change is foreseen by the proposal for a Regulation on a Common European Sales Law.[130] This was the European Commission's response to the political opposition to maximal harmonization in the areas of unfair terms and sale of goods. It came up with the idea of a Regulation that created a Common European Sales Law that parties could opt into. It would only apply in cross-border sales and where

---

[126] R Thaler and C Sunstein, *Nudge: Improving Decisions about Health, Wealth, and Happiness* (New Haven, CT: Yale University Press, 2008).

[127] Case C-52/00 *Commission v France* [2002] ECR I-3827; Case C-154/00 *Commission v Greece* [2002] ECR I-3879; Case C-183/00 *González Sánchez* [2002] ECR I-3901; and Case C-402/03 *SkovÆg* [2006] ECR I-199.

[128] Directive 93/13, Art 8 and Directive 1999/44, Art 8(2).

[129] Over 2,000 amendments were tabled in the European Parliament: see G Howells, 'European Contract Law Reform and European Consumer Law – Two Related but Distinct Regimes' (2011) 7 *European Review of Contract Law* 173; Howells and Schulze, *Modernising and Harmonising Consumer Contract Law* (n 59); H-W Micklitz and N Reich, 'Crónica de una muerte anunciada: The Commission Proposal for a "Directive on Consumer Rights"' (2009) 46 *Common Market Law Review* 471; C Twigg-Flesner and D Metcalfe, 'The Proposed Consumer Rights Directive – Less Haste, More Thought?' (2009) 3 *European Review of Contract Law* 268.   [130] COM(2011) 635 final, 11 October 2011.

parties had chosen it. As it was a Regulation that formed part of the national law of Member States, it was seen as circumventing the Rome I Regulation[131] on the applicable contract law which ensures that in some situations consumers cannot be deprived of their higher levels of mandatory national protection (Article 6(2)). In cross-border situations the argument is that the Common European Sales Law Regulation's rules would form the national level of mandatory protection for such contracts. The political fate of this measure is still in the balance as consumer groups have voiced fierce opposition to the potential loss of higher national protection through an instrument that consumers will in reality have little choice but to accept if that is the only basis on which traders offer to supply goods. However, it is equally to be seen whether traders accept the high standards in the proposal (there are signs that they will seek to water them down, which will make consumers even more opposed to it) or in any event would want to operate a dual regime for domestic and cross-border controls.

12 Enforcement and redress

Consumer protection rules may take the form of regulations typically enforced by public authorities.[132] Enforcement is at the national level and there is no equivalent enforcement role in the consumer protection field for the Commission to the one it plays in the enforcement of competition law. Although patterns vary from State to State and over time, typically consumer safety, marketing practices, and unfair terms are controlled to a large extent by public enforcement. Consumers also have a right of private redress for goods that are of poor quality or cause them harm and to challenge unfair terms. They might also in some circumstances find it more convenient to exercise their right of withdrawal. In some States consumers also have a private right of redress when harmed by unfair commercial practices and one of the influences of Europe has been to encourage debate about expanding this remedy in States where this right is not currently enjoyed.[133] Traditionally the private law remedies for breach of information duties have been weak.[134]

12.1 Methods of enforcement

States have a range of traditions for enforcing regulation – this may involve the criminal law or administrative sanctions. Some directives do, of course, require some specific powers to be available,[135] but for the most part the EU laws normally merely require that States should provide 'adequate and effective means' of ensuring compliance and penalties should be 'effective, proportionate and dissuasive'.[136] It has already been noted

---

[131] Regulation 593/2008 (OJ [2008] L177/6).

[132] In some States there has been a tradition of enforcement by consumer organizations or even trade organization and this mechanism has spread under the influence or European law.

[133] OJ [2010] C46/26. For the UK debate, see Law Commission, *Consumer Redress for Misleading and Aggressive Commercial Practices* (Law Com No 332, 2012).

[134] C Twigg-Flesner and T Wilhelmsson, 'Pre-Contractual Information Duties in the Acquis Communautaire' (2006) 4 *European Review of Contract Law* 441, 465–468.

[135] eg under Directive 2001/95 Member State authorities are entitled to take a number of measures such as banning the marketing of a dangerous product and introduce the accompanying measures required to ensure the ban is complied with (Art 8(1)(e)) or ordering the actual and immediate withdrawal of a dangerous product (Art 8(1)(f)(i)).

[136] As is required in, eg Directive 2011/83, Art 24; Directive 2008/48, Art 23; and Directive 2002/65, Art 11. See also P Rott, 'Effective Enforcement and Different Enforcement Cultures in Europe' in T Wilhelmsson, E Paunio, and A Pohjolainen (eds), *Private Law and the Many Cultures of Europe* (Alphen aan den Rijn: Kluwer Law International, 2007).

that the General Product Safety Directive forced Member States to ensure an agency responsible for consumer safety was in place. The Consumer Protection Cooperation Regulation[137]goes further and requires each Member State to nominate a competent consumer authority to be part of an EU-wide enforcement network that provides for information exchange and mutual assistance. This is a development from the Consumer Injunctions Directive.[138] The idea behind that Directive was that, as well as rationalizing and embedding an EU right to seek injunctions for breach of the consumer *acquis*, cross-border infringements could be addressed by requiring States to give qualified entities (State consumer protection bodies and/or private consumer organizations) from other States access to their injunction procedures. However, the foray of the UK's Office of Fair Trading (OFT) into the Belgian courts in the *Duchesne* case[139] demonstrated how complex that route could be as the already difficult task for the OFT of litigating in a foreign court was made even more complex because of the range of parties involved in different countries giving rise to a plethora of private international law points. In principle the notion of the State where the perpetrator is situated acting against him seems more likely to achieve practical results, and this is hopefully the outcome of greater cooperation under the Consumer Protection Cooperation Regulation. Under the Regulation national authorities can be requested by their counterparts in other States to take all necessary enforcement measures to bring about the cessation or prohibition of the intra-EU infringement without delay.[140]

12.2 Access to justice

Given the relatively small amounts at stake and the high costs of cross-border enforcement,[141] the amount of formal litigation by consumers in this context is likely to be limited. There are EU rules that seek to assist some consumers by providing that proceedings should be brought in their home State courts[142] or ensuring they are not deprived of their home State mandatory consumer protection rules.[143] Often this protection is linked to the consumer being a passive consumer targeted by the trader; though determining when this situation arises in, say, the context of websites, is hard to determine even with some guidance having been provided by the Court.[144] Indeed if the application of these private international law rules is called into question that in itself will involve expensive satellite litigation concerning questions of jurisdiction and choice of law before the substantive issue can be addressed.

The EU has sought to address the cost of litigation. There are some obligations to provide legal aid for cross-border disputes.[145] Also a European small claims procedure[146] has been introduced that in principle provides for a simplified procedure for cross-border disputes which as far as possible relies on a paper-based system. However, the scheme is underused and has revealed some problems, such as language issues, that need more work to

---

[137] Regulation 2006/2004 (OJ [2006] L364/1).   [138] Directive 98/27 (OJ [1998] L166/51).

[139] *Duchesne SA v OFT*, Cass, 2.11.2007, No C.06.0201.F/1.   [140] Regulation 2006/2004, Art 8(1).

[141] COM(2008) 794 final, 27 November 2008, 4.

[142] See now Regulation 1215/2012 (OJ [2012] L351/1) Art 17. Consumers will also benefit from exequatur being abolished so that foreign judgments are automatically enforceable without any special procedure being needed.

[143] For consumer contracts, Regulation 593/2008 (OJ [2008] L177/6) Art 6(2). See also eg Directive 2008/48, Art 22(4); Directive 1999/44, Art 7(2); and Directive 93/13, Art 6(2).

[144] Joined Cases C-585/08 and C-144/09 *Peter Pammer v Reederei Karl Schlüter GmbH & Co KG and Hotel Alpenhof GesmbH v Oliver Heller* [2010] ECR I-12527.   [145] Directive 2002/8 (OJ [2002] L26/41).

[146] Regulation 861/2007 (OJ [2007] L199/1).

redress.[147] Consumers may also be assisted in cross-border contexts by schemes such as the European payment order procedure.[148]

12.3 Alternative dispute resolution

Given the difficulty consumers are likely to face with formal litigation, it is unsurprising that the European Commission has pinned a lot of its hopes on alternative dispute resolution (ADR). It has adopted two recommendations on this topic[149] and the EU has also adopted a Regulation on online dispute resolution for consumer disputes, which is aimed at facilitating the online resolution of disputes.[150] The EU has established a network of advice centres to assist consumers with cross-border disputes (ECC-Net[151] and its financial services counterpart Fin-Net[152]). An important function they have is to channel consumers to appropriate national ADR bodies. Also, a new Directive requires that Member States at least ensure that ADR procedures are available for all consumer disputes.[153]

12.4 Collective redress

There has been much talk about collective redress for consumers. This was sparked by proposals in the competition field[154] and at first was taken up with vigour by those within the Commission responsible for consumer protection. However, whilst some consultation still rumbles on,[155] one senses a lack of enthusiasm to do anything too dramatic in this area. It may even be an area that is best suited to national reforms as one reason many of the civil justice measures only apply to cross-border situations is the reluctance of national legal systems to allow outside interference. Indeed the proposed Recommendation in this area seems like a sensible way forward as it pushes Member States to adopt national procedures respecting common European values.[156] However, there will be a need for Europe to take a stance on collective redress at least to the extent of deciding whether other Member States have to recognize judgments entered following such procedures.

13 Conclusion

When in 1974 Lord Denning made his famous remarks about European law being, for English law, 'like an incoming tide. It flows into the estuaries and up the rivers. It cannot be held back',[157] he was talking about the EEC Treaty and probably would not have

---

[147] X Kramer, 'Small Claim, Simple Recovery? The European Small Claims Procedure and Its Implementation in the Member States' (2011) 12 *ERA Forum* 119. See also the Commission report on Regulation 861/2007 (COM (2013) 795, 19 October 2013) and the proposal to amend the legislation in light of these issues (COM (2013) 794, 19 October 2013).   [148] Regulation 1896/2006 (OJ [2006] L399/1).

[149] Recommendation 98/257/EC (OJ [1998] L115/31) and Recommendation 2001/310 (OJ [2001] L109/56).

[150] Regulation 524/2013 (OJ [2013] L165/1).

[151] http://ec.europa.eu/consumers/ecc/index_en.htm

[152] http://ec.europa.eu/internal_market/fin-net/   [153] Directive 2013/11 (OJ [2013] L165/63).

[154] SEC(2011) 173 final, 4 February 2011; D Fairgrieve and G Howells, 'Collective Redress Procedures – European Debates' in D Fairgrieve and E Lein (eds), *Extraterritoriality and Collective Redress* (Oxford: Oxford University Press, 2012).

[155] COM(2013) 401 final, 11 June 2013: Towards a European Horizontal Framework for Collective Redress.

[156] Commission Recommendation on common principles for injunctive and compensatory collective redress mechanisms in the Member States concerning violations of rights granted under Union Law, C(2013) 3539/3.

[157] *HP Bulmer Ltd v J Bollinger SA* [1974] Ch 401, 418.

foreseen the swathes of secondary legislation which have had a positive tsunami-like effect on national consumer law. For the most part the influence has been positive with EU law allowing the best parts of traditional national consumer law to coexist with the EU imports. Even when it uprooted the UK's venerable Trade Descriptions Act 1968, EU law replaced it with an unfair commercial practices legal regime that is probably better suited to modern trading conditions.

However, there are concerns that the consumer protection character of EU law is being diluted by an obsession with maximal harmonization that threatens national traditions. This is evident in the desire to extend maximal harmonization to areas of private law such as sale and unfair terms in the face of fierce opposition and, when the Commission was defeated, by the attempt to sidestep the result by proposing the Regulation on a Common European Sales Law. Many of the core consumer directives – Consumer Rights, Unfair Contract Terms, Sale, and Unfair Commercial Practices – are now the responsibility of DG Justice rather than the consumer protection directorate DG SANCO. This internal real-location may be mainly the result of an internal power struggle within the Commission, but it risks creating the impression that the consumer protection soul has gone out of EU consumer policy. Rather than the focus being consumer protection, consumer protection is increasingly being integrated into broader civil justice and internal market agendas. For the future it is hard to see many new legislative initiatives being developed – though something more on digital products is likely – and the lessons of behavioural economics may be utilized.[158] Instead the emphasis will be on increasing the effectiveness of enforcement so that consumer confidence to shop in other Member States is enhanced and national borders do not act as shields for rogue traders.

Further reading

S Grundmann, 'The Structure of European Contract Law' (2001) 4 *European Review of Private Law* 505

G Howells and T Wilhelmsson, 'EC and US Approaches to Consumer Protection – Should the Gap be Bridged?'[1997] *Yearbook of European Law* 207

G Howells and T Wilhelmsson, *EU Consumer Law* (Aldershot: Ashgate, 1997)

G Howells and T Wilhelmsson, 'EC Consumer Law – Has It Come of Age?' (2003) 28 *European Law Review* 370

H Micklitz, N Reich, and P Rott, *Understanding EU Consumer Law* (Antwerp: Intersentia, 2009)

H Micklitz, J Stuyck, and E Terryn (eds), *Casebook on Consumer Law* (Oxford: Hart Publishing, 2010)

H Schulte-Nölke, C Twigg-Flesner, and M Ebers, *EU Consumer Law Compendium* (Munich: Sellier, 2008)

R Schulze, 'Precontractual Duties and Conclusion of Contract in European Law' (2005) 6 *European Review of Private Law* 841

P Stone, *EU Private International Law* (2nd edn, Cheltenham: Edward Elgar, 2010)

J Stuyck, 'European Consumer Law after the Treaty of Amsterdam: Consumer Policy in or beyond the Internal Market?' (2000) 37 *Common Market Law Review* 367

---

[158] There were two interesting applications of this in the Consumer Rights Directive on default tick-boxes (Art 22) and surcharges (Art 19).

C Twigg-Flesner, *The Europeanisation of Contract Law* (Abingdon: Routledge-Cavendish, 2008)

C Twigg-Flesner (ed), *The Cambridge Companion to European Union Private Law* (Cambridge: Cambridge University Press, 2010)

S Weatherill, 'The Role of the Informed Consumer in European Community Law' (1994) 2 *Consumer Law Journal* 49

S Weatherill, *EU Consumer Law and Policy* (Cheltenham: Edward Elgar, 2005)

T Wilhelmsson, 'The Abuse of the "Confident Consumer" as a Justification for EC Consumer Law' (2004) 27 *Journal of Consumer Policy* 317

Chapter acknowledgements

I wish to acknowledge the research help provided by Jonathon Watson.

24

EU external action

Geert De Baere

1 Introduction

In a 2010 article in *Time Magazine*, Singaporean scholar Kishore Mahbubani did not pull any punches when describing the EU's position in the world:[1]

---

[1] K Mahbubani, 'Europe's Errors', *Time Magazine*, 8 March 2010.

Europe just doesn't get it. It does not get how irrelevant it is becoming to the rest of the world. And it does not get how relevant the rest of the world is becoming to its future. The world is changing rapidly. Europe continues to drift. I am not exaggerating when I say Europe's obsession with restructuring its internal arrangements is akin to rearranging the deck chairs of a sinking Titanic.

This chapter looks at how the deckchairs are currently arranged, which inevitably involves looking at the ship on which they stand. It starts from the assumption that in order to cast judgement on whether the EU's external policies are effective and consistent (which the image of a drifting or sinking ship would appear to belie) and in general on how the EU has performed as an international actor, it is crucial to understand how the EU is equipped to do so.

The chapter therefore offers an introduction into the law governing how the EU organizes its relations with the outside world.[2] Those relations are both broad in scope and varied in substance. The goods and services that cross the EU's external borders, most of the planes that fly across those borders, much of the pollution that comes from or enters into the EU, the fish caught by EU fishermen outside EU waters – and many more issues besides – are regulated by EU external action law.[3]

The resulting legal framework is of a complexity verging on the byzantine. That is because the Member States, in various ways, want to preserve their competence and control over EU external action on the one hand, but also seek to enhance the EU's external effectiveness and consistency on the other hand. These twin objectives are in obvious tension – if not conflict – but they have each manifested themselves (as has the tension between them) in the multiple rounds of Treaty amendment in various ways.[4]

This chapter explores the resulting complex division of competences between the Member States and the Union and between the different institutions of the Union in the field of external action. The chapter also examines the applicable decision-making procedures, including the procedure for concluding international agreements, and explores the Union's composite system of external representation, illustrating the intricacies involved by looking more closely at EU external environmental policy. Finally, the chapter explores how the Union manages the vertical (between the Union and the Member States) and horizontal (between the different institutions and policy fields of the EU) division of its external competences. While the position of the Union within the wider context of the

---

[2] An earlier attempt can be found in G De Baere, 'The Basics of EU External Relations Law: An Overview of the Post-Lisbon Constitutional Framework for Developing the External Dimensions of EU Asylum and Migration Policy' in M Maes, M-C Foblets, and Ph De Bruycker (eds), *External Dimensions of EU Migration and Asylum Law and Policy/Dimensions Externes du Droit et de la Politique d'Immigration et d'Asile de l'UE* (Brussels: Bruylant, 2011).

[3] This chapter uses the term 'external action' in the same sense as the Treaties, ie as encompassing all external policies of the Union. Those policies include both what this chapter will refer to as 'ordinary EU external action' on the one hand and the common foreign and security policy (CFSP) on the other hand, ie the former First and Second Pillars of the EU before the Lisbon Treaty (see further chapter 2). The chapter occasionally uses the term 'external relations' in the same sense when appropriate (the term is also used twice in the Treaties, ie in Arts 18(4) TEU and 355(3) TFEU, though in the latter case with respect to the Member States and not the Union as such). cf G de Búrca, 'EU External Relations: The Governance Mode of Foreign Policy' in B Van Vooren, S Blockmans, and J Wouters (eds), *The EU's Role in Global Governance: The Legal Dimension* (Oxford: Oxford University Press, 2013) 39–58.

[4] See eg, with respect to the common commercial (ie external trade) policy (CCP) and the doctrine of implied external competences, G De Baere and P Koutrakos, 'The Interactions between the Legislature and the Judiciary in EU External Relations' in P Syrpis (ed), *The Judiciary, the Legislature and the EU Internal Market* (Cambridge: Cambridge University Press, 2012) 244–257.

international legal order and the status of international law within the EU legal order are clearly an important part of the story of the Union's external action,[5] this chapter (with the exception of a limited number of references) only covers the internal EU constitutional law with respect to external action.

2 The foundations of EU external action

2.1 In search of consistency and effectiveness

One of the core tasks of the key new actors of the EU's external action introduced by the Lisbon Treaty, the High Representative of the Union for Foreign Affairs and Security Policy and the European External Action Service (EEAS), is to 'ensure the consistency of the Union's external action'.[6] The drafters of the Treaties clearly realized that consistency in external action would be problematic for the Union, as is evident from the fact that Article 21(3), second paragraph, TEU returns to the issue and provides for the Union to

> ensure consistency between the different areas of its external action and between these and its other policies. The Council and the Commission, assisted by the High Representative of the Union for Foreign Affairs and Security Policy, shall ensure that consistency and shall cooperate to that effect.

Why would consistency or effectiveness be an issue for EU external action? The point of departure in answering that question must be the awareness of a crucial difference between the UK (or indeed most countries) on the one hand, and the EU on the other hand: when considering a response to an international situation, the first question the EU asks itself is not how it could react most effectively, but whether it in fact has the requisite *competence* to act at all and, if so, on what legal basis in the Treaties and through what institution action should be taken. In other words, the Union must always give precedence to considerations of competence over considerations of effectiveness.[7]

2.2 The principle of conferral

In essence, that is because the Union's competences are governed by the principle of conferral as laid down in Article 5(1) and (2) TEU:[8]

> 1. The limits of Union competences are governed by the principle of conferral....
>
> 2. Under the principle of conferral, the Union shall act only within the limits of the competences conferred upon it by the Member States in the Treaties to attain the objectives set out therein. Competences not conferred upon the Union in the Treaties remain with the Member States.

---

[5] eg PJ Kuijper, J Wouters, F Hoffmeister, G De Baere, and T Ramopoulos, *The Law of EU External Relations: Cases, Materials, and Commentary on the EU as an International Legal Actor* (Oxford: Oxford University Press, 2013) chs 5 and 12.

[6] Art 18(4) TEU and Art 3(1) of Council Decision 2010/427/EU of 26 July 2010 establishing the organisation and functioning of the European External Action Service (OJ [2010] L201/30) (EEAS Decision). See further section 5.3.

[7] G De Baere, *Constitutional Principles of EU External Relations* (Oxford: Oxford University Press, 2008) 10 and the literature cited therein.

[8] For more on the concept of EU competences, see chapter 5.

This principle incorporates the idea, fundamental not only in the law of international organizations, but also in the constitutional law of many federal States, that the organization or the federal level of government (here the Union) only has those competences that the Member States have explicitly or impliedly conferred on it in the constitution (here the Treaties). Before contemplating any action, whether internal or external, the Union must therefore first determine whether it actually has competence to do so. This implies essentially two things: (a) the EU is incapable of extending its own competences[9] and (b) it does not have general law-making capacity. Put differently, every single EU action requires one or more legal bases in the Treaties, which must be based on objective factors (including the aim and content of the measure) that are amenable to judicial review,[10] and which determine both the vertical and horizontal division of competences.[11]

2.3 **The distinction between ordinary EU external action and the CFSP**

Crucially, this principle of conferral applies as much to external action as to internal policies.[12] In other words, in its external policies too, the EU only has those competences that the Member States have conferred on it in the Treaties. The Member States also have the liberty to decide the manner in which they confer those competences and how much power they are willing to relinquish, which to a large extent explains why the EU still does not take a united approach to external action. Instead, the EU approaches the subject from two quite different angles, based on the distinction between two core aspects of international relations:[13]

(a) external 'socioeconomic' relations, such as external trade and development cooperation, which fall within what this chapter will refer to as 'ordinary EU external action'. The legal rules governing this area are mostly set out in the TFEU; and

(b) what is commonly called 'high politics' (diplomatic activity and security and defence issues), which fall within the Common Foreign and Security Policy (CFSP). The legal rules governing this area are mostly set out in the TEU.

That distinction also corresponds to that between the former First and Second Pillars of the EU before the Lisbon Treaty (see further chapter 2). The EU's fundamentally different approach to these two areas has persisted after Lisbon, despite the introduction of Title V of the TEU ('General Provisions on the Union's External Action and Specific Provisions on the Common Foreign and Security Policy') and Part Five of the TFEU (entitled simply 'The Union's External Action'), and despite a single set of objectives for EU external action as a whole in Articles 3(5) and 21(2) TEU.[14]

---

[9] See further P Craig, *The Lisbon Treaty: Law, Politics, and Treaty Reform* (Oxford: Oxford University Press, 2010) 156–157.

[10] Case C-137/12 *Commission v Council* ('*Conditional Access Convention*'), judgment of 22 October 2013, nyr, para 52 and the case law cited there.

[11] See Case C-301/06 *Ireland v Parliament and Council* ('*Personal data protection*') [2009] ECR-I-593, para 56. For more on the concept of legal bases, see chapter 5.

[12] Opinion 2/94 *Accession by the Communities to the ECHR* [1996] ECR I-1759, para 24. See also Opinion 2/00 *Cartagena Protocol* [2001] ECR I-9713, para 5.

[13] A Dashwood, M Dougan, B Rodger, E Spaventa, and D Wyatt, *Wyatt and Dashwood's European Union Law* (6th edn, Oxford/Portland, OR: Hart Publishing, 2011) 13.

[14] See also Art 205 TFEU.

It is hardly a novelty to question the assumption that external 'socioeconomic' relations can be easily separated from 'high politics'. Hill has noted that

> the once popular distinction between 'high' and 'low' politics is no longer of much help. High politics – in the sense of serious conflict touching on the state's most basic concerns – can be as much about monetary integration as about territory and the threat of armed attack. Conversely, low politics – in the sense of routine exchanges contained within knowable limits and rarely reaching the public realm – can be observed in NATO [North Atlantic Treaty Organization] or OSCE [Organization for Security and Co-operation in Europe] multilateralism as much as (perhaps more than) in discussions over fish or airport landing rights. Thus the *intrinsic content* of an issue is not a guide to its level of political salience or to the way it will be handled, except in the tautological sense that any issue which blows up into a high-level international conflict (and almost anything has the potential so to do) will lead to decision-makers at the highest level suddenly taking over responsibility.[15]

Yet the distinction persists in the EU's constitutional structure, mainly because most of the Member States want to remain firmly in charge of their 'high politics', or what they choose to regard as such. As the UK Government's 2013 EU competence review dryly puts it:[16]

> The majority of our evidence judged that Member States were firmly in charge of the Common Foreign and Security Policy (CFSP) and Common Security and Defence Policy (CSDP), and could act unilaterally when they judged fit, as the French did in Mali.

Unsurprisingly, the consistency between the various external policies of the EU and the effectiveness of EU external action as a whole remains a challenge.

2.4 The CFSP

As is clear from Title V TEU ('General Provisions on the Union's External Action and Specific Provisions on the Common Foreign and Security Policy'), the Lisbon Treaty has subjected the CFSP to the overall constitutional framework of the EU. The formal abolition of the pillar structure, however, does not imply a complete harmonization of procedures and an integration of all policies under the former Community; instead it essentially leaves the former Second Pillar standing in a modified manner. The post-Lisbon EU Treaty takes into account the different characters of different policies and still permits a substantial amount of differentiation as to how the Union's institutions are involved in law-making. The 2007 Intergovernmental Conference, which led to the adoption of the Lisbon Treaty, decided to drop the idea of one single Constitutional Treaty and to keep the TEU and the (renamed) TFEU as two distinct Treaties, with the CFSP and the European Neighbourhood Policy[17] as the only substantive policies in the TEU. The Lisbon Treaty therefore establishes a single legal order for the Union, but with a more markedly separate sub-order for the CFSP.[18]

---

[15] C Hill, *The Changing Politics of Foreign Policy* (London: Palgrave, 2003) 4.

[16] HM Government, 'Review of the Balance of Competences between the United Kingdom and the European Union: Foreign Policy' (2013) 88, para 6.4.

[17] Art 8 TEU.

[18] See further De Baere, *Constitutional Principles of EU External Relations* (n 7) 209–213.

Moreover, while the ordinary Union framework under the TFEU is governed by the technique of detailed and specific attribution of competences,[19] the present Chapter 2 of Title V TEU on the CFSP remains characterized by an absence of any clear let alone detailed list of what precisely it encompasses. Instead, the allocation of competences in the CFSP consists of the general grant of competence in Article 24(1) TEU, which covers

> all areas of foreign policy and all questions relating to the Union's security, including the progressive framing of a common defence policy that might lead to a common defence.

Article 42(1) TEU in addition provides that the Common Security and Defence Policy (CSDP)

> shall be an integral part of the common foreign and security policy. It shall provide the Union with an operational capacity drawing on civilian and military assets.

The CSDP is to include (Article 42(2) TEU)

> the progressive framing of a common Union defence policy. This will lead to a common defence, when the European Council, acting unanimously, so decides. It shall in that case recommend to the Member States the adoption of such a decision in accordance with their respective constitutional requirements.

The assurance that the CSDP *will* 'lead to a common defence' may at first view appear to contain a much stronger commitment than Article 24(1) TEU, which merely refers to

> the progressive framing of a common defence policy that *might* lead to a common defence.[20]

However, the role of the European Council and the condition that the Member States need to adopt a decision in accordance with their respective constitutional requirements make it clear that not much legal significance should be attached to the phrase 'will lead to a common defence' in Article 42(2) TEU, which should be understood as an aspirational statement of a purely political nature.

Does then the principle of conferral actually apply to the CFSP? Given that, under the previous Treaty framework, the principle of conferral was not explicitly enshrined in the former EU Treaty, but in the first paragraph of then Article 5 EC, some doubted whether the principle applied to the CFSP.[21] Article 5(1) and (2) TEU (see previously), as introduced by the Lisbon Treaty in Title I ('Common Provisions') of the EU Treaty, has now removed all doubt in that regard.

Remarkably, however, the Lisbon Treaty has reinforced the contrast between attribution in ordinary EU external action and in the CFSP by deleting the specific CFSP objectives that before the Lisbon Treaty were listed in ex Article 11(1) TEU, according to which

---

[19] cf A Dashwood, 'The Relationship between the Member States and the European Union/European Community' (2004) 41 *Common Market Law Review* 357, 357 et seq.   [20] Emphasis added.
[21] See the discussion in De Baere, *Constitutional Principles of EU External Relations* (n 7) 105.

the Union was to define and implement a CFSP covering all areas of foreign and security policy, the objectives of which were

- to safeguard the common values, fundamental interests, independence and integrity of the Union in conformity with the principles of the United Nations Charter,
- to strengthen the security of the Union in all ways,
- to preserve peace and strengthen international security, in accordance with the principles of the United Nations Charter, as well as the principles of the Helsinki Final Act[22] and the objectives of the Paris Charter,[23] including those on external borders,
- to promote international cooperation,
- to develop and consolidate democracy and the rule of law, and respect for human rights and fundamental freedoms.

In removing those objectives from the CFSP chapter, the Lisbon Treaty has made the attribution within the CFSP even less detailed and specific than it was before. Instead, Article 21 TEU now contains the overall objectives of EU external action. Article 21(1) TEU provides:

The Union's action on the international scene shall be guided by the principles which have inspired its own creation, development and enlargement, and which it seeks to advance in the wider world: democracy, the rule of law, the universality and indivisibility of human rights and fundamental freedoms, respect for human dignity, the principles of equality and solidarity, and respect for the principles of the United Nations Charter and international law.

Article 21(2) TEU further elaborates these in a rather more comprehensive list of objectives. It provides that the Union is to define and 'pursue common policies and actions', and to 'work for a high degree of cooperation in all fields of international relations, in order to'

(a) safeguard its values, fundamental interests, security, independence and integrity;

(b) consolidate and support democracy, the rule of law, human rights and the principles of international law;

(c) preserve peace, prevent conflicts and strengthen international security, in accordance with the purposes and principles of the United Nations Charter, with the principles of the Helsinki Final Act and with the aims of the Charter of Paris, including those relating to external borders;

(d) foster the sustainable economic, social and environmental development of developing countries, with the primary aim of eradicating poverty;

(e) encourage the integration of all countries into the world economy, including through the progressive abolition of restrictions on international trade;

(f) help develop international measures to preserve and improve the quality of the environment and the sustainable management of global natural resources, in order to ensure sustainable development;

(g) assist populations, countries and regions confronting natural or man-made disasters; and

(h) promote an international system based on stronger multilateral cooperation and good global governance.

---

[22] Conference on Security and Co-operation in Europe Final Act, Helsinki, 1975.
[23] Charter of Paris for a New Europe, Paris 1990.

While some of the old CFSP objectives re-emerge in that list (notably in (a), (b), (c), and (h)), it is important to emphasize that they are objectives common to EU external action in its entirety. That leaves the CFSP with only the most general of competence attributions in Article 24(1) TEU as covering 'all areas of foreign policy and all questions relating to the Union's security'.

Detailed and specific attribution of competences is an important aspect of the principle of conferral as it operates under the TFEU, and its absence in Chapter 2 of Title V of the EU Treaty indicates that the principle applies in a different manner in the CFSP legal order. The Lisbon Treaty has reinforced the contrast between ordinary EU external action and the CFSP in that respect.

3 The existence of EU external competences

3.1 The fundamentals

The former EC Treaty did not contain a general legal basis for external action.[24] Article 281 EC explicitly conferred legal personality on the Community,[25] but the general capacity derived from that article did not constitute an independent legal basis for the adoption of international agreements. However, as a legal person, the Community had the capacity to exercise rights in international legal transactions and enter into obligations over the entire field of its objectives.[26] Contrary to the Community, the pre-Lisbon Union had not been explicitly endowed with legal personality. Nevertheless, ex Article 24 TEU provided the Union with a procedural framework for making international agreements within the spheres of the former Second and Third Pillars concerning the CFSP and Police and Judicial Cooperation in Criminal Matters (PJCCM), respectively, and pre-Lisbon practice tends to suggest that the EU already had legal personality.[27]

With the entry into force of the Lisbon Treaty, Article 47 TEU explicitly confirms the Union's legal personality (merged with the legal personality of the former Community: see Art 1, third paragraph, TEU), thereby removing any lingering doubt in that regard. Furthermore, Article 216(1) TFEU affirms the general capacity of the Union to conclude international agreements. That provision stipulates that the Union may conclude an agreement with one or more third countries or international organizations

(a) where the Treaties so provide; or

(b) where the conclusion of an agreement is 'necessary in order to achieve, within the framework of the Union's policies, one of the objectives referred to in the Treaties, or is provided for in a legally binding Union act or is likely to affect common rules or alter their scope'.

While (a) encompasses the category of competences for the EU to act externally that have been explicitly provided for in the Treaties,[28] (b) is intended as a codification of the Court

---

[24] Contrast Art 101 of the Treaty establishing the European Atomic Energy Community (consolidated version) (EAEC) (OJ [2012] C327/1), which provides: 'The Community may, within the limits of its powers and jurisdiction, enter into obligations by concluding agreements or contracts with a third State, an international organisation or a national of a third State'.   [25] cf the identical Art 184 EAEC.
[26] Case 22/70 *Commission v Council* ('*ERTA*') [1971] ECR 263, paras 13 and 14 and Joined Cases 3, 4 and 6/76 *Cornelis Kramer* ('*Kramer*') [1976] ECR 1279, paras 17 and 18.
[27] eg Council Decision 2001/352/CFSP concerning the conclusion of the Agreement between the European Union and the Federal Republic of Yugoslavia (FRY) on the activities of the European Union Monitoring Mission (EUMM) (OJ [2001] L125/1); Council Decision 2010/53/CFSP of 30 November 2009 concerning the conclusion of the Agreement between Australia and the European Union on the security of classified information (OJ [2010] L26/30).
[28] See further De Baere, *Constitutional Principles of EU External Relations* (n 7) 11–16; P Eeckhout, *EU External Relations Law* (2nd edn, Oxford: Oxford University Press, 2011) 122.

of Justice's case law on implied competences, which were recognized for the first time in *ERTA*.[29]

That case concerned Council proceedings of 20 March 1970 regarding the negotiation and conclusion by the Member States of the then Community, under the auspices of the United Nations Economic Commission for Europe (UNECE), of the European agreement concerning the work of crews of vehicles engaged in international road transport (ERTA in English or AETR in French). The proceedings concerned an arrangement arrived at, not by the Council as an institution of the then Community, but by the Member States meeting in the Council. The Commission requested the annulment of the proceedings, arguing that the Community as such should have concluded this agreement and not the Member States. As there were no relevant explicit external competences for the Community, the case gave the Court the opportunity for the first time to set out its views on whether external competences could perhaps be implied from explicitly conferred internal competences. Implied external competences will be examined more closely in the next section.

3.2 Implied competences

The Treaty provisions regulating external action have always been spread over the entire Treaty, as well as incomplete. Nevertheless, the Lisbon Treaty improved the situation somewhat by introducing Part Five of the TFEU, which can be considered as a step in the direction of improved overall consistency in external action. Attempts to address the lack of explicit legal bases have been made predominantly in two ways:[30] first, explicit legal bases for external competences were added to the Treaties in subsequent amendments; and, secondly, the Court interpreted the existing Treaty provisions so as to allow the Union to develop a viable external action policy, resulting in what is mostly referred to as 'implied external competences'.

The doctrine of implied competences is a well-known principle of municipal constitutional law and of the law of international institutions.[31] Within the EU, implied competences have been relied on mostly with regard to external action. As noted previously, the (extensive and meandering) case law of the Court on implied external competences has now been codified in Article 216(1) TFEU. That provision encompasses three principles, which will be considered in turn. The possibility for implied competences within the CFSP will also be briefly considered.

3.2.1 *ERTA*

The Union 'may conclude an agreement with one or more third countries or international organisations...where the conclusion of an agreement...is likely to affect common rules or alter their scope'. This codifies the *ERTA* principle: the Member States are not allowed to act internationally in a way that would affect existing EU law, because the situation cannot be remedied by merely disapplying the infringing rule. The Member States' competence is thus excluded, which necessitates the existence of EU competences to compensate for the Member States' inability to act. The resulting EU competence is exclusive pursuant to Article 3(2) TFEU.[32]

---

[29] Case 22/70 (n 26) para 17.

[30] EU external competences can also arise from such general legal bases as Arts 114, 115, and 352 TFEU (on the latter provision, see Declaration 41 on Article 352 of the Treaty on the Functioning of the European Union (OJ [2012] C326/352)). See further De Baere, *Constitutional Principles of EU External Relations* (n 7) 29–31 and 58–59.

[31] eg *M'Culloch v The State of Maryland* 17 US 316, 407 (1819) and *Reparation for Injuries suffered in the Service of the United Nations* [1949] ICJ Rep 174, 182.   [32] See section 4.2.1.

3.2.2 Complementarity

The Union 'may conclude an agreement with one or more third countries or international organisations...where the conclusion of an agreement is necessary in order to achieve, within the framework of the Union's policies, one of the objectives referred to in the Treaties'. This codifies the 'complementarity principle',[33] which was spelled out in Opinion 1/76 *European laying-up fund for inland waterway vessels*.[34]

In contrast to *ERTA*, that case concerned a situation where no internal Community legislation (here on the laying-up of barges) existed at the moment the then Community wanted to conclude an agreement with Switzerland. The Community's aim was the rationalization of the economic situation in the inland waterways sector in the Rhine and Moselle basins, and throughout all the Dutch inland waterways and the German inland waterways linked to the Rhine basin, by elimination of short-term overcapacity of the fleet. Given that vessels from Switzerland traditionally participate in navigation on these waterways, it was hard to imagine how that objective could be achieved solely by the establishment of autonomous Community common rules.[35] It was therefore necessary to bring Switzerland into the scheme through an international agreement. Hence the rule that whenever EU law has conferred internal competences on the institutions to attain a specific objective, the Union can enter into the international commitments necessary for attainment of that objective even in the absence of an express provision to that effect.[36]

Internal Union competences are supported by the corresponding external competences only when the latter are truly 'implicit' in the former. This is the case when the internal Union competences cannot reasonably be expected to be effectively exercised without the possibility for the Union to enter into international agreements with third countries on the same subject matter. However, the complementarity principle as codified in Article 216(1) TFEU appears to be wider in scope than the case law on which it is based. In particular, it is not entirely clear whether external action should be necessary for the achievement of the objectives of an explicitly granted competence, or whether the general objectives of EU external action in Article 21 TEU could also give rise to external Union competence on this basis.[37]

3.2.3 Legally binding Union acts

Article 216(1) TFEU also lists the prima facie rather straightforward possibility for the Union to 'conclude an agreement with one or more third countries or international organisations...where the conclusion of an agreement...is provided for in a legally binding Union act', that is to say, in a regulation, a directive, or a decision.[38] That provision will be discussed in its relationship to Article 3(2) TFEU in the next section.

3.2.4 The CFSP

In any event, applying the doctrine of implied competences requires caution and restraint. That is even more the case with respect to the CFSP, especially because the Court for the most part lacks jurisdiction with respect to the provisions in the EU Treaty relating to the

---

[33] A Dashwood, 'The Attribution of External Relations Competence' in A Dashwood and C Hillion (eds), *The General Law of EC External Relations* (London: Sweet & Maxwell, 2000) 127–132.

[34] [1977] ECR 741. But see already *ERTA* (n 26) paras 23–27 and *Kramer* (n 26) paras 30 and 33.

[35] See nevertheless De Baere, *Constitutional Principles of EU External Relations* (n 7) 57–58.

[36] Opinion 1/76 (n 34) para 3; Opinion 2/94 (n 12) para 26.

[37] M Cremona, 'External Relations and External Competence of the European Union: The Emergence of an Integrated Policy' in P Craig and G de Búrca (eds), *The Evolution of EU Law* (2nd edn, Oxford: Oxford University Press, 2011) 225.   [38] Art 288 TFEU.

CFSP and with respect to acts adopted on the basis of those provisions.[39] Moreover, the nature of the attribution as regards the CFSP in Article 24(1) TEU is so broad that an application of the doctrine of implied competences implying all the competences needed for an effective CFSP would lead to an extensive grant of external action competences going far beyond what the EU Treaty permits.

4 The nature of EU external competences

4.1 The fundamentals

One of the more significant novelties introduced by the Lisbon Treaty is Title I of Part One of the TFEU entitled 'Categories and Areas of Union Competence'. Three of those categories as listed in Article 2 TFEU are most relevant for the Union's external action and will be further explored here:[40] exclusive competences,[41] shared competences,[42] and the competence to define and implement a CFSP, including the progressive framing of a CSDP.[43]

The main principles on when the Union is exclusively competent have now been laid down in Article 3 TFEU, the first paragraph of which lists the five explicitly attributed or a priori exclusive competences of the Union:

(a) customs union;
(b) the establishing of the competition rules necessary for the functioning of the internal market;
(c) monetary policy for the Member States whose currency is the euro;
(d) the conservation of marine biological resources under the common fisheries policy;
(e) common commercial policy.

Both the internal and the external aspects of these policies belong to the exclusive competence of the Union. In addition, the second paragraph of Article 3 TFEU provides for the Union to have exclusive competence 'for the conclusion of an international agreement when its conclusion is provided for in a legislative act of the Union or is necessary to enable the Union to exercise its internal competence, or in so far as its conclusion may affect common rules or alter their scope'.[44] While it attempts to codify the case law of the Court on exclusive competences, the criteria listed in Article 3(2) TFEU appear to be neither entirely clear nor sufficiently nuanced and hence in need of further judicial clarification. The Court's existing case law on the nature of EU external competences will therefore need to be taken into account.[45] The different instances of when the Union acquires an exclusive external competence pursuant to Article 3(2) TFEU will be examined in section 4.2.

However, it is important to understand that the EU's competence should be presumed to be non-exclusive, unless there are clear indications to the contrary.[46] Within the category of non-exclusive competences, a distinction should be made between shared competences on the one hand and CFSP competences on the other hand. In turn, within the shared

---

[39] See section 5.2.
[40] See also Art 2(3) and (5) TFEU, which will not be considered further in the present chapter.
[41] Art 2(1) TFEU.   [42] Art 2(2) TFEU.
[43] Art 2(4) TFEU. As noted already, the categories of EU competences are fully examined in chapter 5.
[44] Art 3(2) TFEU.
[45] In that sense, also Opinion of AG Kokott in *Conditional Access Convention* (n 10) points 111–113.
[46] See, to that effect, Case C-370/12 *Pringle*, judgment of 27 November 2012, nyr, paras 120 and 121.

competences, a number of further sub-categories can be distinguished: the shared competences that follow the basic rule, shared competences on the basis of minimum standards, and parallel competences. The coordination by the Union of Member States' competences when EU competences are shared should also be examined in that connection. All these form the subject of section 4.4.

4.2 Exclusive external competence on the basis of Article 3(2) TFEU

4.2.1 *ERTA* exclusivity

Article 3(2) TFEU provides that the Union will have exclusive competence for the conclusion of an international agreement 'insofar as its conclusion may affect common rules or alter their scope'. That reflects the possibility for an EU external competence to become exclusive through the exercise of an EU internal competence. That eventuality is called 'the *ERTA* doctrine' or '*ERTA* exclusivity', which follows the logic of the principle of primacy (ie the priority of EU law over Member States' law),[47] but imposes greater strictures on the international actions of the Member States than primacy does internally.[48]

This manner of acquiring exclusive external competences was recognized for the first time by the Court in the *ERTA* case and further refined, inter alia, in the *Open Skies* cases.[49] The latter cases concerned eight separate actions brought by the Commission under Article 169 EEC (ex Article 226 EC and now Article 258 TFEU) against the UK, Denmark, Sweden, Finland, Belgium, Luxembourg, Austria, and Germany. They concerned various breaches of then Community law arising from the conclusion by those Member States of bilateral air transport agreements with the US. That gave the Court the opportunity to clarify its case law according to which Member States are not to enter into international obligations outside the framework of the Union institutions if these obligations fall within the scope of the common rules, or within an area which is already largely covered by such rules, even if there is no contradiction between those commitments and the common rules.[50] The Court held that if the Union has achieved complete harmonization in a given area, it acquires an exclusive external competence in that area, even in the absence of any express provision authorizing its institutions to negotiate with non-Member States. This is so because the common rules thus adopted could be affected within the meaning of the *ERTA* principle if the Member States retained freedom to negotiate with non-Member States.[51] Both explicit and implied external competences can become exclusive through the exercise by the Union of its competences.

The principles and the complexity involved in their application are well illustrated by the situation in *Open Skies*. There, the Court held that the relevant Community legislation did not govern the granting of traffic rights on intra-Community routes to non-Community carriers nor operating licences of non-Community air carriers which operated within

---

[47] For more on the concept of primacy, see chapter 6. As to whether the principle of primacy applies to the CFSP, see De Baere, *Constitutional Principles of EU External Relations* (n 7) 201–12; and Craig, *The Lisbon Treaty* (n 9) 431–433.

[48] De Baere, *Constitutional Principles of EU External Relations* (n 7) 71–72. See further Case C-114/12 *Commission v Council* (OJ [2012] C138/5), pending.

[49] Case C-466/98 *Commission v UK* [2002] ECR I-9427; Case C-467/98 *Commission v Denmark* [2002] ECR I-9519; Case C-468/98 *Commission v Sweden* [2002] ECR I-9575; Case C-469/98 *Commission v Finland* [2002] ECR I-9627; Case C-471/98 *Commission v Belgium* [2002] ECR I-9681; Case C-472/98 *Commission v Luxembourg* [2002] ECR I-9741; Case C-475/98 *Commission v Austria* [2002] ECR I-9797; and Case C-476/98 *Commission v Germany* [2002] ECR I-9855. The Court confirmed its approach in the 2002 *Open Skies* judgments in Case C-523/04 *Commission v Netherlands* [2007] ECR I-3267.

[50] See eg *Commission v Denmark* (n 49) para 82; *Commission v Germany* (n 49) para 108.

[51] *Commission v Denmark* (n 49) para 84; *Commission v Germany* (n 49) para 110.

the then Community. In other words, the international commitments at issue did not fall within 'an area already covered by Community rules' and hence could not be regarded as affecting those rules. However, Community rules had indirectly but definitely prohibited air carriers of non-member countries operating in the Community from introducing new products or fares lower than the ones existing for identical products. As a consequence, the Community had acquired exclusive competence to enter into commitments with non-member countries relating to that limitation on the freedom of non-Community carriers to set fares and rates.[52] Relevant Community legislation also applied to nationals of non-member countries, where they offer for use or use a computerized reservation system (CRS) in Community territory. The Community thus acquired exclusive competence to contract with non-member countries the obligations relating to CRSs offered for use or used in its territory.[53] Finally, common rules for the allocation of slots at Community airports applied, subject to reciprocity, to air carriers of non-member countries, with the result that the Community had exclusive competence to conclude agreements in that area with non-member countries.[54]

Determining whether and to what extent the Union has exclusive external competence on the basis that the conclusion of an international agreement 'may affect common rules or alter their scope' therefore requires a detailed and often cumbersome analysis. As Advocate General Tizzano put it in his Opinion in *Open Skies*:[55]

> I must point out, however, that in order to establish that the common rules are affected it is not enough to cite general effects of an economic nature which the agreements could have on the functioning of the internal market; what is required instead is to specify in detail the aspects of the Community legislation which could be prejudiced by the agreements.

That requirement can be explained by the fact that the Court needs to steer a very careful course between the desire of the Member States to remain present on the international scene on the basis of their own competences and the need to allow the Union to build a viable (ie effective and consistent) external action policy.

4.2.2 Exclusivity on the basis of a legislative act

Article 3(2) TFEU provides that the Union will have exclusive competence for the conclusion of an international agreement 'when its conclusion is provided for in a legislative act of the Union'.[56] The Lisbon Treaty has thereby codified the Court's case law to that effect. In Opinion 1/94 *GATS and TRIPS*, the Court held that:[57]

> Whenever the [Union] has included in its internal legislative acts provisions relating to the treatment of nationals of non-member countries or expressly conferred on its institutions powers to negotiate with non-member countries, it acquires exclusive external competence in the spheres covered by those acts.

The Court seemed to hold that this *automatically* implied exclusive competence for the Union. That statement does appear to merit some nuance in light of, inter alia, Article 4(3) and (4) TFEU, which ostensibly provide for a type of shared competence without

---

[52] *Commission v Germany* (n 49), para 98.   [53] Ibid, paras 102 and 103.   [54] Ibid, para 106.
[55] Opinion of AG Tizzano in *Open Skies* (n 49) point 77.   [56] cf Art 289(3) TFEU.
[57] [1994] ECR I-5267, para 95; see also *Commission v Denmark* (n 49) para 83; *Commission v Germany* (n 49) para 109.

'pre-emption' (see section 4.4.1), whereby the Union cannot ever prevent the Member States from acting (and vice versa):

3. In the areas of research, technological development and space, the Union shall have competence to carry out activities, in particular to define and implement programmes; however, the exercise of that competence shall not result in Member States being prevented from exercising theirs.

4. In the areas of development cooperation and humanitarian aid, the Union shall have competence to carry out activities and conduct a common policy; however, the exercise of that competence shall not result in Member States being prevented from exercising theirs.

As mentioned previously, Article 216(1) TFEU grants the Union the competence to conclude an agreement with one or more third countries or international organizations where the conclusion of an agreement is 'provided for in a legally binding Union act'. Does the difference in language between Articles 3(2) ('provided for in a legislative act of the Union') and 216(1) TFEU ('provided for in a legally binding Union act') imply that the exclusive nature of the external competence depends on the nature of the procedure by which the internal act granting that competence was adopted? That would indeed seem to be the implication of the wording of those two provisions:[58] if the possibility to conclude an international agreement is provided for in a legally binding Union act, the EU acquires competence to conclude that agreement on the basis of Article 216(1) TFEU. If that same possibility is provided for in a legislative act, the Union acquires *exclusive* competence to conclude that agreement. However, it would seem that even a legislative act cannot grant the Union an exclusive external competence in those areas for which Article 4(3) and (4) TFEU explicitly provides that the Member States cannot be prevented from acting internationally.

4.2.3 Exclusivity on the basis of necessity for the exercise of internal competence

Article 3(2) TFEU provides that the Union will have exclusive competence for the conclusion of an international agreement when this is 'necessary to enable the Union to exercise its internal competence'. That codifies the Court's case law providing for the possibility of exclusivity to arise out of the fact that the internal and external aspects of a policy area can only be exercised effectively together.

The Commission had, for example, argued that such a situation was at hand in *Open Skies*. The Court disagreed. It held that the EC Treaty did not prevent the institutions from arranging, through internal Community rules, concerted action in relation to the US. Furthermore, the EC Treaty equally did not prevent the institutions from prescribing the approach the Member States should take in their external relations, in order to alleviate possible discrimination or distortions of competition resulting from the implementation of the open skies agreements entered into by certain Member States with the US. The Court concluded that it had not been established that the aims of the EC Treaty in the area of air transport could not be achieved by establishing autonomous Community rules.[59] This was confirmed, the Court held, by the fact that in 1992 the Council was able to adopt a set of

---

[58] Perhaps the distinction in wording was introduced to make it clear that this principle cannot give rise to an exclusive competence within the CFSP, given that Art 24(1), second subpara, TEU and Art 31(1) TEU exclude the adoption of legislative acts.

[59] *Commission v Germany* (n 49) para 85; see also Opinion 1/03 *Competence of the Community to conclude the new Lugano Convention on jurisdiction and the recognition and enforcement of judgments in civil and commercial matters* [2006] ECR I-1145, para 123.

measures achieving the internal market in air transport services without feeling the need to enter into any international agreements with the US. That the measures adopted by the Council contained some provisions on the treatment of third-country nationals did not diminish the force of that conclusion in any way. There was, therefore, *in casu* no question of an internal competence that can only be effectively exercised at the same time as the corresponding external competence, and that would render such a competence exclusive in accordance with the Court's reading of Opinion 1/76.[60]

Given that the Court appears to have regarded Opinion 1/76 (see section 3.2) as authority both for the existence and for the exclusive nature of implied external competence, the question arises whether and, if so, how this blurring of the two issues found its way into the TFEU. In particular, how can Article 3(2) TFEU in this respect be distinguished from the fact that the Union 'may conclude an agreement with one or more third countries or international organisations ... where the conclusion of an agreement is necessary in order to achieve, within the framework of the Union's policies, one of the objectives referred to in the Treaties', pursuant to Article 216(1) TFEU.

Perhaps the distinction between existence of implied external competence under Article 216(1) TFEU and the exclusive nature of that competence under Article 3(2) TFEU can be brought back to a distinction the Court arguably appears to have made in part of its case law. On the one hand, there exist situations in which the Union wishes to further, on the external front, internal policy goals, the optimal use of which presupposes an external complement, but which could nonetheless arguably have been sufficiently attained with internal rules only. The Union acquires a non-exclusive external competence in those situations. This is what Opinion 2/92 *Third Revised Decision of the OECD on national treatment* seemed to say[61] and appears to correspond to Article 216(1) TFEU. On the other hand, there may be the rare factual constellations in which the objectives of EU competences could not possibly be achieved without including third countries, through international agreements, into the binding legal framework regulating the situation. The Union would acquire exclusive implied external competences in the case of such an inextricable link,[62] though it is difficult to come up with an example of a situation that would unambiguously fall within that category.[63]

At any rate, neither Article 216(1) TFEU nor Article 3(2) TFEU sufficiently reflect the complexity of the case law on which they are based, especially with regard to the need for an 'inextricable link' in order for 'necessity' to give rise to an exclusive Union competence. The Court of Justice will presumably rely on its pre-codification case law to interpret the text of those two provisions, including, inter alia, what is to be understood under 'necessary'.[64]

4.3 Consequences of exclusive competence

Article 2(1) TFEU provides that when the Treaties confer on the Union exclusive competence in a specific area, only the Union may legislate and adopt legally binding acts. The Member States are only able to do so themselves if they have been so empowered by the Union or for the implementation of Union acts (see the discussion

---

[60] *Commission v Germany* (n 49) paras 86–89.   [61] [1995] ECR I-521, para 32.

[62] The Court omitted a reference to the need for such an inextricable link in Opinion 1/03 (n 59) para 115.

[63] cf Eeckhout, *EU External Relations Law* (n 28) 118, arguing that exclusive implied competences should in fact be confined to the *ERTA* doctrine.

[64] cf De Baere and Koutrakos, 'The Interactions between the Legislature and the Judiciary in EU External Relations' (n 4) 257 and 273.

of implementation by the Member States in sections 5.1 and 5.2). Specifically with respect to external action, it follows from the Court's case law that the exclusivity of the Union's external competence has two main consequences, which are really two sides of the same coin.[65]

(a) First, when the external competence in a certain area is exclusive, the Member States, as the Court put it in *ERTA*, 'no longer have the right, acting individually or even collectively, to undertake obligations with third countries'.[66] The Court also referred to what is now Article 4(3) TEU, enshrining the principle of loyalty and sincere cooperation, and concluded that it would be impossible for the Member States operating outside the institutional framework of the Union to assume responsibilities that might affect or alter the scope of Union rules that have been promulgated for the attainment of Treaty objectives.[67]

(b) Secondly, the Court pointed out in Ruling 1/78 *Draft IAEA Convention on the Physical Protection of Nuclear Materials, Facilities and Transports* that when external Union competence is exclusive:[68]

> the Member States, whether acting individually or collectively, are no longer able to impose on the [Union] obligations which impose conditions on the exercise of prerogatives which thenceforth belong to the [Union] and which therefore no longer fall within the field of national sovereignty.

In other words, the Member States must not attempt to constrain the Union's exercise of its exclusive competence and must cooperate loyally with it in order to facilitate such an exercise.[69]

Exclusivity imposes an obligation on the Member States not to enter into any international agreements that could affect the Union's exclusive competences. In other words, it limits the possibility for law-making by the Member States. They are legally obliged not to exercise their competences to enter into certain international agreements.

There are three main reasons for this:

(a) first, the desire to avoid adverse consequences for the Member States' international liability in case they conclude an international agreement incompatible with EU law;

(b) secondly, the possibility that the existence of an international agreement autonomously concluded by the Member States could prejudice the integrity of the 'coherent system' of rules established by EU law;[70] and

(c) thirdly, the possibility that Member States might block the evolution of EU law by concluding international agreements the subject matter of which is covered by common rules, thus 'freezing' Union law in the state it is in at the moment the agreement is concluded. This explains why even if the intended agreement would be consistent with EU law, the Member States are not allowed to conclude it if it

---

[65] Exclusivity also implies the inapplicability of the principle of subsidiarity: Art 5(3), first subpara, TEU. On that principle, see further chapter 5.   [66] *ERTA* (n 26) para 17.

[67] Ibid, para 22; see further Opinion 1/75 *Draft Understanding on a Local Cost Standard drawn up under the auspices of the OECD* [1975] ECR 1355, 1364.   [68] [1978] ECR 2151, para 32.

[69] cf ibid, paras 33 and 22; *Kramer* (n 26) paras 44–45.

[70] See Opinion 1/03 (n 59), paras 122–133.

falls under exclusive Union competences.[71] Moreover, it is important to understand that competence issues in principle need to be resolved before the intended
international agreement is even negotiated, as it needs to be established who will
negotiate. Given that, in the nature of things, there will be no final text of the
agreement at that point in time, the resolution of the competence question cannot
depend on the existence of an actual conflict between the agreement and the EU
common rules.[72]

However, the Member States retain capacity to conduct international relations both under
national and international law. Exclusive Union competences simply require them not to
act autonomously. This is evident from the text of Article 2(1) TFEU, which provides for
the possibility for the Union to empower the Member States to act in an area in which the
Union enjoys exclusive competence. EU law can therefore authorize the Member States to
act jointly on the international plane even within exclusive external Union competences.[73]
Examples of such empowerment are a number of regulations in which the Union established a procedure for the negotiation and conclusion of agreements between Member
States and third countries concerning jurisdiction, recognition, and enforcement of judgments and decisions in matrimonial matters, matters of parental responsibility, and matters
relating to maintenance obligations, and the law applicable to matters relating to maintenance obligations.[74]

A particular issue arises when an agenda item in an international organization relates
to a subject falling within exclusive Union competence, but where the Union itself has
not managed to become a member of the organization. In such situations, the division of
competences must equally be complied with, and Member States are not to make unilateral proposals, even for non-binding acts. The Court underlined as much with respect to
a proposal Greece submitted to the International Maritime Organization (IMO) Maritime
Safety Committee to examine the creation of check lists or other appropriate tools for
assisting the contracting States of the International Convention for the Safety of Life at Sea
(the SOLAS Convention) in monitoring whether ships and port facilities complied with
certain requirements.[75]

4.4 Non-exclusive competences

4.4.1 Shared competences

The basic rule

'Shared competences', as provided for by Articles 2(2) and 4 TFEU (sometimes referred to
as 'concurrent' competences), can be exercised by the Member States to the extent that the
Union has not exercised, or has decided to cease exercising,[76] its competence. Article 2(2)

---

[71] See also the Opinion of AG Tizzano in *Open Skies* (n 49) points 71–74.

[72] Eeckhout, *EU External Relations Law* (n 28) 86.

[73] See further De Baere, *Constitutional Principles of EU External Relations* (n 7) 59–61.

[74] Council Regulation (EC) No 664/2009 (OJ [2009] L200/46). cf Regulation (EC) No 662/2009 of the
European Parliament and of the Council of 13 July 2009 establishing a procedure for the negotiation and
conclusion of agreements between Member States and third countries on particular matters concerning the
law applicable to contractual and non-contractual obligations (OJ [2009] L200/25). See Eeckhout, *EU External
Relations Law* (n 28) 162.

[75] Case C-45/07 *Commission v Greece* [2009] ECR I-701. See Kuijper et al, *The Law of EU External Relations*
(n 5) 222–225.

[76] See Declaration 18 in relation to the delimitation of competences (OJ [2012] C326/346).

TFEU therefore ties Member States' competences to the evolving exercise of EU competence over time:[77]

> When the Treaties confer on the Union a competence shared with the Member States in a specific area, the Union and the Member States may legislate and adopt legally binding acts in that area. The Member States shall exercise their competence to the extent that the Union has not exercised its competence. The Member States shall again exercise their competence to the extent that the Union has decided to cease exercising its competence.

The effect of this is often referred to as 'occupying the field' or, by analogy with US constitutional doctrine, 'pre-emption'.[78] However, the mechanism is not as generally applicable as it may seem. Apart from the parallel competences discussed further in this section, a number of shared competences preclude the EU from fully harmonizing the law in a certain area, mainly because the Union can only lay down minimum standards.

Minimum standards

A prominent example is Article 193 TFEU, which determines that the substantive environmental measures adopted on the basis of Article 192 TFEU are to be only minimum measures:

> The protective measures adopted pursuant to Article 192 shall not prevent any Member State from maintaining or introducing more stringent protective measures. Such measures must be compatible with the Treaties. They shall be notified to the Commission.

The concept of internal Union minimum standards thus involves the Union harmonizing a certain policy area on the basis of minimum requirements, while leaving the Member States free to adopt more stringent measures. As the Court held in Opinion 1/03, the fact that both the Union rules and the international agreement in question lay down minimum standards:[79]

> may justify the conclusion that the [Union] rules are not affected, even if the [Union] rules and the provisions of the agreement cover the same area.

The requirement that both the Union rules and the international agreement in question lay down minimum standards is necessary in order not to inhibit the development of Union law. If an international agreement lays down an absolute standard, and the Union subsequently decides to raise its minimum standards above the absolute standard of the agreement, a conflict may arise with inevitable consequences for the international responsibility of the Union. External environmental competences and the impact of the fact that they are mostly based on minimum requirements will be further explored in this chapter's case study. As will be illustrated there, the principle of sincere cooperation in Article 4(3) TEU

---

[77] The Member States' unease in that regard caused them to annex to the TEU and TFEU Protocol No 25 on the exercise of shared competence (OJ [2012] C326/307).

[78] See the discussion of the pre-emption doctrine in G De Baere and K Gutman, 'Federalism and International Relations in the European Union and the United States: A Comparative Outlook' in E Cloots, G De Baere, and S Sottiaux (eds), *Federalism in the European Union* (Oxford/Portland, OR: Hart Publishing, 2012) 157–165. However, the Court has not adopted this term, and there is no academic consensus on its usage. Nevertheless, the term has on occasion been used by an Advocate General: see eg the Opinion of AG Ruiz-Jarabo Colomer in Case C-478/07 *Budějovický Budvar* [2009] ECR I-7721, point 93.

[79] Opinion 1/03 (n 59) paras 123 and 127. See also Opinion 2/91 *ILO Convention No 170* [1993] ECR I-1061, para 18. The Court further clarified the impact of minimum standards in Case C-246/07 *Commission v Sweden* ('*PFOS*') [2010] ECR I-3317, para 102. See further case study 24.1.

may nevertheless restrict Member States' actions, even if they are acting within their own sphere of competence.

Parallel competences

'Parallel competences' (a term not used in the Treaties) leave both the Union and the Member States competent to act internationally without one being able definitively to prevent the other from acting. An important example of the latter category[80] is Article 211 TFEU on development cooperation, which states that the Union and the Member States, each within their respective spheres of competence, are to cooperate with third countries and with the competent international organizations. Pursuant to Article 209(2) TFEU, the arrangements for Union cooperation may be the subject of agreements between the Union and the third parties concerned. However, Article 209(2) TFEU ends with the explicit assurance that the external competence described in that article 'shall be without prejudice to Member States' competence to negotiate in international bodies and to conclude international agreements'. Furthermore, Article 4(4) TFEU provides for the exercise of the Union's competence in the areas of development cooperation and humanitarian aid not to result in Member States being prevented from exercising theirs, thus creating parallel competences in those areas.

Coordination of Member States' actions

The Union may in some areas of shared competences adopt measures designed to coordinate Member States' exercise of their competence and the EU's exercise of its competence. For example, in *Open Skies*, the Court countered the Commission's argument that the conclusion of an international agreement was necessary in order to attain objectives of the Treaty that could not be attained by establishing autonomous rules by holding that there was

> nothing in the Treaty to prevent the institutions arranging, in the common rules laid down by them, concerted action in relation to the United States of America, or to prevent them prescribing the approach to be taken by the Member States in their external dealings, so as to mitigate any discrimination or distortions of competition which might result from the implementation of the commitments entered into by certain Member States with the United States of America under open skies agreements.

Following the judgments in *Open Skies*, the EU did indeed adopt legislation coordinating Member States' exercise of their competence with respect to international agreements with third States as regards air traffic rights.[81] Furthermore, on 30 April 2007, the then Community and its Member States and the US signed the Air Transport Agreement designed to replace the bilateral open skies agreements between the US and various EU Member States.[82] The Agreement was provisionally applied from 30 March 2008 for all EU Member States,[83] and amended by a Protocol,[84] signed and provisionally applied on 24 June 2010.[85] The Agreement aims to open access to markets and to maximize benefits for consumers, airlines, labour, and communities on both sides of the Atlantic not just between the initial parties, but also by extending the Agreement to include third

---

[80] See also Art 191(4) TFEU (environmental policy) and Art 219(4) TFEU (monetary policy).

[81] Regulation (EC) No 847/2004 (OJ [2004] L157/7).

[82] Decision 2007/339/EC of the Council and the Representatives of the Governments of the Member States of the European Union, meeting within the Council (OJ [2007] L134/1).

[83] See Art 25(1) of the EU–US Air Transport Agreement.

[84] Decision 2010/465/EU of the Council and the Representatives of the Governments of the Member States of the European Union, meeting within the Council (OJ [2010] L223/1).

[85] See Art 9(1) of the Protocol to the EU–US Air Transport Agreement.

countries,[86] a call to which Norway and Iceland have responded.[87] Besides that, the EU and the Member States have jointly agreed a number of comprehensive treaties with third States on aviation issues, including the liberalization of traffic rights.[88] Due to the shared competence on these issues, these treaties are 'mixed agreements' (ie agreements to which both the EU and the Member States are parties; see section 7.1).

4.4.2 The CFSP

Finally, what type of competence is the CFSP? Could it be argued that Article 4(1) TFEU ('The Union shall share competence with the Member States where the Treaties confer on it a competence which does not relate to the areas referred to in Articles 3 and 6') implies that the CFSP is a shared competence as well? Though a literal reading of Article 4(1) TFEU would seem to have that consequence, in view of Declarations Nos 13 and 14, annexed to the Lisbon Final Act,[89] it appears highly unlikely that the Member States had the intention of subjecting the CFSP to the corollary of shared competences, namely that the Member States can exercise their competence 'to the extent that the Union has not exercised its competence' or 'has decided to cease exercising its competence'.[90]

Moreover, if the CFSP was intended to be a 'shared competence', why then create a separate category of CFSP competence in Article 2(4) TFEU instead of listing it among shared competences in Article 4(2) TFEU and adding a clause to the effect that 'the exercise of that competence shall not result in Member States being prevented from exercising theirs', as was done with regard to research, technological development, space, development cooperation, and humanitarian aid in Article 4(3) and (4) TFEU?

5 Decision-making in EU external action

5.1 The ordinary Union method

The ordinary Union method[91] of decision-making is characterized by

(a) the central role of the Commission in formulating proposals;[92]

(b) qualified majority voting (QMV) in the Council;[93]

(c) involvement of the European Parliament with varying intensity depending on the decision-making procedure, but since Lisbon mostly through the ordinary legislative procedure;[94] and

(d) the role of the Court in ensuring judicial accountability.[95]

---

[86] Art 18(5) of the EU–US Air Transport Agreement.

[87] Decision 2011/708/EU of the Council and of the Representatives of the Governments of the Member States of the European Union, meeting within the Council of 16 June 2011 (OJ [2011] L283/1).

[88] See the Annex to the Communication from the Commission to the European Parliament, the Council, the European Economic and Social Committee and the Committee of the Regions: The EU's External Aviation Policy – Addressing Future Challenges, COM(2012) 556 final.

[89] OJ [2012] C326/345. These two declarations emphasize that the provisions on the CFSP in the TEU do not 'affect' the responsibilities, the existing legal basis, and the powers of the Member States for the formulation and conduct of their foreign policy.

[90] Art 2(2) TFEU, which applies, eg to the common agricultural policy; eg Case C-373/11 *Panellinios Syndesmos Viomichanion Metapoiisis Kapnou*, judgment of 19 September 2013, nyr, paras 26–27. cf Craig, *The Lisbon Treaty* (n 9) 182.

[91] This chapter uses the term 'ordinary Union method' for what formerly was usually referred to as the 'Community method'. [92] Art 17(2) TEU.

[93] Art 16(3) TEU.   [94] Arts 289(1) and 294 TFEU.   [95] Art 19(1) TEU.

This is not the place for an exhaustive analysis of the various aspects of the ordinary Union method.[96] However, a couple of particular points as regards its operation within the field of external action need to be made.

First, as far as autonomous acts are concerned, the Union legal instruments are identical in internal and external policies. The fact that decisions not specifying to whom they are addressed, which formerly fell outside the scope of ex Article 249 EC and were therefore *sui generis*,[97] are now given an explicit legal basis in the fourth paragraph of Article 288 TFEU, would seem to point to there being less need to have recourse to legal instruments outside the scope of that article.

Secondly, the role of the European Parliament in the Union's ordinary external action, while larger than in the CFSP (see section 5.2), is still smaller than with regard to internal Union policies. This was even more the case before the entry into force of the Lisbon Treaty. For example, in the Union's largest and most successful area of external action, the common commercial (ie external trade) policy (CCP), the European Parliament had no formal role in the internal decision-making procedure. The Lisbon Treaty has changed the role of the European Parliament in EU external action in quite important ways, especially with regard to the ordinary EU external action (see further section 6.2). As regards the CCP, Article 207(2) TFEU now provides for the ordinary legislative procedure to apply to measures defining the framework for its implementation. Because Article 218(6)(a)(v) TFEU now provides for the Parliament's consent to be necessary for agreements covering fields to which the ordinary legislative procedure applies, the CCP is now in principle subject to full parliamentary control, both as regards autonomous measures and international agreements.

Thirdly, an all-important point of discussion regarding the ordinary Union method is the procedure followed by the Council for adopting decisions. The options range from unanimity to several forms of majority voting, mostly through QMV.[98]

Fourthly, Union measures are, in the absence of specific provisions to the contrary, to be implemented by the Member States,[99] with due regard to the principle of sincere cooperation in Article 4(3) TEU. In ordinary EU external action, if uniform conditions for implementing legally binding Union acts are required at the Union level, those acts are to confer implementing powers on the Commission, or, in duly justified specific cases, on the Council.[100] In the field of development cooperation, for example, or in programmes such as under the European Neighbourhood and Partnership Instrument,[101] the Commission actively oversees implementation. However, the Commission needs to coordinate in that regard with the High Representative, and the EEAS is to contribute to the programming and management cycle for such instruments. That said, the EEAS has a particular role in the programming, but the management of the Union's external cooperation programmes remains under the responsibility of the Commission, which implements the Union budget[102] and retains the authority over the operational credits.[103]

---

[96] On this issue, see chapter 3 (as regards the political institutions) and chapter 10 (as regards the Court).

[97] See De Baere, *Constitutional Principles of EU External Relations* (n 7) 73–74 and 119–121.

[98] eg Art 207(4) TFEU. On Council voting rules generally, see chapter 4.   [99] Art 291(1) TFEU.

[100] Art 291(2) TFEU.

[101] Regulation (EC) No 1638/2006 of the European Parliament and of the Council (OJ [2006] L310/1).

[102] Art 317 TFEU.

[103] Art 9 EEAS Decision. See further on the EEAS–Commission relationship, J Wouters, G De Baere, B Van Vooren, K Raube, J Odermatt, T Ramopoulos, T Van den Sanden, and Y Tanghe, *The Organisation and Functioning of the European External Action Service: Achievements, Challenges and Opportunities* (Brussels: European Parliament, Directorate-General for External Policies of the Union, Directorate B, Policy Department, 2013) 46–57 (the EP EEAS Study).

Finally, the Court has played a crucial role in the development of Union external action through its case law and its advisory opinions. The most significant contrast with respect to the role of the Court between internal and external matters, apart from its generally more circumspect approach to the latter, is the specific procedure for a preliminary opinion, as laid down in Article 218(11) TFEU:

> A Member State, the European Parliament, the Council or the Commission may obtain the opinion of the Court of Justice as to whether an agreement envisaged is compatible with the Treaties. Where the opinion of the Court is adverse, the agreement envisaged may not enter into force unless it is amended or the Treaties are revised.

There is no similar procedure for determining in advance whether an internal proposal is in accordance with the Treaties. The presence of this procedure with regard to external matters and its absence with respect to internal matters can be explained by the specific needs of external action. The Union cannot afford to conclude an agreement with third countries that will later be found to be infringing the Treaties. For example, in Opinion 2/94, the Court ruled that the then Community could not accede to the European Convention on Human Rights (ECHR)[104] without amendment of the Treaties, thereby providing the necessary impetus for the drafters of the Lisbon Treaty to insert a new Article 6(2) in the EU Treaty stating that the Union is to accede to the ECHR.[105]

Moreover, the Court's normal jurisdiction applies to treaties concluded by the EU, as regards their interpretation and the validity of the decisions to conclude them on the EU's behalf.[106] Article 216(2) TFEU provides for agreements concluded by the Union to be 'binding upon the institutions of the Union and on its Member States'. Such agreements prevail over EU acts,[107] and their provisions form an integral part of the EU legal order as from their entry into force.[108] The direct consequence thereof is that the validity of an EU act may be affected by the fact that it is incompatible with rules of international law when a number of conditions are fulfilled.[109] First, the EU must be bound by those rules;[110] secondly, the nature and the broad logic of the international treaty in question must not preclude the Court from examining the validity of an EU act in light of its provisions;[111] thirdly, the treaty provisions relied upon for the purpose of examining the validity of the EU act in question appear, as regards their content, to be unconditional and sufficiently precise,[112] that is, they contain a clear and precise obligation that is not subject, in its implementation or effects, to the adoption of any subsequent measure.[113]

---

[104] Convention for the Protection of Human Rights and Fundamental Freedoms of 4 November 1950, 213 UNTS 221.

[105] An agreement on the EU's accession to the ECHR was reached in April 2013, and the Court of Justice has been asked whether this agreement is compatible with EU law: Opinion 2/13 (OJ [2013] C260/19), pending. See further chapter 9.

[106] See eg Case C-366/10 *Air Transport Association of America* ('*ATAA*'), judgment of 21 December 2011, nyr, on which see G De Baere and C Ryngaert, 'The ECJ's Judgment in *Air Transport Association of America* and the International Legal Context of the EU's Climate Change Policy' (2013) 18 *European Foreign Affairs Review* 389.   [107] *ATAA* (n 106) para 50.

[108] Case 181/73 *Haegeman* [1974] ECR 449, para 5; and *ATAA* (n 106) para 73.

[109] *ATAA* (n 106) paras 52–55. See further chapter 6.

[110] See Joined Cases 21–24/72 *International Fruit Company* [1972] ECR 1219, para 7.

[111] See Joined Cases C-120/06 P and C-121/06 P *FIAMM v Council and Commission* [2008] ECR I-6513, para 110.   [112] Case C-344/04 *IATA and ELFAA* [2006] ECR I-403, para 39.

[113] See Case 12/86 *Demirel* [1987] ECR 3719, para 14.

5.2 The CFSP

5.2.1 Preparation and adoption

Under the ordinary Union method, with only a few exceptions, nothing can happen without an initiative from the Commission, which as mentioned also has the main responsibility for implementing measures that may be necessary at Union level. By contrast, the formal distinction between the preparation and the adoption of measures is not part of the CFSP. As with respect to ordinary EU external action, CFSP measures are in the first place to be implemented by the Member States.[114] However, where uniform conditions for implementing legally binding CFSP acts are needed, those acts are to confer implementing powers not on the Commission, but on the Council.[115] The Council, its rotating Presidency (held in practice by each Member State in turn for six-month periods),[116] various Council bodies, and now the High Representative have the lead in implementing adopted measures. The Council therefore needed to be equipped with an infrastructure specifically designed for the development and implementation of the CFSP. Moreover, an important and specific feature of the CSDP is that the European Council has become involved not only in setting general guidelines, but in the development of a detailed policy framework.

5.2.2 Legal instruments

While the EU Treaty does not provide for a specific and detailed attribution of competence in the CFSP, it defines the legal instruments that the EU has at its disposal to conduct the CFSP, and develops a specific set of CFSP decision-making procedures. Article 25 TEU states that the Union is to conduct the CFSP by

> (a) defining the general guidelines;
>
> (b) adopting decisions defining:
>
>   (i) actions to be undertaken by the Union;
>
>   (ii) positions to be taken by the Union; and
>
>   (iii) arrangements for the implementation of the decisions referred to in points (i) and (ii);
>
> and by
>
> (c) strengthening systematic cooperation between Member States in the conduct of policy.

Articles 24(1) and 31(1) TEU now also explicitly exclude legislative acts from being adopted within the CFSP.

The possibility for the European Council to adopt 'common strategies' under ex Article 13(2) TEU has now been replaced by Article 22(1) TEU, which provides for the European Council to adopt decisions 'on the strategic interests and objectives of the Union', which are to relate to the CFSP *and* to other areas of the external action of the Union. In other words, Article 22(1) TEU has opened up the possibility for strategic decisions on EU external action in its entirety and not just on the CFSP, thereby remedying the impossibility in that regard under ex Article 13 TEU, which probably played a large part in the demise of the pre-Lisbon common strategies.[117] Nevertheless, despite their potential for contributing to greater consistency in EU external action, no decision under Article 22(1) TEU has yet been adopted.

---

[114] Art 291(1) TFEU.   [115] Art 291(2) TFEU.

[116] On the Council Presidency, see further chapter 3.

[117] De Baere, *Constitutional Principles of EU External Relations* (n 7) 114–115.

5.2.3 Decision-making in the Council

There is a marked distinction between the CFSP and ordinary EU external action with regard to decision-making in the Council. While, pursuant to Article 16(3) TEU, QMV is to be the rule and unanimity the exception since the entry into force of the Lisbon Treaty, Article 31(1) TEU reverses that order within the field of the CFSP: decisions under the CFSP are to be taken by the European Council and the Council acting unanimously, except where Chapter 2 of Title V of the TEU (ie the chapter on the CFSP) provides otherwise.

However, the TEU contains a mechanism to enable a Member State not to take part in a decision without preventing the other Member States from adopting it by unanimity. Pursuant to what is sometimes called 'constructive abstention', when a Member State decides to abstain in a vote, it has the possibility of qualifying this abstention by making a formal declaration,[118] and it will then not be obliged to apply the decision, though it must accept that the decision binds the Union. The Member State in question must also, 'in a spirit of mutual solidarity', refrain from any action likely to conflict with or impede Union action based on the decision on which it has decided to abstain. As with the sincere cooperation obligation of Article 4(3) TEU, the loyalty works both ways: the other Member States have to respect the position of the abstaining Member State. However, differentiation and opting out has its limits. If the Member States wishing to abstain on a specific matter represent at least one-third of the Member States comprising at least one-third of the population of the Union, the decision cannot be adopted. That makes political and legal sense. Council decisions – one might add, especially with regard to external action – should have the support of a substantial number of the members of the Council, or how can it plausibly be claimed that the Union has acted.[119] The mechanism was used, for example, by Cyprus, which abstained on the adoption of the Joint Action setting up the Rule of Law Mission in Kosovo[120] on the ground that it would have preferred an explicit UN Security Council authorization.[121]

By derogation from the unanimity rule in the CFSP, the Council acts by QMV[122]

- when adopting a decision defining a Union action or position on the basis of a decision of the European Council relating to the Union's strategic interests and objectives, as referred to in Article 22(1);

- when adopting a decision defining a Union action or position, on a proposal which the High Representative of the Union for Foreign Affairs and Security Policy has presented following a specific request from the European Council, made on its own initiative or that of the High Representative;

- when adopting any decision implementing a decision defining a Union action or position;

- when appointing a special representative in accordance with Article 33.

---

[118] Art 31(1), second subpara, TEU.

[119] cf RA Wessel, *The European Union's Foreign and Security Policy: A Legal Institutional Perspective* (The Hague/Boston/London: Kluwer Law International, 1999) 144.

[120] Council Joint Action 2008/124/CFSP (OJ [2008] L42/92).

[121] Council Doc CM 448/08 of 4 February 2008. See M Cremona, 'Enhanced Cooperation and the European Foreign and Security and Defence Policy' in JM Beneyto, J Baquero, B Becerril, M Bolle, M Cremona, S Ehret, V López-Ibor, and J Maillo, *Unity and Flexibility in the Future of the European Union: The Challenge of Enhanced Cooperation* (Madrid: CEU Ediciones, 2009) 87. [122] Art 31(2) TEU.

The only significant extension[123] of QMV in the CFSP is the possibility under the second point above. Nevertheless, the default rule of consensus would apply within the European Council in this situation.[124] The same rationale applies to the other possibilities for QMV, which are all, except for the appointment of a special representative, premised on a prior decision having been taken by unanimity or consensus.

Furthermore, under Article 31(2) TEU, second subparagraph, a Member State has the option of preventing a vote when it declares that, 'for vital and stated reasons of national policy, it intends to oppose the adoption of a decision to be taken by qualified majority'. An innovation introduced by the Lisbon Treaty is that the High Representative at this point attempts to avoid referral of the decision to the European Council by searching for a solution acceptable to the objecting Member State. This is to happen 'in close consultation with the Member State involved', and would amount to the High Representative trying his or her best to broker a unanimous decision in the Council, which would make a referral to the European Council superfluous.

However, unanimity has not necessarily always formed a serious obstacle to the development of the CFSP. Indeed, it has often led to decisions based on a wide understanding of the issue and of the advantages and the risks to the Union. QMV does often lead to decisions being taken more speedily, but it does not automatically lead to better decisions.[125]

In sum, there are three CFSP decision-making procedures available for the Council:

- unanimity, which is still the rule, as described in Article 31(1) TEU;
- QMV in the less strict version (Article 16(4) TEU): in the case described in Article 31(2), second indent EU (proposal from the High Representative);
- QMV in the stricter version (Article 238(2) TFEU): in the cases described in Article 31(2), first, third, and fourth indent TEU.

5.2.4 The role of the European Parliament

Article 36 TEU sets out a number of basic possibilities for the Parliament's involvement in the CFSP. The High Representative has to consult the Parliament regularly on 'the main aspects and the basic choices' of the CFSP and the CSDP and 'inform it of how those policies evolve'. She also has to ensure that the views of the European Parliament are 'duly taken into consideration'.[126] Special representatives may be involved in briefing the Parliament. The imprecision in formulating the High Representative's obligations, as exemplified by expressions such as 'main aspects', 'basic choices', and 'regularly' is not encouraging for the Parliament's possibilities for scrutiny. The Parliament can also address questions to the Council or the High Representative or make recommendations to them. Twice a year, it is required to hold a debate on 'progress in implementing' the CFSP, including the CSDP.[127] All in all, the Parliament is kept at a distance from any particular CFSP measure, and can only exercise influence on the general policy choices.[128]

---

[123] See, however, the *passerelle* in Art 31(3) TEU, which authorizes the European Council unanimously to adopt a decision stipulating that the Council is to act by a qualified majority in cases other than those referred to in Art 31(2) TEU.   [124] Art 15(4) TEU.

[125] E Denza, *The Intergovernmental Pillars of the European Union* (Oxford: Oxford University Press, 2002) 170.

[126] On the relationship between the High Representative and the EEAS on the one hand and the European Parliament on the other hand, see EP EEAS Study (n 103) 58–61.   [127] Art 36, para 2, TEU.

[128] De Baere, *Constitutional Principles of EU External Relations* (n 7) 161–166.

5.2.5 The role of the Court of Justice

The role of the Court of Justice forms perhaps the biggest contrast between the CFSP and the rest of the EU legal order: Articles 24(1) TEU and 275 TFEU simply exclude the Court's jurisdiction in the CFSP. There are, however, two exceptions: the Court has jurisdiction[129]

(a) to monitor compliance with Article 40 TEU, which concerns the dividing line between the CFSP and other EU competences (on which, see section 8); and

(b) to rule on proceedings, brought in accordance with Article 263, fourth paragraph, TFEU, reviewing the legality of decisions providing for restrictive measures against natural or legal persons.

5.2.6 Implementation

Under the pre-Lisbon framework, the implementation of CFSP legal instruments by the Member States took place against the background of the solidarity principle in ex Article 11(2) TEU, as was the case with respect to ex Article 10 EC in the Community sphere. Now, Article 4(3) TEU contains one principle of sincere cooperation for the Union as a whole (see further section 7.2), while at the same time, Article 24(3) TEU still contains the specific principle of loyalty for the CFSP:

> The Member States shall support the Union's external and security policy actively and unreservedly in a spirit of loyalty and mutual solidarity and shall comply with the Union's action in this area.
>
> The Member States shall work together to enhance and develop their mutual political solidarity.[130] They shall refrain from any action which is contrary to the interests of the Union or likely to impair its effectiveness as a cohesive force in international relations.
>
> The Council and the High Representative shall ensure compliance with these principles.

More particularly, the Member States have certain duties as regards the implementation of decisions defining actions to be undertaken by the Union and decisions defining positions to be taken by the Union.[131]

In international organizations[132] and at international conferences, as well as in third countries, both the diplomatic and consular missions of the Member States and the Union delegations have to cooperate to ensure implementation of, and compliance with, the decisions defining Union positions and actions adopted pursuant to the CFSP provisions.[133]

5.3 The High Representative and the European External Action Service

With the entry into force of the Lisbon Treaty, the High Representative of the Union for Foreign Affairs and Security Policy, currently Baroness Ashton, replaced both the former High Representative for the CFSP and the Commissioner for external relations.[134]

---

[129] Art 24(1), second subpara, TEU and Art 275, second para, TFEU. See the interpretation of that latter provision in Case T-509/10 *Manufacturing Support & Procurement Kala Naft v Council*, judgment of 25 April 2012, nyr, paras 32–39. This judgment was overturned on other grounds by the Court of Justice: Case C-348/12 P *Council v Manufacturing Support & Procurement Kala Naft*, judgment of 28 November 2013, nyr.

[130] See also Art 222 TFEU (the 'solidarity clause').   [131] Arts 28 and 29 TEU.

[132] See also Art 220 TFEU.   [133] See Art 35, first para, TEU.

[134] See Art 18 TEU. For more on the appointment of the High Representative and her position in the broader institutional context, see chapter 3.

The intention is for her to form a bridge between the CFSP and the other elements of the Union's external action, which is why one of her core tasks is to 'ensure the consistency of the Union's external action'.[135] However, the High Representative has to share the international scene with the President of the European Council, currently Mr Van Rompuy, who 'at his level and in that capacity', is to ensure the external representation of the Union on issues concerning its CFSP, without prejudice to the powers of the High Representative.[136] That probably implies that the President of the European Council is to represent the Union at the level of heads of State and government, while the High Representative ensures representation at ministerial level, which is what on the whole appears to happen in practice.

Article 27(3) TEU provides that in fulfilling his mandate, the High Representative is to be assisted by the EEAS, which is to 'work in cooperation with the diplomatic services of the Member States and shall comprise officials from relevant departments of the General Secretariat of the Council and of the Commission as well as staff seconded from national diplomatic services of the Member States'.

The EEAS was established by a Council decision as a 'functionally autonomous body' of the EU, 'separate from the General Secretariat of the Council and from the Commission' and 'with the legal capacity necessary to perform its tasks and attain its objectives'.[137] This indeterminate status is the result of a compromise between those wanting the EEAS to be an essentially intergovernmental body close to or part of the Council and those preferring it to be close to or part of the Commission. The EEAS was therefore set up as a *sui generis* body 'equidistant' from the Council and the Commission.[138]

The inherent structural complexities of the EEAS are evident from the enumeration of its tasks in the Decision establishing the service.[139] First, the EEAS is to 'support the High Representative in fulfilling his/her mandates',[140] which include conducting the CFSP and CSDP, ensuring the consistency of the EU's external action, presiding over the Foreign Affairs Council,[141] and acting as Vice-President of the Commission. The latter capacity not only includes 'responsibilities incumbent on [the Commission] in external relations' but also 'coordinating other aspects of the Union's external action'.[142] Secondly, the EEAS must 'assist the President of the European Council, the President of the Commission, and the Commission in the exercise of their respective functions in the area of external relations'.[143] Thirdly, the EEAS is to 'support, and work in cooperation with, the diplomatic services of the Member States as well as the General Secretariat of the Council and the services of the Commission, in order to ensure consistency between the different areas of the Union's external action and between those areas and its other policies'.[144] Fourthly, it must 'extend appropriate support and cooperation to the other institutions and bodies of the Union, in particular to the European Parliament'.[145] With the exception of the CFSP/CSDP, this complex set of tasks is determined by reference to *other* EU external actors, and includes a fragile balancing act vis-à-vis ('without prejudice to the normal tasks of') the General Secretariat of the Council and the services of the Commission.[146]

---

[135] Art 18(4) TEU. See also section 2.   [136] Art 15(6) TEU.   [137] Art 1(2) EEAS Decision.
[138] See B Van Vooren, 'A Legal Institutional Perspective on the European External Action Service' (2011) 48 *Common Market Law Review* 501.   [139] See EP EEAS Study (n 103) 18.
[140] Art 2(1) EEAS Decision.
[141] ie the configuration of the Council of Ministers where EU external action is discussed. Pursuant to Art 16(6), third para, TEU, it is to 'elaborate the Union's external action on the basis of strategic guidelines laid down by the European Council and ensure that the Union's action is consistent'.
[142] Art 18(4) TEU.   [143] Art 2(2) EEAS Decision.
[144] Art 3(1) EEAS Decision. cf Art 21(3), second para, TEU.   [145] Art 3(4) EEAS Decision.
[146] EP EEAS Study (n 103) 18.

Adding to this complexity are the numerous cooperative duties listed in Article 3 of the Decision. First, the EEAS must work in cooperation with Member State diplomatic services. Secondly, the EEAS and the services of the Commission are to 'consult each other on all matters relating to the external action of the Union in the exercise of their respective functions, except on matters covered by CSDP', and the EEAS is to 'take part in the preparatory work and procedures relating to acts to be prepared by the Commission in this area'.[147] Thirdly, the Union delegations,[148] that is, the Union's diplomatic representations and as such part of the EEAS, are to 'work in close cooperation and share information with the diplomatic services of the Member States'.[149] Although the reciprocal obligation to share information provided for in the initial draft does not appear in the final text of the Decision, the logic of the principle of sincere cooperation laid down in Article 4(3) TEU indicates that this cannot be only a one-way street.[150]

6 External representation and international agreements

6.1 External representation

A distinction must be made between internal EU decision-making on the one hand and external representation on the other hand, and in particular between the institution that decides the policy line and the institution responsible for representing it externally.[151] In that respect, a balance must be found between the policy-making functions of the Council under Article 16 TEU and Article 17 TEU, which provides that, with the exception of the CFSP and other cases provided for in the Treaties, the Commission is to ensure the Union's external representation. As will be illustrated in case study 24.1, that does not mean that the Commission necessarily decides on the content of the position to be represented. Furthermore, in the CFSP, external representation is ensured by the High Representative (Article 18(2) TEU) and as mentioned previously, 'at his level and in that capacity', by the President of the European Council, without prejudice to the powers of the High Representative (Article 15(6) TEU).

Before the entry into force of the Lisbon Treaty, the Commission represented EU positions concerning the First Pillar, while the Council Presidency represented the Union in other cases, mostly pertaining to the CFSP. However, the Lisbon Treaty removed all explicit references in the Treaties to the role of the Council Presidency in the external representation of the EU. The new Treaty rules (Articles 17 and 27(2) TEU) set a clear framework: the external representation of the EU is ensured by the High Representative in the CFSP, and by the Commission in other external action matters.

While the Lisbon Treaty thus leaves the Council Presidency without a formal role in the external representation of the Union, the Member States retain their sovereignty to conduct their own foreign relations, subject to the rules of the Treaty. The Member States are in principle free to determine their own representation when acting outside the Union institutional framework, as long as they respect the principle of sincere cooperation.

Generally, the attention as regards external representation post-Lisbon has shifted from the CFSP to the notion of shared competences, with regard to which certain issues remain unclear. An example thereof will be examined in case study 24.1.

---

[147] Art 3(2) EEAS Decision.   [148] Art 221 TFEU.   [149] Art 5(9) EEAS Decision.
[150] EP EEAS Study (n 103) 18–19.
[151] See further E Paasivirta, 'The EU's External Representation after Lisbon: New Rule, a New Era?' in P Koutrakos (ed), *The European Union's External Relations a Year After Lisbon* (2011) CLEER Working Papers 2011/3.

The Treaties make no specific mention of the possibility for the EU to take part in international dispute settlement, or of which institution is to represent it in such fora. Nevertheless, agreements to which the Union is a party may include a dispute settlement system, most notably the Dispute Settlement Understanding in Annex 2 of the World Trade Organization (WTO) Agreement.[152] In practice, the Commission Legal Service represents the Union in such international litigation.[153]

6.2 International agreements

With the entry into force of the Lisbon Treaty, Article 218 TFEU introduced one single procedure for negotiating and concluding international agreements over the entire field of Union competences, largely based on the old Community treaty-making procedure in ex Article 300 EC, duly adapted and with a number of exceptions in order to be applicable also to CFSP treaties.

This section describes the different stages of the procedure and the respective roles of the different EU actors involved. While for analytical purposes a distinction between several procedural stages is useful, in practice these stages are not always as clearly separable from each other. This is especially the case with regard to complex negotiations such as the Uruguay Round of the GATT (an important international trade negotiation, during which the scope of the then Community's competences were disputed) leading up to the WTO Agreement, which encompassed several consecutive phases of negotiation.[154]

6.2.1 Negotiation

As under ex Article 300 EC, the procedure under Article 218 TFEU starts with the Commission making a recommendation to the Council,[155] though this is often preceded by exploratory talks in the pre-negotiation stage between the Commission and potential third-country treaty-partners.[156]

By contrast, the ex Article 24 TEU[157] procedure for making international agreements within the spheres of the CFSP and PJCCM was set in motion by the Council, which could authorize the Presidency, assisted by the Commission if necessary, to commence negotiations. The Council, on a recommendation from the Presidency, would then conclude any resulting international agreement.[158] International agreements concluded in accordance with the procedure set out in ex Article 24 TEU bind the institutions of the Union.[159] Nevertheless, an agreement was not to be binding on a Member State whose representative in the Council stated that it had to comply with the requirements of its own constitutional procedure, a possibility that no longer exists after Lisbon.[160]

---

[152]   Agreement Establishing the World Trade Organization, 1867 UNTS 154; 33 ILM 1144 (1994).

[153]   Kuijper et al, *The Law of EU External Relations* (n 5) 62–67.

[154]   See eg JH Jackson, *The World Trading System: Law and Policy of International Economic Relations* (2nd edn, Cambridge, MA/London: MIT Press, 1997) 44–46; P Van den Bossche and W Zdouc, *The Law and Policy of the World Trade Organization: Text, Cases and Materials* (3rd edn, Cambridge: Cambridge University Press, 2013) 79–81.   [155]   Art 218(3) TFEU.

[156]   De Baere, *Constitutional Principles of EU External Relations* (n 7) 79.

[157]   Art 37 TEU now simply provides that the Union may conclude agreements with one or more States or international organizations within the CFSP area.   [158]   Ex Art 24(1) TEU.

[159]   Ex Art 24(6) TEU.

[160]   Ex Art 24(5) TEU. cf nevertheless Art 218(8) TFEU on the agreement on accession of the Union to the ECHR.

However, the Council Presidency, as mentioned previously with respect to external representation, appears to lose out in the evolution from ex Article 24 TEU to Article 218 TFEU. While it had quite an important role in negotiating international agreements in the sphere of the CFSP, its role appears now to have been mostly taken over by the High Representative. Nonetheless, one might presuppose that the Council Presidency will continue to play a role in some form, especially when a proposed international agreement touches upon or includes aspects of Member State competence. Under Article 218(3) TFEU, where the envisaged agreement exclusively or principally concerns the CFSP, the High Representative and not the Commission makes a recommendation to the Council. This is one example of how the Lisbon Treaty, despite the increased consistency due to the unified treaty-making procedure, maintains the differentiation between ordinary EU external action and the CFSP.

Given that a Commission recommendation under Article 218(3) TFEU is not a Commission proposal under Article 293(1) TFEU, the Council does not need to act unanimously to amend it. Furthermore, while the withdrawal by the Commission of a proposal under Articles 293 and 294 TFEU implies an immediate end to the ongoing ordinary legislative procedure, the same would not appear to be the case as regards the withdrawal of a recommendation under Article 218(3) TFEU. The question was at issue during the conflict between the Commission and the Council in the course of the negotiations towards a global ban on mercury, which will be discussed in the case study.[161]

If the Council deems the negotiation of the proposed international agreement in question to be opportune, it adopts a decision authorizing the opening of negotiations and, depending on the subject of the agreement envisaged, nominating the Union negotiator or the head of the Union's negotiating team.[162] Article 218(3) TFEU appears to give the Council a choice,[163] and it will therefore probably let the appointment of the negotiator depend upon what it judges to be the 'centre of gravity' of the agreement. If the Council deems it to be the CFSP, it will most likely appoint the High Representative as negotiator. The Council can also address directives[164] to the negotiator and designate a special committee (which is often a Council working party, ie a Council preparatory committee that performs the 'ground work' in one of the EU's diverse policies, and operates under the aegis of the Committee of Permanent Representatives of the Governments of the Member States (Coreper) or another senior preparatory committee)[165] in consultation with which the negotiations must be conducted. When negotiating the agreement, the negotiator has to consult with special committees appointed by the Council to assist it in this task, and stay within the confines of the negotiating directives given to it by the Council.[166]

---

[161] G De Baere, 'Mercury Rising: The European Union and the International Negotiations for a Globally Binding Instrument on Mercury' (2012) 37 *European Law Review* 648.

[162] Art 218(3) TFEU. Art 218 TFEU spells out who is to submit recommendations under what circumstances, but does not explicitly determine who is to be the negotiator.

[163] See, however, Art 207(3) TFEU (the Commission is the only possible negotiator in the field of the CCP) and Art 219(3) TFEU (the Commission is to be merely 'fully associated with the negotiations' concerning monetary or foreign exchange regime matters).

[164] These directives do not constitute delegated powers from the Council to the Commission and the term 'mandate', though used in daily practice, is therefore inapposite: F Hoffmeister, 'Curse or Blessing? Mixed Agreements in the Recent Practice of the European Union and Its Member States' in C Hillion and P Koutrakos (eds), *Mixed Agreements Revisited: The EU and Its Member States in the World* (Oxford/Portland, OR: Hart Publishing, 2010) 253.

[165] See De Baere, *Constitutional Principles of EU External Relations* (n 7) 131.

[166] Art 218(4) TFEU.

6.2.2 Signature

The signing stage, which may include a decision on the provisional application of the agreement,[167] starts with the negotiator nominated by the Council making a proposal to that effect.[168] It is then up to the Council to decide on the signing of the agreement and hence to approve or disapprove of the negotiator's proposal, acting by QMV, or by unanimity in the same circumstances as regarding the conclusion of the agreement.[169]

6.2.3 Conclusion

The Council concludes the agreement through a decision by QMV, acting on a proposal by the negotiator.[170] Indeed, the first subparagraph of Article 218(8) TFEU specifies that the Council is to act by QMV throughout the procedure. Nonetheless, pursuant to the second subparagraph, a number of exceptions apply. The Council acts unanimously

(a) when the agreement covers a field for which unanimity is required for the adoption of a Union act;[171]

(a) as regards association agreements;[172] and

(b) as regards agreements establishing economic, financial, and technical cooperation[173] with candidate Member States.

A specific case in which the Council is to act unanimously concerns the agreement on accession of the Union to the ECHR.[174] Additionally, the decision concluding this agreement is to enter into force only after it has been approved by the Member States in accordance with their respective constitutional requirements.[175]

Article 207(4) TFEU, which contains a number of specific rules on the negotiation and conclusion of agreements within the sphere of the CCP, adds more exceptions. The Council is to act unanimously as regards agreements in trade in services, the commercial aspects of intellectual property,[176] and foreign direct investment where such agreements include provisions for which unanimity is required for the adoption of internal rules. Moreover, the Council is to act unanimously as regards agreements

(a) in the field of trade in cultural, and audiovisual services, where these agreements risk prejudicing the Union's cultural and linguistic diversity; and

---

[167] cf Art 25 Vienna Convention on the Law of Treaties, 23 May 1969, UN Doc A/Conf.39/27; 1155 UNTS 331. The Vienna Convention does not as such apply to the EU, but its provisions generally reflect international practice and, at least in part, customary international law.   [168] Art 218(5) TFEU.
[169] Art 218(8) TFEU.   [170] Art 218(6) TFEU.
[171] eg in the field of external environmental law, which forms the subject of the case study later in the text, unanimity is required for the limited set of environmental matters listed in Art 192(2) TFEU: '(a) provisions primarily of a fiscal nature; (b) measures affecting: [i] town and country planning, [ii] quantitative management of water resources or affecting, directly or indirectly, the availability of those resources, [iii] land use, with the exception of waste management; (c) measures significantly affecting a Member State's choice between different energy sources and the general structure of its energy supply.' On the difficulties associated with interpreting these exceptions: JH Jans and HHB Vedder, *European Environmental Law after Lisbon* (4th edn, Groningen: Europa Law Publishing, 2012) 59–63.   [172] Art 217 TFEU.
[173] Art 212 TFEU.   [174] Art 6(2) TEU.   [175] Art 218(8) TFEU.
[176] See Case C-414/11 *Daiichi Sankyo and Sanofi-Aventis Deutschland*, judgment off 18 July 2013, nyr, paras 52–53, where the Court clarified that 'of the rules adopted by the European Union in the field of intellectual property, only those with a specific link to international trade are capable of falling within the concept of "commercial aspects of intellectual property" in Article 207(1) TFEU and hence the field of the common commercial policy', which is the case for the Agreement on Trade-Related Aspects of Intellectual Property Rights, 15 April 1994, 1869 UNTS 299; 33 ILM 1197 (1994) (the TRIPS Agreement).

(b) in the field of trade in social, education, and health services, where these agreements risk seriously disturbing the national organization of such services and prejudicing the responsibility of Member States to deliver them.

These are all sensitive areas in which the Member States did not wish to run the risk of the EU concluding an international agreement without the possibility to stop it. A recent illustration of the sensitivity of audiovisual services in particular was provided by the decision of the Council in June 2013 that those services should initially not be part of the negotiation directives for the EU–US trade and investment negotiations, but that the Commission may make recommendations to the Council on possible additional negotiating directives at a later stage.[177] Finally, with respect to agreements in the field of transport, Article 207(5) TFEU simply contains a cross-reference to the Title on transport in the TFEU.[178] Some of the international agreements in that field will be concluded on the basis of exclusive Union competence, while others will follow the format for shared competences, which will often imply that they will be concluded as mixed agreements (ie agreements to which both the EU and the Member States are parties; see section 7.1).

With respect to such agreements, as well as mixed agreements in other fields, a requirement for unanimous voting applies de facto due to the Member States' involvement in the negotiation and ratification of those treaties.

6.2.4 Role of the European Parliament

Article 218(10) TFEU provides for the European Parliament to be immediately and fully informed 'at all stages of the procedure'. Furthermore, parliamentary involvement in the conclusion of international agreements is now the rule, with the exception of agreements relating *exclusively*[179] to the CFSP. In practice the large majority of international agreements concluded by the Union are deemed to fall under one of the categories listed in Article 218(6)(a) TFEU and are subject to consent:[180]

(i)   association agreements;

(ii) the agreement on Union accession to the ECHR;

(iii) agreements establishing a specific institutional framework by organising cooperation procedures;[181]

(iv) agreements with important budgetary implications for the Union;[182] and

(v)   agreements covering fields to which either the ordinary legislative procedure applies,[183] or the special legislative procedure where consent by the European Parliament is required.[184]

---

[177] Commission MEMO/13/564 of 15 June 2013.   [178] Title VI of Part Three TFEU.

[179] Agreements under Art 218 TFEU may include both issues falling under the ordinary EU framework and falling under the CFSP; eg Council Decision 2012/308/CFSP on the accession of the European Union to the Treaty of Amity and Cooperation in Southeast Asia (OJ [2012] L154/1), which is based on a joint legal basis of Arts 31(1) and 37 TEU and Arts 209, 212, and 218(6)(a) and (8), second subpara, TFEU.

[180] See also chapter 4.

[181] Given that most agreements involving a cooperation procedure establish some sort of institutional framework, the latter can hardly be the distinguishing feature of this type of agreement. This category therefore probably refers to international agreements setting up an institutional structure attaining a certain level of complexity, but nonetheless not concluded under the legal basis for association agreements (Art 217 TFEU); eg Council Decision 2006/719/EC of 5 October 2006 on the accession of the Community to the Hague Conference on Private International Law (OJ [2006] L297/1).

[182] See Case C-189/97 *European Parliament v Council* [1999] ECR I-4741, paras 20–32 for the relevant criteria.   [183] Art 294 TFEU.

[184] Art 289(2) TFEU; eg Art 352(1) TFEU, the Union's residual competence. On the scope of the ordinary legislative procedure and special legislative procedures, see further chapter 5.

Category (v) brings about a small revolution in EU external action. Under the second paragraph of ex Article 300(3) EC, that category contained 'agreements *entailing amendment* of an act adopted under the [co-decision] procedure'.[185] Given that consent of the Parliament is now required every time the ordinary legislative procedure *applies* and given the fact that the scope of the ordinary legislative procedure has been significantly enlarged in comparison to the co-decision procedure, Article 218(6)(a)(v) TFEU implies a substantial extension of the power of the European Parliament.

The change is perhaps most dramatic in the CCP where, as mentioned previously, before Lisbon the Parliament had no formal role in internal decision-making and did not even need to be consulted with respect to international trade agreements.[186] Since the entry into force of the Lisbon Treaty, the European Parliament's consent is now required for agreements in the CCP. That much is clear, for example, from the Parliament's refusal to consent to the highly controversial Anti-Counterfeiting Trade Agreement (ACTA).[187]

The Parliament has been keen to demonstrate its increased powers not just in the area of external trade, but in all areas in which its consent is mandatory. For example, shortly after the entry into force of the Lisbon Treaty, the Parliament underlined its greater powers by first withholding its consent to the Agreement between the European Union and the United States of America on the processing and transfer of Financial Messaging Data from the European Union to the United States for purposes of the Terrorist Finance Tracking Program (SWIFT),[188] another controversial international agreement, notably on account of its alleged infringement of the right to protection of personal data, and only agreeing to consent after it felt that its concerns had been taken into account.[189]

Furthermore, Article 218(6)(b) TFEU provides for consultation of the European Parliament to be required in all cases except those for which consent is required pursuant to Article 218(6)(a) TFEU.

6.2.5 Legal instrument

The internal Union instruments used to conclude international agreements are often decisions not specifying to whom they are addressed. As mentioned previously, these are now given an explicit legal basis in the fourth paragraph of Article 288 TFEU. There would therefore be less need than before the entry into force of the Lisbon Treaty to have recourse to legal instruments outside the scope of that article. Nonetheless, regardless of whether the legal instrument by which an international agreement is concluded is listed in Article 288 TFEU or is *sui generis*, it is amenable to judicial review by the Court of Justice.[190]

6.2.6 Decision-making in a body set up by an international agreement

The conclusion by the Union of an 'association agreement' under Article 217 TFEU or another international agreement will sometimes give rise to the establishment of its own decision-making organs within which the Union will wish to take positions. Notable examples include the association agreement with Turkey[191] and the WTO Agreement.

---

[185] Emphasis added.

[186] De Baere, *Constitutional Principles of EU External Relations* (n 7) 75 and 85.

[187] European Parliament legislative resolution of 4 July 2012 (12195/2011 – C7-0027/2012 – 2011/0167(NLE)) (OJ [2013] C349E/552).

[188] European Parliament legislative resolution of 11 February 2010 (05305/1/2010 REV 1 – C7-0004/2010 – 2009/0190(NLE)) (OJ [2010] C341E/100).

[189] European Parliament legislative resolution of 8 July 2010 (11222/1/2010/REV 1 and COR 1 – C7-0158/2010 – 2010/0178(NLE)) (OJ [2011] C351E/453).   [190] *ERTA* (n 26) para 42.

[191] Agreement establishing an Association between the European Economic Community and Turkey – Protocol 1: Provisional Protocol – Protocol 2: Financial Protocol – Final Act – Declarations (OJ [1964] 217/3687, [1973] C113/1, [1977] L361).

Such bodies with the competence to take binding decisions often do so by consensus.[192] The common positions to be defended by the Union need to be established in advance of the meeting at which the decision is scheduled to be taken. Article 218(9) TFEU gives the Council the competence, on a proposal from the Commission or the High Representative, to establish the positions to be adopted on the Union's behalf in such treaty-based bodies, when such a body is 'called upon to adopt acts having legal effects', excluding, however, acts supplementing or amending the institutional framework of the agreement, that is, constitutional decisions *sensu stricto*.

Given that the adoption of binding decisions in such international bodies in effect amounts to a new way of making EU law, the determination of the Union position cannot be left solely to the Commission. These binding decisions do become an integral part of the EU legal system, and at least the involvement of the Council seems therefore necessary,[193] while the European Parliament is to be 'immediately and fully informed', as it is at all stages of the Article 218 TFEU procedure.

7 Managing the vertical division of EU external competences

How is a federal-type structure like the EU[194] to ensure that its policies, while respecting the possibilities for differentiation within and across the several levels of government, remain broadly consistent and coherent, both internally and, which is often considered as at least as important, towards the outside world?

A crucial element in understanding how the current arrangement of the deckchairs on the ship of EU external action affects the Union's ability to have a consistent and effective external policy is to grasp the fact that the Union must do so against the background of 28 Member States retaining a large part of their external sovereignty and consequently their ability to have their own foreign policies. Because of its internally differentiated constitutional structure, the EU has to strive for consistency on two fronts: horizontally between its different institutions, structures, and policies, and vertically, between the EU and its Member States. The Lisbon Treaty has tried to tackle that issue by providing an overarching constitutional framework for the EU's external action, and for the EU in general, through a set of values that are to govern all EU action,[195] as well as a single set of principles and objectives for the entire field of EU external action.[196] The Union must respect those principles and pursue those objectives in the development and implementation of the different areas of the Union's external action, as well as the external aspects of its other policies.[197] The Union must also ensure consistency between the different areas of its external action and between these and its other policies. The Council and the Commission, assisted by the High Representative, are to ensure that consistency and are to cooperate to that effect.[198]

In practice, the Union manages the vertical and horizontal division of external action competences through a combination of pragmatism and principle. While section 8

---

[192] eg Art IX(1) WTO Agreement.

[193] eg Case C-192/89 *Sevince* [1990] ECR I-3461, paras 8–11. This also implies that the Court has jurisdiction to give preliminary rulings on questions of interpretation of such (even non-binding) decisions; eg Case C-188/91 *Deutsche Shell AG v Hauptzollamt Hamburg-Harburg* [1993] ECR I-363, paras 14–18.

[194] See further, R Schütze, *From Dual to Cooperative Federalism: The Changing Structure of European Law* (Oxford: Oxford University Press, 2009) 287–343 and De Baere and Gutman, 'Federalism and International Relations in the European Union and the United States' (n 78). See further chapters 3 and 4.

[195] Art 2 TEU.   [196] Arts 3(5) and 21 TEU, and Art 205 TFEU.

[197] Art 21(3), first subpara, TEU.   [198] Art 21(3), second subpara, TEU.

examines the horizontal division of competences, the present section analyses two constitutional concepts of vital importance for the management of the vertical division of competences: the technique of mixity and the principle of sincere cooperation.

7.1 Mixed agreements

7.1.1 What are mixed agreements?

An introduction into the law of EU external action would not be complete without a few words on the peculiar species called 'mixed agreements', which can be defined as agreements that include among their parties the Union and all or some of the Member States, and which fall partly within the competence of the Union and partly within the competence of the Member States.[199]

7.1.2 Why are there mixed agreements?

Mixed external action is almost invariably the outcome of internal power struggles within the Union, and virtually never the result of a specific demand from a non-Union contracting partner.[200] As Advocate General Sharpston put it, 'the mixed agreement is itself a creature of pragmatic forces – a means of resolving the problems posed by the need for international agreements in a multi-layered system'.[201] Their lack of clarity as to the precise vertical division of competences makes mixed agreements suitable for enabling the Union to act internationally while keeping the competence situation sufficiently vague so as not to affect openly the Member States' external competences. Moreover, an overly precise determination of the respective competences of the Union and the Member States might 'freeze' the Union's competences and hinder its evolving constitutional order. However, the unwillingness of the Union to provide any clear division of competences makes it difficult, particularly for third parties to a mixed agreement, to know who should be held responsible in the event of non-compliance.[202]

The Lisbon Treaty may have reduced the need for mixed agreements. For example, under the previous Treaty framework, if an agreement needed to integrate both First and Second Pillar elements, the preferred solution was often to consider the 'Second Pillar' aspects of the agreement as belonging to Member State competences and resorting to a mixed agreement involving the Community and the Member States.[203] Under Article 218 TFEU, such a 'cross-pillar' agreement can be concluded as one integrated Union agreement while taking into account the differences in procedure between the CFSP and non-CFSP aspects of the agreement.

Another factor that has the potential of reducing the need for mixed agreements is Article 207 TFEU, which (as revised by the Lisbon Treaty) considerably expands the Union's exclusive competence in the CCP.[204] It appears to be intended to cover essentially

---

[199] J Heliskoski, *Mixed Agreements as a Technique for Organizing the International Relations of the European Community and Its Member States* (The Hague/London/New York: Kluwer Law International, 2001) 7. See further, C Hillion and P Koutrakos, *Mixed Agreements Revisited: The EU and Its Member States in the World* (Oxford/Portland, OR: Hart Publishing, 2010).

[200] Eeckhout, *EU External Relations Law* (n 28) 220–221.

[201] Opinion in Case C-240/09 *Lesoochranárske zoskupenie* [2011] ECR I-1255, point 56.

[202] See Eeckhout, *EU External Relations Law* (n 28) 262–264.

[203] De Baere, *Constitutional Principles of EU External Relations* (n 7) 294–298.

[204] Nevertheless, the Court has clarified that the CCP only 'relates to trade with non-member countries, not to trade in the internal market', and the mere fact that an EU act 'is liable to have implications for international

the full scope[205] of the WTO-covered agreements. Not only 'trade in goods and services, and the commercial aspects of intellectual property'[206] are now covered, but also 'foreign direct investment'.

7.1.3 Concluding mixed agreements

There is no specific procedure for concluding mixed agreements, but a practice has developed by which the majority of mixed agreements are negotiated under the Article 218 TFEU procedure (see section 6.2), in combination with a more pronounced presence of Member State representatives, as well as coordination meetings during which the line to be followed by the Commission during the negotiations is decided. For example, notwithstanding the acrimonious battles over the vertical division of competences during the Uruguay Round, the Member States let the Commission act as the negotiator as regards the entire agreement,[207] leaving aside until the end of the negotiations the issue of who was competent – which was then submitted to the Court of Justice.[208]

A mixed agreement has to be ratified by both the Union – which requires going through the normal Article 218 TFEU procedure and, in a clear majority of the cases, includes the formal involvement of the European Parliament – and by every single Member State (if all Member States, as is usual, participate in the agreement), which will have to go through its own constitutional procedures, most often including scrutiny and approval by the Member State parliaments. It does not require much imagination to see that this is liable to be a cumbersome process.

The Union has thus had to develop a strategy to tackle the problems engendered by the potentially long time span between the signing and the entry into force of a mixed agreement. The Council adopted the practice of only concluding a mixed agreement after all Member States have ratified, in order to avoid so-called 'partial mixity'.[209] Apart from this, the Union can also enter into an interim agreement on the Union aspects of the mixed agreement, which can be concluded by a Council decision or can have the agreement provisionally applied from the time of signature, as provided for by Article 218(5) TFEU and Article 25 of the Vienna Convention on the Law of Treaties.[210]

Mixed agreements concluded by the Union form an integral part of the EU legal order, and the Court has jurisdiction to give preliminary rulings concerning the interpretation of such an agreement. In particular, the Court has jurisdiction to define the obligations which the Union has assumed and those which remain the sole responsibility of the Member States in order to interpret the mixed agreement in question.[211]

---

trade' is not enough for it to fall within the CCP. An EU act falls within that policy 'if it relates specifically to international trade in that it is essentially intended to promote, facilitate or govern trade and has direct and immediate effects on trade': *Conditional Access Convention* (n 10) paras 56–57 and the case law cited there.

[205] With the notable exception of transport: Art 207(5) TFEU.

[206] See *Daiichi Sankyo* (n 176), paras 52–53, in which the Court held that the TRIPS Agreement fell within the exclusive competence of the EU in the field of the CCP.

[207] cf P Van den Bossche, 'The European Community and the Uruguay Round Agreements' in JH Jackson and AO Sykes (eds), *Implementing the Uruguay Round* (Oxford: Oxford University Press, 1997) 53–59.

[208] See Opinion 1/94 (n 57).   [209] cf Art 102 EAEC, which expressly provides for this approach.

[210] See n 167. eg Council Decision 2012/196/EC of 13 July 2009 on the signing and provisional application of the Interim Agreement establishing a framework for an Economic Partnership Agreement between the Eastern and Southern Africa States, on the one part, and the European Community and its Member States, on the other part (OJ [2012] L111/1).

[211] *Lesoochranárske zoskupenie* (n 201) paras 30–31 and the case law cited there.

7.2 Sincere cooperation

The duty of loyal cooperation or sincere cooperation, as laid down in Article 4(3) TEU, is of great importance for the Union's external action and for its entire constitutional structure. It requires the Union and the Member States, in full mutual respect, to assist each other in carrying out tasks which flow from the Treaties. The Member States are to take any appropriate measure, general or particular, to ensure fulfilment of the obligations arising out of the Treaties or resulting from the acts of the institutions of the Union and to facilitate the achievement of the Union's tasks and refrain from any measure which could jeopardize the attainment of the Union's objectives. The duty of sincere cooperation is of general application and does not depend either on whether the Union competence concerned is exclusive or on any right of the Member States to enter into obligations towards non-member countries.[212] That duty lies at the basis of the specific duty of cooperation in external matters,[213] which in turn results from the requirement of unity in the international representation of the Union.[214]

Crucially, the duty of cooperation in Union law does not regulate the vertical or horizontal division of competences, but the exercise of those competences.[215] Nevertheless, the Court has been steadily reinforcing the procedural obligations flowing from the duty of loyal cooperation: from the prohibition on submitting a case that falls within the scope of EU law to a non-EU judicial organ,[216] to that on negotiating separate treaties without as much as informing the Commission after the latter has been authorized by the Council to negotiate international agreements with the same third State(s) on the same subject matter,[217] and the prohibition for a Member State to distance itself from an agreed Union strategy by taking action within an international organization that could potentially bind the Union.[218] The procedural duties imposed on Member States by the principle of loyal cooperation cannot be captured in a simple dichotomy of the Member States' ability or inability to act independently. It is clear that the strictures of the duty of cooperation depend crucially on the international context in which the Union and the Member States operate together. The decisive criterion is whether the action of the Member States is likely to hinder or impede the Union's action.

This operation of the duty of cooperation underscores the distinction between the scope of Union law and the scope of Union competences.[219] Indeed, discovering the limits of Union competences is not the same as discovering the limits of the Treaties' scope of application.[220] The duty of cooperation makes this quite clear. Member States and the Union institutions within their respective spheres of competence are under a mutual obligation to cooperate. That is illustrated by the *PFOS* case, which is further considered in the case study.

---

[212] *PFOS* (n 79) paras 69–71 and the case law referred to therein.

[213] Ruling 1/78 (n 68) paras 33–34.   [214] Opinion 2/91 (n 79) para 36.

[215] See C Hillion, '*Tous pour un, un pour tous!* Coherence in the External Relations of the European Union' in M Cremona (ed), *Developments in EU External Relations Law* (Oxford: Oxford University Press, 2008) 28.

[216] Case C-459/03 *Commission v Ireland* ('*Mox Plant*') [2006] ECR I-4635.

[217] Case C-266/03 *Commission v Luxembourg* [2005] ECR I-4805 and Case C-433/03 *Commission v Germany* [2005] ECR I-6985.   [218] *PFOS* (n 79).

[219] See M Cremona, 'Defending the Community Interest: The Duties of Cooperation and Compliance' in M Cremona and B de Witte (eds), *EU Foreign Relations Law: Constitutional Fundamentals* (Oxford: Hart Publishing, 2008) 168.

[220] A Dashwood, 'The Limits of European Community Powers' (1996) 21 *European Law Review* 114.

Case study 24.1: External environmental policy

As a constantly growing policy field with a complex competence structure, external environmental policy provides an excellent testing ground to see the post-Lisbon framework for EU external action in operation.[221]

The protection of the environment is mentioned twice among the basic objectives of the Union's external action.[222] 'Environment' is listed as a shared competence under Article 4(2)(e) TFEU. In particular, the legal bases for EU external environmental law are to be found in Articles 191 and 192 in Title XX of Part Three of the TFEU.[223] Article 193 TFEU[224] further clarifies that measures taken on the basis of Article 192 TFEU are to be minimum requirements. There is an explicit legal basis for EU external action in Article 191(4) TFEU, which provides for the Union and the Member States to cooperate with third countries and with the competent international organizations within their respective spheres of competence, adding that the arrangements for Union cooperation 'may be the subject of agreements between the Union and the third parties concerned'. As is clear from its second subparagraph, measures based on Article 191(4) TFEU leave the Member States' competence to act internationally intact, which implies a parallel competence (see section 4.4.1). However, the Court has severely limited the applicability of that article as a legal basis.[225] As a consequence, ex Article 174(4) EC (now Article 191(4) TFEU) was abandoned as the default legal basis for external environmental agreements. That is, for example, clear from comparing the Commission proposal regarding the Kyoto Protocol, an international agreement linked to the United Nations Framework Convention on Climate Change, which sets internationally binding emission-reduction targets, which was based on ex Article 174(4) EC,[226] and the eventual Council decision, based on ex Article 175(1) EC (now Article 192(1) TFEU).[227] Most substantive measures were based on ex Article 175 EC and will now presumably be based on Article 192 TFEU. The *ERTA* doctrine would in principle appear to apply to such measures.[228]

However, as mentioned previously (see section 4.4.1), minimum standards such as those pursuant to Article 193 TFEU normally give rise to non-exclusive EU competences. The Court further clarified the scope of Article 193 TFEU in the *PFOS* case.[229]

THE *PFOS* CASE

The *PFOS* case concerned infringement proceedings brought by the Commission against Sweden for having unilaterally proposed that perfluoroctane sulfonate (PFOS) be added to Annex A to the Stockholm Convention on Persistent Organic Pollutants.[230] The Stockholm Convention is a multilateral agreement, the objective of which is to protect human health

---

[221] For more on the detail of EU environmental law, see chapter 22. See further on EU external environmental policy, Kuijper et al, *The Law of EU External Relations* (n 5) ch 10.   [222] Art 21(2)(d) and (f) TEU.

[223] Ex Arts 174 and 175 EC.   [224] Ex Art 176 EC.   [225] Opinion 2/00 (n 12) para 44.

[226] Proposal for a Council Decision concerning the approval, on behalf of the European Community, of the Kyoto Protocol to the United Nations Framework Convention on Climate Change and the joint fulfilment of commitments thereunder, COM/2001/0579 final (OJ [2002] 75E/17).

[227] Council Decision 2002/358/EC of 25 April 2002 concerning the approval, on behalf of the European Community, of the Kyoto Protocol to the United Nations Framework Convention on Climate Change and the joint fulfilment of commitments thereunder (OJ [2002] L130/1).

[228] Opinion 2/00 (n 12) paras 44–46.

[229] See further, G De Baere, ' "O, Where is Faith? O, Where is Loyalty?" Some Thoughts on the Duty of Loyal Co-operation and the Union's External Environmental Competences in the Light of the *PFOS* Case' (2011) 36 *European Law Review* 405.   [230] Adopted on 22 May 2001, 40 ILM 532 (2001).

and the environment from Persistent Organic Pollutants (POPs). The first recital in the Preamble to the Convention specifies that POPs possess toxic properties, resist degradation, bioaccumulate, and are transported through air, water, and migratory species across international boundaries and deposited far from their place of release, where they accumulate in terrestrial and aquatic ecosystems. The Convention is a mixed agreement, to which the Union [231] and all Member States are parties.[232]

A Member State is free to adopt measures providing for a higher level of protection within its own jurisdiction. However, proposing such measures within the framework of an international agreement to which the Union is a party, which would imply that the Union may be bound by a more stringent measure with which it did not express its agreement, is quite a different thing and does not fall within the scope of Article 193 TFEU.[233] It is important to appreciate that Sweden was exercising its own competence when it submitted the proposal to list PFOS. However, in doing so, the principle of sincere cooperation (now Article 4(3) TEU) required that it take into account the fact that the Union too is competent in the matter and that a strategy had been agreed within the Council.

THE INTERNATIONAL WHALING COMMISSION

However, if the Union were *not* to be bound by a more stringent measure, the Member States would arguably be free to adopt it or propose it in the relevant international fora. Such a situation would typically occur with respect to an international agreement to which the Union has not acceded, often because the international agreement in question does not permit international organizations to become a party.

An example of this would be the participation of the Member States in the International Whaling Commission (IWC),[234] the international organization competent for the conservation and management of whale stocks. It was set up by the International Convention for the Regulation of Whaling,[235] to which the EU is an observer.[236] EU regulatory activity as regards matters pertaining to whaling does not come under the exclusive common fisheries policy,[237] but under the shared competence on the environment.[238] While Union action

---

[231] Council Decision 2006/507/EC of 14 October 2004 concerning the conclusion, on behalf of the European Community, of the Stockholm Convention on Persistent Organic Pollutants (OJ [2006] L209/1).

[232] *PFOS* (n 79) para 19.   [233] *PFOS* (n 79) para 102.

[234] See Kuijper et al, *The Law of EU External Relations* (n 5) 813–814.

[235] Signed in Washington DC on 2 December 1946, 62 Stat 1716; 161 UNTS 72.

[236] Membership of the IWC is only open to governments that adhere to the Whaling Convention. An amendment to the Whaling Convention allowing the EU to become a member would require the ratification of a protocol by all IWC members. The Commission adopted a proposal in 1992 (COM(92) 316) to negotiate the accession of the Community to the Whaling Convention, but the Council did not follow up on this proposal. In the context of talks about the reform of the IWC, the Commission in 2011 proposed to support proposals addressing the revision of the Convention including the possibility for the EU to become a party to the IWC: COM(2011) 495 final. At its meeting on 19 December 2011, the Council on that basis adopted a Council Decision establishing the position to be adopted on behalf of the European Union, in relation to matters falling within its competence, at the next three meetings of the International Whaling Commission, including the related inter-sessional meetings, with regard to proposals for amendments to the International Convention on the Regulation of Whaling and its Schedule: Council Doc 18153/11.

[237] Art 3(1)(d) TFEU.

[238] Art 4(2)(e) TFEU. Annex I to the TFEU lists the products coming under Art 38 TFEU on the common agriculture and fisheries policy. Chapter 3 mentions 'Fish, crustaceans and molluscs', but not marine mammals. The latter are only mentioned in Chapter 15.04: 'Fats and oil, of fish and marine mammals, whether or not refined'. In any event, EU action on whaling has as a rule been taken under environmental competence.

on whaling has been taken,[239] it would go too far to say that the Union has exercised its competence to such an extent that it has replaced the Member States within the IWC and is consequently bound by its decisions. The Court has put the threshold for that to happen rather high: in order for the Union to be capable of being bound, it must have assumed, and thus had transferred to it, all the powers previously exercised by the Member States that fall within the convention in question.[240] Given that EU action as regards whaling most likely does not meet that threshold, it would seem legitimate for a Member State to vote in favour of any measure proposed within the IWC that would strengthen the protection of whales beyond and above the protection agreed within the Union. That would quite clearly be the case if no position on such a proposal could be reached within the Council.

Would the same count if a position had been reached? Given that the EU is not a party to the Whaling Convention and cannot be bound by the decisions taken by the IWC, it would seem that it must follow from Article 193 TFEU that Member States ought to remain free to support measures enhancing the protection of whales, while being prevented from supporting any measure lowering such protection below the level guaranteed by EU law.[241]

THE MERCURY NEGOTIATIONS

The complexity of EU external environmental competences being what it is, whether and, if so, to what extent a specific issue that forms the subject of international negotiations falls within the competence of the Union or of the Member States is often less than clear. That situation will inevitably lead to competence quarrels between the Union and the Member States and between the EU institutions, all of which are bound by the duty of sincere cooperation in Article 4(3) TEU, a specific institutional application of which is now explicitly contained in Article 13(2) TEU, which provides for the institutions to 'practice mutual sincere cooperation'.

A particularly unseemly example of how things can go awry regardless is the saga surrounding the negotiations for an international binding instrument on mercury.[242] Elemental mercury is a shiny, silver-white metal that is a liquid at room temperature and is or was traditionally used in thermometers.[243] The potentially adverse effects of the presence of mercury in the environment have been well documented. Indeed, recent research has shown substantial economic impacts to the EU from neurocognitive impairment associated with methylmercury (MeHg) exposures. The main source of such exposure is seafood consumption, including many marine species harvested from the global oceans.[244]

Mercury controls have been shown to lead to reductions in fish MeHg concentrations at local scales, but global-scale action is needed to address the mercury problem.[245] Such action was the objective of the negotiations under the United Nations Environment Programme (UNEP) for a global mercury treaty, and the EU wished to take part in the process.

---

[239] eg Council Regulation (EEC) No 348/81 of 20 January 1981 on common rules for imports of whales or other cetacean products (OJ [1981] L39/1); Council Directive 92/43/EEC of 21 May 1992 on the conservation of natural habitats and of wild fauna and flora (OJ [1992] L206/7); Council Regulation (EC) No 338/97 of 9 December 1996 on the protection of species of wild fauna and flora by regulating trade therein (OJ [1997] L61/1).

[240] *ATAA* (n 106) para 63.

[241] See in that sense also L Krämer, 'Negotiating and Voting on Whale Protection within the International Whaling Commission (IWC)' (International Fund for Animal Welfare, 2010) 6–7.

[242] Further De Baere, 'Mercury Rising' (n 161) 640–655.

[243] UNEP Chemicals, 'Global Mercury Assessment' (2002) 40.

[244] EM Sunderland and NE Selin, 'Future Trends in Environmental Mercury Concentrations: Implications for Prevention Strategies' (2013) 12 *Environmental Health* 2.

[245] Ibid, at 'Implications for prevention strategies'.

In its recommendation of 15 July 2009,[246] the Commission suggested that mercury was a substance already regulated to a large extent by existing legislation at Community level. It requested that the Council authorize it to participate, on behalf of the Community in the negotiations, in consultation with the special committee designated by the Council in accordance with the negotiating directives. However, the Council Presidency prepared a text that provided for the EU and its Member States to be represented by the Commission and the rotating Presidency.[247] The Commission took a particularly dim view of that proposed arrangement.

What emerges from the publicly available documents, is that the Commission withdrew its recommendation, which led to an unprecedented institutional crisis. The first session of the intergovernmental negotiating committee (INC) took place in Stockholm from 7 to 11 June 2010. The absence of a decision authorizing the Commission to participate in the negotiations resulted in intense and protracted discussions between the Member States and the Commission on the issue of who should take the floor at the Plenary Session, on behalf of whom, and on what basis. That gave rise to what must have been a baffling spectacle. In addition to an opening statement by the Council Presidency on behalf of the Member States, an opening statement was made by the Commission on behalf of the EU, explaining that it was not in a position to negotiate and that the Member States likewise could not negotiate an instrument that affected internal EU rules. Further statements were then made partly by the Commission on behalf of the EU and partly by the Presidency on behalf of the Member States. The Commission further made it clear that if the Presidency proceeded to intervene on behalf of the Member States, it would likewise continue to take the floor on behalf of the EU. In order to avoid a further eye-wateringly undignified display of disunion, practical arrangements were subsequently agreed for the Presidency to speak on behalf of the Member States on certain topics and for the Commission to speak on behalf of the EU *and* its Member States on other topics.

A compromise was finally reached in late 2010. The Commission was authorized to participate on behalf of the Union in the negotiations on a binding instrument as regards matters falling within the Union's competence and in respect of which the Union has adopted rules.[248] The irony of this unedifying episode is that, in substance, all Member States agree that mercury should be phased out. The mercury negotiations should therefore have been relatively easy from a technical point of view. Nevertheless, all's well that ends well, as the international mercury negotiations culminated in January 2013 in the adoption of the text of a global legally binding instrument on mercury called the Minamata Convention on Mercury.[249]

CONCLUSION

Member States' desire to remain present on the international scene as autonomous actors appears not to have diminished after the entry into force of the Lisbon Treaty. The dispute in the context of the negotiations on a binding instrument on mercury between the

[246] Recommendation from the Commission to the Council on the participation of the European Community in negotiations on a legally binding instrument on mercury further to Decision 25/5 of the Governing Council of the United Nations Environment Programme (UNEP), SEC(2009) 983 final.

[247] Council Doc 9504/10.

[248] Art 1 of the Council Decision on the participation of the Union in negotiations on a legally binding instrument on mercury further to Decision 25/5 of the Governing Council of the United Nations Environment Programme (UNEP), Council Doc 16632/10.

[249] UN Doc UNEP(DTIE)/Hg/CONF/3. In accordance with its Art 31(1), the Convention is to enter into force on the 90th day after the date of deposit of the 50th instrument of ratification, acceptance, approval, or accession.

Commission as defender of increased consistency and efficiency in EU external environmental action through a more unified external representation under its aegis and the Council as the defender of Member State interests is telling in this regard. Mixed representation would appear to be here to stay even after Lisbon, especially in areas of shared competence. The mercury saga is arguably the most flagrant failure yet of post-Lisbon unified international representation and consistent and efficient external action and *PFOS* the most recent judicial reinforcement of the loyalty obligation. However, the international context within which the EU operates may also necessitate the continued presence of Member States in the external representation of EU competences, as the example of the IWC demonstrates.

Finally, it is perhaps a sobering thought that neither the explicit categorization of the Union's competences by the TFEU, nor the structures set-up to provide for a more unified international representation and consistent and efficient external action, nor indeed the reinforcement of loyalty in the Treaties and in the case law, appear to have been able to prevent the mercury debacle. It is therefore as yet unclear whether a more unified international representation and consistent external action, in external environmental policy as in other areas, will remain as elusive a goal in the post-Lisbon era as it has been up to now.

8 Managing the horizontal division of EU external competences

8.1 Pre-Lisbon

The point of departure for the relationship between the First and the Second Pillar under the old Treaty framework was ex Article 1 TEU, which provided that the Union was to be 'founded on the European Communities, *supplemented by* the policies and forms of cooperation established'[250] by the EU Treaty. Following a similar logic, ex Article 47 TEU was designed to preserve the integrity of the Community legal order and provided that nothing in the EU Treaty could affect 'the Treaties establishing the European Communities or the subsequent Treaties and Acts modifying or supplementing them'.

The court had to ensure this, pursuant to ex Article 46 TEU, and did so most notably for external action in *Small Arms and Light Weapons*, a case of great significance for the relationship between First and Second Pillar external action in the pre-Lisbon constitutional framework.[251] The Commission had brought an action seeking the annulment, for lack of competence, of Council Decision 2004/833/CFSP of 2 December 2004 implementing Joint Action 2002/589/CFSP with a view to an EU contribution to the Economic Community of West African States (ECOWAS) in the framework of the Moratorium on Small Arms and Light Weapons.[252] In addition, the Commission raised a plea of illegality, pursuant to ex Article 241 EC (now Article 277 TFEU), against Council Joint Action 2002/589/CFSP[253]

[250] Emphasis added.
[251] Case C-91/05 *Commission v Council* ('*Small Arms and Light Weapons*' or '*SALW*') [2008] ECR I-3651.
[252] OJ [2004] L359/65.
[253] Council Joint Action 2002/589/CFSP of 12 July 2002 on the European Union's contribution to combating the destabilizing accumulation and spread of small arms and light weapons and repealing Joint Action 1999/34/CFSP (OJ [2002] L191/1).

on which the disputed Decision was based. Both pleas were based on the same grounds. The Commission's quarrel was with the fact that the Council had adopted the disputed Decision under the CFSP, whereas the spread of small arms and light weapons is covered by Article 11 of the Cotonou Agreement, which was concluded under then Community competences.[254] The Court held that, in

> providing that nothing in the EU Treaty is to affect the Treaties establishing the European Communities or the subsequent Treaties and Acts modifying or supplementing them, Article 47 EU aims…to maintain and build on the acquis communautaire

and that a measure having legal effects adopted under the CFSP affected the provisions of the EC Treaty 'whenever it could have been adopted on the basis of the EC Treaty'.[255] This was in line with Advocate General Mengozzi's suggestion that ex Article 47 TEU had to be read as providing that 'if an action *could* be undertaken on the basis of the EC Treaty, it *must* be undertaken by virtue of that Treaty'.[256] The Court added that it was unnecessary in this respect to examine whether the measure prevented or limited the exercise by the Community of its competences. The only consideration that mattered is that if the provisions of a CFSP measure, on account of *both their aim and their content*, had as their *main purpose* the implementation of a Community policy, and if they *could properly have been adopted* on the basis of the EC Treaty, those provisions infringed ex Article 47 TEU.[257]

The Court also explicitly held that a combination of legal bases was impossible with regard to a measure that pursues a number of objectives or which has several components falling, respectively, within Community development cooperation policy and within the CFSP, and where neither one of those components is incidental to the other.[258] The Court did not, however, base this conclusion on what would seem to be legally the most convincing argument. The *Titanium dioxide* line of case law, according to which recourse to a dual legal basis is not possible where the procedures laid down for each legal basis are incompatible with each other,[259] created insuperable difficulties for cross-pillar internal measures involving the First and Second Pillars. Whereas CFSP measures were, in principle, to be adopted solely by the Council acting unanimously, development cooperation measures were to be adopted by the Council acting in accordance with the co-decision procedure.[260] Under the *Titanium dioxide* line of case law, these procedures would indeed seem incompatible. However, by not basing its reasoning on the procedural argument but on the position of principle that the Union could not have recourse to a legal basis falling within the CFSP in order to adopt provisions which also fell within a Union competence, the Court appeared to shut the door not only to internal cross-pillar measures with a legal basis in both the First and the Second Pillars, but also to cross-pillar international agreements. Such an approach was not conducive to overall consistency and effectiveness of EU external action in general and development cooperation policy in particular.[261]

---

[254] Partnership Agreement between the members of the African, Caribbean and Pacific Group of States of the one part, and the European Community and its Member States, of the other part, signed in Cotonou on 23 June 2000 (OJ [2000] L317/3).

[255] *SALW* (n 251) paras 58–60.   [256] Opinion in *SALW* (n 251) point 116.

[257] *SALW* (n 251) para 60.   [258] Ibid, para 76.

[259] Case C-300/89 *Commission v Council* ('*Titanium dioxide*') [1991] ECR I-2867, paras 17–21.

[260] Ex Art 251 EC.

[261] De Baere, *Constitutional Principles of EU External Relations* (n 7) 296–297.

8.2 **Post-Lisbon**

The picture has become quite different after the entry into force of the Lisbon Treaty. The third paragraph of Article 1 TEU now provides that the Union is to be founded on the EU Treaty and on the TFEU: 'Those two Treaties shall have the same legal value'.[262] Article 40 TEU now prohibits any *mutual* invasion of territory between the 'Union competences referred to in Articles 3 to 6 of the Treaty on the Functioning of the European Union' (ie the former First Pillar competences) and the CFSP.

However, it is not entirely clear how the Court of Justice might judge whether or not a First Pillar measure has encroached upon the CFSP, because as noted previously, the CFSP under the Lisbon Treaty loses its specific objectives. This makes the Court's objectives-based analysis in *Small Arms and Light Weapons* difficult, if not impossible to undertake. For example, the distinction between 'preserving peace and/or strengthening international security' (CFSP) and 'social and economic development' (development cooperation) would not resolve any border conflict between ordinary external action of the Union and the CFSP. Both would fall under the general objectives of the Union's external action, under Article 21(2)(c) and (d) TEU, respectively.

The matter was before the Court in the post-Lisbon *Legal Basis for Restrictive Measures* case.[263] There, the Court rejected the European Parliament's action for annulment against Council Regulation (EU) No 1286/2009 of 22 December 2009 amending Regulation (EC) No 881/2002 imposing certain specific restrictive measures directed against certain persons and entities associated with Usama bin Laden, the Al-Qaeda network, and the Taliban.[264] The contested Regulation amends Regulation 881/2002[265] to provide for a listing procedure ensuring that the fundamental rights of the defence and in particular the right to be heard are respected, following the Court's judgment[266] in *Kadi and Al Barakaat*.[267] The Court held that the contested Regulation was rightly based on Article 215(2) TFEU, thereby rejecting the European Parliament's argument that the measure ought to have been taken on the basis of Article 75 TFEU, which ensured a greater degree of parliamentary participation through the ordinary legislative procedure.[268]

In doing so, the Court refused to attach any of the objectives of Article 21 TEU specifically to the CFSP, against the advice of Advocate General Bot.[269] It therefore left the question open of how to choose between the CFSP and ordinary external action on the basis of the indications given by the Court in *Small Arms and Light Weapons*. Unless one is willing to adopt Advocate General Bot's approach and sacrifice the Lisbon Treaty's clear aim to infuse more unity in the EU's external action through a set of common objectives, the absence of specific CFSP objectives post-Lisbon makes it considerably more difficult for the Court to apply Article 40 TEU.[270] Perhaps the Court ought from now on to predominantly refer to the actual content of a measure instead of its objectives in order to determine its legal basis. The most viable approach is likely to be for the political institutions and, if

---

[262] See also Art 1(2) TFEU.

[263] Case C-130/10 *Parliament v Council* ('*Legal Basis for Restrictive Measures*' or '*LBRM*'), judgment of 19 July 2012, nyr. See further, G De Baere, 'From "Don't Mention the Titanium Dioxide Judgment" to "I Mentioned It Once, But I Think I Got Away with It All Right": Reflections on the Choice of Legal Basis in EU External Relations after the *Legal Basis for Restrictive Measures* Judgment' (2012–13) 15 *Cambridge Yearbook of European Legal Studies* 537–562.   [264] OJ [2009] L346/42.

[265] Regulation (EC) No 881/2002 (OJ [2002] L139/9).

[266] Joined Cases C-402/05 P and C-415/05 P *Kadi and Al Barakaat International Foundation v Council and Commission* [2008] ECR I-6351. See further Joined Cases C-584/10 P, C-593/10 P and C-595/10 P *Commission, Council and UK v Kadi*, judgment of 18 July 2013, nyr, and chapter 8, case study 8.4 and chapter 9, case study 9.1.

[267] Recital 4 in the Preamble to Regulation 1286/2009.   [268] Art 294 TFEU.

[269] Opinion in *LBRM* (n 263) points 62–63.

[270] Compare Eeckhout, *EU External Relations Law* (n 28) 169, arguing for a nuanced approach.

they cannot agree, for the Court, to determine where the centre of gravity of a measure lies 'all things considered'.[271] The Court has the chance to clarify this issue in a pending action brought by the Parliament against the Council.[272] The Parliament takes the view that a Council Decision, adopted within the CFSP,[273] on the conditions of transfer of suspected pirates and associated seized property from the European Union-led naval force to the Republic of Mauritius and on their conditions after transfer[274] is invalid because it does not relate exclusively to the CFSP, but also to judicial cooperation in criminal matters, police cooperation, and development cooperation, covering fields to which the ordinary legislative procedure applies. Therefore, the agreement should have been concluded after obtaining the European Parliament's consent in accordance with Article 218(6)(a)(v) TFEU. Hence, the Parliament is arguing that the Council has violated the Treaties by failing to choose the appropriate legal basis for the conclusion of the agreement.

What does the equality of the TEU and TFEU (as per the third paragraph of Article 1 TEU and Article 1(2) TFEU) imply for the possibility of legal instruments based on a combined legal basis in the EU Treaty as regards the CFSP and within the TFEU as regards the ordinary external action of the Union? In *Legal Basis for Restrictive Measures*, the Court noted that while Article 75 TFEU provides for the application of the ordinary legislative procedure, which entails QMV in the Council and the Parliament's full participation in the procedure, Article 215(2) TFEU entails merely informing the Parliament. In addition, recourse to Article 215(2) TFEU, unlike recourse to Article 75 TFEU, requires a previous decision in the sphere of the CFSP, the adoption of which, as a general rule, calls for unanimous voting in the Council acting alone.[275] Building on *Titanium dioxide*, the Court then added: 'Differences of that kind are such as to render those procedures incompatible'.[276] In other words, even if the contested regulation does pursue several objectives at the same time or have several components indissociably linked, without one being secondary to the other, the differences in the procedures applicable under Articles 75 and 215(2) TFEU mean that they cannot form a combined legal basis. The Court seemed to take the CFSP procedure necessary to adopt the basic decision under the EU Treaty as integral to the procedure to adopt the subsequent decision under the TFEU. While the Court has thereby not necessarily a priori excluded every combination between the ordinary external action of the EU and the CFSP, it has made such combinations rather unlikely.

9 Conclusion

Rather than merely reshuffling the occasional deckchair, the Union's external action system and by extension the Union as a whole appears to be constantly rebuilding the ship on the open sea, 'never able to dismantle it in dry-dock and to reconstruct it there out of the best materials'.[277] At the same time, Treaty amendment after Treaty amendment, the Union has seen a further development of its external competences and an elaboration of

---

[271] A Dashwood, 'Article 47 TEU and the Relationship between First and Second Pillar Competences' in A Dashwood and M Maresceau (eds), *Law and Practice of EU External Relations: Salient Features of a Changing Landscape* (Cambridge: Cambridge University Press, 2008) 101.

[272] Case C-658/11 *Parliament v Council* (OJ [2012] C58/6), pending. In his Opinion of 30 January 2014, AG Bot takes the view that the decision was rightly founded solely on a CFSP legal basis and accordingly proposes that the Court should dismiss the Parliament's application.

[273] On the basis of Art 37 TEU in combination with Art 218(5) and (6) TFEU.

[274] Council Decision 2011/640/CFSP (OJ [2011] L254/1).   [275] *LBRM* (n 263) para 47.

[276] Ibid, para 48.

[277] cf the metaphor by O Neurath, 'Protocol Sentences' in AJ Ayer (ed), *Logical Positivism* (Glencoe, IL: The Free Press, 1959) 201.

its institutional structure for external action. Furthermore, most actors in the Union have now realized that the fundamentally different approach to ordinary EU external action on the one hand and the CFSP on the other hand, forms a major obstacle to consistent and efficient external action. The need for the Union's socio-economic external action to form a part of one unified policy together with the CFSP was elegantly phrased by Dworkin, who saw it as an example of a valuable shift in political boundaries from smaller and more homogeneous political communities to larger and more diverse ones:[278]

> Both the European nations and the world will gain, I believe, if the EU is able to form a common foreign policy and execute it with the economic power of its community giving strength to its united arm.

Yet, rebuilding the ship remains a challenge, even in the face of evident structural problems. As discussed previously, the nominal abolition of the pillar structure essentially leaves the former Second Pillar in place. Nevertheless, the establishment of the office of the High Representative and of the EEAS is an attempt to bridge the divide between ordinary EU external action and the CFSP. The jury is still out on whether the result is a success, but it cannot be denied that the post-Lisbon institutional system has created opportunities to foster consistency, effectiveness, and continuity in the EU's external action.[279]

From its modest beginnings as a customs union (which contains an essential external aspect by requiring the adoption of a common customs tariff in the relations of the Member States with third countries),[280] the Union has come a long way to the current rather impressive array of external policies. That is a remarkable feat, as the tension between the self-consciousness of the Member States and their constitutional relationship within the Union is especially pronounced in external action, where they remain determined to assert their status as full subjects of the international order.[281] The Union's external action therefore operates as a multi-level system, reflecting the uniqueness of the Union as a body organized along federal lines but with fully fledged States as its component political entities. The complexity this involves is, to a significant degree, unavoidable. It does, however, make the Union an often slightly bewildering international actor for third parties as well as for students of EU external action.

Further reading

M Cremona (ed), *Developments in EU External Relations Law* (Oxford: Oxford University Press, 2008)

M Cremona and B de Witte (eds), *EU Foreign Relations Law: Constitutional Fundamentals* (Oxford/Portland, OR: Hart Publishing, 2008)

A Dashwood and C Hillion (eds), *The General Law of EC External Relations* (London: Sweet & Maxwell, 2000)

A Dashwood and M Maresceau (eds), *Law and Practice of EU External Relations. Salient Features of a Changing Landscape* (Cambridge: Cambridge University Press, 2008)

---

[278] R Dworkin, *Justice for Hedgehogs* (Cambridge, MA/London: Belknap/Harvard, 2011) 382.
[279] EP EEAS Study (n 103) 84.   [280] Art 28 TFEU.
[281] De Baere, *Constitutional Principles of EU External Relations* (n 7) 1.

G DE BAERE, *Constitutional Principles of EU External Relations* (Oxford: Oxford University Press, 2008)

P EECKHOUT, *EU External Relations Law* (2nd edn, Oxford: Oxford University Press, 2011)

R HOLDGAARD, *External Relations Law of the European Community: Legal Reasoning and Legal Discourse* (Austin/Boston/Chicago/New York/The Netherlands: Wolters Kluwer, 2008)

S KEUKELEIRE AND T DELREUX, *The Foreign Policy of the European Union* (2nd edn, Basingstoke: Palgrave Macmillan, 2014)

P KOUTRAKOS, *EU International Relations Law* (Oxford/Portland, OR: Hart Publishing, 2006)

P KOUTRAKOS, *The EU Common Security and Defence Policy* (Oxford: Oxford University Press, 2013)

PJ KUIJPER, J WOUTERS, F HOFFMEISTER, G DE BAERE, AND T RAMOPOULOS, *The Law of EU External Relations: Cases, Materials, and Commentary on the EU as an International Legal Actor* (Oxford: Oxford University Press, 2013)

B VAN VOOREN AND R WESSEL, *EU External Relations Law: Text, Cases and Materials* (Cambridge: Cambridge University Press, 2014)

25

EU criminal law

John R Spencer

1 Introduction

The second section of this chapter examines what EU criminal law consists of (which is not quite what the name suggests), the reasons for its existence, and the mechanism by which it is created. After this, sections 3 to 7 then describe in concrete terms the more important of its practical manifestations. As Member States tend to view control over their criminal law as a central feature of their nationhood, a recurrent theme of the chapter is one of tension – with Member States being torn between the practical necessity for certain problems in the area of criminal law to be dealt with at an EU level, and a deep-seated ideological resistance to this happening. A consequence of this, as we shall see, is that the bulk of the EU instruments of which EU criminal law is composed are designed to help and encourage the criminal justice systems of the various Member States to work together, rather than to impose upon them uniform rules of criminal law or criminal procedure devised by EU law-making institutions: a 'horizontal approach' to the problems of trans-border criminality, rather than a 'vertical approach' of direction from the centre.

2 What is EU criminal law?

The phrase 'EU criminal law'[1] suggests a European criminal code and criminal procedure code, with a European public prosecutor operating in a special set of EU criminal courts: a European version, in other words, of the arrangements that exist in the US. But at present, EU criminal law exists only in a looser sense, in concrete terms comprising five bodies of law governing five distinct but separate matters.

First, there is the body of law creating and regulating a group of European agencies which have been set up to secure the better functioning of criminal justice within the EU. Secondly, there is a body of law designed to facilitate cooperation between the police forces and other law enforcement agencies of the different Member States. Thirdly, there is body of law on what is called *mutual recognition*: rules requiring the criminal justice systems of all Member States to treat as valid and, if called upon, enforce rulings and decisions emanating from the others. Fourthly, there is the body of law the purpose of which is to shape, in certain respects, the substantive criminal law of all Member States. And finally, there is a body of law by which the EU has sought to do the same with criminal procedure. Each of these five areas of EU criminal law will be examined in greater detail in sections 3 to 7 of this chapter.

2.1 Why does EU criminal law exist?

The purposes of the EEC (as the EU formerly was) were originally economic: and at first sight, it is not obvious where criminal law appears on this agenda.

That said, it is obvious that EU law must at least impinge on the criminal law of the Member States in a negative sense, because it takes precedence over national law, including national criminal law, and will therefore override a rule of national criminal law that conflicts with it. So, for example, where EU law provides for free movement of capital, the criminal law of a particular Member State may not penalize the transfer of money from that country to another Member State.[2] A little less obviously, EU law also negatively impinges on national criminal justice systems by prohibiting their use – or their selective non-use – to frustrate the broader policies and purposes of the Union. The TEU requires Member States to 'take any appropriate measures, general or particular, to ensure fulfilment of the obligations arising out of the Treaties resulting from the acts of the institutions of the Union'.[3] Sometimes the obvious 'appropriate measure' is for the Member State concerned to bring its criminal justice system to bear upon the problem; and then a Member State that fails to do so is in breach of this obligation. And so it was that, in 1997, the European Court of Justice condemned France when the government, unwilling to offend French farmers, allowed the police to turn a blind eye to groups of them who took direct action against the importation of fruit and vegetables from other Member

---

[1] For more detailed information on this topic, see A Klip, *European Criminal Law – An Integrative Approach* (2nd edn, Antwerp: Intersentia, 2011); V Mitsilegas, *EU Criminal Law* (Oxford: Hart Publishing, 2009); and S Peers, *EU Justice and Home Affairs Law* (3rd edn, Oxford: Oxford University Press, 2011) chs 9–12.

[2] Joined Cases C-358/93 and C-416/93 *Aldo Bordessa* [1995] ECR I-361.

[3] Art 4(3) TEU; reproducing an obligation already existing by virtue of Art 10 EC.

States (by stopping lorries, beating up the drivers, and damaging or destroying foreign produce).[4]

It is less obvious why EU law should impinge on national criminal law positively, for example by requiring all Member States to pass a law making a certain type of behaviour punishable. What pressures, practical or theoretical, have led to this?

This sort of EU criminal law is sometimes justified as needed to further the fundamental policy of free movement. However, it would be nearer the mark to say that this body of law, or most of it, has been created in response to the unwanted consequences of free movement, rather than in order to promote it. In the wake of the free movement of workers, services, goods, and capital has come a further and unwanted freedom – the free movement of criminals and crime. Free movement makes it easier for a criminal who has committed a crime in one country to decamp to another. And it also leads to an increase in 'trans-border' crimes – for example, smuggling and people-trafficking – where part of the offence takes place in one Member State and part of it in another. To face these problems, the national criminal justice systems of the different Member States must help one another and coordinate their responses. Legal rules are needed at EU level to ensure this happens.

Another factor is the need for rules of criminal law to protect the interests of the EU as an institution. An obvious example is the EU's common currency, hence EU instruments requiring Member States to ensure that their criminal codes penalize counterfeiting the euro.[5] Another is the Union finances. It is concern about these matters which has led, among other things, to the proposal to create a European Public Prosecutor, which is examined later in this chapter (see section 3.4).

There are ideological reasons for the growth of EU criminal law as well as practical ones. Article 67(1) TFEU proclaims an objective of the EU to be the creation of 'an area of freedom, security and justice'. Viewed positively, this is the idea of an area in all parts of which citizens can be sure that the criminal justice system will treat those who come into contact with it with a certain minimum level of humanity, consideration, and efficiency, and it is in this spirit that EU instruments have sought to provide various rights for victims in criminal proceedings.[6] It is also this spirit which, at least in part, has animated the current move towards a series of instruments designed to guarantee various minimum rights for suspects and defendants.

2.2 Tensions

A number of factors combine to make the development of EU criminal law a particularly sensitive issue for the individual Member States.

The first, which tends to colour the attitude of every Member State, is the feeling that there is something about criminal justice which makes it by its very nature something for the nation-State, and the nation-State alone. The power to punish is widely seen as one of the essential attributes of statehood. And it is also felt that the rules determining what types of behaviour should be punishable, and how, should reflect the attitudes and beliefs of the

---

[4] Case C-265/95 *Commission v French Republic* [1997] ECR I-6959. See E Baker, 'Criminal Jurisdiction, the Public Dimension to "Effective Protection" and the Construction of Community–Citizen Relations' (2001) 4 *Cambridge Yearbook of European Legal Studies* 25.

[5] Council Framework Decision of 29 May 2000, 200/383/JHA (OJ [2000] L104/1); Council Regulation (EC) No 1338/2001 of 28 June 2001 laying down measures necessary for the protection of the euro against counterfeiting (OJ [2001] L181/6). See the proposed Directive on this issue, COM(2013) 42, 5 February 2013.

[6] See further section 7.

people of the State concerned, which may differ significantly even as between groups of people as geographically close as the citizens of the different countries of the EU.[7]

These concerns are reflected in the articles of the TFEU conferring competences on the Union to legislate in the area of criminal justice. For example, Article 82(2), which creates a limited power to adopt EU legislation harmonizing rules of criminal procedure, provides that 'Such rules shall take into account the differences between the legal traditions and systems of the Member States'. Similarly, some of these articles incorporate what is usually called the 'emergency brake': the right of any Member State which perceives intended legislation as affecting 'fundamental aspects of its criminal justice system' to call a halt to the process by appealing to the European Council.[8] And similarly, in EU criminal law there seems to be a legislative preference for 'horizontal solutions' over 'vertical solutions': legislation designed to help national criminal justice systems deal with a given problem collectively, rather than superimposing on the national systems a common set of rules, or subjecting them to the authority of a new central body.

A further and more specific source of tension is the diversity between the legal traditions of the different Member States – and, in particular, between the UK and the other countries in the common law tradition, and those which are usually said (at least in the English speaking world) to follow the civil law tradition, the roots of which go back to Roman law.[9] According to some people, the gulf between these two traditions is so wide that even attempts to facilitate cooperation are difficult, and attempts to harmonize are doomed to failure.

How true is this? Though the substantive criminal law of the different Member States is broadly similar,[10] something of a cultural cleavage does exist in relation to criminal procedure. Broadly speaking,[11] continental criminal procedure derives from an inquisitorial tradition, where a criminal court is viewed as an official enquirer whose task it is to find the truth. The criminal procedure of the common law countries on the other hand derives from an accusatorial (or adversarial) tradition in which a criminal court is thought of as a neutral umpire whose role is limited to hearing both sides and deciding if the prosecution has proved the guilt of the defendant beyond all reasonable doubt. But even here, the differences are less significant than is commonly supposed. Over the centuries the criminal procedure systems of continental Europe have been borrowing ideas and institutions from the common law systems, and vice versa.[12] In consequence, the modern criminal procedure of every Member State – including the UK and the Republic of Ireland – is now

---

[7] For these reasons the German Federal Constitutional Court has stated that it would if necessary strike down EU criminal law which conflicted with some principle central to Germany's constitutional identity. See BVerfGE, 2 BvE 2/08 *Gauweiler v Treaty of Lisbon*, 30 June 2009; extracts in English appear in D Chalmers, G Davies, and M Monti, *European Union Law* (2nd edn, Cambridge: Cambridge University Press, 2010) 585.

[8] For more on the notion of an 'emergency brake', see chapter 5.

[9] This bipolar view is of course a huge oversimplification. For a more nuanced view, see chapter 5 of K Zweigert and H Kötz, *An Introduction to Comparative Law*, trans T Weir (3rd edn, Oxford: Clarendon Press, 1998).

[10] A fundamental difference is sometimes said to be that the criminal law in the continental systems is codified whereas in the common law countries it is not. But this is a question of form rather than of substance. Cyprus, a Member State which is part of the common law world, has a criminal code, and likewise most of the common law countries apart from those in Western Europe; and in recent years there have been serious attempts to codify the criminal law in England and in Scotland.

[11] But only very broadly speaking; Italy, eg radically reformed its system of criminal procedure in 1988 with the explicit aim of creating a new system that was adversarial rather than inquisitorial.

[12] See M Delmas-Marty and JR Spencer (eds), *European Criminal Procedures* (Cambridge: Cambridge University Press, 2002) ch 1.

mixed, containing elements from both traditions. Despite this, the notion that the cultural cleavage between the accusatorial and the inquisitorial systems is a serious impediment to the further growth of EU criminal law is widely held. When the Lisbon Treaty (in force 1 December 2009) was negotiated it helped the British government to secure a series of opt-outs which will be examined in the next section of this chapter.

In Eurosceptic circles in the UK, the need to resist the growth of EU criminal law is bolstered by a further belief in what might be called 'the moral superiority of the common law'. This is the notion that the inquisitorial basis of criminal justice in continental Europe is inherently unfair, lacking all the safeguards known and valued in the common law. To anyone familiar with the modern criminal justice systems of continental Europe this is a gross distortion – even accepting that some of the systems, like our own, do have their faults. But distortion as it is, it is advanced as a reason for the UK to resist the growth of EU criminal law: because this would, it is assumed, undermine the common law.[13]

A more extreme version of this theory is that 'Brussels' is planning to impose on Europe a single, uniform system of criminal justice, based upon 'the inquisitorial system', by which the common law with all its historic safeguards would be swept away. Though nonsense, the idea has come to be widely believed[14] – in part, it seems, as a result of misleading and alarmist press coverage of the Corpus Juris project (discussed in section 3.4). When in 2012 a group of 102 Conservative MPs urged the government to opt the UK out of a range of measures in the area of criminal justice (see section 2.3.5) their open letter began by mentioning, as if it were a truth universally acknowledged, 'the EU Commission's ambitions for a pan-European code of Euro Crimes'.

2.3 Evolution and sources

2.3.1 The beginnings: (a) Schengen – alias CISA

The first serious moves towards the creation of EU criminal law took place outside the legal framework of the Community.

Impatient with the current lack of progress towards free movement, in 1985 the transport ministers of France, Germany, Luxembourg, Belgium, and the Netherlands met at Schengen on the river Mosel and signed an agreement designed to lead to the abolition of border controls between the contracting States. In 1990 this agreement led on to a formal convention, usually known as the 'Schengen Convention', or 'CISA' – short for 'Convention Implementing the Schengen Agreement'. In broad outline, CISA provides for the abolition of border checks at the frontiers between the contracting States, together with a swathe of measures intended to compensate for the resulting lack of control.

In the years immediately following, a number of other countries joined.[15] In 1997 the 'Schengen *acquis*' – CISA and the rules and regulations made under it – were 'integrated' into the framework of the EU by a Protocol attached to the Treaty of Amsterdam.[16]

---

[13] Thus legislation to implement the European Arrest Warrant was resisted on the ground that it would result in people facing an inferior form of criminal justice in 'places where the adversarial system does not apply'. See, inter alia, the speech by Oliver Letwin MP, HC 396, col 57 (9 December 2002).

[14] For a striking example, see the article 'The Corpus Juris and the End of British Common Law', ('*The People's Pledge*, 21 April 2011) http://blog.peoplespledge.org/2011/04/21/colin-bullen-corpus-juris-and-the-end-of-br itish-common-law/

[15] Including, incidentally, some which are not members of the EU: Norway, Iceland, and (subsequently) Switzerland and Liechtenstein.

[16] Protocol B; the version attached to the Treaties currently in force is Protocol No 19. For the text of the Schengen *acquis*, see OJ [2000] L239. On the immigration law aspects of the Schengen *acquis*, see chapter 26.

Integration was achieved by giving the Council of Ministers the power to deem the various articles of CISA and subsidiary instruments made under them to have been made under the different competences that the Treaties currently conferred upon the organs of the EC and the EU.[17]

As is well known to those who seek to enter it or leave it, the UK has retained the border controls which it was the main aim of CISA to get rid of. What is less well known, however, is that whilst retaining its border controls, the UK in 2005 then joined in most of the provisions of CISA on enhanced criminal justice and police cooperation which were created to compensate for the loss of them.[18]

2.3.2 The beginnings: (b) Maastricht and the Third Pillar

In 1992 the Maastricht Treaty created alongside the EC a new parallel body called the European Union, endowed with a range of legislative powers in the area of justice and home affairs under a set of constitutional arrangements known as the Third Pillar.[19] The Third Pillar arrangements were intended to be 'intergovernmental' – meaning that the governments of the Member States, rather than the Brussels institutions, were in control. Legislative decisions were made by the Council acting unanimously, so ensuring every Member State a right of veto. And if having signed up to a Third Pillar measure a Member State then failed to implement it, it could not be made the subject of infringement proceedings in the Court of Justice. National courts could seek guidance on the meaning of Third Pillar measures by making references to the Court where the Member State in question had chosen to opt into the procedure permitting this,[20] but some – including the UK – did not.

Initially, a further weakness in the Third Pillar arrangements was the feeble nature of the instruments that could be adopted under it.[21] But in 1997 this changed when the Treaty of Amsterdam added a new weapon to the armoury: framework decisions. These were the Third Pillar equivalent of directives adopted under the First Pillar,[22] and like those, bound the Member States automatically once adopted; though as previously mentioned, there was no legal remedy against Member States which, though in theory bound, chose to disregard them. Once available, framework decisions became the Third Pillar instrument of choice.

2.3.3 Transitional arrangements

It was under these two sets of constitutional arrangements that most of the legal instruments which currently make up the detailed part of EU criminal law were made. Under the Lisbon Treaty they remain in force until they are repealed or replaced. However, after a transitional period of five years, ending on 1 December 2014,[23] an important change will occur, in that the Court of Justice will acquire full jurisdiction over them. This means (among other things) that the Commission will then be able to bring infringement proceedings against Member States that have failed to implement them.

---

[17] Exercised by two Council Decisions of 20 May 1999, 1999/435/EC (OJ [1999] L176/1) and 1999/436/EC (OJ [1999] L176/17).

[18] Council Decision of 22 December 2004 on the putting into effect of parts of the Schengen acquis by the United Kingdom of Great Britain and Northern Ireland (OJ [2004] L395/70).

[19] The powers relating to police and criminal justice were contained in Title VI of the old TEU, Arts 29–42 (as renumbered by the Treaty of Amsterdam). On the 'pillar' system, see further chapter 2.

[20] Art 35 TEU (pre-Lisbon version).

[21] The Council could adopt 'joint positions' and initiate 'joint actions' – and in addition, draw up conventions, which only came into effect if the Member States chose to ratify them.

[22] On the concept of directives, see chapter 5; on their legal effect, see chapter 6.

[23] Protocol No 36, Art 10.

2.3.4 Current arrangements – general

After Lisbon, the main powers of the EU to legislate in criminal justice matters are contained in Chapters 4 and 5 of Title V of Part Three of the TFEU – comprising Articles 82 to 89. Though reflecting the earlier provisions of the old TEU which they replace, they are clearer and more readily intelligible.[24]

Article 82 TFEU deals (in effect) with criminal procedure. Having proclaimed the principle of 'mutual recognition', it provides that, to the furtherance of this end, the EU may (inter alia) 'lay down rules and procedures for ensuring recognition throughout the Union of all forms of judgments and judicial decisions'. And it goes on to provide that, 'to the extent necessary to facilitate mutual recognition', the EU may also adopt directives designed to 'establish minimum rules' in relation to a number of criminal procedure matters: 'mutual admissibility of evidence between Member States', 'the rights of individuals in criminal procedure', 'the rights of victims of crime', and 'any other specific aspects of criminal procedure' which the Council has agreed upon by unanimity, with the consent of the European Parliament.

Article 83 TFEU deals (in effect) with substantive criminal law. It provides that the European Parliament and the Council may enact directives establishing minimum rules concerning the definition of criminal offences and sanctions in those areas of serious crime which have a cross-border dimension or need a concerted effort to deal with them. 'Particularly serious crime' is defined as 'terrorism, trafficking in human beings and sexual exploitation of women and children, illicit drug trafficking, illicit arms trafficking, money laundering, corruption, counterfeiting of means of payment, computer crime and organised crime', plus other types of crime in future determined by the Council, acting unanimously and with the consent of the European Parliament. In addition, the EU may also adopt directives defining crimes and prescribing punishments where 'the approximation of criminal laws and regulations of the Member States proves essential to ensure the effective implementation of a Union policy in an area which has been subject to harmonisation measures'.

Article 84 is a general provision giving the EU authority to help Member States to take action against crime in the field of crime prevention by means other than 'the harmonisation of the laws and regulations of the Member States'.

Article 85 sets out general provisions in relation to Eurojust, the agency designed to help the prosecution authorities of the different Member States coordinate their activities, and Article 86 then goes on to provide a legal basis for the future creation of a European Public Prosecutor. More will be said about these institutions, one actual and the other potential, in section 3.

Articles 87 to 89, comprising Chapter 5 of Title V, confer competences in relation to police cooperation. Article 87 provides that the Union 'shall establish police co-operation', and to this end empowers the EU to legislate on 'the collection, storage, processing, analysis and exchange of relevant information', staff training, staff exchanges, and equipment, and 'common investigative techniques in relation to the detection of serious forms of organised crime'. It then provides a limited power to legislate for 'operational co-operation' between national law enforcement agencies. Article 88 contains general legislative provisions about Europol, the police coordination body, which will be discussed in greater detail in section 3. Finally, Article 89 empowers the Council, by legislation, to make rules about the operation of national police forces and similar agencies beyond their national boundaries.

---

[24] For a detailed analysis, see Peers, *EU Justice and Home Affairs Law* (n 1) para 9.2.4.

The 'measures' which the EU may adopt in the exercise of these competences are the normal ones set out in Article 288 TFEU – namely regulations, directives, decisions, recommendations, and opinions.[25]

The legislative route by which the EU is authorized to make them, however, is less simple to describe. Some, like the power in Article 82(1) to legislate for mutual recognition (see section 5), may be exercised by using the ordinary legislative procedure.[26] Others, like the power to create a European Public Prosecutor contained in Article 86, require a special legislative procedure under which the consent of the European Parliament is first obtained and then in principle a unanimous vote of the Council is required before the matter can go any further; but failing unanimity, nine or more Member States can 'go it alone' by the process known as 'enhanced cooperation'.[27] And legislation designed to harmonize national criminal law or criminal procedure follows a third type of procedure, incorporating what is usually referred to, rather dramatically, as the 'emergency brake'. Here the ordinary legislative procedure is initially followed – but where a Member State 'considers that a draft Directive…would affect fundamental aspects of its criminal justice system' it may refer the matter to the European Council,[28] whereupon the legislative process is suspended. If consensus on the matter is reached at the European Council, the process is resumed. If not, a group of nine or more Member States can then continue on their own – as with the European Public Prosecutor. (So far, the emergency brake remains unpulled.)

Are the legislative powers contained in Title V of the TFEU the limit of the Union's competence in criminal justice matters? Or could legislation in the area of criminal justice also be adopted on the basis of other articles? Under Article 325, for example, the Union can take 'necessary measures' to protect Union finances. Could these include legislation requiring Member States to adjust their criminal law, or criminal procedure? The Commission evidently thinks so, because in July 2012 it put forward a proposal for a new directive in this area, with Article 325 as the proposed legal basis, rather than articles contained in Title V.[29] From the perspective of the Commission, which wants to see this directive adopted, Article 325 has obvious advantages, because the ordinary legislative procedure applies, and the safeguards and limitations that hamper legislation under Title V do not apply. But the Member States, or at least some of them, are unlikely to see the matter in the same light as the Commission.[30]

Before Lisbon, a similar competency issue arose as between the First and the Third Pillars. On one view, the only legislative powers that 'Brussels' enjoyed in the area of criminal justice were those conferred on the (old-style) EU by the Third Pillar, the alternative view being that the legislative competences under the First Pillar permitted at least some criminal justice legislation to be made by the EC too. The issue eventually came before the Court of Justice, which – to the surprise of some – decided that the second view was correct.[31] Given the sensitivities of the Member States over criminal justice matters, it is

---

[25] See chapter 5.   [26] On the types of EU legislative procedure, see chapter 5.

[27] On the concept of enhanced cooperation, see chapter 5.

[28] ie the heads of government of the Member States, the President of the European Council, and the President of the Commission: Art 15(2) TEU. On the European Council, see further chapter 3.

[29] Proposal for a Directive of the European Parliament and of the Council on the fight against fraud to the Union's financial interests by means of criminal law, COM(2012) 363 final, 11 July 2012. On the concept of 'legal basis', see chapter 5.

[30] Indeed, in June 2013, the Council agreed a 'general approach' (ie its agreed position on the proposal, pending negotiations with the European Parliament) on this proposal, in which it took the view that the correct 'legal base' was Art 83 TFEU. See Council Doc 10729/12 (10 June 2012), available at http://register.consilium.europa.eu/pdf/en/13/st10/st10729.en13.pdf

[31] Case C-176/03 *Commission v Council* [2005] ECR 1-7879 and Case C-440/05 *Commission v Council* [2007] ECR 1-9097.

probable that the Court will eventually be required to rule on the similar question that arises under the new arrangements.[32]

2.3.5 Current arrangements – the special position of the UK, 'variable geometry'

Remembering the problems encountered by the UK government when seeking authority from Parliament to implement the Maastricht Treaty, its successor at the time of the Lisbon Treaty sought to ensure that the new arrangements took the UK no further down the route of 'Europeanizing' criminal justice than the Maastricht Treaty had taken it already. The UK government at that time therefore sought to insulate the UK from the two major changes then proposed: (a) the loss of veto entailed in the change from decision-making by unanimity to decision-making by 'QMV' – voting by a qualified majority, and (b) the jurisdiction of the Court of Justice.

From the first of these changes the UK, in company with Ireland, managed to insulate itself by Protocol No 21, under which neither State is bound by any new measures in this area except where it expressly chooses to opt in. This opt-out, it should be noted, applies not only to police and criminal justice measures, but to all measures adopted under any part of Part Three, Title V of the TFEU – which covers border checks, asylum and immigration (see chapter 26), and judicial cooperation in civil matters as well as the topics discussed in this chapter of this book.

Protocol No 21 provides two methods by which the UK or Ireland may opt in to a measure to which it applies. First, within a period of three months of a proposal or initiative being presented to the Council it may give notice that it wishes to join in – thereafter participating in the same way as the other Member States. This means that it is bound by the voting procedures, and their results. Alternatively, it may stand aside until the measure has been adopted, and if it likes the final look of it, ask to be allowed to join in then; at which point it may do so, provided it is able to meet any necessary conditions for participation.[33] In practice there is a third possibility: the UK or Ireland may initially refuse to participate, but express interest in doing so eventually. In this case, it will usually be allowed to take part in the negotiations, though informally and without a vote. If the other Member States are anxious to secure its eventual participation, this will – paradoxically – give the UK or Ireland greater leverage than when they join in at the start; because if the negotiations go against them, they can say 'Unless we get our way on this, we won't join in'.

This time going it alone, the UK also sought to insulate itself from the second of these changes – the acquisition of jurisdiction in this area by the Court of Justice. That the Court would have full jurisdiction over any new measures in the area of police and criminal justice had to be accepted, but the UK negotiators resisted the move to give it jurisdiction over measures adopted under the previous arrangements. Faced by this, the other Member States eventually conceded an arrangement giving the UK the right, at any time up to six months before the end of the five-year transition period, to notify the Council that it will cease to be bound by any remaining Third Pillar measures relating to police and criminal justice when the transition period comes to an end: after which it can seek readmission to such measures, if any, as it later decides it wishes to rejoin. This potential opt-out is contained in Article 10 of Protocol No 36, which deals with a range of transitional measures. Unlike Protocol No 21, it only covers existing measures relating to police and criminal justice, and does not apply to Ireland.

---

[32] G Corstens, 'Criminal Justice in the Post-Lisbon Era' (2011–12) 13 *Cambridge Yearbook of European Legal Studies*, ch 2 assumes that criminal justice legislation can be made on the basis of other articles; Klip, *European Criminal Law* (n 1) 168, believes the question remains open.

[33] The procedure is governed by Art 331 TFEU – one of the provisions on 'enhanced co-operation'.

Exactly what this provision was intended to achieve is not entirely clear[34] but it seems to have been part of a general game-plan to preserve the UK's position as it was under the Maastricht Treaty, rather than a device to enable the UK to denounce it.

In 2012 the UK government came under pressure from the Eurosceptic wing of the Conservative Party, backed by sympathetic newspapers,[35] to use this opt-out to resist 'the EU Commission's ambitions for a pan-European code of Euro-crimes',[36] and, more generally, as the first step in a process of 'repatriating powers from Brussels'. Convinced by these clinching arguments, in September 2012 the UK Prime Minister announced his conversion to this view[37] and some weeks later, the Home Secretary told Parliament that the government was 'minded' for the UK to exercise the opt-out and to negotiate to rejoin individual measures where that was in the national interest:[38] news greeted by the national tabloid the *Daily Express* with the ecstatic headline 'BRITAIN'S FIRST STEP TO EU EXIT'.[39] A nine-month period of silence followed, caused (it was said) by disagreement within the coalition government as to which measures it would be 'in the national interest' to rejoin. During this period the House of Lords EU Committee investigated and concluded that 'the government have not made a convincing case for exercising the opt-out' and that the consequences of doing so would be harmful.[40] Undeterred, in July 2013 the government reaffirmed its previous position, officially invoked the opt-out, and produced the list of Third Pillar measures it would seek to rejoin.[41]

To the uninformed reader, the list appears to be impressive. Of the 130 or so measures to which Protocol No 36 potentially applies,[42] only some 30 would be retained. However, these 30 are the key ones, and they include the European Arrest Warrant, which an important section of the UK's Conservative Party was particularly keen to see abandoned. As this book goes to press, the government is opening negotiations with the EU institutions and the other Member States as to the possibility of rejoining these 30 measures now that the opt-out has been exercised. To simplify a complex legal matter, the rules in the TFEU as to rejoining appear to give the UK the right, within limits, to insist on doing so – but potentially require it to indemnify the other Member States for any incidental expenses this 'in-out' exercise might cause them.[43]

A final point to mention about the post-Lisbon arrangements is the fact that, where the UK opts in to a new criminal justice measure, the government can now implement it by using secondary legislation. Previously, where the implementation of a 'Third Pillar' measure required a change in the law, primary legislation would usually be required. But as

---

[34] See the House of Lords EU Committee, 13th Report of Session 2012–13, 'EU police and criminal justice measures', HL Paper 159, paras 24–29.

[35] See eg P Johnston, 'We have European opt-outs, so why not use them', *Daily Telegraph*, 6 February 2012, and the *Daily Mail* for the same date, *passim*.

[36] See the open letter in the *Daily Telegraph* from 102 Conservative MPs, published on 6 February 2012.

[37] As reported in *The Guardian*, 28 September 2012.   [38] HC 551, col 34 (15 October 2012).

[39] 16 October 2012 (at the bottom of the page 'Daily Express Crusade – GET US OUT OF THE EU').

[40] See n 34.

[41] 'Decision pursuant to Article 10 to the Treaty on the Functioning of the European Union' (Cm 8671, July 2013). The notification of this decision is set out in Council Doc 12750/13 (26 July 2013), available at http://register.consilium.europa.eu/pdf/en/13/st12/st12750.en13.pdf

[42] For an analysis of the measures, and the impact of withdrawing from them, see A Hinarejos, JR Spencer, and S Peers, 'Opting Out of EU Criminal Law – What is Actually Involved?' (2012), CELS Working Paper, New Series, No 1, http://www.cels.law.cam.ac.uk/Media/working_papers/Optout%20text%20final.pdf

[43] For an analysis, see the Statewatch, 'The UK's Planned "Block Opt-Out" from EU Justice and Policing Measures in 2014' (*Statewatch*, 16 October 2012), http://www.statewatch.org/analyses/no-199-uk-opt-out.pdf

amended, section 2(2) of the European Communities Act 1972 now allows the government to use secondary legislation to implement any 'EU obligations', including those in the area of criminal law. This power cannot be used to create new criminal offences that are punishable with more than two years' imprisonment; but, at least in theory, secondary legislation could now be used to implement EU measures requiring rearrangements of criminal procedure, however radical.

3 Organs

3.1 OLAF

The European Anti-Fraud Office is usually known as OLAF, the acronym for its French name, l'Office européen de lutte anti-fraude. The oldest of the EU agencies in the area of criminal justice, it started life in 1988 as UCLAF (Unité de lutte anti-fraude), and was relaunched in 1999 as OLAF, with greater independence, a bigger staff, more extensive powers, and a supervisory body. Its powers and duties are set out in the regulation adopted when it was reconstituted, as since amended.[44] Its office, like that of the Commission to which it is formally attached, is situated in Brussels. As prescribed in the OLAF Regulation, the task of OLAF is to

> conduct administrative investigations for the purpose of fighting fraud, corruption and any other illegal activity affecting the financial interests of the Union. To that end, it shall investigate serious matters relating to the discharge of professional duties constituting a dereliction of the obligations of officials and other servants of the Union.[45]

To this end, it is equipped with wide inquisitorial powers. It is thus an example of the 'vertical' approach to the problems of crime within the EU – a central agency created to deal with problems itself, rather than to help national law enforcement agencies to do so. However, OLAF has no power to prosecute a fraud if it discovers one, and must leave this to the authorities of the Member States concerned; their perceived reluctance to take action is one of the main reasons for the proposal to create a European Public Prosecutor, which is discussed at section 3.4.

If OLAF's internal critics are mainly concerned about its inability to prosecute, its external critics have highlighted other and different matters. One of these is its awkward constitutional position, because OLAF is at once a part of the Commission and the organ responsible for investigating frauds and improper practices within it.[46] Another is the occasional heavy-handedness with which it has exercised its powers – which has led to several well-publicized pieces of litigation.[47]

---

[44] Regulation (EC) No 1073/1999 of the European Parliament and of the Council of 25 May 1999 concerning investigations conducted by the European Anti-Fraud Office (OLAF) (OJ [1999] L136), replaced by Regulation 883/2013 (OJ [2013] L248/1).   [45] Art 1(4).

[46] Mitsilegas, *EU Criminal Law* (n 1) 215–218; X Groussot and Z Popov, 'What's Wrong with OLAF? Accountability, Due Process and Criminal Justice in European Anti-Fraud Policy' (2010) 47 *Common Market Law Review* 605. And see the House of Lords EU Committee, 24th Report of Session 2003–04, 'Strengthening OLAF, the European Anti-Fraud Office', HL Paper 139.

[47] Notably Case T-193/04 *Tillack v Commission* [2006] ECR II-3995. For this and other litigation, see Mitsilegas, *EU Criminal Law* (n 1) and Groussot and Popov, 'What's Wrong with OLAF?' (n 46).

3.2 Europol

Europol,[48] the European Police Office, was created by a Third Pillar convention concluded in 1995 and which came into force in 1998. Since January 2010 Europol's constitutional document has been the Europol Decision, a Council decision adopted before the entry into force of the Lisbon Treaty.[49] Under this document, as before, Europol comprises a Management Board with a representative from every Member State, a Director (with three Deputy Directors), and a Supervising Body. It has legal personality, and its seat is in The Hague.

By Article 3 of the Europol Decision, the purpose of Europol is 'to support and strengthen action by the competent authorities of the Member States and their mutual cooperation in preventing and combating organised crime, terrorism and other forms of serious crime affecting two or more Member States.'

Though the idea of a 'European FBI' has had its supporters,[50] Europol bears little resemblance to the Federal Bureau of Investigation in the US. It is a 'horizontal' body, with no operational powers, the basic task of which is the collection, storage, analysis, and exchange of information about criminals and crimes. To this end, it runs the Europol Information System. Much of the Europol Decision is concerned with the management of this information system, and the issues of data protection that arise from it.

However, Europol can become involved in operational policing to some limited extent. First, by Article 6 of the Decision, Europol staff may participate in 'joint investigation teams' set up by groups of national police forces. Secondly, by Article 7, Europol has the power to make a formal request to a Member State to take action in respect of a particular case. A Member State that receives such a request is obliged to consider it, but is not required to act on it. If it decides not to act on it, however, it must give Europol its reasons, unless to do so would 'harm essential national security interests' or 'jeopardise the success of investigations under way or the safety of individuals'.

In April 2013, a proposal for a new Europol Regulation was put before the Council. Rejecting the advice of the House of Lords EU Committee,[51] the UK government has decided not to opt in. Instead, it is following the policy, described in section 2.3.5, of taking part in the negotiations informally, indicating that it will opt into the final instrument provided the other Member States agree to its demands.[52]

3.3 Eurojust

Eurojust[53] is an EU body which does for public prosecutors much what Europol does for the police.

As such it is the most ambitious of three schemes to support and coordinate their work – the others being the exchange of *magistrats de liaison* (ie public prosecutors seconded

---

[48] Mitsilegas, *EU Criminal Law* (n 1) 161 *et seq*; Klip, *European Criminal Law* (n 1) 387 *et seq*; Peers, *EU Justice and Home Affairs Law* (n 1) 930–934.

[49] Council Decision of 6 April 2009 establishing the European Police Office (Europol) (2009/371/JHA) (OJ [2009] L121/37).   [50] Including Helmut Kohl: see Mitsilegas, *EU Criminal Law* (n 1) 162.

[51] House of Lords EU Committee, 2nd Report of Session 2013–14, 'The UK Opt-In to the Europol Regulation', HL Paper 16.

[52] Statement to the House of Commons by the Minister, James Brokenshire MP, HC 566, col 863 (15 July 2013).

[53] Mitsilegas, *EU Criminal Law* (n 1) 187 *et seq*; Klip, *European Criminal Law* (n 1) 401 *et seq*; Peers, *EU Justice and Home Affairs Law* (n 1) 855–858.

by one Member State to another),[54] and the European Judicial Network – a network of 'national contact points' who, like *magistrats de liaison*, can give practical advice.[55]

Eurojust was created by a Council decision in 2002,[56] its constitution being amended by a second Council decision seven years later,[57] and its legal position then being further regulated by Articles 85 and 86 TFEU.

Like Europol, Eurojust is a legal entity and its official seat is also in The Hague. Its structure is also similar. At a formal level, it is composed of 'one national member seconded by each Member State in accordance with its legal system, being a prosecutor, judge or police officer of equivalent competence'.[58] The resulting 'college' elects a President and Vice-Presidents. Eurojust has a permanent staff, headed by an Administrative Director. Like Europol, it also has an external Supervisory Body.

According to Article 85(1) of the TFEU:

> Eurojust's mission shall be to support and strengthen co-ordination and co-operation between national investigating and prosecuting authorities in relation to serious crime affecting two or more Member States or requiring a prosecution on common bases, on the basis of operations conducted and information supplied by the Member States' authorities and by Europol.

These objectives are elaborated in greater detail by the 2002 Council Decision.[59]

Again like Europol, Eurojust has no power, as such, to require a Member State to investigate a case or institute a prosecution, much less does it have the power to do either of these things itself. By Article 6 of the Decision it may 'ask' a Member State to do either of these things and, indeed, a range of other things as well. These include asking Member States to set up joint investigation teams and, where two Member States are both engaged in investigating or prosecuting the same person, inviting one of them to 'keep off the grass'. Where Eurojust asks a Member State to take a course of action, that Member State is at liberty to refuse – though, as when a Member State refuses to accede to a request from Europol, it must give its reasons, unless to do so would 'harm essential national security interests or would jeopardise the safety of individuals'.[60]

If the formal powers of Eurojust are limited, its usefulness is great. A range of UK law enforcement agencies testified to this in their evidence to the enquiry by the House of Lords EU Committee into the Protocol No 36 opt-out, and even the UK Independence Party (UKIP), which opposes UK membership of the EU, grudgingly accepted that it had 'some utility'.[61] So, unsurprisingly, the instruments constituting Eurojust are included in the list of Third Pillar measures which the UK government wishes to rejoin if the Protocol No 36 opt-out is exercised (see section 2.3.5).

In July 2013 the Commission published a proposal for a new Europol Regulation.[62] It remains to be seen whether, when this is presented to Council, the UK will opt in – or, as

---

[54] Established by the Joint Action of 22 April 1996 (OJ [1996] L105).

[55] Established by the Joint Action of 29 June 1998 (OJ [1998] L191), which was replaced by Council Decision 2008/976/JHA of 16 December 2008 (OJ [2008] L348/130).

[56] Council Decision of 28 February 2002 (OJ [2002] L63/1).

[57] Council Decision 2009/492/JHA of 16 December 2008 on strengthening Eurojust and amending Decision 2002/187/JHA (OJ [2009] L138/14).   [58] Eurojust Decision, Art 2(1) (as amended).

[59] Eurojust Decision, Art 3.

[60] Under the 2002 Decision, Member States could also refuse to give reasons where to do so would 'jeopardise the success of investigations under way', but this phrase was dropped from the 2008 revision.

[61] See n 34, paras 196–198.   [62] COM(2013) 535 final, 17 July 2013.

with the proposed new Europol Regulation, will seek to exert greater leverage by staying outside and indicating that it will join later provided its demands are met.

3.4 **The European Public Prosecutor**

A European Public Prosecutor (alias EPP, or EPPO – European Public Prosecutor's Office) does not exist as yet, but it seems increasingly likely to be created.

The idea was first put forward in 1997 in a document entitled 'CORPUS JURIS – introducing penal provisions for the purpose of the financial interests of the European Union'.[63] This came from a study group set up by the Commission to consider the problem of budgetary fraud, prosecutions for which are currently a matter for the prosecuting agencies of the Member States, some of which show little appetite for it.

This 'vertical solution' was initially unpopular with the Member States and a two-part 'horizontal solution' was put forward as an alternative: a European agency to coordinate the efforts of national prosecutors, plus a system whereby the criminal courts of all Member States would automatically recognize and enforce one another's rulings. This led to Eurojust, discussed at section 3.3, and to the mutual recognition programme, which is discussed later.

Undeterred by the initial response, the Commission continued to press for a European Public Prosecutor. A legal basis for creating an EPPO responsible for prosecuting budgetary frauds was included (as from the entry into force of the Lisbon Treaty) in Article 86 TFEU,[64] and both OLAF and thereafter the Commission did their best to see that the idea remained alive.[65] In July 2013, believing that enough Member States were now in favour for an EPPO to be created as an exercise in enhanced cooperation,[66] the Commission published a detailed proposal.[67] As in the Corpus Juris project, this envisages an EPPO consisting of a network of delegated prosecutors, recruited from national prosecution services and located in their Member States, answering to a chief European Public Prosecutor based in a major European city – and dealing with budgetary fraud offences only.[68] But whereas the Corpus Juris also proposed a uniform code of budgetary fraud offences and a standard set of powers for gathering evidence in relation to them, the EPPO as currently proposed would have to make do with the legal tools provided by the legal system of the Member State where the offence was prosecuted.

A strange postscript is the reaction to this proposal in the UK.[69] In 1998, the Corpus Juris project was discovered by the *Daily Telegraph* and unmasked as a Brussels plot to overthrow the common law. This perspective on the matter was then internalized by the Eurosceptic wing of the Conservative Party. And when in 2011 the UK's European Union Act subjected

---

[63] Published by Editions Economica, Paris; a revised version, produced after further consultation by the group appears in M Delmas-Marty and JAE Vervaele, *The Implementation of the Corpus Juris in the Member States* (Antwerp: Intersentia, 2000).   [64] See section 2.3.4.

[65] In particular, by promoting a study, organized by the Law Faculty at the University of Luxembourg. For details and resulting publications, see http://www.eppo-project.eu/index.php/

[66] As noted earlier, Art 86 provides that, where Member States are not unanimous, a group of nine or more may proceed on their own.

[67] Proposal for a Council Regulation on the establishment of the European Public Prosecutor's Office, COM(2013) 534 final, 17 July 2013.

[68] Under Art 86(4), the European Council, acting unanimously after consulting the Commission, and with the consent of the European Parliament, could extend the EPPO's remit to other serious crimes with a cross-border dimension.

[69] JR Spencer, 'Who's Afraid of the Big, Bad European Public Prosecutor?' (2011–12) 14 *Cambridge Yearbook of European Legal Studies*, ch 14.

future 'surrenders of power to Brussels' to a 'referendum lock', the UK's involvement in any European Public Prosecutor was singled out for specific adverse mention (ie requiring a referendum before the UK could participate). Thus any future UK participation in this project is now effectively precluded.

4 Cooperation between law enforcement agencies

Instruments designed to improve cooperation between national police forces, customs officials, and other law enforcement agencies account for a sizeable part of the body of EU criminal law.[70] Of those currently in force, some are Third Pillar instruments and others derive from Schengen. In terms of substance there are three main types.

The first create databases for the automated exchange of information. Prominent among these is the Schengen Information System (SIS).[71] Under this system, national authorities enter in the database 'alerts' containing outline information about certain persons or objects – for example, that a person is wanted for arrest or extradition, or that a particular object is sought as evidence. The authorities of other Member States can search this database, and if they get a 'hit' can then ask the Member State that issued the alert for further details. There are other schemes as well, including a Customs Information System (CIS) and a Visa Information System (VIS).[72] Another EU scheme, usually known as 'Prüm' because of its origins as an intergovernmental convention concluded outside the EU legislative framework and signed at the German town of Prüm, aims to allow the authorities of one Member State to have direct access to certain crime-related databases held by others.[73]

The second instruments are schemes which give the law enforcement agencies of Member States the right to request information from those of other Member States, and impose a reciprocal duty to supply it. Foremost among these is an instrument usually called the Swedish Framework Decision,[74] which requires Member States to provide information and intelligence to law enforcement agencies from other Member States in the same way as, within that Member State, one agency would make it available to another. Other instruments create specific schemes in relation to particular types of information; for example, a scheme known as ECRIS under which Member States are obliged on request to supply, in a standard shape and form, details of a given person's criminal convictions.[75]

The third are instruments which provide a legal basis for cross-border operations. Of these, the best known is the 2002 Framework Decision on joint investigation teams, or JITs[76] – as used, for example, by the British and the French police to investigate the

---

[70] See generally Peers, *EU Justice and Home Affairs Law* (n 1) 906–924.

[71] The legal basis for which was initially a group of articles in the Schengen Convention (OJ [2000] L239). There is now a second generation of this system, incorporating photographs and fingerprints, which began operations in April 2013, the legal basis for which (as regards its criminal law functions) is Council Decision 2007/533/JHA (OJ [2007] L205/63). On the immigration law aspects of this system, see chapter 26.

[72] See respectively Council Decision 2009/917/JHA (OJ [2009] L323/20) and Council Decision 2008/633/JHA (OJ [2008] L218/129), which applied from 1 September 2013 (OJ [2013] L198/45). For more on the VIS, see chapter 26.

[73] It was incorporated into the EU legal framework by Council Decision 2008/616/JHA of 23 June 2008 (OJ [2008] L210/1).

[74] Council Framework Decision 2006/960/JHA of 18 December 2006 on simplifying the exchange of information and intelligence between law enforcement authorities of the Member States of the European Union (OJ [2006] L386/89).

[75] Council Framework Decision 2009/315/JHA of 26 February 2009 (OJ [2009] L93).

[76] Council Framework Decision 2002/465/JHA of 13 June 2002 (OJ [2002] L162).

mysterious shooting of a British family and a French cyclist in the French Alps in September 2012.[77] Parallel rules concerning customs operations are contained in an earlier instrument usually known as Naples II.[78]

To those trained in systems of constitutional law which allow public authorities freedom of action even where there is no specific legislative basis for it, the significance of some of these instruments might seem less than obvious. Why must we have, for example, an EU instrument providing for joint investigation teams or the exchange of information? Could the police of different Member States not cooperate in such obvious ways without one, on the basis that one good turn deserves another – or may at some future point deserve one? The reason is the risk of the arrangement otherwise infringing national legislation governing, for example, the disclosure of information by the police, or who may carry out certain types of act within the national territory. Where an EU instrument permits these things, all Member States are obliged (at least in theory) to adjust their national legislation accordingly.

In light of this, it is no surprise to see that the most important Third Pillar instruments in this group are among the ones the UK government has said that it wishes to rejoin, now that the Protocol No 36 opt-out has been exercised; although at present, for reasons which are not entirely clear, 'Prüm' is not included in the list.

5 Mutual legal assistance and mutual recognition

5.1 What is mutual recognition?

Mutual recognition is the arrangement whereby the decisions and rulings of the courts and other competent authorities of one legal system are accepted and applied by those of another more or less automatically. This differs from the type of arrangement that traditionally operated between the different nation-States of Europe, whereby such things were a matter of discretion, legal help was given as a favour rather than a duty, and was usually subject to the ultimate control of the executive. Extradition – the traditional arrangement under which wanted persons were recovered from other countries – was in this mould, and likewise 'mutual legal assistance', the traditional arrangement under which lesser forms of active help are sought and given. With these differences in mind, mutual recognition is usually said to follow an 'order model', whereas mutual legal assistance and extradition are said to follow a 'request model'.[79]

In a passive sense, mutual recognition means that the decision or ruling of a criminal court in another country must be given the same status as a decision of another court within the national system. In an active sense, it means that, in addition, active steps must be taken to enforce it. This part of the chapter deals with mutual recognition in the active sense. Three examples of mutual recognition in the passive sense will be discussed in section 7.

At the Tampere Council in 1999 the EU adopted mutual recognition as the way forward for dealing with trans-border crime in Europe – led in this direction by the UK, where mutual recognition has long operated between the different jurisdictions of England and Wales, Scotland, and Northern Ireland. Two years later an ambitious legislative programme

---

[77] http://eurojust.europa.eu/press/PressReleases/Pages/2012/2012-09-21.aspx (*Eurojust*, 21 September 2012).
[78] Council Act of 18 December 1997 drawing up the Convention on mutual assistance and co-operation between customs administrations (Naples II) (OJ [1998] C24/1).
[79] Klip, *European Criminal Law* (n 1) ch 7.

of mutual recognition measures was announced,[80] a substantial part of which has now been carried out.

At the time of writing, there are now eight instruments that provide for mutual recognition in the 'active' sense. These are the Framework Decisions on the European Arrest Warrant[81] and on the European Evidence Warrant,[82] the Framework Decision on the mutual recognition of freezing orders,[83] and the Framework Decision on the mutual recognition of supervision orders 'as an alternative to provisional detention'.[84] Then there are four further instruments relating to the cross-border enforcement of sentences imposed after trial and on conviction. These are the Framework Decision on the mutual recognition of fines,[85] the Framework Decision on the mutual recognition of confiscation orders,[86] the Framework Decision on the mutual recognition of probation orders and other non-custodial penalties,[87] and the Framework Decision on the mutual recognition of prison sentences.[88] And, in addition, a ninth instrument is in the legislative pipeline: a draft Directive to create a European Investigation Order, designed to require the criminal justice systems of the Member States under a general obligation to execute each other's orders relating to the collection of evidence.[89] Of these instruments it is the European Arrest Warrant (EAW) which has had the greatest impact and has provoked the greatest controversy. It is with the EAW that the rest of this section will mainly be concerned.

5.2 The EAW: its origins, and its main features

A number of features of extradition in its traditional form made it slow, costly, and uncertain.[90] First, to back up its request the requesting State had to produce prima facie evidence of guilt. Secondly, it was not available for 'political offences' or 'fiscal offences'. Thirdly, it was subject to a 'dual criminality requirement'; the requesting State had to show that the acts of which the wanted person stood accused would have been criminally punishable in the requested State, had they been committed there. Fourthly, many countries refused on principle to extradite their nationals: among them France, Germany, and Poland – though not, perhaps surprisingly, the UK. Fifthly, the process was political as well as legal, requiring the consent of the executive as well as of the courts. And, sixthly, because its availability in a given case depended on the terms of the extradition treaty (if any) between the requesting and the requested State, it was exceedingly complicated. With the increasing ease and frequency of travel within Europe, and the rapidly increasing number of extradition requests, the situation became intolerable. It was to ease this situation that the EAW was introduced.

---

[80] Programme of measures to implement the principle of mutual recognition of decisions in criminal matters, 2001/C 12/02 (OJ [2001] C12/10).

[81] Council Framework Decision 2002/584/JHA of 13 June 2002 on the European arrest warrant and the surrender procedures between Member States (OJ [2002] L190/1).

[82] Council Framework Decision 2008/978/JHA of 18 December 2008 on the European Evidence Warrant for the purpose of obtaining objects, documents and data for use in proceedings in criminal matters (OJ [2008] L350/72).   [83] Council Framework Decision 2003/577/JHA (OJ [2003] L196/45).

[84] Council Framework Decision 2009/829/JHA (OJ [2009] L294/20).

[85] Council Framework Decision 2005/214/JHA (OJ [2005] L76/16).

[86] Council Framework Decision 2006/783/JHA (OJ [2006] L328/59).

[87] Council Framework Decision 2008/947/JHA (OJ [2008] L337/102).

[88] Council Framework Decision 2008/909/JHA (OJ [2008] L327/27).

[89] For the initial proposal, see OJ [2010] C165/22.

[90] For some facts and figures, see Hinarejos, Spencer, and Peers, 'Opting Out of EU Criminal Law' (n 42) para 96 or JR Spencer 'The European Arrest Warrant' (2003–04) 6 *Cambridge Yearbrook of European Legal Studies*, ch 9.

With the EAW things are now very different. The transfer of suspects and convicted persons between EU Member States is now a purely legal matter, the final decision no longer resting with the executive. The procedure is a summary one, based on the production by the requesting State (renamed the 'issuing State'[91]) of an arrest warrant, not the evidence on the basis of which the warrant was issued. There are time limits: a final decision must be made within ten days where the wanted person consents to surrender and 60 days where he does not. Not only have the exceptions for political or fiscal offences disappeared:[92] the dual criminality requirement is also suppressed for 32 offences set out in what is usually called the Framework Decision List, provided they carry at least three years' imprisonment in the issuing State. And if the basic conditions are met, the requested State (now called the 'executing State') is obliged to surrender the wanted person unless one of a limited number of specified 'grounds for non-execution' listed in the Framework are made out. Significantly, these do not include the fact that the wanted person is a national of the executing State: gone, too, is the nationality exception. And finally, the resulting system is uniform, or nearly so, throughout the whole of the EU – so making it much more user-friendly for those who have to operate it.

The result is that, within Europe, far more wanted people are now handed over than was the case before. In 2003, the last year of the old system, the UK received only 114 extradition requests from the entire world, and only 55 people were surrendered.[93] In 2011/12, by contrast, the UK received 5,832 EAWs, and surrendered 922 persons to other Member States.[94] And the process is much faster. Taking the EU as a whole, it now takes on average around 17 days to hand over a wanted person who consents to his surrender, and around 48 days where he does not: as against around a year, the average time it used to take under the old system.[95]

5.3 Criticisms of the EAW

Of the criticisms that are made about the workings of the EAW, the most serious are two. One is its excessive scope, which enables it to be used in some cases that are trivial, or stale, or both. This problem is graphically illustrated by the much-publicized flood of EAWs emanating from Poland[96] – which worries the UK law enforcement authorities as well as those who speak for the interests of suspects and defendants.

This stems in part from the threshold conditions set out in the Framework Decision, which do not include a general requirement of proportionality – and in consequence of which there is no such requirement in national implementing legislation either. Under Article 2(1) of the Framework Decision, the EAW may be used, subject to the dual criminality requirement, for 'acts punishable by the law of the issuing Member State by a custodial sentence or detention order for a maximum period of at least 12 months or, where

[91] Except by the UK, which in the implementing legislation (Part I of the Extradition Act 2003) stubbornly retains the old terminology in Part I of the Extradition Act 2003.

[92] As between those countries that had ratified it, this had already been abolished by the European Extradition Convention of 1996.

[93] Figures from the Scott Baker Report: S Baker, D Perry, and A Doobay, *A Review of the United Kingdom's Extradition Arrangements* (2011).

[94] 2011/12 figures from Appendix 6 to the House of Lords EU Committee's Report (n 34).

[95] Figures from a report by the Commission to the European Parliament and Council, SEC(2011) 430 final.

[96] According to figures published by the EU Council in May 2011, during 2010 Poland issued 3,753 EAWs – considerably more than Germany, the runner-up, which issued 2,096. According to the Scott Baker Report (n 93), between 2004 and March 2011 the UK surrendered 1,659 persons to Poland – more than four times as many as to its closest competitor, the Netherlands (355).

a sentence has been passed or a detention order has been made, for sentences of at least four months.' As shoplifting is theft, and the maximum penalty for theft is likely to exceed 12 months in every Member State, EAWs are available for use against shoplifters as well as bank-robbers and bandits.

Part of the reason why the EAW is too often used in minor cases is that, as things stand, it is the only instrument available. This means that a State confronted with (say) a minor theft committed by a person who has removed himself to the UK has a choice between issuing an EAW – an instrument designed with grave crimes and organized criminality in mind – and letting the guilty person get away with it. This problem could be solved by creating a workable system for dealing with minor criminality committed across borders. The germ of such a system is already present in the Framework Decision, as yet little used, permitting the cross-border enforcement of fines.[97]

The second serious criticism of the way the EAW works in practice is the fact that it sometimes returns suspects to countries where they then spend excessive periods in prison before trial. This will be the subject of our case study.

Case study 25.1: *Andrew Symeou*

In July 2007 a fight broke out among a group of British youths at a nightclub in a Greek resort, in the course of which one of them, Jonathan Hiles, was killed. Eleven months later, long after the survivors had gone home, the Greek prosecutor issued an EAW accusing Andrew Symeou, a British youth who had been present at the club that night, of homicide. Symeou resisted surrender, claiming that he had been 'fitted up'. The evidence against him, he said, consisted of false statements beaten out of his fellow Britons by the Greek police: an allegation which the young men concerned confirmed. But the Divisional Court, upholding the decision of the judge below, held that, in the absence of any evidence that the Greek prosecutor was acting in bad faith, there were no grounds for resisting the surrender. The truth or falsity of the evidence on the basis of which he was accused, it said, was a matter for the Greek courts to determine.[98] So in July 2009 Symeou was sent to Greece – and there he spent the next two years awaiting trial. For the first ten months of this he was refused bail on the ground that he was not a Greek resident, being held in a prison where the conditions were particularly bad. When the case finally came to trial in June 2011, the court, on the recommendation of the prosecutor, acquitted him. In April 2013 the death was the subject of an inquest in Cardiff, at which Hiles's father accused Symeou of killing his son. A verdict of 'unlawful killing' was returned, the coroner stating that she was certain that Symeou was not the man responsible.

This is an unhappy story, even if justice in the end prevailed. And it has provided fuel to critics of the EAW, who argue on the basis of this case that the UK should withdraw from it.

But was the EAW really the root of the problem here? Even if, as under the old law,[99] the Greek authorities would have had to show a prima facie case in support of an extradition request, the material they had to hand would have satisfied that requirement.[100] Under the previous law, the Home Secretary might have used his discretion to block the extradition. But equally, like the Divisional Court in this case, he might have let it go ahead, saying that

---

[97] See n 85.   [98] *Symeou v Public Prosecutor's Office, Patras* [2009] EWHC 897 (Admin).

[99] The very old law – because as regards most extradition requests emanating from within Europe, the prima facie case requirement had already been abolished as between those countries which had ratified the 1957 European Extradition Convention; one of which was the UK.

[100] *Atkinson v United States* [1971] AC 197.

the truth or falsity of the evidence was a matter for the Greek courts to decide. In other words, the story might have been the same – though more costly and taking even longer.

The root of the problem here, surely, is that the Greek authorities took so long to bring the case to trial, and that Symeou was meanwhile forced to stay in Greece, for much of the time quite needlessly in prison. The injustice of the case would have been much reduced if he had been allowed to spend the period awaiting trial in England. In 2009 the EU adopted a Framework Decision that in theory makes this possible.[101] The deadline for implementing it was 1 December 2012 – but at the time of writing, both Greece and UK have neglected to do so. Long periods of pre-trial detention are a regrettable feature of criminal justice in a number of EU Member States. As we explain in section 7 of this chapter, the EU has expressed concern about this; to which the UK has responded by opposing the idea of EU legislation.

5.4 Mutual recognition: the UK's current position

In popular debate the EAW has been loudly criticized, often on the ground that it means Britons facing continental justice, which many in the UK see as 'inferior' to their own justice system; and the opportunity it provides for getting rid of the EAW was repeatedly put forward as a reason why the UK should exercise the Protocol No 36 opt-out. The UK police, by contrast, see it as a significant weapon in their armoury.[102] It is necessary, they say, not only to ensure that those who flee to Europe after committing crimes in the UK are brought to justice, but also to prevent the UK becoming a safe haven for foreign criminals – a colder version of the 'Costa del Crime' of not-so-blessed memory.[103] In this the police have won the argument, because the Framework Decision on the EAW features on the list of instruments which the government will seek to rejoin if the opt-out is exercised – as indeed do most of the other mutual recognition instruments. But the Home Secretary has promised changes to the UK implementing legislation.[104]

6 Harmonization of substantive criminal law[105]

The last 20 years have seen a rapid growth of European instruments requiring Member States, if they have not already done so, to make various uniform adjustments to their substantive criminal law. In every case, the obligation so imposed is to make a given type of antisocial behaviour punishable; and further duties are usually imposed about the severity of punishment, the categories of person to whom the law applies, and extra-territorial jurisdiction.

The range of matters covered by these instruments is wide and, broadly speaking, covers all the matters which, in the last few years, have agitated public opinion in the Member

---

[101] See n 84.

[102] See in particular the evidence from police sources quoted in the 13th Report of the House of Lords EU Committee (n 34).

[103] Since the EAW, Spain is being progressively emptied of its British criminals. See 'Why Spain's Costa del Crime is now the worst place to go on the run', *Daily Telegraph*, 18 May 2013.

[104] Statement by the Home Secretary, 9 July 2013, available at https://www.gov.uk/government/speeches/home-secretary-oral-statement

[105] Klip, *European Criminal Law* (n 1) ch 4; Peers, *EU Justice and Home Affairs Law* (n 1) ch 10.

States to the point where the media are demanding action and the politicians are promising to provide it. They include instruments on terrorism,[106] drug-dealing,[107] child sexual abuse and pornography,[108] cybercrime,[109] bribery,[110] money-laundering,[111] people-smuggling,[112] people-trafficking,[113] racism and xenophobia,[114] and frauds in relation to electronic payments.[115] With the interests of the EU itself in mind, they also include requiring Member States to make counterfeiting the euro a criminal offence,[116] as well as frauds against the budget.[117]

Worries are sometimes expressed that these instruments impose unreasonable burdens of criminalization on the Member States, and that in the case of the UK they are forcing our criminal law away from its traditional common law patterns. But when the content of these measures is examined it is clear that this not the case. With the exception of bribery and people-trafficking, where the UK legislator was more than willing to extend the law, all the types of conduct at which the instruments are aimed were already criminal offences in all parts of the UK and no adjustment of national law was required to comply with them. And similarly, the maximum penalties that these instruments require are invariably lower than those that UK courts were already entitled to impose.

All this is true not only as regards the types of behaviour and the maximum penalties, but also the range of persons whom the instruments require the Member States to bring within the purview of the offences. A feature of all these instruments is that they require Member States to ensure that criminal liability extends to incitement, aiding and abetting, and attempt, and also that they extend to 'legal persons' – that is, corporations. Though contrary to the traditions of the criminal law of certain Member States, these forms of extended criminal liability are well-established features of the criminal law in all parts of the UK, where they existed long before the EU was created; indeed, far from being examples of 'Brussels' forcing the alien traditions of continental criminal justice on the common law, their presence in these instruments appears to be a cultural transfer in the opposite direction. Pulling the other way, another standard provision in these instruments is an article requiring Member States to create extra-territorial jurisdiction over these offences when committed by their nationals – a feature common in the continental systems, but rare in the UK.[118] However, even this has not obliged the UK to depart from its traditions when it did not wish to do so, because these instruments usually permit those Member States that do not wish to comply with this obligation to avoid it by giving notice to the General Secretariat of the Council and the Commission.

---

[106] Council Framework Decision 2002/475/JHA of 13 June 2002 on combating terrorism (OJ [2002] L164/3). [107] Council Framework Decision 2004/757/JHA (OJ [2004] L335).

[108] Directive 2011/92/EU (OJ [2011] L335/1). [109] Directive 2013/40/EU (OJ [2013] L218/8).

[110] Council Framework Decision 2003/568/JHA (OJ [2003] L192/54).

[111] Council Framework Decision 2001/500/JHA (OJ [2001] L182).

[112] Council Framework Decision 2002/946/JHA (OJ [2002] L328).

[113] Directive 2011/36/EU (OJ [2011] L101/1).

[114] Council Framework Decision 2008/913/JHA (OJ [2008] L328/55).

[115] Council Framework Decision 2001/413/JHA (OJ [2001] L149/1).

[116] Council Framework Decision 2000/383/JHA (OJ [2000] L140/1).

[117] Council Act of 26 July 1995 drawing up the Convention on the protection of the European Communities' financial interests (OJ [1995] C316), http://eur-lex.europa.eu/LexUriServ/LexUriServ.do?uri=CELEX:31995F 1127%2803%29:EN:NOT.

[118] Though not unknown: the Offences Against the Person Act 1861, s 9 creates extra-territorial jurisdiction over homicide committed by British subjects; and s 7 of the Antarctic Act 1994 makes it an offence for a UK national, or a foreign national on a British expedition, to (inter alia) disturb nesting penguins.

Nearly all of these instruments were adopted under the Third Pillar and hence fall within the scope of the Protocol No 36 opt-out. And the UK government's current thinking is that, if the opt-out is exercised, it will not seek to secure the UK's readmission to any of them, apart from one decision dealing with online child pornography.[119] The argument for this position is, in essence, 'there's nothing in any of these for us, so we might as well be shot of them'.

This is a strange position to adopt, for many reasons. It is true that the only concrete benefit the UK derives from this body of instruments is the knowledge that where these things are done in other Member States to victims who are British citizens or UK institutions prosecutions are likely to result, and this is slight. However, turning to the other side of the equation the burdens they impose are non-existent. Our law already complies with all of them. And as it is inconceivable that the UK would ever wish to decriminalize the sorts of conduct at which they are directed, the freedom of action it would supposedly acquire by withdrawing from them is in truth completely worthless. Furthermore, if the government believes that it is somehow contrary to principle for the UK to submit any EU obligation requiring certain forms of behaviour to be criminalized, it is very odd that, just before the Protocol No 36 issue became politically significant, it opted the UK into new (post-Lisbon) EU instruments on people-trafficking, child abuse and pornography, and cybercrime, to none of which the Protocol No 36 opt-out applies.

Here, it looks as if the internal need to make a gesture pleasing to the UK's Eurosceptics has trumped the external need to show international solidarity in fighting forms of crime that tend to have trans-border implications.

7 Harmonization of criminal procedure

Broadly speaking, the EU has adopted legislation affecting the national criminal procedure of the Member States in two different ways. The first is legislation which requires the criminal courts of Member States to take account in current criminal proceedings of steps taken by the criminal justice systems of other Member States in earlier criminal proceedings involving the same person: mutual recognition, but in a passive sense. The second is legislation designed to ensure minimum standards of decent treatment for those who are caught up in criminal proceedings, either as complainants or defendants. In each case, there is a connection – or perceived connection – between the legislation and free movement.

Of passive mutual recognition measures there are three.

The first is a group of articles in the CISA designed to ensure that the 'ne bis in idem' principle, alias the rule against double jeopardy, applies where the case against the defendant has already been dealt with by the criminal justice system of another Member State.[120] The key provision is Article 54 of the Convention, which is as follows:

> A person whose trial has been finally disposed of in one Contracting Party may not be prosecuted in another Contracting party for the same acts provided that, if a penalty has been imposed, it has been enforced, is actually in the process of being enforced or can no longer be enforced under the laws of the sentencing Contracting Party.

[119] Council Decision 2000/375/JHA (OJ [2000] L138).
[120] Mitsilegas, *EU Criminal Law* (n 1) 143 *et seq*; Klip, *European Criminal Law* (n 1) 251 *et seq*; E Sharpston and JM Fernandez-Martin, 'Some Reflections on Schengen Free Movement Rights' (2007–08) 10 *Cambridge Yearbook of European Legal Studies*, ch 15.

The Court of Justice has interpreted this provision widely – holding, for example, that it applies not only where the case has been 'finally disposed of' by a court but also when a public prosecutor, avoiding court proceedings, has closed the file by imposing what is called in English law a conditional caution.[121] This broad approach was said to be justified by the need to encourage free movement: which would be inhibited, it is said, if citizens thought that their criminal past, seemingly behind them, could haunt them with the threat of further punishment when they cross a national border.[122] But Article 54, it should be noted, is only applicable where the criminal proceedings in the other Member State are 'done and dusted'. At present, nothing in EU criminal law bars multiple criminal proceedings for the same offence, if brought simultaneously, not in succession; although a rather vacuous Third Pillar instrument encourages Member States to avoid this situation by consultation.[123]

The second passive mutual recognition instrument is the Framework Decision requiring Member States to give the same weight and effect to previous convictions imposed by the courts of other Member States as they give to previous convictions imposed by their own courts.[124] So where a previous conviction exposes a defendant to the possibility of a higher penalty, this must apply to previous convictions in all other parts of the EU. As with Article 54 of Schengen, the background to this instrument is the policy of free movement – but the aim here is to deal with the consequences, rather than to encourage it. Together with the ECRIS Framework Decision requiring Member States to provide information about criminal records on demand,[125] the object is to make sure that repeat offenders do not transform themselves into first offenders each time they cross a national border.

The third of the passive mutual recognition measures is Article 26(1) of the Framework Decision that created the EAW.[126] This provides that, when sentencing the person it has recovered by using an EAW, the issuing State must deduct from the sentence any period the wanted person spent in prison while the EAW was being executed.

The EU's first attempts to impose minimum standards of decent treatment for the participants in criminal proceedings were directed towards helping complainants – a group whom the legislation, like the media, insists on calling 'victims'.

A Framework Decision on the standing of victims was adopted in 2001,[127] and it was this instrument which, on a reference from a court in Italy, gave rise to the famous *Pupino* decision.[128] Eleven years later this was followed by a Directive,[129] a more elaborate document which will replace the earlier instrument in 2015. This contains no fewer than 22 articles listing specific rights and protections for victims which Member States must ensure are granted by their national systems of criminal procedure. This list is long and here the discussion will be limited to some specific issues only.

Critics of the UK legal system sometimes say that the victim is the criminal justice system's 'forgotten person'. This point is often underlined by comparing the common law systems with some of those in continental Europe, in which the complainant who wishes has

---

[121] Joined Cases C-187/01 and C-385/01 *Hüseyin Gözütok & Klaus Brügge* [2003] ECR I-1345.

[122] See Sharpston and Fernandez-Martin, 'Some Reflections on Schengen Free Movement Rights' (n 120).

[123] Council Framework Decision 2009/948/JHA (OJ [2009] L328).

[124] Council Framework Decision 2008/675/JHA (OJ [2008] L220/32).   [125] See n 75.

[126] See sections 5.2–5.4.   [127] Council Framework Decision 2001/220/JHA (OJ [2001] L82/1).

[128] Case C-105/03 *Pupino* [2005] ECR I-5285, in which the Court of Justice ruled that framework decisions were subject to the same rule as directives, as regards the obligation to interpret national legislation in conformity with them. See further chapter 6.

[129] Directive 2012/29 EU of the European Parliament and of the Council of 25 October 2012 establishing minimum standards on the rights, support and protection of victims of crime, and replacing Council Framework Decision 2001/220/JHA (OJ [2012] L315).

the right to be made an official party – as in France, where he or she can join in a prosecution as a *partie civile*. The 2012 Directive stops short of requiring those Member States where the official status of *partie civile* is unknown to introduce it. However, it does require them to grant complainants a number of rights which, on those systems, would flow from this status automatically. One of these is the right to be heard, which is guaranteed by Article 10, and another, guaranteed by Article 11, is the right to a review of a decision not to prosecute. Had it wished, the UK might perhaps have sidestepped the right to review by reference to a phrase which says the right is be 'in accordance with [the victim's] role in the relevant justice system'. But far from taking this approach, the Crown Prosecution Service has now introduced a formal system of review of decisions of this sort.[130]

Other articles confer on victims rights to various forms of practical protection. Article 23, for example, requires Member States to provide 'measures to avoid unnecessary questioning concerning the victim's private life' and Article 24 requires interviews with child victims to be audiovisually recorded, the resulting interviews to be admissible in evidence.

In addition, the 2011 Directive on people-trafficking[131] requires Member States to ensure that those who are victims of this offence are not then prosecuted for criminal offences which, having been trafficked, they are then forced to commit. In light of this, the Court of Appeal of England and Wales recently quashed the convictions of a group of people who appeared to fall within the scope of this provision – taking the view that a prosecution brought in such circumstances amounted to an abuse of process.[132]

To complete the picture, mention should be made of the 2004 Directive[133] – a First Pillar instrument – which requires all Member States to operate national schemes for compensating the victims of violent crime where they are visitors from other Member States.

Negotiations on a Framework Decision guaranteeing certain minimum rights for defendants began in 2003, shortly after the creation of the EAW.[134] Three years later, however, progress in this direction was abruptly halted when the British government, initially in favour, changed tack and used its political muscle to block it. The reasons for this were never publicly explained, and by the autumn of 2009 the British government had changed its mind again, and was actively backing the Commission in drawing up a 'road map' of proposed new instruments designed to ensure the protection of defendants.[135]

This road map set out a legislative programme containing the following six measures:

(a) an instrument guaranteeing, for those who need it, translation and interpretation;

(b) an instrument guaranteeing the provision, for suspects and defendants, of information about the charges against them, and their rights;

(c) an instrument guaranteeing the provision, within limits, of legal aid and advice;

(d) an instrument guaranteeing detained suspects the right to contact relatives, employers, and consular officials;

---

[130] Victims' Right to Review Scheme, June 2013; details on the CPS website at http://www.cps.gov.uk/victims_witnesses/victims_right_to_review/index.html   [131] See n 113.

[132] *R v L (Children's Commissioner for England and Equality and Human Rights Commission intervening)* [2013] EWCA Crim 991.

[133] Council Directive 2004/80/EC of 29 April 2004 relating to compensation to crime victims (OJ [2004] L261). The UK's opt-out from pre-Lisbon measures does not apply to this Directive.

[134] Green Paper from the Commission, 'Procedural Safeguards for Suspects and Defendants in Criminal Proceedings throughout the European Union', COM(2003)75 final, 19 February 2003; followed by 'A Proposal for a Council Framework Decision on Certain Procedural Rights in Criminal Proceedings throughout the European Union', COM(2004) 328, 28 April 2004.

[135] Resolution of the Council of 30 November 2009 on a Roadmap for strengthening procedural rights of suspected or accused persons in criminal proceedings (OJ [2009] C295/1).

(e) an instrument guaranteeing special safeguards for suspects or accused persons who are vulnerable;

(f) a Green Paper on pre-trial detention.

At the time of writing, work towards implementation of the road map is continuing. Directives have been adopted in respect of measures (a) to (c).[136] To each of measures (a) and (b) the UK has opted in, and it is bound to apply them once the relevant transposition deadlines have passed.[137] The UK has, by contrast, so far refused to opt into the proposal for measure (c) – which will guarantee suspects access to legal advice; though it may opt into the Directive after its adoption, if it decides that the contents are to its taste. Measure (f), the Green Paper on pre-trial detention, was published in June 2011.[138] The UK's reaction to this was to make it plain that the UK would not be in favour of EU legislation in this area;[139] a negative stance which is disappointing, given that over-long periods of pre-trial detention are a vice to which the criminal justice systems of a number of Member States are prone, and – as we saw from the *Symeou* case – a vice which undermines public support for mutual recognition. Discussions on the other road map measures are still at a preliminary stage.

The legal basis on which legal measures to improve the position of victims and defendants have been adopted is Article 82(2) TFEU. This, as we saw earlier, confers on the Union a competence to create legal measures designed to harmonize the criminal procedure of the Member States 'to the extent necessary to facilitate mutual recognition of judgments and judicial decisions and police and judicial co-operation in criminal matters having a cross-border dimension'. At first sight this seems strange: one would have thought that, in the 'area of freedom, security and justice' which Article 67(1) proclaims, ensuring decent treatment for participants in criminal proceedings would be a valid objective in itself, irrespective of its impact (if any) on mutual recognition. However, Article 67(1) must be interpreted in light of the more specific provisions in the later articles. Regrettably, perhaps, these give the EU no power, as such, to require Member States to clean up their criminal justice systems just because their current state of hygiene is imperfect.

8 Conclusion

Because EU criminal law is currently in a state of flux its future shape is difficult to foresee. However, it is thought that two predictions can be safely made. The first is that, as long as free movement prevails within the EU, a body of EU criminal law will be necessary to deal with the unwanted consequences, and that in future there will probably be more of it, not less. The second is that there will continue to be disagreement as to whether the 'horizontal' or the 'vertical' approach should be followed.

---

[136] Directive 2010/64 EU of the European Parliament and of the Council of 20 October 2010 on the right to interpretation and translation in criminal proceedings (OJ [2010] L280/1); Directive 2012/13/EU of the European Parliament and of the Council of 22 May 2012 on the right to information in criminal proceedings (OJ [2012] L142/1); Directive 2013/48/EU of the European Parliament and of the Council of 22 October 2013 on the right of access to a lawyer in criminal proceedings [etc] (OJ [2013] L294/1).

[137] 2 June 2014 in the case of the Directive on information; the Directive on interpretation and translation had to be applied from 27 October 2013.

[138] Strengthening mutual trust in the European judicial area – A Green Paper on the application of EU criminal justice legislation in the field of detention, COM(2011) 327 final, 14 June 2011, available at http://eur-lex.europa.eu/LexUriServ/LexUriServ.do?uri=COM:2011:0327:FIN:EN:PDF

[139] Set out in the 59th Report of Session 2010–12, European Scrutiny Committee, available at http://www.publications.parliament.uk/pa/cm201012/cmselect/cmeuleg/428-liv/42804.htm

From the perspective of the Member States, which tend to resent EU interference with their criminal justice systems, the horizontal approach is usually preferred. However, whether criminal justice is viewed from a 'crime control' perspective or a 'human rights' perspective, there is surely much to be said in favour of the vertical approach. As the EU grows, so the task of coordinating the activities of the national criminal justice systems of the Member States gets harder. And as the *Symeou* case shows, some of those criminal justice systems have worrying defects – defects which, realistically, only a policy of improvement driven from the centre is likely to remove.

Further reading

D CHALMERS, G DAVIES, AND G MONTI, *European Union Law* (2nd edn, Cambridge: Cambridge University Press: 2010) ch 14

A HINAREJOS, J SPENCER, AND S PEERS, 'Opting Out of EU Criminal Law: What is Actually Involved?' (2012), CELS Working Paper, New Series, No 1, http://www.cels.law.cam.ac.uk/Media/working_papers/Optout%20text%20final.pdf

HOUSE OF LORDS EUROPEAN UNION COMMITTEE, 13th Report of Session 2012–13, 'EU Police and Criminal Justice Measures: The UK's 2014 Opt-Out Decision', HL Paper 159

A KLIP, *European Criminal Law – An Integrative Approach* (2nd edn, Antwerp: Intersentia, 2011)

S MIETTINEN, *Criminal Law and Policy in the European Union* (Abingdon: Routledge, 2013)

V MITSILEGAS, *EU Criminal Law* (Oxford: Hart Publishing, 2009)

S PEERS, *EU Justice and Home Affairs Law* (3rd edn, Oxford: Oxford University Press, 2011) chs 9–12

J PRADEL, G CORSTENS, AND G VERMEULEN, *Droit pénal européen* (Paris: Dalloz, 2009)

26

Immigration and asylum

Steve Peers

1 Introduction

Many non-EU citizens visit the EU for a short period, and then leave, yet others stay for longer, sometimes indefinitely. Most enter legally, but some enter without authorization. Some come to join family, to work, or to study, while others enter unwillingly, because they have been trafficked into the territory or are forced by circumstances to leave their country of origin. The EU's involvement in this field of law must not only address these diverse aspects of migration in a coherent way, but also has to manage two distinct but related conflicts: the balance between EU competence in this field and national sovereignty, and the tension between immigration control and the protection of human rights. These two conflicts overlap to the extent that national interior ministries often wish to focus on the perceived security risks of migration, while at least some EU institutions would place a greater priority on human rights protection. Both of these overlapping conflicts will be explored in this chapter.

2 The legal framework

The basic legal framework for the adoption of EU rules on immigration and asylum has changed a number of times, but has moved steadily towards enhanced EU competence and a greater role for the supranational 'Community method'.[1]

2.1 Prior to the Treaty of Amsterdam

Initially, the legal framework in this area was an 'informal intergovernmental' system,[2] during which Member States either agreed Conventions among themselves or adopted non-binding acts such as resolutions or recommendations.[3] Next, following the entry into force of the original Treaty on European Union (TEU, often referred to as the Maastricht Treaty), it became primarily a 'formal intergovernmental system',[4] which set out an official legal framework for the adoption of measures by the Council – either Conventions (which would still need to be ratified by Member States), Joint Positions, or Joint Actions.[5] The legal status of the latter two measures was not defined, and in practice no Conventions on immigration and asylum issues were adopted during this period. Instead, due to disagreements about the intensity and substance of the EU's role in this field, 'soft law' measures such as recommendations and resolutions were still widely used.[6]

The intergovernmental nature of the EU's involvement in these issues during this period was established in particular by the requirement that the Council act unanimously in all cases. Furthermore, there was no obligation even to consult the European Parliament, the Commission had to share its power to make proposals with Member States, and the jurisdiction of the Court of Justice was excluded (except as an option, as regards Conventions).[7] However, when drawing up the original TEU, the Member States favouring a purely intergovernmental approach to these issues compromised with those favouring a more supranational approach, and allowed measures concerning a uniform visa format and a list of the countries whose nationals would need a visa to enter the EU to be adopted by means of the 'Community' process.[8] Perhaps inevitably, there were disputes about the dividing line between the supranational and intergovernmental rules.[9]

---

[1] See S Peers, 'EU Justice and Home Affairs Law (Non-Civil)' in P Craig and G de Búrca (eds), *The Evolution of EU Law* (2nd edn, Oxford: Oxford University Press, 2010) 269–279.

[2] On the concept of intergovernmentalism, see further chapter 2.

[3] See eg the Dublin Convention allocating responsibility for asylum requests (OJ [1997] C254/1).

[4] See Art K to K.9 of the original TEU.

[5] Most Joint Actions and Joint Positions concerned criminal law and policing issues, but for examples in the immigration and asylum field see the Joint Position on the definition of refugee (OJ [1996] L63/2) and the Joint Action on airport transit visas (OJ [1996] L63/8).

[6] See eg the Resolution on the admission of labour migrants (OJ [1996] C274/3).

[7] For analysis, see P Müller-Graff, 'The Legal Bases of the Third Pillar and Its Position in the Framework of the Union Treaty' (1994) 29 *Common Market Law Review* 493.

[8] Art 100c EC, which provided for a Commission monopoly on making proposals, consultation of the European Parliament, and a qualified majority vote in the Council.

[9] One of these cases reached the Court of Justice: Case C-170/96 *Commission v Council* [1998] ECR I-2763, in which the Court ruled that the Joint Action on airport transit visas (n 5) did not 'encroach' upon the Community's power to adopt rules on which non-EU countries' nationals would need a visa to enter the EU.

Moreover, the fairly limited output of the EU in this field during this period stood in contrast to the successful development of a legal framework outside the EU system per se. This was the Schengen Convention, signed by a large group of Member States, which aimed to abolish internal border controls between all of the signatory States and, as a corollary, to strengthen their common external border controls. The signatory States also agreed to adopt a fully common visa policy, and to establish 'flanking' rules on the allocation of asylum applications (which were superseded by the Dublin Convention), irregular migration, and judicial and police cooperation, including the creation of a database known as the Schengen Information System.[10] The Schengen Convention was signed in 1990 and was applied from March 1995; it was not adopted as an EU measure because the UK objected in principle to the abolition of internal border checks between Member States.[11]

2.2 The Treaty of Amsterdam

In order to increase the effectiveness of the EU's action in this area, the Treaty of Amsterdam (in force 1 May 1999) applied the usual 'Community method' to the adoption of immigration and asylum measures (along with civil law measures), subject to a five-year transitional period (ending 1 May 2004) and certain important exceptions.[12] During this transitional period, for most matters the Commission had to share its monopoly of initiative with Member States, the Council still voted unanimously, and the European Parliament was only consulted. After the end of the transitional period, the Commission obtained its usual monopoly over proposing legislation and, for most matters, the Council voted by a qualified majority (QMV) and the European Parliament had powers of co-decision over legislation.[13] However, an important limitation on the role of the Court of Justice in this field (only final courts of the Member States could send references for a preliminary ruling to the Court) was retained even after the transitional period,[14] while the Council also had the power, acting unanimously, to change the rules on the jurisdiction of the Court of Justice, it did not do so.[15]

In light of the reluctance of the UK, Ireland, and Denmark to approve the application of the Community method (even with these delays and exceptions) to this area, those Member States were granted an opt-out. The UK and Ireland could choose, within three months of a proposal being tabled, whether or not they wished to participate in negotiations. If they did not opt in, discussions continued without them. If they opted in but blocked the adoption of the measure concerned, it could be adopted without them. Even

---

[10] See D O'Keeffe, 'The Schengen Convention: A Suitable Model for European Integration?' (1991) 11 *Yearbook of European Law* 185 and J Schutte, 'Schengen: Its Meaning for the Free Movement of Persons in Europe' (1991) 28 *Common Market Law Review* 549.

[11] Moreover, the Court of Justice ruled that there was no legal requirement under EC law to abolish such checks, in the absence of flanking measures such as those set out in the Schengen Convention: Case C-378/97 *Wijsenbeek* [1999] ECR I-6207.

[12] Arts 61–69 EC. For analysis, see D O'Keeffe, 'Can the Leopard Change Its Spots? Visas, Immigration and Asylum following Amsterdam' in D O'Keeffe and P Twomey (eds), *Legal Issues of the Amsterdam Treaty* (Oxford: Hart Publishing, 1999).

[13] The key exception was legal migration, where the Council still voted unanimously after consulting the European Parliament. As regards visas, border controls, and irregular migration, see Art 67(2)–(4) EC and the Council Decision changing the decision-making rules (OJ [2004] L396/45), applicable from 1 January 2005. On this transition, see S Peers, 'Transforming Decision-Making on EC Immigration and Asylum Law' (2005) 30 *European Law Review* 283. As regards asylum, see Art 67(5) EC, inserted by the Treaty of Nice. On the interpretation of this provision, see Case C-133/06 *European Parliament v Council* [2008] ECR I-3189.

[14] Art 68 EC.   [15] Art 67(2) EC, second indent.

if they opted out of discussions initially, they could decide to opt in after a measure was adopted. In practice, the UK and Ireland initially opted in to most measures concerning asylum and irregular migration, but few measures concerning legal migration or visas and border controls. Subsequently, after the end of the transitional period, they opted out of most proposals concerning asylum and irregular migration as well. As for Denmark, it could not participate at all in EU measures in this area, except to the extent that they were connected to ('built upon') the Schengen Convention.

On this point, the Treaty of Amsterdam integrated the Schengen Convention and measures based upon it (referred to as the 'Schengen *acquis*') into the EU legal order, without the participation of the UK and Ireland. Those two Member States had the option to participate in some or all of the Schengen *acquis*, subject to the approval of the Council, acting unanimously. In practice the Council has approved the participation of both the UK and Ireland in the Schengen measures relating to irregular migration, criminal law, and police cooperation,[16] but those Member States are not interested in participating in the 'core' of Schengen, that is, the abolition of internal border controls and the connected common policies on visas and external borders. As a consequence, the Court of Justice has ruled that those Member States cannot participate in any EU acts 'building upon' those core Schengen rules that they have opted out of, notably the creation of an EU borders agency (known in practice as Frontex), the rules on fingerprinting EU citizens who apply for a passport, and full police access to the EU's Visa Information System (on which, see more in section 3.3).[17]

2.3 The Treaty of Lisbon

The Treaty of Lisbon completed the process of applying the usual 'Community' method to this area. The co-decision process, including QMV, now applies to the issue of legal migration, as well as to the issue of visa lists and visa formats (previously the European Parliament was only consulted on these visa issues). This has resulted in agreement upon a number of legal migration proposals that had previously been vetoed by one or more Member State(s).[18] Furthermore, the Treaty also revised (and generally extended) the EU's competence on immigration and asylum issues (see the separate sections later in the chapter). Moreover, the Court of Justice now has its full jurisdiction in this area, which has led to an ongoing increase in the number of immigration and asylum cases referred to the Court.[19]

The Treaty also complemented the rules on the British and Irish opt-outs by new provisions on the possibility of the UK and Ireland being forced to terminate their participation in prior EU measures if they fail to opt in to new measures amending those prior acts.[20] So far these particular rules have not been applied in practice. On the contrary, the EU institutions assume that the UK and Ireland remain bound by legislation in this area that has since been *repealed* by subsequent legislation – on the grounds that the UK and Ireland have not participated in those later measures.[21] Whereas the previous British Labour government

[16] OJ [2000] L131/43 (UK) and OJ [2002] L64/20 (Ireland).
[17] See Case C-77/05 *UK v Council* [2007] ECR I-11459; Case C-137/05 *UK v Council* [2007] ECR I-11593; and Case C-482/08 *UK v Council* [2010] ECR I-10413.
[18] See S Peers, 'Mission Accomplished? EU Justice and Home Affairs Law after the Treaty of Lisbon' (2011) 48 *Common Market Law Review* 661, 673.　　　　　　　[19] See ibid, 682–683.
[20] See S Peers, 'In a World of Their Own? Justice and Home Affairs Opt-Outs and the Treaty of Lisbon' (2007–08) 10 *Cambridge Yearbook of European Legal Studies* 383.
[21] See eg Directive 2011/95 (OJ [2011] L337/9), the second-phase Directive on the qualification for refugee and subsidiary protection status. The UK and Ireland opted out of this Directive, but remain bound by the first-phase Directive on the same subject which it repealed (Directive 2004/83, OJ [2004] L304/12).

went to the Court of Justice to complain about its exclusion from some immigration measures that it wanted to participate in,[22] the current Conservative-led coalition government has conversely gone to the Court to complain that it has been wrongly subjected to EU measures that, in its view, fall within the scope of its opt-out in this area.[23]

3 Visas and border control

3.1 Overview and legal framework

The EU has been more active in the fields of visas and border controls than in any other area of immigration and asylum law, due to the Schengen *acquis* in this area, integrated into EU law in 1999, and the measures which have built upon the Schengen *acquis* since. The key elements of the Schengen system are: the abolition of internal border controls (ie controls at the land, sea, and air borders between States participating in the Schengen rules); the strengthening of external borders (ie borders between Schengen States and non-Schengen States); freedom to travel between the Schengen States for any persons who are legally residing in or visiting those States; and a common short-term visa policy.

The detailed rules on these issues were initially set out in the relevant provisions of the Schengen Convention and the measures implementing it, but these measures have mostly been replaced by a number of EU regulations, in particular those setting out a 'Schengen borders code', establishing an EU agency to assist with border controls (known as Frontex), creating a second-generation version of the previous Schengen Information System (SIS II), listing the third (ie non-EU) countries whose nationals do (or do not) need a visa to enter the EU, setting out a 'visa code', and establishing a Visa Information System (VIS) concerning visa applicants. However, the rules on freedom to travel still appear in the Schengen Convention.[24]

3.2 Border controls

First of all, the Schengen borders code sets out the key rules on the control and surveillance of external borders, as well as the basic obligation to abolish internal border controls between the Member States, subject to limited exceptions.[25] Following the so-called 'Arab Spring' of 2011, concerns about the ability of some Schengen States to play their role controlling the external borders led to a proposal from the Commission to amend the borders code to set out a process by which a State's participation in the Schengen *acquis* could be, in effect, temporarily suspended. While this partial retreat from the principle of free movement met with the approval of Member States, they were

---

[22] See n 17.

[23] Case C-431/11 *UK v Council*, judgment of 26 September 2013, nyr. See also Case C-656/11 *UK v Council* and Case C-81/13 *UK v Council*, both pending. All three cases concern the question of whether the extension to third countries of EU social security rules falls within the scope of the EU's social security powers set out in Art 48 TFEU (which apply to all Member States), or rather the EU's immigration powers (where the opt-out applies). The UK lost the first of these cases, as the Court of Justice held that the social security powers applied to the extension of these social benefits to citizens of Norway, Iceland, and Liechtenstein.

[24] Arts 19–22 Schengen Convention (OJ [2000] L239).

[25] Regulation 562/2006 (OJ [2006] L105/1). On the extent of Member States' remaining power to police the internal borders without infringing the obligation to abolish internal border controls, compare Joined Cases C-188/10 and C-189/10 *Melki and Abdeli* [2010] ECR I-5667 to Case C-278/12 PPU *Adil*, judgment of 19 July 2012, nyr.

insistent that any reintroduction of border controls had to remain within the sole control of Member States, not (as the Commission had proposed) EU institutions. At the
same time, the Council decided to remove the European Parliament from its role as
co-legislator as regards a parallel proposal on the evaluation of Member States' compliance with the Schengen rules.[26] The Parliament's outrage at both developments led to
its refusal to cooperate with the Council as regards these and several other Justice and
Home Affairs (JHA) proposals. Ultimately this deadlock was broken by a deal which gave
a slightly bigger role to the Commission as regards the reintroduction of border controls,
and awarded the European Parliament an indirect role whenever the parallel legislation
was amended.[27]

The application of the borders code is complemented by the Schengen Information
System, originally established by the Schengen Convention, and replaced by SIS II from
April 2013.[28] This provides for a system of issuing alerts for refusal of entry of third-country
nationals who should in principle be refused entry into the entire Schengen area.[29] The
EU institutions are also considering the possible creation of an 'entry-exit system', which
would record the crossing of all third-country nationals across the external Schengen
borders in order to determine which of them had overstayed their permitted time period
to visit.[30]

Furthermore, the Frontex agency has a key role supplementing the Member States' border control authorities. Originally established in 2004, its budget has been hugely increased
and its powers have been enlarged so that it can play a larger role, for instance coordinating return flights and sending rapid action teams to assist Member States facing particular
difficulties controlling their share of the external border.[31] The most recent amendment to
the legislation establishing Frontex also aimed to ensure that its activities were compatible
with human rights obligations – an increasingly important issue in light of the case law of
the European Court of Human Rights (ECtHR).[32]

3.3 **Visa policy**

As for the common visa policy, the original visa list Regulation was adopted in 1995, but
only partially harmonized the list of countries whose nationals needed visas to enter the

---

[26] For these proposals, see respectively COM (2011) 560 and COM (2011) 559, both 16 September 2011.
The Council's argument was that the parallel proposal, which concerned the evaluation of the Schengen system, had to be adopted on the basis of Art 70 TFEU, which confers competence upon the Council to adopt
measures concerning the evaluation of JHA policies, but gives no role for the European Parliament in the
decision-making process.

[27] Regulations 1051/2013 and 1053/2013 (OJ [2013] L295/1 and 27).

[28] Regulation 1987/2006 (OJ [2006] L381/4). On the uses of this system for criminal law and policing purposes, see chapter 25.

[29] See Art 24 of Regulation 1987/2006 (n 28), which sets out the key rules on alerts for refusal of entry.
There are further rules on entry bans in the EU's Returns Directive (see section 4.2). EU free movement law
takes priority over the SIS, so entry bans cannot be issued or enforced as regards third-country national family
members of EU citizens unless the conditions in the free movement rules for refusing entry to such persons
are satisfied: see Case C-503/03 *Commission v Spain* [2006] ECR I-1097.

[30] COM(2013) 95 to 97, 27 February 2013.

[31] Regulation 2007/2004 (OJ [2004] L349/1), as amended by Regulations 863/2007 (OJ [2007] L199/30)
and 1168/2011 (OJ [2011] L304/1). There has been a dispute about the legality of the rules governing Frontex
coordination of Member States' border patrols in the Mediterranean: see further chapter 5.

[32] See the judgment of that Court of 23 February 2012 in *Hirsi v Italy*, nyr, in which it found that the policy
of stopping ships with asylum-seeking passengers in the high seas and returning those passengers to Libya
without considering their asylum claims breached the ECHR.

EU.[33] After the integration of the Schengen *acquis* (which had more fully harmonized visa policy) within the EU legal order in 1999, the Council adopted a Regulation in 2001 which completely harmonized the lists of the countries whose nationals did (or did not) require a visa to cross the external borders.[34] This legislation was subsequently amended a number of times.[35]

The criteria to waive or impose a visa requirement are essentially political, and take into account foreign policy considerations, security risks, and the prospect of irregular migration. Within Europe, the EU legislation permits visa-free entry for nationals of the Western Balkan countries and European micro-States, but requires visas for nationals of Russia, Ukraine, other ex-Soviet countries, and Turkey. But as a compromise, the visa regime for a number of nearby countries has been softened, by means of visa facilitation treaties which simplify the process and reduce the cost of obtaining Schengen visas.[36]

In the Asia/Pacific region, the EU legislation requires visas for nationals of all countries except wealthy countries like Japan, Australia, Korea, Taiwan, and New Zealand. As for the Americas, most countries are exempt from a visa requirement except the majority of Andean countries (nationals of Colombia, Peru, Ecuador, and Bolivia need visas). Finally, nationals of all African and Caribbean countries require visas, with the exception of a few small tropical islands such as Mauritius and Bermuda.

The conditions for obtaining a visa are now set out in the EU's visa code, which also includes provisions on the right to appeal a refusal of a visa.[37] The visa application system is now bolstered by the VIS, which became operational in 2011 and is being rolled out gradually worldwide, starting initially with the North African and Near East regions and extended to Africa and Latin America by 2013.[38]

On the whole, the EU has gradually stepped up the degree of harmonization of visa and border control policies and increased control of entry to EU territory, in particular by means of technical measures (the SIS and VIS) and the enhanced operational role of Frontex.[39] On the other hand, however, the EU visa regime, which increasingly interacts with the EU's external policies and has even come to resemble the EU's hierarchy of trade preferences, is becoming gradually more liberal, in particular with the waiver of visa requirements for Western Balkan countries in 2009 and 2010. However, the EU usually insists on a quid pro quo for the waiver of visa requirements or the conclusion of visa facilitation treaties, in the form of readmission treaties (see further later in the text) and further alignment with EU migration control policy. As regards human rights, EU legislation in this field sets out general rules on this issue, but does not specify concretely how such rights are to be protected in the context of visas and border controls.[40]

---

[33] Regulation 2317/95 (OJ [1995] L234/1).   [34] Regulation 539/2001 (OJ [2001] L82/1).

[35] For a consolidated text, see the annex to chapter 7 of S Peers, E Guild, and J Tomkins (eds), *EU Immigration and Asylum Law* (2nd edn, Leiden: Martinus Nijhoff, 2012), vol 1.

[36] Such treaties are in force with Russia, Georgia, Ukraine, and Moldova; have been signed with Armenia and Cape Verde and agreed with Azerbaijan; and are being negotiated with Belarus. The countries in the Western Balkans also benefited from such treaties from the start of 2008 until the EU waived the visa requirement for them.   [37] Regulation 810/2009 (OJ [2009] L243/1).

[38] Regulation 767/2008 (OJ [2008] L218/60).

[39] See also Regulation 1052/2013 establishing the European Border Surveillance System (Eurosur) (OJ [2013] L295/11).

[40] See Art 26a of the Frontex legislation, inserted by Regulation 1168/2011 (n 31) and Art 3a of the borders code, inserted by Regulation 610/2013 (OJ [2013] L182/1).

4 Irregular migration

4.1 Overview and legal framework

Irregular migration (often referred to as 'illegal' migration) is a subject of great public concern, and 'illegal immigrants' are often demonized as if they were a single category of persons. However, the concept of irregular migration covers a wide variety of situations. Some migrants enter the territory without authorization, either clandestinely without showing themselves to border guards (eg as a stowaway in a lorry) or via official crossing points, but with the use of false or stolen passports or other travel documents. Some enter the territory entirely legally, but then overstay the period of their legal short stay without authorization. Some are even legal residents whose stay on the territory after their residence permit or long-stay visa is withdrawn or not renewed, due to a criminal conviction or alleged security threat, or because the reason they were permitted to enter, is no longer valid (eg they were admitted as a student but have finished their studies). Sometimes a legal resident has a right to, or at least the possibility of, the renewal of his or her residence permit, but that permit expires before it is renewed – either because the person concerned did not apply for a renewal in time, or because, even though he or she applied for a renewal in time, the authorities did not process it in time. In these cases, it is likely that the 'illegal' status of the person concerned will sooner or later be remedied retroactively. Finally, some irregular migrants are would-be asylum seekers whose application for asylum has been definitively rejected.

While some irregular migrants may have the intention of committing serious crimes or even threatening Member States' national security, the large majority are seeking a better life and/or protection from persecution or serious threats in their country of origin. If irregular migrants apply for asylum, their legal status changes (see section 6), although they may again be classified as irregular migrants if their application is definitively rejected. Under some circumstances, an asylum application can excuse a prior breach of immigration law. So as with border controls, there are 'mixed flows' of irregular migrants, some of whom argue that they need international protection and some who do not. Some of the former category will be successful in their claims, but others will not. Even among the latter group, some persons are allowed to stay by Member States, at least for a limited period, on humanitarian grounds (eg they are too ill to travel), or because it is impossible to remove them for practical reasons (eg their State of origin cannot accept their return because their nationality cannot be sufficiently proved), or for other reasons. While in principle those irregular migrants needing protection must be treated differently from those who do not, it is impossible to know in advance which irregular migrants need protection and which do not. Indeed, assessing whether a protection claim is well founded is a separate and complex issue of its own. The status of the persons concerned can change, since an irregular migrant might apply for asylum and a rejected asylum seeker will be considered to be an irregular migrant.

What has the EU done to address these issues? As for the legal framework, Article 67(2) TFEU provides that the EU 'shall frame a common policy on asylum, immigration and external border control, based on solidarity between Member States, which is fair towards third-country nationals.' More specifically, Article 79(1) TFEU sets out the EU's objectives as regards immigration:

> The Union shall develop a common immigration policy aimed at ensuring, at all stages, the efficient management of migration flows, fair treatment of third-country nationals residing legally in Member States, and the prevention of, and enhanced measures to combat, illegal immigration and trafficking in human beings.

While Article 79(1) only requires the EU to be 'fair' toward *legally resident* third-country nationals, Article 67(2) obliges the EU to be 'fair' to third-country nationals in general, not just those who are legally resident.

Article 79(2) TFEU sets out the EU's powers to regulate migration for the 'purposes' set out in Article 79(1). The EU can adopt legislation on

(c) illegal immigration and unauthorised residence, including removal and repatriation of persons residing without authorisation;

(d) combating trafficking in persons, in particular women and children.

Also, Article 79(3) TFEU states that the EU 'may conclude agreements with third countries for the readmission to their countries of origin or provenance of third-country nationals who do not or who no longer fulfil the conditions for entry, presence or residence in the territory of one of the Member States'.

4.2 Adopted legislation

To achieve these objectives, the EU has adopted a number of measures concerning the prevention of irregular migration, the treatment of irregular migrants on the territory, and the expulsion of irregular migrants from the territory. The first category of acts applies in addition to the visa and border control measures discussed previously, and includes rules on carrier sanctions (ie penalizing private companies that transport irregular migrants),[41] the transfer of passenger data,[42] prohibiting and criminalizing the facilitation of irregular authorization and residence,[43] trafficking in persons,[44] and the posting of immigration liaison officers to non-EU countries.[45] The second category of measures comprises rules sanctioning the employers of irregular migrants and rules permitting the stay of victims of trafficking – but on the condition that they help to facilitate criminal prosecutions against their traffickers, and only as long as they are useful for those prosecutions.[46] The third category of measures includes the most important EU measure on irregular migration, the so-called Returns Directive, which regulates the procedure for expelling irregular migrants, including rules on detention, entry bans, and procedural rights.[47] It also includes legislation on the mutual recognition of expulsion orders,[48] transit for expulsion,[49] and joint expulsion flights,[50] as well as readmission treaties with a number of non-EU countries.[51]

---

[41] Art 26 Schengen Convention (n 24), as supplemented by Directive 2001/51 (OJ [2001] L187/45).

[42] Directive 2004/82 (OJ [2004] L261/24).

[43] Directive 2002/90 (OJ [2002] L328/17) and Framework Decision 2002/946 (OJ [2002] L328/1). These rules take priority over the rules in the visa code (n 37) on the revocation of visas issued by another Member State: Case C-83/12 PPU *Vo*, judgment of 10 April 2012, nyr.

[44] Directive 2011/36 (OJ [2011] L101/1).

[45] Regulation 377/2004 establishing an immigration liaison officers' network (OJ [2004] L64/1), as amended by Regulation 493/2011 (OJ [2011] L141/13).   [46] Directive 2004/81 (OJ [2004] L261/19).

[47] Directive 2008/115 (OJ [2008] L348/98). Entry bans are entered into the SIS (see previously).

[48] Directive 2001/40 (OJ [2001] L149/34).   [49] Directive 2003/110 (OJ [2003] L321/26).

[50] OJ [2004] L261/28. See also the role of Frontex in joint expulsions (section 3).

[51] As of 14 October 2013, there were EU readmission treaties in force with Serbia, Bosnia, Macedonia, Montenegro, Albania, Moldova, Russia, Ukraine, Georgia, Pakistan, Sri Lanka, Hong Kong, and Macao. Readmission treaties had been signed with Turkey, Cape Verde, and Armenia and agreed with Azerbaijan; there were active negotiations with Belarus; and there were inactive negotiations with Morocco, Algeria, and China.

As the growing corpus of legislation indicates, the EU has been gradually harmonizing national law as regards control of irregular migration, and moreover it has continually been increasing the degree of control of irregular entry. But as with the EU's visas and borders legislation, there are countervailing tendencies towards human rights protection, in this case due to the role of the Court of Justice – as the following case study indicates.

Case study 26.1: Detention of irregular migrants

While States have increasingly frequently resorted to detention of irregular migrants as a means of deterring them and ensuring they do not abscond during the expulsion procedure, such measures have been criticized on the grounds that the persons concerned have usually not committed any crime (except perhaps the criminal offence of irregular entry, which is only another mechanism of migration control), and that the persons concerned (including children) are sometimes detained for very lengthy periods in unpleasant conditions.[52]

This issue is addressed by international human rights law. Most notably, Article 5(1)(f) of the European Convention on Human Rights (ECHR) permits states to detain a migrant after a 'lawful arrest or detention...to prevent his [or her] effecting an unauthorized entry into the country or of a person against whom action is being taken with a view to deportation'. According to the case law of the ECtHR, detention can be justified as long as expulsion proceedings are underway and are being pursued with 'due diligence'; there is no separate need to show the 'necessity' of this detention, even though such a requirement applies to other grounds of permissible detention set out in Article 5(1) ECHR.[53] This means that detention is no longer justified if the removal is unfeasible, and if an alternative measure to prevent absconding can be applied in practice.[54]

The Returns Directive addresses these detention issues in some detail.[55] According to the Directive, persons subject to return procedures 'may only' be detained 'in order to prepare the return and/or to carry out the removal process, in particular when' there is a risk of absconding or if the person concerned 'avoids or hampers' the return or removal process, 'Unless other sufficient but less coercive measures can be applied effectively in a specific case'. Removal arrangements must be 'in process and executed with due diligence'. Detention can be ordered by administrative or judicial authorities, and must be 'ordered in writing with reasons in fact and law'. If the detention was ordered by administrative authorities, there must be some form of 'speedy' judicial review. There must be regular reviews of detention, either automatically or at the request of the person concerned. The detainee must be released immediately if there is no 'reasonable prospect of removal' or if the conditions for detention no longer exist. Conversely, detention shall be maintained as long as the conditions exist; this shall not exceed six months, except where national law permits a further period of up to one extra year because the removal operation is likely to last longer due to lack of cooperation by the person concerned or delays in obtaining documentation.

The Directive also regulates detention conditions. There must be special facilities 'as a rule' for irregular migrants, and separation from ordinary prisoners if detained in prison. Detainees have the right to contact legal representatives, family members, and consular authorities; there are rules on the situation of vulnerable persons; independent bodies must

---

[52] See generally D Wilsher, *Immigration Detention: Law, History, Politics* (Cambridge: Cambridge University Press, 2012).   [53] See in particular *Chahal v UK* (Appl No 22414/93), ECHR 1996-V1831.
[54] *Mikolenko v Estonia* (Appl No 10664/05), judgment of 8 October 2009.
[55] Arts 15–18 of the Directive (n 47).

be able to visit detention facilities; and information must be given to the persons concerned. There are more detailed rules on the detention of minors and families, although Member States may derogate from certain aspects of the rules concerning speedy judicial review and detention conditions in 'exceptional' situations.

The Court of Justice has been asked on several occasions to interpret these rules. First of all, in the *Kadzoev* judgment,[56] it ruled that the relevant time limits for detention must take into account time served as a detainee before the application of the Directive. Also, a period of detention spent while the removal decision was subject to judicial review had to count towards the time limits. The Court interpreted the concept of a 'reasonable prospect of removal', as meaning that a 'real prospect exists that the removal can be carried out successfully, having regard to' the relevant time limits, and that this prospect 'does not exist where it appears unlikely that the person concerned will be admitted to a third country, having regard to' those time limits. In any event, as the Court pointed out, this ground for releasing the person concerned is irrelevant where the time limits on detention have expired. The Court also ruled that Member States could not keep a person in detention, once the relevant time limit had expired, merely because the detainee does not possess valid documents, his conduct is aggressive, and he has no financial support or accommodation.

Next, in the *El Dridi* judgment,[57] the Court ruled that an irregular migrant could 'only' be detained pursuant to the Directive 'where, in the light of an assessment of each specific situation, the enforcement of the return decision in the form of removal risks being compromised by the conduct of the person concerned'. This judicial rule makes it harder to justify detention than the wording of the Directive, since the Directive does not expressly require an individual assessment of detention decisions, and moreover the Directive states that detention is justified 'in particular' where there is a risk of absconding or avoiding or hampering the removal process. Since the latter two types of behaviour will constitute most or all cases where a third-country national's conduct could compromise the enforcement of a removal decision, the Court of Justice has effectively removed the words 'in particular' from the wording of the Directive. This means, for instance, that a person cannot be initially detained merely because his or her State of origin will probably not cooperate with the removal process. So a detainee can only be detained following an individual assessment of his or her behaviour.

In the same judgment, the Court ruled that the returns process in the Directive was subject to a principle of 'gradation', that is, the process starts by allowing the person concerned the most liberty (a period for voluntary departure) and ends by allowing the least liberty (detention). Even detention 'is strictly regulated... inter alia in order to ensure observance of the fundamental rights of the third-country nationals concerned', in light of the case law of the ECtHR and 'soft law' measures of the Council of Europe. Applying these principles to the facts of the case, the Directive precluded the application of the relevant Italian law, which provided for more possibilities for detention than the Directive (as interpreted by the Court of Justice) permitted. The Court also ruled that the detention provisions of the Directive are directly effective (on the concept of 'direct effect', see chapter 6), which means that anyone detained in breach of the Directive has to be released. Also, the person concerned did not fall within the option for Member States to disapply the Directive to persons who are 'subject to return as a criminal law sanction', because the underlying obligation to leave the territory stemmed from an administrative law decision. Finally, the Court examined the relationship between the Directive and national criminal law, holding that while the Directive did not deprive the Member States of all competence to define criminal law

---

[56] Case C-357/09 PPU [2009] ECR I-11189.   [57] Case C-61/11 PPU [2011] ECR I-3015.

offences relating to irregular migration, Member States nevertheless had to adjust their criminal law legislation to EU rules. In this case, that meant that a custodial sentence for an illegal stay following an expulsion decision could not be imposed on the person concerned before the Member State had first tried to remove him pursuant to the returns process.

The relationship between the Returns Directive and national criminal law was further explored in the Court's third judgment, *Achughbabian*.[58] In this case, the Court pointed out that the Directive did not regulate the initial detention of third-country nationals to determine whether their stay was lawful. National officials have a 'brief but reasonable time' to establish the identity and immigration status of the person concerned, before the rules in the Returns Directive, including the detention rules, start to apply. Once the Directive applies, the detention of the irregular migrant cannot be considered to be an expulsion measure in itself, since the person returned remains on the territory of that Member State while he or she is detained. As in *El Dridi*, the detention of an irregular migrant pursuant to a custodial sentence imposed due to illegal stay was a breach of the Directive, since it delayed the expulsion of the person concerned. Moreover, the Court ruled that Member States could not exclude the application of the Directive to persons who have merely committed the criminal offence of an irregular stay. However, the Court clarified that the sentence in question could always be imposed on the person concerned if the returns process was not carried out.

The net result of these judgments is that EU law has harmonized the issue of immigration detention fairly extensively: detention of irregular migrants is harder to justify and the time limits for detention are more likely to run out. Detention is also expressly linked to human rights protection. Also, Member States cannot impose custodial sentences for illegal stay before they first attempt to enforce a return decision against the person concerned. But there is a catch: the irregular migrants are only protected against serving prison time for the criminal offence of illegal stay if they are returned back to the country they were desperate to leave in the first place. And if they cannot be returned to that country, then they face serving that prison time in addition to any period of immigration detention which they may already have served. Finally, these rules do not apply to the detention of asylum seekers, which is regulated instead by EU asylum legislation.[59]

5 Legal migration

5.1 Overview and legal framework

The EU's involvement in the regulation of legal migration has been more limited than its involvement in other areas of immigration and asylum law. Nevertheless, its role in this area continues to increase, and was facilitated by the switch to QMV in the Council pursuant to the Lisbon Treaty. The key elements of EU policy were set out in the conclusions of the Tampere European Council in 1999, which stated that the EU had to 'ensure fair treatment of third country nationals who reside legally on the territory of its Member States', that 'A more vigorous integration policy should aim at granting them rights and obligations comparable to those of EU citizens', that there was a 'need for approximation' of national law 'on the conditions for admission and residence of third country nationals', and that 'The legal

---

[58]   Case C-329/11, judgment of 6 December 2011, nyr.
[59]   See *Kadzoev* (n 56), in which the Court ruled that the position of asylum seekers is outside the scope of the Returns Directive.

status of third country nationals should be approximated to that of Member States' nationals', with the grant of 'uniform rights...as near as possible to those enjoyed by EU citizens' to a person who 'has resided legally in a Member State for a period of time to be determined and who holds a long-term residence permit'.

Following the entry into force of the Lisbon Treaty, these objectives are reflected in Article 79(1) TFEU, which provides, inter alia, that the EU 'shall develop a common immigration policy aimed at ensuring, at all stages...fair treatment of third-country nationals residing legally in Member States'. To this end, Article 79(2) TFEU gives the EU power to adopt legislation concerning

(a) the conditions of entry and residence, and standards on the issue by Member States of long-term visas and residence permits, including those for the purpose of family reunification;

(b) the definition of the rights of third-country nationals residing legally in a Member State, including the conditions governing freedom of movement and of residence in other Member States.

However, these powers are limited by Article 79(5) TFEU, which specifies that Article 79 'shall not affect the right of Member States to determine volumes of admission of third-country nationals coming from third countries to their territory in order to seek work, whether employed or self- employed'. So, while in principle the EU must aim to establish a 'common immigration policy', including rules on the admission, residence, and rights of third-country nationals legally migrating to the EU, Member States remain free to regulate the numbers of economic migrants coming from third countries.

5.2 Legislation

For some time, in fact, EU legislation did not regulate economic migration at all, and a Commission proposal for comprehensive regulation of this issue was rejected by Member States.[60] Instead, the Commission adopted a 'policy plan' on economic migration,[61] which suggested as an alternative a series of piecemeal measures on this issue. This policy was then implemented by means of the adoption of general legislation on the equal treatment and procedural rights of most economic migrants (the Single Permit Directive),[62] as well as more detailed legislation concerning the admission of certain categories of economic migrants: the Blue Card Directive on highly-skilled migrants,[63] and proposed Directives on intra-corporate transferees and seasonal workers.[64]

As for other categories of legal migrants, the EU has also adopted legislation concerning admission to carry out a research project,[65] and the admission of post-secondary students, school pupils, unpaid trainees, and volunteers.[66] EU Directives also regulate family reunion with legal migrants,[67] as well as (implementing the Tampere objectives) the acquisition of EU long-term residence status for those who have resided legally for more than five years.[68]

---

[60] COM(2001) 386, 11 July 2001.

[61] COM(2005) 669, 21 December 2005; and see the earlier Green Paper (COM(2004) 811, 11 January 2005).

[62] Directive 2011/98 (OJ [2011] L343/1).   [63] Directive 2009/50 (OJ [2009] L155/17).

[64] COM(2010) 378 and 379, 13 July 2010.   [65] Directive 2005/71 (OJ [2005] L289/15).

[66] Directive 2004/114 (OJ [2004] L375/12). The Commission has proposed to merge and amend the latter two Directives: COM(2013) 151, 25 March 2013.   [67] Directive 2003/86 (OJ [2003] L251/12).

[68] Directive 2003/109 (OJ [2004] L16/44). This Directive was later amended, in order to extend its scope to refugees and persons with subsidiary protection: Directive 2011/51 (OJ [2011] L132/1).

Taken as a whole, EU legislation on the initial primary admission of migrants focuses on those who are relatively young, wealthy, and highly skilled, and who are therefore more likely to bring a significant net financial benefit to Member States.

5.3 Case law

The two key themes of this chapter – the extent of EU harmonization and the tension between human rights protection and immigration control – are clearly reflected in the case law of the Court of Justice concerning this legislation. In fact, the European Parliament sued to annul certain provisions of the Family Reunion Directive,[69] on the grounds that human rights were not sufficiently protected by the rules in the Directive allowing Member States to insist on a three-year wait for family reunion and to exclude certain categories of children from the usual rules.[70] The Court of Justice rejected this argument, assessing the Directive particularly in light of the jurisprudence of the ECtHR on Article 8 ECHR concerning the right to family life, which generally does not guarantee a right to admission of family members into the host State.[71] As a general rule, the Court said, the Directive sets a higher standard than this case law, as it guarantees a right of admission for spouses and children; but to the extent that it does not guarantee such a right, Member States are still bound by their ECHR obligations to admit family members in special situations (eg to avoid siblings growing up in different States), and must carry out a case-by-case assessment of any applications for family reunion.

Subsequently, in a case concerning a Moroccan national receiving benefits, who had waited nearly 40 years to obtain family reunion with this wife, the Court ruled that despite the apparent flexibility which the Directive gives to Member States as regards conditions for admission:[72]

> Since authorisation of family reunification is the general rule, the faculty provided for in Article 7(1)(c) of the Directive [ie the condition relating to social assistance] must be interpreted strictly. Furthermore, the margin for manoeuvre which the Member States are recognised as having must not be used by them in a manner which would undermine the objective of the Directive, which is to promote family reunification, and the effectiveness thereof.

Furthermore, 'the concept of "social assistance system of the Member State" is a concept which has its own independent meaning in European Union law and cannot be defined by reference to concepts of national law', and 'the provisions of the Directive...must be interpreted in the light of the fundamental rights and, more particularly, in the light of the right to respect for family life enshrined in both the ECHR and the Charter'. The Court then ruled that the particular Dutch rule setting a social assistance condition breached the Directive. Member States' discretion to reject admission of the family members of migrants with modest incomes was therefore somewhat curtailed.

This can be compared to the Court's judgments concerning the Long-Term Residents' Directive. First of all, in the case of *Kamberaj*,[73] concerning a third-country national from

---

[69] Case C-540/03 *European Parliament v Council* [2006] ECR I-5769.

[70] In fact, few Member States apply these rules: see the Commission's report on the implementation of the Directive (COM (2008) 610, 8 October 2008).

[71] On this case law, see S Peers, 'Family Reunion and Community Law' in N Walker (ed), *Europe's Area of Freedom, Security and Justice* (Oxford: Oxford University Press, 2004) 145–149.

[72] Case C-578/08 *Chakroun* [2010] ECR I-1839, para 43.

[73] Case C-571/10, judgment of 24 April 2012, nyr.

Kosovo applying for housing benefit in Italy, the Court ruled on the interpretation of the equal treatment rules in the Directive. While that Directive gives some effect to the Tampere principle of equal treatment of long-term residents, it conversely leaves a degree of discretion to Member States by specifying that long-term residents are entitled to equal treatment as regards 'social security, social assistance and social protection *as defined by national law*'; moreover, it permits Member States to 'limit equal treatment in respect of social assistance and social protection to core benefits'.[74]

In this case, an Italian regional government had established a different formula for paying housing benefit to third-country nationals as compared to Italian and other EU citizens. Having established that the national rule was discriminatory, the Court ruled that where the EU legislature 'has made an express reference to national law ... it is not for the Court to give the terms concerned an autonomous and uniform definition under [EU] law', as this 'means that the [EU] legislature wished to respect the differences between the Member States concerning the meaning and exact scope of the concepts in question'. Nevertheless, this did not mean that Member States are free to 'undermine the effectiveness' of the equal treatment rule. Also, the Directive had to be interpreted in light of the Charter, which 'recognises and respects the right to social and housing assistance so as to ensure a decent existence for all those who lack sufficient resources, in accordance with the rules laid down by European Union law and national laws and practices'.[75]

As for the possibility to limit the application of equal treatment to 'core benefits', the preamble to the Directive specifies that this concept 'covers at least minimum income support, assistance in case of illness, pregnancy, parental assistance and long-term care', and that 'The modalities for granting such benefits should be determined by national law'. The Court pointed out that although this list did not include housing benefit, it was non-exhaustive, and the reference to 'national law' here applied only to the 'modalities' of granting benefits (the level of benefits, the conditions for receiving them, and the procedural aspects) rather than the definition of 'core benefits'. Moreover, the Italian government had not officially notified any derogation, and any derogations from the general rule of equal treatment had to be interpreted narrowly. So 'core benefits' were those 'which enable individuals to meet their basic needs such as food, accommodation and health'. Finally, if the benefit in question fulfilled the purpose of the right to social and housing assistance set out in the Charter, it could not be denied that it was a 'core benefit'. The Court of Justice then left it to the national court to decide if the benefit in question was indeed a 'core benefit', 'taking into consideration the objective of that benefit, its amount, the conditions subject to which it is awarded and the place of that benefit in the Italian system of social assistance'. Overall, the Court's judgment encouraged the national court to ensure equal treatment as regards housing benefit for long-term residents, and therefore to guarantee that those long-term residents with modest incomes will be able to afford housing.

Secondly, in *Commission v Netherlands*,[76] the Court was asked to rule on whether the Dutch government had breached the Directive by imposing high fees for applications for residence permits made by long-term residents or their family members, including those who exercised the right to move between Member States provided for in the Directive. Even though the Directive did not regulate the issue of application fees – and in fact the Commission's proposal to regulate this issue in its original proposal for the Directive had not

---

[74] Art 11(1)(d) and (4), Directive 2003/109.

[75] Art 34(3). As the Court recognized, the Charter, like the Directive, refers back to national law. See further chapter 9.

[76] Case C-508/10, judgment of 26 April 2012, nyr. See also Case C-502/10 *Singh*, judgment of 18 October 2012, nyr, concerning the interpretation of the exclusions from the scope of the Directive.

been accepted – the Court ruled that Member States' 'discretion' to charge fees 'is not unlimited': Member States cannot 'apply national rules which are liable to jeopardise the achievement of the objectives pursued by a directive and, therefore, deprive it of its effectiveness'. Since the Directive created a right to obtain long-term residence status, and to the rights which stem from that status, if the procedural and substantive conditions set out in the Directive are met, the Dutch government could not charge fees at a level which had 'either the object or the effect of creating an obstacle to…obtaining…long-term resident status'. Applying these criteria, the level of fees being charged breached the Directive. The judgment will be of particular benefit to those long-term residents with modest incomes who would have found it harder to afford the high fees being charged for applications.

It can be seen, in light of both the continued adoption of legislation in this field and the dynamic interpretation of that legislation by the Court of Justice,[77] that the EU's role as regards legal immigration is becoming steadily more significant. The Court has a clear tendency to look for uniform interpretations of EU law, or to constrain Member States' activity by means of the principle of effectiveness where the legislation refers to national law or is silent on an issue. In the Court's view, the legislation aims to confer rights on individuals, and exceptions from those rights must be interpreted narrowly. The overriding importance of human rights also has a continuing impact, not only as regards the right to family reunion but also as regards social rights. Taken as a whole, the case law of the Court of Justice has reduced Member States' power to restrict the benefits of EU legislation on legal migration only to relatively well-off migrants.

6 Asylum

6.1 Overview and legal framework

The definition and status of refugees is set out in the first place in the 1951 UN Convention on the Status of Refugees (referred to as the Geneva Convention in EU law), along with the 1967 Protocol to that Convention.[78] This issue is also affected by other international human rights treaties, in particular the ECHR, which, according to the ECtHR, bans the return of a person to a State in which there is a real risk of suffering torture or other inhuman or degrading treatment as set out in Article 3 ECHR.[79] Since the Geneva Convention does not address all situations in which persons might need some form of protection from return to their country of origin, the concept of 'subsidiary protection' (ie protection outside the scope of that Convention) has been developed. EU law has focused on refugee and subsidiary protection issues, but furthermore there are other forms of protection based on national law and practice, not harmonized by EU law.[80] The Court of Justice has confirmed that Member States can establish and retain such non-harmonized forms of protection, provided that there is no confusion with refugee status.[81]

---

[77] See also Case C-15/11 *Sommer*, judgment of 21 June 2012, nyr where the Court ruled that Member States have only a limited power to restrict third-country students' access to employment pursuant to Directive 2004/114. This judgment particularly benefits those students who need to work to pay for their studies and their other expenses.   [78] All Member States have ratified both measures.

[79] See generally G Goodwin-Gill and J McAdam, *The Refugee in International Law* (3rd edn, Oxford: Oxford University Press, 2007).

[80] See the study by the European Migration Network, 'The Different National Practices Concerning Granting of Non-EU Harmonised Protection Statuses' (EMN, 2010), available at http://www.sisekaitse.ee/pub lic/ERV/synthesis_reports/0_EMN_Synthesis_Report_NonEUharmonised_FinalVersion_January2011.pdf.

[81] Joined Cases C-57/09 and C-101/09 *B and D* [2010] ECR I-10979.

Originally, the Treaty of Amsterdam granted the EU powers to set only 'minimum standards' as regards asylum law.[82] However, EU leaders soon decided, at the Tampere European Council of 1999, that the EU should aim to establish a Common European Asylum System (CEAS), starting with a first round of legislation in the 'short term' (which became known as the 'first phase' of the CEAS), with the intention to establish, 'in the longer term', a 'common asylum procedure and a uniform status for those who are granted asylum valid throughout the Union'.

The first phase of legislation to establish the CEAS was adopted between 2003 and 2005, and consisted of a Directive on the qualification for and content of refugee and subsidiary protection status (the Qualification Directive),[83] a Directive on procedures for applying for refugee status (the Procedures Directive),[84] a Directive on reception conditions for asylum seekers (the Reception Directive),[85] and a Regulation setting out rules to allocate responsibility for each asylum-seeker to a single Member State (the Dublin Regulation).[86] In order to facilitate the application of the latter Regulation, there was also an earlier Regulation establishing 'Eurodac', a system for storing and comparing asylum seekers' fingerprints.[87] There is also a Directive providing for a ready-made system of EU-wide 'temporary protection' in the event of a mass influx of people, but this Directive has never been used in practice.[88]

The EU's next multi-year JHA agenda, the Hague Programme, then set a deadline of 2010 for completing the second phase of legislation to establish the CEAS.[89] However, it did not set any objectives for this second phase. Subsequently, the EU set a new deadline of 2012 to establish the second phase, and also established the twin objectives of raising the level of protection and reducing the large divergences between Member States' recognition rates (ie the percentages of persons whose application for refugee or subsidiary protection status are successful).[90] Following the entry into force of the Lisbon Treaty, the objectives agreed in Tampere are now reflected explicitly in Article 78 TFEU, which first of all requires that

> The Union shall develop a common policy on asylum, subsidiary protection and temporary protection with a view to offering appropriate status to any third-country national requiring international protection and ensuring compliance with the principle of *nonrefoulement*. This policy must be in accordance with the Geneva Convention of 28 July 1951 and the Protocol of 31 January 1967 relating to the status of refugees, and other relevant treaties.

To that end, the European Parliament and the Council

> shall adopt measures for a common European asylum system comprising:
>
> (a) a uniform status of asylum for nationals of third countries, valid throughout the Union;
>
> (b) a uniform status of subsidiary protection for nationals of third countries who, without obtaining European asylum, are in need of international protection;
>
> (c) a common system of temporary protection for displaced persons in the event of a massive inflow;

---

[82] Art 63(1) and (2) EC.   [83] Directive 2004/83 (OJ [2004] L304/12).
[84] Directive 2005/85 (OJ [2005] L326/13).   [85] Directive 2003/9 (OJ [2003] L31/18).
[86] Regulation 343/2003 (OJ [2003] L50/1). The Regulation replaced the Dublin Convention (OJ [1997] C254/1).
[87] Regulation 2725/2000 (OJ [2000] L316/1). The Eurodac system began operations on 15 January 2003 (OJ [2003] C5/2). The Regulation also provides for the mandatory storage of the fingerprints of third-country nationals who cross the border without authorization (to compare those fingerprints with persons who apply for asylum later), and for the optional comparison of the fingerprints of irregular migrants with asylum seekers' fingerprints (to check whether an irregular migrant is the responsibility of another Member State).
[88] Directive 2001/55 (OJ [2001] L212/12).   [89] OJ [2005] C53.   [90] OJ [2010] C115.

(d) common procedures for the granting and withdrawing of uniform asylum or subsidiary protection status;

(e) criteria and mechanisms for determining which Member State is responsible for considering an application for asylum or subsidiary protection;

(f) standards concerning the conditions for the reception of applicants for asylum or subsidiary protection;

(g) partnership and cooperation with third countries for the purpose of managing inflows of people applying for asylum or subsidiary or temporary protection.

In the event, the EU adopted all the legislation to establish the second phase of the CEAS by the summer of 2013.[91] The impact of this legislation, once fully implemented, remains to be seen, but as a whole it provides for further harmonization of national law and additional protection of human rights, taking a modest but significant step towards raising standards in this field, and potentially reducing the divergences in Member States' recognition rates somewhat.[92] Pending the adoption and implementation of this second-phase legislation, the Court of Justice became a significant actor in the field of asylum law, following the removal of the restrictions on its jurisdiction with the entry into force of the Lisbon Treaty.[93]

6.2 Qualification for international protection

The EU's asylum legislation raises a large number of issues, including first of all issues concerning the definition of refugee and subsidiary protection status. As regards both types of protection, a protection need may arise following the applicant's departure from the country of origin (known as protection *sur place*).[94] Also, the 'actors of persecution or serious harm' need not be the State, but may also be private parties, if it can be 'demonstrated' that the State, or parties controlling the State, is 'unable or unwilling' to provide protection against non-State agents.[95] This rule changed the more restrictive interpretation of the Geneva Convention in several Member States, which had traditionally recognized as refugees only those persons fleeing persecution by the State. There is a parallel rule on 'actors of protection', which provides that protection can 'only' be provided by States or parties, including international organizations, controlling all or a substantial part of a State's territory, provided that such bodies are 'willing and able to offer protection'. Such protection must be 'effective and of a non-temporary nature', and is 'generally provided' when the actors of protection 'take reasonable steps to prevent the persecution or suffering of serious harm, inter alia, by operating an effective legal system for the detection, prosecution and punishment of acts constituting persecution or serious harm, and when the applicant has access to such protection'.[96] Furthermore, Member States can apply a concept usually

---

[91] Directive 2011/95 (n 21) (Qualification Directive); Directive 2013/33 on reception conditions (OJ [2013] L180/96); Directive 2013/32 on asylum procedures (OJ [2013] L180/60); the revised Dublin Regulation (Regulation 604/2013, OJ [2013] L180/31); and a revised Eurodac Regulation (Regulation 603/2013, OJ [2013] L180/1). The EU also established a European Asylum Support Office: see Regulation 439/2010 (OJ [2010] L132/11). The 2001 Temporary Protection Directive was not updated.

[92] See S Peers, E Guild, M Garlick, and V Moreno-Lax, *EU Immigration and Asylum Law: Text and Commentary* (2nd edn, Leiden: Martinus Nijhoff, vol 3 forthcoming 2014).   [93] See n 19.

[94] Art 5 Directive 2011/95.   [95] Art 6 Directive 2011/95.

[96] Art 7 Directive 2011/95. This provision was amended by the 2011 Directive to raise the standards of protection and reduce divergences of interpretation. eg some Member States had argued that protection could be provided for by clans: see the Commission's report on the implementation of Directive 2004/83, COM(2010) 314, 16 June 2010.

known as an 'internal flight alternative', if there is a part of a protection-seeker's country of origin which is generally safe,[97] and if that person 'can safely and legally travel to and gain admittance to that part of the country and can reasonably be expected to settle there',[98] taking account of the case law of the ECtHR.[99]

The core definition of a 'refugee' is a person who has 'a well-founded fear of being persecuted for reasons of race, religion, nationality, political opinion or membership of a particular social group'.[100] The EU Directive expands upon both the concept of persecution and the grounds of persecution.[101] On the first point, in a case concerning members of the Ahmadiyya community, who faced attacks and criminalization in Pakistan if they professed their beliefs in public, the Court of Justice clarified the concept of 'persecution'. Even though these asylum seekers could possibly have avoided persecution in their country of origin by refraining from proselytizing to believers in the dominant religion there, and from otherwise practising their beliefs in public, the Court ruled that such persons should not be expected to refrain from public displays of their religion in their country of origin.[102] On the second point, the 2011 amendments to the Directive strengthened the rules relating to gender-based persecution.[103]

As for the definition of subsidiary protection, it must be granted where there are 'substantial grounds...for believing' that the person concerned faces a 'real risk' of 'serious harm', which consists of (a) the death penalty or execution, or (b) torture or other inhuman or degrading treatment or punishment, or (c) a 'serious and individual threat to a civilian's life or person by reason of indiscriminate violence in situations of international or internal armed conflict'.[104] While the first two criteria are based on the established case law of the ECtHR,[105] the meaning of the third criterion was unclear, particularly since it is quite clearly contradictory: how could a person face an *individual* threat by reason of *indiscriminate* violence? The Court of Justice answered this question in a case about Iraqis who feared violent retaliation because they were linked to the US forces then occupying Iraq.[106] In the Court's view, an 'individual' threat could include 'harm to civilians irrespective of their identity, where the degree of indiscriminate violence characterising the armed conflict taking place...reaches such a high level that substantial grounds are shown for believing that a civilian, returned to the relevant country or, as the case may be, to the relevant region, would, solely on account of his presence on the territory of that country or region, face a real risk of being subject to the serious threat referred to in Article 15(c) of the Directive'.

---

[97] Art 8 Directive 2011/95. More precisely, there must be 'no well-founded fear' of persecution and no 'real risk of suffering serious harm', or 'access to protection against persecution or serious harm as defined in Article 7'.

[98] Again, the 2011 Directive amended this rule in order to raise the standards of protection and reduce divergences of interpretation.

[99] See the judgment of that Court in *Salah Sheekh v Netherlands* (Appl No 1948/04), ECHR 2007-I, particularly as regards the ability to travel and settle in the safe part of the country.

[100] Art 2(d) Directive 2011/95, echoing Art 1A(2) of the Geneva Convention.

[101] Arts 9 and 10 Directive 2011/95.

[102] Joined Cases C-71/11 and C-99/11 *Y and Z*, judgment of 5 September 2012, nyr. See also, as regards sexual orientation, Joined Cases C-199–201/12 *X, Y and Z*, judgment of 7 November 2013, nyr.

[103] While the 2004 Directive stated that, as regards the concept of 'particular social group', that 'gender-related aspects *can* be considered, without by themselves alone creating a presumption', the 2011 Directive provides that 'Gender related aspects, including gender identity, *shall* be given due consideration for the purposes of determining membership of a particular social group or identifying a characteristic of such a group' (emphases added).   [104] Arts 2(f) and 15 Directive 2011/95.

[105] See n 79.   [106] Case C-465/07 *Elgafaji and Elgafaji* [2009] ECR I-921.

Once an applicant has been granted refugee or subsidiary protection status, he or she (along with his or her family members) is entitled to the benefits set out in the Qualification Directive, which include a residence permit, access to employment and self-employment, equal treatment with nationals as regards social welfare and health care, and equal treatment with legally resident third-country nationals as regards accommodation.[107] While the first-phase Directive left Member States with an option to give fewer such rights to beneficiaries of subsidiary protection, the second-phase Directive only permits lower standards for such persons as regards social welfare and residence permits.[108]

6.3 Reception conditions for asylum seekers

The Directive on reception conditions regulates such issues as the employment, health care, education, and welfare of asylum seekers during the process of deciding on their application. The second-phase Directive improves standards as compared to the first-phase Directive particularly as regards employment – permitting Member States to require an asylum seeker to wait up to nine months for employment access, whereas the first-phase Directive had permitted a wait of up to 12 months.[109] It also inserted detailed rules on detention of asylum seekers into the Directive. These differ somewhat from the rules on detention of irregular migrants in the Returns Directive (see case study 26.1), in that the grounds for detention are different and there is no express time limit on detention. However, the rules on legal safeguards and detention conditions are quite similar.[110]

6.4 Asylum procedures

Next, the rules on asylum procedures address such issues as legal aid, interviews, the right to an effective remedy (in particular as regards the suspensive effect of appeals), and special procedural rules such as accelerated procedures, the 'safe country of origin' concept, and the 'safe third country' concept (which allow Member States to presume that some countries of origin or transit are safe for all asylum seekers). The second-phase Directive improved standards as regards, for instance, setting a six-month time limit (subject to exceptions) to make a first-instance decision on an application, reducing the number of possible cases subject to accelerated procedures, strengthening the right to an effective remedy, and abolishing the option to apply lower standards as regards the 'safe country of origin' concept.

6.5 Responsibility for applications

Finally, there has been continued controversy concerning the application of the 'Dublin' rules on responsibility for asylum applications, in part because the criteria for responsibility (which in turn assign that responsibility based on family reunion, the issue of a visa or a residence permit, or evidence of crossing a border or remaining on the territory illegally) shifted the burden of dealing with asylum applications towards the EU's external eastern and southern land and sea borders, mostly consisting of poorer Member States. Furthermore, there were widespread concerns that some Member States were systematically not applying many of the basic standards of the Geneva Convention, the ECHR, and

---

[107] Arts 20–34 Directive 2011/95.   [108] Arts 24 and 29 Directive 2011/95.
[109] Art 15 Directive 2013/33; compare to Art 11 Directive 2003/9.
[110] Arts 8–11 Directive 2013/33.

EU law as regards reception conditions, qualification for status, and asylum procedures. Ultimately, the ECtHR ruled that Greece frequently breached Article 3 ECHR (the ban on torture or other inhuman and degrading treatment) due to its low standards on reception conditions (interpreting the ECHR on this point in light of the Reception Directive) and asylum procedures, and that Belgium breached Article 3 ECHR by returning an asylum seeker to Greece despite its knowledge that such breaches were taking place.[111]

In turn, the Court of Justice ruled that while the EU rules were based on mutual trust that each Member State would comply with its human rights obligations, it was possible that the CEAS might 'experience major operational problems in a given Member State, meaning that there is a substantial risk that asylum seekers may, when transferred to that Member State, be treated in a manner incompatible with their fundamental rights'. But the Dublin system could not be suspended following *any* breach of those human rights obligations, but rather where there 'are substantial grounds for believing that there are systemic flaws in the asylum procedure and reception conditions for asylum applicants', leading to a breach of the ban on torture or other inhuman and degrading treatment set out in Article 4 of the EU's Charter of Fundamental Rights. So EU law also prevented sending asylum seekers to Greece pursuant to the Dublin rules.[112] While the Commission proposed to amend the Dublin rules to set out a detailed system for suspending its application in such cases, the final amendment to the legislation only transposed the main elements of the Court's judgment into the text of the revised Regulation.[113]

The problems with the application of the Dublin rules in individual cases can be seen in one reference from a national court to the Court of Justice, concerning the mother of a Chechen refugee in Austria, who sought to join her adult son (and other family members with refugee status there) and apply for asylum herself.[114] This case is particularly tragic, because the applicant's daughter-in-law was raped, contracted HIV, suffered post-traumatic stress disorder and kidney disease, and was unable to look after her three children, who were taken into care as a result. The mother-in-law could look after the children, so they did not have to go into care. However, since she entered the EU via Poland, that country was in principle responsible for her asylum claim under the Dublin rules. Despite the facts of the case, Austria declined to invoke an optional 'humanitarian' exception in the rules, and insisted that the mother-in-law apply for asylum in Poland. Nevertheless, the Court of Justice ruled that on the facts of this case, this exception had to be used, so Austria had to consider her asylum application.

As in other areas, it can be seen that the EU's role in this area is steadily increasing, and indeed is governed by a political and legal objective of establishing a 'common' policy, with a view both to reducing divergences in national policy and increasing standards of human rights protection. Indeed, increasing the role of the EU was formally built in to the concept of a first and second phase of asylum legislation. The second-phase legislation and the case law of the Court of Justice to date both point clearly in the direction of an increasing level of both protection and harmonization, but the EU will still clearly fall short of establishing a 'uniform' concept of asylum law, even following the implementation of the second-phase legislation.

---

[111] *MSS v Belgium and Greece* (Appl No 30696/09), judgment of 21 January 2011, nyr.
[112] Joined Cases C-411/10 and C-493/10 *NS and ME*, judgment of 21 December 2011, nyr.
[113] Art 3(2) Regulation 604/2013.   [114] Case C-245/11 *K*, judgment of 6 November 2012, nyr.

7 Conclusion

In all four areas of immigration and asylum law, the EU's role has been steadily growing. It began with the development of visas and borders rules outside the EU framework, which were integrated into the EU legal framework in 1999 and have been developed significantly (VIS, SIS II, Frontex, visa and border codes) since then. Moreover, since 1999 the EU has adopted both a first and a second phase of legislation concerning the CEAS. In the area of legal migration, the EU began by harmonizing the non-economic aspects of the issue and has subsequently addressed sundry aspects of labour migration. As for irregular migration, the EU's initial piecemeal approach has been supplemented by the adoption of the fairly comprehensive Returns Directive. And these legislative developments have proceeded in pace with the gradual full extension of the Community method of decision-making and judicial control to this area of the law.

The position as regards the tension between human rights protection and immigration control is more mixed. EU legislation and policy on border control and irregular migration, along with technical and operational developments, points clearly towards more control of immigration, but these developments are qualified by human rights exceptions in the borders code, human rights rules in the Frontex legislation, and increased procedural rights for the persons concerned. And the ongoing development of EU legislation on visas, legal migration, and asylum points towards a more liberal approach. There is likely to be a continuing struggle within and between the EU's political institutions and Courts to establish the right balance between migration control and the protection of fundamental rights.

Further reading

H BATTJES, *European Asylum Law and International Law* (Leiden: Martinus Nijhoff, 2006)

N COLEMAN, *European Readmission Policy: Third Country Interests and Refugee Rights* (Leiden: Martinus Nijhoff, 2009)

G GOODWIN-GILL AND J MCADAM, *The Refugee in International Law* (3rd edn Oxford: Oxford University Press, 2007)

K HAILBRONNER, *EU Immigration and Asylum Law – Commentary* (Munich/Oxford/ Baden-Baden: Beck, Hart, Nomos, 2010)

S PEERS, *EU Justice and Home Affairs Law* (3rd edn, Oxford: Oxford University Press, 2011) chs 3–7

S PEERS, E GUILD, M GARLICK, AND V MORENO-LAX, *EU Immigration and Asylum Law: Text and Commentary*, 3 vols (2nd edn, Leiden: Martinus Nijhoff, vols 1 and 2 2012 and vol 3 forthcoming 2014)

A WEISBROCK, *Legal Migration to the European Union* (Leiden: Martinus Nijhoff, 2010)

D WILSHER, *Immigration Detention: Law, History, Politics* (Cambridge: Cambridge University Press, 2012)

Index

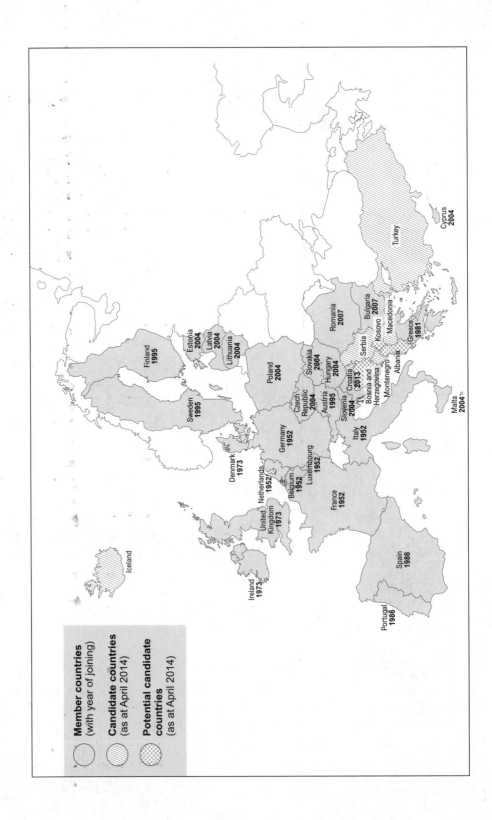

Member countries
(with year of joining)

Candidate countries
(as at April 2014)

Potential candidate
countries
(as at April 2014)

Iceland

Ireland
1973

United
Kingdom
1973

Netherlands
1952

Belgium
1952

Luxembourg
1952

France
1952

Portugal
1986

Spain
1986

Denmark
1973

Germany
1952

Sweden
1995

Finland
1995

Estonia
2004

Latvia
2004

Lithuania
2004

Poland
2004

Czech
Republic
2004

Slovakia
2004

Austria
1995

Hungary
2004

Slovenia
2004

Croatia
2013

Italy
1952

Bosnia and
Herzegovina

Montenegro

Albania

Serbia

Kosovo

Macedonia

Romania
2007

Bulgaria
2007

Greece
1981

Turkey

Cyprus
2004

Malta
2004